August 27–31, 2017
Como, Italy

Association for
Computing Machinery

Advancing Computing as a Science & Profession

RecSys'17

Proceedings of the Eleventh ACM Conference on Recommender Systems

Sponsored by:

ACM SIGCHI

In-cooperation with:

ACM SIGAI, ACM SIGIR, ACM SIGKDD, ACM SIGWEB, & ACM Sigecom

Supported by:

Booking.com, Infinity, Pandora, Huawei, ContentWise, Netflix, Criteo Research, Zalando, Spotify, Amazon, Silver Egg Technology, Politecnico Milano, & Unibz

Association for
Computing Machinery

Advancing Computing as a Science & Profession

The Association for Computing Machinery
2 Penn Plaza, Suite 701
New York, New York 10121-0701

ISBN: 978-1-4503-4652-8 (Digital)

ISBN: 978-1-4503-5674-9 (Print)

Additional copies may be ordered prepaid from:

ACM Order Department
PO Box 30777
New York, NY 10087-0777, USA

Phone: 1-800-342-6626 (USA and Canada)
+1-212-626-0500 (Global)
Fax: +1-212-944-1318
E-mail: acmhelp@acm.org
Hours of Operation: 8:30 am – 4:30 pm ET

RecSys 2017 Chairs' Welcome

It is our great pleasure to welcome you to the *2017 ACM Conference on Recommender Systems (RecSys 2017)*, held in Como, Italy, from August 27th though 31st. The ACM Recommender Systems conference (RecSys) is the premier international forum for the presentation of new research results, systems and techniques in the broad field of recommender systems.

Recommendation is a particular form of information filtering that exploits past behaviors and user similarities to generate a list of information items that is personally tailored to an end-user's preferences. As RecSys brings together the main international research groups working on recommender systems, along with many of the world's leading e-commerce companies, it has become the most important annual conference for the presentation and discussion of recommender systems research.

RecSys 2017, is the eleventh conference in this series. It brings together researchers and practitioners from the academia and industry to present their latest results and identify new trends and challenges in providing recommendation components in a range of innovative application contexts. In addition to the main technical track, RecSys 2017 program features keynote and invited talks, tutorials covering state-of-the-art in this domain, a workshop program, an industrial track and a doctoral symposium.

The program for RecSys 2017 reflects the growth of the Recommender Systems community. For the third time in the history of RecSys we offer two parallel tracks during the three days of the main conference with 106 contributions including 46 technical papers, 9 doctoral symposium papers, 12 industry papers, five tutorials, four keynotes, seven demos and 23 posters. We again offer an extensive pre- and post-conference program with twelve workshops, the RecSys Challenge and the doctoral symposium, which was held at Free University of Bozen-Bolzano on August 25th.

The call for papers attracted a large number of submissions and the program committee reviewed and accepted the following contributions:

Venue or Track	*Reviewed*	*Accepted*	
Long Technical Papers	125	26	20.8%
Short Technical Papers	122	20	16.4%
Doctoral Symposium Papers	15	9	60%
Industry Track Papers	31	12	38.7%
Poster Presentations	45	23	51.1%
Demonstrations	11	7	63.6%

Building on the tradition established by previous years, RecSys 2017 features a strong focus on significant real-world challenges facing industrial practitioners and practical solutions to those challenges. The three industry sessions feature a rich set of talks from: Microsoft, Electronic Arts, Dressipi, Farfetch, Netflix, AirBnB, Skyscanner, CloudAcademy, LinkedIn, Blendle, Aptus and Cheetah Mobile. A wide range of domains are represented in these sessions including eCommerce, news, advertising, recruiting, movies, television, fashion, tourism and eLearning.

This year's conference has truly been a product of the vibrant and supportive community, and the vast cohort of amazing volunteers. We would like to thank all the members of the organizing committee for their generosity, initiative, and brilliant execution. We are tremendously grateful to the 25 senior and 145 regular Program Committee members, who volunteered their time and generated around 750 detailed reviews and 400 discussion comments.

We also extend our deepest gratitude to the many sponsors who generously provided funds and services allowing us support many of the conference events. We thank the organizers and sponsors of the RecSys Challenge, who devoted themselves to organizing this annual competitive event. Finally, we thank all the authors for their contributions in shaping the high-quality content of RecSys 2017, as well as all the conference attendees.

We hope that you find this program interesting and thought-provoking and that the conference provides you with a valuable opportunity to share ideas with other researchers and practitioners from institutions around the world.

Paolo Cremonesi and Francesco Ricci
RecSys 2017 General Chairs

Shlomo Berkovsky and Alexander Tuzhilin
RecSys 2017 Program Chairs

Table of Contents

Paper Session 9: Diversity

Paper Session 10: Conversations

Paper Session 11: Novel and Practical

Paper Session 12: Deep Learning

Paper Session 13: Semantics and Sentiment

Industry Session 1: Games and Travel

Industry Session 2: Interesting Domains

Industry Session 3: Algorithms@Industry

Demonstrations

Workshops and Challenge

Tutorials

Doctoral Symposiums

RecSys 2017 Conference Organization

General Chairs: Paolo Cremonesi (Politecnico di Milano, Italy)
Francesco Ricci (Free University Bozen-Bolzano, Italy)

Program Chairs: Shlomo Berkovsky (CSIRO, Australia)
Alexander Tuzhilin (New York University, USA)

Workshop Chairs: Giovanni Semeraro (University of Bari, Italy)
Marko Tkalčič (Free University Bozen-Bolzano, Italy)

Tutorial Chairs: Li Chen (Hong Kong Baptist University, Hong Kong)
Martha Larson (Radboud University Nijmegen and TU Delft, Netherlands)

Poster and Demo Chairs: Domonkos Tikk (Gravity R&D, Hungary)
Pearl Pu (EPFL, Switzerland)

Industry Chairs: Linas Baltrunas (Netflix, USA)
Alan Said (University of Skövde, Sweden)

Doctoral Symposium Chairs: Robin Burke (DePaul University, USA)
Bart Knijnenburg (Clemson University, USA)

Proceeding Chair: Mehdi Elahi (Free University Bozen-Bolzano, Italy)

Sponsor Chair: Puya Vahabi (Pandora, USA)

Local Arrangement Chair: Emanuele Rabosio (Politecnico di Milano, Italy)

Publicity Chairs: Christoph Trattner (MODUL University Vienna, Austria)
David Elsweiler (University of Regensburg, Germany)

Web Chair Benedikt Loepp (University of Duisburg-Essen, Germany)

Senior Program Committee: Gediminas Adomavicius
Xavier Amatriain
Peter Brusilovsky
Robin Burke
Iván Cantador
Pablo Castells
Li Chen
Martin Ester
Boi Faltings
Alexander Felfernig
Ido Guy

Senior Program Committee (continued):

Alan Hanjalic
Dietmar Jannach
Alexandros Karatzoglou
George Karypis
Joseph Konstan
Yehuda Koren
Bamshad Mobasher
Lior Rokach
Giovanni Semeraro
Bracha Shapira
Harald Steck
Domonkos Tikk
Nava Tintarev
Markus Zanker

Program Committee:

Panagiotis Adamopoulos
Jussara Almeida
Liliana Ardissono
Azin Ashkan
Linas Baltrunas
Justin Basilico
Konstantin Bauman
Joeran Beel
Alejandro Bellogin
András Benczúr
Maria Bielikova
Toine Bogers
Ludovico Boratto
Derek Bridge
Licia Capra
Sylvain Castagnos
James Caverlee
Shuo Chang
Enhong Chen
Elizabeth Daly
Nadja De Carolis
Marco de Gemmis
Ernesto De Luca
Toon De Pessemier
Christian Desrosiers
Tommaso Di Noia
Ernesto Diaz-Aviles
Casey Dugan
Michael Ekstrand
Mehdi Elahi

Program Committee (continued):

Florent Garcin
Franca Garzotto
Yong Ge
Werner Geyer
Jennifer Golbeck
Marcos Goncalves
Guibing Guo
Negar Hariri
Max Harper
Balázs Hidasi
Frank Hopfgartner
Andreas Hotho
Maya Hristakeva
Rong Hu
Neil Hurley
Dmitry Ignatov
Kris Jack
Alejandro Jaimes
Mohsen Jamali
Anthony Jameson
Robert Jaschke
Komal Kapoor
Bart Knijnenburg
Noam Koenigstein
Michal Kompan
Irena Koprinska
Georgia Koutrika
Tsvi Kuflik
Branislav Kveton
Paul Lamere
Martha Larson
Neal Lathia
Danielle Lee
Sang-goo Lee
Sangkeun Lee
Daniel Lemire
Lukas Lerche
Jure Leskovec
Tao Li
Defu Lian
Bin Liu
Huan Liu
Andreas Lommatzsch
Pasquale Lops
Bernd Ludwig

Program Committee (continued):

Leandro Balby Marinho
Luc Martens
Estefanía Martín
Kevin Mccarthy
Wagner Meira
Cataldo Musto
Nadia Najjar
Olfa Nasraoui
Julia Neidhart
Wolfgang Nejdl
Yiu-Kai Ng
Tien Nguyen
Xia Ning
John O'Donovan
Nuria Oliver
Michael O'Mahoney
Vito Ostuni
Javier Parapar
Denis Parra
Jiang Peng
Luiz Pizzato
Till Plumbaum
Josep Pujol
Haggai Roitman
Inbal Ronen
Shaghayegh Sahebi
Alan Said
Olga Santos
Rodrygo Santos
Badrul Sarwar
Markus Schedl
Lars Schmidt-Thieme
Carlos Seminario
Shilad Sen
Guy Shani
Amit Sharma
Yue Shi
Barry Smyth
Maria Soledad-Pera
Oren Somekh
Myra Spiliopoulou
Fabio Stella
Neel Sundaresan
Panagiotis Symeonidis

Program Committee (continued):

Nina Taft
Jiliang Tang
Marko Tkalcic
Paolo Tomeo
Christoph Trattner
Hossein Vahabi
Saúl Vargas
Katrien Verbert
Jian Wang
Jun Wang
Yan Wang
Hannes Werthner
Martijn Willemsen
David Wilson
Le Wu
Hui Xiong
Guandong Xu
Tao Ye
Yong Yu
Quan Yuan
Jie Zhang
Weinan Zhang
Yong Zheng
Hengshu Zhu
Tingshao Zhu
Nivio Ziviani

RecSys 2017 Sponsor & Supporters

Sponsor

SIGCHI

Diamond Supporter:

Booking.com

Platinum Supporter:

infinity

pandora®

HUAWEI

contentwise

NETFLIX

criteo research

zalando

Spotify®

Gold Supporter: amazon

Silver Supporter: SILVER EGG TECHNOLOGY

Institutional donor/supporters logos: POLITECNICO MILANO 1863 unibz

Recommender Systems and the New New Economics of Information

George Loewenstein
Carnegie Mellon University
Pittsburgh, PA, USA
GL20@andrew.cmu.edu

ABSTRACT

George Stigler pioneered the economics of information in the 1960s with his observation that information is a scarce and valuable commodity. Stigler assumed people value information to the extent, and only to the extent, that it helps them to make better decisions, and that people update their beliefs rationally, in response to new information. Stigler won the Nobel prize for his contribution, as did three economists, George Akerlof, Michael Spence and Joseph Stiglitz ten years later. This second wave of research, that came to be called the "new economics of information" adhered to Stigler's assumptions, but examined consequences of asymmetric information – i.e., the fact that interacting individuals often possess different information sets. In this talk I will discuss my research on four phenomena that are key to the information age that don't fit neatly into either wave of economic research on information: curiosity (the desire for information for its own sake), privacy (the desire to withhold information), information avoidance (a phenomenon that Stigler's theory explicitly ruled out), and the desire to share information. The last of these topics is most relevant to recommender systems, so I will devote special attention to it, discussing some of the fundamental motives that drive people to share information.

Author Keywords

Economics of information; information sharing privacy; curiosity; information avoidance;

BIOGRAPHY

George Loewenstein is the Herbert A. Simon University Professor of Economics and Psychology at Carnegie Mellon University. He received his PhD in economics from Yale University in 1985 and since then has held academic positions at The University of Chicago and Carnegie Mellon University, and fellowships at Center for Advanced Study in the Behavioral Sciences, The Institute for Advanced Study in Princeton, The Russell Sage Foundation, The Institute for Advanced Study (Wissenschaftskolleg) in Berlin, and the London School of Economics. His research focuses on applications of psychology to economics, and his specific interests include decision making over time, bargaining and negotiations, psychology and health, privacy, curiosity, information avoidance, law and economics, the psychology of adaptation, the role of emotion in decision making, the psychology of curiosity, conflict of interest, and "out of control" behaviors such as impulsive violent crime and drug addiction. He is one of the founders of the fields of behavioral economics and neuroeconomics.

RecSys '17, August 27-31, 2017, Como, Italy

ACM ISBN 978-1-4503-4652-8/17/08.
DOI: http://dx.doi.org/10.1145/3109859.3109871

Improving Higher Education—Learning Analytics & Recommender Systems Research

George Karypis
Department of Computer Science & Engineering
University of Minnesota, Minneapolis, MN, USA
karypis@umn.edu

ABSTRACT
An enduring issue in higher education is student retention to successful graduation. Studies in the U.S. report that average six-year graduation rates across higher-education institutions is 59% and have remained relatively stable over the last 15 years. For those that do complete a college degree, less than half complete within four-years. Requiring additional terms or leaving college without receiving a bachelor's degree has high human and monetary costs and deprives students from the economic benefits of a college credential (over $1 million in a lifetime and even higher in STEM fields). Moreover, when students do not succeed in graduating, local and national communities struggle to create an educated workforce. Estimates indicate that by 2020 over 64% of the jobs in the U.S. will require at least some post-secondary education. These challenges have been recognized by the U.S. National Research Council, which identified that there is a critical need to develop innovative approaches to enable higher-education institutions retain students, ensure their timely graduation, and are well-trained and workforce ready in their field of study. Failure to do so represents a significant problem as it deprives the U.S. of the highly skilled workforce that it needs to successfully compete in the modern world.

This talk describes various efforts under way to develop "Big Data" methods to analyze in a comprehensive manner, the large and diverse types of education and learning-related data in order to improve undergraduate education. These methods are motivated by and are designed to address various interrelated issues that have a significant impact on college student success and include: (i) academic pathways towards successful and timely graduation from the student perspective; (ii) effective pedagogy by instructors; and (iii) retention and persistence of students from the institutional and advisor perspective. In addition, the talk will discuss areas in which research methods and approaches originally developed by the recommender systems community can be applied to this domain.

Author Keywords
Educational data mining, learning analytics, student modeling.

RecSys'17, August 27–31, 2017, Como, Italy

ACM ISBN 978-1-4503-4652-8/17/08.
DOI: http://dx.doi.org/10.1145/3109859.3109870

BIOGRAPHY
George Karypis is a Distinguished McKnight University Professor and an ADC Chair of Digital Technology at the Department of Computer Science & Engineering at the University of Minnesota, Twin Cities. His research interests span the areas of high performance computing, data mining, recommender systems, information retrieval, bio-informatics, cheminformatics, and scientific computing. His research has resulted in the development of software libraries for serial and parallel graph partitioning (METIS and ParMETIS), hypergraph partitioning (hMETIS), for parallel Cholesky factorization (PSPASES), for collaborative filtering-based recommendation algorithms (SUGGEST), clustering high dimensional datasets (CLUTO), finding frequent patterns in diverse datasets (PAFI), and for protein secondary structure prediction (YASSPP). He has coauthored over 270 papers on these topics and two books ("Introduction to *Protein Structure Prediction: Methods and Algorithms*" (Wiley, 2010) and "Introduction to Parallel Computing" (Publ. Addison Wesley, 2003, 2nd edition)). He is on the editorial boards of many journals and in the program committees of many conferences and workshops on these topics.

Personalization is a Two-Way Street

Ronny Lempel
Outbrain Inc.
Netanya, Israel
rlempel@outbrain.com

ABSTRACT

Recommender systems are first and foremost about matching users with items the systems believe will delight them. The "main street" of personalization is thus about modeling users and items, and matching per user the items predicted to best satisfy the user. This holds for both collaborative filtering and content-based methods. In content discovery engines, difficulties arise from the fact that the content users natively consume on publisher sites does not necessarily match the sponsored content that drives the monetization and sustains those engines. The first part of this talk addresses this gap by sharing lessons learned and by discussing how the gap may be bridged at scale with proper techniques.

The second part of the talk focuses on personalization of audiences on behalf of content marketing campaigns. From the marketers' side, optimizing audiences was traditionally done by refining targeting criteria, basically limiting the set of users to be exposed to their campaigns. Marketers then began sharing conversion data with systems, and the systems began optimizing campaign conversions by serving the campaign to users likely to transact with the marketer. Today, a hybrid approach of *lookalike modeling* combines marketers' targeting criteria with recommendation systems' models to personalize audiences for campaigns, with marketer ROI as the target.

CCS Concepts/ACM Classifiers

• Information systems~Computational advertising • Information systems~Personalization • Information systems~Recommender systems *• Information systems~Content ranking*

Author Keywords

Content discovery; personalization; conversion optimization

BIOGRAPHY

Ronny Lempel joined Outbrain in May 2014 as VP of Outbrain's Recommendations Group, where he oversees the computation and delivery of the company's organic and paid recommendations, as well as the auction mechanisms that run in the paid recommendations' marketplace.

Prior to joining Outbrain, Ronny spent 6.5 years as a Senior Director at Yahoo Labs. Ronny joined Yahoo in October 2007 to open and establish its Research Lab in Haifa, Israel. During his tenure at Yahoo, Ronny led R\&D activities in diverse areas, including Web Search, Web Page Optimization, Recommender Systems and Ad Targeting. In January 2013 Ronny was appointed Yahoo Labs' Chief Data Scientist in addition to his managerial duties.

Prior to joining Yahoo!, Ronny spent 4.5 years at IBM's Haifa Research Lab with the Information Retrieval Group, where his duties included research and development in the area of enterprise search systems. During his tenure at IBM, Ronny managed the Information Retrieval Group for two years.

Ronny received his PhD, which focused on search engine technology, from the Faculty of Computer Science at Technion, Israel Institute of Technology in early 2003. During his PhD studies, Ronny spent two summer internships at the AltaVista search engine.

Ronny has authored over 40 research papers in leading conferences and journals, and holds 18 granted US patents. He regularly serves on program and organization committees of Web-focused conferences, and has taught advanced courses on Search Engine Technologies and Big Data Technologies at Technion.

RecSys'17, August 27–31, 2017, Como, Italy

ACM ISBN 978-1-4503-4652-8/17/08.
DOI: http://dx.doi.org/10.1145/3109859.3109869

Memory Networks for Recommendation

Jason Weston
Facebook AI Research
New York
jasel@fb.com

ABSTRACT
Memory networks are a recently introduced model that combines reasoning, attention and memory for solving tasks in the areas of language understanding and dialogue — where one exciting direction is the use of these models for dialogue-based recommendation. In this talk we describe these models and how they can learn to discuss, answer questions about, and recommend sets of items to a user. The ultimate goal of this research is to produce a full dialogue-based recommendation assistant. We will discuss recent datasets and evaluation tasks that have been built to assess these models abilities to see how far we have come.

CCS Concepts
• **Information systems** → Question answering • **Information systems** → Recommender systems • **Computing methodologies** → Discourse, dialogue and pragmatics • **Computing methodologies** → Natural language generation

Author Keywords
memory-augmented neural networks; dialogue; end-to-end learning

BIOGRAPHY
Jason Weston is a research scientist at Facebook, NY, since Feb 2014. He earned his PhD in machine learning at Royal Holloway, University of London and at AT&T Research in Red Bank, NJ (advisors: Alex Gammerman, Volodya Vovk and Vladimir Vapnik) in 2000. From 2000 to 2001, he was a researcher at Biowulf technologies. From 2002 to 2003 he was a research scientist at the Max Planck Institute for Biological Cybernetics, Tuebingen, Germany. From 2003 to 2009 he was a research staff member at NEC Labs America, Princeton. From 2009 to 2014 he was a research scientist at Google, NY. His interests lie in statistical machine learning and its application to text, audio and images. Jason has published over 100 papers, including best paper awards at ICML and ECML. He was part of the YouTube team that won a National Academy of Television Arts & Sciences Emmy Award for Technology and Engineering for Personalized Recommendation Engines for Video Discovery. He was listed as the 16th most influential machine learning scholar at AMiner and one of the top 50 authors in Computer Science in *Science*.

RecSys'17, August 27–31, 2017, Como, Italy

ACM ISBN 978-1-4503-4652-8/17/08.
DOI: http://dx.doi.org/10.1145/3109859.3109868

Learning to Rank with Trust and Distrust in Recommender Systems

Dimitrios Rafailidis
Department of Computer Science
University of Mons
Mons, Belgium
dimitrios.rafailidis@umons.ac.be

Fabio Crestani
Faculty of Informatics
Università della Svizzera italiana (USI)
Lugano, Switzerland
fabio.crestani@usi.ch

ABSTRACT

The sparsity of users' preferences can significantly degrade the quality of recommendations in the collaborative filtering strategy. To account for the fact that the selections of social friends and foes may improve the recommendation accuracy, we propose a learning to rank model that exploits users' trust and distrust relationships. Our learning to rank model focusses on the performance at the top of the list, with the recommended items that end-users will actually see. In our model, we try to push the relevant items of users and their friends at the top of the list, while ranking low those of their foes. Furthermore, we propose a weighting strategy to capture the correlations of users' preferences with friends' trust and foes' distrust degrees in two intermediate trust- and distrust-preference user latent spaces, respectively. Our experiments on the Epinions dataset show that the proposed learning to rank model significantly outperforms other state-of-the-art methods in the presence of sparsity in users' preferences and when a part of trust and distrust relationships is not available. Furthermore, we demonstrate the crucial role of our weighting strategy in our model, to balance well the influences of friends and foes on users' preferences.

CCS CONCEPTS

•Information systems →Collaborative and social computing systems and tools;

KEYWORDS

Learning to rank; social relationships; collaborative filtering

1 INTRODUCTION

The collaborative filtering strategy has been proved as an effective means for recommender systems, providing similar-minded users with similar recommendations [13]. However, in a real-world scenario the sparsity of users' preferences significantly limits the recommendation accuracy. To overcome the sparsity problem of users' preferences, several models exploit the selections of trust friends to generate trust-based recommendations [8, 18]. In trust-based recommendations, models consider that people tend to rely more on recommendations from friends they trust than on recommendations of anonymous people similar to them [12, 16]. The challenge in trust-based recommender systems is that we have to learn both about users' preferences and trust degrees, as friends do not have necessarily the same preferences [3, 8]. In addition, in online networks users may establish both trust and distrust relationships. For example Epinions[1], an e-commerce site for reviewing and rating products, allows users to evaluate other users based on the quality of their reviews, and form trust and distrust relations with them. In Slashdot[2] users post news and comments, and they can tag other users as friends or foes. The analyses in relevant studies point out that users might accept recommendations from their trusted users, but will certainly not rely on their distrusted foes [27, 29]. Thus, more recently a few attempts have been made to exploit both trust and distrust relationships in recommender systems, in studies such as those reported in [5, 6, 19, 26]. Following the collaborative filtering strategy, these models design different objective functions with trust and distrust relationships to handle the sparsity in users' preferences, assuming that the latent features of users and their friends should be as close as possible, while those of foes as far as possible. However, these methods do not capture well the correlations of users' preferences with friends' trust and foes' distrust degrees, as we will experimentally show in Section 5.

In addition, existing methods that exploit both trust and distrust relationships are mainly focused on the rating prediction problem, aiming to predict the missing ratings of users based on different loss functions. However, several studies point out that focussing on the top-N recommendation problem, that is predicting the products-items that users will see in a ranked recommendation list, reflects more on real-world scenarios [1, 33]. In this respect, several learning to rank models have been introduced to improve the personalized ranking performance directly in the top-N recommendation problem, such as the studies reported in [24, 25, 30]. Moreover, in [4], authors introduce different optimization algorithms to perform push at the top of the list, assuming that what it matters is the performance of the learning to rank models at the top of the list, the recommended items that users will actually see. While there are various attempts to incorporate trust relationships in learning to rank models, such as the studies reported in [3, 15, 20, 21, 33], these models ignore the selections of foes, which play an important role in boosting the recommendation accuracy [7, 28, 29].

[1]http://www.epinions.com/
[2]https://slashdot.org/

RecSys'17, August 27-31, 2017, Como, Italy
 ISBN 978-1-4503-4652-8/17/08...$15.00
DOI: http://dx.doi.org/10.1145/3109859.3109879

To overcome the limitations of existing methods we propose a learning to rank model with trust and distrust relationships, by balancing the influences of friends' and foes' selections on users' preferences. This paper's contributions are summarized as follows:

- We design a learning to rank model, trying to push the relevant items of users and their friends at the top of the recommendation list, while at the same time ranking low the foes' relevant items.
- We propose a weighting strategy to measure the influences of friends and foes. To better capture their trust and distrust degrees with users' preferences, we build an intermediate trust-preference user latent space with friends and their selections, and an intermediate distrust-preference space with foes and their selections.

Our experiments on the Epinions dataset show that the proposed approach outperforms competitive approaches in the presence of preferences' sparsity and when a part of trust and distrust relationships is missing. Also, we demonstrate the importance of our weighting strategy in our learning to rank model to compute the correlations of users' preferences with friends' trust and foes' distrust degrees.

The remainder of the paper is organized as follows. Section 2 reviews the related work, Section 3 defines our ranking problem with trust and distrust relationships and Section 4 details the proposed learning to rank model. Section 5 evaluates the performance of the proposed model against several state-of-the-art methods and, finally, Section 6 concludes the study.

2 RELATED WORK

2.1 Trust-based Recommendations

As trust relationships can leverage the recommendation accuracy, many different strategies have been introduced to exploit the selections of trust friends when producing recommendations. In [12], authors extend the probabilistic matrix factorization of [18] by weighting the user latent factors based on their trust relationships. In [16], a trust-based ensemble method is presented to combine matrix factorization with a trust-based neighbourhood model. In [11], Jamali and Ester combine TrustWalker [10] with a neighbourhood collaborative filtering strategy. In this study, authors run random walks on the trust network, formed by the trust relationships, and then they perform a probabilistic item selection strategy to generate recommendations. Guo et al. [8] extend SVD++ [13], to learn both the user preferences and the influence of her friends. This study considers both friends' ratings and trust degrees to produce recommendations. However, these methods treat the recommendation problem as a rating prediction problem in which different squared loss functions are used to minimize the prediction error. Nonetheless, methods that achieve low rating errors do not necessarily have high ranking performance in the recommendation lists [32]. This occurs because optimizing the predicted values of the ratings may not provide the best recommendation lists in many cases. For instance, if all the low-ranked ratings are predicted very accurately, but significant errors are made on the higher-ranked ratings, then these methods will not provide a high-quality personalized recommendation list to the end-user [1].

2.2 Learning to Rank

Learning to rank methods have been widely studied in recommender systems. The goal is to define a personalized ranking function, and then learn loss functions to improve the ranking performance in the top-N recommendation problem [1]. Representative learning to rank models in recommender systems are CofiRank [30] and CLiMF [25], which use loss functions based on Normalized Discounted Cumulative Gain and Reciprocal Rank, respectively. The Bayesian personalized ranking framework of [24] makes a prediction for every pair of items concerning their relative ordering in the recommendation list. In [4], authors introduce various learning to rank models, which follow different strategies when learning the personalized ranking functions, to account for the fact that users focus on recommendations at the top of the list. However, all the aforementioned learning to rank models do not exploit trust nor distrust relationships in their learning process. Instead, various learning to rank models focus on the ranking performance when generating recommendations with trust relationships. Grimberghe et al. [15] combine Multi-Relational matrix factorization with the Bayesian personalized ranking framework of [24] to model users' feedback both on items and on trust relationships. Zhao et al. [33] present a trust-based Bayesian personalized ranking model that incorporates trust relationships into a pair-wise ranking model, assuming that users tend to assign higher ranks to items that their friends prefer. In [20], a learning to rank model is presented, considering how well the relevant items of users and their friends have been ranked at the top of the list. In [21], authors extend the model of [20] by combing different learning to rank strategies into a joint model to leverage the recommendation accuracy with trust relationships. Chaney et al. [3] infer each user's preferences and the influence of her friends by introducing a Bayesian model that performs Social Poisson factorization. However, all the above learning to rank models ignore users' distrust relationships when generating recommendations.

2.3 Recommendation with Trust and Distrust

Ma et al. [17] present a social regularization method that shares a common user-item matrix, factorized by ratings and social relationships. This work introduces a trust-based, as well as a distrust-based model to exploit trust and distrust relationships in each model separately. The goal of the trust-based model is to minimize the distances of latent features between trust users, while the distrust-based model tries to maximize the latent features' distances between distrust users. Recently, a few attempts have been made to exploit both trust and distrust relationships at the same time in recommender systems. Forsati et al. [6] use trust and distrust relationships in a matrix factorization framework using a hinge loss function. This method assumes that the trust and distrust relationships between users are considered as similarity/dissimilarity in their preferences. Then, the latent features are computed in a manner such that the latent features of foes who are distrusted by a certain user have a guaranteed minimum dissimilarity gap from the worst dissimilarity of friends who are trusted by this same user. In [5], a recommendation strategy is introduced to rank the latent features of users, based on the users' trust and distrust relationships. This method also considers the neutral relationships (users who have no relation to a certain user), aiming to rank the neutral users' latent features after the friends' latent features and before those of foes. In [19] a signed graph is constructed, considering positive and negative weights for the trust and distrust relationships, respectively. Then, a spectral clustering approach is used to generate clusters in the signed graph. The clusters are extracted on condition that users with positive connections should lie close to each other, while users with negative ones should lie far to each other. Following a joint non-negative matrix factorization framework the final recommendations are generated, by co-factorizing the user-item and user-cluster associations. Tang et al. [26] consider a signed graph with trust and distrust relationships and capture local and global information from the signed graph. Local information reveals the correlations among users and her friends/foes, and the global information reveals the reputation of the user in the whole social network, as users tend to trust users with high global reputation. Then, they exploit both local and global information in a matrix factorization technique to compute the recommendations. Nonetheless, none of these studies aim to improve the personalized ranking performance in their learning strategies.

3 PROBLEM DEFINITION

Let $\mathcal{N}$ and $\mathcal{I}$ be the sets of users and items, with $n = |\mathcal{N}|$ being the number of users and $m = |\mathcal{I}|$ the number of items. Our learning to rank model inputs the user-item matrix $\mathbf{R} \in \mathbb{R}^{n\times m}$ with user preferences, expressed by any type of user-item interactions such as ratings, number of views and clicks, and so on. Following the collaborative filtering strategy of matrix factorization, we assume that the recommendations are in the factorized matrix $\hat{\mathbf{R}} \in \mathbb{R}^{n\times m}$ of the user-item interaction matrix $\mathbf{R}$. In addition, we consider two adjacency matrices $\mathbf{A}^+ \in \mathbb{R}^{n\times n}$ and $\mathbf{A}^- \in \mathbb{R}^{n\times n}$, corresponding to the weights of the trust and distrust relationships. Based on the adjacency matrices $\mathbf{A}^+$ and $\mathbf{A}^-$, for each user i we calculate the neighbourhoods $\mathcal{N}_i^+$ and $\mathcal{N}_i^-$ with her friends and foes, respectively. With these settings our problem is formally defined as follows:

Definition 1 (Problem). *Given (i) the friends in the adjacency matrix $\mathbf{A}^+$, (ii) the foes in the adjacency matrix $\mathbf{A}^-$, and (iii) the users' preferences in the user-item interaction matrix $\mathbf{R}$, the goal of the proposed learning to rank model is to compute the factorized matrix $\hat{\mathbf{R}}$, by pushing the relevant items of users and their friends at the top of the recommendation list, and push down the relevant items of foes.*

4 PROPOSED APPROACH

4.1 Learning to Rank Model

Let $\mathcal{X}_i$ and $\mathcal{Y}_i$ be the sets of relevant and irrelevant items of user i. Aiming at improving the ranking performance at the top of the recommendation list, the reverse height of a relevant item x_i is defined as follows [4]:

Definition 2 (Reverse Height). *The reverse height $RH_i(x_i)$ of a relevant item $x_i \in X_i$ in the recommendation list of user i is the number of irrelevant items $y_i \in Y_i$ ranked above x_i.*

Let r_i be the personalized ranking function of user i. According to Definition 1, the reverse height is computed as follows:

$$RH_i(x_i) = \sum_{y_i \in \mathcal{Y}_i} \mathbf{1}\left[r_i(x_i) \leq r_i(y_i)\right] \quad (1)$$

where $\mathbf{1}$ is the indicator function. As the indicator is a not convex function and we have to measure the influences of friends and foes, we take the following surrogate:

$$\begin{aligned} g_i(x_i, y_i) &= r_i(x_i) - r_i(y_i) \\ &+ \frac{1}{|\mathcal{N}_i^+|}\sum_{j\in\mathcal{N}_i^+}\left[\mathbf{W}_{ij}^+\frac{1}{|\mathcal{X}_j|}\sum_{x_j\in\mathcal{X}_j}\left(r_j(x_j) - r_j(y_i)\right)\right] \\ &- \frac{1}{|\mathcal{N}_i^-|}\sum_{v\in\mathcal{N}_i^-}\left[\mathbf{W}_{iv}^-\frac{1}{|\mathcal{X}_v|}\sum_{x_v\in\mathcal{X}_v}\left(r_v(x_v) - r_v(y_i)\right)\right] \end{aligned} \quad (2)$$

where r_j and r_v are the personalized ranking functions of a friend j and a foe v, respectively, and $\mathcal{X}_j$ and $\mathcal{X}_v$ are the sets of items marked as relevant by j and v, accordingly. The term in the middle line of Eq. (2) measures the influence of friends in the surrogate g_i, that is how many relevant items x_j of friend j are ranked above the user's i irrelevant item y_i. Accordingly, the term in the last line of Eq. (2) penalizes the influence of foes based on their relevant items x_v that are ranked above y_i. This means that we have to push the relevant items $x_i \in \mathcal{X}_i$ of user i and $x_j \in \mathcal{X}_j$ of friend j above the irrelevant items $y_i \in \mathcal{Y}_i$ of user i. Also, we have to push down the relevant items $x_v \in \mathcal{X}_v$ of foe v below the irrelevant items y_i. In doing so, the relevant items x_i and x_j will be pushed at the top of the personalized recommendation list of user i and the relevant items x_v will be ranked low.

The weighting matrices $\mathbf{W}^+ \in \mathbb{R}^{n\times n}$ and $\mathbf{W}^- \in \mathbb{R}^{n\times n}$ in Eq. (2) are formally defined as follows:

Definition 3 (Trust Weighting Matrix). *Given a friend $j \in \mathcal{N}_i^+$ of user i and their preferences in the user-item interaction matrix $\mathbf{R}$, each element $\mathbf{W}_{ij}^+$ measures the correlation between j and i, by considering their preferences and trust degree.*

Definition 4 (Distrust Weighting Matrix). *Given a foe $v \in \mathcal{N}_i^-$ of user i and their preferences in $\mathbf{R}$, each element $\mathbf{W}_{iv}^-$ expresses the correlation between v and i, based on their preferences and distrust degree.*

Our weighting strategy to calculate matrices $\mathbf{W}^+$ and $\mathbf{W}^-$ is presented in the subsequent Section 4.2.

In our ranking model, we have to learn the ranking functions r_i, r_j and r_v in a collaborative manner. As previously stated in Section 3, following the collaborative filtering strategy in our model we consider the recommendations in the factorized matrix $\hat{\mathbf{R}} = \mathbf{U}\mathbf{V}^\top$, with $\mathbf{U} \in \mathbb{R}^{n\times k}$ and $\mathbf{V} \in \mathbb{R}^{m\times k}$ being the user and item factor matrices and k the number of latent factors. By taking the respective k-dimensional latent vectors of matrices $\mathbf{U}$ and $\mathbf{V}$, Eq. (2) becomes:

$$\begin{aligned} g_i(x_i, y_i) &= \mathbf{u}_i^\top(\mathbf{v}_{x_i} - \mathbf{v}_{y_i}) \\ &+ \frac{1}{|\mathcal{N}_i^+|}\sum_{j\in\mathcal{N}_i^+}\left[\mathbf{W}_{ij}^+\frac{1}{|\mathcal{X}_j|}\sum_{x_j\in\mathcal{X}_j}\left(\mathbf{u}_j^\top(\mathbf{v}_{x_j} - \mathbf{v}_{y_i})\right)\right] \\ &- \frac{1}{|\mathcal{N}_i^-|}\sum_{v\in\mathcal{N}_i^-}\left[\mathbf{W}_{iv}^-\frac{1}{|\mathcal{X}_v|}\sum_{x_v\in\mathcal{X}_v}\left(\mathbf{u}_v^\top(\mathbf{v}_{x_v} - \mathbf{v}_{y_i})\right)\right] \end{aligned} \quad (3)$$

As the surrogate in Eq. (3) is not convex, we reformulate Eq. (2) as a minimization problem with respect to the latent matrices U and V using the convex logistic function:

$$\min_{\mathbf{U},\mathbf{V}} RH_i(x_i) = \sum_{y_j \in Y_j} \log\left(1 + \exp(-g_i(\mathbf{x}_i, \mathbf{y}_i))\right) \quad (4)$$

In our model we solve the minimization problem in Eq. (4) via gradient descent, using the following update rules at the t-h iteration:

$$\mathbf{u}_i^{t+1} \leftarrow \mathbf{u}_i^t - \eta \frac{\partial RH}{\partial_{\mathbf{u}_i}}, \quad i = 1 \ldots n \quad (5)$$

$$\mathbf{v}_j^{t+1} \leftarrow \mathbf{v}_j^t - \eta \frac{\partial RH}{\partial_{\mathbf{v}_j}}, \quad j = 1 \ldots m \quad (6)$$

where η is the learning parameter and $\partial RH/\partial_{\mathbf{u}_i}$ and $\partial RH/\partial_{\mathbf{v}_j}$ are the respective gradients. When optimizing Eq. (4) the influence of friends' and foes' selections on the user i's preferences might become negative in the surrogate g_i of Eq. (3), that is the case of $P_i < 0$, with the term P_i being equal to:

$\forall i \in \mathcal{N}$

$$\begin{aligned} P_i = & \frac{1}{|\mathcal{N}_i^+|} \sum_{j \in \mathcal{N}_i^+} \left[\mathbf{W}_{ij}^+ \frac{1}{|\mathcal{X}_j|} \sum_{x_j \in \mathcal{X}_j} \left(\mathbf{u}_j^\top (\mathbf{v}_{x_j} - \mathbf{v}_{y_i}) \right) \right] \\ & - \frac{1}{|\mathcal{N}_i^-|} \sum_{v \in \mathcal{N}_i^-} \left[\mathbf{W}_{iv}^- \frac{1}{|\mathcal{X}_v|} \sum_{x_v \in \mathcal{X}_v} \left(\mathbf{u}_v^\top (\mathbf{v}_{x_v} - \mathbf{v}_{y_i}) \right) \right] \end{aligned} \quad (7)$$

Hence, during the optimization of Eq. (4) with the update rules of Eqs. (5)-(6), we define a boolean vector $\mathbf{h}^t \in \{0,1\}^n$ for each iteration t in the gradient descent algorithm, by replacing the surrogate g_i of Eq. (3) with $g_i(x_i, y_i) = \mathbf{u}_i^\top(\mathbf{v}_{x_i} - \mathbf{v}_{y_i}) + \mathbf{h}_i^t P_i$. The i-th entry $\mathbf{h}_i^t$ is calculated as follows: if $P_i < 0$ then $\mathbf{h}_i^t = 0$, and 1 otherwise. Having calculated the factor matrices U and V by minimizing Eq. (4), we compute the factorized matrix $\hat{\mathbf{R}}$ as the product of $\mathbf{U}\mathbf{V}^\top$. Then, for each user i we order the items in the i-th row of $\hat{\mathbf{R}}$ in a descending order, and select the top-N items to generate the final recommendations.

So the challenge in our learning to rank model is how to weigh the influences of friends and foes when optimizing Eq. (4), capturing users' preferences with trust and distrust degrees in the weighting matrices $\mathbf{W}^+$ and $\mathbf{W}^-$.

4.2 Weighting Strategy

Let $\mathbf{U}^+ \in \mathbb{R}^{n \times k^+}$ and $\mathbf{U}^- \in \mathbb{R}^{n \times k^-}$ be the user factor matrices of $\mathbf{A}^+$ and $\mathbf{A}^-$, with k^+ being the number of latent factors of $\mathbf{U}^+$, and k^- the number of latent factors of $\mathbf{U}^-$. We also consider the user factor matrix $\mathbf{U} \in \mathbb{R}^{n \times k}$ of the user-item interaction matrix $\mathbf{R}$. The three user factor matrices U, $\mathbf{U}^+$ and $\mathbf{U}^-$ generate three respective latent spaces, that is a $n \times k$ - dimensional latent space with users' preferences of U, a $n \times k^+$ - dimensional space with trust correlations of $\mathbf{U}^+$ and a $n \times k^-$ - dimensional space with distrust correlations of $\mathbf{U}^-$.

4.2.1 Trust-based Weighting Matrix. As pointed out in several studies, the preferences of trust friends do not necessarily match [3, 8]. Hence, we compute the weighting matrix $\mathbf{W}^+$, to capture users' preferences with their trust correlations in an intermediate *trust-preference user factor* space, formed by a matrix $\mathbf{M}^+ \in \mathbb{R}^{k \times k^+}$ which is defined as follows:

Definition 5 (Trust-Preference User Factor Matrix). *Given the k and k^+ latent dimensions of the n users in U and $\mathbf{U}^+$, the intermediate trust-preference user factor matrix $\mathbf{M}^+$ captures the correlations of users' preferences with friends' trust degrees in an intermediate user latent space, subject to:*

$$\mathbf{W}^+ = \mathbf{U} \times \mathbf{M}^+ \times \mathbf{U}^{+\top} \quad (8)$$

To calculate the user similarities in the latent spaces, we consider the k-dimensional latent vectors u_i in U and the k^+-dimensional vectors u_i^+ in $\mathbf{U}^+$. We define the respective similarity functions s, s^+ and sm^+ in the user latent spaces of U, $\mathbf{U}^+$ and $\mathbf{M}^+$ as follows:

$\forall i \in \mathcal{N}$ and $j \in \mathcal{N}_i^+$

$$s(\mathbf{u}_i, \mathbf{u}_j) = \frac{1}{1 + \exp(-\mathbf{u}_i{}^\top \mathbf{u}_j)} \quad (9)$$

$$s^+(\mathbf{u}_i^+, \mathbf{u}_j^+) = \frac{1}{1 + \exp(-\mathbf{u}_i^{+\top} \mathbf{u}_j^+)} \quad (10)$$

$$sm^+(\mathbf{u}_i, \mathbf{u}_j^+) = \frac{1}{1 + \exp(-\mathbf{u}_i{}^\top \mathbf{M}^+ \mathbf{u}_j^+)} \quad (11)$$

where the product $\mathbf{u}_i^\top \mathbf{M}^+ \mathbf{u}_j^+$ reflects on the embedded distance of $\mathbf{u}_i$ and $\mathbf{u}_j^+$ in the intermediate latent space of $\mathbf{M}^+$. Since users i and j are friends, having (probably) similar preferences, we have to ***maximize*** their similarities in the three latent spaces U, $\mathbf{U}^+$ and $\mathbf{M}^+$. We transform the problem of calculating the intermediate trust-preference user factor matrix into a minimization problem with respect to the user factor matrices U, $\mathbf{U}^+$ and $\mathbf{M}^+$. To achieve this we take the negative natural logarithmic function of the respective similarities. For example, the similarities in the latent space of U are recomputed as follows: $-\sum_{i,j} \log(s(\mathbf{u}_i, \mathbf{u}_j))$. Summarizing, we formulate our minimization problem as the following objective function with respect to the user factor matrices U, $\mathbf{U}^+$ and $\mathbf{M}^+$:

$$\begin{aligned} \min_{\mathbf{U},\mathbf{U}^+,\mathbf{M}^+} L^+(\mathbf{U}, \mathbf{U}^+, \mathbf{M}^+) = & - \sum_{i \in \mathcal{N}, j \in \mathcal{N}_i^+} \log(s(\mathbf{u}_i, \mathbf{u}_j)) \\ & - \sum_{i \in \mathcal{N}, j \in \mathcal{N}_i^+} \log(s^+(\mathbf{u}_i^+, \mathbf{u}_j^+)) - \sum_{i \in \mathcal{N}, j \in \mathcal{N}_i^+} \log(sm^+(\mathbf{u}_i, \mathbf{u}_j^+)) \\ & + \lambda^+ \sum_{c=1}^{k} ||\mathbf{u}_c||_2 + \gamma^+ \sum_{c=1}^{k^+} ||\mathbf{u}_c^+||_2 + \delta^+ ||\mathbf{M}^+||_1 \end{aligned} \quad (12)$$

In the last line, the first two terms are the ℓ_2 norm regularization terms to avoid model overfitting. The third term is the ℓ_1 norm regularization to force the intermediate trust-preference user factor matrix to be sparse, as both the trust relationships in $\mathbf{A}^+$ and the users' preferences in R are sparse. Parameters λ^+, γ^+ and δ^+ control the influences of the respective regularization terms. To optimize the minimization problem in Eq. (12), we use a gradient-based alternating optimization algorithm, that is, we optimize each matrix/variable via gradient descent by fixing the other two [9]. Hence, to compute the three matrices/variables in alternating optimization we calculate the gradients of the objective function in Eq. (12) with respect to matrices U, $\mathbf{U}^+$ and $\mathbf{M}^+$ as follows:

$$\frac{\partial L^+(\mathbf{U},\mathbf{U}^+,\mathbf{M}^+)}{\partial_{\mathbf{u}_i}} = -\sum_{i\in\mathcal{N}, j\in\mathcal{N}_i^+} \frac{\exp(-\mathbf{u}_i{}^\top\mathbf{u}_j)}{1+\exp(-\mathbf{u}_i{}^\top\mathbf{u}_j)}\mathbf{u}_j - \sum_{i\in\mathcal{N}, j\in\mathcal{N}_i^+} \frac{\exp(-\mathbf{u}_i{}^\top\mathbf{M}^+\mathbf{u}_j^+)}{1+\exp(-\mathbf{u}_i{}^\top\mathbf{M}^+\mathbf{u}_j^+)}\mathbf{M}^+\mathbf{u}_j^+ + 2\lambda^+\sum_{c=1}^{k}(\mathbf{u}_i)^c \tag{13}$$

$$\frac{\partial L^+(\mathbf{U},\mathbf{U}^+,\mathbf{M}^+)}{\partial_{\mathbf{u}_i^+}} = -\sum_{i\in\mathcal{N}, j\in\mathcal{N}_i^+} \frac{\exp(-\mathbf{u}_i^{+\top}\mathbf{u}_j^+)}{1+\exp(-\mathbf{u}_i{}^\top\mathbf{u}_j^+)}\mathbf{u}_j^+ - \sum_{i\in\mathcal{N}, j\in\mathcal{N}_i^+} \frac{\exp(-\mathbf{u}_i{}^\top\mathbf{M}^+\mathbf{u}_j^+)}{1+\exp(-\mathbf{u}_i{}^\top\mathbf{M}^+\mathbf{u}_j^+)}\mathbf{u}_i{}^\top\mathbf{M}^+ + 2\gamma^+\sum_{c=1}^{k^+}(\mathbf{u}_i^+)^c \tag{14}$$

$$\frac{\partial L^+(\mathbf{U},\mathbf{U}^+,\mathbf{M}^+)}{\partial_{\mathbf{M}^+}} = -\sum_{i\in\mathcal{N}, j\in\mathcal{N}_i^+} \frac{\exp(-\mathbf{u}_i{}^\top\mathbf{M}^+\mathbf{u}_j^+)}{1+\exp(-\mathbf{u}_i{}^\top\mathbf{M}^+\mathbf{u}_j^+)}\mathbf{u}_i\mathbf{u}_j^{+\top} + \delta^+\sum_{c=1}^{k}\sum_{d=1}^{k^+} sign(\mathbf{M}^+_{cd}) \tag{15}$$

As the ℓ_1 norm regularization term in Eq. (12) is not differentiable at zero, we use the *sign* function in the last term of Eq. (15), with $sign(\mathbf{M}^+_{ij}) = 1$ if $\mathbf{M}^+_{ij} > 0$, $sign(\mathbf{M}^+_{ij}) = -1$ if $\mathbf{M}^+_{ij} < 0$, and 0 otherwise. With the gradients in Eqs.(13)-(15) we optimize the objective function in Eq. (12) via alternating optimization, to compute the trust-preference user factor matrix $\mathbf{M}^+$, and the user factor matrices $\mathbf{U}$ and $\mathbf{U}^+$. Then, based on Eq. (8), we compute the weighting matrix $\mathbf{W}^+$ to capture users' preferences with friends' trust degrees.

4.2.2 *Distrust-based Weighting Matrix.*

To compute the weighting matrix $\mathbf{W}^-$, we calculate the correlations of users' preferences with foes' distrust degrees. We define an intermediate *distrust-preference user factor* matrix as follows:

DEFINITION 6 (DISTRUST-PREFERENCE USER FACTOR MATRIX). *Given the k and k^- latent dimensions of the n users in $\mathbf{U}$ and $\mathbf{U}^-$, the intermediate distrust-preference user factor matrix $\mathbf{M}^- \in \mathbb{R}^{k\times k^-}$ contains the correlations of users' preferences with foes' distrust degrees in an intermediate user latent space, subject to:*

$$\mathbf{W}^- = \mathbf{U}\times\mathbf{M}^-\times\mathbf{U}^{-\top} \tag{16}$$

Accordingly, we have the similarity function s in the latent space of $\mathbf{U}$, and the respective similarity functions s^- and sm^- in $\mathbf{U}^-$ and $\mathbf{M}^-$ as follows:

$\forall i \in \mathcal{N}$ and $v \in \mathcal{N}_i^-$

$$s(\mathbf{u}_i,\mathbf{u}_v) = \frac{1}{1+\exp(-\mathbf{u}_i{}^\top\mathbf{u}_v)} \tag{17}$$

$$s^-(\mathbf{u}_i^-,\mathbf{u}_v^-) = \frac{1}{1+\exp(-\mathbf{u}_i^{-\top}\mathbf{u}_v^-)} \tag{18}$$

$$sm^-(\mathbf{u}_i,\mathbf{u}_v^-) = \frac{1}{1+\exp(-\mathbf{u}_i{}^\top\mathbf{M}^-\mathbf{u}_v^-)} \tag{19}$$

The similarity of the foes' latent vectors have to be ***minimized*** in the user preference latent space in $\mathbf{U}$ and in the intermediate space in $\mathbf{M}^-$, as foes do not have similar preferences [28, 29]. Instead, as users i and v are foes we have to ***maximize*** their similarities in the distrust space of $\mathbf{U}^-$, to express their distrust degree. First we transform the maximization problem of foes' similarity in $\mathbf{U}^-$ as a minimization problem, using the negative natural logarithmic function $-\sum_{i,v}\log(s(\mathbf{u}_i,\mathbf{u}_v))$. Hence, we formulate the following objective function as a minimization problem to compute $\mathbf{U}$, $\mathbf{U}^-$ and $\mathbf{M}^-$:

$$\min_{\mathbf{U},\mathbf{U}^-,\mathbf{M}^-} L^-(\mathbf{U},\mathbf{U}^-,\mathbf{M}^-) = \sum_{i\in\mathcal{N}, v\in\mathcal{N}_i^-} s(\mathbf{u}_i,\mathbf{u}_v) - \sum_{i\in\mathcal{N}, v\in\mathcal{N}_i^-}\log(s^-(\mathbf{u}_i^-,\mathbf{u}_v^-)) + \sum_{i\in\mathcal{N}, v\in\mathcal{N}_i^-} sm^-(\mathbf{u}_i,\mathbf{u}_v^-) + \lambda^-\sum_{c=1}^{k}||\mathbf{u}_c||_2 + \gamma^-\sum_{c=1}^{k^-}||\mathbf{u}_c^-||_2 + \delta^-||\mathbf{M}^-||_1 \tag{20}$$

The respective gradients of the objective function L^- are equal to:

$$\frac{\partial L^-(\mathbf{U},\mathbf{U}^-,\mathbf{M}^-)}{\partial_{\mathbf{u}_i}} = \sum_{i\in\mathcal{N}, v\in\mathcal{N}_i^-} \frac{\exp(-\mathbf{u}_i{}^\top\mathbf{u}_v)}{[1+\exp(-\mathbf{u}_i{}^\top\mathbf{u}_v)]^2}\mathbf{u}_v + \sum_{i\in\mathcal{N}, v\in\mathcal{N}_i^-} \frac{\exp(-\mathbf{u}_i{}^\top\mathbf{M}^-\mathbf{u}_v^-)}{[1+\exp(-\mathbf{u}_i{}^\top\mathbf{M}^-\mathbf{u}_v^-)]^2}\mathbf{M}^-\mathbf{u}_v^- + 2\lambda^-\sum_{c=1}^{k}(\mathbf{u}_i)^c \tag{21}$$

$$\frac{\partial L^-(\mathbf{U},\mathbf{U}^-,\mathbf{M}^-)}{\partial_{\mathbf{u}_i^-}} = -\sum_{i\in\mathcal{N}, v\in\mathcal{N}_i^-} \frac{\exp(-\mathbf{u}_i^{-\top}\mathbf{u}_v^-)}{1+\exp(-\mathbf{u}_i^{-\top}\mathbf{u}_v^-)}\mathbf{u}_v^- + \sum_{i\in\mathcal{N}, v\in\mathcal{N}_i^-} \frac{\exp(-\mathbf{u}_i{}^\top\mathbf{M}^-\mathbf{u}_v^-)}{[1+\exp(-\mathbf{u}_i{}^\top\mathbf{M}^-\mathbf{u}_v^-)]^2}\mathbf{u}_i{}^\top\mathbf{M}^- + 2\gamma^-\sum_{c=1}^{k^-}(\mathbf{u}_i^-)^c \tag{22}$$

$$\frac{\partial L^-(\mathbf{U},\mathbf{U}^-,\mathbf{M}^-)}{\partial_{\mathbf{M}^-}} = \sum_{i\in\mathcal{N}, v\in\mathcal{N}_i^-} \frac{\exp(-\mathbf{u}_i{}^\top\mathbf{M}^-\mathbf{u}_v^-)}{[1+\exp(-\mathbf{u}_i{}^\top\mathbf{M}^-\mathbf{u}_v^-)]^2}\mathbf{u}_i\mathbf{u}_v^{-\top} + \delta^-\sum_{c=1}^{k}\sum_{d=1}^{k^-} sign(\mathbf{M}^-_{cd}) \tag{23}$$

Similarly, with the gradients in Eq.(21)-(23) we optimize Eq. (20) and calculate the three matrices/variables $\mathbf{U}$, $\mathbf{U}^-$ and $\mathbf{M}^-$. Having computed the three matrices we calculate the weighting matrix $\mathbf{W}^-$ in Eq. (16) with users' preferences and foes' distrust degrees.

5 EXPERIMENTS

5.1 Evaluation Setup

We evaluate our experiments on a real-world dataset from Epinions[3] [7], also used in related studies [5, 6, 19]. This dataset contains n=119,867 users, m=676,436 product-items and 12,328,927 ratings, with 452,123 trust and 92,417 distrust relationships. We split the dataset into the training and test sets. Unless stated otherwise, in our experiments we consider the 70% of the ratings as training set, and exploit all trust and distrust relationships. To determine the parameters of each examined model, the training set is further split into two subsets: the cross-validation training set and the cross-validation test set.

To remove user bias from our results, we consider an item as relevant if a user has rated it above her average ratings, and irrelevant otherwise. For users with less than five ratings, we consider

[3] http://www.trustlet.org/epinions.html

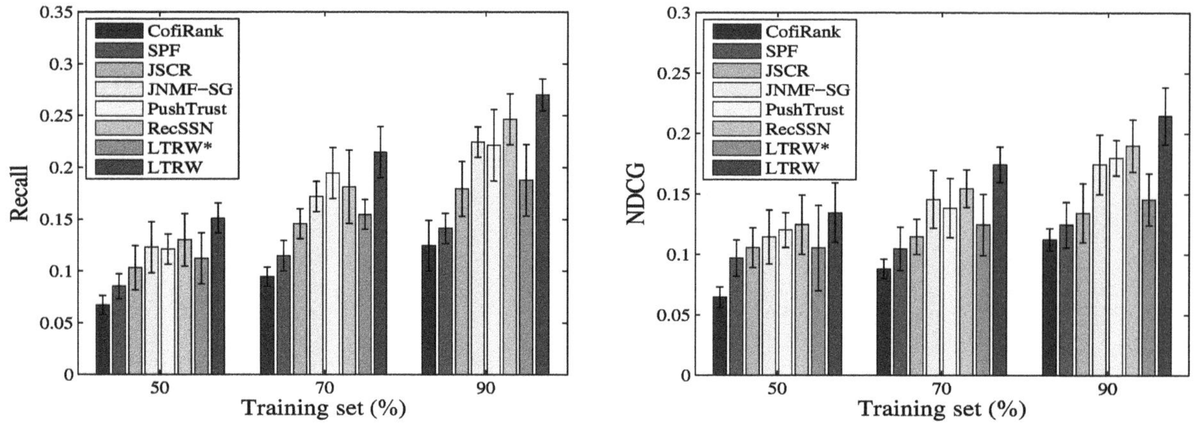

(a) (b)

Figure 1: Effect on (a) recall and (b) NDCG, when varying the size of the training set.

the most highly rated item as relevant. To evaluate the top-N recommendation performance of the examined models we report the ranking-based metrics recall and Normalized Discounted Cumulative Gain (NDCG) [4, 21, 33]. Recall is the ratio of the relevant items in the top-N ranked list over all the relevant items for each user. NDCG measures the ranking of the relevant items in the top-N list. For each user the Discounted Cumulative Gain (DCG) is defined as: $DCG@N = \sum_{j=1}^{N} \frac{2^{rel_j}-1}{\log_2 j+1}$, where rel_j represents the relevance score of item j, that is binary in our case, i.e., relevant or irrelevant. NDCG is the ratio of DCG/iDCG, where iDCG is the ideal DCG value given the ratings in the test set. We repeated our experiment five times, and we report mean values and standard deviations of recall and NDCG over the five runs.

5.2 Compared Methods

We compare our proposed approach with the following baseline methods:

- **CofiRank** [30]: a baseline learning to rank model that ignores users' trust and distrust relationships.
- **SPF** [3]: a trust-based probabilistic model that performs Social Poisson factorization, to match user latent preferences for items with the latent influences of her friends. This model considers only trust relationships.
- **JSCR** [21]: a trust-based learning to rank model that focuses on the top of the list, accounting how well the selections of trust friends have been ranked. This model exploits only trust relationships as well.

We also evaluate the performance of the following trust and distrust-based models:

- **JNMF-SG** [19]: a method that co-factorizes user-item and user-cluster associations, by partitioning users into clusters with a spectral clustering approach based on users' trust and distrust relationships.
- **PushTrust** [5]: a recommendation strategy to compute the latent features of users, based on users' trust and distrust relationships. PushTrust also considers the neutral relationships, aiming to rank the neutral users' latent features after the friends' latent features and before those of the foes.
- **RecSSN** [26]: a recommendation method in social signed networks, that considers trust and distrust relationships when generating recommendations. RecSSN captures both local and global information from the signed graph and then exploits both types of information in a matrix factorization technique with users' preferences.
- **LTRW***: a variant of our approach that avoids the weighting strategy of Section 4.2. In LTRW* we set $\mathbf{W}^+ \leftarrow \mathbf{A}^+$ and $\mathbf{W}^- \leftarrow \mathbf{A}^-$. This variant is used to show the importance of our weighting strategy in our learning to rank model when it is missing.
- **LTRW**: the proposed learning to rank model with our weighting strategy to balance the influences of friends and foes on users' preferences when generating recommendations.

The parameters of the examined methods have been determined via cross-validation (Section 5.1) and in our experiments we report the best results. The parameter analysis of building the trust and distrust-preference user latent spaces in our weighting strategy is further studied in Section 5.6.

5.3 Performance Evaluation

We evaluate the performance of the examined methods by varying the number of ratings in the training set, using all trust and distrust relationships. In this set of experiments we set the length of the recommendation list to top-N=20. Fig. 1(a)-(b) show the effect on recall and NDCG, respectively. We can make the following observations:

- CofiRank has limited performance as it does not exploit users' trust or distrust relationships, thus being negatively affected by the sparsity in users' preferences when reducing the training set sizes. Compared to the baseline method of CofiRank, the trust-based methods SPF and JSCR improve recall and NDCG, as both methods use the selections of trust friends, as well as they capture the users' preferences and the friends' influence in their learning strategies.

- Clearly, the competitive methods of JNMF-SG, PushTrust and RecSSN that generate recommendations with trust and distrust relationships can significantly boost the recommendation accuracy. This indicates that both the selections of friends and foes are important in users' personalized recommendations.
- Evaluated against the proposed LRTW model, the LTRW* variant significantly reduces the recall and NDCG metrics. This occurs because LTRW* does not apply the weighting strategy of Section 4.2, hence it does not learn the influences of users' preferences with friends' trust and foes' distrust degrees. Consequently, the selections of social friends and foes dominate the user's personalized preferences.
- Using the paired t-test ($p < 0.05$), we found out that the proposed LTRW model is superior over all methods, achieving an average relative improvement of 14.67% and 11.25% in terms of recall and NDCG, respectively, compared to the second best method (PushTrust or RecSSN). This happens because LTRW does not only perform the weighting strategy to balance the influences of friends and foes, but also focusses on the ranking performance at the top of the recommendation list. On the contrary, the competitive methods of PushTrust and RecSSN do not account for the ranking performance in their learning strategies.

Fig. 2 shows the effect on recall, with changes in the length of the top-N recommendation list. In this set of experiments we train our models with 70% of the ratings using all social relationships. Again, LTRW beats its competitors in all settings. Evaluated against the second best method, LTRW achieves a relative improvement of 13.48% on average.

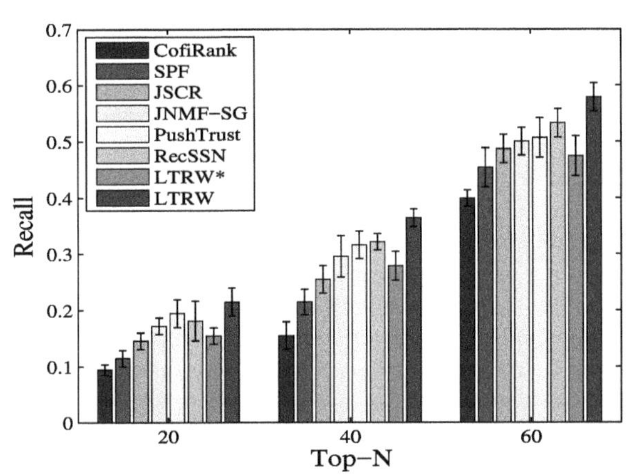

Figure 2: Effect on recall when varying the top-N rec.

5.4 Effect of Missing Social Relationships

In the next set of experiments, we evaluated the performance of the examined models when a part of social relationships is missing. This experiment is performed to measure the performance of models when not all social relationships are available. We ensure that the same percentage of trust and distrust relationships is removed when downsizing the number of relationships. In this set of experiments CofiRank is used for reference as its performance is not affected when varying the percentage of relationships. Fig. 3 presents the effect on recall with top-N=20 with the models trained on 70% of the ratings. We can observe that all social-based models that exploit users' relationships, either trust-based or trust and distrust-based ones, are negatively affected when less relationships are used, having a significant drop on recall. In particular, when exploiting the 75% and 50% of all available relationships the average drops on recall of all social-based methods are 20.26% and 30.94%, respectively. These results indicate that the numbers of trust and distrust relationships play a crucial role in trust-based and trust and distrust-based models when computing recommendations. Evaluated against the second best method our LTRW model maintains the quality of recommendations high, achieving an average improvement of 13.14% in this set of experiments.

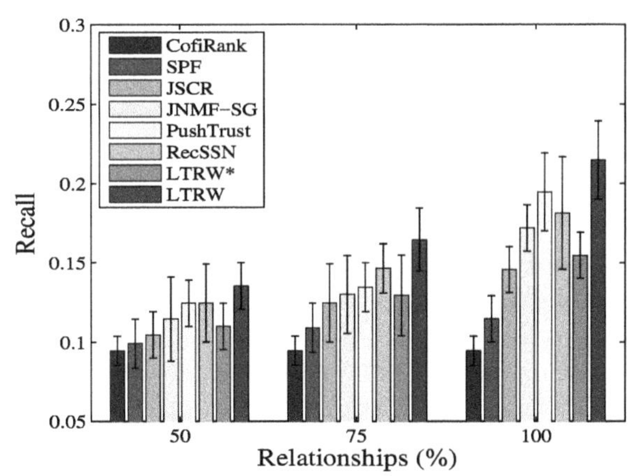

Figure 3: Effect on recall when varying the percentage of social (trust and distrust) relationships.

5.5 Discussion

Exploiting both trust and distrust relationships can clearly leverage the recommendation accuracy. As shown in our experiments all trust and distrust-based models that use the selections of friends and foes outperform the baseline model of CofiRank, and the trust-based models of SPF and JSCR. However, the performances of trust and distrust-based models vary by following different strategies when exploiting users' trust and distrust relationships. JNMF-SG first forms a signed graph based on trust and distrust relationships, and then tries to capture the correlations of friends and foes in the clusters of the graph, on condition that friends and foes should not be clustered together. The final recommendations are produced by co-factorizing the cluster-based associations and the users' preferences. Instead, PushTrust considers the latent features of neutral users, that is users that have no relation to a certain user, and then rank the neutral users' latent features below those of the friends' and above the foes' latent features. However, PushTrust does not focus on the ranking performance at the top of the list in a way that ignores the rankings of friends' and foes' selected items in the list, thus having lower recommendation accuracy than the proposed LTRW model. RecSSN calculates the correlations of users and friends/foes in the signed graph based on friends'/foes' circles in the graph. Also, RecSSN exploits the selections of users that have high reputation in the graph, assuming that users trust the selections of users with high reputation. Nonetheless, RecSSN does not focus on the ranking performance when producing recommendation, as well as does not capture well the correlations of users' preferences with trust degrees in friends' circles and distrust degrees in foes' circles, which explains the limited performance of RecSSN, compared to LTRW.

The proposed LTRW model beats all the competitive trust and distrust-based models in all sets of experiments. LTRW significantly boosts the recommendation accuracy by exploiting two key factors. First it focusses at the ranking performance at the top of the list, by taking into account that users' and friends' relevant items should be ranked high in the list, while those of the foes should be ranked low. In addition, the weighting strategy has a significant contribution to our model, to better capture users' preferences with friends' trust and foes' distrust degrees in the intermediate trust and distrust-preference user latent spaces. Our experiments demonstrate the crucial role of our weighting strategy in the proposed LTRW model, as its LTRW* variant has poor performance with an average relative drop of 27.74% in all experiments.

5.6 Analysis of Trust/Distrust-Preference User Latent Spaces

In this section we study the influence of trust and distrust-preference user latent spaces in the LRTW model, corresponding to matrices $\mathbf{M}^+ \in \mathbb{R}^{k \times k^+}$ and $\mathbf{M}^- \in \mathbb{R}^{k \times k^-}$ of Section 4.2. First, we fix the parameters of the ℓ_2 norm regularization terms $\lambda^+ = \gamma^+ = 1e-04$ in Eq. (12) and $\lambda^- = \gamma^- = 1e-04$ in Eq. (20), as we observed that higher and lower values result in model overfitting and underfitting, respectively. Fig. 4(a)-(b) report the effect on recall, when varying parameters δ^+ and δ^-, having impact on the respective ℓ_1 norm regularization terms of $\mathbf{M}^+$ in Eq. (12) and on $\mathbf{M}^-$ in Eq. (20). LTRW achieves the best performance when we set $\delta^+ = 1e-03$, where higher values of δ^+ force $\mathbf{M}^+$ to be more sparse when optimizing Eq. (12). Similarly, we select $\delta^- = 1e-02$ when computing $\mathbf{M}^-$. An interesting observation is that we fix $\delta^+ < \delta^-$, mainly because the intermediate space $\mathbf{M}^+$ with users' preferences and friends' trust degrees is less sparse than the space of $\mathbf{M}^-$ with user' preferences and foes' distrust degrees, as there are less foes than friends (Section 5.1). This complies with several studies reporting that users tend to establish less distrust relationships than trust ones [26–28].

Fig. 5 presents the effect on recall with changes in the user dimensions of the $k \times k^+$ trust-preference space of $\mathbf{M}^+$ and $k \times k^-$ distrust preference space of $\mathbf{M}^-$. In this set of experiments we vary the user latent dimensions from 10 to 100 by a step of 10. As shown in Fig. 5 the best performance is achieved when $k = 60$, $k^+ = 50$ and

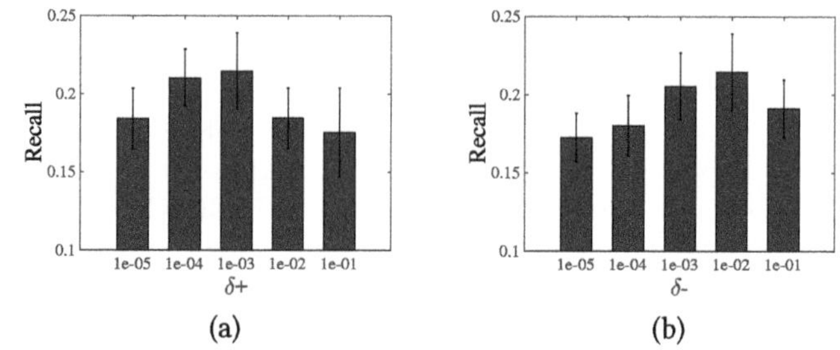

Figure 4: Effect on recall with changes in (a) δ^+ and (b) δ^-.

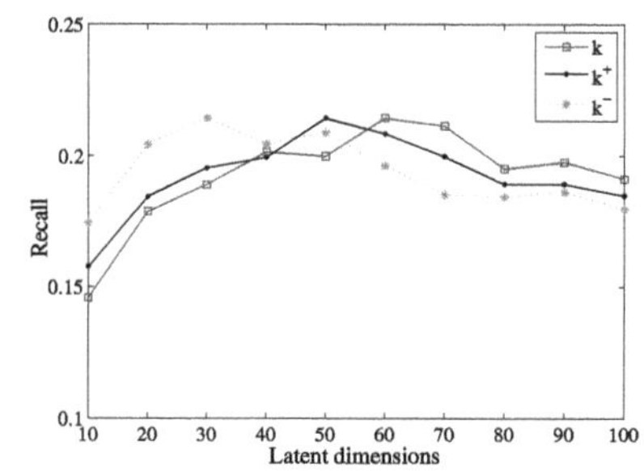

Figure 5: Effect on recall with changes in the user latent dimensions of trust/distrust-preference spaces.

$k^- = 30$, as the model becomes unstable for higher latent dimensions. The model has limited performance when selecting lower latent dimensions, as it does not capture well users' preferences with friends' trust and foes' distrust degrees in the intermediate spaces of $\mathbf{M}^+$ and $\mathbf{M}^-$, respectively.

6 CONCLUSIONS

We presented LTRW, a learning to rank model with trust and distrust relationships, aiming to improve the performance at the top of the list. We introduced a weighting strategy to balance the influences of friends' and foes' selections in our model. In particular we build two intermediate trust/distrust-preference user latent spaces to capture the correlations of users' preferences with friends' trust and foes' distrust degrees, accordingly. Our experiments demonstrate the superiority of the proposed LTRW model over several baselines, achieving a relative improvement of 13.13%, evaluated against the second best model.

Users in recommender systems tend to explore new items, instead of interacting with items they have previously liked in the past, making users' preferences change over time [14, 31]. In addition, while users interact with each other, they establish new relationships and adapt existing ones [2, 27]. This means that users' trust and distrust relationships evolve too. As future work we plan to investigate the performance of our learning to rank model with evolving trust and distrust relationships, to capture users' preference dynamics in recommender systems [22, 23].

ACKNOWLEDGMENTS

Dimitrios Rafailidis was supported by the COMPLEXYS and INFORTECH Research Institutes of University of Mons.

REFERENCES

[1] Charu C. Aggarwal. 2016. *Recommender Systems - The Textbook.* Springer.

[2] Yi Cen, Rentao Gu, and Yuefeng Ji. 2013. Sign Inference for Dynamic Signed Networks via Dictionary Learning. *J. Applied Mathematics* 2013 (2013), 708581:1–708581:10.

[3] Allison June-Barlow Chaney, David M. Blei, and Tina Eliassi-Rad. 2015. A Probabilistic Model for Using Social Networks in Personalized Item Recommendation. In *RecSys.* 43–50.

[4] Konstantina Christakopoulou and Arindam Banerjee. 2015. Collaborative Ranking with a Push at the Top. In *WWW.* 205–215.

[5] Rana Forsati, Iman Barjasteh, Farzan Masrour, Abdol-Hossein Esfahanian, and Hayder Radha. 2015. PushTrust: An Efficient Recommendation Algorithm by Leveraging Trust and Distrust Relations. In *RecSys.* 51–58.

[6] Rana Forsati, Mehrdad Mahdavi, Mehrnoush Shamsfard, and Mohamed Sarwat. 2014. Matrix Factorization with Explicit Trust and Distrust Side Information for Improved Social Recommendation. *ACM Trans. Inf. Syst.* 32, 4 (2014), 17:1–17:38.

[7] Ramanathan V. Guha, Ravi Kumar, Prabhakar Raghavan, and Andrew Tomkins. 2004. Propagation of trust and distrust. In *WWW.* 403–412.

[8] Guibing Guo, Jie Zhang, and Neil Yorke-Smith. 2015. TrustSVD: Collaborative Filtering with Both the Explicit and Implicit Influence of User Trust and of Item Ratings. In *AAAI.* 123–129.

[9] Prateek Jain, Praneeth Netrapalli, and Sujay Sanghavi. 2013. Low-rank Matrix Completion Using Alternating Minimization. In *STOC.* 665–674.

[10] Mohsen Jamali and Martin Ester. 2009. *TrustWalker*: a random walk model for combining trust-based and item-based recommendation. In *KDD.* 397–406.

[11] Mohsen Jamali and Martin Ester. 2009. Using a trust network to improve top-N recommendation. In *RecSys.* 181–188.

[12] Mohsen Jamali and Martin Ester. 2010. A matrix factorization technique with trust propagation for recommendation in social networks. In *RecSys.* 135–142.

[13] Yehuda Koren. 2008. Factorization meets the neighborhood: a multifaceted collaborative filtering model. In *KDD.* 426–434.

[14] Yehuda Koren. 2010. Collaborative filtering with temporal dynamics. *Commun. ACM* 53, 4 (2010), 89–97.

[15] Artus Krohn-Grimberghe, Lucas Drumond, Christoph Freudenthaler, and Lars Schmidt-Thieme. 2012. Multi-relational Matrix Factorization Using Bayesian Personalized Ranking for Social Network Data. In *WSDM.* 173–182.

[16] Hao Ma, Irwin King, and Michael R. Lyu. 2009. Learning to recommend with social trust ensemble. In *SIGIR.* 203–210.

[17] Hao Ma, Michael R. Lyu, and Irwin King. 2009. Learning to recommend with trust and distrust relationships. In *RecSys.* 189–196.

[18] Hao Ma, Haixuan Yang, Michael R. Lyu, and Irwin King. 2008. SoRec: social recommendation using probabilistic matrix factorization. In *CIKM.* 931–940.

[19] Dimitrios Rafailidis. 2016. Modeling trust and distrust information in recommender systems via joint matrix factorization with signed graphs. In *SAC.* 1060–1065.

[20] Dimitrios Rafailidis and Fabio Crestani. 2016. Collaborative Ranking with Social Relationships for Top-N Recommendations. In *SIGIR.* 785–788.

[21] Dimitrios Rafailidis and Fabio Crestani. 2016. Joint Collaborative Ranking with Social Relationships in Top-N Recommendation. In *CIKM.* 1393–1402.

[22] Dimitrios Rafailidis and Alexandros Nanopoulos. 2014. Modeling the dynamics of user preferences in coupled tensor factorization. In *RecSys.* 321–324.

[23] Dimitrios Rafailidis and Alexandros Nanopoulos. 2016. Modeling Users Preference Dynamics and Side Information in Recommender Systems. *IEEE Trans. Systems, Man, and Cybernetics: Systems* 46, 6 (2016), 782–792.

[24] Steffen Rendle, Christoph Freudenthaler, Zeno Gantner, and Lars Schmidt-Thieme. 2009. BPR: Bayesian Personalized Ranking from Implicit Feedback. In *UAI.* 452–461.

[25] Yue Shi, Alexandros Karatzoglou, Linas Baltrunas, Martha Larson, Nuria Oliver, and Alan Hanjalic. 2012. CLiMF: Learning to Maximize Reciprocal Rank with Collaborative Less-is-more Filtering. In *RecSys.* 139–146.

[26] Jiliang Tang, Charu C. Aggarwal, and Huan Liu. 2016. Recommendations in Signed Social Networks. In *WWW.* 31–40.

[27] Jiliang Tang, Yi Chang, Charu Aggarwal, and Huan Liu. 2016. A Survey of Signed Network Mining in Social Media. *ACM Comput. Surv.* 49, 3 (2016), 42:1–42:37.

[28] Jiliang Tang, Xia Hu, Yi Chang, and Huan Liu. 2014. Predictability of Distrust with Interaction Data. In *CIKM.* 181–190.

[29] Patricia Victor, Chris Cornelis, Martine De Cock, and Ankur Teredesai. 2011. Trust- and Distrust-Based Recommendations for Controversial Reviews. *IEEE Intelligent Systems* 26, 1 (2011), 48–55.

[30] Markus Weimer, Alexandros Karatzoglou, Quoc V. Le, and Alexander J. Smola. 2007. COFI RANK - Maximum Margin Matrix Factorization for Collaborative Ranking. In *NIPS.* 1593–1600.

[31] Liang Xiong, Xi Chen, Tzu-Kuo Huang, Jeff G. Schneider, and Jaime G. Carbonell. 2010. Temporal Collaborative Filtering with Bayesian Probabilistic Tensor Factorization. In *SDM.* 211–222.

[32] Xiwang Yang, Harald Steck, Yang Guo, and Yong Liu. 2012. On Top-k Recommendation Using Social Networks. In *RecSys.* 67–74.

[33] Tong Zhao, Julian McAuley, and Irwin King. 2014. Leveraging Social Connections to Improve Personalized Ranking for Collaborative Filtering. In *CIKM.* 261–270.

Metalearning for Context-aware Filtering: Selection of Tensor Factorization Algorithms

Tiago Cunha
Faculdade de Engenharia da Universidade do Porto
Rua Dr. Roberto Frias
Porto, Portugal 4200-465
tiagodscunha@fe.up.pt

Carlos Soares
Faculdade de Engenharia da Universidade do Porto
Rua Dr. Roberto Frias
Porto, Portugal 4200-465
csoares@fe.up.pt

André C.P.L.F. de Carvalho
Universidade de São Paulo, ICMC
Rua Trabalhador Sancarlense
São Carlos, São Paulo, Brasil
andre@icmc.usp.br

ABSTRACT

This work addresses the problem of selecting Tensor Factorization algorithms for the Context-aware Filtering recommendation task using a metalearning approach. The most important challenge of applying metalearning on new problems is the development of useful measures able to characterize the data, i.e. metafeatures. We propose an extensive and exhaustive set of metafeatures to characterize Context-aware Filtering recommendation task. These metafeatures take advantage of the tensor's hierarchical structure via slice operations. The algorithm selection task is addressed as a Label Ranking problem, which ranks the Tensor Factorization algorithms according to their expected performance, rather than simply selecting the algorithm that is expected to obtain the best performance. A comprehensive experimental work is conducted on both levels, baselevel and metalevel (Tensor Factorization and Label Ranking, respectively). The results show that the proposed metafeatures lead to metamodels that tend to rank Tensor Factorization algorithms accurately and that the selected algorithms present high recommendation performance.

CCS CONCEPTS

•**Information systems → Recommender systems;** *Data mining;* •**Computing methodologies → Machine learning;**

KEYWORDS

Context-aware Filtering, Tensor Factorization, Metalearning, Algorithm Selection, Label Ranking

1 INTRODUCTION

Recommender Systems (RSs) deal with the information overload problem by recommending potentially interesting items to users [3]. Several recommendation strategies exist, including Collaborative Filtering (CF) and Context aware Filtering (CAF). In this work, we focus on CAF recommendations, more specifically regarding the usage of Tensor Factorization (TF) algorithms.

RecSys'17, August 27–31, 2017, Como, Italy
 ISBN 978-1-4503-4652-8/17/08...$15.00
DOI: http://dx.doi.org/10.1145/3109859.3109899

Despite the large amount of research dedicated to RS, there are still several challenges that need to be addressed. One of them is how to choose the best CAF algorithm(s) for a given dataset. This study investigates the use of a Metalearning (MtL) approach for CAF algorithm selection. Although the area of algorithm selection for RS has been growing [5, 9, 14, 16, 22, 29], to the best of our knowledge, CAF algorithm selection has never been addressed.

MtL approaches to the algorithm selection problem consist of describing the datasets (i.e. tensors) with quantitative characteristics (i.e. metafeatures) and the relative performance of a set of algorithms. This creates the so called metadata. Learning algorithms can then be applied to this metadata to extract patterns and used them for the selection of the best algorithm(s) for new datasets/problems. MtL approaches are thus organized in base- and metalevels. In this work, the baselevel refers to the CAF recommendation problem using TF and the metalevel is related to the selection of the best ranking of algorithm using Label Ranking (LR).

One of the main challenges of developing MtL approaches is the design of the metafeatures. Metafeatures must 1) contain information about the data that affects the behavior of algorithms and 2) be computationally efficient [7]. Although MtL approaches for CF algorithms have been published [5, 9, 14, 16, 22, 29], given the difference in the structure of the data (matrices vs tensors), a completely new set of metafeatures is required for CAF. Another important issue addressed in this work is related to the type of MtL task. Often, MtL problems are addressed as classification tasks. This means that, given a new problem, a single algorithm is selected. However, it is well-known that this approach has important shortcomings, namely, when the selected algorithm fails, the user is left unsupported [7]. Hence, MtL for algorithm selection should be addressed as a LR task, in which the output is a ranking of candidate algorithms [7]. Thus, the most important contributions are:

- **Label ranking approach to MtL:** metamodels are created using LR to predict a ranking of TF algorithms.
- **Metafeatures for tensors designed using a systematic framework:** tensors are described in an extensive and exhaustive fashion by taking advantage of the tensor's hierarchical structure and slice operations.
- **Interpretation of the metamodel:** the importance of the metafeatures in the performance of the metamodel for selection of TF algorithms is analyzed.

This document is organized as follows: Section 2 presents the theoretical background on all areas involved in this work; Section 3 devotes itself to the proposal of metafeatures for tensors, while Section 4 presents the experimental work undertaken at both the base- and metalevels. The results and their analysis are presented in Section 5, while the conclusions are summarized in Section 6.

2 RELATED WORK

2.1 Recommender Systems

RSs attempt to extract patterns from data, which have the potential to explain and predict recommendations of new items. There are, however, several different strategies to make said recommendations. This work focuses on CF and its extension for CAF through TF.

CF recommendations are based on the premise that a user will probably like the items favored by a similar user. CF employs the feedback from each individual user to recommend items to similar users [50]. Such feedback is represented in a rating matrix, a data structure which is described as $R^{U \times I}$, representing a set of users U, where $u \in \{1, ..., N\}$ and a set of items I, where $i \in \{1, ..., M\}$. Each element of this matrix (R_{ui}) is the feedback provided by user u for item i. The recommendations are typically achieved via Nearest Neighbor [12, 37] or Matrix Factorization techniques [25, 31].

CAF is an extension of CF that uses additional information, for instance time or location, to increase the accuracy of the recommendations [2, 6]. The motivation lies in the premise that the contextual dimensions contains additional useful information to the information in the user and item dimensions in CF. For instance, taking into account the time of the day, the recommendation may capture the difference in music styles a user listens to at work and at home. There are several ways to incorporate contextual information in RS [4], but we focus on the combination of CF and CAF.

Using context in recommendations requires a change in paradigm. The relationship $R : User \times Item \longrightarrow Rating$, is now represented as $R : User \times Item \times Context \longrightarrow Rating$, where $User$ and $Item$ refer to the user and item domains and $Context$ is related to the contextual domain [4]. This change in paradigm is essential to understand why tensors are the ideal data structure for CAF: in the same way the CF paradigm required a matrix (i.e. bidimensional array or 2-order tensor) to hold the feedback values, the most natural representation for the newer paradigm is a 3-order tensor (i.e. multidimensional array).

2.2 Tensor Factorization

The first step for TF is tensor decomposition. This refers to the the way the original tensor is modeled in an intermediary step before the application of the factorization algorithm. The two most popular decomposition methods are CANDECOMP/PARAFAC (CP) [8, 18] and Tucker [45]. Despite the existence of other methods [24], we focus only on these since these are the only ones used in CAF.

The CP decomposition factorizes a tensor into a sum of component rank-one tensors (see Figure 1). Being a rank-one tensor means it can be written as the outer product of N vectors, i.e. $\mathcal{X} = a(1) \circ a(2) \circ ... \circ a(N)$, where $\circ$ represents the outer product. The CP decomposition of a third-order tensor $\mathcal{X} \in \mathbb{R}^{I \times J \times K}$ is [24]:

$$\mathcal{X} \approx \sum_{r=1}^{R} a_r \circ b_r \circ c_r \quad (1)$$

where R is a positive integer and $a_r \in \mathbb{R}^I$, $b_r \in \mathbb{R}^J$ and $c_r \in \mathbb{R}^K$.

The Tucker decomposition transforms a tensor into a core tensor multiplied by a matrix along each mode [24]. Therefore, the decomposition of a tensor $\mathcal{X} \in \mathbb{R}^{I \times J \times K}$ (see Figure 2) is:

$$\mathcal{X} \approx \mathcal{G} \times_1 A \times_2 B \times_3 C = \sum_{p=1}^{P} \sum_{q=1}^{Q} \sum_{r=1}^{R} g_{pqr} a_p \circ b_q \circ c_r \quad (2)$$

where $A \in \mathbb{R}^{I \times P}$, $B \in \mathbb{R}^{J \times Q}$ and $C \in \mathbb{R}^{K \times R}$ are the factor matrices and $G \in \mathbb{R}^{P \times Q \times R}$ is the core tensor. The operator $\times_N$ refers to the N-mode product between the tensor and a matrix.

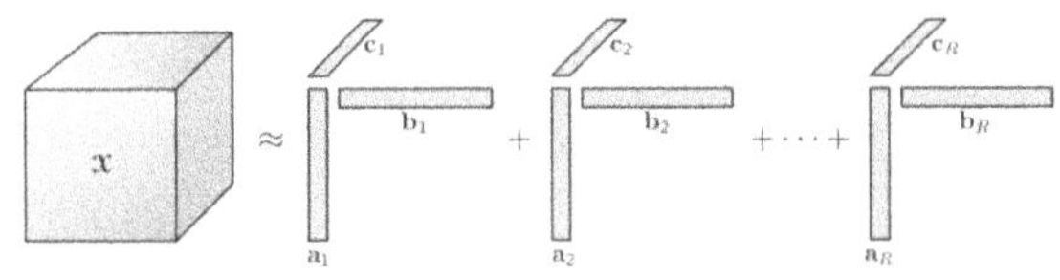

Figure 1: CP decomposition [24].

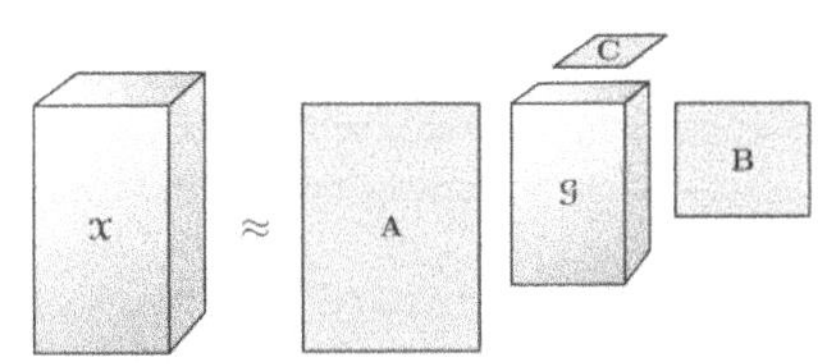

Figure 2: Tucker decomposition [24].

Different decompositions require different algorithms to perform the factorization. While CP is typically approached using Alternating Least Squares (ALS), Tucker decomposition takes advantage of Higher Order Singular Value Decomposition (HOSVD) [24].

2.3 Context aware Filtering with Tensors

CAF using TF has been widely used in the context of RS. The first approaches to apply TF to RS used a HOSVD algorithm and Tucker decomposition, but with different contextual dimensions: time [23] and semantic tags [42, 43]. Recent papers shifted towards the usage of implicit feedback and to replace Tucker by CP decompositions. While some focused the optimization of Mean Average Precision as the loss function [39], others have adapted ALS to perform the factorization [21] and even proposed Bayesian Probabilistic approaches to model the factorization [49]. Some works look at the problem in non-conventional ways: either by applying Factorization Machines instead of TF algorithms [34] or by changing the tensor to a so called Contextual Operating Tensor [28].

2.4 Metalearning

Metalearning (MtL) is concerned with relating characteristics of the data with the behavior of algorithms [46]. It has been extensively used for algorithm selection [27, 33, 35, 36, 41]. The algorithm selection task can be viewed as a learning problem itself, by casting it as a predictive task. For such, it uses a metadataset, where each meta-example corresponds to a dataset. For each meta-example, the predictive features are characteristics (metafeatures) extracted from the corresponding dataset and the targets are the performance (metalabels) of algorithms when applied to the dataset [7].

One of the main challenges in MtL is to define which are the metafeatures that effectively describe how strongly a dataset matches the bias of each algorithm [7]. The MtL literature divides the metafeatures into three main groups [7, 38, 46]:

- statistical and/or information-theoretical measures (obtain numerical data descriptors using standard formulas);
- landmarking-based properties (performance measures obtained from the fast application of algorithms to the datasets);
- model-based characteristics (extraction of properties from fast/simplified models induced from the datasets).

As far as we know, there is no prior work on the algorithm selection for tensors in CAF. There are, however, a few approaches to select CF algorithms [5, 9, 14, 16, 22, 29], which we use as guidelines. Specifically, we inspire ourselves on the statistical and/or information-theoretical measures used in the related work to describe the tensor. However, we must point out the significant gap in difficulty between these two tasks: while in CF one only looks towards describing a matrix, in CAF a much more complex structure is tackled: the tensor. This requires a completely novel and more complex approach. To organize the metafeatures in a more interpretable way, we use a framework [32], described next.

2.5 Systematic metafeatures framework

The systematic metafeatures framework [32] requires three main elements: objects o, functions f and post-functions pf. The process applies each function to each object and, afterwards, each post-function to that outcome in order to generate a single metafeature value. Thus, this framework is represented as: $\{o\}.\{f\}.\{pf\}$. An example is the average sum of ratings for all users.

One important property of this framework is its recursiveness. If one poses the problem in this way, then the outcome of an inner level (IL) application of the framework can be used as the result of an outer level (OL) function. This means that the generic description $\{o\}.\{f\}.\{pf\}$ can be transformed into:

$$\begin{aligned}&\{\text{OL-}o\}.\{\text{OL-}f\}.\{\text{OL-}pf\} = \\ &\{\text{OL-}o\}.\Big[\{\text{IL-}o\}.\{\text{IL-}f\}.\{\text{IL-}pf\}\Big].\{\text{OL-}pf\}\end{aligned} \tag{3}$$

3 METAFEATURES FOR TENSORS

3.1 Tensor basics

Consider a third-order tensor $T \in \mathbb{R}^{U \times I \times C}$ with the dimensions U, I and C, referring specifically to the User, Item and Context dimensions [24]. The dimensions can be characterized as a sequence of ordered and independent elements: $U = (u_x)_{x=1}^{L}$, $I = (i_y)_{y=1}^{M}$ and $C = (c_z)_{z=1}^{N}$, with L, M and N are the maximum number of users, items and contexts, respectively.

Note that by considering only the dimensions U and I, one refers to the CF data structure, i.e. the rating matrix. The contextual dimension C is appended to the tensor, hence enabling another equally important decision factor for the recommendation problem. Each dimension is related to one another in an orthogonal basis, meaning that any point in this data structure is simultaneously mapped on all dimensions. This enables multi-dimensional relationships, which motivate the usage of TF algorithms in CAF [2].

3.2 Tensor slices

In a tensor, data can be queried in several perspectives and with different levels of detail. By selecting specific values on one or more dimensions, one obtains different data structures which contain different patterns. The operation that allows the retrieval of such data structures is known as slice operation [24]. In the context of this work, there are two well defined slice operations, which we name vector-level and matrix-level. The results of such operations are vectors or matrices of ratings, respectively. The slice operations are formalized in Equations 4 and 5 for the matrix and vector-levels, respectively. When an element is not provided, it is represented as $\varnothing$. Considering user u, item i and context c, the different slice operations can be formalized as:

$$\begin{aligned}SLICE(T,u,\varnothing,\varnothing) &= \bigcup_{y=1}^{M}\bigcup_{z=1}^{N} T_{[u,i_y,c_z]} \in \mathbb{R}^{I \times C}\\ SLICE(T,\varnothing,i,\varnothing) &= \bigcup_{x=1}^{L}\bigcup_{z=1}^{N} T_{[u_x,i,c_z]} \in \mathbb{R}^{U \times C}\\ SLICE(T,\varnothing,\varnothing,c) &= \bigcup_{x=1}^{L}\bigcup_{y=1}^{M} T_{[u_x,i_y,c]} \in \mathbb{R}^{U \times I}\end{aligned} \tag{4}$$

$$\begin{aligned}SLICE(T,u,i,\varnothing) &= \bigcup_{z=1}^{N} T_{[u,i,c_z]} \in \mathbb{R}^{C}\\ SLICE(T,u,\varnothing,c) &= \bigcup_{y=1}^{M} T_{[u,i_y,c]} \in \mathbb{R}^{I}\\ SLICE(T,\varnothing,i,c) &= \bigcup_{x=1}^{L} T_{[u_x,i,c]} \in \mathbb{R}^{U}\end{aligned} \tag{5}$$

A representation of the slice operations is shown in Figure 3. Notice that while in Figure 3a, only a specific user u_x is provided, in Figure 3b, an user u_x and an item i_y are both specified. In the first case, the result is a matrix, while the second is a vector.

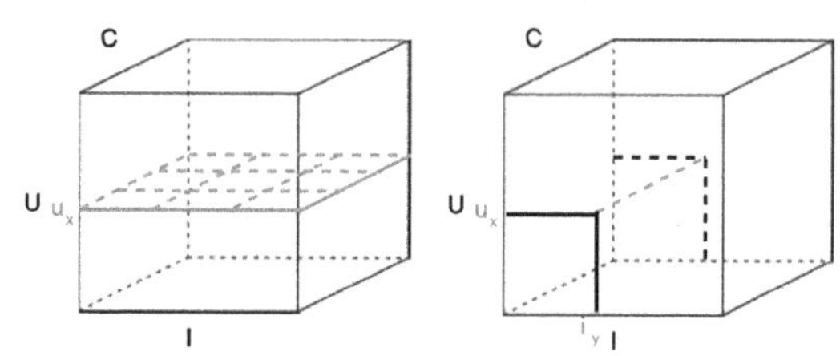

(a) Matrix-level. (b) Vector-level.

Figure 3: Slice operations.

3.3 Metafeatures overview

We now provide an overview of the application of the systematic metafeatures framework (Section 2.5) in terms of objects, functions and post-functions for CAF. The specific details about the metafeatures proposed are given in the following sections.

3.3.1 Objects. Recall that the framework applies functions to a set of objects. Therefore, it is essential to identify suitable objects. An obvious choice of object is the tensor itself. However, since there are few known descriptors for the data structure as whole, one must look beyond. We assume that the vectors and matrices obtained with slice operations (section 3.2) have potential to affect the baselevel algorithm performance. If such assumption is true, then descriptors of these data structures have potential to positively impact the algorithm selection problem. Here, these metafeatures are complemented with global tensor characteristics, such as the Frobenius norm, in order to understand their importance.

The tensor is hierarchically organized in terms of slice operations, as it is described in Figure 4. Three different granularity levels are presented: tensor, matrix and vector. To access the matrix-level data, one fixes one of the dimensions according to a specific element. However, one can also go a granularity level deeper, by providing one additional element of another dimension, reaching the vector-level. It is also possible to go even further, reaching the specific rating. However, this level can be discarded since it cannot be considered a suitable metafeature. By definition, a metafeature is an unique descriptor, representing an aggregated characteristic of a dataset [7]. Since MtL requires several datasets, each with different amounts of users, items and contexts, the metafeatures extracted must be aggregated to create a unique feature which can be extracted in all tensors. Thus, it does not make sense to compute metafeatures based on single values.

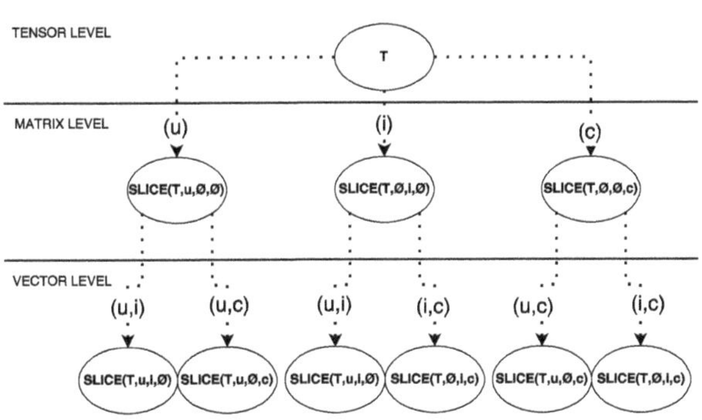

Figure 4: Tensor's structure in terms of slice operations.

Another important aspect of this work is the investigation of relationships among objects and their impact for the selection of algorithms. Hence, besides describing the tensor in several facets, we also attempt to assess the relationships among objects belonging to the same level of slice operations. This approach makes our proposal of metafeatures for CAF a much more difficult problem than it is found in CF [5, 9, 14, 16, 22, 29].

3.3.2 Functions. Following the systematic metafeatures framework, we know that the functions depend on the objects used. Considering the objects studied can be vectors, matrices and the tensor itself, then the task becomes non-trivial. Two properties were identified: the adaptability to the objects and the differentiation between functions that describe a single object or comparisons of objects. The requirements for the different levels in terms of these properties are discussed in Sections 3.4, 3.5 and 3.6.

An important issue concerning our proposal of metafeatures for tensors is that all vectors/matrices to be characterized contain ratings, independently of the type of slice operation employed. This means that since they all share the same data characteristics, one can take advantage of the same functions. This is not true in other MtL scenarios, such as classification and regression [7, 26].

3.3.3 Post-functions. The post-functions to be used must aggregate the result of the application of a function to a set of objects. This means that ideally one should use a large set of statistical properties to describe such outcome. However, due to the combinatorial nature of the framework, this contributes to an explosion of metafeatures to be extracted. Hence, we typically use 3 measures, i.e. one measure for each of the essential elements of univariate analysis: central tendency, dispersion and shape.

3.3.4 Outline. The different metafeatures, organized by level, are described next. The vector-level looks towards describing all the different vectors in a tensor through univariate analysis, yielding structural, statistical and information-theoretical properties. These metafeatures test the assumption that if tensors have different patterns regarding the vectors of one or more dimensions, then the best algorithms will also be different. The matrix-level focuses on describing all the matrices in the tensor through structural and algebraic properties and applies multivariate analysis on the vectors which compose its dimensions. The motivation for these metafeatures lies in testing the assumption that the matrices structure and the relationships among its vectors are informative for the selection of algorithms. This allows to assess whether descriptors of objects or descriptors of interactions among objects hold higher informative power. Lastly, the tensor level extracts structural and algebraic tensor properties and applies multivariate analysis to assess the relationships among its matrices. The motivation for the first is clear: here, we test whether generic tensor descriptors hold informative value which overcomes those of the metafeatures extracted via the remaining slice operations. The second follows the approach also used in the matrix-level.

3.4 Vector-level metafeatures

The vector-level is reached by specific slice operations. We refer to $SLICE(T, u, i, \varnothing)$, $SLICE(T, u, \varnothing, c)$ and $SLICE(T, \varnothing, i, c)$ as **UI**, **UC** and **IC vectors**, respectively. These are the different classes of objects for this metafeatures level.

The functions considered at this level can be categorized according to the properties they represent: structural, statistical and information-theoretical. Structural properties represent the overall dimensions of the vector. We use **size** and **vector sparsity**. Statistical properties characterize the distribution of the ratings. Since this level is concerned with vectors, the metafeatures use functions from univariate analysis [44]. Here, several well defined functions exist: central tendency (**mean**, **mode** and **median**), dispersion (**variance**, **maximum**, **minimum**, **first quartile**, **third quartile** and **standard deviation**) and shape (**skewness** and **kurtosis**). Lastly, one information-theoretical property is used to assess the information within a specific vector: **entropy**.

The post-functions used are: **mean**, **standard deviation** and **skewness**. This creates 126 metafeatures at the vector-level, which can be summarized as:

$$\{\text{UI, UC and IC vectors}\}.\{\text{structural, statistical and information-theoretical properties}\}.\{\text{post-functions}\} \quad (6)$$

3.5 Matrix-level metafeatures

The matrix-level slice operations $SLICE(T, u, \varnothing, \varnothing)$, $SLICE(T, \varnothing, i, \varnothing)$ and $SLICE(T, \varnothing, \varnothing, c)$, are referred to here as **IC**, **UC** and **UI matrices**, respectively. Recall the metafeatures in this level are organized into matrix descriptors and descriptors of the pairwise comparison of the matrix vectors. These are explained next.

3.5.1 Matrix metafeatures. To describe a matrix, structural and algebraic properties can be extracted. Such structural properties are **number of rows**, **number of columns**, **number of ratings**, **matrix sparsity** and the **ratio of rows over columns**. In terms of algebraic properties, only the **norm** can be used for non-square matrices. This limits severely the amount and diversity of properties to extract. To obtain additional properties it is possible to transform the matrix into a squared one, using, for instance, similarity or correlation matrices. Then, properties such as trace, determinant and eigenvalues can be used [19].

Other techniques can also be employed at this stage, such as Matrix Factorization and clustering. These can afterwards be described through a wide range of properties, such as the properties of the factorized matrices or the number and size of clusters found. However, a high computational is expected to compute these metafeatures, which makes them unsuitable for algorithm selection purposes.

The post-functions used at this level are: **mean**, **standard deviation** and **skewness**. Note that 3 properties (number of rows, columns and ratio of rows over columns) are the same for all slices of the same dimension. Therefore, these are not aggregated. The 36 metafeatures produced follow this notation:

$$\{\text{UI, UC and IC matrices}\}.\{\text{structural and algebraic properties}\}.\{\text{post-functions or } \varnothing\} \quad (7)$$

3.5.2 Vector pairwise comparison. These metafeatures describe the relationships among matrix dimensions based on the vectors it contains. The same vectors were already analyzed independently at the vector-level (Section 3.4). Such relationships are assessed using bivariate analysis techniques which do not require dependent variables, since the data used in CAF does not have this property [44].

These pairwise comparisons can be classified as intra or inter-dimensional: while the first focus on comparing, for instance two vectors of users, the other compares a user vector with a context or item vector. This differentiation is required since the nature of the information each of these vectors represents is different (e.g. the ratings of a single user concerning many items vs the ratings of many users concerning a single item).

Intra-dimensional pairwise comparisons always deal with vectors of the same size. This allows more options in terms of functions to be used. We focus on statistical (**correlation**) and information-theoretical (**mutual information**) properties for these problems. On the other hand, since inter-dimensional pairwise comparisons must deal with vectors of different sizes, the functions used are distances between distributions. In this case, one information-theoretical property is obtained via the **Jensen–Shannon divergence**. The post-functions are: **mean**, **standard deviation** and **skewness**. This yields 15 metafeatures, represented as follows:

$$\{\text{rows, columns}\}.\{\text{correlation, mutual inform.}\}.\{\text{post-functions}\}$$
$$\{\text{rows/columns}\}.\{\text{Jensen–Shannon divergence}\}.\{\text{post-functions}\} \quad (8)$$

These metafeatures are computed for all matrices, yielding a very large number of metafeatures, which depends on the size of the dimensions. Since the size of dimensions varies across problem instances, this means that it is not possible to characterize all of them with a vector of metafeatures of the same size. For instance, if we consider all the UI matrices of two tensors, we cannot create assume the amount of features extracted will be the same, since the dimensions can be different. Thus, the framework is applied once more, where the objects are **IC**, **UC** and **UI matrices** and the functions are the outcome of the comparison between vectors. The post-functions used are: **mean**, **standard deviation** and **skewness**. The resulting 135 metafeatures follow this notation:

$$\{\text{UI, UC and IC matrices}\}.\{\text{pairwise comparisons}\}.\{\text{post-functions}\} \quad (9)$$

3.6 Tensor-level metafeatures

Lastly, we describe the tensor-level metafeatures. These are split into those that describe the tensor as a whole and those that are based on pairwise comparisons between its constituent matrices. While the former do not require slice operations, the latter use them to obtain the matrices to be used in the calculations.

3.6.1 Tensor metafeatures. The tensor, which is the object to be processed in the metafeatures framework at this level, can be described by several structural properties: **number of users**, **number of items**, **number of contexts**, **number of ratings**, **tensor sparsity**, **proportion of users over items**, **proportions of users over contexts** and **proportions of items over contexts**. An algebraic operation, the **Frobenius norm**, is also used.

Similarly to Section 3.5.1, other techniques can also be used at this level. The usage of, for instance, multilinear PCA and clustering may extract other types of metafeatures representing different types of patterns that affect the behavior of algorithms. However, the computational cost of these methods make them unsuitable for the algorithm selection problem. Unlike all other metafeatures, these output a single value and, thus, do not require the use of post-functions. Therefore, a total of 9 metafeatures can be formulated:

$$\{\text{tensor}\}.\{\text{structural and algebraic properties}\}.\varnothing \quad (10)$$

3.6.2 Matrix pairwise comparison. The pairwise comparison of matrices uses slice operations to generate three types of objects: **UI**, **UC** and **IC matrices**. Although we can distinguish the intra and inter-dimensional comparisons of matrices (i.e. comparing matrices of the same or different nature), as before, we use the same function: **correlation**. We obtain the correlation between matrices by calculating the correlation between rows of one matrix and columns of another. The result is a matrix of correlation coefficients. Therefore, the only requirements is that the number of rows of the first matrix matches the number of columns of the second one. Due to the nature of the tensor, all matrices have at least one dimension in common. Hence, it is always possible to apply the correlations to any pair of matrices retrieved from the tensor, even if it may be necessary to transpose one or both matrices. Unlike the previous cases, where the same post-functions have been repeated, here we extract only the **maximum** value for each pairwise comparison. The rationale lies in the assumption that only high dependency matters, unlike the previous examples where an overall perspective is essential. The formalization of all 6 metafeatures is:

$$\begin{gathered}\{\text{UI, UC and IC matrices}\}.\{\text{correlation}\}.\{\text{maximum}\}\\ \{\text{UI/UC, UI/IC and UC/IC matrices}\}.\{\text{correlation}\}.\{\text{maximum}\}\end{gathered} \tag{11}$$

Also as in the case of matrix-level metafeatures, the final set of metafeatures is obtained by applying the framework to the intermediate results. In this case, the object is the **tensor** and the function consists of the results of the comparison between matrices. In this case, we obtain a vector of maximum correlations for intra and inter-dimensional comparisons. The results are aggregated using **mean**, **standard deviation** and **skewness**. The formalization of these 18 metafeatures is:

$$\{\text{tensor}\}.\{\text{pairwise comparisons}\}.\{\text{post-functions}\} \tag{12}$$

4 ALGORITHM SELECTION FOR TF

4.1 Baselevel experimental setup

The baselevel is characterized by the datasets, algorithms, evaluation protocol and evaluation measures. The datasets need to be built in such a way that they can be encapsulated in a tensor. Since we are unaware of public datasets specifically for this purpose, we chose to adapt CF datasets. Hence, we searched the available datasets for a common dimension, which could be used as context. We found that the temporal dimension fitted this criteria, since most datasets have the timestamp of the feedback event.

Dimensions must be nominal variables and, since time is a continuous variable, we discretized it. The temporal dimension is divided into a predefined number of bins and each rating event is assigned to the respective bin. The contextual dimension can therefore be described as the sequence of bins. The number of bins used for dimension C are $\{2, 3, 4, 5, 10, 20, 30, 50, 100\}$. Other measurement units could be used, such as day or hour, but we decided to use an approach which could be easily replicated across datasets and that enabled us to have fixed length for the contextual dimension. A total of 34 CF datasets are used from the following domains: Amazon Reviews [30], ConcertTweets [1], MovieLens [17], MovieTweetings [13], Tripadvisor [48] and Yelp [51]. With different binning parameters, this yields 306 datasets.

In terms of TF, this work dwells with CP decomposition (CPD) with several factorization algorithms: CPD, CPD_ALS, CPD_NLS, CPD_RBS and CPD_MINF. The difference between the algorithms lies in the way the optimization process is performed. The CPD_ALS, CPD_MINF, CPD_NLS and CPD_RBS algorithms are optimization-based and use alternating least squares, nonlinear unconstrained optimization, nonlinear least squares and randomized block sampling, respectively. The default version, CPD, is a high-level algorithm which automatically computes an initialization and uses this as a starting point for one or more optimization steps. The implementations from TensorLab [47] was used. In addition, we implemented a baseline algorithm which is an adaptation of the MostPopular version from the CF framework MyMediaLite [15] applied to tensors. The algorithm works by sorting the item ratings for a given user and context to provide the recommendations. This is considered a baseline, since no factorization is involved.

The chosen evaluation protocol is 10-fold cross-validation. The folds are created by splitting the entire dataset of 4-tuples (user, item, context, rating) into ten different groups. Afterwards, each of the nine possible combinations of groups are used to build the tensor and the remaining one to use in the evaluation stage. Since the recommendation follows a Top-N approach [20], the evaluation measures used are Normalized Discounted Cumulative Gain (NDCG), Mean Average Precision (MAP), Mean Reciprocal Rank (MRR) and Area Under the Curve (AUC). While the first three are devoted to ranking accuracy, AUC assesses classification accuracy.

4.2 Metalevel experimental setup

The results obtained at the baselevel, as described in the previous section, are used to create a ranking of the algorithms for each dataset. This ranking is the metatarget (i.e. the dependent variable at the metalevel). Given that baselevel algorithms are evaluated according to multiple measures, a metatarget is generated for each measure. Thus, we have, in fact, multiple metalearning problems, one for each metatarget. The metafeatures for each dataset are also computed, according to the description in Section 3. The values of the metafeatures are the independent variables of the metadata.

Since the goal is to predict a ranking of algorithms, the metalearning problem is addressed as a LR task. The algorithms used at the metalevel (i.e. meta-algorithms) are: kNN and Naive Bayes (NB) [40], Ranking Tree (RT) [10] and the baseline average ranking (AVG). The accuracy of the predicted rankings is measured by computing their correlation to the target ranking, as is usual in LR. The correlation measure used here is Kendall's Tau coefficient. The metalevel performance is estimated using 10-fold cross-validation.

5 RESULTS AND DISCUSSION

5.1 Metalevel evaluation

The results for the performance of the meta-algorithms in all metatargets in terms of Kendall's Tau coefficient are presented in Figure 5. The results show:

- kNN and NB are always the best and worst meta-algorithms. RT beats the baseline only in NDCG and MAP.
- AUC is the metatarget with the worst overall performance, yielding the worst overall correlations coefficients. The performance in NDCG, MAP and MRR metatargets is fairly similar and high, except for the RT meta-algorithm.
- Since kNN is always above the baseline, one can state that our MtL approach is able to predict the rankings of

algorithms. The results are specially important considering the high correlations for the baseline in 3 metatargets.

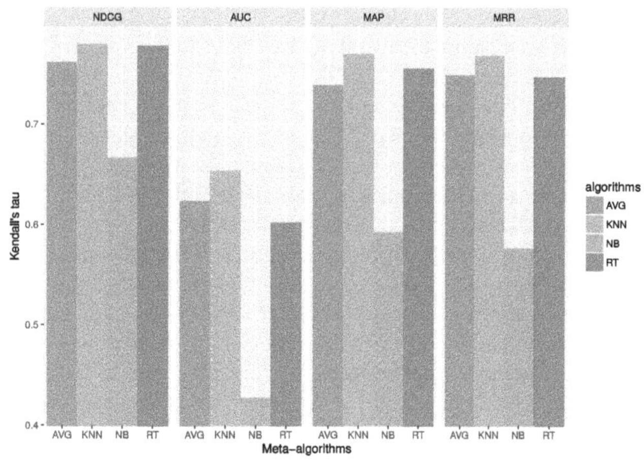

Figure 5: Metalevel evaluation for all meta-algorithms.

To assess whether these results are statistically significant, we use Critical Difference (CD) diagrams [11]. These diagrams rank several methods based on their performance on several datasets. Here, it is applied to the folds of the 10-fold cross validation procedure used on all 4 metatargets. The diagram ranks the algorithms and connects those with differences that are not significantly different (i.e. less than the critical difference, CD). The results are shown in Figure 6 and validate the observations made regarding the meta-algorithms: kNN is better than the baseline and NB; NB is the worst algorithm by far and RT's unstable behavior makes it not statistical significantly different than both kNN and the baseline.

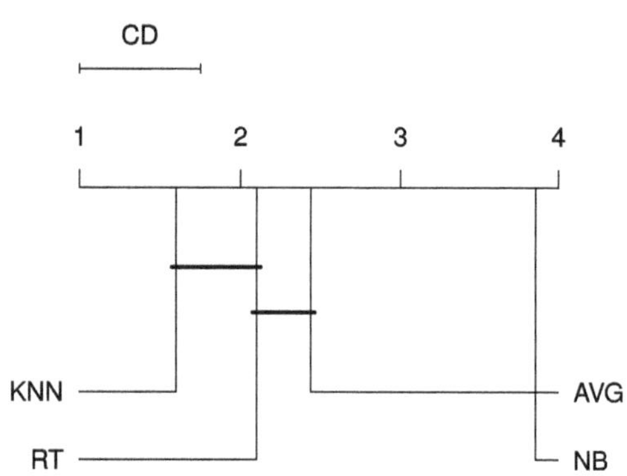

Figure 6: CD diagram for ranking of metamodels.

Based on these results, we further analyzed the behavior of the kNN algorithm. Figure 7 shows Kendall's tau coefficient for $k \in \{1, .., 10\}$ neighbors, separately for the NDCG and AUC metatargets. The baseline is presented in each figure as a horizontal line. Since the results for MRR and MAP are similar to those for NDCG, we do not include them here.

One observes that metamodels beat the baseline for $k > 1$. This shows the robustness of this algorithm for our problem of algorithm selection. However, while for NDCG the performance is fairly constant, in AUC we observe that the performance improves with k. Such variations are dictated by the ranking of algorithms used for training the metamodels, since the metafeatures are the same. This means that the ranking variations in AUC are greater than in NDCG, which makes it a more difficult problem.

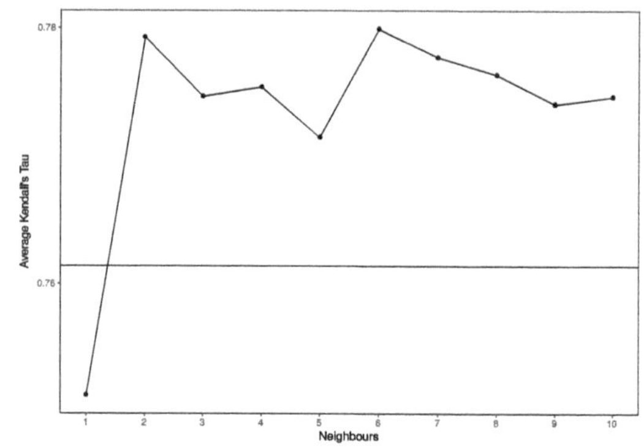

(a) NDCG metatarget.

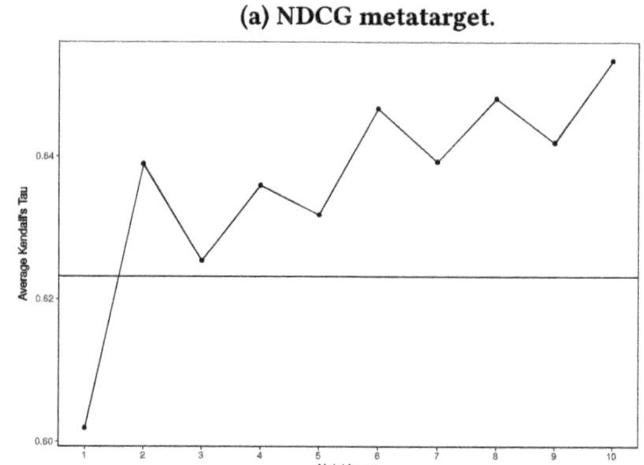

(b) AUC metatarget.

Figure 7: Metalevel evaluation for kNN.

5.2 Baselevel impact

The previous section shows that we can predict the ranking of the algorithms with good accuracy. The question now is whether the use of the algorithms recommended by the metamodel will achieve good baselevel performance. The idea of this evaluation is to simulate different thresholds regarding the number of TF algorithms executed following the ranking order, and to assess the corresponding baselevel performance [7]. A metamodel outperforms the baseline if the performance in a specific threshold is better than the one obtained by average rankings. This mechanism also includes an oracle, which knows beforehand which will be the absolute best algorithm for any case. Therefore, this will create the maximum bound that cannot be beaten (horizontal lines).

Figure 8 presents the baselevel impact for the NDCG and AUC metatargets. Once again, the results for MRR and MAP are not presented as they show the same behavior as NDCG. In both cases is it possible to see that the algorithms recommended by kNN and RT are better than those provided by the baseline recommendation for the top-two algorithms in the predicted rankings. This behavior shows that despite RT not performing well in terms of metalevel evaluation for the AUC and MRR metatargets, the recommendations still yield gains in terms of baselevel performance, on average.

Another interesting observation concerns NB: while for NDCG the performance is worse than the baseline, for AUC it is better. Recalling that this metamodel performed badly in terms of metalevel evaluation, it is surprising to see this behaviour. Once again, this points to the higher difficulty of solving the algorithm selection problem using LR for the AUC metatarget.

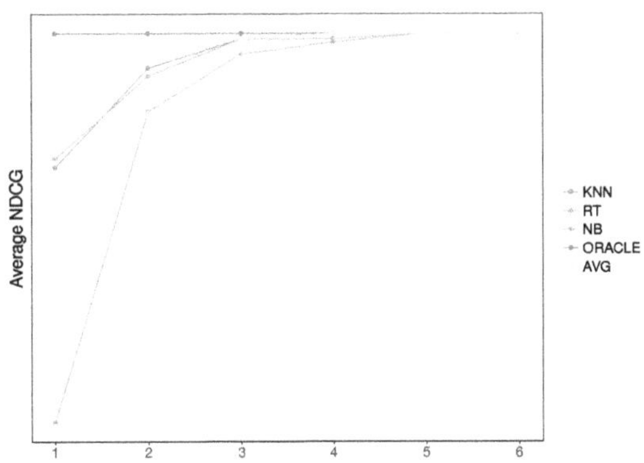

(a) NDCG metatarget.

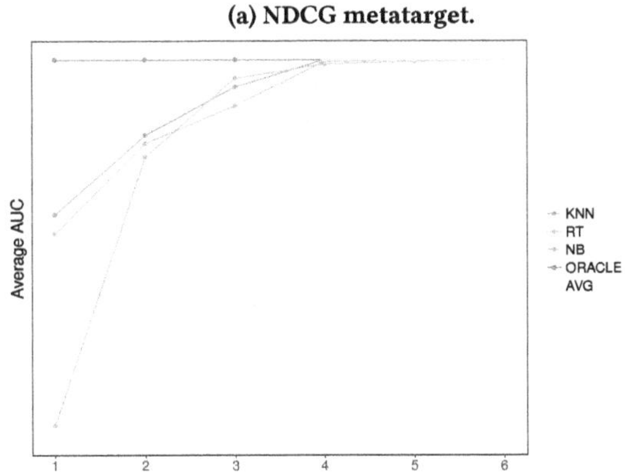

(b) AUC metatarget.

Figure 8: Baselevel impact.

5.3 Importance of metafeatures

Since there is no standard procedure for assessing variable importance in LR, this work uses a simple heuristic approach to address this issue. Using all the metatargets, RT metamodels were trained. Next, the frequency of metafeatures used on those models were computed and ranked. Due to space restrictions, we only summarize the results:

- Most metafeatures are vector pairwise comparisons in nature. Furthermore, their position in the ranking is well established at the top, i.e. 22 out of 24 top metafeatures. This confirms our hypothesis that the characteristics of components of the matrices affect the performance of the CAF methods.
- All other types of metafeatures hold low importance for the problem of algorithm selection. The vector, matrix pairwise comparisons and matrix metafeatures correspond respectively to 6, 2 and 1 of the best metafeatures. This shows the need for future work at these levels.
- More importantly, the metafeatures used to describe the tensor as a whole are not available in the top metafeatures. This, alongside the positive results in both metalevel performance and baselevel impact, validates our approach to use slice operations to create metafeatures for tensors.
- The most represented objects are the UI, IC and UC matrices, respectively with 14, 12 and 7 metafeatures. This is obviously affected by the fact that they are the most frequent type of metafeatures, i.e. the vector pairwise comparison. One notices that IC matrices are represented in 7 out of the top 8 metafeatures.
- The most influential functions are mutual information, correlation and Shannon divergence. There is no clear patterns that distinguishes them, although mutual information is present in 4 of the top 5 metafeatures.

6 CONCLUSIONS AND FUTURE WORK

This work presents the first known approach for algorithm selection for Tensor Factorization algorithms. We follow a Metalearning approach which, given the difference in the nature of the data used in these algorithms in comparison to other algorithm selection tasks previously addressed with metalearning, implies the development of completely new metafeatures to characterize problems. We, thus, propose an extensive and exhaustive set of metafeatures. The metafeatures use slice operations to describe the tensors at several levels of granularity and perspectives. The merits of the proposed approach were validated in a large scale experimental setup. The results have shown that kNN models are capable of solving the problem with statistical significantly better performance than the baseline for all metatargets. In terms of baselevel impact, the models also perform generally better than the baseline. Furthermore, vector pairwise comparison metafeatures have established themselves as the most influential, confirming our hypothesis that these components of the data contain useful information to understand the behavior of TF algorithms. Future work can take several directions: to study contextual dimensions beyond time, include specially designed Tensor Factorization algorithms for Context aware Filtering, study the hyperparameter selection problem, improve and analyze the metafeatures proposed by using more advanced techniques and extend the amount and nature of evaluation measures used in the base- and metalevels.

ACKNOWLEDGEMENTS

This work is financed by the ERDF Fund through the Operational Program for Competitiveness and Internationalization - COMPETE 2020 of Portugal 2020 through the National Innovation Agency (ANI) as part of project 3506. The authors would also like to acknowledge the support from CNPq and FAPESP, Brazilian funding agencies. Special thanks to Hadi Fanaee.

REFERENCES

[1] Panagiotis Adamopoulos and Alexander Tuzhilin. 2014. Estimating the Value of Multi-Dimensional Data Sets in Context-based Recommender Systems. In *8th ACM Conference on Recommender Systems (RecSys 2014)*.

[2] Gediminas Adomavicius, Ramesh Sankaranarayanan, Shahana Sen, and Alexander Tuzhilin. 2005. Incorporating Contextual Information in Recommender Systems Using a Multidimensional Approach. *ACM Transactions on Information Systems* 23, 1 (2005), 103–145.

[3] Gediminas Adomavicius and Alexander Tuzhilin. 2005. Toward the Next Generation of Recommender Systems: A Survey of the State-of-the-Art and Possible Extensions. *IEEE Trans. on Knowl. and Data Eng.* 17, 6 (2005), 734–749.

[4] Gediminas Adomavicius and Alexander Tuzhilin. 2011. Context-Aware Recommender Systems. In *Recommender Systems Handbook*, Paul B. Ricci, Francesco and Rokach, Lior and Shapira, Bracha and Kantor (Ed.). Springer US, Chapter 7, 217–253.

[5] Gediminas Adomavicius and Jingjing Zhang. 2012. Impact of data characteristics on recommender systems performance. *ACM Transactions on Management Information Systems* 3, 1 (2012), 1–17.

[6] J. Bobadilla, F. Ortega, A. Hernando, and A. Gutiérrez. 2013. Recommender systems survey. *Knowledge-Based Systems* 46 (2013), 109–132.

[7] Pavel Brazdil, Christophe Giraud-Carrier, Carlos Soares, and Ricardo Vilalta. 2009. *Metalearning: Applications to Data Mining* (1 ed.). Springer Publishing Company, Incorporated.

[8] J Douglas Carroll and Jih-Jie Chang. 1970. Analysis of individual differences in multidimensional scaling via an n-way generalization of "Eckart-Young" decomposition. *Psychometrika* 35, 3 (1970), 283–319. DOI: http://dx.doi.org/10.1007/BF02310791

[9] Tiago Cunha, Carlos Soares, and André C.P.L.F. de Carvalho. 2016. Selecting Collaborative Filtering algorithms using Metalearning. In *European Conference on Machine Learning and Knowledge Discovery in Databases*. 393–409.

[10] Cláudio Rebelo de Sá, Carlos Soares, Arno Knobbe, and Paulo Cortez. 2016. Label Ranking Forests. *Expert Systems* (2016).

[11] Janez Demšar. 2006. Statistical Comparisons of Classifiers over Multiple Data Sets. *Journal of Machine Learning Research* 7 (2006), 1–30.

[12] Mukund Deshpande and George Karypis. 2004. Item-based top-N recommendation algorithms. *ACM Transactions on Information Systems* 22, 1 (2004), 143–177. DOI: http://dx.doi.org/10.1145/963770.963776

[13] Simon Dooms, Toon De Pessemier, and Luc Martens. 2013. MovieTweetings: a Movie Rating Dataset Collected From Twitter. In *Workshop on Crowdsourcing and Human Computation for Recommender Systems, CrowdRec at RecSys 2013*.

[14] Michael Ekstrand and John Riedl. 2012. When Recommenders Fail: Predicting Recommender Failure for Algorithm Selection and Combination. *ACM Conference on Recommender Systems* (2012), 233–236.

[15] Zeno Gantner, Steffen Rendle, Christoph Freudenthaler, and Lars Schmidt-Thieme. 2011. MyMediaLite: A Free Recommender System Library. In *ACM Conference on Recommender Systems*. 305–308.

[16] Josephine Griffith, Colm O'Riordan, and Humphrey Sorensen. 2012. Investigations into user rating information and predictive accuracy in a collaborative filtering domain. In *ACM Symposium on Applied Computing*. 937–942.

[17] GroupLens. 2016. MovieLens datasets. (2016). http://grouplens.org/datasets/movielens/

[18] A. Harshman. 1970. Foundations of the PARAFAC procedure: Models and conditions for an "explanatory" multimodal factor analysis. (1970).

[19] M Hazewinkel. 2008. *Handbook of Algebra*. Number vol. 5 in Handbook of Algebra. Elsevier Science. https://books.google.pt/books?id=fxiZFOXkIKsC

[20] Jonathan L Herlocker, Joseph a. Konstan, Loren G Terveen, and John T Riedl. 2004. Evaluating collaborative filtering recommender systems. *ACM Transactions on Information Systems* 22, 1 (2004), 5–53. DOI: http://dx.doi.org/10.1145/963770.963772

[21] Balázs Hidasi and Domonkos Tikk. 2012. Fast ALS-based tensor factorization for context-aware recommendation from implicit feedback. In *European Conference on Machine Learning and Knowledge Discovery in Databases*. 67–82.

[22] Zan Huang and Daniel Dajun Zeng. 2011. Why does collaborative filtering work? transaction-based recommendation model validation and selection by analyzing bipartite random graphs. *INFORMS Journal on Computing* 23, 1 (2011), 138–152.

[23] Alexandros Karatzoglou, Xavier Amatriain, Linas Baltrunas, and Nuria Oliver. 2010. Multiverse Recommendation: N-dimensional Tensor Factorization for Context-aware Collaborative Filtering. In *ACM Conference on Recommender Systems*. 79–86.

[24] Tamara G Kolda and Brett W Bader. 2009. Tensor Decompositions and Applications. *SIAM Rev.* 51, 3 (2009), 455–500.

[25] Yehuda Koren, Robert Bell, and Chris Volinsky. 2009. Matrix Factorization Techniques for Recommender Systems. *Computer* 42, 8 (2009), 30–37.

[26] Christiane Lemke, Marcin Budka, and Bogdan Gabrys. 2013. Metalearning: a survey of trends and technologies. *Artificial Intelligence Review* (2013), 1–14.

[27] Christiane Lemke and Bogdan Gabrys. 2010. Meta-learning for time series forecasting and forecast combination. *Neurocomputing* 73, 10-12 (2010), 2006–2016.

[28] Qiang Liu, Shu Wu, and Liang Wang. 2015. COT: Contextual Operating Tensor for Context-Aware Recommender Systems. In *AAAI Conference on Artificial Intelligence*. 203–209.

[29] Pawel Matuszyk and Myra Spiliopoulou. 2014. Predicting the Performance of Collaborative Filtering Algorithms. In *International Conference on Web Intelligence, Mining and Semantics*. 38:1—-38:6.

[30] Julian McAuley and Jure Leskovec. 2013. Hidden Factors and Hidden Topics: Understanding Rating Dimensions with Review Text. In *ACM Conference on Recommender Systems*. 165–172.

[31] István Pilászy, Dávid Zibriczky, and Domonkos Tikk. 2010. Fast ALS-based Matrix Factorization for Explicit and Implicit Feedback Datasets. In *ACM Conference on Recommender Systems*. 71–78.

[32] Fábio Pinto, Carlos Soares, and João Mendes-Moreira. 2016. Towards automatic generation of Metafeatures. In *Pacific Asia Conference on Knowledge Discovery and Data Mining*. 215–226.

[33] Ricardo B C Prudêncio and Teresa B Ludermir. 2004. Meta-learning approaches to selecting time series models. *Neurocomputing* 61 (2004), 121–137.

[34] Steffen Rendle, Zeno Gantner, Christoph Freudenthaler, and Lars Schmidt-thieme. 2011. Fast Context-aware Recommendations with Factorization Machines. In *International ACM SIGIR Conference on Research and Development in Information Retrieval*. 635—-644.

[35] John Rice. 1976. The Algorithm Selection Problem. *Advances in Computers* 15 (1976), 65–118.

[36] André Luis Debiaso Rossi, André Carlos Ponce De Leon Ferreira de Carvalho, Carlos Soares, and Bruno Feres de Souza. 2014. MetaStream: A meta-learning based method for periodic algorithm selection in time-changing data. *Neurocomputing* 127 (2014), 52–64.

[37] Badrul Sarwar, George Karypis, Joseph Konstan, and John Riedl. 2000. Analysis of Recommendation Algorithms for E-Commerce. In *ACM Conference on Electronic commerce*. 158–167.

[38] Floarea Serban, Joaquin Vanschoren, and Abraham Bernstein. 2013. A survey of intelligent assistants for data analysis. *Comput. Surveys* V, 212 (2013), 1–35.

[39] Yue Shi, Alexandros Karatzoglou, Linas Baltrunas, Martha Larson, Alan Hanjalic, and Nuria Oliver. 2012. TFMAP: Optimizing MAP for Top-N Context-aware Recommendation. In *ACM SIGIR Conference on Research and Development in Information Retrieval*. 155–164.

[40] Carlos Soares. 2015. *labelrank: Predicting Rankings of Labels*. https://cran.r-project.org/package=labelrank

[41] Carlos Soares, Pavel B Brazdil, and Petr Kuba. 2004. A Meta-Learning Method to Select the Kernel Width in Support Vector Regression. *Machine Learning* 54, 3 (2004), 195–209. DOI: http://dx.doi.org/10.1023/B:MACH.0000015879.28004.9b

[42] Panagiotis Symeonidis, Alexandros Nanopoulos, and Yannis Manolopoulos. 2008. Tag recommendations based on tensor dimensionality reduction. In *ACM Conference on Recommender Systems*. ACM Press, New York, New York, USA, 43–50. DOI: http://dx.doi.org/10.1145/1454008.1454017

[43] Panagiotis Symeonidis, Alexandros Nanopoulos, and Yannis Manolopoulos. 2010. A Unified Framework for Providing Recommendations in Social Tagging Systems Based on Ternary Semantic Analysis. *IEEE Transactions on Knowledge and Data Engineering* 22, 2 (Feb. 2010), 179–192.

[44] H E A Tinsley and S D Brown. 2000. *Handbook of Applied Multivariate Statistics and Mathematical Modeling*. Elsevier Science. https://books.google.pt/books?id=IIbMnrgTpWMC

[45] Ledyard R Tucker. 1966. Some mathematical notes on three-mode factor analysis. *Psychometrika* 31, 3 (1966), 279–311. DOI: http://dx.doi.org/10.1007/BF02289464

[46] Joaquin Vanschoren. 2010. *Understanding machine learning performance with experiment databases*. Ph.D. Dissertation. Katholieke Universiteit Leuven.

[47] Nico Vervliet, Otto Debals, and L ieven De Lathauwer. 2016. Tensorlab 3.0 - Numerical optimization strategies for large-scale constrained and coupled matrix/tensor factorization. In *Asilomar Conference on Signals, Systems and Computers*. 1733–1738. DOI: http://dx.doi.org/10.1109/ACSSC.2016.7869679

[48] Hongning Wang, Yue Lu, and ChengXiang Zhai. 2011. Latent Aspect Rating Analysis Without Aspect Keyword Supervision. In *Proceedings of the 17th ACM SIGKDD International Conference on Knowledge Discovery and Data Mining (KDD '11)*. ACM, 618–626.

[49] Liang Xiong, Xi Chen, Tzu-Kuo Huang, Jeff Schneider, and Jaime G Carbonell. 2010. Temporal Collaborative Filtering with Bayesian Probabilistic Tensor Factorization. In *SIAM Conference on Data Mining*. 211–222.

[50] Xiwang Yang, Yang Guo, Yong Liu, and Harald Steck. 2014. A survey of collaborative filtering based social recommender systems. *Computer Communications* 41 (2014), 1–10.

[51] Yelp. 2016. Yelp Dataset Challenge. (2016). https://www.yelp.com/dataset_challenge

A Gradient-based Adaptive Learning Framework for Efficient Personal Recommendation

Yue Ning
Virginia Tech
yning@vt.edu

Yue Shi*
Yahoo Research
yueshi@acm.org

Liangjie Hong
Etsy Inc.
lhong@etsy.com

Huzefa Rangwala
George Mason University
rangwala@cs.gmu.edu

Naren Ramakrishnan
Virginia Tech
naren@cs.vt.edu

ABSTRACT

Recommending personalized content to users is a long-standing challenge to many online services including Facebook, Yahoo, Linkedin and Twitter. Traditional recommendation models such as latent factor models and feature-based models are usually trained for all users and optimize an "average" experience for them, yielding sub-optimal solutions. Although multi-task learning provides an opportunity to learn personalized models per user, learning algorithms are usually tailored to specific models (e.g., generalized linear model, matrix factorization and etc.), creating obstacles for a unified engineering interface, which is important for large Internet companies. In this paper, we present an empirical framework to learn user-specific personal models for content recommendation by utilizing gradient information from a global model. Our proposed method can potentially benefit any model that can be optimized through gradients, offering a lightweight yet generic alternative to conventional multi-task learning algorithms for user personalization. We demonstrate the effectiveness of the proposed framework by incorporating it in three popular machine learning algorithms including logistic regression, gradient boosting decision tree and matrix factorization. Our extensive empirical evaluation shows that the proposed framework can significantly improve the efficiency of personalized recommendation in real-world datasets.

CCS CONCEPTS

•**Information systems** → **Personalization; Recommender systems;**

1 INTRODUCTION

Personalized content recommendation plays a key role in online services such as Yahoo, Facebook, LinkedIn and Twitter. User engagements are primarily driven by how content/items are tailored to their personal preferences and interests. In the simplest setting,

*Now at Facebook

RecSys'17, August 27–31, 2017, Como, Italy.

DOI: http://dx.doi.org/10.1145/3109859.3109909

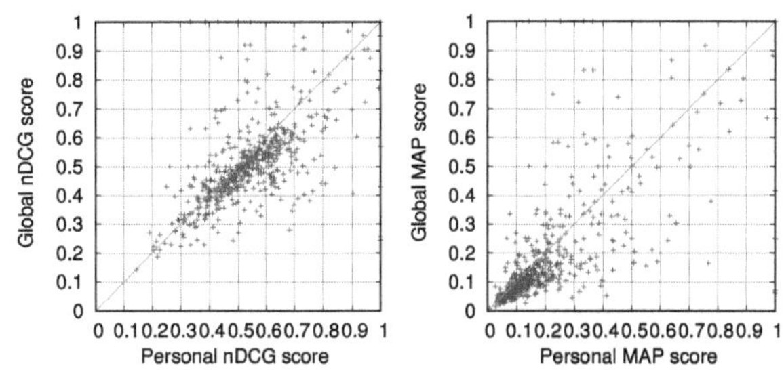

Figure 1: An example of global and personal models. Left figure showcases the nDCG score of users from global (y-axis) and personal (x-axis) models. (Right: MAP score).

when only user-item interactions are available, traditional *collaborative filtering* (CF) methods are usually utilized to produce recommendations. State-of-the-art matrix factorization-based CF models (MF) assume that each user has his/her own latent factors and the recommendation score for a particular user-item pair is a dot-product between user- and item-factors, leading to the effect of personalization. In more complex settings, when richer information or features are available, a common practice is to resort to the paradigm of *learning to rank* (LtR) where a feature vector of each user-item interaction is constructed and a regression/classification model is learned from a large amount of historical interaction data to predict recommendation scores [17]. A wide range of predictive models can be used for LtR, including logistic regression [12, 31] (LogReg), gradient boosting decision tree [11, 13] (GBDT) and LambdaMART [8]. In order to achieve personalization in the LtR setting, heavy feature engineering that characterizes user preferences and interests is usually required and few challenges still remain:

• **Alleviate "average" experience for users.** Although both MF and LtR frameworks provide mechanisms to obtain personalization, they cannot easily leverage individual's data and offer a unique experience for each user. For LtR, a particular model is commonly optimized based on a global objective function. It is therefore an "average" model for everyone and remains suboptimal for individual users [7]. In addition, a global model may be biased to features that are frequent across all interaction data, while an individual user may never have interacted with those features in the past. For MF, while user factors capture user preferences to some degree, item factors are global as one item only has the same set of latent features for all users. Thus, similar to LtR, item factors for a particular item are heavily influenced by how many users have interacted with it. If a user happens to interact with a popular item, the user factors might be "polluted" by the item factors despite of his/her own peculiar preferences. In other words, traditional MF is also a global model.

To demonstrate this effect, we compare the performance of a global model and personal models in terms of normalized Discounted Cumulative Gain (nDCG) and Mean-Average-Precision (MAP), on a dataset from a popular online service, shown in Figure 1. All models are logistic regression, optimizing Click-Through-Rate (CTR). The global model is trained on all users' data where personal models are trained on individuals' own data. Each point on the figure represents a user where X-axis and Y-axis represent nDCG/MAP scores of personal models and a global model respectively. The figure shows that personal models exhibit better performance than global models for most users (72.3% and 73.6% points are in the lower triangle area for nDCG and MAP score). For a small portion of users, the global model tends to have better performance. This observation motivates us to explore the possibility of building personal models by borrowing information from a global model.

• **Generic empirical frameworks for different models.** Multi-task learning (MTL) algorithms have been exploited to tackle the issue mentioned above. Under the context of recommendation, to name a few recent efforts, Generalized Linear Mixed Models [34] and Distributed Personalization [25] are proposed to train a global model and personal models simultaneously. Although these approaches provide opportunities for personalization, they are tied to a particular form of model, in this case, linear model, and the proposed learning (e.g., neighborhood-based collaborative filtering [26], variational inference [27] and etc). Similarly, under the context of information retrieval, MTL have been explored for specific models (e.g., linear model [32] and tree-based boosting method [10]) while no generic framework exists for a wide range of models.

• **Distributed model learning and less access of global data.** Even if most MTL formalisms involve different flavors of personal-level modeling, learning algorithms to solve these problems are usually **global**, meaning that learning algorithms need to access all data during the training, unless sophisticated distributed learning systems are utilized [25]. This is particularly a hurdle for the mobile era where user interaction data is gathered naturally on their mobile devices. For a global model, it requires such data being transmitted to the server-side and to re-train the model there, accruing non-trivial communication costs. On the other hand, personal models can be trained and immediately used on mobile devices, without transmitting data or model updates to devices, resulting in better user experiences with less communication burden.

In this paper, we propose a generic empirical framework to address the aforementioned challenges of learning personal models. The proposed framework provides a lightweight yet effective alternative to MTL for personalization. The framework is generic to a wide variety of machine learning models where we demonstrate three instantiations, LogReg, GBDT, and MF, in this paper. Any learning algorithms relying on gradient information can potentially utilize this framework. Thus, the proposed approach offers a systematic solution to build personal models, not tackling the problem just for a particular model. The central idea of the method is to allow each personal model to leverage information from a global model, to a certain extent, based on the richness of each user's own data. We also show parallel learning procedures that enable us to train personal models at scale. Our contributions in this paper can be summarized as follows:

- We present a novel generic empirical framework for building personal models by leveraging a global model through gradient adaptation, offering a more general personalization approach than MTL.
- We demonstrate three different instantiations of the framework: LogReg, GBDT, and MF, with detailed optimization procedures for building personal models.
- We provide an efficient learning paradigm by exploiting a parallel computing scheme for building large number of personal models.
- Through extensive experiments with a variety of datasets, we show the effectiveness of our framework for improving content recommendation performance.

2 RELATED WORK

We provide a brief overview of state-of-the-art approaches [3, 30] for content recommendation systems as well as MTL for personalization.

Generalized Linear Models: One simple way to build a large-scale content recommendation system is to use generalized linear models to predict responses (e.g., clicks, ratings and etc.) for each user-item feature vector. Recent work [34] demonstrated how to achieve it in an industrial scale. Similar models are used in online advertising as well [2]. Note that, as these models induce global optimization problems, special learning algorithms like ADMM, with sophisticated communication schemes are proposed to solve them.

Tree Boosting: GBDT [13, 14] has been proven effective in many machine learning applications. Together with LambdaMART, tree boosting methods show state-of-the-art performance on many LtR and recommendation tasks [6, 8, 35]. Recently, methods [11] are developed to learn global tree models on large-scale datasets.

Matrix Factorization: MF-based models are widely used for recommendation [19] and assume that there exists a latent vector associated with each user and each item. Also, user and item bias terms are exploited in the optimization [15]. Regression-based LFM [1] and Factorization Machines [28] further extended MF to incorporate arbitrary user and item features. In most cases, gradient descent techniques or alternating least squares (ALS) can be applied to solve the optimization problems. Recent work [7] proposed a customized matrix factorization objective for improved recommendations.

Personalization/Multi-Task Learning: The importance of a personalized application extends to many fields such as social networks [20, 22] and ranking system [29] while social network has also been incorporated in personalization [9]. It is necessary for suggesting relevant/interesting results for users and making distributed computation efficient in mobile side, such as Distributed Matrix Factorization [16]. MTL algorithms have been extensively studied to tackle the problem of personalization in both information retrieval (IR) and recommender systems (RecSys). Here, we highlight a few representative papers. In IR, MTL-style linear ranking model [32] (including feature-hashing methods [33]) and tree-based boosting ranking models [10, 18]) have been proposed to adapt global ranking

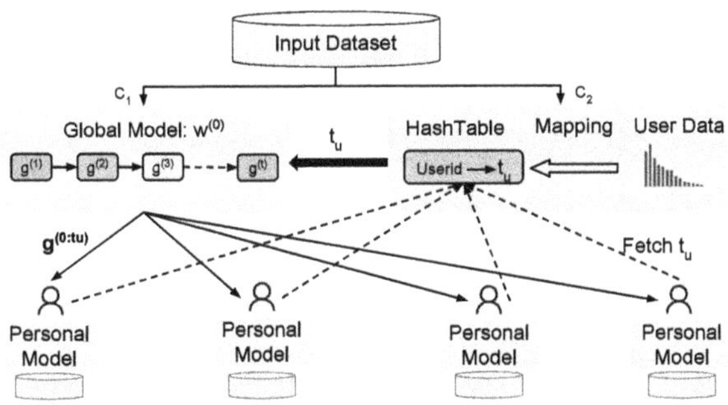

Figure 2: System Framework. Component C_1 trains a global model. Component C_2 generates a hashtable based on users' data distribution. Users request t_u from C_2 and C_1 returns a subsequence of gradients $g^{(0:t_u)}$ to users.

models to user specific ones. In RecSys, early work [26] formulated a MTL based solution for neighborhood-based collaborative filtering methods. Recommending items to users based on *expert* opinions has also been explored [4]. However, most MTL algorithms need to solve global optimization problems. Our propose framework differs from MTL in that personal models can be optimized independently from a global objective function. Also, the generic framework accepts different objective functions.

Curriculum Learning [5] is proposed to solve progressively harder problems, supplying the training examples in a meaningful order may actually lead to improved performance and better convergence. In comparison to Curriculum Learning, our proposed framework focus on efficient learning for personal recommendation models without reordering. It is general and flexible to tailor to different model formalisms.

3 THE PROPOSED FRAMEWORK

A global model is usually learned through an optimization process from all users' data, lacking any personalization. On the contrary, personal models are learned from individuals' data, under the risk of not having enough data to learn stable models. We want to balance these two tradeoffs and design a learning paradigm that adaptively transfers global knowledge to personal models. Figure 2 provides an overview of our framework, that is based on two general assumptions. First, *we assume that both the global model and personal models share the same structure of objective functions.* This assumption is already satisfied by two extreme cases mentioned above. In addition, this assumption also implies that both the global model and personal models can share the same optimization process, which is agnostic to the framework described below. This is a significant advantage over other similar methods such as MTL where optimization algorithms are revised towards more complicated objective functions. Secondly, *we assume the model can be optimized through gradient methods.* This assumption covers a wide range of models including LogReg, GBDT and deep learning models. Note that, our framework does not assume any explicit relationships between global model parameters and personal ones, differing from basic framework of MTL algorithms. This is the key aspect for our proposed approach that allows it to be applicable to multiple learning paradigms.

Algorithm 3.1 Coordination Algorithm

```
input: C (#Groups), (|D_0|, |D_1|, ..., |D_U|), g^(0), g^(1), ..., g^(T)
output: f(u, |D_u|) → t_u
procedure SCHEDULER
    t_1, ..., t_u, ..., t_|U| = 0, u ∈ U
    d_0, d_1, ..., d_U = log |D_0|, log |D_1|, ..., log |D_U|
    Sort (d_0, d_1, ..., d_U) in non-ascending order.
    d_max = max(d_0, d_1, ..., d_U)
    d_min = min(d_0, d_1, ..., d_U)
    s = (d_max − d_min) / C
    for u ∈ U do
        for i ∈ [1, C] do
            if d_u ∈ [d_min + i * s, d_min + (i + 1) * s] then
                p_u = i/C;  t_u = ⌊T * p_u⌋; break
    return {t_u}, u ∈ U
```

During the training process for the global model, gradients at each iteration are saved and transferred to a coordinator for later personal adaptation. The coordinator maintains a mapping between users and gradients. When training a personal model for a given user, we initialize it based on a version of global model and a portion of global gradients that correspond to the training data specific to the user. Then, the personal model extends the training procedure solely based on its own data. The overall learning paradigm is described as follows:

$$\widetilde{\theta}_u = \theta^{(0)} - \eta_1 \sum_{t=1}^{t_u - 1} g^{(t)}(\theta) - \eta_2 \sum_{t=t_u}^{T} g^{(t)}(\theta_u)$$

where θ represents the model parameter, u is the index for one user. In this paradigm, personal models adapt global knowledge by leveraging global gradients, while tailoring themselves to their individual characteristics by concentrating on their own data.

Each user u owns his/her data $\mathcal{D}_u$. The adaptive personalization can be formulated as a learning process, which takes global model gradients and user's data for training a personal model:

$$(\mathcal{G}, \mathcal{D}_u) \xrightarrow{\text{adaptation}} \mathcal{M}_u$$

where $\mathcal{G} = (g^0, g^1, ..., g^T)$ is a series of gradients for updating the global model, and $\mathcal{M}_u$ is the personal model for user u. In the adaptation process, based on user's own dataset $\mathcal{D}_u$, personal models can be learned locally and in parallel. More importantly, users who have insufficient data can still train their models based on global parameters. The generic strategy of our proposed framework is summarized as follows:

(1) Given a dataset of $\mathcal{U}$ users, we learn the global model based on a gradient-based learning algorithm until the iteration T, and save global gradients from each iteration into $\mathcal{G} = (g^0, g^1, ..., g^T)$.

(2) For each user u in $\mathcal{U}$, adaptively distribute a sub-sequence $(g^{0:t_u})$ from global gradients $\mathcal{G}$ based on his/her data $\mathcal{D}_u$.

(3) For each user we locally train a personal model based on the user's data and the adapted global gradients. This step can be implemented in parallel for large-scale data.

Adaptation Mechanism: Assuming, a global model trained with T iterations; for each iteration, model parameters are updated along the opposite direction of their gradient. The gradients are calculated using all the instances in the training set (D^{Tr}). If an

Algorithm 3.2 Adaptive Personal LogReg

input: $\mathcal{D} = (\mathbf{x}_{ui}, y_{ui}), \mathbf{x}_{ui} \in \mathcal{R}^K, y_{ui} \in \{1, 0\}, u \in \mathcal{U}$
output: $\widetilde{\mathbf{W}} = \{\mathbf{w}_u\}, u \in \mathcal{U}$
procedure AP-LogReg($\mathcal{D}$, **W**)
  $(g^{(0)}, g^{(1)}, ..., g^{(T)}) \leftarrow$ Global Training ▷ Eq.1
  HashTable $A[u] = t_u \leftarrow$ Scheduler ($\mathcal{D}$) ▷ Alg. 3.1
  $\widetilde{\mathbf{W}} = \{\}$
  Distribute global gradients $\mathbf{g}^{(0:T)}$
  for user $u \in \mathcal{U}$ **do** ▷ Parallel Computing
    Fetch adapted gradients split t_u from A
    $\widetilde{\mathbf{w}}_u \leftarrow$ LocalTraining($\mathcal{D}_u, g^{(0:t_u)}$) ▷ Eq.3
    $\widetilde{\mathbf{W}} = \widetilde{\mathbf{W}} \cup \widetilde{\mathbf{w}}_u$
  return $\widetilde{\mathbf{W}}$

individual has watched a large amount of specific types of movies, it is more reasonable for the system to recommend personalized movie selections than to recommend popular movies that have been watched by other users. However, given a new user without sufficient historical data, it is safe for the system to recommend well known popular items.

It is difficult to determine a good adaptation locally since the local models for users do not have global knowledge of other users. Under this assumption, a centralized coordinator is designed for distributing global gradients to individual users. Each user is assigned an iteration split t_u given the data distribution across all users. The linear mapping of users data size $|D_u|$ to t_u helps coordinate users. For instance, given C groups of users, the linear mapping adaptation sorts user by their data size in descending order. Then according to the group index, it assigns different subsequences of global gradients to different groups such as $t_u = \lfloor T * \frac{\tau_u}{C} \rfloor$ where τ_u is the group index for user u. For the group with the largest dataset, our method assigns early gradients such as $g^{0:1}$ to this group. The detailed description of the adaptation is presented in Algorithm 3.1.

3.1 Methods

We instantiate the proposed framework to three machine learning models, LogReg, GBDT, and MF, which are widely used for content recommendation. We shall point out that each of these models have individual characteristics, which differentiate it from the others. However, the way we extend these models to their personal versions remains consistent. The demonstration of these three formulations allows us to justify the effectiveness of our proposed framework for learning personal models.

•***Adaptive Logistic Regression***. Generalized linear models, such as LogReg, have been exploited in forecasting users' click events (clicking on advertisements or news articles) [23, 24]. In the LogReg method, the probability of an instance $\mathbf{x}_{ui}$ being positive is estimated by a logistic function, which is $\hat{y}_{ui} = \sigma(\mathbf{w}_u^T \mathbf{x}_{ui})$. And it optimizes the log-likelihood with instances as:

$$\min_{\mathbf{w}} L(\mathbf{w}) = \sum_{d=1}^{N} f(\mathbf{w}) + \lambda r(\mathbf{w}) \tag{1}$$

where $f(\mathbf{w})$ is the negative log likelihood function, $r(\mathbf{w})$ is a regularization function and λ is the coefficient. In our framework, besides

Algorithm 3.3 Adaptive Personal GBDT

input: $\mathcal{D} = (\mathbf{x}_{ui}, y_{ui}), \mathbf{x}_{ui} \in \mathcal{R}^K, y_{ui} \in \{1, 0\}, u \in \mathcal{U}$
Output: $\{\mathcal{H}\}$
procedure AP-GBDT($\mathcal{D}$)
  Initialize the global tree h_0
  $(h^{(0)}, h^{(1)}, ..., h^{(T)}) \leftarrow$ Global Training ▷ Eq.6
  HashTable $A[u] = t_u \leftarrow$ Scheduler($\mathcal{D}$) ▷ Alg. 3.1
  $\mathcal{H} = \{\}$
  Distribute global gradient trees $h^{(0:T)}$ to users
  for user $u \in \mathcal{U}$ **do** ▷ Parallel Computing
    Fetch adapted gradients split t_u from A
    $\widetilde{F}_u \leftarrow$ LocalTraining ($\mathcal{D}_u, h^{(0:t_u)}$) ▷ Eq.7
    $\mathcal{H} = \mathcal{H} \cup \widetilde{F}_u$
  return $\mathcal{H}$

a global parameter $\mathbf{w}$, each user has his/her own local model $\mathbf{w}_u$. First, we train a global model for all users and save gradients at each iterations as $\mathcal{G} = (g^{(0)}, g^{(1)}, ..., g^{(T)})$. Then we initialize each user's parameter by an adaptive global model as, using SGD:

$$\widetilde{\mathbf{w}}_u^{(0)} = \mathbf{w}^{(0)} - \eta_1 \sum_{t=1}^{t_u - 1} g^{(t)}(\mathbf{w}) \tag{2}$$

where each user has a different adaptive t_u. In this case, users with more examples start with an early global parameter (less global gradient descents) and users with less examples start with a relative late global parameter (more global gradient descents). And we update the personal model parameters:

$$\widetilde{\mathbf{w}}_u^{(T)} = \widetilde{\mathbf{w}}_u^{(0)} - \eta_2 \sum_{t=1}^{T - t_u} g^{(t)}(\mathbf{w}_u) \tag{3}$$

Using L_2 regularization in Eq. 1, Eq. 3 is expanded as:

$$\widetilde{\mathbf{w}}_u^{(T)} = \mathbf{w}^{(0)} - \eta_1 \sum_{t=1}^{t_u-1} \sum_{d}^{N} \frac{\partial f}{\partial \mathbf{w}} - \eta_2 \sum_{t=t_u}^{T} \sum_{j}^{N_u} \frac{\partial f}{\partial \mathbf{w}_u} - \eta_1 \lambda \sum_{t=1}^{t_u-1} \mathbf{w} - \eta_2 \lambda \sum_{t=t_u}^{T} \mathbf{w}_u \tag{4}$$

With the above updating rule, it is easy to prove that the adaptive personal method based on gradients is a special case of a general multi-task learning (MTL-LogReg) formula for users as follows:

$$L'(\mathbf{w}_u) = \sum_{j}^{N_u} f(y_{uj}, \hat{y}_{uj}) + \frac{\lambda_1}{2} ||\mathbf{w}_u - \mathbf{w}||^2 + \frac{\lambda_2}{2} ||\mathbf{w}_u||^2 \tag{5}$$

Our application is not limited to only multi-task learning problem. It also fits other algorithms such as Gradient Boosting Decision Tree.

•***Adaptive Gradient Boosting Decision Tree***. Tree boosting has been shown to give state-of-the-art results on many standard classification benchmarks [21]. Unlike LogReg and MF methods, training of Gradient Boosting Decision Tree (GBDT) fits a regression tree h for the residual which is the gradient descent of the loss function. We initialize the estimate as $F(x) = \sum_{u=1}^{U} \sum_{j=1}^{N_u} \frac{y_j}{N}$. During each iteration t in stochastic gradient descent, we calculate the gradient descent $-g(x_j) = y_j - F(x_j)$ and a regression tree h^t is fitted to $-g(x_j)$. In this case, we get $F^t = F^{t-1} + \rho h^{(t-1)}$. The global objective function for GBDT is defined as an additive format:

$$L^{(t)} = \sum_{d}^{N} l(y_d, F_d^{(t-1)} + \rho h^{(t)}) + \Omega(h^{(t)})$$
$$= \sum_{d}^{N} l(y_d, F_d^{(0)} + \rho h^{(0:t)}) + \Omega(h^{(t)}) \tag{6}$$

where $l()$ refers to the loss function such as least square loss, or logistic loss. We apply square loss in our experiment. Global gradient boosting trees are assumed to have more complicated structure than local trees because the global feature space is sparse. In order to avoid overfitting for each user, we add more constraints on the local tree fitting in the regularization part than the global tree regularization.

For adaption, we initialize each user's regression tree from the global regression tree as $\widetilde{F}_u^{(0)}$ and for each personal model, we train the local GBDT as

$$\widetilde{F}_u^{(0)} = F^{(0)} + \rho h^{(0:t_u)}, \ \widetilde{F}_u^{(T)} = \widetilde{F}_u^{(0)} + \rho h_u^{(t_u:T)} \tag{7}$$

Basically, the global GBDT adapted to a user $h^{(0:t_u)}$ generates an initial score for each instance in the user's data. Based on the initial score, the personal GBDT extends training regression trees to fit its own data. Through the adaptation, adaptive GBDT balances the global tree and local trees and also avoids tree combination with different structures.

•***Adaptive Matrix Factorization***. Off-the-shelf algorithms for recommendation systems, such as Matrix Factorization (MF), have been widely applied in various applications such as movies, music, and products. MF assumes each user and item is represented by a global latent vector $\mathbf{q}_u$ and $\mathbf{p}_i$ respectively. The global objective function is defined as:

$$\min_{q_*, p_*, b_*} \sum_{u,i} (r_{ui} - \mu - b_u - b_i - \mathbf{q}_u^T \mathbf{p}_i)$$
$$+ \lambda(||\mathbf{q}_u||^2 + ||\mathbf{p}_i||^2 + b_u^2 + b_i^2) \tag{8}$$

where r_{ui} is the rating score of user u on item i, μ is the global average rating score for current item, b_u and b_i are bias variables for user u and item i.

This optimization problem can be solved by gradient descent technique. For a given training instance r_{ui}, we modify the parameters by moving in the opposite direction of the gradient, yielding:

$$e_{ui} = \mathbf{q}_u^T \mathbf{p}_i + \mu + b_u + b_i - r_{ui} \tag{9}$$

$$g(\mathbf{q}_u) = e_{ui}\mathbf{p}_i + \lambda \mathbf{q}_u, \ g(\mathbf{p}_i) = e_{ui}\mathbf{q}_u + \lambda \mathbf{p}_i \tag{10}$$

$$g(b_u) = e_{ui} + \lambda b_u, \ g(b_i) = e_{ui} + \lambda b_i \tag{11}$$

Observing the SGD solution, the user latent vectors help improve personalization in recommendation. The learning process for updating $\mathbf{q}_u$ is shaped by the global item vector $\mathbf{p}_i$ (Eq.??). Furthermore, the item latent vector is shaped by other users (Eq.10).

For our proposed adaptive learning paradigm, we update the personal user latent models $(\widetilde{\mathbf{q}}_u, \widetilde{b}_u)$ by their own dataset and adaptively use global gradients $g(\mathbf{q}_u), g(\mathbf{p}_i)$ to each user.

$$\widetilde{\mathbf{q}}_u^{(0)} = \mathbf{q}_u^{(0)} - \eta_1 \sum_{t=0}^{t_u} g^{(t)}(\mathbf{q}_u), \widetilde{\mathbf{q}}_u^{(T)} = \widetilde{\mathbf{q}}_u^{(0)} - \eta_2 \sum_{t=0}^{T-t_u} g^{(t)}(\widetilde{\mathbf{q}}_u) \tag{12}$$

$$\widetilde{b}_u^{(0)} = b_u^{(0)} - \eta_1 \sum_{k=0}^{t_u} g^{(t)}(b_u), \widetilde{b}_u^{(T)} = \widetilde{b}_u^{(0)} - \eta_2 \sum_{t=0}^{T-t_u} g^{(t)}(\widetilde{b}_u) \tag{13}$$

Algorithm 3.4 Adaptive Personal MF

```
input: 𝒟 = (u, i, r), u ∈ 𝒰, v ∈ 𝒱, r ∈ ℛ+
output: {Q̃, b̃}
procedure AP-MF(𝒟)
    (P(0), P(1), ..., P(T)) ← Global Training                ▹ Eq.8
    (Q(0), Q(1), ..., Q(T)) ← Global Training                ▹ Eq.8
    HashTable A[u] = t_u ← Scheduler(𝒟)                      ▹ Alg. 3.1
    Q̃ = {}, b̃ = {}
    Distribute global gradients g(q_u)^(0:T), g(P)^(0:T)
    for user u ∈ 𝒰 do                                        ▹ Parallel Computing
        Fetch adapted gradients split t_u from A
        q̃_u, b̃_u ← LocalTraining (𝒟_u, g(q)^(0:t_u), g(P))
                                                             ▹ Eq.12, 13
        Q̃ = Q̃ ∪ q̃_u, b̃ = b̃ ∪ b̃_u
    return (Q̃, b̃)
```

In the global training, we observe that each user latent vector $\mathbf{q}_u$ and item latent vector $\mathbf{p}_i$ are influenced by global instances. In other words, they are influenced by other users' ratings. Both user and item latent vectors are learned and updated through multiple iterations.

In the adaptive personal training, we trace back to an early user latent vector $\widetilde{\mathbf{q}}_u^{(0)}$ which means we adapt global gradients $g^{(0:t_u)}(\mathbf{q}_u)$ and we fix the global item latent vectors $\mathbf{p}_i^{(t)}$. Then we update the user latent vector $\widetilde{\mathbf{q}}_u$ by its own dataset which means the user latent vector is less influenced by the global items and more influenced by its personal rating instances.

In the MF experiment, user and item latent vectors are not easy to be learned if only local data is been exploited. In this case, for comparison, we setup a situation for local-MF that a global MF model is first trained for t iterations and then we send its learned parameters to all users. Local models at user level are initialized by the same global information but they keep updating their user latent vectors locally for multiple runs till convergence.

3.2 Properties

We point out a few properties of the proposed framework in order to understand its usefulness.

•**Generality:** The framework is generic to a variety of machine learning models that can be optimized by gradient-based approaches. Although in the following of the paper our discussion is limited within three use cases, it is straightforward to apply this framework to other models with only a few configuration changes.

•**Extensibility:** The framework is extensible to be used for more sophisticated use cases. First, it is straightforward to extend our framework to incorporate different gradient computation, such as the gradient from a single example or from a mini-batch. Second, it is convenient to extend this framework to the online learning setting, for which we can maintain a window (with fixed size) of gradients from the global model, rather than keeping all the gradients as in the offline setting. Note that in this paper, we focus our presentation and experimentation on the offline setting, while leaving the implementation of this framework for online learning to future work.

Table 1: Dataset Statistics

News Portal				
# users	54845			
# features	351	Movie Ratings		
# click events	2,378,918		Netflix	Movielens
# view events	26,916,620	# users	478920	1721
avg # click events per user	43	# items	17766	3331
avg # events per user	534	sparsity	0.00942	0.039

•**Scalability:** In this framework, the training process of a personal model for one user is independent of all the other users. As such, we can deploy the training process for all the users in an embarassingly parallel manner, making our framework highly scalable. This is useful in the case of mobile device users where the training of personal models can happen on the client side. The training procedure of a global model can be in batch-mode and offline while the training procedure of personal models is parallelizable and online.

The proposed framework is more flexible than conventional MTL algorithms. First, we do not explicit define relationships between global model parameters and personal ones. Second, our approach is straightforward and easy to implement for a wide range of use cases whereas MTL is usually tied to a specific model formalism.

4 EXPERIMENTAL EVALUATION

In this section, we conduct a series of experiments to evaluate the effectiveness of the proposed framework for improving personal models for content recommendation. We first describe the experimental settings including the datasets, evaluation metrics and protocols. Then, we demonstrate the performance of our framework for learning adaptive personal models for LogReg, GBDT, and MF.

4.1 Datasets

The datasets used in our experiments are based on two different domains. One dataset was collected from a main-stream news portal site, which serves news feeds to millions of users. We sampled the event logs from one month in 2016 with user id and article id anonymized. Key statistics of this dataset are presented in Table 1. In this dataset, each example represents an event that a user clicked a news article, or a user viewed but not clicked an article. Note that we take the user click action as a positive label, and the view-but-not-click action as a negative label. Also note that each event is associated with a feature vector. Since this dataset is suitable for ranking content items, we use this dataset to evaluate the LogReg and GBDT-based personal models, which are the major ranking models in real-world applications.

To evaluate the personal models for MF, we use the datasets from the movie domain, i.e., MovieLens 1M dataset and Netflix dataset, which are conventional benchmark datasets in the research community of recommender systems. The statistics of the two datasets are summarized in Table 1.

4.2 Comparative Approaches

We summarize the objective functions for the comparison methods in Table 2. Global models are trained on all users' data. Local models are learned locally on per user's data. MTL represents the approach that users models are averaged by a global parameter. Note that for local-MF, the user vector and item vector are learned globally. We initialize each user model by a trained global model $(\widetilde{q}_u, \widetilde{p}_i, \widetilde{b}_u, \widetilde{b}_i)$ and then we train a localized MF model per user by only using each user's data. The result is evaluated per user.

4.3 Protocol and Metrics

In our experiments, each dataset is split into a training set and a test set. Specifically, for each user we randomly select 80% of his data points to be used in the training set, and leave the rest 20% into the test set. We also use a small fraction of the training set as a validation set to tune the parameters involved in different models. Since LogReg and GBDT are specifically used as ranking models on the news dataset, we adopt the standard ranking metrics from the information retrieval community, i.e., Mean Average Precision (MAP), Mean Reciprocal Rank (MRR), Area Under Curve (AUC), and normalized Discounted Cumulative Gain (nDCG), to evaluate their ranking performance. For evaluating MF-related models on the MovieLens and Netflix datasets, we adopt conventional metrics (as used in the Netflix Prize competition and other public contests), Root Mean Squared Error (RMSE) and Mean Absolute Error (MAE).

In addition to the overall performance, we particularly focus on the performance for different user groups in order to understand the effectiveness of personal models. On the news dataset, we divide users into seven groups based on their data size, indexed from group 1 (smallest) to group 7 (largest). For example, users in group 1 have data points in range $(0, 10)$ and users in group 7 have the range of $(3162, 20000)$. For the MovieLens and Netflix datasets, we sample and then cluster users into five groups and the group with the largest data points in the range of $(200, \infty)$.

4.4 Results

Through the experimental evaluation, we aim to address the following specific research questions: 1) Can we learn personal models from the proposed framework to improve recommendation performance over the global-, local- model and the personalized MTL-models (Sec.4.2)? 2) Can we learn personal models that are adaptive to the characteristics of individual users? 3) Is the proposed framework generally effective for content recommendation across different models and use cases?

4.4.1 Evaluation for Logistic Regression.

Performance Across User Groups. Figure 3 shows the AUC, MRR, MAP and nDCG (averaging across users) scores on test dataset for different LogReg models with varying training epochs. The proposed adaptive LogReg models achieve higher scores on AUC, MAP, MRR, and nDCG with relatively fewer epochs. In terms averaged AUC, MAP, MRR, and nDCG scores across groups, global LogReg models perform the worst compared to other methods.

Performance with Changing # of Training Samples. We compare the performance in terms of AUC score for MTL-LogReg (Eq. 5) and Adaptive-LogReg with # of training samples from 20% to 100% in Figure 4a. Adaptive-LogReg performs better than Global-LogReg, Local-LogReg, and MTL-LogReg in AUC.

4.4.2 Evaluation for Gradient Boosting Decision Tree.

Table 2: Objective functions for different methods.

Model	LogReg	GBDT	MF
Global	$\sum_{d=1}^{N} f(\mathbf{w}) + \lambda\|\|\mathbf{w}\|\|_2^2$	$\sum_{d}^{N} l(y_d, F_d^{(0)} + \rho h^{(0:t)}) + \Omega(h^{(t)})$	$\sum_{u,i}(r_{ui} - \mu - b_u - b_i - \mathbf{q}_u^T \mathbf{p}_i) + \lambda(\|\|\mathbf{q}_u\|\|^2 + \|\|\mathbf{p}_i\|\|^2 + b_u^2 + b_i^2)$
Local	$\sum_{j=1}^{N_u} f(\mathbf{w}_u) + \lambda\|\|\mathbf{w}_u\|\|_2^2$	$\sum_{j}^{N_u} l(y_j, F_j^{(0)} + \rho h^{(0:t)}) + \Omega(h^{(t)})$	$\sum_{i \in N_u}(r_{ui} - \mu - \widetilde{b}_u - \widetilde{b}_i - \widetilde{\mathbf{q}}_u^T \widetilde{\mathbf{p}}_i) + \lambda(\|\|\widetilde{\mathbf{q}}_u\|\|^2 + \|\|\widetilde{\mathbf{p}}_i\|\|^2 + \widetilde{b}_u^2 + \widetilde{b}_i^2)$
MTL	$\sum_{j}^{N_u} f(\mathbf{w}_u) + \frac{\lambda_1}{2}\|\|\mathbf{w}_u - \mathbf{w}\|\|^2 + \frac{\lambda_2}{2}\|\|\mathbf{w}_u\|\|^2$	-	global+$\lambda_2[(\mathbf{q}_u - \mathbf{q})^2 + (\mathbf{p}_i - \mathbf{p})^2 + (b_u - A_u)^2 + (b_i - A_i)^2]$

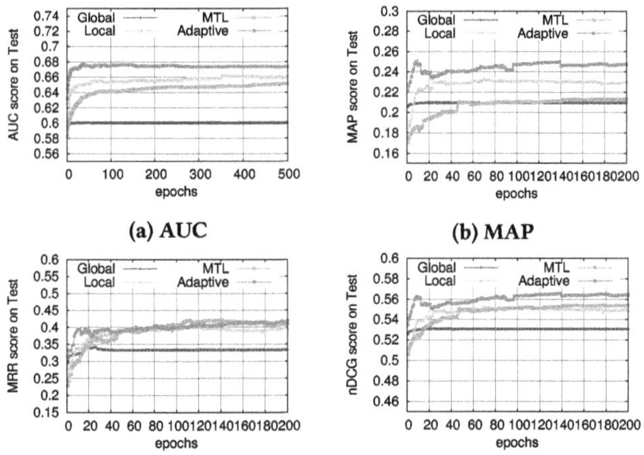

(a) AUC (b) MAP

(c) MRR (d) nDCG

Figure 3: AUC, MAP, MRR and nDCG scores of LogReg models with X-axis as the epochs in the SGD algorithm.

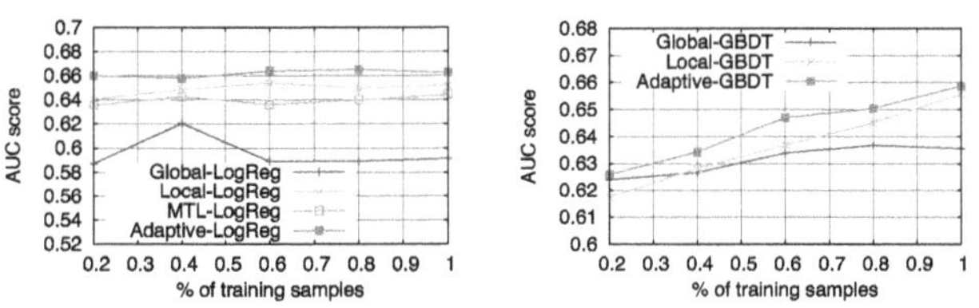

(a) LogReg (b) GBDT

Figure 4: Comparison of Global, Local, and Adaptive models with varying # of training examples.

Performance Across User Groups. Given the space limitation, we only show the MAP score for the groups of users with least data and most data for GBDT models in Figure 5. We observe that adaptive-GBDT outperform both global and local GBDT models in terms of MAP for all groups of users.

Performance with Changing # of Training Samples. We compare the performance in terms of AUC score for Global-GBDT, Local-GBDT, and Adaptive-GBDT with # of training samples from 20% to 100% in Figure 4b. On average of AUC, Adaptive-GBDT performs better than other methods. We also observe that with the increase of training samples, GBDT based methods tend to perform better while LogReg methods achieve relatively stable scores.

Overall Comparison of LogReg and GBDT. In Table 3, we show the average MAP, MRR, and AUC scores across users with respect to different iterations for logistic regression adaptation and GBDT. Global-LogReg is not shown here because it performs the worst as in Fig. 4a. With relatively less iterations, adaptive method outperforms global, local, and MTL in terms of all metrics. Specifically, for AUC score, adaptive-LogReg achieves 4.4% and 2.9% rise compared to the best MTL and local-LogReg models. Adaptive-GBDT outperforms the best globa-GBDT by 1.6% with p-value (=0.003) from a paired t-test experiment.

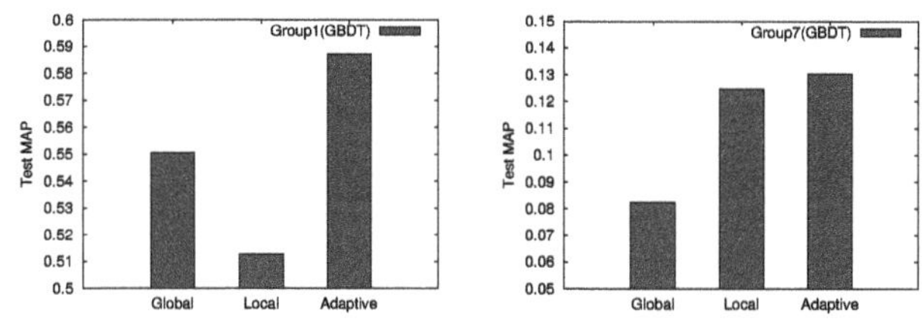

(a) Group 1 (b) Group 7

Figure 5: MAP Comparison of Group 1 (least) and Group 7 (most) for GBDT methods.

4.4.3 Evaluation for Matrix Factorization.

Overall Comparison. In Table 4, we show the average RMSE and MAE scores across groups of users with respect to different values of K (the dimension of latent vectors). In this experiment, global-MF denotes the baseline MF algorithm on the rating data of all users. However, it is not natural to train a local model for each user since the latent vectors $\mathbf{q}, \mathbf{p}$ are updated using a global dataset. Thus we use a different setting as "Local" to denote that we train a global MF model and save the global user latent vectors for each iteration ($\mathbf{U}^{(0)}$ to $\mathbf{U}^{(T)}$) until it converges. Then we use the last model parameter $\mathbf{U}^{(T)}$ to initialize each user model for a localized training process. "Adaptive" indicates the proposed method in the algorithm in Section 3. MTL-MF model is a generalized MTL method on MF. We introduce global parameters ($\mathbf{p}, \mathbf{q}$ and global bias) and regularize the user parameters to be close to global parameter as in the LogReg models. With respect to different choices of K (5, 10, 20), adaptive-MF achieves the best performance (lowest RMSE and MAE values) compared to global-MF, local-MF, and MTL-MF. It outperforms global-MF, local-MF, and MTL-MF by 3.7%, 0.8% and 1.4% (p-values are 0.008, 0.04, 0.002 from paired t-tests) in terms of RMSE(K=5). MTL-MF did not show good performance when ratings on items have a large variance. The model forced the learned item vectors to be similar to the global one.

Performance Across User Groups. Figure 6 shows the quartile analysis of the group level RMSE and MAE for different MF models and for two datasets. We group users in descending order based on their dataset sizes. Comparing to global-MF, both local and adaptive-MF achieve better predictive performance in terms of these two metrics.

Table 3: Performance comparison based on MAP, MRR, AUC and nDCG for LogReg and GBDT. Each value is calculated from the average of 10 runs with standard deviation.

	MTL-LogReg					**Global**-GBDT			
T	MAP	MRR	AUC	nDCG	#Trees	MAP	MRR	AUC	nDCG
20	0.1937(8e-5)	0.3493(4e-4)	0.6226(8e-5)	0.5341(8e-5)	20	0.2094(1e-3)	0.3617(2e-3)	0.6290(1e-3)	0.5329(6e-4)
50	0.2096(4e-5)	0.3834(2e-4)	0.6376(8e-5)	0.5493(4e-5)	50	0.2137(1e-3)	0.3726(1e-3)	0.6341(1e-3)	0.5372(6e-4)
100	0.2104(5e-6)	0.4059(6e-5)	0.6417(9e-7)	0.5512(5e-6)	100	0.2150(8e-3)	0.3769(1e-3)	0.6356(8e-4)	0.5392(6e-4)
200	0.2132(1e-6)	0.4089(7e-5)	0.6459(2e-6)	0.5538(3e-6)	200	0.2161(5e-4)	0.3848(1e-3)	0.6412(6e-4)	0.5415(5e-4)
	Local-LogReg					**Local**-GBDT			
T	MAP	MRR	AUC	nDCG	#Trees	MAP	MRR	AUC	nDCG
20	0.2221(1e-3)	0.3681(6e-3)	0.6469(8e-4)	0.5443(1e-3)	20	0.2262(2e-3)	0.4510(5e-3)	0.6344(3e-3)	0.5604(2e-3)
50	0.2289(2e-3)	0.3890(4e-3)	0.6521(1e-3)	0.5485(1e-3)	50	0.2319(2e-3)	0.4446(4e-3)	0.6505(2e-3)	0.5651(2e-3)
100	0.2308(1e-3)	0.3938(4e-3)	0.6543(9e-4)	0.5504(1e-3)	100	0.2328(1e-3)	0.4465(5e-3)	0.6558(2e-3)	0.5651(2e-3)
200	0.2294(1e-3)	0.3959(2e-3)	0.6555(8e-4)	0.5495(1e-3)	200	0.2322(2e-3)	0.4431(2e-3)	0.6566(1e-3)	0.5649(1e-3)
	Adaptive-LogReg					**Adaptive**-GBDT			
T	MAP	MRR	AUC	nDCG	#Trees	MAP	MRR	AUC	nDCG
20+50	0.2343(3e-4)	0.3919(5e-4)	0.6633(8e-5)	0.5542(2e-4)	20+50	**0.2343**(2e-3)	0.4474(4e-3)	0.6555(2e-3)	0.5661(2e-3)
50+50	0.2353(1e-3)	0.4013(8e-3)	0.6623(7e-4)	0.5559(1e-3)	50+50	0.2325(2e-3)	0.4472(1e-4)	0.6561(8e-4)	**0.5666**(6e-4)
10+200	**0.2454**(5e-5)	**0.4160**(4e-4)	**0.6744**(5e-5)	**0.5643**(4e-5)	10+100	0.2329(2e-3)	0.4423(3e-3)	**0.6587**(1e-3)	0.5650(3e-3)

Table 4: Performance comparison based on RMSE, MAE for MF. NF refers to Netflix and ML refers to MovieLens.

NF	**Global**-MF		**Local**-MF		**MTL**-MF		**Adaptive**-MF	
K	RMSE	MAE	RMSE	MAE	RMSE	MAE	RMSE	MAE
5	0.9343	0.7336	0.907	0.7012	0.9119	0.7148	**0.8991**	**0.6988**
10	0.9215	0.7168	0.8997	0.6933	0.9328	0.7245	**0.8912**	**0.6910**
20	0.9218	0.7166	0.8999	0.6920	0.9208	0.7144	**0.8907**	**0.6892**
ML	**Global**-MF		**Local**-MF		**MTL**-MF		**Adaptive**-MF	
K	RMSE	MAE	RMSE	MAE	RMSE	MAE	RMSE	MAE
5	0.9309	0.7338	0.9254	0.7283	0.9337	0.7365	**0.9188**	**0.724**
10	0.9337	0.7357	0.9253	0.7269	0.9352	0.7401	**0.9178**	**0.7223**
20	0.9348	0.7386	0.9263	0.7285	0.9475	0.751	**0.9184**	**0.7236**

4.4.4 Summary. Based on all the experimental results across three different applications, we do observe that the proposed framework allows us to effectively and efficiently build personal models that lead to improved recommendation performance over either the global model or the local model. This observation confirms a positive answer to our first research question. Based on the results across different user groups in each scenario, we also observe that the proposed framework can adaptively learn personal models by exploiting the global gradients according to individual's characteristic. This observation allows us to answer our second research question affirmatively. Finally, as our experiments demonstrate the usefulness of our framework across a wide scope, in terms of both model classes and application domains, it provides a solid evidence for us to give a positive answer to our third and last research question.

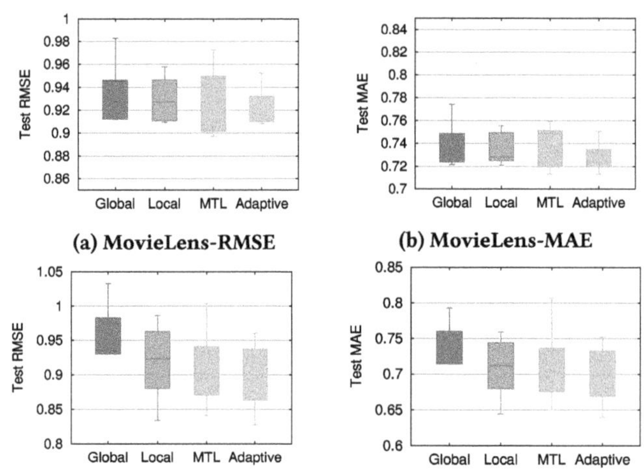

(a) MovieLens-RMSE (b) MovieLens-MAE

(c) Netflix-RMSE (d) Netflix-MAE

Figure 6: RMSE and MAE scores with respect to Global, Local and Adaptive MF models across 5 groups of users.

5 CONCLUSION

In this paper we sought to improve users' experience in personal recommendation where users have varying amount of historical data. We presented a general purpose framework for learning personal models based on adapting the popular gradient descent optimization techniques. We instantiate our proposed framework with three different algorithms and provide training procedures for each of the cases. Through extensive empirical evaluation, we demonstrate the strengths of our proposed framework in terms of predictive performance on real world datasets. In the future, we plan to implement an online learning framework for learning personal models through gradient adaptation. Also, we are interested in studying the effects of adaptive learning rates for users in personal models.

ACKNOWLEDGMENTS

We thank Yahoo Research for its support on this work with an internship. We also thank Ting Chen, Qian Zhao and Qingyun Wu for their helpful discussions. The work was partially supported by NSF Grant No. 1447489.

REFERENCES

[1] Deepak Agarwal and Bee-Chung Chen. Regression-based Latent Factor Models. In *Proceedings of KDD 2009*. 19–28. DOI:http://dx.doi.org/10.1145/1557019.1557029

[2] Deepak Agarwal, Bo Long, Jonathan Traupman, Doris Xin, and Liang Zhang. LASER: A Scalable Response Prediction Platform for Online Advertising. In *Proceedings of WSDM 2014*. 173–182. DOI:http://dx.doi.org/10.1145/2556195.2556252

[3] Xavier Amatriain and Deepak Agarwal. 2016. Tutorial: Lessons Learned from Building Real-life Recommender Systems. In *Proceedings of the 10th ACM Conference on Recommender Systems (RecSys '16)*. ACM, New York, NY, USA, 433–433. DOI:http://dx.doi.org/10.1145/2959100.2959194

[4] Xavier Amatriain, Neal Lathia, Josep M. Pujol, Haewoon Kwak, and Nuria Oliver. 2009. The Wisdom of the Few: A Collaborative Filtering Approach Based on Expert Opinions from the Web. In *Proceedings of the 32Nd International ACM SIGIR Conference on Research and Development in Information Retrieval (SIGIR '09)*. ACM, New York, NY, USA, 532–539. DOI:http://dx.doi.org/10.1145/1571941.1572033

[5] Yoshua Bengio, Jérôme Louradour, Ronan Collobert, and Jason Weston. 2009. Curriculum Learning. In *Proceedings of the 26th Annual International Conference on Machine Learning (ICML '09)*. ACM, New York, NY, USA, 41–48. DOI:http://dx.doi.org/10.1145/1553374.1553380

[6] J. Bennett and S. Lanning. 2007. The Netflix Prize. In *Proceedings of the KDD Cup Workshop 2007*. 3–6.

[7] Alex Beutel, Ed H. Chi, Zhiyuan Cheng, Hubert Pham, and John Anderson. 2017. Beyond Globally Optimal: Focused Learning for Improved Recommendations. In *Proceedings of the 26th International Conference on World Wide Web (WWW '17)*.

[8] Christopher J. C. Burges. 2010. *From RankNet to LambdaRank to LambdaMART: An Overview*. Technical Report. Microsoft Research. http://research.microsoft.com/en-us/um/people/cburges/tech_reports/MSR-TR-2010-82.pdf

[9] Allison J.B. Chaney, David M. Blei, and Tina Eliassi-Rad. 2015. A Probabilistic Model for Using Social Networks in Personalized Item Recommendation. In *Proceedings of the 9th ACM Conference on Recommender Systems (RecSys '15)*. ACM, New York, NY, USA, 43–50. DOI:http://dx.doi.org/10.1145/2792838.2800193

[10] Olivier Chapelle, Pannagadatta Shivaswamy, Srinivas Vadrevu, Kilian Weinberger, Ya Zhang, and Belle Tseng. 2011. Boosted multi-task learning. *Machine Learning* 85, 1 (2011), 149–173. DOI:http://dx.doi.org/10.1007/s10994-010-5231-6

[11] Tianqi Chen and Carlos Guestrin. XGBoost: A Scalable Tree Boosting System. In *Proceedings of KDD 2016*. 785–794.

[12] David R. Cox. 1958. The regression analysis of binary sequences (with discussion). *J Roy Stat Soc B* 20 (1958), 215–242.

[13] Jerome H. Friedman. 2000. Greedy Function Approximation: A Gradient Boosting Machine. *Annals of Statistics* 29 (2000), 1189–1232.

[14] Jerome H. Friedman. 2002. Stochastic gradient boosting. *Computational Statistics & Data Analysis* 38, 4 (2002), 367 – 378. DOI:http://dx.doi.org/10.1016/S0167-9473(01)00065-2 Nonlinear Methods and Data Mining.

[15] Simon Funk. 2006. Netflix Update: Try this at Home. (2006).

[16] Bikash Joshi, Franck Iutzeler, and Massih-Reza Amini. 2016. Asynchronous Distributed Matrix Factorization with Similar User and Item Based Regularization. In *Proceedings of the 10th ACM Conference on Recommender Systems (RecSys '16)*. ACM, New York, NY, USA, 75–78. DOI:http://dx.doi.org/10.1145/2959100.2959161

[17] Alexandros Karatzoglou, Linas Baltrunas, and Yue Shi. 2013. Learning to Rank for Recommender Systems. In *Proceedings of the 7th ACM Conference on Recommender Systems (RecSys '13)*. ACM, New York, NY, USA, 493–494. DOI:http://dx.doi.org/10.1145/2507157.2508063

[18] Gunhee Kim and Eric P. Xing. Time-sensitive Web Image Ranking and Retrieval via Dynamic Multi-task Regression. In *Proceedings of WSDM 2013*. 163–172. DOI:http://dx.doi.org/10.1145/2433396.2433417

[19] Yehuda Koren. Factorization Meets the Neighborhood: A Multifaceted Collaborative Filtering Model. In *Proceedings of KDD 2008*. 426–434. DOI:http://dx.doi.org/10.1145/1401890.1401944

[20] Roy Levin, Hassan Abassi, and Uzi Cohen. 2016. Guided Walk: A Scalable Recommendation Algorithm for Complex Heterogeneous Social Networks. In *Proceedings of the 10th ACM Conference on Recommender Systems (RecSys '16)*. ACM, New York, NY, USA, 293–300. DOI:http://dx.doi.org/10.1145/2959100.2959143

[21] Ping Li. Robust LogitBoost and Adaptive Base Class (ABC) LogitBoost. In *Proceedings of the Twenty-Sixth Conference on Uncertainty in Artificial Intelligence (UAI2010)*. 302–311. https://dslpitt.org/uai/displayArticleDetails.jsp?mmnu=1&smnu=2&article_id=2158&proceeding_id=26

[22] Peter Lofgren, Siddhartha Banerjee, and Ashish Goel. 2016. Personalized PageRank Estimation and Search: A Bidirectional Approach. In *Proceedings of the Ninth ACM International Conference on Web Search and Data Mining (WSDM '16)*. ACM, New York, NY, USA, 163–172. DOI:http://dx.doi.org/10.1145/2835776.2835823

[23] H. Brendan McMahan. 2011. Follow-the-Regularized-Leader and Mirror Descent: Equivalence Theorems and L1 Regularization. In *Proceedings of the 14th International Conference on Artificial Intelligence and Statistics (AISTATS)*.

[24] H. Brendan McMahan, Gary Holt, D. Sculley, Michael Young, Dietmar Ebner, Julian Grady, Lan Nie, Todd Phillips, Eugene Davydov, Daniel Golovin, Sharat Chikkerur, Dan Liu, Martin Wattenberg, Arnar Mar Hrafnkelsson, Tom Boulos, and Jeremy Kubica. Ad Click Prediction: a View from the Trenches. In *Proceedings of KDD 2013*. 1222–1230.

[25] Xu Miao, Chun-Te Chu, Lijun Tang, Yitong Zhou, Joel Young, and Anmol Bhasin. Distributed Personalization. In *Proceedings of KDD 2015*. 1989–1998. DOI:http://dx.doi.org/10.1145/2783258.2788626

[26] Xia Ning and George Karypis. 2010. Multi-task learning for recommender systems. *Journal of Machine Learning Research* 13 (2010), 269–284.

[27] Alexandre Passos, Piyush Rai, Jacques Wainer, and Hal Daumé III. Flexible Modeling of Latent Task Structures in Multitask Learning. In *Proceedings of ICML 2012*. 1103–1110.

[28] Steffen Rendle. 2012. Factorization Machines with libFM. *ACM Trans. Intell. Syst. Technol.* 3, 3, Article 57 (May 2012), 22 pages.

[29] Steffen Rendle, Christoph Freudenthaler, Zeno Gantner, and Lars Schmidt-Thieme. 2009. BPR: Bayesian Personalized Ranking from Implicit Feedback. In *Proceedings of the Twenty-Fifth Conference on Uncertainty in Artificial Intelligence (UAI '09)*. AUAI Press, Arlington, Virginia, United States, 452–461. http://dl.acm.org/citation.cfm?id=1795114.1795167

[30] Dhaval Shah, Pramod Koneru, Parth Shah, and Rohit Parimi. 2016. News Recommendations at Scale at Bloomberg Media: Challenges and Approaches. In *Proceedings of the 10th ACM Conference on Recommender Systems (RecSys '16)*. ACM, New York, NY, USA, 369–369. DOI:http://dx.doi.org/10.1145/2959100.2959118

[31] S. H. Walker and D. B. Duncan. 1967. Estimation of the probability of an event as a function of several independent variables. *Biometrika* 54, 1 (June 1967), 167–179. http://view.ncbi.nlm.nih.gov/pubmed/6049533

[32] Hongning Wang, Xiaodong He, Ming-Wei Chang, Yang Song, Ryen W. White, and Wei Chu. Personalized Ranking Model Adaptation for Web Search. In *Proceedings of SIGIR 2013*. 323–332. DOI:http://dx.doi.org/10.1145/2484028.2484068

[33] Kilian Weinberger, Anirban Dasgupta, John Langford, Alex Smola, and Josh Attenberg. Feature Hashing for Large Scale Multitask Learning. In *Proceedings of ICML 2009*. 1113–1120. DOI:http://dx.doi.org/10.1145/1553374.1553516

[34] XianXing Zhang, Yitong Zhou, Yiming Ma, Bee-Chung Chen, Liang Zhang, and Deepak Agarwal. GLMix: Generalized Linear Mixed Models For Large-Scale Response Prediction. In *Proceedings of KDD 2016*. 363–372. DOI:http://dx.doi.org/10.1145/2939672.2939684

[35] Zhaohui Zheng, Hongyuan Zha, Tong Zhang, Olivier Chapelle, Keke Chen, and Gordon Sun. A General Boosting Method and its Application to Learning Ranking Functions for Web Search. In *Proceedings of NIPS 2008*. 1697–1704.

entity2rec: Learning User-Item Relatedness from Knowledge Graphs for Top-N Item Recommendation

Enrico Palumbo
ISMB
Turin, Italy
EURECOM
Sophia Antipolis, France
palumbo@ismb.it

Giuseppe Rizzo
ISMB
Turin, Italy
giuseppe.rizzo@ismb.it

Raphaël Troncy
EURECOM
Sophia Antipolis, France
raphael.troncy@eurecom.fr

ABSTRACT

Knowledge Graphs have proven to be extremely valuable to recommender systems, as they enable hybrid graph-based recommendation models encompassing both collaborative and content information. Leveraging this wealth of heterogeneous information for top-N item recommendation is a challenging task, as it requires the ability of effectively encoding a diversity of semantic relations and connectivity patterns. In this work, we propose entity2rec, a novel approach to learning user-item relatedness from knowledge graphs for top-N item recommendation. We start from a knowledge graph modeling user-item and item-item relations and we learn property-specific vector representations of users and items applying neural language models on the network. These representations are used to create property-specific user-item relatedness features, which are in turn fed into learning to rank algorithms to learn a global relatedness model that optimizes top-N item recommendations. We evaluate the proposed approach in terms of ranking quality on the MovieLens 1M dataset, outperforming a number of state-of-the-art recommender systems, and we assess the importance of property-specific relatedness scores on the overall ranking quality.

KEYWORDS

hybrid recommender system, node2vec, knowledge graph embeddings, knowledge graph, neural language models, word2vec, learning to rank, linked open data

1 INTRODUCTION

In the last years, research on recommender systems has shown that knowledge graphs are beneficial for hybrid recommender systems, achieving high ranking quality and effectively tackling typical problems of collaborative systems such as data sparsity or new items [5, 28]. A line of work focuses on Linked Open Data knowledge graphs [3], which represent a wealth of freely available multi-domain ontological knowledge and have successfully been used in the past to build recommender systems [7–9, 13]. The crucial point to leverage knowledge graphs to perform item recommendations is to be able to effectively model user-item relatedness from this rich heterogeneous network. To this end, it is highly desirable to opt for approaches that are able to automatically learn user and item representations from an optimization problem on this graph of interactions, minimizing the time-consuming endeavour of feature engineering and leading to better performance [2]. At the same time, it is also beneficial to use a recommendation model whose features have a straight forward interpretation and that can thus be easily adapted to a specific recommendation problem. Last year, node2vec, a new approach to effectively perform feature learning from networks, which combines a flexible random walk strategy with the power of neural language models, has been proposed [11]. However, this approach is not tailored to knowledge graphs, as it does not distinguish among types of entities and of relations, and has never been applied to address recommendation problems. Starting from this work, in this paper, we introduce entity2rec[1], a novel approach to measure user-item relatedness for top-N item recommendation. The contributions of the proposed work can be summarized as follows: (a) we use a knowledge graph encompassing both collaborative information from user feedback and item information from Linked Open Data; (b) we learn property-specific vector representations of knowledge graph entities in a completely unsupervised way via node2vec; (c) we compute property-specific relatedness scores between users and items using the obtained vector representations; (d) we combine the property-specific relatedness scores in a global relatedness score using a supervised learning to rank approach optimizing top-N item recommendation; (e) we evaluate the effectiveness of the proposed approach with respect to four baselines; (f) we remark that, thanks to the explicit semantics of the properties of the knowledge graph, the model is easily adaptable to specific recommendation problems, as the features have a clear interpretation.

2 RELATED WORK

Recommendations using knowledge graphs: in the past years, several works have shown the effectiveness of external knowledge resources to enhance the performance of recommender systems. In [5, 28] the authors start from a graph-based data model encompassing both user feedback and item relations to generate personalized entity recommendations. In [19, 20] the authors adopt a hybrid graph-based data model utilizing Linked Open Data to extract metapath-based feature that are fed into a learning to rank

RecSys '17, August 27–31, 2017, Como, Italy.
© 2017 ACM. 978-1-4503-4652-8/17/08...$15.00
DOI: http://dx.doi.org/10.1145/3109859.3109889

[1] https://github.com/MultimediaSemantics/entity2rec

framework. In [24] the authors propose a content-based recommender system that automatically learns item representations using a feature learning algorithm on a knowledge graph and show the effectiveness of the learned representations in an Item-based K-Nearest Neighbor method.

Feature learning from networks: feature learning from networks is a fundamental step in node and edge classification. Recently, some models have adapted neural language models to networks, resulting in very effective feature learning processes. In general, it has been shown that these methods tend to work better than other dimensionality reduction techniques based on matrix factorization approaches [11]. In Deep Walk [21], the authors learn node representations by simulating random walks on a graph, generating sequences that are successively processed by a neural language model. In [11], the authors propose node2vec, an improvement over Deep Walk, as it adopts a more flexible and sophisticated random walk exploration strategy.

Learning to rank: learning to rank consists in applying machine learning algorithms to learn a ranking function from training data. In this work, we focus on listwise methods, i.e. learning algorithms that are able to directly optimize ranking accuracy metrics from training data. More in detail, we use Adarank [27] and LambdaMart [4]. Adarank is based on boosting, weak learners are iteratively trained to correct the errors of the previous iteration and finally combined together in a linear model. Adarank avoids the problem of the discontinuity of ranking accuracy metrics by optimizing an upper bound of the actual loss function. LambdaMart is the combination of LambdaRank and the boosted tree method MART [10]. The key idea is to optimize the loss function by directly modeling its gradients estimates with respect to the model scores.

3 APPROACH

3.1 Knowledge Graph

In this work, a knowledge graph is defined as a set $K = (E, R, O)$ where E is the set of entities, $R \subset Ex\Gamma xE$ is a set of typed relations between entities and O is an ontology. The ontology O defines the set of relation types ('properties') Γ, the set of entity types Λ, assigns entities to their type $O : e \in E \longrightarrow \Lambda$ and entity types to their related properties $O : \epsilon \in \Lambda \longrightarrow \Gamma_\epsilon \subset \Gamma$. Knowledge graph edges are thus triples $(i, p, j) \in R$ where $i \in E$ and $j \in E$ are entities and $p \in \Gamma$ is a property. In our model, entities include users $u \in U \subset E$ and items $i \in I \subset E \setminus U$. An observed positive feedback between a user and an item (rating $r \geq 4$ in this work) is described by a property not defined by the ontology O, which we name 'feedback'. Thus, $p \in \Gamma_\epsilon^+ = \Gamma_\epsilon \cup$ '$feedback$'. Throughout this work, the ontology O is represented by the DBpedia ontology [1] and we deal with items of the type ϵ ='dbo:Film'. The properties $\Gamma_{dbo:Film}$ related to an entity of the type 'Film' are available online[2].

3.2 Property-specific user-item relatedness

As mentioned in Sec. 1, node2vec [11] has recently shown to be particularly effective at learning vectorial node representations. In a nutshell, node2vec works by simulating a random walk on the

[2] http://mappings.dbpedia.org/server/ontology/classes/Film

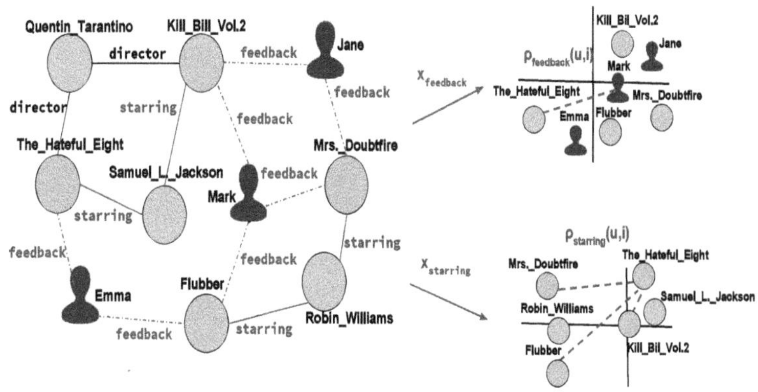

Figure 1: Starting from the knowledge graph K, which contains users (black), items (orange) and other entities (grey), for each property, we generate vector representations x_p with node2vec. The vector representations encode the structure of the graph. For p = 'feedback', we encode collaborative information, users and items are mapped close together in vector space according to their interactions and the relatedness $\rho_{feedback}(u, i)$ can be computed directly. For other properties, such as p = 'starring', we encode content information, items with similar starring actors are embedded close together. The relatedness $\rho_{starring}(u, i)$ has to be computed by averaging the distance from items i' liked by u in the past.

graph, generating sequences of nodes, which are then fed into a neural language model (word2vec [18]) as if they were 'sentences' of a document to learn vector representations of the nodes. From these representations, the relatedness between two nodes can easily be computed using vector similarity measures. However, in a knowledge graph different properties have different semantic values and should have different weights in judging the relatedness between two entities. Films can be related in terms of starring actors and not in terms of subject, share the same director but not the same writer, and processing the whole knowledge graph altogether neglecting the semantics of the properties would not allow to account for this. Thus, we start by learning property-specific vector representation of nodes considering one property at the time. For each property $p \in \Gamma_\epsilon^+$, we define a subgraph K_p as the set of entities connected by the property p, i.e. the triples (i, p, j). Note that for properties where each entity is connected to more than one entity (e.g. 'starring' or 'feedback'), K_p can exhibit complex connectivity patterns. Then, for each K_p independently, we learn a mapping $x_p : e \in K_p \longrightarrow \mathbb{R}^d$, optimizing the node2vec objective function [11]:

$$\max_{x_p} \sum_{e \in K_p} (-\log Z_e + \sum_{n_i \in N(e)} x_p(n_i) \cdot x_p(e)) \quad (1)$$

where $Z_e = \sum_{v \in K_p} \exp(x_p(e) \cdot x_p(v))$ is the per-node partition function and is approximated using negative sampling [18], $N(e) \in K_p$ is the neighborhood of the entity e defined by the node2vec random walk and the optimization is carried out using stochastic gradient ascent over the parameters defining x_p. The optimization attempts to maximize the dot product between vectors of the same neighborhood, i.e. to embed them close together in vector space. Thus, from the vector representations $x_p(e)$, property-specific relatedness scores can be defined as follows:

$$\rho_p(u,i) = \begin{cases} s(x_p(u), x_p(i)) & if\ p = \text{'}feedback\text{'} \\ \frac{1}{|R_+(u)|}\sum_{i' \in R_+(u)} s(x_p(i), x_p(i')) & otherwise \end{cases}$$

where $R_+(u)$ denotes a set of items liked by the user u in the past and s denotes a measure of vector similarity (in this work s = cosine similarity). The features include both collaborative and content information and have a straight-forward interpretation (Fig. 1). When considering p = 'feedback', K is reduced to the graph of user-item interactions and thus $\rho_{feedback}(u,i)$ models collaborative filtering. $\rho_{feedback}(u,i)$ will be high when $x_{feedback}(u)$ is close to the item $x_{feedback}(i)$ in vector space, i.e. when i has been liked by users who have liked the same items of u in the past and are thus tightly connected in the $K_{feedback}$ graph. On the other hand, when p corresponds to other properties of the ontology O the features encode content information. For instance, if p is 'starring', $\rho_{starring}(u,i)$ will be high if $x_{starring}(i)$ is close to items $x_{starring}(i')$, i.e. when i shares starring actors with items that the user u has liked in the past. The hybrid approach is able to tackle the 'new item' issue, as for a new item with no feedback from users, we are still able to compute all the content-based features. For a new user u, the scores $\rho_p(u,i)$ can be computed by averaging the $\rho_p(u',i)$ over all the other users $u' \in U$.

3.3 Global user-item relatedness

For each user-item pair, we are now able to compute all property-specific relatedness scores $\vec{\rho}(u,i) = \{\rho_p(u,i)\}_{p \in \Gamma_e^+}$. We aim to use these scores as features of a global user-item relatedness model that can be used to provide item recommendation. To this end, we define the global user-item relatedness $\rho(u,i;\theta) = f(\vec{\rho}(u,i);\theta)$ as a function f of the property-specific scores $\vec{\rho}(u,i)$ and of a set of parameters θ. The key idea is that of finding the parameters θ that optimize top-N item recommendation as a supervised learning to rank problem [16].

Training data: given a set of users $U = \{u_1, u_2..u_N\}$, each user u_k is associated with a set of items from feedback data $\vec{i_k} = \{i_{k1}, i_{k2}..i_{kn(k)}\}$ where $n(k)$ denotes the number of feedback released by the user u_k and a set of labels $\vec{y_k} = \{y_{k1}, y_{k2}..y_{kn(k)}\}$ denoting the ground truth relevance of items $\vec{i_k}$ (e.g. ratings with explicit feedback or boolean values with implicit feedback). The training set is thus represented as $T = \{(u_k, \vec{i_k}, \vec{y_k})_{k=1}^N\}$.

Ranking function: $\rho(u,i;\theta)$ is a ranking function, meaning that, for each user u_k, the corresponding items $\vec{i_k}$ are sorted according to its score. More formally, $\rho(u,i;\theta)$ induces a permutation of integers $\pi(u_k, \vec{i_k}, \theta)$, corresponding to sorting the list of items $\vec{i_k}$ according its score.

Loss: the agreement $M(\pi(u_k, \vec{i_k}, \theta), \vec{y_k})$ between the permutation $\pi(u_k, \vec{i_k}, \theta)$ induced by $\rho(u,i;\theta)$ and the list of ground truth relevance of items $\vec{y_k}$ can be measured by any information retrieval metric that measures ranking accuracy, such as $P@N$, Mean Average Precision (MAP), NDCG [22]. From this score, a loss function can be easily derived as:

$$C(\theta) = \sum_{k=1}^{N}(1 - M(\pi(u_k, \vec{i_k}, \theta)) \quad (2)$$

Optimization: the learning process has thus the objective of finding the set of parameters θ that minimize the loss function C over the training data:

$$\hat{\theta} = \arg\min_{\theta} C(\theta) \quad (3)$$

The exact form of f, of the loss function C, the set of parameters θ to optimize and the approach used to optimize the loss function depend on the learning to rank algorithm and on the metrics that are optimized. In this work, we use Adarank [27] and LambdaMart [27] as ranking algorithms and we measure $P@N$ and MAP [22].

4 EXPERIMENTAL SETUP

Dataset: the dataset used for the evaluation of the proposed approach is MovieLens 1M[3]. MovieLens 1M [12] is a popular dataset for the evaluation of recommender systems and it contains 1,000,209 anonymous ratings of approximately 3,900 movies made by 6,040 MovieLens users. In a previous work [20], MovieLens 1M items have been mapped to the corresponding DBpedia entities. We leverage these publicly available mappings to make use of Linked Open Data in building the knowledge graph K. Since not every item in the Movielens data has a corresponding DBpedia entity, after this mapping we have 948978 ratings, from 6040 users on 3226 items.

Configuration: first, we define the set of properties p for which the features have to be computed. We start from the properties associated to the class 'Film' by the DBpedia ontology $\Gamma_{dbo:Film}$ and to this set we add 'dct:subject', which relates an entity to a set of possible categories, such as 'American Films'. For each of these properties, we obtain the subgraph K_p through SPARQL [23] queries. The properties for which we obtain a sufficient number of triples (> 15) are those reported in Tab. 3. The subgraph $K_{feedback}$ is derived from the positive ($r \geq 4$) ratings of the MovieLens 1M dataset. The second part of the configuration consists in defining the hyper-parameters of the model, i.e. internal parameters that are not explicitly set by the learning process. For what concerns node2vec, we optimize the parameters P, Q on validation data, experimenting the pairs $(P,Q) \in \{(1,1),(1,4),(4,1)\}$. P, also called *return parameter*, controls the likelihood of returning to a previously visited node. Q, also called *in-out parameter*, controls the probability of moving further away from the source node e. By playing with (P,Q), node2vec achieves a random walk strategy able to approximate a Breadth-First or a Depth-First search. For other parameters, we use the configuration obtained in a previous work, i.e. a walk length $l = 10$, a dimension of the embeddings vector $d = 500$, a number of walks per entity $n = 500$, a context size $k = 10$ and a number of epochs $\eta = 5$. Another hyper-parameter of the proposed approach is the learning to rank model. We experiment two listwise algorithms, AdaRank [27] and LambdaMart [4], on validation data. The implementation of these models is that provided by the software library RankLib[4].

Evaluation protocol: we adopt an evaluation protocol that is similar to RelPlusN [25]. We split the ratings in temporal order, using 80% of data to create a training set and 20% to create a probe set. In the training set, we consider ratings $r \geq 4$ as relevant items and the rest as not relevant. From the probe set, we sample a 4% of data to create a probe validation set and 16% to create a probe test set. Then,

[3] https://grouplens.org/datasets/movielens/1m/
[4] https://sourceforge.net/p/lemur/wiki/RankLib/

P,Q	Ranking model	P@5	P@10	MAP
1,4	**LambdaMart**	**0.0791**	**0.0293**	**0.1717**
4,1	LambdaMart	0.0182	0.0193	0.0570
1,1	LambdaMart	0.0174	0.0188	0.0565
1,4	AdaRank	0.0134	0.0098	0.0278
4,1	AdaRank	0.0078	0.0083	0.0286
1,1	AdaRank	0.0109	0.0098	0.0358

Table 1: Results on the validation set of entity2rec for different combinations of hyper-parameters

Model	P@5	P@10	MAP
entity2rec	**0.2814**	**0.2127**	**0.4232**
MostPop	0.2154	0.1815	0.2907
NMF	0.1208	0.1150	0.1758
SVD	0.0543	0.0469	0.0888
ItemKNN	0.0463	0.0232	0.0990

Table 2: Results on the test set of entity2rec against the baselines

from each of these two datasets, items with rating $r = 5$ are selected and considered as relevant and for each user a number $N = 100$ of other items not rated by the user are randomly sampled as non-relevant examples, creating the validation and the test set. This evaluation protocol allows to avoid the limitations of the TestItems protocol, in which only rated items are ranked [26] and that is thus very different from the context of a real recommender system. Note that the effect of this evaluation protocol is that of underestimating the quality of the recommendations, as the assumption that all unrated items are not relevant is pessimistic. The set of elements liked by a user $R_+(u)$ is defined as the items in the training set with ratings $r = 5$. We measure P@5, P@10 and MAP. As baselines, we use state-of-the-art collaborative filtering algorithms based on Non-Negative Matrix Factorization (NMF) [17], on Singular Value Decomposition [15], ItemKNN with baselines [14] and the Most Popular Items recommendation strategy, which is known to be quite effective on MovieLens due to the power-law distribution of user feedback data [6] (see also Tab. XIV in [19]). The baselines are implemented using the *surprise* python library[5].

5 RESULTS

Comparison with state-of-the-art: the hyper-parameter optimization on validation data shows that LambdaMart performs better than Adarank and that the pair $(P, Q) = (1, 4)$, which corresponds to a walk lingering in the neighborhood of the starting node, approximating Breadth-First-Search, works better than the other pairs. The best score, for every metric, is obtained by the pair $(P, Q) = (1, 4)$ and the model LambdaMart (Tab. 1[6]). Thus, we evaluate this configuration on the test set, comparing it to the NMF, SVD, ItemKNN and Most Popular Items baselines (Sec. 4), outperforming all of them for all the metrics under consideration (Tab. 2).

Feature selection: one of the strengths of the proposed approach is that of using features that have a clear interpretation. In this experiment, we try to evaluate the importance of the selected features

Features	P@5	P@10	MAP
$\rho_{dbo:based\_on}$	0.0529	0.0247	0.0925
$\rho_{dbo:cinematography}$	0.0386	0.0290	0.0794
$\boldsymbol{\rho_{feedback}}$	**0.2317**	**0.1708**	**0.3550**
$\rho_{dbo:director}$	0.0219	0.0211	0.0949
$\rho_{dbo:editing}$	0.0294	0.0305	0.0724
$\rho_{dbo:music\_composer}$	0.0077	0.0040	0.0493
$\rho_{dbo:narrator}$	0.0572	0.0389	0.0834
$\rho_{dbo:producer}$	0.0119	0.0241	0.0498
$\rho_{dbo:starring}$	0.0128	0.0372	0.0728
$\rho_{dct:subject}$	0.0285	0.0326	0.0688
$\rho_{dbo:writer}$	0.0061	0.0216	0.0472
entity2rec	**0.2814**	**0.2127**	**0.4232**

Table 3: Performance of the proposed approach considering one feature at the time

$\rho_p(u, i)$ on the overall ranking quality. To this end, we select one feature at the time and we compute the ranking accuracy (Tab. 3), observing that the feature 'feedback' is by far the best performing one. However, including content-based features improves the overall performance of the system, as can be seen by comparing 'feedback' with 'entity2rec', which includes all the features. We expect this difference to be even more relevant on other datasets affected by a higher sparsity as observed in similar experiments with hybrid recommender systems [19, 28]. It is also worth noting that $\rho_{feedback}$ outperforms all the collaborative filtering baselines of Tab. 2, showing the effectiveness of the proposed approach in learning a measure of user-item relatedness even without content information.

6 CONCLUSIONS

In this work, we propose entity2rec, a new measure of user-item relatedness for top-N item recommendation. Starting from a knowledge graph, property-specific relatedness scores are obtained using a feature learning approach based on neural language models on property-specific subgraphs and then combined through a learning to rank approach to generate a global user-item relatedness measure optimizing top-N item recommendations. This two-stage approach has two major benefits: it allows to configure the system to take into account a specific property when providing recommendations (e.g. recommend movies with similar actors) and it allows to let the learning to rank algorithm implicitly weight the properties to provide recommendations. The results on the MovieLens 1M dataset show that the proposed approach outperforms commonly used collaborative filtering techniques based on matrix factorization, nearest neighbors and the Most Popular items strategy. From the data to the ranking, the feature engineering effort is minimal and the manual intervention is limited to setting and configuring hyper-parameters of the learning process. Future work will involve a more comprehensive evaluation, comparing the model to other hybrid state-of-the-art recommender systems on different domains and datasets, and in a general improvement of the feasibility of the proposed approach in a real recommendation scenario (such as computational time, online updates, context of the recommendations).

[5]http://surprise.readthedocs.io/en/v1.0.2/matrix_factorization.html

[6]Note that the scores obtained on the test set tend to be higher than those on the validation set because the ratio of relevant/non-relevant items is higher in the latter.

REFERENCES

[1] Sören Auer, Christian Bizer, Georgi Kobilarov, Jens Lehmann, Richard Cyganiak, and Zachary Ives. 2007. Dbpedia: A nucleus for a web of open data. In *The semantic web*. Springer, 722–735.

[2] Yoshua Bengio, Aaron Courville, and Pascal Vincent. 2013. Representation learning: A review and new perspectives. *IEEE transactions on pattern analysis and machine intelligence* 35, 8 (2013), 1798–1828.

[3] Christian Bizer, Tom Heath, and Tim Berners-Lee. 2009. Linked data-the story so far. *Semantic Services, Interoperability and Web Applications: Emerging Concepts* (2009), 205–227.

[4] Christopher JC Burges. 2010. From ranknet to lambdarank to lambdamart: An overview. *Learning* 11, 23-581 (2010), 81.

[5] Rose Catherine and William Cohen. 2016. Personalized Recommendations using Knowledge Graphs: A Probabilistic Logic Programming Approach. In *Proceedings of the 10th ACM Conference on Recommender Systems*. ACM, 325–332.

[6] Paolo Cremonesi, Yehuda Koren, and Roberto Turrin. 2010. Performance of recommender algorithms on top-n recommendation tasks. In *Proceedings of the fourth ACM conference on Recommender systems*. ACM, 39–46.

[7] Tommaso Di Noia. 2016. Recommender Systems Meet Linked Open Data. In *International Conference on Web Engineering*. Springer, 620–623.

[8] Tommaso Di Noia, Roberto Mirizzi, Vito Claudio Ostuni, Davide Romito, and Markus Zanker. 2012. Linked open data to support content-based recommender systems. In *Proceedings of the 8th International Conference on Semantic Systems*. ACM, 1–8.

[9] Cristhian Figueroa, Iacopo Vagliano, Oscar Rodríguez Rocha, and Maurizio Morisio. 2015. A systematic literature review of Linked Data-based recommender systems. *Concurrency and Computation: Practice and Experience* 27, 17 (2015), 4659–4684.

[10] Jerome H Friedman. 2001. Greedy function approximation: a gradient boosting machine. *Annals of statistics* (2001), 1189–1232.

[11] Aditya Grover and Jure Leskovec. 2016. node2vec: Scalable feature learning for networks. In *Proceedings of the 22nd ACM SIGKDD International Conference on Knowledge Discovery and Data Mining*. ACM, 855–864.

[12] F Maxwell Harper and Joseph A Konstan. 2016. The movielens datasets: History and context. *ACM Transactions on Interactive Intelligent Systems (TiiS)* 5, 4 (2016), 19.

[13] Houda Khrouf and Raphaël Troncy. 2013. Hybrid event recommendation using linked data and user diversity. In *Proceedings of the 7th ACM conference on Recommender systems*. ACM, 185–192.

[14] Yehuda Koren. 2010. Factor in the neighbors: Scalable and accurate collaborative filtering. *ACM Transactions on Knowledge Discovery from Data (TKDD)* 4, 1 (2010), 1.

[15] Yehuda Koren, Robert Bell, and Chris Volinsky. 2009. Matrix factorization techniques for recommender systems. *Computer* 42, 8 (2009).

[16] Tie-Yan Liu and others. 2009. Learning to rank for information retrieval. *Foundations and Trends® in Information Retrieval* 3, 3 (2009), 225–331.

[17] Xin Luo, Mengchu Zhou, Yunni Xia, and Qingsheng Zhu. 2014. An efficient non-negative matrix-factorization-based approach to collaborative filtering for recommender systems. *IEEE Transactions on Industrial Informatics* 10, 2 (2014), 1273–1284.

[18] Tomas Mikolov, Ilya Sutskever, Kai Chen, Greg S Corrado, and Jeff Dean. 2013. Distributed representations of words and phrases and their compositionality. In *Advances in neural information processing systems*. 3111–3119.

[19] Tommaso Di Noia, Vito Claudio Ostuni, Paolo Tomeo, and Eugenio Di Sciascio. 2016. Sprank: Semantic path-based ranking for top-n recommendations using linked open data. *ACM Transactions on Intelligent Systems and Technology (TIST)* 8, 1 (2016), 9.

[20] Vito Claudio Ostuni, Tommaso Di Noia, Eugenio Di Sciascio, and Roberto Mirizzi. 2013. Top-n recommendations from implicit feedback leveraging linked open data. In *Proceedings of the 7th ACM conference on Recommender systems*. ACM, 85–92.

[21] Bryan Perozzi, Rami Al-Rfou, and Steven Skiena. 2014. Deepwalk: Online learning of social representations. In *Proceedings of the 20th ACM SIGKDD international conference on Knowledge discovery and data mining*. ACM, 701–710.

[22] David Martin Powers. 2011. Evaluation: from precision, recall and F-measure to ROC, informedness, markedness and correlation. *Journal of Machine Learning Technologies* (2011).

[23] Bastian Quilitz and Ulf Leser. 2008. Querying distributed RDF data sources with SPARQL. In *European Semantic Web Conference*. Springer, 524–538.

[24] Jessica Rosati, Petar Ristoski, Tommaso Di Noia, Renato de Leone, and Heiko Paulheim. 2016. RDF graph embeddings for content-based recommender systems. In *CEUR workshop proceedings*, Vol. 1673. RWTH, 23–30.

[25] Alan Said and Alejandro Bellogín. 2014. Comparative recommender system evaluation: benchmarking recommendation frameworks. In *Proceedings of the 8th ACM Conference on Recommender systems*. ACM, 129–136.

[26] Harald Steck. 2013. Evaluation of recommendations: rating-prediction and ranking. In *Proceedings of the 7th ACM conference on Recommender systems*. ACM, 213–220.

[27] Jun Xu and Hang Li. 2007. Adarank: a boosting algorithm for information retrieval. In *Proceedings of the 30th annual international ACM SIGIR conference on Research and development in information retrieval*. ACM, 391–398.

[28] Xiao Yu, Xiang Ren, Yizhou Sun, Quanquan Gu, Bradley Sturt, Urvashi Khandelwal, Brandon Norick, and Jiawei Han. 2014. Personalized entity recommendation: A heterogeneous information network approach. In *Proceedings of the 7th ACM international conference on Web search and data mining*. ACM, 283–292.

On Parallelizing SGD for Pairwise Learning to Rank in Collaborative Filtering Recommender Systems

Murat Yagci
Bogazici University
murat.yagci@boun.edu.tr

Tevfik Aytekin
Bahcesehir University
tevfik.aytekin@bahcesehir.edu.tr

Fikret Gurgen
Bogazici University
gurgen@boun.edu.tr

ABSTRACT

Learning to rank with pairwise loss functions has been found useful in collaborative filtering recommender systems. At web scale, the optimization is often based on matrix factorization with stochastic gradient descent (SGD) which has a sequential nature. We investigate two different shared memory lock-free parallel SGD schemes based on block partitioning and no partitioning for use with pairwise loss functions. To speed up convergence to a solution, we extrapolate simple practical algorithms from their application to pointwise learning to rank. Experimental results show that the proposed algorithms are quite useful regarding their ranking ability and speedup patterns in comparison to their sequential counterpart.

KEYWORDS

Learning to rank; Pairwise loss; Parallel SGD; Personalization

1 INTRODUCTION

Recommendation problem can also be seen as a learning to rank (LtR) problem [6, 9]. Among pointwise [5, 7] and listwise [16] approaches, the pairwise [2, 15] LtR approach attempts to learn from preference information between a pair of items under a certain context [13]. This type of LtR can especially be a good fit for various implicit feedback scenarios since it does not need to ignore or mislabel unknown preferences. Moreover, because it works on item pairs instead of arbitrarily large lists, it can sometimes be more efficient than listwise LtR. Our motivation in this paper is to further improve its scalability to large feedback datasets and streams.

The idea of lock-free parallel SGD has been motivated for different machine learning methods, and applied to matrix completion from sparse feedback data. Two major camps are based on *block partitioning* [12], and *no partitioning* [11]. These approaches are especially interesting for multi-core CPU or GPU processing, and they can be preferable for intensive large-scale memory-based numerical computation.

In this paper, we investigate two shared memory lock-free parallel SGD schemes for personalized pairwise LtR to improve its scalability. We first adapt a block partitioning approach to this setting, and propose the PLtR-B algorithm. We then show that the no partitioning approach is applicable to pairwise LtR as in pointwise LtR [11], and present the PLtR-N algorithm.

We structure our paper as follows: In Section 2, we analyze parallel personalized pairwise LtR, and present the two proposed algorithms. In Section 3, comparative experimental results are provided for the ranking ability of algorithms and the speedup patterns. We conclude in Section 4.

RecSys '17, August 27–31, 2017, Como, Italy

DOI: http://dx.doi.org/10.1145/3109859.3109906

2 METHODS

2.1 Preliminaries on personalized pairwise LtR

Given a set of users, U, and a set of items, I, *personalized pairwise LtR* methods commonly learn from a dataset, $\mathcal{D}$, of triples (u, i, j), where $u \in U$ is the context, and $i, j \in I$. A triple implies a partial personalized ranking such that for a given user u, the ranking $r^i <_u r^j$ holds. In other words, user u prefers item i over item j. In this analysis, unless otherwise stated, we assume that $i \in I_u^+$, $j \in I \setminus I_u^+$, where I_u^+ denotes the set of items interacted by user u in a positive sense. The ultimate goal is to discover full or topmost personalized rankings from available partial rankings.

The typical pairwise error function is in the form :

$$E(\Theta \mid \mathcal{D}) = \sum_{(u,i,j)\in\mathcal{D}} \left\{ L\left(\theta_u, \theta_i, \theta_j\right) + \sum_{\theta_x \in \{\theta_u, \theta_i, \theta_j\}} \lambda_{\theta_x} ||\theta_x||_2^2 \right\}, \quad (1)$$

where Θ represents all model parameters, and λ_{θ_x} is a regularization coefficient. Different loss functions, L, are possible. In this paper, we stick to sigmoid-smoothed pairwise loss and negative log likelihood described in the seminal work, Bayesian personalized ranking (BPR) [15]. The same ideas apply to learning from other differentiable pairwise loss functions, for example, based on hinge loss [2].

In case of BPR with matrix factorization, $L = -\ln \sigma(y_{uij})$, and $y_{uij} = \mathbf{p}_u^\top(\mathbf{q}_i - \mathbf{q}_j)$, where $\mathbf{p}_u, \mathbf{q}_k \in \mathbb{R}^f$ are column vectors in the low-rank component matrices of the factorized user-item preference matrix, $\mathbf{R} \approx \mathbf{P}^\top \mathbf{Q}$. The resulting error function is differentiable with respect to model parameters, and it can be optimized with SGD using a suitable learning rate, γ. The typical procedure is summarized in Algorithm 1. Note that the algorithm often requires multiple passes over the dataset prior to convergence.

Algorithm 1 Personalized pairwise learning to rank

1: **repeat**
2: Sample a tuple (u, i) from positive interaction dataset, $\mathcal{D}^+$;
3: Sample j ;
4: **for all** $\theta_x \in \{\theta_u, \theta_i, \theta_j\}$ **do**
5: $\theta_x = \theta_x - \gamma \frac{\partial}{\partial \theta_x} \{L\left(\theta_u, \theta_i, \theta_j\right) + \lambda_{\theta_x} ||\theta_x||_2^2\}$;
6: **until** convergence

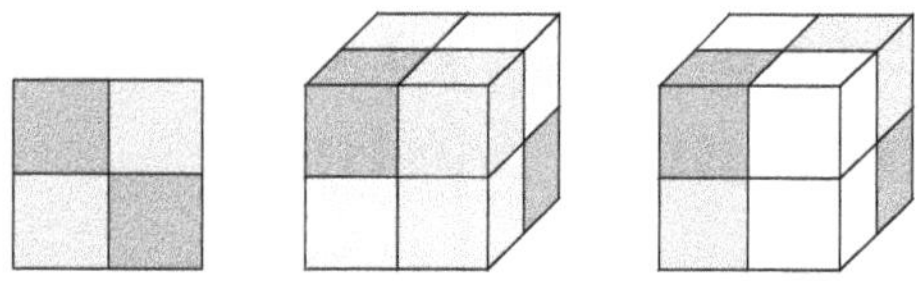

Figure 1: (Left) With 2 processing units, pointwise LtR can be parallelized with such a partitioning of R. Sets of chunks are shown with different colors. (Middle-Right) In pairwise LtR, the second item can be imagined on a third dimension. Two possible partitioning ideas are given.

2.2 Parallel pairwise LtR with block partitioning

For shared memory lock-free parallelization of matrix completion, one idea is block partitioning which partitions a user-item preference matrix, R, into multiple sets of ideally non-overlapping chunks [3, 12]. Then, each processing unit updates one of the chunks in every set which enables a form of parallel processing without using locks. This approach has been originally applied to personalized pointwise LtR scenarios, where updates are based on a single item interaction. In the case of pairwise LtR, a block partitioning solution can be formulated as in Figure 1 regarding the (u, i, j) updates. The block partitioning in the middle does not guarantee non-overlapping sets of chunks. Therefore, we concentrate on the rightmost partitioning approach which forces the (i, j) pairs to be always from the same chunk. This restriction guarantees mutually exclusive updates to both users and items, and it is computationally less expensive. We explain its applicability next.

By slightly modifying the pointwise scheme [12], the following is possible for pairwise LtR: Suppose we have ψ processing units. At each training epoch, we first generate a random permutation of users ($perm_U$) and items ($perm_I$) by shuffling their indexes in place. We then partition all (u, i, j) triples into ψ^2 chunks C_{abc}, where $a, b, c = 1, \ldots, \psi$ such that,

$$a = \left\lfloor \frac{\psi}{|U|} \left(perm_U(u) - 1\right) \right\rfloor + 1, b = \left\lfloor \frac{\psi}{|I|} \left(perm_I(i) - 1\right) \right\rfloor + 1,$$
$$c = \left\lfloor \frac{\psi}{|I|} \left(perm_I(j) - 1\right) \right\rfloor + 1, \quad (2)$$

and the sampled item j is forced to be in a chunk with $c = b$. Note that due to random permutations, users and items corresponding to a chunk are different at each training epoch, which makes this restrictive approach viable.

A set of chunks is updated in a single round and each update round can be decided simply by Algorithm 2. Putting it altogether, the personalized pairwise learning to rank algorithm can be parallelized as in Algorithm 3. We call this algorithm PLtR-B.

Algorithm 2 Deciding the set of chunks in a round

```
for z = 1 to ψ do
    for a = 1 to ψ do
        c = b = (a + z − 1) mod ψ ; {set b = ψ if b == 0} ;
        Add C_abc to Round[z] ;
```

Algorithm 3 Parallel personalized pairwise learning to rank with block partitioning (PLtR-B)

```
1:  for all training epochs do
2:      Generate perm_U and perm_I ;
3:      for all (u, i) in positive interaction dataset, D+ do
4:          Sample j s.t. c = b, and place (u, i, j) in corresponding C_abc ;
5:          {Since c = b, sampling of j can be postponed until line 10, if partitioning step is not performed in a dedicated thread}
6:      Assign C_abc to rounds w.r.t. Algorithm 2 ;
7:      for all Rounds do
8:          for all C_abc in current round in parallel do
9:              for all (u, i, j) ∈ C_abc do
10:                 for all θ_x ∈ {θ_u, θ_i, θ_j} do
11:                     θ_x = θ_x − γ ∂/∂θ_x {L(θ_u, θ_i, θ_j) + λ_θx ||θ_x||_2^2} ;
12:         Synchronize processing units ;
```

We note a few practical concerns regarding the block partitioning solution. First, the chunks in each round need to have a balanced number of training triples in order to fully benefit from parallelization. Random shuffling helps solve this problem, and if necessary, further amendments [18] can be useful. Second, the prior shuffling brings some extra time overhead which can optionally be overcome at the cost of dedicating separate threads [12]. Space overhead is also increased due to auxiliary structures. Third, and importantly, block partitioning imposes a predetermined sampling scheme for (u, i) and j. Therefore, we also investigate the no partitioning approach which can be more versatile for dynamic stream learning environments as well as for pairwise LtR tasks with custom biased sampling schemes [8, 10, 14, 17].

2.3 Parallel pairwise LtR with no partitioning

In this approach, parallel processes can access and write any portion of the shared memory at any time and in a lock-free fashion [11]. Nevertheless, this extreme approach still provides some theoretical guarantees for convergence when the optimization function can be defined as sparse summations, typical of SGD-based personalized LtR. In the case of pairwise LtR, the summation has the sparse form given in (1). This summation induces a hypergraph, $G = (V, E)$. However, unlike a bipartite graph for pointwise LtR, we now have a hypergraph which reflects personalized pairwise item relationships. We illustrate this new hypergraph in Figure 2.

Both $|V|$ and $|E|$ are typically very large with the latter being especially large in the case of pairwise LtR. However, as seen in (1), each summation acts on a single $e \in E$, that is, a very small subset of V, which suggests intuitively that parallel lock-free updates without any partitioning are viable. Following the theoretical analysis in [11], this notion can be formalized using the following statistics of a hypergraph, G:

$$\Omega = \max_{e \in E} |e|,$$
$$\Delta = \frac{\max_{1 \le v \le |V|} |\{e \in E : v \in e\}|}{|E|}, \quad (3)$$
$$\rho = \frac{\max_{e \in E} |\{e' \in E : e' \cap e \neq \emptyset\}|}{|E|},$$

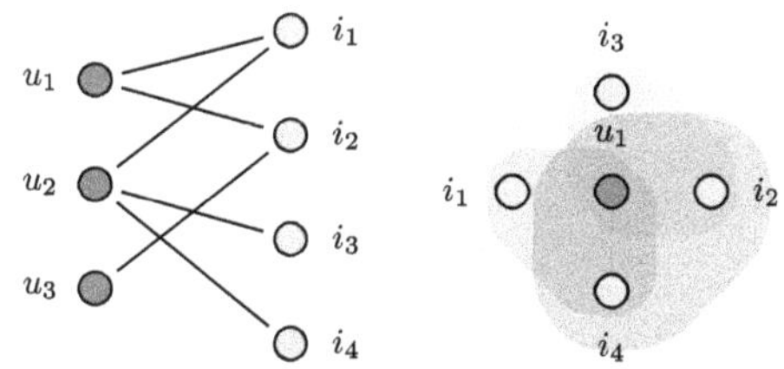

Figure 2: Example hypergraphs showing user-item relationships for pointwise and pairwise LtR respectively. For clarity, the latter is shown for a single user only, where 3-vertex hyperedges capture all possible pairwise item relationships for u_1. Here, $i_1, i_2 \in I^+_{u_1}$ and $i_3, i_4 \in I \setminus I^+_{u_1}$.

where Δ and ρ are measures of vertex regularity and hypergraph sparsity, respectively. When these values are relatively small, parallel updates can bring a highly effective speedup for convergence. In pairwise LtR, $\Omega = 3$, since each e is made up of an (u, i, j) triple. Assume every user makes m interactions, then $|E| = |U| \times m \times (|I| - m)$ triples. Since we have (u, i, j) triples, there can be user and item vertices in the hypergraph. Assume an item is interacted by at most n users. Then, it can be that $\Delta = (|I| - m) \times m/|E|$ regarding user vertices, or $\Delta = [(|I| - m) \times n + m \times (|U| - n)]/|E|$ regarding item vertices. As expected, we see that item vertices determine Δ in many real-life datasets. However, it is not straightforward to make general assumptions about m and n in the worst case. For example, in case $m \ll |I|$, $n \ll |U|$, and $m \approx n$, $\Delta \approx 1/|U| + 1/|I|$ which is close to that of pointwise LtR under similar assumptions. Since $\Omega = 3$, $\rho \leq 3\Delta$. In real-life datasets, the shared memory lock-free approach without any partitioning is effective even when the values of Δ and ρ are relatively high, as shown experimentally in [11] for different machine learning problems including matrix completion in a pointwise LtR setting. We observe in our experiments that in the personalized LtR problem setting, a possible reason behind this situation is that user and item vertex degrees often follow a power law distribution, that is, Δ (maximum normalized vertex degree) can be significantly higher than the values in the modal interval of the normalized vertex degree distribution. In Section 3, we compute these statistics for various datasets and show that the statistics of pairwise LtR are quite similar to those of pointwise LtR.

Algorithm 4 Parallel personalized pairwise LtR with no partitioning (PLtR-N)

```
{Perform following loop in every parallel processing unit}
for all training epochs do
    for all iterations do
        Sample a tuple (u, i) from positive interaction dataset, D+ ;
        Sample j ;
        for all θx ∈ {θu, θi, θj} do
            θx = θx − γ ∂/∂θx {L(θu, θi, θj) + λθx ||θx||_2^2} ;
    Synchronize processing unit if learning rate, γ, changes ;
```

Therefore, we propose to parallelize pairwise LtR without partitioning as given in Algorithm 4. We call this algorithm PLtR-N. As an illustrative example, if we assume ψ processing units and 2ψ total epochs of the learning algorithm, then we see that every processing unit will run 2 epochs instead of a single processing unit running 2ψ epochs.

We note that PLtR-N can be conveniently extended to learn in an incremental fashion with a custom sampling scheme. This has potential benefits like taking time-dependency into account, less memory consumption, and faster convergence in real-life scenarios. For preliminary results, we refer the reader to [17].

Table 1: Basic properties of datasets

	$\|U\|$	$\|I\|$	# of Interactions
ML20M	138,493	27,278	20,000,263
LAST.FM	359,208	159,000	17,177,350

3 EXPERIMENTS

3.1 Datasets and evaluation

We use MovieLens 20M (ML20M) [4], and LAST.FM [1] datasets in our experiments. Basic properties of the final datasets are given in Table 1. Apart from user and item information, the raw interaction datasets contain confidence information in terms of ratings or interaction counts. We use this information to form a test set by leaving one random item out with maximum confidence for every user. We consider the rest as implicit feedback. We also make sure that every user interacts with at least 10 items, and for the LAST.FM dataset that a song is listened to by a user at least twice.

We measure ranking ability of the algorithms using MAP@500 [14], and area under curve (AUC) as described in [15]. Since the results show a similar pattern, we report the latter. Besides ranking evaluation, we illustrate speedup of the algorithms graphically using execution times.

We use a virtual cloud machine having a multi-core Intel Xeon CPU with 12 physical cores, and 16 GB of main memory. There are many ways to implement shared memory parallelism. In this paper, we rely on the Linux operating system and Java (1.7) threads to exploit the available cores. Although this leaves the management of cores to Java virtual machine, we monitor the effectiveness by diagnostic tools. We leave the atomicity of operations to what is available in the system. Guiding source code[1] is provided for reproducibility.

3.2 Statistics of dataset graphs

To complement analysis of PLtR-N in Section 2.3, we enumerate the (u, i, j) triples in the training sets and see that both Δ and ρ are on the order observed in real-life datasets for pointwise LtR. We provide comparative statistics in Table 2 which imply similar convergence properties for pointwise and pairwise LtR.

We also investigate vertex degree distributions of the dataset graphs and compare them with the Δ values in Figure 3. We observe that although the Δ values define an upper bound for normalized vertex degree distributions, the modal intervals of the distributions correspond to much lower values which further support parallel methods like PLtR-N.

[1] github.com/myaged

Table 2: Statistics of dataset graphs for LtR

	Δ	ρ
ML20M - Pointwise LtR	0.0035	$\leq 2\Delta$
ML20M - Pairwise LtR	0.0036	$\leq 3\Delta$
LAST.FM- Pointwise LtR	0.0045	$\leq 2\Delta$
LAST.FM - Pairwise LtR	0.0046	$\leq 3\Delta$

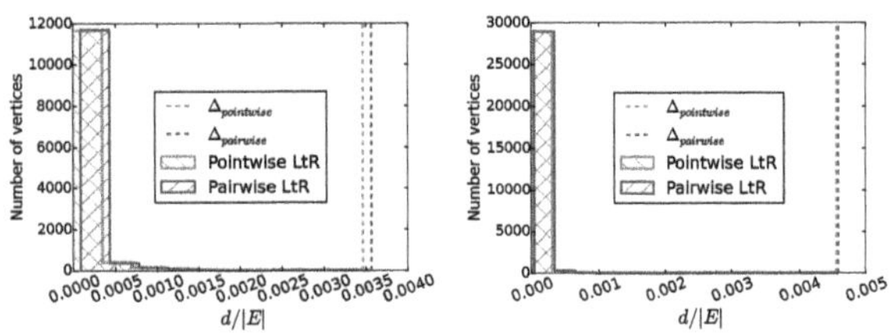

(a) ML20M (b) LAST.FM

Figure 3: Vertex degree (d) distributions in comparison to Δ values for the datasets

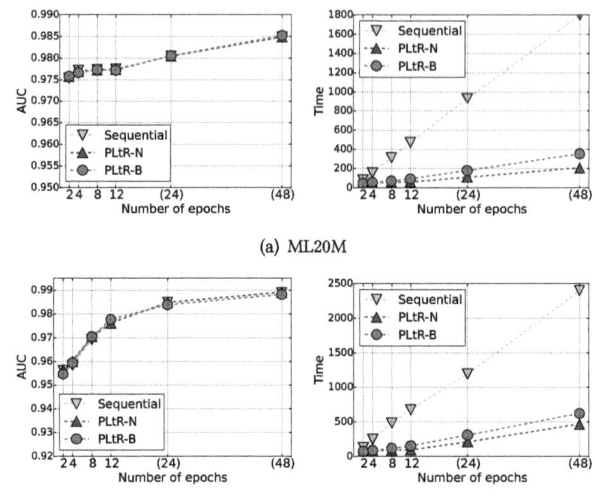

(a) ML20M

(b) LAST.FM

Figure 4: Comparing ranking ability and speedup of algorithms. For 24 and 48 total epochs, both PLtR variants utilize 12 processing units only.

3.3 Evaluation of ranking ability and speedup

Experimental results for PLtR-N up to 12 total epochs are obtained by performing a single epoch in each processing unit. Since we have 12 processing units, we then obtain results for 24, and 48 total epochs by running 2, and 4 epochs at each processing unit respectively. The results are illustrated in Figure 4. The important comparison here is to BPR which performs all epochs sequentially. For both BPR and PLtR-N, the following parameters are found by cross validation in a limited search space: For ML20M, $\gamma = 0.005$ and $f = 20$. For LAST.FM, $\gamma = 0.05$ and $f = 40$. Regularization parameters are found by cross-validation using a search space around $\lambda_{\theta_u} = \lambda_{\theta_i} = 0.0025$, and $\lambda_{\theta_j} = 0.00025$. Initial values in matrices **P** and **Q** are sampled from $\mathcal{N}(0, 0.01)$.

We observe in both datasets that the difference between ranking ability of BPR and PLtR-N is not statistically significant which shows the effectiveness of shared memory lock-free parallelization with no partitioning. On the other hand, the speedup patterns show that PLtR-N scales quite well whereas, as expected, sequential BPR has a linearly increasing execution time with the number of total epochs. Note that since we have 12 processing units in our experimental setup, the increase in PLtR-N execution time for 24 and 48 total epochs is due to the increase in number of epochs per processing unit. These results suggest that PLtR-N can converge much faster without loss of ranking ability, and by making better use of resources at hand.

Experimental results for PLtR-B up to 12 total epochs are obtained by performing ψ parallel updates in each round where ψ is equal to the number of total epochs. For 24 and 48 total epochs, $\psi = 12$. The partitioning is done in the master thread and the parallel processing in worker threads. The parameterization is the same as BPR and PLtR-N. The AUC pattern shows that its convergence is comparable to BPR and PLtR-N. On the other hand, while PLtR-B offers considerable speedup compared to sequential BPR, the speedup pattern is somewhat worse than PLtR-N. Possible reasons include imbalanced chunks in a round, and the partitioning step at master thread. We note that using separate dedicated worker threads for the partitioning step has a potential to improve this speedup.

4 CONCLUSIONS

Personalized pairwise LtR is a powerful approach for learning from relevance feedback datasets. We aim to improve its scalability using state-of-the-art shared memory lock-free parallel SGD schemes. In this direction, we propose two algorithms: PLtR-N and PLtR-B. We show that the usefulness of PLtR-N is due to graph theoretical similarities between pairwise and pointwise LtR for which the shared memory lock-free SGD scheme is known to have good convergence properties. Our experimental results support this analysis further with respect to ranking ability and speedup of the PLtR-N algorithm compared to its sequential counterpart. Block partitioning approach is inherently lock-free for pointwise LtR. We attempt to adapt it for pairwise LtR with the PLtR-B algorithm, and show comparative experimental results to BPR and PLtR-N algorithms. Both PLtR-N and PLtR-B exploit multi-core shared memory architectures, and they are easy to implement which can make them desirable in web-scale applications. They can also facilitate faster testing of pairwise LtR models with different parameterizations, which is a common bottleneck in evaluation design.

We note the following as future work: Although we provide some pointers, the mutual effect of biased sampling schemes and parallelization needs further investigation. Second, GPU-based parallel processing can be exploited for experimental limits of parallelization.

ACKNOWLEDGMENTS

We thank the anonymous reviewers for their comments. This work is supported in part by Bogazici University BAP project no. 13241.

REFERENCES

[1] Oscar Celma. 2010. *Music Recommendation and Discovery in the Long Tail.* Springer.

[2] Ernesto Diaz-Aviles, Lucas Drumond, Lars Schmidt-Thieme, and Wolfgang Nejdl. 2012. Real-time Top-n Recommendation in Social Streams. In *Proceedings of the 6th ACM Conference on Recommender Systems (RecSys '12).* 59–66.

[3] Rainer Gemulla, Erik Nijkamp, Peter J. Haas, and Yannis Sismanis. 2011. Large-scale Matrix Factorization with Distributed Stochastic Gradient Descent. In *Proceedings of the 17th ACM SIGKDD International Conference on Knowledge Discovery and Data Mining (KDD '11).* 69–77.

[4] F. Maxwell Harper and Joseph A. Konstan. 2015. The MovieLens Datasets: History and Context. *ACM Transactions on Interactive Intelligent Systems* 5, 4, Article 19 (2015), 19 pages.

[5] Yifan Hu, Yehuda Koren, and Chris Volinsky. 2008. Collaborative Filtering for Implicit Feedback Datasets. In *Proceedings of the 8th IEEE International Conference on Data Mining (ICDM '08).* 263–272.

[6] Alexandros Karatzoglou, Linas Baltrunas, and Yue Shi. 2013. Learning to Rank for Recommender Systems. In *Proceedings of the 7th ACM Conference on Recommender Systems (RecSys '13).* 493–494.

[7] Yehuda Koren, Robert Bell, and Chris Volinsky. 2009. Matrix Factorization Techniques for Recommender Systems. *Computer* 42, 8 (2009), 30–37.

[8] Lukas Lerche and Dietmar Jannach. 2014. Using Graded Implicit Feedback for Bayesian Personalized Ranking. In *Proceedings of the 8th ACM Conference on Recommender Systems (RecSys '14).* 353–356.

[9] Tie-Yan Liu. 2011. *Learning to Rank for Information Retrieval.* Springer.

[10] Babak Loni, Roberto Pagano, Martha Larson, and Alan Hanjalic. 2016. Bayesian Personalized Ranking with Multi-Channel User Feedback. In *Proceedings of the 10th ACM Conference on Recommender Systems (RecSys '16).* 361–364.

[11] Feng Niu, Benjamin Recht, Christopher Ré, and Stephen J. Wright. 2011. Hogwild: A Lock-Free Approach to Parallelizing Stochastic Gradient Descent. In *Advances in Neural Information Processing Systems.* 693–701.

[12] Benjamin Recht and Christopher Ré. 2013. Parallel stochastic gradient algorithms for large-scale matrix completion. *Mathematical Programming Computation* 5, 2 (2013), 201–226.

[13] Steffen Rendle. 2011. *Context-Aware Ranking with Factorization Models.* Studies in Computational Intelligence, Vol. 330. Springer.

[14] Steffen Rendle and Christoph Freudenthaler. 2014. Improving Pairwise Learning for Item Recommendation from Implicit Feedback. In *Proceedings of the 7th ACM International Conference on Web Search and Data Mining (WSDM '14).* 273–282.

[15] Steffen Rendle, Christoph Freudenthaler, Zeno Gantner, and Lars Schmidt-Thieme. 2009. BPR: Bayesian Personalized Ranking from Implicit Feedback. In *Proceedings of the 25th Conference on Uncertainty in Artificial Intelligence (UAI '09).* 452–461.

[16] Yue Shi, Alexandros Karatzoglou, Linas Baltrunas, Martha Larson, Nuria Oliver, and Alan Hanjalic. 2012. CLiMF: Learning to Maximize Reciprocal Rank with Collaborative Less-is-more Filtering. In *Proceedings of the 6th ACM Conference on Recommender Systems (RecSys '12).* 139–146.

[17] Murat Yagci, Tevfik Aytekin, Hurol Turen, and Fikret Gurgen. 2016. Parallel personalized pairwise learning to rank. In *Proceedings of the 3rd EURO mini conference on From Multiple Criteria Decision Aid to Preference Learning (DA2PL '16).*

[18] Yong Zhuang, Wei-Sheng Chin, Yu-Chin Juan, and Chih-Jen Lin. 2013. A Fast Parallel SGD for Matrix Factorization in Shared Memory Systems. In *Proceedings of 7th ACM Conference on Recommender Systems (RecSys '13).* 249–256.

Controlling Popularity Bias in Learning-to-Rank Recommendation

Himan Abdollahpouri
DePaul University
Chicago, IL, USA
habdolla@depaul.edu

Robin Burke
DePaul University
Chicago, IL, USA
rburke@cs.depaul.edu

Bamshad Mobasher
DePaul University
Chicago, IL, USA
mobasher@depaul.edu

ABSTRACT

Many recommendation algorithms suffer from popularity bias in their output: popular items are recommended frequently and less popular ones rarely, if at all. However, less popular, long-tail items are precisely those that are often desirable recommendations. In this paper, we introduce a flexible regularization-based framework to enhance the long-tail coverage of recommendation lists in a learning-to-rank algorithm. We show that regularization provides a tunable mechanism for controlling the trade-off between accuracy and coverage. Moreover, the experimental results using two data sets show that it is possible to improve coverage of long tail items without substantial loss of ranking performance.

KEYWORDS

Recommender systems; long-tail; Recommendation evaluation; Coverage; Learning to rank

1 INTRODUCTION

Recommender systems have an important role in e-commerce and information sites, helping users find new items. One obstacle to effectiveness of recommenders is in the problem of popularity bias: collaborative filtering recommenders typically emphasize popular items (those with more ratings) much more than other "long-tail" items [13]. Although popular items are often good recommendations, they are also likely to be well-known, therefore recommender systems should seek a balance between popular and less-popular items.

Figure 1 illustrates the long-tail phenomenon in the well-known MovieLens 1M dataset [8]. The y axis represents the number of ratings per item and the x axis shows the product rank. The first vertical line separates the top 20% of items by popularity – these items cumulatively have many more ratings than the 80% long tail items to the right. These "short head" items are the very popular blockbuster movies that garner much more viewer attention. Similar distributions can be found in books, music, and other consumer taste domains.

The second vertical line divides the long tail of the distribution into two parts. The first part we call the *medium tail*: these items are accessible to collaborative recommendation, even though recommendation algorithms often do not produce them. Beyond this point, items receive so few ratings that meaningful cross-user comparison of their ratings becomes noisy and unreliable. For these items, the *distant long tail* or cold-start items, content-based and hybrid recommendation techniques must be employed. Our work in this paper is concerned with collaborative recommendation and therefore focuses on the medium tail.

In this paper, we present a flexible framework for fairness-aware optimization built on the top of a learning to rank algorithm. When applied to long-tail items, this approach enables the system designer to tune the application to achieve a particular tradeoff between ranking accuracy and the inclusion of long-tail items. However, the framework is sufficiently general that it can be used to control recommendation bias for or against any group of items.

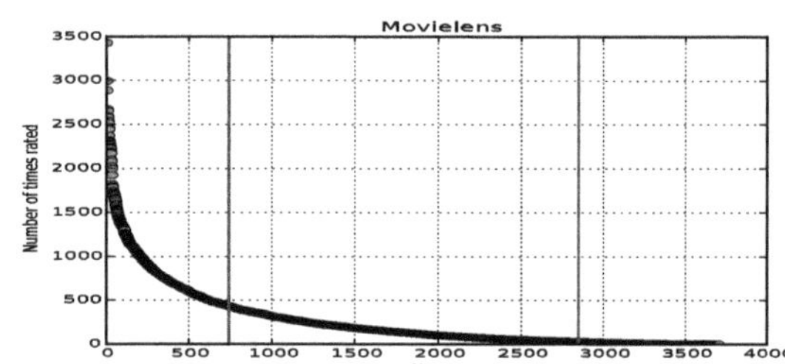

Figure 1: The long-tail of item popularity.

1.1 Related Work

Recommending serendipitous items from the long tail are generally considered to be valuable to users [2, 16], as these are items that users are less likely to know about. Brynjolfsson and his colleagues showed that 30-40% of Amazon book sales are represented by titles that would not normally be found in brick-and-mortar stores [3]. Access to long-tail items is a strong driver for e-commerce growth: the consumer surplus created by providing access to these less-known book titles is estimated at more than seven to ten times the value consumers receive from access to lower prices online.

Long-tail items are also important for generating a fuller understanding of users' preferences. Systems that use active learning to explore each user's profile will typically need to present more long tail items because these are the ones that the user is less likely to have rated, and where user's preferences are more likely to be diverse [12, 15].

Finally, long-tail recommendation can also be understood as a social good. A market that suffers from popularity bias will

RecSys'17, August 27–31, 2017, Como, Italy
 ISBN 978-1-4503-4652-8/17/08...$15.00
DOI: http://dx.doi.org/10.1145/3109859.3109912

lack opportunities to discover more obscure products and will be, by definition, dominated by a few large brands or well-known artists [6]. Such a market will be more homogeneous and offer fewer opportunities for innovation and creativity.

The idea of the long-tail of item popularity and its impact on recommendation quality has been explored by some researchers [3, 13]. In those works, authors tried to improve the performance of the recommender system in terms of accuracy and precision, given the long-tail in the ratings. Our work, instead, focuses on reducing popularity bias and balancing the presentation of items across the popularity distribution.

2 LEARNING TO RANK

We focus on matrix factorization approaches to recommendation in which the training phase involves learning a low rank $n \times k$ latent user matrix P and a low-rank $m \times k$ latent item matrix Q, such that the estimated rating $\hat{r}_{ui}$ can be expressed as $\hat{r}_{ui} = p_u^T q_i$ where p_u^T is the uth row of P, q_i^T is the ith row of Q, and k is the chosen dimension of the latent space. P and Q are learned through the minimization of an accuracy-based objective [10].

Since we are interested in ranking rather than rating prediction, we focus on the learning to rank objective function proposed originally in [9] and further developed in [17]:[1]

$$\sum_{u \in U} \sum_{i \in I} c_{ui} \sum_{j \in I} s_j [(\hat{r}_{ui} - \hat{r}_{uj}) - (r_{ui} - r_{uj})]^2 \quad (1)$$

The role of c_{ui} is to select user-item pairs corresponding to positive feedback from all possible pairs. We consider the implicit feedback case in which $c_{ui} = 0$ if $r_{ui} = 0$, and 1 otherwise. s_j is an importance weighting for item j. In this work, because we are trying to reduce the influence of popular items, we use uniform importance weighting $s_j = 1$, for all j.

3 FAIRNESS-AWARE REGULARIZATION

This work was inspired by recent research by Wasilewski and Hurley [18] in which regularization is used to enhance recommendation diversity in a learning to rank setting, specifically using the RankALS algorithm [17]. The authors calculate a pair-wise dissimilarity matrix D for all pairs of items, demonstrate that intra-list diversity (ILD) can be represented in terms of this matrix, and then experiment with different ways that increased ILD can be made into an optimization objective.

Following a similar approach, we explore the use of regularization to control the popularity bias of a recommender system. We start with an optimization objective of the form:

$$\min_{P,Q} acc(P, Q) + \lambda reg(P, Q) \quad (2)$$

where $acc(.)$ is the accuracy objective, $reg(.)$ is a regularization term, and λ is a coefficient for controlling the effect of regularizer.

Our goal therefore is to identify a regularization component of the objective that will be minimized when the distribution of recommendations is fair. As an initial assumption, we define a *fair recommendation list* as one that achieves a 50/50 balance between medium-tail and short-head items. We intend to generalize this objective in future work.

Wasileski and Hurley start from a dissimilarity matrix D, which contains all pair-wise dissimilarities between items. The regularizer is computed from D in such a way that it pushes the optimization solution towards recommendation lists that balance ranking accuracy with intra-list diversity (ILD).

In our case, we define two sets of items Φ and $\sim\Phi$ corresponding to the short-head and medium-tail items, and define a co-membership matrix D, over these sets. For any pair of items i and j, $d(i, j) = 1$ if i and j are in the same set and 0 otherwise.[2]

Our equivalent for intra-list distance is a measure of the lack of fairness for the two sets of items in a given recommendation list L_u. We define intra-list binary unfairness (ILBU) as the average value of $d(i, j)$ across all pairs of items i, j.

$$ILBU(L_u) = \frac{1}{N(N-1)} \sum_{i,j \in L_u} d(i, j) \quad (3)$$

where N is the number of items in the recommendation list. The fairest list is one that contains equal numbers of items from each set, which can be easily seen: if we start with a balanced distribution and replace an item from Φ with one from $\sim\Phi$, there will be more non-zero pairs and therefore a greater sum over all pairs. Therefore, in this case unlike in [18], the regularizer should be minimized using a positive λ as lower values correspond to an evenly-balanced list.

A more readily interpretable but closely related metric of success we will use for evaluation is the Average Percentage of Tail items (APT) in the recommendation lists, which we define as follows:

$$APT = \frac{1}{|U_t|} \sum_{u \in U_t} \frac{|\{i, i \in (L(u) \cap \sim\Phi)\}|}{|L(u)|} \quad (4)$$

where $|U_t|$ is the number of users in the test set and $L(u)$ is the recommendation list for user u. This measure tells us what percentage of items in users' recommendation lists belongs to the medium tail set.

Note that we do not in our definition of fairness require that each item have an equal chance of being recommended. There are many fewer short-head items and we are, essentially, allocating half of the recommendation list to them.[3] The 50/50 heuristic is a starting point for exploring the effectiveness of our regularization-based technique.

As our ILBU value has the same form as the ILD measure used in [18], we can take advantage of their experience in deriving various regularization terms from it. We chose the LapDQ regularizer, which performed well in Wasilewski and Hurley's experiments: we plan to examine additional regularizers in future work. LapDQ is based on the Laplacian L_D of the D matrix and has the form $tr(Q^T L_D Q)$, where tr is the trace of the matrix. This version of the regularizer only influences the item factors and therefore the p step of the RankALS algorithm, which computes the user factors, is unchanged.

[1]A number of such objectives have been proposed in the literature and the regularization method we propose here could be incorporated with any such pair-wise objective.

[2]We exclude distant long-tail items here. Extending this approach to content-collaborative hybrids is a topic for future work.

[3]Note that it would be possible to adjust the balance between long-tail and short-head items by creating a smaller penalty for larger numbers of short-head items. These possibilities we leave for future work.

For the details of the derivation of the regularizer, readers are referred to [18]. One way to understand the function of *LapDQ* is to note that our D matrix is block-structured, and has the same structure as the adjacency matrix for a graph consisting of two separate components of fully interconnected items. For such a graph, the partition is represented by the eigenvector of the Laplacian corresponding to the largest eigenvalue. In our case, we already know what this partition is – it is the division of the nodes into short-head and medium-tail items. The trace of $Q^T L_D Q$ is the product of each latent factor with the Laplacian of the membership matrix. If the item factors most resemble the partitioning eigenvector – that is, they contain elements from both partitions in opposite signs, then this vector product, and therefore the matrix trace, is minimized. The regularizer therefore pushes each item factor in Q to span both partitions as evenly as possible.

4 EXPERIMENTAL RESULTS

We used two datasets in our experiments. The first is the well-known Movielens 1M dataset that contains 1,000,209 anonymous ratings of approximately 3,900 movies made by 6,040 MovieLens users who joined MovieLens in 2000 [8]. The second dataset is the Epinions dataset, which is gathered from a consumers opinion site where users can review items (such as cars, books, movies, and software) and assign them numeric ratings in the range 1 (min) to 5 (max) [11]. This dataset has total number of 664,824 ratings given by 40,163 users to 139,736 items. In Movielens, each user has a minimum of 20 ratings but in Epinions, there are many users with only a single rated item.

Our examination of the data showed that users with longer profiles were much more likely to have long-tail items in their profiles. From each dataset, we removed users who had fewer than 30 ratings. The retained users were those likely to have rated enough long-tail items so that our objective could be evaluated in a train / test scenario. We also removed distant long-tail items from each dataset, using a limit of 30 ratings. This has a very significant impact on the Epinions dataset, as there is a huge distant part of the tail containing many cold-start products with only one rating.

After the removal of short-profile users and distant long tail items, the Movielens dataset has 5,289 users who rated 2,836 movies with a total number of 972,471 ratings, a reduction of about 3%. Applying the same criteria to the Epinions dataset decreases the data to 157,887 ratings given by 5,383 users to 3,423 items, a reduction of more than 75%.

For the purposes of this experiment, we define the short-head of the distribution (the set Φ) to be the top 20% of the items by rating count. For Movielens, the short-head items were those with more than 400 ratings. In Epinions, a short-head item need only to have more than 46 ratings – which demonstrates the more skewed nature of ratings in the Epinions data.

We used Librec [7], an open source Java framework for recommender system implementation, modified by the inclusion of our regularized version of RankALS. We used a random split of 80% of the data for training and the remaining 20% for testing. For each user in the test set, we recommended a list of 10 items using three different algorithms: most popular(*Pop*), standard ALS (*ALS*) and our fairness-aware regularized ALS (*ALS + Reg*).

We evaluated the results for ranking performance in terms of normalized Discounted Cumulative Gain, nDCG@10. For the fairness-aware aspect of the algorithm, we evaluated the system based on the APT measure, the proportion of medium-tail items in the average recommendation list, and we also measured medium-tail coverage, the total number of items from the medium-tail set that are recommended to any user in the test data. This is a holistic view of how well the system is avoiding popularity bias, but not one that our algorithm attempts to optimize.

Figure 2 shows the trade-off between nDCG@10, the medium-tail proportion, and the total number of medium-tail items covered in the recommendations, evaluated for different values of λ for the Movielens dataset. As expected, increased weight for the regularizer is associated with more tail items in each list, with increased total medium-tail coverage and with lower ranking performance. The APT measure approaches 20% for the highest λ values – corresponding to 2 medium-tail items in each list on average. Without the fairness-aware approach, these lists have only short-head items. Notably, there is a fairly substantial region in which coverage increases with minimal measurable nDCG loss.

On the Movielens dataset at λ =7.0E-5, which seems to be an optimal point in terms of nDCG and medium-tail coverage tradeoff, we see a statistically-significant increase in average medium-tail coverage: 5.6 to 114 ($p <$ 1.0E-5) with statistically-insignificant loss of nDCG: 0.1449 to 0.1441 ($p > 0.25$).

Figure 3 shows a similar pattern for the Epinions dataset. The nDCG performance drops a little more noticeably in this dataset, but there is still a region that has increased medium-tail coverage with minor ranking loss. At λ =2.0E-6, the increase in average medium-tail coverage is smaller, but still significant ($p <$ 1E-4) and the difference in nDCG is not significant at $p > 0.05$, the actual p-value = 0.066.

What we see in these results is similar to the findings of [18], namely that a regularization term incorporating list-wise properties of interest can be incorporated successfully into a learning to rank framework. In Wasilewski and Hurley's work, this was a similarity-based term that enabled them to enhance list-wise diversity; in our case, it is a group-membership-based term that enables us to enhance list-wise coverage of medium tail items.

Note in particular that because this loss function is pair-wise and local to individual recommendation lists, it does not aim to increase catalog coverage in the medium tail directly. It is possible, in a pathological case, to increase list-wise coverage of medium-tail items (i.e. low ILBU / high APT) by providing the same medium-tail items to all users. This minimizes the objective without enhancing medium-tail coverage across the catalog. Our results show that, for these datasets, the optimization of our local objective also increases overall coverage of medium-tail items across the test data.

5 CONCLUSION AND FUTURE WORK

Long-tail items are an important key to practical success for recommender systems. Since short-head items are likely to be well known to many users, the ability to recommend items outside of this band of popularity will determine if a recommender can introduce users to new products and experiences. Yet, it is well-known that recommendation algorithms have biases towards popular items.

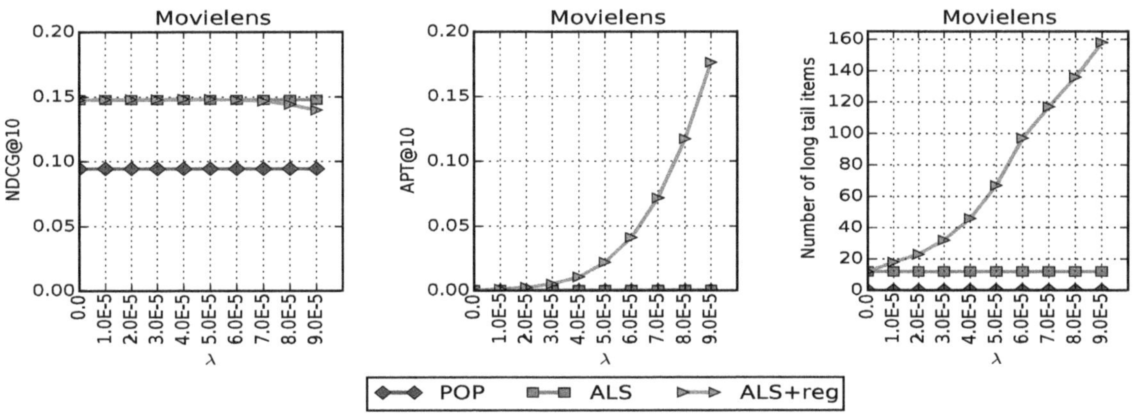

Figure 2: The nDCG, APT, and total long-tail coverage tradeoff (Movielens)

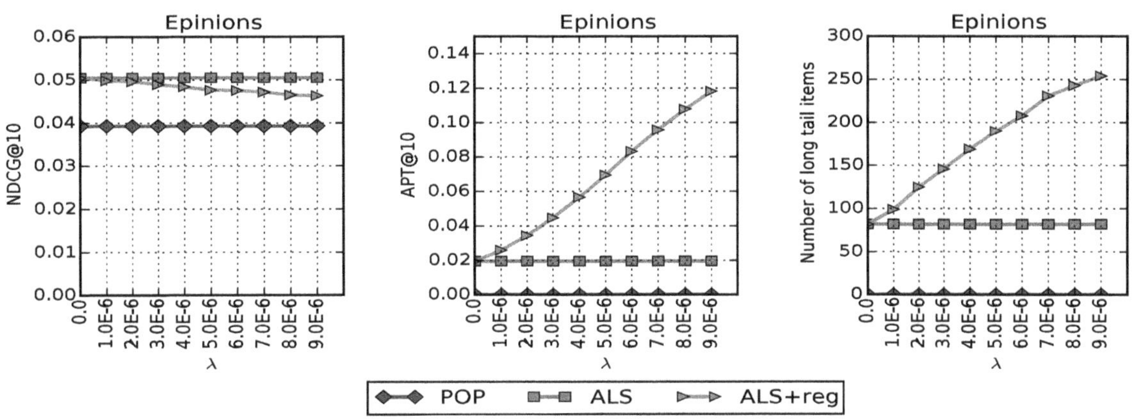

Figure 3: The nDCG, APT, and total long-tail coverage tradeoff (Epinions)

In this paper, we have concentrated on the medium tail – that part of the long tail for which there is sufficient data for collaborative filtering to be effective. Within this set of items, we have shown that it is possible to model the tradeoff between long-tail catalog coverage and ranking accuracy as a multi-objective optimization problem. Our regularization framework, built on related work in diversity optimization, provides a mechanism for tuning the RankALS algorithm to achieve a desired point in this tradeoff space. This fairness-aware regularization approach can, in principle, be applied in any learning algorithm in which the objective is formulated as a pair-wise function of items, such as Bayesian Personalized Ranking [14]. We plan to explore this possibility in future work.

This work suggests a number of other possible extensions. We have defined our objective as a balanced 50/50 presentation of short-head and medium-tail items. However, in some applications, this may be impractical or undesirable. In our future work, we will examine how the co-membership matrix D may be manipulated to target different levels of long-tail item presence (80/20, for example).

Our fairness criterion was formulated relative to two fixed sets. One example of a two-set fairness is in educational recommender systems where the system wants to keep a fair balance between items recommended to females versus those recommended to males [4]. One could imagine generalizing this idea to a situation in which fairness is defined in other ways such as distributing the utilities given to different stakeholders based on some predefined constraints [1]. For example, in [5], the authors discuss a scenario which fairness across multiple product suppliers is sought. In our future work, we will examine if our regularization approach can be extended to encompass this situation as well.

The presence of the distant long tail – items that cannot be integrated into a collaborative filtering framework – suggests the need for a hybrid strategy that incorporates content-based recommendation as well. Content-based recommendation does not depend on peer evaluations and is immune to popularity bias, but may be less effective when content data is noisy or incomplete. Our fairness-aware approach points the way to novel hybrids sensitive to the shape of the popularity distribution.

ACKNOWLEDGMENTS

This work is supported in part by the National Science Foundation under grant IIS-1423368.

REFERENCES

[1] Himan Abdollahpouri, Robin Burke, and Mobasher Bamshad. 2017. Recommender systems as multi-stakeholder environments. In *Proceedings of the 25th Conference on User Modeling, Adaptation and Personalization (UMAP2017)*. ACM, Bratislava, Slovakia, to appear.

[2] Chris Anderson. 2006. *The long tail: Why the future of business is selling more for less.* Hachette Books.

[3] Erik Brynjolfsson, Yu Jeffrey Hu, and Michael D Smith. 2006. From niches to riches: Anatomy of the long tail. *Sloan Management Review* 47, 4 (2006), 67–71.

[4] Robin Burke and Himan Abdollahpouri. 2016. Educational Recommendation with Multiple Stakeholders. In *IEEE/WIC/ACM International Conference on Web Intelligence Workshops (WIW)*. IEEE, Omaha, Nebraska, 62–63.

[5] Robin D. Burke, Himan Abdollahpouri, Bamshad Mobasher, and Trinadh Gupta. 2016. Towards Multi-Stakeholder Utility Evaluation of Recommender Systems. In *Workshop on Surprise, Opposition, and Obstruction in Adaptive and Personalized Systems, UMAP 2016*. 6.

[6] Òscar Celma and Pedro Cano. 2008. From hits to niches?: or how popular artists can bias music recommendation and discovery. In *Proceedings of the 2nd KDD Workshop on Large-Scale Recommender Systems and the Netflix Prize Competition.* ACM, 5.

[7] Guibing Guo, Jie Zhang, Zhu Sun, and Neil Yorke-Smith. 2015. LibRec: A Java Library for Recommender Systems.. In *UMAP Workshops*. 4.

[8] F Maxwell Harper and Joseph A Konstan. 2015. The MovieLens Datasets: History and Context. *ACM Transactions on Interactive Intelligent Systems (TiiS)* 5, 4 (2015), 19.

[9] Michael Jahrer and Andreas Töscher. 2012. Collaborative Filtering Ensemble.. In *KDD Cup*. 61–74.

[10] Yehuda Koren and Robert Bell. 2015. Advances in collaborative filtering. In *Recommender systems handbook*. Springer, 77–118.

[11] Paolo Massa and Paolo Avesani. 2007. Trust-aware recommender systems. In *Proceedings of the 2007 ACM conference on Recommender systems*. ACM, 17–24.

[12] Tien T Nguyen, Pik-Mai Hui, F Maxwell Harper, Loren Terveen, and Joseph A Konstan. 2014. Exploring the filter bubble: the effect of using recommender systems on content diversity. In *Proceedings of the 23rd international conference on World wide web*. ACM, 677–686.

[13] Yoon-Joo Park and Alexander Tuzhilin. 2008. The long tail of recommender systems and how to leverage it. In *Proceedings of the 2008 ACM conference on Recommender systems*. ACM, 11–18.

[14] Steffen Rendle, Christoph Freudenthaler, Zeno Gantner, and Lars Schmidt-Thieme. 2009. BPR: Bayesian personalized ranking from implicit feedback. In *Proceedings of the twenty-fifth conference on uncertainty in artificial intelligence*. AUAI Press, 452–461.

[15] Paul Resnick, R Kelly Garrett, Travis Kriplean, Sean A Munson, and Natalie Jomini Stroud. 2013. Bursting your (filter) bubble: strategies for promoting diverse exposure. In *Proceedings of the 2013 conference on Computer supported cooperative work companion*. ACM, 95–100.

[16] Guy Shani and Asela Gunawardana. 2011. Evaluating recommendation systems. In *Recommender systems handbook*. Springer, 257–297.

[17] Gábor Takács and Domonkos Tikk. 2012. Alternating least squares for personalized ranking. In *Proceedings of the sixth ACM conference on Recommender systems*. ACM, 83–90.

[18] Jacek Wasilewski and Neil Hurley. 2016. Incorporating Diversity in a Learning to Rank Recommender System.. In *FLAIRS Conference*. 572–578.

Educational Question Routing in Online Student Communities

Jakub Macina
Slovak University of Technology
Ilkovicova 2
Bratislava 842 16, Slovakia
jakub.macina@gmail.com

Ivan Srba
Slovak University of Technology
Ilkovicova 2
Bratislava 842 16, Slovakia
ivan.srba@stuba.sk

Joseph Jay Williams
National University of Singapore
13 Computing Drive
Singapore 117417, Republic of Singapore
Harvard University
Cambridge, Massachusetts 02138, USA
williams@comp.nus.edu.sg

Maria Bielikova
Slovak University of Technology
Ilkovicova 2
Bratislava 842 16, Slovakia
maria.bielikova@stuba.sk

ABSTRACT

Students' performance in Massive Open Online Courses (MOOCs) is enhanced by high quality discussion forums or recently emerging educational Community Question Answering (CQA) systems. Nevertheless, only a small number of students answer questions asked by their peers. This results in instructor overload, and many unanswered questions. To increase students' participation, we present an approach for recommendation of new questions to students who are likely to provide answers. Existing approaches to such question routing proposed for non-educational CQA systems tend to rely on a few experts, what is not applicable in educational domain where it is important to involve all kinds of students. In tackling this novel *educational question routing* problem, our method (1) goes beyond previous question-answering data as it incorporates additional non-QA data from the course (to improve prediction accuracy and to involve more of the student community) and (2) applies constraints on users' workload (to prevent user overloading). We use an ensemble classifier for predicting students' willingness to answer a question, as well as students' expertise for answering. We conducted an online evaluation of the proposed method using an A/B experiment in our CQA system deployed in edX MOOC. The proposed method outperformed a baseline method (non-educational question routing enhanced with workload restriction) by improving recommendation accuracy, keeping more community members active, and increasing an average number of their contributions.

CCS CONCEPTS

•**Information systems** →**Recommender systems;** *Personalization; Information extraction; Clustering and classification;* •**Applied computing** →*E-learning;*

KEYWORDS

Question routing, Massive Open Online Courses, Community Question Answering, User Models

1 INTRODUCTION

The expansion of Massive Open Online Courses (MOOCs) could provide the potential for everybody with an internet connection to access educational resources, bringing thousands of students from around the world into a diverse online learning community.

However, a key issue in MOOCs is that many students who enroll do not finish the course. Dropout rates for courses can be as high as 94% [14]. While student completion of MOOCs is a complex issue, previous studies [1, 3] have shown that reduced dropout is associated with: (1) involvement in discussion tools (participating students are more likely to successfully finish the course), and (2) question answering success rate (students are less likely to dropout when a high proportion of discussion forum questions are answered). Discussion tools can reduce dropout by enabling students and course instructors to discuss problems with learning materials, gain deeper insight into a topic, and socialize to build a sense of community [16].

MOOC platforms such as edX[1] and Coursera[2] provide basic built-in discussion forums. Some MOOCs use also additional external discussion tools that incorporate elements of social networking sites, online chats or Community Question Answering (CQA) systems (e.g. [1]). In this work, we focus particularly on CQA systems, such as Stack Overflow[3] and Yahoo! Answers[4], which have been successfully used on the open web, in enterprise domains [13] and they are recently starting to be employed in MOOCs[5] as well. CQA systems are an alternative to standard discussion forums that provide more structured content around questions and their answers. In addition, CQA systems offer more possibilities for collaboration (e.g. best answer selection) and are more community-driven (e.g.

RecSys '17, August 27-31, 2017, Como, Italy
© 2017 ACM. 978-1-4503-4652-8/17/08...$15.00
DOI: http://dx.doi.org/10.1145/3109859.3109886

[1] https://www.edx.org/
[2] https://www.coursera.org/
[3] https://stackoverflow.com/
[4] https://answers.yahoo.com/
[5] E.g. https://cs50.stackexchange.com/

they provide community profiles and possibility to follow activity of other users) [17].

The challenge for MOOC discussion and CQA is that many questions go unanswered, and this proportion of unanswered questions can be as high as 50% [24]. As thousands of students are enrolled, course instructors are overloaded with too many students to serve. Ideally, students themselves could be a resource for answering each other's questions. However, only a small fraction of the student community actually answer questions [1]. Another part of the community (so called lurkers) consumes the content but does not actively contribute in discussion. This reflects the long-tail distribution commonly found in online communities, where a majority of content is created by a minority of users. Two reasons for low participation are (1) many users are not willing to participate, and (2) users who are willing to participate are overloaded with too many questions, and are not able to find the questions of greatest interest for them [4].

We tackle this problem of engaging more students in answering questions in online courses. Our approach is to recommend new questions to those students who are suitable candidates to answer them (so called question routing). To the best of our knowledge, this is the first work investigating question routing (as a task well-known from CQA systems on the open web) in the context of MOOCs. Our main contributions are as follows:

(1) A novel approach to question routing, which addresses the restrictions and novel opportunities of the educational context of MOOCs. While existing methods primarily focus on askers' needs, we take an answerer-oriented approach by considering not only students' expertise, but also willingness to answer a question.
(2) A model of student activity (beyond data about questions and answers) that enables us to involve more students in question answering and reduce the burden on individual users.
(3) An experiment aimed at online evaluation of our question routing method with more than 4600 MOOC students.

This paper is organized as follows. Section 2 reviews state-of-the-art approaches to question routing, and their limitations in educational domains. Section 3 introduces our formulation of the problem of educational question routing. Section 4 describes our method for question routing. Section 5 presents on experimental evaluation of our method in a MOOC.

2 RELATED WORK

CQA systems on the open web raise a wide range of problems in adaptively supporting collaboration among users, for which many recommendation-based solutions have been developed [17]. In this work, we focus on personalized question recommendation. The problem of question recommendation can be seen from two perspectives [23]: (1) providing users with questions which can be beneficial for them, or (2) routing unanswered questions to users who are likely to answer them.

In the first problem of *question recommendation* [21, 24], the task is given a user u to find ordered list of most relevant questions $q_1, ..., q_n$ to the user u. It can be characterized by analogy to product recommendation, where items are questions. Content-based, collaborative filtering or hybrid approaches are applicable here [8]. Question recommendation recommends any type of questions, mostly resolved ones, to all kinds of users. It can be generated on demand or regularly, for example, as a part of a newsletter.

In the second problem of *question routing* [6, 27], given a newly posted question q, the task is to find an ordered list of users $u_1, ..., u_n$ who are most suitable to answer question q. Question routing uses mainly content-based recommendation, since a question only needs to be recommended to users until it is successfully answered. In contrast to question recommendation, question routing recommends *new* questions, that have not yet been answered, and must be achieved with the limited data available after question posting. Question retrieval, i.e. reusing content by automatic identification of semantically similar questions (e.g. [26]), can be used as a supplement to question routing to filter out repeating questions directly at question creation time.

Our work focuses on question routing, because of the potential to support collaboration among students, to involve more of the community in question answering and to increase the amount of students' contributions. The process of question routing in CQA systems can be understood in three phases [7]: (1) construction of a question profile, (2) construction of a user profile, and (3) matching the profiles of questions and users.

The purpose of the question profile is to represent the topic of the question. Models for representing a question include bag-of-words models based on tf-idf, topic models [15, 22] such as Latent Dirichlet Allocation (LDA), and combinations of both [21]. User profiles that capture a user's expertise in a topic can be inferred from the question-answer data from users' previous contributions in CQA system [15, 21]. Previous work has also modeled users' activity [12, 22], when a user is likely to respond [5], and a user's readiness to answer [13]. To match the profiles of questions and users, three main approaches have been used. The first is classification models that predict a match using methods like logistic regression [13] or Support Vector Machines (SVM) [27]. The second is collaborative filtering. For example, Dror [6] proposed a multi-channel hybrid recommender system that combined collaborative filtering and classification. The third is ranking models that draw on work from document retrieval [12, 15, 22].

Current state-of-the-art question routing methods applied in CQA systems on the open web can be characterized as asker-oriented (i.e. primarily focusing on askers' goals). They route new questions only to the best possible answerers (top experts) to satisfy the askers' needs best [6, 12, 15, 22]. In other words, they may overload a small set of experts while the full potential of the community is not utilized (e.g. one third of all answers on Yahoo! Answers are created by junior users not top experts [21]). This asker-oriented attitude may have several significant drawbacks [19]. From sustainability point of view, it is necessary to maintain healthy community ecosystem and utilize the potential of the online community more effectively by involving and satisfying needs of all potential answerers, including novices, lurkers and junior users. This is also especially important in educational domain.

Research work by Luo et al. [13] addressed this sustainability problem by question routing in enterprise CQA system. The uniqueness of their work is in systematically involving inactive users by routing new questions to them. A classification model is used to find best potential answerers. Afterwards, inactive users most similar to the best potential answerers are matched by distance learning utilizing non-QA data from company's internal systems, e.g. current work state. Similarly in our previous work [20], we employed publicly available non-QA data (e.g. users' homepages or profiles on social networking sites) to obtain expertise estimation also for less active users.

To the best of our knowledge, the task of question routing has not been addressed in educational CQA systems yet, although there has been related work on educational CQA more generally. The first question recommendation method designed specifically for MOOCs was proposed by Yang et al. [24]. The main contribution is optimization of predictions given two constraints present in MOOC domain which are limited students' time for participation and adequate knowledge of an answerer to answer a question. It used a context-aware matrix factorization model that exploited three kinds of contextual information – student features, question features and implicit feedback. This approach regularly (e.g. once a week) recommended a list of answered and unanswered questions to all users. This kind of question recommendation may improve question answering success rate, but it does not route questions to individual users. A significant delay is introduced, as newly created questions cannot be immediately routed to suitable answerers. Some progress has been made also in automatically identifying struggling students based on their previous activity [10], gamification in educational CQA system [2] and in identifying low-quality answers that can mislead students [9].

3 INTRODUCTION OF EDUCATIONAL QUESTION ROUTING

Standard question routing solutions are not appropriate for educational domain. At first, educational question answering has a slightly different aim. While the traditional CQA systems stress the importance of asking challenging, unique questions and providing top quality fast answers, in MOOCs, we primarily aim at students' learning. And thus we may accept also more trivial questions and not so perfect and fast answers while students benefit from question answering. Secondly, we need to consider some constraints, students are usually learning about the topic for the first time and in addition they might be in various weeks of the course, thus having different levels of knowledge. At the same time, educational domain brings many additional opportunities in comparison with standard CQA systems on the open web, such as additional information about students (e.g. students' results in the course) and about questions (e.g. interconnection with learning materials).

3.1 Problem characterization

In this paper we introduce a new task of *educational question routing*, which refers to routing of new questions without any answer in educational CQA system to suitable answerers. The goal of educational question routing is to: (1) *decrease information load of users* by accurate recommendations, (2) *engage a greater part of the community in question answering*, and (3) *increase an average number of contributions*. This way educational question routing will also contribute to lower instructor workload and lower dropout rate.

In educational question routing, we should take three factors (constraints) into account: (1) answerers should have appropriate knowledge for answering a question, (2) answerers should have willingness to answer a question, and (3) answerers should not be overloaded with routed questions. The rationale for considering students' adequate expertise is to involve the majority of students (not only top experts) and at the same time recommend them questions with a reasonable difficulty (i.e. not too challenging questions so the necessary quality of the provided answers will be achieved). Some students might have a suitable expertise to answer a question but not all of them are also motivated to actually provide a contribution. Therefore, willingness to answer is also likely to improve the recommendation. And finally, it is necessary to balance recommended questions according to current students' workload, as answering others questions is not students' primary goal.

In educational question routing, we need to tackle two cold-start problems related to questions and users. Firstly, we want to involve students who do not have previous contributions in the CQA system. Thanks to additional possibilities of MOOCs, we are not limited in user modelling (i.e. estimation of expertise and willingness) only at users' previous activities directly in the CQA system. We can exploit several valuable sources of data in the MOOC course. For example, it is possible to estimate student's expertise more accurately by considering knowledge prerequisites for a routed question, such as a previous view of related lecture videos or a sufficient grade for related assignments.

Secondly, only limited data are available about questions at their creation time and we cannot rely on community feedback, such as voting, favorites or comments. However, utilizing information about the asker can help to estimate quantities like question difficulty. We can utilize the so called knowledge gap between an asker and a potential answerer. The knowledge gap denotes a pattern, which was observed by Lin et al. [11], in which the question asked by an expert has a high probability of being difficult and thus can be answered only by other expert users. The same pattern was also observed for users with low expertise and easy questions.

Finally, the method for educational question routing should meet requirements of fast-paced learning environments. It should be designed to route new questions in real-time after question creation. In addition, it should reflect recent activity in the CQA system and MOOC course throughout the period of a course (e.g. when students drop out of the course, the method should not consider them as suitable answerers any more).

3.2 Definitions

Definition 3.1. Categories in MOOCs are organized into a hierarchical structure, where at the first level a course consists of categories representing weeks and at the second level each week consists of categories dedicated to particular topics. This hierarchical structure is usually followed also in discussion tools. Each question is assigned to a particular topic category. If we define Q as the set of all questions in a course, then $Q_{topic} \subseteq Q_{week} \subseteq Q$.

Definition 3.2. Knowledge $K_{u,c}$ is the topical expertise of a user u for answering questions in a category c. In this paper, user knowledge $K_{u,c}$ is estimated as the sum of the total number of contributions in a category c, i.e. answers, comments and votes.

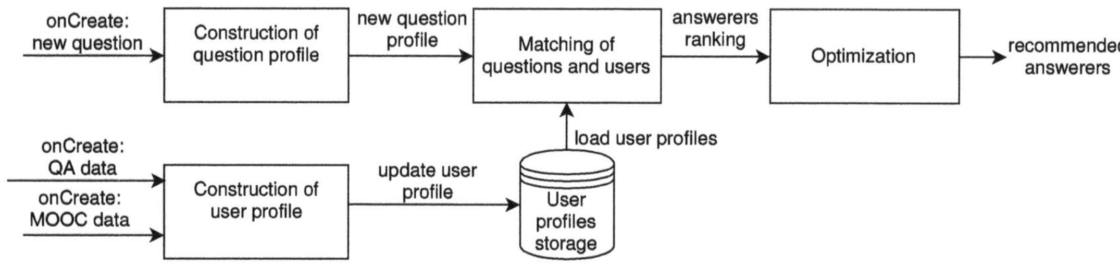

Figure 1: Educational question routing framework.

Definition 3.3. Knowledge gap is the difference in the knowledge of an answerer $K_{answerer,c}$ and knowledge of an asker $K_{asker,c}$ in a category c of a routed question.

Definition 3.4. Workload L_u is the number of questions routed to user u within the recent time period (e.g. during the last 7 days).

4 EDUCATIONAL QUESTION ROUTING FRAMEWORK

An overview of our educational question routing framework is depicted in Figure 1. The inputs for the framework are a new question and users' activities in the CQA system and MOOC. The output for a new question is a list of recommended answerers, sorted by the ranking $r_{u,q}$ of how likely user u is to answer a new question q. The framework is divided into three phases, which are typical for question routing methods, followed by the fourth optimization phase, which is added specifically for educational question routing.

4.1 Construction of question profile

The question profile is created immediately after a new question is posted into the CQA system. It captures the question's content (title and question body), as well as metadata, such as the hierarchy of assigned categories, and information about the asker, who is represented by a user profile (see Section 4.2). Question title and body are concatenated and preprocessed by tokenization, removal of stop words, and stemming. The question text profile θ_q is created as a bag-of-words model with tf-idf weights. The answer profile $\theta_{a,q}$ is created similarly, but since the answer does not have a title the concatenation step is unnecessary. Information about the asker and the categories for week and topic categories are also stored for use in the third question-user matching step.

4.2 Construction of user profile

The user profile is updated after each user activity in the CQA or the MOOC. It consists of two main parts that capture information about the (1) topic of questions a user previously provided answers on, (2) quantity, quality and time distribution of previous user activities carried out in the CQA system or in the MOOC.

Firstly, the user profile models user's interests in particular question topics. A user text profile θ_u is created as a sum of the bag-of-words vectors from question and answer text profiles:

$$\theta_u = \sum_{q \in Q_u} (\theta_q + \theta_{a,q}) \tag{1}$$

where Q_u is the set of questions to which the user provided an answer, θ_q is a question text profile and $\theta_{a,q}$ is an answer text profile of user u for question q.

Secondly, the user profile captures the current level of user activity in the CQA system itself (i.e. number of posted questions, answers, and comments) as well as activity in the MOOC (i.e. number of seen lectures). In addition to level of activity, the user profile captures quality of activity, through earned votes in the CQA system and assignment grades. Quantity and quality of all activities is stored separately for each week and each topic category. As user's activity in the system can vary significantly over time, the user profile also contains time related metrics, such as course registration date and time of last answer.

4.3 Matching of questions and users

The third phase, matching of the question and the user profile, aims to calculate ranking of each user given a new question. Using the profile of a new question and each potential answerer's user profile, we address this as an ensemble of two explicit classification tasks:

(1) Predicting whether a user has sufficient expertise to answer a new question.
(2) Predicting user willingness to answer a new question.

The rationale for splitting the classification into two subtasks is to provide more powerful and flexible global classifier. Moreover, it ensures that both sources of information will be appropriately weighted and used in a global classifier. For example, our approach ensures that expertise features are not the only consideration in question routing at the expense of features that provide a cue to willingness.

The final ensemble ranking combines the predictions of individual classifiers, as the probability of both events occurring – a user having the expertise as well as willingness to answer a new question:

$$P(y = 1) = P(exp = 1) \cdot P(will = 1) \tag{2}$$

where $P(exp = 1)$ is the probability of the positive class for expertise classifier prediction, and $P(will = 1)$ is the probability of the positive class for the willingness classifier. This final probability of each prediction is assigned as the value of $r_{u,q}$ for each user and new question, and used to rank predicted answerers for question routing.

Input features are divided into two groups for each classifier separately: expertise and willingness features (see Table 1). The features dedicated to expertise classification include:

Table 1: Expertise and willingness features, divided into subgroups according to their origin in the CQA system or the MOOC; and according to their type as non-educational (used also by CQA systems on the open web) and educational.

		Non-educational	Educational
Expertise	CQA	question-user text profiles similarity answers count within a week category answers count within a topic category earned votes count within a week category earned votes count within a topic category	overall knowledge gap knowledge gap within a week category knowledge gap within a topic category
	MOOC		average assignments grade portion of seen lectures within a week category portion of seen lectures within a topic category
Willingness	CQA	overall answers/comments/questions count overall earned votes count answers count in the recent period last answer time proportion of days with any activity in CQA	portion of seen questions within a week category portion of seen questions within a topic category
	MOOC	course registration date	portion of days with any activity in MOOC lecture freshness portion of seen lectures within a week category portion of seen lectures within a topic category

(1) simple expertise measures calculated for the question's week/topic category, such as *answers counts* and *earned votes counts,*
(2) *question-user text profiles similarity,* which is calculated as a cosine similarity between the question text profile θ_q and the user text profile θ_u,
(3) *knowledge gap* for the question's week/topic category, which models the level of difficulty for an answerer to answer a new question,
(4) knowledge prerequisites, such as *portion of seen lectures* and student's *average assignments grade* (the rationale is that students who have already seen lectures or have good grades for a question's topic are more likely to have the suitable expertise).

The features for classifying willingness to answer a question include:

(1) simple activity measures, such as *overall answers, questions or comments count,*
(2) *answers count in recent period* which determine the amount of latest activity,
(3) time related metrics, *last answer time* t_u, *lecture freshness* t_l (i.e. time of watching the lecture related to a new question) and *course registration date* t_r (which influences a student commitment as shown by [25]), are processed in relation to time of posting of the new question t_q:

$$t_q - t, \quad t \in \{t_u, t_l, t_r\} \tag{3}$$

(4) *portion of days with any activity in CQA/MOOC* is used to estimate a response time on recommendation,
(5) *portion of seen questions* within the question's week/topic category, which represents student interest in browsing questions in the CQA system,
(6) *portion of seen lectures* within the question's week/topic category, which estimates student activity in the course.

4.4 Optimization

In the last phase of our question routing framework, the constraints are applied similarly as in [13, 24]. Routed questions are balanced by applying a threshold on user's current workload L_u. If L_u is above a threshold, question is not routed to a user u. The goal of the optimization is to not overload users and to involve a greater part of the community in question answering.

5 EXPERIMENTS

This section presents the results of an offline and an online experiment. The goal of both experiments was to evaluate the performance of our educational question routing method. The online experiment enabled us to examine the real-world impact of our question routing method on the student community.

Both experiments were conducted in our open-source CQA system Askalot ported to the edX MOOC platform [18]. We used data from the first half of the course to fine tune parameters of our question routing framework. Then, we used the trained classification models during the online experiment, which was conducted on the second half of the course.

5.1 CQA system and course description

The MOOC course used for our experiments was *QuCryptox Quantum Cryptography*[6] offered by the California Institute of Technology and Delft University of Technology[7]. The course taught basics of quantum cryptography and required advanced knowledge of linear algebra and probability. It lasted 10 weeks from 10th October to 20th December 2016. As the course and the CQA system was available for students also before and after the official course duration, the presented results cover a longer period including two weeks before (26th September 2016) and after (2nd January 2017) course.

[6] https://courses.edx.org/courses/course-v1:CaltechDelftX+QuCryptox+3T2016/
[7] Permission to conduct this research was provided by the course instructors.

Table 2: Statistics on QuCryptox Quantum Cryptography course.

Metric	Quantity
Students enrolled in the course	8115
Students started the course	4618
Users participating in CQA (contributors + lurkers)	1098 (24%)
Users contributing in CQA	377 (8%)
Questions	361
Questions with answer	299 (83%)
Questions with best answer selected	53 (15%)
Answers	386
Comments	476

The course had estimated workload from 6 to 8 hours per week. Each week contained video lectures about several topics followed by quizzes, pen and paper assignments, and coding assignments. Summary statistics about the course are presented in Table 2. The proportion of answered questions was very high during the whole course (84.28% before and 80.30% during the online experiment).

5.2 Baseline

As there is not any other educational question routing method, which we can directly compare with, we used a non-educational variant of our question routing framework as a baseline. It does not consider the educational features, which are listed in Table 1. As we could not afford to overload students in the online experiment by many requests to answer new questions, we applied a workload restriction also on this baseline recommendation. Despite this workload restriction, which is not typical for existing state-of-the-art question routing methods, our selected baseline can be characterized as asker-oriented which is very common in the CQA systems on the open web.

5.3 Offline experiment

Research on methods for question routing are evaluated mostly by offline experiments, while online experiments are conducted very rarely (see [17] for a review). However, offline experiments are limited in several ways. They can only consider users who choose to answer a question as a positive example. However, a user who is a suitable answerer (a positive example) may simply not choose to answer a question if a high-quality answer was already provided by another user. Also, as most available data sets do not provide question views, it is not possible to identify users who see an unanswered question and do not provide any answer (a negative example). Past research therefore considers all users as negative examples, except those who choose to answer a question. Our work addresses these limitations by supplementing the offline evaluation with an ecologically valid online evaluation of our method.

5.3.1 Experimental setup. For training expertise and willingness classifiers, we generated positive ($y = 1$) and negative ($y = 0$) samples from data as defined in Table 3. The ensemble classifier was used to compute whether a question would be routed to a user, and was evaluated by comparision to which users actually answered the question. The optimization step for load balancing was not applied in the offline experiment.

Table 3: Generation of positive and negative samples for expertise classifier and willingness classifier.

	Positive class (class 1)	Negative class (class 0)
Expertise classifier	- answer with positive votes difference - answer which is marked as best answer - answer with positive evaluation from teaching assistant	- answer with negative votes difference - answer with zero votes and another answer was added later - answer with negative evaluation from teaching assistant
Willingness classifier	- answer - comment	- question view without interaction

We performed feature selection by χ^2 selection and filtering out highly correlated features (these features are already removed from Table 1). When selecting appropriate classification algorithms, we required online training, or fast re-training on all previous activities. Particularly, we selected and trained three classifiers - SVM, Random Forest and Logistic Regression. The probability threshold for predicting the positive/negative class of each classifier is found dynamically by maximizing the AUC metric (Area Under the Receiver Operating Curve). We used grid search to find the best combination of parameters and tune the model hyper parameters. We used 10-fold stratified cross validation for evaluating both classification algorithms. Our experiment found that the Random Forest method performed the best on both classification tasks, and so we selected it for both classifiers.

5.3.2 Metrics. We used the following metrics for evaluating our question routing methods for ranking answerers: *Success (S@N)*, *Mean Average Precision (MAP@N)*, *Normalized Discounted Cumulated Gain (nDCG@N)* and *Mean Reciprocal Rank (MRR)*. S@N measures whether any real answerer is among the top N users, while the other metrics are standard in information retrieval.

5.3.3 Results. The results are computed for the whole duration of the course. As shown in Table 4, our educational question routing framework outperformed the baseline approach across all of metrics. If we would recommend new questions to the top 10 most suitable answerers, we would hit at least one actual answerer in 60.1% of all cases, in comparison to the 54.8% achieved by the baseline (see Figure 2).

We explored the feature importance values from the Random Forest classifier. For prediction of user expertise in answering a question, the most important features were similarity of the question and user text profiles, overall knowledge gap, and count of answers. For prediction of user willingness to answer a question, the most important features were the portion of seen questions within a topic category, and the recent period's answers count. Individual classifier AUC performance is $0.67(+/-0.06)$ for the expertise classifier and $0.73(+/-0.06)$ for the willingness classifier.

Table 4: Educational question routing and baseline question routing results for the offline experiment.

Metric	Educational			Baseline		
	N=5	N=10	N=100	N=5	N=10	N=100
S@N	0.418	0.601	0.924	0.369	0.548	0.894
MAP@N	0.221	0.242	0.260	0.193	0.216	0.234
nDCG@N	0.288	0.345	0.413	0.254	0.312	0.384
MRR	0.284			0.259		

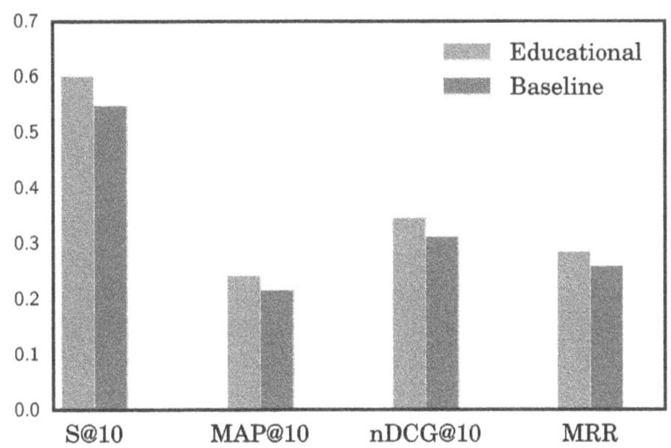

Figure 2: Question routing offline performance results compared to baseline for selected metrics with N=10.

5.4 Online experiment

5.4.1 Experimental setup. We conducted the online experiment as an A/B test in the second half of the QuCryptox Quantum cryptography course, starting from 14th November 2016 (week 6). At the beginning of week 6, the users registered in the CQA system were randomized into three groups of n users, as follows:

(1) *Educational group* (n = 1306). Potential answerers had questions recommended by our educational question routing framework.
(2) *Baseline group* (n = 1306). Users had questions routed by the baseline method.
(3) *Control group* (n = 1306). Users in the control group did not receive any question recommendations.

Randomized assignment was stratified by users' answer counts, to reduce variability. Students who signed up for the course during the online experiment were not included.

Each newly asked question was routed or recommended to the top 10 most suitable users in the educational group and to the top 10 users in the baseline group, using the group's respective question routing method. The constraint on workload L_u for user u was derived from the amount of natural activity of the most active student contributors before the online experiment, and it was set to a maximum of 4 recommendations per 7 days. The recommendation was sent to users as a notification in the CQA system, as well as appearing in the user's dashboard as a personalized list of new recommended questions.

Table 5: Accuracy of question recommendation.

	Educational	Baseline
CTR	23.25%	18.29%
Question routing success rate	15.91%	10.61%

User profiles were updated in real-time and the data loaded for matching questions and users (this ensured users' recent activity was immediately reflected in the question routing, reducing the cold-start problem). Both expertise and willingness classifiers were re-trained each day with the latest data.

5.4.2 Metrics. We evaluated the different conditions (question routing methods) on the following metrics:

- *Click-through rate (CTR)* - The proportion of clicked question recommendations (out of the total number of question recommendations).
- *Question routing success rate* - The proportion of routed questions for which one or more proposed answerer contributed.
- *Users' coverage rate* - The proportion of unique users involved in question routing, because they were selected as a suitable answerer and received a question recommendation (out of the total number of users in the group).
- *Time to answer* - Time in hours for a newly posted question to receive its first answer from a recommended answerer.
- *Answer quality* - This was computed as the difference between the positive and negatives votes by users.

5.4.3 Results. During the online experiment, 132 new questions were routed to potential answerers, resulting into 2640 recommendations. We present results for evaluating the educational question routing goals outlined in Section 3.1.

First, educational question routing needs to decrease the burden on answerers by generating relevant recommendations. One metric for relevant recommendation is a high CTR (see Table 5). The CTR was 23.25% for users in the educational group, but only 18.29% for the baseline group, which was significantly different, $\chi^2(1, N = 2640) = 10.03, p < 0.01$. This difference in CTR of 4.96% means that our method for educational question routing increased the chances of users clicking through by 27%.

A second metric for recommendation quality is the proportion of recommended questions that were answered, or the question routing success rate. The question routing success rate was 15.91% for the educational group, but only 10.61% for the baseline group. While this difference did not reach statistical significance, $\chi^2(1, N = 264) = 1.61, p = 0.20$, this is likely a reflection of the small sample size providing insufficient statistical power to detect differences, as the difference of 5.30% represents an increase of 50% beyond the baseline group. The improvements in recommendation accuracy were achieved by incorporating MOOC data that improved predictions of expertise and willingness to answer questions.

With respect to involving more of the community in educational question routing, we did not observe substantive differences in users' coverage rate, or the proportion of users who answered a recommended question. This rate was 10.72% for the educational group and 10.03% for the baseline group.

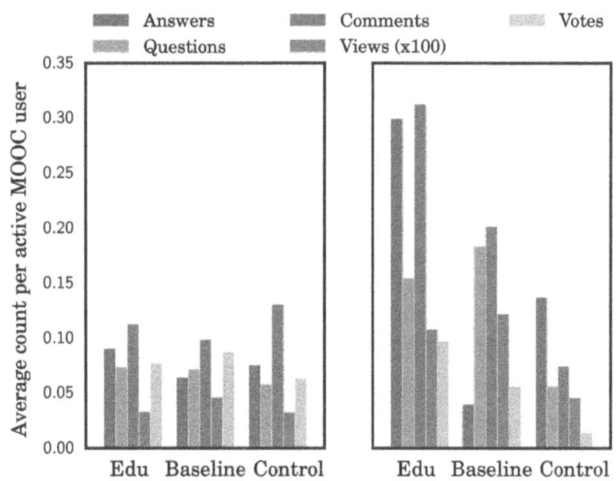

Figure 3: Average amount of activity per active MOOC user before (left) and during (right) the online experiment.

Table 6: Number of contributing CQA users / number of active MOOC users, before and during the online experiment.

	Educational	Baseline	Control
Before	62 / 816 (7.60%)	73 / 812 (8.99%)	74 / 811 (9.12%)
During	40 / 304 (13.16%)	26 / 278 (9.35%)	28 / 321 (8.72%)

In addition to the direct impact of question routing, introducing these methods can also increase overall activity in the CQA system. We report data for each of the three groups, both before and during the online experiment, although the small sample sizes precluded statistical tests. Figure 3 shows the usage behaviors in the CQA system, in terms of posting questions, answers, comments, and viewing and voting on questions. The average count of each behavior was obtained using a similar methodology to [21], where we normalized the absolute numbers of each behavior by the number of active MOOC users in each group (a user is considered as active if he/she had at least one course interaction during the first or second half of the course). The introduction of question routing appears to have led to greater activity in the use of the CQA system, in both the educational and baseline group, relative to the control.

In the Quantum Cryptography course, instructors spent a significant amount of time by collaboration and discussions with students. This high instructors involvement is reflected in the proportion of contributions posted by instructors or teaching assistants, which was 37.28% before the online experiment and only 31.25% during the online experiment. This significant drop confirms that instructors' workload decreased during the online experiment.

To further analyze the impact of question routing and lower instructor load, we verified that it did not have a negative influence on quality of answers and time to answer them. As we stated in Section 3.1, these metrics are not the main subject of optimization (as in the standard question routing methods). However, we do not want these metrics to be reduced at a cost of involving more of the student community or decreasing instructors' workload. The results suggest that the question routing preserves the time to answer and answer quality.

Finally, we evaluated the dropout rate in each user group. We found a minor difference in overall dropout rate from the MOOC (76.72% for educational group vs. 78.71% for baseline). At the same time, we identified a difference in dropout of contributors from the CQA system itself. While in the control group, 21.86% of users stopped contributing to CQA system during the online experiment, it was only 15.61% in the baseline group and even 12.50% in the educational group. This result confirms a positive influence of question routing on keeping users motivated and devoted to question answering. It is also reflected in the proportion of contributing users to CQA system out of active MOOC users (see Table 6), which increased for educational group while it remained rather stable in baseline and control group.

6 CONCLUSIONS

In this paper, we described a new question routing approach for MOOCs. We proposed two innovations which makes our question routing method suitable for an educational domain. Firstly, our approach explicitly models user's willingness to answer the question and combines it with expertise of a user. Secondly, we utilized non-QA data from online course for question routing such as students' grades, activity in the MOOC course and knowledge prerequisites to successfully answer a new question.

There are many additional specifics of MOOCs that provide a possibility for further improvements. Currently, we tackle all types of questions equally. However, in MOOCs some kinds of questions (e.g. those about organizational matters) can be answered only by instructors. If we will be able to automatically and reliable identify them, we can limit the potential answerers to instructors only. Another promising future direction is a better approximation of students knowledge for computing knowledge gap. Finally, applying question routing in MOOC courses with thousands of students brings scalability issues which need to be addressed.

The proposed question routing approach was evaluated by the offline experiment (to fine tune the models and evaluate accuracy of recommendation) and the online experiment (to measure a total impact on the online student community). Based on the comparison with the baseline, it can be concluded that the proposed framework achieved a higher interest of users in the routed questions and engaged more students, who in addition provided more contributions. Moreover, we found out that the recommendations also contributed to the lower dropout rate of active contributors in CQA and to the lower instructors workload.

ACKNOWLEDGMENTS

This work was partially supported by grants No. APVV-15-0508, VG 1/0646/15, KEGA 028STU-4/2017 and "University Science Park of STU Bratislava" ITMS 26240220084, co-funded by the ERDF.

Authors would like to express their sincere gratitude to instructors of Quantum Cryptography course, namely Stephanie Wehner (TU Delft) and Thomas Vidick (Caltech), for their great co-operation and motivation to use Askalot. In addition, authors wish to thank students participating in AskEd team, especially Adrian Huna, for their contribution in making Askalot deployment in edX possible.

REFERENCES

[1] Carlos Alario-Hoyos, Mar Pérez-Sanagustín, Carlos Delgado-Kloos, Hugo A. Parada G, and Mario Munoz-Organero. 2014. Delving into Participants' Profiles and Use of Social Tools in MOOCs. *IEEE Transactions on Learning Technologies* 7, 3 (2014), 260–266.

[2] Chulakorn Aritajati and N. Hari Narayanan. 2013. Facilitating Students' Collaboration and Learning in a Question and Answer System. In *Proceedings of the 2013 Conference on Computer Supported Cooperative Work Companion (CSCW '13)*. ACM, New York, NY, USA, 101–106. DOI: http://dx.doi.org/10.1145/2441955.2441983

[3] Lori Breslow, David E. Pritchard, Jennifer DeBoer, Glenda S. Stump, Andrew D. Ho, and Daniel T. Seaton. 2013. Studying Learning in the Worldwide Classroom: Research into edX's First MOOC. *Research & Practice in Assessment* 8 (2013), 13–25.

[4] C. G. Brinton, M. Chiang, S. Jain, H. Lam, Z. Liu, and F. M. F. Wong. 2014. Learning about Social Learning in MOOCs: From Statistical Analysis to Generative Model. *IEEE Transactions on Learning Technologies* 7, 4 (Oct 2014), 346–359. DOI: http://dx.doi.org/10.1109/TLT.2014.2337900

[5] Tianjian Chen, Jing Cai, Hao Wang, and Yu Dong. 2014. Instant Expert Hunting: Building an Answerer Recommender System for a Large Scale Q&A Website. In *Proceedings of the 29th Annual ACM Symposium on Applied Computing (SAC '14)*. ACM, New York, NY, USA, 260–265. DOI: http://dx.doi.org/10.1145/2554850.2554915

[6] Gideon Dror, Yehuda Koren, Yoelle Maarek, and Idan Szpektor. 2011. I Want to Answer; Who Has a Question?: Yahoo! Answers Recommender System. In *Proceedings of the 17th ACM SIGKDD International Conference on Knowledge Discovery and Data Mining (KDD '11)*. ACM, New York, NY, USA, 1109–1117. DOI: http://dx.doi.org/10.1145/2020408.2020582

[7] Jinwen Guo, Shengliang Xu, Shenghua Bao, and Yong Yu. 2008. Tapping on the Potential of Q&A Community by Recommending Answer Providers. In *Proceedings of the 17th ACM Conference on Information and Knowledge Management (CIKM '08)*. ACM, New York, NY, USA, 921–930. DOI: http://dx.doi.org/10.1145/1458082.1458204

[8] Yutaka Kabutoya, Tomoharu Iwata, Hisako Shiohara, and Ko Fujimura. 2010. Effective Question Recommendation Based on Multiple Features for Question Answering Communities. In *Proceedings of Fourth International AAAI Conference on Weblogs and Social Media*. AAAI, 259–262.

[9] Long T. Le, Chirag Shah, and Erik Choi. 2016. Evaluating the Quality of Educational Answers in Community Question-Answering. In *Proceedings of the 16th ACM/IEEE-CS on Joint Conference on Digital Libraries (JCDL '16)*. ACM, New York, NY, USA, 129–138. DOI: http://dx.doi.org/10.1145/2910896.2910900

[10] Long T. Le, Chirag Shah, and Erik Choi. 2017. Bad Users or Bad Content?: Breaking the Vicious Cycle by Finding Struggling Students in Community Question-Answering. In *Proceedings of the 2017 Conference on Conference Human Information Interaction and Retrieval (CHIIR '17)*. ACM, New York, NY, USA, 165–174. DOI: http://dx.doi.org/10.1145/3020165.3020181

[11] Chih-Lu Lin, Ying-Liang Chen, and Hung-Yu Kao. 2014. Question difficulty evaluation by knowledge gap analysis in Question Answer communities. In *Proceedings of IEEE/ACM International Conference on Advances in Social Networks Analysis and Mining (ASONAM '14)*. IEEE, 336–339.

[12] Mingrong Liu, Yicen Liu, and Qing Yang. 2010. Predicting Best Answerers for New Questions in Community Question Answering. In *Proceedings of the 11th International Conference on Web-age Information Management (WAIM'10)*. Springer, Berlin, Heidelberg, 127–138.

[13] Lin Luo, Fei Wang, Michelle X. Zhou, Yingxin Pan, and Hang Chen. 2014. Who Have Got Answers?: Growing the Pool of Answerers in a Smart Enterprise Social QA System. In *Proceedings of the 19th International Conference on Intelligent User Interfaces (IUI '14)*. ACM, New York, NY, USA, 7–16. DOI: http://dx.doi.org/10.1145/2557500.2557531

[14] Daniel Onah, Jane Sinclair, and Russell Boyatt. 2014. Dropout Rates of Massive Open Online Courses: Behavioural Patterns. *Proceedings of the 6th International Conference on Education and New Learning Technologies (EDULEARN '14)* (2014), 5825–5834.

[15] Fatemeh Riahi, Zainab Zolaktaf, Mahdi Shafiei, and Evangelos Milios. 2012. Finding Expert Users in Community Question Answering. In *Proceedings of the 21st International Conference on World Wide Web (WWW '12 Companion)*. ACM, New York, NY, USA, 791–798. DOI: http://dx.doi.org/10.1145/2187980.2188202

[16] Carolyn Penstein Rosé, Ryan Carlson, Diyi Yang, Miaomiao Wen, Lauren Resnick, Pam Goldman, and Jennifer Sherer. 2014. Social Factors That Contribute to Attrition in MOOCs. In *Proceedings of the First ACM Conference on Learning @ Scale Conference (L@S '14)*. ACM, New York, NY, USA, 197–198. DOI: http://dx.doi.org/10.1145/2556325.2567879

[17] Ivan Srba and Maria Bielikova. 2016. A Comprehensive Survey and Classification of Approaches for Community Question Answering. *ACM Trans. Web* 10, 3, Article 18 (Aug. 2016), 63 pages. DOI: http://dx.doi.org/10.1145/2934687

[18] Ivan Srba and Maria Bielikova. 2016. Design of CQA Systems for Flexible and Scalable Deployment and Evaluation. In *Proceedings of 16th International Conference on Web Engineering (ICWE '16), Lugano, Switzerland, June 6-9, 2016*. Springer, Berlin, Heidelberg, 439–447. DOI: http://dx.doi.org/10.1007/978-3-319-38791-8_30

[19] Ivan Srba and Maria Bielikova. 2016. Why is Stack Overflow Failing? Preserving Sustainability in Community Question Answering. *IEEE Software* 33, 4 (July 2016), 80–89. DOI: http://dx.doi.org/10.1109/MS.2016.34

[20] Ivan Srba, Marek Grznar, and Maria Bielikova. 2015. Utilizing Non-QA Data to Improve Questions Routing for Users with Low QA Activity in CQA. In *Proceedings of the 2015 IEEE/ACM International Conference on Advances in Social Networks Analysis and Mining 2015 (ASONAM '15)*. ACM, New York, NY, USA, 129–136. DOI: http://dx.doi.org/10.1145/2808797.2809331

[21] Idan Szpektor, Yoelle Maarek, and Dan Pelleg. 2013. When Relevance is Not Enough: Promoting Diversity and Freshness in Personalized Question Recommendation. In *Proceedings of the 22nd International Conference on World Wide Web (WWW '13)*. ACM, New York, NY, USA, 1249–1260. DOI: http://dx.doi.org/10.1145/2488388.2488497

[22] Yuan Tian, Pavneet Singh Kochhar, Ee-Peng Lim, Feida Zhu, and David Lo. 2014. Predicting Best Answerers for New Questions: An Approach Leveraging Topic Modeling and Collaborative Voting. In *Social Informatics: SocInfo 2013 International Workshops, QMC and HISTOINFORMATICS, Kyoto, Japan, November 25, 2013, Revised Selected Papers*. Springer, Berlin, Heidelberg, 55–68. DOI: http://dx.doi.org/10.1007/978-3-642-55285-4_5

[23] Fei Xu, Zongcheng Ji, and Bin Wang. 2012. Dual Role Model for Question Recommendation in Community Question Answering. In *Proceedings of the 35th International ACM SIGIR Conference on Research and Development in Information Retrieval (SIGIR '12)*. ACM, New York, NY, USA, 771–780. DOI: http://dx.doi.org/10.1145/2348283.2348387

[24] Diyi Yang, David Adamson, and Carolyn Penstein Rosé. 2014. Question Recommendation with Constraints for Massive Open Online Courses. In *Proceedings of the 8th ACM Conference on Recommender Systems (RecSys '14)*. ACM, New York, NY, USA, 49–56. DOI: http://dx.doi.org/10.1145/2645710.2645748

[25] Diyi Yang, Tanmay Sinha, David Adamson, and Carolyn Penstein Rosé. 2013. Turn on, tune in, drop out: Anticipating student dropouts in massive open online courses. In *Proceedings of the 2013 NIPS Data-driven education workshop*, Vol. 11. 14.

[26] Kai Zhang, Wei Wu, Haocheng Wu, Zhoujun Li, and Ming Zhou. 2014. Question Retrieval with High Quality Answers in Community Question Answering. In *Proceedings of the 23rd ACM International Conference on Conference on Information and Knowledge Management (CIKM '14)*. ACM, New York, NY, USA, 371–380. DOI: http://dx.doi.org/10.1145/2661829.2661908

[27] Tom Chao Zhou, Michael R. Lyu, and Irwin King. 2012. A Classification-based Approach to Question Routing in Community Question Answering. In *Proceedings of the 21st International Conference on World Wide Web (WWW '12 Companion)*. ACM, New York, NY, USA, 783–790. DOI: http://dx.doi.org/10.1145/2187980.2188201

The Magic Barrier Revisited: Accessing Natural Limitations of Recommender Assessment

Kevin Jasberg
Web Science Group
Heinrich-Heine-University Duesseldorf
Duesseldorf, Germany 45225
kevin.jasberg@uni-duesseldorf.de

Sergej Sizov
Web Science Group
Heinrich-Heine-University Duesseldorf
Duesseldorf, Germany 45225
sizov@hhu.de

ABSTRACT

Recommender systems nowadays have many applications and are of great economic benefit. Hence, it is imperative for success-oriented companies to compare various of such systems and select the better one for their purposes. To this end, various metrics of predictive accuracy are commonly used, such as the Root Mean Square Error (RMSE), or precision and recall. All these metrics more or less measure how well a recommender system can predict human behaviour. Unfortunately, human behaviour is always associated with some degree of uncertainty, making the evaluation difficult, since it is not clear whether a deviation is system-induced or just originates from the natural variability of human decision making. At this point, some authors speculated that we may be reaching some Magic Barrier where this variability prevents us from getting much more accurate [12, 13, 24]. In this article, we will extend the existing theory of the Magic Barrier [24] into a new probabilistic but a yet pragmatic model. In particular, we will use methods from metrology and physics to develop easy-to-handle quantities for computation to describe the Magic Barrier for different accuracy metrics and provide suggestions for common application. This discussion is substantiated by comprehensive experiments with real users and large-scale simulations on a high-performance cluster.

CCS CONCEPTS

•**Human-centred computing** →**HCI theory, concepts and models;** User models; User studies; •**Mathematics of computing** →**Distribution functions;**

KEYWORDS

Magic Barrier; Noise; Human Uncertainty; Distribution-Paradigm; Point-Paradigm; RMSE; Ranking Error

1 INTRODUCTION

Recommender systems have become quite essential for our modern information society. Applied within a variety of engines, they predict human behaviour (e.g. ratings a user might give to a specific item) and thus models a user's preferences. In doing so, those algorithms use specific machine learning techniques to learn about one's personal interests and to develop empathy for multiple as well as variable human aspects.

RecSys '17, August 27–31, 2017, Como, Italy.
© 2017 ACM. 978-1-4503-4652-8/17/08...$15.00
DOI: http://dx.doi.org/10.1145/3109859.3109898

Unfortunately, human beings can not be deemed as constant functions. It has recently been shown, that users provide inconsistent ratings when requested to rate same films at different times [13]. This **Human Uncertainty**, as we understand it in this contribution, appears to be a characteristic feature of the cognitive process of decision making which influences its outcome, making it circumstantial and temporally unstable; the outcome appears to be more or less fluctuating randomly when repeating a decision making. Consequently, we may assume that observed decisions are drawn from individual distributions [10].

Accordingly, this complicates the evaluation of recommender systems, since it is not clear whether the difference between a given rating and the prediction is induced by the system or just a matter of Human Uncertainty. If we are able to improve the system-induced prediction quality to such an extent that only the factor of human uncertainty is left, then all visible differences within a quality metric would only exist due to this uncertainty and may vary with each repeated rating trial. This implies that rankings of different (well improved) recommender systems would shuffle with each repetition as well, i.e sound rankings do no longer exist for excellent systems but there is an equivalence class of indistinguishable optimal systems. This leads to the assumption of some Magic Barrier where natural variability may prevent us from getting much more accurate [12].

Motivating Example. As a motivating example, we consider the task of rating prediction, along with the Root Mean Square Error (RMSE) as a widely used metric for prediction quality. In a systematic experiment with real users (described in more detail in forthcoming sections), individuals rated theatrical trailers multiple times. Figure 1a shows that only 35% of all users show constant rating behaviour, whereas about 50% use two different answer categories and 15% of all users make use of three or more categories. Based on these observations, we compute the RMSE for three recommender systems (designed by definition of their predictors π) for each rating trial. Figure 1b depicts the RMSE outcomes and their frequency. It becomes apparent at once that the RMSE itself yields a particular degree of uncertainty, emerged from uncertain user feedback. When ranking these recommender systems, Figure 1b allows for three possible results

$$(R1 \prec R2 \prec R3) \lor (R2 \prec R1 \prec R3) \lor (R1 \prec R3 \prec R2), \quad (1)$$

where the relation $\prec$ denotes "better than". The ranking problem is most obvious for recommender $R1$ as it could be both, the best

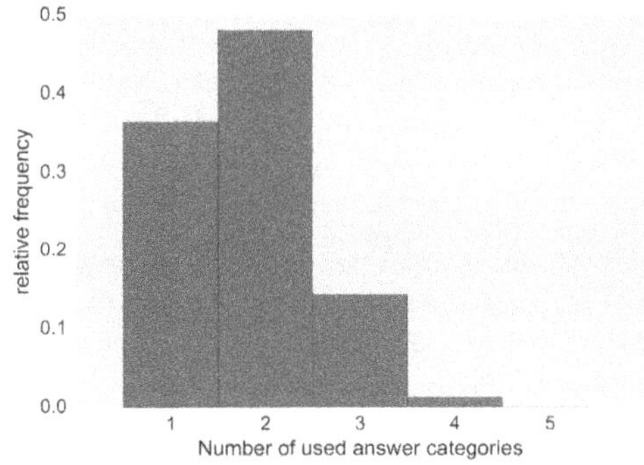

(a) Frequency of used answer categories

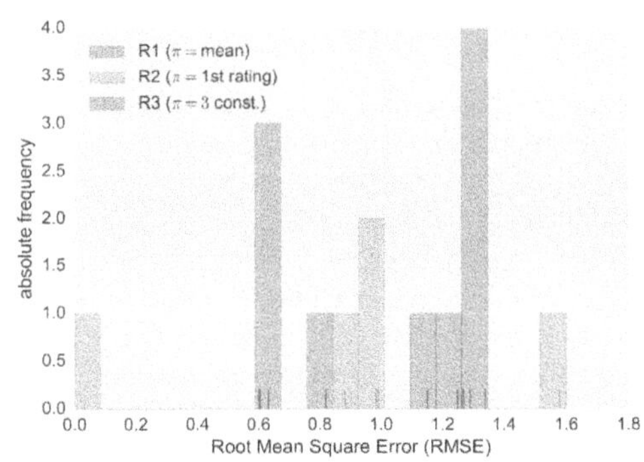

(b) Distribution of RMSE outcomes

Figure 1: Uncertain user ratings and impact on the RMSE

or the worst recommender, although it operates for the same users rating the same items. In addition, it may be possible that further repetitions of ratings would lead to even more ranking possibilities. This naturally implies to deem those RMSE scores as single draws from distributions that are strongly overlapping. As will be revealed later, recommender $R1$ is the Magic Barrier itself. Therefore, our considerations above - the indistinguishability of excellent systems close to the Magic Barrier - hold even for straightforward investigations.

The Problem. The problem of Human Uncertainty - if not explicitly considered - is that any improvement to an existing system or even the assessment of different systems might not be statistically sound. This, in particular, has financial implications when money is invested in the further development of a system but as a result, there is merely an overfitting instead of real improvements. Therefore, the crux is to recognise whether the prediction quality has really improved or is just some random artefact. So there is a need for a decision criterion whether a system still has room for improvements.

For the RMSE in particular, a criterion has recently been developed which allows for a dichotomous consideration (yes or no)[24]. But while the uncertainty of users is considered, its influence on the precise localisation of the Magic Barrier is negated. However, in our example (Fig 1b) we have seen that the RMSE (esp. the Magic Barrier) itself follows a distribution due to Human Uncertainty. As a consequence, systems with an RMSE near the "old" Magic Barrier might already be interfered by this Human Uncertainty and respectively, achieving an RMSE less than the "old" Magic Barrier does not always mean that this system is already interfered. So the question changes from "Is the prediction quality interfered by Human Uncertainty?" to "How likely is it that the prediction quality is interfered by Human Uncertainty?", which allows for more differentiated evaluation of recommender systems.

Our Objective. In this contribution, we present a method by which the Magic Barrier can be estimated for any quality assessment metric. For this purpose, we will embed the Magic Barrier into a complete probabilistic framework and deduce a pragmatic theory through complexity reduction. We aim to generate concrete and action-oriented quantities that can easily be embedded in existing approaches to recommender assessment. We also provide our data records for modelling Human Uncertainty and demonstrate its transferability using the example of Netflix Prize.

2 RELATED WORK

Recommender Systems and Assessment. The central role of recommender systems led to a lot of research and produced a variety of techniques and approaches. A good introduction and overview are given by [16, 23]. For the comparative assessment, different metrics are used to determine the prediction quality, such as the root mean squared error (RMSE), the mean absolute error (MAE), the mean average precision (MAP) along with many others [1, 7, 12]. Although we exemplify our methodology in accordance with the RMSE, the main results of this contribution can be easily adapted for alternative assessment metrics without substantial loss of generality, insofar they require for (uncertain) human input.

Dealing with Uncertainties. The relevance of our contribution arises from the fact that the unavoidable human uncertainty sometimes has a vast influence on the evaluation of different prediction algorithms [3, 5]. The idea of uncertainty is not only related to predictive data mining but also to measuring sciences such as metrology. Recently, a paradigm shift was initiated on the basis of a so far incomplete theory of error [8, 11]. In consequence, measured properties are currently modelled by probability density functions and quantities calculated therefrom are then assigned a distribution by means of a convolution of their argument densities. This model is described in [17]. A feasible framework for computing these convolutions via Monte-Carlo-Simulation is given by [18]. We take this as a basis for our own modelling of uncertainty for addressing similar issues in the field of computer science. To derive a pragmatic and easy to handle theory, we will refer to the Gaussian Error Propagation which is commonly used in physics as well [6, 19, 25].

The Magic Barrier. One of the first works addressing Human Uncertainty and its impact on recommender systems was presented in [13], where users have been proven to give inconsistent ratings on movies. The authors claim that it will never be possible to perfectly predict ratings and that there must exist an upper bound on rating prediction accuracy. Later, this upper bound was mentioned once again in [12] and received the name Magic Barrier, which is still in use nowadays. A first calculation of the Magic Barrier can be found in [24]. Derived by risk function minimisation, the authors defined the Magic Barrier as the square root of the averaged user variances (gathered from repeated ratings). Even though this approach accounts for Human Uncertainty, its influence - namely the uncertainty of the Magic Barrier itself - remains unconsidered. In our contribution, we complete this theory and therefore allow a more differentiated analysis of recommender assessment.

Experimental Designs. The complexity of human perception and cognition can be addressed by means of latent distributions [10]. This idea is widely used in cognitive science and in statistical modelling of ordinal data [14]. We adopt the idea of modelling user uncertainty by means of individual Gaussians following the argumentation in [26] for constructing our individual response models. The methodology applied in our experiments is adopted from experimental psychology [15] and works on repeating rating scenarios for same users-items-pairs as done before in [2].

3 MODELLING A MAGIC BARRIER

In this section, we embed human uncertainty into a mathematical construct and introduce an approach for estimating a Magic Barrier for a given evaluation metric. Although the term "Magic Barrier" is related to the RMSE in particular, such a barrier does basically exist for any metric comparing (uncertain) user inputs with predicted scores. Therefore, we first develop a general framework which will then be illustrated for the RMSE as a prominent example.

3.1 Changing Paradigms

As mentioned above, various experiments [2, 13] along with our own have shown that users are scattering around their true value of preference. Consequently, we may assume that observed decisions are drawn from individual distributions, as a result of complex cognition processes, and influenced by multiple factors (e.g. mood, media literacy, etc.) [10]. Therefrom, a paradigm shift has to be carried out, which is similar to the recent change of perspectives on measurement errors in metrology [8]: Every measurable quantity that is somehow related to human cognition is no longer considered as a single point (point-paradigm) but rather as a whole interval of possible values (set-paradigm) that is somehow distributed (distribution-paradigm). In the context of this paper, we will, therefore, consider user ratings as random variables. On this basis, we develop statistical methodologies that are to be explored hereinafter.

3.2 Composed Quantities

Composed quantities, in this contribution, are quantities Z that compute from a continuous function $Z = g(X_1, \ldots, X_n)$ of large amounts of uncertain arguments X_i (random variables). Hence, Z becomes a random variable itself. This reasoning can be understood heuristically: For each draw, there is a variety of possibilities for a single outcome x_i of a random variable X_i. The outcomes $x_1, \ldots, x_n$ of all random variables altogether result into a single outcome for the composed quantity Z by means of $z = g(x_1, \ldots, x_n)$. Accounting for all the possibilities for $x_1, \ldots, x_n$ (e.g. when repeating draws infinitely) will then result in a variety of possible outcomes z. Thus, the distribution of Z emerges as a convolution of n density functions with respect to the mapping g [17, 18].

3.3 Magic Barrier Estimation

The Magic Barrier is defined as the minimum of an evaluation metric when explicitly accounting for Human Uncertainty. Therefore, we must first specify an optimal recommender by defining its predictors. Then we have to compute the probability density function of the evaluation metric which arises for this optimal recommender.

What is an optimal recommender? The choice of predictors depends on the evaluation metric and the underlying data model. We will demonstrate this by using an example. In the case of the Root Mean Square Error (RMSE)

$$\text{RMSE} = \sqrt{\tfrac{1}{N}\textstyle\sum_{\nu}(X_\nu - \pi_\nu)^2}, \tag{2}$$

the comparison of a rating X_ν and a prediction $\pi_\nu \in \mathbb{R}$ is done via $c(X_\nu) = (X_\nu - \pi_\nu)^2$, whose expectation reaches its minimum when

$$\tfrac{d}{d\pi}\textstyle\sum_{i=0}^{N}(x_i - \pi)^2 = 2 \cdot \sum_{i=0}^{N}(\pi - x_i) = 0 \;\Leftrightarrow\; \pi = \tfrac{1}{N}\sum_{i=0}^{N} x_i \tag{3}$$

where x_i denote the realisations of the random variable X_ν. Hence, the optimal recommender system with respect to the RMSE is defined by $\pi_\nu := \mathbb{E}[X_\nu]$ for each user-item-pair ν.

This might be totally different when considering the Mean Absolute Error (MAE), whose primary comparison is based on the function $c(X_\nu) = |X_\nu - \pi_\nu|$, reaching a minimum for its expectation when π_ν is the median of X_ν. The median corresponds to the expected value, only if a symmetrical distribution is chosen as the underlying data model. Consequently, when assuming all $X_\nu \sim \mathcal{N}(\mu_\nu, \sigma_\nu)$ to be normally distributed (symmetric density function), the optimal recommender system does not differ for the RMSE and the MAE respectively. Having $X_\nu \sim \Gamma(\alpha_\nu, \beta_\nu)$ being gamma-distributed instead, the optimal recommender may be different for both metrics, depending on the extent of asymmetry.

Monte-Carlo-Simulation. Now having the definition of an optimal recommender system, we need to deduce the probability density function of the evaluation metric for this optimum. In theory, this is done by a convolution of all density functions f_i of X_i, but what sounds simple at first, turns out to be quite laborious and inapplicable as demonstrated in [9]. For this reason, metrologists typically apply statistical simulations. In this paper we use **Monte-Carlo-Simulations** as described in [18]: For each of our ratings X_ν, we compute a sample $\mathcal{S}(X_\nu) := \{x_\nu^1, \ldots, x_\nu^\tau\}$ of τ pseudo-random numbers (trials) that are drawn from a distribution (underlying data model). Then, we yield a sample for the evaluation metric $Z = g(X_1, \ldots, X_N)$ via

$$\mathcal{S}(Z) = \left\{z_k = g(x_1^k, \ldots, x_N^k) : k = 1, \ldots, \tau\right\}. \tag{4}$$

Post hoc illustration of this sample by a normed histogram with b bins leads to an approximation for the density of Z.

Although the statistical simulation of convolutions produces excellent results while also being easy to realise, we are facing a blatant run-time problem as soon as we are entering the realm of big data. For example, for $N = 80\,000$ ratings, the simulation already takes up to an hour of runtime using a state-of-the-art computing node. To compute the Magic Barrier on the Netflix test record ($N = 2.8 \cdot 10^6$), we need about 35 hours.

In the following sections, we will derive a pragmatic estimate for the desired density function of the Magic Barrier for arbitrary metrics. With this, we get same results but need only a mere fraction of the simulation runtime. For example, the probability density for the Magic Barrier on the Netflix test record can be computed in less than 80 milliseconds.

Estimation Analytics. Even before the technical possibilities of statistical simulations existed, metrologists had estimated the expected value and the variance of quantities $Z = g(X)$. The core these estimations is to expand $g \in C^{\infty}(\mathbb{R})$ into its Taylor series

$$g(X) = \sum_{k=0}^{\infty} \frac{g^{(k)}(\mu)}{k!} (X - \mu)^k \tag{5}$$

where $g^{(k)}(\mu)$ denotes the kth derivative of g evaluated at the expectation of X. Due to the linearity of the expectation[1], we yield

$$\begin{aligned} \mathbb{E}[g(X)] &= \mathbb{E}\left[\sum_{k=0}^{\infty} \frac{g^{(k)}(\mu)}{k!} (X-\mu)^k\right] = \sum_{k=0}^{\infty} \frac{g^{(k)}(\mu)}{k!} \mathbb{E}\left[(X-\mu)^k\right] \\ &= \sum_{k=0}^{\infty} \frac{g^{(k)}(\mu)}{k!} m_k \end{aligned} \tag{6}$$

where m_k is the k-th central moment. For the variance and its quasi-linearity[2], we yield

$$\begin{aligned} \mathbb{V}[g(X)] &= \mathbb{V}\left[\sum_{k=0}^{\infty} \frac{f^{(k)}(\mu)}{k!} (X-\mu)^k\right] = \sum_{k=0}^{\infty} \left(\frac{f^{(k)}(\mu)}{k!}\right)^2 \mathbb{V}\left[(X-\mu)^k\right] \\ &= \sum_{k=0}^{\infty} \left(\frac{f^{(k)}(\mu)}{k!}\right)^2 (m_{2k} - m_k^2) \end{aligned} \tag{7}$$

where the last line has been simplified by using the common identity $\mathbb{V}[(X-\mu)^k] = \mathbb{E}[(X-\mu)^{2k}] - \mathbb{E}[(X-\mu)^k]^2 = m_{2k} - {m_k}^2$. The usual approximation is to omit terms of higher orders, like

$$\begin{aligned} \mathbb{E}[g(X)] &= g(\mu) + g'(\mu) \cdot m_1 + \ldots \approx g(\mu) \\ \mathbb{V}[g(X)] &= g'(\mu)^2 m_1 + g''(\mu)^2 (m_4 - m_2^2)/4 + \ldots \approx g'(\mu)^2 m_1. \end{aligned}$$

We have so far only considered a smooth function with just one argument in order to guarantee an easy understanding of the methodology. When considering n arguments, we use a Taylor series in more dimensions and yield equivalent results which, together with the assumption of normality, form the Gaussian Error Propagation [6, 19, 25].

4 MAGIC BARRIER FOR THE RMSE

4.1 Application of Gaussian Error Propagation

In this section we will derive closed form approximations for the RMSE and therefore define

$$\mathcal{MB} = g(X_1, \ldots, X_N) := \sqrt{\tfrac{1}{N} \sum_v (X_v - \mathbb{E}[X_v])^2}. \tag{8}$$

Since we have to face multiple arguments, we would usually need a Taylor series in several variables, which is quite ugly for demonstration purposes. Therefore, we first condense all ratings $X_1, \ldots, X_N$ into a single random variable and then use the one-dimensional Taylor approximation. In doing so, we choose Gaussians as the underlying data model for our ratings. By this means, every rating

[1] $\mathbb{E}[aX + b] = a\mathbb{E}[X] + b$ holds for $a, b \in \mathbb{R}$ and arbitrary random variable X
[2] $\mathbb{V}[aX + b] = a^2\mathbb{V}[X]$ holds for $a, b \in \mathbb{R}$ and arbitrary random variable X

$X_v \sim \mathcal{N}(\mu_v, \sigma_v)$ can be written as $X_v = \sigma_v \mathbb{I} + \mu_v$ where $\mathbb{I} \sim \mathcal{N}(0, 1)$. Hence, $Y_v := (X_v - \mathbb{E}[X_v])^2$ receives the expectation

$$\begin{aligned} \mathbb{E}[Y_v] &= \mathbb{E}[(\sigma_v \mathbb{I} + \mu_v - \mu_v)^2] = \mathbb{E}[(\sigma_v \mathbb{I})^2] \\ &= \mathbb{E}[\sigma_v^2 \mathbb{I}^2] = \sigma_v^2 \mathbb{E}[\mathbb{I}^2] = \sigma_v^2 \mathbb{V}[\mathbb{I}] = \sigma_v^2 \end{aligned} \tag{9}$$

as well as the variance

$$\begin{aligned} \mathbb{V}[Y_v] &= \mathbb{V}[(\sigma_v \mathbb{I} + \mu_v - \mu_v)^2] = \mathbb{V}[(\sigma_v \mathbb{I})^2] \\ &= \mathbb{V}[\sigma_v^2 \mathbb{I}^2] = \sigma_v^4 \mathbb{V}[\mathbb{I}^2] = \sigma_v^4 \left(\mathbb{E}[\mathbb{I}^4] - \mathbb{E}[\mathbb{I}^2]^2\right) \\ &= \sigma_v^4 \left(3\mathbb{V}[\mathbb{I}]^2 - \mathbb{V}[\mathbb{I}]^2\right) = 2\sigma_v^4 \end{aligned} \tag{10}$$

We thus obtain a χ^2-distribution for $Z := \frac{1}{N} \sum_v Y_v$ which converges into a Gaussian for a large number N of ratings by means of the central limit theorem. The parameters of this Gaussian are

$$\mathbb{E}[Z] = \mathbb{E}\left[\frac{1}{N} \sum_v Y_v\right] = \frac{1}{N} \sum_v \mathbb{E}[Y_v] = \frac{1}{N} \sum_v \sigma_v^2 \tag{11}$$

$$\mathbb{V}[Z] = \mathbb{V}\left[\frac{1}{N} \sum_v Y_v\right] = \frac{1}{N^2} \sum_v \mathbb{V}[Y_v] = \frac{2}{N^2} \sum_v \sigma_v^4. \tag{12}$$

Now we can consider the Magic Barrier to be the image of the root function of a single random variable, i.e. $\mathcal{MB} = g(X_1, \ldots, X_N) \equiv h(Z) := \sqrt{Z}$ where $Z \sim \mathcal{N}(\frac{1}{N} \sum_v \sigma_v^2, \frac{2}{N^2} \sum_v \sigma_v^4)$. Applying the one-dimensional Taylor approximation from equations 6 and 7 leads to

$$\mathbb{E}[\mathcal{MB}] = \sqrt{\mathbb{E}[Z]} - \frac{\mathbb{V}[Z]}{8\mathbb{E}[Z]^{3/2}} - \ldots \approx \sqrt{\mathbb{E}[Z]} \tag{13}$$

$$\mathbb{V}[\mathcal{MB}] = \frac{\mathbb{V}[Z]}{4\mathbb{E}[Z]} + \frac{\mathbb{V}[Z]^2}{32\mathbb{E}[Z]^3} + \ldots \approx \frac{\mathbb{V}[Z]}{4\mathbb{E}[Z]}. \tag{14}$$

With additional assumption of normality (which is indeed a suitable model, as we will confirm soon), the approximated distribution of the Magic Barrier for the RMSE is

$$\mathcal{MB} \sim \mathcal{N}\left(\sqrt{\frac{1}{N} \sum_v \sigma_v^2}, \frac{1}{2N} \frac{\sum_v \sigma_v^4}{\sum_v \sigma_v^2}\right) \tag{15}$$

where $\mathbb{E}[\mathcal{MB}] \approx (\sum_v \sigma_v^2 / N)^{1/2}$ exactly meets the traditional Magic Barrier as defined in [24] and $\mathbb{V}[\mathcal{MB}] \approx (\sum_v \sigma_v^4)/(2N \sum_v \sigma_v^2)$ represents the traditionally neglected uncertainty of this Magic Barrier, emerged from uncertain user ratings.

4.2 Goodness of Approximation

As mentioned above, the method presented here is merely an approximation, since we omit terms of higher orders. At this point, one may wonder how well this estimate actually matches the true state. To answer this question, we first compare the simulated expectations and variances with the calculated ones in a regression analysis. Concerning the distribution model, we investigate the degree similarity using the Jensen–Shannon-Divergence.

Regression analysis. We keep the following simulations as general as possible. To this end we gradually fix a particular number N of ratings from the set $\{50, 100, 150, 200, 500, 1000\}$ and sample N expectations μ_v uniformly from the interval $[1, 5]$ as well as N variances σ_v^2 uniformly from $[\sigma_{min}^2, \sigma_{max}^2]$. These intervals result from the assumption of five repeated ratings (as happened in our

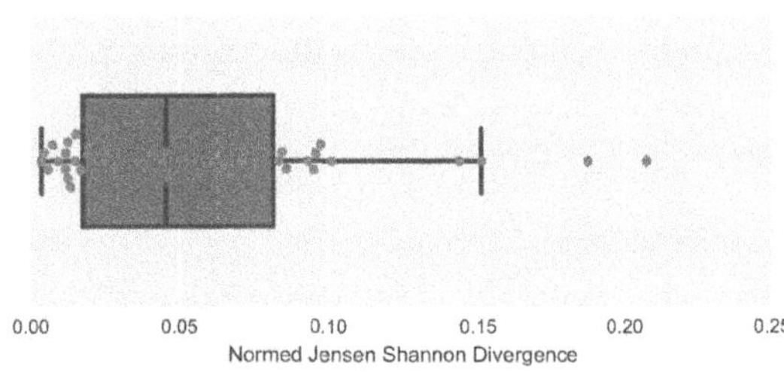

Figure 2: Jensen–Shannon-Divergence for comparing the simulated distribution with a predetermined Gaussian

experiments) with the commonly used 5-star scale. Under these conditions, the positive variance yields limitations[3]

$$\sigma^2_{min} = \text{var}(\{1,1,1,1,2\}) = 0.16 \quad (16)$$

$$\sigma^2_{max} = \text{var}(\{1,1,1,5,5\}) = 3.86 \quad (17)$$

For each pair (μ_v, σ^2_v) we then compute a sample $\mathcal{S}(X_v)$ with $\tau = 10^7$ random numbers drawn from the specified Gaussian to perform the convolution via equation 4. For many repetitions, we receive a lot of simulated expectations/variances to be plotted against the approximated ones by means of linear regression. A perfect match between simulation and approximation would lead to the regression $y = 1 \cdot x + 0$ with correlation coefficient $R^2 = 1$. The results

$$\text{Sim}(\mathbb{E}) = 0.999 \cdot \text{Apr}(\mathbb{E}) - 0.003 \quad (R^2 = 0.99) \quad (18)$$

$$\text{Sim}(\mathbb{V}) = 0.981 \cdot \text{Apr}(\mathbb{V}) + 0.000 \quad (R^2 = 1.00) \quad (19)$$

show that this condition is almost fully achieved and hence we may consider these approximations as appropriate.

Jensen-Shannon-Divergence. When modelling the Magic Barrier, not only the expectation and the variance are of great importance, but rather the entire probability density. While the simulated distribution arises naturally from convolution, it is predetermined for the approximation. Therefore, it is necessary to evaluate the degree of deviation of both distributions. In doing so, we proceed as done in the regression analysis above, but instead of computing means and variances, we transform our samples into discrete probability distributions P_{sim} and P_{apr} and analyse the Jensen-Shannon-Divergence (JSD)

$$\text{JSD}(P_{sim}|P_{apr}) = \frac{1}{2}D_{\text{KL}}(P_{sim}|M) + \frac{1}{2}D_{\text{KL}}(P_{apr}|M) \quad (20)$$

where $D_{\text{KL}}(P_1|P_2) = \sum_i P_1(i)\,\log_2(P_1(i)/P_2(i))$ denotes the Kullback-Leibler-Divergence and $M = \frac{1}{2}(P_{sim} + P_{apr})$. Since we use the base 2 logarithm, the JSD yields the boundaries

$$0 \leq \text{JSD} \leq 2\log(2) \quad \text{or} \quad 0 \leq \frac{\text{JSD}}{2\log(2)} \leq 1 \quad (21)$$

The outcomes for the normed JSD is shown in Figure 2. We observe that the mid-range of all outcomes is located between 0.01 and 0.08 confirming high similarity of the simulated distribution and the assumed Gaussian. There are, however, some outliers which only occur for $N = 50$ ratings. This can be explained by the fact that the RMSE contains the sum of squared normal distributions, which is χ^2-distributed, but quickly converges to the normal distribution for $N > 100$. Thus, the more ratings we have, the more adequate is a Gaussian as the assumed density. For a visual comparison of both distributions, Figure 6 depicts the simulated density as well as the approximation for our experiment with $N = 213$.

[3] Samples are only examples producing the minimum/maximum variance

4.3 Understanding the Magic Barrier

In this section, we will take a closer look at the properties of the Magic Barrier. For this purpose, the individual dependencies of the Magic Barrier and their effects are analysed in a sensitivity analysis. In addition, we will generalise the dichotomous decision criterion from [24] and develop a pragmatic rule of thumb to ascertain whether a deeper consideration of the Magic Barrier seems worthwhile.

Sensitivity analysis. A sensitivity analysis is used to determine how a quantity responds to the variation of its arguments. Therefore, we vary one argument within reasonable boundaries while fixing all the other arguments at the same time.

In Figure 3a and 3b, one can observe the Magic Barrier's reaction to an increasing number N of ratings. It is seen that the expectation remains unaffected by the number of uncertain ratings. Only the extent of the uncertainty raises or lowers the mean value. On a 5-star scale together with five re-ratings, the expected value yields limitations (green and red) due to the minimum and maximum variance possible. The growth behaviour of the expectation under rating uncertainty is asymptotic. However, Figure 3b reveals that the Magic Barrier's variance is heavily impacted by the number of ratings, i.e. the precision of the Magic Barrier even gains when more uncertain ratings are added. The extent of rating uncertainty also leads to boundaries, but this influence gradually disappears for increasing N. A comparison of Figure 3b and Figure 3d reveals that the number of ratings significantly affects the first two decimal places of the variance, whereas the influence of the rating uncertainty affects only the third and fourth decimal places at most. In summary, it can be said that the extent of Human Uncertainty alone is responsible for the location of the Magic Barrier, whilst its spread can be reduced by adding ratings. However, the degree of this improvement decreases very rapidly.

What we have omitted here is the influence of the underlying data model and the applied rating scale. The rating scale limits the variance of a user and thus has a great impact of the possible location of the Magic Barrier. The underlying data model has also a great impact on the Magic Barrier but will be the discussed separately in further research.

Do we need a Magic Distribution? Now having in mind that the variance of the Magic Barrier decreases for large N, one may ask if we really need the Magic Barrier to be a distribution rather that a single score. The answer depends on many factors. First of all, the world of recommender assessment does not entirely consist of large-scale experiments, so that the variance can not be deemed to equal zero. In the case of large-scale experiments, the predefined accuracy of computed scores does matter quite a lot. For example, all RMSE scores were given to the fourth decimal place in Netflix Prize [22]. As shown in the following sections, the standard deviation of the Magic Barrier for the Netflix data set can be assumed to be

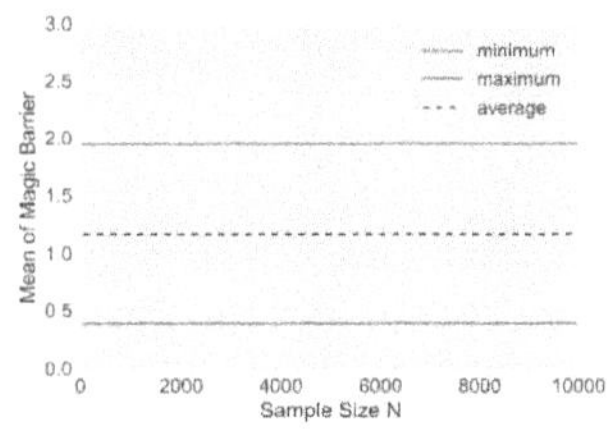

(a) $\mathbb{E}[\mathcal{MB}]$ with respect to N

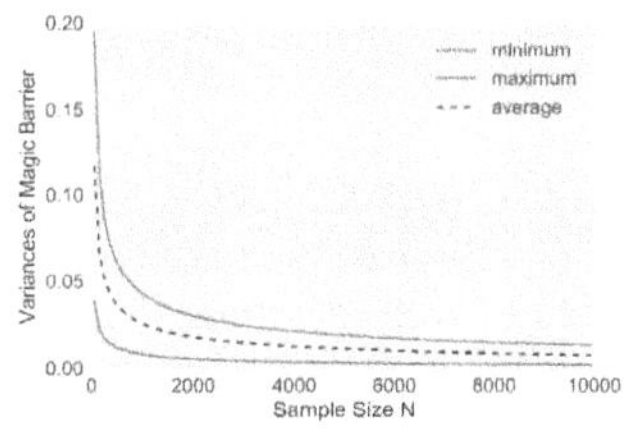

(b) $\mathbb{V}[\mathcal{MB}]$ with respect to N

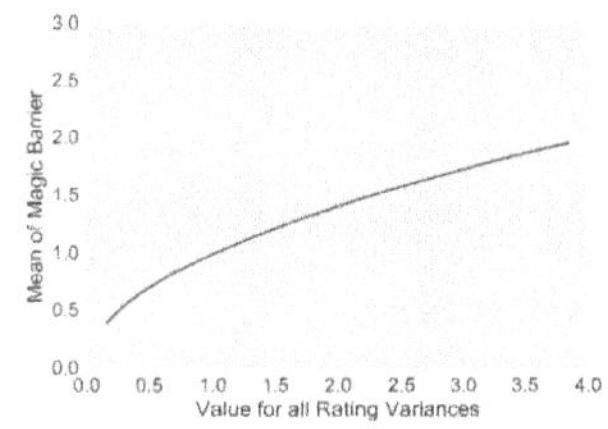

(c) $\mathbb{V}[\mathcal{MB}]$ with respect to σ^2

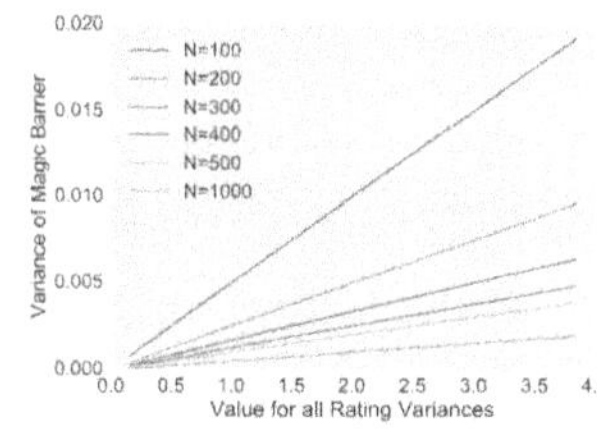

(d) $\mathbb{V}[\mathcal{MB}]$ with respect to σ^2

Figure 3: Sensitivity analysis of the Magic Barrier varying the number of ratings and the extent of rating variances

$\sigma = 0.0007$, which is still seven times larger than the specified rounding accuracy of four decimal places. In this example, we see that even for large data records the effort of considering the Magic Barrier as a distribution is quite meaningful.

Furthermore, we need a non-vanishing variance for a statistically sound decision whether a system can still be improved. Following [24], any improvement of a recommender system is pointless, if the RMSE score is below the Magic Barrier, i.e. $\mathbb{E}[\text{RMSE}] < \mathbb{E}[\mathcal{MB}]$. But since both quantities are distributed, their density functions may nevertheless overlap. Figure 4 illustrates the interference of the Magic Barrier with a recommender system used in our experiments. Although the decision criterion from [24] holds, there is a significant probability that the RMSE outcome is already affected by the Magic Barrier. This probability is given by

$$P(\mathcal{MB} > \text{RMSE}) = \int_{-\infty}^{\infty} f_{\text{RMSE}}(x) \cdot \left(1 - F_{\mathcal{MB}}(x)\right) \mathrm{d}x \qquad (22)$$

where $F_{\mathcal{MB}}(x)$ denotes the cumulative distribution function. In our example from Figure 4, this probability is around 0.33, i.e. the RMSE is interfering with the Magic Barrier in one of three outcomes. For this reason, an analysis of possible improvements can not be answered by a dichotomous decision criterion (yes or no), but has to be answered by means of probabilities (How likely is it that my system can still be improved and what risk am I willing to accept?).

When is a differentiated consideration needed? However, such a differentiated approach is not always worth it. Therefore, it would be useful to have a rule of thumb to find out whether a differentiated consideration is fruitful or not. For example, a possible criterion might be the intersection of the 99%-confidence intervals of the RMSE and the Magic Barrier. Due to normality, further analysis should be taken into consideration, when

$$\mathbb{E}[\mathcal{MB}] + 3\sqrt{\mathbb{V}[\mathcal{MB}]} > \mathbb{E}[\text{RMSE}] - 3\sqrt{\mathbb{V}[\text{RMSE}]}. \qquad (23)$$

By assuming $\mathbb{V}[\mathcal{MB}] \approx \mathbb{V}[\text{RMSE}]$, which usually holds when both quantities are computed on the same data record, this criterion can be simplified to $\mathbb{E}[\text{RMSE}] - \mathbb{E}[\mathcal{MB}] < 6\mathbb{V}[\mathcal{MB}]^{1/2}$.

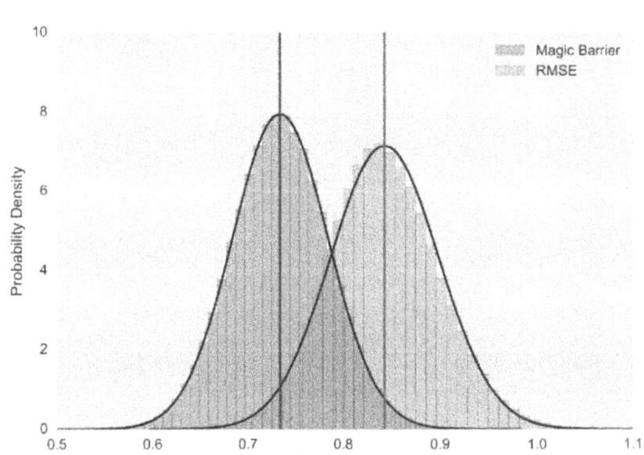

Figure 4: Interference of RMSE with the Magic Barrier

5 EXPERIMENTS

In this section, we examine our theoretical considerations in reality. To this end, we conducted a controlled experiment with real users and measured their uncertainty. We are thus able to support the chosen data model and verify our approximation on a real data set. On this basis, possible applications can be illustrated (e.g. transferring our variances to other situations where no Human Uncertainty was explicitly measured).

5.1 The Experiment

Our experiment is set up with Unipark's[4] survey engine while our participants were committed from the crowdsourcing platform Clickworker[5]. To derive a user's rating distributions, we use the method of re-rating, which was successfully used in [2, 13] before. For this purpose, participants watched theatrical trailers of popular movies and television shows and provided ratings in five repetition trials[6]. User ratings have been recorded for five out of ten fixed trailers so that remaining trailers act as distractors triggering the misinformation effect, i.e. memory is becoming less accurate due to interference from post-event information.

We received a rating tensor $R_{u,i,t}$ with $\dim(R) = (67, 5, 5)$, having $N = 1\,675$ ratings in total, where the coordinates (u, i, t) encode the rating that has been given to item i by user u in the t-th trial. From this record, we derive a unique rating distribution for each user-item-pair by considering tensor-slices in trial-dimension $R_{u,i} := \{R_{u,i,t} | t = 1, \ldots, 5\}$ for which we compute Maximum-Likelihood-Parameters given a predetermined data model (e.g. Gaussians, CUB-Models, etc.). Altogether 67 people from Germany, Austria and Switzerland participated in this experiment. This group can be parted into 57% females and 43% males whose ages range

[4] http://www.unipark.com/de/
[5] https://www.clickworker.de/
[6] A full description can be found on https://anonymity/doubleblind

from 20 to 60 years while over 60% of our participants were aged between 20 and 40. This group also includes a good average of lower, medium and higher educational levels. The rating frequency habits range from "rarely" to "often" in a uniform distribution.

5.2 Data Model and Uncertainties

Proving the data model. In this contribution we opt for Gaussians since they are strongly associated with human characteristics [4] and have also been proven to be appropriate user models in [26]. Additionally, Gaussians exhibit maximum entropy among all distributions with finite mean/variance and support on $\mathbb{R}$. For each recorded item, all tensor slices having a non-vanishing variance are checked for normality by means of a one-sample KS-test [20] with confidence level $\alpha = 0.05$. The null hypothesis was never rejected, allowing to keep the Gaussian distribution as a possible model.

Proving Human Uncertainty. For each of the user-item-pairs $R_{u,i}$, we compute the Gaussian ML-Parameters and consider the variances $\mathbb{V}(R_{u,i})$ as representations of the Human Uncertainty. In our experiment, only few tensor slices contain constant ratings and hence lead to a vanishing variance. Performing an item-wise analysis, the fraction of tensor slices with non-zero variance ranges from 50 to 90% that is, only every second participant is able to reproduce its own decisions for the best case. For the worst case, only one out of ten participants is able to precisely reproduce a rating. Figure 5 depicts the distribution of variances emerged from repeated ratings within our experiment. We observe that the overall variance follows an exponential distribution $\mathbb{V} \sim \text{Exp}(\lambda)$ with parameter $\lambda = 2.11$. This power-law distribution literally means that many users have a low degree of uncertainty while only a few users have a very high degree of uncertainty.

5.3 The Magic Barrier

Figure 3a shows that the expected value of the Magic Barrier depends solely on the Human Uncertainty. For our five-star scale as well as its minimum and maximum variances, the expectation should - when equation 15 holds - be located in the interval $[0.40\,;\,1.55]$. In the case of our experiment, we have $N = 213$ rating distributions with non-vanishing variance. It is clear from Figure 3b that for this sample size, the distribution of the Human Uncertainty has a large impact on the variance of the Magic Barrier. According to equation15, the variance of the Magic Barriers should be found in the interval $[0.0008\,;\,0.0113]$.

On the basis of our data record, the simulation and approximation lead to well matching expectations (ca. 0.733) and variances (ca. 0.003) for the Magic Barrier. It is apparent, that the true values are located near the lower bound of the previously estimated intervals. This can be explained by the power-law distribution, i.e. a lot of variances are near the minimum and only a few have got higher extents. The difference of expectations is about 0.2% while the difference of variances is about 1.2%. The matching between the simulated and the assumed data model of a Gaussian can be clearly confirmed in Figure 6. The corresponding normed JSD is 0.05.

5.4 Application

Implicit Impact on Recommender Assessment. So far we have only discussed the explicit impact on the assessment of recommender systems, that is: How likely is it that a system can still be improved, just before the RMSE solely depends on Human Uncertainty itself. Now we want to investigate the implicit influence, which affects any recommender comparison, even if the corresponding RMSE distributions are not directly overlapping with the Magic Barrier.

In doing so, we generate two copies of the Magic Barrier (as the optimal recommender). Each of these copies is gradually distorted by adding artificial noise to their predictors in such a way that the relative noise difference of both copies remains constant. By increasing the noise for both copies whilst keeping their relative difference constant, we generate an offset (distance from the Magic Barrier). This offset is plotted against the probabilities of error when using the traditional point-paradigm ranking, which is given by the generalisation of equation 22. Figure 7 depicts the family of curves, mapping the distance from the Magic Barrier to the corresponding error probabilities. This distance (x-axis) represents the overall quality of a system, i.e. the larger this quantity, the worse the prediction quality. The colours encode the relative difference Δ of two recommender systems among each other. For the green curve (representing 10% noise of difference), an x-value of 0.15 means

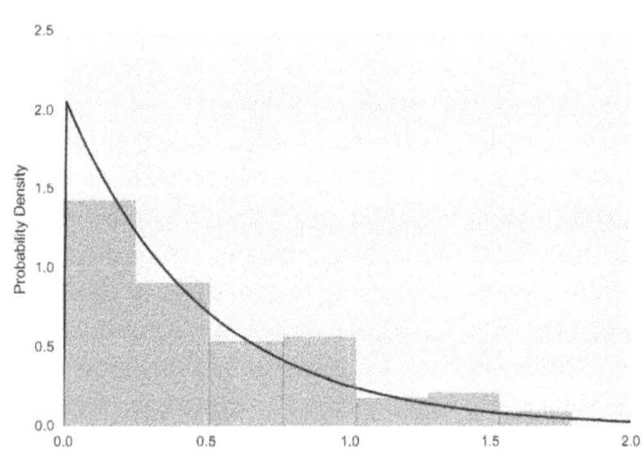

Figure 5: Distribution of variances emerged from repeated ratings within our experiment

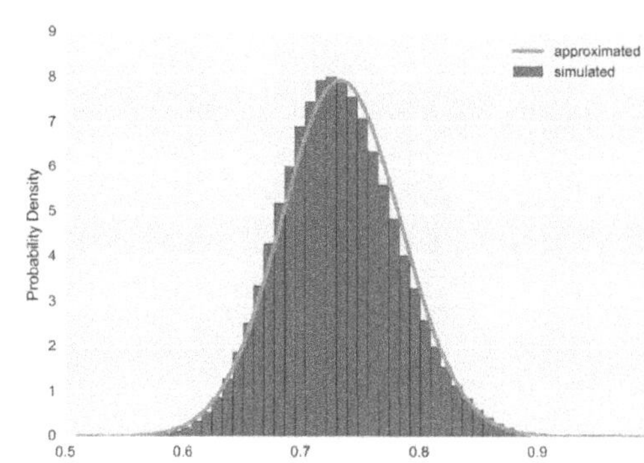

Figure 6: Visual comparison of simulated and approximation Magic Barrier based on experimental data records

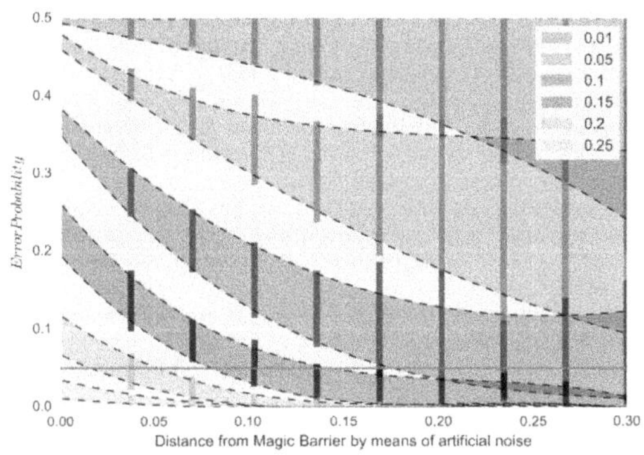

Figure 7: Error Probabilities for ranking systems with constant RMSE difference according to their distance to the Magic Barrier

that system 1 has a noise of 15% whereas system 2 has a noise of 25%. The corresponding y-value indicates the error probability for ranking both systems using the traditional point-paradigm. It is apparent, that two recommender systems can not be brought into a ranking order without considerable error probability if their relative difference is less than 15%, regardless of their basic prediction quality. As a result, we recognise the following: The distance from the Magic Barrier has a great influence on the overlaps in two constantly different recommender systems, i.e. for a fixed difference in prediction quality, they can be distinguished much better if they are bad systems, rather than good ones. On the contrary, the better a system becomes, the more improvement does a revision need, in order to be detected with statistical evidence. This basically means that a recommender system within a repeated process of improvement will certainly reach a prediction quality so that there is probably no sufficiently large amount of optimisation left, in order to distinguish further improvements from the old system with statistical evidence. This convergence is actually the true nature of the Magic Barrier, which could not have been shown without switching perspectives to the distribution paradigm.

Transferability: The Netflix Prize. Unfortunately, existing records have not gathered Human Uncertainty. Therefore, we examine the possibility of applying the findings of our experiment to such data records. To this end, we assume the distribution of Human Uncertainty, emerged from our experiment, to be valid for a larger number of ratings. Under this condition, we will examine possible consequences on Netflix Prize as an example.

The Netflix test record consists of $N = 2.8 \cdot 10^6$ ratings in total. For each of these ratings, we randomly assign a variance drawn from the Pareto distribution in Figure 5. According to this data, the Magic Barrier can be estimated to $\mathcal{MB} \sim \mathcal{N}(0.6687, 0.0007)$. Even though the standard deviation seems small, it is still in the range of Netflix's rounding accuracy of four decimal places. To estimate whether the contest winner [21] might interfere with the Magic Barrier, we use the simplification of Equation 23. Since $\mathbb{E}[\text{RMSE}_{best}] - \mathbb{E}[\mathcal{MB}] = 0.8567 - 0.6687 = 0.1880$ is greater than $6\mathbb{V}[\text{MB}]^{1/2} = 0.1587$, it can be assumed that the Magic Barrier has not yet been reached. In fact, there is still the potential for about 20% of improvement when taking the winner as the reference.

6 DISCUSSION AND CONCLUSIONS

Discussion. In our experiment, the existence of Human Uncertainty is proven and it has been shown that it corresponds to a power-law distribution, i.e. there are many users having a small variance and there are only a few users having a large variance. This implies the existence of an offset within every prediction quality metric that emerges from Human Uncertainty, the so-called Magic Barrier. Having several recommender systems whose RMSEs, for example, are lower than this Magic Barrier, every repetition of the rating proceeding would very likely result into rearrangements of the ranking order, i.e. a reliable ranking can not be built.

In this article, we have lifted an existing theory of this Magic Barrier into a completely probabilistic methodology, providing a generalisation for any quality related metric. Our estimation provides processing of big data in little time while additionally being very precise. With our probabilistic approach, the true nature of the Magic Barrier can be demonstrated: When approaching the Magic Barrier, the distinguishability of many recommender systems automatically decreases, supporting the idea of one equivalence class of optimal systems. Likewise, essential properties of the Magic Barrier have been revealed, for example, the expectation does not change for a higher number of ratings. In contrast, the variance even decreases for an additional number of uncertain ratings and allows to locate the Magic Barrier more precisely. Finally, we have demonstrated the possibility to transfer our results onto other data records in order to make careful predictions of possible interference.

Conclusion. What are the consequences for the assessment of recommender systems in general? The essence of our contribution is the revelation of the following problems:

(1) User feedback always comes along with a particular degree of volatility, denoted Human Uncertainty.
(2) Human Uncertainty creates a barrier from which below any assessment results are just random.
(3) This barrier also implicitly influences recommender assessments; the better our systems become, the more indistinguishable they become.

At this point, it must be said that these problems are not grounded in this new perspective presented here, but have always been present in data analysis. The approach used in this contribution is just able to make these problems visible. Furthermore, these problems do not only occur within our experiments but have also been proven by other authors in different situations of user feedback. This may have far-reaching consequences, especially in the area of the recommender systems, when the selection of a supposedly better system is a monetary decision. For example, financial resources may be invested in improving a system but the improvements achieved are purely random, which remains unnoticed.

For this reason, it becomes crucial to further examine the extent of impact of Human Uncertainty within this field of research. It is also necessary to find proper solutions to these problems, e.g. designing sophisticated mechanisms to identify uncertainty and developing novel strategies to efficiently deal with it. This naturally involves research that connects the fields of behavioural decision making, cognitive psychology and recommender systems to create interdisciplinary synergy effects. We will continue to address these issues in further research.

REFERENCES

[1] Xavier Amatriain (Ed.). 2012. *Workshop on Recommendation Utitlity Evaluation: Beyond RMSE September.* ACM, Dublin, Ireland.

[2] Xavier Amatriain and Josep Pujol. 2009. Rate It Again: Increasing Recommendation Accuracy by User Re-rating. In *Proceedings of the Third ACM Conference on Recommender Systems.* ACM, 173–180.

[3] Xavier Amatriain, Josep M Pujol, and Nuria Oliver. 2009. I like it... i like it not: Evaluating user ratings noise in recommender systems. *International Conference on User Modeling, Adaptation, and Personalization* (2009), 247–258.

[4] F. Gregory Ashby. 1992. *Multidimensional Models of Perception and Cognition (Scientific Psychology Series.* Psychology Press.

[5] Joeran Beel, Marcel Genzmehr, Stefan Langer, Andreas Nürnberger, and Bela Gipp. 2013. A Comparative Analysis of Offline and Online Evaluations and Discussion of Research Paper Recommender System Evaluation. In *Proceedings of the International Workshop on Reproducibility and Replication in Recommender Systems Evaluation (RecSys '13).* 7–14.

[6] Philip Bevington and D. Keith Robinson. 2002. *Data Reduction and Error Analysis for the Physical Sciences* (3rd ed.). McGraw-Hill Education.

[7] Jesús Bobadilla, Fernando Ortega, Antonio Hernando, and Abraham Gutiérrez. 2013. Recommender systems survey. *Knowledge-based systems* 46 (2013), 109–132.

[8] Andy Buffler, Saalih Allie, and Fred Lubben. 2001. The development of first year physics students' ideas about measurement in terms of point and set paradigms. *International Journal of Science Education* 23, 11 (2001), 1137–1156.

[9] F Kenneth Chan. 2011. Miss Distance–Generalized Variance Non-Central Chi Distribution. In *AAS/AIAA Space Flight Mechanics Meeting.* 11–175.

[10] Angela D'Elia and Domenico Piccolo. 2005. A mixture model for preferences data analysis. *Computational Statistics & Data Analysis* 49, 3 (2005), 917–934.

[11] Michael Grabe. 2011. *Grundriss der Generalisierten Gauß'schen Fehlerrechnung.* Springer Berlin Heidelberg.

[12] Herlocker. 2004. Evaluating collaborative filtering recommender systems. *ACM Transactions on Information Systems* 22, 1 (2004), 5–53.

[13] Will Hill, Larry Stead, Mark Rosenstein, and George Furnas. 1995. Recommending and Evaluating Choices in a Virtual Community of Use. In *Proceedings of the SIGCHI Conference on Human Factors in Computing Systems (CHI '95).* 194–201.

[14] Maria Iannario. 2014. Modelling Uncertainty and Overdispersion in Ordinal Data. *Communications in Statistics - Theory and Methods* 43 (2014), 771–786. Issue 14.

[15] Helene Intraub. 1990. Presentation Rate and the Representation of Briefly Glimpsed Pictures in Memory. *Journal of Experimental Psychology* 6, 1 (1990), 1–11.

[16] Dietmar Jannach, Markus Zanker, Alexander Felfernig, and Gerhard Friedrich. 2010. *Recommender Systems: An Introduction.* Cambridge University Press.

[17] JCGM. 2008. *Guide to the Expression of Uncertainty in Measurement.* Technical Report. BIPM.

[18] JCGM. 2008. *Supplement 1 to the GUM - Propagation of distributions using a Monte Carlo method.* Technical Report. BIPM.

[19] HH Ku. 1966. Notes on the use of propagation of error formulas. *J. Res. Nat. Bur. Standards* 70, 4 (1966).

[20] Frank J Massey Jr. 1951. The Kolmogorov-Smirnov test for goodness of fit. *Journal of the American statistical Association* 46, 253 (1951), 68–78.

[21] Netflix. (Oct 25 2016). Netflix Leaderboard. *http://www.netflixprize.com/leaderboard.html* ((Oct 25 2016)).

[22] Netflix. (Oct 25 2016). The Netflix Prize Rules. *http://www.netflixprize.com/rules.html* ((Oct 25 2016)).

[23] Francesco Ricci, Lior Rokach, and Bracha Shapira. 2015. *Recommender Systems Handbook.* Springer.

[24] Alan Said, Brijnesh Jain, Sascha Narr, and Till Plumbaum. 2012. Users and Noise: The Magic Barrier of Recommender Systems. In *User Modeling, Adaptation, and Personalization.* Vol. 7379. Springer Berlin / Heidelberg, 237–248.

[25] John Taylor. 1997. *Introduction to error analysis, the study of uncertainties in physical measurements.* University Science Books.

[26] Yi Zhang and Jonathan Koren. 2007. Efficient bayesian hierarchical user modeling for recommendation system. *Proceedings of the 30th annual international ACM SIGIR conference on Research and development in information retrieval* (2007), 47–54.

Effective User Interface Designs to Increase Energy-efficient Behavior in a Rasch-based Energy Recommender System

Alain Starke
Eindhoven University of Technology
P.O. Box 513
The Netherlands
a.d.starke@tue.nl

Martijn Willemsen
Eindhoven University of Technology
P.O. Box 513
The Netherlands
m.c.willemsen@tue.nl

Chris Snijders
Eindhoven University of Technology
P.O. Box 513
The Netherlands
c.c.p.snijders@tue.nl

ABSTRACT

People often struggle to find appropriate energy-saving measures to take in the household. Although recommender studies show that tailoring a system's interaction method to the domain knowledge of the user can increase energy savings, they did not actually tailor the conservation advice itself. We present two large user studies in which we support users to make an energy-efficient behavioral change by presenting tailored energy-saving advice. Both systems use a one-dimensional, ordinal Rasch scale, which orders 79 energy-saving measures on their behavioral difficulty and link this to a user's energy-saving ability for tailored advice. We established that recommending Rasch-based advice can reduce a user's effort, increase system support and, in turn, increase choice satisfaction and lead to the adoption of more energy-saving measures. Moreover, follow-up surveys administered four weeks later point out that tailoring advice on its feasibility can support behavioral change.

Keywords

Recommender systems; user experience; energy conservation; behavioral change; Rasch model

1 INTRODUCTION

Although most people acknowledge that household energy conservation is important [36], few actually take effective action [17]. Most governments attempt to change consumers' conservation behavior by educating them [10], typically promoting efficiency solutions as installing Solar PV [17, 34]. However, such approaches have had little impact on individual energy-saving behavior [28, 29].

Research in economics and environmental psychology points out that tailored conservation advice is far more effective in increasing energy-efficient behavior [1, 29, 36, 39, 40]. However, tailored advice usually involves expert advisors visiting households [11, 40], which is hard to scale to larger audiences to have a meaningful impact [2].

Recommender systems could play a major role in moving the energy-saving domain forward. Knijnenburg et al. [24] have shown how they can help consumers to make sense of the different energy-saving possibilities. However, they focused predominantly on tailoring the system's preference elicitation method of the (MAUT-based) recommender to the domain knowledge of the user.

It seems that tailoring conservation advice is challenging, as it remains unclear which energy-saving attributes influence one's decision to adopt an energy-saving measure [1, 6, 12]. In particular, commonly described attributes as execution frequency, cost and impact, as used by Knijnenburg et al. [24], are hard to connect to personal characteristics [12]. Moreover, research has presented mixed evidence about the underlying dimensionality of energy conservation [6, 22, 38].

Starke et al. [35] have shown that these issues could be alleviated by presenting energy-saving advice through the psychometric Rasch model [5, 15], which has two interesting properties for recommender systems. First, persons and energy-saving measures are captured onto a single measurement scale [19], ordered respectively on their energy-saving ability and behavioral difficulty [20, 38]. This order is largely determined by engagement frequencies [5, 15]: measures performed by most people have a low behavioral difficulty (e.g. turning off the lights), whereas those performed by fewer people are more difficult (e.g. installing PV cells) [35, 38]. Conversely, persons engaging in more measures usually have a higher ability, and vice versa. Second, Rasch also connects persons and measures formally. It describes the probability of a person performing a certain measure as a function of that person's ability and the measure's difficulty [5, 19]. For instance, a person whose ability is higher than a measure's difficulty level is likely to perform that measure.

Starke et al. [35] developed a Rasch scale of 79 energy-saving measures and found initial evidence that this scale could be used for recommendations. However, two important questions arise from their research. Firstly, they have not tested how tailored advice would hold up against merely using the Rasch ordering without personalization. The scale's difficulty order could already be sufficient for users to find appropriate measures, rather than also taking the user's ability into account. However, such an approach might lead users to focus on popular, low-difficulty measures [33], which are performed by most users [5]. Hence, presenting measures

RecSys '17, August 27-31, 2017, Como, Italy

ACM ISBN 978-1-4503-4652-8/17/08...$15.00
http://dx.doi.org/10.1145/3109859.3109902

tailored to a user's ability level might be more effective, which we will test and show in study 1.

The second question is what type of advice users should be given? In study 2, we investigate how appropriate tailored recommendations and interface design can help people to improve on their energy savings, exploring the trade-off between offering tailored, but easy and feasible measures, which people might already do, versus tailored but more challenging and novel measures.

We will first discuss in more detail the Rasch model and theories on behavioral change that will bring about the research questions for our two studies. Then, we will discuss the 'Saving Aid', our recommender system that will be used in two different versions. Subsequently, we report two large-scale user studies, which test how ability-based advice should be tailored to optimally help users to increase energy savings through the adoption of more energy-saving measures.

2 THEORY

2.1 The Rasch Model

The Rasch model stems from item response theory (IRT) and assumes persons and measures to share a one-dimensional trait for a certain behavioral goal [5, 20]. This trait manifests itself as a formal measurement scale [19], on which persons and measures are ordered on their ability and behavioral difficulty, respectively [38]. Figure 1 depicts how an energy conservation scale can be considered as a two-sided ruler [20], where measures with a low behavioral difficulty are performed generally more often than difficult ones, and vice versa. On the other hand, persons who perform many measures (e.g. person C in figure 1) are assumed to have a higher ability than those performing few (person A) [38].

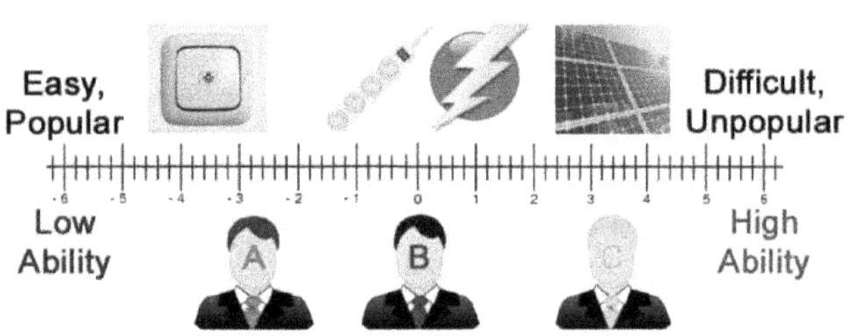

Figure 1: Impression of a Rasch scale of energy-saving measures and persons.

Rasch formalizes the relation between ability and difficulty, describing the probability that a person n performs an energy-saving measure i as the arithmetic difference between that person's energy-saving ability θ and the measure's behavioral difficulty δ [5, 19]:

$$P\{X_{ni} = 1\} = \frac{e^{\theta_n - \delta_i}}{1 + e^{\theta_n - \delta_i}}$$

Figure 2 illustrates for the four energy-saving measures depicted in figure 1 how engagement probability, ability and behavioral difficulty relate to each other. The behavioral difficulty (δ) of a measure is equal to the 50%-engagement probability point of each item-characteristic curve (ICC), which varies between measures. Moreover, the x-axis depicts how different energy-saving abilities (θ), expressed in logistic units or logits, lead to different engagement probabilities (y-axis) for different measures. For instance, a person with energy-saving ability −3 (person A, cf. figure 1) has approximately a 50% probability to regularly turn off the lights (cf. figure 2), but a near zero chance of using green energy or owning solar PV. In contrast, person C (ability = 3.17) has a 50% likelihood of having solar PV installed and is very likely to perform the other three measures as well.

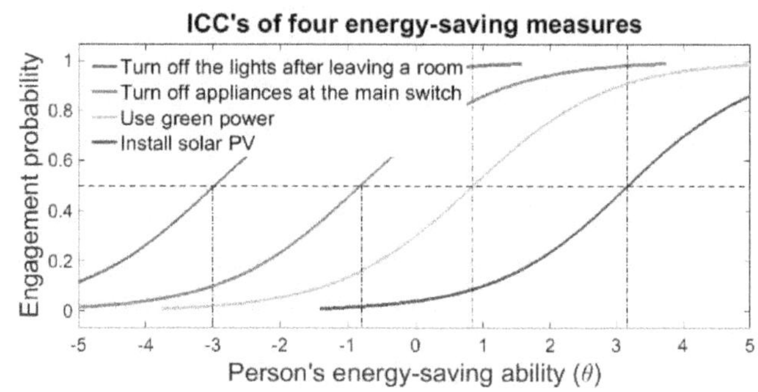

Figure 2: Item-characteristic curves (ICC's) of four energy-saving measures with different behavioral cost levels, yielding different engagement probability levels as a function of a person's energy-saving ability.

The scale's difficulty order can serve as an intuitive tool for those in search of energy-saving possibilities. For example, we could order the measures from very easy (and popular) to very difficult (and infrequently chosen), analogous to showing the most popular items on top of a list, as is commonplace in non-personalized recommender systems [33]. Hence, measures can be considered as a hierarchy of behavioral steps to take towards attaining the goal of saving energy [20], which is an effective representation for users of a recommender system due to its transparency [37].

From a recommender perspective, a classical question arises: would such an ordered scale based on the Rasch model be sufficient or would tailored recommendations outperform such a non-personalized baseline? As tailoring is costly [18], because one needs to know a user's ability before being able to provide good conservation advice, it is important to test its effectiveness.

A person's ability will be a good indicator for where to look for appropriate energy-saving measures on such a scale. Considering the order in figure 1, we should not expect a person who only turns off the lights (e.g. person A) to suddenly install solar PV [38], but rather suggest an intermediate option. The Rasch model prescribes that a person whose ability is equal to a measure's behavioral difficulty has a 50% probability of already performing that measure [5]. Recommending such measures might be a good trade-off between novelty and feasibility, as a person would not perform all measures and they would not be out of reach in terms of behavioral difficulty.

We expect persons to be most motivated to adopt measures with a difficulty level similar to their own ability [32, 35]. This implies that ability-tailored advice might be an effective approach in helping users to attain their energy-saving goals. If a system indicates which measures are the most appropriate rather than users having to browse the scale's order themselves, then these users should experience less effort in looking for measures, thus feeling supported by the system and likewise experience a higher level of choice satisfaction. These expectations lead to our first research question:

RQ1: Using a Rasch scale to promote the adoption of energy-saving measures, is ability-tailored advice more effective and satisfactory, as well as less effortful than a non-personalized ordered set of measures?

2.2 Supporting a User's Conservation Goals

The Rasch model brings a different perspective to how advice can be tailored, which is particularly useful for an energy recommender system. In most recommender domains, systems aim to recommend items that are rather similar to a user's current behavior [9, 14]. However, Ekstrand and Willemsen point out that such an approach is unable to support users who seek behavioral change [14], which is critical for an energy recommender system [24]. Indeed, energy conservation often relies on goals and long-term commitment [2, 8], as well as the need to learn about novel possibilities to change one's current behavior [3, 17], which are not optimally supported by a behavior-based recommender system [14, 23].

Research in persuasive technology has shown how technological interventions can support the user's goals for attaining a better self [7, 14, 16]. For instance in the energy domain, various tools, such as feedback, goal-setting and social comparison, have successfully influenced people's conservation behavior [27, 30, 31]. However, most persuasion tools have yet to move their personalization beyond the message (how-to advice) and towards the content (what-to advice) [4, 21]. A Rasch-based recommender system can contribute to one's self-actualization by pointing out a user's current performance and suggesting where to look next [14, 23]. Moreover, it could also rely on the user's ability to track long-term progress.

We observe two opportunities to persuade users to make more energy-efficient choices. First, to tailor the difficulty level of energy-saving advice in such a way that it supports sustainable behavior, for example by tailoring it either just above or below the user's ability. Second, to encourage sustainable choices through personalized persuasion, for instance by explaining that a slightly challenging measure is a good match for a user by explaining how well it fits [37].

These opportunities touch upon the same aspect, namely the trade-off between a measure's feasibility and novelty [32]. The Rasch model has this trade-off built-in, as relatively easy measures are often perceived as feasible or attractive [32, 35], but are also likely to be already performed and thus not perceived as novel. Similarly, measures just above one's ability are more likely to be novel, but also might be too challenging. However, we expect that adding a persuasive attribute to a suggested measure might increase its perceived feasibility and, in turn, the likelihood it is adopted [16]. For instance, using a score to indicate that a relatively difficult measure is appropriate might increase its perceived feasibility.

We explore this trade-off for ability-tailored advice in the context of an energy recommender system. This leads to a second research question:

RQ2: How should the difficulty level of Rasch-based advice be tailored to be novel and effective, as well as satisfactory and feasible, and can this feasibility also be influenced by persuasive attributes, such as a fit score?

3 THE 'SAVING AID' CONSERVATION TOOL

We examined our research questions in two different energy recommender system studies. Figures 4a and 4b depict the different interfaces of our 'Saving Aid' web shop, which each relied on a Rasch scale of 79 energy-saving measures developed by Starke et al. [35]. Both systems presented information about different measures and their savings, and encouraged users to choose measures which they were willing to take in the four weeks following system use.

3.1 General Procedure

Figure 3 depicts the general procedure of our studies, showing the sequential steps that each user takes when using one of our 'Saving Aid' interfaces. As a first step, each system determined users' energy-saving ability by surveying them on their current conservation behavior, based on the methodology of Starke et al. [35]. This short survey consisted of 13 energy-saving measures, sampled from different difficulty sub-sets across the entire Rasch scale, for which users had to indicate whether they performed each measure or not, or whether a measure was not applicable to their housing situation.

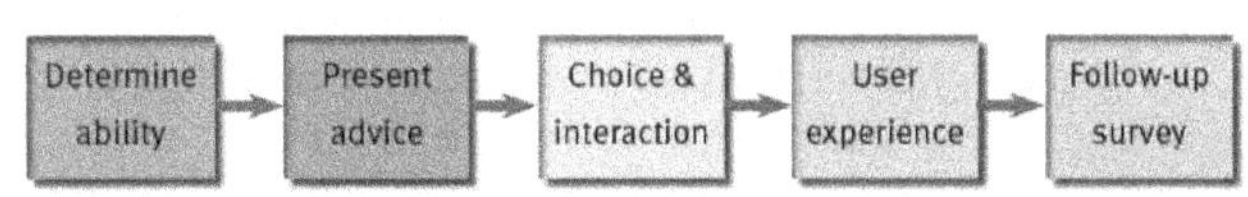

Figure 3: General procedure of our recommender studies. The first four steps were part of our recommender systems, the follow-up survey was sent four weeks later.

Depending on the experimental condition (cf. sections 4.1 & 5.1), advice was presented either in accordance with the user's estimated ability or not. Following this advice, users could interact with the Saving Aid and choose any measure they pleased, as well as review and adjust selected measures in their shopping cart in the upper-right corner of the screen (cf. figure 4a & 4b). Users who confirmed their selection could also opt-in to receive a list of the chosen measures per e-mail.

After finalizing their selection, users were asked to evaluate their system interaction. We examined how users perceived and experienced different interface features through aspects of the framework of Knijnenburg et al. [25, 26]. Perceived support and choice satisfaction were evaluated in both studies, while perceived effort and system satisfaction (study 1), as well as perceived feasibility and novelty (study 2) were study-specific. Finally, four weeks later, we invited all users to a short follow-up survey, in which they were asked to report about the extent to which they performed their chosen measures.

Figure 4a & 4b: The two 'Saving Aid' interfaces employed (Dutch: 'Besparingshulp'), presenting different energy-saving measures. The 'horizontal interface' of study 1 is depicted on the left (4a), in which measures were ordered horizontally, either on ascending or descending order of behavioral difficulty. The 'vertical interface' of study 2 is depicted on the right (4b) and differentiates between three lists of measures: 'basic', 'recommended' (Dutch: 'Aanbevolen'), and 'challenging'. Moreover, in some conditions of the vertical interface, a 'match score' indicated how well a measure fitted the user.

3.2 Unique Interface Aspects

The two systems depicted in Figure 4 have a number of unique interface aspects to examine our research questions. To compare the merits of tailored and non-personalized advice for our first study (cf. RQ1), we employed the 'horizontal interface' shown in figure 4a. The measures were ordered on a horizontal difficulty scale, labeled as ranging from 'easy/popular' to 'challenging/less popular'. Depending on the experimental condition, users were initially presented a particular set of five energy-saving measures, but were free to navigate through all conservation possibilities, either by clicking to see the next measure on the scale or by moving to a different scale position.

In contrast, the 'vertical interface', as shown in figure 4b, addressed RQ2 in study 2. We examined how different levels of ability-based advice and persuasive attributes could lead to more energy-efficient choices. To be able to show a longer list of tailored recommendations, we used a vertical rather than a horizontal interface. The new interface discerned between three lists of energy-saving measures: 'basic', 'recommended' and 'challenging' (cf. figure 4b). Users were initially presented fifteen measures from the 'recommended' list, but were free to navigate both within and between lists. In addition, depending on the experimental condition, users were either shown fit scores or not, indicating how well each measure fitted them.

4 STUDY 1: EFFECTIVENESS OF ABILITY-TAILORED ADVICE

4.1 Research Design

Study 1 investigated whether ability-based advice was more effective and less effortful than a non-personalized approach. Each user of the 'horizontal system' (cf. figure 4a) was assigned to one of four conditions, which determined which five energy-saving measures were initially presented to the user. In this 2x2-research design, we varied the scale's difficulty order (either ascending or descending) and the position on the scale from which measures were initially presented, either tailored (closest to the user's ability) or non-personalized (at the start of the scale, either the most popular or most challenging items). For tailored conditions, three of the five measures were labeled as recommended using a yellow highlight and a star.

4.2 Procedure and Participants

We invited participants from the ThesisTools database to use the Saving Aid depicted in figure 4a. Participants were told they had the opportunity to use a new conservation tool, from which they could choose measures they would like to perform in the four weeks following the study, sent to them per e-mail.

After estimating a user's energy-saving ability (cf. figure 3), the system initially presented five measures, either in accordance with the user's ability or a baseline set. Users could navigate and choose any energy-saving measures they pleased, until confirming their final selection. Subsequently, they were presented a survey on their perceived user experience.

In total, 222 participants completed our web-based experiment and entered a raffle for five 20-euro gift cards. After initial inspection, we excluded 13 participants from analysis, as they did not seem to understand our interface, either choosing all measures which they already performed or making multiple extremely improbable choices from a Rasch model point of view. The remaining sample consisted of 209 participants with a mean age of 44.5 years (SD = 15.8), who chose on average 9.3 energy-saving measures (SD = 8.6), and of which the majority owned a house (63.6%).

Each user was also invited to our follow-up survey, sent approximately four weeks after using the Saving Aid. We sent out invitations to 202 users who had disclosed valid e-mail addresses, from which 78 users (38.6%) replied and indicated to what extent they actually performed their chosen measures.

4.3 Measures

4.3.1 Objective metrics. Several objective metrics could be extracted from the experiment. We derived the users' energy-saving ability from the initial survey of 13 self-reported items. In addition, to measure the choice behavior of our users, we kept track of outcome variables, such as the total number of chosen conservation measures (log-transformed when included in our final model), the average Rasch difficulty level of these measures and the percentage of those measures being reported as performed in our follow-up survey. From the log data of the interface interactions, we calculated the number of chosen items per navigation click as a measure of objective effort.

4.3.2 Subjective measures. We surveyed our users on four subjective constructs: perceived support, perceived effort, system satisfaction and choice satisfaction. For all survey items, users had to indicate on 7-point Likert scales to what extent they agreed with them, which we submitted to a confirmatory factor analysis (CFA) using ordinal dependent variables. Table 1 only reports three user experience constructs, as we could not distinguish system satisfaction from perceived support due to high cross-loadings. The remaining constructs met the guidelines for convergence validity (cf. table 1), as the average variance explained (AVE) was higher than 0.5 [25], but the internal consistency of the perceived effort construct was somewhat questionable, as Cronbach's alpha for this construct was merely 0.69 [15].

Table 1: Survey items in study 1, with factor loadings and robustness scores per user experience construct. Items without loading were excluded from the CFA and SEM.

PERCEIVED EFFORT – survey items ***AVE = 0.511; ALPHA = 0.69***	**Factor Loading**
It took me little effort to use the Saving Aid.	
The Saving Aid takes up a lot of time.	0.804
I quickly understood the functionalities of the Saving Aid.	−0.554
Many actions were required to use the Saving Aid properly.	0.741
The Saving Aid is easy to use.	
PERCEIVED SUPPORT – survey items ***AVE = 0.615; ALPHA = 0.81***	**Factor Loading**
I make better choices using the Saving Aid tool.	0.551
The Saving Aid is helpful to find appropriate measures.	0.608
The Saving Aid does not help to come to a decision.	
The Saving Aid presents the measures in a convenient way.	
Because of the Saving Aid, I could easily choose measures.	0.678
CHOICE SATISFACTION – survey items ***AVE = 0.598; ALPHA = 0.78***	**Factor Loading**
I am happy with the measures I've chosen.	0.574
I think I've chosen the best measures from the list.	
I would have liked to choose different measures than the ones I've chosen.	
It would be fun to perform the chosen measures.	0.550
The measures I've chosen fit me seamlessly.	0.549

4.4 Results

The objective and subjective constructs, as well as relevant interactions were organized into a path model using Structural Equation Modeling (SEM). Figure 5 depicts the model, which fitted adequately[1]: $\chi^2(108) = 191.000$, $p < 0.001$, $CFI = 0.957$, $TLI = 0.949$, $RMSEA = 0.061$, *90%-CI*: [0.046,0.084].

4.4.1 Tailored advice. We examined whether tailored advice would result in more effective and satisfactory recommendations, as was proposed in RQ1. Figure 5 confirms that users receiving tailored advice, compared to non-personalized suggestions, perceived less effort in system use (coef. −0.440, $p < 0.05$). In turn, perceiving less effort also increased perceived system support (coef. −0.767, $p < 0.001$), which also increased the user's satisfaction with the chosen measures (coef. 0.746, $p < 0.001$).

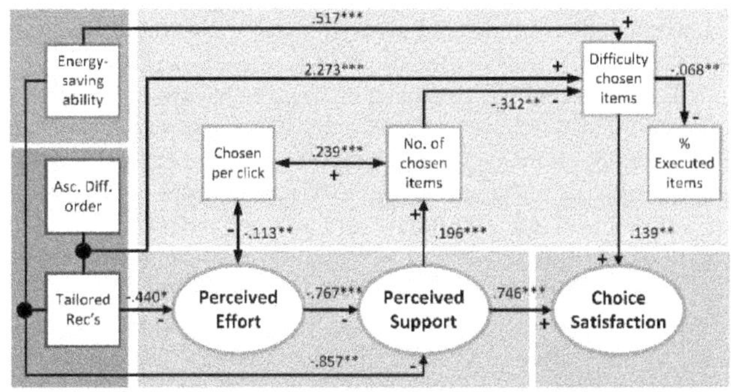

Figure 5: Structural equation model (SEM) for study 1. Numbers on the arrows represent the coefficients. Effects between the subjective constructs are standardized, thus can be considered as correlations. Aspects are grouped by color: Objective system aspects are purple, subjective aspects are green and experience constructs are orange. Behavioral indicators are blue, personal characteristics red [25, 26]. *** $p < 0.001$, ** $p < 0.01$, * $p < 0.05$.

Besides main effects, figure 5 also depicts that tailored advice interacts with energy-saving ability and the scale's difficulty order. We found high-ability users to perceive less support from tailored advice compared to low-ability users (coef. −0.857, $p < 0.01$), possibly because they were more proficient in navigating through the different energy-saving possibilities. Moreover, users facing a scale in ascending order of difficulty chose measures with a higher level of difficulty, when presented tailored advice (coef. 2.273, $p < 0.001$).

This interaction is easier to interpret when inspecting the marginal effects in figure 6. For non-tailored recommendations, the chosen difficulty was higher when facing a scale in descending difficulty order rather than in ascending order (cf. figure 6a), as users were initially recommended difficult measures. Interestingly, this effect almost reversed for tailored advice, which was arguably due to users having a natural tendency to move rightwards on the scale, starting from the recommendations. This implied for a descending difficulty order that users inspected and chose easier measures relative to those recommended, and vice versa for the tailored ascending condition. As choice satisfaction is positively influenced by

[1] In fitting the model, some issues arose with the discriminant validity of perceived effort [25], as it correlated strongly with perceived support and this correlation was slightly higher than the square root of its own explained item variance (AVE). In other words, perceived effort and support are highly correlated constructs, but they were kept in our model as it helped us understand and explain our results better.

both the difficulty level of chosen items and perceived support (cf. figure 5), the marginal effects in figure 6b show an interesting interaction effect. Although the ascending tailored condition was perceived as more satisfying (compared to non-tailored) due to both difficulty and support, the positive effect of perceived support in the descending tailored condition was counteracted by the negative effect of a lower chosen difficulty.

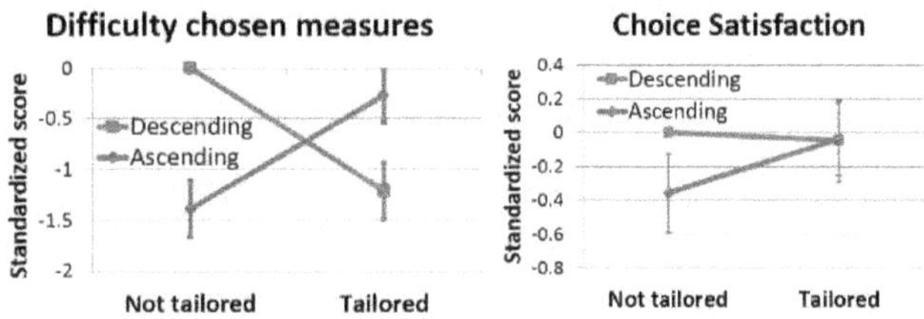

Figure 6a & 6b: Marginal effects of the four experimental conditions on the average difficulty level of chosen measures (6a; on the left), and choice satisfaction (6b; right-hand side). Effects are relative to a baseline of descending & non-tailored. Error bars are 1 std. err.

4.4.2 Mediators: Perceived effort and support. The mediating effort and support constructs depicted in figure 5 had strong behavioral correlates. Effort manifested itself objectively, as users who perceived less effort had also chosen more items for the number of navigation clicks they spent (coef. −0.113, $p < 0.01$). Perceived support also positively affected interaction metrics, as users who perceived higher levels of support also chose more energy-saving measures (coef. 0.196, $p < 0.001$), adhering to earlier findings that a positive user experience can drive energy savings [24]. However, although the difficulty of chosen measures was higher for high-ability users, it decreased if more measures were selected (coef. −0.312, $p < 0.01$).

Figure 5 shows no relation between choice satisfaction and the extent to which users actually performed chosen measures (i.e. '% executed items'). However, we did observe that users mostly followed up on easy measures, as there was a negative relation between the difficulty of chosen system measures and the execution rate four weeks later (coef. −0.068, $p < 0.01$).

4.5 Conclusion

Our path model shows that tailored recommendations positively affect a range of user experience aspects. By reducing both perceived and actual effort, users felt more support, and in turn chose more energy-saving measures and were also satisfied about those choices. This pointed out that providing ability-tailored advice was a more effective approach than merely presenting an ordinal Rasch scale.

The extent to which tailored advice also helps to improve energy savings is less clear from this study. Although more measures were chosen when higher support was perceived, this was against a reduced difficulty level. Moreover, long-term effects in terms of the extent that chosen measures were performed four weeks later, merely showed that users were more likely to perform easier measures.

These findings beg the question whether energy-saving advice should be precisely tailored to a user's ability, or that slightly easier or more difficult advice would be more effective. Hence, presenting tailored, yet slightly more feasible measures might lead to more energy-efficient behavior in the long run. However, users who had chosen relatively difficult measures reported higher levels of choice satisfaction, which could also drive energy savings [24]. Therefore, study 2 examines RQ2, exploring the trade-off between feasibility and novelty for ability-tailored advice.

5 STUDY 2: HOW TO TAILOR THE ADVICE?

5.1 Research Design

Study 2 thus investigated how advice should be tailored to be the most effective, satisfactory and feasible, but also examined whether persuasive attributes can influence this feasibility. All users of our 'vertical system' (cf. figure 4b) were assigned to one out of six conditions, subject to a 2x3-research design. On the one hand, measures were presented either accompanied by a fit score or not. On the other hand, users were initially presented fifteen measures from the 'recommended' tab, which contained measures closest to one out of three levels of ability-difficulty difference: either +1, 0, or -1 logit units (i.e. a relatively low, matching or high difficulty level). By means of these three conditions, we explored the tradeoff between feasibility and novelty/relevance of the measures. Hence, if a user's ability was higher than the item difficulty (+1 logit), users were presented relatively easy measures, which were less novel as users were likely to already perform them (i.e. a 75% probability; cf. figure 2). In contrast, the measures presented at an ability-difficulty difference of -1 logit were more difficult, novel, and relevant, since users were less likely to already perform them (i.e. only a 25%-engagement probability).

The shown fit score, if presented, was a function of the condition's ability-difficulty difference. The top item in the recommended tab would get a fit score close to 100%, while this score decreased for lower-ranked items, following the characteristic curve of the Rasch model (cf. figure 2), with a median value of 77% for the 15th item and most values above 60%. Consequently, measures in the other tabs would show lower fit scores, typically starting at 60-70% and decreasing to 0-1% for items with the largest ability-difficulty difference.

5.2 Procedure and Participants

We invited participants from the ThesisTools participant database to use our 'vertical interface' (cf. figure 4b; only those who did not participate in study 1). The procedure was similar to study 1 and followed the sequential steps depicted in figure 2 (cf. section 3.1): ability estimation, presentation of tailored advice, system interaction and selection of measures, and a user experience survey. Once again, users were free to navigate the entire web shop and could also opt-in to receive the chosen measures via e-mail.

In total, 288 participants completed our experiment and entered a raffle for five web-shop gift cards of 20 euro each. The sample comprised 193 female users (67.0%), 187 home-owners (64.9%), and had a mean age of 39.7 years (SD = 15.0). From this sample, 194 users were also invited to participate in a follow-up survey, four weeks after system use. However, only 46 users (23.7%) indicated to what extent they actually performed their chosen measures.

5.3 Measures

We considered objective measures similar to study 1, such as the total number of chosen measures. Regarding the subjective measures, we considered four constructs: perceived feasibility and perceived novelty (of the recommended measures), as well as perceived support and choice satisfaction. In our final model, perceived novelty was dropped as it suffered from high cross-loadings and including it in our path model deteriorated its fit (cf. section 5.4). Table 2 shows that convergence validity of the other aspects was good, as all AVE values were well above 0.5. Moreover, the internal consistency was good, with high values of Cronbach's alpha.

Table 2: Survey items in study 2, with factor loadings and robustness scores per user experience construct. Items without loading were excluded from the CFA and SEM.

PERCEIVED FEASIBILITY – SURVEY ITEMS *AVE = 0.63; ALPHA = 0.83*	Factor Loading
The recommended measures are hard to perform.	−0.772
I do not have the possibility to perform the recommended measures.	−0.792
The recommended measures are applicable in my home environment.	0.741
It takes little effort to perform the recommended measures.	0.736
PERCEIVED SUPPORT – SURVEY ITEMS ***AVE = 0.775; ALPHA = 0.92***	**Factor Loading**
I make better choices using the saving aid tool.	0.771
The saving aid is helpful to find appropriate measures.	0.918
Because of the saving aid, i could easily choose measures.	0.923
I would like to use the saving aid more often.	0.802
The saving aid is useless.	
CHOICE SATISFACTION – SURVEY ITEMS ***AVE = 0.705; ALPHA = 0.84***	**Factor Loading**
I am happy with the measures I've chosen.	0.674
I think I've chosen the best measures from the list.	
It would be fun to perform the chosen measures.	0.764
The measures I've chosen fit me seamlessly.	0.698

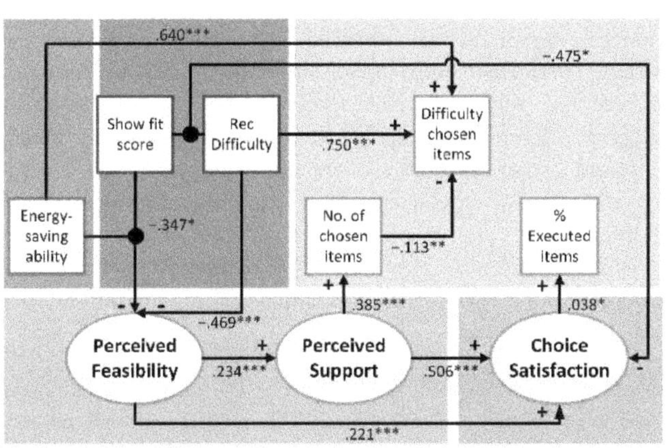

Figure 7: SEM for study 2. Numbers of the arrows represent the coefficients. Effects between the subjective constructs are standardized, thus can be considered as correlations. *** $p < 0.001$, ** $p < 0.01$, * $p < 0.05$.

5.4 Results

All variables were organized into a path model using Structural Equation Modeling (SEM). The model had a good fit: $\chi^2(140)$ = 198.693 $p < 0.001$, *CFI* = 0.992, *TLI* = 0.990, *RMSEA* = 0.046, *90%CI*: [0.034:0.057]. Figure 7 depicts the fitted path model. We coded the three different difficulty conditions as an ordinal variable in our model (different coding showed similar results), while the fit score was encoded as a dummy variable.

5.4.1 Recommendation Difficulty. We examined whether the difficulty of recommendations affected their perceived feasibility and, in turn, users' satisfaction and choice behavior. We found that comparatively difficult 'recommended' lists were perceived as less feasible (coef. −0.469, $p < 0.001$), confirming that easier measures have a higher perceived feasibility [32].

Figure 7 shows that feasibility also affected other objective and subjective measures. Users who perceived recommended items as feasible also experienced a higher choice satisfaction, both through a direct effect (coef. 0.221, $p < 0.001$), as well as through a mediated effect which increased system support (coef. 0.234, $p < 0.001$) and in turn also choice satisfaction (coef. 0.506, $p < 0.001$). Moreover, similar to study 1, users who perceived more support also chose more items (coef. 0.385, $p < 0.001$). Figure 8a supports these findings, illustrating that a lower recommendation difficulty increased the number of items chosen by a user. Figure 8b shows that a similar effect was also observed for choice satisfaction, which on average decreased if recommendation difficulty increased. However, this effect was mainly observed when a fit score was shown, reflected by the significant interaction effect between fit score and recommendation difficulty (coef. -0.475, $p < 0.05$).

As more satisfied users were more likely to actually execute their chosen items four weeks later (coef. 0.038, $p < -0.05$), it was apparent that presenting comparatively easy tailored recommendations led to a better user interface experience, which in turn led to more energy-efficient choices and sustainable behavioral change.

In contrast with study 1, we observed no relation between the chosen difficulty level and follow-up four weeks later. However, we did observe that presenting relatively difficult measures increased the difficulty level of chosen items (coef. 0.750, $p < 0.001$).

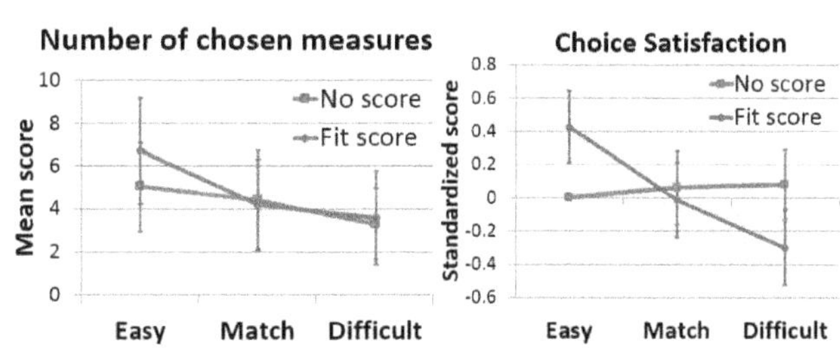

Figure 8a & 8b: The number of chosen measures (8a) and choice satisfaction (8b), as a function of the experimental conditions: fit score (yes or no) and the ability-difficulty difference (easy = +1, match = +0, difficult = -1). Error bars are 1 std. err.

5.4.2 Fit Score. We also examined the effectiveness of presenting a fit score to increase the perceived feasibility, but observed no such main effect. It seems that fit scores reinforced users' preferences for relatively easy measures. Figure 7 shows that high-ability users who were presented a fit score perceived recommended measures as less feasible, as shown by the interaction between these two factors (coef. −0.347, $p < 0.05$). Figure 8b shows that although showing a fit score worsened a user's choice satisfaction for higher levels of recommended difficulty (coef. −0.475, $p < 0.05$), it actually increased choice satisfaction for relatively easy recommendations (compared to showing no fit score). This suggested that fit scores were not successful in motivating users to adopt challenging items, but rather reinforced their current ability levels.

5.5 Conclusion

We investigated how to tailor energy-saving advice to increase its effectiveness and feasibility, and whether this feasibility can be increased by presenting a fit score. We found that ability-tailored recommendations low in difficulty were perceived as more feasible, which made users feel more supported and, in turn, led to more energy-efficient choices and a higher choice satisfaction. In addition, we found that inducing a positive user experience this way, increased the likelihood that users actually performed chosen measures, thus helping them to attain conservation goals, albeit through small behavioral steps in terms of the Rasch scale. This preference for relatively easy measures suggested that users did not mind being presented a recommendation list from which they already performed numerous measures (about 75% of them, according to the Rasch model), compared to a list containing more challenging and novel items with an average engagement probability of 25%. This adhered to earlier research on novelty negatively affecting user satisfaction levels [13].

In addition, we found that presenting a fit score was only effective if the recommended energy-saving measures were relatively easy (cf. figure 7). In fact, showing high fit scores for difficult measures impaired a user's choice satisfaction. Hence, persuasive attributes in our interface were not effective to attain challenging energy-saving goals.

6 DISCUSSION

People often face difficulties in reaching their behavioral goals. To date, most recommender systems are behavior-driven and therefore fail to effectively support those users who wish to accomplish goals for their better selves [14, 23]. In particular, the domain of energy conservation is in need of a tool which helps people to save energy, but research on tailored energy-saving recommendations is limited [24, 35].

We have attempted to fill this gap by using a Rasch scale of energy-saving measures to help users attain their conservation goals [35]. We have established that tailoring energy-saving advice towards a user's ability can reduce a user's perceived effort and increase the feasibility of presented measures. As we also find that users seem to prefer to receive comparatively easy advice which falls just below their own ability [32, 35], we suggest that a user's motivation to save energy is increased the most by making small behavioral steps in terms of the Rasch scale, rather than pushing them to make giant leaps.

This rationale is supported by our findings on the presented fit score. The effectiveness of maximizing fit scores for easy measures might be due to users recognizing presented measures compared to novel suggestions, arguably supporting the credibility of the high fit score and thereby increasing perceived support and satisfaction. In a similar vein, presenting a high fit score for difficult measures might have not been credible and thus deteriorated the interface's efficacy.

The effectiveness of relatively easy ability-tailored advice, especially in terms of feasibility, also suggests that users do not seem to hold particular reasons to not perform certain measures below their own ability level. For example, a person who hardly possesses any electrical appliances might not consider to turn them off at a main switch (cf. figure 1, section 2.1). However, the observed systemic preference for easy measures suggests that this is not the case, and that users might have simply been oblivious to these measures beforehand [3]. However, we do wish to emphasize that ability-tailored advice has shown to be a more effective approach than simply showing the most popular scale items.

Our research is subject to a few limitations. The model fitted in study 1 raises a few concerns regarding the separability of the different constructs. Although this might call for a replication of the study, the outcome of the second study seems to reinforce the findings of the former, as a similar structural model is underlying the results.

Another concern might be that some users might have simply selected a lot of measures and have decided to not perform them. We argue that even though self-report is a delicate measurement method, we have observed small effects of behavioral change four weeks after system use, suggesting that our recommendations and interface have had a positive effect on users' energy-saving behavior.

Finally, the Rasch model has important implications for recommender system research, as well as energy policy. Our Rasch model has shown that a relatively simple personalization algorithm can already yield effective results, which begs the question how an interface using more intricate personalization would perform. Moreover, we have not only measured users' choice behavior, but also checked whether chosen items were actually performed four weeks later. Monitoring a user after system use might be particularly helpful to systems that support behavioral change [14], as it can point out which interface design aspects were effective. However, if a follow-up survey is hard to implement, this research has also shown that system perception constructs can explain a user's choice satisfaction and also correlate with behavioral metrics, which can present a rather complete, triangulated explanation for any effect of system use.

ACKNOWLEDGEMENTS

This work is part of the Research Talent program with project number 406-14-088, which is financed by the Netherlands Organization for Scientific Research (NWO).

We thank Luc Bams, Dennis Dielissen, Tiare Holkema, Lars Middel and Erwin Simons for programming the user interfaces and running the experiments as part of their student projects.

REFERENCES

[1] Abrahamse, W., Steg, L., Vlek, C. and Rothengatter, T. 2005. A review of intervention studies aimed at household energy conservation. *Journal of Environmental Psychology*. 25, 3 (Sep. 2005), 273–291.

[2] Abrahamse, W., Steg, L., Vlek, C. and Rothengatter, T. 2007. The effect of tailored information, goal setting, and tailored feedback on household energy use, energy-related behaviors, and behavioral antecedents. *Journal of Environmental Psychology*. 27, 4 (2007), 265–276.

[3] Benders, R.M.J., Kok, R., Moll, H.C., Wiersma, G. and Noorman, K.J. 2006. New approaches for household energy conservation—In search of personal household energy budgets and energy reduction options. *Energy Policy*. 34, 18 (Dec. 2006), 3612–3622.

[4] Berkovsky, S., Freyne, J. and Oinas-Kukkonen, H. eds. 2012. Influencing Individually: Fusing Personalization and Persuasion. *ACM Trans. Interact. Intell. Syst.* 2, 2 (Jun. 2012), 9:1–9:8.

[5] Bond, T.G. and Fox, C.M. 2006. *Applying the Rasch Model: Fundamental Measurement in the Human Sciences, Second Edition*. Psychology Press.

[6] Boudet, H.S., Flora, J.A. and Armel, K.C. 2016. Clustering household energy-saving behaviours by behavioural attribute. *Energy Policy*. 92, (May 2016), 444–454.

[7] Cialdini, R.B. 2007. *Influence: the psychology of persuasion*. Collins.

[8] Cialdini, R.B. and Trost, M.R. 1998. Social influence: Social norms, conformity and compliance. *The handbook of social psychology, Vols. 1 and 2 (4th ed.)*. D.T. Gilbert, S.T. Fiske, and G. Lindzey, eds. McGraw-Hill. 151–192.

[9] Cosley, D., Lam, S.K., Albert, I., Konstan, J.A. and Riedl, J. 2003. Is Seeing Believing?: How Recommender System Interfaces Affect Users' Opinions. *Proceedings of the SIGCHI Conference on Human Factors in Computing Systems* (New York, NY, USA, 2003), 585–592.

[10] Costanzo, M., Archer, D., Aronson, E. and Pettigrew, T. 1986. Energy conservation behavior: The difficult path from information to action. *American Psychologist*. 41, 5 (1986), 521–528.

[11] Darby, S. 1999. Energy advice–what is it worth. *Proceedings, European Council for an Energy-Efficient Economy Summer Study, paper III*. 5, (1999), 3–5.

[12] Dietz, T., Gardner, G.T., Gilligan, J., Stern, P.C. and Vandenbergh, M.P. 2009. Household actions can provide a behavioral wedge to rapidly reduce US carbon emissions. *Proceedings of the National Academy of Sciences*. 106, 44 (Nov. 2009), 18452–18456.

[13] Ekstrand, M.D., Harper, F.M., Willemsen, M.C. and Konstan, J.A. 2014. User Perception of Differences in Recommender Algorithms. *Proceedings of the 8th ACM Conference on Recommender Systems* (New York, NY, USA, 2014), 161–168.

[14] Ekstrand, M.D. and Willemsen, M.C. 2016. Behaviorism is Not Enough: Better Recommendations Through Listening to Users. *Proceedings of the 10th ACM Conference on Recommender Systems* (New York, NY, USA, 2016), 221–224.

[15] Embretson, S.E. and Reise, S.P. 2000. *Item Response Theory for Psychologists*. Psychology Press.

[16] Fogg, B.J. 2002. *Persuasive Technology: Using Computers to Change What We Think and Do*. Morgan Kaufmann.

[17] Gardner, G.T. and Stern, P.C. 2008. The short list: The most effective actions US households can take to curb climate change. *Environment: science and policy for sustainable development*. 50, 5 (2008), 12–25.

[18] Harper, F.M., Li, X., Chen, Y. and Konstan, J.A. 2005. An Economic Model of User Rating in an Online Recommender System. *SpringerLink* (Jul. 2005), 307–316.

[19] Kaiser, F.G., Byrka, K. and Hartig, T. 2010. Reviving Campbell's Paradigm for Attitude Research. *Personality and Social Psychology Review*. 14, 4 (Nov. 2010), 351–367.

[20] Kaiser, F.G. and Wilson, M. 2004. Goal-directed conservation behavior: the specific composition of a general performance. *Personality and Individual Differences*. 36, 7 (May 2004), 1531–1544.

[21] Kaptein, M., Markopoulos, P., de Ruyter, B. and Aarts, E. 2015. Personalizing persuasive technologies: Explicit and implicit personalization using persuasion profiles. *International Journal of Human-Computer Studies*. 77, (May 2015), 38–51.

[22] Karlin, B., Davis, N., Sanguinetti, A., Gamble, K., Kirkby, D. and Stokols, D. 2014. Dimensions of Conservation Exploring Differences Among Energy Behaviors. *Environment and Behavior*. 46, 4 (May 2014), 423–452.

[23] Knijnenburg, B.P., Sivakumar, S. and Wilkinson, D. 2016. Recommender Systems for Self-Actualization. *Proceedings of the 10th ACM Conference on Recommender Systems* (New York, NY, USA, 2016), 11–14.

[24] Knijnenburg, B.P., Willemsen, M. and Broeders, R. 2014. Smart sustainability through system satisfaction: Tailored preference elicitation for energy-saving recommenders. *Twentieth Americas Conference on Information Systems (AMCIS)* (Georgia, 2014).

[25] Knijnenburg, B.P. and Willemsen, M.C. 2015. Evaluating recommender systems with user experiments. *Recommender Systems Handbook*. Springer. 309–352.

[26] Knijnenburg, B.P., Willemsen, M.C., Gantner, Z., Soncu, H. and Newell, C. 2012. Explaining the user experience of recommender systems. *User Modeling and User-Adapted Interaction*. 22, 4–5 (2012), 441–504.

[27] Mankoff, J., Matthews, D., Fussell, S.R. and Johnson, M. 2007. Leveraging Social Networks To Motivate Individuals to Reduce Their Ecological Footprints. *Proceedings of the 40th Annual Hawaii International Conference on System Sciences* (Washington, DC, USA, 2007), 87–.

[28] McKenzie-Mohr, D. 2000. Fostering sustainable behavior through community-based social marketing. *American Psychologist*. 55, 5 (2000), 531–537.

[29] McMakin, A.H., Malone, E.L. and Lundgren, R.E. 2002. Motivating Residents to Conserve Energy without Financial Incentives. *Environment and Behavior*. 34, 6 (Nov. 2002), 848–863.

[30] Petkov, P., Goswami, S., Köbler, F. and Krcmar, H. 2012. Personalised Eco-feedback As a Design Technique for Motivating Energy Saving Behaviour at Home. *Proceedings of the 7th Nordic Conference on Human-Computer Interaction: Making Sense Through Design* (New York, NY, USA, 2012), 587–596.

[31] Petkov, P., Köbler, F., Foth, M., Medland, R. and Krcmar, H. 2011. Engaging energy saving through motivation-specific social comparison. *CHI'11 Extended Abstracts on Human Factors in Computing Systems* (2011), 1945–1950.

[32] Radha, M., Willemsen, M.C., Boerhof, M. and IJsselsteijn, W.A. 2016. Lifestyle Recommendations for Hypertension Through Rasch-based Feasibility Modeling. *Proceedings of the 2016 Conference on User Modeling Adaptation and Personalization* (New York, NY, USA, 2016), 239–247.

[33] Rashid, A.M., Albert, I., Cosley, D., Lam, S.K., McNee, S.M., Konstan, J.A. and Riedl, J. 2002. Getting to Know You: Learning New User Preferences in Recommender Systems. *Proceedings of the 7th International Conference on Intelligent User Interfaces* (New York, NY, USA, 2002), 127–134.

[34] Schultz, P.W. 2014. Strategies for promoting proenvironmental behavior: Lots of tools but few instructions. *European Psychologist*. 19, 2 (2014), 107–117.

[35] Starke, A., Willemsen, M.C. and Snijders, C. 2015. Saving Energy in 1-D: Tailoring Energy-saving Advice Using a Rasch-based Energy Recommender System. *Proc. 2nd Int. Workshop on Decision Making and Rec. Sys. (DMRS)* (Bolzano, Italy, 2015), 5–8.

[36] Steg, L. 2008. Promoting household energy conservation. *Energy policy*. 36, 12 (2008), 4449–4453.

[37] Tintarev, N. and Masthoff, J. 2007. A Survey of Explanations in Recommender Systems. *2007 IEEE 23rd International Conference on Data Engineering Workshop* (Apr. 2007), 801–810.

[38] Urban, J. and Ščasný, M. 2014. Structure of Domestic Energy Saving: How Many Dimensions? *Environment and Behavior*. (2014), 13916514547081.

[39] Wilson, C. and Dowlatabadi, H. 2007. Models of Decision Making and Residential Energy Use. *Annual Review of Environment and Resources*. 32, 1 (2007), 169–203.

[40] Winett, R.A., Love, S.Q. and Kidd, C. 1982. Effectiveness of an energy specialist and extension agents in promoting summer energy conservation by home visits. *J. Environ. Syst.;(United States)*. 12, 1 (1982).

Evaluating Decision-Aware Recommender Systems

Rus M. Mesas
Universidad Autónoma de Madrid
Madrid, Spain
rusmaria.mesas@estudiante.uam.es

Alejandro Bellogín
Universidad Autónoma de Madrid
Madrid, Spain
alejandro.bellogin@uam.es

ABSTRACT

The main goal of a Recommender System is to suggest relevant items to users, although other utility dimensions – such as diversity, novelty, confidence, possibility of providing explanations – are often considered. In this work, in order to increase the amount of relevant items presented to the user, we analyse how the system could measure the confidence on its own recommendations, so it has the capability of taking decisions about whether an item should be recommended or not. A direct consequence of this design is that the number of suggested items decreases, impacting in some of the beyond-accuracy dimensions (especially, coverage). We present an evaluation of different decision-aware techniques that can be applied to some families of recommender systems, and explore evaluation metrics that allow to combine more than one evaluation dimension. Empiric results show that large precision improvements are obtained when using these approaches at the expense of user and item coverage.

1 INTRODUCTION

Recommender Systems aim at suggesting as many relevant items to the users as possible, although other goals are being considered recently [3]: increasing the diversity or novelty of the recommendations, suggesting items in such a way that it is possible to explain where the recommendation is coming from, increasing the confidence of the user in the system, etc. In this work, we investigate about confidence but from the perspective of the system: what is the confidence a system has in its own recommendations; more specifically, we focus on different methods to embed awareness into the recommendation algorithms about deciding whether an item should be suggested. In this way, we hypothesise the system would only show the more reliable suggestions, hence, increasing the performance of such recommendations, at the expense of, presumably, reducing the number of potential recommendations.

The concept of confidence in recommendation has been applied to different aspects in the field. On the one hand, confidence is defined on the input data, where some authors have studied which combinations of users or (user, item) pairs let generate better recommendations, namely the *profile-level trust* and *item-level trust* approaches from [9], or like in [6], where it is used to interpret the confidence when transforming from implicit data (frequencies) into explicit. On the other hand, we find different mechanisms that help to contextualise the predictions made by the recommendation algorithms. In this way, in [4] a factor is defined (*significance weighting*) that is combined with the user similarity to devalue those cases where such similarity has been computed with not enough data. In a similar fashion, in [1] a method is proposed to filter out recommendations according to the rating deviation received by the items. Previously, in [12], the authors introduced the concepts of support and confidence in case-based recommenders computed from association rules. In parallel, in [8] it was studied how to introduce confidence measures when presenting the recommendations, that is, in the interface the user is interacting with. In that work, even though the confidence metric was very simple (number of ratings observed by the system for one item) it was enough to increase the satisfaction level of the user.

In this paper, we study how the performance of a recommendation algorithm evolves when it decides not to recommend in some situations. If the decision of avoiding a recommendation is sensible – i.e., not random but related to the information available to the system about the target user or item –, the performance is expected to improve at the expense of other quality dimensions such as coverage, novelty, or diversity. This balance is critical, since it is possible to achieve a very high precision recommending only one item to a unique user, which would not be a very useful recommender. Memory-based algorithms are well known for suffering from this issue: if very few neighbours are considered, the coverage is lower, but the recommendations are of higher quality (as observed in terms of error metrics [4]); whereas larger neighbourhoods may increase the likelihood of receiving a noisy recommendation, but the chances of recommending more items are also higher. Because of this, we explore some techniques to combine precision and coverage metrics, an open problem in the area, as stated by some authors [3].

In summary, the contributions of this paper are twofold: a taxonomy of techniques that can be applied to some families of recommender systems allowing to include mechanisms to decide if a recommendation should be generated, and a first exploration to the combination of precision and coverage evaluation metrics.

2 DECISION-AWARE RECOMMENDER SYSTEMS

Modifying recommendation algorithms so that they can decide whether a recommendation should be produced is not an easy task when formulated in a generic way, because each algorithm has different characteristics and hypothesis about the input data and produced suggestions. As a starting point, in this section we shall focus on one of the main types of recommender systems – Collaborative Filtering algorithms.

Different from other works in the literature, our approaches do not exploit or analyse the input data (unlike the works previously mentioned [6, 8]), but intrinsic aspects of the recommendation algorithms or of the components used during prediction are considered, similar to the weights introduced for similarity computation in [4]. More specifically, we exploit the support of the prediction score for nearest-neighbour algorithms (Section 2.1) and the uncertainty in the prediction score for a probabilistic matrix factorisation algorithm (Section 2.2).

RecSys '17, August 27-31, 2017, Como, Italy

ACM ISBN 978-1-4503-4652-8/17/08...$15.00.
https://doi.org/10.1145/3109859.3109888

2.1 Based on prediction support

It is well known that, in order to compute scores for (user, item) pairs, some algorithms use more data than others, depending on the actual users and items under consideration. A paradigmatic example of this situation are the nearest-neighbour recommenders. These algorithms estimate the user preferences based on similar users or items, however, it is required that those neighbours have rated the same item (in the user-based scenario) or that the target user has rated those similar items (in the item-based case).

Indeed, the number of ratings used to predict the user preferences (denoted as *support*) provides an indication of the confidence level the system has about the produced recommendation, since the system cannot trust in the same way a score produced based only on two neighbours or based on one hundred. This is actually the same idea behind the significance weighting approach proposed by Herlocker and colleagues in [4].

Hence, we propose that a nearest-neighbour recommender could decide that **an item is worth a recommendation if at least n out of the k neighbours have participated in the preference computation.** In other words, a prediction would be ignored if less than n neighbours have contributed to the prediction score.

2.2 Based on prediction uncertainty

As described in the previous section, some algorithms compute the prediction scores based on an aggregation of values, usually an average or a weighted average (such as the aforementioned neighbour-based recommenders). Whenever an average is being calculated, it is also possible to compute a standard deviation of the predicted score. When doing this, the standard deviation can be interpreted as a confidence parameter of the algorithm about the score: the larger the deviation, the more uncertainty on the prediction, and hence, the lower the confidence on it.

Hence, we propose that an algorithm, for which it is possible to compute the standard deviation of a prediction score, could decide that **an item is worth a recommendation if the standard deviation of the prediction (*uncertainty*) does not exceed a specified threshold σ_τ.**

More specifically, we apply this approach to a probabilistic matrix factorisation recommender. Although it is possible to apply this strategy to nearest neighbour recommenders, we found this approach is less effective for these algorithms, probably because there is no theoretical formulation for the deviation in those cases.

We describe next how we can compute the standard deviation of a probabilistic matrix factorisation algorithm. For this, we make use of a Bayesian approximation for matrix factorisation proposed in [7]. In this algorithm, the preference scores are computed by approximating a distribution, whose average and deviation should be estimated. Since we need an explicit formulation for the standard deviation, we derived it using mean-field variational inference:

$$Var(r_{ui}) = \tau^2 + \text{trace}\left(\left(\phi_u + \overline{u}\overline{u}^\top\right)\left(\psi_i + \overline{i}\overline{i}^\top\right)\right) - \overline{i}^\top \overline{u}\overline{u}^\top \overline{i} \quad (1)$$

where it is assumed the rating follows a normal distribution with mean $u^\top \cdot i$ and deviation τ, and ϕ_u y $\overline{u}$ represent the covariance matrix and vector of means for user u; ψ_i and $\overline{i}$ denote the same concepts but for item i.

3 EVALUATING DECISION-AWARE RECOMMENDER SYSTEMS

As soon as a recommender system has control over which items should not be recommended for a particular user, it is very likely that the user coverage and the item coverage decrease, even though precision and other accuracy-related metrics increase. For instance, a very high precision could be achieved if an algorithm returns only one (relevant) item for one user, at the expense of a very low coverage. Because of this, it becomes very important to study and define metrics that, somehow, combine precision and coverage, especially in situations of confidence-awareness like the one we propose in this paper.

As noted by Herlocker and colleagues in [5] there is no general coverage metric that, at the same time, gives more weight to relevant items when accounting for coverage, and combines coverage and accuracy measures. Moreover, Gunawardana and Shani mentioned the problem of balancing coverage and accuracy metrics in [3], and leave it as an open issue in the area. We aim to address this problem by combining the values of the different metrics to be compared, especially focused on deriving a metric that assess when a recommender does not return an item.

3.1 F-score or Harmonic Mean

The F-score is an evaluation metric very popular in Machine Learning to combine precision and recall measures. It produces the harmonic mean of both metrics, and it ranges between 0 and 1, 0 being the worst value and 1 the optimal value. Based on this idea, we propose to combine precision and coverage through the harmonic mean, whose general formulation is as follows:

$$F_\beta(P,Q) = (1+\beta^2)\cdot\frac{P\cdot Q}{\beta^2\cdot P + Q} \quad (2)$$

where β is used to control the importance of each metric in the final result: if $\beta = 1$ both metrics P and Q have the same importance, whereas if $\beta < 1$ P is more important than Q.

3.2 G-score or Geometric Mean

Instead of using the harmonic mean, we could also use the geometric mean as follows:

$$G_{\alpha_1,\alpha_2}(P,Q) = (P^{\alpha_1}\cdot Q^{\alpha_2})^{1/(\alpha_1+\alpha_2)} \quad (3)$$

where α_1, α_2 control the importance of each metric. In general, the result obtained for the G-score will always be larger (or equal) to the one obtained for the F-score.

3.3 Correctness

The two metrics defined in the previous sections simply combine the result of some evaluation measures; however we believe this is not enough for the problem we want to address. Typical ranking-based metrics – such as precision – assume that no returning an item which was previously asked to predict a rating for, is an advocate of that item being considered as not relevant by a specific recommendation method. However, this is in contrast with the (desired) situation that a recommender may not provide suggestions in some situations due to a low confidence in the accuracy of such predictions [3, 5].

We propose an evaluation metric that is able to assess when a recommender decides not to recommend a specific item. To do this, we adapt an extension of accuracy proposed in the context of Question Answering by Peñas and Rodrigo in [10]. In that work, the authors assume that there are several questions to be answered by a system, each question has several options, but one (and only one) of those options is correct. If it is possible to give no response for a given question, this action should not be correct, but not incorrect either. Hence, the authors propose a general formulation giving a weight – proportional to the number of correctly answered questions – to the value of unanswered questions.

To apply this evaluation metric to recommendation, we first assume that the set of recommenders we want to compare will receive the same list of items to be ranked, a standard situation shared by many evaluation methodologies [2]. Then, the equivalence between a Question Answering system and a recommender is made – in a user basis – by considering each recommendation algorithm as a different system that will answer (or not) to the questions available, represented as the candidate items to be ranked by a specific methodology. We instantiate four versions of this metric, two of them based on users and two for items:

$$\text{User Correctness}(u, r, N) = \frac{1}{N}\left(TP(u) + TP(u)\frac{NR(u)}{N}\right) \quad (4)$$

$$\text{Recall User Correctness}(u, r, N) = \frac{1}{N}\left(TP(u) + \frac{TP(u)}{|T(u)|}NR(u)\right) \quad (5)$$

$$\text{Item Correctness}(i, r, N) = \frac{1}{|U|}\left(TP(i) + \frac{TP(i)}{|U|}NR(i)\right) \quad (6)$$

$$\text{Recall Item Correctness}(i, r, N) = \frac{1}{|U|}\left(TP(i) + \frac{TP(i)}{|T(i)|}NR(i)\right) \quad (7)$$

where N is the amount of items requested to the recommender r, $TP(u)$ denotes the relevant items recommended to the user, $FP(u)$ the not relevant items being recommended, which combined gives $|T(u)| = TP(u) + FP(u)$; finally, $NR(u) = N - (TP(u) + FP(u))$ denotes the number of unanswered recommendations. The analogous quantities could be defined for the item-based version of the metrics.

4 EXPERIMENTS AND RESULTS

4.1 Experimental Settings

In this paper we have used three datasets from two different domains: two versions of the MovieLens (ML)[1] (ML-100K and ML-1M) dataset and Jester[2]. ML-100K includes 100,000 ratings by 943 users on 1,681 items (movies), ML-1M contains 1,000,209 ratings by 6,040 users on 3,883 movies, and Jester includes 1,710,677 ratings on 150 items (jokes) by 59,132 users. The rating scale on the first two datasets is [1, 5], and on Jester is [−10, 10] (that we moved into [0, 20] to avoid negative ratings).

Some of the algorithms used in the experiments are based on implementations found in RankSys [13], specifically, the nearest-neighbour algorithms and their modifications. The probabilistic matrix factorisation method was implemented by ourselves.

Finally, regarding the evaluation, two publicly available frameworks were used: RankSys and RiVal [11]. On top of the latter framework we implemented the following evaluation metrics: User Space Coverage representing the ratio of users that have received at least one (*USC*) or N (*USC@N*) items as recommendations, Item Space Coverage representing the ratio of items that were recommended to any user by a system returning at most N items (*ISC@N*), and the Correctness metrics as defined in Section 3.3: *UC@N* (User Correctness), *RUC@N* (Recall User Correctness), *IC@N* (Item Correctness) and *RIC@N* (Recall Item Correctness). The RankSys framework was used to obtain novelty and diversity metrics, specifically EPC and AggrDiv [14].

[1] Availlable at https://grouplens.org/datasets/movielens/
[2] Available at http://eigentaste.berkeley.edu/dataset/

4.2 Performance of decision-aware strategies

In this section we evaluate the performance of the different decision-aware strategies presented in Section 2 using the evaluation metrics described in Section 3. When we apply the strategy based on prediction support, the change in coverage is not significant, even though the performance increases slightly; hence, there is no balance to solve, and the algorithm with the highest precision is the clear winner – see in Table 1 the results for ML-100K. User coverage remains almost unchanged until $n \geq 7$, although precision increases even for smaller values of n until $n = 7$. Considering this information, the three versions of the harmonic mean, G, and $G_{2,1}$ all agree on the ranking of the systems, where the best algorithms are those with n equals 5, 6, and 4, in that order. We observe that *UC* and *RUC* do not discriminate much more than that, however, when *IC* and *RIC* are analysed, the best recommenders are not the same as before ($n = 4, 5$) which makes sense because these techniques take the item coverage into account, which decreases more abruptly than the user coverage. Similarly, $G_{1,2}$ also changes the ranking of systems because it gives a higher weight to coverage than precision.

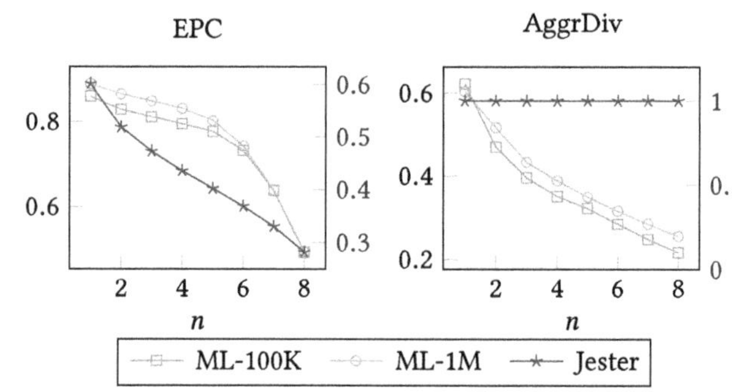

Figure 1: Novelty and diversity metrics at cutoff 10 for a decision-aware strategy based on prediction support. Jester is plotted in the secondary (right) axis.

Figure 1 shows the impact that a decision-aware strategy based on prediction support has on novelty and diversity. We observe that, for larger n, both the diversity and novelty of the lists decrease (which means that the recommended items are more and more popular), except for the Jester dataset. The rationale behind these results is that, when the constraint n becomes more strict, more users are required to have seen (rated) those items, which, in the long term, produces that more popular items are being recommended. This behaviour is consistent for the three analysed datasets.

Now we analyse the decision-aware strategy based on prediction uncertainty. As we show in Table 2, this strategy evidences a strong tradeoff between coverage and precision, since introducing a threshold of 0.82 increases the performance by a factor of 4 but reduces the coverage a 70% with respect to no threshold. This situation is very interesting, because the optimal recommender depends on the evaluation metric: for instance, $\sigma_\tau = 0.84$ obtains the highest value for F_1 and $G_{2,1}$ but not in the other metrics, this is because they are too sensitive to the precision value, since that recommender achieves the second best value. This example evidences the differences between the proposed correctness metrics and the other combination metrics: whereas the latter simply combine two values, the former include further assumptions that, in principle, helps to interpret the comparison between recommenders. Following the previous example, $\sigma_\tau = 0.84$ is preferred over $\sigma_\tau = 0.86$ by F_1, but *UC* inverts this relation; we can infer that $\sigma_\tau = 0.86$ is better suited for deciding when an item should be recommended, since

Table 1: Comparison of performance metrics at cutoff 10 when using a decision-aware strategy based on prediction support, for a nearest-neighbour recommender with $k = 10$ on ML-100K.

n	P	USC	ISC	F_1	F_2	$F_{0.5}$	$G_{1,1}$	$G_{1,2}$	$G_{2,1}$	UC	RUC	IC	RIC
1	0.037	**100.0**	**62.1**	0.070	0.159	0.045	0.191	0.332	0.110	0.037	0.037	0.000	0.015
2	0.133	100.0	46.9	0.234	0.433	0.160	0.364	0.510	0.260	0.133	0.133	0.002	0.021
3	0.188	100.0	39.5	0.317	0.537	0.225	0.434	0.573	0.329	0.189	0.189	0.002	0.026
4	0.230	100.0	35.1	0.374	0.599	0.272	0.480	0.613	0.376	0.234	0.236	0.003	0.029
5	**0.245**	99.7	32.3	**0.393**	**0.618**	**0.288**	**0.494**	**0.624**	**0.391**	**0.259**	**0.266**	**0.003**	**0.029**
6	0.241	96.4	28.5	0.386	0.603	0.284	0.482	0.607	0.383	0.257	0.263	0.003	0.026
7	0.237	85.9	24.8	0.371	0.563	0.277	0.451	0.559	0.364	0.231	0.231	0.002	0.023
8	0.226	66.9	21.7	0.338	0.480	0.260	0.389	0.466	0.324	0.180	0.171	0.002	0.018

Table 2: Comparison of performance metrics at cutoff 10 when using a decision-aware strategy based on prediction uncertainty, for a probabilistic matrix factorisation algorithm on ML-100K.

σ_τ	P	USC	ISC	F_1	F_2	$F_{0.5}$	$G_{1,1}$	$G_{1,2}$	$G_{2,1}$	UC	RUC	IC	RIC
–	0.093	**100.0**	22.7	0.170	0.338	0.113	0.304	0.453	0.205	0.093	0.093	0.001	0.009
0.82	**0.326**	28.2	9.1	0.303	0.290	**0.316**	0.303	0.296	0.311	0.100	0.094	0.001	0.006
0.84	0.283	59.0	15.1	**0.382**	0.484	0.316	0.408	0.462	**0.361**	0.174	0.170	0.002	0.011
0.86	0.214	80.9	19.6	0.338	**0.520**	0.251	**0.416**	0.519	0.333	**0.177**	**0.176**	**0.002**	0.012
0.88	0.181	95.6	22.2	0.304	0.514	0.216	0.415	**0.548**	0.315	0.176	0.176	0.002	**0.013**
0.90	0.165	99.5	24.8	0.283	0.495	0.198	0.405	0.546	0.300	0.165	0.165	0.002	0.013
0.92	0.156	100.0	26.0	0.269	0.480	0.187	0.395	0.538	0.289	0.156	0.156	0.002	0.012
0.94	0.145	100.0	27.3	0.254	0.459	0.175	0.381	0.526	0.276	0.145	0.145	0.002	0.011
0.96	0.139	100.0	28.2	0.245	0.447	0.168	0.373	0.518	0.269	0.139	0.139	0.002	0.011
0.98	0.133	100.0	**28.6**	0.235	0.435	0.161	0.365	0.511	0.261	0.133	0.133	0.002	0.011

we are rewarding unanswered recommendations above incorrect recommendations.

Finally, Figure 2 compares novelty and diversity evolution for different thresholds using a decision-aware strategy based on prediction uncertainty. We observe the same result as in the previous strategy (Figure 1): when the constraints are more strict (σ_τ decreases) both novelty and diversity decrease in the three tested datasets. In this case the rationale is slightly different to what happened before: those items with a lower standard deviation seem to correspond with popular items (like before), however, this constraint really imposes a limit on the number of different items that can be recommended, which ends up producing very low diversity scores.

5 CONCLUSIONS AND FUTURE WORK

In this work we have studied how to increase the user confidence on the system by making the system aware of the decisions taken. For this, we have proposed two strategies to decide if an item should be included in a recommendation list of a specific user, based on the consistency and reliability of the data that will be used by the recommender system to estimate the preferences. These strategies (one based on the support of the prediction and another on its uncertainty) have been evaluated in terms of precision, coverage, novelty, and diversity. We have shown that a balance between these evaluation dimensions – especially between precision and coverage – is critical, and different metrics have been studied to draw conclusions from them.

As a first step towards improving the understanding of this trade-off, we have proposed a family of metrics (correctness) based on the assumption that it is better to avoid a recommendation rather than providing a bad recommendation. However, further analysis is needed in the future, especially to find an objective way to discriminate between these systems and decide which of these metrics correlates better with the user satisfaction. We also aim at extending the correctness family of metrics so that other evaluation dimensions could be combined under the same framework: diversity, novelty, or even other accuracy metrics like nDCG. Additionally, the psychological aspect of the recommendations should also be considered, since if a user expects to receive N recommendations, she may decrease her confidence in the system if less than N recommendations are presented. Moreover, we aim at validating these results in an online setting with real users, in particular, how users value incorrect recommendations in comparison with unanswered/missing recommendations.

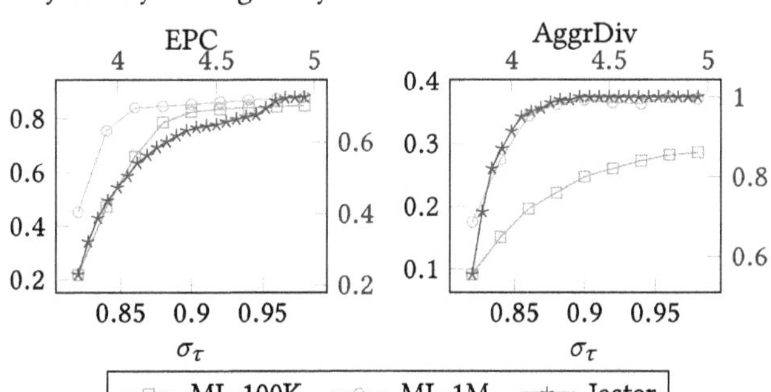

Figure 2: Novelty and diversity metrics at cutoff 10 for a decision-aware strategy based on prediction uncertainty. Jester is plotted in the secondary (right and upper) axis.

Acknowledgments

This work was funded by the national Spanish Government under project TIN2016-80630-P.

REFERENCES

[1] Gediminas Adomavicius, Sreeharsha Kamireddy, and Youngok Kwon. 2007. *Towards more confident recommendations: Improving recommender systems using filtering approach based on rating variance.* Social Science Research Network, 152–157.

[2] Alejandro Bellogin, Pablo Castells, and Ivan Cantador. 2011. Precision-oriented evaluation of recommender systems: an algorithmic comparison. In *Proceedings of the fifth ACM conference on Recommender systems.* ACM, 333–336.

[3] Asela Gunawardana and Guy Shani. 2015. Evaluating Recommender Systems. In *Recommender Systems Handbook.* Springer, 265–308.

[4] Jonathan L. Herlocker, Joseph A. Konstan, and John Riedl. 2002. An Empirical Analysis of Design Choices in Neighborhood-Based Collaborative Filtering Algorithms. *Inf. Retr.* 5, 4 (2002), 287–310.

[5] Jonathan L. Herlocker, Joseph A. Konstan, Loren G. Terveen, and John Riedl. 2004. Evaluating collaborative filtering recommender systems. *ACM Trans. Inf. Syst.* 22, 1 (2004), 5–53. DOI:http://dx.doi.org/10.1145/963770.963772

[6] Yifan Hu, Yehuda Koren, and Chris Volinsky. 2008. Collaborative Filtering for Implicit Feedback Datasets. In *ICDM.* IEEE Computer Society, 263–272.

[7] Yew Jin Lim and Yee Whye Teh. 2007. Variational Bayesian approach to movie rating prediction. In *Proceedings of KDD cup and workshop,* Vol. 7. Citeseer, 15–21.

[8] Sean M. McNee, Shyong K. Lam, Catherine Guetzlaff, Joseph A. Konstan, and John Riedl. 2003. Confidence Displays and Training in Recommender Systems. In *INTERACT.* IOS Press.

[9] John O'Donovan and Barry Smyth. 2005. Trust in recommender systems. In *IUI.* ACM, 167–174.

[10] Anselmo Peñas and Álvaro Rodrigo. 2011. A Simple Measure to Assess Non-response. In *The 49th Annual Meeting of the Association for Computational Linguistics: Human Language Technologies, Proceedings of the Conference, 19-24 June, 2011, Portland, Oregon, USA,* Dekang Lin, Yuji Matsumoto, and Rada Mihalcea (Eds.). The Association for Computer Linguistics, 1415–1424. http://www.aclweb.org/anthology/P11-1142

[11] Alan Said and Alejandro Bellogín. 2014. Rival: a toolkit to foster reproducibility in recommender system evaluation. In *RecSys.* ACM, 371–372.

[12] Barry Smyth, David C. Wilson, and Derry O'Sullivan. 2002. Data Mining Support for Case-Based Collaborative Recommendation. In *AICS (Lecture Notes in Computer Science),* Vol. 2464. Springer, 111–118.

[13] Saúl Vargas. 2015. *Novelty and diversity enhancement and evaluation in Recommender Systems.* Ph.D. Dissertation. Universidad Autónoma de Madrid.

[14] Saúl Vargas and Pablo Castells. 2011. Rank and relevance in novelty and diversity metrics for recommender systems. In *Proceedings of the fifth ACM conference on Recommender systems.* ACM, 109–116.

Using Explainability for Constrained Matrix Factorization

Behnoush Abdollahi
Knowledge Discovery and Web Mining Lab, CECS Department, University of Louisville
Louisville, KY 40292
b.abdollahi@louisville.edu

Olfa Nasraoui
Knowledge Discovery and Web Mining Lab, CECS Department, University of Louisville
Louisville, KY 40292
olfa.nasraoui@louisville.edu

ABSTRACT

Accurate model-based Collaborative Filtering (CF) approaches, such as Matrix Factorization (MF), tend to be black-box machine learning models that lack interpretability and do not provide a straightforward explanation for their outputs. Yet explanations have been shown to improve the transparency of a recommender system by justifying recommendations, and this in turn can enhance the user's trust in the recommendations. Hence, one main challenge in designing a recommender system is mitigating the trade-off between an explainable technique with moderate prediction accuracy and a more accurate technique with no explainable recommendations. In this paper, we focus on factorization models and further assume the absence of any additional data source, such as item content or user attributes. We propose an explainability constrained MF technique that computes the top-n recommendation list from items that are explainable. Experimental results show that our method is effective in generating accurate and explainable recommendations.

1 INTRODUCTION

Machine learning (ML) models are being increasingly used in many sectors, ranging from health and education to e-commerce and criminal investigation. Hence, these algorithmic models are starting to affect the lives of more and more human beings. Examples include risk modeling and decision making in insurance, education (admission and success prediction), credit scoring, healthcare, criminal investigation and predicting recidivism, etc. These models are susceptible to bias that stems from the data itself (attribute or labels are biased) or from systemic social biases that generated the data (e.g. recidivism, arrests). As such, models that are learned from real world data can become unethical if their outputs discriminate, albeit unintentionally, against a certain group of people. While building ethical and fair models seems like the ultimate and ideal goal, the minimum and urgent criterion, that ML models should satisfy, is transparency, and this could be the first step in the direction toward fair and ethical models. Therefore, designing explainable intelligent systems, that facilitate conveying the reasoning behind the results, is of great importance.

When the machine learning model is used in a recommender system, it has been shown that explanations can help users make more accurate decisions; hence, improving user satisfaction and acceptance of recommendations [4, 9, 17]. CF recommender systems provide recommendations to users based on the rating-based similarity between users or items, giving rise to neighborhood-based CF approaches, which can be user-based or item-based. MF methods are accurate CF approaches that map users and items to low-dimensional feature vectors [12]. In most MF-based techniques, predictions are not interpretable and cannot be justified to the user as easily as in neighborhood-based CF methods. One way to communicate explanations would be based on identifying similar users and/or items in the latent space and presenting the most similar users and/or items as the explanation. The drawback of this method is that the way the explanation is generated does not necessarily comply with the learned ML model. This is because the solution to the MF optimization problem does not guarantee that the most similar users to an active user, who have liked the system's suggestion, are necessarily the active user's neighbors in the latent space. It would be very desirable and beneficial to design recommender systems that can give accurate suggestions, which, at the same time, facilitate conveying the reasoning behind the recommendations to the user. However, a main challenge in designing a recommender system is whether to choose an explainable technique with moderate prediction accuracy or a more accurate technique (such as MF) which does not give explainable recommendations.

Our research question is: can we design a Matrix Factorization model for a CF recommender engine that suggests items that are explainable, while recommendations remain accurate? Our current scope is limited to CF recommendations where explanations for recommended items can be generated from the ratings given to these items, by the active user's neighbors or the ratings given by the active user to other items that are similar to the recommended item (known, respectively, as user and item-based neighbor style explanation), as shown in Figure 1.

This article's contribution is a probabilistic formulation that extends our previous Explainable-Matrix Factorization (EMF) model [1], for providing explainable recommendations that can leverage the accurate predictions of MF and the transparency of neighborhood-based CF algorithms. In our method, explainability can be directly formulated based on the rating distribution within the user's or item's neighborhood. If many neighbors have rated the recommended item, or if the user has rated many items that are similar to the recommended item, then this provides a basis upon which to explain the recommendations. We encode the user-item explainability relationship in a graph. While other methods in the literature have used graph structures to find a better representation of data points in lower spaces, we further incorporate the explainability graph in the design of the MF model to be able to generate *explainable* recommendations.

RecSys '17, August 27–31, 2017, Como, Italy.

DOI: http://dx.doi.org/10.1145/3109859.3109913

2 RELATED WORK

There are different ways of classifying explanation styles. Generally neighbor style explanations can be User-Based Neighbor Style Explanation or Item-Based Neighbor Style, also known as Influence Style Explanation [4]. A user-based neighbor-style explanation is based on similar users, and generally is used when the CF method is also a user-based neighborhood style method. An item-based neighbor-style explanation is generally used in item-based CF methods by presenting the items that had the highest impact on the recommender system's decision [3]. In all styles, the data sources employed in the recommendation task, may be different from the data sources used in generating the explanation [4, 5, 9, 18], leading to explanation generation modules that are separate from the recommender system. However, performing the recommendation task based on the items' explainability (thus *integrating* recommendation and explanation) may improve transparency by suggesting interpretable items to the user, while enjoying the powerful prediction of a model-based CF approach. Zhang et al. [19] proposed a model-based CF to generate explainable recommendations based on item features and sentiment analysis of user reviews, as data sources, in addition to the ratings data. Their approach is similar to our method in that the recommendation and explanation modules are *not* separate. In contrast, our approach does *not* require additional reviews for explanation generation. Vig et al. [18] proposed a content-based explanation approach for a CF recommender system, where explanations are generated from community tags, a form of content-based explanation. Herlocker et al. [9] proposed 21 different explanation interfaces for user-based nearest neighbor CF. Gedikli et al. [6] used the same user-based approach as their base recommender system module and compared 10 different existing explanation types and their impact on the perceived level of transparency and hence the satisfaction of the user. Billsus and Pazzani [5] presented a keyword style and influence style explanation approach for their news recommendation system. Recently, Abdollahi and Nasraoui [2] presented an explainable CF approach using Restricted Boltzmann Machines (RBM).

3 PROPOSED METHOD

3.1 Explainability

In neighbor style explanations, the explanation is either *user-based*, i.e. based on the ratings given by similar users to the recommended item, or item-based, i.e. based on ratings given by the active user to similar items, as shown in Figure 1.

For user-based neighbor style explanation, if we divide the counts for each rating value by the total counts, we will obtain the empirical density distribution of the similar users' ratings on the recommended item i. Equivalently, this is the empirical conditional probability of ratings of item i, given the set of similar users for user u, denoted as N_u. For each rating value k in the set of ratings, κ, we can write this probability as:

$$\Pr(r_{v,i} = k | v \in N_u) = \frac{|N_u \cap U_{i,k}|}{|N_u|} \quad (1)$$

where $r_{v,i}$ is the rating of user v to item i and $U_{i,k}$ is the set of users who have given rating k to item i. Using Eq. 1, for each explanation we can calculate the expected value of the ratings given by the similar users to the recommended item i as follows:

$$\mathrm{E}(r_{v,i}|N_u) = \sum_{k \in \kappa} k \times \Pr(r_{v,i} = k | v \in N_u). \quad (2)$$

Your ratings for similar movies

Movie	Your Rating out of 5
L.A. Confidential	4
Air Force One	5
The Game	5
12 Angry Men	3
Carrie	4

Your neighbors' ratings for this movie

Rating	Number of Neighbors
☆	0
☆☆	0
☆☆☆	3
☆☆☆☆	4
☆☆☆☆☆	2

Figure 1: Examples of user-based neighbor style explanation (left), and item-based neighbor style explanation (right).

Similarly, for the item-based neighbor style explanation, the ratings of user u on items that are similar to the recommended item can be used to obtain the empirical conditional probability of user u's ratings on item i. Given the set of similar items to item i, denoted as N_i, we can write this probability as:

$$\Pr(r_{u,j} = k | j \in N_i) = \frac{|N_i \cap I_{u,k}|}{|N_i|} \quad (3)$$

where $I_{u,k}$ is the set of items that were given rating k by user u. Using Eq. 3, the expected value for item-based explanation can be calculated as follows:

$$\mathrm{E}(r_{u,j}|N_i) = \sum_{k \in \kappa} k \times p(r_{u,j} = k | j \in N_i). \quad (4)$$

The expected rating of similar users or similar items gives a reasonable and intuitive measure of goodness or strength of a neighbor style explanation. We furthermore incorporate this value as a soft constraint in a modified cost function whose optimization will favor discovering latent factors that result in recommending items that have higher value for this expected value.

3.2 Explainability Graph

Given a set of users U, a set of items I, and a set of ratings r_{ui} given by user u to item i, we capture the explainability of an item relative to a user in a bipartite graph $G = (V, E)$, with the set of vertices $V = U \cup I$, and the set of edges E from the user nodes $u \in U$ to the item nodes $i \in I$, $E = \{e_{ui} | u \in U, i \in I\}$. The edge weights in the explainability graph are stored in matrix W which represents the explainabilty of the items to the users. Ideally, the edge weights should be higher for items *that can be easily explained* and low in the opposite case. We will try to capture this mutual explainability between an item and a user in an explainability score, $Expl_{u,i}$, which can be either $\mathrm{E}(r_{v,i}|N_u)$ or $\mathrm{E}(r_{u,j}|N_i)$, depending on the particular rationale that is chosen for the explanations. We thus define the *Explainability Matrix*, W, between user-item pairs in the Explainability graph, as follows:

$$W_{u,i} = \begin{cases} Expl_{u,i} & if\ Expl_{u,i} \geq \theta \\ 0 & otherwise \end{cases} \quad (5)$$

where θ denotes a threshold above which we accept item i to be explainable for user u. $W_{u,i}$ thus measures the explainability of item i for user u.

3.3 Explainable-MF

MF is a family of latent factor models that have been used with success in CF recommender system [12]. Using MF, a data matrix,

R, is factored into two lower-rank approximated matrices P and Q, in a joint latent space of dimensionality, f, that is much lower than the typically large number of users or items: $R_{n \times m} \simeq P_{n \times f} Q^T_{f \times m}$. MF algorithms learn the factors $p_u \in \mathbb{R}^f$ and $q_i \in \mathbb{R}^f$, which are the lower-rank representations of user u and item i in dimensionality f [12]. Given the MF definition and the explainability matrix W, we propose an explainable MF, which jointly learns user u and item i's latent vectors, given by p_u and q_i respectively, using as input, the explicit or implicit user interests (ratings or clicks) on the items, as in standard MF models, and using as an additional input, the explainability scores of the items as an additional soft constraint on the reconstruction loss from factorization as input:

$$J = \sum_{u,i \in R} (r_{u,i} - p_u q_i^T)^2 + \frac{\beta}{2}(\| p_u \|^2 + \| q_i \|^2) + \frac{\lambda}{2} \| p_u - q_i \|^2 W_{u,i} \tag{6}$$

where R is the set of user-item pairs for which the ratings are available, $\frac{1}{2}(||p_u||^2 + ||q_i||^2)$ is an $L2$ regularization term weighted by the coefficient β, and λ is an explainability regularization coefficient that controls the smoothness of the new representation and tradeoff between explainability and accuracy. The idea here is that if item i is explainable for user u, meaning $W_{u,i} > \theta$, then their representations in the latent domain should be close to each other ($p_u - q_i$ is close to zero), in order for the objective function to be minimized. Note that the first error term prevents p_u and q_i from vanishing to zero at the same time.

To minimize the objective function, we use stochastic gradient descent, which has been used successfully to solve MF for CF with big data sets [11, 13, 16]. For a given training instance r_{ij}, the updates for $p_u^{(t+1)}$ and $q_i^{(t+1)}$ can be shown to be:

$$\begin{aligned} p_u^{(t+1)} &\leftarrow p_u^{(t)} + \alpha(2(r_{u,i} - p_u q_i^T)q_i - \beta p_u - \lambda(p_u - q_i)W_{u,i}) \\ q_i^{(t+1)} &\leftarrow q_i^{(t)} + \alpha(2(r_{u,i} - p_u q_i^T)p_u - \beta q_i + \lambda(p_u - q_i)W_{u,i}) \end{aligned} \tag{7}$$

where α is the step size. With a proper choice of step size, gradient descent converges to a local minimum.

3.4 Explainability Effect in the Latent Space

The Explainability term used in the objective function J, encourages items, that have higher explainability relative to a user, to be projected close to that user in the latent space, while keeping the rating prediction error small. This can be illustrated for the simple case of two factors with an example. Figure 2 shows a test user, along with all the items, projected in a 2D latent space, learned using both EMF and the standard MF that excludes the explainability constraint. A sample user is shown as one point in black. The items shown in green, are items in the latent space, that have a cosine similarity with the user exceeding 0.7. Red items are explainable items, i.e. they have normalized explainability value larger than 0.7, as calculated using Eq. 2, when $|N_u| = 20$. Both EMF and MF techniques have predicted a sufficient set of relevant items for recommendation. However, the main difference is in the factors learned for the explainable items, shown in red. Using EMF, these explainable (red) items are projected such that they are close and relevant to the user, without decreasing recommendation accuracy. However, using standard MF, the red points are spread throughout the entire latent space, making them less favorable to be recommended.

4 EXPERIMENTAL EVALUATION

We tested our approach on the benchmark MovieLens [7] data which consists of 100, 000 ratings, on a scale of 1 to 5. The data is first split into training and test sets such that 10% of the latest ratings from each user are selected for the test set and the remaining 90% of the ratings are used in the training set. Results are reported over the test ratings.

We compare our results with four CF baseline methods that are most related to our approach: A standard latent factor model— Matrix Factorization

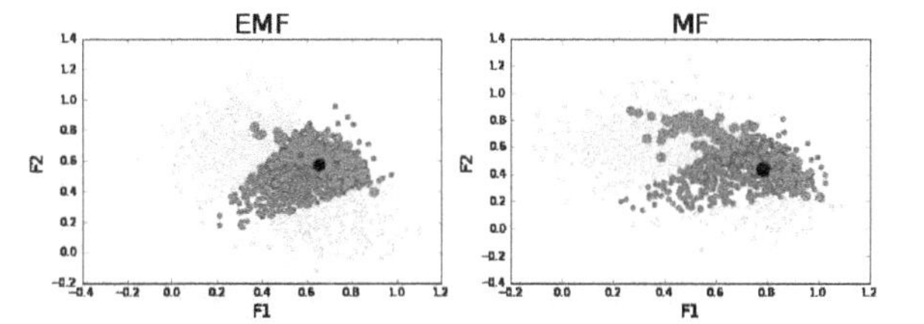

Figure 2: Explainable items (red) and potential recommendations (green) for a sample user (black), along with all the other items (cyan). All are represented in a 2D latent space (f = 2 for visualization purposes). Unlike standard MF, EMF succeeded to learn *explainable* latent item factors among the relevant items for recommendation.

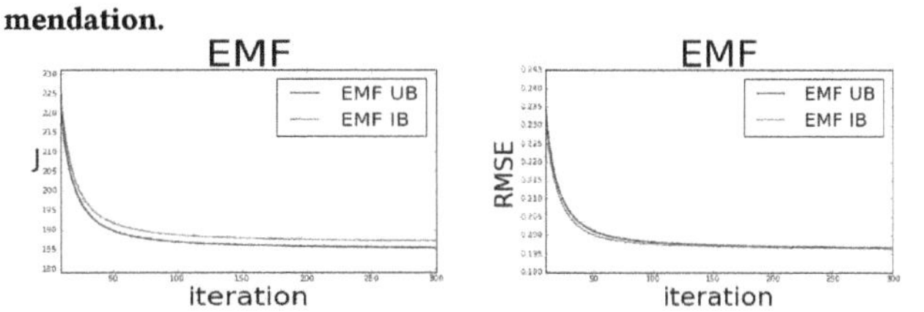

Figure 3: Objective function, J, calculated over the training data in each iteration decreases monotonically (left). RMSE calculated over the test data also decreases in each iteration (right). The setting for this experiment is as follows: $f = 5$, $|N_.| = 20$, $\theta = 0.1$, $\alpha = 0.001$, $\beta = 0.01$, and $\lambda = 0.005$.

(MF) [12], Probabilistic Matrix Factorization (PMF) [14], User-Based (UB) top-n CF [8], and Item-Based (IB) top-n CF [15]. We perform the comparison between our approach and the baselines in terms of top-n recommendation list. Therefore, for the MF-based techniques, the top-n recommendation list for each user is generated by selecting the top-n items with highest dot product between the user and the items' representations in the latent space. Standard UB and IB techniques are the state of the art top-n CF techniques that do not require content data. We use cosine similarity to find the similar users/items when generating W. Ratings are normalized between 0 and 1 and parameters are tuned using cross-validation. Figure 3 shows how the objective function, J, and the Root Mean Square Error (RMSE) decrease in each iteration, eventually converging to the optimal solution.

4.1 Recommender System Evaluation

To evaluate the top-n recommendation results, we use two of the most common top-n metrics: Mean Average Precision (MAP) and Area Under Curve (AUC) at different top-n cutoffs. Table 1 shows the MAP and AUC results when varying the number of factors, f, and also the neighborhood size around users or items, hence collectively denoting this size as $|N_.|$. Other parameters are found using cross-validation: $\alpha = 0.001$, $\beta = 0.01$, $\theta = 0.1$, $\lambda = 0.005$. Both CF techniques, UB and IB, have lower MAP and AUC values compared to other techniques, when varying f. This is because memory based approaches tend to have lower accuracy due to considering only local samples and no latent factors for generating recommendation lists. When increasing f, EMF_{UB} outperforms other approaches. For $f = 5$, MF outperforms both EMF methods. This can be attributed to the impact of the explainability constraint on the learned hidden factors that result in a decrease in accuracy for small f. When varying $|N_.|$, EMF_{IB} outperforms other techniques in most cases, except for $|N_.| = 5$. This is because for small neighborhood size, explainability scores will be very small and the constraint will not have a sufficient impact on the accuracy.

4.2 Explainability Evaluation

To further assess the quality of the proposed approach, it is important to compare the results with other approaches in terms of the explainability

Table 1: Top row: comparison of accuracy when varying f. For EMF_{UB} and EMF_{IB} we set $|N_.| = 50$. Bottom row: comparison of accuracy when varying the number of neighbors. For EMF_{UB}, EMF_{IB}, PMF, and MF we set $f = 10$.

MAP@50						
f	UB	IB	PMF	MF	EMF_{UB}	EMF_{IB}
5	0.009	0.0064	0.0113	0.0149*	0.0108	0.011
10	0.009	0.0064	0.0108	0.0145	0.0157*	0.0112
20	0.009	0.0064	0.0116	0.0143	0.0146*	0.0118
50	0.009	0.0064	0.0126	0.015	0.0165*	0.0138
$\|N_.\|$	UB	IB	PMF	MF	EMF_{UB}	EMF_{IB}
5	0.009	0.0065	0.0108	0.0145*	0.0102	0.0138
10	0.0087	0.0064	0.0108	0.0145	0.0101	0.0197*
20	0.0085	0.0071	0.0108	0.0145	0.009	0.0272*
50	0.0081	0.0077	0.0108	0.0145	0.0105	0.0328*

AUC						
f	UB	IB	PMF	MF	EMF_{UB}	EMF_{IB}
5	0.4988	0.4982	0.5743	0.7129*	0.5616	0.5745
10	0.4988	0.4982	0.5629	0.7033	0.7115*	0.5791
20	0.4988	0.4982	0.563	0.6843	0.6873*	0.5791
50	0.4988	0.4982	0.54	0.5697	0.5984*	0.5019
$\|N_.\|$	UB	IB	PMF	MF	EMF_{UB}	EMF_{IB}
5	0.4759	0.4711	0.563	0.7011	0.7131	0.7707*
10	0.4851	0.4835	0.563	0.7011	0.6787	0.7821*
20	0.489	0.4826	0.563	0.7011	0.6522	0.7872*
50	0.4905	0.4991	0.563	0.7011	0.6855	0.7463*

Table 2: Top row: comparison of accuracy when varying f. For EMF_{UB} and EMF_{IB} we set $|N_.| = 50$. Bottom row: comparison of explainability metrics when varying number of neighbors. For EMF_{UB}, EMF_{IB}, PMF, and MF we set $f = 10$.

MEP@50						
f	UB	IB	PMF	MF	EMF_{UB}	EMF_{IB}
5	0.449	0.551	0.6284	0.7079	0.7080	0.7090*
10	0.449	0.551	0.5412	0.7085	0.7089*	0.7187
20	0.449	0.551	0.3617	0.7187	0.7224	0.7242*
50	0.449	0.551	0.0843	0.5502	0.5845*	0.4011
$\|N_.\|$	UB	IB	PMF	MF	EMF_{UB}	EMF_{IB}
5	0.4831	0.5895	0.5412	0.708	0.7081*	0.708
10	0.4489	0.5516	0.5412	0.708	0.7083	0.7099*
20	0.4195	0.5423	0.5412	0.708	0.7082	0.7087*
50	0.4124	0.5416	0.5412	0.708	0.7083	0.7096*

MER@50						
f	UB	IB	PMF	MF	EMF_{UB}	EMF_{IB}
5	0.054	0.07	0.0706	0.0756	0.0757*	0.073
10	0.054	0.07	0.0622	0.0757	0.0758*	0.0748
20	0.054	0.07	0.0399	0.0778	0.0785*	0.0755
50	0.054	0.07	0.0085	0.0564	0.0569*	0.0362
$\|N_.\|$	UB	IB	PMF	MF	EMF_{UB}	EMF_{IB}
5	0.0583	0.0708	0.062	0.075	0.0756*	0.0729
10	0.0534	0.0701	0.062	0.075	0.0757*	0.0732
20	0.0496	0.0668	0.062	0.075	0.0756*	0.073
50	0.0485	0.0652	0.062	0.075	0.0757*	0.0731

Table 3: varying θ

	EMF_{UB}				EMF_{IB}			
θ	MAP	AUC	MEP	MER	MAP	AUC	MEP	MER
0.2	0.0113	0.5976	0.3287	0.2448	0.0119	0.6027	0.3074	0.0941
0.4	0.0118	0.6156	0.1714	0.2018	0.0111	0.6257	0.1437	0.082
0.6	0.0115	0.6128	0.0713	0.2001	0.0097	0.5574	0.0433	0.0569
1	0.0117	0.6373	0	0	0.0104	0.5831	0	0
Avg.	0.0115	0.6158	0.1429	0.1614	0.0107	0.5922	0.1236	0.0582

of those items that are actually recommended. Note that in this work, we are not proposing a new explanation format that requires user evaluation. However, we can evaluate the top-n recommendations in terms of the explainability of the suggested list. We measure explainability using the MEP and MER metrics [1]. In top-n recommendation, *Explainability Precision (EP)* is defined as the proportion of explainable items in the top-n recommendation list relative to the number of recommended (top-n) items for each user. Similar to the recall metric, *Explainability Recall (ER)* is the proportion of explainable items in the top-n recommendation list relative to the number of *all* explainable items for a given user. In our experiments, EP and ER are calculated using $\theta = 0.01$. Mean EP (MEP) and Mean ER (MER) are reported in Table 2, which are the average values of EP and ER over all users. EMF_{UB} or EMF_{IB} outperform other approaches in terms of MEP, when varying f or $|N_.|$. EMF_{UB} outperforms other techniques in terms of MER, when varying f or $|N_.|$. EMF_{UB} and EMF_{IB} have low MEP and MER results for $f = 50$. This shows that for large f, explainability constraint has counter effect on MEP and MER results. When varying $|N_.|$, EMF_{UB} has higher MER, but lower MEP compared to EMF_{IB} for $|N_.| >= 10$.

To study the effect of the threshold, θ, on the explainability and top-n recommendation accuracy, we trained both EMF models when varying θ, while fixing all the other parameters (Table 3). For both techniques, MEP and MER reach the highest value when the threshold θ is small, and decrease by increasing θ. When $\theta = 1$, almost no user-based or item-based neighbor has high value. This is because users usually tend to rate a small set of items.

5 CONCLUSION

We presented a MF-based recommender system that can suggest items that are relevant and explainable, without any major sacrifice in recommendation accuracy. Our scope, in this work, is limited to CF recommendations where no additional source of data is used in recommendations or in explanations. Thus explainability can be directly formulated based on the rating distribution within the active user's neighborhood or the recommended item's neighborhood. Our rationale is that if many similar users (neighbors) have rated the recommended item, or if the user has rated many items that are similar to the recommended item, then this provides a basis upon which one can explain the recommendations.

We focused our research on CF recommender systems which have been shown to perform better than Content Based (CB) filtering methods [10]. We also focused on user-based or item-based neighbor style explanations and did not use any external data source, relying instead only the ratings. This contribution is important because using *no* external source is one of the main challenges for explainable *pure* CF recommender engines. This, in fact, is one of the main differences between our approach and other approaches in the literature. For this reason, these approaches are not comparable on a fair basis. In the future, we plan to extend our evaluation to include user-based testing and to expand our method to other explanation styles and other recommendation domains.

6 ACKNOWLEDGMENTS

This research was partially supported by KSEF Award KSEF-3113-RDE-017.

REFERENCES

[1] Abdollahi, B., and Nasraoui, O. Explainable matrix factorization for collaborative filtering. In *Proceedings of the 25th International Conference Companion on World Wide Web* (2016), International World Wide Web Conferences Steering Committee, pp. 5–6.

[2] Abdollahi, B., and Nasraoui, O. Explainable restricted boltzmann machines for collaborative filtering. *arXiv preprint arXiv:1606.07129* (2016).

[3] Bilgic, M. Explaining recommendations: Satisfaction vs. promotion. In *In Proceedings of Beyond Personalization 2005, the Workshop on the Next Stage of Recommender Systems Research(IUI2005* (2005), pp. 13–18.

[4] Bilgic, M., and Mooney, R. J. Explaining recommendations: Satisfaction vs. promotion. In *Beyond Personalization Workshop, IUI* (2005), vol. 5.

[5] Billsus, D., and Pazzani, M. J. A personal news agent that talks, learns and explains. In *Proceedings of the third annual conference on Autonomous Agents* (1999), ACM, pp. 268–275.

[6] Gedikli, F., Jannach, D., and Ge, M. How should i explain? a comparison of different explanation types for recommender systems. *International Journal of Human-Computer Studies 72*, 4 (2014), 367–382.

[7] Harper, F. M., and Konstan, J. A. The movielens datasets: History and context. *ACM Transactions on Interactive Intelligent Systems (TiiS) 5*, 4 (2016), 19.

[8] Herlocker, J. L., Konstan, J. A., Borchers, A., and Riedl, J. An algorithmic framework for performing collaborative filtering. In *Proceedings of the 22nd annual international ACM SIGIR conference on Research and development in information retrieval* (1999), ACM, pp. 230–237.

[9] Herlocker, J. L., Konstan, J. A., and Riedl, J. Explaining collaborative filtering recommendations. In *Proceedings of the 2000 ACM conference on Computer supported cooperative work* (2000), ACM, pp. 241–250.

[10] Herlocker, J. L., Konstan, J. A., Terveen, L. G., and Riedl, J. T. Evaluating collaborative filtering recommender systems. *ACM Transactions on Information Systems (TOIS) 22*, 1 (2004), 5–53.

[11] Koren, Y. Factorization meets the neighborhood: a multifaceted collaborative filtering model. In *Proceedings of the 14th ACM SIGKDD international conference on Knowledge discovery and data mining* (2008), ACM, pp. 426–434.

[12] Koren, Y., Bell, R., and Volinsky, C. Matrix factorization techniques for recommender systems. *Computer*, 8 (2009), 30–37.

[13] Paterek, A. Improving regularized singular value decomposition for collaborative filtering. In *Proceedings of KDD cup and workshop* (2007), vol. 2007, pp. 5–8.

[14] Salakhutdinov, R., and Mnih, A. Probabilistic matrix factorization. Citeseer.

[15] Sarwar, B., Karypis, G., Konstan, J., and Riedl, J. Item-based collaborative filtering recommendation algorithms. In *Proceedings of the 10th international conference on World Wide Web* (2001), ACM, pp. 285–295.

[16] Takács, G., Pilászy, I., Németh, B., and Tikk, D. Major components of the gravity recommendation system. *ACM SIGKDD Explorations Newsletter 9*, 2 (2007), 80–83.

[17] Tintarev, N., and Masthoff, J. Designing and evaluating explanations for recommender systems. In *Recommender Systems Handbook*. Springer, 2011, pp. 479–510.

[18] Vig, J., Sen, S., and Riedl, J. Tagsplanations: explaining recommendations using tags. In *Proceedings of the 14th international conference on Intelligent user interfaces* (2009), ACM, pp. 47–56.

[19] Zhang, Y., Lai, G., Zhang, M., Zhang, Y., Liu, Y., and Ma, S. Explicit factor models for explainable recommendation based on phrase-level sentiment analysis. In *Proceedings of the 37th international ACM SIGIR conference on Research & development in information retrieval* (2014), ACM, pp. 83–92.

User Preferences for Hybrid Explanations

Pigi Kouki
UC Santa Cruz
pkouki@soe.ucsc.edu

James Schaffer
U.S. Army Research Laboratory
james.a.schaffer.ctr20@mail.mil

Jay Pujara
UC Santa Cruz
jay@cs.umd.edu

John O'Donovan
UC Santa Barbara
jod@cs.ucsb.edu

Lise Getoor
UC Santa Cruz
getoor@soe.ucsc.edu

ABSTRACT

Hybrid recommender systems combine several different sources of information to generate recommendations. These systems demonstrate improved accuracy compared to single-source recommendation strategies. However, hybrid recommendation strategies are inherently more complex than those that use a single source of information, and thus the process of explaining recommendations to users becomes more challenging. In this paper we describe a hybrid recommender system built on a probabilistic programming language, and discuss the benefits and challenges of explaining its recommendations to users. We perform a mixed model statistical analysis of user preferences for explanations in this system. Through an online user survey, we evaluate explanations for hybrid algorithms in a variety of text and visual, graph-based formats, that are either novel designs or derived from existing hybrid recommender systems.

KEYWORDS

explanations, hybrid recommendations, hybrid explanations

1 INTRODUCTION

Successful recommender systems are integral to many applications ranging from movie recommendations to e-commerce. Effective recommendations must be both accurate and explainable [9, 10, 13, 16]. Hybrid recommender systems, which use a combination of signals such as social connections, item attributes, and user behavior, demonstrate improved recommendation accuracy [4]. However, compared to non-hybrid counterparts, hybrid models are more complex, and present many challenges when explaining recommendations to users. In this work, we study how to provide useful hybrid explanations that capture informative signals from a multitude of data sources without the burden of understanding the complex hybrid model.

Explanatory approaches for traditional, non-hybrid systems rely on a single explanation style (e.g., collaborative, content, knowledge, utility, or social explanation styles) [7]. Existing work has explored user preferences for these single-style explanations [2, 8].

RecSys'17, August 27–31, 2017, Como, Italy.

ISBN 978-1-4503-4652-8/17/08...$15.00.
DOI: http://dx.doi.org/10.1145/3109859.3109915

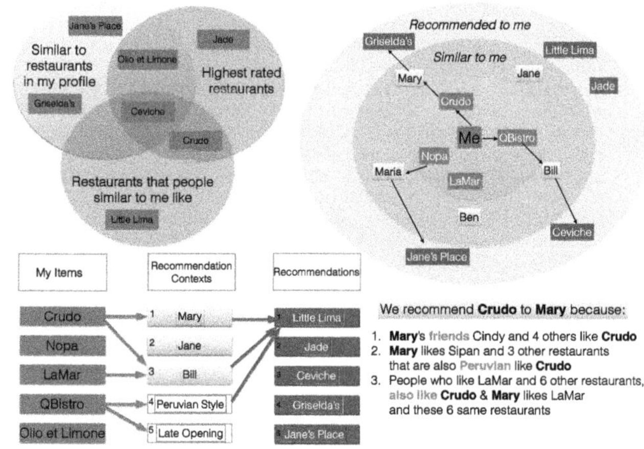

Figure 1: A subset of visualizations presented in our user study of hybrid explanations.

Visualization techniques for explaining recommendations include interfaces with concentric circles [11, 18], Venn diagrams [21], and pathways between columns [3], among many others. Hybrid explanations have been shown to be more effective than single-style explanations [20], but to the best of our knowledge, there is no study that adapts visualization techniques to hybrid recommenders or compares user preferences for hybrid explanations.

In this work, we identify several important dimensions for designing hybrid explanations. Using HyPER [14], a state-of-the-art recommender system, we develop a method for generating explanations from a hybrid model. We conduct a crowdsourced user study (N=200) to evaluate several different design approaches for hybrid explanations. This study answers several fundamental questions about designing hybrid explanations: 1) What visualization is best for hybrid explanations? 2) How should explanations be organized? 3) How much information should be in each explanation? 4) How detailed should each explanation be? Fig. 1 presents a sample of different visualizations that we generated in order to understand user preferences for hybrid explanations (for full details see [15]). This general evaluation strategy can be used to study user preferences for different recommendation domains, such as career sites, music services, and navigational routes.

Our contributions are: 1) a method for generating hybrid explanations from a hybrid recommender system based on a probabilistic programming language, 2) a list of ways explanations can be presented 3) a user evaluation of the different design approaches, and 4) a set of guidelines for designers of hybrid explanation interfaces.

2 RELATED WORK

Several previous studies have considered explanations for recommender systems, demonstrating explanations can increase persuasiveness [8] and satisfaction [25, 26]. To better understand user preferences, research has compared explanation styles [2], combined different explanation styles [24], and considered dimensions such as personalization [25, 26], tags [30], ranking [17], and natural language presentations [5]. In addition to user preferences and design criteria for explanations, several GUIs and visualizations have been proposed for recommendations, including concentric circles (PeerChooser [11, 18]), clustermaps (TalkExplorer [29]), Venn diagrams (SetFusion [21]), and paths among columns (TasteWeights [3, 12]). Extending these ideas, we focus on *hybrid explanations* and study user preferences across designs and interfaces.

3 HYBRID EXPLANATIONS

The first challenge in understanding hybrid explanations is developing a system to translate a hybrid recommender model into a set of component signals and the utility of each component in the model. Here, we use HyPER [14] which makes use of probabilistic soft logic (PSL) [1], a generic probabilistic reasoning framework. We summarize the HyPER model, then describe our approach to converting the model's output to visualizable explanations. Our approach is compatible with any hybrid system with similar output.

The HyPER model is specified using a series of rules in first-order logic syntax defined by the modeler. The rules are used to define a probability distribution over recommendations. For example, to implement user-based collaborative filtering recommendations, the following rule is included in the PSL model:

$$w_{su} : \textsc{SimilarUsers}(u_1, u_2) \land \textsc{Likes}(u_1, i) \Rightarrow \textsc{Likes}(u_2, i)\,. \quad (1)$$

Each rule is associated with a weight, learned from training data, capturing the importance of the rule to the model. In addition to the user-based collaborative filtering rule above, HyPER also includes item-based collaborative filtering rules with mean-centering priors, as well as rules for social-based recommendations using friendships, and content-based rules for using item attributes.

Next, a process known as *grounding* is used to combine the model with data and instantiate a set of propositions. For example, given a dataset with user ratings and a social network, user similarities, item similarities, social relationships, and item attributes are generated as evidence. Together, these ground rules are used by PSL to define a probabilistic graphical model which ranks unseen user-item pairs.

Running inference in HyPER generates recommendations captured by the $\textsc{Likes}$ predicate. After inference is complete, we select the top k items for each user. Then, for each of the top $\textsc{Likes}(u, i)$, we produce associated groundings used during the inference process. For example, in a restaurant recommendation setting, suppose that *Mary*'s top recommended restaurant is *Crudo* (i.e., the predicted value of the unobserved variable $\textsc{Likes}(Mary, Crudo)$ has the highest value among all other predicted values). While inferring the value of $\textsc{Likes}(Mary, Crudo)$, HyPER generated the following *ground* rules:

$$\textsc{Friends}(Mary, Cindy) \land \textsc{Likes}(Cindy, Crudo) \Rightarrow \textsc{Likes}(Mary, Crudo)$$
$$\textsc{Peruvian}(Limon, Crudo) \land \textsc{Likes}(Mary, Limon) \Rightarrow \textsc{Likes}(Mary, Crudo)$$
$$\textsc{SimilarUsers}(Mary, John) \land \textsc{Likes}(John, Crudo) \Rightarrow \textsc{Likes}(Mary, Crudo)$$
$$\textsc{SimilarItems}(Crudo, LaMar) \land \textsc{Likes}(Mary, LaMar) \Rightarrow \textsc{Likes}(Mary, Crudo)$$

Explanation Style	We recommend *Crudo* because:
Social	1. Your friend Cindy likes Crudo
Content	2. You like Peruvian restaurants, like Crudo
User-based	3. Users with similar tastes as you like Crudo
Item-based	4. People who like LaMar, also like Crudo and you like LaMar
Item average rating	5. Crudo is highly rated
User average rating	6. You tend to give high ratings

Table 1: Example of an explanation for a restaurant (Crudo).

Since the groundings are different for each user-item prediction, the resulting explanations are inherently personalized. In Table 1, we present one way of visualizing these groundings using a parser that converts logical rules to natural language. In the next section, we discuss several design considerations and alternative presentations that can be implemented using the set of ground rules.

4 PRESENTATION OF EXPLANATIONS

Given hybrid explanations from HyPER, the next step is designing an interface to present these explanations to users. At a high level, the goal of any presentation style is to improve the user experience. We study the effect of different explanation presentation styles on user experience. To this end, we identify several dimensions for designing interfaces:

- **Presentation (Pres.)**: Natural language (Table 1), rule-based (equation 3), or graphical visualizations.
- **Weighting (Wgt)**: Whether or not explanation weights are displayed.
- **Grouping (Group)**: Whether or not explanations are grouped by style. Each rule can have many groundings in a dataset. For example, do users prefer to be shown the explanation *"Mary's friend Cindy likes Crudo; Mary's friend Josh likes Crudo"* or grouping explanations, *"Mary's friends Cindy and Josh like Crudo."*?
- **Information Density (Dens.)**: Amount of information shown.
- **Aggregation (Aggr.)**: Whether or not rules are aggregated in the grouping case. Do users prefer explanations of the type *"Mary's friends Cindy and 4 others like Crudo."* or *"Mary's friends Cindy, Josh, Rosie, George, Michael like Crudo."*?
- **Meta-explanations (Meta)**: Amount of high-level metadata in explanations (i.e., user similarity, item average rating, and user average rating).
- **Visualization (Visual)**: There are different ways of visualizing hybrid explanations, such as concentric circles [11, 18], Venn diagrams [21], and pathways among columns [3]. For Venn diagrams we used three intersections as suggested in [29]. Pathways among columns was tested with and without display of rules/reasoning.

In addition to the effect of different presentation styles on user experience, we also studied whether users have a specific preference over the *ranking* of the different explanation styles. For example, do users prefer to see social explanations before content-based ones?

5 EVALUATION

We constructed a set of 13 different treatments (Table 2) based on the explanation dimensions described in Section 4. Testing all possible subsets of dimensions was prohibitive, so we chose subsets that we judged as the most informative for explanation design. We

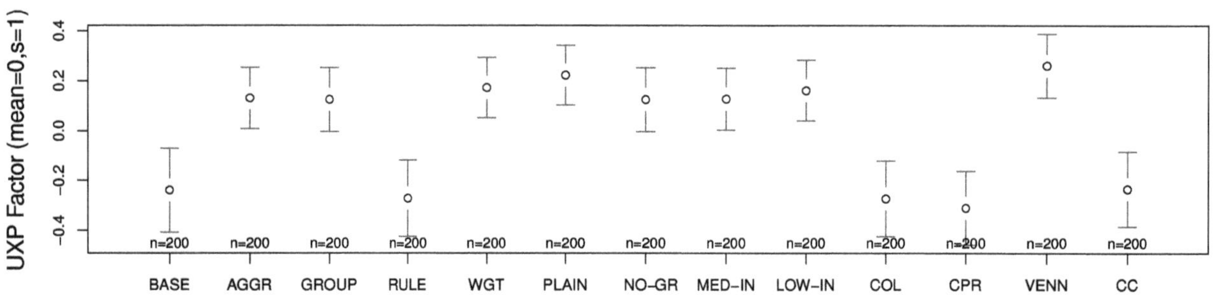

Figure 2: Mean UXP for each treatment. Errors bars are 95% confidence intervals. Treatment descriptions are given in Table 2.

Treat.	Pres.	Wgt	Group	Dens.	Aggr.	Meta
BASE	no exp.	no	no	NA	no	NA
AGGR	english	no	yes	low	yes	low
GROUP	english	no	yes	high	no	low
RULE	rule	no	no	low	no	high
WGT	english	yes	no	low	no	high
PLAIN	english	no	no	low	no	high
NO-GR	english	no	no	med	no	low
MED-IN	english	no	yes	med	no	low
LOW-IN	english	no	yes	low	no	low
		Visual Style				
COL	visual	COLumns + pathways				
CPR	visual	Columns + Pathways with Reasoning				
VENN	visual	VENN diagram				
CC	visual	Concentric Circles				

Table 2: Dimension values for each treatment for the different types of explanations tested.

evaluated explanations for a variety of textual and visual formats. We also included a baseline treatment (BASE) where we presented a recommendation item without any explanation.

We collected 200 samples of within-subjects participant data using Amazon's Mechanical Turk. The design used in our study [19] has been shown to minimize effects of satisficing (e.g., tab-click behavior) in crowdsourced studies. Overall, participants spent between 10 and 30 minutes for the study, 95% of participants were between 18 and 50 years of age, and 42% were male. The data was checked for satisficing users by checking input patterns and timings, however, none of the participants showed indications of violating the assumptions of the study. Each participant was rewarded with $0.5 as incentive.

5.1 Setup

Interface mockups were shown to participants in random order. All the mockups and details of the study can be found in [15]. We ran a synthetic experiment where all users were shown the exact same mockups that were manually generated. Each mockup presented a hybrid explanation for a random user called *"Mary"* for the restaurant *"Crudo"*. For each mockup, we elicited answers for a set of user experience questions, corresponding to understandability, system satisfaction, and perceived persuasiveness (Table 3).

Subjective metrics relating to recommender systems have shown to be strongly correlated (e.g., [22]), thus, confirmatory factor analysis was used to group the question items into a latent user experience variable to allow for simpler presentation of results and eliminate measurement error. A Cronbach's alpha [6] of 0.89 indicates good internal reliability of the constructed user experience (UXP) factor. Average variance extracted (AVE) was 0.64, indicating good convergent validity ($AVE > 0.5$).

Our experiment considered how participants' individual characteristics could affect user experience scores for each treatment. We asked pre-study questions related to visualization familiarity (VF, also shown in Table 3). Analysis showed co-variance between visualization familiarity and user experience was less than 0.5, which indicates good discriminant validity between the constructs.

Users were also given a task to rank different explanation styles according to their preference using a drag and drop interface. Specifically, we showed users the explanations from Table 1 (hiding the style) and asked them to rank these styles from the most to least important. We randomized the order different explanation styles were shown to avoid any order-related biases.

Factor	Question Item Description	R^2	Est.
VF	I am familiar with data visualization.	0.54	0.96
Cronbach: 0.85	I frequently tabulate data with computer software.	0.63	1.20
	I have graphed a lot of data in the past.	0.81	1.38
AVE: 0.60	I am an expert at data visualization.	0.57	1.21
UXP	*Understandability*: The recommendation process is clear to me.	0.73	0.86
Cronbach: 0.87	*Satisfaction*: I would enjoy using this system if it presented recommendations in this way.	0.68	0.82
AVE: 0.64	*Persuasiveness*: The recommendation is convincing.	0.77	0.88

Table 3: The latent VF and UXP factors built on participant responses to subjective questions.

5.2 Results

Figure 2 shows a plot of the mean user experience (factor loadings fixed to 1). To test for differences between the within-subjects treatments, we used structural equation modeling (SEM) [28], which can accommodate latent variables during significance testing, thus eliminating measurement error. We specified two factor models: the first with all within-subjects variables loaded onto a single factor (null hypothesis: no differences between treatments); the second with a factor specified for each of the 13 treatments (hypothesis: treatments cause a change in UXP). The model with a factor specified for each treatment achieved better fit. We used the Akaike Information Criterion (AIC) to estimate the quality of each model (a lower AIC indicates better comparative fit) and achieved

	BASE	AGGR	GROUP	RULE	WGT	PLAIN	NO-GR	MED-IN	LOW-IN	COL	CPR	VENN	CC
β	0.21	0.10	0.18	**0.41**	0.38	0.28	0.35	0.32	0.24	**0.57**	0.33	**0.39**	0.29
Err.	0.08	0.08	0.08	0.09	0.09	0.08	0.09	0.09	0.08	0.09	0.09	0.09	0.08
P	**	0.2	*	***	***	**	***	***	**	***	***	***	***

Table 4: Regressions coefficients (β) in a SEM that examine the relationship between visualization familiarity and observed user experience for each treatment. UXP/VF are latent variables with $\mu = 0, \sigma = 1$, effect sizes (β) on UXP are measured as SD from the mean as VF changes. Significance levels for this table: $^{***}p < .001$, $^{**}p < .01$, $^{*}p < .05$.

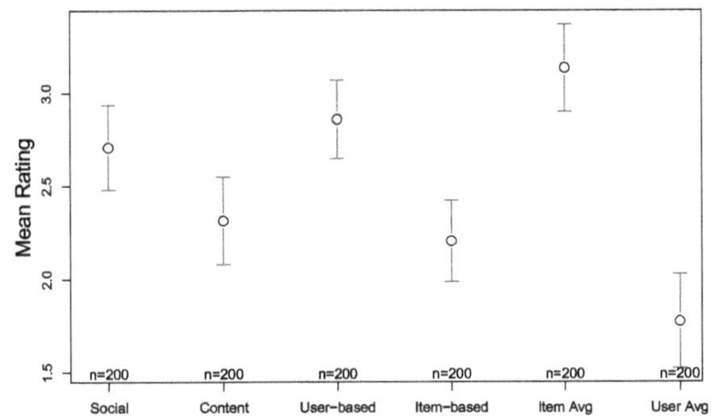

Figure 3: Means of participant ratings (1-6, with 6 being the highest preference) for the explanation style ranking task. Error bars are 95% confidence intervals.

$AIC = 25838$ for the single factor model vs. $AIC = 22908$ for the model with a factor for each treatment. This result indicates that there exist differences in UXP between treatments and thus the null hypothesis is rejected.

Next, we performed post-hoc tests between each treatment using a Raykov change model [23] (this mimics the popular Tukey test [27] while still allowing the use of latent variables). In this method, one factor (treatment) is used as a baseline and a slope is calculated between it and another factor. The post-hoc test showed that the interface using Venn diagrams (VENN) was significantly better than all other visual treatments and the baseline ($p < 0.001$ for BASE, COL,CPR, and CC). VENN also performed significantly better than AGGR, GROUP, NO-GR, MED-IN, and LOW-IN ($\forall\, p < 0.05$). The RULE treatment performed significantly worse than the explanations in plain English, as well as VENN ($\forall\, p < 0.001$). All English treatments performed significantly better than the baseline BASE ($\forall\, p < 0.001$). There was no significant difference between any of the English treatments ($\forall\, p > 0.10$), however, the mean for PLAIN was the highest. Consequently, weights, information density, aggregation, and grouping were also non-significant ($\forall\, p > 0.10$).

Results from the ranking task are shown in Figure 3. For our analysis we converted the ranking into rating data, i.e., the item listed first was given a rating of 6 and the item ranked last received rating 1. Users showed the strongest preference for item average rating explanations, followed by user-based and social explanations. A repeated measures ANOVA revealed differences in rating between the explanation styles ($p < 0.001$). A Tukey post-hoc test showed no statistical difference between social, user-based, and item average rating explanations ($\forall\, p > 0.10$). However, social, user-based, and item average rating were significantly better than item-based and user average rating ($\forall\, p < 0.05$). User-based and item average rating were significantly better than content explanations (both $p < 0.05$).

Finally, we conducted analysis on the relationship between visualization familiarity and user experience. A SEM was built with visualization familiarity regressed onto user experience measurements for each treatment (Table 4). Results indicate that visualization familiarity predicts increased user experience in all treatments, except AGGR. The highest increase in user experience is seen in COL and RULE. Model fit: $N = 200$ with 174 free parameters, $RMSEA = 0.064$ ($CI : [0.058, 0.069]$), $TLI = 0.89, CFI = 0.90$ over null baseline model, $\chi^2(772) = 1397$ (indicate acceptable fit, however, note that overall model fit is not an indicator of whether effects exist between variables).

6 DISCUSSION AND CONCLUSION

We have presented an evaluation of different visualization approaches using hybrid explanations. The results support prior findings [7] that explanations improve the user experience of recommender systems.

More specifically, Venn diagrams outperform all other visual interfaces and five of seven English interfaces, but are difficult to adapt to more than three sources. Natural language approaches were preferable to rule groundings from HyPER. Our experiments did not show a statistically significant difference across dimensions such as weights, information density, aggregation, or grouping in these explanations. This suggests that most plain English explanations may perform more or less the same in recommendation settings. Our results indicated that social, user-based, and item average rating explanations were the preferred explanation styles by users. Furthermore, we have established a reliable scale, as evidenced by Cronbach's α, for visualization familiarity which might be used to tailor explanation styles to individual users.

Additionally, we discovered that color-blind users ($N = 14$) rated the RULE interface higher in terms of UXP than the rest of the sampled population, with marginal significance ($\beta = 0.15, p = 0.051$). The mockup for this interface used a fairly intense violet color which may have been difficult to read for all but the colorblind users. While the colorblind sample was not large enough to change the results of the study, it highlights the need to accommodate these types of users when evaluating UXP for recommender systems.

The mockups that we showed to the users were manually produced and not generated by the HyPER system. As a result, the study was synthetic and did not support personalization. In future work we plan to analyze factors such as the quality of the recommendation and whether the user agrees and connects with the evidence. To this end, we plan to use HyPER's output, implement the best performing interfaces from our study (Venn, English PLAIN) and run a more comprehensive user case study in a lab setting to better understand effectiveness, efficiency, and user satisfaction of the explanatory system. One open question is determining effective methods for ranking explanations. We plan to compare several ranking strategies by designing interactive interfaces that support personalization.

REFERENCES

[1] S. Bach, M. Broecheler, B. Huang, and L. Getoor. 2017. Hinge-Loss Markov Random Fields and Probabilistic Soft Logic. *Journal of Machine Learning Research (JMLR)* (2017).

[2] M. Bilgic and R. Mooney. 2005. Explaining Recommendations: Satisfaction vs. Promotion. In *Proceedings of Beyond Personalization 2005: A Workshop on the Next Stage of Recommender Systems Research at the 2005 International Conference on Intelligent User Interfaces.*

[3] S. Bostandjiev, J. O'Donovan, and T. Höllerer. 2012. TasteWeights: A Visual Interactive Hybrid Recommender System. In *Proceedings of the Sixth ACM Conference on Recommender Systems (RecSys '12).* 35–42.

[4] R. Burke. 2007. Hybrid Web Recommender Systems. In *The Adaptive Web.* Springer.

[5] S. Chang, M. Harper, and L. Terveen. 2016. Crowd-Based Personalized Natural Language Explanations for Recommendations. In *Proceedings of the 10th ACM Conference on Recommender Systems (RecSys '16).* 175–182.

[6] L. Cronbach. 1951. Coefficient Alpha and the Internal Structure of Tests. *Psychometrika* 16, 3 (1951), 297–334.

[7] F. Gerhard and Z. Markus. 2011. A Taxonomy for Generating Explanations in Recommender Systems. *AI Magazine* 32, 3 (2011).

[8] J. Herlocker, J. Konstan, and J. Riedl. 2000. Explaining Collaborative Filtering Recommendations. In *Proceedings of the 2000 ACM Conference on Computer Supported Cooperative Work (CSCW '00).* 241–250.

[9] D. Jannach and G. Adomavicius. 2016. Recommendations with a Purpose. In *Proceedings of the 10th ACM Conference on Recommender Systems (RecSys '16).* 7–10.

[10] D. Jannach, P. Resnick, A. Tuzhilin, and M. Zanker. 2016. Recommender Systems — Beyond Matrix Completion. *Commun. ACM* 59, 11 (2016), 94–102.

[11] A. Kangasrääsiö, D. Glowacka, and S. Kaski. 2015. Improving Controllability and Predictability of Interactive Recommendation Interfaces for Exploratory Search. In *Proceedings of the 20th International Conference on Intelligent User Interfaces (IUI '15).* 247–251.

[12] B. Knijnenburg, S. Bostandjiev, J. O'Donovan, and A. Kobsa. 2012. Inspectability and Control in Social Recommenders. In *Proceedings of the Sixth ACM Conference on Recommender Systems (RecSys '12).* 43–50.

[13] J. Konstan and J. Riedl. 2012. Recommender Systems: From Algorithms to User Experience. *User Modeling and User-Adapted Interaction* 22, 1-2 (2012), 101–123.

[14] P. Kouki, S. Fakhraei, J. Foulds, M. Eirinaki, and L. Getoor. 2015. HyPER: A Flexible and Extensible Probabilistic Framework for Hybrid Recommender Systems. In *Proceedings of the 9th ACM Conference on Recommender Systems (RecSys '15).* 99–106.

[15] P. Kouki, J. Schaffer, J. Pujara, J. O'Donovan, and L. Getoor. 2017. Supplemental Material: User Preferences for Hybrid Explanations. (2017). https://linqspub.soe.ucsc.edu/basilic/web/Publications/2017/kouki:recsys17:sup-mat/kouki-recsys17-sup-mat.pdf

[16] S. McNee, J. Riedl, and J. Konstan. 2006. Being Accurate is Not Enough: How Accuracy Metrics Have Hurt Recommender Systems. In *CHI '06 Extended Abstracts on Human Factors in Computing Systems (CHI EA '06).* 1097–1101.

[17] K. Muhammad, A. Lawlor, and B. Smyth. 2016. On the Use of Opinionated Explanations to Rank and Justify Recommendations. In *Proceedings of the 29th International Florida Artificial Intelligence Research Society Conference (FLAIRS '16).* 554–559.

[18] J. O'Donovan, B. Smyth, B. Gretarsson, S. Bostandjiev, and T. Höllerer. 2008. PeerChooser: Visual Interactive Recommendation. In *Proceedings of the SIGCHI Conference on Human Factors in Computing Systems (CHI '08).* 1085–1088.

[19] D. Oppenheimer, T. Meyvis, and N. Davidenko. 2009. Instructional manipulation checks: Detecting satisficing to increase statistical power. *Journal of Experimental Social Psychology* 45, 4 (2009), 867–872.

[20] A. Papadimitriou, P. Symeonidis, and Y. Manolopoulos. 2012. A Generalized Taxonomy of Explanations Styles for Traditional and Social Recommender Systems. *Data Min. Knowl. Discov.* 24, 3 (2012), 555–583.

[21] D. Parra, P. Brusilovsky, and C. Trattner. 2014. See What You Want to See: Visual User-driven Approach for Hybrid Recommendation. In *Proceedings of the 19th International Conference on Intelligent User Interfaces (IUI '14).* 235–240.

[22] P. Pu, L. Chen, and R. Hu. A user-centric evaluation framework for recommender systems. In *Proceedings of the 5th ACM conference on Recommender systems (RecSys '11).*

[23] T. Raykov. 1992. Structural models for studying correlates and predictors of change. *Australian Journal of Psychology* 44, 2 (1992), 101–112.

[24] P. Symeonidis, A. Nanopoulos, and Y. Manolopoulos. 2009. MoviExplain: A Recommender System with Explanations. In *Proceedings of the Third ACM Conference on Recommender Systems (RecSys '09).* 317–320.

[25] N. Tintarev and J. Masthoff. 2007. Effective Explanations of Recommendations: User-centered Design. In *Proceedings of the 1st ACM Conference on Recommender Systems (RecSys '07).* 153–156.

[26] N. Tintarev and J. Masthoff. 2012. Evaluating the Effectiveness of Explanations for Recommender Systems. *User Modeling and User-Adapted Interaction* 22, 4-5 (2012), 399–439.

[27] J. Tukey. 1949. Comparing individual means in the analysis of variance. *Biometrics* (1949), 99–114.

[28] J. Ullman and P. Bentler. 2003. *Structural equation modeling.* Wiley Online Library.

[29] K. Verbert, D. Parra, P. Brusilovsky, and E. Duval. 2013. Visualizing Recommendations to Support Exploration, Transparency and Controllability. In *Proceedings of the 18th International Conference on Intelligent User Interfaces (IUI '13).* 351–362.

[30] J. Vig, S. Sen, and J. Riedl. 2009. Tagsplanations: Explaining Recommendations Using Tags. In *Proceedings of the 14th International Conference on Intelligent User Interfaces (IUI '09).* 47–56.

Secure Multi-Party Protocols for Item-Based Collaborative Filtering

Erez Shmueli
Tel Aviv University
Tel Aviv, Israel
shmueli@tau.ac.il

Tamir Tassa
The Open University
Ra'anana, Israel
tamirta@openu.ac.il

ABSTRACT

Recommender systems have become extremely common in recent years, and are utilized in a variety of domains such as movies, music, news, products, restaurants, etc. While a typical recommender system bases its recommendations solely on users' preference data collected by the system itself, the quality of recommendations can significantly be improved if several recommender systems (or vendors) share their data. However, such data sharing poses significant privacy and security challenges, both to the vendors and the users. In this paper we propose secure protocols for distributed item-based Collaborative Filtering. Our protocols allow to compute both the predicted ratings of items and their predicted rankings, without compromising privacy nor predictions' accuracy. Unlike previous solutions in which the secure protocols are executed solely by the vendors, our protocols assume the existence of a mediator that performs intermediate computations on encrypted data supplied by the vendors. Such a mediated setting is advantageous over the non-mediated one since it enables each vendor to communicate solely with the mediator. This yields reduced communication costs and it allows each vendor to issue recommendations to its clients without being dependent on the availability and willingness of the other vendors to collaborate.

CCS CONCEPTS

•Information systems → Collaborative filtering; •Security and privacy → Privacy-preserving protocols;

KEYWORDS

Item-based collaborative filtering, Distributed computing, Privacy

1 INTRODUCTION

The explosion of information that is available to users over the World Wide Web was the main driving force in the emergence of recommendation systems that aim at helping users find their needles in the haystack [23]. One of the main techniques on which recommendation systems are based is collaborative filtering (CF) [8]. CF predicts the preferences of users based on the preferences of the community (rather than on the users' characteristics). Specifically, CF methods use large databases that store information regarding rating or purchasing history of users in the community. These data are modeled as a matrix over the set of users (rows) and items (columns), where the entry for a given user u and a given item b is either binary (indicating whether user u purchased item b or not), or a rating that u gave to b.

CF is broadly classified into memory-based and model-based approaches. The memory-based approach is either user-based, in the sense that recommendations for a given user u are derived from the preferences of users that are similar to u, or item-based, i.e., u is offered items which are similar to those that he purchased or liked in the past. The similarity between users or items is defined by some metric between the corresponding rows or columns, respectively, in the user-item matrix. The item-based approach is more suitable for deployment in e-commerce sites, due to its better scalability, and, indeed, it is one of the most widely deployed CF techniques [6].

Since memory-based approaches utilize the entire matrix of past ratings or purchases, some of them do not scale well. In such cases, model-based approaches may be more applicable. In model-based approaches, the original user-item matrix is used to train a compact model, which is then used for prediction. The model is developed by artificial intelligence techniques (e.g., Bayesian classification) or by linear algebraic techniques (e.g., SVD). While item-based methods have comparable performance to that of model-based methods when predicted ratings are the required output, the former methods tend to show better performance when the required output is the top h items for a given user [6]. Furthermore, item-based recommendations are more easily interpretable to the user.

Instead of basing their recommendations to their clients solely on their own databases, vendors may significantly improve the quality of their recommendations by sharing their user-item preferential data [3]. However, such sharing poses significant privacy and security challenges. Indeed, commercial organizations may be reluctant to share their proprietary data about past users' purchases or ratings as it may serve competing entities. In addition, the users' privacy might be hindered if personal information about their past activities which they provided to one commercial entity would be handed over by that entity to other entities.

Privacy-preserving collaborative filtering (PPCF) enables the practice of CF without leaking private information. One class of PPCF algorithms is based on techniques such as data perturbation or generalization. The outputs issued by such algorithms may differ from the outputs of their non-privacy preserving counterparts, due to the noise that they introduce to the training data. Another class of PPCF algorithms is based on cryptographic techniques, such as homomorphic encryption or secret sharing. Employing

RecSys'17, August 27–31, 2017, Como, Italy.
 ISBN 978-1-4503-4652-8/17/08...$15.00.
DOI: http://dx.doi.org/10.1145/3109859.3109881

cryptographic techniques, rather than data perturbation, offers better privacy-preservation and it enables issuing the same output as in the the underlying non-privacy preserving algorithm.

In this paper we propose protocols of Secure Multiparty Computation (SMC) for PPCF. We focus on the vertical distribution case, where each of the collaborating vendors (denoted $V_1, \ldots, V_K$) offers a different subset of items to the same underlying population of users. The discussion of the horizontal distribution setting, in which $V_1, \ldots, V_K$ offer the same set of items but each vendor serves a distinct subset of users, is deferred to the full version of this paper due to lack of space. We design privacy-preserving protocols for computing predicted ratings and rankings.

Most previous PPCF solutions are protocols that are executed solely by the vendors. Our protocols, on the other hand, involve a mediator, T. Having such a mediator reduces the need of the vendors to communicate with each other only to the offline (and infrequent) phase in which a model of similarity between items is built; in the online phase, where vendors need to issue predicted ratings and rankings to their clients, each vendor communicates directly vis-à-vis T and does not need to communicate with other vendors. Such a mediated setting is advantageous over the non-mediated setting since it entails reduced communication costs. More importantly, each vendor can issue recommendations to its clients without "bothering" all other vendors each time or be dependent on their availability and willingness to collaborate.

The paper is organized as follows. We begin with a review of related work (Section 2). We then provide the necessary background on item-based CF and cryptographic methods (Section 3). Our PPCF protocols are described in Section 4. We present our experimental evaluation in Section 5, and conclude in Section 6.

2 RELATED WORK

Privacy-preserving collaborative filtering (PPCF) enables the practice of CF without leaking private information. We proceed to overview several recent PPCF works. Interested readers may refer to [4, 7] for a more comprehensive survey.

Polat and Du [19] discuss how to provide predictions for single items in case of a vertical distribution scenario with two vendors. In another study of theirs [20], they show how to offer top recommendations in both the horizontal and vertical distribution scenarios without deeply violating the vendors' privacy. They concentrate on the case of two vendors, and the case of binary user-item data. Jeckmans et al. [11] considered a case of horizontal distribution between two vendors, V_1 and V_2. They considered an asymmetric setting in which V_2 collaborates with V_1 so that V_1 can offer to its clients better recommendations, while V_2 does not benefit at all from such a collaboration. All of the above works are based on user-based CF, i.e., the recommendations to u are derived from the items that users similar to u liked. The studies that we describe next follow (like us) the item-based approach.

Basu et al. [2] propose algorithms for a privacy-preserving execution of an item-based CF scheme that is based on the Slope One predictor [15]. The work which is closest to ours is that of Yakut and Polat [33]. To the best of our knowledge, it is the only other work that deals with item-based CF which is based on the cosine-similarity score. They concentrated on the case of two vendors and considered the arbitrary distribution scenario. A main vehicle by which they obtain privacy is by introducing fake ratings into the distributed matrix. Hence, as opposed to our algorithms that issue exactly the same outputs as their non-privacy preserving counterparts, the outputs of the algorithms in [33] are inaccurate, and in order to enhance the privacy, greater levels of noise must be introduced, what implies a further reduction of accuracy.

All of the above studies are non-mediated. Hence, whenever a vendor wishes to compute predicted ratings or rankings, all other vendors need to be available and cooperating. Also, except [2], they concentrate on the case of $K = 2$ vendors; a natural extension of those schemes to a general K (to enable better recommendations) entails high communication costs. Such challenges do not exist in the mediated setting, where any single vendor communicates (in the online phase) only with the mediator.

3 PRELIMINARIES

3.1 Item-based collaborative filtering

Here we provide a brief introduction to item-based CF [22]. A more comprehensive discussion is given in [6].

Let $U = \{u_1, \ldots, u_N\}$ be a set of users and $B = \{b_1, \ldots, b_M\}$ be a set of items (say, books). The user-item rating matrix, R, is an $N \times M$ matrix where $R(n, m)$ is the rating that u_n gave to b_m, a value which is usually taken from a small range of positive integers, say $\{1, 2, 3, 4, 5\}$, and $R(n, m) = 0$ if u_n did not rate b_m. Item-based CF consists of two phases: an offline phase, in which the matrix R is used to learn a model of similarity between items; and an online phase in which that model is used to predict user ratings or to rank items according to their potential appeal to a given user. (The offline phase should be repeated periodically in order to update the similarity scores according to the changes in U, B, and R.)

The similarity model is an $M \times M$ symmetric matrix S where $S(\ell, m)$ is the similarity score between items b_ℓ and b_m, $\ell, m \in [M] := \{1, 2, \ldots, M\}$. Let $\mathbf{c}_m = (R(n, m) : n \in [N])$ denote hereinafter the mth column in the user-item rating matrix R, $m \in [M]$. Then the similarity scores are defined in Definition 3.1.[1]

Definition 3.1. Assume that $\ell, m \in [M]$ and set $\mathbf{c}_{\ell|m} := \mathbf{c}_\ell \cdot \xi(\mathbf{c}_m)$; namely, $\mathbf{c}_{\ell|m} := (\mathbf{c}_{\ell|m}(1), \ldots, \mathbf{c}_{\ell|m}(N))^t$ is the projection of the ℓth column of the user-item rating matrix R on the subset of users that rated both items b_ℓ and b_m. Then the cosine similarity score is

$$S(\ell, m) = \frac{\langle \mathbf{c}_\ell, \mathbf{c}_m \rangle}{\|\mathbf{c}_{\ell|m}\| \cdot \|\mathbf{c}_{m|\ell}\|} . \quad (1)$$

The similarity scores are used to predict u_n's rating of b_m as follows. Let (a) $N_q(m)$ be the set of indices of the q items with highest $S(\cdot, m)$ (for some preset, typically small, $q < M$); (b) $N_q^+(m) := \{\ell \in N_q(m) : S(\ell, m) > 0\}$; (c) $\mathbf{s}_m$ be the vector for which $\mathbf{s}_m(\ell) = S(\ell, m)$ if $\ell \in N_q^+(m)$ and $\mathbf{s}_m(\ell) = 0$ for $\ell \in [M] \setminus N_q^+(m)$; (d) $\overline{R(b_m)}$ be b_m's average rating; (e) $\mathbf{r}_n$ be the nth row of the matrix R; and (f) $\bar{\mathbf{r}}_n$ be the vector of u_n's adjusted ratings, i.e. $\bar{\mathbf{r}}_n(m) =$

[1] Notation agreements: (a) If r is a nonnegative integer then $\xi(r) = 0$ if $r = 0$ and $\xi(r) = 1$ otherwise. (b) If $\mathbf{x}$ is a vector and f is a function then $f(\mathbf{x})$ is the vector in which $f(\mathbf{x})(\cdot) = f(\mathbf{x}(\cdot))$. (c) If $\mathbf{x}$ and $\mathbf{y}$ are vectors then $\langle \mathbf{x}, \mathbf{y} \rangle$ is their inner product, while $\mathbf{x} \cdot \mathbf{y}$ is the vector in which $(\mathbf{x} \cdot \mathbf{y})(\cdot) = \mathbf{x}(\cdot) \cdot \mathbf{y}(\cdot)$.

$(R(n,m)-\overline{R(b_m)})\cdot\xi(R(n,m))$, $m\in[M]$. Then

$$P(u_n,b_m):=\overline{R(b_m)}+\frac{\langle \mathbf{s}_m,\bar{\mathbf{r}}_n\rangle}{\langle \mathbf{s}_m,\xi(\mathbf{r}_n)\rangle}\,. \tag{2}$$

If the denominator in Eq. (2) equals zero, $P(u_n,b_m)$ is set to $\overline{R(b_m)}$. (There exist several variants of the similarity score and prediction formula. We focus here on the variant suggested in [6], which performs best. The adjustment of our protocols to other variants is straightforward.)

Sometimes, instead of showing to u_n his predicted rating on some item, the goal is to present to him the h items which are most likely to appeal to him, without predicted ratings. To that end, one produces a *ranking* of all items that u_n had not rated so far in order to extract from it the top h items, for some $h\ge 1$. One approach is to base the ranking on the items' predicted ratings (Eq. (2)). However, a simpler ranking procedure produces better results (see [6, Section 2.3]). Let $I(n)$ be the subset of indices of items that u_n already rated. Define for each $m\in[M]\setminus I(n)$ the score

$$\hat{s}(m)=\sum_{\ell\in I(n)\cap N_q(m)} S(\ell,m)\,. \tag{3}$$

Then, the top h items to be recommended to u_n are those with the highest value of $\hat{s}(m)$.

3.2 Cryptographic building blocks

An encryption function $\mathcal{F}$ is called (additively) *homomorphic* if for every two plaintexts, m_1 and m_2, $\mathcal{F}(m_1+m_2)=\mathcal{F}(m_1)\cdot\mathcal{F}(m_2)$. When the encryption function is randomized (in the sense that $\mathcal{F}(m)$ depends on m as well as on a random string) then $\mathcal{F}$ is called *probabilistic*. The semantically secure Paillier cipher [18] is both homomorphic and probabilistic. In our protocols, $V_1,\ldots,V_K$ jointly generate the key pair in a homomorphic and probabilistic encryption function $\mathcal{F}$; they notify T of the encryption key, but keep the decryption key private. (In order to jointly generate a random key pair, the vendors only need to generate a random bit string of the same length as the key; this can be done, say, if every vendor chooses its own random string and then they all engage in a secure summation protocol.)

Another building block of secure multi-party computation that we shall need is that of secure division. Tassa and Bonchi [26] considered a setting that involves three parties, P_1, P_2 and H. P_i, $i=1,2$, holds a private integer a_i, and the goal is to let H recover the real quotient a_1/a_2 but not the values of a_1 and a_2. Towards that end, P_1 and P_2 jointly generate a random real number $X\sim Z$ where Z is the distribution on $[1,\infty)$ with probability density function $f_Z(x)=x^{-2}$; then they jointly generate a random $g\sim U(0,X)$, and they send to H the values ga_i, $i=1,2$, which H proceeds to divide in order to recover $q=a_1/a_2$. The masking multiplier g prevents H from learning a_i, but it can still recover q. The selection of the probability distribution from which g is drawn is made in order to minimize the information that H can extract from ga_i on a_i. Here we use this idea as follows: T holds two encrypted values $\mathcal{F}(a_1)$ and $\mathcal{F}(a_2)$ and it wishes to allow a vendor V_k to get the quotient $q=a_1/a_2$ so that no one reveals a_1 nor a_2. To that end it sends to V_k the values $b_i:=\mathcal{F}(a_i)^g$, $i=1,2$, for a random g that was generated as described above. Since $\mathcal{F}$ is homomorphic then $b_i:=\mathcal{F}(ga_i)$. V_k decrypts the two received values and gets $\mathcal{F}^{-1}(b_i)=ga_i$, $i=1,2$, which it then proceeds to divide in order to get q.

4 PPCF PROTOCOLS

Here we deal with the vertical distribution scenario, where each vendor owns a different subset of R's columns. In Sections 4.1 and 4.2 we describe the computations and protocols that are performed in the offline phase and involve all of the vendors $V_1,\ldots,V_K$, as well as the mediator T. Then, we describe the online phase in which a given vendor V_k submits queries to T towards computing the predicted rating of some user u_n for an item b_m, $P(u_n,b_m)$, Eq. (2) (Section 4.3), or getting the top h items for a given user u_n (Section 4.4). The online phase is carried out solely by V_k and T. Namely, the participation of all vendors is required only in the offline and less frequent phase.

User ordering. The vendors jointly decide on a random ordering of U, which is kept secret from T. Hereinafter, u_n denotes the nth user in that ordering.

Item ordering. The vendors jointly decide on a random ordering of the unified item set B. Let $I_k\subset[M]$ denote the subset of indices of V_k's items in that ordering, $k\in[K]$. T is notified of I_k, $k\in[K]$, but apart from that the ordering is kept secret from T. If $M_k:=|I_k|$ is the number of items offered by V_k, $k\in[K]$, then for every $m\in I_k$, the vector $\mathbf{c}_m$ (the mth column in the user-item rating matrix R) is known only to V_k.

We note that in order to select those random orderings, all that is needed is to select a common random seed; such a common random seed can be generated as described in Section 3.2.

Privacy. The goal of each vendor V_k is to protect its own proprietary data, being the sub-matrix $R_k:=\{R(n,m):n\in[N],m\in I_k\}$, from V_j, $j\neq k$, and T. Ideally, no such party should gain any information on R_k from its view during the execution of our protocols, beyond what can be inferred from its own input and the output of the protocol. However, while such perfect security is achievable for any problem of SMC (by invoking generic solutions such as Yao's garbled circuit construction [34]), when looking for *practical* solutions, some relaxations of the notion of perfect privacy are usually inevitable, provided that the leaked information is deemed benign. Examples for such studies are numerous and span various domains of distributed computing, e.g. association rule mining [13, 25, 31], anonymization [27, 28, 35], computation on distributed graphs [1] or constraint optimization [9, 10, 14, 29, 30]. In fact, also all PPCF studies that were reviewed in Section 2 offer protection to the private data, but that protection is not perfect. The protocols that we present here are also privacy-preserving in that sense. For each of our protocols we discuss its privacy-preservation and identify the excess information that they may leak, and explain why such leakage of information is benign. Our protocols rely solely on standard cryptographic building blocks, as described in Section 3.2; this offers a significant advantage as they can be readily implemented on top of standard libraries.

We make here an assumption which is common in PPCF literature: all parties are semi-honest and do not collude. Semi-honesty means that the parties follows the protocols' specifications but try to extract from their view information on the inputs of their peers.

(See, for instance, [12, 24, 35] for a discussion and justification of that assumption.)

4.1 Offline model construction

The split $[M] = \bigcup_{k=1}^{K} I_k$ induces a split of the similarity matrix S into K^2 blocks, $S_{j,k}$, $j, k \in [K]$, where the dimensions of the block $S_{j,k}$ are $M_j \times M_k$. The K diagonal blocks, $S_{k,k}$, $k \in [K]$, consist of similarity scores between pairs of items that are offered by the same vendor. Each V_k can compute by itself the block $S_{k,k}$ and send it to T. The computation of $S_{j,k}$, where $j \neq k$, depends on inputs from V_j and V_k. Protocol 1 enables that computation.

Assume that b_ℓ is one of the items offered by V_j and b_m is one of V_k's items. Protocol 1 is executed by V_j, V_k and T towards the goal of T learning $S(\ell, m)$. The protocol relies on a sub-protocol SSP for Secure Scalar Product. If $\mathbf{x}$ is a vector held by V_j and $\mathbf{y}$ is a vector held by V_k, then an execution of SSP with those two inputs ends with T learning $\langle \mathbf{x}, \mathbf{y} \rangle$, and nothing further, while both V_j and V_k remain oblivious of the input vector of the other vendor.

First, V_j (where $j < k$) selects a random multiplier $g_{\ell,m}$ (Step 1). Then they execute SSP towards T receiving $z_1 = g_{\ell,m} \cdot \langle \mathbf{c}_\ell, \mathbf{c}_m \rangle$ (Step 2). In Steps 3 and 4 T gets $z_2 = g_{\ell,m} \cdot \langle \mathbf{c}_\ell^2, \xi(\mathbf{c}_m) \rangle$ and $z_3 = g_{\ell,m} \cdot \langle \xi(\mathbf{c}_\ell), \mathbf{c}_m^2 \rangle$. Since $z_2 = g_{\ell,m} \cdot \|\mathbf{c}_{\ell|m}\|^2$ and $z_3 = g_{\ell,m} \cdot \|\mathbf{c}_{m|\ell}\|^2$, we infer by Eq. (1) that in Step 5 T recovers $S(\ell, m)$. (If the denominator in that quotient is zero, a case that occurs when no two users rated both items, the similarity score is set to zero.)

Protocol 1 Computing the similarity score for a single pair of items.

Require: V_j holds the vector $\mathbf{c}_\ell$ for item b_ℓ;
V_k holds the vector $\mathbf{c}_m$ for item b_m.
1: V_j selects a random integer multiplier $g_{\ell,m}$.
2: $T \leftarrow z_1 := SSP(g_{\ell,m} \cdot \mathbf{c}_\ell, \mathbf{c}_m)$.
3: $T \leftarrow z_2 := SSP(g_{\ell,m} \cdot \mathbf{c}_\ell^2, \xi(\mathbf{c}_m))$.
4: $T \leftarrow z_3 := SSP(g_{\ell,m} \cdot \xi(\mathbf{c}_\ell), \mathbf{c}_m^2)$.
5: T sets $S(\ell, m) := z_1/\sqrt{z_2 z_3}$ if $z_2 z_3 \neq 0$, and $S(\ell, m) = 0$ otherwise.
Ensure: T gets $S(\ell, m)$.

Secure computation of scalar products of private vectors is a fundamental problem in SMC, as it serves a basic building block for many other secure protocols (see e.g. [32] and the references therein). Protocol 1 can be executed with any SSP sub-protocol. We find the protocol of Du and Zhan [5] most fitting in our context, since their protocol is designed for the mediated setting which we consider; namely, two parties hold each of the input vectors and the scalar product goes to a mediator. In addition, because it relies on a mediator, it solves the problem with perfect security without resorting to expensive cryptographic means, thus implying low computational and communication costs.

Protocol 1 ends with T having the similarity score $S(\ell, m)$ between a single pair of items offered by V_j and V_k. V_j and V_k have to perform Protocol 1 in parallel for all $\ell \in I_j$ and $m \in I_k$. That parallelized version of Protocol 1 has to be run by all $\binom{K}{2}$ pairs of vendors.

Privacy. By using a secure SSP sub-protocol (such as the one in [5]), none of the vendors may infer any information on inputs of other vendors. As for T, the usage of random multipliers prevents it from learning the terms in the numerator and denominator of Eq. (1). T does learn the similarity scores between items, but, owing to the random item ordering, it cannot link those scores to the relevant pair of items.

(Due to page limitation, we omit the computational and communication cost analysis of all our protocols.)

A concluding remark. The similarity scores $S(\ell, m)$ are real-valued and in the next phase they need to be used in computing predicted ratings and rankings in a privacy-preserving manner. In doing so, it is necessary to subject them to encryption. Since encryption functions are applied on discrete integer domains, T translates all real values s in the matrix S into integer values by mappings of the form $s \mapsto \hat{s} := \lfloor Ls + 0.5 \rfloor$, where L is a large integer.

4.2 In preparation to the online phase

The computation of predicted ratings depends on $\bar{\mathbf{r}}_n$ and $\xi(\mathbf{r}_n)$, see Eq. (2). The vectors $\bar{\mathbf{r}}_n$ are real-valued. We translate them into integer-valued vectors $\hat{\mathbf{r}}_n$, where $\hat{\mathbf{r}}_n(m) := \lfloor L\bar{\mathbf{r}}_n(m) + 0.5 \rfloor$, and L is a large integer as described in the concluding remark of Section 4.1. Then, in the online phase, the predicted ratings will be computed as follows:

$$P(u_n, b_m) := \overline{R(b_m)} + \frac{1}{L} \cdot \frac{\langle \mathbf{s}_m, \hat{\mathbf{r}}_n \rangle}{\langle \mathbf{s}_m, \xi(\mathbf{r}_n) \rangle} . \quad (4)$$

Up to negligible rounding errors, Eq. (4) issues the same predictions as Eq. (2) while relying only on integer values.

Protocol 2 is designed so that at its completion T holds an $\mathcal{F}$-encryption of the vectors $\hat{\mathbf{r}}_n$ and $\xi(\mathbf{r}_n)$, for all $n \in [N]$, where $\mathcal{F}$ is the homomorphic encryption function that can be decrypted by the vendors only. Owing to the security of the $\mathcal{F}$-encryption, this protocol keeps the information owned by the vendors protected from T.

Protocol 2 Conveying to T encryptions of user-rating vectors.

Require: Each V_k, $k \in [K]$, holds $R(n, m)$ for all $n \in [N]$ and $m \in I_k$.
1: Each V_k computes for each $m \in I_k$ the average rating of b_m, $\overline{R(b_m)} = \frac{\sum_{n \in [N]} R(n,m)}{\sum_{n \in [N]} \xi(R(n,m))}$.
2: Each V_k computes the adjusted user-item matrix over its items, $\overline{R(n,m)} := \left(R(n,m) - \overline{R(b_m)} \right) \cdot \xi(R(n,m))$, $n \in [N]$, $m \in I_k$.
3: Each V_k computes $\hat{R}(n,m) = \lfloor L\overline{R(n,m)} + 0.5 \rfloor$, $n \in [N]$, $m \in I_k$.
4: Each V_k sends to T the matrices $(\mathcal{F}(\hat{R}(n,m)) : n \in [N], m \in I_k)$ and $(\mathcal{F}(\xi(R(n,m))) : n \in [N], m \in I_k)$.
5: T concatenates the K received matrices.
Ensure: T gets $\mathcal{F}(\hat{\mathbf{r}}_n)$ and $\mathcal{F}(\xi(\mathbf{r}_n))$, $\forall n \in [N]$.

Privacy. In Protocol 2 only the mediator T gets information. That information is encrypted by $\mathcal{F}$, and therefore it is protected from T and can only be used, by applying homomorphic arithmetic later on, to produce other $\mathcal{F}$-encrypted values that will be sent back to the vendors. No party (be it a vendor, the mediator, or an eavesdropper) receives any part of the user-item matrix R which it does not own.

Note that practical deployments of our protocols should be enhanced with standard security mechanisms. In particular, each party should create its own pair of private and public keys, and get from a Certificate Authority a corresponding certificate. Then, each message must be signed by the sender and encrypted under the receiver's public key. Such standard security layers are essential when implementing *any* SMC protocol, and they come *on top* of the SMC protocol. They are essential in order to prevent eavesdropping, masquerading, and other well-known attacks on communication systems.

4.3 Computing predicted ratings

In this phase, any vendor V_k, $k \in [K]$, can submit a query to T for the predicted rating of a single user $u \in U$ of an item b offered by V_k. Such queries are answered, in a privacy preserving manner, by Protocol 3. In the protocol we rely upon the following lemma.

Lemma 4.1. *Let $\mathcal{F}$ be a homomorphic encryption function and let $\mathbf{x}$ and $\mathbf{y}$ be two N-dimensional integer vectors. Denote $(\mathcal{F}(\mathbf{x}))^{\mathbf{y}} := \prod_{n=1}^{N} \mathcal{F}(\mathbf{x}(n))^{\mathbf{y}(n)}$. Then $(\mathcal{F}(\mathbf{x}))^{\mathbf{y}} = \mathcal{F}(\langle \mathbf{x}, \mathbf{y} \rangle)$.*

Protocol 3 begins with V_k submitting a query to T (Step 1); the query includes an index $n \in [N]$ of a user $u_n \in U$ and an index $m \in I_k$ of an item b_m that V_k offers. Then, T computes the set $N_q^+(m)$ (see Section 3.1); those are the indices $\{\ell_1, \ldots, \ell_t\}$ of the $t \le q$ items in $B \setminus \{b_m\}$ (not necessarily from among those offered by V_k) that have the highest and positive similarity scores against b_m (Step 2). T then sets $\mathbf{s}_m$ to be the mth column of the similarity matrix, where all entries not corresponding to the above $N_q^+(m)$-items are zeroed (Step 3). Those steps can be carried out just once for each item, so that the results can be used in future queries for the same item.

In Step 4 T selects a random multiplier g (as explained in Section 3.2) that will obfuscate from V_k the values of the numerator and the denominator in the quotient in Eq. (4), but will enable V_k to compute that quotient. Recall that, owing to Protocol 2, T has the vectors $\mathcal{F}(\hat{\mathbf{r}}_n)$ and $\mathcal{F}(\xi(\mathbf{r}_n))$ for u_n. Then, relying on Lemma 4.1, T computes in Step 5 the $\mathcal{F}$-encryption x of the scalar product $x' := g \cdot \sum_{i=1}^{t} S(\ell_i, m)\hat{\mathbf{r}}_n(\ell_i)$, as well as the $\mathcal{F}$-encryption y of the scalar product $y' := g \cdot \sum_{i=1}^{t} S(\ell_i, m)\xi(\mathbf{r}_n(\ell_i))$. It sends those values to V_k who proceeds to decrypt them (Step 6) and then use them in Eq. (4) to get the predicted rating (Step 7). (Recall that the average rating for each item b_m, $m \in I_k$, can be computed by V_k alone and was already computed in Protocol 2.)

Privacy. The only party who receives information in Protocol 3 is V_k. It receives the numerator and denominator in the quotient in Eq. (4) that determines the desired predicted rating. Since both values are obfuscated by a random multiplier that T generates, V_k only receives their quotient but it does not learn the value of neither of them beyond what is implied by that quotient.

4.4 Computing the most recommended items

Here we discuss the case where in the online phase, instead of showing to the user u_n predicted ratings for items that he had not rated so far, V_k presents to him a list of the h items, yet unrated by u_n, which are most likely to appeal to him. In view of our discussion in Section 3.1, such a computation would be carried out by V_k and T as follows: if $I(n)$ is the subset of indices of items that u_n already rated, then V_k will select the h indices $m \in I_k \setminus I(n)$ for which $\hat{s}(m) = \sum_{\ell \in I(n) \cap N_q(m)} S(\ell, m)$, Eq. (3), are largest, where $S(\ell, m)$ are the scaled integral similarity scores that T got as a result of Protocol 1.

Protocol 3 Computing a predicted rating of $u \in U$ for an item offered by V_k.

1: V_k sends to T a query $(n, m) \in [N] \times I_k$.
2: T computes the set $N_q^+(m) := \{\ell_1, \ldots, \ell_t\}$.
3: T sets an M-dimensional vector $\mathbf{s}_m$ where $\mathbf{s}_m(\ell) = S(\ell, m)$ if $\ell \in N_q^+(m)$ and $\mathbf{s}_m(\ell) = 0$ otherwise.
4: T selects a random integer multiplier g.
5: T sends to V_k the two scalar values $x = \mathcal{F}(\hat{\mathbf{r}}_n)^{(g \cdot \mathbf{s}_m)}$ and $y = \mathcal{F}(\xi(\mathbf{r}_n))^{(g \cdot \mathbf{s}_m)}$.
6: V_k computes $x' := \mathcal{F}^{-1}(x)$ and $y' := \mathcal{F}^{-1}(y)$.
7: V_k sets $P(u_n, b_m) = \overline{R(b_m)} + x'/Ly'$ if $y' \neq 0$, and $P(u_n, b_m) = \overline{R(b_m)}$ otherwise.

Ensure: V_K gets $P(u_n, b_m)$.

Protocol 4 performs that computation in a privacy-preserving manner. It starts by V_k submitting a query to T (Step 1). In Steps 2-4, T generates an $\mathcal{F}$-encryption of $\hat{s}(m)$ for all $m \in I_k$, multiplied by a random integer multiplier g, as described in Section 3.2. Indeed, by Eq. (3) and Lemma 4.1, and the fact that $\xi(\mathbf{r}_n)$ is a binary vector with $\xi(\mathbf{r}_n)(\ell) = 1$ if and only if $\ell \in I(n)$, it follows that $\mathbf{x}(m) = \mathcal{F}(g\hat{s}(m))$ for all $m \in I_k$.

Next (Step 5), T computes an M_k-dimensional vector $\mathbf{y}$ such that $\mathbf{y}(m) = \mathcal{F}(1)$ if $m \in I_k \cap I(n)$ (namely, if u_n already rated that item) and $\mathbf{y}(m) = \mathcal{F}(0)$ if $m \in I_k \setminus I(n)$. T generates the vector $\mathbf{y}$ by taking the restriction of the vector $\mathcal{F}(\xi(\mathbf{r}_n))$ (that T received in Protocol 2) to I_k and multiplying each of its entries by a fresh random encryption of 0. Because $\mathcal{F}$ is homomorphic, such an operation changes only the ciphertext value but not the underlying plaintext. The reason for this seemingly redundant operation will be clarified below.

Next, T sends a random permutation of the vectors $\mathbf{x}$ and $\mathbf{y}$ to V_k, who decrypts them into $\mathbf{x}'$ and $\mathbf{y}'$, respectively (Steps 6-7). Hence, $\mathbf{x}'$ holds a permutation of the values $g\hat{s}(m)$, for all items $m \in I_k$, while $\mathbf{y}'$ holds a corresponding permutation of 0 and 1 values that identify those items which u_n had already rated. Since T had scrambled the latter ciphertexts (by multiplying each one of them with a fresh random encryption of 0), V_k can only distinguish between rated and unrated items, but it cannot distinguish between items within either one of those two subsets. (If T had not multiplied each $\mathcal{F}(\xi(\mathbf{r}_n)(m))$ with a fresh encryption of zero, then V_k would have been able to reverse engineer the random permutation π by comparing the entries of $\mathbf{y}$ with the encrypted entries of $\xi(\mathbf{r}_n)$ that it had sent to T earlier in Step 4 in Protocol 2.) V_k proceeds to find the indices of the h yet unrated items with largest $g\hat{s}(m)$ (and hence also largest $\hat{s}(m)$) and sends them to T (Step 8). T responds by letting V_k know the original indices of those items (Step 9). Those are the items to be presented to the user u_n as the top-h recommended items.

Privacy. The values of the scores $\hat{s}(m)$ are hidden from V_k by the random multiplier g. However, using that mechanism alone

Protocol 4 Computing for u_n the top h yet unrated items offered by V_k.

1: V_k sends to T a query $n \in [N]$.
2: For each $m \in I_k$, T defines an M-dimensional vector $\mathbf{s}_m$ where $\mathbf{s}_m(\ell) = S(\ell, m)$ if $\ell \in N_q(m)$ and $\mathbf{s}_m(\ell) = 0$ otherwise.
3: T selects a random integer multiplier g.
4: T computes an M_k-dimensional vector $\mathbf{x}$ where $\mathbf{x}(m) = \mathcal{F}(\xi(\mathbf{r}_n))^{(g \cdot \mathbf{s}_m)}$, $\forall m \in I_k$.
5: T computes an M_k-dimensional vector $\mathbf{y}$, where $\mathbf{y}(m) = \mathcal{F}(\xi(\mathbf{r}_n)(m)) \cdot \mathcal{F}(0)$, $\forall m \in I_k$.
6: T generates a secret and random permutation π over I_k and sends to V_k the vectors $\pi(\mathbf{x})$ and $\pi(\mathbf{y})$.
7: V_k computes $\mathbf{x}' := \mathcal{F}^{-1}(\pi(\mathbf{x}))$ and $\mathbf{y}' := \mathcal{F}^{-1}(\pi(\mathbf{y}))$.
8: V_k sends to T the set of indices $\{m_1, \ldots, m_h\}$ in which $\mathbf{y}'(\cdot) = 0$ and $\mathbf{x}'(\cdot)$ are largest.
9: T sends back to V_k the set of original indices $\{\pi^{-1}(m_1), \ldots, \pi^{-1}(m_h)\}$ in a new random order.

Ensure: V_K gets the indices in $I_k \setminus I(n)$ of the top h items to be recommended to u_n.

would have leaked to V_k the ratios between the scores $\hat{s}(m)$. In order to reduce such information leakage (even though the ratio between $\hat{s}(m_1)$ and $\hat{s}(m_2)$ is arguably non-sensitive), we introduced two additional mechanisms. One is the random permutation π which prevents V_k from associating a given masked score $g\hat{s}(m)$ to an item b_m. The other mechanism is the ciphertext scrambling that T did in Step 5, as we explained above. The combination of those two mechanisms allows V_k and T to find the h items which are yet unrated by u_n and have the largest $\hat{s}(m)$ scores, without disclosing to V_k information on the scores $\hat{s}(m)$ of the items that it offers.

5 EXPERIMENTS

Experimental setting. All experiments were run on a 13-inch MacBook Pro with a 3.0GHz dual-core Intel Core i7 CPU and 16GB of RAM. The algorithms were implemented in Java as an extension to the open source LibRec library[2].

Datasets. We used four publicly available datasets: MovieLens 100K, MovieLens 1M, MovieLens 20M, and FilmTrust. Table 1 reports their main characteristics: number of users N, number of items M, number of ratings $numR$, density (%) $D := \frac{numR}{NM} \times 100$, and the rating scale.

Table 1: Dataset characteristics

dataset	N	M	$numR$	density	scale
MovieLens 100K	943	1682	10^5	6.30%	[1,5]
MovieLens 1M	6040	3706	10^6	4.47%	[1,5]
MovieLens 20M	138000	27000	$2 \cdot 10^7$	0.54%	[1,5]
FilmTrust	1508	2071	35497	1.14%	[.5,4]

Methodology. In each experiment we randomly split the $numR$ input ratings into training (70%) and testing (30%) sets. We then simulated a vertical distribution between K vendors by randomly splitting the complete user-item matrix R into K (almost) equal-sized sub-matrices, vertically. Namely, if R is of dimensions $N \times M$, we split it into K matrices of (almost equal) dimensions $N \times M_k$, where $M_k \in \{\lfloor M/K \rfloor, \lceil M/K \rceil\}$, $k \in [K]$. We then ran the PPCF protocols on this distributed data and computed the performance of the resulting recommender system when trying to predict the ratings or rankings of the testing data from the training data. We repeated this process ten times, each time with new and independent random choices. Finally, we report the average performance over those ten runs.

In the first two experiments, we compare the performance of our protocols for predicting ratings and rankings to the protocol of Yakut and Polat (YP) [33], which is the only other item-based PPCF protocol that is directly comparable to ours. Since the latter protocol is designed for the case $K = 2$, our next experiments are carried out on vertical splits of the user-item matrices into two random vertical sub-matrices.

One of the tools which YP utilizes in order to offer privacy is by adding fake ratings. Assume that V_k has a sub-matrix of dimensions $N \times M_k$ that includes $numR_k$ actual ratings. Then V_k replaces p% of the remaining $NM_k - numR_k$ entries with fake ratings, $k = 1, 2$. The value of the fake ratings can be set in several ways. One of the suggestions made in [33], which we adopt herein, is that each V_k uses the global mean rating over all rated entries in its sub-matrix.

Experiment 1. We compared the accuracy of our Protocol 3 for predicting ratings to that of YP. We applied Protocol 3 for each of the testing entries and then computed the MAE over all testing entries (in both sites of V_1 and V_2). We did a similar test with the prediction protocol YP, with several values of p (the percentage of fake ratings). Finally, we used a baseline algorithm that simply predicts for each user u and item b that $P(u, b) = \overline{R(b)}$, where $\overline{R(b)}$ is the average rating given to item b. Figure 1 shows the resulting errors as obtained on each of our datasets. (Recall that the shown values are averaged over ten random and independent runs.) As can be seen, the accuracy of YP with $p = 0$ coincides with that of our Protocol 3, but such a version of YP is non-private. Increasing p to higher values that would provide better hiding of each vendor's data results in higher errors, that in the two MoviLens datasets even became higher than that of the naïve (and perfectly secure) item-mean predictor. To summarize, our protocols, which base their security on cryptographic means, rather than randomization, offer higher security than YP; in addition, the output of our protocols (as opposed to YP) fully coincides with the non-secure algorithm.

Experiment 2. Next, we compared the quality of ranking as offered by our Protocol 4, to the quality of rankings which are derived from computing predicted ratings, by either our Protocol 3 or by YP [33]. The comparison is made by the AUC (Area Under the Receiver Operating Curve) measure; AUC values range from 0.5 (worst) to 1 (best).

Let $I_{k,n}$ deote the set of items offered by V_k which u_n had rated, and their corresponding entries in R were selected for training. We follow the usual practice of generating rankings over all items in the complement set, $I^c_{k,n} := I_k \setminus I_{k,n}$, and then comparing that ranking to the baseline ranking, in which all items in $I^c_{k,n}$ which u_n had rated are considered positive and all other items in $I^c_{k,n}$ are considered negative. Specifically, for each $m \in I^c_{k,n}$ we computed

[2] http://www.librec.net

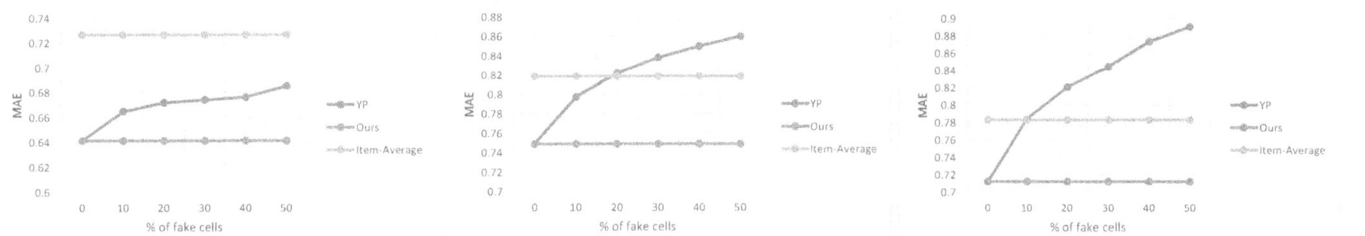

Figure 1: Rating prediction: FilmTrust (left), MovieLens 100K (center) and MovieLens 1M (right)

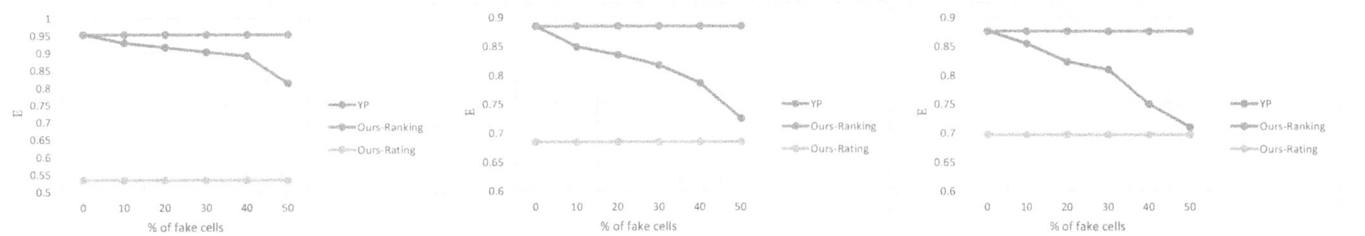

Figure 2: Ranking prediction: FilmTrust (left), MovieLens 100K (center) and MovieLens 1M (right)

three scores: its predicted rating by Protocol 3, its predicted rating by YP, and the score $\hat{s}(m)$, Eq. (3), by which Protocol 4 ranks. By thus we get three sequences of scores which induce three rankings over $I^c_{k,n}$. We compared each of those rankings to the above described baseline ranking. Letting $E_{k,n}$ denote the AUC value obtained for one of those three rankings, we finally compute the average value $E = \left(\sum_{k=1}^{2} \sum_{n=1}^{N} E_{k,n}\right)/2N$. Figure 2 shows the average of E, for each of the three scoring functions, over ten random runs. As can be seen, Protocol 4, which is designed for issuing rankings, issues significantly better rankings than rankings based on the predicted ratings of either Protocol 3 or YP.

Experiment 3. We conclude with runtime experimentation. We measured the cryptographic overhead on both the mediator T and a typical vendor V_k in the offline and online phases. For encryption we used the Paillier cryptosystem [18] implemented in Java[3]. Table 2 shows the runtime overheads in each of the three datasets, when they are distributed evenly and vertically among $K = 5$ vendors[4], in hours(h), minutes(m), seconds(s), and miliseconds(ms).

In the offline phase, we focus only on Protocol 2. We ignore Protocol 1 for two reasons. First, the actual runtime depends on the selection of the SSP sub-protocol. Second, if one chooses the SSP protocol of [5], which is most fitting in our setting, then it involves no cryptographic operations, and hence the privacy-induced overhead is negligible. Protocol 2 entails cryptographic overhead only on the vendors, as they need to encrypt their matrix entries. The overhead is considerable. In the three datasets apart from the largest one, MovieLens 20M, the offline computation time takes from 14.5 minutes up to 3.4 hours. However, as that phase is run only once in a period (say, once a week), and since the required computations can be easily parallelized, such overhead is reasonable.

In the largest dataset, MovieLens 20M, the situation is different. A direct application of Protocol 2 would take several days. Hence, for datasets of such dimensions we perform the following economization. The values that V_k has to encrypt in Protocol 2 are $\hat{R}(n, m)$ (see its definition in Step 3 of Protocol 2) and $\xi(R(n, m))$, for all $n \in [N]$, $m \in I_k$. But 99.46% of those values are just zero, as implied by the sparsity of the MovieLens 20M dataset (see Table 1). While we stressed earlier the importance of using a probabilistic encryption function that would hide from T the pattern of plaintexts underneath the encryption, performing such a large number of repeated encryptions is too extreme. (A direct application of Protocol 2 would encrypt the value zero $1.48 \cdot 10^9$ times, since that is the number of zeros in the matrices $\hat{R}(n, m)$ and $\xi(R(n, m))$ for each vendor in the vertical distribution scenario that we consider for that dataset.)

In order to dramatically decrease the runtime, we created, for each vendor, a "dictionary" of $\sqrt{2NM_k}$ random and independent encryptions of zero. Then, whenever we had to create a random encryption of zero, we picked two elements from the dictionary and multiplied them (without picking the same pair twice). That way, we were able to generate the needed number of zero encryptions without repeating the same ciphertext twice. Since the cost of multiplication is much smaller than that of encryption, the resulting runtime was reduced to only 48 minutes.

For the online phase we used $q = 80$. (Recall that q is the size of the item-neighborhoods which are used in predicting ratings

[3] www.csee.umbc.edu/~kunliu1/research/Paillier.html

[4] The times in the Rating column are independent of K. Those in the Offline and Ranking columns are inversely proportional to K, under the assumption of even distribution.

and rankings.) The overhead for predicting ratings (Protocol 3) is negligible. The overhead for ranking (Protocol 4) is much larger, since for ranking, it is needed to compute a score for all items (while in rating a score needs to be computed only for a single item). But despite the fact that the runtimes for computing rankings are high (few seconds in the three smaller datasets and over one minute, in total, in the largest dataset), such runtimes are no show-stoppers for three reasons: (a) The computations of T as well as those of V_k can be parallelized so that by dedicating several machines for performing the costly cryptographic operations it is possible to reduce the computation time. (b) Presenting the top h recommended items for a user may be a service which is offered at the initiation of the vendor (as opposed to one that is triggered by a demand of the user). In such a case, once the vendor identifies a user as an active consumer who should be presented with such recommendations, it may start this computation and present the issued recommendations to the user when they become available. (c) V_k may define upfront for u_n a subset of items $I_k(n) \subset I_k$ that could be of interest for him (say, based on his history or demographics) and then notify T of that subset. Then, T could compute $\mathbf{x}(m)$ and $\mathbf{y}(m)$ only for $m \in I_k(n)$. The resulting runtime, for both T and V_k, will consequently reduce by a factor of $M_k/|I_k(n)|$.

Table 2: Cryptographic runtime overheads

Dataset	Offline	Rating		Ranking	
	V_k	T	V_k	T	V_k
MovieLens 100K	14.5m	13.1ms	5.1ms	2.6s	1.7s
MovieLens 1M	3.4h	15.8ms	5.1ms	5.8s	3.8s
MovieLens 20M	48m(*)	15.1ms	5.1ms	42.8s	34s
FilmTrust	37.2m	13.4ms	5.1ms	3.3s	2.1s

6 CONCLUSION

We devised herein secure multi-party protocols for executing item-based PPCF over distributed datasets. In this extended abstract we focused on the vertical distributed setting; the horizontal case is deferred to the full version. Our protocols rely on a mediator. Such a mediator is essential since, without it, the different vendors would need to constantly be online and be ready to serve requests by other vendors. Our protocols issue exactly the same results as their non-privacy preserving counterparts, and they protect each vendor's data from other vendors as well as from the mediator. Our protocols rely solely on existing cryptographic arsenal; this offers a significant advantage as they can be readily implemented on top of standard libraries.

This study suggests several future research directions: (a) Enhancing our protocols so that they offer privacy even if some of the interacting parties do not act honestly, or collude. To the best of our knowledge, none of the existing PPCF studies had considered such settings. (b) Generalizing our protocols to deal with an arbitrary distribution setting (i.e, not a purely vertical or a purely horizontal split). (c) Examining the applicability of our techniques to other CF algorithms, such as matrix factorization-based algorithms and their extensions (e.g. [21]) and compare their performance to that of existing privacy-preserving matrix factorization algorithms, such as [16, 17].

REFERENCES

[1] Gilad Asharov, Francesco Bonchi, David García-Soriano, and Tamir Tassa. 2017. Secure Centrality Computation Over Multiple Networks. In *WWW*. 957–966.

[2] Anirban Basu, Jaideep Vaidya, and Hiroaki Kikuchi. 2012. Perturbation Based Privacy Preserving Slope One Predictors for Collaborative Filtering. In *IFIPTM*. 17–35.

[3] Iván Cantador, Ignacio Fernández-Tobías, Shlomo Berkovsky, and Paolo Cremonesi. 2015. Cross-domain recommender systems. In *Recommender Systems Handbook*. 919–959.

[4] Fran Casino, Constantinos Patsakis, Domenec Puig, and Agusti Solanas. 2013. On Privacy Preserving Collaborative Filtering: Current Trends, Open Problems, and New Issues. In *ICEBE*. 244–249.

[5] Wenliang Du and Justin Zhijun Zhan. 2002. A practical approach to solve Secure Multi-party Computation problems. In *Workshop on New Security Paradigms*. 127–135.

[6] Michael D. Ekstrand, John Riedl, and Joseph A. Konstan. 2011. Collaborative Filtering Recommender Systems. *Foundations and Trends in Human-Computer Interaction* 4, 2 (2011), 175–243.

[7] Arik Friedman, Bart P Knijnenburg, Kris Vanhecke, Luc Martens, and Shlomo Berkovsky. 2015. Privacy aspects of recommender systems. In *Recommender Systems Handbook*. 649–688.

[8] David Goldberg, David A. Nichols, Brian M. Oki, and Douglas B. Terry. 1992. Using Collaborative Filtering to Weave an Information Tapestry. *Commun. ACM* 35, 12 (1992), 61–70.

[9] Tal Grinshpoun and Tamir Tassa. 2014. A privacy-preserving algorithm for distributed constraint optimization. In *AAMAS*. 909–916.

[10] Tal Grinshpoun and Tamir Tassa. 2016. P-SyncBB: A Privacy Preserving Branch and Bound DCOP Algorithm. *J. Artificial Intelligence Research* 57 (2016), 621–660.

[11] Arjan Jeckmans, Qiang Tang, and Pieter H. Hartel. 2012. Privacy-preserving collaborative filtering based on horizontally partitioned dataset. In *International Conference on Collaboration Technologies and Systems*. 439–446.

[12] Wei Jiang and Chris Clifton. 2006. A secure distributed framework for achieving k-anonymity. *The VLDB Journal* 15 (2006), 316–333.

[13] Murat Kantarcioglu and Chris Clifton. 2004. Privacy-preserving distributed mining of association rules on horizontally partitioned data. *IEEE Transactions on Knowledge and Data Engineering* 16 (2004), 1026–1037.

[14] Thomas Léauté and Boi Faltings. 2013. Protecting Privacy through Distributed Computation in Multi-agent Decision Making. *J. Artificial Intelligence Research* 47 (2013), 649–695.

[15] Daniel Lemire and Anna Maclachlan. 2005. Slope One Predictors for Online Rating-Based Collaborative Filtering. In *SDM*. 471–475.

[16] Kartik Nayak, Xiao Shaun Wang, Stratis Ioannidis, Udi Weinsberg, Nina Taft, and Elaine Shi. 2015. GraphSC: Parallel Secure Computation Made Easy. In *IEEE Symposium on Security and Privacy*. 377–394.

[17] Valeria Nikolaenko, Stratis Ioannidis, Udi Weinsberg, Marc Joye, Nina Taft, and Dan Boneh. 2013. Privacy-preserving matrix factorization. In *CCS*. 801–812.

[18] Pascal Paillier. 1999. Public-Key Cryptosystems Based on Composite Degree Residuosity Classes. In *Eurocrypt*. 223–238.

[19] Huseyin Polat and Wenliang Du. 2005. Privacy-Preserving Collaborative Filtering on Vertically Partitioned Data. In *PKDD*. 651–658.

[20] Huseyin Polat and Wenliang Du. 2008. Privacy-preserving top-N recommendation on distributed data. *Journal of the Association for Information Science and Technology* 59 (2008), 1093–1108.

[21] Steffen Rendle, Christoph Freudenthaler, Zeno Gantner, and Lars Schmidt-Thieme. 2009. BPR: Bayesian personalized ranking from implicit feedback. In *UAI*. 452–461.

[22] Badrul M. Sarwar, George Karypis, Joseph A. Konstan, and John Riedl. 2001. Item-based collaborative filtering recommendation algorithms. In *WWW*. 285–295.

[23] J. Ben Schafer, Joseph A. Konstan, and John Riedl. 1999. Recommender systems in e-commerce. In *EC*. 158–166.

[24] Assaf Schuster, Ran Wolff, and Bobi Gilburd. 2004. Privacy-preserving association rule mining in large-scale distributed systems. In *CCGRID*. 411–418.

[25] Tamir Tassa. 2014. Secure Mining of Association Rules inHorizontally Distributed Databases. *IEEE Transactions on Knowledge and Data Engineering* 26 (2014), 970–983.

[26] Tamir Tassa and Francesco Bonchi. 2014. Privacy Preserving Estimation of Social Influence. In *EDBT*. 559–570.

[27] Tamir Tassa and Dror J. Cohen. 2013. Anonymization of Centralized and Distributed Social Networks by Sequential Clustering. *IEEE Transactions on Knowledge and Data Engineering* 25 (2013), 311–324.

[28] Tamir Tassa and Ehud Gudes. 2012. Secure distributed computation of anonymized views of shared databases. *Transactions on Database Systems* 37, Article 11 (2012).

[29] Tamir Tassa, Roie Zivan, and Tal Grinshpoun. 2015. Max-Sum Goes Private. In *IJCAI*. 425–431.

[30] Tamir Tassa, Roie Zivan, and Tal Grinshpoun. 2016. Preserving Privacy in Region Optimal DCOP Algorithms. In *IJCAI*. 496–502.
[31] Jaideep Vaidya and Chris Clifton. 2002. Privacy preserving association rule mining in vertically partitioned data. In *KDD*. 639–644.
[32] I-Cheng Wang, Chih-Hao Shen, Justin Zhan, Tsan-sheng Hsu, Churn-Jung Liau, and Da-Wei Wang. 2009. Toward Empirical Aspects of Secure Scalar Product. *IEEE Transactions on Systems, Man, and Cybernetics, Part C* 39 (2009), 440–447.
[33] Ibrahim Yakut and Huseyin Polat. 2012. Arbitrarily distributed data-based recommendations with privacy. *Data & Knowledge Engineering* 72 (2012), 239–256.
[34] Andrew C. Yao. 1982. Protocols for secure computation. In *FOCS*. 160–164.
[35] Sheng Zhong, Zhiqiang Yang, and Rebecca N. Wright. 2005. Privacy-enhancing k-anonymization of customer data. In *PODS*. 139–147.

Modeling the Assimilation-Contrast Effects in Online Product Rating Systems: Debiasing and Recommendations

Xiaoying Zhang
The Chinese University of Hong Kong
xyzhang@cse.cuhk.edu.hk

Junzhou Zhao
The Chinese University of Hong Kong
junzhouzhao@gmail.com

John C.S. Lui
The Chinese University of Hong Kong
cslui@cse.cuhk.edu.hk

ABSTRACT

The *unbiasedness* of online product ratings, an important property to ensure that users' ratings indeed reflect their true evaluations to products, is vital both in shaping consumer purchase decisions and providing reliable recommendations. Recent experimental studies showed that distortions from historical ratings would ruin the *unbiasedness* of subsequent ratings. How to "*discover*" the distortions from historical ratings in each *single* rating (or at the micro-level), and perform the "*debiasing operations*" in real rating systems are the main objectives of this work.

Using 42 million real customer ratings, we first show that users either "*assimilate*" or "*contrast*" to historical ratings under different scenarios: users conform to historical ratings if historical ratings are not far from the product quality (assimilation), while users deviate from historical ratings if historical ratings are significantly different from the product quality (contrast). This phenomenon can be explained by the well-known psychological argument: the "*Assimilate-Contrast*" theory. However, none of the existing works on modeling historical ratings' influence have taken this into account, and this motivates us to propose the *Historical Influence Aware Latent Factor Model* (HIALF), the first model for real rating systems to capture and mitigate historical distortions in each *single* rating. HIALF also allows us to study the influence patterns of historical ratings from a modeling perspective, and it perfectly matches the assimilation and contrast effects we previously observed. Also, HIALF achieves significant improvements in predicting subsequent ratings, and accurately predicts the relationships revealed in previous empirical measurements on real ratings. Finally, we show that HIALF can contribute to better recommendations by decoupling users' real preference from distorted ratings, and reveal the intrinsic product quality for wiser consumer purchase decisions.

1 INTRODUCTION

Online rating system is perhaps one of the most important modules in a wide variety of contemporary web applications ranging from e-commerce websites [18, 27] to online video/news platforms [7, 31]. Such online rating systems allow users to rate items (e.g., products, videos, etc.) they have recently consumed, and these ratings can help subsequent users in making decisions on whether to consume this item or not. In order to have correct subsequent decision making, the *unbiasedness* of ratings, a property to ensure that users' ratings indeed reflect their true evaluations to the product, is crucial. Furthermore, unbiased users' ratings are also important to recommender systems so that they can provide reliable recommendations.

However, recent experimental studies [3, 19, 22, 30] showed that the disclosed historical ratings would ruin the *unbiasedness* of subsequent ratings, making them inaccurate to convey users' intrinsic evaluations to products. Such distortions bring both *macro-level* and *micro-level* effects. At the macro level, the distortions from historical ratings will make overall rating distribution deviate from the intrinsic product quality, thereby misleading subsequent consumers to wrong purchase decisions [19, 22, 30]. At the micro level (or at the granularity of each single rating), the distortion in the rating provides an adulterated view of user's preference for the product, weakening recommender systems' ability to provide high-quality recommendations [3]. As in [3], even for products with the same quality, users tend to rate higher when they observe high historical ratings as compared to low historical ratings. Thus, when a user rates a product high under high historical ratings, the high rating may not suggest the user's high preference to the product anymore, since it may be the result of high historical ratings.

Recently, Wang et al. [28] studied the macro-level influence from historical ratings. However, to debias the historical distortions in recommendations, we need a *micro-level* model to characterize the historical ratings' influence in each *single* rating. Previously, several works [2, 13] tried to mitigate the micro-level historical ratings' influence with an assumption that we know *users' intrinsic ratings*, the ratings given when users couldn't observe historical ratings. However, their models are inapplicable in real rating systems where users' intrinsic ratings are usually latent. To the best of our knowledge, there is no work to characterize and debias the micro-level influence from historical ratings in real rating systems. The main challenge is that people do not fully understand how historical ratings affect the user who gives the next rating.

Present work. The goal of this work is to develop a model for *real rating systems* to accurately characterize and debias the influence from historical ratings in each *single* rating microscopically. To handle the challenge mentioned before, we analyze real ratings to understand how historical ratings affect user's rating behavior.

In this work, we first analyze a dataset of 42 million ratings from *Tripadvisor* and *Amazon*. We find that users either *assimilate* or *contrast* to historical ratings under different scenarios: a user tends to give a rating similar to historical ratings when historical ratings are not far from the product quality (assimilation), while deviating from historical ratings when historical ratings differ significantly from the product quality (contrast). In fact, this phenomenon can be well explained by the "*Assimilate-Contrast*" theory [4] in psychology.

RecSys '17, August 27-31, 2017, Como, Italy

ACM ISBN 978-1-4503-4652-8/17/08...$15.00
https://doi.org/10.1145/3109859.3109885

Then, we find that the previous works [2, 13, 28] were unable to explain our empirical results. Thus we propose *Historical Influence Aware Latent Factor Model* (HIALF), the first model designed for *real rating systems* to capture and mitigate the *micro-level* influence from historical ratings. In HIALF, we do not make any assumptions about influence patterns of historical ratings, but we discover the most likely influence pattern from data. The discovered influence patterns via HIALF match perfectly with the assimilation and contrast effects in empirical observations. Compared with previous methods, HIALF reveals the closest fitting to the relationships observed in previous empirical measurements on real ratings, and significantly reduces the mean-squared error (MSE) in predicting subsequent ratings, i.e., up to 39% as compared with HEARD [28] and 12% as compared with the standard latent factor model [21].

Finally, we demonstrate two applications of HIALF. HIALF enables us to separate users' intrinsic interests from historical distortions, leading to better product recommendations. Also, we can directly compare products by their intrinsic qualities, without being misguided by distorted historical ratings.

Contributions. Overall, we make the following contributions:

- **Observations.** We first reveal the assimilation and contrast effects in user's rating behavior caused by historical ratings. We also provide an explanation for our observations by a well-known psychological theory (Section 2).
- **Modeling.** We develop the first model (HIALF) for real rating systems to characterize and mitigate historical distortions in each single rating microscopically (Section 3).
- **Performance.** The discovered influence patterns of historical ratings via HIALF perfectly match the assimilation and contrast effects in observations. Moreover, HIALF achieves significantly improvements in predicting subsequent ratings, and accurately fits the relationships revealed in empirical measurements on real ratings (Section 4).
- **Applications.** HIALF can contribute to better recommendations by separating users' intrinsic interests from historical distortions. It can also facilitate wiser purchase decisions by revealing the intrinsic product quality (Section 5).

2 HOW HISTORICAL RATINGS AFFECT THE NEXT SINGLE RATING

We conduct empirical measurements on real world datasets to study how historical ratings affect its next single rating. In this section, we first describe these rating datasets, then we discuss how to measure the impact of historical ratings on its next rating. Finally, we propose an explanation of our empirical observations, and verify that the existing works [2, 13, 28] cannot explain our observations, which motivates us to design a model for real rating systems to depict the micro-level historical ratings' influence in the next section.

2.1 Rating Datasets

We first introduce two large scale public available rating datasets from Amazon[1] and TripAdvisor[2], respectively.

Amazon is a popular e-commerce website that allows users to review and rate products they recently consumed, e.g., books, clothes, etc. In the Amazon dataset [18], we focus on ratings of the top four largest categories: books, movies, electronics, and clothes. These four categories cover about 48.8% of all products, and 50.4% of all ratings on Amazon. The dataset spans from May 1996 to July 2014.

TripAdvisor is a popular travel website that provides reviews and ratings of travel-related contents, e.g., hotels, restaurants, etc. We use the entire ratings on it from April 2001 to September 2012 [26].

Table 1 summarizes the basic statistics of our dataset.

Table 1: Summary of rating datasets.

category	# products	# users	# ratings
Amazon-books	2, 370, 585	8, 026, 324	22, 507, 155
Amazon-clothes	1, 503, 384	3, 117, 268	5, 748, 920
Amazon-electronics	498, 196	4, 261, 096	7, 824, 482
Amazon-movies	208, 321	2, 088, 620	4, 607, 047
TripAdvisor	12, 730	781, 329	1, 621, 956

2.2 Empirical Measurements and Observations

We conduct empirical measurements on the above datasets to study how historical ratings affect its next rating.

Let $r_{p,i}$ denote the i-th rating of product p, and let $\mathcal{H}_{p,i} \triangleq (r_{p,1}, \ldots, r_{p,i-1})$ denote a sequence of $i-1$ ratings of product p received before $r_{p,i}$ (in the chronological order of receiving time). $\mathcal{H}_{p,i}$ will be referred to as the *historical ratings* of $r_{p,i}$.

We want to measure how historical ratings $\mathcal{H}_{p,i}$ affect its next rating $r_{p,i}$. Intuitively, there are two factors that could affect a user's decision on rating a product: (1) the product quality; (2) other users' ratings/reviews to which the user was exposed.

The first factor is latent and around the average of ratings given by a large population who were not exposed to historical ratings [25]. To process our dataset, we group products with similar average ratings into one group such that each group has a maximum deviation of 0.2 in the average rating. For example, consider the two selected groups of products with average ratings in [2.9, 3.1] and [3.9, 4.1], and we assume the first (second) group has an *approximately true quality* of 3 (4). We only consider groups containing more than 100 products and on average, each dataset has 10 groups.

Then, in each product group, for each rating $r_{p,i}$, we first calculate its *prior expectation* formed on historical ratings $\mathcal{H}_{p,i}$: $e_{p,i} = \frac{1}{i-1}\sum_{k=1}^{i-1} r_{p,k}$, resulting in a pair $(e_{p,i}, r_{p,i})$[3]. We find that a set of pairs $\{(\dot{e}, \dot{r}_1), \ldots, (\dot{e}, \dot{r}_k)\}$ have the same prior expectation $\dot{e}$, but the ratings $\{\dot{r}_1, \ldots, \dot{r}_k\}$ are given by thousands of different users. We aggregate ratings $\{\dot{r}_1, \ldots, \dot{r}_k\}$ to get $\bar{r} = \frac{1}{k}\sum_{i=1}^{k} \dot{r}_i$. Thus, the resulting list $\{(\dot{e}, \bar{r})\}$ describes how prior expectation $\dot{e}$ affects its next rating $\bar{r}$, on average, in this product group. Finally, we plot the relationship between prior expectation $\dot{e}$ and the average of the next rating $\bar{r}$ for each selected product group in Figure 1. Relationships in other groups are similar with the two selected groups.

Some may argue that the user's personal taste is another factor that affects the user's rating. However, the user's personal taste will not affect the plotted relationships, because for each prior expectation $\dot{e}$, we aggregate thousands of users' ratings to obtain the average of the next rating $\bar{r}$, the aggregated distortions of thousands of users' personal tastes will be insignificant and can be ignored.

[1] https://www.amazon.com
[2] https://www.tripadvisor.com
[3] In all our analysis, we round $e_{p,i}$ to one decimal place.

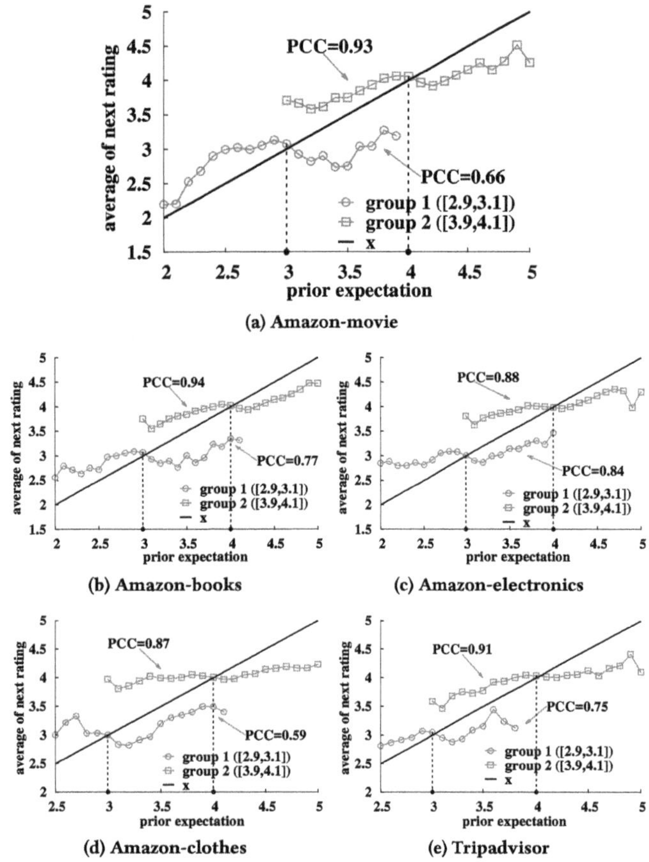

(a) Amazon-movie

(b) Amazon-books

(c) Amazon-electronics

(d) Amazon-clothes

(e) Tripadvisor

Figure 1: Relationship between prior expectation $\dot{e}$ and the average of the next rating $\bar{r}$. The group 1 (group 2) contains products with average ratings in [2.9, 3.1] ([3.9, 4.1]). We observe that products' historical ratings do affect its next rating, and each curve with □ (∘) is divided into two parts by the group's *approximately true quality* (3 for group 1, and 4 for group 2).

Observations. We obtain two main observations from Figure 1:

- Products' historical ratings do affect the next rating. For example, in Figure (1a), the Pearson correlation coefficient of group 1 (products with average ratings in [2.9, 3.1]) and group 2 (products with average ratings in [3.9, 4.1]) are 0.66 and 0.93 respectively. In general, the Pearson correlation coefficients (PCC) are in the range [0.59, 0.94], this reflects a positive correlation between prior expectation and the next rating.
- Each curve with □ (∘) is divided into two parts by the group's *approximately true quality* (3 for group 1, and 4 for group 2). The black line represents a hypothetical linear relationship between prior expectation and its next rating, i.e., the user will give a 4-star rating as long as his prior expectation is 4. Take the group 2 in Figure (1a) as an example, when prior expectation is below the group's approximately true quality of 4, it will receive a rating higher than the prior expectation, on average; and when prior expectation is above the group's approximately true quality of 4, it will receive a rating lower than the prior expectation, on average. It is important to note that this phenomenon is *consistent* among all groups of products in our dataset, and it is interesting to find an explanation of this result.

2.3 Proposed Explanation of Observations

Let us now answer two fundamental questions: (1) why do historical ratings influence its next rating? (2) why does the influence of historical ratings behave consistently like those in Figure 1?

One possible answer to the first question is that different historical ratings lead the user to form different prior expectations for the product, which impact the user's overall satisfaction with the product (the given rating). Before consuming a product, a customer usually refers to previous aggregated ratings to see whether the product really meets his needs. At this stage, he forms his "prior expectation" for that product. Using the customer satisfaction theory [20], user's prior expectation of the product and the product quality together determine the user's satisfaction on the product. Thus, different historical ratings lead to different prior expectations, which in turn affect the next single rating.

To answer the second question, we refer to three well-known psychological theories [4] which describe how the user's prior expectation for the product and the product quality together determine the user's overall satisfaction with the product. Figure (2a) shows the sample representations of three theories. The product quality is 3 and is represented by the line parallel with x axis.

- **"Assimilate" theory**: The user's satisfaction of the product is always similar to his prior expectation (the orange line with △).
- **"Contrast" theory**: The customer will magnify the difference between his prior expectation for the product and the product quality; i.e., if his prior expectation is below (above) the product quality, the user will evaluate the product more (less) favorably than the product quality (the purple line with ∘).
- **"Assimilate-Contrast" theory**: If the disparity between his prior expectation and the product quality can be accepted by the user (in $[\theta, \sigma]$ in Figure (2a)), the user's satisfaction with the product assimilates to his prior expectation; otherwise, the difference between the prior expectation and the product quality tends to be magnified (the red line with □).

One interesting question is which theory can explain our empirical observations. To answer this question, we combine all groups with the same average rating range in five datasets. For example, Figure (2b) illustrates the relationship for all products with average ratings in [2.9, 3.1]. We choose this group because its approximately true quality is in the middle of the rating scale of *Amazon* and *Tripadvisor*. One can see that the relationship follows the *"Assimilate-Contrast"* theory in that (1) prior expectation has a positive correlation with its next rating (contradicting with the *"Contrast"* theory), and (2) when prior expectation is in [1, 1.8) and (4.6, 5], the average of the next rating diverges from the increasing trend in [1.8, 4.6] (contradicting with the *"Assimilate"* theory).

Hypothesis Test. Let us now design a statistical hypothesis test to see whether the *"Assimilate-Contrast"* theory can explain our observations in general. The *"Assimilate-Contrast"* theory differs from the other two theories because its slope changes when the difference between prior expectation and the product quality is large, for example, when prior expectation is in $[1, \theta)$ and $(\sigma, 5]$ in Figure (2a). In our test, each data point is a pair (e, r_e), where e is the prior expectation, and r_e is the rating given under e. Thus, we can construct four sets. The set $C_1 (C_3)$ contains all data points

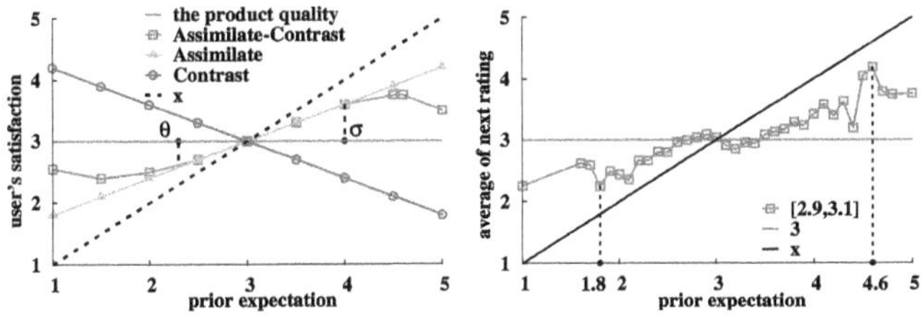

(a) (b)

Figure 2: (a) Sample representations of three theories. (b) Relationship between prior expectation and the average of the next rating in products with average ratings in $[2.9, 3.1]$ **in all five datasets.**

with prior expectation e much smaller (larger) than the product quality q, $C_1 = \{(e, r_e)|e < \theta < q\}$ ($C_3 = \{(e, r_e)|e > \sigma > q\}$). The set $C_2(C_4)$ contains data points with prior expectation e smaller (larger) than but near the product quality q, $C_2 = \{(e, r_e)|\theta < e < q\}$ ($C_4 = \{(e, r_e)|q < e < \sigma\}$). Then, we calculate the slope between $(\theta, \bar{r}_\theta)$ and each point in $C_1(C_2)$, putting it in $S_1(S_2)$, i.e., $S_i = \{\frac{r_e - \bar{r}_\theta}{e - \theta}|(e, r_e) \in C_i\}, i = 1, 2$. Here, $\bar{r}_\theta$ is the average of ratings under prior expectation θ. Similarly, we calculate the slope between $(\sigma, \bar{r}_\sigma)$ and each point in $C_3(C_4)$, getting $S_3(S_4)$. We will discuss how we set θ and σ in the next paragraph. If the *"Assimilate-Contrast"* theory holds, the mean of $S_1(S_3)$ should be smaller than the mean of $S_2(S_4)$. Otherwise, the mean of $S_1(S_3)$ equals to the mean of $S_2(S_4)$. We use student t-test to examine whether there exists a significant difference between the mean of $S_1(S_3)$ and $S_2(S_4)$.

Specifically, we first group products with similar average ratings as before. In each group, we divide the $\{(e, r_e)\}$ pairs into distinct partitions such that pairs in each partition share a unique prior expectation. We discretize real-valued e by equal-interval partition, i.e., prior expectations in $[a - \epsilon, a + \epsilon]$[4] are taken as the same prior expectation as a. Then, we get $S_i, i = 1, 2, 3, 4$ and apply the student t-test [5]. We use Welch-Satterthwaite approximation [23] to get the degrees of freedom. Let $\hat{\theta}$ ($\hat{\sigma}$) be the fourth smallest (largest) prior expectations, then we set $\theta = \min\{\hat{\theta}, q - 1\}$, and $\sigma = \max\{\hat{\sigma}, q + 1\}$. The null hypothesis in our test is that there exists no statistically significant difference between the mean of $S_1(S_3)$ and $S_2(S_4)$, while the alternate hypothesis is that the mean of $S_1(S_3)$ is smaller than the mean of $S_2(S_4)$. We test all hypothesis at the 0.05 significance level. We observe that 11 out of 12 groups reject the null hypothesis of the t-test between S_1 and S_2, and 7 out of 8 groups reject the null hypothesis of the t-test between S_3 and S_4. Since almost all groups reject the null hypothesis, the *"Assimilate-Contrast"* theory is a more appropriate theory to explain how customers are affected by historical ratings.

2.4 Deficiencies of existing works

Next, we show that existing works on modeling historical ratings' influence [2, 13, 28] fail to explain our previous observations.

In our dataset, users' intrinsic ratings are latent, thus we are unable to build the model in [2, 13]. Wang et al. [28] developed HEARD to model how historical ratings $\mathcal{H}_{p,i}$ influence the general rating distribution after next M ratings $x_{p,i+M}$ at the macro level. Here, for a one-to-K star rating system, $x_{p,i+M} \triangleq [x^{(1)}_{p,i+M}, \ldots, x^{(K)}_{p,i+M}]$, where $x^{(k)}_{p,i+M}$ represents the proportion of level-k ratings in the first $(i + M - 1)$ ratings of the product p. Note that the goal of HEARD is fundamentally different from ours. However, given historical ratings $\mathcal{H}_{p,i}$, the probabilistic model of HEARD can reveal the probability $P(r_{p,i} = k|\mathcal{H}_{p,i}), \forall k \in \{1, \ldots, K\}$. Hence, HEARD can be taken as a model to predict the next rating $r_{p,i}$ given its history $\mathcal{H}_{p,i}$. Thus, we perform experiments to see whether HEARD can reveal our previous observations. Specifically, we first train HEARD with each dataset. Then, we select the same groups of products in each dataset as in Figure 1. In each selected group, for each rating, given its historical ratings $\mathcal{H}_{p,i}$, we use HEARD to predict the next rating $r^H_{p,i} = argmax_k P(r_{p,i} = k|\mathcal{H}_{p,i})$. We also calculate its prior expectation $e_{p,i} = \frac{1}{i-1}\sum_{k=1}^{i-1} r_{p,k}$ based on real ratings, obtaining a pair $(e_{p,i}, r^H_{p,i})$. Finally, for each distinct prior expectation e, we calculate the average of the next HEARD-generated ratings under e, denoting as r^H_e.

Before checking the slope changes as in hypothesis tests, we first check whether the resulting list $\{(e, r^H_e)\}$ meets $r^H_e \leq e$, when $e \geq q$, as in Figure 1. Here q refers to the approximately true quality of the product group. Let E^+_q denote those prior expectations larger than q: $E^+_q = \{e|e - q \geq 0\}$. We calculate the average deviation from e to r^H_e when $e \geq q$: $d^H = \frac{1}{|E^+_q|}\sum_{e \in E^+_q}(e - r^H_e)$. Let r^*_e be the average of the next *real* rating given under prior expectation e. We also calculate the average deviation from e to r^*_e when $e \geq q$, which we denote as d^*. Note that d^* is always positive in the real rating datasets, because $r_e \leq e$, when $e \geq q$ in Figure 1. We present d^H and d^* in both groups on all five datasets in Table 2. From Table 2, we observe that all d^H are negative and significantly different from the positive d^*. For example, in *Amazon-books*, for all e, on average, HEARD predicts a larger r^H_e than e in both groups ($d^H < 0$), while in real ratings, r_e should be smaller than e ($d^* > 0$). This already suggests that HEARD *fails* to explain our observations in real rating datasets, and there is no need for the hypothesis tests. The deficiency of HEARD is because HEARD mainly focuses on the macro-level historical ratings' influence in overall rating distribution, rather the micro-level historical influence in each singe rating.

Table 2: d^H and d^* on all five datasets.

category	HEARD (d^H)		real ratings (d^*)	
	group 1	group 2	group 1	group 2
Amazon-books	-0.7899	-0.4305	0.5697	0.3681
Amazon-clothes	-0.8629	-0.4438	0.3733	0.4396
Amazon-electronics	-0.4944	-0.4421	0.4202	0.3868
Amazon-movies	-0.8194	-0.4332	0.5333	0.3913
TripAdvisor	-0.5097	-0.2339	0.2784	0.4368

3 PROPOSED MODEL

In this section, we describe in detail the *Historical Influence Aware Latent Factor Model* (HIALF) which leverages previous observations to characterize the micro-level influence from historical ratings in real rating systems. Our objectives are: (1) to model the influence of historical ratings so as to do a better prediction of the next rating; (2) to reveal the intrinsic qualities of products and users' intrinsic preference so to do a better job in product recommendations.

[4] we set $\epsilon = 0.1$.

[5] We discard groups containing less than 100 products and prior expectations followed by less than 100 ratings due to their low statistical reliability.

3.1 Preliminary: Latent Factor Model

One can first consider using the classical latent factor (LF) model [21] to predict the rating $r_{u,p}$ for user u and product p as:

$$r_{u,p} = g + b_u + b_p + {\boldsymbol{x_u}}^T \boldsymbol{y_p} \tag{1}$$

Here g is the overall rating for an arbitrary user and product; b_u and b_p denote the user and item bias, respectively; $\boldsymbol{x_u}$ and $\boldsymbol{y_p}$ represent vectors of latent features for user u and product p.

We need to emphasize that the standard latent factor model cannot explain our empirical observations because it does not consider factors due to the effects of historical ratings to subsequent ratings. We mention the standard latent factor model because HIALF is an enhanced version of the LF model.

3.2 Historical Influence Aware Latent Factor Model (HIALF)

Let the term *user u's experienced quality of product p* refer to product p's quality in user u's view. We use $h_{p,i}$ to represent the distortion from historical ratings $\mathcal{H}_{p,i}$.

In HIALF, the i-th rating of product p given by user u is mainly taken as a combination of two factors: (1) user u's experienced quality of product p, denoted as $q_{u,p}$; (2) the distortion from historical ratings $h_{p,i}$. The first factor is determined by product p's intrinsic quality and user u's overall interest in product p. We model it by

$$q_{u,p} = g + b_p + {\boldsymbol{x_u}}^T \boldsymbol{y_p} \tag{2}$$

According to previous observations, the second factor $h_{p,i}$ depends on the discrepancy between $q_{u,p}$ and the prior expectation formed on the historical ratings (i.e., $e_{p,i}$). Thus, we use a categorical function $\boldsymbol{\beta}(x)$ to represent the induced bias when the difference between $e_{p,i}$ and $q_{u,p}$ is x, i.e., $x = e_{p,i} - q_{u,p}$. We call $\boldsymbol{\beta}(x)$ as *the disconfirmation bias curve.* Moreover, applying Latané's theory [14], the size of historical ratings $|\mathcal{H}_{p,i}|$ will boost the distortion $h_{p,i}$. For example, 100 historical ratings will exert a larger influence on the next rating than only 1 historical rating. Thus, let $f(x)$ be a scaling function to represent the magnitude of impact by historical ratings of size x. We have:

$$h_{p,i} = f(|\mathcal{H}_{p,i}|)\boldsymbol{\beta}(e_{p,i} - q_{u,p}) \tag{3}$$

All in all, HIALF predicts $\hat{r}_{p,i,u}$ for the i-th rating of product p given by user u as follows:

$$\begin{aligned} \hat{r}_{p,i,u} &= b_u + q_{u,p} + \alpha_u h_{p,i} \\ &= g + b_u + b_p + {\boldsymbol{x_u}}^T \boldsymbol{y_p} + \alpha_u f(|\mathcal{H}_{p,i}|)\boldsymbol{\beta}(e_{p,i} - q_{u,p}) \end{aligned} \tag{4}$$

Here, $g, b_u, b_p, \boldsymbol{x_u}, \boldsymbol{y_p}$ take on the same roles as in the basic latent factor model; α_u models how easily user u will be influenced by historical ratings. A larger α_u means that user u is easier to be affected. Next, we describe how to model $\boldsymbol{\beta}(x)$, $f(x)$, and give a more realistic formula of $e_{p,i}$.

Modeling the disconfirmation bias curve $\boldsymbol{\beta}(x)$. We use a data-driven approach to model $\boldsymbol{\beta}(x)$, i.e., we do not constrain the form of $\boldsymbol{\beta}(x)$ (i.e., to be linear or quadratic). Instead, we learn the most appropriate format from data. We expect the learned $\boldsymbol{\beta}(x)$ can match the assimilation and contrast effects in previous observations.

Online rating systems usually have a limited rating range. For example, *Amazon* and *Tripadvisor* adopt one-to-five-star rating system. Thus, $x = e_{p,i} - q_{u,p}$ is in a fixed known range $[x_a, x_b]$. For

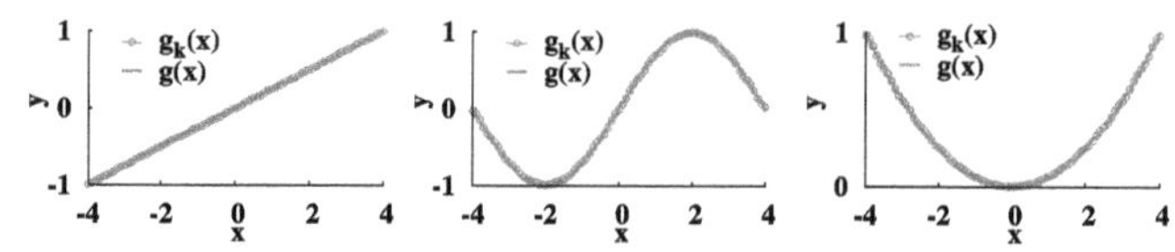

(a) (b) (c)

Figure 3: Using kernel function to approximate three different functions with x in $[-4, 4]$: (a) $g(x) = \frac{x}{4}$; (b) $g(x) = \sin(\frac{\pi x}{4})$; (c) $g(x) = (\frac{x}{4})^2$. In kernel function, we use $\{x_1, \ldots, x_n\} = \{-4, -3.5, -3, \ldots, 3, 3.5, 4\}$ and $\kappa = 10$.

example, on both *Amazon* and *Tripadvisor*, $x \in [-4, 4]$ since both $e_{p,i}$ and $q_{u,p}$ are in $[1, 5]$. In this work, we use non-parametric kernel regression [29] to model $\boldsymbol{\beta}(x)$.

In kernel regression, given a set of i.i.d. samples $\{(x_i, y_i)\}_{i=1}^n$ from model $y_i = g(x_i) + \epsilon_i$, where ϵ_i represents the noise from the standard normal distribution, we can approximate $g(x)$ by a kernel function $g_k(x) = \frac{\sum_{i=1}^n w(x, x_i) \cdot y_i}{\sum_{i=1}^n w(x, x_i)}$. The term $w(x, x_i)$ gives a greater weight to x that is closer to x_i, and we select $w(x, x_i) = exp(-\kappa(x - x_i)^2)$, where κ controls the smoothness of the function. Figure 3 shows examples using kernel methods to approximate three different $g(x)$ with x in $[-4, 4]$, and $g_k(x)$ always gives a good approximation to $g(x)$.

Thus, if we can get a set of samples $\{(e_l, v_l)\}_{l=1}^n$ from the disconfirmation bias curve, i.e., $v_l = \boldsymbol{\beta}(e_l) + \epsilon_l$, where ϵ_l represents the noise from the standard normal distribution, we represent $\boldsymbol{\beta}(x)$ as:

$$\boldsymbol{\beta}(x) = \frac{\sum_{l=1}^n w(x, e_l) \cdot v_l}{\sum_{l=1}^n w(x, e_l)} \tag{5}$$

To obtain the set of samples $\{(e_l, v_l)\}_{l=1}^n$, we let $\{e_1, \ldots, e_n\}$ be uniformly distributed in the known range of x ($[x_a, x_b]$), i.e., in our dataset, we set $\{e_1, \ldots, e_n\} = \{-4, -3.5, \ldots, 3.5, 4\}$. And we take $\{v_1, \ldots, v_n\}$ as parameters and learn them from data.

Modeling magnifying curve $f(x)$. Intuitively, the more historical ratings exist, the larger the magnifying effect will be. The previous psychological study [14] showed that the slope of $f(x)$ decreases as x increases, but the slope remains positive. In this work, we use the following *magnitude function* $f(x)$ to describe the magnifying effect of historical ratings with a size x.

$$f(x) = \frac{a}{1 + exp(-b * x)} - \frac{a}{2} \tag{6}$$

The first component is a sigmoid function while the second component (subtracting $a/2$) is to ensure that $f(0) = 0$, because when we do not have any historical ratings, no magnifying effect exists.

Modeling prior expectation $e_{p,i}$. In previous measurements, we used the average of historical ratings as prior expectation $e_{p,i}$. In reality, users focus more on recent ratings instead of all ratings of a product. Hence, we represent $e_{p,i}$ by the following general formula:

$$e_{p,i} = \frac{\sum_{k=1}^{i-1} \xi(i-k) \cdot r_{p,k}}{\sum_{k=1}^{i-1} \xi(i-k)} \tag{7}$$

Here, $\xi(d) = exp(-\gamma * d)$ denotes an exponential triggering kernel, which models the decay of influence; $r_{p,k}$ is the k-th real rating of product p; γ controls the extent to which users prefer recent ratings. If γ is 0, then $e_{p,i}$ is exactly the average of historical ratings. A larger γ means that users focus more on recent ratings. In our case, γ is set by cross-validation.

3.3 Model Inference

Overall, our goal is to solve the following optimization problem:

$$\min_{\Theta} \sum_{(p,i,u)\in\mathcal{K}} (r_{p,i,u} - \hat{r}_{p,i,u})^2 + \lambda_{rec}(b_u^2 + b_p^2 + ||\boldsymbol{x_u}||_2^2 + ||\boldsymbol{y_p}||_2^2) + \lambda_f(a^2 + b^2) + \lambda_\beta(\sum_l v_l^2) + \lambda_\alpha(\alpha_u^2)$$

Here, $\Theta = \{g, \{b_u\}, \{b_p\}, \{\boldsymbol{x_u}\}, \{\boldsymbol{y_p}\}, \{\alpha_u\}, a, b, \{v_l\}\}$; $r_{p,i,u}$ is the real rating; $\hat{r}_{p,i,u}$ is the predicted rating by HIALF (Equation (4)); $\mathcal{K}$ contains all (p, i, u) pairs, and a pair (p, i, u) represents that the i-th rating of product p in the dataset is given by user u. Using this objective function, we aim to make $\hat{r}_{p,i,u}$ as close as possible to the real rating $r_{p,i,u}$. $\lambda_{rec}, \lambda_f, \lambda_\beta, \lambda_\alpha$ are regularization hyperparameters to prevent overfitting. We use stochastic gradient descent (SGD) algorithm to learn parameters, which is widely used in previous works [8, 11, 12], due to its efficiency.

4 EXPERIMENTS

We conduct experiments on real rating datasets (Table 1) to compare the performance of our model (HIALF) with state-of-the-art models. We compare different models by evaluating: (1) how accurate a model could predict the subsequent ratings, and (2) how well a model could fit the previous empirical observations in real ratings.

4.1 Validating The Disconfirmation Bias Curve

One important thing we need to check is whether the disconfirmation bias curve $\boldsymbol{\beta}(x)$ meets with the *"Assimilate-Contrast"* theory because this will dictate the accuracy of HIALF.

As in Figure 4, all learned $\boldsymbol{\beta}(x)$ perfectly match the *"Assimilate-Contrast"* theory. $\boldsymbol{\beta}(x)$ on *Amazon-books, Amazon-movie, Amazon-electronics* and *Tripadvisor*, have similar formats with the sample representation of the *"Assimilate-Contrast"* theory in Figure (2a). $\boldsymbol{\beta}(x)$ on *Amazon-clothes* also follows the theory: in the range $[0, 1]$, the bias roughly equals to difference between prior expectation and the product quality, while deviating it out of the range.

We also notice that $\boldsymbol{\beta}(x)$ is close to 0 for some x, for example, x in $[-4, -3]$ or $[3, 4]$ in Figure (4a). There are two possible reasons. For one thing, x seldom achieves values in these ranges. Take $x = -3$ as an example, it means that a user takes an inferior product in others' views (i.e., forming a prior expectation as 1-star) as a good 4-star product. In reality, such large discrepancy rarely occurs. With a high probability, an inferior product in many users' view is truly a bad product. Then with constraints on value of v_l (i.e., λ_β), $\boldsymbol{\beta}(x)$ in the above ranges is close to 0. For another, from a psychological point of view, as mentioned in [32], if users find others' opinions highly contradict with their own opinions, they may tend to insist on their own opinions.

4.2 Predicting Subsequent Ratings

For the rating sequence of each product, we split it into the training subsequence and the testing subsequence, and put the two subsequences into the training set and the testing set, respectively. We train the model on the training set, and validate the model on the testing set in terms of mean squared error (MSE). We compare HIALF with several state-of-the-art models: HEARD [28], latent factor (LF) model [21], and also a variant of HIALF model, denoted

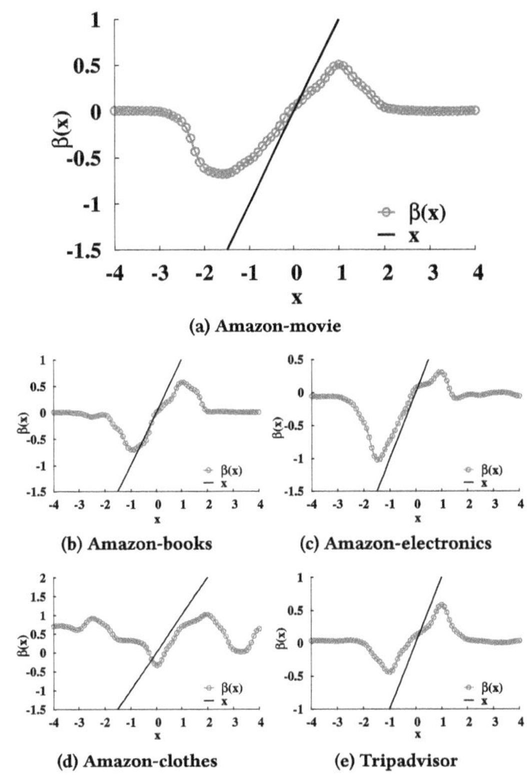

Figure 4: The learned disconfirmation bias curve $\boldsymbol{\beta}(x)$. All $\boldsymbol{\beta}(x)$ perfectly match the *"Assimilate-Contrast"* theory.

by HIALF-AVG. In HIALF-AVG, prior expectation is taken as the average of historical ratings without emphasis on recent ratings.

Results. Table 3 shows that our model significantly outperforms alternatives on all datasets. On average, HIALF achieves a 33% reduction in MSE compared to HEARD, and a 6% reduction to LF.

Note that improvements over LF are bounded by the extent to which ratings in the dataset are affected by historical ratings. We apply curve fitting to all lines in Figure 1 with a linear model $y = ax + b$. Here, the slope a represents the average increase in the next rating when prior expectation moves from x to $x + 1$, thus a larger a implies the larger distortions from prior expectations (historical ratings). The average slope of two fitting curves in *Amazon-movie* is the largest (0.34), while *Amazon-clothes* reveals the smallest average slope as 0.22. In other words, *Amazon-movie* suffers the largest distortions from historical ratings, while *Amazon-clothes* suffers the smallest historical distortions. From Table 3, HIALF has the most significant benefits on *Amazon-movie* over LF and the least benefits on *Amazon-clothes* over LF. Furthermore, HIALF is consistently more accurate than HIALF-AVG, because users focus more on recent ratings when shaping prior expectations.

4.3 Fitting Empirical Observations

Next, we re-do the empirical measurements in Section 2 with the predicted ratings by HEARD, LF, HIALF, respectively. Note that an accurate model should reveal a similar relationship as in our previous observations in real ratings.

Table 3: *MSE* on five datasets

	Amazon-movie	Amazon-books	Amazon-electronics	Amazon-clothes	Tripadvisor
HEARD	1.5826	1.5548	3.1170	2.1550	1.3135
LF	1.2794	1.0777	1.9634	1.4123	1.0074
HIALF-AVG	1.2054	1.0619	1.9357	1.3985	0.9805
HIALF	**1.1194**	**1.0318**	**1.8764**	**1.3759**	**0.9405**
benefits of HIALF over HEARD	29.27%	32.83%	39.80%	35.17%	28.40%
benefits of HIALF over LF	12.51%	4.26%	4.43%	2.58%	6.64 %

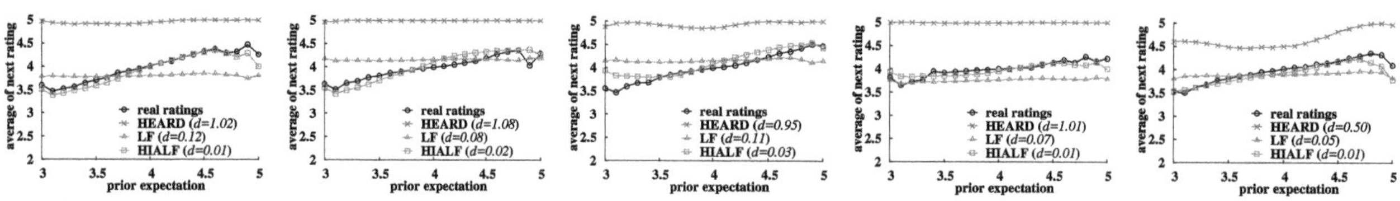

(a) Amazon-movie (b) Amazon-electronics (c) Amazon-books (d) Amazon-clothes (e) Tripadvisor

Figure 5: Relationship between prior expectation (defined in Equation (7)) and the average of the next rating. A smaller d implies a better fitting.

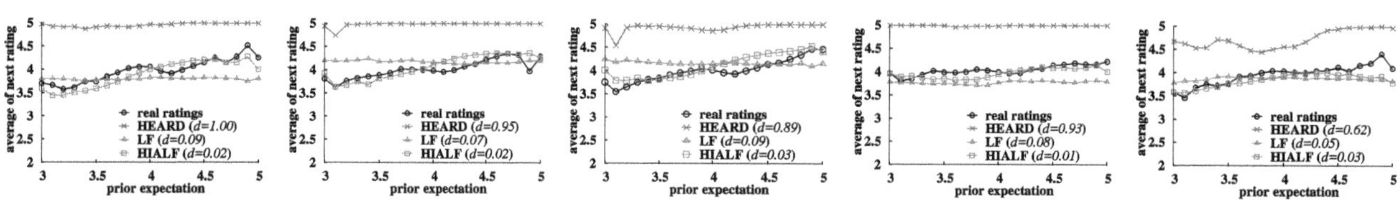

(a) Amzon-movie (b) Amazon-electronics (c) Amazon-books (d) Amazon-clothes (e) Tripadvisor

Figure 6: Relationship between prior expectation (the average of historical ratings) and the average of the next rating. A smaller d implies a better fitting.

Due to the page limit, we only describe the experimental steps on HIALF here. Experiments on other models are similar. For each dataset, we first model it using HIALF. Then, we select the same groups of products as in Figure 1. In each selected group, for each rating, given its history $\mathcal{H}_{p,i}$, we use HIALF to predict the next rating $r_{p,i}^{HIALF}$. We also calculate its prior expectation $e_{p,i}$ based on real ratings, getting one pair $(e_{p,i}, r_{p,i}^{HIALF})$. We consider two types of $e_{p,i}$ here: (1) the average of historical ratings; (2) the one defined in Equation (7) that focuses more on recent ratings. Finally, for each type of $e_{p,i}$, we plot the relationship between prior expectation and the average of the next HIALF-generated rating. Figure 5 shows the results with prior expectation defined in Equation (7), while prior expectation in Figure 6 is the average of historical ratings. Here, we only plot the relationship for the group of products with average ratings in [3.9, 4.1] in each dataset because this group contains more products. Similar patterns are also found in other groups of products.

Summary of results. Both Figure 5 and Figure 6 indicate that HIALF provides the best fit to previous observations in real ratings. Take Figure (5a) and Figure (6a) as examples. The black lines with ○ are the relationship between prior expectation and the average of the next rating in real ratings, and we can find our model HIALF (red line with □) fits the relationship of real ratings the best, as compared to LF (blue line with △) and HEARD (the purple line with ×). We also define a quantative metric to measure the difference between relationship in real ratings and in ratings generated by model A (where A can be HEARD/LF/HIALF) as: $d = \frac{\sum_{e \in E}(r_e - r_e^A)^2}{|E|}$, where E contains all distinct prior expectation e, r_e is the average of real ratings under e, and r_e^A is the average of model A-generated ratings under e. HIALF also reveals the smallest d, implying the closest fitting to empirical observations in real ratings. The latent factor model (LF) reveals relationships that are approximately parallel to the x axis, since LF does not consider the factors of distortions from historical ratings. HEARD is too optimistic since it always tends to predict high ratings when prior expectations are larger than 3.

5 APPLICATIONS

In this section, we apply HIALF to improve recommendations and to help users to make wiser consuming decisions.

5.1 Debiased Recommender System

Using HIALF, one can easily obtain users' and products' intrinsic features $(b_p, b_u, \boldsymbol{x_u}, \boldsymbol{y_p})$ without any contamination from historical ratings. Thus, base on these intrinsic features, for a product p that user u has not consumed, we can generate a recommendation score:

$$rec(p, u) = g + b_p + b_u + \boldsymbol{x_u}^T \boldsymbol{y_p} \tag{8}$$

here $g, b_p, \boldsymbol{x_u}, \boldsymbol{y_p}, b_u$ are learned parameters in HIALF. Products with high recommendation scores are those potential products that user u may like, and therefore we recommend these products to user u. We call a recommender system using the above methodology as *debiased recsys*.

We compare *debiased recsys* with the standard latent factor model (LF) since HIALF is built on top of the latent factor model. Note that HIALF is orthogonal to other techniques to improve recommendations, such as modeling evolution of users' expertise [17], modeling

Table 4: RMSE on five datasets

category	LF	debiased recsys
Amazon-movie	1.0639	**1.0465**
Amazon-books	0.9125	**0.8922**
Amazon-electronics	1.2273	**1.2083**
Amazon-clothes	1.1239	**1.1034**
Tripadvisor	1.1919	**1.1776**

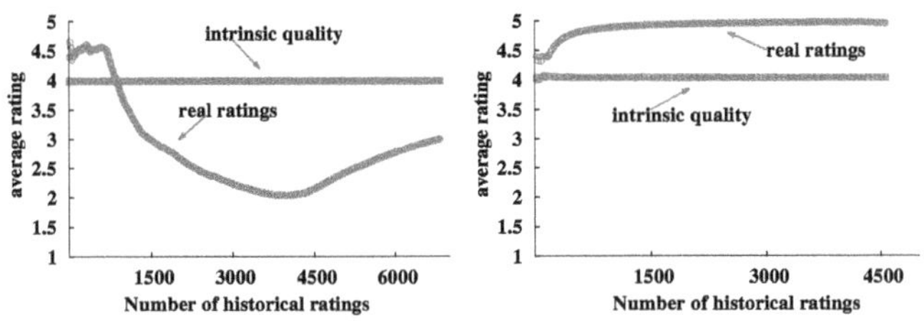

(a) sample product 1 (b) sample product 2

Figure 7: Two products with similar intrinsic quality have different rating growth histories, leading to significantly distinct ratings.

temporal dynamics [12], etc. For the future work, we can combine HIALF with the above techniques for further improvements.

We take the set of ratings without historical ratings as the ground truth. We train HIALF with the rest of ratings using the same hyperparameters ($\lambda_\beta, \lambda_f, etc.$) as in Section 4.2. We report the Root Mean Square Error (RMSE) on the ground truth in Table 4. RMSE is widely used to evaluate the quality of recommendations [8, 11, 12].

As in Table 4, *debiased recsys* consistently reveals smaller RMSE than LF, implying that it can provide better recommendations.

5.2 Exposing The Intrinsic Product Quality

The intrinsic quality of a product is around the aggregated collective ratings given by a large group of users who were not exposed to historical ratings [25]. With HIALF, we can also easily get the intrinsic quality of product p, which we denote as q_p^*, by factoring out the distortions from historical ratings.

$$q_p^* = \sum_i (g + b_p + \mathbf{x}_{\tilde{u}(p,i)}{}^T \mathbf{y}_p) \tag{9}$$

Here $\tilde{u}(p, i)$ is the user who gave the i-th rating of product p.

We use the case study in Figure 7 to illustrate the significance of revealing the intrinsic qualities of products. Figure 7 shows the dynamics of the average rating of two selected products in *Amazon-movie*. These two products have similar intrinsic quality (around 4) and similar initial ratings. Note that initial ratings suffer small historical distortions. However, after they experienced a sequence of ratings with different trends, the average rating of product 1 and product 2 are 3.2 and 4.9 respectively (differ at about 1.7). This shows the impact of historical ratings' distortions. With HIALF, one can perform debiasing operation and obtain the intrinsic quality so that users will not be misguided by historical ratings.

6 RELATED WORK

Biases in rating system. Users' ratings are often *biased*, due to a variety of causes, such as ratings from spammers [15] or water-armies [1], evolution of users' expertise [17], temporal dynamics [12], dimensional biases [9], biases across categories [10], biases due to algorithms [24] etc. In this paper, we focus on a different kind of bias caused by influence from historical ratings.

Experiments on historical ratings' influence. Recent studies [3, 19, 22, 30] found that the disclosed historical ratings would distort subsequent ratings. Experiments [19, 30] revealed that small positive manipulations would encourage more positive future ratings, creating accumulative herding that boosts the final average ratings. Even for products with the same quality, users tend to rate higher when they are displayed with higher historical ratings [3, 22]. Our work is motivated by the above findings, however, our goal is to model rather than to test the influence from historical ratings.

Modeling historical ratings' influence. Previous works [2, 13] have attempted to mitigate the *micro-level* influence from historical ratings. However, their models were developed for specially designed rating systems, and one needs to know users' ratings given when users cannot see historical ratings, which is usually latent in reality. Wang et al. [28] then developed a more practical model (HEARD) to characterize the macro-level influence from historical ratings on *Amazon*, i.e., how historical ratings of a product will affect its general rating distribution after 100 ratings. The goal is different from our work since we aim to capture the microscopic influence, i.e., how historical ratings will affect its next single rating.

Social network-based influence. Several works [5, 6] also modeled and debiased the influence in social network, i.e., *peer effects*. Peer effects are interactive and more credible, i.e., users and their friends will influence each other and users often trust each other. The historical ratings are usually generated by strangers, and only previous ratings can influence the subsequent ratings. The difference between these two types of influence makes our work differ from this line of works.

7 CONCLUSION AND FUTURE WORK

In this paper, using 42 million ratings from *Tripadvisor* and *Amazon*, we first reveal and explain the assimilation and contrast effects in users' given ratings caused by historical ratings. Then we propose HIALF, the first model for real rating systems to characterize the *micro-level* influence from historical ratings in each single rating. We demonstrate the effectiveness of HIALF in predicting subsequent ratings, capturing dynamics in real ratings, and providing better recommendations, and further revealing products' intrinsic qualities for subsequent wiser decisions on purchasing products.

There are several directions for future work. First, besides ratings, review texts also contain a lot of information. The recent work [16] has combined reviews and ratings for better recommendations. Thus one can further improve the HIALF model by incorporating useful information embedded in the review texts. Also, HIALF is orthogonal to other factors in ratings, such as evolution of user's expertise [17], temporal dynamics [12], etc. Considering these factors may contribute to a better model, we plan to do this in our future work.

ACKNOWLEDGMENTS

The authors would like to thank anonymous reviewers for their valuable comments. This work is supported in part by the GRF 14208816 and Huawei Research Grant.

REFERENCES

[1] 2017. Internet Water Army. https://en.wikipedia.org/wiki/Internet_Water_Army. (2017). (accessed March 2017).

[2] Gediminas Adomavicius, Jesse Bockstedt, Shawn Curley, and Jingjing Zhang. 2014. De-biasing user preference ratings in recommender systems. In *IntRS Workshop@RecSys 2014*. 2–9.

[3] Gediminas Adomavicius, Jesse Bockstedt, Shawn P. Curley, and Jingjing Zhang. 2016. Understanding Effects of Personalized vs. Aggregate Ratings on User Preferences. In *IntRS Workshop@RecSys 2016*. 14–21.

[4] Rolph E Anderson. 1973. Consumer dissatisfaction: The effect of disconfirmed expectancy on perceived product performance. *Journal of marketing research* (1973), 38–44.

[5] Abhimanyu Das, Sreenivas Gollapudi, Rina Panigrahy, and Mahyar Salek. 2013. Debiasing social wisdom. In *Proceedings of the 19th ACM SIGKDD international conference on Knowledge discovery and data mining*. ACM, 500–508.

[6] Anirban Dasgupta, Ravi Kumar, and D Sivakumar. 2012. Social sampling. In *Proceedings of the 18th ACM SIGKDD international conference on Knowledge discovery and data mining*. ACM, 235–243.

[7] James Davidson, Benjamin Liebald, Junning Liu, Palash Nandy, Taylor Van Vleet, Ullas Gargi, Sujoy Gupta, Yu He, Mike Lambert, Blake Livingston, et al. 2010. The YouTube video recommendation system. In *Proceedings of the fourth ACM conference on Recommender systems*. ACM, 293–296.

[8] Rana Forsati, Iman Barjasteh, Farzan Masrour, Abdol-Hossein Esfahanian, and Hayder Radha. 2015. Pushtrust: An efficient recommendation algorithm by leveraging trust and distrust relations. In *Proceedings of the 9th ACM Conference on Recommender Systems*. ACM, 51–58.

[9] Yong Ge and Jingjing Li. 2015. Measure and Mitigate the Dimensional Bias in Online Reviews and Ratings. (2015).

[10] Fangjian Guo and David B Dunson. 2015. Uncovering Systematic Bias in Ratings across Categories: a Bayesian Approach. In *Proceedings of the 9th ACM Conference on Recommender Systems*. ACM, 317–320.

[11] Yehuda Koren. 2008. Factorization meets the neighborhood: a multifaceted collaborative filtering model. In *Proceedings of the 14th ACM SIGKDD international conference on Knowledge discovery and data mining*. ACM, 426–434.

[12] Yehuda Koren. 2009. Collaborative filtering with temporal dynamics. In *Proceedings of the 15th ACM SIGKDD international conference on Knowledge discovery and data mining*. ACM, 447–456.

[13] Sanjay Krishnan, Jay Patel, Michael Franklin, and Ken Goldberg. 2014. Social influence bias in recommender systems: a methodology for learning, analyzing, and mitigating bias in ratings. In *Proceedings of the 8th ACM Conference on Recommender systems*. 137–144.

[14] Bibb Latané. 1981. The psychology of social impact. *American psychologist* 36, 4 (1981), 343.

[15] Ee-Peng Lim, Viet-An Nguyen, Nitin Jindal, Bing Liu, and Hady Wirawan Lauw. 2010. Detecting product review spammers using rating behaviors. In *Proceedings of the 19th ACM international conference on Information and knowledge management*. ACM, 939–948.

[16] Guang Ling, Michael R Lyu, and Irwin King. 2014. Ratings meet reviews, a combined approach to recommend. In *Proceedings of the 8th ACM Conference on Recommender systems*. ACM, 105–112.

[17] Julian McAuley and Jure Leskovec. 2013. From Amateurs to Connoisseurs: Modeling the Evolution of User Expertise through Online Reviews. In *WWW'13: Proceedings of the 22ed International World Wide Web Conference*.

[18] Julian McAuley, Rahul Pandey, and Jure Leskovec. 2015. Inferring networks of substitutable and complementary products. In *Proceedings of the 21th ACM SIGKDD International Conference on Knowledge Discovery and Data Mining*. ACM, 785–794.

[19] Lev Muchnik, Sinan Aral, and Sean J Taylor. 2013. Social influence bias: A randomized experiment. *Science* 341, 6146 (2013), 647–651.

[20] Richard L Oliver. 2014. *Satisfaction: A behavioral perspective on the consumer*. Routledge.

[21] Francesco Ricci, Lior Rokach, and Bracha Shapira. 2011. *Introduction to recommender systems handbook*. Springer.

[22] Matthew J Salganik, Peter Sheridan Dodds, and Duncan J Watts. 2006. Experimental study of inequality and unpredictability in an artificial cultural market. *science* 311, 5762 (2006), 854–856.

[23] Franklin E Satterthwaite. 1946. An approximate distribution of estimates of variance components. *Biometrics bulletin* 2, 6 (1946), 110–114.

[24] Patrick Shafto and Olfa Nasraoui. 2016. Human-Recommender Systems: From Benchmark Data to Benchmark Cognitive Models. In *Proceedings of the 10th ACM Conference on Recommender Systems*. ACM, 127–130.

[25] James Surowiecki, Mark P Silverman, et al. 2007. The wisdom of crowds. *American Journal of Physics* 75, 2 (2007), 190–192.

[26] Hongning Wang, Yue Lu, and ChengXiang Zhai. 2011. Latent aspect rating analysis without aspect keyword supervision. In *Proceedings of the 17th ACM SIGKDD international conference on Knowledge discovery and data mining*. ACM, 618–626.

[27] Jian Wang and Yi Zhang. 2013. Opportunity Models for E-commerce Recommendation: Right Product, Right Time. In *SIGIR*.

[28] Ting Wang, Dashun Wang, and Fei Wang. 2014. Quantifying herding effects in crowd wisdom. In *Proceedings of the 20th ACM SIGKDD international conference on Knowledge discovery and data mining*. ACM, 1087–1096.

[29] Larry Wasserman. 2013. *All of statistics: a concise course in statistical inference*. Springer Science & Business Media.

[30] Tim Weninger, Thomas James Johnston, and Maria Glenski. 2015. Random voting effects in social-digital spaces: A case study of reddit post submissions. In *Proceedings of the 26th ACM conference on hypertext & social media*. ACM, 293–297.

[31] Ming Yan, Jitao Sang, and Changsheng Xu. 2015. Unified YouTube Video Recommendation via Cross-network Collaboration. In *ICMR*.

[32] Haiyi Zhu and Bernardo A Huberman. 2014. To switch or not to switch: understanding social influence in online choices. *American Behavioral Scientist* 58, 10 (2014), 1329–1344.

Fairness-Aware Group Recommendation with Pareto-Efficiency

Lin Xiao
Tsinghua University
Institute of Interdisciplinary Information Sciences,
jackielinxiao@gmail.com

Zhang Min*
Tsinghua University
Department of Computer Science and Technology,
z-m@tsinghua.edu.cn

Zhang Yongfeng
University of Massachusetts Amherst
College of Information and Computer Science,
yongfeng@cs.umass.edu

Gu Zhaoquan
Guangzhou University, and The University of HongKong
Department of Computer Science,
demin456@gmail.com

Liu Yiqun
Tsinghua University
Department of Computer Science and Technology,
yiqunliu@tsinghua.edu.cn

Ma Shaoping
Tsinghua University
Department of Computer Science and Technology,
msp@tsinghua.edu.cn

ABSTRACT

Group recommendation has attracted significant research efforts for its importance in benefiting a group of users. This paper investigates the Group Recommendation problem from a novel aspect, which tries to maximize the satisfaction of each group member while minimizing the unfairness between them. In this work, we present several semantics of the individual utility and propose two concepts of social welfare and fairness for modeling the overall utilities and the balance between group members. We formulate the problem as a multiple objective optimization problem and show that it is NP-Hard in different semantics. Given the multiple-objective nature of fairness-aware group recommendation problem, we provide an optimization framework for fairness-aware group recommendation from the perspective of Pareto Efficiency. We conduct extensive experiments on real-world datasets and evaluate our algorithm in terms of standard accuracy metrics. The results indicate that our algorithm achieves superior performances and considering fairness in group recommendation can enhance the recommendation accuracy.

1 INTRODUCTION

Group recommendation is to recommend items to groups of users whose preferences can be different from each other. The applications of group recommendation are frequently seen in real life and on the web, for example, families have to decide which TV program to watch; Social network websites [31] encourage users to build up social groups and share contents within groups; and E-Commerce websites like Groupon recommend coupons to groups of users for sales promotion. Other scenarios include music/movie group recommendation [7], and restaurant recommendations to groups [19].

The research of group recommendation was first seen in [6], which introduces a group recommender system called Polylens to recommend movies to groups of users. Previous studies on group recommendation deal with the problem on two kinds of groups: persistent and ephemeral groups [22]. The persistent groups refer to groups with consistent structures and historical records of interactions between groups and items [30] [13] [28]; while ephemeral groups can be formed ad hoc and the users may just constitute the groups for the first time [2] [39] [22]. For recommendation to persistent groups, the group can be seen as a virtual user and the personalized recommendation algorithms can be applied since the interactions between groups and items are available. But for recommendations to ephemeral groups, the historical interactions do not exist and the recommendation can only be generated from the aggregation of the individual preferences. In this paper, we concentrate on the general scenario of making recommendations to ephemeral groups.

Previous studies on group recommendation focus on recommending one item at a time. Various preference aggregation functions are applied to find a consensus between the users on a single item. Some important semantics have been proposed for the evaluation [1], [31] [26]. In this way, the group recommendation algorithms evaluate how an item satisfies a group of users and select the Top K items which satisfy the group most as recommendation. However, as pointed out in [21], the best item according to this function may still leave some users feeling dissatisfied and slighted.

In this paper, we look at the problem from a different perspective of user utility in the group recommendation. The user utility is determined by how relevant the recommended items are to the user. Therefore only when the K recommended items are decided can we know the utility of the user achieved from the items. We propose to evaluate the user satisfaction with utility function and further consider the overall social welfare (the sum of user utilities inside the

*Corresponding Author

RecSys'17, August 27–31, 2017, Como, Italy.
 ISBN 978-1-4503-4652-8/17/08...$15.00.
DOI:http://dx.doi.org/10.1145/3109859.3109887

group) and fairness (the balance of user utilities inside the group) to evaluate the quality of group recommendation.

Evaluating user satisfaction from each individual's perspective can be found in some studies [36] [21]. This modeling makes it possible to explicitly evaluate the imbalances between users in terms of their satisfactions achieved from the group recommendation.

More specifically, we model the individual satisfaction about the recommendation by considering the relevance of each recommended item to the user. Meanwhile, we adopt the semantics originating from Social Choice Theory [35] [3] and fairness measure [14] to combine the individual satisfactions as the fairness of group recommendation. We formulate the fairness-aware group recommendation problem as a multiple objective optimization problem and provide a theoretical analysis to show that it is NP-Hard. We further provide a multiple objective optimization framework which preserves Pareto efficiency between multiple objectives.

The remaining of the work is organized as follows: the next section introduces some important related work about group recommendation and multiple objective optimization; Section 3 presents the detailed modeling of user utilities, social welfare and fairness, then we introduce the problem formulation of fairness-aware group recommendation; We propose Pareto-effcient algorithms to solve the problem with scarlarization approaches in Section 4; We conduct extensive experiments on real-world datasets with different types of groups and evaluate the recommendation quality with typical accuracy metrics in Section 5. Finally, we get to the conclusion in Section 6.

2 RELATED WORK

In this section, we introduce some important studies about group recommendation and multiple objective optimization.

2.1 Group Recommendation

The studies of group recommendation can be categorized into two aspects based on the types of groups [22]. Groups with consistent structures and historical interactions are often referred as persistent groups while the groups formed by users ad-hoc are referred as ephemeral groups. Making recommendations to persistent groups is closer to personalized recommendation, considering that each group can be seen as a user and personalized recommendation techniques can be applied [30] [13] [28]. In our work, we focus on ephemeral group recommendations.

The recommendation to ephemeral groups is much more difficult since there exist no interactions between groups and items thus the group can not be seen as a virtual user. Existing studies on ephemeral group recommendations focus on preference aggregation methods that aggregate the individual preferences of group members as a group preference. The collaborative filtering approaches are utilized to generate the individual preferences first and various preference aggregation functions are used to aggregate the individual preferences into group preferences.

The combination of Collaborative Filtering approaches and group recommendation is reflected in some previous studies: [2], [40], [20] and [37]. Various aggregation functions have been proposed for prefrence aggregation, most of them come from the social choice theory [3]. The important semantics are Average and Least Misery, which are widely adopted in group recommendation studies [1], [2], [29], [32] and [22]. The similarity between our work and previous studies is that both of them compute the individual preferences first. The difference is that our work considers the satisfactions of users from the perspective of each individual and tries to maximize the overall satisfaction while maintaining fairness between them. While existing studies model the relevance of a single item to the group and fairness is not explicitly modeled.

It is assumed that user influences exist in the group decision process, the studies concerning with user influences include [17], [34], [23], [39] and [22]. Some probabilistic models have been proposed to capture the user preferences and their influences in the group. The basic assumption of these studies is that users should be treated differently in group recommendation and the concept of influence is proposed to capture the heterogeneity. In our work, users also have to make compromises with each other in order to achieve better fairness in group recommendation, which is similar to heterogeneous influences in spirit (considering that treating users the same may lead to suboptimal solutions in terms of fairness). Some studies incorporate social relationships into the group recommendation, including [32], [10] and [38]. Social relationships can be useful in enriching the user preferences [32] and some studies incorporates both social and content interests in group recommender systems to enhance the recommendation quality.

There are few studies on the fairness issues in group recommendation. Some previous studies concern with this problem from the perspective from game theory and voting theory: [12], [18], [4], [5] and [16]. Some group recommendation studies treat the group decision process as non-cooperative games and try to find equilibria of the games as feasible recommendations. Some other studies treat the group decision process as a voting campaign and use voting mechanisms to find a proper recommendation through a voting process. However, these approaches do not explicitly consider fairness in the recommendation modeling and the trade-off between overall satisfaction and fairness is unclear.

A similar study on fairness in group recommendation is [21], where user fairness is modeled as how satisfied the user is with the group recommendation. [21] tries to maximize the predefined fairness so that the number of users who find the recommendation is fair is maximized. In this paper, we look at the fairness from a different perspective, we model the balance between user utilities with the group recommendation as fairness and hope to find a proper trade-off between the overall user utilities (social welfare)and the differences between them (fairness).

There are several differences between this work and [21]: First, the fairness semantics are different in two studies. In our work, we first define the individual utility given a recommendation to the group and then treat the imbalances between group members' utilities as the metric of fairness. We argue that the fairness proposed in [21] sometimes may cause extreme unfairness to the users. Consider the the case when a group of ten users are recommended with an item, eight of them are satisfied with the item while two of them hate the item. According to [21], the fairness is 0.8 which means quite a majority of group members find the recommendation "fair". However the remaining two users who dislike the item are ignored in this semantic. In our proposal, the fairness is relatively low since two users suffer from the recommendation severely (both least misery and min-max fairness care about the least satisfied user). Second, [21] concerns with maximization of fairness in group recommendation while our work considers the group recommendation from a multi-objective perspective (optimizing fairness and social welfare simultaneously). Third, [21] evaluates the performances of group recommendation with self-defined metrics while this work evaluates the quality of group recommendation with widely-used accuracy metrics. Moreover, this work provides a general framework for defining fairness with individual utility and an optimizing framework with Pareto efficiency. Therefore the similar procedure can be extended to other fairness semantics in group recommendation.

2.2 Multi-Objective Optimization

The studies on multi-objective optimization are rich and various approaches have been proposed [9]. One important feature of multiple objective optimization is that (usually) there does not exist a solution that satisfies all the objectives simultaneously. In that case, the objective functions are conflicting, and there exist a (possibly infinite) number of Pareto optimal solutions. A solution is called Pareto efficient, if none of the objective functions can be improved without degrading some of the other objectives. Notice that there are multiple solutions that satisfy the Pareto Optimality, the set of all Pareto optimal solutions is named as Pareto Front.

Various ways have been proposed to solve the Pareto Front, including A Priori approaches and A posteriori methods. The first approache aims to scalarize the objectives into a single objective function; while the second approach uses evolutionary algorithms [41] to update the solutions by iterations.

Some studies have considered multiple objectives in personalized recommendation tasks, including [27], [15], [25]. In [25], multiple objectives including accuracy, diversity and novelty are simultaneously considered and a pareto front is found to satisfy the mentioned objectives. There are few studies on optimizing multiple objectives in group recommendation and we are among the first to optimize both overall satisfaction and fairness in group recommendation through a multiple-objective optimization framework.

3 FAIRNESS-AWARE GROUP RECOMMENDATION MODELING

3.1 Individual Utility Modeling

In recommender systems, the preferences of users are learnt from their historical interactions with items. Given a new item, the relevance of the item to a user can be predicted with Collaborative Filtering methods [33] [24]. In the group recommendation process, we first compute the relevances of candidate items to each user. In this way, we get a full user-item interaction matrix where each entry (between user u and item i) reflects the pairwise relevance as $rel(u,i) \in [rel_{min}, rel_{max}]$ where rel_{max} and rel_{min} represent the ranges of relevance values.

The utility function $U(u,I)$ of user u given the recommendation I is a function of the relevances of recommended items $rel(u,i)$, $\forall u, i \in I$ to the user:

Definition 3.1. **Individual Utility:** The individual utility of user u in group G when a set of items I ($|I| = K$) are recommended to the group, is a function $U(u,I) : U \times I \rightarrow [0,1]$ of the relevances $rel(u,i)$ where $i \in I$. Some semantics are presented as follows:

(1) Average: $U(u,I) = \frac{1}{K \times rel_{max}} \sum_{i \in I} rel(u,i)$
(2) Proportionality: $U(u,I) = \frac{\sum_{i \in I} rel(u,i)}{\sum_{i \in I(u,K)} rel(u,i)}$

where $I(u,K)$ denotes the set of items which are among the top-K favourite items of user u. Notice that the relevance of an item to a user can be binary or fractional. When the relevance is 1 for an item from the top-K favourite items, the utility following proportionality semantic becomes the ratio of top-K favorite items of the user in the group recommendation list.

3.2 Social Welfare and Fairness Modeling

For evaluating the overall satisfaction of users about group recommendation quality, we aggregate all the individual utilities as social welfare and further consider fairness as the extent of imbalance between their individual utilities.

Definition 3.2. **Social Welfare:** The Social Welfare (denoted as $SW(g,I)$) is the overall utility of all users inside the group g given a group recommendation I:

$$SW(g,I) = \frac{1}{|g|} \sum_{u \in g} U(u,I), \forall g, I$$

The fairness depicts how imbalanced the users are satisfied with the recommendation. Therefore it should reflect the comparison between the utilities of users inside the group.

Definition 3.3. **Fairness:** Given a group recommendation I to group g, the fairness (denoted as $F(g,I)$) is a function of $U(u,I), \forall u \in g$, $\forall I$. Some semantics are summarized as follows:

$$Least\ Misery: F_{LM}(g, I) = \min\{U(u, I), \forall u \in g\}$$
$$Variance: F_{Var}(g, I) = 1 - Var(\{U(u, I), \forall u \in g\})$$
$$Jain's\ Fairness: F_J(g, I) = \frac{(\sum_{u \in g} U(u, I))^2}{|U| \cdot \sum_{u \in g} U(u, I)^2}$$
$$Min - Max\ Ratio: F_M(g, I) = \frac{\min\{U(u, I), \forall u \in g\}}{\max\{U(u, I), \forall u \in g\}}$$

Variance Fairness and Jain's Fairness [14] encourage the group members to achieve close utilities between each other; while Least Misery Fairness and Min-Max Ratio emphasise the gap between the least and highest utilities of group members. Despite the differences of the Fairness in definitions, the consensus intuition of these metrics is to minimize the difference between the individual utilities of group members. We formulate the fairness-aware group recommendation problem as follows:

PROBLEM 1. *Given a group of users U and a set of items $\tilde{I}$, the group recommendation aims to recommend a set $I \in \tilde{I}$ of K items to maximize the social welfare $SW(U, I)$ and fairness $F(U, I)$.*

However, it is difficult to optimize the fairness metrics in group recommendations. We analyze the computational complexity of optimizing the fairness metric and present the results here:

THEOREM 3.4. *The Least Misery fairness and Min-Max Ratio fairness maximization problems are NP-Hard.*

PROOF. Without loss of generality, we consider a restricted version of the problem where the matrix consists of integer 0s or 1s and has even number of columns. Consider the decision version of the fairness optimization problem: is there a recommendation I of K items for the group g so that $F_{LM}(g, I) \geq \frac{1}{K}$, $F_{Var}(g, I) \geq \frac{1}{K}$? This is equivalent to the problem: **given a matrix A whose entry is either 0 or 1 and the sum of each row is K, is there a selection of K columns such that the sum of each row with selected columns is greater than 1?**

We reduce the problem to 3SAT problem, which is a famous NP-Hard problem. The 3SAT problem is given arbitrary formulas, determining the satisfiability of a formula in conjunctive normal form where each clause is limited to three literals. For any given instance $C_1 \wedge C_2 \wedge ...C_n$ where each clause consists of three literals $C_i = x_{i1} \vee x_{i2} \vee x_{i3}, \forall i = 1, 2, .., n$.

we construct a matrix A like this: first, we construct m rows where each of them corresponds to a literal and then n rows where each of them corresponds to a clause. Then we construct 2m columns where first m columns corresponds to the literals x_i and the next m columns corresponds to literals $\neg x_i$. For the first m rows, we set $A_{i,i}$ and $A_{i,i+m}$ to 1 and the rest of the entries to 0; for the next m+n rows, we set the entries in row m+j corresponding to the each literal in clause c_j to 1 and the rest entries to 0. For example, given a formula, the construction of the matrix is shown in Fig. 1.

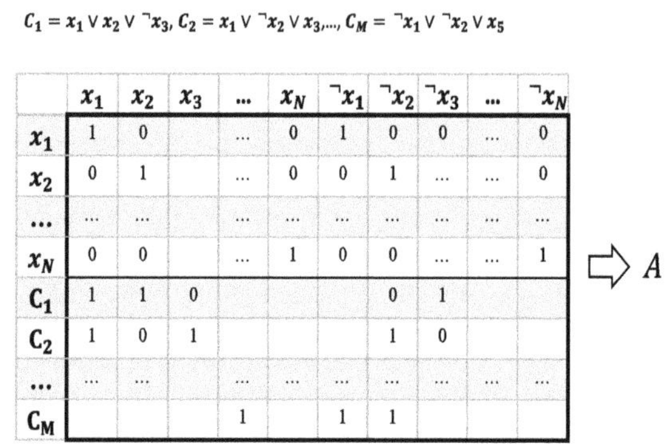

Figure 1: An example for SAT reduction

Now we show that given any true instance of one problem, it corresponds to the true instance of the other problem:

"3SAT $\Rightarrow$ Fairness Maximization": given a positive instance of 3SAT, we know that each literal x_i is either 1 or 0, which means the first m rows satisfy the requirement; for the remaining n rows, in order to guarantee the clause to be true, at least one of the literal should be true, which means at least one entry of 1 should be selected. In summary, the requirement is satisfied.

"Fairness Maximization $\Rightarrow$ 3SAT": given a positive instance of MMFM, consider the first m rows, either the literal x_i or $\neg x_i$ is 1, which coincides with the satisfiability of any clause; For the remaining n rows, at least one entry with value 1 is selected, as the construction shows, the corresponding clause is true. Since each row corresponds to a clause, all the clauses are true, which makes the whole formula to be true. □

3.3 Problem Formulation

The scalar concept of "optimality" does not apply directly in the multi-objective setting. Here the notion of Pareto optimality is used to depict the optimality. Consider a solution S of multiple objective optimization problem, where each objective function is denoted as $f_i, i = 1, 2, ..., p$, therefore the values of the objective functions for solution S correspond to a vector: $(S_1, S_2, ..., S_p)$. A solution S' dominates solution S if $\forall i \in [1, p]$, $S_i \leq S'_i$ and $\exists j \in [1, p]$, $S_j < S'_j$.

Definition 3.5. **Pareto Optimal and Pareto Front:** A solution S is Pareto Optimal if and only if there exists no other solution S' that dominates S. The set of all Pareto optimal solutions is referred to as the Pareto Front.

Scarlarization is a typical method for solving a Pareto-Efficient solution for multiple objective solution. The scarlarization scheme is to assign weights to each objective and use the weighted sum of different objective functions as a single objective for proximity:

$$\lambda \cdot SW(g, I) + (1 - \lambda) \cdot F(g, I) \quad (1)$$

It is easy to see that when $0 < \lambda < 1$, the optimal solution to the scalarized single objective optimization problem is Pareto Optimal. Given that optimizing the single objective of

Algorithm 1 Greedy Algorithm for Fairness-Aware Recommendation to Groups

Input: A given group: G, A set of Items: I, Length of Recommendation List: K;

1: Initialize $L = \emptyset$;
2: **while** $Length(L) < K$: **do**
3: Select an item $j \in I \setminus L$ that maximizes $\lambda \cdot SW(g, L \cup j) + (1 - \lambda) \cdot F(g, L \cup j)$;
4: Add item j to the list L: $L = L \cup j$;
5: **end while**
6: Output the recommendation list L;

fairness is NP-Hard, we look for efficient heuristic algorithms for the fairness-aware group recommendation problem.

4 OPTIMIZATION FRAMEWORK WITH PARETO EFFICIENCY

In this section, we formally introduce the optimization framework for fairness-aware group recommendation problem. Two ways are presented to achieve the Pareto-Efficient solutions, including scalarization with greedy algorithms and scalarization with integer programming.

Given the scalarized single objective optimization problem, we still face a NP-Hard problem as proved in last section. We propose a greedy algorithm for the scalarized problem which applies to all the proposed semantics of user utilities and fairness. The basic idea of greedy algorithm is to select an item that achieves the highest fairness when it is added to the current recommendation list. The detailed algorithm is illustrated in Alg. 1.

An important advantage of Greedy algorithm is the computational efficiency. Notice that solving an optimization problem can be time-consuming, it is even more complex to solve a non-convex optimization problem. However the Greedy algorithm gradually selects one item in each iteration, the algorithm runs K iterations to generate a final recommendation, which is more time-efficient.

Notice that some semantics for fairness are relatively simple in form, we can adopt integer programming techniques to solve the problem. We use $X_j \in \{0, 1\}, \forall j \in I$ to denote whether item $j \in I$ is recommended to the group. The recommendation process can be formulated into integer programming problems according to the individual utility and fairness semantics. We list the integer variable representation of the individual utilities:

- Average: $U(u, I) = \sum_{j \in I} rel(u, j) X_j$;
- Proportionality: $U(u, I) = \frac{\sum_{j \in I} rel(u,j) X_j}{\sum_{j \in I(u,k)} rel(u,j)}$.

Given these representations for individual utility functions, we can reformulate the problem of group recommendation into an integer program:

$$\begin{aligned} \max.\ & \lambda \cdot SW(g, I) + (1 - \lambda) \cdot F(g, I) \\ s.t.\ & \sum_i X_i = K \\ & X_i \in \{0, 1\} \end{aligned} \tag{2}$$

Algorithm 2 Integer Programming Based Algorithm for Fairness Aware Recommendation to Groups

Input: A given group: G, A set of Items: I, Length of Recommendation List: K;

1: Formulate the Recommendation problem as an integer programming following Eqn. 4;
2: Solve the Relaxed convex programming with Boundary Constraints, denote the solution as $X_j, \forall j \in I$;
3: Select K items I_m^K with greatest values of X_j;
4: Output the recommendation list $L = \{X_j \in I_m^K\}$;

For LM fairness semantic, the integer programming can be formulated as:

$$\begin{aligned} \max.\ & \lambda \cdot SW(g, I) + (1 - \lambda) \cdot \frac{1}{K} U_{min} \\ s.t.\ & \sum_i X_i = K \\ & U(u, I) \geq U_{min}, \forall u \in g \\ & X_i \in \{0, 1\} \end{aligned} \tag{3}$$

For Min-Max fairness semantic, the integer programming can be formulated as:

$$\begin{aligned} \max.\ & \lambda \cdot SW(g, I) + (1 - \lambda) \cdot \frac{U_{min}}{U_{max}} \\ s.t.\ & \sum_i X_i = K \\ & U(u, I) \geq U_{min}, \forall u \in g \\ & U(u, I) \leq U_{max}, \forall u \in g \\ & X_i \in \{0, 1\} \end{aligned} \tag{4}$$

For the variance and Jain's fairness semantics, the objective function can be directly reformulated by rewriting $F(u, I)$ with $U(u, I)$. The integer program is usually NP-Hard and very difficult to solve with an optimal solution. We can relax the binary constraint of integer variables to fractional variables with boundary constraints ($0 \leq X_i \leq 1$) and solve the relaxed program with a fractional solution. Then we round them into integers. Some semantics like Least Misery and Variance fairness ($\min_{u \in g} U(u, I)$ and $Var(\{U(u, I), \forall u \in g\})$) are relatively simple. Thus the objective function becomes convex and the relaxed program can be solved with an optimal solution. The algorithm based on integer programming is presented in Alg.2.

5 EXPERIMENT

We conduct extensive experiments on real-world datasets to evaluate our algorithms in terms of typical recommendation accuracy metrics. Moreover, we also exploit the impact of trade-offs on the item recommendation accuracy.

5.1 Experiment Settings

We choose the real-world datasets Movielens and MoviePilot for experiments. The Movielens dataset contains the interactions between individual users and items but has no groups, therefore we construct groups from the individual users with typical methods following previous work [2], [8]

Table 1: Statistics of the datasets.

Dataset	#Users	#Items	#Interactions	#Groups
Movielens	6,040	3,907	1,000,067	\
MoviePilot	171,670	23,974	4,391,822	290

and [21]. The users in MoviePilot dataset may share movie rental accounts with each other and those sharing same account form a group. There are a considerable number of users in MoviePilot dataset, only 602 users share accounts with others. Most of the groups contain only two users and the maximum size of the groups is four. The details of the datasets are listed in Table. 1.

In our experiments, we use five-fold cross-validation for Movielens where four folds are used for training and the remaining fold is used as testing set. The dataset of MoviePilot comes from the challenge of CAMRA and We thus use the training set to learn the model and rank all the non-rated items for each user and compare to the evaluation set for both the recommendation tasks. For datasets that contain only individual interactions with items, we generate three kinds of groups to conduct the experiments, including random user groups (RG), similar user groups (SG) and diverse user groups (DG). In order to generate these groups based on user similarities, we first compute the similarities of users based on their historical interactions with the items; then we randomly select G users for G groups and greedily select the most (least) similar user to each SG (DG) group from the remaining users. For each group, we set the group size as eight and 100 groups are generated for each dataset. We also alter the group size to evaluate its impacts.

We adopt the cosine similarity between the ratings given by two users to compute the similar and diverse user groups. For the missing individual preferences on items, we adopt state-of-the-art approach BPR [24] to make predictions on the Top-K favourite items of each user [1]. For the Top-K group recommendation task, we first compute the Top K most relevant items $I(u, K)$ for each individual user u and set their relevances with two semantics:

- Binary Semantic: $rel(u,i) = 1, \forall u, i \in I(u,k)$ and $rel(u,i) = 0, \forall u, i \notin I(u,k)$;
- Borda Semantic: $rel(u,i) = |\{j | rank(u,j) < rank(u,i), \forall j \in I(u,k)\}|$, $\forall u, i \in I(u,k)$, where $rank(u,i)$ is the ranking of item i in the Top-K personalized recommendation list for user u.

We also conduct experiments to show the performances of item recommendation to groups, some important metrics are adopted:

$$Rec@K = \frac{\sum_{i=1}^{K} rel_i}{\min(K, |y_u^{test}|)}; Prec@K = \frac{\sum_{i=1}^{K} rel_i}{K};$$

$$DCG@K = \sum_{i=1}^{K} \frac{2^{rel_i} - 1}{log_2(i+1)}; NDCG@K = \frac{DCG@K}{IDCG@K}$$

Meanwhile, we also adopt F score to evaluate the recommendation performances, which is a coordination of both

[1]We adopt the implementation of BPR from Librec [11]

Table 4: Performances Comparisons on MoviePilot with Borda Relevance, $K = 10$

Metrics	LM Ranking	Ave Ranking	SPGreedy	EFGreedy	Greedy-LM	Greedy-Var
Prec@K	0.0385	0.0467	0.0003	0.0013	0.0484	**0.0488**
Rec@K	0.0762	0.0910	0.0003	0.0020	0.0942	**0.0945**
F@K	0.0512	0.0617	0.0003	0.0016	0.0639	**0.0644**
NDCG@K	0.2376	0.2450	0.0008	0.0077	**0.2507**	0.2502

Table 5: Performances Comparisons on MoviePilot with Borda Relevance, $K = 20$

Metrics	LM Ranking	Ave Ranking	SPGreedy	EFGreedy	Greedy-LM	Greedy-Var
Prec@K	0.0423	0.0456	0.0008	0.0011	0.0464	**0.0465**
Rec@K	0.1483	0.1603	0.0015	0.0046	0.1636	**0.1639**
F@K	0.0658	0.0710	0.0010	0.0018	0.0723	**0.0724**
NDCG@K	0.2825	0.2901	0.0025	0.0080	0.2910	**0.2915**

precision and recall:

$$F@K = \frac{2Rec@K \cdot Prec@K}{Rec@K + Prec@K}$$

$rel_i = 1/0$ indicates whether the item at rank i in the Top-K recommendation list is in the test set. y_u^{test} denotes the items rated by user u in the testing set. The notion **IDCG** means the maximum possible **DCG** through ideal ranking.

We compare the performances of our algorithm with some existing state-of-art baselines, including:

- LM Ranking Algorithm [2]: this algorithm ranks the items based on the Least Misery relevances and recommend the Top-K items;
- Ave Ranking Algorithm [2]: this algorithm ranks the items based on the Average relevances and recommend the Top-K items;
- SPGreedy Algorithm [21]: this algorithm proposes a fairness metric called proportionality and greedily selects items to maximize the fairness;
- EFGreedy Algorithm [21]: this algorithm proposes a fairness metric called envy-freeness and greedily selects items to maximize the fairness;
- Greedy-LM (proposed in this paper): this algorithm is our proposed greedy algorithm for Least Misery fairness-aware group recommendation;
- Greedy-Var (proposed in this paper): this algorithm is our proposed greedy algorithm for Variance fairness-aware group recommendation.

5.2 Performance on Recommendation

We further investigate the performance of our algorithm on item recommendation tasks. We first utilize a state-of-art collaborative ranking method to generate the user's preference on unrecommended items as an ordering list. Then we adopt Proportionality as individual utility and different fairness metrics for recommendation. When making recommendations to the groups, an item may have been rated by one user while the others have not. We set the relevances of items to zeros for users who have rated them.

Table 2: Performances of GreedyAlg-Var under different λ on MovieLens with Borda Relevance (Rand Group, Sim Group and Div Group), $|G| = 8$, $K = 10$

λ, RG	0	0.1	0.2	0.3	0.4	0.5	0.6	0.7	0.8	0.9	1
F@K	0.0260	0.0817	0.0877	0.0953	0.1019	0.1041	0.1046	0.1053	0.1058	0.1062	0.1062
NDCG@K	0.0697	0.2200	0.2287	0.2334	0.2394	0.2423	0.2440	0.2421	0.2459	0.2478	0.2476
λ, SG	0	0.1	0.2	0.3	0.4	0.5	0.6	0.7	0.8	0.9	1
F@K	0.0103	0.0519	0.0631	0.0759	0.0772	0.0792	0.0799	0.0816	0.0821	0.0841	0.0819
NDCG@K	0.0335	0.1577	0.1691	0.1906	0.2003	0.2031	0.2072	0.2091	0.2079	0.2108	0.2079
λ, DG	0	0.1	0.2	0.3	0.4	0.5	0.6	0.7	0.8	0.9	1
F@K	0.0292	0.0656	0.0714	0.0848	0.0925	0.0950	0.0959	0.0978	0.0990	0.0983	0.0960
NDCG@K	0.0767	0.1715	0.1839	0.2076	0.2185	0.2246	0.2218	0.2237	0.2251	0.2248	0.2228

Table 3: Performances of GreedyAlg-Var under different λ on MovieLens with Binary Relevance (Rand Group, Sim Group and Div Group), $|G| = 8$, $K = 10$

λ, RG	0	0.1	0.2	0.3	0.4	0.5	0.6	0.7	0.8	0.9	1
F@K	0.0193	0.0452	0.0477	0.0596	0.0851	0.0985	0.1015	0.1032	0.1047	0.1059	0.1017
NDCG@K	0.0584	0.1505	0.1547	0.1722	0.2076	0.2322	0.2406	0.2377	0.2389	0.2419	0.2357
λ, SG	0	0.1	0.2	0.3	0.4	0.5	0.6	0.7	0.8	0.9	1
F@K	0.0088	0.0294	0.0328	0.0479	0.0678	0.0725	0.0739	0.0761	0.0785	0.0786	0.0757
NDCG@K	0.0317	0.1102	0.1168	0.1442	0.1720	0.1803	0.1836	0.1872	0.1923	0.1931	0.1834
λ, DG	0	0.1	0.2	0.3	0.4	0.5	0.6	0.7	0.8	0.9	1
F@K	0.0202	0.0414	0.0433	0.0551	0.0753	0.0879	0.0893	0.0884	0.0887	0.0895	0.0889
NDCG@K	0.0574	0.1386	0.1441	0.1623	0.1904	0.2063	0.2132	0.2094	0.2092	0.2052	0.2051

We select the values of λ uniformly from the interval $[0, 1]$ and generate recommendation lists for different scenarios. A 10% sample of the dataset is used as validation set to choose the parameter λ. We compare the performances of comparative algorithms with different semantics of relevances on three types of groups and the results are presented in Fig. 2 and Fig. 3.

The experimental results show that considering fairness in item recommendation leads to better accuracy, regardless of which type of groups is considered. It is an interesting finding since fairness is not directly related to recommendation accuracy. The possible reason is that considering fairness can make up for the imbalance between users' satisfactions and users who are less satisfied can get higher utilities so that the overall accuracy is improved. Meanwhile, we find that the improvements of recommendation accuracy are not the same on all types of groups.

We also compare the performances under different choices of λ, the results are presented in Table. 3. The variance fairness maximization tries to minimize the difference between the utilities of users and considering the fairness at a proper level is important for recommendation accuracy. The empirical performances show that setting λ to 0.8 to 0.9 leads to the best results. Since maximizing fairness alone may harm the satisfaction of users (when recommending commonly disliked items to the group, the fairness is high but the overall social welfare is low), this finding is reasonable.

We also conduct experiments on the MoviePilot dataset where users can share a same movie rental account and those users form a movie rental group. Notice that the groups in this dataset usually contain only two users, therefore the setting is closer to personalized recommendation than the setting of Movielens. Comparing the performances of group recommendation with binary and borda semantics for relevance, we find that using the borda semantic preserves the comparative differences between items thus leads to better performances, especially when the group size is small. Due to the better performances on borda semantic on small groups, we present the results of MoviePilot with borda semantic with $K = 10$ and $K = 20$ in Table. 4 and Table. 5.

The results from the table indicate that our algorithms still achieve superior performances. Since the groups in MoviePilot are real, the results show that the group decision process does involve the coordination of individual users and considering fairness in the process can improve the recommendation accuracy. As the groups in MoviePilot are small and the improvements of our algorithm are more significant when groups are large in size, our algorithm can be more useful in other real-life groups whose sizes are larger.

6 CONCLUSION

In this paper, we investigate how fairness can be modeled in group recommendation and its impact on the quality of recommendation. More specifically, we propose various semantics for user individual utility and further model fairness as a proximity of how balanced the utilities of users are when group recommendations are given. Based on the proposed utilities and fairness, we consider the fairness-aware group recommendation problem and prove its NP-Hardness. In order to optimize both user utility and fairness in group recommendation, we propose a general optimization framework based on Pareto Efficiency. We conduct extensive experiments on real-world datasets to evaluate the performance of

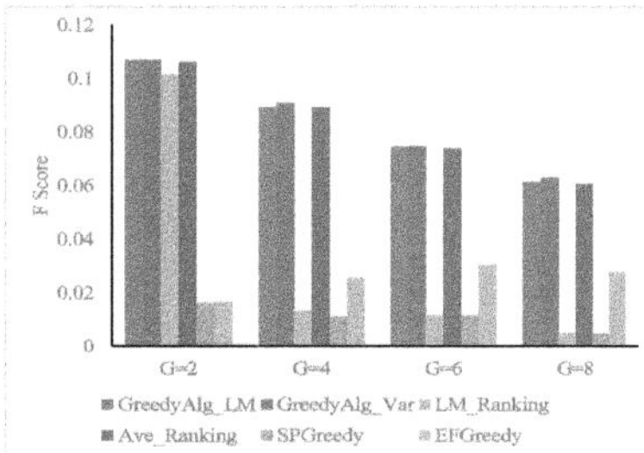

(a) Borda Relevance, Rand Groups

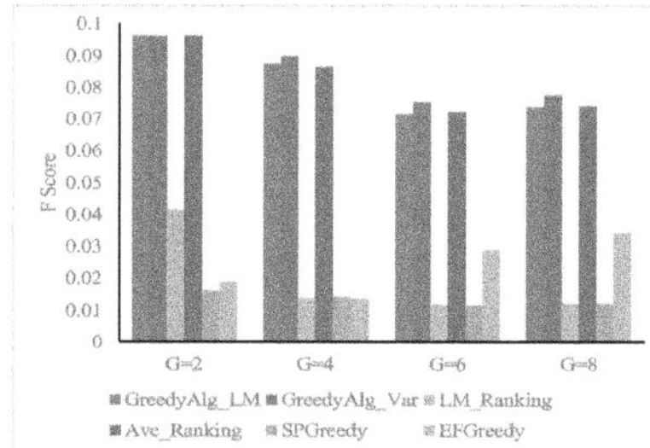

(b) Binary Relevance, Rand Groups

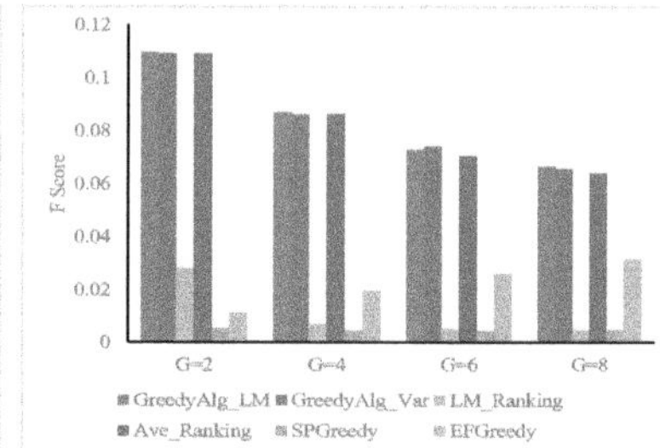

(c) Borda Relevance, Sim Groups

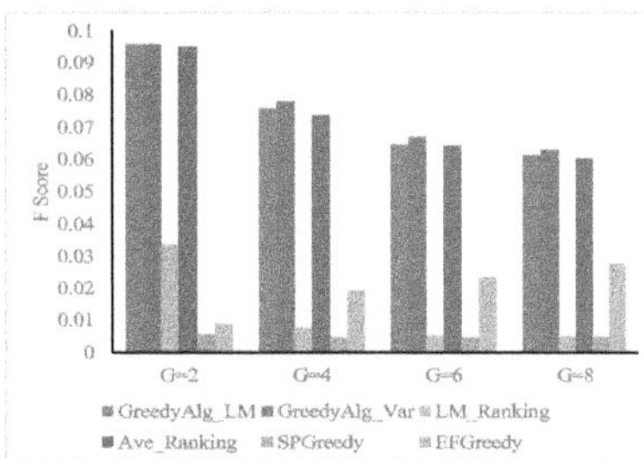

(d) Binary Relevance, Sim Groups

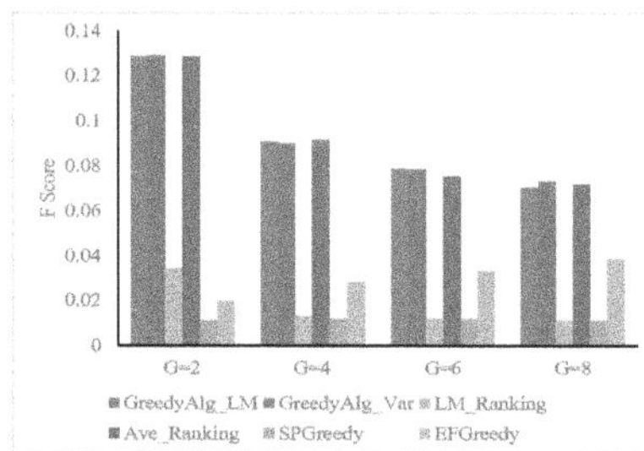

(e) Borda Relevance, Div Groups

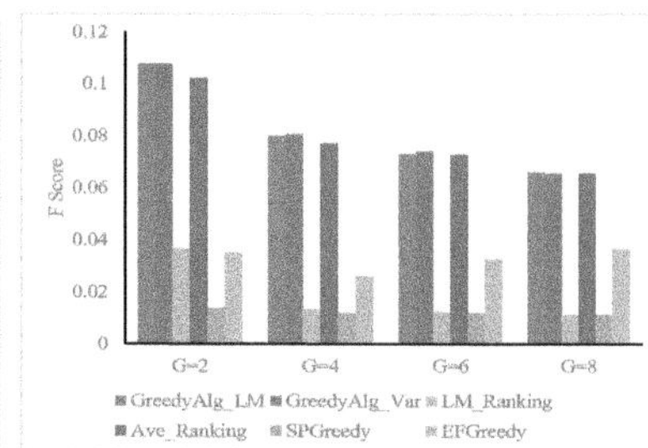

(f) Binary Relevance, Div Groups

Figure 2: F@10 with different group sizes on MovieLens

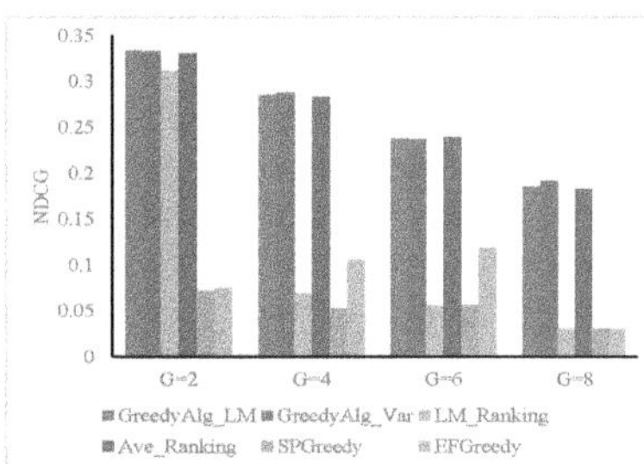

(a) Borda Relevance, Rand Groups

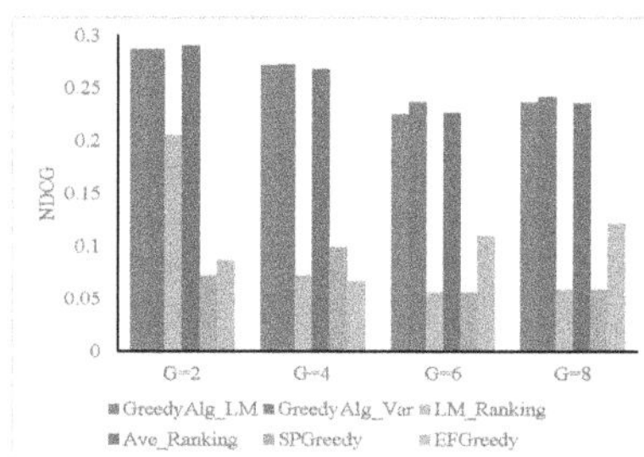

(b) Binary Relevance, Rand Groups

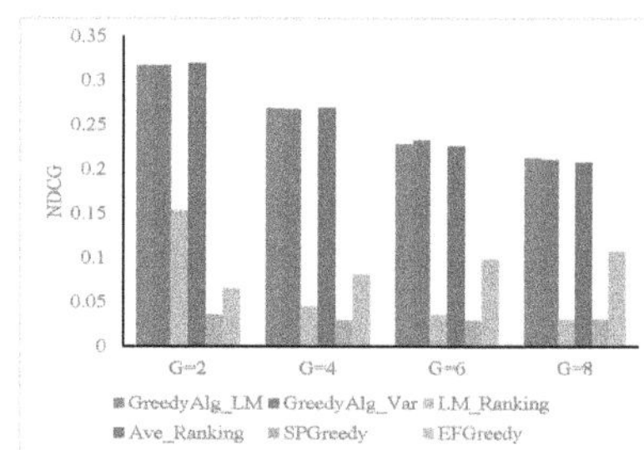

(c) Borda Relevance, Sim Groups

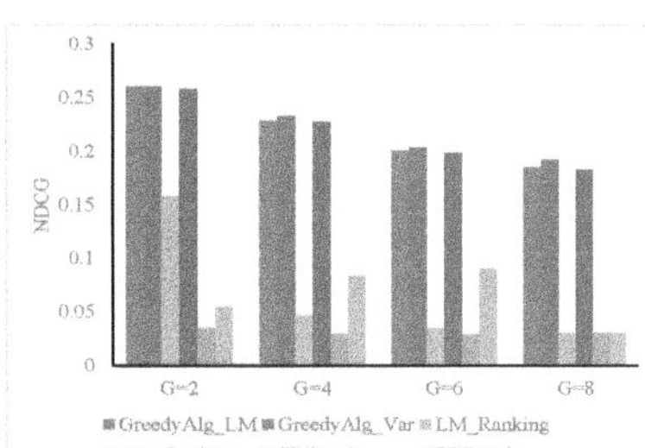

(d) Binary Relevance, Sim Groups

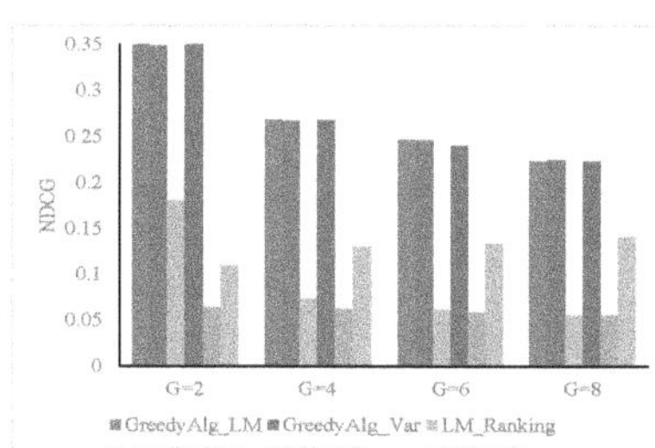

(e) Borda Relevance, Div Groups

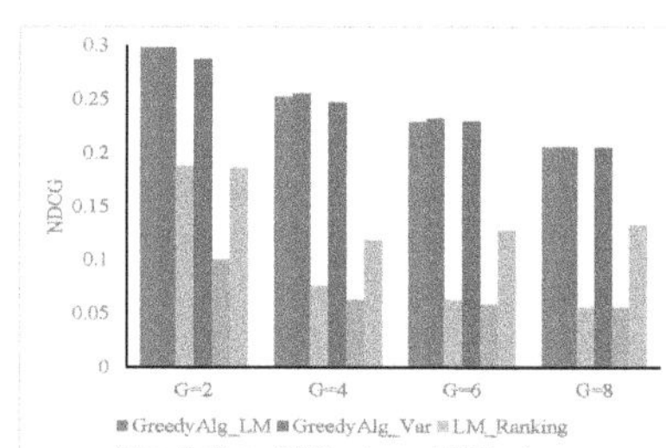

(f) Binary Relevance, Div Groups

Figure 3: NDCG@10 with different group sizes on MovieLens

group recommendation in terms of accuracy. The results indicate that considering fairness can improve the quality of group recommendation.

7 ACKNOWLEDGEMENT

This work is supported by Natural Science Foundation of China (Grant No. 61532011, 61672311) and National Key Basic Research Program (2015CB358700). Part of the work is sponsored by the Center for Intelligent Information Retrieval. Meanwhile it is supported in part by the Hong Kong Scholars Program.

REFERENCES

[1] S. Amer-Yahia, S. B. Roy, A. Chawlat, G. Das, and C. Yu. Group recommendation: Semantics and efficiency. *Proc. VLDB Endow.*, 2(1), Aug. 2009.

[2] L. Baltrunas, T. Makcinskas, and F. Ricci. Group recommendations with rank aggregation and collaborative filtering. In *Proceedings of the fourth ACM conference on Recommender systems*, pages 119–126. ACM, 2010.

[3] F. Brandt, V. Conitzer, and U. Endriss. Computational social choice. *Multiagent systems*, pages 213–283, 2012.

[4] L. A. Carvalho and H. T. Macedo. Generation of coalition structures to provide proper groups' formation in group recommender systems. In *Proceedings of the 22nd International Conference on World Wide Web*, pages 945–950. ACM, 2013.

[5] L. A. M. C. Carvalho and H. T. Macedo. Users' satisfaction in recommendation systems for groups: an approach based on noncooperative games. In *Proceedings of the 22nd International Conference on World Wide Web*, pages 951–958. ACM, 2013.

[6] D. Cosley, J. A. Konstan, and J. Riedl. Polylens: A recommender system for groups of user. In *In ECSCW*, 2001.

[7] A. Crossen, J. Budzik, and K. J. Hammond. Flytrap: Intelligent group music recommendation. In *IUI '02*, New York, NY, USA, 2002. ACM.

[8] T. De Pessemier, S. Dooms, and L. Martens. Design and evaluation of a group recommender system. In *Proceedings of the sixth ACM conference on Recommender systems*, pages 225–228. ACM, 2012.

[9] K. Deb, K. Sindhya, and J. Hakanen. Multi-objective optimization. In *Decision Sciences: Theory and Practice*, pages 145–184. CRC Press, 2016.

[10] M. Gartrell, X. Xing, Q. Lv, A. Beach, R. Han, S. Mishra, and K. Seada. Enhancing group recommendation by incorporating social relationship interactions. In *Proceedings of the 16th ACM international conference on Supporting group work*, pages 97–106. ACM, 2010.

[11] G. Guo, J. Zhang, Z. Sun, and N. Yorke-Smith. Librec: A java library for recommender systems. In *UMAP Workshops*, 2015.

[12] F. Guzzi, F. Ricci, and R. Burke. Interactive multi-party critiquing for group recommendation. In *Proceedings of the fifth ACM conference on Recommender systems*, pages 265–268. ACM, 2011.

[13] L. Hu, J. Cao, G. Xu, L. Cao, Z. Gu, and W. Cao. Deep modeling of group preferences for group-based recommendation. In *AAAI*, pages 1861–1867, 2014.

[14] R. Jain, D.-M. Chiu, and W. R. Hawe. *A quantitative measure of fairness and discrimination for resource allocation in shared computer system*, volume 38. Eastern Research Laboratory, Digital Equipment Corporation Hudson, MA, 1984.

[15] T. Jambor and J. Wang. Optimizing multiple objectives in collaborative filtering. In *Proceedings of the fourth ACM conference on Recommender systems*, pages 55–62. ACM, 2010.

[16] M. Kompan and M. Bieliková. Voting based group recommendation: How users vote. In *HT (Doctoral Consortium/Late-breaking Results/Workshops)*, 2014.

[17] X. Liu, Y. Tian, M. Ye, and W.-C. Lee. Exploring personal impact for group recommendation. In *Proceedings of the 21st ACM international conference on Information and knowledge management*, pages 674–683. ACM, 2012.

[18] L. Naamani Dery, M. Kalech, L. Rokach, and B. Shapira. Iterative voting under uncertainty for group recommender systems. In *Proceedings of the fourth ACM conference on Recommender systems*, pages 265–268. ACM, 2010.

[19] E. Ntoutsi, K. Stefanidis, K. Nørvåg, and H.-P. Kriegel. Fast group recommendations by applying user clustering. In *ER'12*, Berlin, Heidelberg, 2012. Springer-Verlag.

[20] W. Pan and L. Chen. Gbpr: Group preference based bayesian personalized ranking for one-class collaborative filtering. In *IJCAI*, volume 13, pages 2691–2697, 2013.

[21] S. Qi, N. Mamoulis, E. Pitoura, and P. Tsaparas. Recommending packages to groups. In *Data Mining (ICDM), 2016 IEEE 16th International Conference on*, pages 449–458. IEEE, 2016.

[22] E. Quintarelli, E. Rabosio, and L. Tanca. Recommending new items to ephemeral groups using contextual user influence. In *Proceedings of the 10th ACM Conference on Recommender Systems*, pages 285–292. ACM, 2016.

[23] J. A. Recio-Garcia, G. Jimenez-Diaz, A. A. Sanchez-Ruiz, and B. Diaz-Agudo. Personality aware recommendations to groups. In *Proceedings of the third ACM conference on Recommender systems*, pages 325–328. ACM, 2009.

[24] S. Rendle, C. Freudenthaler, Z. Gantner, and L. Schmidt-Thieme. Bpr: Bayesian personalized ranking from implicit feedback. In *Proceedings of the twenty-fifth conference on uncertainty in artificial intelligence*, pages 452–461. AUAI Press, 2009.

[25] M. T. Ribeiro, A. Lacerda, A. Veloso, and N. Ziviani. Pareto-efficient hybridization for multi-objective recommender systems. In *Proceedings of the sixth ACM conference on Recommender systems*, pages 19–26. ACM, 2012.

[26] F. Ricci, L. Rokach, and B. Shapira. *Introduction to recommender systems handbook*. Springer, 2011.

[27] M. Rodriguez, C. Posse, and E. Zhang. Multiple objective optimization in recommender systems. In *Proceedings of the sixth ACM conference on Recommender systems*, pages 11–18. ACM, 2012.

[28] I. Ronen, I. Guy, E. Kravi, and M. Barnea. Recommending social media content to community owners. In *Proceedings of the 37th international ACM SIGIR conference on Research & development in information retrieval*, pages 243–252. ACM, 2014.

[29] S. B. Roy, S. Thirumuruganathan, S. Amer-Yahia, G. Das, and C. Yu. Exploiting group recommendation functions for flexible preferences. In *Data Engineering (ICDE), 2014 IEEE 30th International Conference on*, pages 412–423. IEEE, 2014.

[30] A. Said, S. Berkovsky, and E. W. De Luca. Group recommendation in context. In *Proceedings of the 2nd Challenge on Context-Aware Movie Recommendation*, pages 2–4. ACM, 2011.

[31] A. Salehi-Abari and C. Boutilier. Preference-oriented social networks: Group recommendation and inference. In *RecSys '15*, New York, NY, USA, 2015. ACM.

[32] A. Salehi-Abari and C. Boutilier. Preference-oriented social networks: Group recommendation and inference. In *Proceedings of the 9th ACM Conference on Recommender Systems*, pages 35–42. ACM, 2015.

[33] B. Sarwar, G. Karypis, J. Konstan, and J. Riedl. Item-based collaborative filtering recommendation algorithms. In *Proceedings of the 10th International Conference on World Wide Web*, WWW '01, pages 285–295, New York, NY, USA, 2001. ACM.

[34] S. Seko, T. Yagi, M. Motegi, and S. Muto. Group recommendation using feature space representing behavioral tendency and power balance among members. In *Proceedings of the fifth ACM conference on Recommender systems*, pages 101–108. ACM, 2011.

[35] A. Sen. Social choice theory. *Handbook of mathematical economics*, 3:1073–1181, 1986.

[36] P. Skowron, P. Faliszewski, and J. Lang. Finding a collective set of items: From proportional multirepresentation to group recommendation. *Artificial Intelligence*, 241:191–216, 2016.

[37] X. Wang, R. Donaldson, C. Nell, P. Gorniak, M. Ester, and J. Bu. Recommending groups to users using user-group engagement and time-dependent matrix factorization. In *AAAI*, pages 1331–1337. AAAI Press, 2016.

[38] M. Ye, X. Liu, and W.-C. Lee. Exploring social influence for recommendation: a generative model approach. In *SIGIR*, pages 671–680. ACM, 2012.

[39] Q. Yuan, G. Cong, and C.-Y. Lin. Com: a generative model for group recommendation. In *Proceedings of the 20th ACM SIGKDD international conference on Knowledge discovery and data mining*, pages 163–172. ACM, 2014.

[40] W. Zhang, J. Wang, and W. Feng. Combining latent factor model with location features for event-based group recommendation. In *KDD*, pages 910–918. ACM, 2013.

[41] E. Zitzler and L. Thiele. Multiobjective evolutionary algorithms: a comparative case study and the strength pareto approach. *IEEE transactions on Evolutionary Computation*, 3(4):257–271, 1999.

A Novel Recommender System for Helping Marathoners to Achieve a New Personal-Best

Barry Smyth
Insight Centre for Data Analytics
School of Computer Science
University College Dublin, Ireland
barry.smyth@ucd.ie

Pádraig Cunningham
Insight Centre for Data Analytics
School of Computer Science
University College Dublin, Ireland
padraig.cunningham@ucd.ie

ABSTRACT

We describe a novel application for recommender systems – helping marathon runners to run a new personal-best race-time – by predicting a challenging, but achievable target-time, and by recommending a tailored race-plan to achieve this time. A comprehensive evaluation of prediction accuracy and race-plan quality is provided using a large-scale dataset with almost 400,000 runners from the last 12 years of the Chicago marathon.

CCS CONCEPTS

• **Information systems** → **Personalization**; *Data analytics*;

KEYWORDS

Recommender systems, sports analytics

1 INTRODUCTION

Marathon running is a popular mass-participation sport that attracts millions of runners, from all walks of life, to our city streets. Running a marathon is hard and completing the 42.2 kms on race-day is the final stage, after months of training. But running a marathon is also incredibly rewarding, and for many it is an opportunity to push themselves to a new *personal-best* finish-time.

Running a marathon personal-best needs careful planning. It starts with a target-time to aim for; a time that is not so easy that you will feel untested, but also not so hard that you run the risk of ruining your race because you hit the wall. Various race predictors exist to help runners predict their likely finish-times, based on factors including gender, age, experience, past races, even training and strategy; see [3, 12, 17]. However, they usually base their predictions on shorter races and are not specifically tuned for helping runners to predict the *stretch-goal* that a personal-best represents. And none help the runner when it comes to planning how to achieve this time.

A race-plan — how a runner paces their race — is critically important, especially in an endurance event (see [2, 4, 11]), and considerable research has been devoted to understanding pacing in the marathon [7, 9, 16]. In this work we argue that a target finish-time alone is not enough to ensure marathon success: runners need a race-plan or *pacing plan* to achieve this time, a segment by segment plan for how fast or slow they should run, given the characteristics of the course, so that they will meet the target-time. For example, some runners may plan to run *even-splits*, rarely varying their pace throughout the race. Others will aim for *positive-splits*, running a slower second-half compared to the first, while others will aim for *negative-splits*, running a faster second-half. We argue that such coarse-grained strategies do not go far enough. A good pacing plan will help a runner to manage their effort throughout the race, segment by segment, hill by hill This is especially important during the crucial early stages of the marathon, when many go out too fast, and helps to reduce the risk of hitting the wall later in the race.

The main contribution of this work is to introduce a novel recommender system for helping marathon runners to identify, and plan for, new personal-best (*PB*) finish-times. We describe how to construct suitable *training cases* from conventional race-records, and how to use these cases to *predict* a *PB* time and *recommend* a tailored pacing plan. We evaluate the results using data from the last 12 years of the Chicago marathon.

RecSys '17, August 27-31, 2017, Como, Italy

ACM ISBN 978-1-4503-4652-8/17/08...$15.00
https://doi.org/10.1145/3109859.3109874

2 RECOMMENDING A PERSONAL-BEST

In this section we describe how to transform marathon race data into suitable training cases for generating *PB* predictions and their corresponding race-plans.

2.1 From Races to Cases

The starting point for this work is a marathon *race-record*, a set of *split-times* at regular intervals. Most big-city marathons provide 5km split-times, which we use here.

Our solution adopts a Case-Based Reasoning (CBR) approach: CBR seeks to solve a new problem by reusing and adapting the solutions to similar, past problems; see [1, 8, 13]. Here the 'problem' we want to solve is to predict a *PB* marathon (that is, a finish-time and a race plan) for a runner based on a suboptimal (*non personal-best* or *nPB*) race. The *nPB* race acts as the *problem description* while the runner's *PB* race is the *problem solution* [14]. A runner with data for n past races provides us with $n-1$ problem-solution cases, corresponding to the $n-1$ non *PB*s, each paired with the runner's identified *PB*. Thus, each case is a $\langle nPB, PB \rangle$ pair and the *PB* can be used as the basis of a *PB* time and race plan for other runners who have run races similar to the *nPB*. An example case is shown in Figure 1. The *nPB* and *PB* races have the same representation. The most fundamental feature is the average pace with the race profile represented as deviations from this baseline.

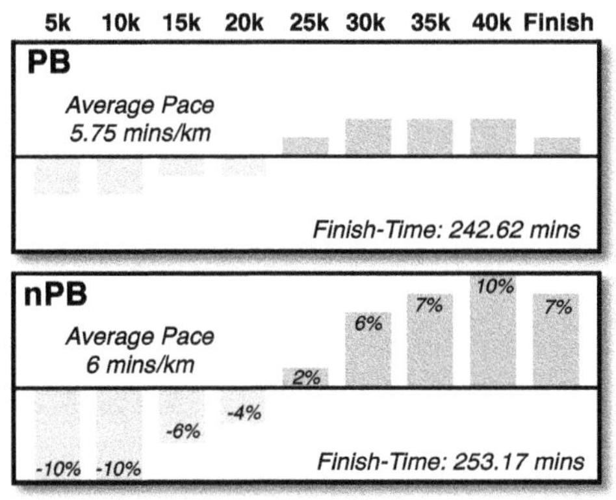

Figure 1: Sample case with *nPB* and *PB* times and pacing.

More formally, given a *repeat* runner r with race-records, $m_1, \ldots m_n$, we identify the personal-best as the race with the fastest finish-time; this may not be their true personal-best, but it represents their best race within the available data. We generate $n-1$ race cases by pairing each *nPB* race with this *PB* race; see Equation 1.

$$c_{ij}(r, m_i, m_j) = \left\langle nPB_i(r, m_i), PB(r, m_j) \right\rangle \quad (1)$$

Figure 1 shows a sample case with a 253-minute *nPB* and a 242-minute *PB*. The *nPB* is characterised by a much more varied pacing profile; the runner started fast and finished slow. In contrast, their *PB* race is much more evenly paced, neither starting out too fast, nor finishing too slow, and completing their race with a modest positive-split and an 11-minute *PB*.

2.2 Predicting a Best Achievable PB Time

We treat the task of determining a challenging but achievable *PB* time as a prediction problem. The intuition is that the features of *nPB* races are predictive of future *PB* times. Thus, we use the *nPB* parts of race-cases as training data and the *PB* times as the target prediction feature. In Section 3 we evaluate a number of standard machine learning algorithms for this.

2.3 Recommending Suitable Race Plans

Next we need to recommend a suitable race-plan for achieving this *PB* time. For the purpose of this work, a race-plan is a sequence of paces during each of the (5km) race segments; rather than using *actual* paces we focus on *relative* paces for the purpose of race-plan recommendation. To generate a plan we identify the k cases whose *PB* times are closest to the predicted *PB* time. These cases correspond to runners who managed to achieve a similar *PB*, to the one predicted for the current runner. The assumption is that the *PB* pacing profiles for these k runners provide a basis for the new race-plan. For now we generate a plan based on the mean relative segment paces for the k cases; obviously this is just one of a range of strategies that will be considered as part of future work.

3 EVALUATION

We use an evaluation dataset of marathon records from the last 12 years of the Chicago marathon. There are 387,077 individual race records for 287,906 unique runners (45% female). From these we produce 99,171 race cases involving pairs of *nPB* and *PB* races. We use 10-fold cross-validation to evaluate the PB predictions and race-plan recommendations. For the former we calculate the percentage difference between the predicted PB and actual PB of each test case. And to evaluate race-plans we compute the similarity between the recommended plan and the actual race-plan as the mean percentage difference between race segment paces. We test 3 standard machine learning algorithms for prediction — linear regression (*Reg*), *kNN* (with $k = 10$), and elastic nets (*EN*) — each of these will typically generate different PB predictions, which in turn will lead to different race-plan recommendations.

	Reg		*kNN*		*EN*	
	Err	*Sim*	*Err*	*Sim*	*Err*	*Sim*
M	5.20	92.75	5.25	92.61	5.38	92.58
F	4.78	93.49	4.87	93.33	4.96	93.31

Table 1: Summary results for *Reg*, *kNN*, and *EN*.

3.1 Prediction Error & Plan Similarity

Table 1 shows the mean prediction error and race-plan similarity for these algorithms, for men and women. We can see error rates of about 5%, lower for women than men, and race-plans that are more than 90% similar to the actual *PB* plans, again slightly better for women than for men. These prediction errors are competitive with those reported by [17], albeit for the different problem of *personal-best* prediction, rather than regular race-time prediction, and without the benefit of training and injury data, but with more race data. In what follows we will present more detailed results for *Reg* (the other algorithms behave similarly) leaving further algorithmic tuning and evaluation as a matter for future work.

3.2 Ability as Finish-Time

Figure 2(a) & (b) shows the prediction error and plan similarity for runners with different (*nPB*) finish-times. Error and similarity tend to deteriorate for increasing finish-times. For example, we can generate PB predictions for fast 180-minute marathoners within about 2.5% of actual PB times, but the error grows to over 4% for 240-minute finishers, before plateauing around 5% after the 300-minute mark. Similarly, recommended race-plans become less and less like the actual race-plans, as finish-times increase.

Thus, faster runners may be more predictable, and this hints that their race cases may be of higher quality than those of slower runners, a point that we will return to presently. Female runners enjoy better predictions and more similar plan recommendations than males, which is consistent with research [9, 16] on the better pacing discipline of female runners, making their races more predictable.

3.3 Personal-Best Difference

How does performance vary with differences between *nPB* and *PB* finish-times? Are runners with closer *nPB* and *PB* times easier to predict? Figure 2(c) & (d) show how *PB Difference* impacts prediction

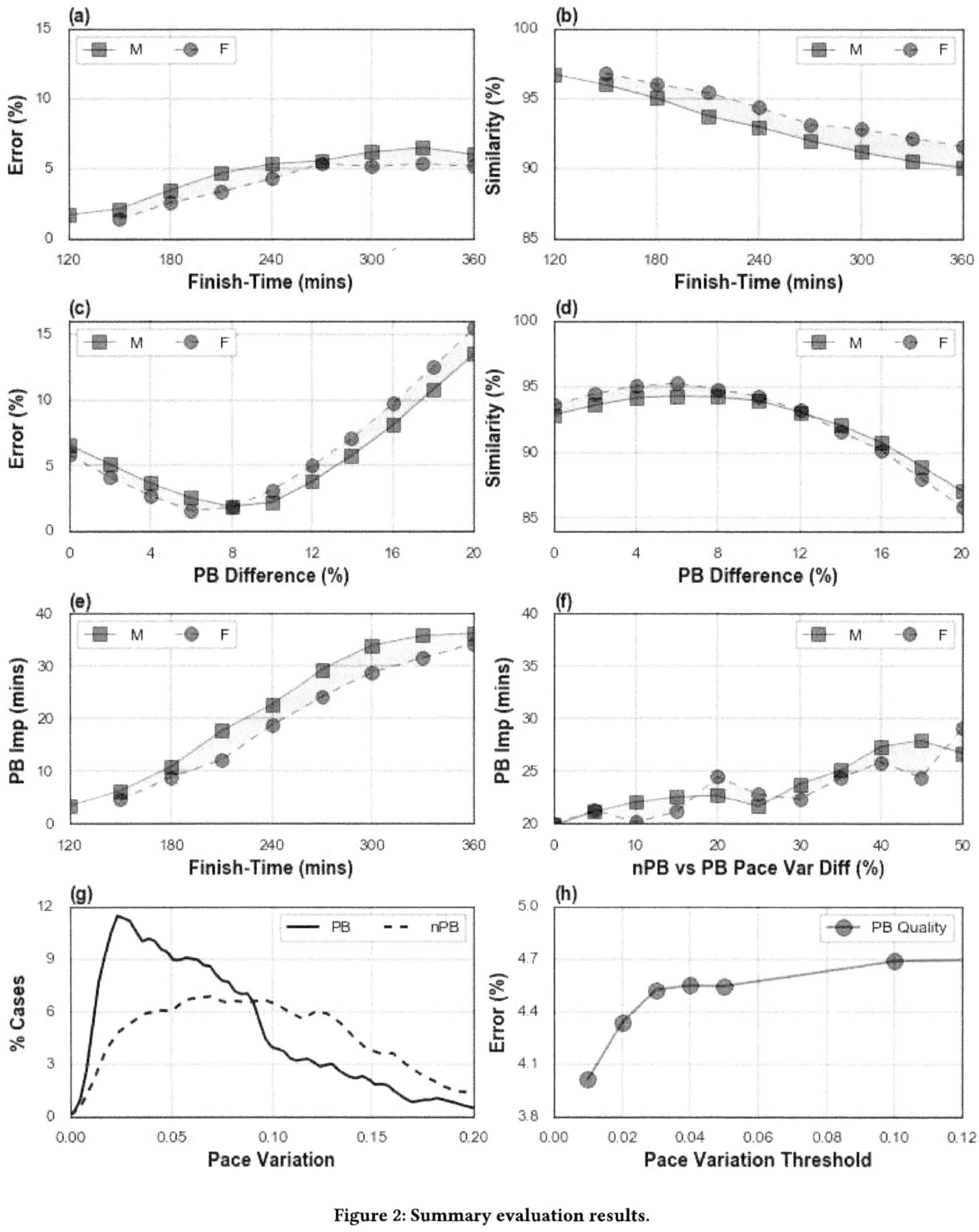

Figure 2: Summary evaluation results.

error and plan similarity; note, a *PB Difference* of 10% means the *PB* time is 10% *faster* than the *nPB* time. Runners with very similar (<4%), or very different (>12%), *nPB* and *PB* races are more difficult to predict, and recommend for, with the best performance seen for *PB Difference* values of about 7-8%.

Low *PB Difference* runners tend to be either: (a) faster, regular marathoners enjoying modest incremental improvements; or (b) slower, infrequent runners registering marginal gains, and who are less motivated by a new personal-best. In combination this makes these runners more difficult to model. On the other hand the high *PB Difference* runners are more difficult to predict for, because they are registering unusually large *PB* improvements.

3.4 Personal-Best Improvements

More concretely, Figure 2(e) shows the actual PB improvements predicted for various finish-times. For example, 240-minute *nPB* runner is predicted a 20-minute faster *PB* (+/- 5 or 6 minutes) under the right conditions.

Another factor that impacts *PB* improvement is the difference in *pace variation* between a runner's races; we can measure pace variation as the coefficient of variation of the segment paces of a race. More even pacing is usually associated with better quality races and larger differences between the pace variation of *nPB* and *PB* races usually means that the *nPB* race is a poor one (lots of pace variation, perhaps indicating the runner hit the wall) relative to a higher quality *PB* race, with a lot less variation. Such a case should exhibit more scope for improvement, which is what we see in Figure 2(f); cases with similar pace variations predict 20 minute *PB* improvements where as cases with greater pace variation differences predict 25-30 minute improvements.

3.5 On Case Quality

This suggests not all cases are created equally. In Figure 2(g) — pace variation histograms for *nPB* and *PB* races — we see, not surprisingly, that *PB*'s exhibit less pace variation than *nPBs*. Thus, using pace variation as a measure of race quality, we can filter cases, for quality, by excluding those whose *PB* pace variation exceeds a minimum threshold.

When we do this for different thresholds, in Figure 2(h), we see a marked effect on prediction error. For race-cases with high quality *PBs* (pace variation threshold < 3%) the prediction error is low, and it disimproves steadily as this threshold.increases, because lower quality cases are included. For example, when we admit cases with *PB* pace variations of up to 0.1 the error is 4.7% compared to just under 4% when we only admit more evenly paced *PB* races (pace variation = 0.01), a relative increase in error of almost 20%

4 DISCUSSION

In this paper we have described a novel use-case for recommender systems: helping marathon runners to achieve a personal-best in a future race by providing them with a challenging but achievable goal-time and an actionable race-plan to achieve it. Our results show that accuracte predictions can be made and that high-quality race-plans can be recommended, at least in the sense that these predictions and recommendations are close matches for the properties of the PB's that test runners have completed. This work is related to a growing interest in the application of recommender systems and similar technolgies to areas such as personal health and wellbeing; see for example [5, 6, 10, 15].

As always there is room for improvement. While prediction error rates are low, they increase for slower runners; for those finishing after the 4-hour mark, predictions, which come with an error rate of 5+%, are likely to be 12+ minutes off relative to the 'true' PB time. These runners stand to benefit most, from this system and, therefore, they stand to suffer most from growing error rates. This speaks to the need for more effective prediction methods that can provide for more stable, lower error rates across all finish-times. To do this we will explore further algorithms and feature-sets in the future, paying particular attention to the benefit of including enriched race histories as part of our training cases.

Another important matter to bear in mind concerns the nature of the evaluation itself. By design our measure of prediction success, and recommendation quality, is the personal-best race eventually run by a test runner. Since this race was completed without the benefit of this recommender system it raises the question of whether these runners may have achieved even faster PBs had they received our predictions and race-plans? This is certainly a valid question and, not doubt there was room for improvement for many of these runners, even during their PB races. Whether our approach can drive even further improvement remains to be seen, and this can only be tested by evaluating the outcomes of races where runners have had the benefit of these recommendations. Another opportunity for future research.

5 CONCLUSIONS

The main contribution of this work is a novel application for recommender systems: helping marathoners to achieve personal-best times by predicting a challenging, yet achievable, target-time for their next race, and by recommending a tailored race-plan for achieving it. Evaluation results show strong prediction performance when tested against historical *PB* times.

This short paper is less about the sophistication of the prediction/recommendation algorithms used – we use straightforward techniques, which offer considerable room for tuning and improvement – and more about the novel domain, race representation, and the dual tasks of prediction and recommendation. Going forward, as mentioned above, we plan to explore the potential for further algorithmic improvements, including, for instance, using multiple *nPB* races within *PB* cases to evaluate the benefits more comprehensive race histories, or by harnessing auxialliary data such as training or injury data. We will also apply these methods to other endurance sports, such as cycling, and look to leverage additional performance data such as heart-rate and power-meter readings as further indicators of effort, and also to provide more detailed race-plans to athletes.

ACKNOWLEDGMENTS

Supported by Science Foundation Ireland through the Insight Centre for Data Analytics, under grant number SFI/12/RC/2289, and by Accenture Labs, Dublin.

REFERENCES

[1] Agnar Aamodt and Enric Plaza. 1994. Case-Based Reasoning: Foundational Issues, Methodological Variations, and System Approaches. *AI Commun.* 7, 1 (1994), 39–59. https://doi.org/10.3233/AIC-1994-7104

[2] Bertrand Baron, Farouck Moullan, Fabien Deruelle, and Timothy D Noakes. 2009. The role of emotions on pacing strategies and performance in middle and long duration sport events. *British Journal of Sports Medicine* (2009).

[3] Francesco Bartolucci and Thomas Brendan Murphy. 2015. A finite mixture latent trajectory model for modeling ultrarunners' behavior in a 24-hour race. *Journal of Quantitative Analysis in Sports* 11, 4 (2015), 193–203.

[4] Deryn Bath, Louise A Turner, Andrew N Bosch, Ross Tucker, Estelle V Lambert, Kevin G Thompson, and Alan St Clair Gibson. 2012. The effect of a second runner on pacing strategy and RPE during a running time trial. *International journal of sports physiology and performance* 7, 1 (2012), 26–32.

[5] Shlomo Berkovsky and Jill Freyne. 2013. Food Recommendations: Biases that Underpin Ratings. In *Proceedings of the 3rd Workshop on Human Decision Making in Recommender Systems in conjunction with the 7th ACM Conference on Recommender Systems (RecSys 2013), Hong Kong, China, October 12, 2013.* 42. http://ceur-ws.org/Vol-1050/paper8.pdf

[6] Shlomo Berkovsky, Jill Freyne, and Mac Coombe. 2012. Physical Activity Motivating Games: Be Active and Get Your Own Reward. *ACM Trans. Comput.-Hum. Interact.* 19, 4 (2012), 32:1–32:41. https://doi.org/10.1145/2395131.2395139

[7] Matthew P Buman, Britton W Brewer, and Allen E Cornelius. 2009. A discrete-time hazard model of hitting the wall in recreational marathon runners. *Psychology of Sport and Exercise* 10, 6 (2009), 662–666.

[8] Pádraig Cunningham, Barry Smyth, and Neil J. Hurley. 1995. On the use of CBR in optimisation problems such as the TSP. In *Case-Based Reasoning Research and Development, First International Conference, ICCBR-95, Sesimbra, Portugal, October 23-26, 1995, Proceedings.* 401–410. https://doi.org/10.1007/3-540-60598-3_36

[9] Robert O Deaner, Rickey E Carter, Michael J Joyner, and Sandra K Hunter. 2014. Men are More Likely than Women to Slow in the Marathon. *Med Sci Sports Exerc* 4, 3 (2014), 607–616.

[10] Elizabeth Dunford, Helen Trevena, Chester Goodsell, Ka Hung Ng, Jacqui Webster, Audra Millis, Stan Goldstein, Orla Hugueniot, and Bruce Neal. 2014. FoodSwitch: a mobile phone app to enable consumers to make healthier food choices and crowdsourcing of national food composition data. *JMIR mHealth and uHealth* 2, 3 (2014), e37.

[11] Carl Foster, Matthew Schrager, Ann C Snyder, and Nancy N Thompson. 1994. Pacing strategy and athletic performance. *Sports Medicine* 17, 2 (1994), 77–85.

[12] Peter S Riegel. 1981. Athletic Records and Human Endurance: A time-vs.-distance equation describing world-record performances may be used to compare the relative endurance capabilities of various groups of people. *American Scientist* 69, 3 (1981), 285–290.

[13] Barry Smyth. 2007. Case-Based Recommendation. In *The Adaptive Web, Methods and Strategies of Web Personalization.* 342–376. https://doi.org/10.1007/978-3-540-72079-9_11

[14] Barry Smyth and Pádraig Cunningham. 2017. Running with Cases: A CBR Approach to Running Your Best Marathon. In *Proceedings of the 25th International Conference on Case-Based Reasoning ICCBR 2017)*, David W. Aha and Jean Lieber (Eds.). Springer International Publishing, 360–374".

[15] Maria Alice L. Thé, Ronda C. Bell, Katia G. Camargo, Rosina Weber, Alejandro Martins, and Ricardo M. Barcia. 2000. *Case-Based Reasoning for Nutrition Consulting.* Springer London, London, 180–190. https://doi.org/10.1007/978-1-4471-0465-0_11

[16] Nicholas William Trubee. 2011. *The Effects of Age, Sex, Heat Stress, and Finish Time on Pacing in the Marathon.* Ph.D. Dissertation. University of Dayton.

[17] Andrew J Vickers and Emily A Vertosick. 2016. An empirical study of race times in recreational endurance runners. *BMC Sports Science, Medicine and Rehabilitation* 8, 1 (2016), 26.

Recommending Personalized News in Short User Sessions

Elena Viorica Epure*
CRI, Panthéon-Sorbonne
Paris, France
Elena.Epure@malix.univ-paris1.fr

Benjamin Kille*
DAI-Lab, TU Berlin
Berlin, Germany
benjamin.kille@dai-labor.de

Jon Espen Ingvaldsen
IDI, NTNU
Trondheim, Norway
jonespi@idi.ntnu.no

Rebecca Deneckere
CRI, Panthéon-Sorbonne
Paris, France
Rebecca.Deneckere@univ-paris1.fr

Camille Salinesi
CRI, Panthéon-Sorbonne
Paris, France
Camille.Salinesi@univ-paris1.fr

Sahin Albayrak
DAI-Lab, TU Berlin
Berlin, Germany
sahin.albayrak@dai-labor.de

ABSTRACT

News organizations employ personalized recommenders to target news articles to specific readers and thus foster engagement. Existing approaches rely on extensive user profiles. However frequently possible, readers rarely authenticate themselves on news publishers' websites. This paper proposes an approach for such cases. It provides a basic degree of personalization while complying with the key characteristics of news recommendation including news popularity, recency, and the dynamics of reading behavior. We extend existing research on the dynamics of news reading behavior by focusing both on the progress of reading interests over time and their relations. Reading interests are considered in three levels: short-, medium-, and long-term. Combinations of these are evaluated in terms of added value to the recommendation's performance and ensured news variety. Experiments with 17-month worth of logs from a German news publisher show that most frequent relations between news reading interests are constant in time but their probabilities change. Recommendations based on combined short-term and long-term interests result in increased accuracy while recommendations based on combined short-term and medium-term interests yield higher news variety.

CCS CONCEPTS

• **Information systems → Data analytics**; **Content ranking**; **Web log analysis**; *Data stream mining*; *Personalization*;

KEYWORDS

News reading behavior, News reading interests, Recommender system, Personalization, Markov processes, Stationarity analysis

*Both authors contributed equally to this work.

RecSys '17, August 27–31, 2017, Como, Italy

ACM ISBN 978-1-4503-4652-8/17/08...$15.00
https://doi.org/10.1145/3109859.3109894

1 INTRODUCTION

The digital transformation has been a game changer for legacy news media. Keeping readers loyal has become highly competitive for publishers as their new business models rely on advertisement or related revenues [28]. Personalized recommendation has emerged as a popular way to tackle this challenge by automatically suggesting news to online readers. However, creating effective solutions faces particular constraints [15, 27]. Large publishers release hundreds of news daily, implying that they must deal with fast-growing numbers of items that get quickly outdated and irrelevant to most readers. News readers exhibit more unstable consumption behavior than users in other domains such as entertainment. External events affect, e.g. breaking news, affect readers interests [15]. In addition, the news domains experiences extreme levels of sparsity.

Existing news recommender solutions address these challenges to some extent. Most of them suggest fresh and popular news. Some consider the dynamics of news reading behavior. However, they rely on the availability of rich user profiles for personalized recommendations. Still, many publishers lack this knowledge, unlike news aggregators' services [2, 6] or company blogs [31], as readers tend to consume online news without authentication. Cross-device and cross-browser tracking are technicly challenging endevaors. Thus, in practice, publishers observe relatively short sessions with fewer than ten clicks on average [9, 10, 27].

As per-user models are unsuitable in short sessions, we propose a new approach to recommendation which ensures basic personalization. The approach combines crowd reading behavior over time and the current user session. Thereby, we model crowd reading behavior for different time frames. When providing recommendations, should the models from the same day, from the last weeks, or from the last months be used? In the current work, we analyze the dynamics of the crowd news reading behavior and its effect on recommendations. We show that such design choices can significantly affect the outcome.

This work includes four contributions. First, we extend the existing distinction between short- and long-term reading behavior as we establish medium-term reading behavior. The reading behavior concerns readers' interests, which are linked to news categories. Section 2 conveys a detailed description. Second, we identify reading episodes and derive models specifically reflecting engage reading. Third, we assess the dynamics of the crowd reading behavior, complementary to related studies in news media. Specifically, we focus on the evolution of the relations between news categories rather than on standalone categories. Fourth, we compare three recommendation policies in terms of performance and news variety: (a) a policy based merely on short-term behavior; (b) a policy integrating short- and medium-term behaviors; (c) a policy integrating short- and long-term behaviors. Experiments are conducted with real data from a German news publisher, spanning 17 months. The long period is chosen to account for fluctuations caused by seasonal or other types of effects.

Our findings show that in reading episodes users are likely to read news within the same category. The relations between news categories are stable in time as the most likely target categories from a given source stay the same. However, their priorities, represented by transition probabilities, change every 1 to 4 months. Augmenting the short-term behavior with knowledge about the long- and medium-term behavior improves recommendations. The policy combining short- and long-term interests yields higher accuracy than combining short- and medium-term interests. Contrarily, combining short- and medium-term interests yields higher variety.

Further, the formalization of the proposed approach is presented. The experiments are described in Section 3 and discussed in Section 4, followed be the related work in Section 5. Finally, conclusions are drawn and directions for future works are indicated.

2 DEFINING READING BEHAVIOR IN NEWS

We consider an online environment in which a publisher provides a collection of news articles to interested readers. Let $\mathcal{U} = \{u_m\}_{m=1}^{M}$ represent the increasing set of visitors. Further, let $\mathcal{I} = \{i_n\}_{n=1}^{N}$ represent the increasing collection of news articles. The publisher observes how visitors act on the website. In particular, the publisher keeps track of events whenever a visitor reads an article. Let $\theta = (\theta_u, \theta_i, \theta_t, \theta_c)$ represent such an event where the individual variables refer to visitor, article, time, and context. The publisher observers a sequence of events $\Theta = \{\theta^{(\alpha)}\}_{\alpha=1}^{A}$ such that $\theta_t^{(\alpha)} < \theta_t^{(\alpha+1)}, \forall\alpha$. We represent the reading behavior of individual users as $\Theta_u = \{\theta : \theta_u = u\}$. We assume that visitors have limited time and desire to read articles. In particular, the number of news articles a visitor is willing to read is $X \ll N$.

The publisher tries to engage visitors by providing a small set of suggestions, every time an article is read. Formally, the publisher employs a policy π which takes a given event $\theta^{(\alpha)}$ and automatically produces a ranked list of suggestions $S^{(\alpha)} = \{s_k \,|s_k \in I\}_{k=1}^{K}$. The publisher monitors how visitors react upon the received suggestions in order to drive policy improvement. The policy that produced the suggestions gets credited with the reward R whenever a visitor reads any of the suggested articles:

$$R(\pi, \theta^{(\alpha)}, S^{(\alpha)}) = \begin{cases} 1 & \text{if } \exists\beta > \alpha, \theta^{(\beta)} \in (\Theta_u \cap S^{(\alpha)}) \\ 0 & \text{otherwise} \end{cases} \tag{1}$$

For practical purposes, the publisher disregards future events if the visitor is inactive for more than a specified time τ_u. Publishers can employ a variety of policies $\pi \in \Pi$. Their objective is to find the policy that maximizes the cumulative rewards:

$$\pi^* = \arg\max_{\pi\in\Pi} \sum_{\theta\in\Theta} R(\pi, \theta, S). \tag{2}$$

We investigate three policies: (a) the short-term news reading; (b) the long- and short-term news reading; (c) the medium- and short-term news reading. These are further described.

Editors put the most recent and significant news at the start of newspapers. Analogously, our first policy suggests articles which have been popular recently. We refer to this policy as *baseline* and it corresponds to the short-term news reading interests. The baseline has associated a list L of fixed size ϵ. As the system observes another event, θ_i is added to L. If adding θ_i exceeds ϵ, the oldest element is dismissed. Thereby, L continuously stores the most recently read articles. At the same time, the more popular an article is, the more often it will appear in L. The baseline policy suggests elements from L, most recently added and different from the article being currently read by the user u. Also, the recommendation has an implicit popularity bias as the probability of choosing a list of articles $S^{(\alpha)}$ depends on $f_{i|L}, i \in S^{\alpha}$, the frequency of article i in L.

The remaining two policies enrich the baseline with information about the news reading process—how readers transition between news categories. A stochastic process models a random system changing over time. Formally, if D is a subinterval of $[0, \infty)$, a continuous-time stochastic process is a set of random variables $\{X_d\}, d \in D$. If we restrict $D = \mathbb{N}_0$, we obtain a discrete-time stochastic process. Let $\Xi = \{\xi\}_{v=1}^{V}$ be the finite set of news categories, corresponding to the random variables of the news reading process. Let $\xi(\theta_i)$ refer to the category assigned to the article i. Hence, we can transform the reading behavior of an individual user u, $\Theta_u = (\theta^{(1)}, \theta^{(2)}, \ldots, \theta^{(\alpha)})$ into a sequence of categories: $\Xi_u = (\xi(\theta_i^{(1)}), \xi(\theta_i^{(2)}), \ldots, \xi(\theta_i^{(\alpha)}))$. The Markov property characterizes a stochastic process whose current state captures all information necessary to compute the probability of the next state [21]. For the news reading behavior, this is formally defined as:

$$\begin{aligned} &\Pr[X_{d+1} = \xi_v | X_d = \xi_w, X_{d-1} = \xi_{w-1}, \ldots, X_0 = \xi_{w_0}] = \\ &\Pr[X_{d+1} = \xi_v | X_d = \xi_w] = p_{ij}, \forall d \in \mathbb{N}_0, \xi_{w_0}, \ldots, \xi_w, \xi_v \in \Xi \end{aligned} \tag{3}$$

A transition matrix over all permutations of two categories ($|\Xi| = V$) represents the dynamics of such as system:

$$T = \begin{bmatrix} p_{11} & \cdots & p_{1V} \\ p_{21} & \cdots & p_{2V} \\ \vdots & \ddots & \vdots \\ p_{V1} & \cdots & p_{VV} \end{bmatrix} \quad p_{vw} \geq 0, \sum_{w}^{\xi_w\in\Xi} p_{vw} = 1, \quad \forall v, \xi_v \in \Xi \tag{4}$$

The transition probabilities p_{vw} can be estimated from observations as the ratio between the frequency of transitions from category ξ_v to category ξ_w and the total number of transitions from ξ_v. If the transition matrix T stays constant as the system evolves, the stochastic process is referred to as *First-Order Markov Process*.

We use the defined reading behavior process to create a new recommendation policy on top of the baseline. For each category ξ, there is a separate list L_ξ used to model short-term reading interests. For each event θ, we determine the category $\xi(\theta_i) = \xi_v$. Subsequently, we select the most likely category for the next article: $\xi^* = \arg\max_{p_{vw}} T$ and return suggestions from L_{ξ^*}. We distinguish the medium-term news reading interests from the long-term ones based on the observations used for estimating T. The matrix corresponding to the long-term behavior contains all the

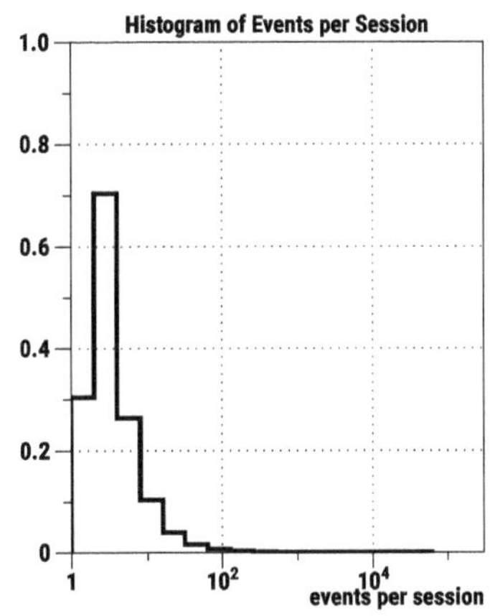

Figure 1: Histogram of events per session (log scale)

existing observations. The matrix corresponding to the medium-term behavior contains observations from a limited period only.

3 EXPERIMENTS

The research questions we address in this paper are:

Q_1 How stable in time is the news reading behavior, modeled as Markov processes over news categories?

Q_2 How do different strategies of combining long-, medium- and short-term news reading interests in a recommender compare in terms of performance and news variety?

3.1 Data Description

The data set is provided by a German news publisher that accommodates on average 3 million visits per week. It consists of ≈ 196.6 million events, which span 475 days from August 2014 to December 2015. Data from June 16 to June 27, 2015 is missing due to technical problems with the logging system. An event is generated and logged when an article is accessed on the news publisher's website. The events are logged with the following information: the user session's identifier, the event's time-stamp, and the article's link and meta-data, which includes the associated categories. The categories are manually assigned by editors, each time an article is uploaded on the website, and are a set of pre-established keywords (see Table 1). We rely on editors' experiences to assign categories in a consistent manner. Most of the user sessions have less than 10 events as shown in Figure 1.

3.2 Data Transformation

Before the experiments, the data has been pre-processed. First, we eliminated events associated to the default session. This session captures all events with cookies disabled such that individual users cannot be tracked. Second, we chronologically sorted the events within sessions. Third, we segmented sessions into reading episodes. Therein, we cut session if events occurred in less than 60 s or longer than 3600 s apart. These thresholds were set after observing and questioning our personal circle about the time spent on article reading. Other sources also suggest an average of 20 min per article[1].

The transition matrices over news categories have been computed as follows. Consecutive events in a reading episode become a transition, the first being the source, the second the target. Multiple transitions emerge if either source or target event have several categories assigned. In this case, the Cartesian product of the source and target category sets is calculated, each obtained element becoming a transition.

3.3 News Reading Dynamics

The first research question aims to assess the dynamics of the news reading behavior modeled as a Markov process over news category. We have analyzed the stationarity of the Markov process using a method based on the χ^2 statistical test [3]. The method starts with computing the transition matrix for the complete period τ and the transition matrices for all consecutive sub-intervals $t \in \tau$. Then, these local transition matrices are tested against the overall transition matrix for statistical difference. We formulate the null hypothesis and the alternative hypothesis:

$H_0 : \forall t \in \tau : p_{vw|t} = p_{vw} \leftrightarrow H_a : \exists t \in \tau : p_{vw|t} \neq p_{vw}$

- p_{vw} denotes the estimated transition probability from state ξ_v to state ξ_w for the entire period τ;
- $p_{vw|t}$ denotes the estimated transition probability from state ξ_v to state ξ_w only for the sub-periods $t \in \tau$;

Given that there are at least two positive values in each row v of the overall transition matrix T, the χ^2 test is computed as follows:

$$Q = \sum_{t \in \tau} \sum_{\xi_v \in \Xi} \sum_{\xi_w \in \Xi_v} z_{v|t} \frac{(p_{vw|t} - p_{vw})^2}{p_{vw}} \approx \text{asy}\chi^2\left(\sum_{\xi_v \in \Xi} (a_v - 1)(b_v - 1) \right) \quad (5)$$

- $z_{v|t}$ denotes the number of observed transitions from state ξ_v in sub-period t, it could be 0;
- $\Xi_v = \{w : p_{vw} > 0, \xi_w \in \Xi\}, \xi_v \in \Xi$; contains all target states observed from state ξ_v for the entire period τ;
- Q has an asymptotic chi-squared distribution (asyχ^2) with the number of degrees of freedom computed as sum over all states $\xi_v \in \Xi$ by considering two terms: a_v is the number of sub-periods t for which transitions from state ξ_v are observed; $b_v = |\Xi_v|$ is the number of positive values in the row v of the transition matrix for the entire period τ.

The test could be also adjusted to assess how much a certain sub-period t differs from the complete period τ. In this case, the outer sum in (Eq. 5) has 2 terms ($|\tau| = 2$): the period t and the transition matrix computed for all the other periods from τ except t.

The first prerequisite to conduct the stationarity analysis on our data set is to decide the magnitude of the sub-periods t: days, weeks or months. Periods spanning days or weeks were excluded. In a descriptive analysis, we observed that breaking news changes the local reading pattern. Also, we randomly selected consecutive days and weeks, and ran the stationarity test. The results showed a significant matrix variance (p-value $p < 0.001$). Consistent with

[1] http://contentmarketinginstitute.com/2016/01/visitors-read-article/

Table 1: News categories and associated codes

Cars, Motor, Traffic	1	Science, Communication	2	Games, Virtual World, Toys	3
Politics, Business, Economics	4	Travel, Tourism, Navigation	5	TV, Radio, Video, Photo	6
General News	7	Professional, Career	8	Computers, Technology	9
Family, Education, Leisure	10	Banking, Finance, Insurance	11	Health, Sports, Nutrition	12
Real Estate, Home, Gardening	13	People, Relationships	14	Fashion, Lifestyle, Culture	15

this, Bickenbach and Bode [3] claim that while more granular sub-samples are preferred, they should not be too small. Otherwise, non-stationarity could emerge from the test, even though the process is Markov [3]. Eventually, the sub-periods t were set to 1 month.

When working with matrices of millions of events, a difference caused by few thousands transitions is not necessarily significant. However, as the Chi-Square test is very sensitive to the number of observations, it could yield non-stationarity [12]. For this reason, we decided to correct the transition frequencies by a factor of 0.001. The values were brought from big-data (millions) to a magnitude equivalent to what has been observed in similar studies (thousands) [3]. After correction, the frequencies still reached tens of thousands, which we consider a representative sample size.

3.4 Recommendation Policy Comparison

The second research question aims to compare the three policies introduced in Section 2 in terms of recommendation performance and ensured news variety. Publishers focus on maintaining the engagement of their readers. Thus, one way to measure performance is through the cumulative rewards $R(\pi, \Theta)$. Frequently, they normalize the rewards by the number of requests to obtain the click-through rate (CTR) = $\frac{1}{|\Theta|}\sum_{\theta\in\Theta} R(\pi, \theta, S)$. More sophisticated evaluation metrics such as the ranking-based ones—normalized discounted cumulative gain or mean reciprocal rank— exist but they cannot be applied in conditions with insufficient user feedback.

Besides monitoring how well readers' preferences are met, we look at the overall variety of suggestions. Having a more diverse set of suggestions can lead to readers experiencing serendipity. Let $S^{(A)}$ refer to all recommendations produced by applying the policy π to the upcoming events Θ. Further, we define the number of times an article i is recommended: $v_i = \sum_{s\in S^{(A)}} \mathbb{I}(s = i)$, where $\mathbb{I}$ refers to the indicator function which returns 1 if the condition applies and 0 otherwise. Finally, let $I^{(K)}$ refer to the K items with highest v_i. We quantify overall news variety as,

$$\delta = 1 - \frac{\sum_{i\in I^{(K)}} v_i}{|S^{(A)}|}. \quad (6)$$

In other words, the number of recommendations subsumed by elements of $I^{(K)}$ is normalized by the total number of recommendations and subtracted from 1. Thus, $\delta \in [0, 1]$ with $\delta = 0$ referring to the case that all readers received the identical K suggestions and $\delta = 1$ signaling that all readers received disjoint sets of suggestions.

We use the same data for this evaluation as has been used for the stationarity analysis in the previous section. This allows us to have a sound and transparent base for comparing the recommender outcomes, especially for changing periods or strongly deviating months. The evaluation follows a sliding-window approach. First, the three news recommendation algorithms are initialized with 10 000 events from September 2014 and the initial transition matrix is computed for August 2014. Subsequently, all events are processed in chronological order. Each recommendation algorithm computes a list of $K = 4$ suggestions. The choice of 4 suggestions corresponds to the number of suggestions displayed on the website of the news publisher. Then, for each user associated with the suggestions, it is checked whether they accessed one of the recommended articles within an hour. Having exceeded the 1 h limit, the suggestions are discarded. Then, the cumulative rewards and news variety are hourly computed. This yields a total of 11 355 measurements.

4 RESULTS AND DISCUSSION

This section presents the results of our experimentation. Section 4.1 is devoted to the stationarity analysis. Section 4.2 shows the observation regarding the recommendation policies.

4.1 News Reading Dynamics

We assessed the stationarity of the news reading behavior, modeled as a Markov process over news categories, for the entire period of August, 2014–December, 2015. Using the Chi-Square test (Equation 5), we obtained $Q = 8709.744$ with df $= 1778$ degrees of freedom, leading to the rejection of H_0 ($p < 0.01$). Thus, the transition probabilities fluctuate during the 17-month period. Further, we have checked whether longer periods exhibit stationary patterns. For getting better insights into how to find these periods, and whether they existed, we used the Chi-Square test (Equation 5) adjusted for computing individual period difference: $|\tau| = 2$; the first sum term is t, the assessed month; the second sum term is the rest of the period τ except this month. Then, the resulting Q values per month were plotted. Thereby, we observed a major structural break from March 2015 to April 2015. Then, the test was re-run for the period August 2014 and March 2015 still rejecting H_0 with $Q = 1124.85, \text{df} = 938, p < 0.01$. However, when Q values for each month of this period were plotted, a potential strong similarity has been observed between September, 2014 and February, 2015. Indeed, the Chi-Square test confirmed this similarity, accepting the null hypothesis with $Q = 700.51, \text{df} = 645, p > 0.05$. We repeated this procedure for the period April, 2015–December, 2015. Finally, the following homogeneous periods have been discovered:

- Sep. 2014–Feb. 2015: $Q = 700.5, \text{df} = 645, p > 0.05$,
- Apr. 2015–Jul. 2015: $Q = 6.56, \text{df} = 48, p > 0.99$,
- Sep. 2015–Oct. 2015: $Q = 14.95, \text{df} = 55, p > 0.99$,
- Nov. 2015–Dec. 2015: $Q = 62.16, \text{df} = 47, p > 0.05$.

Figure 2 is consistent with these findings. The y-axis represents the transition probabilities greater than 0.05 from category 7—General News, to all news categories; the x-axis reflects the month.

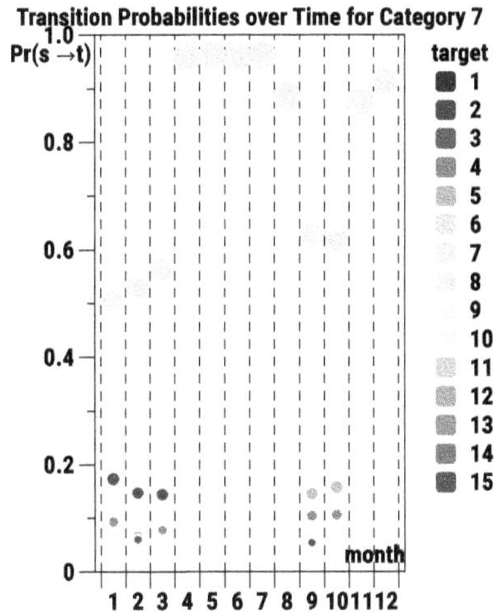

Figure 2: Probabilities per month for transitions from General News—code 7, to all categories in 2015.

The discovered homogeneous periods become visible: the circles for the months within this period line up almost horizontally. Further, we noticed a tendency to read within the same category. The highest transition probability corresponds to category 7, same as the source. Finally, it appears that few target categories are preferred to be read next, after the source category, over the entire period: Science, Communication—code 2; Politics, Business Economics—code 4; Travel, Tourism, Navigation—code 5. However, their priority changes in time. For instance, travel and tourism news are read most frequently together with the general news in the beginning of the year (January–March). We created visualizations for other source categories as well observing similar results (figures omitted for space reason).

Often, in solutions, the model stationarity is taken for granted. However, these results show that news reading behavior has both stable and dynamic parts. The most preferred news categories read after a given category seem to be stable. By contrary, the transitions between these news categories are stationary for limited periods of time, with some singular months with strongly deviating patterns (e.g. August, 2014 and 2015). Consequently, the preceding month appears to be often a suitable base for recommendation, except for the months with strongly deviating reading patterns or starting a homogeneous period. Being able to identify the cause of these changes and predict them could be very useful for adjusting dynamically the recommendation. We contemplate that various factors could influence news reading behavior: changes in human habits induced by seasons, structural changes of news publishers' websites or very important news events spanning longer periods.

4.2 Recommendation Policy Comparison

Figure 3 presents the performance results of the proposed strategies for recommendation: short-term interests only (baseline (B)), short- and long-term interests (transition complete (T_c)), short- and medium-term interests (transition 1 month (T_1)). On the left-hand side, each curve reflects the proportion of per-hour measurements, y-value, exhibiting a maximum response rate of x-value. For instance, baseline intersects the ordinate at ≈ 0.27, meaning that about 27 % of per-hour measurements have associated a 0.0 % response rate. Alternatively, T_c achieves in about 80 % of the cases a response rate up to 10 %. Thus, a more distant curve from the top left corner is preferred. The right-hand side of Figure 3 shows the pair-wise comparison of the recommendation strategies: transition 1 month vs. baseline, transition complete vs. baseline, and transition 1 month vs. transition complete. The x-axis conveys the per-hour measurements in chronological order, the left-most point being the first hour of September 1, 2014, the right-most point the last hour of December 31, 2015. The y-axis values illustrate the difference between the response rates of each pair of measurements. Positive values are shown in blue and negative ones in red.

Both T_1 and T_c achieve higher response rates on average than the baseline. T_c performs similarly to or even better than T_1. Analyzing the granular measurements, we observe that T_1 falls short of T_c in particular during the months: March, May, November and December, 2015. The subpar performance of T_1 could be explained for March—strongly deviating month from February 2015, its base of prediction, and November—the first month of a new homogeneous period so different than October 2015. Nonetheless, May and December, 2015 have associated low response rates even though they were very similar to their preceding months. This outcome could be explained by what happens in the second part of the recommendation, when the short-term interests strategy is used. The dynamic data structures of articles are sensitive to the latest crowd reading behavior. It appears that there is a division among the crowd reading interests, hypothetically caused by the co-existence of multiple strongly influential news, competing in popularity. Another interesting aspect is that sometimes strongly deviating months or the last months of homogeneous periods are a good base for prediction such as March, July and August, 2015. This indicates that even if the overall reading behavior changes, the most likely transition from a given source category stays consistent. Therefore, even for time-variant periods, the target category associated to a source appears stable.

Further, Figure 4 plots the histogram with news variety measurements for T_1 and T_c, hourly computed with Equation 6 and K set to 4. We observe that T_1 varies suggestions better than T_c as shown by the right-most peak in Figure 4. The long-term interests represent the transition probabilities in the long-run between news categories. Aligned with the literature [6, 34], this reading behavior converges to few most preferred categories chosen in recommendations. However, such behavior is not sensitive to local strong trends such as season-induced changes that could temporally modify the most likely transitions. Contrarily, the medium-term interests strategy is able to overcome this, leading to a higher news variety.

4.3 Reflections on News Recommendation

The proposed solution shows that categories provide noticeable improvements despite their simplistic nature and a fair level of personalization when rich user data is missing. Categorical information is readily available, thus it could be implemented as-is in other news recommendations setups.

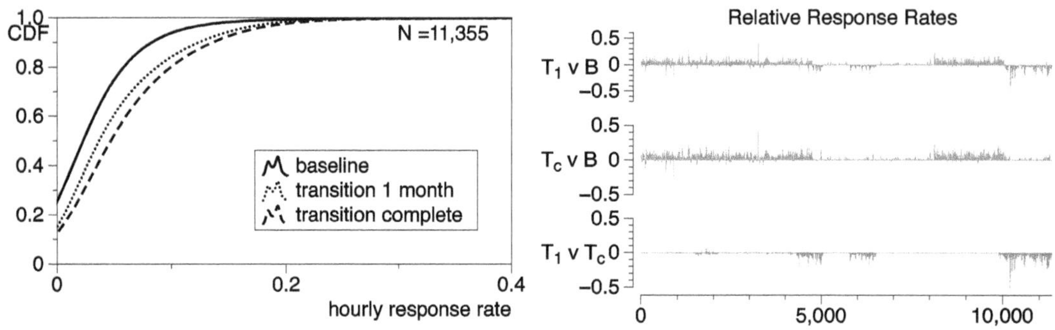

Figure 3: The left-hand side shows the cumulative distribution function (CDF) of the hourly response rates for the compared recommenders. The right-hand side shows the pair-wise comparison. Long and medium-term interests improve the results over short-term interests only. The strategy based on the long and short-term interests yields consistently the best results.

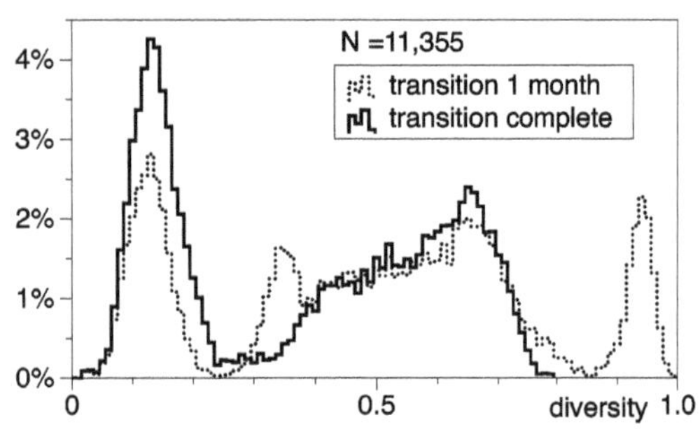

Figure 4: Analysis of the news variety ensured by T_1 and T_c. The two histograms show the distribution across the spectrum. T_1 has a peak of very high variety, which T_c lacks.

Its simplicity ensures scalability and maintainability; the crowd-based models for recommendations and the lack of authentication ensures high privacy. Data sparsity is not an issue as the proposed hybrid solution uses categories, which are limited and mostly stable in time, and the dynamic data structures are pruned to store a fixed number of articles. The proposed analysis of news reading dynamics could support decisions about which data to use for building models.

Our experiments show that by varying the time horizon publishers can trade some accuracy for news variety. Accuracy reflects how well the news recommender anticipates readers' preferences. Variety indicates to what degree readers are exposed to different articles. Which should publishers prioritize? Mark Thompson (CEO of the *New York Times*) [33] lists major challenges that news publishers face as they compete online. Revenue from printed newspapers declines. Publishers have to counteract the downward trend by attracting users online. Hereby, they cannot negotiate as comfortably as they used to for the printed news. Digital social media sites constitute the major players in digital advertising. Thus, successfully harnessing users' attention is crucial to generate online revenues. This suggests focusing on accuracy. Give readers what they want to read to keep their sessions alive. At the same time, news consumption affects society, economy, and politics. Rasmus Kleis Nielsen (Director of Research, *Reuters*) [29] finds that world-wide people prefer personalized news recommendations. Still, he points out that this may create "filter bubbles". These are spaces in which people consume similar news, reinforcing their existing believes and opinions. They represent a serious danger to social, economic, and political discourse as they prevent exposure to deviating opinions. This favors news variety over accuracy. Finding the right balance between both aspects remains a major challenge for publishers to address in the future. Maximizing profits may lead to social divides. Optimizing news variety may yield economic damage to the publisher. Publishers may have to find additional sources of revenue to compensate reduced accuracy. Readers may have to spend money to have access to high-quality journalism.

5 LITERATURE REVIEW

Traditionally, recommender solutions are of grouped into two types [1, 14, 19]. A content-based recommender suggests items similar to previously liked ones. A collaborative recommender suggests items by comparing user preferences. Hybrid solutions are frequently reported to perform best in the news domain [2, 4, 6, 20, 24–26].

5.1 News Reading Interests

News readers' interests are seldom expressed explicitly. Common approaches discover readers' interests from click behavior and articles' categories [23]. In some cases, the categories of the articles are already defined in advance and represented as contextual meta-data [6, 9, 10]. In other cases, categories are discovered automatically and represented either as more granular vocabularies associated to the categories [2, 4, 25], or keywords defining general, well-known topics such as sport or politics [24, 26, 37]. In most of these works, once known, recommenders use the categories as explicit knowledge. Other approaches do not infer users' interests but incorporate them implicitly as built-in features. For instance, Billsus et al. [4] and Li et al. [24] address short-term interests through standard content-based components by recommending articles similar to what users recently read.

Multiple authors distinguish short-term and long-term interests [4, 24, 26]. The long-term interests are considered by most of related works as the users' genuine interests which are less likely to change over time. Contrarily, the short-term interests are discovered from the most recent reading behavior and could represent deviations from the long-term interests triggered by momentary events such as breaking news or interesting reading discoveries. Billsus et al. [4] prioritize the short-term interests model in the formulation of recommendations in Google News as they claim it is more sensitive to changes. In a follow-up work on the Google News system, Liu et al. [26] showed that the short-term interests of an individual user follow closely the short-term interests of the general public. Consequently, in this updated solution, they use the unpersonalized model to address the short-term interests, and the individual user's past reading behavior for predicting categories within the long-term interests. Another mechanism for manipulating the changes in users' preferences is decaying older interests in favor of the newest ones [6, 24].

We distinguish between short- and long-term news reading interests as well, but we implement them differently. The short-term interests are implicitly captured by providing recommendations according to the real-time popularity distribution of the news, most recently read by the crowd. The long-term behavior is explicitly captured with transitions over news categories, dynamically maintained. We also introduce a new type of behavior corresponding to the medium-term interests. Additionally, our models are created per-crowd and from data reflecting engaged reading.

5.2 News Recency, Popularity, and Variety

While some news articles could be relevant even weeks or months after their publication, others get quickly outdated for the majority of users. Thus, recency and popularity are often considered in news recommendation [2, 4, 6, 9, 20, 25].

Billsus et al. [4] report that their recommender takes a list of articles as input, which have been selected in advance by several criteria including recency. Likewise, in the work of Li et al. [24] a probabilistic graphical model is built with recent articles. Furthermore, Das et al. [6] choose to re-build the recommender models every hour in order to present the freshest information to the users. They use a covisitation metric in recommendation that captures the relative popularity (what is the most popular article visited together with the current read article). Similarly, in Yahoo's news aggregator, articles are selected to represent both new and popular events [2]. For this, they consider articles' timestamps and key events identified through the events' count distribution within the selected article set [2]. Liang et al. [25] set a higher weight to the most recent articles from those discovered by using models for short and long-term interests. External knowledge from Twitter can also be used to determine popularity [7, 20, 30].

While popularity and recency are common news features included in recommender systems, variety is mentioned as a future work in some papers [4, 6] or less relevant in some others [2, 9]. The users' long-term interests model used in [4] does not vary the recommendations for users with similar profiles but per user. Das et al. [6] limit the news variety to the cluster of similar users. Li et al. [24] handle news variety explicitly through random walks in the user-item affinity graph created in advance. Likewise, a probabilistic model is proposed in [19] to address this aspect. In contrast, having analyzed the transition matrices extracted from the CLEF NewsREEL 2014 competition data set, Doychev et al. [9] show that users tend to read news from the same category. Moreover, few dominant categories and clicks between these categories account for the majority of items that are read [9]. Driven by similar reasons, Ahmed et al. [2] provide recommendations within the same category—story, but they also focus to some extent on other tangential categories as they claim users are interested in different aspects of an event (e.g. political, economic).

In the short-term reading policy, we consider popularity and recency, without any external sources. As for news variety, we do not prioritize it for categories, but we ensure that two readers are likely to be recommended different articles in a short time window.

5.3 Session-based Recommendation

Session-based recommender systems focus on sessions rather than on complete user profiles. Shani et al. [32] highlight the session-based character of recommender systems deployed in business setups. They move the underlying model from a matrix completion task toward a *Markov Decision Process* (MDP). Businesses encounter session-based recommender systems in domains including music [38], products [18], and news [23]. Deep learning architectures have been applied to session-based recommendation (cf. Hidasi et al. [17], and Tan et al. [22]), achieving promising results. Still, they involve a multitude of parameters to optimize. Our method circumvents the efforts to tune as many parameters albeit sacrificing accuracy to some degree.

In our solution, sessions are analyzed and split in reading episodes in case of too short or long reading times between consecutive events. Related works that approached the session splitting to some degree are [25, 39]. Nonetheless, the former considers fast browsing only, setting a time within 3 s to 250 s, while the later splits in sub-sessions of 30 min, without reasoning on clicks.

5.4 Process Models for Recommendation

Several works model news recommender solutions as probabilistic graphical problems [2, 24, 31]. Li et al. [24] consider the states in the process being both users and articles and the possible transitions are user to article, article to article and article to user. They populate the transition matrix with similarity scores between articles and between users and articles [24]. Ahmed et al. [2] use a transition graph with three types of states: views, clicks, and documents where the views are considered latent variables. The probability of a click to happen is conditioned on the current document, current view, and the previous click [2]. Sahoo et al. [31] choose a Hidden Markov Model where users are the observed variables and the latent classes represent globally preferred consumption patterns per month. Yang et al. [39] propose a topic-aware Markov model for recommending web pages. Segments of sessions—consecutive web page visits, are transformed to temporal states while sequences of articles of the same topic become topical states. The prediction of a page to a user considers the similarity to other users and the probability of observing the user's session containing the predicted page [39].

Though effective, the presented models are difficult to maintain with an increasing number of clicks, users, and items. Categories in our approach are a more stable choice. Also, these solutions rely on much longer sessions. Yang et al. [39] report an average of 3700 clicks per user and others in the news domain [24–26] select only authenticated sessions of minimum 10 clicks. As per-user models are likely unsuitable in short sessions, we aggregate knowledge on news consumption over time and introduce personalization in sessions. Compared with the other works, Sahoo et al. [31] also uses successfully a global model with personalization based on users' cases, but with reported high computational costs.

5.5 News Reading Behavior Analysis

In order to learn more about users' reading behavior and lead the design of the news recommenders, certain works performed high-scale user log analysis over time [11, 24, 26].

Li et al. [24] compared the reading behavior regarding long- and short-term interests. They considered short-term interests being the categories preferred by users within a time window of three days and similarly, the long-term interests were associated with a time period of 15 days. Moreover, three groups of users were created based on the click frequency and separately analyzed. The approach they used for comparison was to plot the Kullback-Leibler (KL) divergence scores, averaged per group, and computed between two consecutive periods for each user. Results showed that long-term goals are quite stable while the short-term ones vary significantly. Liu et al. [26] conducted their analysis by visually projecting the differences between categories' distribution for each user, for each two consecutive months, and also the click distribution for each category per month. The news categories are general topics such as world news, sport, entertainment, and the distribution is represented by the averaged number of clicks per category. They discovered that the current preferences of users change, that the general public interests follow the big events trend (e.g. national news are read more during elections) and, to certain extent, that the individual users' interests follow those of the general public. Esiyok et al. [11] analyzed immediate transitions between categories.

Compared to these works, we assess the dynamics of the news reading behavior through the stationarity of the Markov process across news categories. To our knowledge, we are the first to investigate the evolution of news categories relations over time.

6 CONCLUSION AND FUTURE WORKS

With the digital transformation, news has started being created and delivered by many entities besides news publishers. News consumers are exposed nowadays to increased sources of information and setups. In this highly competitive ecosystem, news publishers have sought ways to engage existing and attract new readers. Hence, personalized news recommendation has become a key element in their strategy. The proposed solutions aimed to ensure the delivery of fresh and interesting news, taking into consideration the dynamics of reading interests.

Still, limited research has tackled news personalization in hybrid recommenders when extensive user profile are unavailable. Most of the news publishers face this issue as the website authentication is a rare habit among online readers and the cookie-identification has its limits. In this paper, we prove that a recommender based on the dynamics of reading behavior, news popularity, and recency can provide a basic level of personalization and comply with the main domain constraints revealed by the related solutions. Specifically, we design and compare three variants of news recommendation centered on short-, medium-, and long-term reading interests. The short-term interests are captured at the article level, by recommending news recently read by the crowd, biased by popularity. The medium- and long-term interests are captured at the news category level, by predicting the next category to be read from the current user session and the Markov process over all categories. Moreover, the dynamics of the news reading behavior modeled as transitions between news categories is assessed over an extensive period.

The proposed research questions are addressed through experimentation with real data from a German news publisher. First, news readers appear to stay loyal to certain categories, which are frequently read together within a reading episode. Nonetheless, the priority for these relations, captured by transitions, changes in months possibly because of seasons, popular events lasting longer time, or structural changes in publishers' websites. Second, augmenting a short-term interests recommendation policy with the long- or medium-term behavior leads to higher response rates. Considering the transitions between news categories from the previous month leads to a higher variety than the long-term transitions.

Several limits could be identified nonetheless. The proposed solution handles cold start well on the user side. Still, it cannot immediately recommend new items until they have been read at least once. Moreover, the dynamic data structures storing articles can have the popularity manipulated artificially, propagating thus a fake filter bubble. Currently, the recommendation of news could be sometimes redundant as the solution checks only the user's most recent read. Parameters are present in the solution: ϵ the size of article buffers per category, the thresholds involved in the identification of reading episodes. Future work should explore other values of these parameters and their effect on recommendations. Online evaluation will show how well this approach performs under real-life conditions. Also, evaluation with additional data sets and with different session-based recommenders is required.

More content and context features could be considered in the future extending the proposed approach. In the current solution, the news categories are manually associated to the articles by editors or journalists. An alternative approach is to use more of the news content data directly. If humans are biased or inconsistent in their tagging practices, algorithms for category assignment could assist them or augment in the back-end the manually attached category set. Solutions for classifying news articles into categories or representing the data items in terms of semantic entities with links to conceptual abstractions have already been proposed [2, 5, 8, 25].

External sources of knowledge such as social media could be explored for identifying the most recent trends and injecting news variety in recommendations by external drivers [13, 16, 36]. Suggestions at the category level in the form of a time-line is another option to be explored [35]. For this, the variety of the recommended categories should be ensured. The literature revealed that there is a lack of agreement about how short- and long-term interests are defined. For instance, long-term is limited to 15 days in [24] and to a month in [26]. However, in order to more easily integrate conclusions emerging from various studies, a sound, well-documented framework should be proposed. Finally, our approach could be applicable to other domains where the item consumption is sequential within the same session, and items have a relevant feature associated or inferred. This could be the case for music or job recommendation.

REFERENCES

[1] Gediminas Adomavicius and Alexander Tuzhilin. 2005. Toward the Next Generation of Recommender Systems: A Survey of the State-of-the-Art and Possible Extensions. *Transactions on Knowledge and Data Engineering* 17, 6 (2005), 734–749.

[2] Amr Ahmed, Choon Hui Teo, S V N Vishwanathan, and Alex Smola. 2012. Fair and Balanced : Learning to Present News Stories. In *WSDM.* 333–342.

[3] F. Bickenbach and E. Bode. 2003. Evaluating the Markov Property in Studies of Economic Convergence. *International Regional Science Review* 26, 3 (2003), 363–392. DOI: http://dx.doi.org/10.1177/0160017603253789

[4] Daniel Billsus and Michael J Pazzani. 2007. Adaptive News Access. In *The Adaptive Web*, Peter Brusilovsky, Alfred Kobsa, and Wolfgang Nejdl (Eds.). Springer, Chapter 18, 550–570.

[5] Michel Capelle, Alexander Hogenboom, Alexander Hogenboom, and Flavius Frasincar. 2013. Semantic News Recommendation Using WordNet and Bing Similarities Categories and Subject Descriptors. In *Symposium on Applied Computing.* 296–302.

[6] Abhinandan Das, Mayur Datar, Ashutosh Garg, and Shyam Rajaram. 2007. Google News Personalization: Scalable Online. In *WWW.* 271–280.

[7] Gianmarco De Francisci Morales, Aristides Gionis, and Claudio Lucchese. 2012. From Chatter to Headlines: Harnessing the Real-time Web for Personalized News Recommendation. In *Proceedings of the Fifth ACM International Conference on Web Search and Data Mining (WSDM '12).* ACM, New York, NY, USA, 153–162. DOI: http://dx.doi.org/10.1145/2124295.2124315

[8] Marco de Gemmis, Pasquale Lops, Cataldo Musto, Fedelucio Narducci, and Giovanni Semeraro. 2015. *Semantics-Aware Content-Based Recommender Systems.* Springer US, Boston, MA, 119–159. DOI: http://dx.doi.org/10.1007/978-1-4899-7637-6_4

[9] Doychin Doychev, Aonghus Lawlor, Rachael Rafter, and Barry Smyth. 2014. An Analysis of Recommender Algorithms for Online News. In *CLEF (Working Notes).* 825–836.

[10] E. V. Epure, J. E. Ingvaldsen, R. Deneckere, and C. Salinesi. 2016. Process Mining for Recommender Strategies Support in News Media. In *Proceedings of the 10th International Conference on Research Challenges in Information Science (RCIS).* IEEE.

[11] Cagdas Esiyok, Benjamin Kille, Brijnesh-Johannes Jain, Frank Hopfgartner, and Sahin Albayrak. 2014. Users' Reading Habits in Online News Portals. In *Proceedings of the 5th Information Interaction in Context Symposium (IIiX '14).* ACM, New York, NY, USA, 263–266. DOI: http://dx.doi.org/10.1145/2637002.2637038

[12] Anna Frankfort-Nachmias, ChavaLeon-Guerrero. 2006. *Social Statistics for a Diverse Society.* Pine Forge Press.

[13] Qi Gao, Fabian Abel, Geert-Jan Houben, and Ke Tao. 2011. Interweaving Trend and User Modeling for Personalized News Recommendation. In *IEEE/WIC/ACM International Conferences on Web Intelligence and Intelligent Agent Technology.* IEEE, 100–103. DOI: http://dx.doi.org/10.1109/WI-IAT.2011.74

[14] Florent Garcin, Kai Zhou, Boi Faltings, and Vincent Schickel. 2012. Personalized News Recommendation Based on Collaborative Filtering. In *Proceedings of the IEEE/WIC/ACM International Joint Conferences on Web Intelligence and Intelligent Agent Technology (WI-IAT '12).* IEEE Computer Society, Washington, DC, USA, 437–441.

[15] Jon Atle Gulla, Bei Yu, Özlem Özgöbek, and Nafiseh Shabib. 2015. Third International Workshop on News Recommendation and Analytics (INRA 2015). In *Proceedings of the 9th ACM Conference on Recommender Systems.* ACM, 345–346.

[16] Anat Hashavit, Roy Levin, Ido Guy, and Gilad Kutiel. 2016. Effective Trend Detection within a Dynamic Search Context. In *Proceedings of the 39th International ACM SIGIR conference on Research and Development in Information Retrieval.* ACM, 817–820.

[17] Balázs Hidasi, Alexandros Karatzoglou, Linas Baltrunas, and Domonkos Tikk. 2015. Session-based Recommendations with Recurrent Neural Networks. In *Proceedings of the International Conference on Learning Representations.*

[18] Wenxing Hong, Lei Li, and Tao Li. 2012. Product Recommendation with Temporal Dynamics. *Expert systems with applications* 39, 16 (2012), 12398–12406.

[19] Amin Javari and Mahdi Jalili. 2015. A Probabilistic Model to Resolve Diversity–Accuracy Challenge of Recommendation Systems. *Knowledge and Information Systems* 44, 3 (2015), 609–627. DOI: http://dx.doi.org/10.1007/s10115-014-0779-2

[20] Nirmal Jonnalagedda, Susan Gauch, Kevin Labille, and Sultan Alfarhood. 2016. Incorporating Popularity in a Personalized News Recommender System. *PeerJ Computer Science* 2 (2016), e63.

[21] J.G. Kemény and J.L. Snell. 1960. *Finite Markov Chains.* Van Nostrand.

[22] Yong Kiam Tan, Xinxing Xu, and Yong Liu. 2016. Improved Recurrent Neural Networks for Session-based Recommendations. *arXiv preprint arXiv:1606.08117* (2016).

[23] Lihong Li, Wei Chu, John Langford, and Robert E. Schapire. 2010. A Contextual-Bandit Approach to Personalized News Article Recommendation. In *Proceedings of the 19th International Conference on World Wide Web (WWW '10).* ACM Press, New York, New York, USA. DOI: http://dx.doi.org/10.1145/1772690.1772758

[24] Lei Li, Li Zheng, Fan Yang, and Tao Li. 2014. Modeling and Broadening Temporal User Interest in Personalized News Recommendation. *Expert Systems with Applications* 41, 7 (2014), 3168–3177.

[25] Ting-Peng Liang and Hung-Jen Lai. 2002. Discovering User Interests from Web Browsing Behavior: An Application to Internet News Services. In *HICSS.* IEEE Computer Society, 203.

[26] Jiahui Liu, Peter Dolan, and Elin Rønby Pedersen. 2010. Personalized News Recommendation Based on Click Behavior. In *Proceedings of the International Conference on Intelligent User Interfaces.* 31–40.

[27] Andreas Lommatzsch. 2014. Real-Time News Recommendation Using Context-Aware Ensembles. In *Proceedings of the 36th European Conference on IR Research (ECIR '14).* Springer, 51–62. DOI: http://dx.doi.org/10.1007/978-3-319-06028-6_5

[28] Nic Newman. 2017. Overview and Key Findings of the 2016 Report. (2017). http://digitalnewsreport.org/survey/2016/overview-key-findings-2016/.

[29] Rasmus Kleis Nielsen. 2016. People Want Personalised Recommendations (Even as they Worry about the Consequences). In *Digital News Report.*

[30] Owen Phelan, Kevin McCarthy, and Barry Smyth. 2009. Using Twitter to Recommend Real-time Topical News. In *Proceedings of the Third Conference on Recommender Systems (RecSys '09).* ACM, New York, NY, USA, 385–388. DOI: http://dx.doi.org/10.1145/1639714.1639794

[31] Nachiketa Sahoo, Param Vir Singh, and Tridas Mukhopadhyay. 2012. A Hidden Markov Model for Collaborative Filtering. *MIS Q.* 36, 4 (Dec. 2012), 1329–1356.

[32] Guy Shani, David Heckerman, and Ronen I Brafman. 2005. An MDP-Based Recommender System. *Journal of machine Learning research* (2005).

[33] Mark Thompson. 2016. The Challenging New Economics of Journalism. In *Digital News Report.*

[34] Emily Thorson. 2008. Changing Patterns of News Consumption and Participation. *Information, Communication & Society* 11, 4 (2008), 473–489. DOI: http://dx.doi.org/10.1080/13691180801999027

[35] Giang Tran, Mohammad Alrifai, and Eelco Herder. 2015. Timeline summarization from relevant headlines. In *European Conference on Information Retrieval.* Springer International Publishing, 245–256.

[36] David Vallet, Shlomo Berkovsky, Sebastien Ardon, Anirban Mahanti, and Mohamed Ali Kafaar. 2015. Characterizing and Predicting Viral-and-Popular Video Content. In *Proceedings of the 24th ACM International on Conference on Information and Knowledge Management.* ACM, 1591–1600.

[37] X. Wu, F. Xie, G. Wu, and W. Ding. 2011. Personalized News Filtering and Summarization on the Web. In *Proceedings of the 23rd International Conference on Tools with Artificial Intelligence.* IEEE, 414–421. DOI: http://dx.doi.org/10.1109/ICTAI.2011.68

[38] Diyi Yang, Tianqi Chen, Weinan Zhang, Qiuxia Lu, and Yong Yu. 2012. Local Implicit Feedback Mining for Music Recommendation. In *Proceedings of the sixth ACM conference on Recommender systems.* ACM, 91–98.

[39] Qingyan Yang, Ju Fan, Jianyong Wang, and Lizhu Zhou. 2010. Personalizing Web Page Recommendation via Collaborative Filtering and Topic-Aware Markov Model. In *Proceedings of the International Conference on Data Mining (ICDM '10).* IEEE Computer Society, 1145–1150. DOI: http://dx.doi.org/10.1109/ICDM.2010.28

Personalizing Session-based Recommendations with Hierarchical Recurrent Neural Networks

Massimo Quadrana
Politecnico di Milano, Milan, Italy
massimo.quadrana@polimi.it

Alexandros Karatzoglou
Telefonica Research, Barcelona, Spain
alexk@tid.es

Balázs Hidasi
Gravity R&D, Budapest, Hungary
balazs.hidasi@gravityrd.com

Paolo Cremonesi
Politecnico di Milano, Milan, Italy
paolo.cremonesi@polimi.it

ABSTRACT

Session-based recommendations are highly relevant in many modern on-line services (e.g. e-commerce, video streaming) and recommendation settings. Recently, Recurrent Neural Networks have been shown to perform very well in session-based settings. While in many session-based recommendation domains user identifiers are hard to come by, there are also domains in which user profiles are readily available. We propose a seamless way to personalize RNN models with cross-session information transfer and devise a Hierarchical RNN model that relays end evolves latent hidden states of the RNNs across user sessions. Results on two industry datasets show large improvements over the session-only RNNs.

CCS CONCEPTS

• **Information systems → Recommender systems;** • **Computing methodologies → Neural networks;**

KEYWORDS

recurrent neural networks; personalization; session-based recommendation; session-aware recommendation

1 INTRODUCTION

In many online systems where recommendations are applied, interactions between a user and the system are organized into sessions. A session is a group of interactions that take place within a given time frame. Sessions from a user can occur on the same day, or over several days, weeks, or months. A session usually has a goal, such as finding a good restaurant in a city, or listening to music of a certain style or mood.

Providing recommendations in these domains poses unique challenges that until recently have been mainly tackled by applying conventional recommender algorithms [10] on either the last interaction or the last session (session-based recommenders). Recurrent Neural Networks (RNNs) have been recently used for the purpose of session-based recommendations [7] outperforming item-based methods by 15% to 30% in terms of ranking metrics. In *session-based recommenders*, recommendations are provided based solely on the interactions in the current user session, as user are assumed to be anonymous. But in many of these systems there are cases where a user might be logged-in (e.g. music streaming services) or some form of user identifier might be present (cookie or other identifier). In these cases it is reasonable to assume that the user behavior in past sessions might provide valuable information for providing recommendations in the next session.

A simple way of incorporating past user session information in session-based algorithm would be to simply concatenate past and current user sessions. While this seems like a reasonable approach, we will see in the experimental section that this does not yield the best results.

In this work we describe a novel algorithm based on RNNs that can deal with both cases: (i) *session-aware recommenders*, when user identifiers are present and propagate information from the previous user session to the next, thus improving the recommendation accuracy, and (ii) *session-based recommenders*, when there are no past sessions (i.e., no user identifiers). The algorithm is based on a Hierarchical RNN where the hidden state of a lower-level RNN at the end of one user session is passed as an input to a higher-level RNN which aims at predicting a good initialization (i.e., a good context vector) for the hidden state of the lower RNN for the next session of the user.

We evaluate the Hierarchical RNNs on two datasets from industry comparing them to the plain session-based RNN and to item-based collaborative filtering. Hierarchical RNNs outperform both alternatives by a healthy margin.

2 RELATED WORK

Session-based recommendations. Classical CF methods (e.g. matrix factorization) break down in the session-based setting when no user profile can be constructed from past user behavior. A natural solution to this problem is the item-to-item recommendation approach [11, 16]. In this setting an item-to-item similarity matrix is precomputed from the available session data, items that are often clicked together in sessions are deemed to be similar. These similarities are then used to create recommendations. While simple, this method has been proven to be effective and is widely employed. Though, these methods only take into account the last click of the user, in effect ignoring the information of the previous clicks.

RecSys'17, August 27–31, 2017, Como, Italy.
 978-1-4503-4652-8/17/08...$15.00
DOI: http://dx.doi.org/10.1145/3109859.3109896

Recurrent Neural Models. RNNs are the deep models of choice when dealing with sequential data [12]. RNNs have been used in image and video captioning, time series prediction, natural language processing and much more. Long Short-Term Memory (LSTM) [9] networks are a type of RNNs that have been shown to work particularly well, it includes additional gates that regulate when and how much to take the input into account and when to reset the hidden state. This helps with the vanishing gradient problem that often plagues the standard RNN models. Slightly simplified version of LSTM – that still maintains all their properties – are Gated Recurrent Units (GRUs) [3] which we use in this work.

RNNs were first used to model session data in [7]. The recurrent neural network is trained with a ranking loss on a one-hot representation of the session (clicked) item-IDs. The RNN is then used to provide recommendations after each click for new sessions. This work only focused on the clicked item-IDs in the current session while here we aim at modeling the user behavior across sessions as well. RNNs were also used to jointly model the content or features of items together with click-sequence interactions [8]. By including item features extracted for example, from the thumbnail image of videos or the textual description of a product, the so-called parallel-RNN model provided superior recommendation quality wrt. 'plain' RNNs. In [19], authors proposed data augmentation techniques to improve the performance of the RNN for session-based recommendations, these techniques have though the side effect of increasing training times as a single session is split into several sub-sessions for training. RNNs have also been used in more standard user-item collaborative filtering settings where the aim is to model the evolution of the user and items factors [20] [4] where the results are though less impressive, with the proposed methods barely outperforming standard matrix factorization methods. Finally a sequence to sequence model with a version of Hierarchical Recurrent Neural Networks was used for generative context-aware query suggestion in [17].

3 MODEL

In this section we describe the proposed Hierarchical RNN (*HRNN* henceforth) model for personalized session-based recommendation.

3.1 Session-based Recurrent Neural Network

Our model is based on the session-based Recurrent Neural Network (RNN henceforth) model presented in [7]. RNN is based on a single Gated Recurrent Unit (GRU) layer that models the interactions of the user within a session. The RNN takes as input the current item ID in the session and outputs a score for each item representing the likelihood of being the next item in the session.

Formally, for each session $S_m = \{i_{m,1}, i_{m,2}, ..., i_{m,N_m}\}$, RNN computes the following session-level representation

$$s_{m,n} = GRU_{ses}\left(i_{m,n}, s_{m,n-1}\right), \ n = 1, ..., N_m - 1 \quad (1)$$

where GRU_{ses} is the *session-level* GRU and $s_{m,n}$ its hidden state at step n, being $s_{m,0} = 0$ (the null vector), and $i_{m,n}$ is the one-hot vector of the current item ID [1].

The output of the RNN is a score $\hat{r}_{m,n}$ for every item in the catalog indicating the likelihood of being the next item in the session (or, equivalently, its relevance for the next step in the session)

$$\hat{r}_{m,n} = g\left(s_{m,n}\right), \ n = 1, ..., N_m - 1 \quad (2)$$

where $g(\cdot)$ is a non-linear function like softmax or tanh depending on the loss function. During training, scores are compared to a one-hot vector of the next item ID in the session to compute the loss. The network can be trained with several ranking loss functions such as cross-entropy, BPR [14] and TOP1 [7]. In this work, the TOP1 loss always outperformed other ranking losses, so we consider only it in the rest of the paper. The **TOP1** loss is the regularized approximation of the relative rank of the relevant item. The relative rank of the relevant item is given by $\frac{1}{N_S} \cdot \sum_{j=1}^{N_S} I\{\hat{r}_{s,j} > \hat{r}_{s,i}\}$ where $r_{s,j}$ is the score of a sampled 'irrelevant item'. $I\{\cdot\}$ is approximated with a sigmoid. To force the scores of negative examples ('irrelevant items') towards zero a regularization term is added to the loss. The final loss function is as follows: $L_s = \frac{1}{N_S} \cdot \sum_{j=1}^{N_S} \sigma\left(\hat{r}_{s,j} - \hat{r}_{s,i}\right) + \sigma\left(\hat{r}^2_{s,j}\right)$

RNN is trained efficiently with session-parallel mini-batches. At each training step, the input to GRU_{ses} is the stacked one-hot representation of the current item ID of a batch of sessions. The session-parallel mechanism keeps the pointers to the current item of every session in the mini-batch and resets the hidden state of the RNN when sessions end. To further reduce the computational complexity, the loss is computed over the current item IDs and a sample of negative items. Specifically, the current item ID of each session is used as positive item and the IDs of the remaining sessions in the mini-batch as negative items when computing the loss. This makes explicit negative item sampling unnecessary and enables popularity-based sampling. However, since user-identifiers are unknown in pure session-based scenarios, there are good chances that negative samples will be 'contaminated' by positive items the user interacts with in other sessions.

3.2 Personalized Session-based Hierarchical Recurrent Neural Network

Our *HRNN* model builds on top of RNN by: (i) adding an additional GRU layer to model information across user sessions and to track the evolution of the user interests over time; (ii) using a powerful user-parallel mini-batch mechanism for efficient training.

3.2.1 Architecture. Beside the session-level GRU, our *HRNN* model adds one *user-level* GRU (GRU_{usr}) to model the user activity across sessions.

Figure 1 shows a graphical representation of *HRNN*. At each time step, recommendations are generated by GRU_{ses}, as in RNN. However, when a session ends, the user representation is updated. When a new session starts, the hidden state of GRU_{usr} is used to initialize GRU_{ses} and, optionally, propagated in input to GRU_{ses}.

Formally, for each user u with sessions $C^u = \{S^u_1, S^u_2, ..., S^u_{M_u}\}$, the user-level GRU takes as input the session-level representations $s^u_1, s^u_2, ..., s^u_{M_u}$, being $s^u_m = s^u_{m,N_m-1}$ the last hidden state of GRU_{ses} of each user session S^u_m, and uses them to update the user-level representation c^u_m. Henceforth we drop the user superscript u to unclutter notation. The user-level representation c_m is updated as

$$c_m = GRU_{usr}\left(s_m, c_{m-1}\right), \ m = 1, ..., M_u \quad (3)$$

where $c_0 = 0$ (the null vector). The input to the user-level GRU is connected to the last hidden state of the session-level GRU. In this

[1] To simplify the explanation we use a notation similar to [17].

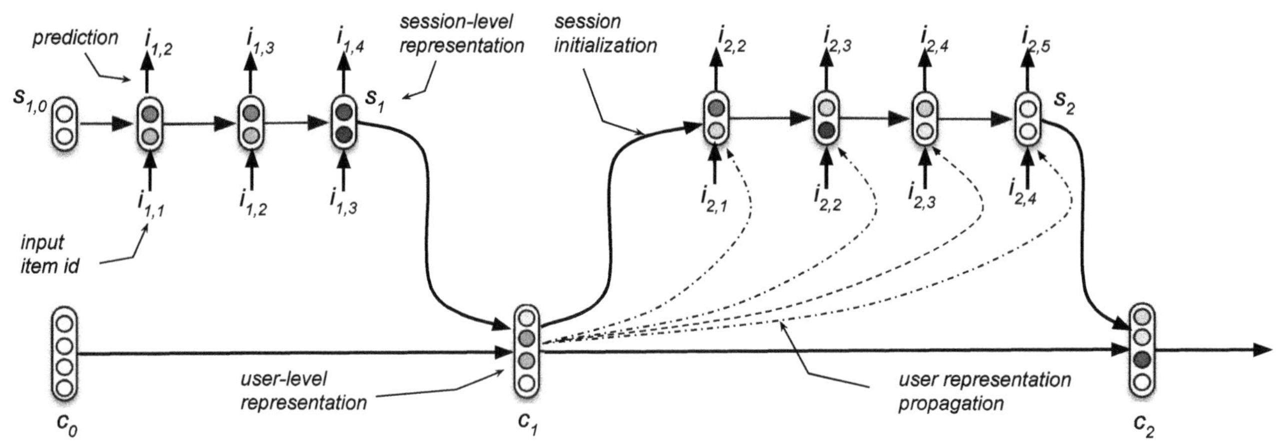

Figure 1: Graphical representation of the proposed Hierarchical RNN model for personalized session-based recommendation. The model is composed of an hierarchy of two GRUs, the session-level GRU (GRU_{ses}) and the user-level GRU (GRU_{usr}). The session-level GRU models the user activity within sessions and generates recommendations. The user-level GRU models the evolution of the user across sessions and provides personalization capabilities to the session-level GRU by initializing its hidden state and, optionally, by propagating the user representation in input.

way, the user-level GRU can track the evolution of the user across sessions and, in turn, model the dynamics user interests seamlessly. Notice that the user-level representation is kept *fixed* throughout the session and it is updated only when the session ends.

The user-level representation is then used to initialize the hidden state of the session-level GRU. Given c_m, the initial hidden state $s_{m+1,0}$ of the session-level GRU for the following session is set to

$$s_{m+1,0} = \tanh(W_{init}c_m + b_{init}) \quad (4)$$

where W_{init} and b_{init} are the initialization weights and biases respectively. In this way, the information relative to the preferences expressed by the user in the previous sessions is transferred to the session-level. Session-level representations are then updated as follows

$$s_{m+1,n} = GRU_{ses}\left(i_{m+1,n}, s_{m+1,n-1}\,[, c_m]\right),\; n = 1, ..., N_{m+1} - 1 \quad (5)$$

where the square brackets indicate that c_m can be *optionally* propagated in input to the session-level GRU.

The model is trained end-to-end using back-propagation [15]. The weights of GRU_{usr} are updated only between sessions, i.e. when a session ends and when the forthcoming session starts. However, when the user representation is propagated in input to GRU_{ses}, the weights of GRU_{usr} are updated also within sessions even if c_m is kept fixed. We also tried with propagating the user-level representation to the final prediction layer (i.e., by adding term c_m in Equation 2) but we always incurred into severe degradation of the performances, even wrt. simple session-based RNN. We therefore discarded this setting from this discussion.

Note here that the GRU_{usr} does not simply pass on the hidden state of the previous user session to the next but also learns (during training) how user sessions evolve during time. We will see in the experimental section that this is crucial in achieving increased performance. In effect GRU_{usr} computes and evolves a user profile that is based on the previous user sessions, thus in effect personalizing the GRU_{ses}. In the original RNN, users who had clicked/interacted with the same sequence of items in a session would get the same recommendations; in *HRNN* this is not anymore the case, recommendations will be influenced by the the users past sessions as well.

In summary, we considered the following two different *HRNN* settings, depending on whether the user representation c_m is considered in Equation 5:

- *HRNN Init*, in which c_m is used only to initialize the representation of the next session.
- *HRNN All*, in which c_m is used for initialization and propagated in input at each step of the next session.

In *HRNN Init*, the session-level GRU can exploit the historical preferences along with the session-level dynamics of the user interest. *HRNN All* instead enforces the usage of the user representation at session-level at the expense of a slightly greater model complexity. As we will see, this can lead to substantially different results depending on the recommendation scenario.

3.2.2 Learning. For the sake of efficiency in training, we have edited the session-parallel mini-batch mechanism described in [8] to account for user identifiers during training (see Figure 2). We first group sessions by user and then sort session events within each group by time-stamp. We then order users at random. At the first iteration, the first item of the first session of the first B users constitute the input to the *HRNN*; the second item in each session

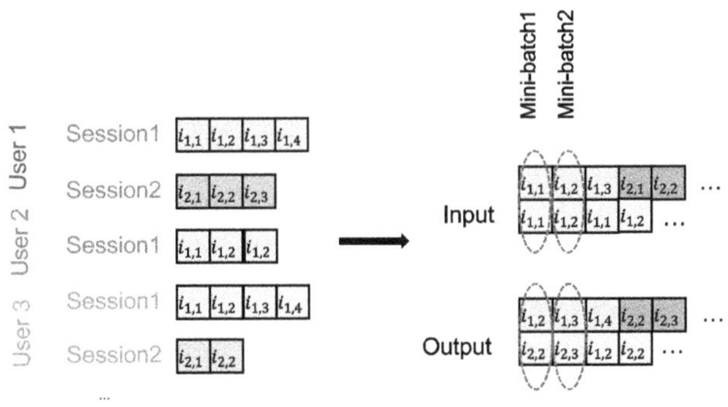

Figure 2: User-parallel mini-batches for mini-batch size 2.

Dataset	XING	VIDEO
Users	11,479	13,717
Items	59,297	19,218
Sessions	89,591	133,165
Events	546,862	825,449
Events per item†	6/9.3/14.4	9/43.0/683.7
Events per session†	4/6.1/5.5	4/6.2/8.2
Sessions per user†	6/7.8/4.8	7/9.8/7.8
Training - Events	488,576	745,482
Training - Sessions	78,276	120,160
Test - Events	58,286	79,967
Test - Sessions	11,315	13,605

Table 1: Main properties of the datasets (†median/mean/std).

constitute its output. The output is then used as input for the next iteration, and so on. When a session in the mini-batch ends, Equation 3 is used to update the hidden state of GRU_{usr} and Equation 4 to initialize the hidden state of GRU_{ses} for the forthcoming session, if any. When a user has been processed completely, the hidden states of both GRU_{usr} and GRU_{ses} are reset and the next user is put in its place in the mini-batch.

With user-parallel mini-batches we can train *HRNN*s efficiently over users having different number of sessions and sessions of different length. Moreover, this mechanism allows to sample negative items in a user-independent fashion, hence reducing the chances of 'contamination' of the negative samples with actual positive items. The sampling procedure is still popularity-based, since the likelihood for an item to appear in the mini-batch is proportional to its popularity. Both properties are known to be beneficial for pairwise learning with implicit user feedback [13].

4 EXPERIMENTS

In this section we describe our experimental setup and provide an in-depth discussion of the obtained results.

4.1 Datasets

We used two datasets for our experiments. The first is the XING [2] Recsys Challenge 2016 dataset [1] that contains interactions on job postings for 770k users over a 80-days period. User interactions come with time-stamps and interaction type (click, bookmark, reply and delete). We named this dataset XING. The second dataset is a proprietary dataset from a Youtube-like video-on-demand web site. The dataset tracks the videos watched by 13k users over a 2-months period. Viewing events lasting less than a fixed threshold are not tracked. We named this dataset VIDEO.

We manually partitioned the interaction data into sessions by using a 30-minute idle threshold. For the XING dataset we discarded interactions having type 'delete'. We also discarded repeated interactions of the same type within sessions to reduce noise (e.g. repeated clicks on the same job posting within a session). We then preprocessed both datasets as follows. We removed items with support less than 20 for XING and 10 for VIDEO since items with low support are not optimal for modeling. We removed sessions having < 3 interactions to filter too short and poorly informative sessions, and kept users having ≥ 5 sessions to have sufficient cross-session information for proper modeling of returning users.

The test set is build with the last session of each user. The remaining sessions form the training set. We also filtered items in the test set that do not belong to the training set. This partitioning allows to run the evaluation over users having different amounts of historical sessions in their profiles, hence to measure the recommendation quality over users having different degrees of activity with the system (see Section 4.3.1 for an in-depth analysis). We further partitioned the training set with the same procedure to tune the hyper-parameters of the algorithms. The characteristics of the datasets are summarized in Table 1.

4.2 Baselines and parameter tuning

We compared our *HRNN* model against several baselines, namely Personal Pop (PPOP), Item-KNN, RNN and RNN Concat:

- Personal Pop (PPOP) recommends the item with the largest number of interactions by the user.
- Item-KNN computes an item-to-item cosine similarity based on the co-occurrence of items within sessions.
- RNN adopts the same model described in [7]. This model uses the basic GRU with a TOP1 loss function and session-parallel minibatching: sessions from the same user are fed to the RNN independently from each other.
- RNN Concat is the same as RNN, but sessions from the same user are concatenated into a single session[3].

We optimize the neural models for TOP1 loss using AdaGrad [5] with momentum for 10 epochs. Increasing the number of epochs did not significantly improve the loss in all models. We used dropout regularization [18] on the hidden states of RNN and *HRNN*. We applied dropout also to GRU_{ses} initialization for *HRNN* (Equation 4). We used single-layer GRU networks in both levels in the hierarchy, as using multiple layers did not improve the performance. In order to assess how the capacity of the network impacts the recommendation quality, in our experiments we considered both *small* networks

[2]https://www.xing.com/en

[3]We experimented with a variant of this baseline that adds a special 'separator item' to enforce the separation between sessions; however, it did not show better performance in our experiments.

Model	Batch size	Dropout	Learning rate/ Momentum
RNN (*small*)†	100	0.2	0.1/0.1
RNN (*large*)†	100	0.2	0.1/0.0
HRNN All (*small*)	100	0.1/0.1/0.2	0.1/0.2
HRNN All (*large*)	50	0.0/0.2/0.2	0.05/0.3
HRNN Init (*small*)	50	0.0/0.1/0.0	0.1/0.0
HRNN Init (*large*)	100	0.1/0.2/0.2	0.1/0.1

Table 2: Network hyper-parameters on XING († RNN and RNN Concat share the same values).

with 100 hidden units per GRU layer and *large* networks with 500 hidden units per GRU layer.

We tuned the hyper-parameters of each model (baselines included) on the validation set using random search [2]. To help the reproducibility of our experiments, we report the hyper-parameters used in our experiments on the XING dataset in Table 2 [4]. Dropout probabilities for *HRNN*s are relative to the user-level GRU, session-level GRU and initialization in this order. The optimal neighborhood size for Item-KNN is 300 for both datasets.

Neural models were trained on Nvidia K80 GPUs equipped with 12GB of GPU memory[5]. Training times vary from ~5 minutes for the small RNN model on XING to ~30 minutes for the large *HRNN All* on VIDEO. Evaluation took no longer than 2 minutes for all the experiments. We want to highlight that training times do not significantly differ between RNN and *HRNN*s, with *HRNN All* being the most computationally expensive model due to the higher complexity of its architecture (see Figure 1).

4.3 Results

We evaluate wrt. the sequential next-item prediction task, i.e. given an event of the user session, we evaluate how well the algorithm predicts the following event. All RNN-based models are fed with events in the session one after the other, and we check the rank of the item selected by the user in the next event. In addition, *HRNN* models and RNN Concat are *bootstrapped* with all the sessions in the user history that precede the testing one in their original order. This step slows down the evaluation but it is necessary to properly set the internal representations of the personalized models (e.g., the user-level representation for *HRNN*s) before evaluation starts. Notice that the evaluation metrics are still computed only over events in the test set, so evaluation remains fair. In addition, we discarded the first prediction computed by the RNN Concat baseline in each test session, since it is the only method capable of recommending the first event in the user sessions.

As recommender systems can suggest only few items at once, the relevant item should be amongst the first few items in the recommendation list. We therefore evaluate the recommendation quality in terms of Recall@5, Precision@5 and Mean Reciprocal Rank (MRR@5). In sequential next-item prediction, Recall@5 is equivalent to the hit-rate metric, and it measures the proportion of cases out of all test cases in which the relevant item is amongst the top-5 items. This is an accurate model for certain practical scenarios where no recommendation is highlighted and their absolute order does not matter, and strongly correlates with important KPIs such as CTR [6]. Precision@5 measures the fraction of correct recommendations in the top-5 positions of each recommendation list. MRR@5 is the reciprocal rank of the relevant item, where the reciprocal rank is manually set to zero if the rank is greater than 5. MRR takes the rank of the items into account, which is important in cases where the order of recommendations matters.

Table 3 summarizes the results for both XING and VIDEO datasets. We trained each neural model for 10 times with different random seeds and report the average results[6]. We used Wilcoxon signed-rank test to assess significance of the difference between the proposed *HRNN* models and the state-of-the-art session-based RNN and the naïve personalization strategy used by RNN Concat.

Results on XING. On this dataset, the simple personalized popularity baseline is a very competitive method, capable of outperforming the more sophisticated Item-KNN baseline by large margins. As prior studies on the dataset have already shown, users' activity within and across sessions has a high degree of repetitiveness. This makes the generation of 'non-trivial' personalized recommendations in this scenario very challenging [1].

This is further highlighted by the poor performance of session-based RNN that is always significantly worse than PPOP independently of the capacity of the network. Nevertheless, personalized session-based recommendation can overcome its limitations and achieve superior performance in terms of Recall and Precision with both small and large networks. *HRNN*s significantly outperform RNN Concat in terms of Recall and Precision (up to +3%/+1% with small/large networks), and provide significantly better MRR with large networks (up to +5.4% with *HRNN All*). Moreover, *HRNN*s significantly outperform the strong PPOP baseline of ~11% in Recall and Precision, while obtaining comparable MRR. This is a significant result in a domain where more trivial personalization strategies are so effective.

The comparison between the two *HRNN* variants does not highlight significant differences, excluded a small (~2%) advantage of *HRNN All* over *HRNN Init* in MRR. The differences in terms of Recall and Precision are not statistically significant. Having established the superiority of *HRNN*s over session-based recommendation and trivial concatenation, we resort to the VIDEO dataset to shed further light on the differences between the proposed personalized session-based recommendation solutions.

Results on VIDEO. The experiments on this dataset exhibit drastically different results from the XING dataset. Item-KNN baseline significantly outperforms PPOP, and session-based RNN can outperform both baselines by large margins. This is in line with past results over similar datasets [7, 8].

RNN Concat has comparable Recall and Precision with respect to session-based RNNs and interestingly significantly better MRR

[4]The source code is available at https://github.com/mquad/hgru4rec.

[5]We employed Amazon EC2 *p2.xlarge* spot instances in our experiments.

[6]The random seed controls the initialization of the parameters of the network, which in turn can lead substantially different results in absolute terms. Even though, we have not observed substantial differences in the relative performances of neural models when using different random seeds.

		XING			VIDEO		
		Recall@5	**MRR@5**	**Precision@5**	**Recall@5**	**MRR@5**	**Precision@5**
	Item-KNN	0.0697	0.0406	0.0139	0.4192	0.2916	0.0838
	PPOP	0.1326	**0.0939**	0.0265	0.3887	0.3031	0.0777
small	RNN	0.1292	0.0799	0.0258	0.4639	0.3366	0.0928
small	RNN Concat	*0.1358*	*0.0844*	*0.0272*	0.4682	0.3459	0.0936
small	*HRNN All*	*0.1334*†	*0.0842*	*0.0267*†	*0.5272*	*0.3663*	*0.1054*
small	*HRNN Init*	*0.1337*†	*0.0832*	*0.0267*†	*0.5421*	*0.4119*	*0.1084*
large	RNN	0.1317	0.0796	0.0263	0.5551	0.3886	0.1110
large	RNN Concat	*0.1467*	*0.0878*	*0.0293*	0.5582	*0.4333*	*0.1116*
large	*HRNN All*	***0.1482***†	*0.0925*	***0.0296***†	0.5191	0.3877	0.1038
large	*HRNN Init*	***0.1473***†	*0.0901*	***0.0295***†	***0.5947***	***0.4433***	***0.1189***

Table 3: Results of Recall, MRR and Precision for $N = 5$ on the XING and VIDEO datasets. *small* networks have 100 hidden units for RNNs and 100+100 for *HRNNs*; *large* networks have 500 hidden units for RNNs and 500+500 for *HRNNs*). All the networks have statistically significant different (ssd.) results from the baselines (Wilcoxon signed-rank test $p < 0.01$). Networks ssd. from RNN are in italic; *HRNNs* ssd. from RNN Concat are underlined. Best values are in bold. All differences between *HRNNs* are significant excluded the values marked with † superscript.

when large networks are used. This suggest that straight concatenation does not enhance the retrieval capabilities of the RNN recommender but strengthens its ability in ranking items correctly.

However, *HRNN Init* has significantly better performance than all baselines. It significantly outperforms all baselines and RNNs (up to 6.5% better Recall and 2.3% MRR wrt. RNN Concat with large networks). In other words, also in this scenario the more complex cross-session dynamics modeled by *HRNN* provide significant advantages in the overall recommendation quality. We will investigate on the possible reasons for these results in the following sections. It is worth noting that *HRNN All* performs poorly in this scenario. We impute the context-enforcing policy used in this setting for the severe degradation of the recommendation quality. One possible explanation could be that the consumption of multimedia content (videos in our case) is a strongly session-based scenario, much stronger than the job search scenario represented in XING. Users may follow general community trends and have long-term interests that are captured by the user-level GRU. However, the user activity within a session can be totally disconnected from her more recent sessions, and even from her general interests (for example, users having a strong general interest over extreme-sport videos may occasionally watch cartoon movie trailers). *HRNN Init* models the user taste dynamics and lets the session-level GRU free to exploit them according to the actual evolution of the user interests within session. Its greater flexibility leads to superior recommendation quality.

4.3.1 Analysis on the user history length. We investigate deeper the behavior of Hierarchical RNN models. Since we expect the length of the user history to have an impact on the recommendation quality, we breakdown the evaluation by the number of sessions in the history of the user. This serves as a proxy for the 'freshness' of the user within the system, and allows to evaluate recommenders under different amounts of historical information about the user modeled by the user-level GRU before a session begins. To this purpose, we partitioned user histories into two groups: 'Short' user histories having ≤ 6 sessions and 'Long' user histories having 6 or more. The statistics on the fraction of sessions belonging to each group for both datasets are reported in Table 4. Since our goal is to measure the impact of the complex cross-session dynamics used in *HRNN* wrt. traditional RNN, we restrict these analysis to RNN-based recommenders in the *large* configuration. For each algorithm, we compute the average Recall@5 and MRR@5 per test session grouped by history length. The analysis on Precision@5 returns similar results to Recall@5, so we omit it here also for space reasons. To enhance the robustness of the experimental results, we run the evaluation 10 times with different random seeds and report the median value per algorithm. Figure 3 shows the results on XING. As the length of the user history grows, we can notice that Recall slightly increases and MRR slightly decreases in MRR for all methods, session-based RNN included. The relative performance between methods does not changes significantly between short and long user histories, with *HRNN All* being the best performing model with 12% better Recall@5 and 14-16% better MRR@5 wrt. session-based RNN. *HRNN Init* has performance comparable to RNN Concat and *HRNN All* in accordance to our previous findings.

History length	XING	VIDEO
Short (≤ 6)	67.00%	53.69%
Long (> 6)	33.00%	46.31%

Table 4: Percentage of sessions in each history length group.

Figure 4 shows the results on VIDEO. Recall of all methods – session-based RNN included – improves with the length of the user history. MRR instead improves with history length only for RNN Concat and *HRNN Init*. This highlights the need for effective personalization strategies to obtain superior recommendation quality at session-level for users that heavily utilize the system. Moreover, the performance gain of *HRNN Init* wrt. session-based RNN grows from 5%/12% (short) to 7%/19% (long) in Recall@5/MRR@5, further highlighting the quality of our personalization strategy. Coherently with our previous findings, *HRNN All* does not perform well in

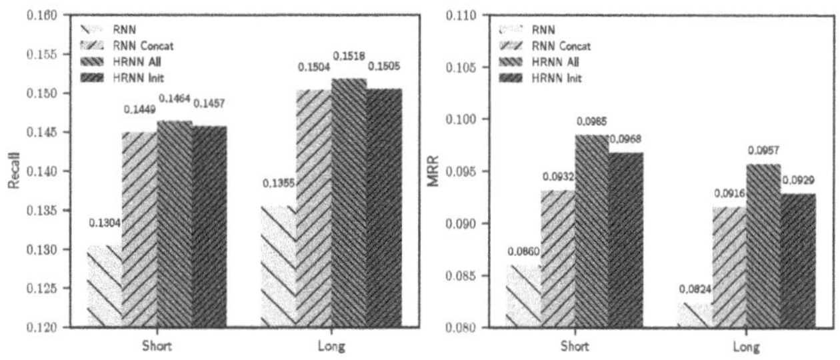

Figure 3: Recall@5 and MRR@5 on XING grouped by user history length.

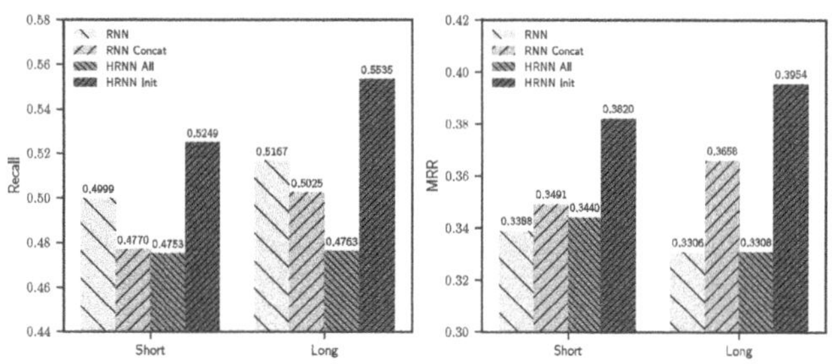

Figure 4: Recall@5 and MRR@5 on VIDEO grouped by user history length.

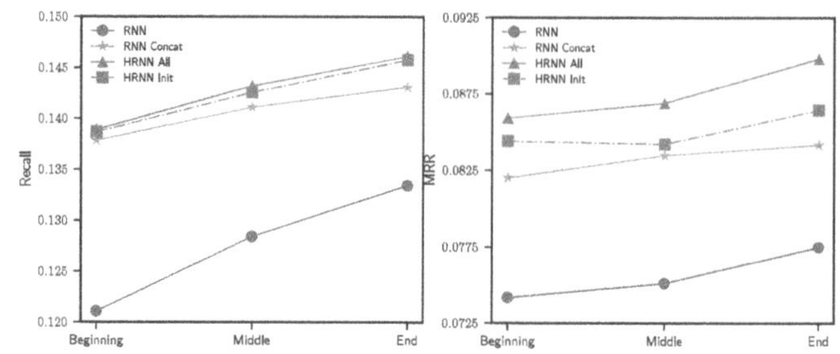

Figure 5: Recall@5 and MRR@5 on XING for different positions within session.

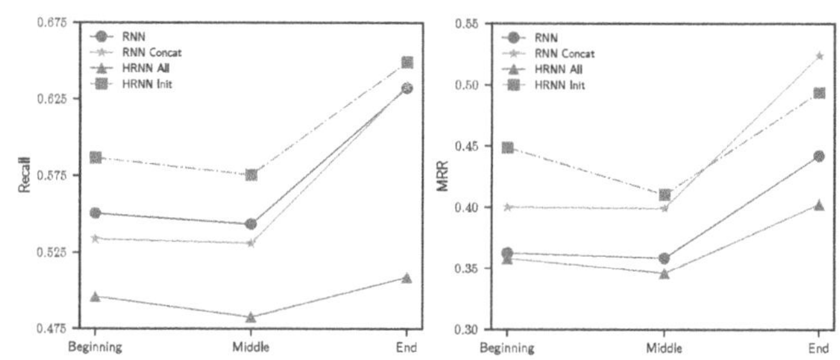

Figure 6: Recall@5 and MRR@5 on VIDEO for different positions within session.

this scenario, and its performances are steady (or even decrease) between the two groups.

In summary, the length of the user history has a significant impact on the recommendation quality as expected. In loosely session-bounded domains like XING, in which the user activity is highly repetitive and less diverse across sessions, enforcing the user representation in input at session-level provides slightly better performance over the simpler initialization-only approach. However, in the more strongly session-based scenario, in which the user activity across sessions has a higher degree of variability and may significantly diverge from the user historical interest and tastes, the simpler and more efficient *HRNN Init* variant has significantly better recommendation quality.

4.3.2 Analysis within sessions. Here we breakdown by number of events within the session in order to measure the impact of personalization within the user session. We limit the analysis to sessions having length ≥ 5 (6,736 sessions for XING and 8,254 for VIDEO). We compute the average values of each metric groped by position within the session (Beginning, Middle and End). Beginning refers to the first 2 events of the session, Middle to the 3rd and 4th, and End to any event after the 4th. As in the previous analysis, we focus on RNN-based models in the *large* configuration and report the median of the averages values of each metric computed over 10 runs with different random seeds. Results for Recall@5 and MRR@5 are shown in Figure 5 and Figure 6 for XING and VIDEO respectively.

On XING, the performance of all methods increses with the number of previous items in the session, suggesting that the user context at session-level is properly leveraged by all RNN-based models. However, there is a wide margin between personalized and 'pure' session-based models. Both *HRNN*s have similar Recall@5 and are comparable to RNN Concat. Interestingly, the gain in MRR@5 of *HRNN All* wrt. to both RNN and RNN Concat grows with the number of items processed, meaning that in this scenario the historical user information becomes more useful as the user session continues. *HRNN Init* has constantly better MRR that RNN Concat, with wider margins at the beginning and at the and of the session.

On VIDEO, the behavior within session is different. We can notice that both Recall and MRR increase between the beginning and end of a session as expected. *HRNN Init* exhibits a large improvement over RNN and RNN Concat at the beginning of the session (up to 10% better Recall and 25% better MRR). This conforms with the intuition that past user activity can be effectively used to predict the first actions of the user in the forthcoming session with greater accuracy. After the first few events the gain in Recall of personalized over pure session-based models reduces, while the gain in MRR stays stable. In other words, after a few events, the session-level dynamics start to prevail over longer-term user interest dynamics, making personalization strategies less effective. However, personalization still provides superior ranking quality all over the session, as testified by the higher MRR of both *HRNN Init* and RNN Concat over RNN. It is important to notice that better recommendations at beginning of a session are more impactful than later in the session because they are more likely to increase the chances of retaining the user. Finally, *HRNN All* is always the worse method, further underpinning the superiority of the *HRNN Init* variant.

	VIDEOXXL		
	Recall@5	**MRR@5**	**Precision@5**
RNN	0.3415	0.2314	0.0683
RNN Concat	0.3459	0.2368	0.0692
HRNN All	0.3621	0.2658	0.0724
HRNN Init	**0.4362**	**0.3261**	**0.0872**

Table 5: Results on the VIDEOXXL dataset for small networks. Best values are in bold.

4.3.3 Experiments on a large-scale dataset. We validated *HRNN*s over a larger version of the VIDEO dataset used in the previous experiments. This dataset is composed by the interactions of 810k users on 380k videos over the same 2 months periods, for a total of 33M events and 8.5M sessions. We then applied the same preprocessing steps used for the VIDEO dataset. We named this dataset VIDEOXXL. Due to our limited computational resources, we could only test small networks (100 hidden units for RNN and for 100+100 *HRNN*s) on this large-scale dataset. We run all RNNs and *HRNN*s once using the same hyper-parameters learned on the small VIDEO dataset. Although not optimal, this approach provides a first approximation on the applicability of our solution under a more general setting. For the same reason, we do not provide an exhaustive analysis on the experimental results as done for the smaller datasets. To speed up evaluation, we computed the rank of the relevant item compared to the 50,000 most supported items, as done in [8].

Results are summarized in Table 5 and confirm our previous findings on the small VIDEO dataset. RNN Concat is not effective and performs similarly to session-based RNN. On the other hand, Hierarchical RNNs outperform session-based RNN by healty margins. In particular, *HRNN Init* outperforms session-based RNN by ~28% in Recall@5 and by ~41% in MRR@5. These results further confirm the effectiveness of the *HRNN* models presented in this paper, and further underpin the superiority of *HRNN Init* over the alternative approaches for personalized session-based recommendation.

5 CONCLUSIONS AND FUTURE WORK

In this paper we addressed the problem of personalizing session-based recommendation by proposing a model based Hierarchical RNN, that extends previous RNN-based session modeling with one additional GRU level that models the user activity across sessions and the evolution of her interests over time. *HRNN*s provide a seamless way of transferring the knowledge acquired on the long-term dynamics of the user interest to session-level, and hence to provide personalized session-based recommendations to returning users. The proposed *HRNN*s model significantly outperform both state-of-the-art session-based RNNs and the other basic personalization strategies for session-based recommendation on two real-world datasets having different nature. In particular, we noticed that the simpler approach that only initializes the session-level representation with the evolving representation of the user (*HRNN Init*) gives the best results. We delved into the dynamics of session-based RNN models within and across sessions, providing extensive evidences of the superiority of the proposed *HRNN Init* approach and setting new state-of-the-art performances for personalized session-based recommendation.

As future works, we plan to study attention models and the usage of item and user features as ways of refining user representations and improve session-based recommendation even further. We also plan to investigate personalized session-based models in other domains, such as music recommendation, e-commerce and online advertisement.

REFERENCES

[1] *RecSys Challenge '16: Proceedings of the Recommender Systems Challenge*, New York, NY, USA, 2016. ACM.

[2] James Bergstra and Yoshua Bengio. Random search for hyper-parameter optimization. *J. Mach. Learn. Res.*, 13:281–305, February 2012.

[3] Kyunghyun Cho, Bart van Merriënboer, Dzmitry Bahdanau, and Yoshua Bengio. On the properties of neural machine translation: Encoder–decoder approaches. In *SSST-8: 8th Workshop on Syntax, Semantics and Structure in Statistical Translation*, pages 103–111, 2014.

[4] Robin Devooght and Hugues Bersini. Collaborative filtering with recurrent neural networks. *arXiv preprint arXiv:1608.07400*, 2016.

[5] John Duchi, Elad Hazan, and Yoram Singer. Adaptive subgradient methods for online learning and stochastic optimization. *The Journal of Machine Learning Research*, 12:2121–2159, 2011.

[6] B. Hidasi and D. Tikk. Fast ALS-based tensor factorization for context-aware recommendation from implicit feedback. In *ECML-PKDD'12, Part II*, number 7524 in LNCS, pages 67–82. Springer, 2012.

[7] Balázs Hidasi, Alexandros Karatzoglou, Linas Baltrunas, and Domonkos Tikk. Session-based recommendations with recurrent neural networks. *CoRR*, abs/1511.06939, 2015.

[8] Balázs Hidasi, Massimo Quadrana, Alexandros Karatzoglou, and Domonkos Tikk. Parallel recurrent neural network architectures for feature-rich session-based recommendations. In *Proceedings of the 10th ACM Conference on Recommender Systems*, RecSys '16, pages 241–248, New York, NY, USA, 2016. ACM.

[9] Sepp Hochreiter and Jürgen Schmidhuber. Long short-term memory. *Neural computation*, 9(8):1735–1780, 1997.

[10] Noam Koenigstein and Yehuda Koren. Towards scalable and accurate item-oriented recommendations. In *Proceedings of the 7th ACM Conference on Recommender Systems*, RecSys '13, pages 419–422, New York, NY, USA, 2013. ACM.

[11] G. Linden, B. Smith, and J. York. Amazon.com recommendations: Item-to-item collaborative filtering. *Internet Computing, IEEE*, 7(1):76–80, 2003.

[12] Zachary C Lipton, John Berkowitz, and Charles Elkan. A critical review of recurrent neural networks for sequence learning. *CoRR*, 1506.00019, 2015.

[13] Steffen Rendle and Christoph Freudenthaler. Improving pairwise learning for item recommendation from implicit feedback. In *Proceedings of the 7th ACM International Conference on Web Search and Data Mining*, WSDM '14, pages 273–282, New York, NY, USA, 2014. ACM.

[14] Steffen Rendle, Christoph Freudenthaler, Zeno Gantner, and Lars Schmidt-Thieme. Bpr: Bayesian personalized ranking from implicit feedback. In *Proceedings of the Twenty-Fifth Conference on Uncertainty in Artificial Intelligence*, UAI '09, pages 452–461, Arlington, Virginia, United States, 2009. AUAI Press.

[15] D. E. Rumelhart, G. E. Hinton, and R. J. Williams. Neurocomputing: Foundations of research. chapter Learning Internal Representations by Error Propagation, pages 673–695. MIT Press, Cambridge, MA, USA, 1988.

[16] Badrul Sarwar, George Karypis, Joseph Konstan, and John Riedl. Item-based collaborative filtering recommendation algorithms. In *WWW:01: 10th Int. Conf. on World Wide Web*, pages 285–295, 2001.

[17] Alessandro Sordoni, Yoshua Bengio, Hossein Vahabi, Christina Lioma, Jakob Grue Simonsen, and Jian-Yun Nie. A hierarchical recurrent encoder-decoder for generative context-aware query suggestion. In *Proceedings of the 24th ACM International on Conference on Information and Knowledge Management*, pages 553–562. ACM, 2015.

[18] Nitish Srivastava, Geoffrey Hinton, Alex Krizhevsky, Ilya Sutskever, and Ruslan Salakhutdinov. Dropout: A simple way to prevent neural networks from overfitting. *J. Mach. Learn. Res.*, 15(1):1929–1958, January 2014.

[19] Yong Kiam Tan, Xinxing Xu, and Yong Liu. Improved recurrent neural networks for session-based recommendations. In *Proceedings of the 1st Workshop on Deep Learning for Recommender Systems*, DLRS 2016, pages 17–22, New York, NY, USA, 2016. ACM.

[20] Chao-Yuan Wu, Amr Ahmed, Alex Beutel, Alexander J. Smola, and How Jing. Recurrent recommender networks. In *Proceedings of the Tenth ACM International Conference on Web Search and Data Mining*, WSDM '17, pages 495–503, New York, NY, USA, 2017. ACM.

3D Convolutional Networks for Session-based Recommendation with Content Features

Trinh Xuan Tuan
NextSmarty R&D
Hanoi, Vietnam
tuantx@nextsmarty.com

Tu Minh Phuong*
Department of Computer Science
Posts and Telecommunications Institute of Technology
Hanoi, Vietnam
phuongtm@ptit.edu.vn

ABSTRACT

In many real-life recommendation settings, user profiles and past activities are not available. The recommender system should make predictions based on session data, e.g. session clicks and descriptions of clicked items. Conventional recommendation approaches, which rely on past user-item interaction data, cannot deliver accurate results in these situations. In this paper, we describe a method that combines session clicks and content features such as item descriptions and item categories to generate recommendations. To model these data, which are usually of different types and nature, we use 3-dimensional convolutional neural networks with character-level encoding of all input data. While 3D architectures provide a natural way to capture spatio-temporal patterns, character-level networks allow modeling different data types using their raw textual representation, thus reducing feature engineering effort. We applied the proposed method to predict add-to-cart events in e-commerce websites, which is more difficult then predicting next clicks. On two real datasets, our method outperformed several baselines and a state-of-the-art method based on recurrent neural networks.

CCS CONCEPTS

• **Information systems → Recommender systems**;

KEYWORDS

Convolutional neural networks; session-based recommendation; recommender systems

ACM Reference format:
Trinh Xuan Tuan and Tu Minh Phuong. 2017. 3D Convolutional Networks for Session-based Recommendation with Content Features. In *Proceedings of RecSys'17, August 27–31, 2017, Como, Italy*, , 9 pages.
DOI: http://dx.doi.org/10.1145/3109859.3109900

1 INTRODUCTION

In order to generate personalized recommendations, traditional recommender systems rely on user profiles created from purchase histories, explicit ratings or other kinds of past interactions such as views, comments etc. For a given user, collaborative filtering (CF) approaches make predictions based on users with similar profiles [7] or by computing hidden factors of users and items with matrix factorization methods [15]. On the other hand, content based approaches recommend items based on their similarity to those present in the profile [2]. In either case, informative user profiles are assumed to be available. Unfortunately, this is often not the case in real-life applications. To create a profile, the user must be identified across sessions, for example by authentication. In practice, however, many e-commerce websites allow users to browse and even make purchases without authentication. Although there are other methods for user identification, e.g. by using cookies or fingerprinting techniques, the applicability of those methods is limited because of their relatively low reliability and privacy concerns. In addition, the creation of an informative profile requires the user to have enough interactions with the system in the past. This is often not satisfied, as many retail websites have small percentage of returning users, i.e. most users have only one visit or purchase.

When user profiles are not available, a typical solution is to base recommendations on session data, e.g. session clicks. These data have two important characteristics. First, session clicks are sequential in nature and the order of clicks may contain information of user intent. Second, clicked items are often associated with metadata such as names, categories, and descriptions, which provide additional information about user taste. In the absence of user profiles, it is important to exploit these two characteristics to draw more information from data. Therefore, a session-based recommendation method should have the following desired properties:

- The method should be able to model sequential patterns in streams of clicks. Previously, a popular method for session-based recommendation is item-to-item kNN. This method makes recommendation based only on item co-occurrences, completely ignoring click orders. There are other methods that use transition probabilities but they consider only the last click, ignoring information from past clicks. Recent findings show that explicitly taking into account the sequential nature of clicks and considering all past events result in improved recommendations [6, 11].
- The method should provide a simple way to represent and combine item IDs with metadata. Usually an item is associated with features of different types. For example, a product may have a numerical product ID, textual name/description, and it may belong to one or more categories from some category hierarchy. Most existing methods perform feature extraction and selection for each type of feature independently, or even construct an independent model for each feature

*Also with FPT Software Research Lab.

RecSys'17, August 27–31, 2017, Como, Italy

DOI: http://dx.doi.org/10.1145/3109859.3109900

type and then combine their outputs [12]. This requires a lot of effort for feature engineering and may fail to capture interactions between features. It would be more convenient to have a general way to represent different feature types and jointly model their interactions.

In this work, we propose a session-based recommendation method with these two desired properties. The method uses a 3D convolutional neural network (3D CNN) [13, 24] to capture sequential patterns in streams of clicks and associated features. It considers item IDs and all content features including hierarchical categories as texts and represent the resulting textual data with a character-level model [28]. A deep 3D CNN provides a natural way to jointly model temporal and content patterns that are indicative of purchasing intentions. At the same time, representing all features at character level frees us from the need of time consuming feature engineering and can be applied for different types of features. We empirically show that character-level encoding, combined with 3D CNN, can deliver competitive recommendation accuracy. In addition, unlike previous works that use 1-hot encoded vector for numerical item-IDs and words [12], character-level encoding results in much more compact representation for input. And, unlike other works that learn item embeddings [23], our model does not require any embedding layer. Given that both 1-hot representation of words and item embeddings results in large numbers of parameters, our model has substantially fewer parameters than previous deep neural network models for session-based recommendation.

Most existing methods for session-based recommendation predict the next click and present to the user a short list of top predictions. While predicting the next click is appropriate for news and media sites, it is not enough for retail websites. In the latter case, it is more useful to predict and recommend the list of products the user intents to buy. This will reduce browsing time, focus the user on potential products, and thus increase the purchase probability. However, directly predicting purchased items is more difficult than predicting the next click and requires appropriate organization of training data from session logs. Here we show that the proposed 3D CNN, if trained appropriately, is able to predict add-to-cart items with relatively high accuracy. Specifically, when user clicks on some item, this click and all the previous clicks of the current session (if any) are given as input, from which the model will predict a short list of items the user is likely to add to cart and present them as a recommendation.

We experimentally evaluated the proposed method on product recommendation in two retail websites, where each product is associated with textual descriptions and categories. We compared our method with several baselines and a leading session-based recommendation method using recurrent neural networks. The results show that our method achieved superior performance, while requiring less feature engineering steps.

In summary, our contributions are as follows:

- We propose a 3D CNN model for session-based recommendation, which allows jointly modeling sequential pattern of session clicks and different content features of items. The model can predict add-to-cart items based on the past clicks of the current session.
- We propose using character-level representation for all types of features, which frees us from feature engineering steps and reduces the number of model parameters. Experiments demonstrate the effectiveness of the proposed method.

2 RELATED WORK

Collaborative and content-based filtering

Collaborative filtering (CF) and content-based filtering (CBF) are two main groups of approaches used in recommender systems. The most popular CF algorithms are matrix factorization and nearest neighbor methods. Given a matrix of user-item ratings, matrix factorization [15] finds vectors of hidden factors for each user and each item so that, for each user-item pair, the inner product of their vectors closely approximates their original rating value, if this rating exists. The missing ratings are then computed as inner products of respective user and item vectors. Nearest neighbor methods [7] utilize the similarity between users based on user-item interactions to form a neighborhood for an active user, based on which recommendations are generated for the user. Symmetrically, it is possible to utilize similarity between items and compute item neighborhood, which is known as item-based recommendation [5, 22]. While matrix factorization and user-based kNN require user profiles in forms of user-item interactions, item-based nearest neighbor methods can be modified to work in session-based recommendation settings, in which items frequently appearing together in sessions are considered similar.

Content-based methods use content features of items to calculate similarities between them and recommend items similar to ones the user preferred in the past [2]. An advantage of CBF methods is their ability in handling new items, for which few or no user interactions exist. CF and CBF can be combined in so called hybrid systems to utilize the strengths of both methods [1]. Our work here also combines content feature with session clicks to boost the prediction accuracy.

Deep leaning

Deep learning has delivered state-of-the-art results in computer vision [16, 18], speech recognition [8], and several other application domains [17]. Two most popular deep learning models are convolutional neural networks (CNN) and recurrent neural networks (RNN). Other deep learning models include autoencoders, restricted Boltzman machines (RBMs), and fully connected networks with multiple hidden layers [17]. Deep learning methods have also been shown to be successful for recommendation tasks. A pioneering work along this direction was presented by Salakhutdinop et al. [21], in which several layers of RBMs are stacked together to deliver a better accuracy than a CF algorithm using singular value decomposition. Wang et al. [27] propose a hybrid method, in which they use a network of stacked denoising autoencoders to extract features from textual descriptions of items. The extracted features are then incorporated into a CF model to alleviate the problem when user-item interaction data are sparse. Van den Oord et al. [25] proposed a somewhat similar hybrid method, which uses deep learning to learn features from content descriptions of songs, which are then incorporated into a CF model to tackle the data sparsity problem. The difference is that they use CNNs for feature learning rather than autoencoders. Our method also uses CNNs and content features, but our CNN model allows capturing both spatial and temporal patterns, which is important for sequential nature of session clicks. Recently, Covington et al. [4] describe the system Google uses for video recommendation in Youtube. The system consists of a layer for learning user and item embeddings. These embeddings with other features such as time, video freshness etc. are then fed to several fully embedded layers to generate a distribution over millions of videos, from which top videos are recommended.

Session-based recommendation

Conventional CF and CBF do not work well in session-based settings, where user profiles are not available. A natural approach for this situation is item-based recommendation [5, 22], in which two items are deemed to be similar if they are frequently clicked together in the same sessions. Note that, this is slightly different from original item-based CF, in which two items are considered similar if they receive similar settings from the same set of users. While simple, item-based methods have been shown to be effective and widely deployed. A drawback of item-based recommendation is that it does not consider click order and generates predictions based only on the last click. Rendle et al. [20] propose so called Factorized Personalized Markov Chains to model sequential behaviors as a transition graph of items, which they use to predict next-basket items. Their work is similar to ours in that they predict next-basket items. However, unlike our work, they do that based only on previous baskets of the same user, while we make predictions based on all previous clicks without user identity. Figueiredo et al. [6] propose a Bayesian generative model to model click sequences. Their method is a generic method for any settings where data are sequences of events, which include session clicks. Learning item embeddings is another approach applicable for session-based recommendation. Inspired by learning word distributional representation in NLP, methods of this approach learn embeddings for items by training a shallow neural network to predict next purchased item in a transaction [9, 26]. The authors of [26] also leverage item metadata to regularize item embeddings, which makes it relevant to content-based approaches. Following successful applications of deep learning models in recommendation, Hidasi et al. [11] propose a pioneering work on using deep learning for session-based recommendation, in which they use RNN to model whole sequences of session click IDs. This work was then elaborated by Tan et al. [23], where they use a similar RNN architecture but with other loss functions and training data generation methods. In a later work, Hidasi et al. [12] extend their previous work by combining rich features of clicked items such as item IDs, textual descriptions, and images. They use different RNNs to represent different types of features and train those networks in a parallel fashion. Our work is relevant to [12] in that we combine features of different type for better session-based recommendation. However, our method uses a totally different model (3D CNN) and encoding method, which provide improved accuracy while simplify feature engineering steps.

3 METHODS

In this section we describe in detail the character-level representation for input data and the 3D CNN architecture for modeling both temporal and spatial patterns in sequences of clicks with associated content features. This is followed by an explanation of training procedure and training data preparation.

Let $[c_1, c_2, ..., c_n]$ $(n \geq 2)$ denote the sequence of item-viewing clicks for a given session, where c_i $(i = 1..n)$ is the ID of the i-th clicked item. In each session, there are zero or more clicks immediately followed by add-to-cart events (i.e. the viewed items are added to cart). Let $[a_1, a_2, ..., a_n]$ be an indicator vector so that $a_i = 1$ if c_i is added to cart, and $a_i = 0$ otherwise. For any given prefix $[c_1, c_2, ..., c_t]$ $(t = 1..n{-}1)$ of the session, the recommendation task is to predict subsequent add-to-cart items if such occur in the rest of the session, i.e. to predict $c_i | t < i \leq n, a_i = 1$. Note that this formulation is different from that of previous works, in which the task is to predict subsequent clicks rather than add-to-cart items [6, 11]. Predicting add-to-cart events, while more challenging, is more useful for e-commerce websites, as it guides users directly to items of highly probable purchase. We also assume that each item has a numerical ID, textual name and descriptions, and belongs to a category defined by the website owner. Here, we seek to find a model that takes into account all these information when making predictions.

3.1 Character-level Representation of Input

Inspired by the success of character-level CNNs in NLP [14, 28], we represent IDs and other item features using character-level encoding, which we describe in this section.

Let V denote the vocabulary of characters (alphabet) of size $|V|$. Suppose an item feature f is given as a sequence of characters $[v_1, v_2, ..., v_k]$, where k is the length of f . Then the character-level encoding of feature f is given by matrix $U^f \in \mathbb{R}^{|V| \times k}$, where the element at i-th row and j-th column is equal to 1 if v_j corresponds to i-th entry in V, and is equal to 0 otherwise. In other words, the j-th column of U^f is the 1-hot encoded vector of character v_j. In this work, we use vocabulary V of 55 characters, including all lower case characters from English alphabet, 10 digit characters, and several other characters. The characters are shown below:

```
abcdefghijklmnopqrstuvwxyz0123456789 -,
;.!?:"'/\|_@#$%
```

For each clicked item, we represent the associated features as follows.

- *Item ID.* A numerical ID is simply treated as a sequence of digit characters.
- *Name and descriptions.* It is straightforward to concatenate item name and descriptions which are already sequences of characters. In practice, the name is usually long enough and already provides a concise and informative description of an item, for example " iPhone 7 Smart Battery Case - Black". Therefore, we use only names and ignore additional descriptions to save computation time and reduce model size.
- *Category.* Categories are usually organized in a hierarchy by the website owner. To utilize the information encoded in the hierarchy, we concatenate the current category with all its ancestors up to the root and use the resulting sequence of characters as category feature, for example "apple/iphone/iphone7/accessories".

Given character-level encoded matrices for each type of features, we stack the matrices on top of each other to form a final matrix of

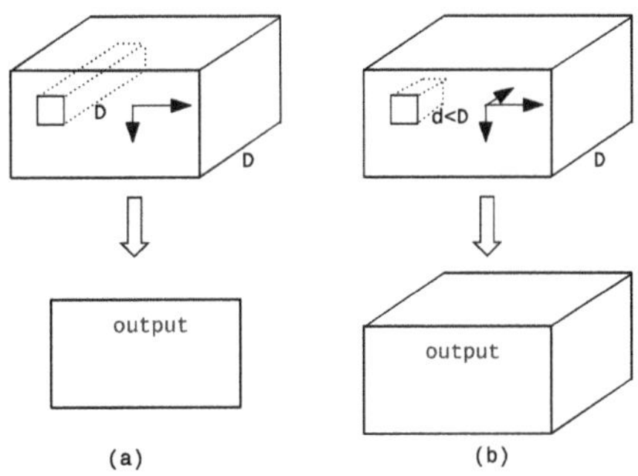

Figure 1: 2D and 3D convolution operations applied to multiple frames. a) 2D convolution results in 2D output. b) 3D convolution results in 3D output.

$X \in \mathbb{R}^{m \times n}$, where $m = |V| * F$ with F being the number of feature types (3 in this case), and n is the length of the longest feature (see figure 2 for an illustration). We set n to 150 in our experiments, ignoring characters beyond this limit. If a feature length is shorter than n then we add columns with all zeros to the right to get a matrix with exactly n columns.

3.2 3D CNN Architecture

Convolutional neural networks (CNNs) [18] are a type of neural network architectures that have achieved state-of-the-art results in computer vision , speech recognition and have been shown to be competitive in several NLP tasks [3, 17]. By applying convolution operations (known as kernels or filters) at different levels of granularity, a CNN can extract features that are useful for learning tasks and reduce the need of manual feature engineering. This characteristic is desired in our problem, where the goal is to extract from streams of clicks useful patterns, which are predictive of add-to-cart events. A pattern can be a sequence of clicks, a sequence of categories, a sequence of name parts, or their combination.

Traditional deployment of CNNs for computer vision mainly involves spatial convolutions, which are known as 2D CNNs. Our recommendation settings, however, involve both spatial and temporal information, which need to be modeled jointly. To achieve this, we adopt the 3D network architecture, originally introduced for video data [13, 24]. A main difference of a 3D network is that convolution and pooling are performed in all three dimensions (i.e. spatio-temporally), while in 2D networks they are performed spatially in two dimensions, even if the input is 3-dimensional. Figure 1 illustrates the difference between 2D and 3D architectures for 3-dimensional input. In the case of 2D networks, the 3D input volume collapses into a 2D structure right after the first convolution layer, thus loosing all temporal information. For 3D networks, the temporal information is preserved for subsequent convolution layers.

In this section, we describe the architecture of 3D CNNs for session-based recommendations. Figure 2 give a detailed illustration of the first layers, and Figure 3 shows the whole architecture of the proposed model. Recall that, for a click i, we represent the ID, name, and category using one character-level encoded matrix $U_i \in \mathbb{R}^{m \times n}$

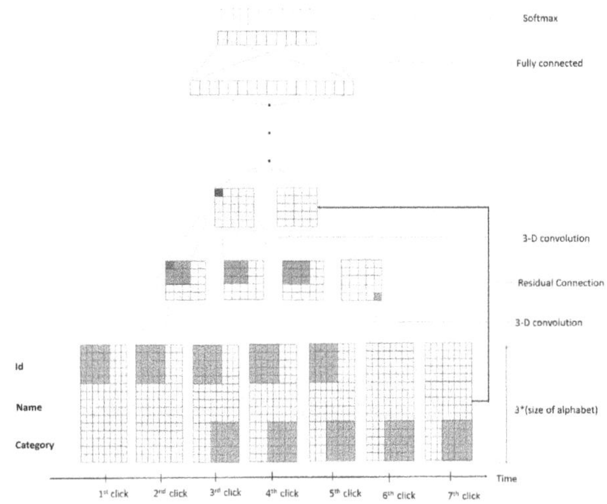

Figure 2: Illustration of the first and last layers.

(see the previous section). Inspired by computer vision terminology we will call such a matrix "frame". Then, a sequence of clicked is represented by putting corresponding frames side by side. As the result, we get a cube $U \in \mathbb{R}^{m \times n \times d}$, where d is the number of clicks. This will serve as the first feature map for the model.

We use a model consisting of several convolution layers stacked together. In each convolution stage, we perform a 3D convolution between a 3D kernel and the feature map at this stage, after which we add a bias and perform a nonlinear transformation to obtain a new feature map (Rectified Linear Unit [ReLU] was used as the linear transformation function for all layers). There are several kernels for each convolution stage, resulting in the corresponding number of feature maps for the next layer.

A recent work of He et al. [10] has shown the advantages of using residual connection in CNNs. We also employ this technique, adding residual connections to several convolution stages. There are two types of residual connections: (i). Identity connection applied to input and output of the same dimensions (solid line shortcuts in figure 3). (ii) The projection connection (dotted line), used to perform spatial downsampling by 1x1 convolution with a stride of 2. The filter shape in the first layer is [5,size of alphabet,5] and the stride is [2,2,2] (corresponding to [width, height, depth]). In the subsequent layers we use filters and average pooling of shape [3,3,3], and alternate between two stride shapes of [1,1,1] and [2,2,2] (see the figure). There are 16 filters in the first convolution stage. For the subsequent layers, we vary the of number of filters following two rules: (1) if the output height, width are the same as the input, the number of filter remain unchanged. (2). If the output height and width are halved, the number of filter is doubled. There is only one pooling layer before the fully connected layer. We use both L2 regularization and dropout with probability of 0.5 for the fully connected layer to prevent over fitting.

Our model uses classification-based output, where the output O' is a vector of probabilities over the items. This is achieved by using a softmax layer, trained to minimize a cross-entropy loss. For a given click, let $C_A = c_i$ be the set of subsequent add-to-cart items. We can

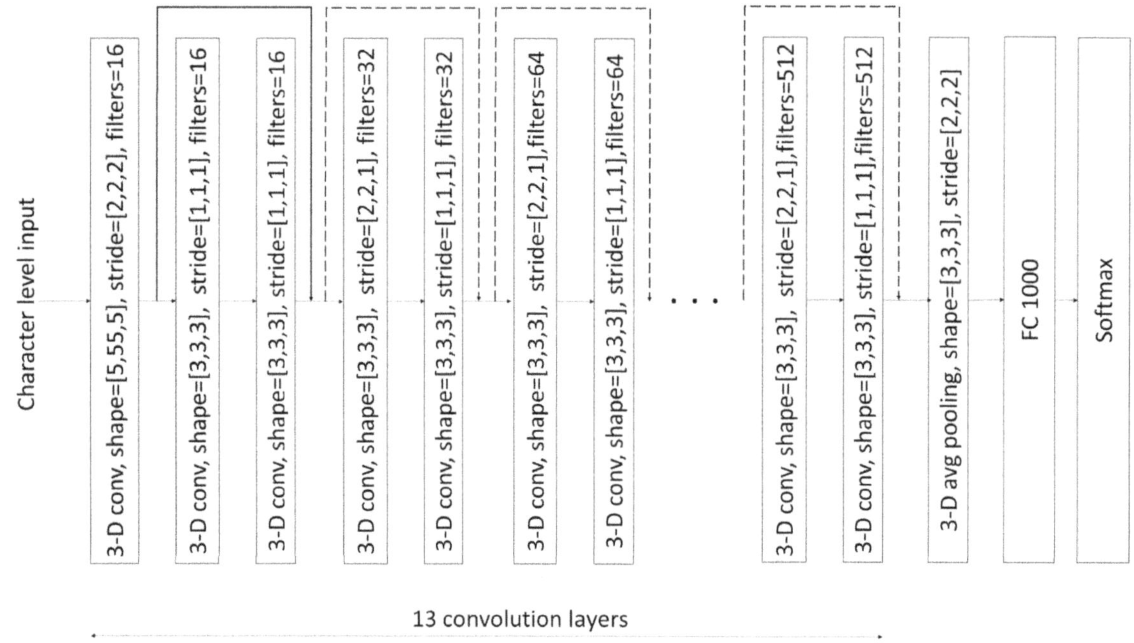

Figure 3: Architecture of the 3D CNN model with detailed information for each layer. Solid lines correspond to residual identity connections. Dotted lines correspond to residual projection connections.

represent C_A as a $|C_A|$-hot vector O of size N (N is the number of items), so that elements corresponding to C_A members are set to 1 and the others are set to zeros. The model is trained to minimize the cross-entropy loss between O and O'. At prediction, the items are presented as a ranked list according to their predicted probabilities. From the list we use top K items for a recommendation.

3.3 Training

In this section we describe the procedure for preparing training data. For each session containing at least one add-to-cart item, we use all prefixes up to the last add-to-cart item as training sequences. For each such training sequence, all subsequent add-to-cart item IDs are used as corresponding training labels (see figure 4 for an illustration). Since a 3D CNN model must have a fixed temporal size (which we set to 7 in our experiments), we process training sequences that are shorter or longer than seven clicks as follows. For shorter sequences, we use right padding, i.e. adding frames with all zeros to the right, to get the required number of frames. For a longer sequence, we remove some clicks to retain the required number of clicks. There are three options to remove clicks:

- Remove the first clicks. This means only the last clicked items are used as input. The assumption behind this method is that the most recent clicks have more impact on add-to-cart decision.
- Remove the last clicks: only the first clicked items are retained. The assumption is that the first impression is more important while later clicks are less important.
- Remove the middle clicks and retain the same number of the first and last clicks. This combines the above two assumptions.

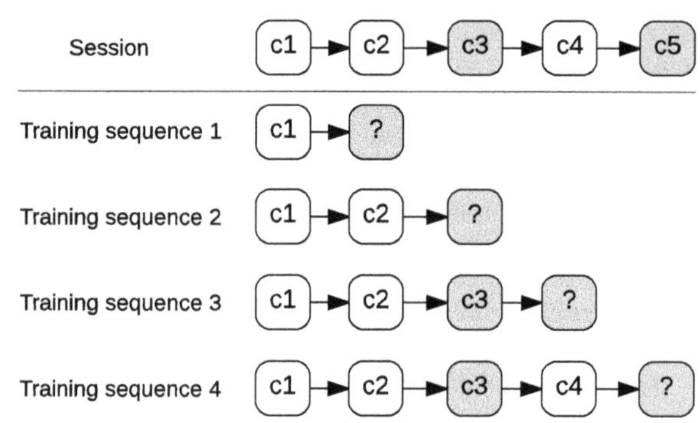

Figure 4: Generation of training sequences. Normal clicks are shown in white, clicks with add-to-cart are shown in blue. For each training sequence, the labels to predict are all subsequent add-to-cart clicks.

The same processing is applied at prediction time.

4 EXPERIMENTS AND RESULTS

In this section, we evaluate the performance of the proposed method compared to state-of-the-art session based recommendation algorithms on two datasets. We also reports results for different settings and parameter values.

Table 1: Statistics of the datasets

Datasets	JEWELRY	ELECTRONICS
Training set		
Sessions	42,698	30,982
Clicks	604,176	319,829
Sequences	591,884	307,135
Test set		
Sessions	4,966	4,421
Clicks	71,304	46,361
Sequences	69,135	45,127
Items	8,086	4,520

4.1 Experimental Setup

Datasets

We evaluated the proposed method on two proprietary datasets. The datasets were collected from two retail websites of small to medium size. The first dataset consists of product view events of a website selling jewelry products. The view events immediately followed by add-to-cart events were specially marked. The data were collected for a period of about three months without holiday or sale seasons. We will refer to this dataset as JEWELRY. The second dataset consists of product viewing clicks of a website selling electronics products over a period of three months. Similar to the first dataset, the view events with following add-to-cart were marked. We refer to this dataset as ELECTRONICS. Both sites only had simple recommendation in forms of most popular and new coming products. Note that the products in two datasets belong to two different domains of different characteristics. While jewelry is usually considered hedonic products (pleasure-oriented consumption), electronics products are more utilitarian (goal-oriented consumption) [19].

We removed all sessions not containing any add-to-cart event. We also removed sessions with only one click followed by an add-to-cart event because they are not suitable for session-based recommendation. We filtered items that were not added to cart in any session of the experimented period. For each product, its name (used as descriptions) and category name were retrieved and transformed to lower-case. Table 1 summarizes the statistics of the two datasets.

Setup

We used the sessions of the last ten days to form the test set and all remaining sessions for training. From session clicks, training and test sequences were generated as described in section 3.3. Each test sequence is fed to the trained model, from which a ranking over items is returned. We evaluated the experimented methods on how well they predicted subsequent add-to-cart clicks from each test sequence. In real-life settings, a recommender system presents to a user a short list of top-N recommended items. An accurate recommendation should contain actual add-to-cart items in this list. Thus, the first evaluation metrics here is recall@N. For a test sequence, recall@N is the number of actual subsequent add-to-cart items among top-N recommended items divided by the number of all subsequent actual add-to-cart items. We report recall@N averaged over all sequences in the test set.

The second metrics used in evaluation is Mean Reciprocal Rank (MRR@N), which is the average of reciprocal ranks of actual add-to-cart items with a rank set to zero if it exceeds N. MRR@N measures how well a recommender system assigns a higher rank for an actual item, thus is more sensitive than recall@N for ranking within top-N ranked items. We computed recall@N and MRR@N for N = 5, 10, 20, which correspond to different sizes of recommendation panels in webpages.

We conducted hyperparameter search on ELECTRONICS dataset, using a validation set consisting of the last 10% sessions from the training set. The optimal hyperparameters tuned on ELECTRONICS validation set were then used in all experiments. Specifically, we trained our model using mini-batches of size 250 with Adam optimizer and learning rate of 0.001. The model was trained for 100 epochs. The weights were initialized using truncated Gaussian with zero mean and standard deviation of 0.1. The length of each feature is limited to 150 characters. This length was enough for the longest category path in both datasets.

Baselines

We compared our method with the following session-based recommendation methods.

- Item-based kNN. The first, and very competitive baseline is Item-based kNN. This is a simple, yet effective method, which is widely deployed in practice. In this method, two item are considered similar if they co-occur frequently in different sessions. Because the problem is to predict subsequent add-to-cart events, we calculate the similarity between each item and only add-to-cart items. In prediction, the method outputs top-N items, which are most similar to the current clicked one.
- ID-RNN. This method [11] uses RNN to model session clicks and require only item IDs. The method was reported to deliver substantial improvement over Item-based kNN. We used the implementation provided by the authors ID-RNN with default parameters (https://github.com/hidasib/GRU4Rec). Although ID-RNN was originally proposed for next click recommendation, it is straightforward to train ID-RNN to predict subsequent add-to-cart items by using such items as training labels.
- Parallel-RNN. This method [12], proposed by the same authors of ID-RNN, also uses RNN but extend the model to consider textual descriptions of items and associated images, in addition to IDs as in ID-RNN. This is a leading method for session-based recommendation, which has been reported to be very effective in combining data of several types. Parallel-RNN is the most closely related to our method as it can combine different item features by combining different RNNs, trained on those features. We re-implemented Rich-RNN in TensorFlow with parameters corresponding to the best performance in their paper (bag-of-word TF-IDF for text, hidden unit of size 500+500, parallel networks, Interleaving training). Like in the case of ID-RNN, we trained Parallel-RNN to predict add-to-cart items by using such items as training

Table 2: Comparison of methods for shortening long sequences on JEWELRY dataset.

Shortening method	Recall@5	Recall@10	Recall@20
Only first clicks	0.3212	0.4005	0.4754
Only last clicks	0.3302	0.4078	0.4830
First and last clicks	0.3412	0.4152	0.4892

Table 3: Comparison of methods for shortening long sequences on ELECTRONICS dataset

Shortening method	Recall@5	Recall@10	Recall@20
Only first clicks	0.3662	0.4101	0.4734
Only last clicks	0.3654	0.4178	0.4810
First and last clicks	0.3907	0.4227	0.4894

labels. We used the same ID, names, and categories data as used with our method.

We could not compare our method with TribeFlow [6] because there is no obvious way to train TribeFlow to predict add-to-cart events.

4.2 Results

The first experiment was designed to evaluate the methods used in shortening long sessions to fit the width of the first network layer. For CNNs, this processing is necessary but can lead to information lost. Recall that we remove clicks from long sessions in three ways: remove the first, last, and medium clicks (see section 3.3). We applied these methods to process long sequences in both training and prediction and measured corresponding Recall@N for each method. The Recall@N values for three methods and two datasets are shown in Table 2 and Table 3. As can be seen, removing the medium clicks results in the highest Recall, while removing the first and last clicks result in lower Recall values, especially for top-5 recommendation. This patterns are similar across datasets. These results suggest that the first and last clicks are more important for predicting add-to-cart events than those in the middle. While the first clicks may be indicative of user intent when entering the site, the last ones may be indicative of user convergence on the items of interest. Middle clicks are likely be performed for exploration purposes. Based on these results, in the remaining experiments, we retained only the first and last clicks from long sequences.

In the next experiment, we evaluated the effectiveness of the proposed model in predicting add-to-cart items. This task is more difficult than predicting the next click because the distance between the current and add-to-cart click is usually much longer. To measure how the model is effective in recommending distant add-to-cart events we used the trained model to predict the last add-to-cart clicks in sessions of different lengths from the test set. For a test session of a given length, we generated all prefixes as described in section 3.3, used them as input for predicting the last add-to-cart item, and recorded Recall and MRR of the predictions. We used the Recall and MRR values, averaged over all prefixes as the measures of recommendation effectiveness for this session. This experiment

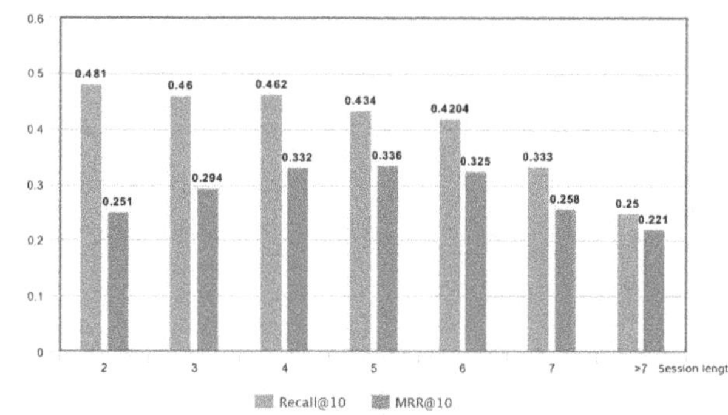

Figure 5: Effect of session length on accuracy. Shown for ELECTRONICS dataset.

was performed on ELECTRONICS dataset. Figure 5 shows averaged Recall@10 and MRR@10 as measures of recommendation effectiveness for each session length. As expected, Recall value gradually decreases as session length grows. For sessions of more than seven clicks, the Recall@10 drops to 0.25, compared to Recall@10 of 0.48 for sessions with two clicks. There are two possible explanations for this phenomenon. First, in a short session, the user is probably more focused and has stronger intent toward some items. Second, it is more difficult to predict something more distant in the future, which is the case in long sessions. At the same time, Recall@10 score of 0.25 for sessions with more than seven clicks is still impressive, showing that one fourth of actual add-to-cart items correctly appear among top-10 recommended. A somewhat less expected result is MRR@10, which achieved the highest value for sessions of length 5 and lower values for shorter and longer sessions. Despite this surprising result, the model achieved averaged MRR@10 of 0.22 for long sessions, which is encouraging for a challenging task like predicting distant add-to-cart events.

In the next experiment, we compared our model with baselines described in the previous section. In addition to the model using all item features (referred to as *3D-CNN Full*), we also measured the accuracy of the 3D CNN model using only IDs as input (referred to as *3D-CNN ID*). The results of experimented models on JEWELRY and ELECTRONICS datasets are summarized in Table 4 and 5 respectively. As can be seen from the tables, the deep learning models consistently outperformed the Item-based kNN baseline in terms of both Recall and MRR at all threshold values (5, 10, 20), despite the fact that Item-based kNN is a very competitive baseline. An interesting observation is the competitive performance of 3D-CNN ID, as compared to ID-RNN. Although the 3D CNN model with ID data achieved lower Recall and MRR scores than ID-RNN on the first dataset, it outperformed ID-RNN on the second dataset, in terms of most metrics, with only one exception - the Recall@20 score. This is interesting because RNNs are usually considered to be more suitable than CNNs in modeling sequential data. We believe the competitiveness of CNN in this case comes from the use of 3D convolution.

Models that combine names and categories with IDs, namely Parallel-RNN and 3D-CNN Full, achieved higher Recall and MRR

Table 4: Results on JEWELRY dataset. The best results for each metrics are shown in bold.

Method	Recall			MRR		
	Recall@5	Recall@10	Recall@20	MRR@5	MRR@10	MRR@20
Item-based kNN	0.2211	0.2990	0.3317	0.1476	0.1608	0.16341
ID-RNN	0.2512	0.3542	0.3944	0.1618	0.1774	0.1798
Parallel-RNN	0.3241	0.4095	0.4874	0.1754	0.1865	0.1923
3D-CNN ID	0.2365	0.2947	0.3650	0.1534	0.1616	0.1668
3D-CNN Full	**0.3412**	**0.4152**	**0.4892**	**0.1883**	**0.1934**	**0.1986**

Table 5: Results on ELECTRONICS dataset. The best results for each metrics are shown in bold.

Method	Recall			MRR		
	Recall@5	Recall@10	Recall@20	MRR@5	MRR@10	MRR@20
Item-based kNN	0.2859	0.3679	0.4108	0.1950	0.2059	0.2106
ID-RNN	0.2907	0.3708	0.4461	0.2025	0.2151	0.2208
Parallel-RNN	0.3469	0.4061	0.4861	0.2059	0.2162	0.2233
3D-CNN ID	0.3333	0.3795	0.4234	0.2478	0.2550	0.2580
3D-CNN Full	**0.3907**	**0.4227**	**0.4894**	**0.2781**	**0.2840**	**0.2883**

values than those using only IDs, across all datasets and metrics. This confirms the effectiveness of combining different features to improve recommendation accuracy.

The 3D CNN model using different features (3D-CNN Full) consistently outperformed other experimented models including state-of-the-art Parallel-RNN, in terms of all evaluation metrics, on both datasets. The superiority of 3D-CNN Full over Parallel-RNN is specially significant for top-5 and top-10 recommendation, as illustrated by Recall@5 and Recall@10 values. This has been observed in both datasets. The difference between two models, however, is not significant for Recall@20. 3D-CNN Full still achieved higher Recall@20 scores, but the difference is negligible. It is worth noticing that high Recall scores for top-5 and top-10 are specially important when the area for recommendation in a webpage is limited, and only a small number of items can be displayed. On ELECTRONICS dataset, 3D-CNN Full achieved much higher MRR scores than Parallel-RNN, for all three threshold values. The difference between MRR scores of two methods is smaller on JEWELRY dataset, but the margin is still substantial for MRR@5 and MRR@10.

5 CONCLUSION

We have introduced a 3D CNN model for session-based recommendation. The proposed model allows combining different item features such as ID, name, and metadata. This is achieved by two recipes: 1) using character-level encoding for all features; and 2) using CNN with 3D convolutions. We have shown that character-level encoding is applicable for important types of item features. More importantly, it frees us from most feature engineering steps. As a side effect, character-level encoding results in networks with fewer parameters as compared to 1-hot encoding of words, for example. 3D convolution allows jointly extracting temporal and spatial features, which is desired in modeling session data. We have presented experimental results with datasets from real e-commerce websites. The results demonstrate the effectiveness of our method in predicting add-to-cart events. This setting, although important in e-commerce, was not well explored previously. The proposed method outperformed all baselines including a state-of-the-art RNN based method. Traditionally, RNNs have been widely considered the model of choice for sequential data. The effectiveness of our method, in addition to existing successful applications of 3D CNN for video and time series data, suggest that 3D CNNs are also a suitable architecture for modeling sequential data, especially when sequence elements are associated with complex features. Finally, although the current model uses only ID and metadata, it is straightforward to incorporate other features such as timestamp or indication of past add-to-cart events from the same session. By doing this, the method can be easily extended to model co-purchase patterns, which have been shown to be useful in practice.

ACKNOWLEDGMENTS

This work was supported in part by FPT.

REFERENCES

[1] Ngo Xuan Bach, Nguyen Do Hai, and Tu Minh Phuong. 2016. Personalized recommendation of stories for commenting in forum-based social media. *Information Sciences* 352 (2016), 48 – 60.

[2] Marko Balabanović and Yoav Shoham. 1997. Fab: Content-based, Collaborative Recommendation. *Commun. ACM* 40, 3 (mar 1997), 66–72. DOI: https://doi.org/10.1145/245108.245124

[3] Ronan Collobert, Jason Weston, Léon Bottou, Michael Karlen, Koray Kavukcuoglu, and Pavel Kuksa. 2011. Natural Language Processing (Almost) from Scratch. *J. Mach. Learn. Res.* 12 (nov 2011), 2493–2537. http://dl.acm.org/citation.cfm?id=1953048.2078186

[4] Paul Covington, Jay Adams, and Emre Sargin. 2016. Deep Neural Networks for YouTube Recommendations. In *Proceedings of the 10th ACM Conference on Recommender Systems (RecSys '16)*. ACM, New York, NY, USA, 191–198. DOI: https://doi.org/10.1145/2959100.2959190

[5] Mukund Deshpande and George Karypis. 2004. Item-based top- N recommendation algorithms. *ACM Transactions on Information Systems* 22, 1 (jan 2004), 143–177. DOI: https://doi.org/10.1145/963770.963776

[6] Flavio Figueiredo, Bruno Ribeiro, Jussara M Almeida, and Christos Faloutsos. 2016. TribeFlow: Mining & Predicting User Trajectories. In *Proceedings of the 25th International Conference on World Wide Web (WWW '16)*. International World

Wide Web Conferences Steering Committee, Republic and Canton of Geneva, Switzerland, 695–706. DOI: https://doi.org/10.1145/2872427.2883059

[7] David Goldberg, David Nichols, Brian M Oki, and Douglas Terry. 1992. Using Collaborative Filtering to Weave an Information Tapestry. *Commun. ACM* 35, 12 (dec 1992), 61–70. DOI: https://doi.org/10.1145/138859.138867

[8] Alex Graves, Abdel-rahman Mohamed, and Geoffrey Hinton. 2013. Speech recognition with deep recurrent neural networks. In *Acoustics, speech and signal processing (icassp), 2013 ieee international conference on*. IEEE, 6645–6649.

[9] Mihajlo Grbovic, Vladan Radosavljevic, Nemanja Djuric, Narayan Bhamidipati, Jaikit Savla, Varun Bhagwan, and Doug Sharp. 2015. E-commerce in Your Inbox: Product Recommendations at Scale. In *Proceedings of the 21th ACM SIGKDD International Conference on Knowledge Discovery and Data Mining (KDD '15)*. ACM, New York, NY, USA, 1809–1818. DOI: https://doi.org/10.1145/2783258.2788627

[10] Kaiming He, Xiangyu Zhang, Shaoqing Ren, and Jian Sun. 2016. Deep Residual Learning for Image Recognition. In *The IEEE Conference on Computer Vision and Pattern Recognition (CVPR)*.

[11] Balázs Hidasi, Alexandros Karatzoglou, L. Baltrunas, and Domonkos Tikk. 2016. Session-based recommendations with recurrent neural networks. In *International Conference on Learning Representations*.

[12] Balázs Hidasi, Massimo Quadrana, Alexandros Karatzoglou, and Domonkos Tikk. 2016. Parallel Recurrent Neural Network Architectures for Feature-rich Session-based Recommendations. In *Proceedings of the 10th ACM Conference on Recommender Systems (RecSys '16)*. ACM, New York, NY, USA, 241–248. DOI: https://doi.org/10.1145/2959100.2959167

[13] S Ji, W Xu, M Yang, and K Yu. 2013. 3D Convolutional Neural Networks for Human Action Recognition. *IEEE Transactions on Pattern Analysis and Machine Intelligence* 35, 1 (jan 2013), 221–231. DOI: https://doi.org/10.1109/TPAMI.2012.59

[14] Yoon Kim, Yacine Jernite, David Sontag, and Alexander M. Rush. 2016. Character-aware Neural Language Models. In *Proceedings of the Thirtieth AAAI Conference on Artificial Intelligence (AAAI'16)*. AAAI Press, 2741–2749. http://dl.acm.org/citation.cfm?id=3016100.3016285

[15] Yehuda Koren, Robert Bell, and Chris Volinsky. 2009. Matrix Factorization Techniques for Recommender Systems. *Computer* 42, 8 (aug 2009), 30–37. DOI: https://doi.org/10.1109/MC.2009.263

[16] Alex Krizhevsky, Ilya Sutskever, and Geoffrey E Hinton. 2012. ImageNet Classification with Deep Convolutional Neural Networks. In *Proceedings of the 25th International Conference on Neural Information Processing Systems (NIPS'12)*. Curran Associates Inc., USA, 1097–1105. http://dl.acm.org/citation.cfm?id=2999134.2999257

[17] Yann LeCun, Yoshua Bengio, and Geoffrey Hinton. 2015. Deep learning. *Nature* 521, 7553 (2015), 436–444.

[18] Y. LeCun, B. Boser, J. S. Denker, D. Henderson, R. E. Howard, W. Hubbard, and L. D. Jackel. 1990. Handwritten Digit Recognition with a Back-Propagation Network. In *Advances in Neural Information Processing Systems*. Morgan Kaufmann, 396–404.

[19] Dokyun Lee and Kartik Hosanagar. 2016. When Do Recommender Systems Work the Best?: The Moderating Effects of Product Attributes and Consumer Reviews on Recommender Performance. In *Proceedings of the 25th International Conference on World Wide Web (WWW '16)*. International World Wide Web Conferences Steering Committee, Republic and Canton of Geneva, Switzerland, 85–97. DOI: https://doi.org/10.1145/2872427.2882976

[20] Steffen Rendle, Christoph Freudenthaler, and Lars Schmidt-Thieme. 2010. Factorizing Personalized Markov Chains for Next-basket Recommendation. In *Proceedings of the 19th International Conference on World Wide Web (WWW '10)*. ACM, New York, NY, USA, 811–820. DOI: https://doi.org/10.1145/1772690.1772773

[21] Ruslan Salakhutdinov, Andriy Mnih, and Geoffrey Hinton. 2007. Restricted Boltzmann Machines for Collaborative Filtering. In *Proceedings of the 24th International Conference on Machine Learning (ICML '07)*. ACM, New York, NY, USA, 791–798. DOI: https://doi.org/10.1145/1273496.1273596

[22] Badrul Sarwar, George Karypis, Joseph Konstan, and John Riedl. 2001. Item-based Collaborative Filtering Recommendation Algorithms. In *Proceedings of the 10th International Conference on World Wide Web (WWW '01)*. ACM, New York, NY, USA, 285–295. DOI: https://doi.org/10.1145/371920.372071

[23] Yong Kiam Tan, Xinxing Xu, and Yong Liu. 2016. Improved Recurrent Neural Networks for Session-based Recommendations. In *Proceedings of the 1st Workshop on Deep Learning for Recommender Systems (DLRS 2016)*. ACM, New York, NY, USA, 17–22. DOI: https://doi.org/10.1145/2988450.2988452

[24] Du Tran, Lubomir Bourdev, Rob Fergus, Lorenzo Torresani, and Manohar Paluri. 2015. Learning Spatiotemporal Features with 3D Convolutional Networks. In *Proceedings of the 2015 IEEE International Conference on Computer Vision (ICCV) (ICCV '15)*. IEEE Computer Society, Washington, DC, USA, 4489–4497. DOI: https://doi.org/10.1109/ICCV.2015.510

[25] Aäron Van den Oord, Sander Dieleman, and Benjamin Schrauwen. 2013. Deep Content-based Music Recommendation. In *Proceedings of the 26th International Conference on Neural Information Processing Systems (NIPS'13)*. Curran Associates Inc., USA, 2643–2651. http://dl.acm.org/citation.cfm?id=2999792.2999907

[26] Flavian Vasile, Elena Smirnova, and Alexis Conneau. 2016. Meta-Prod2Vec: Product Embeddings Using Side-Information for Recommendation. In *Proceedings of the 10th ACM Conference on Recommender Systems (RecSys '16)*. ACM, New York, NY, USA, 225–232. DOI: https://doi.org/10.1145/2959100.2959160

[27] Hao Wang, Naiyan Wang, and Dit-Yan Yeung. 2015. Collaborative Deep Learning for Recommender Systems. In *Proceedings of the 21th ACM SIGKDD International Conference on Knowledge Discovery and Data Mining (KDD '15)*. ACM, New York, NY, USA, 1235–1244. DOI: https://doi.org/10.1145/2783258.2783273

[28] Xiang Zhang, Junbo Zhao, and Yann LeCun. 2015. Character-level Convolutional Networks for Text Classification. In *Proceedings of the 28th International Conference on Neural Information Processing Systems (NIPS'15)*. MIT Press, Cambridge, MA, USA, 649–657. http://dl.acm.org/citation.cfm?id=2969239.2969312

Modeling User Session and Intent with an Attention-based Encoder-Decoder Architecture

Pablo Loyola*
The University of Tokyo
Tokyo, Japan
pablo@weblab.t.u-tokyo.ac.jp

Chen Liu
Rakuten Institute of Technology
Tokyo, Japan
chen.liu@rakuten.com

Yu Hirate
Rakuten Institute of Technology
Tokyo, Japan
yu.hirate@rakuten.com

ABSTRACT

We propose an encoder-decoder neural architecture to model user session and intent using browsing and purchasing data from a large e-commerce company.

We begin by identifying the source-target transition pairs between items within each session. Then, the set of source items are passed through an encoder, whose learned representation is used by the decoder to estimate the sequence of target items. Therefore, as this process is performed pair-wise, we hypothesize that the model could capture the transition regularities in a more fine grained way. Additionally, our model incorporates an attention mechanism to explicitly learn the more expressive portions of the sequences in order to improve performance. Besides modeling the user sessions, we also extended the original architecture by means of attaching a second decoder that is jointly trained to predict the purchasing intent of user in each session. With this, we want to explore to what extent the model can capture inter session dependencies.

We performed an empirical study comparing against several baselines on a large real world dataset, showing that our approach is competitive in both item and intent prediction.

KEYWORDS

Recommender Systems, Recurrent Neural Networks, Attention Mechanisms

1 INTRODUCTION

Recommender systems have received a vast amount of interest in recent years, as a natural consequence of the increasing complexity and scale of web services and e-commerce platforms. These models have varied over time, but in general can be classified as *behavior-based* or *content-based.* The former takes historical data from browsing and purchasing activity, considering an explicit time component from which predictive models can be computed. On the other hand, content-based approaches generate a feature space from where items can be mapped and their similarity is derived by means of an ad-hoc metric. Moreover, approaches such as collaborative filtering [17] aimed to combine both trying to construct item relationships based on co-purchasing activity.

Besides choosing the type of method to generate the recommendations, there is also an inherent challenge on how the data is represented and how we feed it to the chosen model. In any statistical learning setting, it is known that the representation of the data has a considerable impact on performance, and that different representations can entangle different explanatory factors [3]. We consider this issue is specially relevant in e-commerce, as we are in the presence of a highly multimodal and usually noisy setting, where a single item can be represented from different perspectives, such as its purchasing activity, content, rating or reviews information, among others. Finding meaningful representations for users is also challenging, given the heterogeneity of sessions and difficulty on estimating motivations from indirect sources.

Recently, the success that representation learning approaches have achieved on fields such as computer vision and speech recognition has naturally motivated their application in a recommender setting. These methods aim at automatically learn distributed feature representations from the data as an alternative to handcrafted feature engineering [8]. Within this paradigm, recurrent neural networks (RNN) have emerged as powerful tools to model sequential data [6]. Recent approaches on recommender systems have incorporated these models, mainly for user session prediction [10]. While these models have provided relevant insights, we consider there is room for improvement, as session prediction is inherently a sequential problem. Moreover, from our exploratory analysis using standard recurrent architectures for session modeling, we found that they worked well when the number of items remains relatively small, But when we tested in a more realistic setting, increasing the dataset impacted negatively on the performance.

As an alternative to current models that use one network to model sessions, in this work we propose to explore a neural architecture based on the encoder decoder paradigm [21], which was initially designed for machine translation [4]. This model consists of two recurrent neural networks that work in a symbiotic way. We begin by identifying the source-target transition pairs between items within each session. Then, the set of source items are passed through an encoder, whose learned representation is used by the decoder to estimate the sequence of target items. Therefore, as this process is performed pair-wise, and both networks are jointly trained end-to-end, we hypothesize that this model could capture the transition regularities in a more comprehensive fine grained way than using a single network. At the core of our model we incorporated an attention mechanism to explicitly learn the more

*Work done while the author was an intern at Rakuten Institute of Technology

RecSys'17, August 27–31, 2017, Como, Italy
© 2017 ACM. ISBN 978-1-4503-4652-8/17/08...$15.00
DOI: http://dx.doi.org/0.1145/3109859.3109917

expressive portions of the sequences in order to improve performance.

While characterizing the distributional regularities of the transition within sessions represents a relevant input for generating recommendations, we consider that it is necessary to incorporate the user intent, for instance, if the user will just browse or perform a purchase within the session. We consider this factor of high relevance, as it provides an explicit feedback and more comprehensive context. To explore the feasibility of that idea, we attached a second decoder to the proposed model, which is jointly trained to estimate the likelihood of a purchase event for a given session. With this, we are also interested in assessing the flexibility of the architecture in the sense of its ability to incorporate other data sources to complement user modeling.

We performed an empirical study on user activity from a large scale e-commerce platform. We compared the performance of our model against three baselines, one of them a recurrent architecture. The results show that our model is competitive, especially as we increase the item space, where baseline performance decreases. Additionally, results on intent prediction suggest the feasibility of the idea, opening a new opportunity for further research.

In summary, we proposed a recurrent architecture that is able to provide relevant item predictions at session based level and it is flexible enough to incorporate additional tasks, such as intent estimation.

2 RELATED WORK

Recent advances in representation learning mainly from vision and natural language processing have been adapted to an e-commerce setting, with the goal of improving the accuracy of product recommendations [8].

In terms of how to generate recommendations through representation learning, literature shows attempts in categories ranging from a content-based and collaborative filtering to temporal and hybrid models. The main theme covering these methods is the construction of a feature learner to obtain unified user-item representations, which are then used for recommendations.

One of the first approaches was proposed on the field of music recommendation, where van den Oord et al [23] developed a model inspired on previous work in feature learning from audio signal [9] to learn latent factors which are used for training a classifier. In [25], Wang et al. proposed *collaborative deep learning*, a Bayesian model that combine both feature learning from product content information and collaborative filtering from the user ratings.

In a more recent work, Covington et al [7] used a deep architecture to learn unified representations for users and videos to generate recommendations on Youtube. In this case, taking into consideration factors such as scale, freshness and noise, the authors propose a system conformed by two neural networks, the first one in charge of choosing candidates and the second one is used to rank them. Both networks receive embeddings of learned features which passes through a series of non-linearities.

The problem of learning combined representation from users and products has been also studied by Zheng et al in [26], where the authors focused on unifying item reviews to learn item features and the history of reviews written by users to learn user behaviour. The learned representations are merged in a share layer that match users and items to perform recommendations.

The second line of research consists of considering the time as the main component and modeling the sequences of items the user visits. From understanding that sequence, these models are able to provide a prediction about the next item. In the case of using recurrent neural networks, we can mention the work by Hidasi et al [10], where the authors proposed a recurrent architecture to generate session-based recommendations, specifically by training a gated recurrent unit (GRU) based network [4] through a session parallel mini-batch process to avoid the need to restrict session length. Additionally, they presented a loss function that considers the ranking of relevant items. The same authors proposed an extension in [11] in which they incorporate other dimensions of product information such as image features, by implementing a parallel recurrent architecture, on which the information is merged to perform a more comprehensive prediction. More recently, Tan et al [22] proposed an extension to [10] based on data augmentation and adding the ability to directly predict embedding vectors instead of item id.

In [19], Song et al proposed an architecture that combines both long-term and short-term temporal user preferences which are modeled through different stepwise long short term memory (LSTM) networks [12].

3 PROPOSED APPROACH

We assume the availability of a set of user activity, both in terms of browsing sessions and purchasing events. Our goal is to develop a model capable of computing session based recommendations, by predicting the next item based on the past activity.

We rely on a recurrent architecture to learn feature representations and encode the transition dependencies at a distributional level.

Let us assume a sequence of items representing an user session in the form $s = \{i_1, i_2, \ldots, i_N\}$. From that, we define a transition as the pair of two consecutive items, (i_{j-1}, i_j), where the first element is called *source* and the second, *target*. Then, the set of item transition pairs for s, P_s will be given by $P_s = \{(i_1, i_2), (i_2, i_3), \ldots, (i_{N-1}, i_N)\}$. We subsequently obtain the group of sources $S_s = \{i_1, \ldots, i_{N-1}\}$ and targets $T_s = \{i_2, \ldots, i_N\}$. Additionally, for each session, we can obtain a binary feature indicating if there is a purchasing event or not.

Therefore, we can formalize our problem as trying to learn a model M, such as $M : S_s \longrightarrow T_s$. As this can be seen as a sequential modeling problem, a recurrent model can be trained for this task in a way that we can find a set of parameters θ that maximizes the likelihood of a element in the target set t_i given an input coming from the sources set s and the currently history of sequence , t_1^{i-1}, $\prod P(t_i | t_1^{i-1}, s; \theta)$. We propose to parametrize model M with an encoder-decoder architecture, more commonly known as *sequence to sequence* [21], which was initially proposed for neural machine translation [5], but recently its use has been expanded successfully outside the field of natural language processing[24].

The generic architecture assumes two recurrent neural networks working together [15]. The first one, the encoder, receives the input sequence and generates a fixed length representation c =

$q(h_1, \ldots, h_T)$, where q is a non-linear function and h_i is the hidden state of the encoder at time i.

For the encoder, a bidirectional RNN [18] is used, which reads the sequence forward and backwards, generating two sets of hidden states. Therefore, the representation for a given internal state h_j is the concatenation of both vectors, $h_j = [\overrightarrow{h_j}; \overleftarrow{h_j}]$. In our setting, the encoder reads the sequence of elements coming from the *source* set. With this, we are able to obtain a fixed length representation of the whole sequence.

Then, the second network, the decoder, takes the output of the encoder and uses it as the initial state from which it starts to estimate the sequence of elements coming from the *target* sequence. In our setting, the decoder RNN is unidirectional. This network works by, at each time step i, computing its internal states as $d_i = f(d_{i-1}, c_i)$, where d_{i-1} represents the decoder state at time i_1. We also treat c_i as an *attention* mechanism [2], to encapsulate the portions of the *source* sequence that has more expressive power. In this case, this vector is the result of the weighted sum of all encoder internal states:

$$c_i = \sum_{j=1}^{T} \alpha_{i,j} h_j \tag{1}$$

where the weights $\alpha_{i,j}$ are learned by an additional feed forward neural network that is jointly trained with the rest of the components of the system:

$$\alpha_{i,j} = \frac{exp(e_{i,j})}{\sum_{k=1}^{T} exp(e_{i,k})} \tag{2}$$

$$e_{i,k} = g(s_{i-1}, h_k) \tag{3}$$

where g is parametrized with a feed forward neural network. This configuration is shown in the upper part of Figure 1, where A represents the attention mechanism the computes c_i.

Finally, we experimented with an explicit transfer of information between the two networks, which is shown the bottom part of Figure 1. We called this process *alignment* and consists of passing both y_{i-1}, the previous emitted label associated to the set of target items (represented by a purple line) and h_i, internal state computed by the encoder at time i, to the decoder. Note the that we are making an explicit alignment between internal states from both networks and therefore the expression for the decoder state will be $d_i = f(d_{i-1}, y_{i-1}, h_i, c_i)$.

3.1 Adding Session Intent

While being able to represent and estimate the distributional characteristics of item transitions among sessions is our primary goal, another key element that could provide additional and useful insights for user understanding is the actual action that the user performed during the session under study or on the future activity. In that sense, of special interest is to know if the user is likely to *purchase* or just *browse*. We define those two actions as part the *intent* of the user. In order to incorporate this additional element, we propose to modify the encoder-decoder architecture by adding a second decoder, which is also jointly trained with the rest of the system. This second decoder takes the output from the encoder and it is configured to output only one element, which is associated

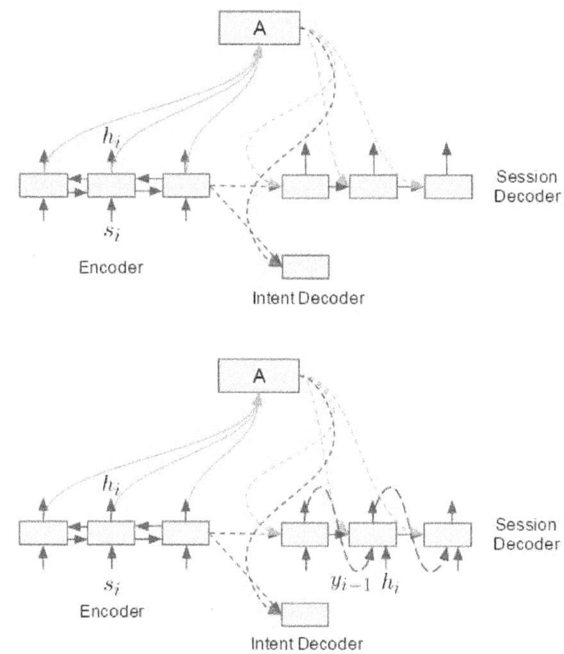

Figure 1: Proposed model for session and intent modeling with attention (top) and attention + alignments (bottom).

to the class *purchase* or *browse* and can be modeled as a binary variable.

It must be noted that instead of RNN for this element, we could have just used another feed forward network, because strictly we are not trying to generate sequential output. But our exploratory analysis showed that in fact the use of a recurrent architecture performed better. We hypothesize this is because as the cost of both decoders are backpropagated jointly to the encoder at training time, costs from the same nature could generate a smoother learning signal. However a more comprehensive answer might require further analysis.

For the *intent* decoder, we also compute a context, which is passed along with the output from the encoder. The resulting architecture can be seen in Figure 1, where the red line represents the contribution from the attention mechanism . In terms of the intent we want to model, we propose to try two configurations. In the first place, we try to predict the intent in the current session, which means, just from the sequence transitions, estimate of any of the elements in the sequence will be purchased or not. For the second configuration, we obtained the intent from the next session that the user generated. With this, we wanted to explore if it is possible for the model to relate events that are temporally delayed, i.e., if there is a connection between the sequence of elements explored and the action in the immediate future.

4 EMPIRICAL STUDY

We designed and implemented and empirical study to test the validity and practical use of the proposed approach.

4.1 Data

We obtained a subset of the user activity from a large scale e-commerce system. Our total set consists of 9 million user sessions. Each session is conformed by the sequence of items browsed by the user and their respective time stamp, session id and user id. The set of unique items contained in our dataset reaches the approximately 400.000. We also collected the purchasing activity within the same period of time, allowing us to compute the intent of each session.

We divided the full dataset into training, and testing using a 80:20 proportion. From the training set, we took 10% as a validation set, which was used for hyper parameter selection.

4.2 Baselines

We compare the proposed approach against three baselines:

Item-KNN: This method provides an item recommendation based on its co-occurrence with other items along sessions and it is computed as a function of the number of co-occurrences of item pairs within sessions and the number of session that contains that item pair.

BPR-MF: Matrix factorization method that optimizes a pair wise ranking function through stochastic gradient descent [16]. We followed [10] in the sense of obtained an estimation of the feature representation for each item through averaging past occurrences.

GRU4Rec: Method proposed by Hidasi et al [10], which consists of a GRU-based architecture that iteratively read session items predicting the next one through a pair wise ranking function.

For each method we computed two metrics to measure performance. In the first place, Recall20, which provides the proportion of predictions which contain the ground truth among the top-20 items. Additionally we reported the mean reciprocal rank (MRR), which is a more strict metric as it explicitly considers the order of a set of candidates provided by a model. In this case we also consider a top 20 ranking.

4.3 Experimental Settings

We implemented our approach on top of the Tensorflow library [1]. Hyperparameter optimization was conducted on the validation set where we explored variations on the type of cell used (LSTM or GRU) and the number of units. From that process we decided to use LSTM with 100 units. For training we set the batch size on 32 and a Dropout [20] of 0.5 as regularization. We experimented with batch normalization [14], but we did not observe relevant improvement, while it had a considerable overhead on the time consumption. We tested several optimization methods, and the best cost-effective performance was obtained with Adam [13].

In the case of the baselines, we adapted a publicly available implementation [10]. In the case of GRU4Rec, we studied variations related to the number of hidden units and the loss function. We used the same validation set to perform hyperparameter optimization.

5 RESULTS AND DISCUSSION

Item session prediction results are shown in Table 1, where we called our method EDRec. From them, we can see that the proposed approach on average outperforms the presented baselines. Specifically in terms of MRR, we observe that the model tends to order the resulting candidates in a more effective way than the other approaches. We hypothesize that the memory component of the recurrent models allows them to retain more effectively the order, and, in the particular case of the proposed encoder-decoder architecture, the use of additional matching mechanisms such as alignment and attention increase the chances of model long term dependencies.

Table 1: Recall and MRR for the different approaches presented and their variations.

Model	Recall@20	MRR@20
Item-KNN	0.327	0.139
BPR-MF	0.310	0.135
GRU4Rec	0.3481	0189
GRU4Rec (cross-entropy)	0.3506	0.207
EDRec	0.3775	0.214
EDRec w/ alignment	0.3905	0.249
EDRec w/ alignment and attention	0.3914	0.231

Regarding the intent estimation, our results show an accuracy of the 67 % when we try to predict the intent in the current session, but it drops to 61.2% when we try to estimate the intent of the next session for a given user. We think these results are caused due to the natural imbalance of the data, as the purchase intent is seen in approximately the 30% of the sessions in the dataset.

We also studied the change in the performance as we increase the amount of data, both in terms of number of feasible items and also number of sessions. In this case, we observed that, on our dataset, initially both GRU4Rec and our approach behave similarly, but when we start using approximately 70% of our dataset, GRU4Rec performance showed no increment, while our model performance kept increasing up to the point we used our entire dataset. We consider that this partial result that could enable a deeper analysis in the future related to the scalability of the models, and how to allow them to keep learning when the possible space of items to predict become extremely large.

Another element worth mentioning is the time associated to the execution of the studied models. In this case, we can see a clear overhead in the proposed approach, requiring up to two times more time to reach convergence. We consider this fact as a natural consequence of the more complex mechanics of the model. Therefore there is an explicit trade-off to be considered.

6 CONCLUSION AND FUTURE WORK

In this work, we proposed an encoder-decoder architecture for modeling user sessions in an e-commerce setting. Our initial study shows that our approach is able to reach state of the art results, while it is flexible enough to incorporate additional task, such as the way we propose to jointly predict the user intent. For future work, we consider necessary extending the scale of the empirical study in order to provide a better support and also explore if more data dimensions could be incorporated to enhance the analysis.

REFERENCES

[1] Martín Abadi, Ashish Agarwal, Paul Barham, Eugene Brevdo, Zhifeng Chen, Craig Citro, Greg S Corrado, Andy Davis, Jeffrey Dean, Matthieu Devin, and others. 2016. Tensorflow: Large-scale machine learning on heterogeneous distributed systems. *arXiv preprint arXiv:1603.04467* (2016).

[2] Dzmitry Bahdanau, Kyunghyun Cho, and Yoshua Bengio. 2014. Neural machine translation by jointly learning to align and translate. *arXiv preprint arXiv:1409.0473* (2014).

[3] Yoshua Bengio, Aaron Courville, and Pascal Vincent. 2013. Representation learning: A review and new perspectives. *IEEE transactions on pattern analysis and machine intelligence* 35, 8 (2013), 1798–1828.

[4] Kyunghyun Cho, Bart Van Merriënboer, Dzmitry Bahdanau, and Yoshua Bengio. 2014. On the properties of neural machine translation: Encoder-decoder approaches. *arXiv preprint arXiv:1409.1259* (2014).

[5] Kyunghyun Cho, Bart Van Merriënboer, Caglar Gulcehre, Dzmitry Bahdanau, Fethi Bougares, Holger Schwenk, and Yoshua Bengio. 2014. Learning phrase representations using RNN encoder-decoder for statistical machine translation. *arXiv preprint arXiv:1406.1078* (2014).

[6] Junyoung Chung, Caglar Gulcehre, KyungHyun Cho, and Yoshua Bengio. 2014. Empirical evaluation of gated recurrent neural networks on sequence modeling. *arXiv preprint arXiv:1412.3555* (2014).

[7] Paul Covington, Jay Adams, and Emre Sargin. 2016. Deep neural networks for youtube recommendations. In *Proceedings of the 10th ACM Conference on Recommender Systems*. ACM, 191–198.

[8] Ian Goodfellow, Yoshua Bengio, and Aaron Courville. 2016. *Deep learning*. MIT Press.

[9] Philippe Hamel and Douglas Eck. 2010. Learning Features from Music Audio with Deep Belief Networks.. In *ISMIR*, Vol. 10. Utrecht, The Netherlands, 339–344.

[10] Balázs Hidasi, Alexandros Karatzoglou, Linas Baltrunas, and Domonkos Tikk. 2015. Session-based recommendations with recurrent neural networks. *arXiv preprint arXiv:1511.06939* (2015).

[11] Balázs Hidasi, Massimo Quadrana, Alexandros Karatzoglou, and Domonkos Tikk. 2016. Parallel Recurrent Neural Network Architectures for Feature-rich Session-based Recommendations. In *Proceedings of the 10th ACM Conference on Recommender Systems (RecSys '16)*. ACM, New York, NY, USA, 241–248. DOI: http://dx.doi.org/10.1145/2959100.2959167

[12] Sepp Hochreiter and Jürgen Schmidhuber. 1997. Long short-term memory. *Neural computation* 9, 8 (1997), 1735–1780.

[13] Diederik Kingma and Jimmy Ba. 2014. Adam: A method for stochastic optimization. *arXiv preprint arXiv:1412.6980* (2014).

[14] César Laurent, Gabriel Pereyra, Philémon Brakel, Ying Zhang, and Yoshua Bengio. 2016. Batch normalized recurrent neural networks. In *Acoustics, Speech and Signal Processing (ICASSP), 2016 IEEE International Conference on*. IEEE, 2657–2661.

[15] Bing Liu and Ian Lane. 2016. Attention-Based Recurrent Neural Network Models for Joint Intent Detection and Slot Filling. *Interspeech 2016* (2016), 685–689.

[16] Steffen Rendle, Christoph Freudenthaler, Zeno Gantner, and Lars Schmidt-Thieme. 2009. BPR: Bayesian personalized ranking from implicit feedback. In *Proceedings of the twenty-fifth conference on uncertainty in artificial intelligence*. AUAI Press, 452–461.

[17] Badrul Sarwar, George Karypis, Joseph Konstan, and John Riedl. 2001. Item-based collaborative filtering recommendation algorithms. In *Proceedings of the 10th international conference on World Wide Web*. ACM, 285–295.

[18] Mike Schuster and Kuldip K Paliwal. 1997. Bidirectional recurrent neural networks. *IEEE Transactions on Signal Processing* 45, 11 (1997), 2673–2681.

[19] Yang Song, Ali Mamdouh Elkahky, and Xiaodong He. 2016. Multi-rate deep learning for temporal recommendation. In *Proceedings of the 39th International ACM SIGIR conference on Research and Development in Information Retrieval*. ACM, 909–912.

[20] Nitish Srivastava, Geoffrey E Hinton, Alex Krizhevsky, Ilya Sutskever, and Ruslan Salakhutdinov. 2014. Dropout: a simple way to prevent neural networks from overfitting. *Journal of Machine Learning Research* 15, 1 (2014), 1929–1958.

[21] Ilya Sutskever, Oriol Vinyals, and Quoc V Le. 2014. Sequence to sequence learning with neural networks. In *Advances in neural information processing systems*. 3104–3112.

[22] Yong Kiam Tan, Xinxing Xu, and Yong Liu. 2016. Improved recurrent neural networks for session-based recommendations. In *Proceedings of the 1st Workshop on Deep Learning for Recommender Systems*. ACM, 17–22.

[23] Aaron Van den Oord, Sander Dieleman, and Benjamin Schrauwen. 2013. Deep content-based music recommendation. In *Advances in neural information processing systems*. 2643–2651.

[24] Oriol Vinyals, Meire Fortunato, and Navdeep Jaitly. 2015. Pointer networks. In *Advances in Neural Information Processing Systems*. 2692–2700.

[25] Hao Wang, Naiyan Wang, and Dit-Yan Yeung. 2015. Collaborative deep learning for recommender systems. In *Proceedings of the 21th ACM SIGKDD International Conference on Knowledge Discovery and Data Mining*. ACM, 1235–1244.

[26] Lei Zheng, Vahid Noroozi, and Philip S. Yu. 2017. Joint Deep Modeling of Users and Items Using Reviews for Recommendation. In *Proceedings of the Tenth ACM International Conference on Web Search and Data Mining (WSDM '17)*. ACM, New York, NY, USA, 425–434. DOI: http://dx.doi.org/10.1145/3018661.3018665

Sequential User-based Recurrent Neural Network Recommendations

Tim Donkers
University of Duisburg-Essen
Duisburg, Germany
tim.donkers@uni-due.de

Benedikt Loepp
University of Duisburg-Essen
Duisburg, Germany
benedikt.loepp@uni-due.de

Jürgen Ziegler
University of Duisburg-Essen
Duisburg, Germany
juergen.ziegler@uni-due.de

ABSTRACT

Recurrent Neural Networks are powerful tools for modeling sequences. They are flexibly extensible and can incorporate various kinds of information including temporal order. These properties make them well suited for generating sequential recommendations. In this paper, we extend Recurrent Neural Networks by considering unique characteristics of the Recommender Systems domain. One of these characteristics is the explicit notion of the user recommendations are specifically generated for. We show how individual users can be represented in addition to sequences of consumed items in a new type of Gated Recurrent Unit to effectively produce personalized next item recommendations. Offline experiments on two real-world datasets indicate that our extensions clearly improve objective performance when compared to state-of-the-art recommender algorithms and to a conventional Recurrent Neural Network.

CCS CONCEPTS

• **Information systems → Recommender systems;** • **Computing methodologies → Artificial intelligence;**

KEYWORDS

Recommender Systems, Deep Learning, Neural Networks, Recurrent Neural Networks, Sequential Recommendations

ACM Reference format:
Tim Donkers, Benedikt Loepp, and Jürgen Ziegler. 2017. Sequential User-based Recurrent Neural Network Recommendations. In *Proceedings of RecSys '17, Como, Italy, August 27-31, 2017,* 9 pages.
https://doi.org/10.1145/3109859.3109877

1 INTRODUCTION

The majority of today's *Recommender Systems* (RS) [41] relies on algorithms that are designed under the assumption that user preferences are static patterns [29, 50]. *Collaborative Filtering* (CF) [28] approaches, both neighborhood- and model-based, have proved immensely useful without any consideration of time. However, assuming consumption events to be independent from each other precludes taking advantage of the temporal dynamics that naturally exist in user behavior [50]. Thus, despite the practical success of time-agnostic models, it seems promising to investigate whether the inclusion of temporal aspects can improve effectiveness. For instance, many commercial goods are only bought during a specific season. Music songs are played in succession according to, among others, the user's current mood or the desire for diversity, and are often arranged in playlists. Fictional series are typically consumed one episode after another, before any other content is considered. In contrast to the conception prevailing in many RS, individual data points used in temporal or sequential recommendations thus cannot be assumed independent and uniformly distributed, as they typically form correlated sequences. Several ways exist to approach this issue, e.g. by extending conventional time-independent algorithms [e.g. 7, 27], integrating time as a contextual factor [e.g. 22, 24], or by applying sequence-based methods primarily used in other domains [e.g. 42]. Still, many approaches ignore that generating recommendations is an inherently time-dependent task and focus only on achieving increasingly accurate predictions.

Compared to other areas, sequence modeling has overall been less explored in RS research due to the long-lasting focus on time-agnostic models. This gap may also be explained by the unique nature of the recommendation problem. Although heavily influenced by Machine Learning [41], many modern techniques successfully applied in other domains cannot easily be transfered to RS. This is particularly true for techniques from a research field currently attracting much attention, *Deep Learning* (DL). DL allows to solve problems of representation learning, i.e. automatically discovering adequate representations of data without manual feature engineering [10]. These representations are expressed in terms of stacked, hierarchically ordered simpler representations. While DL is widely used with considerable success in areas such as Natural Language Processing [6, 11, 12, 33, 36] or Image Processing [16, 30, 47], it has only rarely been applied to the recommendation problem. The few exceptions focus on purposes other than sequential recommending, e.g. using DL as a preprocessing step to conventional techniques [49, 52]. Even if they consider consumption sequences [13, 18, 19, 48, 53, 54], they often have other limitations.

RecSys '17, August 27-31, 2017, Como, Italy

ACM ISBN 978-1-4503-4652-8/17/08...$15.00
https://doi.org/10.1145/3109859.3109877

Recurrent Neural Networks (RNN) represent a specific form of DL models which possess several properties that make them attractive for sequence modeling [10]. In particular, they are capable of incorporating input from past consumption events, allowing to derive a wide range of sequence-to-sequence mappings. In order to consider time as a first class factor for modeling user preferences in RS, RNNs thus constitute a promising family of techniques. One shortcoming of simple variants, however, is the limited number of input variables that can effectively be handled [2]. Gated architectures [6] are designed to overcome this limitation by including gating units trained to control information flow through the network, thereby learning to keep information over a long period of time. Both *Long Short-Term Memory* (LSTM) [9, 20] and *Gated Recurrent Unit* (GRU) [5, 6] networks have shown advantages in real-world applications. Gated RNNs, however, have not been designed with the recommendation domain in mind. In particular, they are not optimized for taking interaction between user and system into account. As mentioned above, first attempts have been made to use DL for sequential recommending [13, 18, 19, 48, 53, 54]. Yet, they tend to reuse standard networks without modifications. As a result, the models usually have no notion about the specification of a target sequence, i.e. that respective RS have no mechanism to consider the fact that a sequence of consumed items is unique to an individual user. The networks treat every single sequence equivalently, thus learning global consumption behavior, but are unable to (deeply) integrate user-specific information.

In this paper, we propose a novel DL approach to address the sequential recommendation problem. First, relying on the benefits of gated RNNs, we model the temporal dynamics of consumption sequences. Second, through a novel gated architecture with additional input layers, we explicitly represent the individual user in such a network. These user-based GRUs are uniquely designed and optimized for the purpose of generating personalized next item recommendations. We theoretically and empirically show that not only out-of-the-box RNNs, but especially our approach using a novel gated architecture, may outperform state-of-the-art recommender algorithms as well as their time-dependent counterparts with respect to objective performance when predicting sequences. Offline experiments conducted on two real-world datasets indicate significant improvements when comparing our approach to common baseline RS algorithms and to a conventional RNN.

The remainder of this paper is organized as follows: First, we discuss relevant work related to sequential recommending and to applying DL in RS research. Second, we present our approach of user-based RNNs for RS. Next, we describe how we evaluated this approach in offline experiments. Finally, we conclude the paper and discuss potential future work.

2 RELATED WORK

User representation in RS is often designed as a statistically stationary process where every expressed preference is assumed to be fixed over time [29, 50]. However, relational data in real-world scenarios are often evolving and exhibit strong temporal patterns [55]. Time may therefore be considered an important contextual dimension also in RS [4]. Generating recommendations in a time-independent manner may in contrast result in estimations of preferences based on user-item relations that are no longer valid. This lack of adaptability with respect to one of the most natural properties of user behavior has motivated several approaches that integrate temporal dynamics[1]. In the following, we discuss the most important ones, and especially those most closely related to ours that also exploit DL techniques as a means to generate sequential recommendations.

2.1 Towards Sequential Recommendations

To adequately reflect user interests, functions that rank items according to some notion of utility are today considered most suitable for generating personalized recommendations [14]. Advances in RS research suggest that implicit feedback thereby often provides more comprehensive and extensive insights into user behavior than explicit ratings [39]. Fitting a static model to data naturally depending on dynamic processes approximates an improper data-generating function [42]. For this reason, several methods exist to incorporate temporal information into RS at some stage, which can be differentiated as follows [50]:

- *Time-aware RS* consider time as a contextual feature during the training phase. Timestamps serve as an additional source of information by which the model is enriched. The rationale behind is that user behavior underlies certain habits and regularities that repeat in regular time intervals, consequently allowing a more accurate prediction of similar patterns in the future.
- *Time-dependent RS* consider user preference data as chronologically ordered sequences, assuming that the most intrinsic property is that time establishes an order of the events. Input is required in chronological form, while exact time spans do not need to be taken into account. The algorithms consequently do not aim at modeling time as being cyclic, but rather at adapting to changes.

Existing time-aware methods include pre- and post-filtering [1] as well as Tensor Factorization [24]. In general, statistical models explicitly designed to predict sequences as used, for example, in automated playlist generation [3], may also be applied. However, they typically do not aim at modeling higher-order long-term dependencies. Eventually, time-dependent RS are conceptually closest to the definition of time used throughout this paper. Therefore, in the following, we focus on attempts that utilize chronological input data. By incrementally training models based on recency, the respective

[1] See one of the extensive surveys for an overview [e.g. 4, 50].

systems may capture, among others, continuous temporal dynamics such as concept drifts [26], changes in item popularity, or virtually any effect observable in sequential data.

Many approaches extend conventional CF techniques, for instance, by translating k-NN methods. In [18], it has been parenthetically shown that an unpersonalized variant of item-based k-NN achieves reasonably good results in sequence prediction tasks. Under an assumption similar to the Markov property, each prediction only depends on the item the user has previously consumed. In [7], a fully personalized time-discounted version has been proposed by extending k-NN with an exponential decaying component that penalizes items consumed a long time ago. Other approaches use time as a means for determining similarities, e.g. when consumption events are close together [17] or lie within a sliding window employed over the most recent sessions [35].

Matrix Factorization (MF) [29] algorithms have also been adapted. For example, baseline predictors can be added to the original framework to account for temporal dynamics [27]. Similar to their time-aware counterparts, sequential MF models have been extended to Tensor Factorization [55]. The dimensions contain time intervals so that the tensor can be seen as a periodic collection of ratings over time. Others have turned the MF problem into a graph-based model [38], integrated a Markov model for predicting the next shopping basket [40], or generalized existing temporal MF approaches to latent time series models [57]. Overall, the variant proposed in [23] comes closest to the definition we use: The authors model temporal order by means of a time window that includes feature vectors of previously consumed items. Thus, both collaborative interactions and time series aspects of the collaborative data can be taken into account.

2.2 Deep Learning in RS Research

The approaches discussed before constitute extensions of established time-agnostic recommendation methods. DL techniques such as RNNs can also be considered useful for sequential recommending as they are specifically designed for modeling temporal aspects. Despite the advantages of such techniques, only few neural network approaches have yet been generally proposed in RS research—most of them not focused on sequential recommendations.

One of the first attempts that only uses a shallow network structure is presented in [43]. Here, two-layered undirected graphical models called Restricted Boltzmann Machines are used to model user ratings for the prediction task. Deep neural networks have in contrast primarily been applied in preprocessing steps to conventional RS techniques. In [49], for instance, features are extracted from unstructured content, here raw music data. These features then serve as input to conventional CF in order to improve its performance. In [52], DL is performed on generic content-based information. The resulting deep feature representation is used as an enhancement to address the sparsity problem occurring in CF. More specific data, e.g. tag-based user and item profiles, have been embedded into a deep feature space in order to approach the hardly controllable dynamics of underlying tag corpora [56]. For that, the authors model similarities between users and potential target items by inferring a deep semantic model. Finally, some approaches actually exploit user interaction behavior. For example, for the purpose of generating adaptive user interfaces, i.e. recommending next actions based on similar interaction patterns found in the user base, GRUs have been used to embed learned interaction patterns together with users and interaction elements [46].

Only few works have yet used DL to explicitly generate sequential recommendations in a self-contained manner. The proposed approaches thereby often only focus on modeling consumption sequences without explicitly representing individual users [13, 18, 19, 48]. For instance, the applicability of the approach presented in [18] is restricted to sessions only. While user representation remains uncovered, the authors introduce a variant of a GRU model that utilizes pair-wise loss functions. In [48], this approach is extended by means of a priori data augmentation in form of sequence preprocessing. In addition, to reduce influence of outdated properties, essentially two models are trained: The first one on the complete dataset, which is then used to initialize the second one subsequently trained only on a subset of newer samples. Only recently, the RNN from [18] has been merged with feature-rich content information [19]: Item one-hot vectors and vectors of extracted features (e.g. corresponding to images of the respective items) are simultaneously treated as input to a GRU layer.

Few exceptions also consider user-related aspects [53, 54], but lack a deep integration of user vectors into the gating process. In [53], the RNN framework is extended by solving two recommendation problems and then merging the outputs: First, information is recurrently extracted from consumed item sequences. Second, specific user concepts are distinguished in a feed-forward manner. As a result, user characteristics are only considered independently from sequence properties. In [54], the authors train individual RNNs to model user and item evolution separately. The outputs from both networks are subsequently coupled with further auxiliary parameters capturing stationary concepts in order to predict user ratings. This architecture requires learning two RNNs such that user and item properties can yet again only loosely be intertwined.

3 USER-BASED RECURRENT NEURAL NETWORKS

Generating sequential recommendations relies on the assumption that individual data points form correlated sequences. Vectorized abstractions of user preferences or behavioral patterns are valuable information sources that can help to improve recommendation quality. In the previous section, we have discussed several existing methods for formalizing a sequential problem in the context of time-dependent recommendations. In the following, we elaborate on how we consider temporal dynamics in RS using DL techniques, and present a novel gated architecture for RNNs using specialized

GRUs that allows us to seamlessly integrate user-related information into the model.

The explicit notion of user information distinguishes our work from other DL approaches proposed for RS that usually focus on consumption sessions without explicitly representing the user. Compared to the few exceptions that already integrate user-related information (see Section 2), our approach is the first to deeply integrate user vectors into the gating process.

3.1 Recurrent Neural Networks for RS

First, for generating sequential recommendations, we need to concretize the generalized, domain-independent formulation of RNNs and transfer it to RS. RNNs, especially when augmented with gating layers, are powerful tools for modeling sequences of any kind[2]. We rely on a variant of RNNs that produces an output $\mathbf{o}^{(t)} \in \mathbb{R}^{|I|}$ at each time step via an affine transformation of the current hidden state $\mathbf{h}^{(t)} \in \mathbb{R}^{n}$:

$$\mathbf{o}^{(t)} = T_{n,|I|}\mathbf{h}^{(t)}, \tag{1}$$

where $T_{k,l} : \mathbb{R}^k \to \mathbb{R}^l$ is an affine transformation of the form $\mathbf{Wx} + \mathbf{b}$. In conventional RNNs, the computation of a hidden state is defined as a function of the previous hidden state and an input vector. In the context of RNNs for RS, we define this input vector $\mathbf{i}^{(t)} \in \{0,1\}^{|I|}$ as a one-hot vector where the only index different from zero corresponds to the index of a particular item.

3.2 User-based Gated Recurrent Units

Now, in order to integrate user characteristics into the model, we first define a one-hot user variable $\boldsymbol{\upsilon}^{(t)} \in \{0,1\}^{|\Upsilon|}$ with Υ being the set of users. We assume the data to be comprised of user-item tuples such that $\boldsymbol{\upsilon}$ can be interpreted as an indicator of the user consuming item $\mathbf{i}$ at a certain time step t in the sequence. Based on this, we extend the original definition (see [e.g. 6]) of the hidden state:

$$\mathbf{h}^{(t)} = f(\mathbf{h}^{(t-1)}, \mathbf{i}^{(t)}, \boldsymbol{\upsilon}^{(t)}; \boldsymbol{\theta}) \tag{2}$$

The network's predictive power may benefit from explicitly memorizing concepts about the user inside the recurrent cells. In the following, we discuss several realizations of (2) that architecturally modify the original recurrent unit[3]. By incorporating a user variable $\boldsymbol{\upsilon}^{(t)}$, we can thus deeply integrate user-related information into the network.

3.2.1 Linear User Integration. Linear user integration is comparable to strategies of considering context for gated units. For instance, in [34], word-related topic vectors are incorporated into a neural network language model to improve performance. Similarly, $\boldsymbol{\upsilon}^{(t)}$ can be viewed as an additional input layer that is connected to the gated units. Thereby, it can influence decisions about forgetting certain pieces of information or updating hidden states:

$$\begin{bmatrix}\mathbf{u}\\ \mathbf{r}\end{bmatrix} = \begin{bmatrix}\sigma\\ \sigma\end{bmatrix} T_{3n,2n} \begin{bmatrix}\mathbf{h}^{(t-1)}\\ \mathbf{E}_i\mathbf{i}^{(t)}\\ \mathbf{E}_\upsilon\boldsymbol{\upsilon}^{(t)}\end{bmatrix}, \tag{3}$$

where σ is the logistic sigmoid. $\mathbf{E}_i \in \mathbb{R}^{|I|\times n}$ and $\mathbf{E}_\upsilon \in \mathbb{R}^{|\Upsilon|\times n}$ are embedding matrices that map one-hot vectors into a densified information space. This kind of densification via projection is widely applied in DL research (see [e.g. 32, 33]).

While the gating processes inside the hidden units deal with temporal aspects of the data, non-temporal structures can be exploited by including embedding. In the embedded space, items that appear in similar contexts are also spatially close. For notational simplicity, we assume that the embedding dimension is equal to the hidden dimension n although this does not necessarily has to be the case.

Besides influencing update and reset gates, the user vector can also be included in the calculation of hidden states. For this, we first calculate a state update vector $\mathbf{k} \in \mathbb{R}^n$:

$$\begin{aligned}\mathbf{k} = \tanh(\, & T_{n,n}\,\mathbf{r} \odot \mathbf{h}^{(t-1)}\\ & + T_{n,n}\mathbf{E}_i\mathbf{i}^{(t)}\\ & + T_{n,n}\mathbf{E}_\upsilon\boldsymbol{\upsilon}^{(t)}\,),\end{aligned} \tag{4}$$

where tanh is the hyperbolic tangent and $\odot$ represents element-wise multiplication.

Subsequently, we can leakily integrate $\mathbf{k}$ into the hidden state update mechanism subject to $\mathbf{u}$:

$$\mathbf{h}^{(t)} = (1_n - \mathbf{u}) \odot \mathbf{h}^{(t-1)} + \mathbf{u} \odot \mathbf{k}, \tag{5}$$

where 1_n is a vector of ones.

While $\mathbf{i}^{(t)}$ changes with every time step, consumption sequences are unique to only a single user, i.e. $\boldsymbol{\upsilon}^{(t)}$ remains constant. Generalized properties of each item in the sequence relate to the consuming user by feeding back succeeding losses to parameters conditioned by this particular $\boldsymbol{\upsilon}^{(t)}$. As a result, trained user-related parameters are representing superordinate concepts. This means, parameters corresponding to $\boldsymbol{\upsilon}^{(t)}$ express the user's general preference structure. Figure 1 depicts such a linear user GRU cell.

3.2.2 Rectified Linear User Integration. The linear integration of $\boldsymbol{\upsilon}^{(t)}$ allows the recurrent cell to condition the activation based on user characteristics. However, repeatedly applying the same user vector increases redundancy that might lead to undesired effects like higher sensitivity to underfitting and non-zero predictions for all user-item pairs since the particular network parameters are trained with respect to unchanging input over a long series of steps.

Furthermore, user-related parameters might not be equally important at every step in time. Some recommendations might be sufficiently derived only based on item vectors without considering a user component. For example, one can assume that users will consume all parts of a movie trilogy in a row. Thus, cells should learn to selectively set focus on different parts of the user representation. We use a leaky

[2] For a general introduction to RNNs, please refer to [e.g. 31].
[3] We use GRUs due to notational simplicity, although all principles can easily be transferred to LSTM in analogous form.

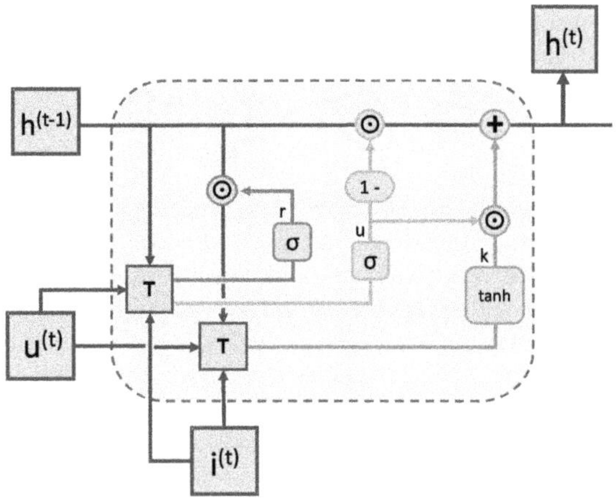

Figure 1: Linear user-based GRU cell: In addition to the item input vector i, the user representation $\boldsymbol{v}$ is included.

integrator inspired by rectified linear units [15] to attach weight to the transformed components of $\boldsymbol{v}^{(t)}$:

$$(\mathbf{E}_v \boldsymbol{v}^{(t)})_l \leftarrow \begin{cases} 0, & \text{if } (\mathbf{E}_v \boldsymbol{v}^{(t)})_l < \kappa_{1,l} \\ \omega(\mathbf{E}_v \boldsymbol{v}^{(t)})_l, & \text{if } \kappa_{1,l} < (\mathbf{E}_v \boldsymbol{v}^{(t)})_l < \kappa_{2,l} \\ (\mathbf{E}_v \boldsymbol{v}^{(t)})_l, & \text{else} \end{cases}, \tag{6}$$

where l refers to a particular entry of vector $\mathbf{E}_v \boldsymbol{v}^{(t)}$. $\boldsymbol{\kappa}_1 \in \mathbb{R}^n$ and $\boldsymbol{\kappa}_2 \in \mathbb{R}^n$ are threshold parameter vectors conditioned on previous hidden state as well as item and user vector:

$$\begin{bmatrix} \boldsymbol{\kappa}_1 \\ \boldsymbol{\kappa}_2 \end{bmatrix} = T_{3n,2n} \begin{bmatrix} \mathbf{h}^{(t-1)} \\ \mathbf{E}_i \mathbf{i}^{(t)} \\ \mathbf{E}_v \boldsymbol{v}^{(t)} \end{bmatrix} \tag{7}$$

The thresholds dynamically ensure that only relevant parts of the user representation are exploited to produce network output. User-specific concepts can thus be shut off if there is reason to assume that the current input should be handled independently. Note that very important concepts, i.e. high values in $\mathbf{E}_v \boldsymbol{v}^{(t)}$, are only discarded if there is a strong indication of orthogonality, i.e. high values for $\boldsymbol{\kappa}_1$.

In cases where a component is only important to a certain degree, i.e. $\kappa_{1,l} < (\mathbf{E}_v \boldsymbol{v}^{(t)})_l < \kappa_{2,l}$, it might be advantageous not to turn it off completely, but only to limit its throughput. For this purpose, we also integrate a leaky variant with $\omega \in [0, 1]$. Update and reset cells are then calculated according to (3) with the filtered user component. The leaky integrator is included in the cell shown in Figure 2.

3.2.3 Attentional User Integration. As already derived in Section 3.2.1, the user component represents stable concepts as opposed to the current input vector $\mathbf{i}^{(t)}$ that rather expresses short-term aspects. The rectified linear user integration is only designed to impede the user component when necessary. As an alternative, the network could adaptively shift focus between user and item aspects. For instance, the

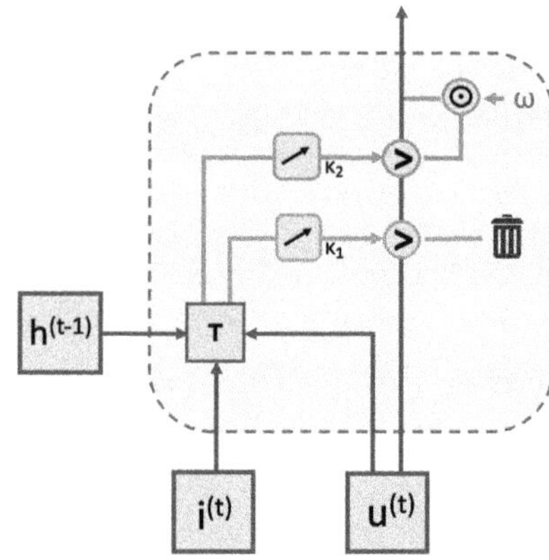

Figure 2: The rectified linear gating process detached from the complete cell: Item and user vectors as well as previous hidden state are concatenated and mapped linearly twice in order to calculate κ_1 and κ_2. Components of the user vector that are element-wise smaller than the corresponding values in κ_1 are discarded. Components smaller than κ_2 are diminished by element-wise multiplication with ω.

user component's influence should be low at $t=0$ when no information about the user is present, and progressively increase afterwards as the sequence is further propagated. Moreover, at times, a consumed item might be out of the ordinary and would decrease succeeding estimation quality. In such cases, resorting to a stable user representation and excluding the outlier could attenuate or even annul its impact.

We therefore propose an adaptive approach that includes a new kind of gated cell that regulates the gating process. Let $\boldsymbol{\xi} \in \mathbb{R}^n$ be the attentional regulation gate:

$$\boldsymbol{\xi} = \sigma(T_{n,n}\mathbf{h}^{(t-1)} + T_{n,n}\mathbf{E}_i \mathbf{i}^{(t)} + T_{n,n}\mathbf{E}_v \boldsymbol{v}^{(t)}) \tag{8}$$

We use logistic sigmoid as a squashing function to leakily regulate the proportion of item and user focus. In contrast to a linear user-based GRU cell, item and user vectors are now weighted by $\boldsymbol{\xi}$:

$$\begin{bmatrix} \mathbf{u} \\ \mathbf{r} \end{bmatrix} = \begin{bmatrix} \sigma \\ \sigma \end{bmatrix} T_{3n,2n} \begin{bmatrix} \mathbf{h}^{(t-1)} \\ (1_n - \boldsymbol{\xi}) \odot \mathbf{E}_i \mathbf{i}^{(t)} \\ \boldsymbol{\xi} \odot \mathbf{E}_v \boldsymbol{v}^{(t)} \end{bmatrix} \tag{9}$$

Furthermore, the hidden state's update mechanism is not only dependent on $\mathbf{i}^{(t)}$ and $\boldsymbol{v}^{(t)}$, but also on $\boldsymbol{\xi}$:

$$\begin{aligned} \mathbf{k} = \tanh(& T_{n,n}\, \mathbf{r} \odot \mathbf{h}^{(t-1)} \\ & + T_{n,n}\, (1_n - \boldsymbol{\xi}) \odot \mathbf{E}_i \mathbf{i}^{(t)} \\ & + T_{n,n}\, \boldsymbol{\xi} \odot \mathbf{E}_v \boldsymbol{v}^{(t)}) \end{aligned} \tag{10}$$

The state update vector $\mathbf{k}$ is then integrated analogously to (5). In contrast to (4), the attentional gate $\boldsymbol{\xi}$ now acts as a leaky integrator that can choose to completely ignore the user aspect (extremely low sigmoids) or simply copy it (extremely high sigmoids), see Figure 3. Informally speaking, the gate regulates the extent to which users are considered as opposed to items. Note that parameters for the attention gate should be initialized with values close to zero such that the network behaves similar to a standard GRU at the beginning of the training phase, and then may gradually shift focus. Thus, the network will not explicitly focus on the user component until it has learned to do so.

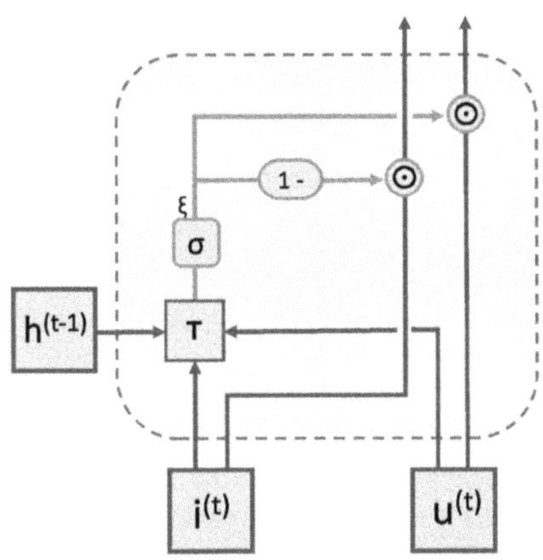

Figure 3: The attentional layer ξ detached from the complete cell: Item and user vectors as well as previous hidden state are concatenated and mapped with sigmoid squashing to form a gate that controls information flow between item and user component. Low sigmoids increase the throughput of item-related components, high sigmoids support the user side.

4 EVALUATION

To objectively justify our theoretical models derived in the previous section, we conducted several offline experiments. In particular, we aimed at answering the question how our novel user-based RNN approach with its different variants to deeply integrate user information performs on the sequential recommendation task when compared to a conventional RNN as well as state-of-the-art recommendation techniques.

Hence, we compared our three user-based networks (i.e. using linear, rectified linear, and attentional user integration) with a standard GRU network without any of our proposed extensions[4]. We also considered the following baselines: We trained time-independent item-based k-NN as well as its time-dependent exponentially decaying counterpart [7]. Moreover, using the BPR learning criterion [39], we trained a standard MF [29] as well as a sequential MF [23] variant.

4.1 Methodology

In the following, we describe the evaluation metrics and datasets we used, as well as the algorithmic setup.

[4]We implemented the different variants using *TensorFlow* (https://www.tensorflow.org/), an open source software framework especially designed for building deep neural networks as data flow graphs. For all experiments, we used ECP P2 instances provided by *Amazon Web Services* (https://aws.amazon.com/), which are powerful scalable instances designed for GPU-based operations using CUDA.

4.1.1 Metrics. Based on temporally ordered lists of consumed items, our objective is to correctly predict the next item a target user will likely consume. The ground truth at a particular time step is therefore represented by a single user-item tuple. To present the user with adequate recommendations, the target item should be among the first few recommended items. In accordance with recent RS research, we thus use the following evaluation metrics:

- MRR@k (*Mean Reciprocal Rank*) is defined as the average of the reciprocal ranks of the desired items [51]. The rank is set to zero if it is above k.
- *Recall@k* is defined as the fraction of cases where the item actually consumed in the next event is among the top k items recommended [37].

We set $k = 20$, as it appears desirable from a user's perspective to expect the target among the first 20 items [18].

4.1.2 Datasets. We ran our approach as well as all the baselines on the following two real-world datasets:

- *MovieLens 10M:* The MovieLens 10M dataset[5] consists of 10 000 054 ratings assigned to 10 681 movies by 71 567 users. In order to mimic implicit data, we binarized all ratings independent of their value, considering them as positive feedback as it has been done in [e.g. 39]. Using the timestamps provided, we thus got an ordered sequence of consumption events for each user. The dataset contains only sequences with a minimum length of 20, making further preprocessing of the training set unnecessary. The average sequence length is 115. We aimed at predicting the next movie to watch.
- *LastFM 1K Users:* The LastFM 1K Users dataset[6] contains user-timestamp-artist-song tuples collected via the LastFM API. The dataset has a total of 19 150 868 data points for 992 users. Due to computational reasons we performed our evaluation on a 10 % subsample. The resulting average sequence length is 1 738. We aimed at predicting the next song title.

We split each dataset into three parts: First, the major fraction of every sequence serves as training data. Second, we use a validation set during training to measure performance on unseen data. These validation results determine, for instance, early stopping used in the learning phase to avoid overfitting [21]. Third, we use a distinct test set to measure actual performance after learning is completed. The training set consists of the first 90 % of every user consumption sequence. The remaining 10 % of each sequence are split evenly into validation and test set while maintaining the order. As it is common practice in RS research, items not seen during training are filtered out from validation and test set.

4.1.3 Hyperparameter and Network Setup. Table 1 shows all hyperparameters we set for our experiments based on extensive pretesting with grid search.

For the RNN variants, we propagate mini-batch based learning with batch size of 1000. We use shallow networks

[5]https://grouplens.org/datasets/movielens/
[6]http://www.dtic.upf.edu/~ocelma/MusicRecommendationDataset/

Table 1: Hyperparameter values for all algorithms used in our experiments on the two datasets.

Parameter	Value	Parameter	Value
Item-based k-NN		**General GRU**	
Nearest Neighbors	100	Batch size	1000
Exp. Dec. Item-based k-NN		Layers	1
Decaying Constant	1	Hidden Units	1000
Matrix Factorization		Unfold Dimension	20
Latent Factors	20	Dropout	0.8
Iterations	30	Gradient Cap	5.0
Learning Rate	0.01	Iterations	10
Seq. Matrix Factorization		Learning Rate	0.001
Window Size	2	**User-based GRU**	
		User Dropout	0.5

Table 2: MRR@20 and Recall@20 for all baselines as well as our proposed user-based RNN variants.

	MovieLens		LastFM	
	MRR@20	Recall@20	MRR@20	Recall@20
Baselines				
Item-based k-NN	0.036 39	0.121 42	0.044 38	0.101 26
Exp. Dec. Item-based k-NN	0.042 31	0.128 53	0.055 94	0.167 24
Matrix Factorization	0.011 92	0.077 44	0.032 89	0.127 23
Seq. Matrix Factorization	0.015 50	0.107 30	0.027 69	0.112 24
Standard GRU	0.047 30	0.157 73	0.143 74	0.202 69
User-based RNN				
Linear User-based GRU	0.052 51	0.160 28	0.182 52	0.249 20
Rectified Linear User-based GRU	0.059 01	0.186 97	**0.191 54**	0.254 09
Attentional User-based GRU	**0.062 55**	**0.205 40**	0.187 31	**0.254 85**

of depth 1 with hidden dimensionality 1000 that is unfolded for 20 time steps. Stacking multiple hidden recurrent layers on top of each other to create depth [8, 12, 44] did not improve overall performance in our pretests. According to [36], depth in RNNs introduces capabilities to represent different timescales. When trained on the datasets we used, the networks however did not seem to benefit from this property.

For regularization, we apply Dropout [58] with a keep probability of 0.8 for item and 0.5 for user vectors. We use a gradient cap of 5.0 to clip large gradients that might otherwise lead to skip over minima. Furthermore, we introduce a L^2 parameter norm penalty on user side in order to control for redundancy. Its contribution weight is set to 0.01. Regarding the matrices embedding the one-hot encoded input vectors, we set the dimension equal to the hidden dimension. Weight matrices and biases are initialized randomly with values drawn from $[-0.1, 0.1]$. We run training for 10 iterations.

Linear and attentional user integration do not require setting any further parameters. In case of rectified linear user integration, grid search indicated to set $\omega = 0.2$, i.e. diminished user-related concepts are only considered by 20 % of their original magnitude.

Pretests also indicated that the RNNs are trained best with Adam optimizer [25] using a learning rate of 0.001 against Cross Entropy loss. For this, we normalize output vectors $\mathbf{o}^{(t)}$ via softmax function in order to produce a valid probability distribution.

4.2 Results

Table 2 shows the results received after training the baselines as well as our DL models on both datasets.

The RNNs yield results superior to the baselines in terms of both metrics. On the MovieLens dataset, there is a substantial gain in objective performance compared to the next best baseline. Namely, there is an improvement of 12 % in MRR@20 and 23 % in Recall@20, respectively, when comparing exponentially decaying item-based k-NN to the standard GRU. On the LastFM dataset, the differences in ranking quality become even more apparent (at least 157 % improvement in terms of MRR@20, 21 % in Recall@20).

Integrating user information significantly improves statistical power in GRU networks. All user-based RNN variants outperform the standard GRU network that does not consider user information. In particular, the integration variant that performs best in terms of MRR@20, i.e. attentional on the MovieLens and rectified linear on the LastMF dataset, leads to an improvement of 32 % or 33 %, respectively. For Recall@20, there is similar gain with results 30 % better on the MovieLens, and 28 % better on the LastFM dataset.

Taking a closer look at the results for the user-based RNNs, attentional user integration achieves the overall best results. Only on the LastFM dataset, MRR@20 is slightly lower than for the rectified linear variant. In all other cases, the attentional realization outperforms the others.

Finally, concerning the baselines, item-based k-NN is better at modeling sequences than MF. Even sequential MF achieves clearly inferior results than the original item-based k-NN without any temporal extensions. As a side note, while the temporal item-based k-NN generally outperforms its time-independent counterpart, sequential MF seems not beneficial compared to standard MF on the LastFM dataset.

4.3 Discussion

Overall, the results indicate that RNNs clearly outperform other recommending approaches when it comes to generating sequential recommendations. As earlier experiments by others suggested [e.g. 18, 48], even out-of-the-box RNNs achieve superior results with respect to widely used evaluation metrics when compared to state-of-the-art item-based k-NN or MF approaches. This is particularly true for their derivatives specifically extended to consider temporal effects.

By deeply integrating user information, we were able to personalize the sequence prediction task. The experiments suggest that our networks are able to learn the implicit relations between events more effectively when passing in externally encoded information about users. Nonetheless, the advantages of exploiting temporal dynamics in combination with user information seem to depend on the background data. For instance, the relative performance gain is much higher on the LastFM than on the MovieLens dataset. Considering the nature of the datasets, this is however not surprising: During one session, users generally listen to more than one song in a row, e.g. they consume playlists or whole albums at once, and factors such as the user's mood determine which title is likely to be consumed next. Thus, similar to the underlying grammar in Natural Language Processing, there exist inherent dependencies between succeeding events that can be exploited. Such relations are much less obvious when recommending movies as people in this case generally do not consume multiple items in immediate succession. Furthermore, sequences in the MovieLens dataset can be considered more artificially, as they do not describe actual consumption events at certain points in time, but reproduce the process of actively providing feedback in form of ratings. Still, there seem to be some implicit connections between the events that can be captured by the networks: Even with such a dataset, RNNs achieve superior results for predicting the next item compared to baseline techniques.

Regarding the different variants of user integration, rectified linear and attentional realization yield generally better results than the linear one. This indicates that regulating redundancy of user input in fact appears to be beneficial. The mechanism seems to support cells in controlling information flow more accurately. In both of the advanced variants, influence of the user variable can be diminished when necessary, thus restricting its impact and preventing overgeneralization. Thereby, it is important to note that integrating user information does not come along with considerably higher runtime requirements. In particular, the user-based RNNs can be trained in almost same amount of time as a standard GRU network. For instance, on the MovieLens dataset the number of processed input tuples per second was on average 24 917 for the Standard GRU, 22 887 for the Linear User-based GRU, 22 840 for the Rectified Linear User-based GRU, and 22 822 for the Attentional User-based GRU. In general, as earlier work on RNNs in RS research has shown [e.g. 18], training the models with sufficient computational power can be done in reasonable time.

5 CONCLUSIONS AND OUTLOOK

With the rise of DL in the past decade, RNNs have become practical and powerful tools for large-scale supervised learning of sequences. This progress has become most apparent in Natural Language Processing where they have set several new benchmarks outperforming techniques that have been considered state-of-the-art for a long time. Similar to other works, the promising results from our experiments show that RNNs allow to take a novel perspective on applications such as RS that were originally designed in a time-agnostic manner. Our novel approach proposed in this paper allows generating personalized suggestions while time is considered as a first class factor, thereby significantly improving recommendation quality. The way we formulate RNNs enables us to model user behavior and to capture dependencies between consumption events more adequately than with established recommendation techniques that often fail at appropriately representing temporal dynamics in user interests.

Gated recurrent networks have set records in accuracy on many tasks in recent years. Noteworthy, these advances result from novel or extended architectures rather than from fundamentally novel algorithms [31, 45]. This also applies to our user-based RNNs: We essentially adopted the original architecture to take the unique characteristics of the recommendation domain into account. Our specific extensions have then shown to increase statistical expressiveness: Deeply integrating a user representation leads to significant improvements when predicting user behavior such as watching movies or listening to music. Including a user-specific layer, the networks seem capable of learning concepts that are unique to a certain user. Since changing inputs are related to a user vector that remains constant over the course of a particular sequence, the networks learn to represent global user concepts explicitly, rather than implicitly as it would be the case in conventional gated units. Hence, the networks can distinguish between user preferences more accurately.

We have presented a DL-based framework that is particularly designed to generate personalized next item recommendations, thereby independent of techniques used in contemporary RS research. In future work, we plan to additionally integrate state-of-the-art recommendation techniques such as MF into the design space of RNNs, e.g. in form of contextual variables. By this means, we would be able to combine the best of both worlds while also extending the scope of applicability. Also, this might be helpful for better supporting situations where the user's consumption sequence is rather short, e.g. at cold-start. Moreover, we aim at taking varying time intervals into account. RNNs are designed for modeling sequential data with no notion of time spans between succeeding events. Especially for recommendation tasks, however, time deltas can be extremely valuable information. For instance, if two consumption events are distant from each other, the first item might not be a good predictor because user preference likely has changed over time. In this context, a comparison with statistical models particularly designed for predicting sequences would also be of interest. Finally, as interactive approaches are more and more discussed in RS research, it seems promising to examine ways of increasing control and transparency also in DL-based RS.

REFERENCES

[1] L. Baltrunas and X. Amatriain. 2009. Towards time-dependant recommendation based on implicit feedback. In *CARS '09*.

[2] Y. Bengio, P. Frasconi, and P. Simard. 1993. The problem of learning long-term dependencies in recurrent networks. In *ICNN '93*. IEEE, 1183–1188.

[3] G. Bonnin and D. Jannach. 2015. Automated generation of music playlists: Survey and experiments. *ACM Comput Surv* 47, 2 (2015), 26:1–26:35.

[4] P. G. Campos, F. Díez, and I. Cantador. 2014. Time-aware recommender systems: A comprehensive survey and analysis of existing evaluation protocols. *User Model User-Adap* 24, 1-2 (2014), 67–119.

[5] K. Cho, B. Van Merriënboer, D. Bahdanau, and Y. Bengio. 2014. On the properties of neural machine translation: Encoder-decoder approaches. In *SSST '14*.

[6] J. Chung, C. Gulcehre, K. Cho, and Y. Bengio. 2014. Empirical evaluation of gated recurrent neural networks on sequence modeling. In *Deep Learning Workshop at NIPS '14*.

[7] Y. Ding and X. Li. 2005. Time weight collaborative filtering. In *CIKM '05*. ACM, 485–492.

[8] S. El Hihi and Y. Bengio. 1995. Hierarchical recurrent neural networks for long-term dependencies. In *NIPS '95*. 493–499.

[9] F. Gers. 2001. *Long short-term memory in recurrent neural networks.* Ph.D. Dissertation. University of Hannover.
[10] I. Goodfellow, Y. Bengio, and A. Courville. 2016. *Deep learning.* MIT Press.
[11] A. Graves. 2013. Generating sequences with recurrent neural networks. (2013).
[12] A. Graves, A. Mohamed, and G. Hinton. 2013. Speech recognition with deep recurrent neural networks. In *ICASSP '13.* IEEE, 6645–6649.
[13] A. Greenstein-Messica, L. Rokach, and M. Friedman. 2017. Session-based recommendations using item embedding. In *IUI '17.* ACM, 629–633.
[14] A. Gunawardana and G. Shani. 2009. A survey of accuracy evaluation metrics of recommendation tasks. *J Mach Learn Res* 10 (2009), 2935–2962.
[15] K. He, X. Zhang, S. Ren, and J. Sun. 2015. Delving deep into rectifiers: Surpassing human-level performance on imagenet classification. In *ICCV '15.* 1026–1034.
[16] K. He, X. Zhang, S. Ren, and J. Sun. 2016. Deep residual learning for image recognition. In *CVPR '16.* IEEE, 770–778.
[17] C. Hermann. 2010. Time-based recommendations for lecture materials. In *EdMedia '10.* 1028–1033.
[18] B. Hidasi, A. Karatzoglou, L. Baltrunas, and D. Tikk. 2015. Session-based recommendations with recurrent neural networks. In *ICLR '16.*
[19] B. Hidasi, M. Quadrana, A. Karatzoglou, and D. Tikk. 2016. Parallel recurrent neural network architectures for feature-rich session-based recommendations. In *RecSys '16.* ACM, 241–248.
[20] S. Hochreiter and J. Schmidhuber. 1997. Long short-term memory. *Neural Comput* 9, 8 (1997), 1735–1780.
[21] T. Hofmann. 2001. Unsupervised learning by probabilistic latent semantic analysis. *Mach Learn* 42, 1-2 (2001), 177–196.
[22] T. Hussein, T. Linder, W. Gaulke, and J. Ziegler. 2014. Hybreed: A software framework for developing context-aware hybrid recommender systems. *User Model User-Adap* 24, 1-2 (2014), 121–174.
[23] A. Karatzoglou. 2011. Collaborative temporal order modeling. In *RecSys '11.* ACM, 313–316.
[24] A. Karatzoglou, X. Amatriain, L. Baltrunas, and N. Oliver. 2010. Multiverse recommendation: N-dimensional tensor factorization for context-aware collaborative filtering. In *RecSys '10.* ACM, 79–86.
[25] D. Kingma and J. Ba. 2015. Adam: A method for stochastic optimization. In *ICLR '15.*
[26] R. Klinkenberg and T. Joachims. 2000. Detecting concept drift with support vector machines. In *ICML '00.* Morgan Kaufmann, 487–494.
[27] Y. Koren. 2010. Collaborative filtering with temporal dynamics. *Commun ACM* 53, 4 (2010), 89–97.
[28] Y. Koren and R. Bell. 2015. *Recommender systems handbook.* Springer, Chapter Advances in collaborative filtering, 77–118.
[29] Y. Koren, R. Bell, and C. Volinsky. 2009. Matrix factorization techniques for recommender systems. *IEEE Computer* 42, 8 (2009), 30–37.
[30] A. Krizhevsky, I. Sutskever, and G. E. Hinton. 2012. Imagenet classification with deep convolutional neural networks. In *NIPS '12.* 1097–1105.
[31] Z. C. Lipton, J. Berkowitz, and C. Elkan. 2015. A critical review of recurrent neural networks for sequence learning. (2015).
[32] T. Mikolov, K. Chen, G. Corrado, and J. Dean. 2013. Efficient estimation of word representations in vector space. *Workshop at ICLR '13.*
[33] T. Mikolov, I. Sutskever, K. Chen, G. S. Corrado, and J. Dean. 2013. Distributed representations of words and phrases and their compositionality. In *NIPS '13.* 3111–3119.
[34] T. Mikolov and G. Zweig. 2012. Context dependent recurrent neural network language model. In *SLT '12.* 234–239.
[35] O. Nasraoui, J. Cerwinske, C. Rojas, and F. Gonzalez. 2007. Performance of recommendation systems in dynamic streaming environments. In *SDM '07.* SIAM, 569–574.
[36] R. Pascanu, C. Gulcehre, K. Cho, and Y. Bengio. 2014. How to construct deep recurrent neural networks. In *ICLR '14.*
[37] D. M. Powers. 2011. Evaluation: From precision, recall and F-measure to ROC, informedness, markedness and correlation. *J Mach Learn Tech* 2, 1 (2011), 37–63.
[38] S. Rallapalli, L. Qiu, Y. Zhang, and Y.-C. Chen. 2010. Exploiting temporal stability and low-rank structure for localization in mobile networks. In *MobiCom '10.* ACM, 161–172.
[39] S. Rendle, C. Freudenthaler, Z. Gantner, and L. Schmidt-Thieme. 2009. BPR: Bayesian personalized ranking from implicit feedback. In *UAI '09.* AUAI Press, 452–461.
[40] S. Rendle, C. Freudenthaler, and L. Schmidt-Thieme. 2010. Factorizing personalized Markov chains for next-basket recommendation. In *WWW '10.* ACM, 811–820.
[41] F. Ricci, L. Rokach, and B. Shapira. 2015. *Recommender systems handbook* (2nd ed.). Springer.
[42] N. Sahoo, P. V. Singh, and T. Mukhopadhyay. 2012. A hidden Markov model for collaborative filtering. *MIS Quarterly* 36, 4 (2012), 1329–1356.
[43] R. Salakhutdinov, A. Mnih, and G. E. Hinton. 2007. Restricted Boltzmann machines for collaborative filtering. In *ICML '07.* ACM, 791–798.
[44] J. Schmidhuber. 1992. Learning complex, extended sequences using the principle of history compression. *Neural Comput* 4, 2 (1992), 234–242.
[45] J. Schmidhuber. 2015. Deep learning in neural networks: An overview. *Neural Networks* 61 (2015), 85–117.
[46] H. Soh, S. Sanner, M. White, and G. Jamieson. 2017. Deep sequential recommendation for personalized adaptive user interfaces. In *IUI '17.* ACM, 589–593.
[47] C. Szegedy, W. Liu, Y. Jia, P. Sermanet, S. Reed, D. Anguelov, D. Erhan, V. Vanhoucke, and A. Rabinovich. 2015. Going deeper with convolutions. In *CVPR '15.* IEEE, 1–9.
[48] Y. K. Tan, X. Xu, and Y. Liu. 2016. Improved recurrent neural networks for session-based recommendations. In *DLRS '16.* ACM, 17–22.
[49] A. van den Oord, S. Dieleman, and B. Schrauwen. 2013. Deep content-based music recommendation. In *NIPS '13.* 2643–2651.
[50] J. Vinagre, A. M. Jorge, and J. Gama. 2015. An overview on the exploitation of time in collaborative filtering. *Data Min Knowl Disc* 5, 5 (2015), 195–215.
[51] E. M. Voorhees. 1999. The TREC-8 question answering track report. In *TREC '99.* 77–82.
[52] H. Wang, N. Wang, and D.-Y. Yeung. 2015. Collaborative deep learning for recommender systems. In *KDD '15.* ACM, 1235–1244.
[53] C. Wu, J. Wang, J. Liu, and W. Liu. 2016. Recurrent neural network based recommendation for time heterogenous feedback. *Knowl-Based Syst* 109 (2016), 90–103.
[54] C.-Y. Wu, A. Ahmed, A. Beutel, A. J. Smola, and H. Jing. 2017. Recurrent recommender networks. In *WSDM '17.* ACM, 495–503.
[55] L. Xiong, X. Chen, T.-K. Huang, J. Schneider, and J. Carbonell. 2010. Temporal collaborative filtering with bayesian probabilistic tensor factorization. In *SDM '10.* SIAM, 211–222.
[56] Z. Xu, C. Chen, T. Lukasiewicz, Y. Miao, and X. Meng. 2016. Tag-aware personalized recommendation using a deep-semantic similarity model with negative sampling. In *CIKM '16.* ACM, 1921–1924.
[57] H.-F. Yu, N. Rao, and I. S. Dhillon. 2015. High-dimensional time series prediction with missing values. (2015).
[58] W. Zaremba, I. Sutskever, and O. Vinyals. 2014. Recurrent neural network regularization. (2014).

Translation-based Recommendation

Ruining He
UC San Diego
r4he@cs.ucsd.edu

Wang-Cheng Kang
UC San Diego
wckang@eng.ucsd.edu

Julian McAuley
UC San Diego
jmcauley@cs.ucsd.edu

ABSTRACT

Modeling the complex interactions between users and items as well as amongst items themselves is at the core of designing successful recommender systems. One classical setting is predicting users' personalized sequential behavior (or 'next-item' recommendation), where the challenges mainly lie in modeling 'third-order' interactions between a user, her previously visited item(s), and the next item to consume. Existing methods typically decompose these higher-order interactions into a combination of *pairwise* relationships, by way of which user preferences (user-item interactions) and sequential patterns (item-item interactions) are captured by separate components. In this paper, we propose a unified method, *TransRec*, to model such third-order relationships for large-scale sequential prediction. Methodologically, we embed items into a 'transition space' where users are modeled as *translation* vectors operating on item sequences. Empirically, this approach outperforms the state-of-the-art on a wide spectrum of real-world datasets. Data and code are available at https://sites.google.com/a/eng.ucsd.edu/ruining-he/.

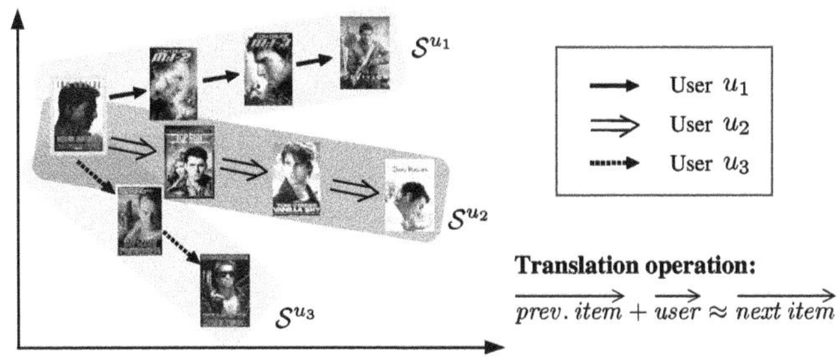

Figure 1: *TransRec* as a sequential model: Items (movies) are embedded into a 'transition space' where each user is modeled by a *translation* vector. The transition of a user from one item to another is captured by a user-specific translation operation. Here we demonstrate the historical sequences S^{u_1}, S^{u_2}, and S^{u_3} of three users. Given the same starting point, the movie *Mission: Impossible I*, u_1 went on to watch the whole series, u_2 continued to watch drama movies by Tom Cruise, and u_3 switched to similar action movies.

1 INTRODUCTION

Modeling and predicting the *interactions* between users and items, as well as the *relationships* amongst the items themselves are the main tasks of recommender systems. For instance, in order to predict *sequential* user actions like the next product to purchase, movie to watch, or place to visit, it is essential (and challenging!) to model the *third-order* interactions between a user (u), the item(s) she recently consumed (i), and the item to visit next (j). Not only does the model need to handle the complexity of the interactions themselves, but also the scale and inherent sparsity of real-world data.

Traditional recommendation methods usually excel at modeling two-way (i.e., pairwise) interactions. There are Matrix Factorization (MF) techniques [8] that make use of inner products to model the compatibility between user-item pairs (i.e., user preferences). Likewise, there are also (first-order) Markov Chain (MC) models [23] that capture transition relationships between pairs of adjacent items in sequences (i.e., sequential dynamics), often by way of factorizing the transition matrix in favor of generalization ability. For the task of sequential recommendation, researchers have made use of scalable tensor factorization methods, such as Factorized Personalized Markov Chains (FPMC) proposed by Rendle *et al.* [20]. FPMC models third-order relationships between u, i, and j by the *summation* of two pairwise relationships: one for the compatibility between u and the next item j, and another for the sequential continuity between the previous item i and the next item j. Ultimately, this is a combination of MF and MC (see Section 3.5 for details).

Recently, there have been two lines of works that aim to improve FPMC. Personalized metric embedding methods replace the inner products in FPMC with Euclidean distances, where the metricity assumption—especially the triangle inequality—enables the model to generalize better [4, 13, 28]. However, these works still adopt the framework of modeling the user preference component and sequential continuity component separately, which may be disadvantageous as the two components are inherently correlated.

Another line of work [26] makes use of operations like average/max pooling to *aggregate* the representations of the user u and the previous item i, before their compatibility with the next item j is measured. These works partially address the issue of modeling the dependence of the two key components, though are hard to interpret and can not benefit from the generalization ability of metric embeddings.

In this paper, we aim to tackle the above issues by introducing a new framework called *Translation-based Recommendation* (*TransRec*). The key idea behind *TransRec* is presented in Figure 1: Items are embedded as points in a (latent) 'transition space'; each user is represented as a 'translation vector' in the same space. Then, the third-order interactions mentioned earlier are captured by a personalized translation operation: the coordinates of previous item i, plus the translation vector of u determine (approximately) the coordinates of the next item j, i.e., $\vec{\gamma}_i + \vec{t}_u \approx \vec{\gamma}_j$. Finally, we

RecSys'17, August 27–31, 2017, Como, Italy.
 ISBN 978-1-4503-4652-8/17/08...$15.00.
DOI: http://dx.doi.org/10.1145/3109859.3109882

model the compatibility of the (u, i, j) triplet with a distance function $d(\vec{\gamma}_i + \vec{t}_u, \vec{\gamma}_j)$. At prediction time, recommendations can be via nearest-neighbor search centered at $\vec{\gamma}_i + \vec{t}_u$.

The advantages of such an approach are three-fold: (1) *TransRec* naturally models third-order interactions with only a *single* component; (2) *TransRec* also enjoys the generalization benefits from the implicit metricity assumption; and (3) *TransRec* can easily handle large sequences (e.g., millions of instances) due to its simple form. Empirically, we conduct comprehensive experiments on a wide range of large, real-world datasets (which are publicly available), and quantitatively demonstrate the superior recommendation performance achieved by *TransRec*.

In addition to the sequential prediction task, we also investigate the strength of *TransRec* at tackling item-to-item recommendation where pairwise relations between items need to be captured, e.g., suggesting a shirt to match a previously purchased pair of pants. State-of-the-art works for this task are mainly based on metric or non-metric embeddings (e.g., [5, 11]). We empirically evaluate *TransRec* on eight large co-purchase datasets from *Amazon* and find it to significantly outperform multiple state-of-the-art models by using the translation structure.

Finally, we introduce a new large, sequential prediction dataset, from *Google Local*, that contains a large corpus of ratings and reviews on millions of businesses around the world.

2 RELATED WORK

General recommendation. Traditional approaches to recommendation ignore sequential signals in the system. Such systems focus on modeling user preferences, and typically rely on Collaborative Filtering (CF) techniques, especially Matrix Factorization (MF) [22]. For implicit feedback data (like purchases, clicks, and thumbs-up), point-wise and pairwise methods based on MF have been proposed. Point-wise methods (e.g., [6, 16, 17]) assume all non-observed feedback to be negative and factorize the user-item feedback matrix. In contrast, pairwise methods (e.g., [18, 19, 21]) make a weaker assumption that users simply prefer observed feedback over unobserved feedback and optimize the pairwise rankings of (positive, non-positive) pairs.

Modeling temporal dynamics. Several works extend general recommendation models to make use of timestamps associated with feedback. For example, early similarity-based CF (e.g., [3]) uses time weighting schemes that assign decaying weights to previously-rated items when computing similarities. More recent efforts are mostly based on MF, where the goal is to model and understand the historical *evolution* of users and items, e.g., Koren *et al.* achieved state-of-the-art rating prediction results on *Netflix* data, largely by exploiting temporal signals [7, 8]. The sequential prediction task we are tackling is related to the above, except that instead of directly using those timestamps, it focuses on learning the sequential relationships between user actions (i.e., it focuses on the *order* of actions rather than the specific time).

Sequential recommendation. Scalable sequential models usually rely on Markov Chains (MC) to capture sequential patterns (e.g., [4, 20, 26]). Rendle *et al.* proposed to factorize the third-order 'cube' that represents the transitions amongst items made by users. The resulting model, Factorized Personalized Markov Chains (FPMC), can be seen as a combination of MF and MC and achieves good performance for next-basket recommendation.

Table 1: Notation

Notation	Explanation
$\mathcal{U}, \mathcal{I}$	user set, item set
u, i, j	user $u \in \mathcal{U}$, items $i, j \in \mathcal{I}$
$\mathcal{S}^u$	historical sequence of user u: $(\mathcal{S}^u_1, \mathcal{S}^u_2, \cdots, \mathcal{S}^u_{\lvert\mathcal{S}^u\rvert})$
Φ	transition space; $\Phi = \mathbb{R}^K$
Ψ	a subspace in Φ; $\Psi \subseteq \Phi$
$\vec{\gamma}_i$	embedding vector associated with item i; $\vec{\gamma}_i \in \Psi$
$\vec{t}$	(global) translation vector $\vec{t} \in \Phi$
$\vec{t}_u$	translation vector associated with user u; $\vec{t}_u \in \Phi$
$\vec{T}_u$	$\vec{T}_u = \vec{t} + \vec{t}_u$; $\vec{T}_u \in \Phi$
β_i	bias term associated with item i; $\beta_i \in \mathbb{R}$
$\vec{f}_i$	explicit feature vectors associated with item i
$d(x, y)$	distance between x and y

There are also works that have adopted metric embeddings for the recommendation task, leading to better generalization ability. For example, Chen *et al.* introduced Logistic Metric Embeddings (LME) for music playlist generation [2], where the Markov transitions among different songs are encoded by the distances among them. Recently, Feng *et al.* further extended LME to model personalized sequential behavior and used pairwise ranking for predicting next points-of-interest [4]. On the other hand, Wang *et al.* recently introduced the Hierarchical Representation Model (HRM), which extends FPMC by applying aggregation operations (like max/average pooling) to model more complex interactions. We will give more details of these works in Section 3.5.2.

Our work differs from the above in that we introduce a *translation*-based structure which naturally models the third-order interactions between a user, the previous item, and the next item for personalized Markov transitions.

Knowledge bases. Although different from recommendation, there has been a large body of work in knowledge bases that focuses on modeling multiple, complex relationships between various entities. Recently, partially motivated by the findings made by word2vec [12], translation-based methods (e.g., [1, 10, 27]) have achieved state-of-the-art accuracy and scalability, in contrast to those achieved by traditional embedding methods relying on tensor decomposition or collective matrix factorization (e.g., [14, 15, 24]). Our work is inspired by those findings, and we tackle the challenges from modeling large-scale, personalized, and complicated sequential data. This is the first work that explores this direction to the best of our knowledge.

3 THE TRANSLATION-BASED MODEL

3.1 Problem Formulation

We refer to the objects that users ($\mathcal{U}$) interact with in the system as items ($\mathcal{I}$), e.g., products, movies, or places. The *sequential*, or 'next-item,' prediction task we are tackling is formulated as follows. For each user $u \in \mathcal{U}$ we have a sequence of items $\mathcal{S}^u = (\mathcal{S}^u_1, \mathcal{S}^u_2, \cdots, \mathcal{S}^u_{\lvert\mathcal{S}^u\rvert})$ that u has interacted with. Given the sequence set from all users $\mathcal{S} = \{\mathcal{S}^{u_1}, \mathcal{S}^{u_2}, \cdots, \mathcal{S}^{u_{\lvert\mathcal{U}\rvert}}\}$, our objective is to predict the next item to be 'consumed' by each user and generate recommendation lists accordingly. Notation used throughout the paper is summarized in Table 1.

3.2 The Proposed Model

We aim to build a model that (1) naturally captures personalized sequential behavior, and (2) easily scales to large, real-world datasets. Methodologically, we learn a transition space $\Phi = \mathbb{R}^K$, where each item i is represented with a point/vector $\vec{\gamma}_i \in \Phi$. $\vec{\gamma}_i$ can be *latent*, or transformed from certain explicit features of item i, e.g., the output of a neural network. In this paper we take $\vec{\gamma}_i$ as latent vectors.

Recall that the historical sequence $\mathcal{S}^u$ of user u is a series of transitions u has made from one item to another. To model the *personalized* sequential behavior, we represent each user u with a *translation* vector $\vec{t}_u \in \Phi$ to capture u's inherent intent or 'long-term preferences' that influenced her to make these decisions. In particular, if u transitioned from item i to item j, what we want is

$$\vec{\gamma}_i + \vec{t}_u \approx \vec{\gamma}_j,$$

which means $\vec{\gamma}_j$ should be a nearest neighbor of $\vec{\gamma}_i + \vec{t}_u$ in Φ according to some distance metric $d(x, y)$, e.g., $\mathcal{L}_1$ distance.

Note that we are uncovering a metric space where (1) *neighborhood* captures the notion of similarity and (2) *translation* encapsulates various semantically complex transition relationships amongst items. In both cases, the inherent triangle inequality assumption plays an important role in helping the model to generalize well, as it does in canonical metric learning scenarios. For instance, if users tend to transition from item A to two items B and C, then *TransRec* will also put B close to C. This is a desirable property especially when data sparsity is a major concern. One plausible alternative is to use the inner product of $\vec{\gamma}_i + \vec{t}_u$ and $\vec{\gamma}_j$ to model their 'compatibility.' However, this way item B and C in our above example might be far from each other because inner products do not guarantee the triangle inequality condition.

Due to the sparsity of real-world datasets, it might not be affordable to learn separate translation vectors $\vec{t}_u$ for each user. Therefore we add another translation vector $\vec{t}$ to capture 'global' transition dynamics across all users, and we let

$$\vec{T}_u = \vec{t} + \vec{t}_u.$$

This way $\vec{t}_u$ can be seen as an offset vector associated with user u. Although doing so yields no additional expressive power,[1] the advantage is that $\vec{t}_u$'s of *cold-start* users will be regularized towards 0 and we are essentially using $\vec{t}$—the 'average' behavior—to make predictions for these users.

Finally, the probability that a given user u transitions from the previous item i to the next item j is predicted by

$$\begin{aligned} &Prob(j \mid u, i) \propto \beta_j - d(\vec{\gamma}_i + \vec{T}_u, \vec{\gamma}_j), \\ &\text{subject to} \quad \vec{\gamma}_i \in \Psi \subseteq \Phi, \quad \text{for } i \in \mathcal{I}. \end{aligned} \tag{1}$$

Ψ is a subspace in Φ, e.g., a unit ball, a technique which has been shown to be helpful for mitigating 'curse of dimensionality' issues (e.g., [1, 10, 27]). In the above equation a single bias term β_j is added to capture overall item popularity.

[1]Note that we can still learn personalized sequential behavior as users are being parameterized separately.

Ranking Optimization. Given a user and the associated historical sequence, the ultimate goal of the task is to rank the ground-truth item j higher than all other items ($j' \in \mathcal{I} \setminus j$). Therefore it is a natural choice to optimize the pairwise ranking between j and j' by (e.g.) Sequential Bayesian Personalized Ranking (S-BPR) [20]. To this end, we optimize the total order $>_{u,i}$ given the user u and the previous item i in the sequence:

$$\begin{aligned} \widehat{\Theta} &= \arg\max_{\Theta} \ \ln \prod_{u \in \mathcal{U}} \prod_{j \in \mathcal{S}^u} \prod_{j' \notin \mathcal{S}^u} Prob(j >_{u,i} j' | \Theta)\, Prob(\Theta) \\ &= \arg\max_{\Theta} \sum_{u \in \mathcal{U}} \sum_{j \in \mathcal{S}^u} \sum_{j' \notin \mathcal{S}^u} \ln \sigma(\widehat{p}_{u,i,j} - \widehat{p}_{u,i,j'}) - \Omega(\Theta), \end{aligned} \tag{2}$$

where i is the preceding item[2] of j in $\mathcal{S}^u$, $\widehat{p}_{u,i,j}$ is a shorthand for the prediction in Eq. (1), Θ is the parameter set $\{\beta_{i \in \mathcal{I}}, \vec{\gamma}_{i \in \mathcal{I}}, \vec{t}_{u \in \mathcal{U}}, \vec{t}\}$, and $\Omega(\Theta)$ is an $\mathcal{L}_2$ regularizer. Note that according to S-BPR, the probability that the ground-truth item j is ranked higher than a 'negative' item j' (i.e., $Prob(j >_{u,i} j' | \Theta)$) is estimated by the sigmoid function $\sigma(\widehat{p}_{u,i,j} - \widehat{p}_{u,i,j'})$.

3.3 Inferring the Parameters

Initialization. Item embeddings $\vec{\gamma}_{i \in \mathcal{I}}$ and $\vec{t}$ are randomly initialized to be unit vectors. $\beta_{i \in \mathcal{I}}$ and $\vec{t}_{u \in \mathcal{U}}$ are initialized to be zero.

Learning Procedure. The objective function (Eq. (2)) is maximized by stochastic gradient ascent: First, we uniformly sample a user u from $\mathcal{U}$. Then, a 'positive' item j and a 'negative' item j' are uniformly sampled from $\mathcal{S}^u \setminus \mathcal{S}^u_1$ and $\mathcal{I} \setminus \mathcal{S}^u$ respectively. Next, parameters are updated via stochastic gradient ascent:

$$\Theta \leftarrow \Theta + \epsilon \cdot \left(\sigma(\widehat{p}_{u,i,j'} - \widehat{p}_{u,i,j}) \frac{\partial(\widehat{p}_{u,i,j} - \widehat{p}_{u,i,j'})}{\partial \Theta} - \lambda_\Theta \cdot \Theta \right),$$

where ϵ is the learning rate and λ_Θ is a regularization hyperparameter. Finally, we re-normalize $\vec{\gamma}_i$, $\vec{\gamma}_j$, and $\vec{\gamma}_{j'}$ to be vectors in Ψ. For example, if we let Ψ be the unit $\mathcal{L}_2$-ball, then $\vec{\gamma} \leftarrow \vec{\gamma}/\max(1, \|\vec{\gamma}\|)$. The above steps are repeated until convergence or until the accuracy plateaus on the validation set.

3.4 Nearest Neighbor Search

At test time, recommendation can be made via nearest neighbor search. A small challenge lies in handling bias terms: First, we replace β_j with $\beta'_j = \beta_j - \max_{k \in \mathcal{I}} \beta_k$ for $j \in \mathcal{I}$. Shifting the bias terms does not change the ranking of items for any query. Next, we absorb β'_j into $\vec{\gamma}_j$ and get $\vec{\gamma}'_j = (\vec{\gamma}_j; \sqrt{-\beta'_j})$ for (squared) $\mathcal{L}_2$ distance, or $\vec{\gamma}'_j = (\vec{\gamma}_j; \beta'_j)$ for $\mathcal{L}_1$ distance. Finally, given a user u and an item i, we obtain the 'query' coordinate $(\vec{\gamma}_i + \vec{T}_u; 0)$, which can then be used for retrieving nearest neighbors in the space of $\vec{\gamma}'_j$.

3.5 Connections to Existing Models

3.5.1 Knowledge Graphs. Our method is inspired by recent advances in knowledge graph completion, e.g., [1, 10, 25, 27, 29], where the objective is to model multiple types of relations between pairs of entities, e.g., Turing was born in England ('was_born_in' is the relation between 'Turing' and 'England'). One state-of-the-art technique (e.g., [1, 10, 27]) is embedding entities as points and relations as *translation* vectors such that the relationship between

[2]Here j can not be the first item in the sequence $\mathcal{S}^u$ as it has no preceding item.

two entities is captured by the corresponding translation operation. In the previous example, if we represent 'Turing,' 'England,' and 'was_born_in' with vectors $\overrightarrow{head}$, $\overrightarrow{tail}$, and $\overrightarrow{relation}$ respectively, then the following is desired: $\overrightarrow{head} + \overrightarrow{relation} \approx \overrightarrow{tail}$.

In recommendation settings, items are analogous to 'entities' in knowledge graphs. Our key idea is to represent each user as one particular type of 'relation' such that it captures the personalized reasons a user transitions from one item to another.

3.5.2 Sequential Models. State-of-the-art sequential prediction models are typically based on (personalized) Markov Chains. FPMC is a seminal model proposed by [20], whose predictor consists of two key components: (1) the inner product of user and item factors (capturing users' inherent preferences), and (2) the inner product of the factors of the previous and next item (capturing sequential dynamics). FPMC is essentially the combination of MF and factorized MC:

$$Prob(j \mid u, i) \propto \langle \vec{M}_u, \vec{N}_j \rangle + \langle \vec{P}_i, \vec{Q}_j \rangle, \tag{3}$$

where user embeddings $\vec{M}_u$ and item embeddings $\vec{N}_j$, $\vec{P}_i$, $\vec{Q}_j$ are parameters learned from the data.

Recently, Personalized Ranking Metric Embedding (PRME) [4] was proposed to improve FPMC by learning two metric spaces: one for measuring user-item affinity and another for sequential continuity. It predicts according to:

$$Prob(j \mid u, i) \propto -\left(\alpha \cdot \|\vec{M}_u - \vec{N}_j\|_2^2 + (1-\alpha) \cdot \|\vec{P}_i - \vec{P}_j\|_2^2\right), \tag{4}$$

which replaces inner products in FPMC by distances. As argued in [2, 4], the underlying metricity assumption brings better generalization ability. However, like FPMC, PRME still has to learn two closely *correlated* components in a separate manner, using a hyperparameter α to balance them.

Another recent work, Hierarchical Representation Model (HRM) [26], tries to extend FPMC by using an *aggregation* operation (max/average pooling) to blend users' preferences ($\vec{M}_u$) and their recent activities ($\vec{N}_i$):

$$Prob(j \mid u, i) \propto \langle \text{aggregation}(\vec{M}_u, \vec{N}_i), \vec{N}_j \rangle. \tag{5}$$

Although the predictor can be seen as modeling the third-order interactions with a single component, the aggregation is hard to interpret and does not reap the benefits of using metric embeddings as PRME does.

TransRec also falls into the category of Markov Chain models; however, it applies a novel *translation*-based structure in a metric space, which enjoys the benefits of using a single, interpretable component as well as a metric space.

4 EXPERIMENTS

4.1 Datasets and Statistics

To fully evaluate the capability and applicability of *TransRec*, in our experiments we include a wide range of publicly available datasets varying significantly in domain, size, data sparsity, and variability/complexity.

Table 2: Statistics (in ascending order of item density).

Dataset	#users ($\vert\mathcal{U}\vert$)	#items ($\vert\mathcal{I}\vert$)	#actions	avg. #actions /user	avg. #actions /item
Epinions	5,015	8,335	26,932	5.37	3.23
Automotive	34,316	40,287	183,573	5.35	4.56
Google	350,811	505,516	2,591,026	7.39	5.13
Office	16,716	22,357	128,070	7.66	5.73
Toys	57,617	69,147	410,920	7.13	5.94
Clothing	184,050	174,484	1,068,972	5.81	6.13
Cellphone	68,330	60,083	429,231	6.28	7.14
Games	31,013	23,715	287,107	9.26	12.11
Electronics	253,996	145,199	2,109,879	8.31	14.53
Foursquare	43,110	13,335	306,553	7.11	22.99
Flixter	69,485	25,759	8,000,971	115.15	310.61
Total	**1.11M**	**1.09M**	**15.5M**	-	-

Amazon.[3] The first group of datasets, comprising large corpora of reviews and timestamps on various products, were recently introduced by [11]. These data are originally from *Amazon.com* and span May 1996 to July 2014. Top-level product categories on *Amazon* were constructed as separate datasets by [11]. In this paper, we take a series of large categories including 'Automotive,' 'Cell Phones and Accessories,' 'Clothing, Shoes, and Jewelry,' 'Electronics,' 'Office Products,' 'Toys and Games,' and 'Video Games.' This set of data is notable for its high sparsity and variability.

Epinions.[4] This dataset was collected by [30] from *Epinions.com*, a popular online consumer review website. The reviews span January 2001 to November 2013.

Foursquare.[5] Is originally from *Foursquare.com*, containing a large number of check-ins of users at different venues from December 2011 to April 2012. This dataset was collected by [9] and is widely used for evaluating next point-of-interest prediction methods.

Flixter.[6] A large, dense movie rating dataset from *Flixter.com*. The timespan is from November 2005 to November 2009.

Google Local. We introduce a new dataset from *Google* which contains 11,453,845 reviews and ratings from 4,567,431 users on 3,116,785 local businesses (with detailed name, hours, phone number, address, GPS, etc.). There are as many as 48,013 categories of local businesses distributed over five continents, ranging from restaurants, hotels, parks, shopping malls, movie theaters, schools, military recruiting offices, bird control, mediation services (etc.). Figure 2 shows the number of reviews and businesses associated with each of the top 1,000 popular categories. The vast vocabulary of items, variability, and data sparsity make it a challenging dataset to examine the effectiveness of our model. Although not the goal of our study, this is also a potentially useful dataset for location-based recommendation.

For each of the above datasets, we discard users and items with fewer than 5 associated actions in the system. In cases where star-ratings are available, we take all of them as users' positive feedback,

[3]http://jmcauley.ucsd.edu/data/amazon/
[4]http://jmcauley.ucsd.edu/data/epinions/
[5]https://archive.org/details/201309_foursquare_dataset_umn
[6]http://www.cs.ubc.ca/~jamalim/datasets/

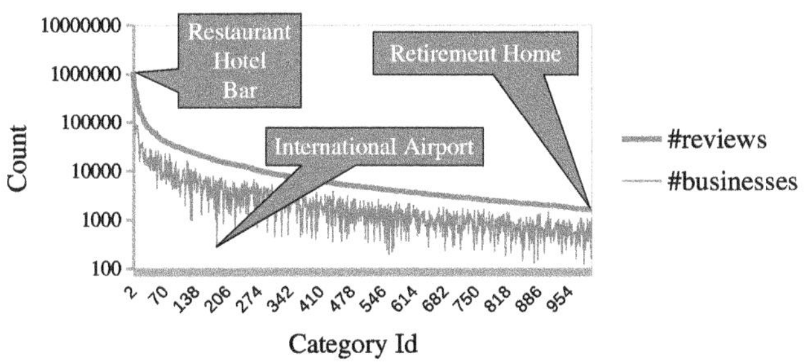

Figure 2: Number of reviews and local businesses associated with the top 1,000 popular categories from *Google Local*.

since we are dealing with implicit feedback settings and care about purchases/check-in actions (etc.) rather than the specific ratings. Statistics (after pre-processing) are shown in Table 2.

4.2 Comparison Methods

PopRec: This is a naïve baseline that ranks items according to their popularity, i.e., it recommends the most popular items to users and is not personalized.
Bayesian Personalized Ranking (BPR-MF) [19]: BPR-MF is a state-of-the-art item recommendation model which takes Matrix Factorization as the underlying predictor. It ignores the sequential signals in the system.
Factorized Markov Chain (FMC): Captures the 'global' sequential dynamics by factorizing the item-to-item transition matrix (shared by all users), but does not capture personalized behavior.
Factorized Personalized Markov Chain (FPMC) [20]: Uses a predictor that combines Matrix Factorization and factorized Markov Chains so that personalized Markov behavior can be captured (see Eq. (3)).
Personalized Ranking Metric Embedding (PRME) [4]: PRME models personalized Markov behavior by the summation of two Euclidean distances (see Eq. (4)).
Hierarchical Representation Model (HRM) [26]: HRM extends FPMC by using aggregation operations like max pooling to model more complex interactions (see Eq. (5)). We compare against HRM with both max pooling and average pooling, denoted by HRM_{max} and HRM_{avg} respectively.
Translation-based Recommendation (*TransRec*): Our method, which unifies user preferences and sequential dynamics with translations. In experiments we try both $\mathcal{L}_1$ and squared $\mathcal{L}_2$ distance [7] for our predictor (see Eq. (1)).

Table 3 examines the properties of different methods. The ultimate goal of the baselines is to demonstrate (1) the performance achieved by state-of-the-art sequentially-unaware item recommendation models (BPR-MF) and purely sequential models without modeling personalization (FMC); (2) the benefits of combining personalization and sequential dynamics in a 'linear' (FPMC) and non-linear way (HRM), or using metric embeddings (PRME); and (3) the strength of *TransRec* using translations.

[7] Note that this can be seen as optimizing an $\mathcal{L}_2$ distance space, similar to the approach used by PRME [4].

Table 3: Models. P: Personalized? S: Sequentially-aware? M: Metric-based? U: Unified model of third-order relations?

Property	PopRec	BPR-MF	FMC	FPMC	HRM	PRME	*TransRec*
P	✘	✔	✘	✔	✔	✔	✔
S	✘	✘	✔	✔	✔	✔	✔
M	✘	✘	✘	✘	✘	✔	✔
U	✘	✘	✘	✘	✔	✘	✔

4.3 Evaluation Methodology

For each dataset, we partition the sequence $\mathcal{S}^u$ for each user u into three parts: (1) the most recent one $\mathcal{S}^u_{|\mathcal{S}^u|}$ for test, (2) the second most recent one $\mathcal{S}^u_{|\mathcal{S}^u|-1}$ for validation, and (3) all the rest for training. Hyperparameters in all cases are tuned by grid search with the validation set. Finally, we report the performance of each method on the test set in terms of the following ranking metrics:
Area Under the ROC Curve (AUC):

$$AUC = \frac{1}{|\mathcal{U}|} \sum_{u \in \mathcal{U}} \frac{1}{|\mathcal{I} \setminus \mathcal{S}^u|} \sum_{j' \in \mathcal{I} \setminus \mathcal{S}^u} \mathbf{1}(R_{u,g_u} < R_{u,j'}),$$

Hit Rate at position 50 (Hit@50):

$$Hit@50 = \frac{1}{|\mathcal{U}|} \sum_{u \in \mathcal{U}} \mathbf{1}(R_{u,g_u} \le 50),$$

where g_u is the 'ground-truth' item associated with user u at the most recent time step, $R_{u,i}$ is the rank of item i for user u (smaller is better), and $\mathbf{1}(b)$ is an indicator function that returns 1 if the argument b is *true*; 0 otherwise.

4.4 Performance and Quantitative Analysis

Results are collated in Table 4. Due to the sparsity of most of the datasets in consideration, the number of dimensions K of all latent vectors in all cases is set to 10 for simplicity; we investigate the importance of the number of dimensions in our parameter study later. Note that in Table 4 datasets are ranked in ascending order of item density. The last column (%Improv.) demonstrates the percentage improvement of *TransRec* over the strongest baseline for each dataset. The main findings are summarized as follows:

BPR-MF and FMC achieve considerably better results than the popularity-based baseline in most cases, in spite of modeling personalization and sequential patterns in isolation. This means that uncovering the underlying user-item and item-item relationships is key to making meaningful recommendations.

FPMC and HRM are essentially combinations of MF and FMC. FPMC beats BPR-MF and FMC mainly on relatively dense datasets like *Toys*, *Foursquare*, and *Flixter*, and loses on sparse datasets—possibly due to the large number of parameters it introduces. From Table 4 we see that HRM achieves strong results amongst all baselines in most cases, presumably from the aggregation operations.

PRME replaces the inner products in FPMC by distance functions. It beats FPMC in most cases, though loses to HRM due to different modeling strategies. Note that like FPMC, PRME turns out to be quite strong at handling dense datasets like *Foursquare* and *Flixter*. We speculate that the two models could benefit from

Table 4: Ranking results on different datasets (higher is better). The number of latent dimensions K for all comparison methods is set to 10. The best performance in each case is underlined. The last column shows the percentage improvement of *TransRec* over the best baseline.

Dataset	Metric	PopRec	BPR-MF	FMC	FPMC	HRM_{avg}	HRM_{max}	PRME	$\text{TransRec}_{\mathcal{L}_1}$	$\text{TransRec}_{\mathcal{L}_2}$	%Improv.
Epinions	*AUC*	0.4576	0.5523	0.5537	0.5517	0.6060	0.5617	0.6117	0.6063	0.6133	0.3%
	Hit@50	3.42%	3.70%	3.84%	2.93%	3.44%	2.79%	2.51%	3.18%	4.63%	20.6%
Automotive	*AUC*	0.5870	0.6342	0.6438	0.6427	0.6704	0.6556	0.6469	0.6779	0.6868	2.5%
	Hit@50	3.84%	3.80%	2.32%	3.11%	4.47%	3.71%	3.42%	5.07%	5.37%	20.1%
Google	*AUC*	0.5391	0.8188	0.7619	0.7740	0.8640	0.8102	0.8252	0.8359	0.8691	0.6%
	Hit@50	0.32%	4.27%	3.54%	3.99%	3.55%	4.59%	5.07%	6.37%	6.84%	32.5%
Office	*AUC*	0.6427	0.6979	0.6867	0.6866	0.6981	0.7005	0.7020	0.7186	0.7302	4.0%
	Hit@50	1.66%	4.09%	2.66%	2.97%	5.50%	4.17%	6.20%	6.86%	6.51%	10.7%
Toys	*AUC*	0.6240	0.7232	0.6645	0.7194	0.7579	0.7258	0.7261	0.7442	0.7590	0.2%
	Hit@50	1.69%	3.60%	1.55%	4.41%	5.25%	3.74%	4.80%	5.46%	5.44%	4.0%
Clothing	*AUC*	0.6189	0.6508	0.6640	0.6646	0.7057	0.6862	0.6886	0.7047	0.7243	2.6%
	Hit@50	1.11%	1.05%	0.57%	0.51%	1.70%	1.15%	1.00%	1.76%	2.12%	24.7%
Cellphone	*AUC*	0.6959	0.7569	0.7347	0.7375	0.7892	0.7654	0.7860	0.7988	0.8104	2.7%
	Hit@50	4.43%	5.15%	3.23%	2.81%	8.77%	6.32%	6.95%	9.46%	9.54%	8.8%
Games	*AUC*	0.7495	0.8517	0.8407	0.8523	0.8776	0.8566	0.8597	0.8711	0.8815	0.4%
	Hit@50	5.17%	10.93%	13.93%	12.29%	14.44%	12.86%	14.22%	16.61%	16.44%	15.0%
Electronics	*AUC*	0.7837	0.8096	0.8158	0.8082	0.8212	0.8148	0.8337	0.8457	0.8484	1.8%
	Hit@50	4.62%	2.98%	4.15%	2.82%	4.09%	2.59%	3.07%	4.89%	5.19%	12.3%
Foursquare	*AUC*	0.9168	0.9511	0.9463	0.9479	0.9559	0.9523	0.9565	0.9631	0.9651	0.9%
	Hit@50	55.60%	60.03%	63.00%	64.53%	60.75%	61.60%	65.32%	66.12%	67.09%	2.7%
Flixter	*AUC*	0.9459	0.9722	0.9568	0.9718	0.9695	0.9687	0.9728	0.9727	0.9750	0.2%
	Hit@50	11.92%	21.58%	22.23%	33.11%	32.34%	30.88%	40.81%	35.52%	35.02%	-13.0%

the considerable amount of additional parameters they use when data is dense.

TransRec outperforms other methods in nearly all cases. The improvements seem to be correlated with:

Variability. *TransRec* achieves large improvements (32.5% and 24.7% in terms of Hit@50) on *Google* and *Clothing*, two datasets with the largest vocabularies of items in our collection. Taking *Google* as an example, it includes all kinds of restaurants, bars, shops (etc.) as well as a global user base, which requires the ability to handle the vast variability.

Sparsity. *TransRec* beats all baselines especially on comparatively sparser datasets like *Epinions*, *Automotive*, and *Google*. The only exception is in terms of Hit@50 on *Flixter*, the *densest* dataset in consideration. We speculate that *TransRec* is at a disadvantage by using fewer parameters (than PRME) especially when K is set to a small number (10). As we demonstrate in Section 4.6, we can achieve comparable results with the strongest baseline when increasing the model dimensionality.

In addition, we empirically find that (squared) $\mathcal{L}_2$ distance typically outperforms $\mathcal{L}_1$ distance, though the latter also beats baselines in most cases.

4.5 Convergence

In Figure 3 we demonstrate (test) AUCs with increasing training iterations on four datasets with varying sparsity—*Automotive*, *Electronics*, *Foursquare*, and *Flixter*. *Automotive* is representative of sparse datasets in our collection. Simple baselines like FMC and BPR-MF converge faster than other methods on sparse datasets, presumably due to the relatively simpler dynamics they capture. FPMC also converges fast on such datasets as a result of its tendency to overfit (recall that we terminate once no further improvements are achieved on the validation set). On denser datasets like *Electronics*, *Foursquare*, and *Flixter*, all methods tend to converge at comparable speeds due to the need to unravel denser relationships amongst different entities.

4.6 Sensitivity

For the three densest datasets—*Electronics*, *Foursquare*, and *Flixter*—we also experimented with different numbers of dimensions for user/item representations. We increase K from 10 to 100 and present AUC and Hit@50 values on the test set in Figure 4. *TransRec* still dominates other methods on *Electronics* and *Foursquare*. As for *Flixter*, from the rightmost subfigure we can see that in terms of Hit@50 the gap between *TransRec* ($\mathcal{L}_2$) and PRME, the strongest baseline on this data, closes as we increase the dimensionality.

4.7 Implementation Details

To make fair comparisons, we used stochastic gradient ascent to optimize pairwise rankings for all models (except PopRec) with a fixed learning rate of 0.05. Regularization hyperparamters are selected from $\{0, 0.001, 0.01, 0.1, 1\}$ (using the validation set). We did not make use of the dropout technique mentioned in the HRM

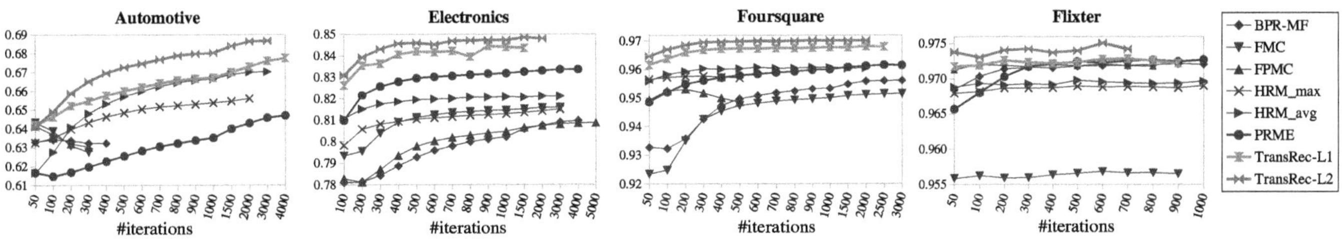

Figure 3: Convergence: Test AUCs on four datasets as the number of training iterations increases (K = 10).

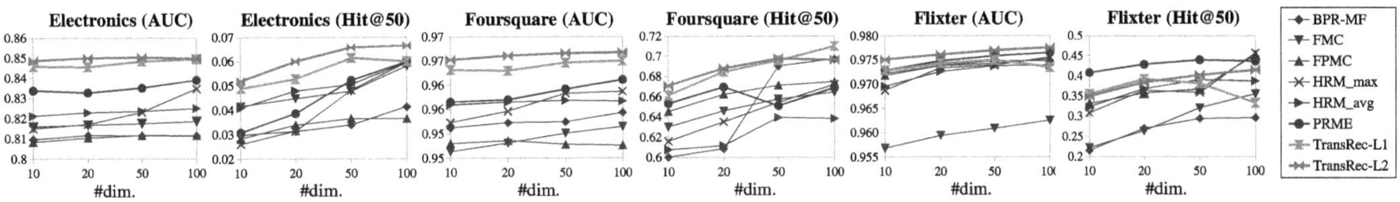

Figure 4: Sensitivity: Accuracy variation on the three densest datasets with increasing dimensionality (i.e., K).

paper to make it comparable to other methods. For PRME, we selected α from $\{0.2, 0.5, 0.8\}$. 0.2 was found to be the best in the PRME paper, which is consistent with our own observations. For *TransRec*, we used the unit $\mathcal{L}_2$-ball as our subspace Ψ. We also tried using the unit $\mathcal{L}_2$-sphere (i.e., the surface of the ball), but it led to slightly worse results in practice.

4.8 Recommendations

In Figure 5 we demonstrate some recommendations made by *TransRec* (K = 10) on *Electronics*. We randomly sample a few users from the datasets and show their historical sequences on the left, and demonstrate the top-1 recommendation on the right. As we can see from these examples, *TransRec* can capture long-term dynamics successfully. For example, *TransRec* recommends a tripod to the first user who appears to be a photographer. The last user bought multiple headphones and similar items in history; *TransRec* recommends new headphones after the purchase of an iPod accessory. In addition, *TransRec* also captures short-term dynamics. For instance, it recommends a desktop case to the fifth user after the purchase of a motherboard. Similarly, the sixth user is recommended a HDTV after recently purchasing a home theater receiver/speaker.

Figure 5: Recommendations made for a random sample of seven users by *TransRec* on *Electronics* data.

4.9 Item-to-item recommendation

By removing the personalization element, *TransRec* can straightforwardly be adapted to handle item-to-item recommendation, another classical setting where recommendations are made in the context of a specific item, e.g., recommending items that are likely to be purchased together. This setting is analogous to the knowledge graph completion task in that relationships among different items need to be modeled.

4.9.1 Datasets and Evaluation Methodology. We use 8 large datasets representing *co-purchase* relationships between products from *Amazon* [11]. They are a variety of top-level *Amazon* categories; to make the task more challenging, we only consider edges that connect two different top-level subcategories within each of the above datasets (e.g., recommending complementary items rather than substitutes). Statistics of these datasets are collated in Table 5.

Note that in these datasets edges are *directed*, e.g., it makes sense to recommend a charger/backpack after a customer purchases a laptop, but not the other way around.

Features. To further evaluate *TransRec*, we consider testing its capability here as a *content*-based method. To this end, we extract Bag-of-Words (BoW) features from each product's review text. In short, for each dataset we removed stop-words and constructed a dictionary comprising the 5,000 most frequent nouns or adjectives

Table 5: Statistics (in ascending order of #edges).

Dataset	Full name	#items	#edges
Office	Office Products	130,006	52,942
Home	Home & Kitchen	410,244	122,955
Games	Video Games	50,210	314,124
Electronics	Electronics	476,004	549,914
Automotive	Automotive	320,116	637,814
Movies	Movies & TV	200,941	648,256
Cellphone	Cell Phones & Accessories	319,678	667,918
Toys	Toys & Games	327,699	948,729
Total		**2.23M**	**3.94M**

or adjective-noun bigrams. These features have been shown to be effective on this data [5].

Evaluation Methodology. For each of the above datasets, we randomly partition the edges with an 80%/10%/10% train/validation/test split. Validation is used to select hyperparameters and performance is reported on the test set. Again we report AUC and Hit@10 (see Section 4.3). Here we use 10 for the hit rate because, as we show later, item-to-item recommendation proves simpler than personalized sequential prediction.

4.9.2 *The Translation-based Model.* Here we adopt a *content*-based version of *TransRec*, to investigate its ability to tackle explicit features. Let $\vec{f_i}$ denote the explicit feature vector associated with item i. We add one additional embedding layer $E(\cdot)$ on top of $\vec{f}$ to project items into the 'relational space' Φ. Formally, *TransRec* makes predictions according to

$$Prob(j \mid i) \propto -\, d\left(E(\vec{f_i}) + \vec{t}, E(\vec{f_j})\right),$$

$$\text{subject to} \quad E(\vec{f_i}) \in \Psi \subseteq \Phi, \quad \text{for } i \in \mathcal{I}.$$

$E(\cdot)$ could be a linear embedding layer, a non-linear layer like a neural network, or even some combination of latent and content-based representations.

4.9.3 *Baselines.* We mainly compare against two related models based on metric (or *non*-metric) embeddings. These are state-of-the-art *content*-based methods for item-to-item recommendation and have demonstrated strong results on the same data [5, 11]. The complete list of baselines is as follows:

Weighted Nearest Neighbor (WNN): WNN measures the 'dissimilarity' between pairs of items by a weighted Euclidean distance in the raw feature space: $d_{\vec{w}}(i,j) = \|\vec{w} \circ (\vec{f_i} - \vec{f_j})\|_2^2$, where $\circ$ is the Hadamard product and $\vec{w}$ is a parameter to be learned.

Low-rank Mahalanobis Transform (LMT) [11]: A state-of-the-art embedding method for learning the notion of compatibilities among different items. LMT learns a single low-rank Mahalanobis transform matrix W to embed all items into a relational space within which the distance between items is measured to make predictions: $d_W(i,j) = \|W\vec{f_i} - W\vec{f_j}\|_2^2$.

Mixtures of Non-metric Embeddings (Monomer) [5]: Monomer extends LMT by learning *mixtures* of low-rank embeddings to uncover more complex reasons to explain the relationships between items. It relaxes the metricity assumption used by LMT and can naturally handle directed relationships.

Table 6: Accuracy for co-purchase prediction.

Dataset	Metric	WNN	LMT	Monomer	TransRec	%Improv.
Office	*AUC*	0.6952	0.8848	0.8736	0.9437	6.7%
	Hit@10	1.45%	3.08%	1.96%	12.69%	312.0%
Home	*AUC*	0.6696	0.9101	0.8841	0.9482	4.2%
	Hit@10	2.24%	4.46%	0.63%	8.80%	97.3%
Games	*AUC*	0.7199	0.9423	0.9239	0.9736	3.3%
	Hit@10	2.64%	4.19%	0.59%	7.78%	85.7%
Electronics	*AUC*	0.7538	0.9316	0.9299	0.9651	3.5%
	Hit@10	1.78%	2.59%	0.29%	5.32%	105.4%
Automotive	*AUC*	0.7317	0.9054	0.9152	0.9490	3.7%
	Hit@10	1.20%	1.97%	0.36%	4.48%	127.4%
Movies	*AUC*	0.7668	0.9536	0.9516	0.9730	1.9%
	Hit@10	2.84%	4.37%	0.99%	6.19%	41.7%
Cellphone	*AUC*	0.6867	0.7932	0.8445	0.9127	8.1%
	Hit@10	0.80%	0.94%	0.04%	2.42%	157.5%
Toys	*AUC*	0.7529	0.9216	0.9353	0.9552	2.1%
	Hit@10	2.27%	2.67%	0.59%	3.99%	49.4%

4.9.4 *Quantitative Results and Analyses.* For fair comparison, we adopted the setting in [5], so that we use 100 dimensions for the relational spaces of LMT and *TransRec*; 5 spaces each with 20 dimensions are learned for Monomer. For simplicity, in our experiments we used squared $\mathcal{L}_2$ distance and $\Psi = \Phi$ for *TransRec*, i.e., no constraints on the vector $E(\vec{f})$. Also, a linear embedding layer is used as the function E to make it more comparable with our baselines. Experimental results are collated in Table 6. Our main findings are summarized as follows: (1) *TransRec* outperforms all baselines in all cases considerably, which indicates that translation-based structure seems to be stronger at modeling relationships among items compared to purely distance-based methods. This is also consistent with the findings from knowledge base literature (e.g., [1, 10, 27]). (2) *TransRec* tends to lead to larger improvements for sparse datasets like *Office*, in contrast to the improvements on denser datasets like *Toys* and *Games*.

5 CONCLUSION

We introduced a scalable *translation*-based method, *TransRec*, for modeling the semantically complex relationships between different entities in recommender systems. We analyzed the connections of *TransRec* to existing methods and demonstrated its suitability for modeling third-order interactions between users, their previously consumed item, and their next item. In addition to the superior results achieved on the sequential prediction task on a wide spectrum of large, real-world datasets, we also investigated the strength of *TransRec* at tackling item-to-item recommendation. The success of *TransRec* on the two tasks suggests that translation-based architectures are promising for general-purpose recommendation problems.

In addition, we introduced a large-scale dataset for sequential (and potentially geographical) recommendation from *Google Local*, that contains detailed information about millions of local businesses (e.g., restaurants, malls, shops) around the world as well as ratings and reviews from millions of users.

REFERENCES

[1] Antoine Bordes, Nicolas Usunier, Alberto Garcia-Duran, Jason Weston, and Oksana Yakhnenko. 2013. Translating embeddings for modeling multi-relational data. In *Proceedings of the Advances in Neural Information Processing Systems (NIPS)*. 2787–2795.

[2] Shuo Chen, Josh L. Moore, Douglas Turnbull, and Thorsten Joachims. 2012. Playlist prediction via metric embedding. In *Proceedings of the ACM SIGKDD Conferences on Knowledge Discovery and Data Mining (SIGKDD)*. 714–722.

[3] Yi Ding and Xue Li. 2005. Time weight collaborative filtering. In *Proceedings of the ACM International Conference on Information and Knowledge Management (CIKM)*. 485–492.

[4] Shanshan Feng, Xutao Li, Yifeng Zeng, Gao Cong, Yeow Meng Chee, and Quan Yuan. 2015. Personalized ranking metric embedding for next new POI recommendation. In *Proceedings of the International Joint Conference on Artificial Intelligence (IJCAI)*. 2069–2075.

[5] Ruining He, Charles Packer, and Julian McAuley. 2016. Learning compatibility across categories for heterogeneous item recommendation. In *IEEE International Conference on Data Mining (ICDM)*. 937–942.

[6] Yifan Hu, Yehuda Koren, and Chris Volinsky. 2008. Collaborative filtering for implicit feedback datasets. In *Proceedings of the IEEE International Conference on Data Mining (ICDM)*. 263–272.

[7] Yehuda Koren. 2010. Collaborative filtering with temporal dynamics. *Commun. ACM* 53, 4 (2010), 89–97.

[8] Yehuda Koren, Robert Bell, and Chris Volinsky. 2009. Matrix Factorization techniques for recommender systems. *Computer* 42, 8 (2009), 30–37.

[9] Justin J. Levandoski, Mohamed Sarwat, Ahmed Eldawy, and Mohamed F. Mokbel. 2012. LARS: A location-aware recommender system. In *Proceedings of the IEEE International Conference on Data Engineering (ICDE)*. 450–461.

[10] Yankai Lin, Zhiyuan Liu, Maosong Sun, Yang Liu, and Xuan Zhu. 2015. Learning entity and relation embeddings for knowledge graph completion. In *Proceedings of the AAAI Conference on Artificial Intelligence (AAAI)*. 2181–2187.

[11] Julian J. McAuley, Christopher Targett, Qinfeng Shi, and Anton van den Hengel. 2015. Image-based recommendations on styles and substitutes. In *Proceedings of the International ACM SIGIR Conference on Research and Development in Information Retrieval (SIGIR)*. 43–52.

[12] Tomas Mikolov, Ilya Sutskever, Kai Chen, Greg S Corrado, and Jeff Dean. 2013. Distributed representations of words and phrases and their compositionality. In *Proceedings of the Advances in Neural Information Processing Systems (NIPS)*. 3111–3119.

[13] Joshua L. Moore, Shuo Chen, Douglas Turnbull, and Thorsten Joachims. 2013. Taste over time: the temporal dynamics of user preferences. In *Proceedings of the International Society for Music Information Retrieval Conference (ISMIR)*. 401–406.

[14] Maximilian Nickel, Volker Tresp, and Hans-Peter Kriegel. 2011. A three-way model for collective learning on multi-relational data. In *Proceedings of the International Conference on Machine Learning (ICML)*. 809–816.

[15] Maximilian Nickel, Volker Tresp, and Hans-Peter Kriegel. 2012. Factorizing yago: scalable machine learning for linked data. In *Proceedings of the International Conference on World Wide Web (WWW)*. 271–280.

[16] Xia Ning and George Karypis. 2011. SLIM: Sparse linear methods for top-n recommender systems. In *Proceedings of the IEEE International Conference on Data Mining (ICDM)*. 497–506.

[17] Rong Pan, Yunhong Zhou, Bin Cao, Nathan N. Liu, Rajan Lukose, Martin Scholz, and Qiang Yang. 2008. One-class collaborative filtering. In *Proceedings of the IEEE International Conference on Data Mining (ICDM)*. 502–511.

[18] Steffen Rendle and Christoph Freudenthaler. 2014. Improving pairwise learning for item recommendation from implicit feedback. In *Proceedings of the ACM International Conference on Web Search and Data Mining (WSDM)*. 273–282.

[19] Steffen Rendle, Christoph Freudenthaler, Zeno Gantner, and Lars Schmidt-Thieme. 2009. BPR: Bayesian personalized ranking from implicit feedback. In *Proceedings of the Conference on Uncertainty in Artificial Intelligence (UAI)*. 452–461.

[20] Steffen Rendle, Christoph Freudenthaler, and Lars Schmidt-Thieme. 2010. Factorizing personalized markov chains for next-basket recommendation. In *Proceedings of the International Conference on World Wide Web (WWW)*. 811–820.

[21] Steffen Rendle and Lars Schmidt-Thieme. 2010. Pairwise interaction tensor factorization for personalized tag recommendation. In *Proceedings of the ACM International Conference on Web Search and Data Mining (WSDM)*. 81–90.

[22] Francesco Ricci, Lior Rokach, Bracha Shapira, and Paul Kantor. 2011. *Recommender systems handbook*. Springer US.

[23] Richard Serfozo. 2009. *Basics of applied stochastic processes*. Springer Science & Business Media.

[24] Ajit P. Singh and Geoffrey J. Gordon. 2008. Relational learning via collective matrix factorization. In *Proceedings of the ACM SIGKDD Conferences on Knowledge Discovery and Data Mining (SIGKDD)*. 650–658.

[25] Théo Trouillon, Johannes Welbl, Sebastian Riedel, Éric Gaussier, and Guillaume Bouchard. 2016. Complex embeddings for simple link prediction. In *Proceedings of the International Conference on Machine Learning (ICML)*. 2071–2080.

[26] Pengfei Wang, Jiafeng Guo, Yanyan Lan, Jun Xu, Shengxian Wan, and Xueqi Cheng. 2015. Learning hierarchical representation model for nextbasket recommendation. In *Proceedings of the International ACM SIGIR Conference on Research and Development in Information Retrieval (SIGIR)*. 403–412.

[27] Zhen Wang, Jianwen Zhang, Jianlin Feng, and Zheng Chen. 2014. Knowledge graph embedding by translating on hyperplanes. In *Proceedings of the AAAI Conference on Artificial Intelligence (AAAI)*. 1112–1119.

[28] Xiang Wu, Qi Liu, Enhong Chen, Liang He, Jingsong Lv, Can Cao, and Guoping Hu. 2013. Personalized next-song recommendation in online karaokes. In *Proceedings of the ACM Conference on Recommender Systems (RecSys)*. 137–140.

[29] Bishan Yang, Wen-tau Yih, Xiaodong He, Jianfeng Gao, and Li Deng. 2015. Embedding entities and relations for learning and inference in knowledge bases. In *Proceedings of the International Conference on Learning Representations (ICLR)*. 1–13.

[30] Tong Zhao, Julian McAuley, and Irwin King. 2014. Leveraging social connections to improve personalized ranking for collaborative filtering. In *Proceedings of the ACM International Conference on Information and Knowledge Management (CIKM)*. 261–270.

MPR: Multi-Objective Pairwise Ranking

Rasaq Otunba
Inf. Sci. & Tech. Dept.
George Mason University
Fairfax, Virginia, USA
rotunba@gmu.edu

Raimi A. Rufai
Hybris Marketing
SAP Labs, Inc.
Montreal, Quebec, Canada
raimi.rufai@sap.com

Jessica Lin
Computer Science Dept.
George Mason University
Fairfax, Virginia, USA
jessica@gmu.edu

ABSTRACT

The recommendation challenge can be posed as the problem of predicting either item ratings or item rankings. The latter approach has proven more effective. Pairwise learning-to-rank techniques have been relatively successful. Hence, they are popularly used for learning recommender model parameters such as those in collaborative filtering (CF) models. The model parameters are learned by optimizing close smooth approximations of the non-smooth information retrieval (IR) metrics such as Mean Area Under ROC curve (AUC).

Targeted campaigns are an alternative to item recommendations for increasing conversion. The user ranking task is referred to as audience retrieval. It is used in targeted campaigns to rank push campaign recipients based on their potential to convert. In this work, we consider the task of efficiently learning a ranking model that provides item recommendations and user rankings simultaneously. We adopt pairwise learning for this task. We refer to our approach as *multi-objective pairwise ranking* (MPR).

We describe our approach and use experiments to evaluate its performance.

CCS CONCEPTS

•Information systems →Personalization; •Computing methodologies →Learning to rank;

KEYWORDS

Collaborative filtering; recommendations; audience retrieval

ACM Reference format:
Rasaq Otunba, Raimi A. Rufai, and Jessica Lin. 2017. MPR: Multi-Objective Pairwise Ranking. In *Proceedings of RecSys'17, August 27–31, 2017, Como, Italy.*, 9 pages.
DOI: http://dx.doi.org/10.1145/3109859.3109903

1 INTRODUCTION

Recommendation is a vital part of services rendered by many content providers either as a primary service or as an ancillary one. Search engine providers like Google recommend non-personalized results to search queries as a main service while other institutions such as Amazon recommend similar content to initially searched content as an ancillary service. Personalization refers to recommending content tailored to each user's preferences. Personalization can boost conversion. Most existing personalization systems provide item recommendations. Item recommendation continues to be an attractive research area especially after the Netflix Price a decade ago [15]. Some of the existing methods for item recommendation predict ratings while others predict item rankings. It has been shown that predicting item rankings leads to better item recommendations [1, 28, 29]. The recent proliferation of content on social media platforms has also led to increased interest in tailoring content for consumers. An example is Twitter recently experimenting with sorting tweets by interest rather than the current reverse chronological ordering. Facebook also continues to tweak its news feed ranking algorithm for improved personalization.

Targeted marketing push campaigns can also help increase conversion. An example application is in marketing where products are recommended to potential customers. Customers are ranked based on their potential to engage in product push campaigns. The task of ranking users in this manner is considered ranking from implicit feedback since users typically click or act on the delivered campaign as opposed to rating the campaign. Many techniques have been proposed for item ranking based on implicit feedback [11, 21]. The user ranking problem (aka audience retrieval) in targeted campaigns is gaining more attention under the umbrella of computational advertising [17]. The need for increased conversion is driving the research for more effective campaigns. While item recommendation engines have been successfully used for audience retrieval and even led to increased click-to-open rates (CTOR) of push campaigns [27], techniques specifically designed for audience retrieval have proven more effective [16, 17, 20, 31].

We propose a solution for simultaneous item recommendation and audience retrieval in this work. Our proposed solution avoids training two different systems. In particular, we consider our proposed solution as a framework for combining an item ranking algorithm with an audience retrieval one. We refer to it as a *multi-objective ranking algorithm* (MPR). The combination maintains the same asymptotic time bounds as its constituent ranking algorithms. We adopt the pairwise learning-to-rank approach for implicit feedback in this work because of its success. The remainder of this paper is organized as follows. In Section 2, we summarize related work. In Section 3, we give the necessary background for the rest of the paper. We describe the two algorithms in Sections 4 and 5. We validate our approach with experiments on popular datasets in Section 6 and discuss the results in Sections 7 and 8. Finally, we conclude by summarizing the work and hinting on possible directions of future work in Section 9.

RecSys'17, August 27–31, 2017, Como, Italy.

ISBN 978-1-4503-4652-8/17/08...$15.00.
DOI: http://dx.doi.org/10.1145/3109859.3109903

2 RELATED WORK

The inputs to a personalized recommender system include users, items, and feedback. The feedback can be implicit in the form of observed actions such as clicks and views or explicit in the form of ratings. Implicit feedback is often more readily available than explicit feedback. The approaches to recommendations can be knowledge-based, content-based or collaborative. Knowledge-based recommendation takes the context and domain knowledge into consideration. In content-based recommenders, recommendation is based on matches between user profiles and item characteristics. Content filtering enjoys industry success at companies like Pandora by recommending musical content based on user profiles. A challenge to content based recommenders is the lack of information in some instances.

The most prominent of these approaches, collaborative filtering (CF), on the other hand, uses ratings or implicit feedback. In item recommendations, user-based CF considers users' historical actions on items as well as the actions of similar users. Item-based CF however considers historical actions of users on similar items. Content-based recommendation and CF can be combined in a hybrid setting [30]. Matrix factorization (MF)-CF performs better than kNN-CF in general [15]. In this work, we focus on MF-CF for this reason even though our techniques are adaptable to kNN-CF.

Many recommendation algorithms provide item recommendations using a machine learning technique. This often involves learning a model by optimizing it with respect to a rating prediction objective function such as the mean squared error or (a smooth version of) a ranking objective function such as AUC.

Some existing item recommendation techniques have been used for audience retrieval. Robinson [24] addresses the audience retrieval problem using the traditional user-based CF technique. There are other techniques specifically designed for audience retrieval. Sandeep et al. [20] proposed techniques for maximizing campaign conversions by using multiple user actions, including search queries, page views, ad clicks, etc. A conversion for a given campaign is a transaction, initiated by the campaign, that generates revenue. Yandong et al. [17] combined the information about a campaign and a set of *seed users* who converted in a previous campaign to maximize conversions. Bhargav et al. [31] claimed user-campaign feedback is insufficient for audience retrieval due to sparsity. They instead used user-product preferences in a collaborative setting for audience retrieval. Their technique called *focused matrix factorization model* (FMF) is an extension of the popular Bayesian personalized ranking (BPR) [22] algorithm. Haishan et al. [16] attempted to expand an existing targeted audience by identifying new users with similar attributes.

3 BACKGROUND

In this section, we define notations and preliminaries that will be used in the rest of the article. We also give an overview of CF recommender systems, objective functions, and the RankNet cost function.

3.1 Notations and Preliminaries

We denote the set of all users by U and the set of all items by I. A user interaction with an item is recorded as 1 to represent implicit feedback. A lack of implicit feedback is not recorded at all, since it might imply either a lack of interest in the item or merely a missing value. In many other systems, unobserved feedback is considered negative. The latter approach causes the trained model to predict unseen feedback as negative even when it could just be missing. The set of all user implicit feedback, $U \times I$, is denoted by S. $S_{training}$ is the training set and S_{test} is the test set. We denote users that prefer item i by U_i^+, users that do not prefer i by U_i^- and the overall ranking of users per item i by U_i. We denote items preferred by user u by I_u^+, items not preferred by user u by I_u^- and the overall ranking of items for user u by I_u. The actual components (users and items) are represented by a matrix $\mathbf{X}$ where x_{ui} is the feedback of user u on item i. The vector $\mathbf{x_u}$ denotes the interactions of user u in $\mathbf{X}$. In MF, $\mathbf{X}$ is factorized into low rank matrices $\mathbf{P}$ for users and $\mathbf{Q}$ for items. Henceforth, we refer to the values of $\mathbf{P}$ and $\mathbf{Q}$ as model parameters. Matrices and vectors are represented in bold font. We denote predicted ranking of items for user u by $\hat{I}_u$ and predicted ranking of users per item i by $\hat{U}_i$. We define $\hat{x}_{ui}$ as a real-valued function that predicts the preference of user u of item i based on model parameters. For item ranking, we denote by $\hat{x}_{uij}$ the predicted relative preference of user u of item i over item j based on model parameters. More formally,

$$\hat{x}_{uij} = \hat{x}_{ui} - \hat{x}_{uj}. \quad (1)$$

Similarly, we denote by $\hat{y}_{kvw}$ the predicted relative preference of user v of item k compared to user w based on model parameters. In formal notation,

$$\hat{y}_{kvw} = \hat{y}_{kv} - \hat{y}_{kw}. \quad (2)$$

3.2 Overview of CF Recommender Systems

Recommender models represent the relationship between input parameters (users, items, and feedback) and the desired output (ratings or implicit feedback). We now review the two CF models: neighborhood-based and latent factor systems. Our proposed technique is applicable to both models. The CF models are differentiated by how $\hat{x}_{ui}$ is derived. Other hybrid variants such as factorized neighborhood [13, 14] are derived from these two CF models. These models could be learned using machine learning algorithms such as stochastic gradient descent (SGD) and alternating least squares (ALS). The SGD method is one of the most popular first-order iterative optimization algorithms. SGD is popularly used in learning-to-rank algorithms.

3.2.1 Latent Factor Models. The two low-rank factor matrices $\mathbf{P}$ and $\mathbf{Q}$ are typically learned using SGD. These matrices are expected to better represent the features of items and users. This is a form of dimensionality reduction. The value $\hat{x}_{ui}$ is typically computed as the dot product of the user latent vector $\mathbf{p_u}$ and the item latent vector $\mathbf{q_i}$.

$$\hat{x}_{ui} = \mathbf{p_u^T} . \mathbf{q_i} \quad (3)$$

Some state-of-the-art techniques compute $\hat{x}_{ui}$ with sophisticated approaches such as deep neural networks. The authors of [9] for example replaced the typical dot product with a deep neural network (multi-layer feed-forward neural network). One wonders if other neural network architectures might yield better results.

3.2.2 Neighborhood Systems. Neighborhood systems can be either *memory-based* or *model-based.* Each of these can be either user-based k-nearest-neighbor (userkNN) or item-based k-nearest-neighbor (item-kNN) [4]. In userkNN, given some k, $\hat{x}_{ui}$ is computed as the weighted sum of the feedback of the k users most similar to user u on item i, where similarity is computed according to some *similarity measure.* In itemkNN, given some k, $\hat{x}_{ui}$ is computed as the weighted sum of the feedback of user u on the k items most similar to item i. ItemKNN is known to outperform [25] userKNN because the item neighborhood is sparse [19]. We describe only itemKNN below, but userKNN is analogous. We define the predicted feedback of user u on item i as:

$$\hat{x}_{ui} = \sum_{j \in C_i \wedge j \neq i} f(x_{uj}), \tag{4}$$

where C_i is the index set of the k items most similar to i and f is a weight function based on the similarity of i to j. Common similarity measures are the Jaccard, Cosine etc. The cosine vector similarity c_{ij} between items i and j is computed by:

$$c_{ij} = \frac{|U_i^+ \cap U_j^+|}{\sqrt{|U_i^+|.|U_j^+|}}. \tag{5}$$

So far, we have described the *memory-based* neighborhood method. In the model-based neighborhood systems, prediction is done on model parameters. An example similarity function used in model-based neighborhood systems is the sparse aggregation coefficients [19]. In such systems, $\hat{x}_{ui}$ is computed as:

$$\hat{x}_{ui} = \sum_{j \in C_i \wedge j \neq i} f(\hat{x}_{uj}), \tag{6}$$

where $\hat{x}_{uj} = \mathbf{p_u}^T.\mathbf{w_j}$ and $\mathbf{w_j}$ is a learned vector coefficient of item j in an n x n matrix $\mathbf{W}$.

3.3 Objective Functions

Learning the parameters of recommender model involves optimizing an objective function, typically including a regularization term to avoid over-fitting. Objective functions can be *point-wise, pair-wise* or *list-wise.* In each case, the objective function can be one of a number of loss functions, including the square loss [15], log loss [21], hinge loss [23] etc. We denote the objective function to be optimized by $L(\cdot)$.

3.3.1 Point-wise Objective Function. The goal of a point-wise objective function is to minimize the overall error of predicting the feedback a user u would give an item i. A point-wise objective [15] function can be expressed schematically as:

$$\sum_{u \in U} \sum_{i \in I} L(x_{ui}, \hat{x}_{ui}) \tag{7}$$

where L is some loss function and x_{ui} is the actual feedback of user u on item i.

3.3.2 Pair-wise objective function. The goal a pair-wise objective function is to minimize the overall error of predicting the feedback of a user u that prefers item i compared to another item j with (missing implicit feedback). This is particularly suitable for predicting rankings rather than ratings. An example of this is the work of Rendle et al. [21] for item recommendations.

$$\sum_{u \in U} \sum_{i \in I_u^+} \sum_{j \in I_u^-} L(x_{uij}, \hat{x}_{uij}) \tag{8}$$

3.3.3 List-wise objective function. The goal of a list-wise objective function is to minimize the overall error of predicting the ranking of items in I for each user u in U. This is less common than pair-wise and point-wise approaches. An example of this for item recommendations is proposed by Shi et al. [26] and Huang et al. [12].

$$\sum_{u \in U} L(I_u, \hat{I}_u) \tag{9}$$

3.4 RankNet

The RankNet probabilistic cross-entropy cost function is a pairwise ranking objective function widely used in many machine learning algorithms [3]. The cross-entropy between two entities can be intuitively described as a measure of uncertainty in a system with respect to two entities. The goal of minimizing the cross-entropy cost function is to reduce the amount of uncertainty of the model in ranking two items. The cross-entropy cost function is known to improve the performance of machine learning algorithms e.g. DNN [5]. Hence, we adopt the RankNet function in our techniques. The RankNet cost function can also be described as a measure of the prediction error from swapping two correctly ranked items. The RankNet cost function combines the pairwise cross-entropy cost and the logistic sigmoid of the difference of the item relevance scores. Given a user u and two items i and j, the RankNet loss L_{uij} is written as:

$$L_{uij} = -\overline{P}_{uij} \ln P_{uij} - (1 - \overline{P}_{uij}) \ln\big(1 - P_{uij}\big), \tag{10}$$

where P_{uij} is defined as

$$\frac{1}{1 + e^{-\hat{x}_{uij}}}, \tag{11}$$

i.e. the probability that user u prefers an item i to item j is modeled by the logistic sigmoid function. Given a user u and a pair of items i and j, without loss of generality, let us assume that u always prefers item i to j. The probability of this event is denoted by $\overline{P}_{uij} = 1$. By substituting $\overline{P}_{uij}$ and P_{uij} in Equation (10), we obtain

$$L_{uij} = \ln\Big(1 + e^{-\hat{x}_{uij}}\Big). \tag{12}$$

The derivative of L_{uij} with respect to $\hat{x}_{uij}$ is:

$$\frac{\partial L_{uij}}{\partial \hat{x}_{uij}} = \frac{-1}{1 + e^{\hat{x}_{uij}}}. \tag{13}$$

4 AUDIENCE RETRIEVAL

We give a pairwise ranking algorithm for audience retrieval here. It is straightforward to derive an item ranking equivalent. We describe our optimization criterion which we refer to as AR-OPT for easy reference and its derivative. We also explore the analogy of AR-OPT to the AUC metric.

4.1 AR-OPT Optimization Criterion

We define the likelihood of estimating the model parameters **P** and **Q** given that a user v would prefer an item k more strongly than another user w. Formally, this likelihood is equivalent to the probability, $\Pr(y_{kvw}|\mathbf{P},\mathbf{Q})$. In terms of the cross entropy cost function, $\mathcal{L}(\mathbf{P},\mathbf{Q}|y_{kvw})$, the likelihood function can be expressed as

$$\mathcal{L}(\mathbf{P},\mathbf{Q}|y_{kvw}) = \Pr(y_{kvw}|\mathbf{P},\mathbf{Q}) \tag{14}$$

$$= e^{-L_{kvw}}. \tag{15}$$

Since maximizing the likelihood estimate (MLE) is equivalent to minimizing the negative log-likelihood , we can define our audience retrieval optimization criterion, AR-OPT, in terms of the negative log-likelihood function as

$$\textit{AR-OPT} = -\ln \prod_{k\in I, v\in U_k^+, w\in U_k^-} e^{-L_{kvw}} \tag{16}$$

$$= \prod_{k\in I, v\in U_k^+, w\in U_k^-} L_{kvw} \tag{17}$$

$$= \sum_{k\in I}\sum_{v\in U_k^+}\sum_{w\in U_k^-} \ln\left(1+e^{-y_{kvw}}\right) \tag{18}$$

$$(\mathbf{P}_{MLE},\mathbf{Q}_{MLE}) = \arg\min_{\mathbf{P},\mathbf{Q}} \textit{AR-OPT} \tag{19}$$

$$(\mathbf{P}_{MAP},\mathbf{Q}_{MAP}) = \arg\min_{\mathbf{P},\mathbf{Q}} \{\textit{AR-OPT}\cdot\Pr(\mathbf{P},\mathbf{Q})\} \tag{20}$$

where MAP is the maximum a posteriori estimate derived from Bayesian inference which takes priors of **P** and **Q** into account. $\Pr(\mathbf{P},\mathbf{Q})$ is the prior distribution before optimization. Since in this work, we assumed $\Pr(\mathbf{P},\mathbf{Q})$ to be uniform, the two solutions in Equation (19) and Equation (20) coincide. We further express *AR-OPT* as:

$$\textit{AR-OPT} = \sum_{k\in I}\sum_{v\in U_k^+}\sum_{w\in U_k^-} \left\{\ln\left(1+e^{-\hat{y}_{kvw}}\right) + \left\{\frac{\lambda_P}{2}||\mathbf{p_v}||_F^2 + \frac{\lambda_P}{2}||\mathbf{p_w}||_F^2 + \frac{\lambda_Q}{2}||\mathbf{q_k}||_F^2\right\}\right\} \tag{21}$$

where λ is the regularization hyper-parameter introduced to avoid overfitting. The partial derivatives of AR-OPT are:

$$\frac{\partial}{\partial \mathbf{q_k}}\textit{AR-OPT} = \sum_{k\in I}\sum_{v\in U_k^+}\sum_{w\in U_k^-} \frac{\partial L_{kvw}}{\partial \hat{y}_{kvw}}\cdot\frac{\partial}{\partial \mathbf{q_k}}\hat{y}_{kvw} + \lambda_Q\mathbf{q_k} \tag{22}$$

$$\frac{\partial}{\partial \mathbf{p_v}}\textit{AR-OPT} = \sum_{k\in I}\sum_{v\in U_k^+}\sum_{w\in U_k^-} \frac{\partial L_{kvw}}{\partial \hat{y}_{kvw}}\cdot\frac{\partial}{\partial \mathbf{p_v}}\hat{y}_{kvw} + \lambda_P\mathbf{p_v} \tag{23}$$

$$\frac{\partial}{\partial \mathbf{p_w}}\textit{AR-OPT} = \sum_{k\in I}\sum_{v\in U_k^+}\sum_{w\in U_k^-} \frac{\partial L_{kvw}}{\partial \hat{y}_{kvw}}\cdot\frac{\partial}{\partial \mathbf{p_w}}\hat{y}_{kvw} + \lambda_P\mathbf{p_w} \tag{24}$$

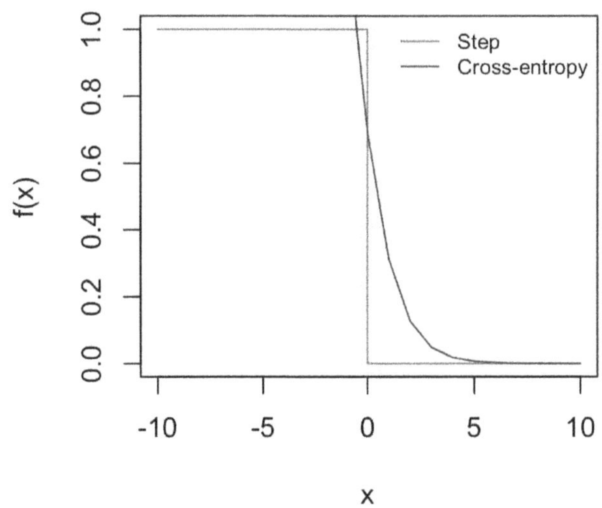

Figure 1: The RankNet cross entropy cost function and the Heaviside step function

4.1.1 Analogy to AUC. Pairwise learning algorithms including the ones presented in this work ultimately aim to maximize the number of correctly ranked pairs. The receiver operating characteristic (ROC) curve depicts the number of correctly ranked pairs more closely. AUC is sometimes criticized for not penalizing incorrect rankings. Nonetheless, it is still widely considered to be a good measurement of click-through rate [6]. Mean AUC over all items and all users is defined as:

$$AUC = \sum_{k\in I}\sum_{v\in U_k^+}\sum_{w\in U_k^-} z_k * \delta(\hat{y}_{kvw}) \tag{25}$$

where the above expression implicitly defines AUC *gain* and z_k is the normalization constant:

$$z_k = \frac{1}{|I||U_k^+||U_k^-|} \tag{26}$$

and $\delta(x)$ is the Heaviside function:

$$\delta(\hat{y}_{kvw}) = \begin{cases}1, & \text{if } \hat{y}_{kvw} > 0\\ 0, & \text{otherwise}\end{cases} \tag{27}$$

We can express AUC loss as:

$$AUC_{loss} = 1 - \sum_{k\in I}\sum_{v\in U_k^+}\sum_{w\in U_k^-} z_k * \delta(\hat{y}_{kvw}) \tag{28}$$

$$= \sum_{k\in I}\sum_{v\in U_k^+}\sum_{w\in U_k^-} z_k * (1-\delta(\hat{y}_{kvw})) \tag{29}$$

Equation (18) has a similar structure to Equation (29) if we ignore the normalization constant z_k in the latter. We observe that minimizing the RankNet cost function is equivalent to minimizing the AUC loss i.e. $1-\delta(\hat{y}_{kvw})$.

$$1-\delta(\hat{y}_{kvw}) = \begin{cases}0, & \text{if } \hat{y}_{kvw} > 0\\ 1, & \text{otherwise}\end{cases} \tag{30}$$

Figure 1 shows the similarity in the shapes of the above step function and the RankNet cross-entropy cost function.

4.2 Audience Retrieval Learning Algorithm

Our audience retrieval algorithm (AR) uses SGD with the optimization criterion introduced above to learn the model parameters **P** and **Q**. The task of pairwise ranking is to predict $\mathbf{p}_\mathbf{k}^T\mathbf{q}_\mathbf{v} - \mathbf{p}_\mathbf{k}^T\mathbf{q}_\mathbf{w}$ for user v on preferred item k and another user w with no preference for item k. So, we have two models to update: **P** and **Q**. The vectors $\mathbf{p}_\mathbf{k}$ and $\mathbf{q}_\mathbf{v}$ are row feature vectors of the item and user latent factor matrices respectively. For an f-ranked matrix **P** (and **Q**), the vector $\mathbf{p}_\mathbf{k}$ (and $\mathbf{q}_\mathbf{u}$) is f-dimensional. The partial derivatives of $\hat{y}_{kvw}$ are given as:

$$\frac{\partial}{\partial \mathbf{q}_\mathbf{k}}\hat{y}_{kvw} = \mathbf{p}_\mathbf{v} - \mathbf{p}_\mathbf{w} \tag{31}$$

$$\frac{\partial}{\partial \mathbf{p}_\mathbf{v}}\hat{y}_{kvw} = \mathbf{q}_\mathbf{k} \tag{32}$$

$$\frac{\partial}{\partial \mathbf{p}_\mathbf{w}}\hat{y}_{kvw} = -\mathbf{q}_\mathbf{k} \tag{33}$$

Note that the partial derivatives given in Equations (31) to (33) direct the path that SGD takes to arrive at the optimal solution. The pseudocode of AR is given in Algorithm 1.

Algorithm 1 AR(I, U)

1: **Output:** Optimized matrices **P** and **Q**
2: initialize learning rate η, **P** and **Q**
3: **repeat**
4: draw k, v, w from I, U_k^+, U_k^- uniformly
5: $\mathbf{q}_\mathbf{k} \leftarrow \mathbf{q}_\mathbf{k} - \eta * \frac{\partial}{\partial \mathbf{q}_\mathbf{k}} \textit{AR-OPT}$
$\mathbf{p}_\mathbf{v} \leftarrow \mathbf{p}_\mathbf{v} - \eta * \frac{\partial}{\partial \mathbf{p}_\mathbf{v}} \textit{AR-OPT}$
$\mathbf{p}_\mathbf{w} \leftarrow \mathbf{p}_\mathbf{w} - \eta * \frac{\partial}{\partial \mathbf{p}_\mathbf{w}} \textit{AR-OPT}$
6: **until** convergence or maximum number of iterations
7: **return P, Q**

Note that the updates to the model parameters in Line 5 are performed concurrently and take a step in the stochastic descent towards the optimal solution. In Line 4 of Algorithm 1, we draw k from I such that neither U_k^+ nor U_k^- is empty. This takes time $O(t|I|)$, where $t \in (0,1)$ is the proportion of new items not currently preferred by anyone. The retrieval of the two sets U_k^+ and U_k^- takes $O(|U|)$. The time complexity of AR is thus $O(s(t|I| + |U|)) = O(s(|I|+|U|))$ where s is the number of times the loop in Algorithm 1 is executed.

5 MULTI-OBJECTIVE PAIRWISE RANKING

We propose MPR as a combination of AR and its item pairwise ranking equivalent. We define the objective function *MPR-OPT* as the weighted sum of the item ranking objective function *IR-OPT* and the audience retrieval objective function *AR-OPT*. This approach is sometimes called *linear scalarization* [18].

$$\textit{MPR-OPT} = \alpha \textit{AR-OPT} + (1-\alpha)\textit{IR-OPT} \tag{34}$$

where α is a scalarization hyperparameter for trading off between the constituent objective functions. It is obvious from the above equation that:

$$\frac{\partial}{\partial \mathbf{q}_\mathbf{k}}\textit{MPR-OPT} = \alpha\frac{\partial}{\partial \mathbf{q}_\mathbf{k}}\textit{AR-OPT}, \tag{35}$$

$$\frac{\partial}{\partial \mathbf{p}_\mathbf{v}}\textit{MPR-OPT} = \alpha\frac{\partial}{\partial \mathbf{p}_\mathbf{v}}\textit{AR-OPT}, \tag{36}$$

$$\frac{\partial}{\partial \mathbf{p}_\mathbf{w}}\textit{MPR-OPT} = \alpha\frac{\partial}{\partial \mathbf{p}_\mathbf{w}}\textit{AR-OPT}, \tag{37}$$

$$\frac{\partial}{\partial \mathbf{p}_\mathbf{u}}\textit{MPR-OPT} = (1-\alpha)\frac{\partial}{\partial \mathbf{p}_\mathbf{u}}\textit{IR-OPT}, \tag{38}$$

$$\frac{\partial}{\partial \mathbf{q}_\mathbf{i}}\textit{MPR-OPT} = (1-\alpha)\frac{\partial}{\partial \mathbf{q}_\mathbf{i}}\textit{IR-OPT}, \tag{39}$$

$$\frac{\partial}{\partial \mathbf{q}_\mathbf{j}}\textit{MPR-OPT} = (1-\alpha)\frac{\partial}{\partial \mathbf{q}_\mathbf{j}}\textit{IR-OPT}. \tag{40}$$

We defined *AR-OPT* and its partial derivatives in Equations (21) to (24). We define IR-OPT and its derivatives as

$$\textit{IR-OPT} = \sum_{u\in U}\sum_{i\in I_u^+}\sum_{j\in I_u^-}\Big\{\ln\Big(1+e^{-\hat{x}_{uij}}\Big) + \Big\{\frac{\lambda_P}{2}||\mathbf{p}_\mathbf{u}||_F^2 + \frac{\lambda_Q}{2}||\mathbf{q}_\mathbf{i}||_F^2 + \frac{\lambda_Q}{2}||\mathbf{q}_\mathbf{j}||_F^2\Big\}\Big\}. \tag{41}$$

The partial derivatives of IR-OPT are defined as

$$\frac{\partial \textit{IR-OPT}}{\partial \mathbf{p}_\mathbf{u}} = \sum_{u\in U}\sum_{i\in I_u^+}\sum_{j\in I_u^-}\frac{\partial L_{uij}}{\partial \hat{x}_{uij}}.\frac{\partial}{\partial \mathbf{q}_\mathbf{k}}\hat{x}_{uij} + \lambda_P\mathbf{p}_\mathbf{u} \tag{42}$$

$$\frac{\partial \textit{IR-OPT}}{\partial \mathbf{q}_\mathbf{i}} = \sum_{u\in U}\sum_{i\in I_u^+}\sum_{j\in I_u^-}\frac{\partial L_{uij}}{\partial \hat{x}_{uij}}.\frac{\partial}{\partial \mathbf{q}_\mathbf{i}}\hat{x}_{uij} + \lambda_Q\mathbf{q}_\mathbf{i} \tag{43}$$

$$\frac{\partial \textit{IR-OPT}}{\partial \mathbf{q}_\mathbf{j}} = \sum_{u\in U}\sum_{i\in I_u^+}\sum_{j\in I_u^-}\frac{\partial L_{uij}}{\partial \hat{x}_{uij}}.\frac{\partial}{\partial \mathbf{q}_\mathbf{j}}\hat{x}_{uij} + \lambda_Q\mathbf{q}_\mathbf{j} \tag{44}$$

Algorithm 2 MPR(I, U)

1: **Output:** Optimized matrices **P** and **Q**
2: initialize α, η, **P** and **Q**
3: **repeat**
4: draw u, i, j from U, I_u^+, I_u^- uniformly
5: $\mathbf{p}_\mathbf{u} \leftarrow \mathbf{p}_\mathbf{u} - \eta * \frac{\partial}{\partial \mathbf{p}_\mathbf{u}} \textit{MPR-OPT}$
$\mathbf{q}_\mathbf{i} \leftarrow \mathbf{q}_\mathbf{i} - \eta * \frac{\partial}{\partial \mathbf{q}_\mathbf{i}} \textit{MPR-OPT}$
$\mathbf{q}_\mathbf{j} \leftarrow \mathbf{q}_\mathbf{j} - \eta * \frac{\partial}{\partial \mathbf{q}_\mathbf{j}} \textit{MPR-OPT}$
6: draw k, v, w from I, U_k^+, U_k^- uniformly
7: $\mathbf{q}_\mathbf{k} \leftarrow \mathbf{q}_\mathbf{k} - \eta * \frac{\partial}{\partial \mathbf{q}_\mathbf{k}} \textit{MPR-OPT}$
$\mathbf{p}_\mathbf{v} \leftarrow \mathbf{p}_\mathbf{v} - \eta * \frac{\partial}{\partial \mathbf{p}_\mathbf{v}} \textit{MPR-OPT}$
$\mathbf{p}_\mathbf{w} \leftarrow \mathbf{p}_\mathbf{w} - \eta * \frac{\partial}{\partial \mathbf{p}_\mathbf{w}} \textit{MPR-OPT}$
8: **until** convergence or maximum number of iterations
9: **return P, Q**

Algorithm 2 gives the pseudocode of the MPR algorithm. Each set of updates of the model parameters is done concurrently. Note that sampling in Line 6 is independent of that in Line 4. The sampling of items and users in Line 4 and Line 6 are done similarly to Line 4 of Algorithm 1 .

Let s be the number of times the loop in the Algorithm 2 is executed. The time complexity of MPR is $O(s(t|I|+|U|+r|U|+|I|)) =$

$O(s(|I| + |U|))$, where s and t are as defined for AR and $r \in (0, 1)$ is the proportion of new users. The three algorithms AR, BPR, and MPR have the same worst-case time and space bounds. However, the constant embedded in the time complexity of MPR might be slightly higher due to the extra updates to the model parameters in each iteration.

We have already provided the partial derivatives of $\hat{y}_{kvw}$ in Equations (31) to (33). The partial derivatives of $\hat{x}_{uij}$ are given below:

$$\frac{\partial}{\partial \mathbf{p_u}} \hat{x}_{uij} = \mathbf{q_i} - \mathbf{q_j} \tag{45}$$

$$\frac{\partial}{\partial \mathbf{q_i}} \hat{x}_{uij} = \mathbf{p_u} \tag{46}$$

$$\frac{\partial}{\partial \mathbf{q_j}} \hat{x}_{uij} = -\mathbf{p_u} \tag{47}$$

6 EXPERIMENTS

Our goal is to determine if MPR is able to compete on both tasks of item ranking and audience retrieval, while maintaining the same complexity as the other ranking algorithms.

6.1 Evaluation Metrics

Mean AUC was described earlier. We describe the other metrics used for evaluations here from an audience retrieval perspective. We leave out the description of metrics for item ranking because they are trivial to derive. Evaluations are done on both audience retrieval and item ranking. All Metrics are computed for top 10 except where stated e.g. P@5 is precision for top 5.

6.1.1 *Recall.* Recall at truncation level k, $R@k$ is defined as:

$$R@k = \sum_{k=1}^{r} \frac{rel_k}{r} \tag{48}$$

where r is the total number of relevant users and rel_k is the binary relevance label of the k-th user.

6.1.2 *Mean Average Precision.* MAP is a measure of the precision of users at every rank. MAP over all users for all items is evaluated as:

$$MAP = \frac{1}{|S_{test}|} \sum_{i \in S_{test}} \frac{1}{n} \sum_{i=1}^{n} rel_i \sum_{k=1}^{i} \frac{rel_k}{k} \tag{49}$$

where $\sum_{k=1}^{i} \frac{rel_k}{k}$ is the precision at k, $P@k$.

6.1.3 *Mean Normalized Discounted Cumulative Gain.* NDCG is a measure of the overall relevance of users based on rank. Correctly ranked users at the top are highly regarded and vice versa. NDCG over all users for all items is evaluated as:

$$NDCG = \frac{1}{|S_{test}|} \sum_{i \in S_{test}} \frac{DCG}{IDCG} \tag{50}$$

where $IDCG$ is the ideal ranking DCG and

$$DCG@K = \sum_{i=1}^{K} \frac{2^{rel_i} - 1}{ln(i+1)} \tag{51}$$

where rel_i is the relevance label of the user ranked i-th.

Table 1: Datasets

Dataset	#Users	#Items	#Ratings
Yahoo	7,642	11,915	211,231
MovieLens	6,040	3,706	1,000,209
Eachmovie	72,916	1,628	2,811,983

6.1.4 *Mean Reciprocal Rank.* MRR is a measure of how high the topmost relevant user is ranked. MRR over all users for all items is evaluated as:

$$MRR = \frac{1}{|S_{test}|} \sum_{i \in S_{test}} \frac{1}{rank_i} \tag{52}$$

where $rank_i$ is the rank of the highest ranked relevant user.

6.2 Comparison Baselines

We compare MPR with AR and three other algorithms. The first is a simple non-personalized baseline algorithm that ranks users and items by popularity called MostPop i.e. ranking is done by item popularity for item ranking and ranking is done by user popularity for audience retrieval. We consider another item ranking algorithm referred to as BPR [21] to check the effectiveness of a model optimized for item ranking on item ranking and audience retrieval. The last baseline is the state-of-the-art algorithm referred to as element-wise Alternating Least Squares (eALS) [10], which optimizes for ratings prediction.

6.3 Experimental Repeatability

We perform the experiments with a publicly available recommendation engines framework called LibRec[1] [7]. LibRec contains implementations of many state-of-the-art recommendation algorithms. We implemented our contributions in LibRec and the artifacts (software, datasets, and manuscripts) for our experiments in this work are publicly available at [2]. We evaluate the proposed methods against the baselines with 5-fold Leave-One-Out-Cross-Validation. We experimented with different values of model hyperparameters such as the learning rate and regularization parameters till we obtained the best performance for all algorithms. We set α to 0.5 for equally weighted sum for our experiments.

6.4 Datasets

All three datasets used for the experiments are available in the public domain. A summary of these datasets can be found in Table 1. We further describe them below. All the datasets contain explicit ratings but we set all positive ratings to 1 as the only valid class for implicit feedback. Implicit feedback in this work is used for both item ranking and audience retrieval. All the datasets contain user identifiers, item identifiers, and ratings.

6.4.1 *Yahoo! Movies User Ratings Dataset.* This dataset was retrieved from the Yahoo! Webscope Program released for validation of recommender systems. It contains the Yahoo! Movies community's preferences for different movies. The movies are rated on a scale from A+ to F. All users in this datasets have rated at least 10

[1]https://www.librec.net
[2]https://goo.gl/HhqQHd

Table 2: Yahoo Results on Item Ranking

Metrics	AR	MPR	BPR	MostPop	eALS
P@5	0.089	**0.170**	0.144	0.127	**0.177**
P@10	0.076	**0.133**	0.120	0.095	**0.136**
R@5	0.100	0.209	0.167	0.165	**0.223**
R@10	0.169	0.317	0.277	0.247	**0.329**
AUC	0.891	**0.965**	**0.965**	0.950	0.936
MAP	0.104	**0.210**	0.174	0.164	**0.220**
NDCG	0.320	**0.443**	0.410	0.388	**0.444**
MRR	0.213	**0.380**	0.322	0.319	**0.389**
#Wins	0	3.0	0.5	0	**4.5**

Table 3: Yahoo Results on Audience Retrieval

Metrics	AR	MPR	BPR	MostPop	eALS
P@5	**0.101**	**0.101**	0.064	0.065	0.082
P@10	**0.075**	**0.076**	0.049	0.045	0.061
R@5	**0.155**	**0.162**	0.076	0.100	0.104
R@10	**0.212**	**0.218**	0.104	0.129	0.140
AUC	**0.908**	**0.914**	0.869	0.795	0.773
MAP	**0.135**	**0.142**	0.077	0.071	0.093
NDCG	**0.326**	**0.334**	0.256	0.248	0.270
MRR	**0.252**	**0.256**	0.163	0.166	0.202
#Wins	**4**	**4**	0	0	0

movies and all movies are rated by at least one user. We refer to this dataset simply as Yahoo.

6.4.2 Movielens Dataset. MovieLens dataset [8] is a publicly available dataset used for research in different fields such as education, research, and industry. The dataset was obtained from the MovieLens website (http://movielens.org), a website run by the GroupLens Research lab at the University of Minnesota. MovieLens runs a free personalized movie recommendation engine based on CF for recommending movies to users. We denote this dataset by MovieLens for easy reference.

6.4.3 EachMovie Dataset. This dataset has been used in many research works. It was obtained from the EachMovie collaborative filtering service created for experimental purposes as part of a research project at the Digital Equipment Corporation (DEC) Systems Research Center. We refer to this dataset as EachMovie for convenience.

7 RESULTS

We describe our observations from the results in Tables 2 to 7. The winning algorithm per metric is emboldened in each row of all tables. We assume a margin of error of 0.005, hence the winning algorithm has to be greater than the next winner by at least a margin of 0.01. #Wins represents the number of wins per algorithm. In the case of a tie between k algorithms, each algorithm is assigned a Wins of $1/k$. We split observations on the results per task below.

Table 4: MovieLens Results on Item Ranking

Metrics	AR	MPR	BPR	MostPop	eALS
P@5	0.140	**0.396**	**0.386**	0.211	**0.393**
P@10	0.128	**0.345**	**0.338**	0.182	**0.343**
R@5	0.024	**0.100**	**0.095**	0.041	**0.098**
R@10	0.044	**0.163**	**0.157**	0.067	**0.161**
AUC	0.831	**0.937**	**0.935**	0.858	0.927
MAP	0.079	**0.240**	**0.230**	0.102	**0.241**
NDCG	0.427	**0.603**	**0.594**	0.459	**0.602**
MRR	0.283	**0.626**	0.612	0.391	**0.625**
#Wins	0	**3**	2.5	0	2.5

Table 5: MovieLens Results on Audience Retrieval

Metrics	AR	MPR	BPR	MostPop	eALS
P@5	**0.364**	**0.359**	0.157	0.202	**0.362**
P@10	**0.321**	**0.316**	0.138	0.177	**0.318**
R@5	**0.061**	**0.066**	0.021	0.033	**0.059**
R@10	**0.099**	**0.104**	0.035	0.050	**0.095**
AUC	**0.917**	**0.920**	0.804	0.815	0.907
MAP	**0.181**	**0.188**	0.069	0.085	**0.183**
NDCG	**0.553**	**0.559**	0.424	0.448	**0.552**
MRR	**0.574**	**0.577**	0.320	0.406	**0.572**
#Wins	**2.8**	**2.8**	0	0	2.3

Table 6: EachMovie Results on Item Ranking

Metrics	AR	MPR	BPR	MostPop	eALS
P@5	0.230	**0.405**	0.392	0.227	0.369
P@10	0.183	**0.321**	**0.313**	0.172	0.301
R@5	0.227	**0.362**	0.348	0.202	0.343
R@10	0.317	**0.506**	0.491	0.265	0.487
AUC	0.900	**0.980**	**0.980**	0.944	0.963
MAP	0.278	**0.445**	0.427	0.259	0.419
NDCG	0.531	**0.682**	0.668	0.522	0.657
MRR	0.444	**0.688**	0.666	0.457	0.632
#Wins	0	7	1	0	0

Table 7: EachMovie Results on Audience Retrieval

Metrics	AR	MPR	BPR	MostPop	eALS
P@5	0.480	**0.564**	0.159	0.317	0.525
P@10	0.421	**0.483**	0.160	0.235	0.438
R@5	**0.085**	**0.093**	0.005	0.048	0.078
R@10	**0.119**	**0.128**	0.012	0.057	0.104
AUC	**0.972**	**0.973**	0.905	0.897	0.963
MAP	0.223	**0.255**	0.079	0.097	0.222
NDCG	0.655	**0.683**	0.480	0.524	0.650
MRR	0.716	**0.807**	0.274	0.671	0.782
#Wins	1.5	**6.5**	0	0	0

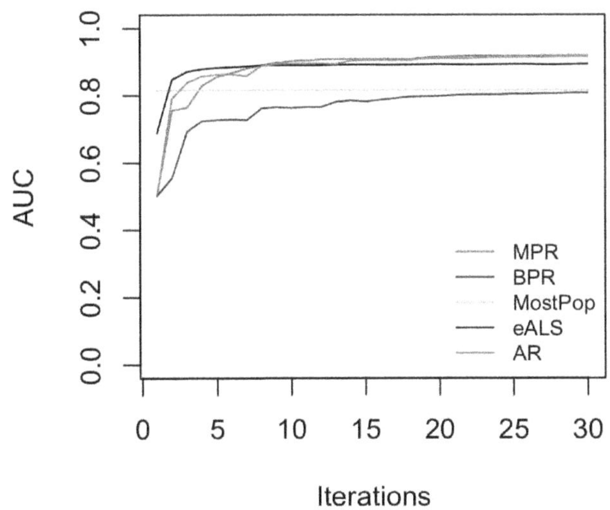

Figure 2: Convergence of all algorithms to the optimum AUC on the MovieLens dataset for audience retrieval

7.1 Item Ranking

eALS, followed closely by MPR, outperforms the other algorithms on Yahoo on all metrics except AUC where BPR competes more with MPR. BPR comes in third place on Yahoo. MPR wins on MovieLens, followed closely by BPR and eALS on all metrics. MPR clearly outperforms the other techniques on EachMovie, while BPR comes in second. MostPop and AR perform the worst on all datasets.

7.2 Audience Retrieval

AR ties with MPR on Yahoo. AR ties with MPR on MovieLens with eALS coming closely after them. MPR is the clear winner on EachMovie. AR consistently scores high on AUC across all the datasets. BPR and MostPop performed the worst across datasets.

7.3 Significance test

Our null hypothesis is that MPR is no better than any of the other algorithms. We used the Wilcoxon signed rank test to compare all algorithms with MPR with a p-value = 0.01. We account for the correlation of the metrics used by controlling for false discovery rate (FDR) [2] with $q^* = 0.01$. All algorithms in comparison with MPR have p-value < 0.00001, so we are able to reject the null hypothesis even with the control for FDR.

8 DISCUSSION

The results in Section 7 show that MPR performs the best overall on both tasks. It clearly outperforms all the other algorithms on EachMovie, the largest of the datasets. The experiments also show that a simple equally weighted sum can be an effective multi-objective optimization technique. MPR competes well on the metrics where it does not outperform the other algorithms. We initially set out to check if MPR would compete favorably with the item ranking algorithms on the item ranking task and also with the audience retrieval algorithms on the audience retrieval task. However, MPR exceeded that expectation by performing better on item ranking and audience retrieval than the respective item ranking and audience retrieval algorithms on most of the datasets. We believe MPR performs so well on both tasks because it is optimized for both tasks. For either task, MPR is able to draw on extra latent information that other algorithms could not.

On the AUC metric, we make a few observations across datasets. MPR consistently performs well even when it is outperformed on the other metrics. BPR consistently performs well on the task of item ranking, while AR performs consistently well on the task of audience retrieval. This can be explained by the optimization of a smooth approximation to AUC in BPR, MPR, and AR. MPR minimizes AUC loss for all tasks. BPR maximizes AUC gain for item ranking while AR maximizes AUC gain for audience retrieval. As expected, BPR performs well on item ranking because it is optimized for it, but does poorly on audience retrieval since it is not optimized for it. Similarly, AR performs well on audience retrieval because it is optimized for it but does poorly on item ranking as it not optimized for it.

eALS performs very well on item ranking for the Yahoo dataset and decently overall. This can be explained by the fact that eALS is a rating prediction technique and it is not optimized for any metric in particular nor for either task. We are not too surprised by the lackluster performance of MostPop as it is a naive approach with no personalization. However, MostPop performed better than BPR on audience retrieval in most instances. MostPop also performed better than AR on item ranking in some instances.

In order to demonstrate the convergence of algorithms, we include Figure 2 here to show how each algorithm converges with respect to AUC on the MovieLens dataset. MostPop has no convergence rate since there is no training at all. eALS converges quickly but MPR and AR continue to converge to a higher AUC. The faster convergence of eALS is not surprising as this was already demonstrated by its creators in [10].

9 CONCLUSION

We have presented a multi-objective pairwise ranking (MPR) algorithm that performs simultaneous item ranking and audience retrieval without compromising efficiency. The experiments on different popular datasets and metrics show the effectiveness of MPR.

We noted that MPR's margin of victory on the EachMovie dataset is so large that we would like to explore the reasons for it on this dataset in a future work. We would like to investigate the performance of other multi-objective optimization algorithms such as multi-gradient descent algorithm (MGDA) and the *Lagrangian* multiplier method. We also plan to extend our study to more datasets. Although we use the audience retrieval algorithm described earlier and its item ranking equivalent in this work for demonstration, MPR is an extensible framework that can accommodate the combination of different item ranking and audience retrieval techniques. It would be interesting to explore different weights for the item ranking objective function and audience retrieval techniques in future work. We believe MPR is also adaptable to online processing and parallelization similar to its constituent ranking algorithms. We would like to perform experiments to show these.

REFERENCES

[1] S. Balakrishnan and S. Chopra. Collaborative ranking. In *Proceedings of the Fifth ACM International Conference on Web Search and Data Mining*, WSDM '12, pages 143–152, New York, NY, USA, 2012. ACM.
[2] Y. Benjamini and Y. Hochberg. Controlling the False Discovery Rate: A Practical and Powerful Approach to Multiple Testing. *Journal of the Royal Statistical Society. Series B (Methodological)*, 57(1):289–300, 1995.
[3] C. Burges, T. Shaked, E. Renshaw, A. Lazier, M. Deeds, N. Hamilton, and G. Hullender. Learning to rank using gradient descent. In *Proceedings of the 22Nd International Conference on Machine Learning*, ICML '05, pages 89–96, New York, NY, USA, 2005. ACM.
[4] M. Deshpande and G. Karypis. Item-based top-n recommendation algorithms. *ACM Trans. Inf. Syst.*, 22(1):143–177, Jan. 2004.
[5] I. Goodfellow, Y. Bengio, and A. Courville. *Deep Learning*. MIT Press, 2016.
[6] T. Graepel, J. Q. n. Candela, T. Borchert, and R. Herbrich. Web-Scale Bayesian Click-Through rate Prediction for Sponsored Search Advertising in Microsoft's Bing Search Engine. In *Proceedings of the 27th International Conference on Machine Learning*, pages 13–20, Haifa, 2010.
[7] G. Guo, J. Zhang, Z. Sun, and N. Yorke-Smith. Librec: A java library for recommender systems. In *Posters, Demos, Late-breaking Results and Workshop Proceedings of the 23rd Conference on User Modeling, Adaptation, and Personalization (UMAP 2015), Dublin, Ireland, June 29 - July 3, 2015.*, 2015.
[8] F. M. Harper and J. A. Konstan. The movielens datasets: History and context. *ACM Trans. Interact. Intell. Syst.*, 5(4):19:1–19:19, Dec. 2015.
[9] X. He, L. Liao, H. Zhang, L. Nie, X. Hu, and T.-S. Chua. Neural collaborative filtering. In *Proceedings of the 26th International Conference on World Wide Web*, WWW '17, New York, NY, USA, 2017. ACM.
[10] X. He, H. Zhang, M.-Y. Kan, and T.-S. Chua. Fast matrix factorization for online recommendation with implicit feedback. In *Proceedings of the 39th International ACM SIGIR Conference on Research and Development in Information Retrieval*, SIGIR '16, pages 549–558, New York, NY, USA, 2016. ACM.
[11] Y. Hu, Y. Koren, and C. Volinsky. Collaborative filtering for implicit feedback datasets. In *Proceedings of the 2008 Eighth IEEE International Conference on Data Mining*, ICDM '08, pages 263–272, Washington, DC, USA, 2008. IEEE Computer Society.
[12] S. Huang, S. Wang, T.-Y. Liu, J. Ma, Z. Chen, and J. Veijalainen. Listwise collaborative filtering. In *Proceedings of the 38th International ACM SIGIR Conference on Research and Development in Information Retrieval*, SIGIR '15, pages 343–352, New York, NY, USA, 2015. ACM.
[13] S. Kabbur, X. Ning, and G. Karypis. Fism: Factored item similarity models for top-n recommender systems. In *Proceedings of the 19th ACM SIGKDD International Conference on Knowledge Discovery and Data Mining*, KDD '13, pages 659–667, New York, NY, USA, 2013. ACM.
[14] Y. Koren. Factorization meets the neighborhood: A multifaceted collaborative filtering model. In *Proceedings of the 14th ACM SIGKDD International Conference on Knowledge Discovery and Data Mining*, KDD '08, pages 426–434, New York, NY, USA, 2008. ACM.
[15] Y. Koren, R. Bell, and C. Volinsky. Matrix factorization techniques for recommender systems. *Computer*, 42(8):30–37, Aug. 2009.
[16] H. Liu, D. Pardoe, K. Liu, M. Thakur, F. Cao, and C. Li. Audience expansion for online social network advertising. In *Proceedings of the 22Nd ACM SIGKDD International Conference on Knowledge Discovery and Data Mining*, KDD '16, pages 165–174, New York, NY, USA, 2016. ACM.
[17] Y. Liu, S. Pandey, D. Agarwal, and V. Josifovski. Finding the right consumer: Optimizing for conversion in display advertising campaigns. In *Proceedings of the Fifth ACM International Conference on Web Search and Data Mining*, WSDM '12, pages 473–482, New York, NY, USA, 2012. ACM.
[18] R. T. Marler and J. S. Arora. The weighted sum method for multi-objective optimization: new insights. *Structural and Multidisciplinary Optimization*, 41(6):853–862, 2010.
[19] X. Ning and G. Karypis. Slim: Sparse linear methods for top-n recommender systems. In *2011 IEEE 11th International Conference on Data Mining*, pages 497–506, Dec 2011.
[20] S. Pandey, M. Aly, A. Bagherjeiran, A. Hatch, P. Ciccolo, A. Ratnaparkhi, and M. Zinkevich. Learning to target: What works for behavioral targeting. In *Proceedings of the 20th ACM International Conference on Information and Knowledge Management*, CIKM '11, pages 1805–1814, New York, NY, USA, 2011. ACM.
[21] S. Rendle, C. Freudenthaler, Z. Gantner, and L. Schmidt-Thieme. Bpr: Bayesian personalized ranking from implicit feedback. In *Proceedings of the Twenty-Fifth Conference on Uncertainty in Artificial Intelligence*, UAI '09, pages 452–461, Arlington, Virginia, United States, 2009. AUAI Press.
[22] S. Rendle and L. Schmidt-Thieme. Online-updating regularized kernel matrix factorization models for large-scale recommender systems. In *Proceedings of the 2008 ACM Conference on Recommender Systems*, RecSys '08, pages 251–258, New York, NY, USA, 2008. ACM.
[23] J. D. M. Rennie and N. Srebro. Fast maximum margin matrix factorization for collaborative prediction. In *Proceedings of the 22Nd International Conference on Machine Learning*, ICML '05, pages 713–719, New York, NY, USA, 2005. ACM.
[24] G. Robinson. Automated collaborative filtering in world wide web advertising, July 24 1997. WO Patent App. PCT/US1996/020,429.
[25] B. Sarwar, G. Karypis, J. Konstan, and J. Riedl. Item-based collaborative filtering recommendation algorithms. In *Proceedings of the 10th International Conference on World Wide Web*, WWW '01, pages 285–295, New York, NY, USA, 2001. ACM.
[26] Y. Shi, M. Larson, and A. Hanjalic. List-wise learning to rank with matrix factorization for collaborative filtering. In *Proceedings of the Fourth ACM Conference on Recommender Systems*, RecSys '10, pages 269–272, New York, NY, USA, 2010. ACM.
[27] J. van Rijn and J. Braams. National client email report, May 2015.
[28] M. Volkovs and R. S. Zemel. Collaborative ranking with 17 parameters. In F. Pereira, C. J. C. Burges, L. Bottou, and K. Q. Weinberger, editors, *Advances in Neural Information Processing Systems 25*, pages 2294–2302. Curran Associates, Inc., 2012.
[29] M. Weimer, A. Karatzoglou, Q. V. Le, and A. J. Smola. Cofi rank - maximum margin matrix factorization for collaborative ranking. In J. Platt, D. Koller, Y. Singer, and S. Roweis, editors, *Advances in Neural Information Processing Systems 20*, pages 1593–1600, Cambridge, MA, 2007. MIT Press.
[30] S. Xu, S. Wu, and L. Wang. Personalized semantic ranking for collaborative recommendation. In *Proceedings of the 38th International ACM SIGIR Conference on Research and Development in Information Retrieval*, SIGIR '15, pages 971–974, New York, NY, USA, 2015. ACM.
[31] J. Yuan, B. Kanagal, V. Josifovski, L. Garcia-Pueyo, A. Ahmed, and S. Pandey. Focused matrix factorization for audience selection in display advertising. In *Proceedings of the 2013 IEEE International Conference on Data Engineering (ICDE 2013)*, ICDE '13, pages 386–397, Washington, DC, USA, 2013. IEEE Computer Society.

An Elementary View on Factorization Machines

Sebastian Prillo
Universidad de Buenos Aires
sprillo@dc.uba.ar

ABSTRACT

Factorization Machines (FMs) are a model class capable of learning pairwise (and in general higher order) feature interactions from high dimensional, sparse data. In this paper we adopt an elementary view on FMs. Specifically, we view FMs as a sum of simple surfaces - a hyperplane plus several squared hyperplanes - in the original feature space. This elementary view, although equivalent to that of low rank matrix factorization, is geometrically more intuitive and points to some interesting generalizations. Led by our intuition, we challenge our understanding of the inductive bias of FMs by showing a simple dataset where FMs *counterintuitively* fail to learn the weight of the interaction between two features. We discuss the reasons, and mathematically formulate and prove a form of this limitation. Also inspired by our elementary view, we propose modeling *intermediate orders of interaction*, such as 1.5-way FMs. Beyond the specific proposals, the goal of this paper is to expose our thoughts and ideas to the research community in an effort to take FMs to the next level.

KEYWORDS

ANOVA kernel; Factorization Machines; Machine Learning; Recommender Systems

1 INTRODUCTION

Factorization Machines (FMs), introduced by Steffen Rendle in [6] are a supervised learning model class which excels at learning pairwise feature interactions from sparse data. The origin of FMs lies in matrix factorization models commonly used in recommender system tasks. However, FMs are different in that they are not limited to specific types of data - they are a *general* predictor.

FMs are best understood by considering the following second-order polynomial model:

$$\hat{y}(x) := w_0 + \sum_{i=1}^{n} w_i x_i + \sum_{i=1}^{n}\sum_{j=i+1}^{n} w_{i,j} x_i x_j \tag{1}$$

and then demanding that the pairwise interaction weight matrix $W = (w_{i,j})_{1 \le i,j \le n}$ have low-rank representation $W = VV^T$ where $V \in \mathbb{R}^{n \times k}$ (we ignore the diagonal terms in W); k is of course typically chosen to be much smaller than n. The FM model equation thus is:

$$\hat{y}(x) := w_0 + \sum_{i=1}^{n} w_i x_i + \sum_{i=1}^{n}\sum_{j=i+1}^{n} \langle v_i, v_j \rangle x_i x_j \tag{2}$$

where $w_0 \in \mathbb{R}$, $w \in \mathbb{R}^n$ and v_i is the i-th row of $V \in \mathbb{R}^{n \times k}$.

A widely adopted interpretation of FMs is that they work by embedding each feature in a k dimensional vector space and then expressing the weight of the interaction between two features as the similarity of their vector embeddings. In [6], Rendle uses this interpretation to explain how FMs can learn user preferences from a small toy dataset of user-movie ratings.

We focus instead on the following reformulation of FMs. As Rendle has shown himself [6, Lema 3.1], the FM model equation can be rewritten as:

$$\hat{y}(x) := w_0 + \sum_{i=1}^{n} w_i x_i + \frac{1}{2}\sum_{f=1}^{k}\left(\left(\sum_{i=1}^{n} v_{i,f} x_i\right)^2 - \sum_{i=1}^{n} v_{i,f}^2 x_i^2\right) \tag{3}$$

Rendle uses this reformulation to prove that FMs can be computed in linear time $O(nk)$ and thus efficiently trained. However, this reformulation has further meaning: it shows that FMs are (roughly) nothing more than the sum of a hyperplane plus k squared hyperplanes in the original feature space. This is our *elementary view*.

Inspired by our elementary view, we make our first contribution by showing a simple dataset where FMs counterintuitively fail to learn the weight of the interaction between two features. We discuss why this happens and dig deeper into the inductive bias of FMs, hopefully shedding some light on the way they work, and how we can use them better.

For our second contribution, we show how we might go about modeling *intermediate orders* of interaction, such as 1.5-way FMs. Several generalizations of FMs have been proposed in the past, including Higher-Order FMs (HOFM) [2, 6], Field-Aware FMs (FFMs) [5] and Convex FMs [1], however, to the best of our knowledge, intermediate-order FMs represent a novel concept.

2 ASYMMETRY OF FACTORIZATION MACHINES

2.1 Discussion

An obvious consequence of viewing FMs as the sum of a hyperplane plus k squared hyperplanes in the original feature space is that FMs exhibit some form of asymmetry with respect to the response variable. Let us make this clear by means of an example: Suppose we want to train a classifier to distinguish cats from dogs. Label 'cat' as the positive class and 'dog' as the negative class. Train a FM (say with logistic link function). Now reverse the class labels (make 'dog'

RecSys '17, August 27-31, 2017, Como, Italy

ACM ISBN 978-1-4503-4652-8/17/08...$15.00
https://doi.org/10.1145/3109859.3109892

the positive class and 'cat' the negative class) and train another FM. *Then these two FMs will perform differently*, and the reason for this does not have to do with the fact that the FM optimization problem is non-convex: it rather has to do with the fact that FMs' hypothesis space is different from its 'negative'. Formally, if FM^+ is the family of functions defined by equation 3, then by 'its negative' we mean the family $FM^- = \{-f : f \in FM^+\}$.

The fact that FMs exhibit this form of asymmetry is by no means a problem, but since it is not the typical case for a general predictor, it raises some questions regarding FMs' inductive bias. After some thought, we have come up with a simple toy dataset to show how this asymmetry might impact FMs. Consider the following dataset, which portrays the impact of several factors on life expectancy:

smokes	sedentary life	unhealthy diet	life expectancy
0	0	0	10
1	0	0	8
0	1	0	8
0	0	1	8
1	1	0	2
1	0	1	2

We purposefully omitted the observation $(0, 1, 1, 2)$ from the dataset to use it as our test case. Following Rendle's exact same line of argument as in [6, Parameter Estimation Under Sparsity], replacing 'Bob' by 'sedentary life', 'Charlie' by 'unhealthy diet', 'Star Wars' by 'smokes', and 'rating' by 'life expectancy', we get this claim: "*'sedentary life' and 'unhealthy diet' will have similar factor vectors v_2 and v_3 because both have similar interactions with 'smokes' (v_1) for predicting 'life expectancy'* ". In other words, v_2 and v_3 must be similar. But this implies that the inner product between v_2 and v_3 must be positive, and hence the pairwise weight for sedentary life and unhealthy diet must be positive. This is the opposite of what we were expecting! What went wrong?

Let us explain the previous example with concrete numbers. To make our point we will consider $k = 1$, but as we will prove, a similar result holds in higher dimensions. The FM model equation for $k = 1$ is:

$$\hat{y}(x) = w_0 + w_1x_1 + w_2x_2 + w_3x_3 + v_1v_2x_1x_2 + v_1v_3x_1x_3 + v_2v_3x_2x_3 \tag{4}$$

where $w_i, v_i \in \mathbb{R}$. Let us fit this FM to the data and see what it learns about the pairwise interaction between the features 'sedentary life' and 'unhealthy diet'; our intuition demands this weight to be negative. Note that the weights for the pairwise interactions are v_1v_2, v_1v_3 and v_2v_3, whose product is a perfect square. Thus, if the FM infers from the data that smoking and having a sedentary life should have a negative impact on life expectancy, and similarly that smoking and having an unhealthy diet should have a negative impact on life expectancy, then the FM **must** conclude that having a sedentary life and an unhealthy diet should have a positive impact on life expectancy. For example, the FM could learn the weights

$$(w_0, w_1, w_2, w_3, v_1, v_2, v_3) = (10, -2, -2, -2, -2, 2, 2)$$

which fit the data, but will surprisingly predict a life expectancy of 10 for point $(0, 1, 1)$. Note that if we reverse the effect of the independent variables on the dependent variable, say by multiplying the life expectancy by -1, then the FM can learn weights

$$(w_0, w_1, w_2, w_3, v_1, v_2, v_3) = (-10, 2, 2, 2, 2, 2, 2)$$

and correctly predict a value of -2 for point $(0, 1, 1)$.

In the general case ($k \geq 1$), it is not necessarily true that if $\langle v_1, v_2 \rangle$ and $\langle v_1, v_3 \rangle$ are negative, then $\langle v_2, v_3 \rangle$ is positive. For larger values of k, the high-dimensionality of the embedding space allows the vectors to accommodate in more sophisticated ways. However, the following result holds:

Theorem 2.1. *Given $n + 2$ vectors in $\mathbb{R}^n$ ($n \geq 1$), there are two whose inner product is non-negative.*

Proof. We prove the proposition by induction on n. For $n = 1$ it is trivial. Suppose it is true for some $n - 1 \geq 1$ and let us prove it for n. Let $v_1, v_2, \ldots, v_{n+2}$ be $n + 2$ vectors in $\mathbb{R}^n$. If $v_1 = 0$ we are done, so suppose otherwise. If any of the other v_i ($i \neq 1$) forms a non-obtuse angle with v_1 we are also done, so suppose $\langle v_i, v_1 \rangle < 0$ for all $i \neq 1$. Write $v_i = \langle v_i, v_1 \rangle \frac{v_1}{|v_1|^2} + u_i$ where $u_i \in \langle v_1 \rangle^{\perp}$. Then $u_2, u_3, \ldots, u_{n+2}$ are $n + 1$ vectors in an $n - 1$-dimensional space isomorphic to $\mathbb{R}^{n-1}$, so by the inductive hypothesis there exist $2 \leq s < t \leq n + 2$ such that $\langle u_s, u_t \rangle \geq 0$. Since $\langle v_s, v_1 \rangle, \langle v_t, v_1 \rangle$ are both negative it follows that $\langle v_s, v_t \rangle = \left\langle \langle v_s, v_1 \rangle \frac{v_1}{|v_1|^2} + u_s, \langle v_t, v_1 \rangle \frac{v_1}{|v_1|^2} + u_t \right\rangle = \frac{\langle v_s, v_1 \rangle \langle v_t, v_1 \rangle}{|v_1|^2} + \langle u_s, u_t \rangle > \langle u_s, u_t \rangle \geq 0$, and we are done. □

As a corollary, given a Factorization Machine with embedding of dimension k, for any $k + 2$ chosen features there will always be two whose pairwise interaction weight is non-negative. This is an easy to grasp result showing a limitation of FMs. Of course, the result is false if 'non-negative' is changed by 'non-positive', which displays the asymmetric nature of FMs.

Our analysis raises some questions regarding the inductive bias of FMs: we would like to know intuitively what criterion FMs are using to infer the pairwise interaction weights, and why this criterion is asymmetric. To answer this question, it is again convenient to look at the case $k = 1$ (larger values of k are just meant to generalize this intuition to higher dimensions) and consider a graph on n vertices, one vertex per feature. Let the edge between two vertices be assigned the weight of the pairwise interaction between those features. Assume for simplicity that all weights are non-zero. Then FMs can model precisely those graphs where:

(1) For every cycle of even length, the two alternating products of edge weights are equal.
(2) For every cycle of odd length, the product of its weights is positive.

From this, it is clear that FMs (with $k = 1$) have only n degrees of freedom: fix the weights of a spanning tree and an edge forming an odd cycle (in a way that does not violate condition 2), and from the above restrictions all other weights are uniquely determined. FM^- changes (2) to read 'for every cycle of odd length, the product of its weights is **negative**'. FMs 'fail' in our toy dataset because our intuition want us to infer from two negative edges in a triangle a third negative edge, but the inductive bias of FMs will do the exact opposite.

Explaining why this issue does not arise during Rendle's explanation of the toy user-movie dataset is a bit more subtle, and has to do with the fact that in this dataset the pairwise weights that are only ever exercised are induced by a bipartite graph with users on one side and movies on the other, but FM^+ and FM^- are equally expressive in this context. Formally, $FM^+ = FM^-$ when we restrict the domain of the functions in FM^+ and FM^- to the set X of vectors $x \in \{0,1\}^{U+I}$ ($U, I \in \mathbb{N}$ fixed) such that exactly one of $x_1, \dots, x_U$ is 1, and exactly one of $x_{U+1}, \dots, x_{U+I}$ is 1. The proof for this is easy: if $f \in FM^+$ is parametrized by the weights $(w_0, \dots, w_n, v_1, \dots, v_{U+I})$ as in equation 2, then $-f \in FM^+$, parametrized by the weights $(-w_0, \dots, -w_n, -v_1, \dots, -v_U, v_{U+1}, \dots, v_{U+I})$, hence $FM^+ = FM^-$.

2.2 Exploiting or addressing asymmetry

The previous discussion suggests a trivial trick to try to improve the performance of FMs: since $FM^+ \neq FM^-$ (except specific cases as the one discussed), *just by reversing the response variable in the dataset* (which is equivalent to training a model from FM^- instead of FM^+) the performance of FMs might improve. Ensembling models from FM^+ and FM^- might be another good idea.

If we talk about 'fixing' the asymmetry of FMs, some good ideas can be taken from the work of [3]. Indeed, we can consider:

$$\hat{y}(x) = w_0 + \sum_{i=1}^{n} w_i x_i + \frac{1}{2}\sum_{f=1}^{k} \lambda_i \Big(\big(\sum_{i=1}^{n} v_{i,f} x_i\big)^2 - \sum_{i=1}^{n} v_{i,f}^2 x_i^2 \Big) \quad (5)$$

where $\lambda_i \in \mathbb{R}$. Since the absolute value of λ_i can be absorbed into the right hand factor, this hypothesis space as expressive as limiting each λ_i to take the value -1 or 1. From our elementary point of view, the squared hyperplanes can now be either added or subtracted. A middle ground approach which does not require fitting λ is to just force half the λ_i in equation 5 to be 1 and the other half to be -1. Although this might sound ad-hoc, it has a nice mathematical interpretation: it is the same as the original FM model equation (2) but with a $\frac{k}{2}$ (assume k even) dimensional feature embedding in $\mathbb{C}^{\frac{k}{2}}$ (hence $V \in \mathbb{C}^{n \times \frac{k}{2}}$), with the real inner product replaced by the bilinear form $\langle a+bi, c+di \rangle = \langle a,c \rangle + i\langle b,c \rangle + i\langle a,d \rangle - \langle b,d \rangle$ for $a,b,c,d \in \mathbb{R}^{\frac{k}{2}}$, and then taking the real part from the resulting equation. It is tempting to call these *complex FMs*.

Interestingly, equation 5 is closely related to the following model, also derived from [3]:

$$\hat{y}(x) := w_0 + \sum_{i=1}^{n} w_i x_i + \sum_{i=1}^{n}\sum_{j=i+1}^{n} \langle u_i, v_j \rangle x_i x_j \quad (6)$$

where $w_0 \in \mathbb{R}$, $w \in \mathbb{R}^n$ and $U, V \in \mathbb{R}^{n \times k}$. In essence, the asymmetry we have discussed is directly related to the positive semi-definiteness of the pairwise interaction weight matrix W. By relaxing the representation of W from $W = VV^T$ to $W = UV^T$, the positive semi-definiteness of W is bypassed. The results in [3] suggest that the models defined by equations 5 and 6 should be of comparable performance when the embedding size of the former is twice the one of the latter.

3 INTERMEDIATE-ORDER FACTORIZATION MACHINES

3.1 Motivation

The essence of FMs lies in the distributive law: when squaring a hyperplane pairwise interaction terms arise naturally, and similarly when cubing a hyperplane 3-way interaction terms arise. Of course, this also generates some unwanted terms such as $v_i^2 v_j x_i^2 x_j$ which we must deal with. But clearly, *there is nothing stopping us from exponentiating a hyperplane to an arbitrary d-th power.* By doing so, we can interpret it as giving rise to d-way interactions.

3.2 Formalization

To formalize this idea, it is convenient to speak in terms of kernels. As stated in [2, 3], the FM model equation (3) is equivalent to

$$\hat{y}(x) = w_0 + \langle w, x \rangle + \sum_{f=1}^{k} \mathcal{K}_f(c_f, x) \quad (7)$$

where $\mathcal{K}_f = \mathcal{A}_2$ are ANOVA kernels of degree 2, and c_f is the f-th column of V. Similarly, 3-way FMs are a combination of ANOVA kernels of degree 2 and 3. In general, the ANOVA kernel $\mathcal{A}_m$ of degree m is responsible for capturing interactions of order m. Thus, the goal of building intermediate-order FMs translates to that of extrapolating $\mathcal{A}_m$ to non-integral values of m. Of course, the discrete nature underlying the definition of $\mathcal{A}_m$ makes it hard to do so directly. However, by expressing $\mathcal{A}_m$ in terms of simpler quantities we can try to achieve our goal. These simpler quantities will be precisely powers of hyperplanes, as discussed in our initial motivation, among others.

Specifically, let $\mathcal{D}_m(x,y) = \sum_{i=1}^{n} x_i^m y_i^m$ be the 'power sum' kernel of degree m. That is, if e_m and p_m are respectively the elementary and power sum symmetric polynomials of degree m in n variables, and $\circ$ is the Hadamard product, then we have $\mathcal{D}_m(x,y) = p_m(x \circ y)$ and $\mathcal{A}_m(x,y) = e_m(x \circ y)$. Since the p_i ($1 \le i \le n$) form a basis for the ring of symmetric polynomials over $\mathbb{Q}$ - of which e_m is such an element - then e_m admits a unique representation as a polynomial in the p_i, and in turn $\mathcal{A}_m$ admits a unique representation as polynomial in the $\mathcal{D}_i$. For instance, $\mathcal{A}_2 = \frac{1}{2}(\mathcal{D}_1^2 - \mathcal{D}_2)$ and $\mathcal{A}_3 = \frac{1}{6}(\mathcal{D}_1^3 - 3\mathcal{D}_2\mathcal{D}_1 + 2\mathcal{D}_3)$. These identities are derived in [3, Lemma 3], but the connection with the ring of symmetric polynomials was not identified. Thus, in general, for all m we have an essentially unique representation

$$\mathcal{A}_m = \sum_{i=1}^{s} q_i \prod_{j=1}^{t_i} \mathcal{D}_{m_{i,j}} \quad (8)$$

where $s \in \mathbb{N}_0, q_i \in \mathbb{Q}, t_i \in \mathbb{N}, m_{i,j} \le n$. With this, let us define the extrapolation of $\mathcal{A}_m$ to order $d \in \mathbb{R}$ by

$$\mathcal{A}_{m \to d} = \sum_{i=1}^{s} q_i \prod_{j=1}^{t_i} \operatorname{sign}(\mathcal{D}_{m_{i,j}}) \big|\mathcal{D}_{m_{i,j}}\big|^{\frac{d}{m}} \quad (9)$$

Note that this extrapolation is consistent in the sense that $\mathcal{A}_m = \mathcal{A}_{m \to m}$ for all $m \in \mathbb{N}$, and, furthermore, $\mathcal{A}_{m \to d}$ is homogeneous of degree d, meaning $\mathcal{A}_{m \to d}(\lambda x, y) = \operatorname{sign}(\lambda^m)|\lambda|^d \mathcal{A}_{m \to d}(x,y)$. Please note that our extrapolation is by no means the only nor the best way to do this. We believe that there might be a better way to extrapolate $\mathcal{A}_m$ to non-integral values of m, perhaps in a way that seamlessly unifies all the ANOVA kernels of different degrees. We think an affirmative answer to this question would be a major breakthrough in our understanding of Factorization Machines.

3.3 Extrapolating 2-way FMs

When $m = 2$ we have $\mathcal{A}_m = \frac{1}{2}\mathcal{D}_1\mathcal{D}_1 - \frac{1}{2}\mathcal{D}_2$ and hence equation 9 leads to $\mathcal{A}_{2\to d} = \frac{1}{2}(|\mathcal{D}_1|^d - \mathcal{D}_2^{\frac{d}{2}})$. Thus, we can extrapolate 2-way FMs to d-way FMs by considering

$$\hat{y}(x) := w_0 + \sum_{i=1}^{n} w_i x_i + \frac{1}{2}\sum_{f=1}^{k}\left(\left|\sum_{i=1}^{n} v_{i,f}x_i\right|^d - \left(\sum_{i=1}^{n} v_{i,f}^2 x_i^2\right)^{\frac{d}{2}}\right) \quad (10)$$

Let us extend our previous definitions and denote FM_d^+ the family of functions defined by equation 10, and $FM_d^- = \{-f : f \in FM_d^+\}$.

3.4 Implementation

Adapting 2-way FMs to support equation 10 is easy in the case of SGD learning. We believe it might not be possible to do so efficiently in the case of ALS and MCMC learning, because the key property of multi-linearity, which leads to multi-convexity, is lost. See [7] for a full exposition on these learning procedures applied to FMs.

Perhaps surprisingly, when $d \geq 1$, equation 10 has continuous partial derivatives with respect to the $v_{i,f}$, given by:

$$\frac{\partial}{\partial v_{i,f}}\hat{y}(x) = \frac{d}{2}x_i \operatorname{sign}(D_1)|D_1|^{d-1} - \frac{d}{2}v_{i,f}x_i^2 D_2^{\frac{d-2}{2}}$$

where $D_1 = \mathcal{D}_1(c_f, x)$ and $D_2 = \mathcal{D}_2(c_f, x)$. This is similar to the derivatives of 2-way FMs and can also be computed efficiently with minor modifications to the code. The only caveat is that exponentiating a floating point number to an arbitrary exponent is *a priori* a slow operation, but this can be overcome by restricting ourselves to suitable values of d, such as $d \in \{1.25, 1.50, 1.75, \dots\}$ for which exponentiation can be efficiently computed by taking only square roots. Note also that equation 10 can be easily differentiated with respect to d, allowing us to learn the interaction level from the data if we wish.

4 RESULTS

We modified the libFM implementation [7] to support intermediate-order FMs as defined by equation 10. We ran experiments on the Movielens 100k dataset[1] [4]; the dataset contains 10^5 ratings from 943 users on 1682 movies. We trained d-way FMs for $d \in \{1.25, 1.5, 1.75, 2\}$. We set $k = 4$, and after some experimentation settled on a learning rate of 0.01, regularization of 0.075 and initialization standard deviation of 10^{-5}, which seem to work well for these models. For each model, given a random number seed, we trained it on each of the five 80/20 c.v. splits `u*.base`,`u*.test` provided by the owners of the dataset. We trained for 200 iterations (enough for the models to overfit) and considered the best validation RMSE obtained during these 200 iterations. We then averaged this validation RMSE over the 5 folds. Finally, for this statistic we plotted the mean and a confidence interval corresponding to two standard deviations, computed from 30 runs with different seeds: $1 \leq seed \leq 30$. This whole experiment was run twice, the second time by first multiplying the response variable by -1.

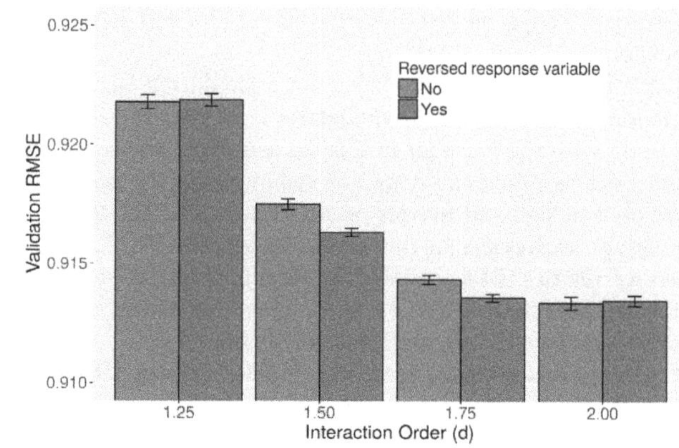

Figure 1: Effect of interaction order and reversal of the response variable on RMSE.

Several of the observations we made in this paper are reflected in the results. First of all, since the dataset consists of only two categorical variables, we have $FM_2^+ = FM_2^-$, as we have proven, and this is supported by the confidence intervals for $d = 2$ which considerably overlap. On the other hand, it is not necessarily true that $FM_d^+ = FM_d^-$ for $d \neq 2$ (our proof fails in this case), and indeed when reversing the response variable, our 1.5 and 1.75-way FMs see a boost in RMSE. Finally, we can see that 1.75-way FMs are competitive with 2-way FMs on this dataset. It is worthwhile to mention that we trained linear models which achieved an RMSE of 0.942, so even 1.25-way FMs perform significantly better than plain linear models.

We tried training these d-way FMs for $2 < d < 3$ but surprisingly, as soon as $d > 2.1$, SGD gets stuck in what appears to be a plateau with high training RMSE, only ever escaping. This seems to align with another behavior we observed, where for $1 < d < 2$, the smaller the value of d, the faster the progress SGD makes in the first iterations: it takes 2-way FMs roughly 40 iterations to reach the same RMSE as 1.25-way FMs in 10 iterations. It looks like smaller values of d might make the optimization problem more amenable for SGD by altering the curvature of the error surface, but this will require further investigation.

5 CONCLUSION

In this paper we explored an elementary view on FMs. This gave us immediate insights: we explored the asymmetry of FMs, which allowed us to better understand their inductive bias, and we proposed the modeling of intermediate orders of interaction, an abstract concept. We showed preliminary results supporting the value of our ideas. However, our work leaves several open questions: for instance, our way of modeling intermediate-order interactions feels perfectible. Our hope is that these ideas can be taken by the research community and ripened to evolve FMs to the next level.

[1] https://grouplens.org/datasets/movielens/100k/

REFERENCES

[1] Mathieu Blondel, Akinori Fujino, and Naonori Ueda. 2015. Convex Factorization Machines. In *Proceedings, Part II, of the European Conference on Machine Learning and Knowledge Discovery in Databases - Volume 9285 (ECML PKDD 2015)*. Springer-Verlag New York, Inc., New York, NY, USA, 19–35. https://doi.org/10.1007/978-3-319-23525-7_2

[2] Mathieu Blondel, Akinori Fujino, Naonori Ueda, and Masakazu Ishihata. 2016. Higher-Order Factorization Machines. In *Advances in Neural Information Processing Systems 29*, D. D. Lee, M. Sugiyama, U. V. Luxburg, I. Guyon, and R. Garnett (Eds.). Curran Associates, Inc., 3351–3359. http://papers.nips.cc/paper/6144-higher-order-factorization-machines.pdf

[3] Mathieu Blondel, Masakazu Ishihata, Akinori Fujino, and Naonori Ueda. 2016. Polynomial Networks and Factorization Machines: New Insights and Efficient Training Algorithms. In *Proceedings of the 33rd International Conference on International Conference on Machine Learning - Volume 48 (ICML'16)*. JMLR.org, 850–858. http://dl.acm.org/citation.cfm?id=3045390.3045481

[4] F. Maxwell Harper and Joseph A. Konstan. 2015. The MovieLens Datasets: History and Context. *ACM Trans. Interact. Intell. Syst.* 5, 4, Article 19 (Dec. 2015), 19 pages. https://doi.org/10.1145/2827872

[5] Yuchin Juan, Yong Zhuang, Wei-Sheng Chin, and Chih-Jen Lin. 2016. Field-aware Factorization Machines for CTR Prediction. In *Proceedings of the 10th ACM Conference on Recommender Systems.*

[6] Steffen Rendle. 2010. Factorization Machines. In *Proceedings of the 2010 IEEE International Conference on Data Mining.*

[7] Steffen Rendle. 2012. Factorization Machines with libFM. *ACM Trans. Intell. Syst. Technol.* 3 (2012).

Expediting Exploration by Attribute-to-Feature Mapping for Cold-Start Recommendations

Deborah Cohen*
Google Research
Tel-Aviv, Israel
debbycohen@gmail.com

Michal Aharon, Yair Koren, and Oren Somekh
Yahoo Research, Haifa, Israel
(michala,yairkoren,orens)@yahoo-inc.com

Raz Nissim*
General Motors
Advanced Technical Center
Herzliya, Israel
raz.nissim@gm.com

ABSTRACT

The item cold-start problem is inherent to collaborative filtering (CF) recommenders where items and users are represented by vectors in a latent space. It emerges since CF recommenders rely solely on historical user interactions to characterize their item inventory. As a result, an effective serving of new and trendy items to users may be delayed until enough user feedback is received, thus, reducing both users' and content suppliers' satisfaction. To mitigate this problem, many commercial recommenders apply random exploration and devote a small portion of their traffic to explore new items and gather interactions from random users. Alternatively, content or context information is combined into the CF recommender, resulting in a hybrid system. Another hybrid approach is to learn a mapping between the item attribute space and the CF latent feature space, and use it to characterize the new items providing initial estimates for their latent vectors.

In this paper, we adopt the attribute-to-feature mapping approach to expedite random exploration of new items and present LearnAROMA - an advanced algorithm for learning the mapping, previously proposed in the context of classification. In particular, LearnAROMA learns a Gaussian distribution over the mapping matrix. Numerical evaluation demonstrates that this learning technique achieves more accurate initial estimates than logistic regression methods. We then consider a random exploration setting, in which new items are further explored as user interactions arrive. To leverage the initial latent vector estimates with the incoming interactions, we propose DynamicBPR - an algorithm for updating the new item latent vectors without retraining the CF model. Numerical evaluation reveals that DynamicBPR achieves similar accuracy as a CF model trained on all the ratings, using 71% less exploring users than conventional random exploration.

KEYWORDS

Recommendation systems, collaborative-filtering, random exploration, item cold-start problem

*This work was done while Deborah and Raz were with Yahoo Research, Haifa, Israel.

RecSys'17, August 27–31, 2017, Como, Italy.
© 2017 ACM. ISBN 978-1-4503-4652-8/17/08...$15.00.
DOI: http://dx.doi.org/10.1145/3109859.3109880

1 INTRODUCTION

In recent years, recommendation technologies have become an essential tool for matching relevant content and services to users. Whether these are news items, movies, mobile apps, or even ads, recommender systems usually use historical user interactions and stated preferences, and content information to characterize their items. Techniques that rely on content information are known as *content-based* [18], while techniques that rely solely on historical users interactions, such as clicks, skips and ratings, are known as *collaborative filtering* (CF) [14]. Notably, CF techniques require no domain knowledge or content analysis and excel at exploiting popularity trends, which drive much of the observed user interactions and typically would be completely missed by content based approaches. In addition, relying directly on user behavior allows uncovering complex and unexpected patterns that would be difficult or impossible to profile using known data attributes. Therefore, CF attracted much attention in recent years, resulting in significant progress and adoption by many commercial systems.

Since CF recommenders rely only on historical user interactions to characterize their entities, the lack of such data for new entities imposes an inherent problem known as the *cold-start problem*. Hence, without sufficient historical user data, CF-based recommenders cannot reliably model new entities. Despite the fact that users and items have similar representations in the latent space, the users and items cold-start problems are essentially different. The main difference comes from the ability to interview new users when joining a service in order to bootstrap their modeling. Besides, in most settings the number of users is much larger than the number of items. Hence, a typical item usually gets more ratings than an individual user provides.

To mitigate the CF item cold-start problem, a few known approaches are usually applied. The most common method, used by many commercial web-scale recommenders, is random exploration, where a small random portion of the user traffic is devoted to explore new items. Then, the resulting user feedback is used to model the new items. This approach is simple but inefficient, since the matching between users and items is almost arbitrary and recent work shows that carefully selecting the exploring users is beneficial [1, 6]. Another common approach to combat the item cold-start issue is to utilize item attributes in addition to the users feedback resulting in a *hybrid* recommender. Numerous ways to integrate the item attributes into the CF model have been suggested over the years. The basic principle driving this approach is that new items share attributes with mature items. Therefore, the recommender can characterize the latter with latent vector representations of their attributes and provide an initial representation for the new items. Another approach which exploits item attributes as well, but in an implicit way, is presented in [8]. In particular, the authors train a CF model and then learn a linear mapping between the item attributes space and the CF latent space. Once the mapping is set, it is used to provide an initial estimate for the new items latent vectors.

In this paper, we address the CF item cold-start problem and adopt a hybrid approach. The presentation is formulated in terms of item cold-starts since this problem is typically more challenging. However, the derivations and algorithms can be directly applied to user cold-starts as well. Inspired by the approach of [8], we consider item attributes to CF latent space mappings. In particular, in order to learn the linear mapping between attributes and latent features, we present LearnAROMA, a variant of the AROMA (Adaptive Regularization Of MAtrix models) algorithm, presented in [4, 5] in the context of linear classification. The key principle of AROMA is that instead of maintaining a single weight matrix, it considers a Gaussian distribution over possible models. Moreover, while [8] considers an initial estimate to the new item latent vectors only, we also consider a random exploration setting where users interactions with the new items are arriving. For this setting, we present a simple algorithm, DynamicBPR, that updates the new items latent vectors with the incoming interactions, using a regularized maximum likelihood convex objective. Our approach does not require to retrain the CF model, which would be inefficient in large scale systems. Finally, we test our LearnAROMA based initial estimate and update algorithm DynamicBPR using the MovieLens2K dataset, which includes genre, and crew information in addition to users ratings, and demonstrate their benefits over several baselines. The main contributions of this work are:

- The LearnAROMA algorithm for learning items attributes to latent space mapping, that provides an initial estimate of new items latent vectors.
- The DynamicBPR algorithm for updating new items latent vectors during random exploration, leveraging their initial estimate with incoming users' interactions, without retraining the whole CF model.
- Numerical evaluation that demonstrates the superiority of the LearnAROMA algorithm over the LearnMap algorithm of [8]. In addition, the DynamicBPR algorithm is shown to achieve similar accuracies to those achieved by retraining the whole model, requiring far less interactions compared to random exploration.

The rest of the paper is organized as follows. In Section 2, we review related work. Section 3 formulates the item cold-start problem and sets our goals. In Section 4, we describe LearnMap, an item attributes to latent space mapping approach, to mitigate the CF item cold-start problem. An alternative algorithm to learn this mapping, LearnAROMA, is elaborated in Section 5. Section 6 formulates the exploration setting and presents the DynamicBPR algorithm that dynamically updates the latent vectors. Numerical evaluation results are presented in Section 7. We conclude and consider future work in Section 8.

2 RELATED WORK

Several approaches have recently been proposed, that aim at mitigating the inherent item cold-start problem in CF recommenders. These can be divided into two main categories; pure CF systems that gather exploratory feedback from users on new items, and hybrid approaches that combine content-based and CF recommendation techniques.

2.1 Pure CF Techniques

A naive common approach for this first category is to use an exploration bucket, where randomly selected users are exposed to the new item, generating feedback for the latter. This simple and inefficient approach can be improved by selecting the most useful users, who are more likely to be interested in the new items [6], or who will provide the best characterization for them [1, 15]. Unfortunately, these approaches require user cooperation.

Other CF techniques address the wide sense cold-start users, that is infrequent users with few ratings [13, 22]. In this setting, the users latent vectors express similarities depending on the items rated by the user. However, these can obviously not be applied to the narrow sense cold-starts problem, where no ratings are available for new entities (see [21] for online update of items with few ratings).

Another approach that combines exploration-exploitation simultaneously, is based on *multi-armed bandit* (MAB) where presenting an item to a user in a specific context is abstracted as pulling a MAB arm with some uncertain reward (cf., [3] and references therein). However, these methods become very complex when the item inventory is large (e.g., typical ad inventory can reach 200K items).

2.2 Hybrid Techniques

Hybrid techniques alleviate the need for users' help by exploiting content information. Several strategies can be adopted for creating hybrid techniques: working directly in the item and user attribute space [10, 11, 16, 17]; incorporating item attributes into the latent space [19]; mapping the attribute space to the CF latent space in order to estimate new items' latent vectors [2, 8].

Avoiding asking real users for their help, [17] uses artificial users or bots implementing various heuristics, in part based on content information, to generate synthetic data. A stochastic hybrid approach, where the joint distribution of users vote vector is modeled using a *Boltzmann machine*, is presented in [10, 11].

In [2], a similar framework as in [22] is considered, where the mean prior of the item and user latent vectors are expressed as linear functions of their corresponding known attributes. Here, given the ratings and attributes, the goal is to find the maximum likelihood estimate of the parameters that define the mapping between the attribute and latent domains. In addition, the authors consider an incremental learning setting where for each batch of observations, the current posterior becomes prior and is combined with the data likelihood to provide an updated posterior.

A general approach referred to as *factorization machines* is presented in [19]. Special cases of the factorization machines include but are not limited to the traditional *matrix factorization* (MF), SVD++ (see [13]), nearest neighbor models and attribute-aware models. In the latter case, each attribute is associated with a latent vector which are directly included in the feature vectors.

A hybrid MF-CF and content-based technique is adopted in [8]. The goal is to learn the mapping function between the entities (items) attribute space and their latent space. The factorization model is first trained on the known ratings. Then, two learning approaches are suggested; the first is a *K-Nearest Neighbor* (KNN) mapping where the new latent vectors are weighted averages of the features of the k closest neighbors in the attribute space. The second approach assumes that the latent vectors are linear functions of the attributes. Once the mapping functions are found, the latent vector of a new entity with known attributes can be computed and new item-user scores can be derived by taking the inner product between corresponding user-item latent vectors (see also [23] where the mapping approach is used sub-optimally as a baseline).

3 PROBLEM FORMULATION

In this section, we present the recommendation model and formulate the item cold-start issue. We then describe our generic framework and MF model training.

3.1 Model Description

Consider a system with N users and M items, including M_1 mature items and M_2 new items (cold-starts), so that $M = M_1 + M_2$. Each item is associated with a known $L \times 1$ binary attribute vector $\mathbf{a}_j$ that contains the item content information (e.g., for movies: genres, actors and directors). For example, consider a recommender system for movies including the movies *The Butterfly Effect* and *Toy Story* and the following $L = 4$ genres: *Animation, Comedy, Drama, Fantasy.* If we assign consecutive indices in alphabetical order to both the movies and genres, the resulting attributes vectors are $\mathbf{a}_1 = [0\ 0\ 1\ 0]^T$ and $\mathbf{a}_2 = [1\ 1\ 0\ 1]^T$. Attributes representation is not restricted to a binary set and the mapping derived here for binary attributes, for the sake of simplicity, can be extended to other attributes forms.

Let S be the $N \times M$ binary feedback matrix, with $S_{ij} = 1$ if user i has provided positive feedback on item j; otherwise $S_{ij} = 0$. Positive feedback refers to any user-item interaction, e.g. rating or click, while negative feedback indicates a lack of interaction. Denote the set of items for which user i has provided positive feedback by $I_i^+ = \{j|S_{ij} = 1\}$ and the set of items for which user i has not provided feedback by $I_i^- = \{j|S_{ij} = 0\}$. The feedback for mature items, namely S_{ij}, for $1 \le j \le M_1$ is assumed to be known, whereas it is dynamically discovered for new (or cold-start) items, $M_1 < j \le M$, one user-item interaction at a time.

In terms of items, our dataset is divided between mature and new items. For new items, we distinguish between users that provide feedback allowing for dynamic training and test users. We thus divide the dataset into 3 parts, as shown in Fig. 1. The first group $\mathcal{A}_1$ constitutes the model training group and is composed of the N users and the M_1 mature items. The second group $\mathcal{A}_2$ is composed of N_1 users and the M_2 new items for dynamic training. Lastly, the third group $\mathcal{A}_3$ represents the test group and includes the remaining interactions (or feedback) between the $N_2 = N - N_1$ users and M_2 new items.

Our goal is twofold. First, we provide an initial estimate for the latent vectors of new items, before any feedback for them is acquired. Second, we dynamically update these latent vectors with respect to sequentially incoming feedback without retraining the model.

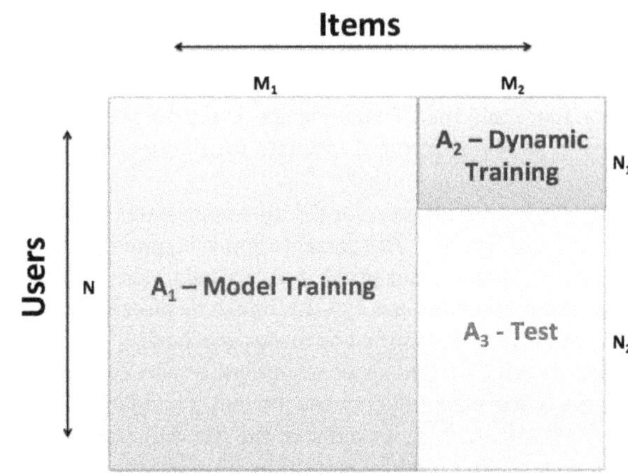

Figure 1: Dataset division.

3.2 High-Level Framework

Our approach includes three stages. The first is a traditional MF that trains a static and stable model composed of users and mature items, as described earlier. This stage results in latent vectors $\mathbf{u}_i, 1 \le i \le N$ and $\mathbf{v}_j, 1 \le j \le M_1$, for users and items, respectively. The second stage derives a mapping between item content-based attributes $\mathbf{a}_j$ and latent vectors $\mathbf{v}_j$ computed in the previous stage, yielding a mapping matrix $\mathbf{W}$. Using the attribute-to-feature mapping, we can then compute initial latent vectors $\hat{\mathbf{v}}_j^0 = \mathbf{W}\mathbf{a}_j$ for new items, or cold-starts, namely $M_1 < j \le M$. The last stage dynamically updates the new mapped latent vectors $\hat{\mathbf{v}}_j$ from new feedback on cold-starts items. This dynamic training of cold-start items does not require retraining the mature model, but only expands it to include new items.

In the next section, we describe the MF approach we adopt. In Sections 4 and 5, we present two attribute-to-feature mapping methods. Last, in Section 6, we show how the latent vectors can be dynamically updated.

3.3 BPR-MF Model Training

The principle of MF is to represent both items and users in a common latent space, which aims at capturing patterns of users feedback on items. More specifically, the latent vectors $\mathbf{u}_i, 1 \le i \le N$ and $\mathbf{v}_j, 1 \le j \le M_1$, for users and items, respectively, are inferred from the feedback such that the corresponding score of user i to item j is estimated by their inner product

$$\hat{y}_{ij} = \langle \mathbf{u}_i, \mathbf{v}_j \rangle + b_i + b_j = \sum_{k=1}^{K} u_{ik} v_{jk} + b_i + b_j. \quad (1)$$

Here, K is the latent space dimension, u_{ik} (v_{jk}) denotes the kth latent factor (or latent feature) of vector $\mathbf{u}_i$ ($\mathbf{v}_j$), and b_i and b_j are the biases of user i and item j, respectively. These users-items scores are used to rank the items for a specific user.

Specifically, we consider the *Bayesian personalized ranking* (BPR) [20] framework, used for model training with implicit feedback. The key idea is to consider entity pairs instead of single entities in the loss function, allowing the interpretation of positive-only data as partial ranking data and canceling the impact of entity bias. Here, we consider pairs of items per user, where the first item received positive feedback from the user and the second one did not. The BPR-MF optimization criterion, expressed as follows

$$\max_{\mathbf{u}_i,\mathbf{v}_p,\mathbf{v}_q,b_p,b_q} \sum_{i,p,q\in\mathcal{A}_1} \ln\frac{1}{1+e^{-\hat{x}_{ipq}}} - \lambda\left(||\mathbf{u}_i||^2 + ||\mathbf{v}_p||^2 + ||\mathbf{v}_q||^2\right) - \lambda_b\left(b_p^2 + b_q^2\right) \quad (2)$$

is a non-convex optimization problem. Here, $\lambda, \lambda_b > 0$ are regularization parameters, $\mathcal{A}_1 = \left\{(i,p,q) | p \in I_i^+ \wedge q \in I_i^-\right\}$ and

$$\hat{x}_{ipq} = \hat{y}_{ip} - \hat{y}_{iq}. \quad (3)$$

Note that in this case, the user bias b_i in (1) cancels out; thus, we do not consider user biases.

As the optimization criterion (2) is differentiable, an obvious choice for maximization is gradient descent. Since full gradient descent suffers from slow convergence, the stochastic approach is adopted in [20]. It has been empirically shown [20] that the order in which the training pairs are traversed is crucial. In particular, an item-wise or user-wise traverse approach leads to poor convergence whereas the proposed bootstrap sampling method, that is drawing user-items triples uniformly at random, converges much faster. In order to learn the BPR-MF model, we thus use the LearnBPR algorithm from [20], summarized in Algorithm 1.

Algorithm 1 LearnBPR

Input:
$S(\mathcal{A}_1)$ - feedback of N users on M_1 mature items
$\mathbf{v}_j, b_j, 1 \le j \le M_1$ - mature items latent vectors and biases
α, α_b - update step sizes
λ, λ_b - regularization parameters
Output:
$\mathbf{u}_i, 1 \le i \le N$ - users latent vectors

repeat
  draw (i,p,q) from $\mathcal{A}_1$
  $\hat{x}_{ipq} \leftarrow \hat{y}_{ip} - \hat{y}_{iq}$
  for $1 \le k \le K$ **do**
    $u_{ik} \leftarrow u_{ik} + \alpha\left(\frac{e^{-\hat{x}_{ipq}}}{1+e^{-\hat{x}_{ipq}}}(v_{pk} - v_{qk}) - \lambda u_{ik}\right)$
    $v_{pk} \leftarrow v_{pk} + \alpha\left(\frac{e^{-\hat{x}_{ipq}}}{1+e^{-\hat{x}_{ipq}}}u_{ik} - \lambda v_{pk}\right)$
    $v_{qk} \leftarrow v_{qk} + \alpha\left(-\frac{e^{-\hat{x}_{ipq}}}{1+e^{-\hat{x}_{ipq}}}u_{ik} - \lambda v_{qk}\right)$
    $b_p \leftarrow b_p + \alpha_b\left(\frac{e^{-\hat{x}_{ipq}}}{1+e^{-\hat{x}_{ipq}}} - \lambda_b b_p\right)$
    $b_q \leftarrow b_q + \alpha_b\left(-\frac{e^{-\hat{x}_{ipq}}}{1+e^{-\hat{x}_{ipq}}} - \lambda_b b_q\right)$
  end for
until convergence

4 ATTRIBUTE-TO-FEATURE MAPPING

The first stage of the training, described in Section 3.3, is a traditional BPR-MF whose output are latent vectors $\mathbf{u}_i$ for each user $1 \le i \le N$ and $\mathbf{v}_j$ for each mature item $1 \le j \le M_1$. The next training stage maps the item attribute vectors $\mathbf{a}_j$ to the item latent space, such that

$$\mathbf{v}_j = \mathbf{h}(\mathbf{a}_j), \quad (4)$$

for some function $\mathbf{h} : \mathbb{Z}_2^L \to \mathbb{R}^K$, where $\mathbb{Z}_2 = \{0,1\}$. We focus on a linear mapping, where the mapping function is represented by a $K \times L$ matrix. In this stage, we learn the mapping matrix $\mathbf{W}$.

In this case, the inner product between latent vectors becomes

$$\hat{y}_{ij} = \langle \mathbf{u}_i, \mathbf{v}_j \rangle = \mathbf{u}_i^T \mathbf{W} \mathbf{a}_j. \quad (5)$$

The convex optimization criterion with respect to $\mathbf{W}$ is then expressed as follows

$$\max_{\mathbf{W}} \sum_{i,p,q\in A} \ln\frac{1}{1+e^{-\hat{x}_{ipq}}} - \lambda||\mathbf{W}||_F, \quad (6)$$

where $||\cdot||_F$ denotes the *Frobenius norm* and $\hat{x}_{ipq} = \hat{y}_{ip} - \hat{y}_{iq}$, with $\hat{y}_{ip}$ and $\hat{y}_{iq}$ defined in (5).

In order to learn the mapping matrix $\mathbf{W}$, the LearnMap algorithm from [8], summarized in Algorithm 2 for completeness, uses a gradient descent approach. In the algorithm description, $\mathbf{w}^k$ denotes the kth row of $\mathbf{W}$.

Algorithm 2 LearnMap

Input:
$S(\mathcal{A}_1)$ - feedback of N users on M_1 mature items
$\mathbf{u}_i, 1 \le i \le N$ - users latent vectors
$\mathbf{a}_j, 1 \le j \le M_1$ - mature items attribute vectors
α - update step size
λ - regularization parameter
Output:
$\mathbf{W}$ - $K \times L$ attribute-to-feature mapping matrix

repeat
  draw (i,p,q) from $\mathcal{A}_1$
  $\hat{x}_{ipq} \leftarrow \hat{y}_{ip} - \hat{y}_{iq}$
  for $1 \le k \le K$ **do**
    $\mathbf{w}^k \leftarrow \mathbf{w}^k + \alpha\left(\frac{e^{-\hat{x}_{ipq}}}{1+e^{-\hat{x}_{ipq}}}u_{ik}(\mathbf{a}_p - \mathbf{a}_1) - \lambda\mathbf{w}^k\right)$
  end for
until convergence

Once $\mathbf{W}$ is learnt, the resulting item latent vectors are then given by

$$\hat{\mathbf{v}}_j^0 = \mathbf{W}\mathbf{a}_j. \quad (7)$$

The mapped item latent vectors $\hat{\mathbf{v}}_j^0$, for $M_1 < j \le M$, are our initial estimate for new, or cold-start, items.

It is noted that the linear approach can be extended to non-linear mapping to account for interactions between attributes. However, we found that non-linear mappings (e.g., quadratic polynomial mapping) yield marginal improvement.

5 AROMA-BASED MAPPING

In this section, we present an alternative mapping learning algorithm based on the *adaptive regularization of matrix models* (AROMA) algorithm, presented in [4] in the context of linear classification. The matrix approach AROMA extends its vector version *adaptive regularization of weights* (AROW) [5] to learn a weight matrix $\mathbf{W}$ and its corresponding confidence coefficient matrix Σ. The key idea of AROW is that instead of maintaining a single weight vector $\mathbf{w}$, it considers distribution over possible models. In particular, AROW maintains a Gaussian distribution over vectors denoted by $\mathcal{N}(\mathbf{w}, \Sigma)$.

5.1 Preliminaries

The goal of AROMA is to learn a linear similarity measure between pairs of objects - here, items and users - in the form $S_W(\mathbf{u}, \mathbf{a}) = \mathbf{u}_i^T \mathbf{W} \mathbf{a}_j$. A weak supervision setup is adopted where training is based on relative similarity. In particular, at the tth round, a triplet $\mathbf{u}_t = \mathbf{u}_i$, for some $1 \le i \le N$, $\mathbf{a}_t^+ \in I_i^+, \mathbf{a}_t^- \in I_i^-$ is sampled. The objective is to order the similarity measures of the objects $\mathbf{a}_t^+, \mathbf{a}_t^-$ with a safety margin

$$S_W(\mathbf{u}_t, \mathbf{a}_t^+) \ge S_W(\mathbf{u}_t, \mathbf{a}_t^-) + 1. \quad (8)$$

To learn a scoring function that obeys (8), the authors use the following *squared-hinge loss*, or L2 loss,

$$\ell_W^2(\mathbf{u}_t, \mathbf{a}_t^+, \mathbf{a}_t^-) = \left(\max\{0, 1 - \mathbf{u}_t^T \mathbf{W}(\mathbf{a}_t^+ - \mathbf{a}_t^-)\}\right)^2, \quad (9)$$

which is a common alternative to the ℓ_1 loss in binary classification. Two special covariance matrix cases are considered. The first assumes a diagonal covariance matrix Σ which leads to a diagonal mapping matrix $\mathbf{W}$. We thus focus on the second case, referred to as factored covariance [4]. This approach models the distribution of mapping matrices based on factorizing the covariance matrix to capture separately correlations in the "input" (right side of the mapping matrix, i.e., attributes in our setting) and in the "output" (left side, i.e., latent vectors) [4]. To that end, the authors in [4] use the definition of a *matrix variate normal distribution* [12]. In Definition 5.1, $\otimes$ denotes the *Kronecker product*.

Definition 5.1. A random matrix $\mathbf{X} \in \mathbb{R}^{K \times L}$ is said to have a matrix variate normal distribution with mean matrix $\mathbf{W} \in \mathbb{R}^{K \times L}$ and covariance matrix $\Omega \otimes \Lambda$, where $\Omega \in \mathbb{R}^{K \times K}$ and $\Lambda \in \mathbb{R}^{L \times L}$ are both symmetric and positive semidefinite (PSD), if $\mathrm{vec}(\mathbf{X}) \sim \mathcal{N}(\mathrm{vec}(\mathbf{W}), \Omega \otimes \Lambda)$. Matrix variate normal distributions are denoted by $\mathcal{N}(\mathbf{W}, \Omega \otimes \Lambda)$.

The same unconstrained objective of AROW [5] to update the model parameters $\mathbf{W}$ and Σ is adopted and revisited in [4] for the AROMA matrix settings. In the matrix variate normal distribution case, the convex objective becomes

$$\begin{aligned} D_{KL}&(\mathcal{N}(\mathbf{W}, \Omega \otimes \Lambda) || \mathcal{N}(\mathbf{W}_{t-1}, \Omega_{t-1} \otimes \Lambda_{t-1})) \\ &+ \frac{1}{2r}\left(\max\{0, 1 - \mathbf{u}^T \mathbf{W}(\mathbf{a}^+ - \mathbf{a}^-)\}\right)^2 + \\ &\qquad \frac{1}{2r}(\mathbf{u}^T \Omega \mathbf{u})((\mathbf{a}^+ - \mathbf{a}^-)^T \Lambda (\mathbf{a}^+ - \mathbf{a}^-)), \quad (10) \end{aligned}$$

where $r > 0$ is a regularization parameter and D_{KL} denotes the *Kullback-Leibler* divergence. The first summand of the objective ensures that the parameters do not change radically from round to round. The middle summand penalizes classification errors. As hinted by the last summand which aims at minimizing the eigenvalues of the confidence matrix $\Sigma = \Omega \otimes \Lambda$, the more examples, the higher the confidence should be.

Denote $\mathbf{a}_t = \mathbf{a}_t^+ - \mathbf{a}_t^-$. The global minimum of the objective (10) was shown to be obtained by the following update rule [4],

$$\mathbf{W}_t = \mathbf{W}_{t-1} + \frac{\max\{0, 1 - \mathbf{u}_t^T \mathbf{W}_{t-1} \mathbf{a}_t\}}{\mathbf{u}_t^T \Lambda_{t-1} \mathbf{u}_t \mathbf{a}_t^T \Omega_{t-1} \mathbf{a}_t + r} \Lambda_{t-1} \mathbf{u}_t \mathbf{a}_t^T \Omega_{t-1}, \quad (11)$$

$$\Omega_t = \Omega_{t-1} - \frac{\mathbf{u}_t^T \Lambda_{t-1} \mathbf{u}_t}{(\mathbf{u}_t^T \Lambda_{t-1} \mathbf{u}_t)(\mathbf{a}_t^T \Omega_{t-1} \mathbf{a}_t) + Kr} \Omega_{t-1} \mathbf{a}_t \mathbf{a}_t^T \Omega_{t-1}, \quad (12)$$

$$\Lambda_t = \Lambda_{t-1} - \frac{\mathbf{a}_t^T \Omega_{t-1} \mathbf{a}_t}{(\mathbf{a}_t^T \Omega_{t-1} \mathbf{a}_t)(\mathbf{u}_t^T \Lambda_{t-1} \mathbf{u}_t) + Lr} \Lambda_{t-1} \mathbf{u}_t \mathbf{u}_t^T \Lambda_{t-1}. \quad (13)$$

5.2 LearnAROMA Mapping

In our case, instead of minimizing the squared-hinge loss ℓ_W^2, we wish to maximize the logarithm of the sigmoid function, namely

$$\ln \frac{1}{1 + e^{-\mathbf{u}^T \mathbf{W} \mathbf{a}}}, \quad (14)$$

or alternatively, we want to minimize

$$\ln\left(1 + e^{-\mathbf{u}^T \mathbf{W} \mathbf{a}}\right), \quad (15)$$

Unfortunately, using (15) as the second summand of the objective (10) does not lead to an analytically solvable update for $\mathbf{W}$. Therefore, we propose to **approximate** (15) by the hinge loss function given by

$$\max\{0, 1 - \mathbf{u}^T \mathbf{W} \mathbf{a}\} \quad (16)$$

rather than the squared-hinge loss used in (10). As shown in Fig. 2, the two losses are similar.

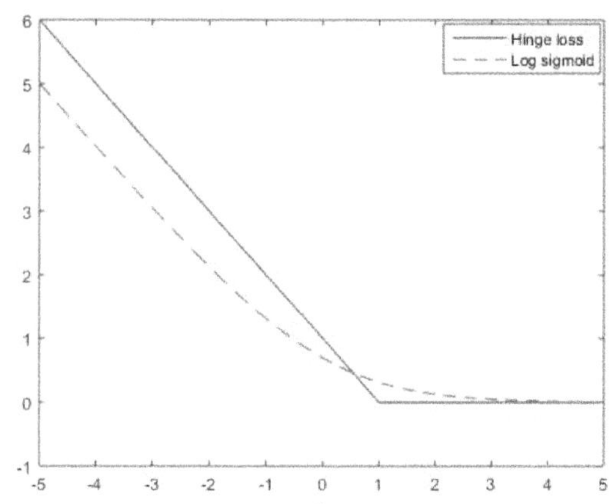

Figure 2: Hinge loss vs. natural logarithm of a sigmoid function.

In this case, the update rule for $\mathbf{W}$ (11) reduces to

$$\mathbf{W}_t = \mathbf{W}_{t-1} + \frac{1}{2r} \Lambda_{t-1} \mathbf{u}_t \mathbf{a}_t^T \Omega_{t-1}, \quad (17)$$

if $\mathbf{u}_t^T \mathbf{W} \mathbf{a}_t < 1$. Otherwise, no update is required. The updates concerning the covariance matrix components (12) and (13) remain unchanged. Our modified AROMA is summarized in Algorithm 3.

Again, once $\mathbf{W}$ is estimated, the resulting item latent vectors are then given by (7).

5.3 Complexity Analysis

LearnMap requires storing the $K \times L$ matrix $\mathbf{W}$ and thus requires a memory of KL. The time complexity of each stochastic gradient descent update is KL as well. LearnAROMA uses a total memory of $KL + K^2 + L^2$ to store the mean matrix $\mathbf{W}$ and the covariance matrices Ω and Λ. The time complexity of each step is $KL + K^2 + L^2$ as well since it involves addition to all elements of the matrices.

Algorithm 3 LearnAROMA

Input:
$S(\mathcal{A}_1)$ - feedback of N users on M_1 mature items
$\mathbf{u}_i$, $1 \le i \le N$ - users latent vectors
$\mathbf{a}_j$, $1 \le j \le M_1$ - mature items attribute vectors
r - regularization parameter
Output:
$\mathbf{W}$ - $K \times L$ attribute-to-feature mapping matrix

repeat
  draw (i, p, q) from $\mathcal{A}_1$
  define $\mathbf{u}_t = \mathbf{u}_i$, $\mathbf{a}_t = \mathbf{a}_p - \mathbf{a}_q$
  if $\mathbf{u}_t^T \mathbf{W} \mathbf{a}_t < 1$ **then**
    update $\mathbf{W}_t$ using (17)
  end if
  update Ω_t using (12)
  update Λ_t using (13)
until convergence

6 EXPEDITING RANDOM EXPLORATION

Consider a new item (cold-start) $j \in \mathcal{A}_2$. Our initial estimate for its latent vector is solely content-based since we do not have any ratings yet for this item and is given by $\hat{\mathbf{v}}_j^0 = \mathbf{W}\mathbf{a}_j$, where $\mathbf{W}$ is obtained using either mapping presented in Section 4 or 5. We now dynamically update the item latent vector estimate as well as its bias with each new rating. We considered estimating the cold-start items bias using content-based mapping, similarly to our latent vector estimation, but this approach did not yield good results.

The BPR-MF criterion is applied on couple of items, one positive and one negative. Therefore, for each new positive feedback, we draw a negative item from the training set for the user who provided the feedback, and vice versa.

For a positive feedback, we denote $j = p$. The optimization criterion is then given by

$$\max_{\hat{\mathbf{v}}_p, \hat{b}_p} \sum_i \ln \frac{1}{1 + e^{-\hat{x}_{ipq}}} - \lambda \|\hat{\mathbf{v}}_p - \hat{\mathbf{v}}_p^0\|^2 - \lambda_b \hat{b}_p^2. \tag{18}$$

Here i denotes t exploring users, chosen randomly from $\mathcal{A}_2$, that rated the new item p, and $\hat{x}_{ipq} = \hat{y}_{ip} - \hat{y}_{iq} = \mathbf{u}_i^T \hat{\mathbf{v}}_p - \mathbf{u}_i^T \mathbf{v}_q + \hat{b}_p - b_q$ where q denotes the drawn negative item for the corresponding user, namely it holds that $q \in I_i^-$. The optimization criterion for a negative ranking is obtained by inverting the roles of both items. If necessary, a traditional regularizer is added to avoid overfitting by controlling the norm of the latent vector, that is $\lambda_1 \|\hat{\mathbf{v}}_p\|^2$. The resulting DynamicBPR algorithm is shown in Algorithm 4. DynamicBPR is applied to each cold-start item separately, as new interactions with this item are arriving. In the algorithm description, $\mathcal{A}_2(t)$ includes t raws randomly chosen from $\mathcal{A}_2(t)$. Note, that no more than t ratings are used to characterize the new item. In addition, we note that since the users latent vectors are fixed, the optimization is performed only with respect to the items latent vector and is convex. Therefore, convergence is guaranteed.

It is worth mentioning that this online approach does not require retraining the mature model, but only trains the cold-start item latent vectors separately. We also considered updating the mapping matrix along with the items latent vectors, but this method did not yield any significant improvement. This suggests that, given enough mature items and users, the mapping is not drastically changed by new arriving entities.

Algorithm 4 DynamicBPR

Input:
$\hat{\mathbf{v}}_j^0 = \mathbf{W}\mathbf{a}_j$ - new item j initial latent vector, $j \in \mathcal{A}_2$
$\mathcal{A}_2(t)$ - t raws randomly chosen from $\mathcal{A}_2$
$\mathbf{u}_i$, $1 \le i \le N$ - users latent vectors
α, α_b - update step sizes
λ, λ_b - regularization parameter
Output:
$\hat{\mathbf{v}}_j^t$ - new item j estimated latent vector

repeat
  draw a user i from $\mathcal{A}_2(t)$
  if $j \in I_i^+$ **then**
    draw $q \in I_i^-$ from $\mathcal{A}_1$ and set $p = j$
  else
    draw $p \in I_i^+$ from $\mathcal{A}_1$ and set $q = j$
  end if
  $\hat{x}_{ipq} \leftarrow \hat{y}_{ip} - \hat{y}_{iq}$
  if $j \in I_i^+$ **then**
    for $1 \le k \le K$ **do**
      $\hat{v}_{pk} \leftarrow \hat{v}_{pk} + \alpha \left(\frac{e^{-\hat{x}_{ipq}}}{1+e^{-\hat{x}_{ipq}}} u_{ik} - \lambda \left(\hat{v}_{pk} - \hat{v}_{pk}^0 \right) \right)$
    end for
    $\hat{b}_p \leftarrow \hat{b}_p + \alpha_b \left(\frac{e^{-\hat{x}_{ipq}}}{1+e^{-\hat{x}_{ipq}}} - \lambda_b \hat{b}_p \right)$
  else
    for $1 \le k \le K$ **do**
      $\hat{v}_{qk} \leftarrow \hat{v}_{qk} + \alpha \left(-\frac{e^{-\hat{x}_{ipq}}}{1+e^{-\hat{x}_{ipq}}} u_{ik} - \lambda \left(\hat{v}_{qk} - \hat{v}_{qk}^0 \right) \right)$
    end for
    $\hat{b}_q \leftarrow \hat{b}_q + \alpha_b \left(-\frac{e^{-\hat{x}_{ipq}}}{1+e^{-\hat{x}_{ipq}}} - \lambda_b \hat{b}_q \right)$
  end if
until convergence

7 NUMERICAL EVALUATION

This section presents our numerical evaluation and demonstrates the two aspects of our random exploration expedition approach. First, we evaluate the initial estimate of the new items latent vectors using LearnMap and LearnAROMA. Then, we examine the online update of these vectors with DynamicBPR while feedback on the new items is arriving.

7.1 Dataset

We use the MovieLens2K dataset released by HetRec 2011.[1] This dataset provides ratings values which we convert to binary feedback, assuming that users tend to rate movies they have watched [8]. If movie j is rated by user i, then $j \in I_i^+$, namely any rating is considered as positive feedback. If movie j is not rated by user i, then $j \in I_i^-$. We consider $N = 2113$ users and $M = 6590$ movies and randomly split the dataset so that $N_1 = 0.2N$ and $M_2 = 0.2M$ (see Fig. 1); that is, the number of users in the test set correspond to 80% of the total number of users and the cold-start items are 20%

[1] http://grouplens.org/datasets/hetrec-2011

Set	Users	Items	Events
$\mathcal{A}_1$	$N = 2113$	$M_1 = 5328$	845761
$\mathcal{A}_2$	$N_1 = 421$	$M_2 = 1262$	18554
$\mathcal{A}_3$	$N_2 = 1692$	$M_2 = 1262$	95003

Table 1: Dataset split

of the total number of movies. Table 1 summarizes the dimensions of the resulting model training set $\mathcal{A}_1$, dynamic training set $\mathcal{A}_2$, and test set $\mathcal{A}_3$. In the table, *Events* refer to the number of positive feedback.

The latent space dimension is set to $K = 12$.[2] We consider genres as movies attributes. The attribute vector $\mathbf{a}_j$ are binary vectors of size $L = 20$, with the lth entry equals 1 if the movie exhibits the lth attribute and 0 otherwise. We observed that exploiting additional attributes such as movie directors or actors does not significantly improve the mapping performance, as previously seen in [8]. Therefore, we focus only on genres as attributes.

Our algorithms were implemented using the MyMediaLite[3] recommender system library, presented in [9]. The library is free/open source software, distributed under the terms of the GNU General Public License.

7.2 Performance Metric

Throughout the simulations, we adopt the *area under curve* (AUC) per user, which is a common ranking accuracy measure, as evaluation metric [7]. The AUC per user measures the ratio of pairs correctly ranked with respect to the total number of evaluated pairs in the test set and is defined as

$$\mathrm{AUC} = \sum_{(i,p,q)\in\mathcal{A}_3} \frac{1}{N_2|I_i^+||I_i^-|}\delta(\hat{x}_{ipq}), \qquad (19)$$

where $\delta(x) = 1$ if $x \geq 0$ and $\delta(x) = 0$ otherwise.

7.3 BPR-MF Model and Mapping Training

We first consider a scenario deprived of cold-starts, as a baseline. Here, we perform the BPR-MF model training using LearnBPR algorithm (see Section 3.3) on both $\mathcal{A}_1$ and $\mathcal{A}_2$ and use $\mathcal{A}_3$ for testing (i.e., "weak generalization" setting). We then learn the attribute to latent space linear mapping, using either the LearnMap algorithm of [8] (see Section 4) or the LearnAROMA algorithm of Section 5. Both the users and items latent vectors as well as the attribute-to-feature mappings are learnt on the sets $\mathcal{A}_1$ and $\mathcal{A}_2$. We consider both linear and quadratic mappings. However, since the quadratic approach does not significantly improve the ranking performance and add complexity overhead, we only focus on linear mapping.

The latent vectors in LearnBPR are initialized using a Gaussian distribution $\mathcal{N}(0, 0.1)$. The mapping matrix entries are initialized to 0 in both LearnMap and LearnAROMA. In the latter, the covariance matrices Ω and Λ are initially set to the $K \times K$ and $L \times L$ identity matrices, respectively. The hyperparameters are chosen via a basic grid search. For LearnBPR, we use $\alpha = \alpha_b = 0.05$, $\lambda = 0.02$ and $\lambda_b = 0$. For LearnMap, we use $\alpha = 0.05$, $\alpha_b = 0.05$, $\lambda = 0.01$ and $\lambda_b = 0.05$. For LearnAROMA, we set $r = 100$.

[2] Increasing the latent space dimension did not yield significant improvements on performance.

[3] http://ismll.de/mymedialite

Method	AUC per user
LearnBPR	0.86029
LearnMap	0.84710
LearnAROMA	0.84989

Table 2: Accuracies for "weak generalization" setting (no cold-start)

Method	AUC per user
LearnMap	0.61123
LearnAROMA	0.62811

Table 3: Accuracies for "strong generalization" setting (cold-start)

Table 2 presents the AUC per user of the three algorithms over the test set $\mathcal{A}_3$: LearnBPR, LearnMap and LearnAROMA. Examining Table 2, we observe that the LearnBPR outperforms the two other algorithms that are replacing the items latent vectors $\mathbf{v}_j$ with their mapping-based estimates $\hat{\mathbf{v}}_j = \mathbf{W}\mathbf{a}_j$. This is not surprising since the two mapping based algorithms includes fewer degrees of freedom. Moreover, the results also reveals that the LearnAROMA algorithm is slightly more accurate than the LearnMap algorithm. It is noted that we report these results just to demonstrate that the mapping is well trained using both algorithms and provides recommendations that are only 1.5% less accurate than the "upper bound" accuracy provided by the LearnBPR algorithm.

7.4 Initial Latent Vectors Estimates

We return to our original setting and investigate the performance of the mappings presented in Sections 4 and 5 with respect to new items. Here, we perform the BPR-MF model training and learn the mapping on the set $\mathcal{A}_1$. Then, the cold-starts latent vectors of new items $M_1 < j \leq M$ are computed using (7) (i.e., "strong generalization" setting). Table 3 presents the AUC per user using the initial latent vectors estimates of the new items over the test set $\mathcal{A}_3$.

The results reveal that learning the mapping with the LearnAROMA algorithm provides a 2.7% lift in AUC for new items over the LearnMap algorithm of [8]. Since our approach outperforms LearnMap, it is obviously also better than the baselines presented in [8] (i.e., KNN and linear based methods [8]). We note that random initialization of the latent vectors yields AUC = 0.5 as expected.

7.5 Dynamic Update

Lastly, we demonstrate our approach for expediting random exploration, where we receive a predefined number of exploring users (randomly chosen) interactions with the new items, taken from $\mathcal{A}_2$ (i.e., "strong generalization" setting). The test results calculated over $\mathcal{A}_3$ are presented with respect to the number of available user feedback, either positive or negative, for each item, averaged over $M_2 = 1262$ items. We apply our DynamicBPR algorithm using three

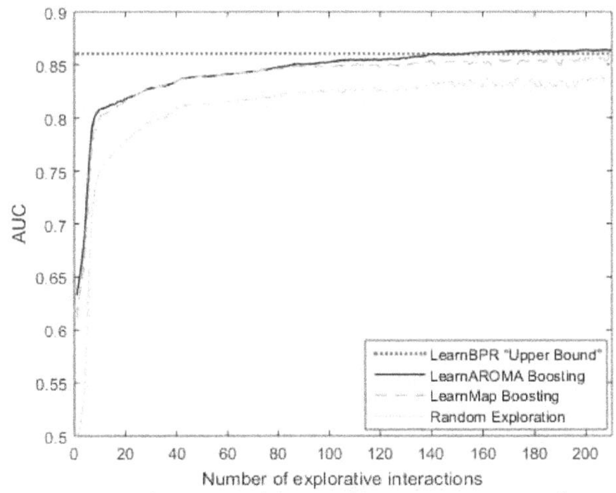

Figure 3: Expediting random exploration using attribute-to-feature mapping

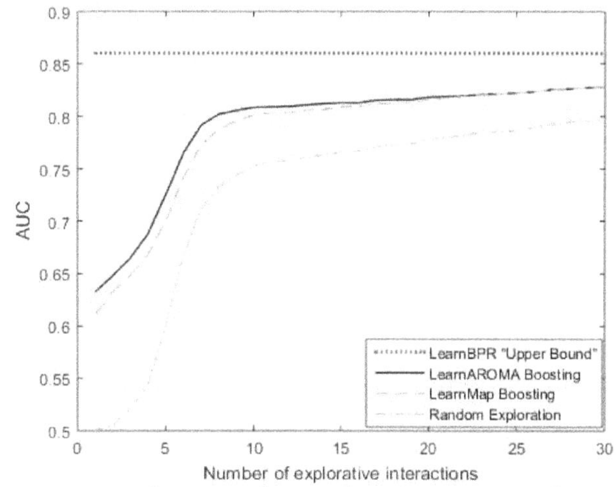

Figure 4: Expediting random exploration using attribute-to-feature mapping (zoom-in).

different initial estimations for the cold-start latent vectors: random $\mathcal{N}(0, 0.1)$, LearnMap (Algorithm 2) and LearnAROMA (Algorithm 3).

Figure 3 presents the AUC accuracies as functions of the number of explorative interactions of all three methods along with the LearnBPR baseline described in Section 7.3 that serves as an "upper bound". We observe that the LearnAROMA based DynamicBPR performance approaches the BPR-MF trained on both $\mathcal{A}_1$ and $\mathcal{A}_2$, namely with no cold-start items. In particular, the LearnAROMA based DynamicBPR reaches 95% accuracy of the LearnBPR "upper bound" using on average 71% less explorative interactions when compared to random exploration (21 vs. 72 interactions). In addition, the LearnAROMA achieves higher accuracy level than that achieved by LearnMap for large number of interactions when exploration reaches saturation and more interactions yield only marginal improvements.

Finally, we focus on the initial phase of the exploration where the benefits of our LearnAROMA based DynamicBPR are more pronounced. Accordingly, Fig. 4 presents a zoom-in of Fig. 3 into the low number of interaction region. Examining the figure, the superiority of our approach over the LearnMap of [8] and especially over random exploration is evident. In addition, we note that LearnAROMA is significantly less sensitive to the choice of hyperparameters in LearnBPR than the LearnMap algorithm. That is, LearnAROMA would yield similar performance even if the model training phase was not performed with optimal hyperparameters, whereas the performance of LearnMap would decrease.

Additional experiment results where we have also updated the mappings individually for each new item with the incoming interactions showed no significant improvements on performance and are thus not presented here.

8 CONCLUDING REMARKS

In this work we consider ways to expedite new item exploration using item attributes in MF-CF based recommenders. In particular, we adopt the approach of [8] where an attribute-to-feature mapping is learnt and used to provide an initial representation for new items, i.e., an initial estimate for their latent vectors. Similarly to [8], we also consider a linear mapping. However, to do so, we adapt the AROMA [4] algorithm, that performs convex optimization for weight matrix estimation in the context of binary classification, to the ranking problem. The resulting algorithm, referred to as LearnAROMA, allows us to learn the attribute to feature mapping. Then, we provide an initial estimate for the new item latent vectors and continue to the exploration phase where users interactions are arriving. To leverage the initial latent vector estimation with the incoming ratings, we present DynamicBPR, a simple update algorithm based on a regularized maximum likelihood convex objective.

Numerical evaluation reveals that our LearnAROMA algorithm provides better initial characterization of the new items than the LearnMAP algorithm of [8] and shows a 2.7% lift in AUC. In addition, we demonstrate the expedition of the exploration phase where our simple update algorithm DynamicBPR achieves comparable accuracies as those provided by a model fully trained with all ratings (an "upper bound" on accuracy) for a rather modest number of exploring users when compared to random exploration. In particular, our algorithm requires on average 71% less exploring users than random exploration to reach a 95% accuracy.

In this work, we consider a random exploration setting where random users are selected to explore the new items (see Section 6). Nevertheless, the benefits of smart exploration, where users who are more likely to interact with the new item are selected for exploration, were recently demonstrated in [6]. In future work, we plan to combine the user selection methods of [6] and the latent vector update algorithm of Section 6 and evaluate the overall lift in performance. Another possible extension of this work is to exploit the estimated confidence matrix along with the mapping, to tune the regularization parameter of DynamicBPR. Indeed, items with attributes for which our mapping has a higher confidence level are likely to have better initial estimate and thus should have a higher regularization term.

REFERENCES

[1] O. Anava, S. Golan, N. Golbandi, Z. Karnin, R. Lempel, O. Rokhlenko, and O. Somekh. 2015. Budget-constrained item cold-start handling in collaborative filtering recommenders via optimal design. *Proc. WWW* (2015).

[2] D. Argawal and B.-C. Chen. 2009. Regression-based Latent Factor Models. *Proc. KDD* (2009).

[3] Olivier Chapelle and Lihong Li. 2011. An empirical evaluation of thompson sampling. In *Advances in neural information processing systems*. 2249–2257.

[4] K. Crammer and G. Chechik. 2012. Adaptive regularization of weight matrices. *Int. Conf. on Machine Learning* (2012).

[5] K. Crammer, A. Kulesza, and M. Dredze. 2009. Adaptive regularization of weight vectors. *NIPS* (2009).

[6] D. Drachsler-Cohen, O. Somekh, S. Golan, M. Aharon, O. Anava, and N. Avigdor-Elgrabli. 2015. ExcUseMe: asking users to help in item cold-start recommendations. *Proc. RecSys* (2015).

[7] Tom Fawcett. 2006. An introduction to ROC analysis. *Pattern recognition letters* 27, 8 (2006), 861–874.

[8] Z. Gantner, L. Drumond, C. Freudenthaler, S. Rendle, and L. Shmidt-Thieme. 2010. Learning Attribute-to-Feature Mappings for Cold-Start Recommendations. *ICDM'10: Proceedings of the 10th IEEE international conference on data mining* (2010).

[9] Z. Gantner, S. Rendle, C. Freudenthaler, and L. Shmidt-Thieme. 2011. MyMediaLite: a free recommender system library. *Proceeding of the fifth ACM conference on Recommender systems* (2011), 305–308.

[10] A. Gunawardana and C. Meek. 2008. Tied Boltzmann machines for cold starts recommendations. *Proc. RecSys* (2008).

[11] A. Gunawardana and C. Meek. 2009. A unified approach to building hybrid recommender systems. *Proc. RecSys* (2009).

[12] A. K. Gupta and D. K. Nagar. 1999. Matrix variate distributions. *Chapman and Hall/CRC* (1999).

[13] Y. Koren. 2008. Factorization meets the neighborhood: a multifaceted collaborative filtering model. *Proc. KDD* (2008).

[14] Y. Koren and R. Bell. 2010. Advances in collaborative filtering. In *Recommender systems handbook*. Springer, 145–186.

[15] N. Liu, X. Meng, C. Liu, and Q. Yang. 2011. Wisdom of the better few: cold start recommendation via representative based rating elicitation. *Proc. RecSys* (2011).

[16] S.-T. Park and W. Chu. 2009. Pairwise preference regression for cold-start recommendation. *Proc. RecSys* (2009).

[17] S.-T. Park, D. Pennock, O. Madani, N. Good, and D. DeCoste. 2006. Naive filterbots for robust cold-start recommendations. *KDD'06: Proceedings of the 12th ACM SIGKDD international conference on knowledge discovery and data mining* (2006).

[18] Michael J. Pazzani and Daniel Billsus. 2007. Content-based recommendation systems. In *The adaptive web*. Springer, 325–341.

[19] S. Rendle. 2012. Factorization machines with libFM. *ACM* (2012).

[20] S. Rendle, C. Freudenthaler, Z. Gantner, and L. Shmidt-Thieme. 2009. BPR: Bayesian personalized ranking from implicit feedback. *UAI* (2009).

[21] Steffen Rendle and Lars Schmidt-Thieme. 2008. Online-updating regularized kernel matrix factorization models for large-scale recommender systems. In *Proceedings of the 2008 ACM conference on Recommender systems*. ACM, 251–258.

[22] R. Salakhutdinov and A. Mnih. 2008. Probabilistic matrix factorization. *NIPS* (2008).

[23] Martin Saveski and Amin Mantrach. 2014. Item cold-start recommendations: learning local collective embeddings. In *Proceedings of the 8th ACM Conference on Recommender systems*. ACM, 89–96.

Additive Co-Clustering with Social Influence for Recommendation

Xixi Du
Beijing Key Lab of Traffic Data Analysis and Mining
Beijing Jiaotong University
Beijing, China 100044
15120391@bjtu.edu.cn

Huafeng Liu
Beijing Key Lab of Traffic Data Analysis and Mining
Beijing Jiaotong University
Beijing, China 100044
15120419@bjtu.edu.cn

Liping Jing
Beijing Key Lab of Traffic Data Analysis and Mining
Beijing Jiaotong University
Beijing, China 100044
lpjing@bjtu.edu.cn

ABSTRACT

Recommender system is a popular tool to accurately and actively provide users with potentially interesting information. For capturing the users' preferences and approximating the missing data, matrix completion and approximation are widely adopted. Except for the typical low-rank factorization-based methods, the additive co-clustering approach (ACCAMS) is recently proposed to succinctly approximate large-scale rating matrix. Although ACCAMS efficiently produces effective recommendation result, it still suffers from the cold-start problem. To address this issue, we propose a **S**ocial **I**nfluence **A**dditive **C**o-**C**lustering method (SIACC) by making use of user-item rating data and user-user social relations.

The main idea of SIACC is to extract the social influences from the social network, integrate them to additive co-clustering for effectively determining the user clusters and item clusters, minimize the loss error by backfitting the residuals of data approximation in the previous iteration, and finally improve the recommendation performance. In order to take advantage of social influence, we present a **g**raph-regularized **w**eighted-**F**uzzy **C**-**M**eans algorithm (gwFCM) to cluster users. gwFCM has ability to identify user groups from both rating and social information. Specifically, gwFCM makes sure that a pair of users have similar cluster membership if they have direct social relation (denoted as local social influence), and that the user with higher reputation (denoted as global social influence) plays a dominate role in clustering process. The reasonable user clusters obtained by gwFCM can benefit the item clustering, which will leverage the additive co-clustering processing and further improve the recommendation performance. A series of experiments on three real-world datasets have shown that SIACC outperforms the existing popular recommendation methods (PMF and ACCAMS) and social recommendation methods (SoReg, TrustMF, Locabal and SPF), especially on the cold-start users recommendation and running time.

CCS CONCEPTS

•Information systems →Recommender systems; Clustering and classification;

KEYWORDS

Recommendation System, Additive Co-Clustering, Social Influence, Cold-Start Users

1 INTRODUCTION

As an indispensable technique to tackle the information overload problem, recommender system is nowadays ubiquitous in various domains and e-commerce platforms. It aims to provide the online users with the potentially interesting information, such as recommendation of products at Amazon, books/movies/musics at Douban, research articles at CiteULike and etc. A high quality recommendation system can not only capture users' individualized preferences, but also increase both satisfaction for users and revenue for content providers.

Among the existing recommendation methods, matrix approximation techniques, including low-rank matrix factorization and additive co-clustering, are widely adopted in the academia and the industry. The low-rank matrix factorization is a typical model-based collaborative filtering approach [1], which is relatively simple and effective. This kind of methods attempt to automatically predict the interest of users through matrix factorization [2, 21]. Even though these methods have promising results, they are faced with two main challenges: cold-start and computation complexity. When there are a large amount of users or items, they have to incur the cost of latent factor identification from the high-dimension matrix. Furthermore, these methods can not provide satisfactory recommendations for cold-start users or cold-start items.

In order to improve the performance on cold-start users, researchers have demonstrated that recommendation models with the aid of social relations can provide better recommendations. This kind of recommendation is based on the social rationale, i.e., the user's interest is affected by his/her connected neighbors. To date, a series of matrix factorization based social recommendation methods have been proposed by taking available social relations as constraints to design models. For example, the social relations are employed to adjust the latent user factor [6, 14] and latent user preference [5] respectively, or determine the user latent factor by simultaneously factorizing user-user social matrix and user-item rating matrix [8, 15, 23, 27, 28]. Although these methods take advantage of the social relations to improve the recommendation accuracy, the additional social information makes the model more complicated and slows down the recommendation process, i.e., their computational complexity increases with the increasing size of users and items.

RecSys'17, August 27–31, 2017, Como, Italy

ISBN 978-1-4503-4652-8/17/08...$15.00
DOI: http://dx.doi.org/10.1145/3109859.3109883

For handling large-scale user-item rating data, Beutel et al. [3] recently proposed an additive co-clustering model to succinctly approximate the rating matrix (ACCAMS). ACCAMS takes linear combinations of co-clusterings to encode the factorial nature of large-scale matrix without incurring the cost of high-dimension matrix factorization. ACCAMS has been theoretically and empirically proved efficient, however, it only considers the preference matrix and still suffers from cold-start problem. Therefore, in this work, we present a Social Influence Additive Co-Clustering method (SIACC) by making use of user-item rating data and social relations among users to improve the prediction quality and speed up the recommendation process.

The main idea of SIACC is to integrate the social influence to the ACCAMS. Firstly, the global and local social influence of users are extracted from social network. Global social influence indicates the reputation of each user in the whole social network. Local social influence reveals the correlations between users and their neighborhoods in the social network. Secondly, a graph-regularized weighted fuzzy c-means clustering algorithm (gwFCM) is proposed to identify the user clusters and the corresponding cluster centers. In gwFCM, the local social influence is used to constraint the user cluster membership via a graph regularizer term so that a pair of users obtain similar cluster memberships if they have local social influence. The global social influence of each user is used to weight data fitting term so that the user with higher reputation plays a dominate role in clustering process. Thirdly, the item clusters are identified by applying k-means (KM) clustering algorithm on the user cluster centers. Following ACCAMS, SIACC iteratively applies gwFCM and KM to minimizing the approximation error by backfitting the residuals of the data approximation in the previous iteration.

The rest of the paper is organized as follows. The related work about matrix approximation-based recommendation systems is discussed in Section 2. Section 3 gives the proposed SIACC recommendation framework for rating matrix approximation, including the new user clustering algorithm (gwFCM) which exploits both rating data and social influence. In Section 4, we give the details of experiments on three real-world datasets and discuss the results. Finally, a brief conclusion and future work are given in Section 5.

2 RELATED WORK

Before reviewing the matrix approximation techniques for recommendation systems, we first introduce notations used in this paper. Suppose there are n users and m items. Let $R = \left[R_{ij}\right]_{n\times m}$ denote the user-item rating matrix. If the i-th user gives a rating to the j-th item, R_{ij} is the rating score, otherwise $R_{ij} = 0$. Users can establish social relations to each other. The unknown cell set in R is denoted as Ω, i.e., the values of R_Ω have to be predicted. Let $A = [A_{iz}]_{n\times n}$ denote the user-user social relations where $A_{iz} = 1$ if the i-th and z-th users have social relation, otherwise $A_{iz} = 0$. Next, we will discuss the popular matrix factorization and additive co-clustering recommendation approaches.

2.1 Matrix Factorization

Matrix factorization (MF) techniques have been widely employed for recommendation systems [2, 10, 21, 22]. The basic idea of these approaches is employing low-rank matrix factorization on the rating matrix R to identify the user factor and item factor, which can be implemented by solving the following optimization problem,

$$\min \frac{1}{2}\Big(\sum_{R_{ij}\neq 0} (R_{ij} - {h_i}^{\mathrm{T}} b_j)^2 + \lambda(\|H\|_F^2 + \|B\|_F^2)\Big). \tag{1}$$

where $H = [h_1, h_2, \cdots, h_n] \in \mathbb{R}^{r\times n}$ with h_i indicating the i-th user in the latent space, $B = [b_1, b_2, \cdots, b_m] \in \mathbb{R}^{r\times m}$ with b_j indicating the j-th item, and r is the number of features in the latent space. Then, the incomplete rating matrix R can be approximated by $H^T B$, and the unknown component R_{ij} can be estimated by $h_i^T b_j$.

The MF-based recommendation methods usually assume that users are independent and identically distributed, which ignores the connection among users. Meanwhile, they can not provide satisfactory recommendations to the users having few or no rating information. Recently, more and more researchers investigated the social recommendation based on the social rationale, i.e., the user's social neighbors can affect his/her preference. The main idea is to integrate the social relations into the MF model via two strategies. The first strategy mainly factorizes the rating matrix and adjusts the latent user factor (H) [6, 8, 9, 13, 14, 16] or latent user preference [5] by his/her neighbors. The second strategy simultaneously factorizes rating matrix and social matrix to identify the latent user/item factor (H) [15, 23, 27, 28]. Even though these methods improve the prediction quality, the social relation information makes the models more complicated and aggravates the computational complexity of model training process.

2.2 Additive Co-Clustering

Recently, Beutel et al. [3] presented an additive co-clustering model to approximate the rating matrix succinctly (ACCAMS). To predict the missing values of rating matrix R, ACCAMS aims to iteratively learn s stencils $\left\{S(T^l, c^l, d^l)\right\}_{l=1}^{s}$ and approximate R via

$$\min_{\{T^l, c^l, d^l\}} \left\| R - \sum_{l=1}^{s} S\left(T^l, c^l, d^l\right)\right\|_F^2 \tag{2}$$

In the l-th iteration, $c^l \in \{1, \ldots k_n\}^n$ is a user-cluster index vector, $d^l \in \{1, \ldots k_m\}^m$ is a item-cluster index vector, k_n is the number of user clusters, and k_m for item clusters. The user and item clusters are determined by applying k-means on the l-th input data R^l, where $R^{l+1} = R^l - S^l$ (with $R^1 = R$) as follows.

$$\min \sum_{i=1}^{n} \sum_{k=1}^{k_n} U_{ik} \left\|R_{i\cdot}^l - X_{k\cdot}\right\|_2^2 \tag{3}$$

where$X = [X_{kj}] \in \mathbb{R}^{k_n\times m}$ with $X_{k\cdot}$ is the center of the k-th cluster, $U = [U_{ik}] \in \mathbb{R}^{n\times k_n}$ (s.t. $U_{ik} \in \{0,1\}$, $\sum_{k=1}^{k_n} U_{ik} = 1\ \forall i$) is the user cluster membership matrix, $U_{ik} = 1$ denotes that the i-th user belongs to the k-th cluster, otherwise $U_{ik} = 0$. In this case, user-cluster index vector c^l can be identified by

$$c_i^l = \{k | U_{ik} = 1\}, i = 1, \ldots n. \tag{4}$$

Similarly, the item clusters and d^l can be identified by applying k-means on the user cluster centers X. The template $T^l \in \mathbb{R}^{k_n\times k_m}$ is generated according to c^l, d^l and the input data R^l, so that T_{pq}^l

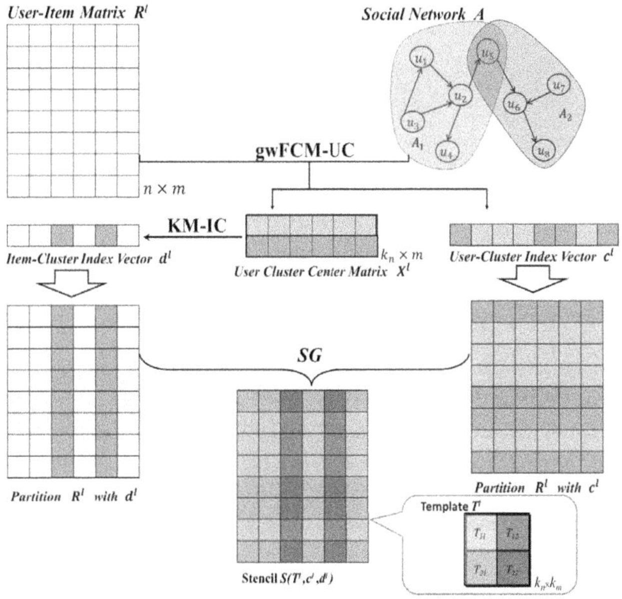

Figure 1: The Framework of SIACC Recommendation.

is the mean of $\{R^l_{ij}|c^l_i = p, d^l_j = q\}$. Finally, the rating that the i-th user gives to the j-th item can be predicted by $\sum_{l=1}^{s} S(T^l, c^l, d^l)_{ij} = \sum_{l=1}^{s} T^l_{pq}$.

Although ACCAMS has been proved efficient and effective for recommendation, it still has some drawbacks. Firstly, each user is required to have a distinct membership to one single cluster because of k-means, however, ambiguity may exist in real world datasets, thus it is necessary to allow each user have memberships in all clusters. Secondly, only the sparse user-item preference information is used in ACCAMS, which results in cold-start problem like the classical MF model. In order to solve these problems, we will propose a new social influence additive co-clustering recommendation framework (SIACC) to make use of both user preference information and user social information, and efficiently approximate the incomplete user-item rating matrix.

3 THE PROPOSED SIACC RECOMMENDATION METHOD

The key step of ACCAMS is to get the user and item clusters, so that users in the same cluster are likely to share similar tastes. Although the user-item rating data can provide some preference clues to find the user clusters, it is limited due to its sparsity. The booming online social networking websites, as complementary resources, offer more opportunities to mine the correlations between users. In social network, social relations are established according to the users' trust of one another. Such social relations include two perspectives: local and global. From the local view, according to social correlation theories [17, 19], the user correlations indicate that users who have direct social relations usually share similar tastes with each other. From the global view [18], the user correlations indicate that the users with higher reputation in social network, to a large extent, influence other users' decision when they seek suggestions. In literatures, more and more researches focus on exploiting such correlations to improve the performance of recommendation [23], but most of them focus on local social correlations [6, 8, 9, 13, 14, 16, 27, 28].

In this section, we will present a social influence additive co-clustering recommendation framework (SIACC) as shown in Figure 1. It aims to integrate the global and local user correlations into additive co-clustering for efficiently approximate the incomplete rating matrix. SIACC is an iterative matrix approximation process including three parts: user clusters generation (gwFCM-UC), item clusters generation (kM-IC), and stencil generation (SG), which will be described next.

3.1 User Cluster Generation (gwFCM-UC)

In real applications, one user may have various tastes. For example, a young person may like soap opera as well as war movie. Similarly, in social network A (as shown in Figure 1), the user u_5 may belong to the left social community as well as the right community. Thus, ambiguity really exists in the user's cluster membership. Given the input data R^l in the l-th iteration, for capturing such ambiguity, we adopt fuzzy c-means [7] instead of k-means as the base clustering method to find the user clusters by minimizing

$$\sum_{i=1}^{n}\sum_{k=1}^{k_n} U_{ik}^{\beta} \left\|R^l_{i\cdot} - X_{k\cdot}\right\|_2^2 \tag{5}$$

Here $\beta \geqslant 1$ is the fuzzy factor, and its value is set as 2 following [7]. $X \in \mathbb{R}^{k_n \times m}$ is the user cluster center set, $U \in \mathbb{R}^{n \times k_n}$ (s.t., $U_{ik} \in [0, 1]$, $\sum_{k=1}^{k_n} U_{ik} = 1, \forall i$) is the user cluster membership matrix with component U_{ik} indicating the probability that the i-th user belongs to the k-th cluster.

According to social influence theory[18], the global perspective of social relation reveals the reputation of a user in the whole social network, the user with high reputation usually has a greater influence. In other words, user reputation plays an important role in recommendation just like celebrity effect [23]. Following [20], the reputation of each user can be calculated via

$$\omega_i = \frac{1}{1 + log(r_i)}, \tag{6}$$

where $r_i \in [1, n]$ donates the the i-th user's reputation rank which can be obtained by the most popular algorithm (e.g., PageRank). For example, $r_i = 1$ indicates that the i-th user has the highest reputation in the whole social network, then its reputation ω_i should have the largest value. In this case, we can weight each user when determining the user clusters by minimizing

$$\sum_{i=1}^{n}\sum_{k=1}^{k_n} \omega_i U_{ik}^{2} \left\|R^l_{i\cdot} - X_{k\cdot}\right\|_2^2, \tag{7}$$

having the same constraints with (5). This weighted FCM has ability to let the users with higher reputation dominate the whole clustering process.

Meanwhile, social correlation theories[17] indicate that users with similar tastes are more likely to be socially connected. In other words, users with stronger social correlations are more likely to share similar interests than those who have weak or no correlations. Researchers have shown that exploiting such direct social relations among connected users can improve the recommendation quality [6, 8, 9, 13, 14, 16, 23, 27]. Following [26], such social relation strength (denoted as $Q \in \mathbb{R}^{n \times n}$) can be measured via the user preference cosine similarity as follows.

$$Q_{iz} = \begin{cases} \frac{\sum_j R_{ij} R_{zj}}{\sqrt{\sum_j R_{ij}^2}\sqrt{\sum_j R_{zj}^2}} & u_i \text{ connected with } u_z, \text{ i.e., } A_{iz} = 1, \\ 0 & otherwise \text{ i.e., } A_{iz} = 0. \end{cases} \tag{8}$$

Recall the weighted fuzzy c-means model (7), it outputs a cluster membership vector for each user, then we can enforce the local social correlations on the cluster membership vectors of the corresponding pair of users (the i-th and z-th users) via minimizing

$$\sum_{i,z} Q_{iz} \|U_{i\cdot} - U_{z\cdot}\|_2^2 \tag{9}$$

This term is also called graph regularizer [4]. Minimizing this term can make the user memberships have the similar local structure with that demonstrated in the social relation strength Q.

By combining (7) and (9), the user clusters can be identified by integrating global and local social influence into fuzzy c-means by minimizing

$$\begin{aligned} J_u = &\sum_{i=1}^{n}\sum_{k=1}^{k_n} \omega_i U_{ik}^2 \left\|R_{i\cdot}^l - X_{k\cdot}\right\|_2^2 \\ &+ \lambda \sum_{i,z} Q_{iz} \|U_{i\cdot} - U_{z\cdot}\|_2^2 \end{aligned} \tag{10}$$

s.t:

$$U_{ik} \in [0,1], \forall i,k; \qquad \sum_{k=1}^{k_n} U_{ik} = 1, \forall i. \tag{11}$$

where the parameter λ is introduced to control the contributions of rating information and social influence to user clustering process, which can be tuned via cross-validation technique. We call this model as graph-regularized and weighted FCM (gwFCM).

Minimizing (10) is a constrained optimization problem, which can be solved using Lagrange Multiplier Method. Its Lagrange function is

$$\begin{aligned} J_u = &\sum_{i=1}^{n}\sum_{k=1}^{k_n} \omega_i U_{ik}^2 \left\|R_{i\cdot}^l - X_{k\cdot}\right\|^2 \\ &+ \lambda \sum_{i,z} Q_{iz} \|U_{i\cdot} - U_{z\cdot}\|^2 + \eta_i \left(\sum_{k=1}^{k_n} U_{ik} - 1\right) \end{aligned} \tag{12}$$

where η_i is Lagrange Multiplier.

The local minimum about U and X is the point where the first-order derivative is 0 as follows.

$$\frac{\partial J_u}{\partial X_{kj}} = -2 \sum_{i=1}^{n} \omega_i U_{ik}^2 \left(R_{ij}^l - X_{kj}\right) = 0 \tag{13}$$

$$\begin{aligned} \frac{\partial J_u}{\partial U_{ik}} = &\, 2\omega_i U_{ik} \left\|R_{i\cdot}^l - X_{k\cdot}\right\|_2^2 \\ &+ 2\lambda \sum_{z} Q_{iz} (U_{ik} - U_{zk}) + \eta_i = 0 \end{aligned} \tag{14}$$

By substituting η_i, we can get the iterative formula for updating X_{kj} and U_{ik}:

$$X_{kj} = \frac{\sum_{i=1}^{n} \omega_i R_{ij}^l U_{ik}^2}{\sum_{i=1}^{n} \omega_i U_{ik}^2} \tag{15}$$

$$U_{ik} = \frac{\sum_{c=1}^{k} \omega_i \left\|R_{i\cdot}^l - X_{c\cdot}\right\|_2^2 + \lambda \sum_z Q_{iz} U_{zk}}{\omega_i \left\|R_{i\cdot}^l - X_{k\cdot}\right\|_2^2 + \lambda \sum_z Q_{iz}} \tag{16}$$

Once having the user cluster membership U, the user cluster index vector c^l can be determined by

$$c_i^l = p, \text{ where } p = \arg\max_k \{U_{ik}\}_{k=1}^{k_n}. \tag{17}$$

3.2 Item Cluster Generation (KM-IC)

The set of user cluster centers ($X \in \mathbb{R}^{k_n \times m}$), to some extent, represents the current rating matrix R^l in a high level. Thus, for the sake of computational simplicity, we apply k-means on the user cluster centers X instead of the original data R^l to find the item clusters by minimizing

$$\min \sum_{j=1}^{m}\sum_{k=1}^{k_m} V_{jk} \left\|X_{\cdot j} - Y_{\cdot k}\right\|_2^2 \tag{18}$$

s.t.

$$V_{jk} \in \{0,1\}, \forall j,k; \qquad \sum_{k=1}^{k_m} V_{jk} = 1, \forall j.$$

Here $Y \in \mathbb{R}^{k_n \times k_m}$ is the item cluster center set, $V \in \mathbb{R}^{m \times k_m}$ is the user cluster indicator matrix with component $V_{jk} = 1$ if the j-th item belongs to the k-th cluster, otherwise $V_{jk} = 0$. In this case, we can determine the item cluster index vector d^l by

$$d_j^l = q, \text{ where } V_{jq} = 1. \tag{19}$$

3.3 Stencil Generation (SG)

Following [3], we can generate the stencil $S(T^l, c^l, d^l)$ according to c^l, d^l and the input data R^l. More specifically, the template T^l is a $k_n \times k_m$ matrix, and its (p,q)-th cell value is calculated by

$$T_{pq}^l = mean\left\{R_{ij}^l | c_i^l = p, d_j^l = q\right\} \tag{20}$$

Then the stencil $S \in \mathbb{R}^{n \times m}$ can be identified via

$$S\left(T^l, c^l, d^l\right)_{ij} = T_{c_i^l d_j^l}^l. \tag{21}$$

For each iteration, after obtaining the stencil $S(T^l, c^l, d^l)$, we can calculate the residual between the input data R^l and the stencil, which is used as the input data for the next co-clustering iteration, i.e.,

$$R^{l+1} = R^l - S\left(T^l, c^l, d^l\right). \tag{22}$$

3.4 SIACC Recommendation

By iteratively co-clustering the residual between input data and the corresponding stencil, we can minimize the loss between the original rating matrix R and the linear-combination of all stencils. In other words, the user-item rating matrix R can be well approximated by the linear-combination of stencils and then do recommendation. The process of stencil generation will be repeated until the stopping condition is satisfied, as shown in Algorithm

1. The linear combination of stencils can be taken as an additive model of co-clustering on both users and items.

Algorithm 1 SIACC Recommendation Method

Require: Rating matrix R with n users and m items, social network A, number of user clusters k_n, number of item clusters k_m, number of stencils s, set of unknown cells Ω.
  Compute the reputation ω_i for each user via (6) based on A;
  Compute social relation strength matrix Q via (8) based on A and R;
  Set $R^1 = R, \hat{R}_\Omega = 0$;
  for $l = 1$ to s **do**
    Compute user-cluster index vector c^l and user cluster centers X from R^l and Q via (17) and (15);
    Compute item-cluster index vector d^l from X via (19);
    for $p, q \in \{1, \dots k_n\} \times \{1, \dots k_m\}$ **do**
      Calculate the template T^l_{pq} using (20);
    end for
    Fill in the stencil $S\left(T^l, c^l, d^l\right)$ via (21);
    $R^{l+1} \leftarrow R^l - S\left(T^l, c^l, d^l\right)$;
    $\hat{R}_\Omega = \hat{R}_\Omega + S\left(T^l, c^l, d^l\right)_\Omega$.
  end for
  Output the predicated values $\hat{R}_\Omega$ on unknown cells.

The space complexity of the proposed SIACC framework depends on the size of stencil. Its cost includes storing user-cluster index vector c, item-cluster index vector d and template T, and finally has a upper bound $(n \log_2 k_n + m \log_2 k_m + 32 k_n k_m)$ bits [3]. Comparing with the MF-based model with $32(n+m)r$ bits (the value of each user/item on each latent feature is recorded as a float with 32 bits), SIACC needs fewer space because in real application the number of latent features r is usually larger than the clusters $32 \log_2 k_n$ and $32 \log_2 k_m$.

For running time, the main computation complexity of SIACC is to iteratively find c, d and template T. In each iteration, the time of updating c is $O\big((nnz(R) + nnz(Q))k_n\big)$, the time of updating d is $O(mk_nk_m)$, the time of updating T is $O(k_nk_m)$, thus the total computation complexity is $O\big(s(nnz(R) + nnz(Q) + mk_m)k_n\big)$ with s stencils. Comparing with the MF-based social recommendation model (e.g., Locabal [23]) with $O\big(t\,(nnz(R) + nnz(Q))\,r\big)$ (t is the number of iterations), SIACC is much faster because in real application r is usually larger than k_n and k_m, and t is much greater than s. In next section, we will demonstrate the computation complexity using a series of experiments.

4 EXPERIMENTS

In this section, we will demonstrate the effect of parameters on SIACC, and the recommendation performance of the proposed SIACC by comparing it with four popular existing recommendation methods on three real-world datasets.

4.1 Dataset

In order to sufficiently validate the performance of SIACC, we consider the recommendation data including social information among users such as Ciao[1], Epinions[2], and Douban[3] which are usually used in literatures. The preference/rating scores in these three datasets are in five levels (from 1 to 5). The relations in the first two datasets are recorded in a who-trust-whom social network, i.e., a directed trust network, while in Douban, the relations are from friendship between users, i.e., they are recorded in a undirected network. In the experiments, we ignore the effect of direction, i.e., all social networks are considered as undirected networks. The details of three datasets are listed in Table 1. It can be seen that both rating matrix and social network are sparse, which exacerbates the difficulties of recommendation.

Table 1: Summary of experimental datasets

	Ciao	Epinions	Duban
♯ users (n)	7,375	49,290	129,490
♯ items (m)	106,797	139,738	58,541
♯ ratings	284,086	664,824	16,830,839
♯ relations	111,781	487,183	1,692,952
rating density	0.036%	0.010%	0.222%
social density	0.2055%	0.0201%	0.0202%

Five-fold cross-validation technique is used for training and testing. Specially, each data set is randomly split into five equal sized subsets, four subsets are used as the training set and the left one as testing set in each fold. Five folds are conducted to ensure all subsets are tested, and the average test performance is recorded as the final results.

4.2 Methodology

To comparatively demonstrate the performance of our method, the classical matrix factorization-based collaborative filtering method (PMF) [21] and the additive co-clustering model (ACCAMS) [3] are taken as baselines which only consider rating information to do recommendation. Since SIACC takes both rating and social information into account, it can be taken as social recommendation. The existing social recommendation methods can be roughly divided into two categories according to the usage of social information, thus four representative methods (two from each category) are used as baselines to compare SIACC. Among them SoReg [16] and SPF[5] employ the social relations to adjust the latent user factors. TrustMF[28] and Locabal [23] simultaneously factorize social matrix and rating matrix to learn the common latent user factor.

The optimal experimental settings for all methods are determined either by experiments or suggested by previous works. In the PMF, SoReg, and Locabal, the number of features in latent space is 10 for three datasets. The regularization parameter on latent factors is 0.001 for Douban, and 0.1 for Ciao and Epinions for these three methods. The parameter to control the contribution of social information is set to 1 in SoReg and Locabal. For ACCAMS, we tuned its parameters including number of user clusters k_n, number of item clusters k_m and number of stencils s.

[1] http://www.jiliang.xyz/trust.html
[2] http://www.trustlet.org/downloaded_epinions.html
[3] https://www.cse.cuhk.edu.hk/irwin.king.new/pub/data/douban

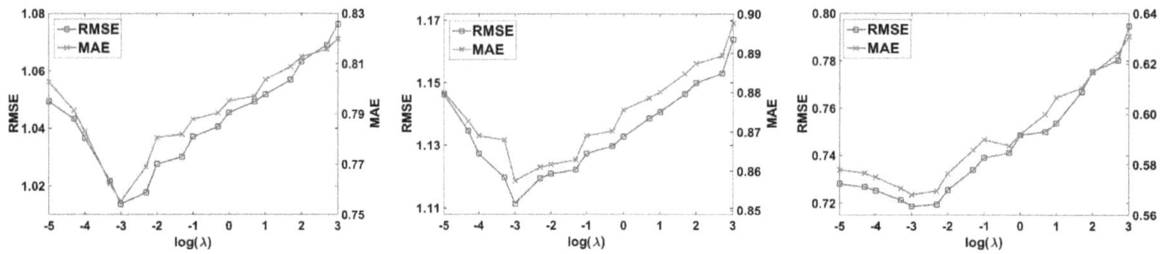

(a) Ciao (b) Epinions (c) Douban

Figure 2: Effect of parameter λ on SIACC for (a) Ciao, (b) Epinions and (c) Douban datasets in terms of RMSE and MAE.

Table 2: Comparisons of different recommendation methods from two views (All Users and Cold-Start (CS) Users).

	Datasets	Metrics	PMF	SoReg	TrustMF	Locabal	SPF	ACCAMS	SIACC
All Users	Ciao	MAE	0.8256	0.7964	0.7650	0.7561	0.7658	0.8084	**0.7554**
		RMSE	1.1310	1.0919	1.0309	1.0214	1.0330	1.0615	**1.0138**
	Epinions	MAE	1.1206	1.0506	1.0369	0.9374	1.0225	0.8971	**0.8515**
		RMSE	1.3654	1.3034	1.2859	1.1548	1.2489	1.1701	**1.1115**
	Douban	MAE	0.6230	0.6163	0.5931	0.5757	0.5976	0.5818	**0.5679**
		RMSE	0.7699	0.7636	0.7340	0.7190	0.7373	0.7309	**0.7183**
CS Users	Ciao	MAE	0.9343	0.9179	0.8493	0.8296	0.8593	0.7965	**0.7394**
		RMSE	1.1876	1.1548	1.0852	1.0774	1.0879	1.0441	**1.0221**
	Epinions	MAE	1.3508	1.2525	1.2459	1.0877	1.1062	0.9445	**0.8856**
		RMSE	1.4477	1.3492	1.3357	1.2651	1.2961	1.2207	**1.1971**
	Douban	MAE	0.8433	0.7952	0.7245	0.7244	0.7373	0.6570	**0.6389**
		RMSE	1.0239	0.9789	0.8881	0.8836	0.9180	0.8344	**0.8323**

In order to validate the prediction quality, two well known evaluation metrics, Root Mean Square Error(RMSE) and Mean Absolute Error(MAE), are adopted in experiments, which are defined by:

$$RMSE = \sqrt{\frac{1}{|\Omega|}\sum_{i,j}(R_{ij} - \hat{R}_{ij})^2} \tag{23}$$

$$MAE = \frac{1}{|\Omega|}\sum_{i,j}\left|R_{ij} - \hat{R}_{ij}\right| \tag{24}$$

where Ω is the unknown cells set and $|\Omega|$ is the number of test ratings. R_{ij} is the true rating value that the i-th user gave to the j-th item in testing data. $\hat{R}_{ij}$ is the predicted value from different methods. The smaller RMSE and MAE values indicate better recommendation result.

4.3 Results and Discussion

In the proposed SIACC method, there are four parameters to tune, including λ in (10) to trade off the contribution of rating information and social information on user clustering, and three parameters to generate the stencil (number of user clusters k_n, number of item clusters k_m and number of stencils s). Thus, the first experiments are conducted to test the effects of these parameters. Then a series of experiments are conducted to compare SIACC with the existing four methods on recommendation quality and running time.

4.3.1 Effect of parameter λ: Figure 2 shows the effect of regularizer parameter λ on three datasets. The results demonstrate that SIACC performs better as λ increases, reaches the best value at round $\lambda = 0.001$ for three datasets, and then decreases in performance as λ grows larger. We believe this is because a smaller λ can not efficiently make use of the social information to determine the user clusters, while a larger λ may ignore the importance of preference information, thus decreasing the efficacy of the recommendation. These results confirm that social information is helpful to cluster users and further improve the recommendation performance.

4.3.2 Effect of parameters k and s: For the sake of simplicity, we set $k_n = k_m = k$ in experiments following [3]. The effect of both k and s on SIACC is shown in Figure 3 for two sparse datasets (Ciao and Epinions). From Figure 3, it can be seen that the performance is destroyed when s is large, the main reason is that more stencils will overfit the training data. Meanwhile, we find that SIACC is relatively stable under varying k when fixing s. Thus, small k is enough to approximate the rating matrix.

4.3.3 Comparing with existing methods: In order to deep investigate the performance of recommendation, we compare SIACC with the baselines from two views. First, All Users view indicates that all ratings of unknown set Ω as the testing set. Second, Cold-start Users (CS Users) view means that the users who rate less than five items will be involved in the testing set. The best results are marked

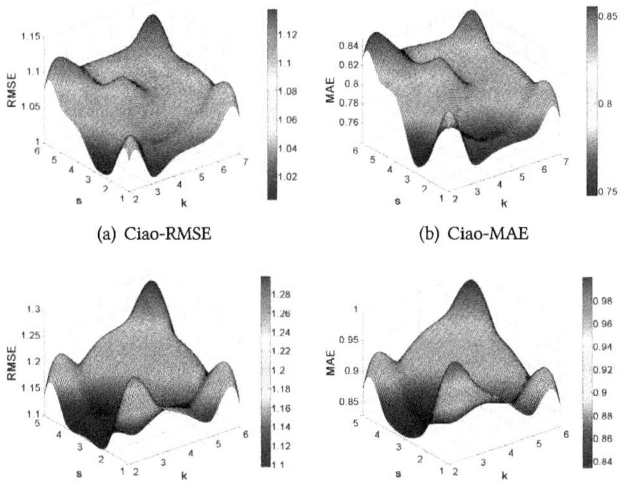
(a) Ciao-RMSE (b) Ciao-MAE

(c) Epinions-RMSE (d) Epinions-MAE

Figure 3: Effect of parameters $k = k_n = k_m$ and s on SIACC for Ciao and Epinions datasets in terms of RMSE and MAE.

in bold as shown in Table 2. It can be seen that SIACC consistently outperforms the baselines. In the first category of social recommendation methods, SPF is better than SoReg. In the second category, Locabal outperforms TrustMF, which means that considering both local and global social influence is more useful than only considering local social influence. Thus, the following comparisons focus on SIACC and PMF, ACCMAS, SPF, and Locabal.

The relative improvements that SIACC achieves relative to four baselines on three datasets are calculated. Since it is challenging to recommend items to cold-start users, we take the cold-start users as an example, as shown in Figure 4. Obviously, SIACC performs better than ACCAMS, which demonstrates that social relations benefit the additive co-clustering process. SIACC is superior to the existing social recommendation methods (Locabal and SPF), which means that integrating global and local social influence into additive co-clustering framework is more useful than into the matrix factorization model to approximate the rating matrix.

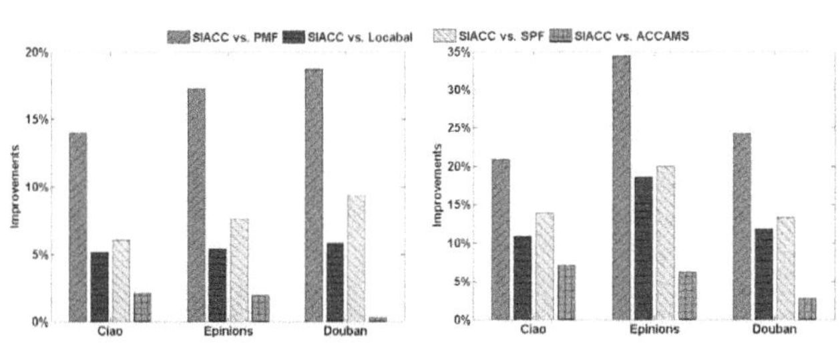

(a) RMSE (b) MAE

Figure 4: The relative improvements of SIACC vs. four baselines on could-start users in three datasets in terms of (a) RMSE and (b) MAE.

Even though the relative improvements are small, small improvements can lead to significant differences of recommendations in practice [11]. Thus, we assess the statistical significance using t-test. Table 3 lists the p-value between SIACC and four baselines for MAE on the cold-start users in three datasets. To be excited, the p values are 0.006 or better for all cases. Similarly, p values are 0.01 or better for RMSE, thus we can say SIACC significantly improve the recommendation performance.

Table 3: Statistical significance (p-value) obtained by SIACC vs. four baselines for MAE on Cold-Start Users.

Datasets	vs. PMF	vs. Locabal	vs. SPF	vs. ACCAMS
Ciao	5.54E-07	1.59E-04	2.12E-05	6.42E-03
Epinions	4.06E-09	9.22E-10	4.97E-10	1.66E-04
Douban	2.56E-11	2.99E-08	1.29E-04	4.93E-03

Table 4: Comparisons of SIACC vs. Locabal on three datasets in terms of running time (seconds).

	Ciao	Epinions	Douban
Locabal	302.37	871.32	1592.91
SIACC	113.37	219.52	932.60

Finally, we evaluate the efficiency of SIACC by comparing it with Locabal, because these two methods consider both global and local social influence. Meanwhile, Locabal is the best social recommendation method among the baselines. These two algorithms are implemented in C++ at the hots with Intel(R) Xeon(R) 2.0GHz CPU E7-4820 v2 having 64GB memory. The operating system is Red Hat Enterprise Linux. Table 4 lists the average running time of five times (for 5-fold corss-validation) on three datasets. Again, the proposed SIACC is faster than Locabal, and the performance improvements of SIACC over Locabal are 1.7× or better. This result demonstrates that additive co-clustering framework is much efficient than low-rank factorization on matrix approximation even integrating extra information, which is consistent to the result obtained in [3].

5 CONCLUSIONS AND FUTURE WORK

In this paper, we proposed a new social influence additive co-clustering method for social recommendation. Both global and local social relations among users are effectively integrated into co-clustering process to generate user/item clusters and stencils. This strategy can iteratively co-cluster the residual between input data and the corresponding stencil, and then minimize the loss between rating matrix and the linear combination of stencils. The unknown rating values can be effectively and efficiently predicted by linear combining the stencils. The experiments on benchmark datasets have shown that SIACC consistently and significantly outperforms the popular existing methods.

In this work, we ignore the directional property of social network, however, it plays an important role to identify the social relations [27]. Meanwhile, only the direct social relations are considered here, indirect social relations (for the users who are not directly connected) [12, 24] have been proved useful for social recommendation. Thus, it is interesting to consider them to extend SIACC. Furthermore, we could integrate other available information such as reviews and item content, like [25], to design more effective and explainable recommender systems. Last but not least, we plan to design a model to simultaneously clustering users and items instead of the current two-phase strategy.

ACKNOWLEDGMENTS

The authors would like to thank Alex Beutel for discussion on co-clustering programming and experiments constructing. This work was partially supported by the NSFC Grant (61375062, 61632004) and CCF-Tencent Open Research Fund (RAGR20150116).

REFERENCES

[1] G. Adomavicius and A. Tuzhilin. 2005. Toward the next generation of recommender systems : A survey of the state-of-the-art and possible extensions. *IEEE Transactions on Knowledge and Data Engineering* 17, 6 (2005), 734–749.

[2] M. Aharon, M. Elad, and A. Bruckstein. 2006. SVD: An Algorithm for Designing Overcomplete Dictionaries for Sparse Representation. *IEEE Transactions on Signal Processing* 54, 11 (2006), 4311–4322.

[3] A. Beutel, A. Ahmed, and A. Smola. 2015. ACCAMS: Additive Co-Clustering to Approximate Matrices Succinctly. In *Proceedings of International Conference on World Wide Web*. 119–129.

[4] D. Cai, X. He, J. Han, and T. Huang. 2011. Graph regularized non-negative matrix factorization for data representation. *IEEE Transactions on Pattern Analysis and Machine Intelligence* 33, 8 (2011), 1548–1560.

[5] A. Chaney, D. Blei, and T. Eliassi-Rad. 2015. A probabilistic model for using social networks in personalized item recommendation. In *Proceedings of ACM Conference on Recommender Systems*. 43–50.

[6] G. Guo, J. Zhang, and N. Yorkesmith. 2015. TrustSVD: Collaborative Filtering with Both the Explicit and Implicit Influence of User Trust and of Item Ratings. In *Proceedings of AAAI Conference on Artificial Intelligence*. 123–129.

[7] R. Hathaway and J. Bezdek. 2001. Fuzzy c-means clustering of incomplete data. *IEEE Transactions on Systems Man and Cybernetics Part B Cybernetics* 31, 5 (2001), 735–744.

[8] M. Jamali and M. Ester. 2010. A matrix factorization technique with trust propagation for recommendation in social networks. In *Proceedings of ACM Conference on Recommender Systems*. 135–142.

[9] M. Jiang, P. Cui, R. Liu, Q. Yang, F. Wang, W. Zhu, and S. Yang. 2012. Social contextual recommendation. In *Proceedings of ACM Conference on Information and Knowledge Management*. 45–54.

[10] L. Jing, P. Wang, and L. Yang. 2015. Sparse probabilistic matrix factorization by Llaplace distribution for collaborative filtering. In *Proceedings of the International Conference on Artificial Intelligence*. 1771–1777.

[11] Y. Koren, R. Bell, and C. Kolinsky. 2010. Factor in the neighbors: scalable and accurate collaborative filtering. *ACM Transactions on Knowledge Discovery from Data* 4, 1 (2010), 1–24.

[12] H. Li, D.Wu, W. Tang, and N. Mamoulis. 2015. Overlapping community regularization for rating prediction in social recommender systems. In *Proceedings of ACM Conference on Recommender Systems*. 27–34.

[13] H. Li, D. Wu, and N. Mamoulis. 2014. A revisit to social network-based recommendation systems. In *Proceedings of ACM Special Interest Group on Information Retrieval*. 1239–1242.

[14] H. Ma, I. King, and M. Lyu. 2009. Learning to recommend with social trust ensemble. In *Proceedings of International ACM SIGIR Conference on Research and Development in Information Retrieval*. 203–210.

[15] H. Ma, H. Yang, M. Lyu, and I. King. 2008. SoRec:social recommendation using probabilistic matrix factorization. In *Proceedings of ACM Conference on Information and Knowledge Management*. 931–940.

[16] H. Ma, D. Zhou, C. Liu, M. Lyu, and I. King. 2011. Recommender systems with social regularization. In *Proceedings of ACM Web Search and Web Data Mining*. ACM, 287–296.

[17] P. Marsden and N. Friedkin. 1993. Network studies of social influence. *Sociological Methods and Research* 22, 1 (1993), 127–151.

[18] P. Massa. *Trust in E-services: Technologies, Practices and Challenges*. IGI Publishing.

[19] L. McPherson and J. Cook. 2001. Birds of a feather: homophily in social networks. *Annual Review of Sociology* 27, 1 (2001), 415–444.

[20] L. Page, S. Brin, R. Motwani, and T. Winograd. 1999. *Bringing order to the web.* Technical Report. Technical Report 1999-66, Stanford InfoLab.

[21] R. Salakhutdinov and A. Mnih. 2007. Probabilistic matrix factorization. In *Proceedings of International Conference on Machine Learning*. 880–887.

[22] R. Salakhutdinov and A. Mnih. 2008. Bayesian probabilistic matrix factorization using Markov chain Monte Carlo. In *Proceedings of International Conference on Machine Learning*. 880–887.

[23] J. Tang, X. Hu, H. Gao, and H. Liu. 2013. Exploiting local and global social context for recommendation. In *Proceedings of International Joint Conference on Artificial Intelligence*.

[24] J. Tang, S. Wang, X. Hu, D. Yin, Y. Bi, Y. Chang, and H. Liu. 2016. Recommendation with social dimensions. In *Proceedings of AAAI Conference on Artificial Intelligence*. 251–257.

[25] C. Wu, A. Beutel, A. Ahmed, and A. Smola. 2016. Explaining reviews and ratings with PACO: poisson additive co-clustering. In *Proceedings of International Conference on World Wide Web*. 127–128.

[26] R. Xiang, J. Neville, and M. Rogati. 2010. Modeling relationship strength in online social networks. In *Proceedings of International Conference on World Wide Web*. 981–990.

[27] B. Yang, Y. Lei, J. Liu, and D. Liu. 2016. Social collaborative filtering by trust. *IEEE Transactions on Pattern Analysis and Machine Intelligence, online publication* (2016).

[28] B. Yang, L. Yu, D. Liu, and J. Liu. 2013. Social collaborative filtering by trust. In *Proceedings of International Joint Conference on Artificial Intelligence*. 2747–2753.

Folding: Why Good Models Sometimes Make Spurious Recommendations

Doris Xin*
University of Illinois at Urbana-Champaign
201 N Goodwin Ave
Urbana, Illinois 61801
dorx0@illinois.edu

Nicolas Mayoraz
Google Research
1600 Amphitheatre Parkway
Mountain View, California 94043
nmayoraz@google.com

Hubert Pham
Google Research
1600 Amphitheatre Parkway
Mountain View, California 94043
hubertpham@google.com

Karthik Lakshmanan
Google Research
1600 Amphitheatre Parkway
Mountain View, California 94043
lakshmanan@google.com

John R. Anderson
Google Research
1600 Amphitheatre Parkway
Mountain View, California 94043
janders@google.com

ABSTRACT

In recommender systems based on low-rank factorization of a partially observed user-item matrix, a common phenomenon that plagues many otherwise effective models is the interleaving of good and spurious recommendations in the top-K results. A single spurious recommendation can dramatically impact the perceived quality of a recommender system. Spurious recommendations do not result in serendipitous discoveries but rather cognitive dissonance. In this work, we investigate *folding*, a major contributing factor to spurious recommendations. Folding refers to the unintentional overlap of disparate groups of users and items in the low-rank embedding vector space, induced by improper handling of missing data. We formally define a metric that quantifies the severity of folding in a trained system, to assist in diagnosing its potential to make inappropriate recommendations. The *folding metric* complements existing information retrieval metrics that focus on the number of good recommendations and their ranks but ignore the impact of undesired recommendations. We motivate the folding metric definition on synthetic data and evaluate its effectiveness on both synthetic and real world datasets. In studying the relationship between the folding metric and other characteristics of recommender systems, we observe that optimizing for goodness metrics can lead to high folding and thus more spurious recommendations.

KEYWORDS

collaborative filtering; matrix factorization; folding; evaluation metric; MNAR

*Work done while the author was at Google Research.

RecSys'17, August 27–31, 2017, Como, Italy.
 ISBN 978-1-4503-4652-8/17/08.
DOI: http://dx.doi.org/10.1145/3109859.3109911

1 INTRODUCTION

Recommender systems based on collaborative filtering propose items to users by generalizing from sparse observed user-item affinities. Prior to live deployment, system developers measure the quality of recommenders using offline metrics that typically treat the recommendation problem as a regression or ranking problem. Regression metrics (e.g., RMSE, MAE) measure how accurately the system can predict the affinity of some hold-out user-item affinities, whereas ranking metrics (e.g., Precision@K, MAP) measure how well hold-out observations intersect with predicted recommendations, for each user. Such metrics are one-sided: they are only *goodness* metrics, focused on measuring recommendation performance based on observed data, while ignoring the possible presence and range of inappropriate recommendations.

In the development of production recommendation systems, disregarding bad recommendations is a critical issue, as a single inappropriate recommendation, even surrounded by many excellent ones, can have a disastrous impact on user experience. Furthermore, not all bad recommendations are equally undesirable. For example, when recommending movies to a user that mostly watches animated Disney movies, a recommendation set that consists of relevant animated videos, along with a PG romantic comedy, is perhaps questionable. Arguably far worse are recommendations with those same animated movies but alongside an NC-17 horror movie. This issue is exacerbated in cold-start situations, where the model makes predictions for new items when much of the interaction data is unobserved.

The above scenarios arise because observed data is not uniformly distributed among user-item pairs. In most applications, we do not have explicit ratings from clearly unrelated pairs, e.g., between a child viewer and an horror movie. Hence, classical goodness metrics focused on evaluation against observed data cannot effectively detect and differentiate the scenarios above. This problem is related to the issue of data *missing not at random* (MNAR), well studied in the recommendation system literature [19]. Proposed solutions so far include building models that are explicitly aware of bias in the training data [27] and focusing on the recommendations at the top [2], yielding models that are less likely to score inappropriate recommendations highly. However, to the best of our knowledge, there has been little attention devoted to designing a *badness* metric that captures the range of inappropriate recommendations. The lack of labeled data for bad user-item pairs explains the inherent complexity in designing a badness metric, and identifying specific inappropriate user-item pairs for such a metric is no simpler than solving the original regression problem.

Spurious estimations are predictions that are not well-supported by the observations from which the model is trained. Thus, they are artifacts of the model rather than being inherent to the data. It is important to note that these are different from diverse recommendations, where the recommendations are explicitly aimed at satisfying a diversity objective that leads to serendipitous discoveries. By contrast, spurious estimations are made by the recommender model due to lack of associated data. Semantically, spurious recommendation could mean that an item is inappropriate for user (e.g., horror films to children).

We propose the *folding metric* as a measure of badness with respect to unobserved data in a recommendation model. The metric pursues an approach based on inferring the geometry of the embedding space that results from matrix factorization. In the matrix factorization setting, users and items are embedded in a vector space such that elements with high affinity are near in the space by some distance metric, and dissimilar items are far apart. However, as we will demonstrate, when missing data is not handled properly, the resultant space can embed similar users and items to be well-positioned with respect to each other, but place or *fold* those elements in the same region as another unrelated group of coherent users and items. Two groups are unrelated if their members have never interacted with each other. When generating recommendations for a user by returning its nearest-neighbors in the embedding space, folding leads to spurious recommendations. Using synthetic data, we illustrate how the folding metric complements a goodness metric. Optimizing solely for goodness can lead to models with high folding, which in turn translates to more inappropriate recommendations.

In our experiments, we evaluate the folding metric on the MovieLens dataset [7] and empirically show that it is robust to different estimations of the likelihood of user-item interactions, which is a prerequisite to the folding metric.

2 PRELIMINARIES

A set of m users and n items for which we have some observed ratings $a_{ij} \in \mathbb{R}$ constitutes the setting of a regression problem in collaborative filtering. The observed ratings a_{ij} partially define a matrix $\boldsymbol{A} \in \mathbb{R}^{m \times n}$, where $\Omega \subset \{1, \ldots, m\} \times \{1, \ldots, n\}$ denotes the set of observed entries of $\boldsymbol{A}$, and typically $|\Omega| \ll mn$. These observations can be explicit user-item ratings, or they can reflect the number of exposures and interactions (e.g., click through rate).

The goal of a recommender system is to estimate which unobserved entries have the largest latent values in any given row $\boldsymbol{a}_i$ of $\boldsymbol{A}$. A popular approach is to assume that the unknown underlying process generating observations defines a low-rank k matrix. The goal is then to approximate the partially defined matrix $\boldsymbol{A}$ with a low-rank matrix $\boldsymbol{U}^\top \boldsymbol{V}$ where $\boldsymbol{U} \in \mathbb{R}^{k \times m}, \boldsymbol{V} \in \mathbb{R}^{k \times n}$, by solving the following optimization problem:

$$\min_{\boldsymbol{U},\boldsymbol{V}} \|\boldsymbol{W} \odot (\boldsymbol{A} - \boldsymbol{U}^\top \boldsymbol{V})\|_F^2 + \lambda(\|\boldsymbol{U}\|_F^2 + \|\boldsymbol{V}\|_F^2), \quad (1)$$

where $\boldsymbol{W} \in \mathbb{R}_+^{m \times n}$ is a weight matrix, $\odot$ denotes the Hadamard matrix product, $\|\cdot\|_F$ represents the Frobenius norm, and $\lambda \geq 0$ is a regularization parameter.

The problem in Equation (1) is well defined if for each $(i,j) \notin \Omega$, either $w_{ij} = 0$, or a_{ij} is predetermined. Handling missing data by selecting the appropriate w_{ij} and a_{ij} for $(i,j) \notin \Omega$ is of crucial importance to any factorization-based recommendation algorithm. In regression problems, unobserved entries are set to a prior. Common choices for the prior are a global constant and functions of i and/or j. For example, in a user-movie rating scenario, users have mostly watched and rated movies they like, hence the prior for all ratings should be lower than the global average observed ratings.

2.1 Weighting the Unknown

Various propositions for $\boldsymbol{W}$ have led to a broad range of algorithms. On one end of the spectrum, setting $\boldsymbol{W} = \boldsymbol{1}$ and $a_{ij} = 0, \forall (i,j) \notin \Omega$ in Equation (1) converts the problem to an SVD decomposition of $\boldsymbol{A}$ (under $\lambda = 0$). This approach is known to lead to recommendations that can be quite poor when $\boldsymbol{A}$ is very sparse, because the loss function is dominated by the unobserved data. In practice, a sparsity rate of 10^{-3} or lower is common, thus making this approach inapplicable in most settings. On the other end of the spectrum, the unobserved data can be ignored all together by setting

$$\boldsymbol{W} = \boldsymbol{1}^{\Omega},$$

where $\boldsymbol{1}^{\Omega}$ is the indicator matrix of the set Ω such that $\boldsymbol{1}^{\Omega}_{ij} = 1$ for $(i,j) \in \Omega$ and 0 otherwise. As we will demonstrate in Section 4, this can lead to spurious recommendations.

[12] shows that attributing a small uniform weight to all unobserved data leads to success on the Netflix Prize, by setting

$$\boldsymbol{W} = \boldsymbol{1}^{\Omega} + \alpha \boldsymbol{W}^0, \quad (2)$$

where $\alpha > 0$ is a meta-parameter that controls the importance attributed to the unobserved user-item pairs. This meta-parameter α needs careful tuning. A reasonable choice for α is in the order of the sparsity rate of $\boldsymbol{A}$, thereby sharing evenly the total weight of the observed and unobserved data in Equation (1). Different choices for $\boldsymbol{W}^0 \in \mathbb{R}^{m \times n}$ have been studied in [12], where $\boldsymbol{W}^0$ is the all-ones matrix; in [24], where $\boldsymbol{W}^0$ is rank 1; and in [25], where $w_{ij} = c_i c_j$ with multiple options for c_i and c_j.

2.2 Optimization Strategies

The optimization problem in Equation (1) has been widely studied in the literature in the context of collaborating filtering and recommender systems, and the proposed solutions broadly fall into two categories: weighted alternating least square solvers (WALS) and stochastic gradient descent solvers (SGD).

WALS presents the considerable advantage of taking into account the full matrix $\boldsymbol{A}$, down-weighting appropriately the unobserved entries, often leading to more accurate models [30]. According to [12] and [24], as long as the weight matrix is of the simple form of Equation (2), WALS solvers are able to handle large matrices.

The main advantage of SGD is flexibility. For example, SGD naturally supports (i) various cost functions beyond squared loss (e.g. logistic loss, SoftMax + cross-entropy), (ii) non-linearity (e.g. in the form of hidden layers of a deep neural network), and (iii) integration of meta data (e.g. user geo-location or movie language or genre). However, the efficiency of SGD relies heavily on negative sampling (selecting for each batch some $(i,j) \notin \Omega$ and setting $w_{ij} > 0$), and many sampling strategies have been proposed [13, 23]. For this reason, SGD algorithms become slow to converge for very large and extremely sparse problems, and the largest problems that can be solved by SGD in reasonable time are orders of magnitude smaller than the sizes mentioned above handled by WALS.

We have done extensive comparisons between WALS and SGD in other contexts, and for appropriate negative sampling strategies aimed at emulating the same weight of unobserved data α, the optimal solution reached by SGD is qualitatively the same as the one obtained by WALS, with the latter being typically much faster. Therefore, in all our experiments in this paper, we use a WALS solver to optimize Equation (1).

3 FOLDING

3.1 The Folding Phenomenon: A Case Study

To establish some intuition on the folding problem, consider the toy example user-movie ratings matrix A shown in Figure 1. Rows of A represent users while columns denote movies. Users rate movies on a scale of 1 to 5 with 5 being the most favorable. Whitespace in the matrix indicates unobserved ratings.

Matrix factorization based techniques assume that the user-rating pairs are generated from a low-rank process. In this example we explicitly define the underlying process in terms of user and item groups, visualized by the block structure in Figure 1(a). Note that this block structure can be extracted from real datasets by rearranging the rows and columns to place similar rows/columns next to each other. Movies are grouped by either their genres or language, while users are grouped by the genres of movies they've watched, with the exception that i) some popular Family/Action/Romantic films have been rated by users in more than one block and ii) only bilingual users have rated Japanese films.

Figure 1(b) depicts A, the matrix containing observed ratings for some user-movie pairs. Users are more likely to rate movies they enjoy than not, echoing the same observed trend in the MovieLens dataset. The optimization problem in Equation (1) is solved for A^o, the centered version of A (the mean rating is subtracted), using WALS with $a^o_{ij} = 0 \; \forall (i,j) \notin \Omega$, embedding dimension $k = 3$, and weight on the unobserved $\alpha = 0$. Figure 1(c) shows $A^* = U^\top V$, the approximation of A^o using the WALS solutions. Let $\bar{B}$ be the masking matrix that has 0 for the dark blocks in Figure 1(a) and 1 everywhere else. Figure 1(d) shows $(A^* - A^o) \odot \bar{B}$, the difference between the predicted ratings and the actual ratings for the blocks without user-movie interactions. The large positive errors are due to folding.

Figure 2 visualizes the embedding vectors to provide insight into the embedding space geometry underlying the folding phenomenon. It shows a 2D projection of the 3D WALS embedding vectors in U and V. For visual clarity, we only show the subset of user groups that are most impacted by folding. The embedding vectors exhibit a few undesired characteristics: i) embedding vectors for horror films are close to embedding vectors for children, who have rated nothing but family films; ii) action fans are placed in closer proximity to Japanese films than action films, when none have previously rated any Japanese films. We refer to this phenomenon in which disparate groups are collapsed onto the same region in the embedding space as folding.

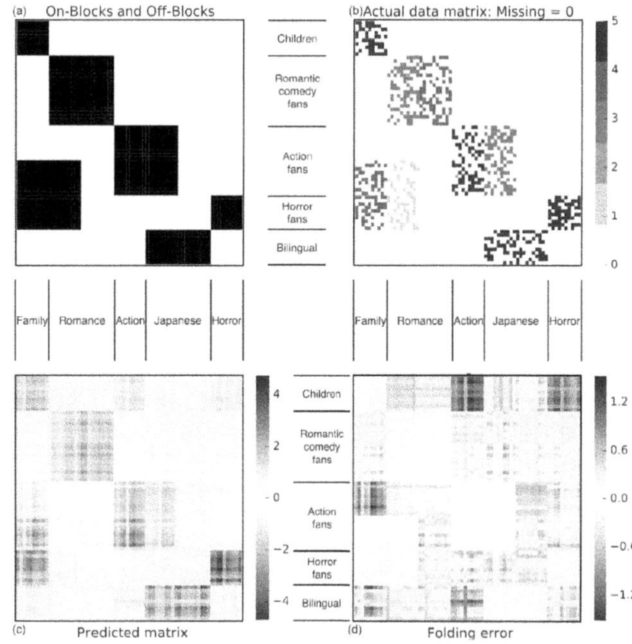

Figure 1: Synthetic User-Movie Ratings.

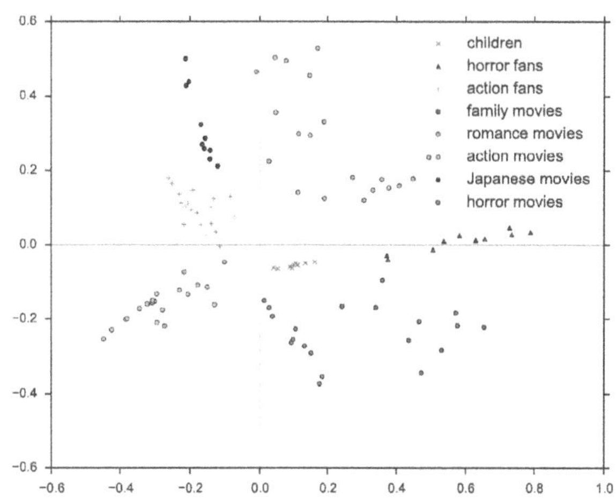

Figure 2: Embedding Vectors for User and Movies in Figure 1

In a typical recommender system powered by low-rank matrix factorization, the standard method for generating recommendations, after the embedding vectors are trained, is to take the top-K items, excluding previously rated items, with embedding vectors that achieve the highest cosine similarity (or dot product) with a given user vector. The predicted matrix shown in Figure 1(c) illustrates the ramifications: for children, while the family movie group is recovered correctly, other groups of movies are ranked too high (action, horror) and some of these movies are bound to creep in the top-K recommendations.

Recommending an uninteresting family film to a child is far less of an offense than recommending a horror film. Determining the impact of a bad recommendation is hinged upon our ability to discern why a user-item rating is missing from the observation set Ω. The Missing Not At Random (MNAR) principle postulates that not all user-item pairs have equal likelihood of being unobserved. As shown in Figure 1, the likelihood is tied to the consumption pattern – for a given user, a movie in a genre she has regularly rated is much less likely to have a missing rating than in a genre she has never interacted with before. We capture the missing data mechanism via *relatedness*, to be discussed in Section 3.4.

3.2 An Example of Folding using MovieLens

A concrete example of folding is shown in Table 1 using the MovieLens data [7]. Treating the recommendation problem as a regression problem with a_{ij} being the star rating user i gave to movie j, we solve the optimization problem in Equation (1) twice, once ignoring all missing data (setting $\alpha = 0$ in Equation (2)), and once using $\alpha = 0.001$, and $a_{ij} = 2\ \forall(i,j) \notin \Omega$). The MovieLens data is first partitioned into training and hold-out, and Equation (1) is optimized using the training data alone.

According to the mean squared error (MSE) measured on the hold-out set, the solution obtained while ignoring the missing data is quantitatively better than the one using the missing data. However, a cosine-based nearest neighbors analysis clearly reveals folding in the first case, indicated by high-ranking inappropriate recommendations reported in Table 1. The query movie "Cinderella" is a musical targeting children and youth. The second set, composed predominantly of comedies and adolescent drama, is thus more fitting than the crime thrillers and drama for a mature audience in the first set, even though the cosine measures are higher in the first set.

3.3 Causes of Folding

Folding is best explained by partitioning the unobserved data into related and unrelated missing values. A related user-item pair is unobserved for potentially multiple reasons. For example, the user might not interact with an item due to lack of exposure but would otherwise have an opinion about that item, or perhaps the item is extremely popular and the missing observation denotes implicit negative affinity. Together with Ω, the set of observed user-item pairs, the missing related data form the related user-item pairs. Each related missing user-item pair can take any rating value. In Figure 1, the related missing user-item pairs are the missing entries in the populated blocks of the data matrix in (b). Serendipitous recommendations are always about unobserved related data.

Recs Ignoring Missing Data		**Recs Using Missing Data**	
Movie	Cosine	Movie	Cosine
Cinderella (1997) Children|Fantasy|Musical|Romance	1	**Cinderella (1997)** Children|Fantasy|Musical|Romance	1
Ransom (a.k.a. The Terrorists) (1975) Crime|Thriller	0.912	27 Dresses (2008) Comedy|Romance	0.821
Memoirs of a Geisha (2005) Drama|Romance	0.909	Twilight (2008) Drama|Fantasy|Romance|Thriller	0.810
Hairspray (2007) Comedy|Drama|Musical	0.897	Made of Honor (2008) Comedy|Romance	0.780
Monster House (2006) Adventure|Animation|Children|Comedy|Drama|Fantasy|Mystery	0.895	High School Musical 2 (2007) Comedy|Drama|Musical|Romance	0.771
Cold Mountain (2003) Drama|Romance|War	0.892	House Bunny, The (2008) Comedy	0.764
Millions (2004) Children|Comedy|Crime|Drama|Fantasy	0.890	Step Up (2006) Drama|Romance	0.761
Seven Pounds (2008) Drama	0.890	P.S. I Love You (2007) Comedy|Drama|Romance	0.761
Tuesdays with Morrie (1999) Drama	0.889	Fool's Gold (2008) Action|Adventure|Comedy|Romance	0.738
Bobby (2006) Drama	0.888	Nanny Diaries, The (2007) Comedy|Drama|Romance	0.735

Table 1: Top 9 recommendations for the movie Cinderella according to a two different models.

In contrast, an unrelated missing user-item pair characterizes a user who has no interest in an item (e.g., children and horror films or Japanese films and non-speakers). Unrelated missing data often constitute the vast majority of the missing observations, due to some inherent structure in the data generation process: user-item consumption is naturally limited by region, languages, or it is artificially restricted by targeting. In the example of Section 3.1, the unrelated missing observations are all the user-item pairs outside of the dark blocks in Figure 1(a).

Folding pertains to falsely assigning high affinity to unrelated missing data. By contrast, identifying similarities in related missing data is considered generalization by the model from known data. When a model folds, it leads to spurious recommendations, often inter-leaved with good recommendations, which makes the issue hard to detect. The likelihood of a model to fold is exacerbated by the fact that the indicator matrix $\mathbf{1}^{\Omega}$ is often close to a block sparse matrix (as in Figure 1), due to implicit partitioning of users and items based on metadata such as countries, languages, interests, etc– most viewers will watch movies with either the sound track or subtitles in a language they understand; many music listeners are interested in 2-3 genres of music; online shoppers are shown ads about items from a small pool of topics targeted to them.

To illustrate how such situation can lead to folding, consider the simplified scenario where $\mathbf{1}^{\Omega}$ is K-block-diagonal, inducing a partition of users into K populations and items into K groups. When unobserved data are ignored ($\alpha = 0$), there are no constraints between users in population k and items in group $l \neq k$. Hence, Equation 1 can split into K independent sub-problems. In any optimal solution the embedding vectors of users and items of a population k are organized in specific positions with respect to each-other, but they can fold on top of users and items of population $l \neq k$.

3.4 Relatedness

The folding metric is based upon the notion of *relatedness* between a user i and an item j, which captures the likelihood of interaction between i and j, regardless of the rating. Pairwise relatedness between users and items can be modeled in a matrix $\boldsymbol{R} \in [0,1]^{m \times n}$. Such a matrix is usually not available and needs to be estimated first. Section 4 explores and evaluates one way to estimate $\boldsymbol{R}$ for the specific case of MovieLens data, along with a generic approach, which is described next.

One can compute a low-rank approximation of the binary matrix $\mathbf{1}^{\Omega}$, and then apply a coefficient-wise monotonic transformation (e.g. translation + normalization) to get $\boldsymbol{R}$ in $[0,1]^{m \times n}$. This approximation can be done using WALS with a high unobserved weight parameter α (e.g. $\alpha = 1$), or simply using SVD. The rank should ideally be just large enough to capture the underlying hidden structure of $\mathbf{1}^{\Omega}$, but small enough not to encode any noise. This low-rank approximation is a form of smoothing of $\mathbf{1}^{\Omega}$ with the desired property that for a majority of user-item pairs, r_{ij} is large if $(i,j) \in \Omega$ and small otherwise. However, r_{ij} can also be somewhat large if user i and item j are not directly connected, i.e., $(i,j) \notin \Omega$, but closely related in the bipartite graph defined by Ω. Conversely, this approach also allows for cases where r_{ij} is small for $(i,j) \in \Omega$, which is a desirable property in the case of noisy data.

3.5 The Folding Metric Definition

Definition 3.1. Given a measure of relatedness $\boldsymbol{R}$, the folding metric $F_{\boldsymbol{R}}$, which assesses the propensity of a user-item similarity measure S to cause spurious recommendations, is defined as

$$F_{\boldsymbol{R}}(S) = \frac{1}{mn} \sum_{i,j} \max(0, s_{ij} - r_{ij})$$

The asymmetry due to $\max(0, \cdot)$ causes the folding metric to be only a badness measure: folding increases when unrelated pairs are considered similar but is not affected when related pairs are rated as dissimilar. First, related pairs are taken care of by goodness metrics (which are always used jointly with the folding metric), as they are likely supported by observed ratings. Second, predicting low ratings on related pairs is legitimate and does not contribute to folding.

In the context of matrix factorization, the similarity measure S is defined over the factors $(\boldsymbol{U}, \boldsymbol{V})$. Its exact definition can vary based on the application, but a reasonable choice is the cosine similarity between user vector $\boldsymbol{u}_i$ and an item vector $\boldsymbol{v}_j$. Note that given Definition (3.1), (i,j) pairs with negative s_{ij} make no contribution to the folding metric, regardless of the value for $r_{ij} \in [0,1]$.

The folding metrics $F_{\boldsymbol{R}}(S)$ and $F_{\boldsymbol{R}}(S')$ for different similarity measures S and S' are comparable only if S and S' have similar distributions. For example, the folding value of a cosine similarity and the folding value of a dot-product similarity are both interesting in their own rights, but cannot be compared.

3.6 Relationship to Other Metrics

In this section we discuss the relationship between the folding metric and existing metrics for evaluating recommender systems. Below, let Ω_i^R denote the set of related items to user i, and let Ω_i^U denote the set of unrelated items to user i.

3.6.1 Precision. Precision is applicable only in the context of recommending good items, a task with a binary objective. During offline evaluation for this task, a fraction of the items rated favorably by the user is held out from the training set, and the model is measured on its ability to retrieve the hold-out set. Traditionally, missing observations are treated as negatives in such evaluations, which require negative labels. That is, recommending an item not in the hold-out set is considered a false positive. Since most applications only recommend to the users a small fraction of all available items, precision is commonly measured on only the top-K recommendations, in a variant known as precision@K,

$$\text{Precision@}K = \frac{TP}{K} = 1 - \frac{FP}{K}$$

where TP is the number of true positives and FP is the number of false positives corresponding to the number of missing observations in the standard treatment.

While the folding metric operates mainly in a space orthogonal to the focus of precision, high folding can negatively impact performance measured by precision@K. By the MNAR principle, $E[P_{obs}(i,j)] \gg E[P_{obs}(i,k)]$ for movie j in the related set Ω_i^R vs. movie k in the unrelated set Ω_i^U, where $P_{obs}(u,v)$ denotes the probability of observing a rating for movie v by user u. Let $\mathbf{y}_i$ be a recommendation set consisting of K items and $P_{FP}(i,j)$ denote the likelihood of user-item pair (i,j) being a false positive. Since all missings are regarded as negatives by precision, $E[P_{FP}(i,j)] \propto E[1 - P_{obs}(i,j)]$, which implies

$$E[\text{Precision@}K] \propto \sum_{y \in \mathbf{y}_i} E[P_{obs}(i,y)]$$

For two recommendations sets $\mathbf{y}_i$ and $\mathbf{y}'_i$ of size K such that $|\mathbf{y}_i \cap \Omega_i^U| > |\mathbf{y}'_i \cap \Omega_i^U|$, i.e. $\mathbf{y}_i$ suffers more from folding,

$$\sum_{y \in \mathbf{y}_i} E[P_{obs}(i,y)] < \sum_{y \in \mathbf{y}'_i} E[P_{obs}(i,y)],$$

implying that $\mathbf{y}_i$ with higher folding has lower precision@K in expectation. However, for a given value of precision, folding can take on a range of values because precision does not distinguish between related and unrelated missings. Folding is more severe with top-K results containing unrelated missings than related missings.

3.6.2 Ranking Based. One major drawback to precision/recall is that they are not sensitive to the position of the true positives in the ranked list for the top-K results. Ranking based metrics such as discounted cumulative gain (DCG) is designed to measure the system's ability to prioritize good recommendations over the bad ones. DCG@K, the analog to precision/recall@K, is defined as

$$DCG@K = \sum_{i=1}^{K} \frac{2^{r(i)} - 1}{\log_2(i+1)}$$

where $r(i)$ indicates the relevance of the item at position i. A common choice for r is a binary indicator for observed interaction between a user and an item. As with precision/recall, missing items have a relevance of 0, effectively acting as a negative. For recommendation sets that have the same precision, the ones that have the positives positioned towards the top of the list have higher DCG.

DCG@K is also negatively impacted by high folding. The interleaving of $g \in \Omega_i^R$ and $b \in \Omega_i^U$ pushes down the ranks of positives, resulting in a lower DCG. The MNAR assumption implies $E[r(g)] > E[r(b)]$. Since DCG also does not distinguish between related and unrelated missings, the value for the folding metric can vary significantly between models with the same DCG.

3.6.3 RMSE. Root mean squared error (RMSE) is the standard choice for evaluating recommender systems on regression tasks such as user rating prediction. While the metrics above heed some notion of negatives, RMSE does not consider them at all. For the @K metrics above, a false negative occupies a spot that could have been filled with a true positive, thus lowering the metric. For RMSE, any value can be placed on the missing entries without affecting the objective. Our experiments suggest that when constrained by embedding dimensions, systems that optimize for RMSE predict high values on Ω_i^U, which indicates higher folding, to achieve more accurate predictions for Ω_i^R.

4 EXPERIMENTS

To separate the study of folding from the estimation of the relatedness matrix $\boldsymbol{R}$, we first report experiments on synthetic data, where the relatedness is known as part of the data generation process. Then, we illustrate folding on models trained on the MovieLens dataset.

4.1 Assessing Folding on Synthetic Data

The experiments reported below involve 5000 users and 6000 items. The low-rank process that defines user consumption patterns is generated by partitioning users into 5 groups of sizes varying from 400 to 1600 and items into 10 groups of sizes from 100 to 1400. Out of the 50 blocks in {user groups} × {item groups}, a quarter of them are marked as *on-blocks* (dark blocks in Figure 1(a)), which connect *related* users and items. These on-blocks are selected randomly such that any user or item is in at least one on-block. The remaining blocks are *off-blocks*, connecting *unrelated* users and items. Each block is further divided into 2 x 2 sub-blocks, and each sub-block is assigned a random integer in $[1, 5]$ representing user-item ratings. From the low-rank process mask, 25% of the user-item pairs in the on-blocks are randomly selected as part of the observed dataset, along with 2.5% of the entries in the off-blocks (assigned random ratings) to simulate noise. 25% of the observed dataset is held out for testing, excluding noisy entries. We repeat this data generation process 100 times, and Figure 3 reports means and standard deviations among these 100 experiments. In each experiment, the $\{0, 1\}$ matrix of on/off blocks is used as the relatedness matrix $\boldsymbol{R}$, i.e., $r_{i,j} = 1$ if and only if the user i and item j pair belongs to an on-block. Each full data matrix in $\{0, \ldots, 5\}^{5000\times6000}$ is factored using WALS, with a regularization parameter $\lambda = 0.1$ while varying k, the embedding dimension, and α, the weight on unobserved user-item pairs. Figure 3 shows the RMSE measured on hold-out data and the folding metric measured on all user-item pairs for different combinations of k and α. Folding is calculated for the cosine similarity between user and item embeddings.

Note that since in these datasets $\frac{3}{4}$ of the blocks are off-blocks, $r_{i,j} = 0$ for $\frac{3}{4}$ of the user-item pairs in expectation. The maximum folding value is 0.75 when the model assigns maximum cosine similarity $s_{i,j} = 1$ to every unrelated pair. If the expected cosine similarity over the unrelated pairs is just average ($s_{i,j} = 0.5$) the folding measure is 0.375.

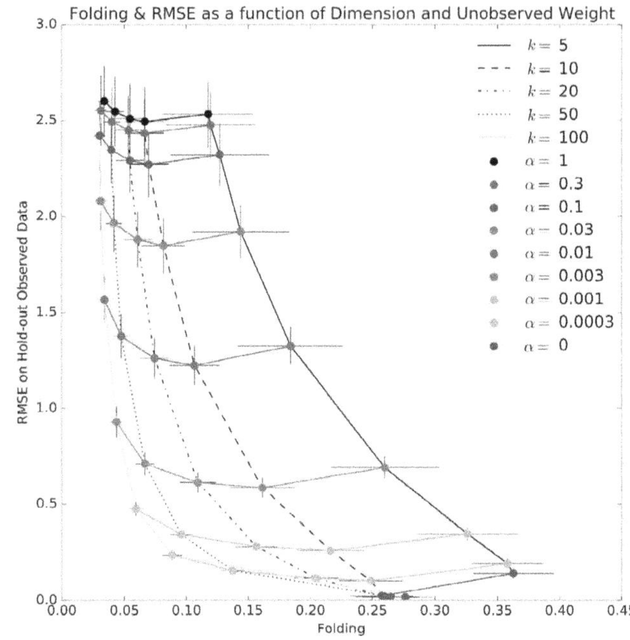

Figure 3: Negative correlation between RMSE and Folding, varying dimension k and unobserved weight α.

For any fixed embedding dimension k, decreasing the weight on unobserved data α improves the error rate on hold-out data but deteriorates the folding metric. This trend is more pronounced in lower dimensions, as the model does not have enough resolution to represent the data well. Ignoring the numerous unobserved pairs naturally leads to more folding. Similarly, fixing α and decreasing k worsens the folding metric, as the information is more compressed, but improves the error rate, as overfitting decreases, up to the point where the model underfits.

Optimizing only for RMSE yields $k = 10$ and $\alpha = 0$ as optimal hyperparameters. However, they lead to $F_{\boldsymbol{R}} > 0.25$, which indicates that many user-item pairs in off-blocks are considered similar. This is unreasonable for both the synthetic data generation process and real-world datasets. Hyperparameter tuning is a multi-objective problem, and in practice, the right balance between RMSE and folding is application-specific.

4.2 Assessing Folding on Real Data

The MovieLens 10M dataset contains 10M ratings for 10,681 movies by 71,567 users, yielding a sparsity rate of 1.3% [7]. We center the observed ratings $\boldsymbol{A}$ by subtracting the global average from all ratings and set the unobserved entries a_{ij} to 0. We randomly select 10% of all observed entries to be held out from training for testing. The optimization problem in Equation (1) is then solved using the training data and WALS with regularization $\lambda = 10$ while varying the embedding dimension k and unobserved weight α.

Computing the folding metric requires a definition of $\boldsymbol{R}$, the relatedness between all users and all items. Following the proposition in Section 3, we approximate $\mathbf{1}^{\Omega}$ using a rank l factorization $\boldsymbol{X}^\top \boldsymbol{Y}$, with $\boldsymbol{X} \in \mathbb{R}^{l\times m}$ and $\boldsymbol{Y} \in \mathbb{R}^{l\times n}$, using WALS with a high weight of

$\alpha = 1$ for unobserved ratings. Using this factorization, we define relatedness $\boldsymbol{R}^{\text{CF}}$ as

$$r_{ij}^{\text{CF}} = \max(0, \text{cosine}(\boldsymbol{x}_i, \boldsymbol{y}_j)) . \tag{3}$$

In our experiments, the $\boldsymbol{R}^{\text{CF}}$ matrices produced by setting l to 15, 30 and 35 lead to identical conclusions. All following results are obtained using $l = 30$.

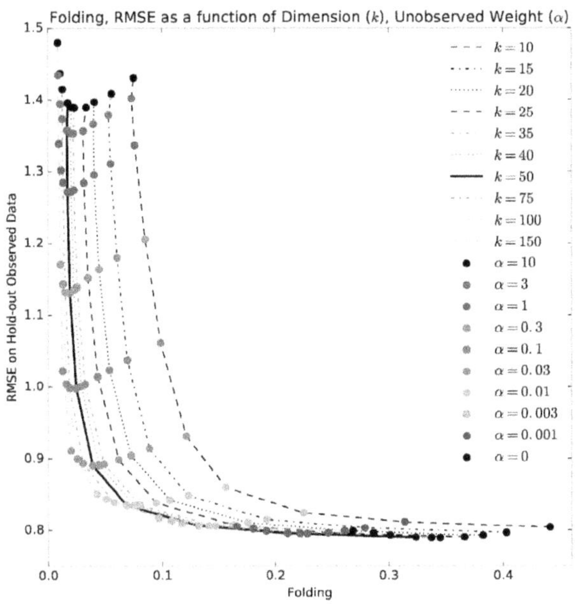

Figure 4: RMSE vs Folding on the MovieLens dataset.

Figure 4 shows the relationship between folding and RMSE as functions of k and α. RMSE is evaluated on hold-out data. We observe a negative correlation between RMSE and folding, which express two opposing goals. Consistent with the synthetic data, for any fixed dimension k, decreasing α improves RMSE, which drops rapidly from 1.5 to 0.9 with little increase in folding. However, once α is below 0.03, minor improvements in RMSE come at a heavy cost on folding. This suggests a compromise that would be overlooked when only RMSE is optimized. For any fixed α, increasing the dimension k reduces folding, as the embeddings gain more degrees of freedom. For left to right, the curves appear in order of decreasing k. Points with the same α and different k form parabolic curves in this order because both overfitting in the high dimensional regime and underfitting in the low dimensional regime lead to generalization error. The local minimum is consistently achieved at $k = 50$ (bold) for different values of α, which suggests that 50 is the closest to the true rank among our choices of embedding dimensions.

The best RMSE in our results is comparable to the state of the art on the same dataset (0.771 reported by [31]). However, all RMSE values ≤ 0.8 are obtained from low α (missing data is largely ignored) and associated with high folding measure ≥ 0.2. This suggests that the best-RMSE models have high propensity to make spurious recommendations like the ones in the first set of movies in Table 1.

From an information theoretic standpoint, k presents an upper bound on the amount of information that can be encoded in the embedding space. The model can choose to devote the information content to recovering the observed entries, avoiding overprediction on unrelated pairs, or a combination of both. Recovering observations and avoiding overpredictions are at odds with each other under limited model complexity. Suppose three distinct user-item groups exist in a dataset but the model is only capable of encoding two. The model can encode the two largest groups and omit the smallest, or it can merge two groups together so that observations in all three groups are recovered. In the former, the model misses out on all observation in the smallest group but does not fold; in the latter, the model overpredicts on unrelated user-item pairs that separate the two merged groups, leading to folding. This is the root cause behind the negative correlation observed between RMSE and folding.

4.3 Robustness of the Folding Metric

As mentioned in Section 4.2, comparing the folding metric obtained from different dimensions l of the approximate factorization of $\mathbf{1}^{\Omega}$ leads to similar results. To further demonstrate the robustness of the folding metric to estimations of $\boldsymbol{R}$, we compare the folding metric computed using $\boldsymbol{R}$ derived from a factorization-based estimation (using $l = 30$) with using a metadata-based approach.

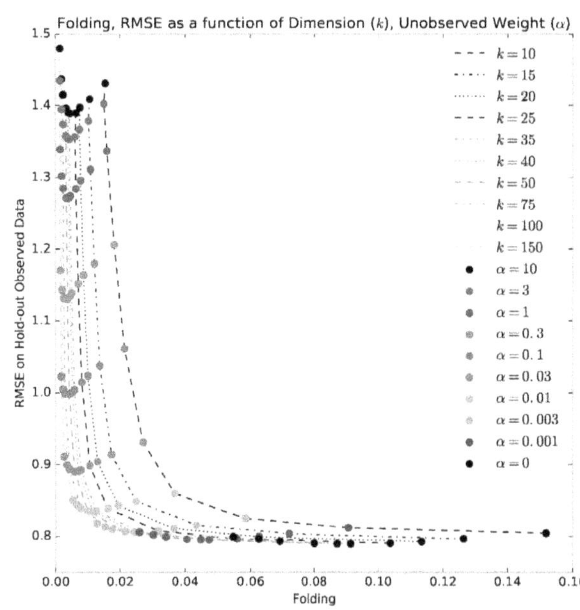

Figure 5: RMSE vs Folding on the MovieLens dataset, using genre embeddings for relatedness.

The MovieLens dataset [7] contains genre metadata, which can also form a basis for user-item relatedness. Each movie belongs to one or more of 18 genres. A simple model maps each movie j to an 18-dimensional vector, where y_{jd} is 1 if movie j belongs to genre d, and 0 otherwise. Each user is mapped onto the same space where x_{id} is the fraction of movies of genre d rated by user i. The relatedness $\boldsymbol{R}^{\text{genre}}$ is then defined by applying Equation (3) to the genre vectors.

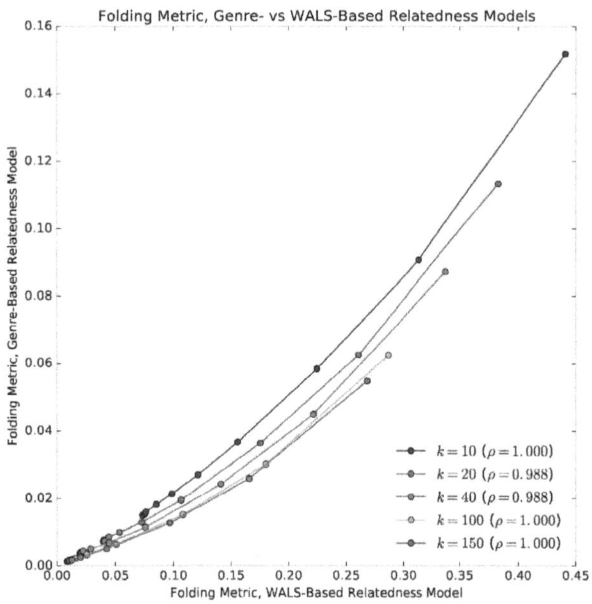

Figure 6: Folding metrics based on different estimates of R are strongly correlated.

Figure 5 shows the resulting parametric curves in the folding-RMSE space. The behavior is similar to the relationship between RMSE and folding in the case of the factorization-based estimation. In fact, the two choices for R lead to folding measures that are strongly monotonic, as shown in Figure 6. Each point in the plot represents a WALS model trained with a specific k and α. The set of models shown in Figure 6 is identical to the set in Figure 4. Points with the same k are connected to demonstrate the monotonicity between the folding measures obtained using the two choices for R, evidenced by Spearman's $\rho \approx 1$.

5 RELATED WORK

The success of matrix factorization techniques in the Netflix Prize competition [17] popularized their use in modern recommender systems. One major strength of such approaches over their predecessors is the ability to incorporate implicit feedback, in contrast to explicit user-item ratings. Effectively augmenting recommender systems with implicit feedback requires understanding the nature of missing entries in the user-item matrix.

[19, 21] apply the missing data theory to address the issue of missing observations, and [21] establishes through a user study that data is missing not at random (MNAR), as users report to deliberately avoid rating certain groups of items, in hopes of improving their recommendations. [5, 8, 11, 12, 18, 20, 24, 25, 27, 29] investigate methods to distinguish missing data due to avoidance vs. lack of exposure. [11, 18, 27] propose to capture the missing data mechanism through a dedicated model that determines implicit negatives used for training the recommender system. [8] studies the low-rank nature of the missing data model and provides performance bounds derived from the low-rank assumption. [5, 12, 24] use heuristic approaches to weight the missing entries such that the matrix-factorization optimization objective is influenced by mispredictions on missing data, effectively treating missing data as weak implicit negative feedback. On the other hand, [29] provides alternative objectives designed to counter the bias introduced by MNAR data. Through comparative evaluations, authors in [20] conclude that MNAR algorithms outperform algorithms that assume data is missing at random (MAR). The proposed folding metric uses a low-rank similarity model that reflects the missing data mechanism to identify models that are prone to the pitfalls of MNAR data.

Effective offline evaluation, a challenge in recommendation model learning, has generated a great deal of research interest in recent years. Choosing the wrong evaluation metric can lead to suboptimal models for the recommendation task at hand [6]. The matter is complicated by the MNAR nature of data, which calls for evaluation frameworks that can differentiate different types of missing data. [6, 10, 28] provide surveys of existing metrics and their effectiveness on different recommendation tasks. [3] shows that for the top-N task, where the model predicts the N items with which a user is most likely to interact, algorithms that optimize for RMSE perform significantly worse than PureSVD (SVD with missing entries imputed as 0s). This result motivates our choices for ground truth similarity discussed earlier. [26] shows that measuring model performance on missing entries helps avoid bias introduced when considering only observed data. Our work complements existing metrics by measuring the severity of mispredictions on implicit unobserved data.

[15, 16, 22] study recommender system quality from a user-centric perspective. User satisfaction is often captured by a serendipity metric, complementary to the folding metric that quantifies bad user experience. [1, 4, 14] explore ways by which serendipity is measured and its inverse relationship to other metrics. [9] advocates for systems that provide explanations for its recommendations to improve user experience. The folding metric helps explain, to the system developers, potential causes of negative user experience.

6 CONCLUSION AND FUTURE WORK

Real-world recommender systems are often constrained by partially observed user-item interactions yet must generalize recommendations to unobserved user-item settings. We propose the folding metric to quantify the likelihood of producing incongruous recommendations while performing such generalizations. The key to this metric is the fact that not all generalizations are created equal. We have studied the metric in the low-rank matrix factorization context with WALS solvers, where unrelated items can be in close proximity in the embedding space due to lack of observations that explicitly force them apart. Our experiments with the MovieLens dataset [7] show that RMSE is negatively correlated with the folding metric, revealing that the best models trade off incremental RMSE gains for increasing folding costs. Experiments also affirm that the folding metric is robust to approaches used to estimate user-item relatedness, yielding similar results when using genre metadata as a proxy for relatedness vs. low-rank factorization. In future work, we aim to study the folding metric in the context of SGD solvers and develop negative sampling strategies that can effectively address folding in those systems.

REFERENCES

[1] Panagiotis Adamopoulos and Alexander Tuzhilin. 2015. On unexpectedness in recommender systems: Or how to better expect the unexpected. *ACM Transactions on Intelligent Systems and Technology* (2015).

[2] Konstantina Christakopoulou and Arindam Banerjee. 2015. Collaborative Ranking with a Push at the Top. *International World Wide Web Conference (WWW)* (2015).

[3] Paolo Cremonesi, Yehuda Koren, and Roberto Turrin. 2010. Performance of recommender algorithms on top-n recommendation tasks. In *RecSys*. ACM.

[4] Mouzhi Ge, Carla Delgado-Battenfeld, and Dietmar Jannach. 2010. Beyond accuracy: evaluating recommender systems by coverage and serendipity. In *RecSys*. ACM.

[5] Quanquan Gu, Jie Zhou, and Chris Ding. 2010. Collaborative filtering: Weighted nonnegative matrix factorization incorporating user and item graphs. In *International Conference on Data Mining*. SIAM.

[6] Asela Gunawardana and Guy Shani. 2009. A survey of accuracy evaluation metrics of recommendation tasks. *Journal of Machine Learning Research* (2009).

[7] F. Maxwell Harper and Joseph A. Konstan. 2015. The MovieLens Datasets: History and Context. *ACM Transactions on Interactive Intelligent Systems* (2015).

[8] Elad Hazan, Roi Livni, and Yishay Mansour. 2015. Classification with Low Rank and Missing Data. In *ICML*.

[9] Jonathan L Herlocker, Joseph A Konstan, and John Riedl. 2000. Explaining collaborative filtering recommendations. In *CSCW*. ACM.

[10] Jonathan L Herlocker, Joseph A Konstan, Loren G Terveen, and John T Riedl. 2004. Evaluating collaborative filtering recommender systems. *ACM Transactions on Information Systems (TOIS)* (2004).

[11] José Miguel Hernández-Lobato, Neil Houlsby, and Zoubin Ghahramani. 2014. Probabilistic Matrix Factorization with Non-random Missing Data. In *ICML*.

[12] Yifan Hu, Yehuda Koren, and Chris Volinsky. 2008. Collaborative filtering for implicit feedback datasets. In *International Conference on Data Mining (ICDM)*. IEEE.

[13] Sébastien Jean, Kyunghyun Cho, Roland Memisevic, and Yoshua Bengio. 2015. On Using Very Large Target Vocabulary for Neural Machine Translation. *Association for Computational Linguistics* (2015).

[14] Noriaki Kawamae. 2010. Serendipitous recommendations via innovators. In *SIGIR*. ACM.

[15] Bart P Knijnenburg, Martijn C Willemsen, Zeno Gantner, Hakan Soncu, and Chris Newell. 2012. Explaining the user experience of recommender systems. *User Modeling and User-Adapted Interaction* (2012).

[16] Joseph A Konstan and John Riedl. 2012. Recommender systems: from algorithms to user experience. *User Modeling and User-Adapted Interaction* (2012).

[17] Yehuda Koren, Robert Bell, and Chris Volinsky. 2009. Matrix factorization techniques for recommender systems. *IEEE Computer* (2009).

[18] Dawen Liang, Laurent Charlin, James McInerney, and David M Blei. 2016. Modeling user exposure in recommendation. In *International Conference on World Wide Web (WWW)*.

[19] Roderick JA Little and Donald B Rubin. 2014. *Statistical analysis with missing data*. John Wiley & Sons.

[20] Benjamin M Marlin and Richard S Zemel. 2009. Collaborative prediction and ranking with non-random missing data. In *RecSys*. ACM.

[21] Benjamin M. Marlin, Richard S. Zemel, Sam Roweis, and Malcolm Slaney. 2007. Collaborative Filtering and the Missing at Random Assumption. In *Uncertainty in Artificial Intelligence (UAI)*. AUAI Press.

[22] Sean M McNee, John Riedl, and Joseph A Konstan. 2006. Making recommendations better: an analytic model for human-recommender interaction. In *CHI extended abstracts on Human factors in computing systems*. ACM.

[23] Andriy Mnih and Koray Kavukcuoglu. 2013. Learning word embeddings efficiently with noise-contrastive estimation. In *NIPS*.

[24] Rong Pan and Martin Scholz. 2009. Mind the Gaps: Weighting the Unknown in Large-scale One-class Collaborative Filtering. In *KDD*. ACM.

[25] Rong Pan, Yunhong Zhou, Bin Cao, Nathan N. Liu, Rajan Lukose, Martin Scholz, and Qiang Yang. 2008. One-Class Collaborative Filtering. In *ICDM*. IEEE Computer Society.

[26] Bruno Pradel, Nicolas Usunier, and Patrick Gallinari. 2012. Ranking with non-random missing ratings: influence of popularity and positivity on evaluation metrics. In *RecSys*. ACM.

[27] Tobias Schnabel, Adith Swaminathan, Ashudeep Singh, Navin Chandak, and Thorsten Joachims. 2016. Recommendations as treatments: Debiasing learning and evaluation. *arXiv preprint arXiv:1602.05352* (2016).

[28] Guy Shani and Asela Gunawardana. 2011. Evaluating recommendation systems. In *Recommender systems handbook*. Springer, 257–297.

[29] Harald Steck. 2010. Training and testing of recommender systems on data missing not at random. In *KDD*. ACM.

[30] Hsiang-Fu Yu, Mikhail Bilenko, and Chih-Jen Lin. 2017. Selection of Negative Samples for One-class Matrix Factorization. In *SDM*. SIAM.

[31] Yin Zheng, Bangsheng Tang, Wenkui Ding, and Hanning Zhou. 2016. A Neural Autoregressive Approach to Collaborative Filtering. In *ICML*.

Chemical Reactant Recommendation Using a Network of Organic Chemistry

John Savage*
Nuritas, Ireland

Akihiro Kishimoto
IBM Research, Ireland

Beat Buesser
IBM Research, Ireland

Ernesto Diaz-Aviles†
Libre AI Labs, Ireland

Carlos Alzate
IBM Research, Ireland

ABSTRACT

This paper focuses on the task of recommending to the chemist candidate molecules (reactants) necessary to synthesize a given target molecule (product), which is a novel application as well as an important step for the chemist to find a synthesis route to generate the product. We formulate this task as a link-prediction problem over a so-called Network of Organic Chemistry (NOC) that we have constructed from 8 million chemical reactions described in the US patent literature between 1976 and 2013. We leverage state-of-the-art factorization algorithms for recommender systems to solve this task. Our empirical evaluation demonstrates that Factorization Machines, trained with chemistry-specific knowledge, outperforms current methods based on similarity of chemical structures.

CCS CONCEPTS

• **Information systems → Recommender systems;**

KEYWORDS

Chemistry; reactant recommendation; link-prediction

1 INTRODUCTION

Chemistry is a scientific field where humans have to gain experience and intuition over many decades to be able to routinely discover new insights. The number of experienced chemists is small and a limiting factor in large industries like pharmaceuticals, nutrition, or materials that rely heavily on synthetic manufacturing of chemical molecules. Next to other factors this includes finding a feasible reaction pathway to synthesize a target molecule. Due to the significant human effort only a small number of feasible synthesis routes are usually discovered out of an incredibly large combinatorial space of possible chemical reactions, which limits the discovery of new and the optimization of exiting drugs and materials. Despite 40 years of efforts, e.g., [2, 9, 10, 15], computer aided design has not been successful to instigate widespread routine use by chemists. This can be attributed in part to the difficulty of building the generalized chemistry knowledge required for plausible analyses [15]. Currently, the main tools for designing synthesis routes are the Network of Organic Chemistry (NOC) [9] and rule-based synthesis planners [15]. The NOC is limited by the fact that it can only provide information on previously known reactions, while rule-based synthesis planners require rules designed by experienced humans and therefore can be overly rigid.

While collaborative filtering has been commonly used to recommend commodity items such as movies and music to a large number of users [12, 13], this paper is as far as we know the first attempt to employ such recommender systems to provide professional level decision support in chemistry. The main difficulty in using recommender systems in chemistry is the definition of recommendation accuracy. For movie recommendations or other similar applications, the cost of a bad recommendation is low. However, in chemistry the recommendation of a poor molecule could result in days or weeks of wasted time and money for a chemist.

This paper focuses on the task of recommending candidate reactants that could be used to synthesize a target product. We formulate this task as a link-prediction problem over a large-scale graph based on the NOC, a graph representation of the reactions in a database. New links predicted in the NOC contain the reactants recommended to a chemist for further consideration. Unlike the NOC, our approach can help the chemist find a new synthetic route. In addition, our approach can do so without using predefined over-rigid rules of the rule-based synthesis planners.

We apply to the NOC two factorization models that learn personalized ranking [21], which are closely related to collaborative filtering: one based on Matrix Factorization [12], and the second based on Factorization Machines (FMs) [20]. We enhance our models with chemical fingerprints representing chemistry-specific knowledge about the structure and properties of molecules.

We have constructed our NOC based on 8 million chemical reactions extracted from the US patent literature between 1976 and 2013 for performance evaluation. Our results indicate that FMs in combination with chemical fingerprints perform better than the similarity baseline which justifies further research to improve the accuracy based on collaborative filtering for applications in chemistry.

2 OUR APPROACH

Our approach regards chemical products and reactants as users and items of the recommender system, respectively, and attempts to recommend an item (i.e., reactant) to a user (i.e., product designed by a chemist). The product can be either an existing molecule or new molecule which does not exist yet in the world.

*This work was performed while Savage was an intern at IBM Research, Ireland.
†This work was performed while Diaz-Aviles was affiliated with IBM Research, Ireland.

RecSys '17, August 27-31, 2017, Como, Italy

ACM ISBN 978-1-4503-4652-8/17/08...$15.00
https://doi.org/10.1145/3109859.3109895

We first construct a large-scale NOC graph from many chemical reaction equations, then learn a model over NOC based on factorization models, and predict a link from a product to a reactant. We further add fingerprints of chemical molecules as attributes to the model, thus counteracting the cold-start problem of collaborative filtering, that is, for the case of which the target product has a new molecule structure is not therefore available in NOC.

Construction of NOC

Both products and reactants are represented as nodes in the large-scale NOC graph. We construct NOC as shown previously [1]. A directed link from node A to node B indicates that product B is synthesized from reactant A. For example, suppose that reaction $H_2 + O_2 \rightarrow H_2O$ is available. Then, NOC includes three nodes H_2O, H_2 and O_2 with two links $H_2 \rightarrow H_2O$ and $O_2 \rightarrow H_2O$.

Using all molecules that appear in all reactions results in constructing NOC with many connections to small, common, relatively uninteresting molecules, and leads to returning unmeaningful recommendations. For example, including H_2O in NOC and recommending it to a chemist is not insightful even if H_2O is used for a synthesis of the target.

As a simple yet practical choice, in each reaction we choose the heaviest reactant and heaviest product and connect these two molecules in NOC, since these heavy molecules tend to have complicated structures. An ideal way would be to construct a function that accurately evaluates the importance of the molecules in the reaction and include only important ones, which is future work.

NOC does not distinguish the reactants from the products, since a molecule can be a product as well as a reactant in practice. When a chemist selects a node in a graph, that node is marked as a product the chemist needs to synthesize. If the chemist designs a new product, it is added to NOC and marked as a product. The remaining nodes are the reactants that could be recommended to the chemist.

Chemical Fingerprints

A lot of work has been done in the chemoinformatics community on representing molecules *in silico* for the purposes of searching through chemical databases for similar molecules [26], since similar molecules often share common chemical characteristics. The molecular fingerprints used for this purpose represent molecules as bit vectors which indicate the presence or absence of molecular substructures. Our approach integrates the fingerprints with the factorization models to effectively capture the characteristics of the chemistry domain (see the next subsection).

Among many choices in the literature, we chose to use the MACCS fingerprint that is one of the most simple, standard versions [3], because it is readily available in open source chemoinformatics codes such as Open Babel [18]. The MACCS fingerprint consists a list of 166 chemical structures, such as a carbon atom, a carbon-oxygen bond or a benzene ring, represented as a bit vector of length 166, with bits set to 1 if the structure is present in the molecule.

Factorization Models

Our approach regards NOC as a training set. With this training set, our approach learns a model based on factorization models. We assume that the same reactant would be used if two products have similar sets of the reactants used to synthesize them in the past.

In the reactant recommendation task, positive training examples (i.e., successful reactions) are available such as in scientific reporting [5] and patent literature. However, no negative examples (i.e., failed reactions) are usually publicly available as global knowledge. In addition, considering the feature vector size and the number of available examples, our approach needs to perform machine learning under sparsity. We employ and evaluate the following two approaches that attempt to resolve these issues.

Matrix Factorization based on BPR. Bayesian Personalized Ranking (BPR) is a Matrix Factorization (MF) approach that deals with the case where only positive training examples are available [21]. In BPR, training examples are constructed as $D = \{(u, i, j)\}$, where i is an item already used by user u (i.e. known successful reaction) and j is an item which has not been used by u yet (i.e., unobserved whether a reaction will be successful or failed). That is, BPR only assumes that for each user an observed item is preferred to an unobserved item. Then, when two unobserved items are given to a user, BPR attempts to predict which item is preferred by that user. That is, by training a model with D, rather than calculating an accurate preference score of a single item, BPR attempts to accurately rank a pair of two unobserved items for each user by learning model parameters based on maximum a posteriori estimation.

We employ standard MF combined with BPR as Rendle et al. present [21]. Let q_i and p_u be two vectors representing the latent factors of item i and user u, respectively. The score of recommending item i to user u is approximated by the dot product: $\hat{r}_{ui} = q_i^{\top} p_u$.

The major issue in using this pure collaborative filtering technique in these scenarios is the cold-start problem, where there are not enough user-item interactions to provide good preference score estimates [6]. This is particularly important in the use case presented here, as the molecules chemists are interested in synthesizing have generally not been seen before. To solve the cold-start problem, we added attributes of users or items based on chemical fingerprints, bit vectors that capture characteristics of a molecules.

To incorporate fingerprints into MF, we used the Linear Mapping method from [6]. This method sets the number of factors to the number of attributes N_a and learns a mapping from the user (product) attributes to user factors, as well as the item (reactant) factors, and approximates the true user-item score matrix as before.

Factorization Machines. We also employ Factorization Machines (FMs) [19], since FMs are known to be able to address the problem with huge sparsity, which is the case of our recommendation task. We use FM combined with aforementioned BPR to perform the ranking task with only positive training examples [20].

FMs inherit advantages of both MF and Support Vector Machines (SVMs) [25]. Like SVMs, since FMs work as a general predictor with any real valued feature vector, we can easily add chemistry-specific features to FMs. Like MF, FMs model all interactions between variables using factorized parameters.

In the FM model, the users and items are represented in a feature vector $\mathbf{x}$ along with any other features deemed useful and the outcome y as the rating, or 1 in the case of positive training examples.

Table 1: Details of Dataset.

# Reactants	# Products	# Reactions
700,000	800,000	8,000,000

The model then becomes:

$$\hat{y} = w_0 + \sum_{i=1}^{n} w_i x_i + \sum_{i=1}^{n} \sum_{j=i+1}^{n} \langle \mathbf{v}_i, \mathbf{v}_j \rangle x_i x_j \quad (1)$$

with the model parameters to be estimated being: $w_0 \in \mathfrak{R}, \mathbf{w} \in \mathfrak{R}^n, \mathbf{V} \in \mathfrak{R}^{n \times k}$, and $\langle \cdot, \cdot \rangle$ is the dot product.

As shown in Figure 1, our feature vector consists of the user (product) elements, item (reactant) elements, and attributes. Each element in the feature vector is either 1 or 0. If a reaction in NOC indicates that reactant R is used to synthesize product P, the bits are set corresponding to P and R in the product and reactant elements, respectively. We use the fingerprints of a product and a reactant as attributes of FMs.

product	reactant	MACCS
one-hot encoding	one-hot encoding	fingerprint

Figure 1: Factorization Machines features.

3 EMPIRICAL EVALUATION

For our empirical evaluation we use a reaction database from the text mining of US patents from 1976–2013 provided by Lowe[1] [16].

The full reaction database was split in time to test whether knowledge of all previously patented reactions could predict reactions patented in the future. The split was made at January 1st 2013, and the numbers of reactions in the split are shown in Table 1.

With the training done on a random 100,000 subset of the full training data, the predictions were tested on the reactions in 2013. An ideal prediction would have a high recall@N for low N, and we set $N = 10$. We also show the results for the area under the receiver operating characteristic curve (AUC) as this is analogous to the metric that BPR optimizes on.

We do not show the precision@N, since it may not be a good measure of prediction quality. Note that the training and test set are not a "gold-standard", there may be many molecules that are good recommendations for a given molecule but are not included in the reactions in the training or test set.

We compared the performance of BPR-based MF and FMs. We also included an approach that recommends molecules that are similar to the target product, calculated by Jaccard similarity using the MACCS fingerprints.

We set the size of the latent dimensions in FMs to $k = 128$, and the latent vector size in MF to $k = 16$. We chose these numbers by cross validation in preliminary experiments. In case of MF with the attributes, the size of the latent vector was identical to the size of the MACCS fingerprint (i.e., $k = 166$). All algorithms were implemented by using libFM [20] and MyMediaLite [7]. The experiments were run on a Linux/GNU machine with 2.6GHz 12-core processor with 80GB of RAM.

[1] https://bitbucket.org/dan2097/patent-reaction-extraction/downloads

Results

We conducted a first round of experiments in a highly sparse NOC using all reactions and products in the dataset (either rare or common). Then, we conducted a set of experiments in a more realistic setting based on a denser NOC, which uses reactions with products that have been created more than 10 times in the patent dataset.

Highly Sparse NOC. We start with the results under sparsity. In this setting the MF approach underperformed the similarity-based recommendation, followed by the results of FMs that performed slightly better.

Recall@10 and AUC shown in Figure 2 clearly indicate that Matrix Factorization performed poorly. For pure MF the recall@10 score was zero, indicating that MF completely failed to recommend meaningful reactants due to the sparsity of the dataset. Since patents mainly file molecules that have new chemical structures, there are many examples of pairs of molecules appearing only once in the literature.

The similarity-based approach performs well since many reactions tend change only a small part of the chemical structure of a reactant to synthesize products. However, the low recall@10 score of 0.26 indicates that similarity-based approaches are not sufficient for reactant prediction. The AUC score indicates that MF had a problem training its parameters well enough to perform a good prediction. MF could not overcome the cold-start problem due to the fact the attribute interactions are learned on a per-reactant basis. As we can see from the performance of the similarity-based approach, the attributes of chemicals should interact consistently in reactions, and so we should be able to learn the parameters for these interactions and apply them globally, which we can do using Factorization Machines.

Figure 3 compares FMs against the similarity-based approach. "FM with attributes" indicates that FMs include the MACCS fingerprints as attributes, as in Figure 1. We also included an FM model that uses only fingerprints in its feature vector, denoted as "FM with ONLY attributes". With this FM model, we intended to evaluate the performance without the collaborative filtering characteristics.

FMs performed much better than MF. The high AUC scores indicate the success of model training. The full FM model returned a slightly better recall@10 score than the similarity-based approach (0.27 versus 0.26). When only the fingerprints were used for the FMs, the FM model worsened the recall@10 score. This shows that FMs exploiting the connectivity of NOC is important for improving their predictive power.

The reason why the full FM model achieved only small improvement to the similarity-based recommendation can be explained again by the data sparsity of the patent dataset caused by many reactions that appear only once.

Dense NOC. In practice, NOC would be more connected as the more common reactions would be included. Chemists would repeatedly use these reactions, and such common reactions would help connect the peripheral reactions to construct the core of the network.

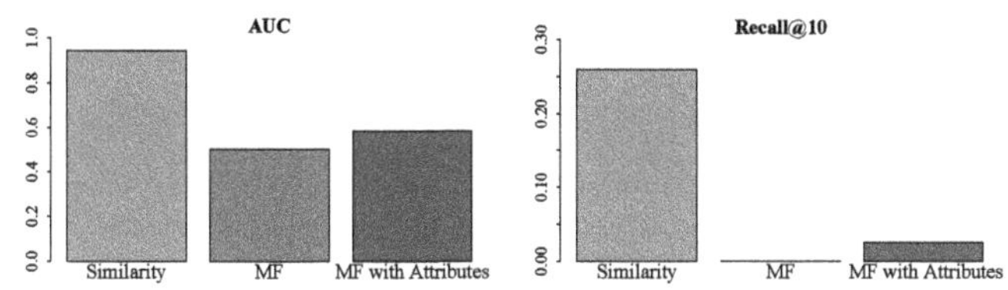

Figure 2: MF results on a sparse NOC.

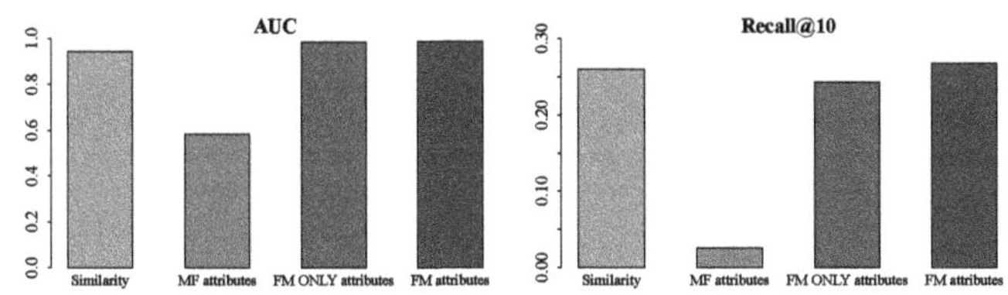

Figure 3: FMs results on a sparse NOC.

To approximate this scenario, we constructed NOC by only using reactions with products that have been created more than 10 times in the patent dataset.

Figure 4 shows the results of training the FMs on this denser NOC. The FM model with no attribute features shows that simple collaborative filtering performs better than similarity-based recommendation (recall@10 0.20 vs 0.13) in this denser network. FM with ONLY attributes performed closely to the similarity-based recommender (recall@10 = 0.14).

The full FM model successfully yielded a much better recall@10 score (0.36), showing the additive performance of the collaborative filtering and chemical attributes modeling. The full FM model inherits advantages of both MF and chemistry-specific knowledge. The former advantage of FMs accounts for the network connectivity of NOC by performing collaborative filtering, while the latter means it can learn about interactions between chemical structures in each pair of molecules. In this general dataset, it will learn parameters so it performs comparably to the similarity-based approach. However, in datasets containing limited numbers of reaction types, it should learn interactions specific to those reaction types.

4 RELATED WORK

Collaborative filtering has attracted great interest in recommender systems for movie rental and streaming platforms, internet-based retailers, etc. See [12, 13] for the literature review about the Matrix Factorization algorithm and its variants.

Computer aided design has been investigated for several tasks in chemistry since many decades with first rules of organic chemistry by Corey in 1969 [2]. The work closely related to our approach is graph-based analysis of existing reactions, reaction pathway discovery based on rule-based synthesis planners, and chemical reaction prediction, which we review below.

Grzybowski et al. [9] have generated the Network of Organic Chemistry (NOC), a graph representation of the chemical reactions for analyzing existing reactions [8, 14]. However, the NOC can only provide information on previously known reactions.

Several researchers have developed rule-based synthesis planners that return a reaction pathway to synthesize a target molecule designed by the chemist e.g., [10, 15]. But rule-based synthesis

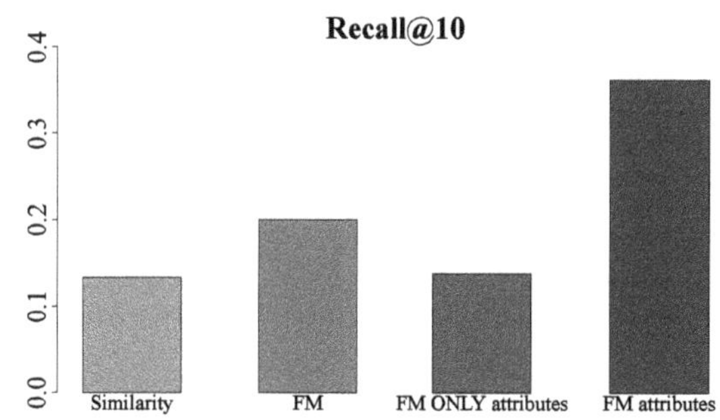

Figure 4: FMs results on a dense NOC.

planners rely heavily on reaction templates that describe the substructures of reactants and products of known reactions. While parameters of the reaction templates can be tuned by machine learning [24], rule-based synthesis planners are not able to find pathways that would require previously unseen reaction templates.

There are approaches to predict reactions to synthesize a new chemical product from given reactants, e.g., [11, 23], including the development of novel fingerprints [22]. However, these approaches do not enable the chemists to specify the target products they are interested in synthesizing. In contrast, our task is to predict for a given target molecule a ranked list of candidate reactants to synthesize the target molecule. In other worlds, our approach solves a so-called inverse problem to reaction prediction, while reaction problem is a forward problem. The results on reaction template parameter tuning [24] imply that our inverse problem would be more difficult to solve than their forward problem.

Other related work includes approaches to discover new enzyme reactions in the biology network [17, 27]. These approaches predict new links only between existing enzymes by addressing only the forward problem in the biology network (i.e., predicting an enzyme reaction in a normal direction).

5 CONCLUSIONS AND FUTURE WORK

We presented an approach to adapt factorization-model-based link-prediction techniques to the task of recommending chemical reactants to the chemists. Our approach based on FMs with chemical fingerprints showed promising results, especially when performing reactant predictions in highly-connected NOC, where the chemists would work on more commonly than the very sparse set of patent documents.

Our recall@10 scores indicate that the accuracy of the prediction still needs to be improved. On the other hand, since this is the first attempt to apply factorization models to the reactant recommendation domain in chemistry, followup research will appear which would achieve significant improvements. Ideas yet to explore as future work include:

- an incorporation of recently developed chemical fingerprints learned by Deep Learning (e.g., [4]),
- a combination with rule-based planners and reaction prediction technologies, and
- a better approach to extracting important molecules from reactions to include them in NOC.

REFERENCES

[1] Kyle J. M. Bishop, Rafal Klajn, and Bartosz A. Grzybowski. 2006. The core and most useful molecules in organic chemistry. *Angewandte Chemie - International Edition* 45, 32 (2006), 5348–5354. https://doi.org/10.1002/anie.200600881

[2] E. J. Corey and W. T. Wipke. 1969. Computer-assisted design of complex organic syntheses. *Science* 166, 3902 (October 1969), 178–92. https://doi.org/10.1126/science.166.3902.178

[3] Joseph L. Durant, Burton A. Leland, Douglas R. Henry, and James G. Nourse. 2002. Reoptimization of MDL Keys for Use in Drug Discovery. *Journal of Chemical Information and Modeling* 42, 6 (November 2002), 1273–1280. https://doi.org/10.1021/ci010132r

[4] David K. Duvenaud, Dougal Maclaurin, Jorge Aguilera-Iparraguirre, Rafael Gómez-Bombarell, Timothy Hirzel, Alán Aspuru-Guzik, and Ryan P. Adams. 2015. Convolutional Networks on Graphs for Learning Molecular Fingerprints. In *Proceeedings of the 28th Annual Conference on Neural Information Processing Systems*. 2224–2232.

[5] Kerry Dwan, Douglas G. Altman, Juan A. Arnaiz, Jill Bloom, An-Wen Chan, Eugenia Cronin, Evelyne Decullier, Philippa J. Easterbrook, Erik Von Elm, Carrol Gamble, Davina Ghersi, John P. A. Ioannidis, John Simes, and Paula R. Williamson. 2008. Systematic review of the empirical evidence of study publication bias and outcome reporting bias. *PloS one* 3, 8 (January 2008), e3081. https://doi.org/10.1371/journal.pone.0003081

[6] Zeno Gantner, Lucas Drumond, Christoph Freudenthaler, Steffen Rendle, and Lars Schmidt-Thieme. 2010. Learning attribute-to-feature mappings for cold-start recommendations. In *Proceedings of the 10th IEEE International Conference on Data Mining*. 176–185. https://doi.org/10.1109/ICDM.2010.129

[7] Zeno Gantner, Steffen Rendle, Christoph Freudenthaler, and Lars Schmidt-Thieme. 2011. MyMediaLite: A Free Recommender System Library. In *5th ACM International Conference on Recommender Systems (RecSys 2011)*.

[8] Chris M. Gothard, Siowling Soh, Nosheen A. Gothard, Bartlomiej Kowalczyk, Yanhu Wei, Bilge Baytekin, and Bartosz A. Grzybowski. 2012. Rewiring Chemistry: Algorithmic Discovery and Experimental Validation of One-Pot Reactions in the Network of Organic Chemistry. *Angewandte Chemie International Edition* 51, 32 (2012), 7922–7927. https://doi.org/10.1002/anie.201202155

[9] Bartosz A. Grzybowski, Kyle J. M. Bishop, Bartlomiej Kowalczyk, and Christopher E. Wilmer. 2009. The 'wired' universe of organic chemistry. *Nature Chemistry* 1, 1 (April 2009), 31–6. https://doi.org/10.1038/nchem.136

[10] Abraham Heifets and Igor Jurisica. 2012. Construction of New Medicines via Game Proof Search. In *Proceedings of the 26th AAAI Conference on Artificial Intelligence*, Vol. 2. 1564–1570. http://www.scopus.com/inward/record.url?eid=2-s2.0-84868287208

[11] Matthew A. Kayala and Pierre Baldi. 2011. A Machine Learning Approach to Predict Chemical Reactions. In *Proceeding of the 25th Annual Conference on Advances in Neural Information Processing Systems*. 747–755. http://papers.nips.cc/paper/4356-a-machine-learning-approach-to-predict-chemical-reactions.pdf

[12] Yehuda Koren, Robert Bell, and Chris Volinsky. 2009. Matrix Factorization Techniques for Recommender Systems. *IEEE Computer* 42, 8 (2009), 30–37.

[13] Yehuda Koren and Robert M. Bell. 2015. *Recommender Systems Handbook*. Springer, Chapter Advances in Collaborative Filtering, 77–118.

[14] Mikolaj Kowalik, Chris M. Gothard, Aaron M. Drews, Nosheen A. Gothard, Alex Weckiewicz, Patrick E. Fuller, Bartosz A. Grzybowski, and Kyle J. M. Bishop. 2012. Parallel optimization of synthetic pathways within the network of organic chemistry. *Angewandte Chemie (International ed. in English)* 51, 32 (August 2012), 7928–32. https://doi.org/10.1002/anie.201202209

[15] James Law, Zsolt Zsoldos, Aniko Simon, Darryl Reid, Yang Liu, Sing Yoong Khew, A. Peter Johnson, Sarah Major, Robert A. Wade, and Howard Y. Ando. 2009. Route Designer: A Retrosynthetic Analysis Tool Utilizing Automated Retrosynthetic Rule Generation. *Journal of Chemical Information and Modeling* 49, 3 (2009), 593–602. https://doi.org/10.1021/ci800228y

[16] Daniel M. Lowe. 2012. *Extraction of Chemical Structures and Reactions from the Literature*. Ph.D. Dissertation. University of Cambridge.

[17] Aditya Krishna Menon and Charles Elkan. 2011. Link prediction via matrix factorization. *Machine Learning and Knowledge Discovery in Databases* 6912 (2011), 437–452. https://doi.org/10.1007/978-3-642-23783-6_28

[18] Noel M. O'Boyle, Michael Banck, Craig A. James, Chris Morley, Tim Vandermeersch, and Geoffrey R. Hutchison. 2011. Open Babel: An open chemical toolbox. *Journal of Cheminformatics* 3, 1 (January 2011), 33. https://doi.org/10.1186/1758-2946-3-33

[19] Steffen Rendle. 2010. Factorization Machines. In *Proceedings of the 10th IEEE International Conference on Data Mining*. 995–1000. https://doi.org/10.1109/ICDM.2010.127

[20] Steffen Rendle. 2012. Factorization Machine with libFM. *ACM Transactions on Intelligent Systems and Technology* 3, 3 (2012), 1–22. https://doi.org/10.1145/2168752.2168771

[21] Steffen Rendle, Christoph Freudenthaler, Zeno Gantner, and Lars Schmidt-Thieme. 2009. BPR : Bayesian Personalized Ranking from Implicit Feedback. In *Proceedings of the 25th Conference on Uncertainty in Artificial Intelligence*, Vol. cs.LG. 452–461. arXiv:1205.2618 http://dl.acm.org/citation.cfm?id=1795167

[22] Nadine Schneider, Daniel M. Lowe, Roger A. Sayle, and Gregory A. Landrum. 2015. Development of a novel fingerprint for chemical reactions and its application to large-scale reaction classification and similarity. *Journal of Chemical Information and Modeling* 55, 1 (2015), 39–53. https://doi.org/10.1021/ci5006614

[23] Marwin H. S. Segler and Mark P. Waller. 2017. Modelling Chemical Reasoning to Predict and Invent Reactions. *Chemistry – A European Journal* 1521, 3765 (2017).

[24] Marwin H. S. Segler and Mark P. Waller. 2017. Neural-Symbolic Machine Learning for Retrosynthesis and Reaction Prediction. *Chemistry – A European Journal* 1521, 3765 (2017).

[25] Vladimir N. Vapnik. 1998. *Statisical Learning Theory*. Wiley.

[26] Peter Willett, John M. Barnard, and Geoffrey M. Downs. 1998. Chemical Similarity Searching. *Journal of Chemical Information and Modeling* 38, 6 (November 1998), 983–996. https://doi.org/10.1021/ci9800211

[27] Yoshihiro Yamanishi, Jean-Philippe Vert, and Minoru Kanehisa. 2005. Supervised enzyme network inference from the integration of genomic data and chemical information. *Bioinromatics* 21 (2005), 468–477.

Fewer Flops at the Top: Accuracy, Diversity, and Regularization in Two-Class Collaborative Filtering

Bibek Paudel
Department of Informatics
University of Zurich
Zurich, Switzerland
paudel@ifi.uzh.ch

Thilo Haas
University of Zurich
Zurich, Switzerland
thilo@thilohaas.ch

Abraham Bernstein
Department of Informatics
University of Zurich
Zurich, Switzerland
bernstein@ifi.uzh.ch

ABSTRACT

In most existing recommender systems, implicit or explicit interactions are treated as positive links and all unknown interactions are treated as negative links. The goal is to suggest new links that will be perceived as positive by users. However, as signed social networks and newer content services become common, it is important to distinguish positive from negative preferences. Even in existing applications, the cost of negative recommendations could be high when people are looking for new jobs, friends, or places to live.

In this work, we develop novel probabilistic latent factor models to recommend positive links and compare them with existing methods on five different openly available datasets. Our models are able to produce better ranking lists and are effective in the task of ranking positive links at the top, with fewer negative links (flops). Moreover, we find that modeling signed social networks and user preferences this way has the advantage of increasing the diversity of recommendations. We also investigate the effect of regularization on the quality of recommendations, a matter that has not received enough attention in the literature. We find that regularization parameter heavily affects the quality of recommendations in terms of both accuracy and diversity.

CCS CONCEPTS

•**Information systems** →**Recommender systems;** *Information extraction;* Document filtering; •**Human-centered computing** →*Social networks;*

KEYWORDS

matrix factorization, positive and negative recommendations, collaborative filtering, diverse recommendations
DOI: http://dx.doi.org/10.1145/3109859.3109916

1 INTRODUCTION

Collaborative Filtering has found use in a wide range of applications from movies to book recommendation, and from job suggestion to matchmaking. In essence, these models produce personalized ranking lists for users such that the choices perceived as positive by the user are ranked towards the top of her list. They do so by differentiating previous *positive* choices from *all other* choices of the user. In other words, user preference is modeled as a binary variable: known positive preferences are treated as positive, while unknown or negative preferences are treated as negative preferences. The personalized ranking thus generated for the user is only concerned with the benefit of putting positive items at the top of the list. Since both negative and unknown items are clubbed together, these systems treat the cost of them appearing at the top of the list as the same.

This assumption may be flawed in many cases. Consider a choice that costs more than a few minutes of time wasted by listening to a bad song. Jobs, education, cities to live, or friends to make are some choices that require a user to be more invested. In such cases, it is undesirable to recommend negative items high in the ranked list, since the user would not appreciate them. Unknown and negative items cannot be treated as having the same cost in this setting. We would like to have a system that puts choices perceived as positive by the user at the top of her ranking list, while at the same time having as few negative choices (flops) as possible at the top of that list. This is the focus of our work in this paper.

Increasingly, negative feedback is becoming more common in the setting of both explicit and implicit feedback. Examples of explicit negative feedback are buttons like *dislike* and *downvote* on popular online services, whereas skipping to the next song within few seconds of listening to it can be considered an example of implicit negative feedback. In the latter example, skipping a song may not necessarily imply dislike, but rather an act of trying to find a familiar song. The problem of interpreting implicit signals is tricky and needs careful problem-specific consideration.

Negative and positive links also feature in other domains, most notably social networks. In case of signed social networks, two nodes can have a relationship that is labeled as positive or negative. Examples of positive relations may include friendship or trust, and mistrust maybe an example of negative relation. People choose to follow or friend other people in social networks, indicating positive preference. In other cases, they choose to block, unfriend or mute, as an expression of negative preference.

Naturally, as in item-recommender systems, a link recommendation service has to be able to differentiate these important distinctions. Failing to separate negative preferences from positive ones may make the service unattractive to the user, reducing its usability and ultimately efficiency. Again, the goal – as in recommender systems – is to rank other people in the social network in a way that positive links appear at the top, with fewer negative links.

In this work, we propose novel techniques to achieve the goal stated above. Specifically, our main contributions are: (a) we define

RecSys '17, August 27–31, 2017, Como, Italy.
© 2017 ACM. 978-1-4503-4652-8/17/08…$15.00
DOI: http://dx.doi.org/10.1145/3109859.3109916

the problem of Two-Class Collaborative Filtering (TCCF) (b) we develop new probabilistic latent factor models to deal with the TCCF problem: TC-MF (Two-Class Matrix Factorization) and its variation TC-MF1, and S-MF (SoftMax Matrix Factorization), (c) we show with results in five different datasets and in comparison with other state-of-the-art methods that our approach is able to generate rankings with positive items at the top and negative at the bottom.

We find that modeling signed social networks and user preferences this way has advantages other than ranking accuracy: our recommendations are more diverse whilst consistently being among the best in terms of recommendation accuracy, a quality desirable in recommender systems. We also investigate the effect of regularization parameter in the quality of recommendations, a matter that has not received enough attention in the literature. We find that regularization parameter significantly affects both accuracy and the diversity of recommendations.

2 PROBLEM DEFINITION

Our work is general enough to be applied to any domain with pairwise (dyadic) interaction between nodes. This includes the settings of recommender systems and social network link prediction. Graphs and matrices lend themselves as general frameworks to model such data and relationships.

Consider a set of nodes V and a set of directed edges between them E, forming a graph $G(V, E)$. Depending on the dataset, G could be bi-bipartite, in which case the set of left-vertices and right-vertices are M and N respectively. In the case of a user-item graph, M denotes the set of users and N the set of items and $V = M \cup N$. For example, in a movie recommendation system, N could be the set of movies available in the system. In such cases, the edge set is $E \subseteq M \times N$. In the case of a social network, there is only one type of node: the users of the network and the edge set is: $E \subseteq V \times V$. For simplicity, in both cases, we'll refer to the graph as user-item graph or *interaction graph*.

When the graph is not bi-bipartite, the set of nodes that have at least one incoming edges is treated as N and the set of nodes that have at least one outgoing edge is treated as M. Although these are not disjoint sets, from the view of each node in M, all the other nodes can be considered as items and from the view of each node in N, all other nodes can be considered as users. The cardinality of these sets are denoted as $|M|$ and $|N|$. A single edge is denoted as an ordered pair $(i, j) \in E$ such that $i \in M, j \in N$, or simply as $e_{i,j}$. Additionally, each edge in the graph has a label among $L_{obs} = \{+1, -1\}$. All pairs in $\{M \times N\} \setminus E$ (absent/possible edges) have the label 0 (or ?) indicating unknown label. The complete set of labels is then: $L = L_{obs} \cup \{0\} = \{+1, -1, 0\}$. The label of an edge can be denoted in functional form as: $f_L : V \times V \rightarrow L$. Although the datasets we use will only have these three categorical labels, the term *rating* will be used interchangeably with labels. Relationships between nodes are also referred to as interactions, feedbacks, or links. Links are called positive links or negative links based on their labels. The feedback dataset set can also be modeled as a matrix: $\mathbf{P} \in \{+1, -1, 0\}^{|M| \times |N|}$ and defined as: $p_{i,j} = f_L(e_{i,j})$.

The matrix $\mathbf{P}$ is called the user-item matrix or simply *interaction/feedback matrix*. A subset of the edges from E are separated as training set E_{tr}, correspondingly a training matrix $\mathbf{R}$ can be defined with entries $r_{i,j}$. Based on $\mathbf{R}$, our goal is then to learn a model that ranks the nodes in N for each node in M, with the goal that potentially negative links are at the bottom and potentially positive links at the top of the ranking.

This is the **Two-Class Collaborative Filtering Problem.**

One way of measuring such a ranking is using the AUC measure. For any given user (in M), consider the training set as: $(n_i, l_i)_{i=1}^{n}$ where $n_i \in N$ and $l_i \in L_{obs}$. Let $\mathcal{P} = \{n_i \mid l_i = 1\}$ be the set of positive training samples and $\mathcal{N} = \{n_i \mid l_i = -1\}$ be the set of negative samples. AUC is then defined as:

$$AUC = \frac{1}{|\mathcal{P}|\,|\mathcal{N}|} \sum_{n_i \in \mathcal{P}} \sum_{n_j \in \mathcal{N}} \delta(f(n_i) > f(n_j)) \tag{1}$$

where $\delta(f)$ is an indicator function which is 1 if f is satisfied and 0 otherwise. The AUC in (1) measures how many positive items are ranked above negative items and normalizes it by the total number of possible pairs. Its value is 1 for a perfect ranking (i.e., each positive item is ranked above all negative items) and 0.5 for a random ranking. AUC is the value of the Wilcoxon-Mann-Whitney statistic [7]. Note that this AUC is slightly different when used to rank only positive items- in that case it suffices to rank positive items above all the other items.

Another measure, proposed in [19] is called the Generalized AUC (GAUC). Unlike AUC in (1), GAUC also considers the relative ranking of positive items and negative items with respect to the class of unknown items. Specifically, it is highest when all positive items are ranked at the top, all unknown items are ranked in the middle and the negative items are ranked at the bottom. Similar to above, consider the training set $(n_i, l_i)_{i=1}^{n}$ with l_i now defined to include unknown labels: $l_i \in L$. The set of samples with unknown labels is $\mathcal{O} = \{n_i \mid l_i = 0\}$. Then GAUC is:

$$GAUC = \frac{1}{|\mathcal{P}| + |\mathcal{N}|}\Big(\frac{1}{|\mathcal{O}| + |\mathcal{N}|} \sum_{n_i \in \mathcal{P}} \sum_{n_s \in \mathcal{O} \cup \mathcal{N}} \delta(f(n_i) > f(n_s)) + \frac{1}{|\mathcal{O}| + |\mathcal{P}|} \sum_{n_j \in \mathcal{N}} \sum_{n_t \in \mathcal{O} \cup \mathcal{P}} \delta(f(n_j) > f(n_t))\Big) \tag{2}$$

3 RELATED WORK

Broadly, our work in this paper can be compared with previous work in the domain of recommender systems and social network link recommendation using matrix factorization. We discuss previous work from these areas in this section.

Collaborative Filtering [2, 6, 16] was used early on in recommendation systems. Most of these systems deal with explicit feedback datasets. These include numeric rating (usually 1-5) provided by a user to express her preference to the items. Such methods try to model the dataset as completely as possible. The missing values in the interaction matrix are filled using user's mean rating or global mean rating. The aim is to learn a model from a partially observed dataset that is close to the original rating matrix.

One-Class Collaborative Filtering (OCCF) was introduced by [13]. OCCF relaxed the need to model the data completely and to differentiate between different kinds of preferences. In OCCF, separating known positive preferences from unknown or negative preferences is enough because the goal is to recommend links of positive class only. In this way, incomplete matrices with 1 and ? can be used to model the input dataset and predict positive links.

Modeling interaction data as a binary matrix in this way has found widespread use and popularity. OCCF forms the backbone of many online services that suggest next movie to watch or a new restaurant to try. Similar systems are also used for link recommendation in social networks.

Matrix Factorization techniques aim to find two low-dimensional factor matrices to approximate and complete the missing values in **R** based on some loss function. Their application in Recommender Systems has been reviewed in [11]. Probabilistic Matrix Factorization [10, 17, 18] has shown to outperform vanilla Matrix Factorization. Bayesian Personalized Ranking [15] (BPRMF) is another matrix factorization method that aims to maximize the pairwise ranking between positive and negative items. This translates to maximizing the AUC (Area Under the ROC curve) and thus fits more naturally to the ranking task than the usually adopted approach of minimizing the loss over the positive items alone.

Similar to [8], Logistic Matrix Factorization [10] factorizes the observed user-item rating matrix **R** into two low dimensional matrices **A** and **B**, but using a logistic loss instead of squared loss.

We argue that it is often equally important to distinguish negative links from positive ones. Our focus in this work is to rank positive links at the top and negative links at the bottom for each user's ranked list.

GAUC-OPT [19] is a recently introduced model that aims to do so by optimizing a pairwise ranking measure called the Generalized AUC (GAUC) as in (2). Our work is motivated by the problem introduced in [19], who in turn extended the work by [15]. Previously, [13] considered a different but related problem of balancing the extent of treating missing values as negative examples. They don't try to distinguish between missing and negative examples, but treat all missing values as negative examples. Their focus is to balance positive and negative examples by introducing several weighting schemes. The Matrix Factorization techniques introduced above employ models similar to [13], with the weighing of the implicit feedbacks. Different from our work, in [15], the focus is on differentiating positive links from all other links; the optimization depends on sampling triplets from positive and unknown preferences, whereas we use different latent factor formulations.

In this work, we focus on probabilistic latent factor models in order to solve the problem of the Two Class Collaborative Filtering. Our models are distinctively different from these approaches. Unlike the models discussed above, we explicitly model the probability of positive and negative link in our likelihood function, enabling the model to better differentiate between those two classes. We use a probabilistic approach, i.e., estimate the probability of positive and negative feedback and use it for ranking. Ranking links this way automatically places positive items at the top and negative at the bottom, meaning that items with unknown preferences will appear in the middle. This is not the case with other existing latent factor models. Our results show that this modeling choice is indeed beneficial and improves performance compared to other models.

4 TWO CLASS COLLABORATIVE FILTERING

Latent factor models decompose the training matrix $\mathbf{R}^{|M|\times|N|}$ into two low dimensional factor matrices $\mathbf{A}^{|M|\times k}$ and $\mathbf{B}^{k\times|N|}$ with $k < |M|$, $k < |N|$, such that their product approximates the original matrix **R** according to some loss function.

In other words, if $E(.)$ is some loss function, then the goal is to minimize $E(\mathbf{R}, \mathbf{AB}) + \lambda(\mathbf{A}, \mathbf{B})$, where $\lambda(\mathbf{A}, \mathbf{B})$ is regularization term to prevent overfitting. Typically, squared loss is used, which allows for quick analytical solution in the form of Alternating Least Squares (ALS) by fixing one factor at a time [8].

ALS based methods have proved to be useful in both tasks: rating prediction and ranking. Since we are dealing with more than one class in this work, we take a probabilistic approach that helps us directly model the probability of a user liking or disliking a link. In that, we opt for a logistic loss function as a natural choice instead of a squared loss function. This means that we can't use ALS based optimization, but have to move towards the local minima using a gradient based approach.

Matrix Factorization with logistic loss has been described in [18] and recently in [10]. In this scenario, the probability that a user interacts with an item is modeled according to the logistic function as follows:

$$p(r^+_{u,i} \mid a_u, b_i, \beta_u, \beta_i) = \frac{\exp(a_u b_i^T + \beta_u + \beta_i)}{1 + \exp(a_u b_i^T + \beta_u, +\beta_i)} \quad (3)$$

The terms β_u and β_i are bias factors associated with each user u and item i, and account for the differences among users and items respectively. The vectors a_u's and b_i's are rows and columns of the factor matrices **A** and **B**.

Under the assumption that all observed ratings $r_{u,i}$ in **R** are independent, it optimizes the following likelihood function, where α defines a weighting factor to balance between positive and unknown ratings as suggested by [8]:

$$p^{LK} = \prod_{(u,i)\in M\times N} p(r^+_{u,i} \mid a_u, b_i, \beta_u, \beta_i)^{\alpha r_{u,i}} \\ (1 - p(r^+_{u,i} \mid a_u, b_i, \beta_u, \beta_i)) \quad (4)$$

To distinguish between unknown and negative feedback, we explicitly account for negative classes within the likelihood function and introduce three models: i) Two-Class Matrix Factorization 1 (TC-MF1), ii) Two-Class Matrix Factorization (TC-MF), and iii) Softmax Matrix Factorization (S-MF). While TC-MF1 and TC-MF are adaptations of the existing probabilistic matrix factorization methods, S-MF introduces a novel way to approach the problem. In S-MF, we use two separate latent features for each item, corresponding to positive and negative preferences. Thus S-MF needs to learn twice as many parameters per item compared to the two other models.

Next we describe our new models and formulate their optimization schemes using the log likelihood function according to [9], which are able to directly capture the user's preference towards positive and negative items.

4.1 TC-MF1

The goal of TC-MF1 is first to differentiate between positive and negative or unknown feedback and second to use the resulting matrix factorization to provide a probability measure for classifying positive and negative feedback. To distinguish between the positive and negative items, we denote the probability that a user u likes link i as $p(r^+_{ui} \mid a_u, b_i, \beta_u, \beta_i)$ and the probability that u dislikes link k as: $p(r^-_{uk} \mid a_u, b_k, \beta_u, \beta_k) = 1 - p(r^+_{uk} \mid a_u, b_k, \beta_u, \beta_k)$. For better readability we omit the conditionals in the remainder of this paper, defining the probabilities simply as $p(r^+_{ui})$ and $p(r^-_{uk})$. We also use $\mathcal{F}$ to represent the matrix factorization results, $\mathcal{F} := a_u b_i^T + \beta_u + \beta_i$

This model differs from [10] in the definition of the likelihood function. We only consider the probability of a negative rating for truly negative or unknown samples within the likelihood function, instead of for every rating being considered. We therefore only account for the loss of false positives, whereas [10] also accounts for the loss of true positives. With this adaption we expect the model to perform better in arranging truly positive samples on top of a user's ranking list.

With f_L as defined in Section 2, $\mathcal{F}$ as defined above, and δ as an indicator function, we consider the following likelihood function:

$$p^{LK} = \prod_{(u,i)\in M\times N} p(r^+_{ui})^{\delta(f_L(u,i)=+1)}(1-p(r^+_{ui}))^{1-\delta(f_L(u,i)=+1)}$$

The resulting log-likelihood function is:

$$\log p^{LK} = \sum_{(u,i)\in M\times N} \delta(f_L(u,i)=+1)\mathcal{F} - \log(1+\exp(\mathcal{F}))$$

4.2 TC-MF

In this approach, we use a different likelihood function to account for the probability of a negative rating only if the given user rated this item negative. We include positive and negative feedback and ignore unknown feedback within the likelihood function.

This is different from the objective for [10] described above: we are explicitly modeling the probability of the user's preference of being positive or negative in our likelihood function, whereas the former model only assigns different weights to the probability of a user's preference for an item to be positive.

We expect that TC-MF can better differentiate between positive and negative feedback because of this modeling choice.

With f_L, $\mathcal{F}$, and δ as defined previously, we consider the following likelihood function:

$$p^{LK} = \prod_{(u,i)\in M\times N} p(r^+_{u,i})^{\delta(f_L(u,i)=+1)}(1-p(r^+_{u,i}))^{\delta(f_L(u,i)=-1)} \tag{5}$$

And the resulting log-likelihood function, when expanded is:

$$\log p^{LK} = \sum_{(u,i)\in M\times N} \delta(f_L(u,i)=+1)\mathcal{F} - \big(\delta(f_L(u,i)=+1)+\delta(f_L(u,i)=-1)\big)\log(1+\exp(\mathcal{F})) \tag{6}$$

For both TC-MF1 and TC-MF, following (6), we aim to maximize the following objective function, with additional L-2 regularization terms:

$$\max_{a,b,\beta_u,\beta_i} \sum_{(u,i)\in M\times N} \log p^{LK} - \frac{\lambda}{2}\|a\|_2 - \frac{\lambda}{2}\|b\|_2 \tag{7}$$

4.3 S-MF

The above models, being extensions of the One-Class Collaborative Filtering models, can only differentiate positive links from negative links by estimating a single probability term $p(r^+_{ui})$. Intuitively, capturing the signals in the unknown links (?), together with positive (+) and negative (−) links should provide a richer model. To better model the Two-Class Collaborative Filtering problem, we assume that each item has a positive latent factor and another negative latent factor. This is shown as a graphical model in Fig. 1. Each user has a single latent factor that interacts with both latent factors of each item. This model assumes each user-item interaction to be part of one of the three classes: +, −, or 0. Modeling the problem this way, we can estimate the probabilities for a positive or negative preference towards an item.

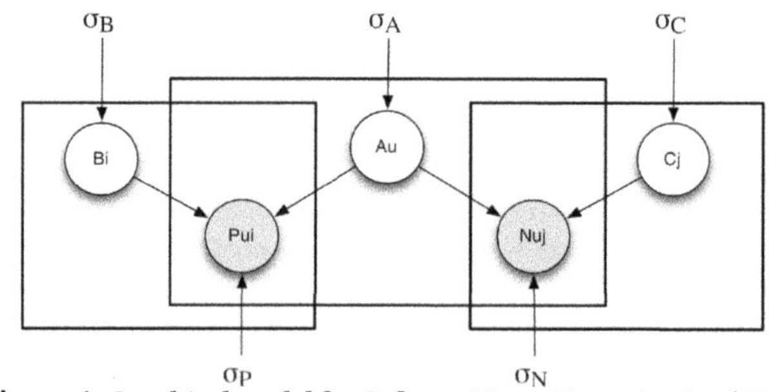

Figure 1: Graphical model for Softmax Matrix Factorization (S-MF)

We will learn a combination of two independent logistic regressions, representing positive (P) and negative (N) item membership with common latent user features **A**, as well as positive (**B**) and negative latent item features (**C**).

$$\text{Positive (P): } \hat{\mathbf{R}}^+ = \mathbf{A}\mathbf{B}^\mathrm{T} + \beta_\mathrm{i}^+ + \beta_\mathrm{u}$$

$$\text{Negative (N): } \hat{\mathbf{R}}^- = \mathbf{A}\mathbf{C}^\mathrm{T} + \beta_\mathrm{i}^- + \beta_\mathrm{u}$$

We denote the probability that user u likes item i as:

$$p(r^+_{ui} \mid a_u, b_i, c_i, \beta_i^+, \beta_i^-, \beta_u) = \frac{\exp(a_u b_i^T + \beta_i^+ + \beta_u)}{1+\exp(a_u b_i^T + \beta_i^+ + \beta_u)+\exp(a_u c_i^T + \beta_i^- + \beta_u)}$$

And the probability that user u dislikes item k as:

$$p(r^-_{uk} \mid a_u, b_k, c_k, \beta_k^+, \beta_k^-, \beta_u) = \frac{\exp(a_u c_k^T + \beta_j^- + \beta_u)}{1+\exp(a_u b_k^T + \beta_k^+ + \beta_u)+\exp(a_u c_k^T + \beta_k^- + \beta_u)}$$

And therefore the probability that it is unknown if the user u likes or dislikes the item j as:

$$p(r^0_{uj} \mid a_u, b_j, c_j, \beta_j^+, \beta_j^-, \beta_u) = 1 - p(r^+_{uj} \mid a_u, b_j, c_j, \beta_j^+, \beta_j^-, \beta_u) - p(r^-_{uj} \mid a_u, b_j, c_j, \beta_j^+, \beta_j^-, \beta_u)$$

Again, for simplicity we omit the conditionals and denote the probabilities as $p(r^+_{ui})$, $p(r^-_{ui})$, and $p(r^0_{ui})$. Given the following likelihood function with symbols as defined previously:

$$p^{LK} = \prod_{(u,i)\in M\times N} p(r^+_{ui})^{\delta(f_L(u,i)=+1)} p(r^-_{ui})^{\delta(f_L(u,i)=-1)} p(r^0_{ui})^{\delta(f_L(u,i)=0)}$$

we get this logistic likelihood function which we want to maximize:

$$\log P^{LK} = \sum_{(u,i)\in M\times N} \delta(f_L(u,i)=+1)(a_u b_i^T + \beta_i^+ + \beta_u) + \delta(f_L(u,i)=-1)(a_u c_i^T + \beta_i^- + \beta_u) - \log\left(1 + e^{a_u b_i^T + \beta_i^+ + \beta_u} + e^{a_u c_i^T + \beta_i^- + \beta_u}\right)$$

Optimization. In order to maximize the logistic likelihood functions for all three methods described above, we first find their partial derivatives in terms of the user and item latent factors. We use the gradients to update the user and item factors iteratively. We

	M/N	Edges	Density	+Links
Slashdot	7,896/9,504	305,583	0.004	75.74%
WikiVote	6,129/2,384	103,185	0.007	76.89%
MovieLens	6,040/3,706	998,087	0.044	54.56%
Yelp	6,945/11,274	316,162	0.004	57.64%
BookCrossing	3,398/14,841	306,669	0.006	28.78%

Table 1: Statistics of the evaluated datasets.

begin with random factors and at each step we keep the user factors constant while updating the item factors. In the next step we keep the item factors constant while updating the user factors. This alternating gradient approach is used until convergence or until a certain number of iterations have been made.

The gradients of user and item factors can be derived from the expressions above; we include them in a supplementary document for space reasons[1].

5 EXPERIMENTS AND EVALUATION

In this section we provide a detailed description of our evaluation scheme. We want to investigate the following: (a) overall (listwise) ranking accuracy and ranking quality at two ends of the list (top-k and bottom-k), which are necessary for many applications, (b) recommendation diversity of different models, (c) behavior of different models with the change in model parameter, viz. number of latent factors k, and regularization constant λ, (d) performance of the more complex S-MF model as more training data is available. Recall that S-MF has twice as many parameters for each item. More details about our evaluation is available at https://github.com/uzh/tccf.

5.1 Setup

First we introduce the datasets, evaluation measures, and baseline methods we compare with.

Datasets and Train/Test Splits. We evaluate our models on five well-known and open datasets: Slashdot [12], WikiVote [3], MovieLens [2], BookCrossing [20], and Yelp [3] (restaurants only). The first two are signed directed social networks and the others are from the recommender systems domain. In order to have sufficient training and test data, we make sure that each node has received and given a certain number of feedbacks.

The Slashdot dataset contains feedback of users as Friends (positive link) or Foes (negative link) by other users. WikiVote comprises information about users voting for (positive link) or against (negative link) admin candidates in the Wikipedia community voting.

Unlike Slashdot and WikiVote, other datasets do not have explicit negative feedback, but user preference is expressed as a numeric rating value (e.g., between 1 and 5). To convert numeric ratings into positive and negative feedback, we subtract each rating of a user by the mean rating provided by the user over all items. An alternative is to consider high ratings (e.g., 4-5) as positive and low ratings (1-2) as negative. However, some users may have a high rating bias and only provide ratings between 3 and 5. By applying mean-removal from each user's ratings, we address this problem and convert numeric ratings to user specific positive or negative preference over items.

The properties of the resulting datasets are described in Table 1. We can see that MovieLens is the least sparse dataset and all datasets other than BookCrossing have a higher proportion of positive feedbacks. The frequency distribution of positive and negative links is shown in Figure 2. The distribution is long tailed for both positive and negative links, but towards the tail all datasets other than BookCrossing have even fewer negative links.

For evaluations, we create five different test and train splits of each dataset. Each test split is generated by randomly sampling 30% of the total feedbacks such that in the resulting training split: (a) every node (user) has given at least five positive and three negative feedbacks, and (b) every nodes (item) has received at least one positive and one negative feedback. We train the models on the training sets and generate rankings. The models then are evaluated based on how many links in the test set are successfully predicted at the relevant ends (top or bottom) of the ranked lists. All evaluations are performed by doing 5-fold cross validation over these splits and taking average value for each measurement.

Evaluation Measures. Apart from AUC and GAUC measures introduced in Section 2, we use other common measures to evaluate the performance of our models. **AUC** and **GAUC** describe the quality of the entire ranking list by quantifying how better it is from a random ordering. Although they are useful measures to compare different models, for most applications only a small subset of the ranking is ever used. User experience with search engines, social networks or recommender systems involves interaction with such small personalized rankings, usually including 10-20 suggestions.

Our goal is to generate a ranking of links such that more positive links and few negative links (flops) feature at the top of the list. In other words, we want to simultaneously have two different types of links at the two ends of the ranked list.

A *positive hit* (or true positive) and a *negative hit/flop* (or true negative) are a positive- and a negative link from the test set, respectively. Precision at top-k (**P@k**) counts the number of hits among the top-k links of the ranked list divided by the cut-off level k. Similarly, Precision at bottom-k (**P@-10**) is the number of negative hits in the bottom-k divided by k. Hit Rate at top-k (**H@k**) is the total number of positive hits predicted by the model at top-k divided by the number of users. Likewise, Hit Rate at bottom-k (**H@-k**) is the total number of negative hits at bottom-k divided by the number of users.

Apart from having many positive links at the top, it is also desirable to have fewer flops at the top. We measure this quality using **NI@k**, which is calculated as $\frac{\#\text{negative links at top-k}}{k}$.

All the above measures are concerned with the accuracy of ranking. A good recommendation system is one that additionally provides the users with diverse suggestions. Item Coverage at top-k (**IC@k**) measures the total number of unique suggestions on the top-k recommendation for all users divided by the total number of recommendable links. Similarly, we measure the average popularity of recommended links at top-k by **Id@k** (Item-degree). A very high Id@k means that mostly well-known suggestions are made to the users. These *blockbuster* suggestions are probably already known to the users. Therefore, a very high Id@k is not a desirable quality. A more detailed discussion of recommendation diversity and diversity measures can be found in [1, 4, 14].

The values of P@k, H@k, AUC, GAUC and NI@k reported in this section are averaged over all users. Higher values P@k, H@k, AUC, and GAUC indicate better ranking, while a lower value of

[1]Supplementary document http://www.merlin.uzh.ch/publication/show/15001
[2]http://grouplens.org/datasets/movielens/1m/
[3]http://www.ics.uci.edu/~vpsaini/

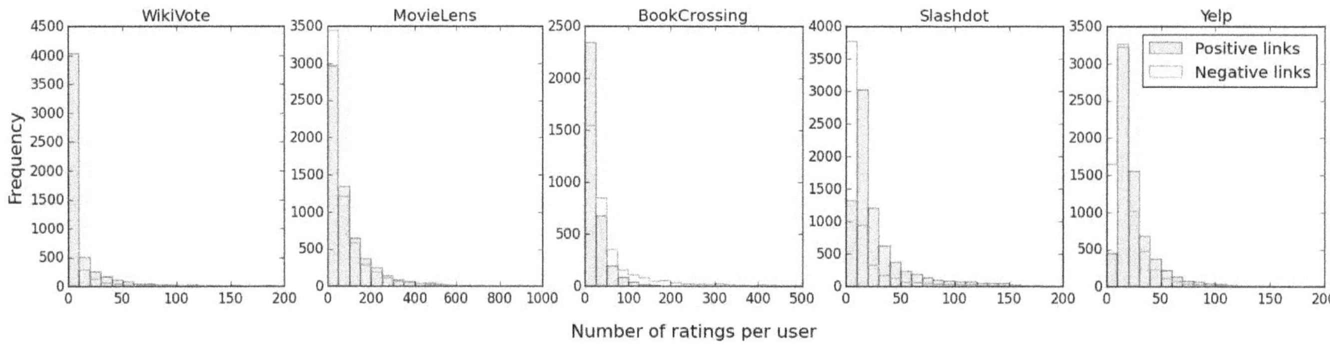

Figure 2: Distribution of different types of links per user. The horizontal axis shows the number of links per user and the vertical axis shows the frequency. As an example, for WikiVote, the number of users with 0-10 negative links is about 2,500.

NI@k is desirable. For IC@k, a higher value is desirable, while for Id@k a lower value is desirable.

Baselines and Parameters. We compare our methods with BPRMF [15], GAUC-OPT [19], and Matrix Factorization [18] model with logistic loss [10]. All of these methods have the same parameter k, which is the number of latent factors. Similarly, they all use the regularization constant λ and BPRMF has additional regularizer for negative item factors, which is $\lambda/10$. In order to be fair to the compared systems, we evaluated with parameters similar to [19], as well as some additional ones. We ran experiments with $\lambda \in \{0.001, 0.01, 1, 5, 10, 20, 50, 100\}$. Similarly, we varied the number of factors within $k \in \{10, 30, 50, 70, 90\}$. We also varied learning rates between 0.001 and 0.01. For TC-MF1, TC-MF, S-MF and MF, we used AdaGrad [5] with a single parameter of $\gamma = 1$ instead of using different learning rates. We want to see if our models performs well without searching on a lot of different parameter settings. We ran all models until convergence or a maximum of 30 iterations.

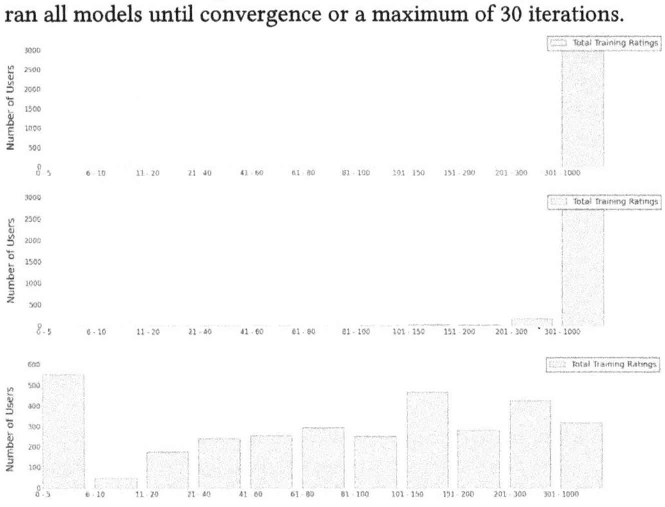

Figure 3: Median Item Degree at top-k (Id@5) on Slashdot dataset. From top to bottom: BPRMF, TC-MF, and S-MF. S-MF recommends links from all bands while others recommend many popular links.

5.2 Result and Discussion

We now present the result of our experimental evaluations and compare the performance of our methods with the state-of-the-art methods.

Model	AUC	GAUC	P@5	P@10	P@-5	P@-10	NI@5	H@5	H@10	IC@5	Id@5
Slashdot											
TC-MF	**0.77**	**0.68**	**0.09**	**0.07**	**0.029**	**0.027**	**0.002**	**0.30**	**0.41**	0.027	580.34
TC-MF1	0.60	0.59	0.07	0.06	0.001	0.001	0.005	0.25	0.36	0.025	662.79
S-MF	0.58	0.56	0.01	0.01	0.005	0.002	0.004	0.07	0.10	**0.236**	**137.4**
MF	0.68	0.63	0.07	0.06	0.023	0.019	0.004	0.27	0.37	0.019	786.08
BPRMF	0.61	0.60	0.08	0.06	0.001	0.001	0.004	0.29	0.40	0.001	801.67
GAUC-OPT	0.68	0.62	0.05	0.05	0.013	0.012	0.003	0.18	0.27	0.211	163.73
WikiVote											
TC-MF	0.65	0.64	0.02	0.03	**0.016**	**0.016**	0.008	0.10	0.18	0.06	60.29
TC-MF1	0.64	0.64	0.03	0.03	0.001	0.001	0.008	0.12	0.24	**0.4**	83.40
S-MF	0.69	0.67	0.04	0.04	0.013	0.012	0.009	0.17	0.26	0.369	61.56
MF	**0.74**	**0.69**	0.02	0.03	0.004	0.004	**0.003**	0.10	0.19	0.299	**57.6**
BPRMF	0.62	0.63	**0.07**	**0.06**	0.001	0.001	0.023	**0.27**	**0.39**	0.005	148.69
GAUC-OPT	0.66	0.62	0.04	0.04	0.007	0.008	**0.003**	0.16	0.28	0.398	78.29
MovieLens											
TC-MF	0.74	0.64	0.17	0.16	0.032	0.030	0.019	0.49	0.63	0.072	1439.26
TC-MF1	0.65	0.58	0.18	0.17	0.001	0.001	0.038	0.51	0.66	0.010	1861.91
S-MF	0.82	0.81	0.13	0.12	**0.041**	**0.043**	0.038	0.43	0.56	**0.442**	967.83
MF	**0.84**	**0.83**	0.07	0.07	0.005	0.006	0.016	0.25	0.39	0.256	**740.72**
BPRMF	0.68	0.58	**0.21**	**0.20**	0.000	0.000	0.036	**0.60**	**0.75**	0.051	1442.08
GAUC-OPT	0.69	0.62	0.14	0.13	**0.041**	0.041	**0.015**	0.55	0.55	0.335	882.58
Yelp											
TC-MF	0.64	0.60	**0.01**	**0.01**	**0.005**	**0.004**	0.003	0.05	0.10	0.0009	238.3
TC-MF1	0.59	0.57	**0.01**	**0.01**	0.000	0.000	0.004	0.05	0.09	0.041	236.42
S-MF	0.57	0.56	**0.01**	**0.01**	0.004	**0.004**	0.004	0.04	0.07	**0.39**	55.56
MF	**0.75**	**0.72**	0.00	0.00	0.000	0.000	**0.001**	0.02	0.03	0.309	**47.99**
BPRMF	0.60	0.58	**0.01**	**0.01**	0.000	0.000	0.005	**0.07**	**0.12**	0.002	209.29
GAUC-OPT	0.54	0.53	**0.01**	**0.01**	0.002	0.002	0.003	0.04	0.08	0.29	74.51
BookCrossing											
TC-MF	0.52	0.56	0.01	0.01	**0.033**	**0.028**	0.003	0.03	0.04	0.0007	74.93
TC-MF1	0.50	0.55	0.00	0.00	0.006	0.006	0.005	0.01	0.02	**0.312**	32.35
S-MF	0.55	0.58	0.00	0.00	0.010	0.007	0.008	0.02	0.03	0.19	55.56
MF	**0.70**	**0.71**	0.00	0.00	0.001	0.001	**0.001**	0.00	0.00	0.068	**6.2**
BPRMF	0.50	0.42	**0.02**	**0.02**	0.000	0.001	0.024	**0.08**	**0.14**	0.001	92.37
GAUC-OPT	0.52	0.52	0.00	0.00	0.013	0.013	0.003	0.02	0.03	0.235	42.63

Table 2: Performance for parameters corresponding to the maximum value of GAUC. Measures above the dotted line indicate the performance of our models for each dataset.

Listwise and Top-k Ranking. We present the result of all evaluated methods for their parameter values corresponding to maximum GAUC in Table 2. The best measure in each column is bold-faced. From Table 2, we can see that TC-MF and S-MF are often better than BPRMF and GAUC-OPT in terms of list-wise measures (AUC and GAUC). While MF outperforms our models in listwise measures, it performs poorly in the top-k measure at the top (P@5, P@10, H@5, H@10) and bottom (P@-5, P@-10) of the list. Although BPRMF performs better at ranking positive items at the top of the list, we can see that TC-MF has much lower proportion of flops at the top of the list (NI@5). For example, in case of WikiVote and BookCrossing datasets, BPRMF has about three to eight times more flops at the top of the list compared to TC-MF, and two to three times more compared to S-MF. Recall that the BookCrossing dataset has more

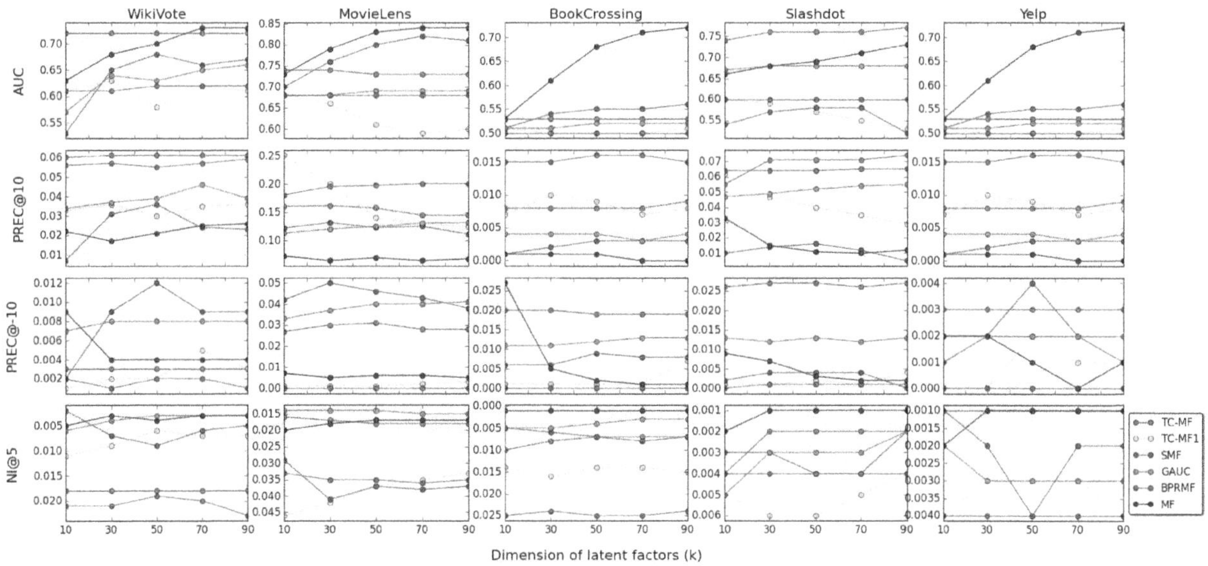

Figure 4: AUC, Prec@10, Prec@-10, and NI@5 at different values of k (dimension of latent factors). Note that the y-axis for NI@5 has been inversed, so that the highest curve indicates the best performance.

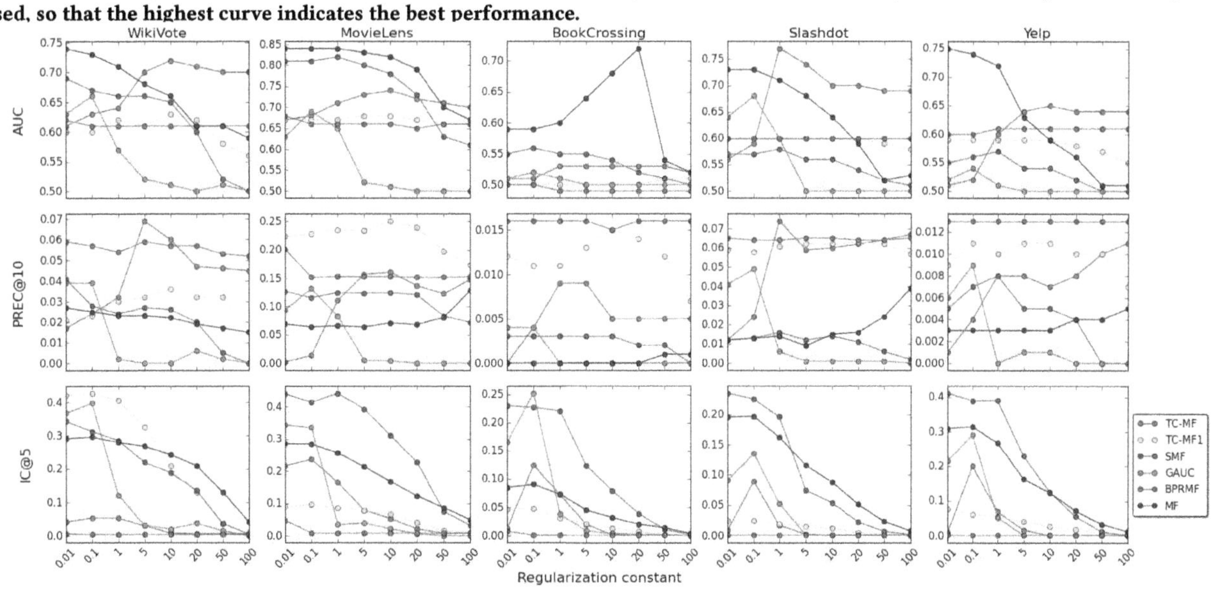

Figure 5: AUC, Prec@10, and IC@5 at different values of λ (regularization constant).

negative links than positive ones. Similarly, while GAUC-OPT is good at ranking negative items at the bottom, it is not as good in distinguishing positive items. On datasets other than MovieLens, S-MF also has fewer flops at the top of the list (NI@5) compared to BPRMF.

For ranking negative links at the bottom of the list (P@-5, P@-10), our models do better than others for all datasets. Similarly, in case of the very sparse Slashdot dataset, TC-MF outperforms every other model. For the remaining datasets, they are among the top or second-top performing model across both positive and negative ranking measures towards the top and bottom of the ranking list. We also observe TC-MF usually performs better than S-MF. As S-MF is more complex, we expect it to model the problem better and generate superior ranking than TC-MF. However, since S-MF also has to learn a lot more parameters than TC-MF, the sparsity of training data might affect the former's performance. We investigate this issue later in this section. From the above discussion, we can suggest that our models are suitable for a general ranking task, as well as the task of TCCF at both ends of the list, i.e., more positive items and fewer flops at the top of the list.

Recommendation Diversity. As described in Section 5.1, we measure recommendation diversity in terms of Item Coverage (IC@5) and median degree of recommended links in the top-k list (Id@5). A lower value of IC@5 is not desirable as it means that few common links appear in the top-5 ranking for many users. Likewise, a higher value of Id@5 is not desirable since it suggests that very-popular links are being suggested to the users, which might suggest a boring recommendation of blockbuster items.

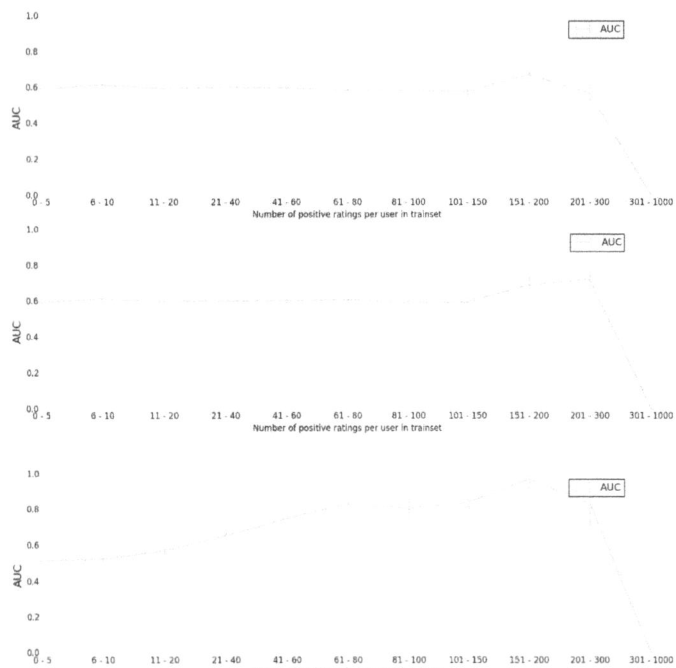

Figure 6: AUC for users with varying amount of training data on the Slashdot dataset, from top to bottom: BPRMF, TC-MF, and S-MF.

From Table 2, we see that BPRMF has very low IC@5 values for all datasets, while S-MF and TC-MF recommend more low-degree links and are better in IC@5 measure. Although BPRMF performs better in P@5 and H@5, it seems to achieve this by recommending few popular links to all users, which we can observe in the Id@5 column. In Figure 3, we show the frequency distribution of Id@5 for BPRMF, TC-MF, and S-MF on the Slashdot dataset. While S-MF recommends items from all bands, other methods recommend mostly popular items only. This behavior holds across other datasets too, but we omit them here for space reasons. Thus, we can see that our model produces more diverse recommendations.

Variation with k and λ. We plot the variation of four different measures with the model parameter (dimension of latent features, k) in Figure 4, by choosing the best performing regularization constant λ for each model. Notice that the y-axis for NI@5 is inverted, which means that a higher curve indicates better performance.

From Figure 4, we see that at $k = 10$, TC-MF has the highest AUC on all datasets and is stable across different values of k. The advantage of using fewer dimensions is cheaper storage and more compressed representation of the dataset, allowing quick computation of recommendation lists. The other interpretation is that TC-MF is not able to exploit higher dimension features to capture more nuances in the dataset. In other words, it indicates that TC-MF is a simple model with the ability to generalize well with few parameters, i.e., without over-fitting. The AUC values of S-MF and MF improve as k increases.

For P@10, the best models across multiple k values are BPRMF, TC-MF1 and TC-MF. Likewise, for P@-10, the best models are SMF, GAUC-OPT, and TC-MF. BPRMF has consistently low values for NI@5, indicating higher proportion of flops at the top of the list.

In Figure 5, we choose the best value of k for each model and plot the variation of three different measures with the regularization parameter λ. The most revealing finding from Figure 5 is that as the regularization parameter λ increases, Item Coverage $IC@5$ decreases and approaches 0. Most previous work using matrix factorization methods only report their best performance using any regularization parameter, but this finding suggests that the choice of regularization parameter is an important consideration. A limited set of regularization parameters might produce a better recommendation in terms of some measure like AUC, while at the same time being very limited in terms of diversity. For this reason we evaluate with $\lambda \in \{0.001, 0.01, 1, 5, 10, 20, 50, 100\}$, while regularization parameters only above 1 are reported in [19] . In Figure 5, we see that a higher AUC value is possible at the cost of a low recommendation diversity. We can also see that S-MF has higher diversity as well as higher accuracy (AUC) and modest top-k performance (P@10) at lower values of λ. On the other hand, BPRMF has higher accuracy values, but at the cost of diversity.

Performance of S-MF with more training data. As we discussed in the above sections, while S-MF does good in some measures on some datasets, it still underperforms other models despite being a more complex model. S-MF needs to learn twice as many parameters for each item compared to the other models. We would like to investigate if lack of training data because of the skewed rating distribution explains this difference in performance. In Figure 6, we present the AUC values of three top-performing models BPRMF, TC-MF, and SMF on the Slashdot dataset for users with varying number of positive links in the training set.

We can observe from this figure that the AUC performance for other models remains relatively flat throughout, while it gradually increases and approaches 1.0 for S-MF as more training data is available. This behavior is also observed in other datasets. This suggests that S-MF is able to produce a better ranking as more training data is available.

6 CONCLUSION

In this paper, we described the Two Class Collaborative Filtering Problem. Ranking positive items at the top of a ranking list is important, but so is being able to distinguish negative items (flops) and rank fewer of them at the top. This problem has only recently received attention because of the increased availability of negative feedback and research on signed social networks. A related problem is that of producing a ranking list with higher diversity, i.e., of links that are not already well-known. In other words, it is important for recommendation systems to generate rankings that are both accurate on the one hand, and not boring on the other hand.

We introduced new probabilistic latent factor models that are able to perform well on the above defined TCCF problem. Specifically, TC-MF model is an extension of the esiting MF model that is simple, yet more accurate in the TCCF task than existing models. The more complex S-MF model produces better rankings but it needs more training data to do so. Our models also produce more diverse and non-blockbuster recommendations.

In the future, we're interested to look into improving the predictive performance of these model. We also want to incorporate side information to make them more robust and perform better with fewer training data.

REFERENCES

[1] Gediminas Adomavicius and YoungOk Kwon. 2012. Improving aggregate recommendation diversity using ranking-based techniques. *IEEE Transactions on Knowledge and Data Engineering* 24, 5 (2012), 896–911.

[2] John S Breese, David Heckerman, and Carl Kadie. 1998. Empirical analysis of predictive algorithms for collaborative filtering. In *Proceedings of the Fourteenth conference on Uncertainty in artificial intelligence*. Morgan Kaufmann Publishers Inc., 43–52.

[3] Moira Burke and Robert Kraut. 2008. Mopping up: modeling wikipedia promotion decisions. In *Proceedings of the 2008 ACM conference on Computer supported cooperative work*. ACM, 27–36.

[4] Pablo Castells, Neil J Hurley, and Saul Vargas. 2015. Novelty and diversity in recommender systems. In *Recommender Systems Handbook*. Springer, 881–918.

[5] John Duchi, Elad Hazan, and Yoram Singer. 2011. Adaptive subgradient methods for online learning and stochastic optimization. *Journal of Machine Learning Research* 12, Jul (2011), 2121–2159.

[6] David Goldberg, David Nichols, Brian M Oki, and Douglas Terry. 1992. Using collaborative filtering to weave an information tapestry. *Commun. ACM* 35, 12 (1992), 61–70.

[7] James A Hanley and Barbara J McNeil. 1983. A method of comparing the areas under receiver operating characteristic curves derived from the same cases. *Radiology* 148, 3 (1983), 839–843.

[8] Yifan Hu, Yehuda Koren, and Chris Volinsky. 2008. Collaborative filtering for implicit feedback datasets. In *2008 Eighth IEEE International Conference on Data Mining*. Ieee, 263–272.

[9] Gareth James, Daniela Witten, Trevor Hastie, and Robert Tibshirani. 2014. *An Introduction to Statistical Learning: With Applications in R*. Springer Publishing Company, Incorporated.

[10] Christopher C Johnson. 2014. Logistic matrix factorization for implicit feedback data. In *NIPS 2014 Workshop on Distributed Machine Learning and Matrix Computations*.

[11] Yehuda Koren, Robert Bell, and Chris Volinsky. 2009. Matrix factorization techniques for recommender systems. *Computer* 8 (2009), 30–37.

[12] Cliff AC Lampe, Erik Johnston, and Paul Resnick. 2007. Follow the reader: filtering comments on slashdot. In *Proceedings of the SIGCHI conference on Human factors in computing systems*. ACM, 1253–1262.

[13] Rong Pan, Yunhong Zhou, Bin Cao, Nathan N Liu, Rajan Lukose, Martin Scholz, and Qiang Yang. 2008. One-class collaborative filtering. In *2008 Eighth IEEE International Conference on Data Mining*. IEEE, 502–511.

[14] Bibek Paudel, Fabian Christoffel, Chris Newell, and Abraham Bernstein. 2016. Updatable, Accurate, Diverse, and Scalable Recommendations for Interactive Applications. *ACM Trans. Interact. Intell. Syst.* 7, 1, Article 1 (Dec. 2016), 34 pages. DOI: http://dx.doi.org/10.1145/2955101

[15] Steffen Rendle, Christoph Freudenthaler, Zeno Gantner, and Lars Schmidt-Thieme. 2009. BPR: Bayesian personalized ranking from implicit feedback. In *Proceedings of the twenty-fifth conference on uncertainty in artificial intelligence*. AUAI Press, 452–461.

[16] Paul Resnick, Neophytos Iacovou, Mitesh Suchak, Peter Bergstrom, and John Riedl. 1994. GroupLens: an open architecture for collaborative filtering of netnews. In *Proceedings of the 1994 ACM conference on Computer supported cooperative work*. ACM, 175–186.

[17] Ruslan Salakhutdinov and Andriy Mnih. 2008. Bayesian probabilistic matrix factorization using Markov chain Monte Carlo. In *Proceedings of the 25th international conference on Machine learning*. ACM, 880–887.

[18] Ruslan Salakhutdinov and Andriy Mnih. 2011. Probabilistic matrix factorization. Citeseer.

[19] Dongjin Song and David A Meyer. 2015. Recommending Positive Links in Signed Social Networks by Optimizing a Generalized AUC.. In *AAAI*. 290–296.

[20] Cai-Nicolas Ziegler, Sean M McNee, Joseph A Konstan, and Georg Lausen. 2005. Improving recommendation lists through topic diversification. In *Proceedings of the 14th international conference on World Wide Web*. ACM, 22–32.

Geographical Diversification in POI Recommendation: Toward Improved Coverage on Interested Areas

Jungkyu Han
Waseda University
Tokyo, Japan
han.jungkyu@akane.waseda.jp

Hayato Yamana
Waseda University
Tokyo, Japan
yamana@waseda.jp

ABSTRACT

In recommending POIs(Point-Of-Interests), factors such as the diversity of the recommended POIs are as important as accuracy for providing a satisfactory recommendation. Although existing diversification methods can help POI recommender systems suggest more diverse POIs, they lack "geographical diversification," which results in the concentration of the supposedly "diverse" recommended POIs on "a small portion" in areas where the target-user is most active. This is caused by the neglect of POI locations in the diversification, i.e., existing diversification methods try to diversify the categories of recommended items. However, geographical diversification is essential for users whose activity interests comprise many sub-areas and who require a variety of recommended POIs encompassing all their activity interests. In this paper, we propose a novel *proportional geographical diversification* method that recommends a variety of POIs located in the activity district of a user such that the variety of sub-areas in the district is proportional to the frequency of his/her activity in each sub-area. We compare the performance of the proposed method with existing diversification methods using real datasets. The evaluation result shows that no method except the proposed one can significantly increase geographical diversity at the expense of tolerable accuracy loss.

CCS CONCEPTS

• **Information systems → Information retrieval diversity**;

KEYWORDS

POI recommendation; Diversity; Geographical diversity;

ACM Reference format:
Jungkyu Han and Hayato Yamana. 2017. Geographical Diversification in POI Recommendation: Toward Improved Coverage on Interested Areas. In *Proceedings of RecSys'17, August 27–31, 2017, Como, Italy*, , 5 pages.
DOI: http://dx.doi.org/10.1145/3109859.3109884

1 INTRODUCTION

While recommending items, the diversity of the recommended items is as important as the recommendation accuracy. For instance, books that span a variety of categories (genres) would interest an user more than books from a single popular category[30]. In recommending POIs(Point-Of-Interests), in addition to the diversity of POI categories, *geographical diversification (geo-diversifiation)* or the diversity of POI locations can also be considered. For example, when a user visits both a shopping area and an office area habitually, recommending POIs from both areas is better than recommending POIs from only one of the areas.

Geo-diversity is particularly useful in recommending POIs that are located in a user's activity districts such as near his/her workplace or along his/her commute line that consists of many sub-areas frequently visited by the user. Because of routine visits to activity districts[6], the various sub-areas in the district have similar visit probability regardless of the user's current location. Therefore, recommending POIs that are located near the current location - a popular form of mobile application - is less useful. Instead, recommending POIs by assuming that the user interest is distributed over many sub-areas in the district achieves a more satisfactory result. In contrast, a recommender that merely recommends POIs from only a small portion of the sub-areas will lose user interest. Although existing diversification methods[30][7][19] are capable of diversifying the category of POIs, they lack "geo-diversification," which results in the concentration of supposedly "diverse" recommended POIs on "a small portion" of the sub-areas where the target-user is most active.

To address the problem, we propose a novel *proportional geographical diversification* method that recommends a variety of POIs located in an user's activity district such that the variety of sub-areas located in a district is proportional to the frequency of user activity in each sub-area. The proposed technique can also be applied to any POI recommender system that has already been deployed.

We describe related work in Section 2. A detailed description of geographic diversification is provided in Section 3. We report the evaluation results and conclude our paper in Section 4 and Section 5, respectively.

2 RELATED WORK

Our study is related to POI recommendation and recommendation result diversification. In this section, we briefly describe POI recommendation studies followed by a review of the current diversification methods.

POI recommendation: Most POI recommendation methods integrate aspects unique to POI with memory-based [24][27][26] or model-based Collaborative Filtering (CF) [5][15][8][16][10][25]. More specifically, aspects such as *user activity density over areas* [24][28][5][15][27], *suitable time of visit for each POI*[8][26], visiting trend of the public in each visited area[16][10][25], and social

RecSys'17, August 27–31, 2017, Como, Italy

ISBN 978-1-4503-4652-8/17/08...$15.00
DOI: http://dx.doi.org/10.1145/3109859.3109884

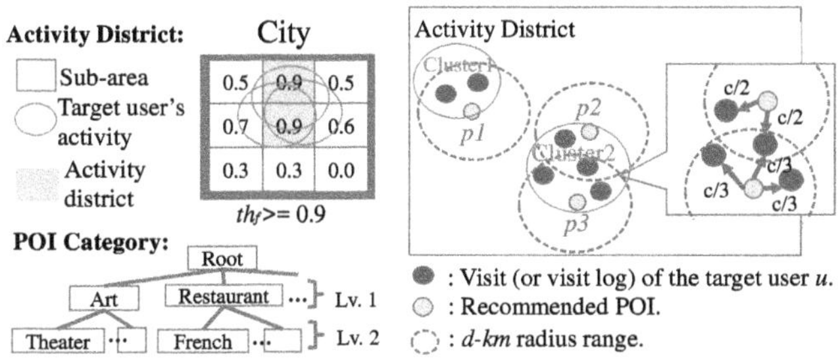

(a) Activity district, POI Category (b) Geo-diversification

Figure 1: Activity district, POI category, and Geo-Div.

connections [24][28][5] were studied to improve POI recommendation performance. The above mentioned aspects were integrated with the design and evaluated with regard to improving the recommendation accuracy. Therefore, it is not clear if the existing POI recommendation studies can be directly applied to the geo-diversification problem that we are attempting to solve.

Result diversification: The concept of result diversification has been introduced to recommendation systems from the field of IR [30][22].

Re-ordering methods[30][7][19][2][12][3] achieve diversification by re-ordering the items in the recommendation list(*RecList*). An ordered RecList of the n items calculated from a base recommender is re-ordered on the basis of a given diversification objective, and then, the top-k ($k < n$) items in the re-ordered list are presented to the user as the final RecList. Since re-ordering methods are mainly designed for item "category" diversification, they are not directly applicable to "location" diversification. A specific group of re-ordering methods[30][2][3] that are based on pair-wise item distance can be applied to the location diversification objective by defining the "distance" as the geographic distance between two POIs. However, as a result, these methods simply recommend POIs that are located far from each other.

Modification of the CF algorithms to handle diversity has been proposed[11][17][1][18][21][23]. For instance, *Hurley et al.* [11] proposed a personalized ranking method that incorporates pair-wise dissimilarity of the items in the RecList. Graph-based diversification methods[13] and clustering-based diversification methods[29][14] that adopt graph and clustering algorithms, respectively, for recommended item diversification were also studied. However, these studies also did not consider the location of items. Furthermore, the cost incurred in applying these techniques to POI recommender systems that have already been deployed is high in comparison to applying re-ordering methods because "core" recommender algorithms must be modified.

3 GEOGRAPHICAL DIVERSIFICATION

In this section, we first define the important terms that are used in the following discussion, and then describe the proposed geo-diversification. We use lower case u to refer to the recommendation target user. Hereafter, *RecPOIs* represent individual POIs that need to be recommended, and *RecList* refers to the entire list of POIs to be recommended.

3.1 Activity district and POI recommendation

We first define u's activity district that indicates the set of the sub-areas frequently visited by u. In other words, the activity district represents the set of sub-areas where u's activity density is greater than a pre-defined threshold.

Sub-area: Sub-area $\boldsymbol{a}$ **indicates a 0.5** $\boldsymbol{km} \times$ **0.5** $\boldsymbol{km}$ **squared area** that covers a partial geographic area of a given city (ct). Upper case A indicates the set of all non-overlapping sub-areas that satisfy $ct = \sum_{a \in A} a$.

Activity Density: Activity density $\boldsymbol{\hat{d}_{u,a} \in [0,1]}$ in Eq.(1) indicates the estimated value of how frequently u visits a sub-area a, normalized for each u. Therefore, $\hat{d}_{u,a}$ becomes 1 (or 0) iff a is the most frequent (or rarest) visited sub-area of u. Here, $d_{u,a}$ in Eq.(1) indicates u's visit-probability density to a, which is calculated by using an Adaptive Density Kernel [28].

$$\hat{d}_{u,a} = \frac{log(d_{u,a} - \min_{a' \in A} d_{u,a'} + 1)}{log(\max_{a' \in A} d_{u,a'} - \min_{a' \in A} d_{u,a'} + 1)} \qquad (1)$$

Activity District: We formally define the **activity district for each** $\boldsymbol{u}$ **as** $\boldsymbol{AD_u = \{a \in A | \hat{d}_{u,a} \geq th_f\}}$, as shown in the upper part of Figure 1a. RecPOIs are selected from the POIs located in $\forall a \in AD_u$. The goal of using AD_u is to find out all the sub-areas where u visits with some frequency. If th_f is too large, only one sub-area is selected. On the other hand, if th_f is too small, all the sub-areas in the city are selected. We empirically use $th_f = 0.9$ after manually evaluating the distribution of u's visit logs and the corresponding AD_u of randomly sampled users.

POI recommendation: A POI recommendation for u indicates a suggestion made to u that consists of k POIs selected from the POIs located in $\boldsymbol{AD_u}$.

3.2 Proportional geo-diversification

To achieve geo-diversification, **(R1)** the RecPOIs should be positioned in locations that are near to those visited by u. In addition, **(R2)** the ratio of the RecPOIs in some location should be proportional to the ratio of u's visits to the nearby locations. As shown in Figure 1b, we recommend three POIs to u who visited Cluster1 twice and Cluster2 four times, one POI was located close to Cluster1 and two POIs were located close to Cluster2.

To realize (R1) and (R2), we assign a distributable cover value c to each recommendable POI. When a POI p is considered as a RecPOI, c of p is evenly divided and distributed to each of u's visits located nearby (in the callout in Figure 1b). For each visit, if there are multiple RecPOIs located nearby, the distributed values from the RecPOIs are accumulated. In the ideal case, by recommending POIs that make all accumulated values on the visits equal, we can roughly satisfy (R1) and (R2) because the same proportion of RecPOIs are located nearby for each visit.

Alg. 1 and Table 1 describe the details of the aforementioned distribution procedure and the adopted symbols, respectively. A log $l \in < user, time, POI >$ is maintained on geographic space by using the location of *POI* in l. We use raw logs instead of activity density in Eq.(1) for each sub-area because sub-area based averaging is too

Table 1: Symbols

SYM	Explanation	SYM	Explanation
T_u	The set of u's visit logs located in AD_u.	s_l	The accumulated cover value on visit log l.
$R_{k,u}$	The set of k RecPOIs for u.	n_{NR}	The accumulated cover value could not be distributed to none of visit logs
d_p	The d-km radius range from POI p.	c_p	The cover value c possesed by POI p.
k	The number of RecPOIs.	v_l	The accumulated cover value on visit log l in the ideal case. $\forall_{l \in T_u} v_l = 1$.

Algorithm 1 Distributing c of each RecPOI to the user visits

procedure DISTRIBUTE-$c(T_u, R_{k,u}, d, k)$
Output: s_l and v_l for each $l \in T_u$, and n_{NR};
$\forall_{l \in T_u}(s_l \leftarrow 0, v_l \leftarrow 1)$, $n_{NR} \leftarrow 0$, $\forall_{p \in R_{k,u}} c_p \leftarrow |T_u|/k$;
for each POI $p \in R_{k,u}$ **do**
$loglist \leftarrow getLogs\_In\_Range\_d_p(d_p, T_u)$;
$count \leftarrow getTheNumberOfLogs(loglist)$;
if $count < 1$ **then** $n_{NR} \leftarrow n_{NR} + c_p/|T_u|$;
else, for each l in $loglist$ **do** $s_l \leftarrow s_l + c_p/count$;

coarse to locate RecPOIs.

To measure the uniformness of the cover value distribution over $\forall_{l \in T_u} s_l$, we use the proportionality metric PR_g (Eq.(2), $PR_g \in [0.0, 1.0]$) proposed by *Dang et al.*[7]. PR_g is the complement of the disproportionality metric DP_g (Eq.(3)) divided by its possible maximum value. Both the metrics are calculated using the result of Alg.1. Here, we write only $R_{k,u}$ in the input parentheses of the metrics for representing the expression concisely. Owing to the initial value assigned to c_p in Alg. 1, $\forall_{l \in T_u} v_l = 1$. f_l indicates the validity flag of disproportionality for log l. The value of f_l is 1 if $v_l \geq s_l$ and 0 otherwise. When the values of c_ps from all RecPOIs $p \in R_{k,u}$ are not uniformly distributed over the logs $l \in T_u$, DP_g becomes to 1, and hence, PR_g approaches 0.

$$PR_g(R_{k,u}) = 1 - DP_g(R_{k,u})/(|T_u| + 1/2) \tag{2}$$

$$DP_g(R_{k,u}) = \sum_{l \in T_u} f_l \cdot (v_l - s_l)^2 + n_{NR}^2/2 \tag{3}$$

3.3 Objective Function

In most of the re-ordering algorithms described in Section 2, re-ordering is carried out by greedy selection; the item(POI) that achieves maximum increment of the diversification objective at a given selection trial is selected from the item list calculated by a base recommender and then placed in the tail of the RecList[30][7][19]. We adopt re-ordering as it decouples diversification from the base recommender, and therefore is flexible enough to apply to already deployed POI recommender systems.

Eq.(4) represents the diversification objective of our proposed method. $rel(i)$ indicates the relevance score for POI i and $div_g(i, R)$ indicates the $PR_g(R_{k,u})$ increment by adding i to the RecList R at a given time point. For $rel(i)$, we use the score calculated for i by the base recommender. $\lambda \in [0.0, 1.0]$ denotes the diversity weight.

$$obj_{GeoD}(i, R) = rel(i)^{1-\lambda} \cdot div_g(i, R)^{\lambda} \tag{4}$$

$$div_g(i, R) = max(0, PR_g(\{i\} \cup R) - PR_g(R)) \tag{5}$$

4 EVALUATION

4.1 Dataset and Algorithms

For evaluation, we tested POI recommendations for the cities of Phoenix and Las Vegas in the USA using publicly available *Yelp Dataset Challenge* [1]. We selected cities that had the largest portions of visit logs in the dataset. POIs visited by less than five users were discarded from the dataset. Furthermore, only visit logs by users who had at least 20 visit logs in the target city were considered such users are more likely to have many sub-areas. As a result 20,723 POIs and 472,972 visit logs from 8,341 users for Phoenix, and 6,725 POIs and 197,368 visit logs from 8,812 users for Las Vegas were used.

The dataset provides a hierarchical category of POIs as shown in the bottom part of Figure 1a. We use the Lv.2 category in the category tree. For the distance of the two categories of POI i and j, we use Eq.(6) proposed by *Castillo et al.*[4]. cat_i indicates the category that i belongs to, and $sp(cat_i, cat_j)$ indicates the length of the shortest path between category cat_i and cat_j in the category tree. When more than one category is assigned to i or j, we take the minimum value of $sp(cat_i, cat_j)$ from all possible combinations.

$$dissim_{cat}(i, j) = 1 - 1/(1 + sp(cat_i, cat_j)) \tag{6}$$

The evaluation was carried out using 3-fold cross validation. The POIs that appear in u's training set or the POIs that are not located in AD_u are discarded from u's test set. In the test, for each u, a RecList is calculated from the POIs located in AD_u. As a result, on average, 7,217 users in Phoenix and 2,454 users in Las Vegas got recommendations in a single validation. Using re-ordering methods described in Section 2, a base recommender calculates n POIs for u, and then k out of the n calculated POIs are recommended by a given diversification method. We use $n = 80$, $k = 20$, and $d = 0.5km$ for re-ordering and *geo-diversity*.

We used *Ye et al.*'s method[24] as the base POI recommender (**Geo_UCF**) tuned to maximize the Recall metric[9]. We selected the algorithm because Geo_UCF is a pioneering work in POI recommendation that is referred by many other works and shows better accuracy(Recall) in our pre-evaluation as compared to other state-of-the-art proposals[28][10]. With respect to diversification, we evaluated two state-of-the-art category diversification methods, *Vargas et al.*[19] (**Binom**) and *Dang et al.*[7](**PM2**), list diversification methods based on pair-wise item dissimilarity in the RecList (**LD-cat** and **LD-geo**, the objective function is found in Eq.(2) of [19]), and our proposed method(**Geo-div**). LD-cat uses category distance in Eq.(6), and LD-dist uses km as the distance between the locations of two POI i, j to calculate pairwise item dissimilarity. For comparison, we also evaluate the random recommender (**Random**), which recommends POIs randomly and the popularity recommender (**Pop**), which recommends top-k popular POIs.

4.2 Evaluation Metric

We evaluate the algorithms using five metrics: *Recall@x*[9], *ILD@x*[30], *EPC@x*[20], *PRg@x*(Eq.(2)), and *PRg-r@x*. These metrics are calculated for each test user and, except for *PRg-r@x*, the average values obtained for all the test users are reported for each metric. For

[1] https://www.yelp.com/dataset_challenge

PRg-r@x, the average of test users whose *PRg-r@x* value is greater than zero is reported.

Recall@x is an accuracy metric. In Eq.(7), *GT* indicates the set of the all ground truth POIs and RET_x represents the set of ground truth POIs included in the top-x POIs in the RecList. *ILD@x*(Eq.(8), a variation of ILS in [30]) measures pairwise category dissimilarity of the top-x POIs in the RecList. R_x in Eq.(8) indicates the set of the top-x POIs in the RecList. We measure two versions of ILD: $ILD_{cat}@x$ used Eq.(6) and $ILD_{geo}@x$ used *km* distance as $dissim(i, j)$, respectively. *EPC@x* is a novelty metric proposed by *Vargas et al.*[20]. A high *EPC@x* value indicates that the less-popular ground-truth POIs are located in the top part of the top-x POIs in the RecList. *PRg@x* indicates the value of PR_g calculated with the top-x POIs in the RecList. *PRg-r@x* carried out the same calculation as *PRg@x*, but with the ground truth POIs in the top-x POIs in the RecList. All of the metrics except for *ILD-geo* are in the [0.0, 1.0] range, where a value of 1 indicates the best performance in each metric.

$$Recall@x = |RET_x|/|GT| \tag{7}$$

$$ILD@x = \sum_{i,j \in R_x \wedge i \neq j} dissim(i, j)/(|R_x| \cdot (|R_x| - 1)) \tag{8}$$

Table 2: Experimental results (Phoenix)

Alg.	*Recall@5*	*ILD-(cat,geo)@5*	*EPC@5*	*PRg@5*	PRg-r@5
Random	0.006	**0.387, 1.851**	**0.796**	0.301	0.157
Pop	0.054	0.314, 1.394	0.211	0.306	0.158
Geo_UCF[24]	**0.067**	0.303, 1.382	0.372	0.420	0.202
Geo_UCF_PRg[24]	0.062	0.314, 1.047	0.445	**0.518**	**0.251**
PM2[7]	0.057	0.286, 1.519	0.510	0.426	0.189
Binom(0.5)[19]	**0.067**	0.321, 1.388	0.375	0.421	0.201
Binom(0.9)	0.065	0.374, 1.424	0.395	0.424	0.197
LD-cat(0.5)[Eq.(3) of [19]]	0.062	**0.400**, 1.445	0.402	0.427	0.196
LD-geo(0.5)[Eq.(3) of [19]]	0.047	0.340, 2.573	0.407	0.329	0.146
LD-geo(0.9)	0.039	0.350, **2.594**	0.420	0.308	0.133
Geo-Div(0.5)	0.060	0.322, 1.650	0.475	0.719	0.271
Geo-Div(0.9)	0.054	0.333, 1.821	**0.524**	**0.812**	**0.280**
Alg.	***Recall@10***	***ILD-(cat,geo)@10***	***EPC@10***	***PRg@10***	**PRg-r@10**
Random	0.012	**0.387, 1.853**	**0.795**	0.394	0.126
Pop	0.092	0.320, 1.485	0.292	0.412	0.146
Geo_UCF	**0.111**	0.316, 1.431	0.428	0.516	0.173
Geo_UCF_PRg	0.101	0.327, 1.064	0.489	**0.594**	**0.203**
PM2	0.098	0.292, 1.537	0.539	0.525	0.164
Binom(0.5)	**0.110**	0.325, 1.435	0.429	0.516	0.173
Binom(0.9)	0.105	0.367, 1.468	0.446	0.524	0.171
LD-cat(0.5)	0.093	**0.400**, 1.504	0.465	0.535	0.167
LD-geo(0.5)	0.086	0.344, 2.162	0.458	0.466	0.134
LD-geo(0.9)	0.066	0.355, **2.181**	0.480	0.441	0.117
Geo-Div(0.5)	0.095	0.336, 1.654	0.524	0.867	**0.222**
Geo-Div(0.9)	0.089	0.342, 1.673	**0.563**	**0.888**	0.220
Alg.	***Recall@20***	***ILD(cat,geo)@20***	***EPC@20***	***PRg@20***	**PRg-r@20**
Random	0.024	**0.388, 1.855**	**0.795**	0.462	0.097
Pop	0.151	0.333, 1.526	0.375	0.477	0.122
Geo_UCF	**0.178**	0.330, 1.482	0.489	0.588	0.141
Geo_UCF_PRg)	0.154	0.343, 1.081	0.534	**0.647**	**0.155**
PM2	0.164	0.300, 1.556	0.576	0.594	0.135
Binom(0.5)	**0.177**	0.333, 1.481	0.489	0.589	0.141
Binom(0.9)	0.165	0.357, 1.495	0.494	0.595	0.138
LD-cat(0.5)	0.130	**0.398**, 1.520	0.514	0.619	0.130
LD-geo(0.5)	0.152	0.346, 1.894	0.505	0.571	0.123
LD-geo(0.9)	0.121	0.356, **1.916**	0.530	0.558	0.108
Geo-Div(0.5)	0.155	0.345, 1.587	0.562	**0.875**	**0.165**
Geo-Div(0.9)	0.149	0.347, 1.584	**0.590**	**0.875**	0.161

*The value in () in Alg. column indicates the adopted diversification weight.
**Bold faced in Alg. column indicates the proposed method and the best performance in other columns.
***Avg. and Med. of $|AD_u|$ for all target users in Phoenix are 103 and 86 respectively.

4.3 Results and Discussion

The results are shown in Table 2. The two cities show similar trends. Owing to space limitations we only report the results from Phoenix. For the algorithms that control the weight ([0.0, 1.0]) on the diversification, we list the results of 0.5 and 0.9 except for LD-cat that showed nearly identical performance from a weight of 0.5. We also report the performance of Geo_UCF(**Geo_UCF_PRg**) tuned for maximizing *PRg@x* using increased weight on the estimated visit probability of u at a given POI location. When we compare Random, Pop, Geo_UCF, and Geo_UCF_PRg, Random achieves the highest *ILD-cat*, *ILD-geo*, and *EPC* owing to the randomly selected POIs, but has the lowest *Recall*. Pop has lower *ILD-geo*, and a *PRg* similar to that of Random. The performance of Pop indicates a concentration of the RecPOIs in a small portion of the area, and RecPOIs do not cover all the locations visited by u. The higher *Recall* and *PRg* measures in Geo_UCF and Geo_UCF_PRg as compared to the other two show the usefulness of personalization. However, interestingly, Geo_UCF_PRg has the lowest *ILD-geo* amongst all the evaluated algorithms despite its high *PRg*. One possible explanation is that Geo_UCF_PRg concentrates the RecPOIs in a small portion of u's active areas.

Among the diversification algorithms, PM achieves high *Recall* and *EPC*, but has low *ILD-cat*. Binom achieves both high *Recall* and high *ILD-cat* but has low *EPC*. The high *EPC* of PM is achieved because PM recommends POIs in the preferable categories of u, and the preferable categories deviated somewhat from the categories that popular POIs included. However, the concentration on the preferable categories lowered *ILD-cat*. Binom avoids over-concentration on certain categories, in other words, recommends POIs in less preferable categories, which results in high *ILD-cat* but low *EPC*. LD-cat and LD-geo work well in their objective and showed good performance in *ILD-cat* and *ILD-geo* metrices, respectively.

None of the diversification methods significantly improve *PRg* in comparison with Geo_UCF except for Geo-Div. High *PRg* and *PRg-r* of Geo-Div support Geo-Div's superiority, not only in terms of *PRg* that improves RecPOIs, but also on *PRg* improvement exhibited by the accurately predicted POIs. Although LD-geo has the highest *ILD-geo*, it cannot achieve high *PRg* improvement because LD-geo simply recommends POIs that are located far from each other. The *Recall* of Geo-Div(0.5) is not significantly lower than that of the other diversification methods, and is greater than that of Pop. Geo-Div also has high *EPC*. One possible explanation is that Geo-Div recommends POIs from a variety of areas, and therefore avoids recommending many popular RecPOIs located in a small portion of popular areas. The results show that Geo-Div is one of the best options when we need geo-diversification in POI recommendation. However, Geo-Div does not consider category diversification, and therefore does not significantly improve *ILD-cat*.

5 CONCLUSION

In this paper, we introduced the concept of geo-diversification and proposed a geo-diversification method for POI recommendation. Experimental results showed that our method achieves superior geo-diversification at the expense of tolerable accuracy loss. In future studies, we will carry out user studies to understand user perception about geo-diversification. We also plan on reinterpreting existing concepts of diversity in the context of POI recommendation and integrating the concepts on geo-diversification.

REFERENCES

[1] P. Adamopoulos and A. Tuzhilin. 2014. On Over-specialization and Concentration Bias of Recommendations: Probabilistic Neighborhood Selection in Collaborative Filtering Systems. In *Proc. of the 8th ACM Conference on Recommender Systems (RecSys '14)*. ACM, 153–160.

[2] I. Benouaret and D. Lenne. 2016. A Package Recommendation Framework for Trip Planning Activities. In *Proc. of the 10th ACM Conference on Recommender Systems (RecSys '16)*. 203–206.

[3] J. Carbonell and J. Goldstein. 1998. The Use of MMR, Diversity-based Reranking for Reordering Documents and Producing Summaries. In *Proc. of the 21st Annual International ACM SIGIR Conference on Research and Development in Information Retrieval (SIGIR '98)*. 335–336.

[4] L. Castillo, E. Armengol, E. Onaindía, L. Sebastiá, J. González-boticario, A. Rodríguez, S. Fernández, J.D. Arias, and D. Borrajo. 2008. SAMAP. An user-oriented adaptive system for planning tourist visits. *Expert Systems with Applications* (2008).

[5] C. Cheng, H. Yang, I. King, and M. R. Lyu. 2012. Fused Matrix Factorization with Geographical and Social Influence in Location-based Social Networks. In *Proc. of the Twenty-Sixth AAAI Conference on Artificial Intelligence (AAAI'12)*. 17–23.

[6] E. Cho, S. A. Myers, and J. Leskovec. 2011. Friendship and Mobility: User Movement in Location-based Social Networks. In *Proceedings of the 17th ACM SIGKDD International Conference on Knowledge Discovery and Data Mining (KDD '11)*. 1082–1090.

[7] V. Dang and W. B. Croft. 2012. Diversity by Proportionality: An Election-based Approach to Search Result Diversification. In *Proc. of the 35th International ACM SIGIR Conference on Research and Development in Information Retrieval (SIGIR '12)*. 65–74.

[8] H. Gao, J. Tang, X. Hu, and H. Liu. 2013. Exploring Temporal Effects for Location Recommendation on Location-based Social Networks. In *Proc. of the 7th ACM Conference on Recommender Systems (RecSys '13)*. 93–100.

[9] J. L. Herlocker, J. A. Konstan, L. G. Terveen, and J. T. Riedl. 2004. Evaluating Collaborative Filtering Recommender Systems. *ACM Trans. Inf. Syst.* 22, 1 (Jan. 2004), 5–53.

[10] L. Hu, A. Sun, and Y. Liu. 2014. Your Neighbors Affect Your Ratings: On Geographical Neighborhood Influence to Rating Prediction. In *Proc. of the 37th International ACM SIGIR Conference on Research & Development in Information Retrieval (SIGIR '14)*. 345–354.

[11] N. Hurley. 2013. Personalised Ranking with Diversity. In *Proc. of the 7th ACM Conference on Recommender Systems (RecSys '13)*. 379–382.

[12] N. Hurley and M. Zhang. 2011. Novelty and Diversity in Top-N Recommendation – Analysis and Evaluation. *ACM Trans. Internet Technol.* 10, 4, Article 14 (March 2011), 30 pages.

[13] O. Küçüktunç, E. Saule, K. Kaya, and Ü. V. Çatalyürek. 2014. Diversifying Citation Recommendations. *ACM Trans. Intell. Syst. Technol.* 5, 4, Article 55 (Dec. 2014), 21 pages.

[14] L. Li, D. Wang, T. Li, D. Knox, and B. Padmanabhan. 2011. SCENE: A Scalable Two-stage Personalized News Recommendation System. In *Proc. of the 34th International ACM SIGIR Conference on Research and Development in Information Retrieval (SIGIR '11)*. 125–134.

[15] B. Liu, Y. Fu, Z. Yao, and H. Xiong. 2013. Learning Geographical Preferences for Point-of-interest Recommendation. In *Proc. of the 19th ACM SIGKDD International Conference on Knowledge Discovery and Data Mining (KDD '13)*. 1043–1051.

[16] Y. Liu, W. Wei, A. Sun, and C. Miao. 2014. Exploiting Geographical Neighborhood Characteristics for Location Recommendation. In *Proc. of the 23rd ACM International Conference on Conference on Information and Knowledge Management (CIKM '14)*. 739–748.

[17] K. Niemann and M. Wolpers. 2013. A New Collaborative Filtering Approach for Increasing the Aggregate Diversity of Recommender Systems. In *Proc. of the 19th ACM SIGKDD International Conference on Knowledge Discovery and Data Mining (KDD '13)*. 955–963.

[18] A. Said, B. Fields, B. J. Jain, and S. Albayrak. 2013. User-centric Evaluation of a K-furthest Neighbor Collaborative Filtering Recommender Algorithm. In *Proc. of the 2013 Conference on Computer Supported Cooperative Work (CSCW '13)*. 1399–1408.

[19] S. Vargas, L. Baltrunas, A. Karatzoglou, and P. Castells. 2014. Coverage, Redundancy and Size-awareness in Genre Diversity for Recommender Systems. In *Proc. of the 8th ACM Conference on Recommender Systems (RecSys '14)*. 209–216.

[20] S. Vargas and P. Castells. 2011. Rank and Relevance in Novelty and Diversity Metrics for Recommender Systems. In *Proc. of the Fifth ACM Conference on Recommender Systems (RecSys '11)*. 109–116.

[21] S. Vargas and P. Castells. 2014. Improving Sales Diversity by Recommending Users to Items. In *Proc. of the 8th ACM Conference on Recommender Systems (RecSys '14)*. 145–152.

[22] S. Vargas, P. Castells, and D. Vallet. 2011. Intent-oriented Diversity in Recommender Systems. In *Proc. of the 34th International ACM SIGIR Conference on Research and Development in Information Retrieval (SIGIR '11)*. 1211–1212.

[23] L. Wu, Q. Liu, E. Chen, N.J. Yuan, G. Guo, and X. Xie. 2016. Relevance Meets Coverage: A Unified Framework to Generate Diversified Recommendations. *ACM Trans. Intell. Syst. Technol.* 7, 3, Article 39 (Feb. 2016), 39:1–39:30 pages.

[24] M. Ye, P. Yin, W.-C. Lee, and D.-L. Lee. 2011. Exploiting Geographical Influence for Collaborative Point-of-interest Recommendation. In *Proc. of the 34th International ACM SIGIR Conference on Research and Development in Information Retrieval (SIGIR '11)*. 325–334.

[25] H. Yin, Y. Sun, B. Cui, Z. Hu, and L. Chen. 2013. LCARS: A Location-content-aware Recommender System. In *Proc. of the 19th ACM SIGKDD International Conference on Knowledge Discovery and Data Mining (KDD '13)*. 221–229.

[26] Q. Yuan, G. Cong, Z. Ma, A. Sun, and N.M. Thalmann. 2013. Time-aware Point-of-interest Recommendation. In *Proc. of the 36th International ACM SIGIR Conference on Research and Development in Information Retrieval (SIGIR '13)*. 363–372.

[27] J.-D. Zhang and C.-Y. Chow. 2013. iGSLR: Personalized Geo-social Location Recommendation: A Kernel Density Estimation Approach. In *Proc. of the 21st ACM SIGSPATIAL International Conference on Advances in Geographic Information Systems (SIGSPATIAL'13)*. 334–343.

[28] J.-D. Zhang and C.-Y. Chow. 2015. GeoSoCa: Exploiting Geographical, Social and Categorical Correlations for Point-of-Interest Recommendations. In *Proc. of the 38th International ACM SIGIR Conference on Research and Development in Information Retrieval (SIGIR '15)*. 443–452.

[29] M. Zhang and N. Hurley. 2009. Novel Item Recommendation by User Profile Partitioning. In *Proc. of the 2009 IEEE/WIC/ACM International Joint Conference on Web Intelligence and Intelligent Agent Technology - Volume 01 (WI-IAT '09)*. 508–515.

[30] C.-N. Ziegler, S. M. McNee, J. A. Konstan, and G. Lausen. 2005. Improving Recommendation Lists Through Topic Diversification. In *Proc. of the 14th International Conference on World Wide Web (WWW '05)*. 22–32.

Understanding How People Use Natural Language to Ask for Recommendations

Jie Kang
University of Minnesota
kangx385@umn.edu

Kyle Condiff
University of Minnesota
cond0155@umn.edu

Shuo Chang*
Quora, Inc.
schang@quora.com

Joseph A. Konstan
University of Minnesota
konstan@umn.edu

Loren Terveen
University of Minnesota
terveen@umn.edu

F. Maxwell Harper
University of Minnesota
max@umn.edu

ABSTRACT

The technical barriers for conversing with recommender systems using natural language are vanishing. Already, there are commercial systems that facilitate interactions with an AI agent. For instance, it is possible to say "what should I watch" to an Apple TV remote to get recommendations. In this research, we investigate how users initially interact with a new natural language recommender to deepen our understanding of the range of inputs that these technologies can expect. We deploy a *natural language interface* to a recommender system, we observe users' first interactions and follow-up queries, and we measure the differences between speaking- and typing-based interfaces. We employ qualitative methods to derive a categorization of users' first queries (objective, subjective, and navigation) and follow-up queries (refine, reformulate, start over). We employ quantitative methods to determine the differences between speech and text, finding that speech inputs are typically longer and more conversational.

CCS CONCEPTS

• **Human-centered computing** → *Natural language interfaces*; • **Information systems** → *Recommender systems*;

KEYWORDS

recommender systems; natural language recommenders; critiquing; voice; speech; virtual assistants; qualitative methods; user study.

ACM Reference format:
Jie Kang, Kyle Condiff, Shuo Chang, Joseph A. Konstan, Loren Terveen, and F. Maxwell Harper. 2017. Understanding How People Use Natural Language to Ask for Recommendations. In *Proceedings of RecSys '17, Como, Italy, August 27-31, 2017,* 9 pages.
https://doi.org/10.1145/3109859.3109873

*Affiliated with the University of Minnesota during this project.

ACM ISBN 978-1-4503-4652-8/17/08...$15.00
https://doi.org/10.1145/3109859.3109873

1 INTRODUCTION

"Hey Netflix, I want to watch an action movie ... spy-thriller ... maybe something like the Bourne Identity ... no, something less violent and more intellectual ... OK, show me the preview for Argo."

The above quote exemplifies an interaction pattern that we believe is coming to recommender systems in the near future. The user speaks to a device — in this case, a television screen — which incorporates each statement into a recommendation request. The request is matched against the user's preferences and globally-known properties of the database to find the most relevant results. As the results are presented on-screen, the user evaluates the results (potentially helping to clarify what he or she is looking for, which may be fuzzy) and issues a follow-up request to help the system find better results.

Several of the requirements to build a system like this are already in place. For example, set-top boxes from Amazon, Apple, and Comcast already listen for users to issue verbal commands or search for content. Some even allow users to ask for recommendations, though these features are currently incredibly shallow and limited. (Asking the Apple TV for "what should I watch tonight" results in a non-personalized list of content with the response "I hear these are worth checking out".) The piece that is missing from the current generation of natural language recommenders like these is the deep one: the ability to understand the nuanced intention of recommendation requests and to translate that intention into the right results.

This research serves to address a basic gap in our knowledge: though we can contrive examples like the one above to demonstrate the nuance of user requests, we do not know how people will actually speak or type to a fluent natural language recommender system. Therefore, we conducted and report on a study of users' *first interactions* with a new natural language recommendation-finding feature built into an established recommender system. By structuring our study around these first interactions, we seek to understand the goals that users might have, the types of queries they might issue, or how they might choose to express follow-up queries to refine results. To build natural language recommenders that respond to a full range of queries, we must begin to understand what the full range might be.

This paper is structured as follows. We first describe related work, with a focus on conversational recommenders, user goals in information retrieval, and prior comparisons of typing and speech. We then describe a prototype natural language recommender and an experiment that we used to collect recommendation-seeking requests. We follow this with three sections that constitute our primary contributions: (a) a qualitative analysis of recommendation-seeking goals in first queries, (b) a qualitative analysis of follow-up requests, and (c) a quantitative analysis of differences between text and speech modalities. We conclude with a discussion of the implications of these findings for designers of natural language recommenders.

As a further contribution, we make our experimental dataset publicly available [14]. In conducting this research, we collected recommendation-seeking queries, follow-up queries, and survey responses from 347 users of an established recommender system. This dataset is the first of its kind, and can be used to seed system-building or to facilitate subsequent studies on natural-language recommender systems.

2 RELATED WORK

One of the directions of this work — to explore the question of how voice and text compare in recommendation-seeking requests — builds on prior results in comparing text with speech. Most relevant is an analysis of the semantic and syntactic differences between spoken and typed-in queries using mobile search engine logs [9]. That work reveals that spoken queries are "closer to natural language", and are more often phrased as questions. Research on mobile search has contributed other relevant results, including a related finding that spoken queries are more "natural" and longer [6], a frequency analysis of mobile search categories [13], and a categorization of voice transcription errors and subsequent query reformulation strategies [12]. Early CSCW work investigated the differences between speech and text in annotating documents, finding that speech led to more effective communication of higher-level concepts, while text was superior at low-level comments [3]. Recent work has shown that technological barriers to voice input and transcription are disappearing [23].

Surprisingly little research has been done on the use of natural language (typed or spoken) in recommender systems. There has, however, been substantial work around the related topic of "conversational recommenders" [21, 26], where the user and the system engage with one another to iteratively refine a query. For instance, researchers have explored "critiquing" interfaces that offer users the chance to offer suggestions like "More like item A, but cheaper" [15]. However, little of this work involves natural language. One notable exception is the Adaptive Place Advisor [8], an early natural language conversational recommender, where the user and the recommender system engage in a natural text-based dialogue to narrow down a set of restaurant recommendations. This work was later extended to become a spoken dialogue recommender system based on a personalized user model [28].

In this work we explore how people use natural language to express a recommendation-seeking goal. Several notable recommender systems papers have proposed a set of goals or intentions that recommender systems should support. For instance, the human-recommender interaction (HRI) model [16] proposes terminology for describing a user-centric view of a recommender system, and is based on a hierarchy of user goals and tasks. This work explicitly recognizes that users are not always able to fully express their information needs; they label this uncertainty factor "concreteness". One of the most highly-cited papers on evaluating recommender systems [10] proposes a set of user tasks that categorize user goals in a recommender system; those goals (e.g., "find good items" and "just browsing") are at a higher level of abstraction from the goals studied here. In general, recommender systems research has focused more on supporting these high-level tasks, as opposed to designing for or understanding lower-level, goal-driven recommendation seeking tasks [25].

The field of information retrieval (IR) has contributed more research on understanding lower-level information seeking goals. Several highly-cited papers contribute categorizations of how users interact with search engines. Perhaps the most influential categorization [2] proposes three types of user goals in search: "navigational" (to reach a particular site), "informational" (to acquire information), and "transactional" (to locate services). Rose and Levinson extended this understanding by manually coding a set of 1,500 queries from AltaVista, adding a second level of categorization, and describing a frequency analysis of the different user goals [22]. Subsequent work used machine learning methods to infer these user goals across seven search datasets [11].

3 DATA COLLECTION

To investigate the use of a natural language recommendation-seeking interface, we built an experimental voice-based search interface into MovieLens[1], an established movie recommendation site, and asked site members to use it and provide feedback. This section describes the context of the study, the methods for collecting user responses, and the attributes of the final dataset that we use for subsequent analysis.

3.1 Experimental Site

MovieLens provides personalized movie recommendations for its members. The user experience is largely oriented around the process of finding movies to watch: members rate the movies they've seen to receive personalized recommendations based on those ratings. MovieLens does not offer any sort of natural language search features, though the site has a prominent "omnisearch" widget that allows users to search for a title, tag, or person.

We augmented MovieLens with an experimental interface that allows users to speak (or type) to the system. The system responds to the user request with a list of ten movies. To illustrate, the user might say "great car chases", and the system might return "Mad Max: Fury Road" and nine other movies that feature cars, chases, and/or greatness.

To be clear: building a state-of-the-art natural language query engine for movies is out of scope for this research project. Such a system would require substantial domain-specific investment at each level of the system architecture from voice recognition that understands actors' names to keyword extraction that is tuned to the particular needs of movie searches. Our goal here is a system that works "well enough" to allow us to answer our research questions — a method employed in prior HCI research, e.g. [30]. Though we considered deploying a "Wizard of Oz" recommender, we wish to promote ecological validity by giving subjects a system that "feels real" and can be used at the place and time of their choosing. To

[1] http://movielens.org

Figure 1: A screenshot of the voice input interface.

promote this validity, we recruited subjects with the promise of trying "an experimental feature" that we are considering bringing to MovieLens.

To build the prototype, we combine several off-the-shelf components with custom server-side search logic. On the client (web browser) side, we incorporate a voice input widget and voice-to-speech service from Wit.ai (https://wit.ai) to accept users' speech. The interface requires the user to click a button to start and end the process of collecting voice input. We immediately send the audio to wit.ai, which converts the audio to text. We allow users to view the results and to re-try or edit the results manually if the transcription results in errors, or if their microphone is not working.

We send the transcribed query to the MovieLens server to produce a list of the most relevant movies using custom search logic. Our process first uses AlchemyAPI (http://www.alchemyapi.com) to extract keywords from the query string, then searches for movies with titles, actors, directors, genres, or tags that match those extracted keywords. Movies with more matches get higher scores.

See the Data Collection Results section below for experimental evaluation of the quality of the recommender's results.

3.2 Subject Recruitment, Conditions, and Tasks

To evaluate user query behavior, we recruited MovieLens users by email. To bring in users with at least minimal familiarity with MovieLens, we emailed only users who had logged in during the previous six months and who had rated enough movies (15) to unlock personalized recommendations. Users who clicked on the link in the email were logged in to MovieLens and shown an experimental consent form; subjects were given the chance to immediately opt-out or stop at any time. This experiment was approved by our research institution's IRB.

We include just two experimental conditions: `speaking` or `typing`. Users in the speaking condition submit their queries by speaking at their computer or device, while users in the typing condition submit their queries by typing into an input box. Our assignment is not random, because some users do not have a working microphone attached to their computer. Therefore, our assignment is based on the strategy visualized in Figure 2. Subjects who cannot use a microphone are put in the typing condition. Subjects who can use the microphone are assigned randomly to the speaking condition (75% chance) or the typing condition (25% chance). There is a possibility that users with working microphones are different from users without working microphones (e.g., they might be more tech-savvy), and we examine this potential bias below.

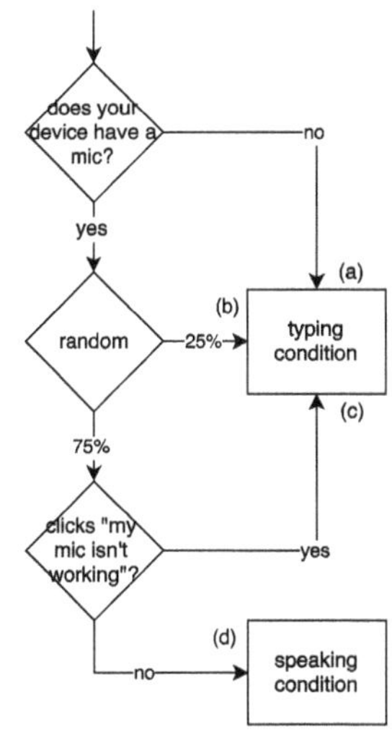

Figure 2: Method for assigning subjects to the `speaking` or `typing` condition. We first ask subjects if they have a working microphone. Users who say "no" are put into the typing condition (a), while users who say "yes" are randomly assigned to typing (b) or speaking. Users who are assigned to the speaking condition can click "my microphone isn't working" to fall back to the typing condition (c), or they can use the voice interface (d).

We ask consenting subjects to complete several tasks in sequence, summarized in Figure 3. All subjects begin the study by interacting with the typing- or speaking-based natural language input interface with the prompt "I can help you find movies. What are you looking for?" (see Figure 1). Once the subject submits a query, the system responds with ten search results and a short survey asking subjects to rate "how well do these results match what you were looking for" (on a 5 point "very poor" to "excellent" scale). Subjects who rate the results overall as "very poor" or "poor" are asked to explain how the results could be improved using free text input; subjects who rate the results as "fair" or better are asked to express a *follow-up query* (the interface prompts: "I can improve these results. Tell me more about what you want."). Finally, all subjects are surveyed about several factors, including how they hope the feature would work in MovieLens and their experience with other voice recognition interfaces. We state the specific wording of individual survey questions alongside results below.

3.3 Data Collection Results

We emailed 9,972 MovieLens members on May 12, 2016 and collected data through May 24; 544 consented to participate (5.5%). We collect at most one response per subject. For each subject, we consider their input to be "valid" if it is non-empty and not a testing or nonsense query (our coding methods are described below). For example, we exclude the user queries "testing one two three testing one two three" (testing), "xx" (nonsense), and "blah blah blah blah blah blah blah blah" (nonsense). Further, we discard any queries from the speaking condition where the user completely rewrote

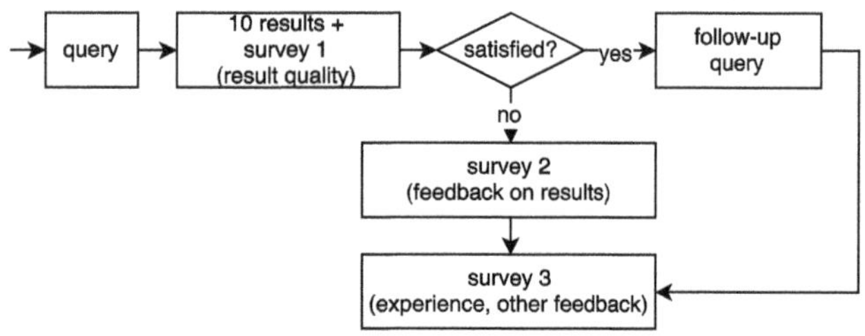

Figure 3: Flow chart describing subjects' experimental tasks.

Dataset	Total	Speaking
`input sample`	347	95 (27.4%)
`survey sample`	224	65 (29.0%)
`follow-up input sample`	151	43 (28.5%)

Table 1: Number of subjects (total, and in the speaking condition) in each dataset.

the transcribed speech using the text area, as it is not clear if these queries are representative of speech or text input. Resultantly, this excludes all users who received an empty transcription from wit.ai.

After these filtering steps, our dataset contains 347 valid queries, which we label the `input sample`. These queries were generally short in terms of character count (median 14, average 18.0) and word count (median 2, average 3.1). While 195/347 (56.4%) subjects reported having a working microphone, only 95/347 (27.4%) are in the speaking condition. This number is much lower than the expected value (~146) given the 75% random assignment rate; this is explained by two factors: (a) 40 users who manually switched into the typing condition by clicking the "my microphone isn't working" button after trying the microphone, and (b) a higher dropout rate in the speaking condition due to users who give up (and therefore do not click "send") after receiving one or more low-quality transcriptions.

We further divide subjects into two additional datasets to analyze survey responses and follow-up queries. 224/347 (64.6%) of the subjects provided complete survey responses, which we label the `survey sample`. 151/347 (43.5%) of the subjects provided a valid follow-up query, which we label the `follow-up input sample`. See Table 1 for an overview of the size of each dataset.

Overall, subjects tended to rate the quality of the MovieLens search results as "fair" — 156/224 (69.6%) of subjects reported that the results matched what they were looking for at fair or better, while the others reported "very poor" (12.9%) or "poor" (17.4%).

4 FIRST QUERIES

We code the queries from the `input sample` in several ways to facilitate frequency analysis and other forms of quantitative analysis on the dataset of transcribed user queries. Generally, we follow the inductive, open coding approach described in [18] for analyzing open-ended comments through constant comparison [7], which is based on grounded theory methods [1]. Specifically, four of the researchers involved in this project read through the dataset of user queries together, assigning new codes or refining old codes as we went. Our goal is to describe the queries in terms that will be useful to recommender system designers in our content domain.

Once we had developed a stable hierarchy of codes, two researchers separately coded 187 random responses to measure consistency and to help calibrate their coding practice (Cohen's kappa across 14 codes on 187 responses: avg=0.87; min=0.72; max=1.0). To determine the final coding used in this analysis, the two researchers then both coded *all* of the responses, then discussed and resolved disagreements.

4.1 Recommendation Goals

Inspired by classic work on categorizing web search [2, 22], we seek to understand users' underlying goals for interacting with the recommender. Similar to a search engine dedicated to searching across the web, a natural language-based interaction in a recommender system is a means to achieving a goal — in this case to find great movies to watch or to browse information about movies they are already interested in. Users express their queries in different ways in order to achieve this goal.

As with [22], our inductive coding method leads to a hierarchy of user goals, summarized in Table 2. We develop three top-level goals: objective, subjective, and navigation.

We define an *objective* goal as a request that can be answered without controversy. These goals seek to filter the movie space by specifying an attribute such as a genre, an actor, or a release date. These types of objective goals are often easy to answer using the sort of information that is typically available on movie websites. However, we find many examples of objective goals that cannot be easily answered using a typical database of movie information. We label these goals as seeking "deep features", indicating that users wish to filter movies by nuanced or specific criteria. Some examples of requests including deep features are "apocalyptic special effects" and "a movie about berlin wall".

We define a *subjective* goal as a request that involves judgment, uncertainty, and/or personalization. While objective goals tend to act as boolean filters (a movie either stars Brad Pitt or it does not), subjective goals are a more natural fit with a scoring or ordering algorithm. For instance, the query "interesting characters" might apply to many movies, some more strongly than others. Answering subjective queries — much like objective deep features — is difficult, because neither metadata databases nor recommender systems may track how much "clever plot" or "sad" a movie has.

We divide subjective goals into three common sub-types. Emotion requests tend to specify a particular feeling that a movie invokes in the viewer, e.g. "cheerful comedy". Quality requests are either explicit about wanting good/best movies (e.g., "Some *good* dystopic sci-fi would be nice."), or specify the aspects of the movie that make it good (e.g., "*classic* sci-fi movies'). Finally, movie-based requests seek related movies, e.g., "something like Pulp Fiction". We consider movie-based requests to be subjective rather than objective, because there is no objective and universally-held metric to determine the similarity between any two movies [5].

A *navigation* goal is the simplest of the three — the user wants to see one or more particular movies, so they state part or all of a title. Some examples in our dataset are "the social network" (which matches one movie) and "Star Wars" (which matches a series).

Recommendation Goal	Description	Examples
1. objective	My goal is to find movies based on their known, non-controversial attributes concerning...	
1.1 genre	...the type or category of movie	"superhero movies"
1.2 deep features	...uncommonly tracked features concerning plot, setting, or other nuanced characteristics	"movies with open endings or plot twists"
1.3 people	...the people who star in or participate in making the movie	"Brad Pitt"
1.4 release date	...when the movie was released	"can you find me a funny romantic movie made in the 2000s?"
1.5 region	...where in the world the movie is from	"british murder mystery"
1.6 language	...the primary language of the movie	"show me a list of german movies"
2. subjective	My goal is to find movies based on a quality judgment concerning...	
2.1 emotion	...the feeling of the movie	"sad movie"
2.2 quality	...the enjoyable parts of the movie	"interesting characters, clever plot"
2.3 movie-based	...the relationship to another movie	"what would you recommend to a fan of Big Lebowski?"
3. navigation	My goal is to find a particular movie by its title	"blade runner"

Table 2: Hierarchy of coded recommendation goals. A query can have more than one. E.g., "funny romantic movie made in the 2000s" codes as genre ("romantic"), quality ("funny"), and release date ("2000s").

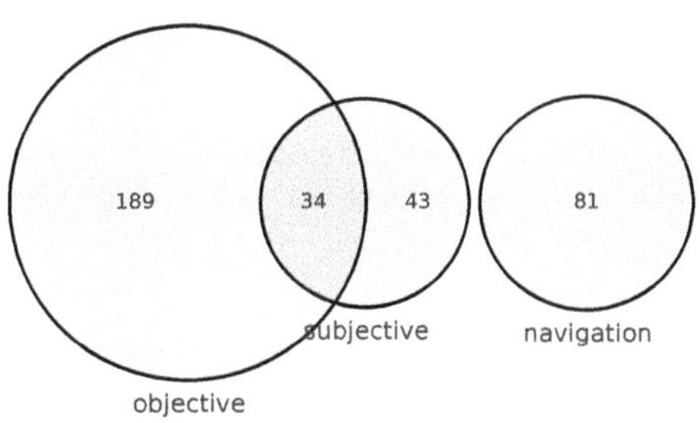

Figure 4: Venn diagram of top-level recommendation goals, which demonstrates how objective and subjective queries overlap, while navigation queries are independent.

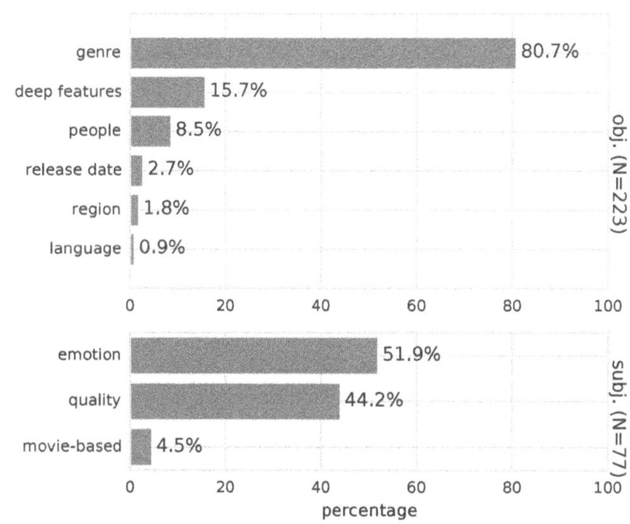

Figure 5: Percentage of objective (top) and subjective (bottom) requests containing the shown second-level goals. These goals are not mutually exclusive, therefore the bars in each chart sum to greater than 100%.

Unlike Rose and Levinson [22], our hierarchy of goals is not per-query exclusive; it is often the case that a single request contains several different goals. Users typically seek to intersect these multiple goals. For example, the query "drama movies with happy ending" combines two objective goals ("drama" genre, "happy ending" deep feature); the user wishes to find a movie with all of these qualities. We only observe two queries (2/343 = 0.6%) using the word "or", and only one of these appears to be requesting a union of multiple different goals ("movies with open endings or plot twists"). See Figure 4 for a visualization of the overlap between top-level goals, and Figure 5 for a visualization of the frequency of second-level goals in our data.

4.2 Other Coded Properties of Responses

We encoded several other properties of user responses that serve to improve our understanding of natural language queries. The coding methods, including the methods for measuring inter-rater reliability, are identical to those described above.

Conversational. Some queries are phrased as though the user is conversing with a human; we code these queries as conversational. Examples include "I'm looking for a hard sci-fi movie" and "find a movie like eternal sunshine of the spotless mind". These phrasings indicate a willingness to engage in a dialogue with a software agent. We found that 24.8% of the queries in our dataset are conversational.

Number of Modifiers. One measure of query complexity is the number of modifiers the query contains, where each modifier serves to filter or reorder the results. For example, "I'm looking for a movie that's not sad" has a single modifier ("not sad"), while "biographic dramas" has two ("biographic" [*sic*], "dramas"). Our earlier coding of recommendation goals is different from this metric because a request might have multiple components of the same type of goal (e.g., "spy thriller" and "adventure and drama" each contain two genre goals). In our dataset, 69.7% of the queries have a single modifier, 23.9% of the queries have two modifiers, 6.1% have three, and 0.3% have four (the maximum in our data).

Recommend. Some queries in our dataset explicitly seek recommended movies. Some examples are "a good movie" and "I'm looking for the best sci fi horror movie". Contrast these queries with the majority of queries where the desire for recommended movies is implicit ("looking for horror movies"), uncertain ("buddy cop movies" might seek the best movies in this genre, or a comprehensive view), or probably missing (navigation queries like "28 days later" seek a single movie, not a list). Only 4.4% of the queries in our dataset are explicit about seeking recommendations.

5 FOLLOW-UP QUERIES

Subjects who rate their search results as "fair" or better are asked to express a *follow-up query* with the prompt: "I can improve these results. Tell me more about what you want." This prompt is designed to elicit a second query, this time informed by a set of 10 search results. In this section, we qualitatively analyze queries from the subjects who complete this step (the `follow-up input sample`).

Unlike subjects' first queries, where their goals are typically explicit and recognizable, follow-up queries are commonly ambiguous with respect to their goals. For instance, a subject whose first query is "Science Fiction" and whose follow-up query is "Horror" could plausibly either be specifying an additional genre filter, or could be starting a new search.

Because of this ambiguity, in this analysis we adopt qualitative methods to identify *themes*, using word repetition and key-words-in-context methods [24]. Two coders went through the entire dataset to identify themes using these methods. The coders then discussed the emergent themes, integrated them, and extracted high-quality examples of each theme from the dataset.

In considering these findings, it is important to recognize that some subjects' initial query goals were met better than others. It is likely that the quality of the recommendations [20] affects subjects' follow-up behavior, but we do not investigate that link here.

5.1 Refine

Subjects commonly use the follow-up query to refine the initial query towards a more specific result (N=62, 41.1%). These subjects assume the system remembers their initial query, and specify *additional criteria* that they wish the recommender to consider.

Refine with further constraints. Many refinement queries suggest that the subject is still interested in the initial query, and wishes to further constrain the universe of the search space. Several examples follow (we denote the initial query with **1**, and the follow-up query with **2**):

1: a mystery drama with a suspenseful ending
2: something from the last few years

1: An action movie with a sense of humour
2: more sitcom less absurd

Refine with clarification. Other refinement queries reflect a disappointment with the initial results. These subjects attempt to help the digital assistant by providing more information:

1: Horror
2: More true horror instead of drama/ thriller

1: i'm looking for a great arts picture
2: this should really be an indie movie

5.2 Reformulate

Other subjects use the follow-up prompt to reformulate their initial query (N=34, 22.5%). These subjects appear to remain interested in their original query, but wish to *completely restate* the query to improve the recommendations. These subjects do not assume that the recommender remembers their last query, and typically reuse some portion of the original language.

Reformulate with further constraints. As with the refine queries, some subjects appear to reformulate to further narrow the set of results:

1: i'm looking for a romantic comedy
2: i'd like a romantic comedy that was created after the year 2000

1: i'm looking for time travel movie
2: I'm looking for a time travel movie that i haven't seen before

Reformulate with clarification. Other subjects reformulate queries in an attempt to encourage the system to better results:

1: a romantic comedy with a happy ending
2: romantic comedy with tensions between the couple but ends well

1: 28 days later
2: Movies like "28 days later"

5.3 Start Over

The third major theme we discovered in follow-up queries is that subjects want to start a new query (N=55, 36.4%), even though the experimental prompt says "*tell me more* about what you want" (emphasis not in the interface). These subjects may be experimenting with the system, or may realize that their first query is not at all what they are looking for:

1: mad max fury road
2: finding dory

1: red violin
2: new documentaries

6 SPEAKING VS. TYPING

The above analysis combines the recommendation-seeking queries from two modalities: speaking and typing. In this section we consider the differences in queries between these two modalities.

6.1 Subject Bias and Group Selection

We assign users in our experiment to either a `speaking` or a `typing` condition. However, our assignment procedure is non-random, as we wish to include users with no working microphone. Therefore, there are potential behavioral biases in our dataset between users in the different assignment pipelines. For instance, users who self-report no microphone might be more likely to be working on a desktop computer (vs. a portable device) or they might have less experience overall interacting with speech-activated interfaces.

See Table 3 for a summary of the number of users in each assignment category; the assignment process is shown above in Figure 2. There are three ways of reaching the typing condition, and only one way to reach the speaking condition.

We find evidence of several differences between users in the different assignment categories, which affects our subsequent analysis. We describe these findings in some detail as they reveal several interesting differences in self-reported experience and behavioral patterns. We test differences using a likelihood-ratio chi-squared test for categorical data, or a wilcoxon test for numerical data.

Subjects without a microphone self-report less frequent use of voice assistant technologies. Our survey contains the question "how often do you use a voice assistant (e.g., Google Now, Siri, etc.)?", with a six point response scale: "never" (0), "rarely" (1), "a few times a month" (2), "a few times a week" (3), "once a day" (4), "multiple times a day" (5). Subjects with a microphone (typing-random, typing-mic-not-working, and speaking-random) answered this question similarly (N=144, p=0.656). However, subjects without a microphone answered with lower scores (N=256, p<0.001). For instance, 50% of these users responded with "never" as compared with 21%-25% of subjects in the other three groups.

There are observable behavioral differences among the three assignment categories that feed into the typing condition. There are a few ways in which these three groups of subjects (a-c) behave similarly: they input approximately the same length queries (p=0.748), with a similar proportion of navigation (p=0.839) and objective (p=0.387) features. However, we find differences in the proportion of subjective features (typing-mic=10.0%, typing-mic-not-working=25.0%, typing-no-mic=28.9%; p=0.008), and conversational queries (typing-mic=6.7%, typing-mic-not-working=32.5%, typing-no-mic=19.1%; p=0.003). Subjects in group typing-mic-not-working also took longer (medians in seconds: typing-mic=17.5, typing-mic-not-working=42, typing-no-mic=20, p<0.001), though this may be explained by additional time spent determining the microphone failure and switching into the typing condition.

Due to these differences between assignment categories, we restrict this analysis to subjects in `typing-random` (N=60) and `speaking-random` (N=95). These groups are randomly assigned, and they report similar experience with voice assistant technologies (% subjects reporting 3 or higher: speaking-random=29.2%, typing-random=31.8%; p=0.386).

6.2 Results

Speaking to the recommender leads to longer queries than typing (medians in characters: speaking=19, typing=12.5; p<0.001). Related, we find that subjects in the speaking condition were much more likely to make conversational requests (proportion conversational queries: speaking=40.0%, typing=4.0%; p<0.001).

Speaking to the recommender takes more time (medians in seconds: speaking=39, typing=17.5; p<0.001). This effect may be due to time spent correcting transcription errors; possibly, the effect would disappear with a perfect voice recognition system.

Speaking leads to more queries with objective deep features (speaking=14.7%, typing=5.0%; p=0.047), and more subjective movie-based queries (speaking=5.3%, typing=0.0%; p=0.025). Other second-level type features have similar ratios between the two groups and do not show statistically significant differences in our dataset. Additionally, we did not find statistically significant differences between the two groups in terms of proportion of queries with objective (speaking=67.4%, typing=70%), subjective (speaking=17.9%, typing=10.0%), or navigation (speaking=22.1%, typing=23.3%) queries.

7 DISCUSSION

In this work, we use a prototype movie recommendation interface to learn more about how users might structure recommendation-seeking queries. Our work demonstrates both similarities and differences in how users approach recommendation and search. Our taxonomy of recommendation goals includes the concept of "navigational" queries that was developed to understand search behavior [2, 11, 27]. However, since recommendation is typically single-site, unlike web search, the other search goals from the information retrieval literature ("informational" and "transactional") are less applicable. Instead, we have chosen to model the characteristics by which users appear to filter and prioritize content — using "objective" and "subjective" criteria. Subjective queries, in particular, are interesting to consider, as they do a poor job of filtering, but provide an important signal to guide ranking. These differences highlight the shortcomings of applying current-generation search technology to the problem of natural language recommendations, and point to some of the key challenges that recommender systems researchers must overcome in developing next-generation systems.

Several prominent features of our recommendation-seeking taxonomy — namely, "objective deep features" and "subjective" features — are not easily handled by traditional recommendation algorithms. Deep features (e.g., "plot twists") are objective, but are out of the scope of entity metadata typically tracked. Subjective features (e.g., "great acting") are even more difficult, as they model opinion rather than objective truth. In our experiment, 15% of the queries contain "deep features", while 22% contain "subjective" features, underscoring their importance. One possible direction is the use of text-mining algorithms — such as the Tag Genome [29] or word2vec [17] — on unstructured text such as reviews. However, the prominence of these complex features points to a fascinating line of future work where systems combine the notion of "recommended items" with the user's contextual search for aspects such as "not violent" or "great acting".

In this research, we offered subjects the chance to follow-up their initial query, prompting "I can improve these results. Tell me

assignment category	N (input)	N (survey)	condition	has mic?	mic working?
(a) typing-no-mic	152	112	typing	no	N.A.
(b) typing-random	60	44	typing	yes	N.A.
(c) typing-mic-not-working	40	28	typing	yes	no
(d) speaking-random	95	72	speaking	yes	yes

Table 3: Four ways that users could be assigned to the typing or speaking condition. (a-d) correspond to the flowchart shown in Figure 2. Due to measured biases (explained in the text), we restrict our analysis of typing vs. speaking to groups b and d.

more about what you want." Given these instructions, we think it is surprising that many subjects issue "start-over" or "reformulate" queries. To explain this finding, we might look to information foraging theory [19] to indicate poor information scent [4] in the ten recommendations, or we might look to individuals' tendencies towards orienteering or teleporting search behaviors [27]. It is also possible that this behavior is a force of habit: frequent repeated use of search engines has trained us to understand that each query is a new query. We find that it is frequently difficult to disambiguate refine, reformulate, and start over queries, because the classification depends on the user's latent intent. Systems supporting natural language follow-up queries will have a difficult time inferring this intent, though it is critically important for determining the best recommendations. Interfaces or algorithms that naturally facilitate this disambiguation is an interesting area of future work.

While the future may bring nearly perfect voice recognition, the present offers tools that commonly make transcription errors. For ease of experimentation, to increase the pool of experimental subjects, and to avoid transcription errors such as these, researchers may wish to study natural language interfaces using typing as a surrogate for speaking. In this research, we find some key differences between these two modalities: speaking leads to longer, more conversational queries that are more likely to contain objective deep features ("plot twist") and subjective movie-based features ("movies like The Terminal"). Therefore, when text is used as a surrogate for speech, it will lead to somewhat different patterns of input, which may affect research results in some contexts.

7.1 Limitations and Future Work

Our work is based on the behavior of subjects who are seeking *movie* recommendations, and therefore it is unclear which of the findings presented here will generalize to other domains. We speculate that several of our high-level findings extend beyond the movie domain. For example, a variety of recommenders may find users expressing objective features to filter results along with subjective features to prioritize results. Also, there is nothing domain-specific to our finding that users more conversational in their queries when speaking than when typing. It is future work to confirm this speculation and to compare our current findings with natural language recommendation-seeking behaviors in other domains.

We cannot be certain that our small sample (N=347) is representative of the larger population of movie-recommendation seekers. Adding subjects from outside our experimental site – or simply expanding the pool of subjects from our site – might change the results of our frequency analysis or even reshape the outcome of our qualitative coding process. Our goal, given the scarcity of prior work on this topic, is to develop an initial, broad understanding of user behavior with a natural language recommender, which is served by a small sample. It is future work to expand this study to many users across sites to drill in on these results to further understand topics such as recommendation-seeking vocabularies or machine learning to infer recommendation-seeking goals.

Fundamentally, though we wish to explore an "open-ended" recommendation prompt, we found in internal testing that we could not simply use a Google-style interface (just an unlabeled box and a button) because users did not understand it. Therefore, we included a prompt designed to evoke a "virtual assistant" like Alexa or Cortana, stating "I can help you find movies. What are you looking for?" This prompt shapes the pattern of responses in an uncertain way. Future work might explore how different prompts — such as those employed by the Facebook Messenger-based movie recommender chatbot "And Chill" (andchill.io) — impact user requests.

8 CONCLUSION

In this paper, we describe a prototype natural language interface to a recommender system that prompts the user to open-ended recommendation requests. We study users' first interactions with the system to encourage users to express what they want, rather than the queries they know will work in a particular system.

We make several contributions to our understanding of recommender systems. To our knowledge, this is the first work to describe user recommendation requests in a natural language interface. To make sense of these requests, we contribute a taxonomy of user recommendation goals; the top-level goals are objective, subjective, and navigational. We also describe a dataset of follow-up requests, finding that while people use this second input to refine their initial request in a "critiquing" style, many others reformulate their query or start over. We study the differences between text and speech modalities, finding that speech leads users to longer, more conversational queries with more objective "deep features" and subjective "movie-based" features.

We collected a dataset of 347 users' first queries, follow-up queries, and survey responses, which we have released as an open dataset [14]; we hope this dataset will be a useful complement to this paper for systems-builders and researchers in developing the next generation of recommendation technology.

9 ACKNOWLEDGMENTS

This material is based on work supported by the National Science Foundation under grants IIS-0964695, IIS-1017697, IIS-1111201, IIS-1210863, and IIS-1218826, and by a grant from Google.

REFERENCES

[1] Andreas Bohm. 2004. Theoretical Coding: Text Analysis in Grounded Theory. In *A companion to qualitative research*. 270.

[2] Andrei Broder. 2002. A Taxonomy of Web Search. *SIGIR Forum* 36, 2 (Sept. 2002), 3–10. https://doi.org/10.1145/792550.792552

[3] Barbara L. Chalfonte, Robert S. Fish, and Robert E. Kraut. 1991. Expressive Richness: A Comparison of Speech and Text As Media for Revision. In *Proceedings of the SIGCHI Conference on Human Factors in Computing Systems (CHI '91)*. ACM, New York, NY, USA, 21–26. https://doi.org/10.1145/108844.108848

[4] Ed H. Chi, Peter Pirolli, Kim Chen, and James Pitkow. 2001. Using Information Scent to Model User Information Needs and Actions and the Web. In *Proceedings of the SIGCHI Conference on Human Factors in Computing Systems (CHI '01)*. ACM, New York, NY, USA, 490–497. https://doi.org/10.1145/365024.365325

[5] Lucas Colucci, Prachi Doshi, Kun-Lin Lee, Jiajie Liang, Yin Lin, Ishan Vashishtha, Jia Zhang, and Alvin Jude. 2016. Evaluating Item-Item Similarity Algorithms for Movies. In *Proceedings of the 2016 CHI Conference Extended Abstracts on Human Factors in Computing Systems (CHI EA '16)*. ACM, New York, NY, USA, 2141–2147. https://doi.org/10.1145/2851581.2892362

[6] Fabio Crestani and Heather Du. 2006. Written Versus Spoken Queries: A Qualitative and Quantitative Comparative Analysis. *J. Am. Soc. Inf. Sci. Technol.* 57, 7 (May 2006), 881–890. https://doi.org/10.1002/asi.v57:7

[7] Jane Dye, Irene Schatz, Brian Rosenberg, and Susanne Coleman. 2000. Constant Comparison Method: A Kaleidoscope of Data. *The Qualitative Report* 4, 1 (Jan. 2000), 1–10.

[8] Mehmet H. Göker and Cynthia A. Thompson. 2000. Personalized Conversational Case-Based Recommendation. In *Advances in Case-Based Reasoning*, Enrico Blanzieri and Luigi Portinale (Eds.). Number 1898 in Lecture Notes in Computer Science. Springer Berlin Heidelberg, 99–111. DOI: 10.1007/3-540-44527-7_10.

[9] Ido Guy. 2016. Searching by Talking: Analysis of Voice Queries on Mobile Web Search. In *Proceedings of the 39th International ACM SIGIR Conference on Research and Development in Information Retrieval (SIGIR '16)*. ACM, New York, NY, USA, 35–44. https://doi.org/10.1145/2911451.2911525

[10] Jonathan L. Herlocker, Joseph A. Konstan, Loren G. Terveen, and John T. Riedl. 2004. Evaluating Collaborative Filtering Recommender Systems. *ACM Trans. Inf. Syst.* 22, 1 (Jan. 2004), 5–53. https://doi.org/10.1145/963770.963772

[11] Bernard J. Jansen, Danielle L. Booth, and Amanda Spink. 2008. Determining the informational, navigational, and transactional intent of Web queries. *Information Processing & Management* 44, 3 (May 2008), 1251–1266. https://doi.org/10.1016/j.ipm.2007.07.015

[12] Jiepu Jiang, Wei Jeng, and Daqing He. 2013. How Do Users Respond to Voice Input Errors?: Lexical and Phonetic Query Reformulation in Voice Search. In *Proceedings of the 36th International ACM SIGIR Conference on Research and Development in Information Retrieval (SIGIR '13)*. ACM, New York, NY, USA, 143–152. https://doi.org/10.1145/2484028.2484092

[13] Maryam Kamvar and Shumeet Baluja. 2006. A Large Scale Study of Wireless Search Behavior: Google Mobile Search. In *Proceedings of the SIGCHI Conference on Human Factors in Computing Systems (CHI '06)*. ACM, New York, NY, USA, 701–709. https://doi.org/10.1145/1124772.1124877

[14] Jie Kang, Kyle Condiff, Shuo Chang, Joseph A. Konstan, Loren Terveen, and F. Maxwell Harper. 2017. Understanding How People Use Natural Language to Ask for Recommendations: Query Dataset. (June 2017). http://conservancy.umn.edu/handle/11299/188687 type: dataset.

[15] Lorraine McGinty and James Reilly. 2011. On the Evolution of Critiquing Recommenders. In *Recommender Systems Handbook*, Francesco Ricci, Lior Rokach, Bracha Shapira, and Paul B. Kantor (Eds.). Springer US, 419–453. DOI: 10.1007/978-0-387-85820-3_13.

[16] Sean M. McNee, John Riedl, and Joseph A. Konstan. 2006. Making Recommendations Better: An Analytic Model for Human-recommender Interaction. In *CHI '06 Extended Abstracts on Human Factors in Computing Systems (CHI EA '06)*. ACM, New York, NY, USA, 1103–1108. https://doi.org/10.1145/1125451.1125660

[17] Tomas Mikolov, Ilya Sutskever, Kai Chen, Greg S Corrado, and Jeff Dean. 2013. Distributed Representations of Words and Phrases and their Compositionality. In *Advances in Neural Information Processing Systems 26*, C. J. C. Burges, L. Bottou, M. Welling, Z. Ghahramani, and K. Q. Weinberger (Eds.). Curran Associates, Inc., 3111–3119.

[18] Hendrik Müller, Aaron Sedley, and Elizabeth Ferrall-Nunge. 2014. Survey Research in HCI. In *Ways of Knowing in HCI*, Judith S. Olson and Wendy A. Kellogg (Eds.). Springer New York, 229–266. DOI: 10.1007/978-1-4939-0378-8_10.

[19] Peter Pirolli and Stuart Card. 1999. Information foraging. *Psychological Review* 106, 4 (1999), 643–675. https://doi.org/10.1037/0033-295X.106.4.643

[20] Pearl Pu, Li Chen, and Rong Hu. 2011. A User-centric Evaluation Framework for Recommender Systems. In *Proceedings of the Fifth ACM Conference on Recommender Systems (RecSys '11)*. ACM, New York, NY, USA, 157–164. https://doi.org/10.1145/2043932.2043962

[21] Francesco Ricci, Lior Rokach, and Bracha Shapira. 2011. Introduction to Recommender Systems Handbook. In *Recommender Systems Handbook*, Francesco Ricci, Lior Rokach, Bracha Shapira, and Paul B. Kantor (Eds.). Springer US, 1–35. DOI: 10.1007/978-0-387-85820-3_1.

[22] Daniel E. Rose and Danny Levinson. 2004. Understanding User Goals in Web Search. In *Proceedings of the 13th International Conference on World Wide Web (WWW '04)*. ACM, New York, NY, USA, 13–19. https://doi.org/10.1145/988672.988675

[23] Sherry Ruan, Jacob O. Wobbrock, Kenny Liou, Andrew Ng, and James Landay. 2016. Speech Is 3x Faster than Typing for English and Mandarin Text Entry on Mobile Devices. *arXiv:1608.07323 [cs.HC]* (Aug. 2016).

[24] Gery W. Ryan and H. Russell Bernard. 2003. Techniques to Identify Themes. *Field Methods* 15, 1 (Feb. 2003), 85–109. https://doi.org/10.1177/1525822X02239569

[25] J. Ben Schafer, Dan Frankowski, Jon Herlocker, and Shilad Sen. 2007. Collaborative Filtering Recommender Systems. In *The Adaptive Web*, Peter Brusilovsky, Alfred Kobsa, and Wolfgang Nejdl (Eds.). Number 4321 in Lecture Notes in Computer Science. Springer Berlin Heidelberg, 291–324. DOI: 10.1007/978-3-540-72079-9_9.

[26] B. Smyth, L. McGinty, J. Reilly, and K. McCarthy. 2004. Compound Critiques for Conversational Recommender Systems. In *IEEE/WIC/ACM International Conference on Web Intelligence, 2004. WI 2004. Proceedings.* 145–151. https://doi.org/10.1109/WI.2004.10098

[27] Jaime Teevan, Christine Alvarado, Mark S. Ackerman, and David R. Karger. 2004. The Perfect Search Engine is Not Enough: A Study of Orienteering Behavior in Directed Search. In *Proceedings of the SIGCHI Conference on Human Factors in Computing Systems (CHI '04)*. ACM, New York, NY, USA, 415–422. https://doi.org/10.1145/985692.985745

[28] Cynthia A. Thompson, Mehmet H. Göker, and Pat Langley. 2004. A Personalized System for Conversational Recommendations. *J. Artif. Int. Res.* 21, 1 (March 2004), 393–428.

[29] Jesse Vig, Shilad Sen, and John Riedl. 2012. The Tag Genome: Encoding Community Knowledge to Support Novel Interaction. *ACM Trans. Interact. Intell. Syst.* 2, 3 (Sept. 2012), 13:1–13:44. https://doi.org/10.1145/2362394.2362395

[30] Steve Whittaker, Julia Hirschberg, Brian Amento, Litza Stark, Michiel Bacchiani, Philip Isenhour, Larry Stead, Gary Zamchick, and Aaron Rosenberg. 2002. SCANMail: A Voicemail Interface That Makes Speech Browsable, Readable and Searchable. In *Proceedings of the SIGCHI Conference on Human Factors in Computing Systems (CHI '02)*. ACM, New York, NY, USA, 275–282. https://doi.org/10.1145/503376.503426

Defining and Supporting Narrative-driven Recommendation

Toine Bogers
Department of Communication & Psychology
Aalborg University Copenhagen
Denmark
toine@hum.aau.dk

Marijn Koolen
Huygens ING
Netherlands
marijn.koolen@huygens.knaw.nl

ABSTRACT

Research into recommendation algorithms has made great strides in recent years. However, these algorithms are typically applied in relatively straightforward scenarios: given information about a user's past preferences, what will they like in the future? Recommendation is often more complex: evaluating recommended items never takes place in a vacuum, and it is often a single step in the user's more complex background task. In this paper, we define a specific type of recommendation scenario called narrative-driven recommendation, where the recommendation process is driven by both a log of the user's past transactions as well as a narrative description of their current interest(s). Through an analysis of a set of real-world recommendation narratives from the LibraryThing forums, we demonstrate the uniqueness and richness of this scenario and highlight common patterns and properties of such narratives.

KEYWORDS

Narrative-driven Recommendation, Query-driven Recommendation, Complex Recommendation, Conversational Recommenders

ACM Reference format:
Toine Bogers and Marijn Koolen. 2017. Defining and Supporting Narrative-driven Recommendation. In *Proceedings of RecSys'17, August 27–31, 2017, Como, Italy,* 5 pages.
DOI: http://dx.doi.org/10.1145/3109859.3109893

1 INTRODUCTION

Over the past decade, recommendation algorithms for ratings prediction and item ranking have steadily matured with matrix factorization and other latent factor models emerging as the state-of-the-art algorithms to apply in both existing and new domains. However, these algorithms are typically applied in relatively straightforward and static scenarios: given information about a user's past item preferences, can we predict whether they will like a new item or rank all unseen items based on predicted interest?

In reality, recommendation is often a more complex problem: the evaluation of a list of recommended items never takes place in a vacuum, and is often a single step in the user's more complex background need. These needs place a variety of constraints on which recommendations are interesting to the user and when they are appropriate. There is relatively little research on how to elicit rich information about these complex background needs or how to incorporate them into the recommendation process. In this paper, we focus on one particular scenario where users provide more information about their recommendation needs than just a log of their past preferences. We define a specific scenario called *narrative-driven recommendation* (NDR), where the recommendation process is driven by both a log of the user's past transactions as well as a narrative description of their current need and the context of use. An example of such a narrative request is the following: *"I'm looking for manly books about manly issues, that aren't too gritty, but make you think as much as you laugh. So far these examples I have on my bookshelf: 'About a Boy' and 'High Fidelity' by Nick Hornby, 'Train Man' by Hitori Nakano. Have you any other manly books for manly men such as I?"* (ID-B24040). It describes both different aspects of the desired books as well as providing an overview of relevant past preferences.

We argue that NDR represents a distinct scenario for recommender systems research that requires more study. One reason for this are the lessons that these narrative descriptions can teach us about recommendation in general. In addition, specific fields like conversational recommendation could also benefit from a better understanding of narrative descriptions of user needs and vice versa. This paper represents a first step in the study of NDR through the following contributions:

(1) A principled, operational definition of NDR.
(2) A motivation of NDR as a meaningful research problem by providing a quantitative analysis of its prevalence and composition.
(3) An analysis of the common patterns and properties of narrative recommendation requests to guide future research.

The rest of this paper is organized as follows. We define NDR and explain how it differs from other tasks in Section 2. Section 3 discusses the relevant related work. Section 4 then provides evidence for the importance of this recommendation scenario and attempts to map the common patterns and properties present in these rich narratives. We conclude in Section 5.

2 NARRATIVE-DRIVEN RECOMMENDATION

The focus of this paper is on supporting *narrative-driven recommendation*, which can be seen as a complex recommendation scenario where the recommendation process is driven by both a log of the user's past transactions as well as a narrative description of their current needs or interests. That is, what would make suggested items relevant to them and why are they requesting recommendations, i.e., what is the background task and context? Example scenarios could include explicitly soliciting recommendations for

RecSys'17, August 27–31, 2017, Como, Italy

978-1-4503-4652-8/17/08…$15.00
DOI: http://dx.doi.org/10.1145/3109859.3109893

a contextual need, steering generic recommendations towards a current interest, or posting a narrative description of their need on a forum, asking other forum members for suggestions.

This type of recommendation could also be seen as a form of personalized search. Recent years have indeed seen a convergence of information access paradigms. Back in 1992, Belkin already discussed the similarities between information filtering and IR [3] and more recently Furner [9] also argued that recommendation and retrieval are two sides of the same coin. The aim of this paper is not to debate whether recommendation is simply query-free search or whether search is in fact query-driven recommendation. We do, however, wish to argue that this information access problem can be effectively studied from a recommendation perspective, and to present an operational definition of NDR. We argue that NDR has two essential components:

(1) **Information about user preferences** One of the main data sources for recommendation are transaction logs containing user preferences. These can either be expressed explicitly by the user in the form of ratings or they can be captured implicitly in the form of usage information, e.g., which books has the user read? Naturally, other data sources can also be integrated into recommendation algorithms, such as information about the users, the items, or the relationships between them. However, for NDR we believe that only user preference data is essential for defining this as a recommendation problem as opposed to search. We argue that these are scenarios where a user has little trouble identifying which items are broadly relevant for them, but would instead like to know which ones are closest to their preferences, preferably with an explanation of why.

(2) **Narrative description of user need** The other component in NDR is a textual description of the user's recommendation need. One of the major differences between personalized search and NDR is the length of description provided to the system: instead of a set of 3-4 query terms [23], we are typically dealing with a longer description of one or more natural language sentences in NDR. Often, such narratives describe the type(s) of items that the user would find interesting or relevant as well as (part of) the context for requesting the recommendations. Users tend to mention one or more aspects that separate the interesting and relevant items from the irrelevant ones. Narratives combining multiple relevance aspects can be seen as complex examples of constraint-based recommendation [8], such as users who are looking for bestseller novels set in World War II for their book club. Another way users can describe which type(s) of items they would like, is by providing positive or negative example items in the hope that other users familiar with one or more of these items can identify the latent properties that connect these items to relevant unseen items. These examples can also be seen as a sparse representation of user preferences. Many narratives also describe the context (of use) for the desired recommendations: is the user asking for suggestions for a friend, is it part of a larger background task such as triggering discussion in a book club, or should it help pass the time during traveling? This element may not always be present nor necessary to provide accurate recommendations.

We wish to argue that *both* of these components have to be present for the scenario to involve NDR. An example of such an NDR need is this example from the movie domain, where the user is looking for *"films where a regular person (not a cop, spy, etc) has a mystery to solve, not related to crime or conspiracies, but still has to do "detective work" following clues and leads. An example would be last year's Walter Mitty, where the protagonist tracks down a photographer to recover a photo negative he needs. Any ideas?"* (ID-M225531765). In this case, the user describes the plot and genre elements that single out which movies could be relevant. By providing a positive example, the user indicates that this example should take precedence over their general user preferences. In cases without specific examples, the user's preferences should typically play a bigger role.

A scenario where we only have a narrative description without any information about user preferences is an example of complex search, whereas recommendation based on user preference information without a narrative description is traditional recommendation. Another, perhaps obvious requirement, is that the user must have a need for recommendations, as opposed to a *known-item* need where the user is looking for a specific item, but not able to remember the essential metadata to locate it again [14]. This allows us to formulate the following definition of NDR:

Narrative-driven recommendation is a recommendation scenario that contains (1) a narrative description of the aspects of items desired by the users ($\geq$ 1 sentence) along with an optional context of use; and (2) information about user preferences, either in the form of a transaction log of user preferences or user-provided positive and/or negative examples of other items. The narrative must describe a open request for recommendations as opposed to locating a specific item.

3 RELATED WORK

One avenue of related research is the work on query-driven recommendation. Adomavicius et al. [1, 2] introduced REQUEST, a structured query language for customizing recommendations, which can be used to specify more complex recommendation needs than just "give me items I would like", although it does not consider textual representations of recommendation needs. Hariri et al. [12] proposed a query-driven context-aware recommender system that provides recommendations based on a user's preference profile, adapted to a given situation or context that represents short-term interests or needs of a user in a given situation.

Narrative descriptions of needs and interests are typical of (human) conversational recommendation, where one person describes the kind of items they like and what they would be interested in, and others come up with suggestions and possibly explanations for why. In this sense, NDR is related to conversational and critiquing-based recommender systems, which aim to elicit more information about user needs through dialog and interaction [6, 20, 21].

Narrative requests for recommendation share similarities with product reviews in terms of their composition and complexity, in that they cover different aspects of a product with the author describing likes and dislikes. O'Mahony and Smyth [22] investigated ways of recommending reviews that offer contrasting views to help users choose between items while Dong et al. [7] extracted topical and sentiment information from reviews to identify the most informative reviews. The key difference between reviews and narrative requests is that reviews represent an evaluation of *experienced items*, whereas requests describe *unspecified items* that would fit the user's current interests.

There is a renewed focus in Information Retrieval on complex search tasks and how best to support them [11, 18]. Some of these tasks are found on the boundary between search and recommendation [17]. Complex narratives have been used in interactive IR [10] to study how users perform complex search. They are also commonly used in IR evaluation and test collection building to guide assessors [13]. However, Koolen et al. [19] found that the narratives that are written to assess artificially created topics for IR evaluation are different in nature from the narratives that users write when they ask peers for recommendations. The Social Book Search campaigns at INEX [16] and CLEF [15] found complex, narrative-focused information needs to be common in online book discussion forums, such as GoodReads and LibraryThing. We build on their work in this paper. Finally, Bogers [4] performed a similar analysis of narrative movie requests on a collection of IMDB forum threads.

4 ANALYZING NARRATIVE REQUESTS

4.1 How common are they?

Our aim with this paper is not to convince the reader that NDR is as common as regular recommendation. Formulating an explicit request takes more effort by the user than deriving implicit interests from their transactions does. The same is true for explicit user preferences: ratings and reviews are harder to come by than usage information, due to the effort required. However, NDR is not a niche problem either. Users are perhaps not as vocal about it and might simply give up before asking their peers, but we believe that if NDR systems were available, we would see many more users trying to express their complex needs, interests and preferences to such systems. Even if it were a niche problem, an analysis of such narratives could still teach us about what people might need from recommender systems in general, but cannot (yet) express.

However, there are places on the Web where we can expect to find people expressing such complex requests and where they turn to other people for help in solving their problems that current systems cannot offer: discussion forums. In this paper, we use the book domain as the setting for our analysis, but note that other domains have similar forums, such as the IMDB message boards for movies (*I Need To Know*[1] and *Lists & Recommendations*[2]), and the subreddit *Tip of My Tongue*[3] for all kinds of items.

We analyze narratives asking for recommendations on the LibraryThing (LT) discussion forums. LT is a social cataloging website with an active user community dedicated to all aspects of book cataloging, reading, and discussion. The forums are for any kind of discussion about books, with no specific group for narrative requests as they occur in many different groups. Currently, there are close to 190,000 threads in the LT forums[4], of which many are dedicated to book clubs and reading challenges. For the SBS Mining Track [5] a random sample of 3,934 threads were annotated, of which 13.1% (n = 517) were book request narratives, showing that needs for recommendations are common. It also means there are potentially nearly 25,000 book request narratives on LT already. It is worth noting that GoodReads has many more users (55 million)[5] than LT (2 million). We assume that the GoodReads user base is not fundamentally different in the complexity of the recommendation needs, so potentially many more users with similar needs exist. Since many book readers use neither platform, the total user base for NDR is potentially even larger in the book domain alone.

In this paper, we re-use a collection of 115,899 LT discussion threads originally used for the INEX 2014 Social Book Search Track [16], which contains all threads initiated between August 15, 2006 and November 6, 2012. Figure 1 shows the temporal distribution of thread starting dates (blue bars) as well as distribution of starting dates of narrative request threads (red line) from 2006 to 2011. In this period, an average of 51 threads were started every day. The number of narrative requests threads per month is significantly lower, because only around 13% of all threads contain narrative requests and because these frequencies represent a small sample of all request narratives. Data for the year 2012 was excluded from Figure 1 due to a bug in the crawler not dealing properly with a change in the thread format. However, narrative requests from 2012 were included in the rest of the analysis in this paper, because they occurred in the same proportion to all threads as the 2006-2011 data. Figure 1 shows that thread creation frequencies in general have stayed relatively constant, and that the posting frequency of requests for book recommendations follow the general trends pretty well ($r = 0.532, p < .001$). Forum activity in general is higher around the holiday periods, probably because users have more time to read and discuss reading on the LT forums.

4.2 What do they look like?

In the previous section we showed that NDR is a common scenario and, as such, deserves our attention. In this section we analyze these recommendation narratives to uncover common patterns in the kinds of aspects and contexts people describe in them. To this end, we annotated a random sample of the first posts of 1,457 narrative LT requests[6] according to whether they (1) represent a known-item search or a narrative recommendation request, (2) are at least a full sentence, (3) mention example books or authors, and (4) mention the context of use (i.e., does the reader have a specific purpose for the requested book recommendations)?

4.2.1 Narrative length. Our analysis of narrative length revealed that posts below 70 characters consist mainly of one or two short conversational sentences, and ask for topical suggestions without adding any further detail to the request. An example of such a narrative is *"YA books about Time Travel. Any recommendations?"* (ID-B64934). However, there are only 30 such posts. For 8 of these, the message body only contains the words *any suggestions* or *any recommendations* and the request is covered by the thread title. Note that for narrative length we only consider the message body. The mean (median) length of a narrative is 527 (417) characters.

[1] http://www.imdb.com/board/bd0000001/threads/, last accessed February 17, 2017
[2] http://www.imdb.com/board/bd0000122/threads/, last accessed February 17, 2017
[3] https://www.reddit.com/r/tipofmytongue/, last accessed April 1, 2017
[4] http://www.librarything.com/zeitgeist, last accessed March 30, 2017
[5] https://www.goodreads.com/about/us, last accessed on March 30, 2017
[6] Available at http://social-book-search.humanities.uva.nl/#/overview

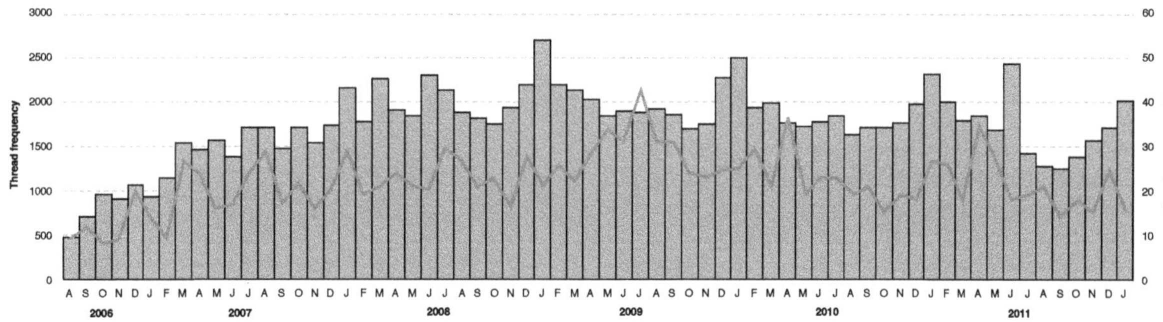

Figure 1: Thread creation frequency on the LibraryThing forums over time (blue bars, left axis), measured by the number of unique threads initiated each month. The red line (right axis) shows the creation frequency of narrative request threads.

Table 1: Distribution of examples and context-of-use over the 974 narrative requests.

		Context *Yes*	Context *No*	Total
Examples	*Yes*	209	352	561
	No	170	243	413
Total		379	595	974

Table 2: Aspect distribution and overlap in 742 requests

	A	C	E	F	M	N	S
Accessibility	*137*	96	41	48	28	8	27
Content		*598*	157	267	176	26	98
Engagement			*196*	88	40	11	24
Familiarity				*326*	74	17	45
Metadata					*179*	11	25
Novelty						*34*	10
Socio-cultural							*133*

4.2.2 Examples & Context of use. As per our definition of NDR in Section 2, we do not consider known-item requests to be examples of valid recommendation needs. Of the 1,457 forum requests, 483 (or 33.2%) are known-item needs, leaving 974 pure narrative requests. Table 1 shows a further breakdown of these 974 requests according to whether they include examples and/or an intended context of use. This gives us a better understanding of how common the different elements of narrative requests are. Users provide at least one relevant example in 58% of these narratives and an intended context of use in 39% of all cases. There are 209 (21%) narratives that contain both examples and the context of use. It is important to note that most of the 243 narratives that do not provide either, are not traditional recommendation needs as these requests still provide a long narrative describing the user's need.

4.2.3 Narrative aspects. The final element of our exploratory analysis focuses on the aspects that make recommended items relevant to the user. We used a comprehensive set of annotations for a subset of the 1,457 narratives, taken from the Suggestion task of the INEX Social Book Search evaluation campaign [16]. These topics were labeled according to eight relevance aspects, seven of which were previously identified by Reuter [24] and defined in more detail by Koolen et al. [17]: Content, Metadata, Familiarity (e.g. related to a previous reading experience), Engagement, Accessibility (e.g. language, difficulty, availability), Novelty and Socio-cultural relevance (i.e., related to the socio-cultural background of the user). We leave out the requests that have a Known-item aspect, because it represents a pure *search* task and requires different system support, leaving 742 requests for analysis. While different classification schemes could also be applied to our narrative requests, they provide a first step towards a meaningful differentiation between narratives and thereby the development of recommendation algorithms for coping with these different aspects.

Table 2 shows the distribution and co-occurrence statistics of these seven aspects over the 742 topics. Most narratives have a Content aspect where the user describes preferred characteristics of any next book(s) to read. The second-most frequent aspect is Familiarity, where narratives contain either examples of previously read books or authors and a request for similar, complementary or dissimilar items, or explicit references to previous reading experiences (e.g., books that scarred the requester or made them think). Many narratives combine Familiarity with Metadata, Content or Engagement, where the user desires focused recommendations based on examples, but is also trying to express what it is about those examples that they found salient, so using temporary 'mini-profiles' based on those examples alone is not enough. In narratives with a Novelty aspect, user express a preference for something different from what is in their profile, yet the profile may still reflect preferences for style, difficulty, language, and other aspects.

We claim that our analysis demonstrates the complexity of these narrative requests. To develop recommender systems that can support this kind of recommendation scenario, one significant challenge is coming up with solutions to transform such requests into useful input for recommendation algorithms. One way could be to define a list of interface features that allow a user to express such complex needs in a machine-readable way. Another way could be to use text mining techniques to extract such features automatically.

5 DISCUSSION & CONCLUSIONS

We believe that the time is ripe in the recommender systems field to start diverting some of its research attention to investigating more complex recommendation scenarios. Narrative-driven recommendation represents such a scenario. Its combination of traditional recommendation based on user preferences combined with a focused narrative description of the user's current interest(s) and context of use calls for new approaches that merge the best of different information access paradigms, such as recommendation, search, and text mining. NDR is not a niche problem: we believe that the tens of thousands of examples already available on the Web represent just the tip of the iceberg when it comes to more focused recommendation needs that existing systems cannot adequately meet. NDR is perhaps not as common as regular interaction with recommender systems, but this is partly the result of the inability of current systems to meet more complex recommendation needs. A better understanding of these narrative needs can teach us more about how to approach recommendation in general as well as help benefit other recommendation scenarios. Forums are just one way of eliciting complex recommendation needs. Conversational recommendation, for instance, is another elicitation technique that shares many of the underlying problems with NDR: how can we use natural language understanding to better extract the relevant signals that represent the underlying complex need? NDR are a promising resource, because they could enable easy offline experimentation with such techniques.

Promising directions for future work could therefore be to use text mining to extract more meaning from the narratives as well as the development of hybrid recommenders that can tackle both the user preference and narrative components. Another direction could be the development of interfaces to elicit these complex aspects from the users directly, bringing it closer to true conversational recommendation. Finally, in addition to books and movies [4] other domains should be studied as well, such as product discussion forums, travel forums, gaming forums, and so on.

REFERENCES

[1] Gediminas Adomavicius, Alexander Tuzhilin, and Rong Zheng. 2005. RQL: A Query Language For Recommender Systems. (2005). http://hdl.handle.net/2451/14109

[2] Gediminas Adomavicius, Alexander Tuzhilin, and Rong Zheng. 2010. REQUEST: A Query Language for Customizing Recommendations. *Information Systems Research* 22, 1 (2010).

[3] Nicholas J. Belkin and W. Bruce Croft. 1992. Information Filtering and Information Retrieval: Two Sides of the Same Coin? *Communications of the ACM* 35, 12 (1992), 29–38.

[4] Toine Bogers. 2015. Searching for Movies: An Exploratory Analysis of Movie-related Information Needs. In *Proceedings of iConference 2015*. iDEALS.

[5] Toine Bogers, Iris Hendrickx, Marijn Koolen, and Suzan Verberne. 2016. Overview of the SBS 2016 Mining Track. In *Working Notes of CLEF 2016 - Conference and Labs of the Evaluation forum, Évora, Portugal, 5-8 September, 2016*. 1053–1063.

[6] Konstantina Christakopoulou, Filip Radlinski, and Katja Hofmann. 2016. Towards Conversational Recommender Systems. In *Proceedings of the 22nd ACM SIGKDD International Conference on Knowledge Discovery and Data Mining*. ACM, 815–824.

[7] Ruihai Dong, Markus Schaal, Michael P O'Mahony, and Barry Smyth. 2013. Topic Extraction from Online Reviews for Classification and Recommendation. In *Proceedings of the Twenty-Third international joint conference on Artificial Intelligence*. AAAI Press, 1310–1316.

[8] Alexander Felfernig, Gerhard Friedrich, Dietmar Jannach, and Markus Zanker. 2015. Constraint-Based Recommender Systems. In *Recommender Systems Handbook*, Francesco Ricci, Lior Rokach, and Bracha Shapira (Eds.). Springer, 161–190.

[9] Jonathan Furner. 2002. On Recommending. *Journal of the American Society for Information Science and Technology* 53, 9 (2002), 747–763.

[10] Maria Gäde, Mark Michael Hall, Hugo C. Huurdeman, Jaap Kamps, Marijn Koolen, Mette Skov, Toine Bogers, and David Walsh. 2016. Overview of the SBS 2016 Interactive Track. In *Working Notes of CLEF 2016 - Conference and Labs of the Evaluation forum, Évora, Portugal, 5-8 September, 2016*. 1024–1038.

[11] Maria Gäde, Mark Michael Hall, Hugo C. Huurdeman, Jaap Kamps, Marijn Koolen, Mette Skov, Elaine Toms, and David Walsh. 2015. First Workshop on Supporting Complex Search Tasks. In *Proceedings of the First International Workshop on Supporting Complex Search Tasks co-located with the 37th European Conference on Information Retrieval (ECIR 2015), Vienna, Austria, March 29, 2015.*

[12] Negar Hariri, Bamshad Mobasher, and Robin Burke. 2013. Query-driven Context-aware Recommendation. In *Proceedings of the 7th ACM conference on Recommender systems*. ACM, 9–16.

[13] Donna Harman and Ellen M. Voorhees. 2006. TREC: An Overview. *ARIST* 40, 1 (2006), 113–155.

[14] Bernard J. Jansen, Danielle L. Booth, and Amanda Spink. 2008. Determining the Informational, Navigational, and Transactional Intent of Web Queries. *Information Processing & Management* 44, 3 (2008), 1251–1266.

[15] Marijn Koolen, Toine Bogers, Maria Gäde, Mark M. Hall, Iris Hendrickx, Hugo C. Huurdeman, Jaap Kamps, Mette Skov, Suzan Verberne, and David Walsh. 2016. Overview of the CLEF 2016 Social Book Search Lab. In *Experimental IR Meets Multilinguality, Multimodality, and Interaction - 7th International Conference of the CLEF Association, CLEF 2016, Évora, Portugal, September 5-8, 2016, Proceedings.* 351–370.

[16] Marijn Koolen, Toine Bogers, Jaap Kamps, Gabriella Kazai, and Michael Preminger. 2014. Overview of the INEX 2014 Social Book Search Track. In *Working Notes for CLEF 2014 Conference, Sheffield, UK, September 15-18, 2014*. 462–479.

[17] Marijn Koolen, Toine Bogers, Jaap Kamps, and Antal van den Bosch. 2015. Looking for Books in Social Media: An Analysis of Complex Search Requests. In *ECIR '15: Proceedings of the 37th European Conference on Information Retrieval (Lecture Notes in Computer Science)*, Vol. 9022. Springer, 184–196.

[18] Marijn Koolen, Jaap Kamps, Toine Bogers, Nicholas J. Belkin, Diane Kelly, and Emine Yilmaz. 2017. Current Research in Supporting Complex Search Tasks. In *Proceedings of the Second Workshop on Supporting Complex Search Tasks co-located with the ACM SIGIR Conference on Human Information Interaction & Retrieval (CHIIR 2017), Oslo, Norway, March 11, 2017*. 1–4.

[19] Marijn Koolen, Jaap Kamps, and Gabriella Kazai. 2012. Social Book Search: Comparing Topical Relevance Judgements and Book Suggestions for Evaluation. In *CIKM '12: Proceedings of the 21st ACM International Conference on Information and Knowledge Management*, Xue-wen Chen, Guy Lebanon, Haixun Wang, and Mohammed J. Zaki (Eds.). ACM, 185–194.

[20] Tariq Mahmood and Francesco Ricci. 2009. Improving Recommender Systems with Adaptive Conversational Strategies. In *Proceedings of the 20th ACM Conference on Hypertext and Hypermedia*. ACM, 73–82.

[21] Lorraine McGinty and James Reilly. 2011. On the Evolution of Critiquing Recommenders. In *Recommender Systems Handbook*, Francesco Ricci, Lior Rokach, Bracha Shapira, and Paul B. Kantor (Eds.). Springer, 419–453.

[22] Michael P O'Mahony and Barry Smyth. 2010. A Classification-based Review Recommender. *Knowledge-Based Systems* 23, 4 (2010), 323–329.

[23] Greg Pass, Abdur Chowdhury, and Cayley Torgeson. 2006. A Picture of Search. In *InfoScale '06: The First International Conference on Scalable Information Systems.*

[24] Kara Reuter. 2007. Assessing Aesthetic Relevance: Children's Book Selection in a Digital Library. *JASIST* 58, 12 (2007), 1745–1763.

Recommending Product Sizes to Customers

Vivek Sembium
Amazon Development Center India
viveksem@amazon.com

Rajeev Rastogi
Amazon Development Center India
rastogi@amazon.com

Atul Saroop
Amazon Development Center India
asaroop@amazon.com

Srujana Merugu*
srujana@gmail.com

ABSTRACT

We propose a novel latent factor model for recommending product size fits {Small, Fit, Large} to customers. Latent factors for customers and products in our model correspond to their physical true size, and are learnt from past product purchase and returns data. The outcome for a customer, product pair is predicted based on the difference between customer and product true sizes, and efficient algorithms are proposed for computing customer and product true size values that minimize two loss function variants. In experiments with Amazon shoe datasets, we show that our latent factor models incorporating personas, and leveraging return codes show a 17-21% AUC improvement compared to baselines. In an online A/B test, our algorithms show an improvement of 0.49% in percentage of Fit transactions over control.

CCS CONCEPTS

•**Information systems** →**Collaborative filtering; Recommender systems;**

KEYWORDS

Personalization, Hinge Loss, Recommendation, Latent Factors, Ordinal Loss

1 INTRODUCTION

Product categories such as shoes and apparel have huge sizing variations across brands and locales, which makes it difficult to pick the right size for a desired product. For example, the catalog size to physical size mapping convention for Reebok is: 6 = 15cm, 7 = 17cm, 8 = 21cm, while that for Nike is: 6 = 16cm, 7 = 18cm, 8 = 22cm. Poorly chosen fits and wasteful strategies on part of the customers (e.g. buying multiple sizes of a product and returning the rest) result in very high return rates. A large number of customers also shy away from purchasing online in these product categories due to the effort involved in choosing the right sized product. Hence, e-commerce companies such as Amazon have a huge interest in being able to automatically provide highly accurate sizing guidance about products to customers.

*Work done while author was at Amazon.

RecSys '17, August 27–31, 2017, Como, Italy.

978-1-4503-4652-8/17/08.
DOI: http://dx.doi.org/10.1145/3109859.3109891

In the size recommendation problem, a customer implicitly provides the context of a desired product by viewing the detail page of a product and requires a recommendation for the appropriate size variant of the product. For example, the customer might be viewing the detail page of Nike Women's Tennis Classic shoe and needs to choose from 10 different size variants corresponding to sizes from 6 to 15. Thus, given the context of a desired product, our objective is to recommend the appropriate size variant for a customer.

The problem of recommending sizes to customers is challenging due to the following reasons:

- *Data sparsity.* Typically, a small fraction of customers and products account for the bulk of purchases. A majority of customers and products have very few purchases.
- *Cold start.* The environment is highly dynamic with new customers and products (that have no past purchases) for which size recommendation need to be generated.
- *Multiple personas.* Many users tend to shop for their families (e.g., spouses, children) and occasionally even purchase gifts for friends. Thus, a customer account may have multiple underlying personas with widely varying sizes. In order to make accurate size recommendations, it is important to separate out these personas and learn the individual sizes for each customer persona.

In this paper, we propose a novel latent factor model for determining how a product of certain size fits a customer, i.e., {Small, Fit, Large}. Latent factors for customers and products in our model correspond to their physical true sizes (e.g. for dimensions like length and width), and are learnt from past product purchase and returns data. The true (latent) sizes of customers and products are used to predict the fit outcome for each product purchased by a customer. Specifically, for each (customer, product) purchase transaction, our model outputs a score that is a (linear) function of the difference between customer and product true sizes, which is then used to predict the outcome. We present a construction that reduces a loss function with ordinal outcomes to a new loss function with binary outcomes. We define Hinge loss and Logistic loss variants, and propose efficient algorithms with linear time complexity for computing customer and product true size values that minimize the two loss variants.

We show how features of customers (e.g. demographic information such as age, gender, past return rates) and products (e.g. brand, catalog size, category) can be incorporated into our model to handle data sparsity and cold start scenarios involving (new) customers and products for whom we have very few or no purchase transactions. Finally, we extend our formulation to address the case where each customer corresponds to multiple personas and propose a hierarchical clustering algorithm to discover the different underlying personas for each customer. In experiments with Amazon shoe datasets, we show that our latent factor models incorporating personas, and leveraging return codes show a 17-21% AUC improvement compared to baselines. Furthermore, our algorithms can learn customer and product true sizes from large datasets containing millions of purchase transactions in a few minutes.

The remainder of the paper is organized as follows. After surveying prior work on recommendations and latent factor models in Section 2, we formally define our size recommendation problem in Section 3. In Section 4, we reduce our ordinal regression problem to multiple binary classification problems, and consider different binary loss function variants such as Hinge loss and Logistic loss. In Section 5, we propose efficient algorithms with linear time complexity for computing customer and product true size values that minimize the two loss variants. We show how our algorithms can be extended to leverage customer and product features, handle multiple personas within each customer account, and infer multi-dimensional true size vectors for customers and products in Sections 6-8. We compare our proposed product size recommendation algorithms to baselines on real-life Amazon Shoes data in Section 9, and offer concluding remarks in Section 10.

2 RELATED WORK

There is a vast body of research on latent factor models. The most predominant techniques are based on matrix factorization. [1, 2, 14]. Subsequently, there have been many extensions such as [5] to model general non-gaussian distributions, [6] based on tensor factorization, [4, 6] for dynamic extensions to capture varying user preferences, [7, 8] based on bilinear models, among many others. There have also been Bayesian approaches for recommendation systems [3, 9, 10], and techniques that leverage additional information like product meta data, user reviews and so on [12, 13].

The above-mentioned prior work on the general recommendation problem is based on learning a context independent representation. It learns latent factors with information aggregated across multiple contexts. The size recommendation problem is a special case of the general recommendation problem, where the only context of interest is the semantics of physical size of customers and products in a transaction, and its relationship to the physical fitment provided by the customer ({`Small`, `Fit`, `Large`}). Clearly, the general recommendation problem is not suitable for size recommendation as the learnt context independent representation has potential loss in information due to aggregation across contexts (such as personas).

We also note that there has been research on context aware recommender systems such as [17, 18], tensor factorization based recommender systems such as [15, 16] and physical context based recommender systems such as [19]. These techniques are not suitable for size recommendation that involves recommending a single precise size that best fits the customer, and leveraging ordinal information such as the catalog size ordering of products and customer returns data indicating product fitment for the customer. The physical context in these approaches refers to the current state of the user and the environment such as weather, humidity, location etc., but are not suitable to model the physical context of size and its relationship to the customer return data.

Our proposed model is also closely related to paired comparison models such as the Thurstone model [21] and Bradley-Terry model [20], which deal with modeling the outcomes of comparison between pairs of entities. These models are often used in psychometrics for comparing choices and in sports ratings (e.g., Elo ratings for chess) for comparing player performances. As in the current problem formulation, the goal is to estimate a latent factor (e.g., goodness of a choice, player's ability) associated with the entities such that the difference in the latent factor values determines the comparison outcome. However, the latent factors in traditional paired comparison models are only single dimensional unlike the proposed model that allows multi-dimensional latent vectors. The proposed model also extends the paired-comparison models by allowing weighting along the different dimensions, inclusion of feature effects, and handling sub-entities (e.g., personas within a customer account).

3 SIZE RECOMMENDATION PROBLEM

A product in categories such as shoes or apparel has multiple sizes. We will refer to the product as *parent* product and the different size variations as *child* products of the parent product. We will denote the set of all child products by $\mathcal{P}$ and the set of all customers by C. We have access to the set of past customer transactions $\mathcal{D}$ where each transaction in $\mathcal{D}$ is a triple of the form (customer, child product, return code). Specifically, each transaction has the form (i, j, y_{ij}) where i is the customer making the purchase, j is the purchased child product, and y_{ij} is either `Fit` if the customer does not return the product, or the return code provided by the customer when returning the purchased product, which can be `Small` or `Large`. For each child product j, we also have access to the catalog size c_j provided by the manufacturer.

In this paper, our objective is to recommend for a (customer, parent product) pair, the child product with the best size fit. We do this by inferring the true (latent) sizes of customers and child products using past transactions in $\mathcal{D}$. Let s_i denote the true size for customer i and t_j be the true size for child product j. Once we have the true sizes, we recommend the child product j whose true size t_j is closest to the customer's true size s_i. To simplify the presentation, in the remainder of the paper, we will refer to child products as simply products.

As mentioned earlier, we leverage past customer transactions in $\mathcal{D}$ to deduce true sizes for customers and products. Intuitively, if $\mathcal{D}$ contains a transaction $(i, j, \texttt{Fit})$, then the true sizes s_i and t_j must be close, that is, $|s_i - t_j|$ must be small. On the other hand, if transaction $(i, j, \texttt{Small}) \in \mathcal{D}$, then the customer true size s_i must be much larger than the product true size t_j, or alternately, $s_i - t_j$ must be large. Similarly, if transaction $(i, j, \texttt{Large}) \in \mathcal{D}$, then the customer true size s_i must be much smaller than the product true size t_j, or alternately, $t_j - s_i$ must be large. Let $f_w(s_i, t_j) = w \cdot (s_i - t_j)$ be our (linear) model with weight parameter $w \geq 0$. Furthermore, let $L(y_{ij}, f_w(s_i, t_j))$ be a loss function that takes on large values (and thus penalizes s_i, t_j values) for transactions (i, j, y_{ij}) such that: (1) $y_{ij} = \texttt{Fit}$ and $|f_w(s_i, t_j)|$ is large (exceeds a threshold value), (2)

y_{ij} = Small and $f_w(s_i, t_j)$ is a large negative quantity (falls below a threshold value), or (3) y_{ij} = Large and $f_w(s_i, t_j)$ is a large positive quantity (exceeds a threshold value). Then, what we seek are true size values s_i, t_j that minimize the loss function over transactions in $\mathcal{D}$.

The size recommendation problem can thus be formally stated as follows:

Problem Statement: Given past customer transactions $\mathcal{D}$, catalog sizes $\{c_j\}$ for products, and loss function $L(y_{ij}, f_w(s_i, t_j))$ for transactions $(i, j, y_{ij}) \in \mathcal{D}$, compute true sizes $\{s_i\}$ for customers and $\{t_j\}$ for child products such that $\mathcal{L} = \sum_{(i,j,y_{ij}) \in \mathcal{D}} L(y_{ij}, f_w(s_i, t_j))$ is minimized. □

In the following sections, we first define different loss functions $L(y_{ij}, f_w(s_i, t_j))$, and then present algorithms for computing true sizes and parameter values that minimize the loss functions. We initially assume single-dimensional size values, and later in Section 8, we show how our schemes can be generalized to handle multi-dimensional size vectors.

4 LOSS FUNCTIONS

The values of the outcome y_{ij} in each transaction are one of Small, Fit or Large. There is an inherent ordering among these values and so it is preferable to model our loss function minimization problem as an ordinal regression problem. Li and Lin [11] present a detailed discussion on deriving loss functions appropriate for outcomes with multiple discrete ordered levels by reducing the ordinal regression problem to multiple binary classification problems. The construction expresses loss function L with ordinal outcomes Small, Fit and Large in terms of a new loss function L^{bin} with binary outcomes in $\{-1, +1\}$.

$$L(y_{ij}, f_w(s_i, t_j)) = \begin{cases} L^{bin}(+1, f_w(s_i, t_j) - b_2) & \text{if } y_{ij} = \texttt{Small} \\ (L^{bin}(-1, f_w(s_i, t_j) - b_2) & \\ +L^{bin}(+1, f_w(s_i, t_j) - b_1)) & \text{if } y_{ij} = \texttt{Fit} \\ L^{bin}(-1, f_w(s_i, t_j) - b_1) & \text{if } y_{ij} = \texttt{Large} \end{cases} \tag{1}$$

Above b_1 and b_2 are threshold parameters with $b_2 > b_1$ that split the model score $f_w(s_i, t_j)$ line into three segments such that a model score greater than b_2 corresponds to Small, a score less than b_1 corresponds to Large, and scores in between b_1 and b_2 correspond to Fit. As a result, if y_{ij} = Small then we want the model score $f_w(s_i, t_j)$ to be greater than b_2 and so we assign a positive class label (+1) to $f_w(s_i, t_j) - b_2$. On the other hand, if y_{ij} = Fit then we want the model score $f_w(s_i, t_j)$ to be less than b_2 and so we assign a negative class label (−1) to $f_w(s_i, t_j) - b_2$.

We can use any of the binary loss functions such as Hinge loss $L^{hinge}(y, \hat{y}) = \max\{0, 1 - y \cdot \hat{y}\}$ or Logistic loss $L^{logistic}(y, \hat{y}) = \log(\frac{1}{1+e^{-y \cdot \hat{y}}})$ for the binary loss function L^{bin}. Substituting L^{hinge} for L^{bin} in Equation (1) above, we get the following loss function values for Hinge loss:

ALGORITHM 1: Algorithm for computing customer and product true sizes.

ComputeTrueSizes(C, $\mathcal{P}$, $\mathcal{D}$, $\{c_j\}$)

```
1: for each product j, t_j = c_j.
2: w = 1; b_1 = −1; b_2 = +1.
3: while (not converged) and (numIterations < maxIterations) do
4:    for each customer i, s_i = argmin_{s_i}(L | {t_j}, w, b_1, b_2).
5:    for each product j, t_j = argmin_{t_j}(L | {s_i}, w, b_1, b_2).
6:    w, b_1, b_2 = argmin_{w,b_1,b_2}(L | {s_i}, {t_j}).
7: end while
8: return {{s_i}, {t_j}, w, b_1, b_2}.
```

$$L(y_{ij}, f_w(s_i, t_j)) = \begin{cases} \max\{0, 1 - f_w(s_i, t_j) + b_2)\} & \text{if } y_{ij} = \texttt{Small} \\ (\max\{0, 1 + f_w(s_i, t_j) - b_2)\} & \\ + \max\{0, 1 - f_w(s_i, t_j) + b_1)\}) & \text{if } y_{ij} = \texttt{Fit} \\ \max\{0, 1 + f_w(s_i, t_j) - b_1)\} & \text{if } y_{ij} = \texttt{Large} \end{cases} \tag{2}$$

The Hinge loss function values for Fit, Small and Large transactions with respect to customer true size s_i are shown in Figures 1, 2 and 3, respectively.

Similarly, substituting $L^{logistic}$ for L^{bin} in Equation (1) above gives us the following loss function values for Logistic loss:

$$L(y_{ij}, f_w(s_i, t_j)) = \begin{cases} \log(\frac{1}{1+e^{-f_w(s_i,t_j)+b_2}}) & \text{if } y_{ij} = \texttt{Small} \\ (\log(\frac{1}{1+e^{f_w(s_i,t_j)-b_2}}) & \\ + \log(\frac{1}{1+e^{-f_w(s_i,t_j)+b_1}})) & \text{if } y_{ij} = \texttt{Fit} \\ \log(\frac{1}{1+e^{f_w(s_i,t_j)-b_1}}) & \text{if } y_{ij} = \texttt{Large} \end{cases} \tag{3}$$

5 ALGORITHMS FOR COMPUTING TRUE SIZES

In this section, we present algorithms for computing true size values $\{s_i\}$ for customers and $\{t_j\}$ for products (as well as the optimal scaling factor w, and the thresholds b_1, b_2) that minimize $\mathcal{L} = \sum_{(i,j,y_{ij}) \in \mathcal{D}} L(y_{ij}, f_w(s_i, t_j))$ for different loss functions such as Hinge Loss and Logistic Loss.

5.1 Hinge Loss

We consider Hinge loss because it can be optimized more efficiently and it also provides an upper bound on the zero one loss resulting in good generalization error bounds. Our algorithm (see Algorithm 1) computes true size values in an iterative manner with each iteration split into three phases that focus on computing customer true sizes while keeping product true sizes and parameter values fixed (Phase 1), computing product true sizes while keeping customer true sizes and parameter values fixed (Phase 2), and computing parameter values while keeping product and customer true sizes fixed (Phase 3). We describe the three phases in detail below.

For each product j, the true size t_j is initialized to the catalog size c_j (e.g. provided by the manufacturer). Furthermore, the thresholds b_1 and b_2 are initialized to -1 and +1, respectively, and the scaling factor w is initialized to 1. The algorithm terminates once the true

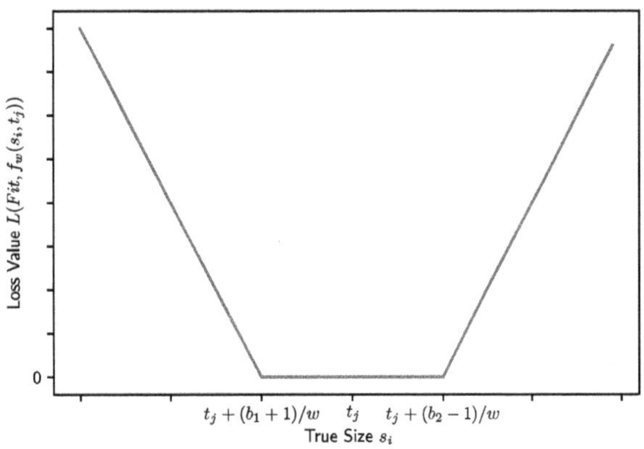

Figure 1: Hinge loss value for a `Fit` transaction vs s_i.

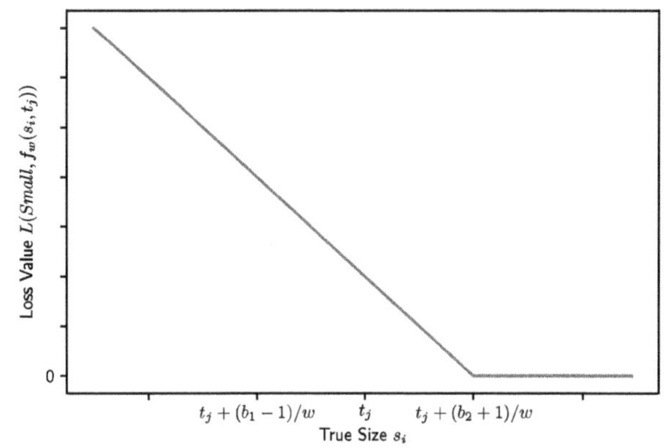

Figure 2: Hinge loss value for a `Small` transaction vs s_i.

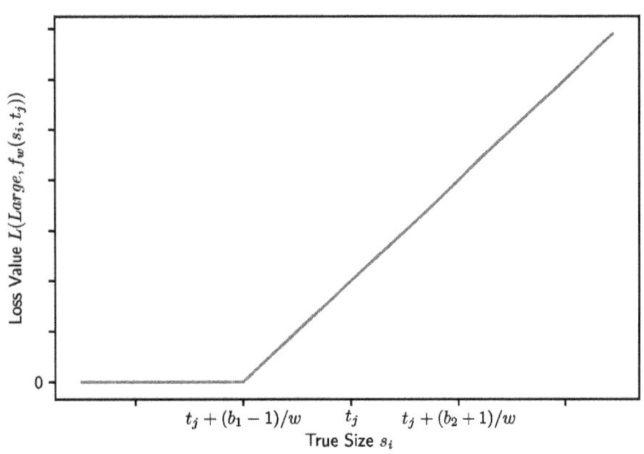

Figure 3: Hinge loss value for a `Large` transaction vs s_i.

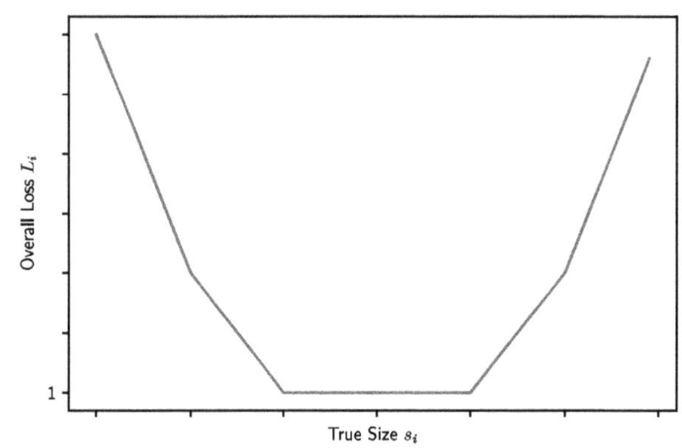

Figure 4: Illustrative overall hinge loss vs s_i.

size values converge or the number of iterations exceeds the max number of iterations.

Phase 1: Computing customer true sizes $\{s_i\}$. Figure 4 shows how the loss function $L(y_{ij}, f_w(s_i, t_j))$ value varies with s_i for Hinge loss (see Equation (2)). As can be seen, the slope of the loss function changes at $t_j + \frac{b_1-1}{w}$ for y_{ij} = `Large` (Figure 3), at $t_j + \frac{b_1+1}{w}$ and $t_j + \frac{b_2-1}{w}$ for y_{ij} = `Fit` (Figure 1), and at $t_j + \frac{b_2+1}{w}$ for y_{ij} = `Small` (Figure 2). Furthermore, the loss function is convex and its slope only increases as s_i is increased.

Now, lets look at the overall loss function $\mathcal{L} = \sum_{(i,j,y_{ij})\in\mathcal{D}} L(y_{ij}, f_w(s_i, t_j))$. This does not have any (direct) coupling between customer sizes s_i and so s_i values that minimize the overall loss function can be computed independently. Specifically, for each s_i, we seek the size value that minimizes $\mathcal{L}_i = \sum_{(i,j,y_{ij})\in\mathcal{D}} L(y_{ij}, f_w(s_i, t_j))$ which is the sum of loss function values $L(y_{ij}, f_w(s_i, t_j))$ over products j purchased by i. Thus,

$$\begin{aligned}\mathcal{L}_i = &\sum_{(i,j,y_{ij})\in\mathcal{D}\wedge y_{ij}=\texttt{Small}} \max\{0, 1 - f_w(s_i, t_j) + b_2\} \\ &+ \sum_{(i,j,y_{ij})\in\mathcal{D}\wedge y_{ij}=\texttt{Fit}} (\max\{0, 1 + f_w(s_i, t_j) - b_2\} \\ &\qquad + \max\{0, 1 - f_w(s_i, t_j) + b_1\}) \\ &+ \sum_{(i,j,y_{ij})\in\mathcal{D}\wedge y_{ij}=\texttt{Large}} \max\{0, 1 + f_w(s_i, t_j) - b_1\}\end{aligned}$$

We now present an efficient scheme with time complexity linear in the size of $\mathcal{D}$ for computing the optimal s_i value that minimizes $\mathcal{L}_i$. Let

$$\begin{aligned}\mathcal{S}_i =& \{t_j + \frac{b_2+1}{w} | (i,j,y_{ij}) \in \mathcal{D} \wedge y_{ij} = \texttt{Small}\} \\ &\cup \{t_j + \frac{b_1+1}{w}, t_j + \frac{b_2-1}{w} | (i,j,y_{ij}) \in \mathcal{D} \wedge y_{ij} = \texttt{Fit}\} \\ &\cup \{t_j + \frac{b_1-1}{w} | (i,j,y_{ij}) \in \mathcal{D} \wedge y_{ij} = \texttt{Large}\}\end{aligned}$$

Observe that $\mathcal{L}_i$ is continuous, piecewise linear in s_i and convex (since it is the sum of convex loss functions). Figure 4 shows the value of $\mathcal{L}_i$ as the value of s_i is varied. As can be seen, the slope of $\mathcal{L}_i$ is non-decreasing as s_i is increased and transition points for the slope occur at s_i values in $\mathcal{S}_i$. Thus, the optimal s_i value that minimizes $\mathcal{L}_i$ can be determined by traversing the values in $\mathcal{S}_i$ in increasing order and selecting s_i to be the smallest value where the slope of $\mathcal{L}_i$ becomes non-negative.

Phase 2: Computing product true sizes $\{t_j\}$. Similar to customer true size estimation, for each product j, we need to find the size value that minimizes the sum of loss function values $\mathcal{L}'_j = \sum_{(i,j,y_{ij})\in\mathcal{D}} L(y_{ij}, f_w(s_i, t_j))$ over customers i who purchase j. Let

$$\begin{aligned}\mathcal{S}'_j =& \{s_i - \frac{b_2+1}{w} | (i,j,y_{ij}) \in \mathcal{D} \wedge y_{ij} = \texttt{Small}\}\\ &\cup \{s_i - \frac{b_1+1}{w}, s_i - \frac{b_2-1}{w} | (i,j,y_{ij}) \in \mathcal{D} \wedge y_{ij} = \texttt{Fit}\}\\ &\cup \{s_i - \frac{b_1-1}{w} | (i,j,y_{ij}) \in \mathcal{D} \wedge y_{ij} = \texttt{Large}\}\end{aligned}$$

The optimal t_j value that minimizes $\mathcal{L}'_j$ can be determined by traversing values in $\mathcal{S}'_j$ is increasing order and selecting the value where the slope of $\mathcal{L}'_j$ becomes non-negative.

Phase 3: Computing model parameter values $\{w, b_1, b_2\}$. Once the true sizes of customers and products are estimated, we fix them and estimate optimal values of the scaling factor w and thresholds b_1, b_2 that minimize $\mathcal{L}$ using any gradient descent algorithm (e.g. SGD).

5.2 Handling General Loss Functions

In the previous subsection, we presented an efficient algorithm for computing customer and product true size values when the loss function is Hinge loss. We can compute true size values $\{s_i\}$ for customers and $\{t_j\}$ for products that minimize $\mathcal{L}$ for other loss functions such as logistic loss (see Equation (3)) as well. Our algorithm is iterative, and in each iteration, alternates between computing s_i, t_j values and parameters w, b_1 and b_2. Specifically, in each iteration, the algorithm first uses gradient descent to compute s_i, t_j values with fixed w, b_1, b_2 values, and then uses gradient descent to compute w, b_1, b_2 values with fixed s_i, t_j values.

6 LEVERAGING CUSTOMER AND PRODUCT FEATURES

We can improve the accuracy of our model, combat data sparsity and handle cold start scenarios by leveraging additional information in the form of user features such as age, gender, Prime subscription, etc. and product features such as brand, category, product type, etc. Our new (linear) model with customer and product features x_{ij} is $f_w = w \cdot (s_i - t_j) + w_x \cdot x_{ij}$ – here w_x are the weights for features x_{ij}. Previous iterative algorithms for Hinge loss and Logistic loss can be extended to learn the weight parameters w_x for features as follows. In each iteration, the algorithms first compute s_i, t_j values (using the algorithms described in Sections 5.1 and 5.2 for Hinge loss and Logistic loss, respectively), and then use gradient descent to compute w, w_x, b_1, b_2 values with fixed s_i, t_j values.

ALGORITHM 2: Algorithm for computing customer persona and product true sizes.

ComputeTrueSizesPersonas(C, $\mathcal{P}$, $\mathcal{D}$, $\{c_j\}$)

```
for each product j, t_j = c_j.
w = 1; b_1 = −1; b_2 = +1.
while (not converged) and (numIterations < maxIterations) do
    for each customer i do
        Cluster purchase transactions (i, j, y_ij) of i in D into clusters
        C_1, ..., C_k.
        for each cluster C_l, replace every transaction (i, j, y_ij) ∈ C_l
        with (i_l, j, y_ij) ∈ D.
    end for
    for each customer persona i_l,
    s_il = argmin_{s_il}(L|{t_j}, w, w_x, b_1, b_2).
    for each product j, t_j = argmin_{t_j}(L|{s_il}, w, w_x, b_1, b_2).
    w, w_x, b_1, b_2 = argmin_{w, w_x, b_1, b_2}(L|{s_il}, {t_j}).
end while
return {{s_il}, {t_j}, w, b_1, b_2}.
```

7 HANDLING PERSONAS

In practice, a customer account may be shared by multiple individuals with different sizes, for e.g., different family members including children and adults. Thus, learning a single true size per customer account may lead to inaccurate true size estimates. In this section, we present a hierarchical clustering algorithm for identifying the personas within each customer account and grouping together the purchase transactions in $\mathcal{D}$ for each persona.

Algorithm 2 describes our algorithm for handling personas when computing customer and product true sizes. The algorithm is similar to Algorithm 1 except for the two points below:

- At the start of each iteration, for each customer i, the customer transactions $(i, j, y_{ij}) \in \mathcal{D}$ with `Fit` outcome are clustered based on the purchased product true sizes t_j. (The true sizes t_j are initialized to the catalog sizes c_j.) A hierarchical agglomerative clustering algorithm is used to cluster the customer's transactions. The algorithm iteratively merges clusters as long as the standard deviation of each merged cluster does not exceed a threshold σ_{max}. (σ_{max} is a hyper-parameter which is tuned by cross validation.) Let $C_1, \ldots, C_k$ be k clusters obtained as a result of clustering the `Fit` transactions belonging to customer i. Further, let m_l be the mean of t_j values for transactions in cluster C_l. Next, the `Small` and `Large` transactions (i, j, y_{ij}) of customer i are assigned to one of the k clusters as follows: (1) If y_{ij} = `Small`, then the transaction is added to cluster C_l where l is the index of the cluster with the smallest m_l value greater than t_j, and (2) If y_{ij} = `Large`, then the transaction is added to cluster C_l where l is the index of the cluster with the largest m_l value less than t_j. The k clusters $C_1, \ldots, C_k$ correspond to transactions of personas for customer i.
- After the clustering step, let $C_1, \ldots, C_k$ be k clusters corresponding to personas for customer i. We treat each persona with transactions in the lth cluster C_l as a separate customer i_l. Thus, all transactions $(i, j, y_{ij}) \in \mathcal{D}$ belonging to

cluster C_l are replaced with transactions (i_l, j, y_{ij}) where i_l is the new customer corresponding to the persona for cluster C_l. The algorithms described in Sections 5 and 6 are then run on the new set of transactions belonging to customer personas to compute the true size values $\{s_{i_l}\}, \{t_j\}$ and parameters w, w_x, b_1, b_2.

8 EXTENSION TO MULTI-DIMENSIONAL SIZES

We can extend our techniques to infer multi-dimensional true size vectors for customers and products. The various dimensions capture different aspects related to size such as length and width for shoes, or waist and length for jeans. We define $f_{\mathbf{w}}(\mathbf{s_i}, \mathbf{t_j})$ for a 2 dimensional formulation as follows: $f_{\mathbf{w}}(\mathbf{s_i}, \mathbf{t_j}) = w_1(s_{i_1} - t_{j_1}) + w_2(s_{i_2} - t_{j_2})$, where w_1 and w_2 represent length and width scaling parameters, respectively, s_{i_1} and s_{i_2} represent customer length and width, respectively, and t_{j_1} and t_{j_2} represent product length and width, respectively.

We assume a transaction with physical fitment "Fit" corresponds to a product fitting the customer on both length and width dimensions. Correspondingly, the Algorithm 1 can be first applied to learn the customer true width s_{i_2} using only "Fit" transactions (ignoring step 6). Then a modified version of Algorithm 1 that (1) initializes the learnt customer width (s_{i_2}) and manufacturer provided catalog sizes (t_{j_1}, t_{j_2}), and (2) updates sizes s_{i_1}, s_{i_2}, t_{j_1} and t_{j_2} followed by model parameters w_1 and w_2 in that order using a procedure similar to Section 5.1. The above procedure can similarly be extended to any given d-dimensional customer and product vectors.

9 EXPERIMENTS

In order to measure the performance of our proposed models, we evaluated our techniques on offline Amazon Shoes datasets, and also carried out an online A/B test for the Mobile & Tablet experience. Our offline experimental setup is described in Section 9.1, while Section 9.2 provides details about the data and offline experimental results. The results from the online A/B test is noted in Section 9.3.

9.1 Offline Experimental Setup

For measuring performance of our models on offline datasets, we compare our results against a baseline model that uses the catalog size as a proxy for the latent size of a product and estimates a customers latent size as the average of all catalog sizes for that customer's transactions with a *fitSuitabilityCode* of `Fit`. However, note that the offline datasets are restrictive in nature for our setting. In such a setup, since our recommended sizes were never shown to the customer, we never get to know the customer's response to our recommendations. The only datapoint that we observe is the transaction that the customer carried out and the resultant *fitSuitabilityCode* of the transaction. Hence, in the offline setting we compare size recommendation schemes by their ability to predict the *fitSuitabilityCode* outcome of unseen transactions. We equate such an ability to the power of a classifier which takes the learnt latent product and customer sizes of the size recommendation algorithm as input and predicts the *fitSuitabilityCode* class of the transaction as the output. We carry out a time-based split of available customer transactions into training and test set to closely reflect online scenario where transactions up-to a certain time can be used for predicting future transactions. The size recommendation algorithm (ours and the baseline) learn customer and product true sizes on the training set. We also learn logistic regression (Linear) and Random Forest (RF) classifiers which then take the learnt customer and product latent sizes as input and produce *fitSuitabilityCode* as output. Performance of such Linear and RF classifiers on the test set are then used to compare the performance of our algorithm with that of the baseline.

9.2 Offline experiments with Softlines shoes data

Data Analysis: We collected transactions data for customers, transactions were represented in terms of the following attributes - *customerId*, *productId* and *fitSuitabilityCode* $\in$ {`Small`, `Fit`, `Large`}. We used the first 80% of transactions in temporal order for training while the remaining were used as the test set. We collected transactions data for customers for six product categories labeled A-F for proprietary reasons. The number of transactions in each dataset is shown in Table 2. Each transaction is represented in terms of the following attributes – customerID, productID, fitSuitabilityCode $\in$ {`Small`, `Fit`, `Large`}.

In our datasets, catalog size for all products varies between 4 and 20 on the US sizing scheme, with 0.5 size intervals. We plot the histogram of count of products and transactions respectively for different catalog sizes in Figures 5 and 6. In order to safeguard proprietary information, we do not report the actual product and transaction counts for different catalog sizes in Figures 5 and 6, respectively. While these plots tend to indicate that the customers may have a slight bias towards buying full catalog sizes over half sizes, but such behavior could be a manifestation of half sizes being out-of-stock at the time of purchase as well. And since we do not record in-stock availability of various catalog sizes at the time of a customer's purchase, we cannot pinpoint the exact root cause for the full sizes being more popular than half sizes, at least not based on the data that we have. Also, for categories except "C", most customer purchases are for catalog sizes between 7 and 10. For the "C" category, the popular catalog sizes are between sizes 8 and 12. The number of transactions is extremely small for sizes greater than 14 and is almost negligible for products with sizes more than 17.

We plot the histograms of number of products and customers respectively with different transactions counts in Figures 7 and 8. In order to safeguard proprietary information, we do not report the actual product and transaction counts for different catalog sizes in Figures 7 and 8, respectively. Note that a majority of products and customers have fewer than 3 transactions in the training data.

Offline Experimental Results: Table 1 summarizes the results of our experiments on various offline datasets. Performance of Algorithm 1 (described in Section 5.1) with and without personas are compared with the baseline method discussed in Section 9.1 (Baseline) and a baseline method which has information about personas (Baseline Persona). Logistic Regression (Linear) and Random Forest (RF) based classifiers are then built based on the output of each of the algorithms, and then their performance is compared on the basis of the weighted AUC of the resulting classifier, as discussed in Section 9.1. From Table 1, we can make the following inferences:

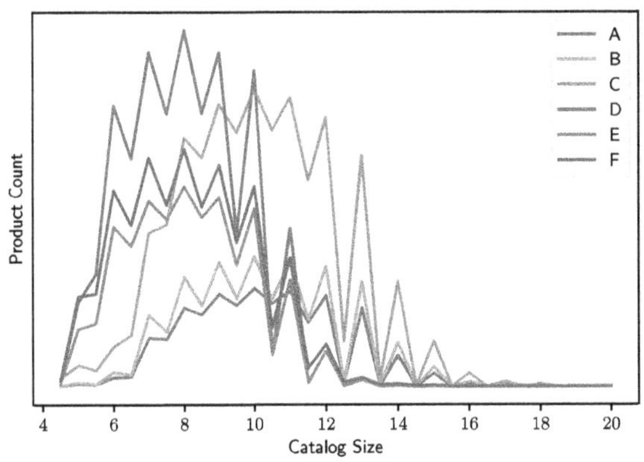

Figure 5: product count across catalog size.

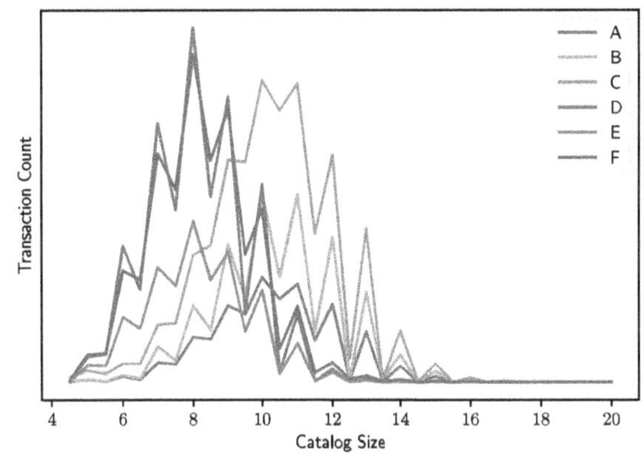

Figure 6: Transaction count across catalog size.

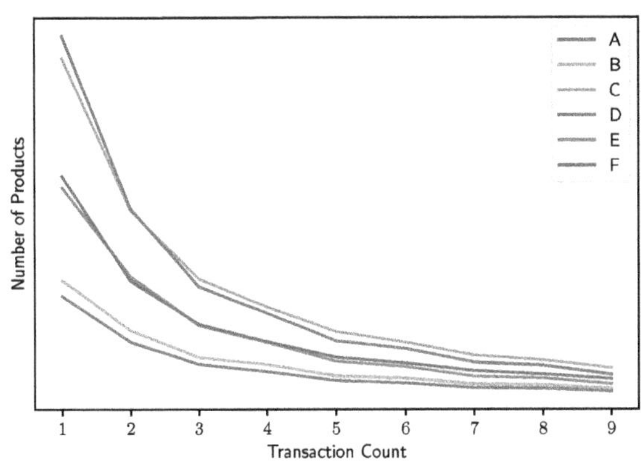

Figure 7: Histogram of products with transaction count.

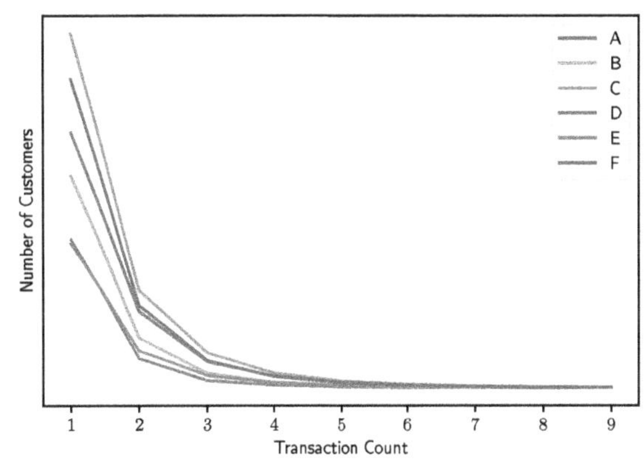

Figure 8: Histogram of customers with transaction count.

Dataset	Baseline RF	Baseline Persona Linear	Baseline Persona RF	Algorithm 1 Linear	Algorithm 1 RF	Algorithm 1 Persona Linear	Algorithm 1 Persona RF
A	0.6%	0%	0%	16.4%	17.2%	17.9%	**18.1%**
B	2.1%	0.4%	2.1%	20.3%	21.3%	**21.3%**	20.5%
C	3.8%	1.9%	1.9%	15.7%	16.1%	**18.4%**	17.8%
D	2.7%	1.2%	1.6%	20.0%	20.2%	**21.3%**	20.7%
E	1.5%	0.2%	0.6%	15.8%	15.6%	**17.4%**	**17.4%**
F	2.5%	2.7%	2.3%	18.1%	17.3%	**18.5%**	17.3%

Table 1: Summary of offline experimental results. We report the percentage improvements in weighted AUC over an above Baseline Linear AUC values for each dataset.

A	B	C	D	E	F
10.4M	17M	33.2M	25M	12.9M	27M

Table 2: Summary of transaction count for all datasets.

(1) Algorithm 1 has 17-21% higher AUC compared to the baseline method and (2) Modeling Personas boosts the AUC of Algorithm 1 further up-to 2.3%.

9.3 Online A/B test Results

Based on the output of Algorithm 1, we ran an online A/B test against an incumbent size recommendation algorithm as control in the US marketplace for Mobile and Tablet experience. The incumbent algorithm is a proprietary algorithm that groups products into clusters based on co-purchase frequency. Thus, product pairs that are bought by a large set of customers end up in the same cluster. A measure of central tendency based on the catalog sizes of products participating in each of the clusters is used to assign the cluster and its participating products a latent size. Recommendations to customers are then carried out in the latent size space. Conceptually, Algorithm 1 also tries to achieve a similar result, though in a more principled manner. The results of the online A/B test showed that we are able to achieve an improvement of 0.49% (p-value < 0.001) in the percentage of `Fit` transactions over control, which also translates into a reduction of the same magnitude in the number of return transactions.

10 CONCLUSION

In this paper, we proposed a novel latent factor model for predicting product size fits based on the difference between customer and product (latent) true sizes. We devised efficient algorithms for computing customer and product true size values by minimizing two loss function variants, and proposed a hierarchical clustering algorithm to discover the underlying personas for each customer. On Amazon shoe datasets, our latent factor model has an AUC that is 17-21% higher compared to baselines. In an online A/B test, our algorithms show an improvement of 0.49% in percentage of Fit transactions over control.

REFERENCES

[1] Ruslan Salakhutdinov and Andriy Mnih. Probablistic Matrix Factorization. NIPS 2008.
[2] Yehuda Koren, Robert Bell and Chris Volinsky. Matrix Factorization Techniques for Recommender Systems. IEEE Computer 2009.
[3] P. K. Gopalan, L. Charlin, and D. Blei. Content-based recommendations with Poisson factorization. "In Advances in Neural Information Processing Systems", pages 3176-3184, 2014.
[4] Dynamic Poisson Factorization, by Laurent Charlin, Rajesh Ranganath, James McInerney and David M. Blei, ACM Conference on Recommender Systems, Recsys 15
[5] A Framework for Matrix Factorization based on General Distributions, by Josef Bauer and Alexandros Nanopoulos, ACM Conference on Recommender Systems, Recsys 14
[6] Modeling the Dynamics of User Preferences in Coupled Tensor Factorization by Dimitrios Rafailidis and Alexandros Nanopoulos, ACM Conference on Recommender Systems, Recsys 14
[7] Wei Chu and Seung-Taek Park. Personalized Recommendation on Dynamic Content Using Predictive Bilinear Models. WWW 2009.
[8] Deepak Agarwal and Bee-Chung Chen. Regression based Latent Factor Models. KDD 2009.
[9] Bayesian latent variable models for collaborative item rating prediction, Morgan Harvey, ACM International Conference on Information and Knowledge Management, CIKM 2011.
[10] Bayesian probabilistic matrix factorization using Markov chain Monte Carlo, Ruslan Salakhutdinov, Andriy Mnih, International Conference on Machine Learning, ICML 2008.
[11] Ling Li and Hsuan-Tien Lin. Ordinal Regression by Extended Binary Classification.Neural Information Processing Systems, NIPS 2006.
[12] J. McAuley and J. Leskovec. Hidden factors and hidden topics: understanding rating dimensions with review text. ACM Conference on Recommender Systems, Recsys 2013.
[13] Meta-Prod2Vec – Product Embeddings Using Side-Information for Recommendation by Flavian Vasile, Elena Smirnova, Alexis Conneau, ACM Conference on Recommender Systems, Recsys 16
[14] Asynchronous Distributed Matrix Factorization with Similar User and Item Based Regularization, Bikash Joshi, Franck Iutzeler, Massih-Reza Amini, ACM Conference on Recommender Systems, Recsys 16
[15] Alexandros Karatzoglou, Xavier Amatriain, Linas Baltrunas, and Nuria Oliver. 2010. Multiverse recommendation: n-dimensional tensor factorization for context-aware collaborative filtering. In Proceedings of the fourth ACM conference on Recommender systems (RecSys '10). ACM, New York, NY, USA, 79-86. DOI=http://dx.doi.org/10.1145/1864708.1864727
[16] Atsuhiro Narita, Kohei Hayashi, Ryota Tomioka, and Hisashi Kashima. 2011. Tensor factorization using auxiliary information. In Proceedings of the 2011 European conference on Machine learning and knowledge discovery in databases - Volume Part II (ECML PKDD'11), Dimitrios Gunopulos, Thomas Hofmann, Donato Malerba, and Michalis Vazirgiannis (Eds.), Vol. Part II. Springer-Verlag, Berlin, Heidelberg, 501-516.
[17] Panniello, Umberto, et al. "Experimental comparison of pre-vs. post-filtering approaches in context-aware recommender systems." Proceedings of the third ACM conference on Recommender systems. ACM, 2009.
[18] Adomavicius, Gediminas, and Alexander Tuzhilin. "Context-aware recommender systems." Recommender systems handbook. Springer US, 2015. 191-226.
[19] Karen Church, Barry Smyth, Paul Cotter, and Keith Bradley. 2007. Mobile information access: A study of emerging search behavior on the mobile Internet. ACM Trans. Web 1, 1, Article 4 (May 2007). DOI=http://dx.doi.org/10.1145/1232722.1232726
[20] Bradley, R.A. and Terry, M.E. (1952). Rank analysis of incomplete block designs, I. the method of paired comparisons. Biometrika, 39, 324–345.
[21] Thurstone, L.L. (1959). The Measurement of Values. Chicago: The University of Chicago Press.

Practical Lessons from Developing a Large-Scale Recommender System at Zalando

Antonino Freno
Zalando SE
Berlin, Germany
antonino.freno@zalando.de

ABSTRACT

Developing a *real-world* recommender system, i.e. for use in large-scale online retail, poses a number of different challenges. Interestingly, only a small part of these challenges are of algorithmic nature, such as how to select the most accurate model for a given use case. Instead, most technical problems usually arise from *operational constraints*, such as: adaptation to novel use cases; cost and complexity of system maintenance; capability of reusing pre-existing signal and integrating heterogeneous data sources.

In this paper, we describe the system we developed in order to address those constraints at Zalando, which is one of the most popular online fashion retailers in Europe. In particular, we explain how moving from a collaborative filtering approach to a learning-to-rank model helped us to effectively tackle the challenges mentioned above, while improving at the same time the quality of our recommendations. A fairly detailed description of our software architecture is provided, along with an overview of the algorithmic approach. On the other hand, we present some of the offline and online experiments that we ran in order to validate our models.

CCS CONCEPTS

• **Information systems → Recommender systems**; *Learning to rank*; • **Computing methodologies** → Batch learning; Regularization;

KEYWORDS

learning to rank; large-scale learning; recommender system architecture

1 INTRODUCTION

Zalando (http://www.zalando.com/) provides a unique hub for digital fashion content in Europe. In the online shop, machine-learned product recommendations are disseminated over many different contexts, ranging from general navigation aid on the homepage to personalized sorting in the catalog and item-to-item recommendations on product detail pages. In order to keep up with an ever-changing market and the constantly growing customer needs, algorithmic progress has always been a crucial requirement for our recommendation services. Yet, when viewed from the trenches of online retail industry, recommender systems development assumes a significantly different shape than we are used to think from an academic perspective.

From a scientific point of view, research on machine-learned recommender systems tries to identify *optimal* recommendation algorithms. Here, optimality is typically defined in terms of *maximum achievable accuracy* (possibly weighted by computational efficiency) with respect to specific recommendation goals, settings, and constraints. Accuracy is measured by a number of different metrics, which formally measure the quality of recommendations in terms of the ranking they induce on a set of candidate items. However, real-world recommender systems, such as those powering all major e-commerce platforms, have to face a sensibly different question, i.e. how to *maximize business value* in the long term. In this context, the notion of business value has at least two different sides. On the one hand, we want to generate value for our customers, e.g. in terms of user engagement, retention, conversion rate, revenue, and related performance indicators. On the other hand, we want to generate internal value, in terms of the long-term profitability of our technology assets. Here, profitability means *operational excellence*, on at least three different dimensions: (*i*) possibility of adapting the recommender system to novel use cases; (*ii*) cost and complexity of the involved maintenance; (*iii*) capability of capitalizing on pre-existing signal and effectively integrating newly available data sources. In this sense, an optimal recommender system is one that achieves operational excellence along at least these three dimensions, while also generating value for customers.

Back in the past, most of the recommendation contexts on Zalando were powered by machine learning models based on collaborative filtering (CF). As we tried to improve on these models and replace them by more sophisticated approaches, we carefully redesigned our system by keeping in mind the three guidelines of operational excellence mentioned above. To this purpose, we moved to a recommendation framework based on learning to rank (L2R). In this paper, we provide an in-depth overview of our L2R architecture. In particular, we discuss how the chosen framework enabled our recommendation stack to address operational concerns. Our goal is to stress the importance of treating the operational quality of recommender systems as a major criterion for the scientific analysis of those systems. We believe that by achieving a tighter integration of operational and algorithmic concerns, faster and more

RecSys '17, August 27-31, 2017, Como, Italy

ACM ISBN 978-1-4503-4652-8/17/08...$15.00
https://doi.org/10.1145/3109859.3109897

Figure 1: Item-based recommendations on a product detail page.

effective technology transfer can be achieved for the outcome of recommender systems research. In Sec. 2, we describe the main contexts where we serve recommendations in the fashion store. Sec. 3 reviews the theoretical framework underlying our machine learning system, whereas the system architecture is illustrated in Sec. 4. Sec. 5 presents some results from offline and online experiments. Finally, in Sec. 6 we draw some conclusions and sketch directions for future research.

2 USE CASES AND APPROACH

In Secs. 2.1–2.3 we review three different recommendation contexts from the Zalando web store. At the same time, we sketch the backbone of our modeling approach.

2.1 Item-based Recommendations

The first type of recommendations we serve at Zalando are the ones available on product detail pages, namely the ones usually presented in a "Similar items" carousel. These recommendations are not necessarily personalized, in that they simply model the relevance of additional candidate products with respect to the item that the user is currently checking out (i.e. the main subject of the currently open page). An example is provided in Fig. 1.

The way we model the relevance of candidate products for a given reference item is via the scoring function s:

$$s(\boldsymbol{i}_i, \boldsymbol{i}_j) = \varphi(\psi^I(\boldsymbol{i}_i, \boldsymbol{i}_j)) \tag{1}$$

Figure 2: Personalized recommendations on the Zalando home.

where $\boldsymbol{i}_i$ is the reference item, and $\boldsymbol{i}_j$ is a candidate product for which we want to compute the relevance score. Once we score all relevant candidates $\boldsymbol{i}_j$, we rank them by score, and then recommend the top k.

The key ingredients to define are on the one hand the scoring function φ, and on the other hand ψ^I, which combines the base article and the candidate recommendation into the feature vector to be fed into ϕ. We will address the definition of ϕ in Sec. 3.2. While ϕ will be estimated by a general L2R routine, ψ^I encodes instead some of our domain knowledge by specifying how the attributes of $\boldsymbol{i}_i$ and $\boldsymbol{i}_j$ interact to one another. For example, if articles have a color attribute, their interaction $\psi^I(\boldsymbol{i}_i, \boldsymbol{i}_j)$ might contain an attribute specifying whether the two articles have the same color or not. Another interaction attribute might be given by the price difference of the two products, and so on. Therefore, we refer to ψ^I as an *interaction function*. Virtually, there is no limit to the type and quantity of interaction attributes we can encode into our model, as long as the information required to calculate them is available from the attributes of the input items. And of course, whenever relevant to the task at hand, non-relational attributes from the interacting items (e.g. the popularity of candidate articles) can also be incorporated into ψ^I.

2.2 Personalized Recommendations

General personalized recommendations are served to customers whenever no specific context or intention is assumed for the current context. For example, we serve personalized recommendations on the Zalando home page, usually presenting them in a "Recommended for you" box.

The scoring function for personalized recommendations can be modeled as follows:

$$s(\boldsymbol{u}_i, \boldsymbol{i}_j) = \varphi(\psi^U(\boldsymbol{u}_i, \boldsymbol{i}_j)) \tag{2}$$

where $\boldsymbol{u}_i$ is a user, and $\boldsymbol{i}_j$ is the candidate product we want to score with respect to $\boldsymbol{u}_i$. The key difference between Eq. 1 and Eq. 2 is that now, the function ψ^U has to model the interaction between user and article attributes (rather than an article-to-article interaction). For example, if we know the user's favorite brand, we can encode a boolean attribute specifying whether the brand of $\boldsymbol{i}_j$ is the same as $\boldsymbol{u}_i$'s favorite brand. In other words, ψ^U encapsulates the feature-engineering side of our user-to-item recommendation model.

2.3 Personalized Item-based Recommendations

Another recommendation context arises when we attempt to personalize the recommendations we show in product detail pages, such as the ones that appear in the carousel already displayed in Fig. 1. In this case, there are three different entities to be accounted for in our scoring function, namely the user $\boldsymbol{u}_i$, the base article $\boldsymbol{i}_j$, and the candidate product $\boldsymbol{i}_k$:

$$s(\boldsymbol{u}_i, \boldsymbol{i}_j, \boldsymbol{i}_k) = \varphi(\psi^{U,I}(\boldsymbol{u}_i, \boldsymbol{i}_j, \boldsymbol{i}_k)) \tag{3}$$

To address this context, we have to leverage both item-to-item and user-to-item interactions, or possibly come up with ternary interaction attributes. For example, we might simply define $\psi^{U,I}$ as a concatenation of the values returned by the previously defined functions ψ^I and ψ^U, i.e. $\psi^{U,I}(\boldsymbol{u}_i, \boldsymbol{i}_j, \boldsymbol{i}_k) = (\psi^U(\boldsymbol{u}_i, \boldsymbol{i}_k), \psi^I(\boldsymbol{i}_j, \boldsymbol{i}_k))$. Also, we might want to include ternary interaction attributes. For example, we can have a boolean feature specifying whether the user's most frequently purchased brand, the base item's brand, and the candidate article's brand are all the same or not, or a real-valued feature calculating the fraction of pairs (x, y) from the set $\{(\boldsymbol{u}_i, \boldsymbol{i}_k), (\boldsymbol{i}_j, \boldsymbol{i}_k)\}$ such that x and y can be assigned to the same brand.

3 LEARNING TO RANK

We now review the L2R framework underlying our recommender system. In Sec. 3.1, we summarize some of the vast literature available on the topic, whereas Sec. 3.2 outlines the approach we use to estimate our models from data.

3.1 Related Work

L2R approaches are usually classified into three broad families: pointwise, pairwise, and listwise methods [16]. Pointwise models attempt to estimate the relevance score of each item as an independent data point. The supervision for learning the relevance score is typically extracted from previously (e.g. manually) ranked lists of candidates, by using the positions of candidates within the lists as the respective labels. At prediction time, the items returned for a query are sorted according to their scores. Linear or logistic regression are examples of scoring functions used in pointwise methods. Pairwise approaches score ordered pairs of items instead of individual items. Here, the goal is to learn the correct order of these pairs. In other words, the goal is to score the more relevant items higher than less relevant ones. The advantage of this approach over pointwise methods is that it does not require to learn absolute relevance scores. RankSVM [12, 13] is one of the most popular pairwise models. It formalizes ranking as a binary classification problem for item pairs and uses support vector machines as the underlying classifier. Another one is Rank Logistic Regression [21]. RankBoost [10] is also a pairwise model, where the ranking is learned through boosting. The idea is to construct a sequence of "weak" rankers in an iterative fashion, and then to predict ranks using a linear combination of the weak learners. Finally, listwise approaches rely on ranked lists as training examples. In particular, they try to minimize a loss function defined over full lists instead of ordered pairs sampled from those lists. ListNet [4] is a listwise ranking algorithm, which performs gradient descent over a loss function based on cross-entropy. AdaRank [24] is also a listwise approach, based instead on boosting. Gradient-boosted trees (GBTs) have recently become quite popular in learning to rank [3, 19]. Although GBTs have been shown to outperform simpler approaches (such as linear models), training them over web-scale datasets can be very expensive. Moreover, scoring latency is a serious issue for GBTs whenever we are not able to precompute and cache predictions. An alternative model, which is very suitable for the large-scale setting, is the WSABIE algorithm [22], which relies on low-dimensional embeddings and data sub-sampling. Yet another model is given by ElasticRank [9], inspired by a former approach known as LambdaRank [2]. ElasticRank inherits from LambdaRank the idea of weighting the loss function by a listwise penalization scheme. The loss is minimized by stochastic gradient descent, where the training algorithm is allowed to perform only one pass through the training data. Moreover, the special focus of this model is given by sparsity-inducing regularization schemes.

3.2 Ranking Loss Minimization

Let our training sample be a set $\mathcal{X}$ containing the pairs $(\boldsymbol{x}_1^+, \boldsymbol{x}_1^-), \ldots, (\boldsymbol{x}_n^+, \boldsymbol{x}_n^-)$, where each pair $(\boldsymbol{x}_i^+, \boldsymbol{x}_i^-)$ is such that $\boldsymbol{x}_i^+$ should be ranked higher than $\boldsymbol{x}_i^-$. If the setting is given by personalized recommendation, as described in Sec. 2.2, each training pair will be defined as follows:

$$(\boldsymbol{x}_i^+, \boldsymbol{x}_i^-) = (\psi^U(\boldsymbol{u}_j, \boldsymbol{i}^+), \psi^U(\boldsymbol{u}_j, \boldsymbol{i}^-)) \tag{4}$$

where item $\boldsymbol{i}^+$ is more relevant to user $\boldsymbol{u}_j$ than item $\boldsymbol{i}^-$. Relevance labeling might be obtained in several different ways, via implicit or explicit feedback. For example, $\boldsymbol{u}_j$ might have clicked (or purchased) $\boldsymbol{i}^+$ but not $\boldsymbol{i}^-$, assuming that both items where available in the same candidate set. Or, $\boldsymbol{u}_j$ might have explicitly labeled some articles, by rating them or placing them in a wishlist. The way we sample user feedback clearly depends on the available data (and especially on the quality and limitations of user feedback tracking), the specific use case, and possibly on computational requirements, and it is tuned for each application both by offline and online experimentation. The definition given in Eq. 4 can easily be cast to suitable forms for the item-based and personalized item-based recommendation setting, respectively.

For each training pair $(\boldsymbol{x}_i^+, \boldsymbol{x}_i^-)$, our ranking loss is defined as follows:

$$\ell(\boldsymbol{x}_i^+, \boldsymbol{x}_i^-; \varphi) = \max\left\{0, \varphi(\boldsymbol{x}_i^-) - \varphi(\boldsymbol{x}_i^+) + \epsilon\right\} \tag{5}$$

for some slack parameter $\epsilon \geqslant 0$. Different choices are possible other than the hinge loss specified in Eq. 5, e.g. the logistic loss $\log\{1 + \exp(\varphi(\boldsymbol{x}_i^+) - \varphi(\boldsymbol{x}_i^-))\}$. For our applications, we found the hinge loss completely satisfying.

Given a training pair $(\boldsymbol{x}_i^+, \boldsymbol{x}_i^-)$, we can optimize the parameters in φ by minimizing the ranking loss over $(\boldsymbol{x}_i^+, \boldsymbol{x}_i^-)$. This task can be accomplished via standard (sub-)gradient descent methods. Any choice for the parametric form of φ, ranging from simple linear regression to a multilayer perceptron, will be compatible with the ranking metric we are adopting as long as we are able to compute the corresponding (sub-)gradients. Throughout our applications, we assume a linear form for the scoring function ϕ, i.e. $\varphi(\boldsymbol{x}) = \boldsymbol{w}^\top \boldsymbol{x}$.

This is not only practical from the computational point of view, but it also preserves the convexity of the ranking loss defined in (5), which is a convenient property for the purpose of parameter optimization.

In order to induce sparsity in the learned scoring function, i.e. to completely drop some components in the weight vector $\boldsymbol{w}$, we can add ℓ_1-based regularization to the loss defined in Eq. 5. The resulting objective function will be convex, with both theoretical guarantees and efficient optimization schemes [20]. As previously advocated in the large-scale setting [17], we additionally consider a squared ℓ_2-term, hence leading to the following ranking loss:

$$\ell^*(\boldsymbol{x}_i^+,\boldsymbol{x}_i^-;\varphi_{\boldsymbol{w}}) = \ell(\boldsymbol{x}_i^+,\boldsymbol{x}_i^-;\varphi_{\boldsymbol{w}}) + \lambda_1\|\boldsymbol{w}\|_1 + \frac{1}{2}\lambda_2\|\boldsymbol{w}\|_2^2 \qquad (6)$$

where λ_1 and λ_2 are non-negative hyperparameters determining, respectively, the weight of the ℓ_1 and ℓ_2 penalties within the overall loss. The resulting regularization model is usually referred to as elastic-net [25]. It is worth stressing that, for our web-scale application, sparsity is an extremely important requirement for the learned model. The reason is that, to extract useful signal from the available training data, we often need to exploit very high-dimensional feature representations, e.g. by considering all possible pairwise interactions of categorical attributes through a one-hot encoding scheme. This easily leads to feature vectors having billions of components. Therefore, dropping as many irrelevant features as possible is especially useful both to improve generalization and to reduce the memory footprint (and possibly the latency) of the learned model.

In order to learn our parameter vector from a training set $\mathcal{X} = \{(\boldsymbol{x}_1^+,\boldsymbol{x}_1^-),\dots,(\boldsymbol{x}_n^+,\boldsymbol{x}_n^-)\}$, we use gradient descent to address the following, averaged regularized problem:

$$\min_{\boldsymbol{w}} \frac{1}{n}\sum_{i=1}^{n} \ell(\boldsymbol{x}_i^+,\boldsymbol{x}_i^-;\varphi_{\boldsymbol{w}}) + \lambda_1\|\boldsymbol{w}\|_1 + \frac{1}{2}\lambda_2\|\boldsymbol{w}\|_2^2 \qquad (7)$$

In our applications, the number of training data points is typically in the order of several millions. To cope with the dataset size, we distribute the training load over several workers using the in-memory cluster computing capabilities offered by Apache Spark (http://spark.apache.org/). This way, we can easily calculate and sum up the gradient of ℓ^* over the full dataset in no more than a couple of seconds, and hence perform a few hundreds of gradient descent iterations in just a few minutes.

As proposed in [15], we can simply enforce sparsity by adding a pruning operation to gradient descent. The pruning step, scheduled every k gradient iterations, simply consists of setting to 0 all the weights w_i such that, for a chosen threshold θ, $|w_i| < \theta$. Clearly, the higher the value we choose for θ, the sparser the model will become. The experiments reported in [9] show that this simple technique performs surprisingly well as compared to way more sophisticated approaches available from the literature [7, 23]. Therefore, we adopt such regularization scheme as our default choice.

4 SYSTEM ARCHITECTURE

This section provides an overview of our system architecture. Our stack is fully deployed on Amazon AWS (https://aws.amazon.com/), and it is organized into a collection of offline jobs on the one hand, and a group of online services

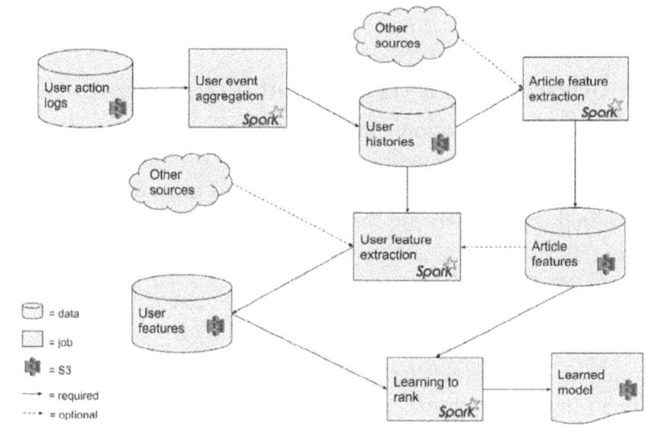

Figure 3: A diagram of our offline jobs: event aggregation, feature extraction, and learning to rank.

on the other hand. Sec. 4.1 describes the former, whereas the web services are presented in Sec. 4.2. A critical outlook is then proposed in Sec. 4.3.

4.1 Offline Jobs

Let us look at how we organize all of the necessary batch calculations into a graph of interdependent offline jobs. Here, the goal is to produce and persist all data that will be necessary in order for the live recommendation engine to serve fresh results to our visitors. The jobs architecture is depicted in Fig. 3.

Everything starts from user action logs, which record every action performed by our customers on the Zalando web store. The first job aggregates all actions on a per-user basis. The difficulty here is that the volume of server logs is massive and distributed over multiple locations. Therefore, we cannot afford to crunch and re-aggregate all of this data every time we need to retrieve actions for a given customer. Pre-aggregation of customer actions allows subsequent jobs to selectively retrieve the relevant information in a much more convenient way.

Once the user histories have been aggregated, they are used for two purposes. On the one hand, we can extract a number of dynamic article features (i.e. quantities that change over time), such as number of clicks received by a product within a given time window, number of purchases, and so on. Here, we might be tempted to extract such features directly from the (non-aggregated) event logs. The drawback of such an idea is that it would prevent us from filtering out undesirable data points, such as events generated by robots or crawlers, which pollute our data by introducing noise and distorting their distribution. These problematic events can typically be identified only once we analyze the behavior of the respective cookies/user identifiers, and this behavior only materializes once the relevant event sets are aggregated and some basic statistics are derived from them.

On the other hand, we extract a wide range of user attributes, such as time elapsed since the user was last active on the shop, how the user choices are distributed over different product brands, or the price distribution of purchased articles. User feature extraction

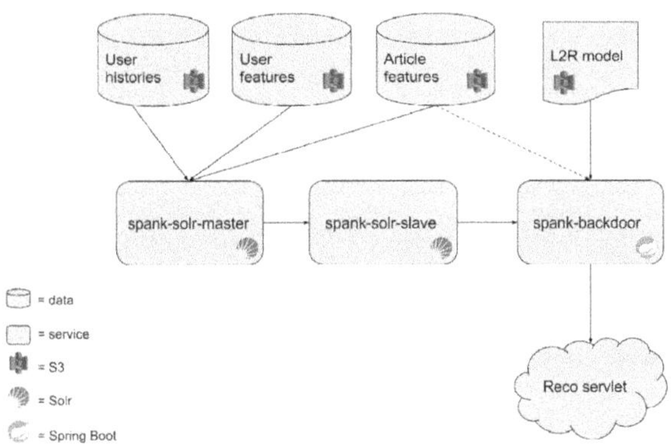

Figure 4: A diagram of our web services: data indexing, real-time ranking, and post-processing. 'Spank' is the name we use to refer to our content-based recommendation stack.

can also exploit already computed article features. For example, if we want to measure how user purchases are affected by product popularity, then for each purchase, we need to check how popular the corresponding product was at the time it was purchased (e.g. in terms of click-through rate).

Finally, the L2R job estimates the scoring function from the extracted historical data, relying on both user and article features. A dedicated job has to be run for each different recommendation setup (i.e. for each one of the different models specified in Eqs. 1–3), since they lean on different data representations and features. The learned scoring functions are then deployed to our live ranking services.

The full offline job pipeline is run at short, regular intervals (e.g. daily). This is important to ensure that new events ingested in our browsing logs can contribute to the calculation of user and article features, as well as to the adaptation of the machine-learned scoring function to drifting data distributions.

4.2 Web Services

The purpose of our recommendation services is to provide a RESTful API [8], returning sorted sets of results for queries that conform to one of the following use cases: (*i*) get top-k recommendations for item $\boldsymbol{i}_i$; (*ii*) get top-k recommendations for user $\boldsymbol{u}_i$; (*ii*) get top-k recommendations for user $\boldsymbol{u}_i$ and item $\boldsymbol{i}_j$. These patterns correspond to the three use cases described in Sec. 2. A diagram of our online architecture is given in Fig. 4.

The first step in setting up our live recommendation stack is to make the user and article data available for real-time processing, as they are originally stored in large, distributed batches. To this aim, we index our data into Apache Solr (http://lucene.apache.org/solr/), which allows us to retrieve single feature vectors by (user/article) id within an average latency of less than 5 milliseconds. Our Solr service is set up with a master/slave architecture. That is, the master server only takes care of indexing data coming from the offline jobs whenever new batches become available, which is a computationally expensive operation. On the other hand, the slaves mirror the content available from the master by mere data replication, and they expose it to the ranking engine for real-time querying. This way, we make sure that the computational load incurred while indexing new data batches will not affect the latency of Solr queries, which would have a tremendous impact on the responsiveness of the recommendation API.

A second component of the live system is given by the ranking servlet, exposing the recommendation API mentioned above. We refer to this component as the *backdoor engine*, for the following reason. As illustrated in Fig. 4, the backdoor service does not serve directly customer requests. Such requests go first to the stack labeled as 'Reco servlet', which then forwards the relevant requests to the backdoor engine. The goal behind this choice is to separate the problem of calculating and ranking recommendations from the problem of post-processing (e.g. filtering or rendering) them for the final customers. Such post-processing tasks are both complex to perform and extrinsic to the genuine recommendation problem, as they typically come from *ad hoc* business requirements or from interoperating with external services, such as sales, campaigns, hand-coded rules, advertising, de-duplication, front-end restrictions, and so on. Therefore, the backdoor-based architecture frees up the recommendation engine from the complexity of managing extrinsic logic, hence streamlining both software development and system operation work.

As shown in the diagram, the L2R model artifact can be loaded directly from the location where it is saved by the offline jobs, i.e. it does not need any sort of indexing, since this artifact is nothing but a self-contained weight-vector (possibly enriched with some additional configuration). This happens as soon as the backdoor servlet is started, while the model is also immediately refreshed whenever more recent artifacts become available. On the other hand, article features can be usefully cached in the same servlet, to a more or less significant extent. Caching will be crucial to minimize serving latency. Differently from user data, which have to be queried according to more unpredictable patterns, article queries tend to be generated according to a power-law distribution, because of the popularity patterns which are intrinsic to fashion shopping. Because of this, we can not only achieve relatively high cache-hit rates, but also initialize the cache with the most popular articles whenever new instances are added to the stack, which will be immensely beneficial to the initial responsiveness of these instances.

4.3 Discussion

We now proceed to discuss, in Secs. 4.3.1–4.3.3, how the system presented so far copes, respectively, with the three operational concerns motivating our general approach.

4.3.1 Adaptation to Diverse Use cases. As described in Sec. 2, product recommendation takes different forms as soon as we move through different contexts, e.g. depending on whether personalization is involved, whether a reference article is currently the focus, and so on. Therefore, being able to seamlessly adapt the available infrastructure to the different use cases is crucial to maximize the value of the adopted recommendation technology. This is the main consideration we had in mind when choosing a model such that only one specific component (i.e. the interaction function ψ) has to be modified whenever we tackle a new context. ψ^I, ψ^U, and $\psi^{U,I}$ are self-contained, plug and play modules, which are completely decoupled from anything but the offline L2R job and the online backdoor servlet. Of course, these last two components need to be aware of which interaction function has to be loaded for each specific use case. But the logic of the encompassing system remains completely untouched whenever we move from one context to another.

4.3.2 System Operation. Maintaining a recommendation architecture can require significant efforts, for a variety of reasons. The amount of data to be processed, both for offline modeling and for online serving, is typically huge, which requires distributed processing infrastructure on both sides. Also, because of the system complexity and the need to continuously improve over time (in order to tackle new challenges and meet continuously evolving customer needs), the system components need to be easily replaceable and modifiable, while avoiding the risk of breaking the whole system whenever a local change is operated. While the system described in Secs. 4.1–4.2 takes a non-trivial *cognitive* effort to be operated and mastered, it does not require *expensive* operations whenever a component has to be modified in some way. For example, extracting some more user features from the historical data only requires a change in the corresponding feature extraction job, and the outcome will be automatically available for all subsequent stages, independent on when and how the other components will start using the new input. Similarly, adding one more L2R job, e.g. in order to move from non-personalized to personalized item-based recommendations, only requires to implement and add one job to the offline pipeline, without affecting any other component, and independent of whether and when the new model will go live. In other words, while designing the presented architecture, we strived to decouple as much as possible all different system components, so that the cost of operating the whole system could be minimized by isolating the scope of the most typically required interventions. Furthermore, the sharp separation between offline and online stack encapsulates the live system from unpredictable, possibly breaking changes happening in any of the ingested data sources, allowing us to detect the problem from its impact on the offline jobs, and to fix it before it starts affecting our customers through its downstream effects.

4.3.3 Exploitation of Pre-existing Signal. Whenever new data sources become available or whenever new signal can be exploited from a (possibly pre-existing) predictive model, the novel information can be homogeneously fed into the L2R engine in the form of additional features. Such an incremental modeling approach can lead to continuous improvement in recommendation quality, due to the seamless exploitation of the novel information. As we will illustrate in Sec. 5, we found this strategy to generate a lot of momentum in the process of replacing the engines currently used in production by increasingly accurate ones.

An extremely simple example of how we incorporated a pre-existing recommender into L2R is given by how we integrated the output of our previous CF engine for item-to-item scoring. Here, we just started to ingest the predicted item-to-item relevance into the article feature-extraction job, so that the similarities were made available to the interaction function ψ^I as pre-calculated features. A more sophisticated example of how we added a new type of signal is offered by the integration of a Word2Vec-based article embedding model [18]. For the purpose of article recommendation, we

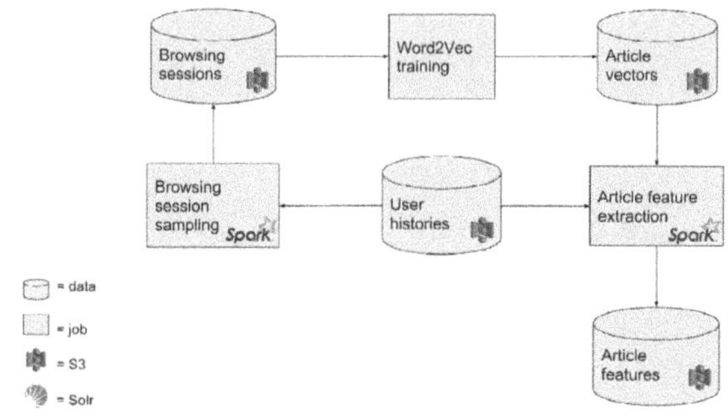

Figure 5: Integration of Word2Vec-based article embeddings into our offline pipeline: the entry point is provided by the article feature extraction job.

were interested in extracting a latent-vector representation of our products, by capturing the contextual relation of article views with the articles explored within the same browsing sessions. To this purpose, we simply model sessions as sequences of article views, and have a Word2Vec learning routine run on these sequences. The job flow is described in Fig. 5. As shown in the diagram, a simple entry point for the new embeddings into our offline job graph is provided by the feature extraction job for articles. The new data source is thereby made available to the L2R stage.

5 EXPERIMENTAL RESULTS

As Zalando is mainly focused on online shopping, the most reliable way for us to choose between competing recommendation algorithms and models is by comparing their live (i.e. online) performance in terms of a number of metrics, such as click-through rate, customer conversion rate, number of sales, generated revenue, effective catalog size [11], and additional indicators as well. However, when the candidates for online testing are too many, the only way to prioritize the different options is given by offline testing, i.e. by measuring the performance of the alternative models on historical data. The advantage of offline experiments is not only that the same data can be used to benchmark an arbitrary number of models, but also that poor models can be prevented from hurting our customers by exposing inaccurate recommendations. Moreover, whenever a new machine learning model is developed, extensive hyperparameter tuning and hypothesis testing needs to be done on validation data. Performing this task on online data is simply prohibitive both in terms of time and in terms of business risk. On the other hand, the drawback of offline testing is both that it suffers from bias (as the historical data are generated by the very same models we are trying to supersede), and that it does not capture all subtleties involved in a live system (such as the interaction with other components, the impact on user experience of higher/lower latencies, and so on). Therefore, we usually select between competing models by first deciding, through offline experimentation, which ones we want to benchmark in a live setting, and then by running dedicated A/B tests to determine whether the current production model should be replaced by a new one.

The purpose of this section is to illustrate how we learned one of the lessons discussed in the previous sections, namely the one considered in Sec. 4.3.3. One point that became clear to us both via offline and online experimentation is that focusing on the feature-based model described so far allows us to significantly speed-up algorithmic innovation, throughout our recommendation use cases, via inherently incremental improvements. The reason is that, without forcing us to go for the operational risk and expense of substituting new systems for the current production model, the adopted L2R framework makes room for a seamless integration of heterogeneous models and data sources, by merging all of them into the final scoring model in the form of additional features. Secs. 5.1–5.2 give an example of how this incremental benefit was detected and brought live in one of our personalized recommendation contexts, namely on the Zalando Home.

5.1 Offline Experiment

One way to test the ranking accuracy of a given recommendation engine from historical data is the following. We build our training set by sampling browsing sessions from user action logs, covering whatever time interval is suitable for training our algorithms. Typically, we use data from at least 7 consecutive days, going up at most to 4 consecutive weeks. Then, if our training sample extends to day d at latest, we use day $d + 1$ for testing. For hyperparameter tuning, day d is actually held out of the training data, so that it can be used to build a validation set, and the algorithms are trained using data generated no later than on day $d-1$. Such a training sample is enough to provide several millions of user sessions, whereas for the test set we usually subsample about half a million sessions. To construct test queries from a user session, we proceed as follows. All articles that the user clicks on (or purchases) within the session are labeled as relevant items, i.e. as items that the ranking/recommendation algorithm should rank/recommend on top of anything else. Then, we check the position of the relevant items in the top-k recommendation lists produced by the competing algorithms, and we measure the corresponding ranking accuracy.

Our chosen metric for this measurement is normalized discounted cumulative gain (NDCG) at k [6]. A formal comparison of different evaluation metrics goes beyond the scope of this paper. However, it is worth mentioning that, on our datasets, alternative metrics (such as precision or recall at k) usually give consistent indications about which models are most accurate. NDCG is a normalized version of the following metric:

$$DCG@k(\boldsymbol{r}, \boldsymbol{l}) = \sum_{i=1}^{\min\{k,n\}} \frac{2^{l_i} - 1}{\log_2(r_i) + 1} \tag{8}$$

where $\boldsymbol{r} = (r_1, \ldots, r_n)$ is the ranking induced by a given algorithm on n candidate products, and l_i is the relevance label of the i-th product in the list. We set the relevance label to 1 if the product was clicked/purchased, whereas $l_i = 0$ otherwise. DCG has non-negative values, and larger DCG values correspond to better rankings. NDCG normalizes the right-hand side of Eq. 8, dividing it by the DCG of a perfect ranking, i.e. the ranking induced by the relevance labels themselves.

As we started experimenting with L2R, the very first feature to use was simply the score calculated by the pre-existing CF engine.

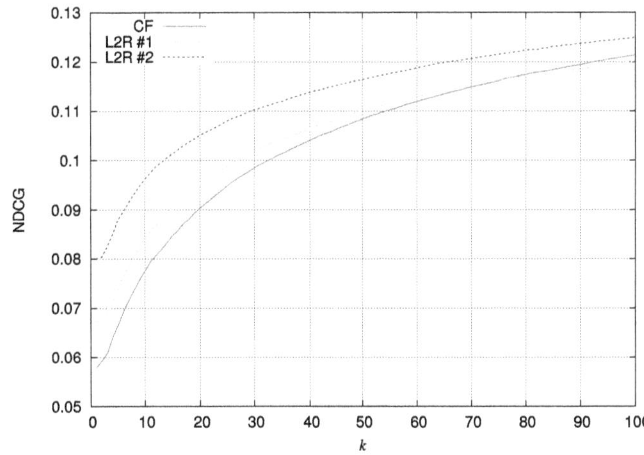

Figure 6: ***NDCG@k*** **measurements on a one-day traffic sample for: (*i*) CF; (*ii*) L2R using CF-based features plus static product attributes (L2R #1); (*iii*) L2R model using all the features from L2R #1 plus Word2Vec-based similarity (L2R #2).**

Basically, the CF engine was an adaptation of the approach presented in [1]. As a number of static article features were available from our product catalog, such as brand, price, category, colors, and a variety of high-level tags, we simply added all such attributes to the L2R model. To this purpose, we engineered several types of attribute interactions and encoded them into our ψ^U function, using the strategy described in Sec. 2.2. We then compared this first version of our L2R model (L2R #1) to the CF baseline, leading to the NDCG measurements plotted in Fig. 6.

As the figure shows, L2R #1 achieves some noticeable improvement over CF, although the ranking deteriorates for large values of k. We notice that the measurement was seen to be statistically significant, as the experiment was repeated on several occasions, for different data samples. The evidence was enough for us to set up and run an A/B test, which we describe in Sec. 5.2. It is important to note that, in order to see the mentioned improvement in NDCG, it was not enough to add a bunch of features to the CF score, as described above, and then just hope for the learned model to regularize away all noise while learning the optimal scoring. Instead, extensive feature selection was necessary, which we performed by repeated cross-validation on held-out data. Unfortunately, when the features are poorly engineered, or just too noisy, the model accuracy can be hurt to a more or less significant extent, and regularization does not seem to be enough to isolate the good signal from noise.

Once the Word2Vec-based article embeddings were available from our modeling pipeline, we also started to experiment with features extracted from the embeddings. The simplest way to engineer such a feature into ψ^U is, for example, to calculate the cosine similarity between the latent vector representation of the candidate product and a suitable vector representation of the user. As a heuristic, the user vector might be calculated as the average of the article vectors from the relevant shopping history. We then add the new feature to the ones already used in L2R #1, and refer to the resulting model as L2R #2. As plotted in Fig. 6, L2R #2 significantly improves over L2R #1. Presumably, this happens because the newly

Country	ΔCTR	ΔCR> 0 & $p < 0.1$
#1	+15.22%	×
#2	+20.44%	✓
#3	+33.13%	×
#4	+23.93%	×
#5	+37.88%	✓

Table 1: Click-through rate and conversion rate results from A/B tests run over five different countries. Country names are masked in order to not disclose possibly sensitive information. L2R is used for treatment, while CF is used for the control group.

engineered feature conveys signal which is not captured by the pre-existing features. This makes the L2R #2 model a second, even more promising candidate for further A/B testing (which is currently work in progress). As the Word2Vec model requires a dedicated training routine to be run, relying on specific hyperparameter tuning, the chosen hyperparameters turn out to have a non-trivial effect on the accuracy of the final L2R model. However, a convenient property of the used L2R framework is that, while we observed a poor hyperparameter setup to make the Word2Vec-based similarity completely inaccurate if used as a stand-alone article-relevance predictor, using it instead as one of several L2R input features makes the final predictions way more robust to inaccuracies in the learned embeddings. In particular, if we refer to the plot in Fig. 6, what we observed is that, for less accurate settings of the Word2Vec hyperparameters, the NDCG curve of L2R #2 would get closer and closer to L2R #1, without however falling below that level. On the other hand, we did not see a stand-alone prediction model based only on the Word2Vec similarity coming anywhere close to the CF baseline.

5.2 Online Experiments

Offline NDCG measurements do not tell us with certainty how the L2R model will impact our business performance indicators in production. Therefore, we ran some A/B tests in order to compare L2R to the CF baseline. The tested L2R model is L2R #1 from the previous section (i.e. not including Word2Vec-based features, which were not yet available when the online tests were run). The tests concern the Zalando Home, where general personalized recommendations are shown to visitors (along with other content) as hints for navigation. The metrics we used for the evaluation were mainly click-through rate (CTR) and conversion rate (CR). The former is defined as the fraction of displayed recommendations that receive at least one-click, while the latter is the fraction of visitors who end up making at least one purchase during the relevant time window. The results are summarized in Table 1 for five different countries. To avoid disclosing any sensitive information with respect to our business performance, for CTR we report the relative difference between control (CF) and treatment group (L2R), whereas for CR, instead of mentioning explicit values, we report whether a statistically significant improvement ($p < 0.1$) was achieved or not. For an overview of the A/B testing methodology on the web and the involved significance calculations, we refer the reader to [14].

As shown in the table, the treatment group consistently outperforms control in CTR. All CTR measurements were statistically significant, where the p values very quickly converged to 0. An interesting point to remark is that, although the gap between L2R and CF is significantly positive everywhere, different countries display a noticeably different behavior in this respect, as the relative difference between the two algorithms exhibits a relatively large variance over different domains. This country-specific behavior is the reason why it is extremely important to run a dedicated test for each involved domain, in order to avoid making false (and financially risky) generalizations. On the other hand, our previous experience with the subtleties of fashion shopping shows that CR, as compared to CTR, is much more difficult to increase by mere algorithmic change. Nevertheless, CR increases significantly in two out of the five reported experiments, i.e. in countries #2 and #5, while it does not deviate significantly from the control in all other experiments. Besides the metrics discussed here, we also monitored additional revenue- and engagement-based measurements, which also showed, overall, either an improvement or no statistically significant difference. Therefore, the L2R engine was rolled out to production in all involved domains. In our interpretation, the key strategy by which L2R superseded CF in our production systems is by enriching the signal provided by CF through the integration of additional data sources into the final predictions, rather than discarding the old system and building on entirely different foundations.

6 CONCLUSIONS AND FUTURE WORK

In this paper, we argued that the operational challenges involved in running recommender systems in the real world should be included as major dimensions in a formal analysis of such systems. In particular, we sketched three basic criteria by which such an analysis should be conducted, namely (*i*) flexibility of the system with respect to different use cases, (*ii*) cost of operations, and (*iii*) ease of integration of heterogeneous signal. To illustrate the importance of these criteria, we showed how they inspired us to redesign the recommender systems at Zalando from the ground up.

Although several directions are open for further development, we wish to mention one which is especially appealing as a next step, namely to complement our system with deep learning-based signal. Deep neural networks were recently shown to have significant potential also in the recommendation domain [5]. In particular, they promise to alleviate the burden of the feature engineering process, which unfortunately requires, in our current setup, a non-trivial amount of manual work and quite a few iterations in order to deliver satisfying results.

7 ACKNOWLEDGMENTS

I am extremely grateful to everyone in the Recommendation Team at Zalando for the outstanding help and support they provided throughout all phases of this project. A special thought goes out to my friend Ilaria Castelli.

REFERENCES

[1] Fabio Aiolli. 2013. Efficient top-n recommendation for very large scale binary rated datasets. In *Seventh ACM Conference on Recommender Systems, RecSys '13,*

Hong Kong, China, October 12-16, 2013, Qiang Yang, Irwin King, Qing Li, Pearl Pu, and George Karypis (Eds.). ACM, 273–280.
[2] Christopher J. C. Burges, Robert Ragno, and Quoc Viet Le. 2006. Learning to Rank with Nonsmooth Cost Functions. In *Advances in Neural Information Processing Systems (NIPS)*. 193–200.
[3] Christopher J. C. Burges, Krysta Marie Svore, Paul N. Bennett, Andrzej Pastusiak, and Qiang Wu. 2011. Learning to Rank Using an Ensemble of Lambda-Gradient Models. In *Proceedings of the Yahoo! Learning to Rank Challenge, held at ICML 2010, Haifa, Israel, June 25, 2010*. 25–35.
[4] Zhe Cao, Tao Qin, Tie-Yan Liu, Ming-Feng Tsai, and Hang Li. 2007. Learning to rank: from pairwise approach to listwise approach. In *Proceedings of the 24th International Conference on Machine learning (ICML 2007)*. ACM, New York, NY, USA, 129–136.
[5] Paul Covington, Jay Adams, and Emre Sargin. 2016. Deep Neural Networks for YouTube Recommendations. In *Proceedings of the 10th ACM Conference on Recommender Systems (RecSys '16)*. ACM, New York, NY, USA, 191–198.
[6] Bruce Croft, Donald Metzler, and Trevor Strohman. 2009. *Search Engines: Information Retrieval in Practice*. Addison-Wesley, Boston (MA).
[7] John C. Duchi and Yoram Singer. 2009. Efficient Online and Batch Learning Using Forward Backward Splitting. *Journal of Machine Learning Research* 10 (2009), 2899–2934.
[8] Roy Thomas Fielding. 2000. *Architectural Styles and the Design of Network-based Software Architectures*. Ph.D. Dissertation. University of California, Irvine.
[9] Antonino Freno, Martin Saveski, Rodolphe Jenatton, and Cédric Archambeau. 2015. One-Pass Ranking Models for Low-Latency Product Recommendations. In *Proceedings of the 21th ACM SIGKDD International Conference on Knowledge Discovery and Data Mining, Sydney, NSW, Australia, August 10-13, 2015*. ACM, 1789–1798.
[10] Yoav Freund, Raj Iyer, Robert E. Schapire, and Yoram Singer. 2003. An Efficient Boosting Algorithm for Combining Preferences. *Journal of Maching Learning Research* 4 (2003), 933–969.
[11] Carlos A. Gomez-Uribe and Neil Hunt. 2016. The Netflix Recommender System: Algorithms, Business Value, and Innovation. *ACM Trans. Management Inf. Syst.* 6, 4 (2016), 13:1–13:19.
[12] Ralf Herbrich, Thore Graepel, and Klaus Obermayer. 2000. Large Margin Rank Boundaries for Ordinal Regression. In *Advances in Large Margin Classifiers*, Smola, Bartlett, Schölkopf, and Schuurmans (Eds.). MIT Press, Chapter 7, 115–132.
[13] Thorsten Joachims. 2002. Optimizing Search Engines Using Clickthrough Data. In *Proceedings of the Eighth ACM SIGKDD International Conference on Knowledge Discovery and Data Mining*. ACM, New York, NY, USA, 133–142.
[14] Ron Kohavi, Roger Longbotham, Dan Sommerfield, and Randal M. Henne. 2009. Controlled experiments on the web: survey and practical guide. *Data Mining and Knowledge Discovery* 18, 1 (2009), 140–181.
[15] John Langford, Lihong Li, and Tong Zhang. 2009. Sparse Online Learning via Truncated Gradient. *Journal of Machine Learning Research* 10 (2009), 777–801.
[16] Tie-Yan Liu. 2009. Learning to Rank for Information Retrieval. *Foundations and Trends in Information Retrieval* 3, 3 (2009), 225–331.
[17] H Brendan McMahan, Gary Holt, D Sculley, Michael Young, Dietmar Ebner, Julian Grady, Lan Nie, Todd Phillips, Eugene Davydov, Daniel Golovin, et al. 2013. Ad click prediction: a view from the trenches. In *Proceedings of the 19th ACM SIGKDD international conference on Knowledge discovery and data mining (KDD 2013)*. ACM, 1222–1230.
[18] Tomas Mikolov, Ilya Sutskever, Kai Chen, Gregory S. Corrado, and Jeffrey Dean. 2013. Distributed Representations of Words and Phrases and their Compositionality. In *Advances in Neural Information Processing Systems (NIPS 2013)*, Christopher J. C. Burges, Léon Bottou, Zoubin Ghahramani, and Kilian Q. Weinberger (Eds.). 3111–3119.
[19] Ananth Mohan, Zheng Chen, and Kilian Q. Weinberger. 2011. Web-Search Ranking with Initialized Gradient Boosted Regression Trees. In *Yahoo! Learning to Rank Challenge*. 77–89.
[20] S. Negahban, P. Ravikumar, M. J. Wainwright, and B. Yu. 2009. A unified framework for high-dimensional analysis of M-estimators with decomposable regularizers. In *Advances in Neural Information Processing Systems 22 (NIPS 2009)*, Y. Bengio, D. Schuurmans, J. D. Lafferty, C. K. I. Williams, and A. Culotta (Eds.). 1348–1356.
[21] D. Sculley. 2009. Large scale learning to rank. In *NIPS Workshop on Advances in Ranking*.
[22] Jason Weston, Samy Bengio, and Nicolas Usunier. 2011. WSABIE: Scaling Up to Large Vocabulary Image Annotation. In *IJCAI 2011, Proceedings of the 22nd International Joint Conference on Artificial Intelligence, Barcelona, Catalonia, Spain, July 16-22, 2011*. 2764–2770.
[23] Lin Xiao. 2010. Dual Averaging Methods for Regularized Stochastic Learning and Online Optimization. *Journal of Machine Learning Research* 11 (2010), 2543–2596.
[24] Jun Xu and Hang Li. 2007. AdaRank: A Boosting Algorithm for Information Retrieval. In *SIGIR '07: Proceedings of the 30th Annual International ACM SIGIR Conference on Research and Development in Information Retrieval*. ACM, New York, NY, USA, 391–398.
[25] H. Zou and T. Hastie. 2005. Regularization and variable selection via the elastic net. *Journal of the Royal Statistical Society. Series B* 67, 2 (2005), 301–320.

Exploiting Socio-Economic Models for Lodging Recommendation in the Sharing Economy

Raul Sanchez-Vazquez
Department of Computer Science
Universidade Federal de Minas Gerais
Belo Horizonte, MG, Brazil
raulsanchez@dcc.ufmg.br

Jordan Silva
Department of Computer Science
Universidade Federal de Minas Gerais
Belo Horizonte, MG, Brazil
jordan@dcc.ufmg.br

Rodrygo L. T. Santos
Department of Computer Science
Universidade Federal de Minas Gerais
Belo Horizonte, MG, Brazil
rodrygo@dcc.ufmg.br

ABSTRACT

Recent years have witnessed the emergence of sharing economy marketplaces, which enable users to share goods and services in a peer-to-peer fashion. A prominent example in the travel industry is Airbnb, which connects guests with hosts, allowing both to exchange cultural experiences in addition to the economic transaction. Nonetheless, Airbnb guest profiles are typically sparse, which limits the applicability of traditional lodging recommendation approaches. Inspired by recent socio-economic analyses of repurchase intent behavior on Airbnb, we propose a context-aware learning-to-rank approach for lodging recommendation, aimed to infer the user's perception of several dimensions involved in choosing which lodging to book. In particular, we devise features aimed to capture the user's price sensitivity as well as their perceived value of a particular lodging, the risk involved in choosing it rather than other available options, the authenticity of the cultural experience it could provide, and its overall perception by other users through word of mouth. Through a comprehensive evaluation using publicly available Airbnb data, we demonstrate the effectiveness of our proposed approach compared to a number of alternative recommendation baselines, including a simulation of Airbnb's own recommender.

KEYWORDS

Lodging Recommendation; Context Awareness; Learning to Rank; Consumption Behavior; The Sharing Economy

1 INTRODUCTION

The travel industry has largely adopted the Internet as one of its main sales channels, helping customers find information in order to plan their trip [19]. As a result, specialized e-tourist agencies evolved and became popular services that simplified the travel planning process [2, 5], helping travelers with personalized assistance. Naturally, recommender systems (RS) have also been proposed to tackle problems in the travel domain [3, 18], allowing users to have a customized interaction with online platforms. Recently, the travel industry has been reshaped by the so-called sharing economy, which introduced online marketplaces with innovative consumption modalities that stand in sharp contrast to their traditional counterparts [1, 12, 15]. Such consumption modalities are characterized by user-to-user transactions in a peer-to-peer (P2P) fashion, with the online marketplace serving as a mediator [15].

Airbnb[1] is a prominent representative of the sharing economy and the largest P2P lodging provider, allowing users to list, search, and rent lodgings, enabling guests to benefit from the advice of local hosts. Researches have studied P2P lodging and found important peculiarities that substantially distinguish it from a traditional hotel lodging scenario [15, 22, 25, 39]. In particular, P2P lodging has been described as more than just a hotel substitute for three main reasons: (1) P2P lodging provides a much more dynamic ecosystem as lodging supply can rapidly respond to changes in demand, (2) P2P lodging serves a wider range of use cases due to the increased diversity and geographical coverage of lodging supply, (3) P2P lodging customers give importance to cost savings, utility, trust, and familiarity, shaping unique customer preferences. At the same time, as illustrated in Figure 1 for the Airbnb dataset used in our experiments, guest profiles are typically small, with 80% of the users having fewer than 5 bookings in their profile. As a result, the user-lodging matrix is extremely sparse (99.9997%), which hinders an accurate modeling of users' distinctive preferences.

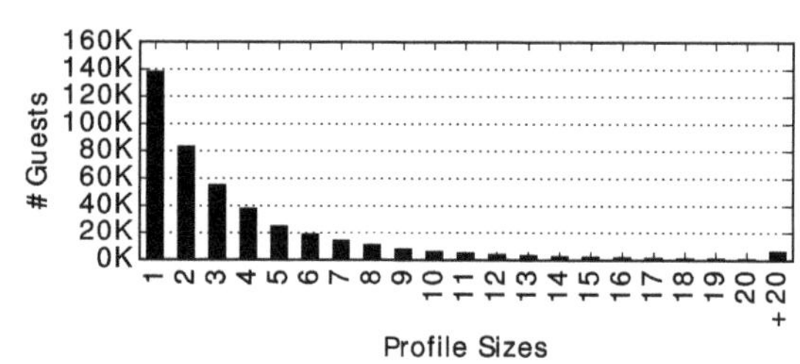

Figure 1: Profile size distribution of Airbnb users.

Inspired by recent socio-economic analyses of consumption behavior on Airbnb, we propose a context-aware learning-to-rank approach for lodging recommendation. Our approach tackles the aforementioned challenges by modeling several contextual dimensions associated with guests' decision of which lodgings to book. In particular, we devise features to capture guests' price sensitivity as well as their perceived value of a particular lodging option, the risk involved in choosing it rather than other available options, the

[1] https://www.airbnb.com/

RecSys '17, August 27–31, 2017, Como, Italy.

DOI: http://dx.doi.org/10.1145/3107411.3107471

authenticity of the experience it could provide, and its overall perception by online guests' word of mouth. Through a comprehensive evaluation using publicly available data from Airbnb, we demonstrate the effectiveness and robustness of our approach in contrast to effective baselines from the literature as well as a simulation of Airbnb's own recommender. Moreover, through an ablation study, we provide further evidence to support or refute existing theories of lodging consumption behavior in the sharing economy. To the best of our knowledge, our approach is the first to address lodging recommendation in a sharing economy marketplace.

Our main contributions are three-fold:

(1) A novel lodging recommendation approach that models the socio-economic context around available lodgings as contextual features for learning to rank.
(2) A test collection and evaluation methodology for lodging recommendation in the sharing economy.
(3) A comprehensive evaluation of the proposed approach in a case study using Airbnb.

In the remainder of this paper, Section 2 discusses related work on lodging recommendation. Section 3 details our proposed context-aware learning-to-rank approach for tackling this problem. Sections 4 and 5 describe the experimental setup and the results of the empirical evaluation of our approach. Lastly, Section 6 provides our concluding remarks and directions for future work.

2 RELATED WORK

According to surveys in RS [3, 11, 18], there are multiple works aiming to assist tourists and travelers in their planning process. Concretely, these different approaches recommend one or more of the following items: travel destinations, touristic attractions, recreational activities, accommodations, and eatery venues. The majority of these works recommends lodgings in conjunction with (or constrained to) other items, leaving it unclear how to apply them to pure lodging recommendation. While no previous work has tackled lodging recommendation in the sharing economy to the best of our knowledge, in the following, we describe related approaches for the more traditional problem of hotel recommendation.

Saga et al. [31] proposed to use an undirected hotel-guest graph obtained from booking transactions. The graph is converted into a preference transition network, i.e., a graph G with hotels as nodes, and with two hotel nodes h_i and h_j having an edge between them if users that booked h_i are likely to book h_j. Recommendation is performed in two stages. First, the user explicitly selects an initial hotel h to produce a list of neighboring nodes as candidates. Then, each candidate hotel h_i is scored by $f(h_i) = in_i - out_i - C^2$, where in_i and out_i are the in- and out-degree of the candidate hotel h_i in G, whereas the factor C quantifies previous recommendations of the same hotel, in order to promote novelty in the ranking.

Levi et al. [21] characterized the hotel domain as a cold-start scenario. They assumed that users give more importance to reviews written by similar users than reviews written by users with different background, where similarity is defined in terms of nationality, travel intention (single, couple, family, group, and business), and preferences on hotel traits (location, service, food, room, etc.). In their work, hotels are modeled as feature vectors using the words (features) contained in their reviews. In addition, they extract features for each nationality, travel intention, and hotel trait. Hotel recommendation is performed by aggregating the importance assigned to each feature by users with similar preferences as the target user. A crowdsourcing experiment using Amazon Mechanical Turk showed evidence of the usefulness of mining reviews to identify typical types of user for any given hotel.

Zhang et al. [40] proposed a hybrid approach to hotel recommendation. By modeling users and hotels in latent topic spaces, they produce user and hotel similarity matrices. These matrices are then leveraged when factorizing the user-hotel rating matrix. Data normalization is performed by taking into account each user's traveling mode (single, couple, group, family, business, and others). The final step produces recommendation using maximal marginal relevance [7], a diversification technique, which reduces redundancy while maintaining relevance. Relatedly, PCA-ANFIS [26] tackles recommendation when hotels possess ratings in various aspects (e.g. value, rooms, location, cleanliness, check in/front desk, service, and business services). Such ratings are used to create a 3-dimension tensor, corresponding to: users, items, and the multiple ratings. The tensor is used to cluster users and for each individual cluster dimensionality reduction is achieved. A second step consists of training multiple ANFIS, a neural network that integrates fuzzy logic principles, to predict overall ratings in each cluster. Their experiments demonstrated that PCA-ANFIS leads to improvements in predictive accuracy of tourism multi-criteria prediction.

3 CONTEXTUAL SOCIO-ECONOMIC MODELS FOR LODGING RECOMMENDATION

Given a user u and a target location l, a lodging recommender must rank the lodgings $\mathcal{I}$ in the surroundings of l, prioritizing those where u would like to sojourn. Recommender systems typically leverage information on users, items, or interactions between users and items. As illustrated in Figure 1, Airbnb guest profiles are severely sparse, which limits the applicability of traditional collaborative or content-based approaches. On the other hand, as discussed in Section 2, existing hotel recommendation approaches ignore the economic drivers that motivate users to consume lodgings in the sharing economy. In order to overcome these challenges, we propose a context-aware learning-to-rank approach for lodging recommendation, aimed to exploit the socio-economic context around available lodgings as multiple ranking features.

Our approach is inspired by recent socio-economic studies in the domain of Airbnb. In particular, Liang [22] analyzed five aspects of users' recurrent consumption of Airbnb lodgings:

(1) **Perceived Value**, the trade-off between the benefits versus the cost of each available lodging;
(2) **Perceived Risk**, the assessment of all possible negative outcomes derived from booking the lodging;
(3) **Price Sensitivity**, the extent to which the price of a lodging affects a guest's booking behavior;
(4) **Perceived Authenticity**, the extent to which a guest feels like natively living at the lodging place; and
(5) **Electronic-Word-of-Mouth**, informal opinions that frame the judgment of other users towards the lodging.

In the following, we model each of these consumption behavior aspects as a preference dimension represented by multiple ranking features. Table 1 lists all 176 features[2] used to represent each candidate lodging in our approach, which capture the socio-economic context of an available lodging in different ways.

Table 1: Lodging recommendation features. The "input" column denotes whether each feature is estimated based upon candidate item *i*, item context *c*, or both.

feature class	input	qty
Perceived Value (PV)		
Pricing	*i*	6
Property type	*i*	21
Room type	*i*	3
Bed type	*i*	5
Equipments	*i*	4
Property capacity	*i*	1
Guests allowed	*i*	1
Amenities	*i*	40
Nearby venues	*c*	3
Nearby venues check-ins (min, max, avg, med)	*c*	12
Nearby venues distance (min, max, avg, med, norm.)	*i, c*	24
Perceived Risk (PR)		
Cancellation policy	*i*	5
Ratings	*i*	7
Reviews (std, norm.)	*i*	2
Nearby lodgings	*c*	1
Nearby lodgings reviews (avg, std)	*c*	2
Price Sensitivity (PS)		
Histogram lodgings prices (avg, skw, kur)	*c*	3
Sampled lodgings prices (avg, skw, kur)	*c*	3
Price (normalized)	*i, c*	3
Perceived Authenticity (PA)		
Authenticity score (avg, med, min, max, skw, kur)	*i*	6
Electronic Word of Mouth (EWoM)		
Sentiment score (avg, med, min, max, skw, kur)	*i*	24
Grand total		176

3.1 Perceived Value (PV)

Perceived Value (PV) quantifies the cost-benefit trade-off of a lodging. In particular, the cost of a lodging is measured by multiple numeric features conveying different pricing policies (e.g., daily, weekly, monthly price) as well as special fees including a security deposit or a fee for external visitors. On the other hand, the benefit of a lodging is conveyed by categorical features such as property type (e.g., apartment, house, loft), room type (private, shared, entire home), bed type (airbed, couch, futon, real bed, pull-out sofa), numerical features such as property capacity and number of available equipments (e.g., bathrooms, bedrooms, beds), and indicator features, such as whether external guests are allowed or which amenities (e.g., cable tv, doorman, dryer) the lodging provides.

Many studies demonstrate the importance of points of interest for touristic involvement, which has been shown to influence the selection of travel destinations [14, 27, 35]. To further quantify the benefit offered by a lodging, we propose to characterize its surroundings, by leveraging data from a location-based social network. In particular, using the Foursquare API,[3] we obtain information about up to 50 nearby venues from three different Foursquare categories: food, art & entertainment, and travel & transportation. We delimit the sampling radius based on findings on human time and distance perception: 500 m for eatery venues (accessible by a 5 minutes walk [4, 36]) and 1.5 km for entertainment and travel venues (accessible by a 15 minutes car drive[4][5] [20, 33]).

In addition to the total number of nearby venues in each category, we summarize distributions of two properties of these venues: number of check-ins and distance from the candidate lodging. Each of these distributions is encoded into multiple numeric features using different summary statistics, such as minimum, maximum, average, and median. Finally, just as psychological maps shape geographical boundaries in people's minds [29], the perceived distance from a lodging to popular venues may differ from their actual physical distance. In order to quantify this intuition, we propose to normalize the distance to express that customers are more willing to travel longer distances in order to reach popular venues. We achieve such a normalization by dividing the distance to a venue by the number of check-ins that the venue possesses.

3.2 Perceived Risk (PR)

Previous studies highlighted Perceived Risk (PR) as one of the key factors that affect repurchase intention on Airbnb [22]. Following a classical risk taxonomy [17], users take a *performance risk* as they cannot experience a lodging prior to their arrival, a *financial risk* as they may incur in cancellation fees, and a *physical risk* as they rarely know the host. In many online environments, risk symptoms can be alleviated through different mechanisms. In our scenario, we propose to quantify a lodging's performance risk through numerical features quantifying its received ratings on several aspects (cleanliness, accuracy, value, check-in, location, communication, and overall experience). In turn, financial risk is conveyed by a categorical feature indicating the available booking cancellation policies. Lastly, physical risk is quantified by measuring the popularity of the lodging, as well as the average and standard deviation of the popularity of nearby lodgings. These summary statistics are further used to normalize each lodging's raw popularity.

3.3 Price Sensitivity (PS)

Price Sensitivity (PS) is arguably one of the most important factors, broadly and intuitively accepted as a decisive motivator in consumers' behavior [9, 10, 34]. Airbnb users may present a high degree of PS as choosing a lodging requires a vivid exploration of multiple price options. Indeed, it has been shown that PS increases the more users are aware of the price dispersion of a given product [9]. Therefore, to model this preference dimension, we propose to summarize the price distribution of all candidate lodgings in a target location. To this end, we consider two price distributions: a price histogram displayed on the Airbnb search interface (see

[2] See [32] for further details.

[3] https://developer.foursquare.com/

[4] https://bitre.gov.au/publications/2015/files/is_073

[5] http://www.census.gov/hhes/commuting

Figure 2) and a price distribution sampled from the set of candidate lodgings. To quantify a guest's perception of these price distributions, they are both summarized using multiple statistics, including average, skewness, and kurtosis. In addition, these distributions' average and standard deviation are used to standardize each lodging's raw price. Standardized prices can be interpreted as how cheaper or more expensive a lodging is compared to nearby alternatives.

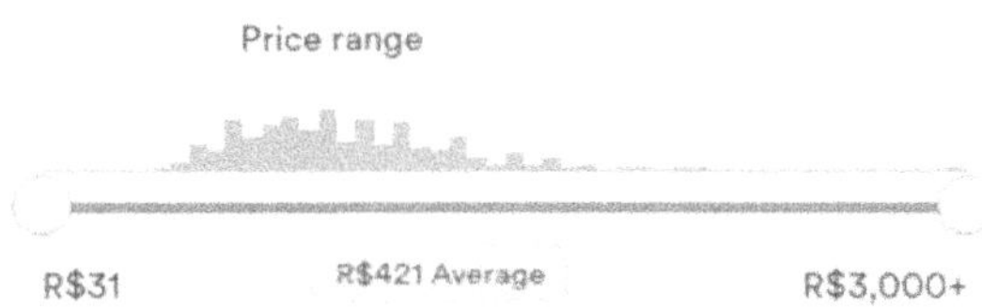

Figure 2: Airbnb price histogram.

3.4 Perceived Authenticity (PA)

Perceived Authenticity (PA) measures the extent to which a lodging offers a truly local living experience [22]. To quantify PA, we propose to mimic the way reviews are used by guests to sense authenticity as perceived (and reported) by other guests. To this end, we hand-build an authenticity lexicon comprising words that convey an authentic experience. The authenticity lexicon was built by reading several reviews and manually selecting words that usually appear when a user explicitly expresses a sense of PA. The lexicon can be seen in Table 2 and is composed of a total of 33 words.

Table 2: Handbuilt authenticity lexicon.

live	experience	authentic	share	truly	unique
real	recommend	welcome	talk	meet	friend
warm	community	explore	advice	connect	people
charm	communicate	discover	help	home	feel
place	neighborhood	genuine	time	chat	cozy
useful	hospitality	nearby			

An authenticity score for a review is estimated as the likelihood that it generates the authenticity lexicon. To this end, we use a standard language modeling approach with Dirichlet smoothing [28] after applying standard text processing techniques (lowercasing, stopword removal, Hunspell stemming). Finally, after producing a distribution of authenticity scores for the reviews associated with a lodging, we compute various authenticity scores for the lodging itself by using multiple summary statistics (average, median, minimum, maximum, skewness, and kurtosis).

3.5 Electronic Word of Mouth (EWoM)

In P2P lodging websites, reviews are the most common manifestation of Electronic Word of Mouth (EWoM) [22]. Indeed, guests are aware that their personal opinion on a lodging may help frame the perception of other users regarding the quality of this lodging [37], ultimately playing an key role in the booking decision process.

To take the pulse of Airbnb users towards individual lodgings, we propose to leverage standard sentiment analysis techniques. In particular, we use Vader [16], a state-of-the-art sentiment analysis tool, to extract four sentiment polarity scores from each review: positiveness, negativeness, neutrality, and a compound score. For a given lodging, EWoM scores are then produced by aggregating the various polarity scores associated with its reviews. Once again, we use multiple summary statistics to this end (average, median, minimum, maximum, skewness, and kurtosis).

3.6 Contextual Learning

Sections 3.1 through 3.5 presented multiple contextual models for lodging recommendation inspired by recently proposed socio-economic theories of consumption behavior on Airbnb. To further leverage these models for tackling the lodging recommendation problem, we resort to learning to rank [23]. In particular, our goal is to learn a ranking model $f : \mathcal{X} \rightarrow \mathcal{Y}$ mapping the input space $\mathcal{X}$ into the output space $\mathcal{Y}$. Our input space includes n learning instances $\{\vec{X}_j\}_{j=1}^{n}$, where $\vec{X}_j = \Phi(u_j, l_j, \mathcal{I}_j)$ is a feature matrix representation (produced by a feature extractor Φ) of a sample of lodgings $\mathcal{I}_j$ retrieved for user u_j near target location l_j. As described in Table 1, we consider a total of 176 features organized into five broad preference dimensions. In turn, our output space $\mathcal{Y}$ comprises n label vectors $\{\vec{Y}_j\}_{j=1}^{n}$, where $\vec{Y}_j$ provides relevance labels for each lodging $i \in \mathcal{I}_j$. To learn an effective ranking model f, we use LambdaMART [38], a gradient boosted regression tree learner, which represents the current state-of-the-art in learning to rank [8].

4 EXPERIMENTAL SETUP

This section describes the experimental setup that supports the evaluation of our context-aware learning to rank approach for lodging recommendation introduced in Section 3. In particular, we aim to answer the following research questions:

Q1. How effective is our lodging recommendation approach?
Q2. How do different features contribute to our approach?
Q3. How do our results relate to lodging consumption theories?

In the following, we describe the test collection used in our experiments, the baselines used for comparison and the procedure undertaken to train and test them as well as our own models.

4.1 Test Collection

Our experiments are conducted using publicly available data collected between March and September 2016 from Airbnb for two target cities: New York City, USA (NYC) and London, UK (LON). The crawled dataset includes lodgings geographically spread over each city. For each lodging, we obtain a structured representation of its description, along with the entire history of reviews it received from guests up to the time of crawl. For each guest, we further obtain a sample of up to 10 of the most recent reviews received from hosts all over the world. Because hosts may have multiple lodgings on offer, we further crawl the list of lodgings offered by each host to reconcile the precise lodging in each guest's history. Table 3 provides summary statistics of the produced dataset, which is available upon request. Percentages are relative to Airbnb's claimed numbers of guests and lodgings in the world, except for the number of transactions, which is extrapolated proportionally to the average number of transactions per lodging in the dataset.

Table 3: Salient statistics of the recommendation dataset.

	NYC	LON	World	Airbnb
# Guests	219.9 k	223.1 k	9.25 M (31.9%)	60.0 M
# Lodgings	17.3 k	22.1 k	0.48 M (26.3%)	2.0 M
# Transactions	250.5 k	266.7 k	15.70 M (15.4%)	49.2 M

Our test collection comprises multiple test cases of the form $\langle u, l, t, \mathcal{I}, i^* \rangle$, where u is a target guest, l is the location where the guest wishes to sojourn, t is the time of the recommendation request, $\mathcal{I}$ is a set of candidate items within a radius of 2 km of l, and $i^* \in \mathcal{I}$ is the lodging originally booked by u, which should be promoted by a lodging recommender. In each city, we sample 1,500 test cases geographically distributed across the city. In order to simulate the exploratory nature of a guest seeking lodging in a given location l, we replicate each test case five times, varying the candidate set $\mathcal{I}$ each time within the original radius of 2 km. These five distinct test cases portray the guest u using an interactive map to browse and explore the listing supply around the neighborhood of l, where he or she wishes to sojourn. All five simulations are included in our evaluation as independent test cases, totaling $1,500 \times 5 = 7,500$ test cases per city, 15,000 test cases overall.

4.2 Training & Test Procedure

Sorting the test cases in our test collection by their booking date in ascending order, we split the test collection into 12 disjoint folds with roughly the same number of test cases each. As illustrated in Figure 3, evaluation is performed in a sliding window comprising five folds across eight evaluation rounds. In all rounds, the first four folds are used for training different models in a 4-fold cross validation, whereas the fifth fold is used for testing trained models. Hyperparameter tuning is performed via grid search using the training folds of the first round. Ranking effectiveness is measured using Mean Reciprocal Rank (MRR) on the test folds across all rounds. Statistical significance is verified using a paired t-test with $\alpha < 0.05$ with Bonferroni correction for multiple comparisons.

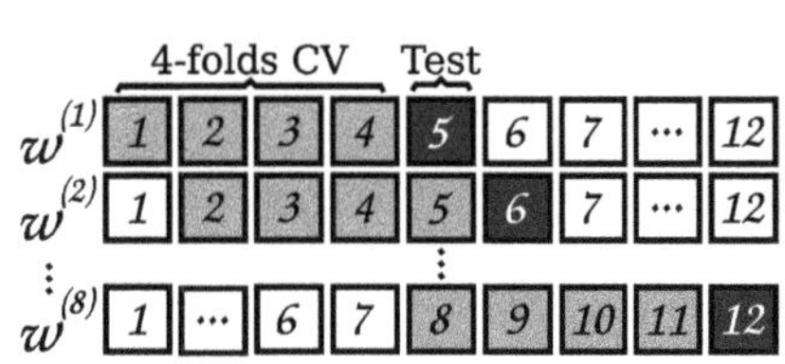

Figure 3: Sliding time windows.

4.3 Recommendation Baselines

We contrast our approach to three effective baselines:

(1) **Popularity** is a bias-centric model based on the lodging's booking count. Ties are solved by randomly sorting conflicting items [6].
(2) **Airbnb** consists of the non-personalized ranking produced by Airbnb's own recommender given the same input as all the other recommenders in our evaluation.
(3) **Bayesian Personalized Ranking Matrix Factorization** (BPRMF) [30] is a state-of-the-art matrix factorization approach for top-n recommendation.

5 RESULTS & DISCUSSIONS

In this section, we empirically evaluate our contextual learning-to-rank approach for lodging recommendation (CLLR, for short) in sharing economy marketplaces. In the following, we address each of the three research questions stated in Section 4 in turn.

5.1 Model Effectiveness

In this section, we address *Q1*, by analyzing the effectiveness of CLLR in contrast to the baselines introduced in Section 4.3: Popularity, BPRMF, and Airbnb. Table 4 shows MRR figures along with 95% confidence intervals for each baseline and our CLLR model. The lowest performance is attained by BPRMF, followed closely by the Popularity recommender, resulting in a statistical tie. These findings highlight the difficulties of collaborative recommenders to deal with the sparsity problem [31, 40]. Airbnb's recommender delivers a competitive performance, attaining the best MRR among the considered baselines. Finally, our CLLR model attains the highest MRR, significantly outperforming all three baselines, as denotes by the ▼ symbol alongside each baseline.

Table 4: MRR of CLLR vs multiple baselines.

	BPRMF	Popularity	Airbnb	CLLR
MRR	0.0215▼	0.0231▼	0.0328▼	**0.0400**
CI (95%)	0.0014	0.0015	0.0018	0.0021

To improve our understanding of the effectiveness of CLLR, Figure 4 shows MRR figures across all eight test folds at different points in time, with error bars denoting 95% confidence intervals for the means at the various points. For all but one test fold, CLLR consistently outperforms all baseline recommenders. Red stars indicate that CLLR performed statistically better ($\alpha = 0.05$) than all baselines, whereas blue stars denote statistical significance for all but one of Airbnb or Popularity ($\alpha = 0.05$). The only exception is the test fold of the fourth round, where Airbnb was the top performer.

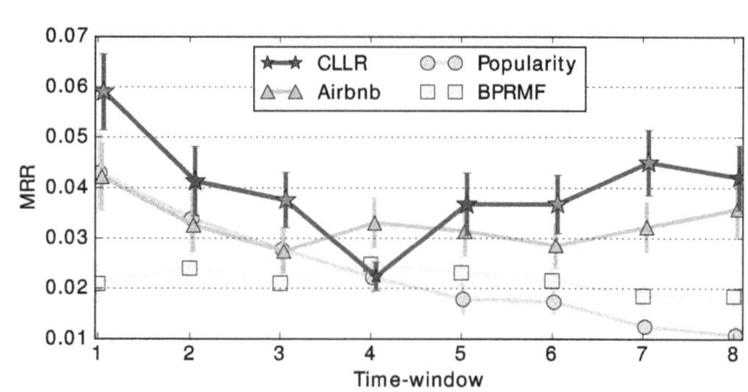

Figure 4: MRR by time window.

To better understand the drop in performance at the fourth round in Figure 4, we perform an ablation study, by discarding information that potentially misled CLLR into making wrong predictions, and hence causing the observed decay in performance. To this end, Figure 5 shows MRR figures attained by CLLR and five variants, each omitting one preference dimension at a time, namely, PV, PR, PS, PA, EWoM. Once again, error bars denotes 95% confidence intervals for the mean performance of each model at each point in time. As observed from the figure, at the fourth test round, removing the preference dimensions PS, PA, and PR (red markers) considerably improves the performance of the model. In particular, the fourth time window includes training data comprising bookings made between 10/2015-03/2016 and testing data comprising bookings made in 04/2016. This observation suggests that these dimensions may have hindered the model's generalization capabilities on this particular time window, perhaps influenced by a seasonal behavior (e.g., most of the training data are in the winter, whereas test data resides in spring) or an anomalous event (e.g., currency fluctuations). Nonetheless, further analysis is required to narrow down which subsets of features in the affected preference dimensions underperformed and what caused them to do so.

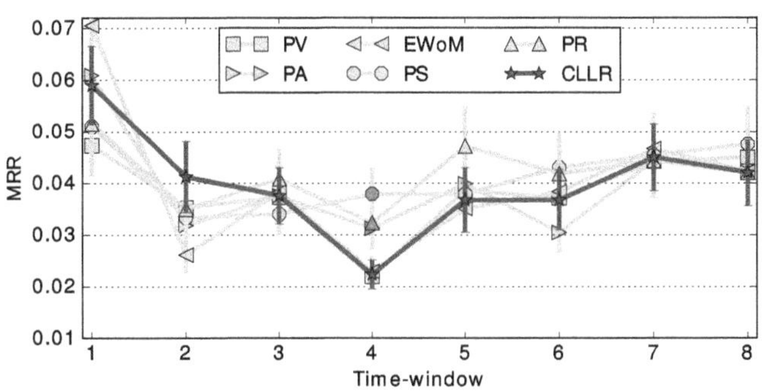

Figure 5: MRR by time window.

To further assess the robustness of CLLR in terms of the information it leverages, Table 5 shows consolidated MRR figures of the CLLR variants previously shown in Figure 5, however averaged across all eight test rounds. Intuitively, we would expect that the removal of certain preference dimensions would result in a significant loss in effectiveness. Nevertheless, none of the CLLR variants significantly differ from the complete model using all preference dimensions according to a two-tailed paired t-test with $\alpha < 0.05$. Recalling *Q1*, this result attests the effectiveness of CLLR and its robustness to noise due to eventual abnormalities in training.

Table 5: MRR after removing individual dimensions.

	PV	PR	PS	PA	EWoM
MRR	0.0383	0.0418	0.0412	0.0397	0.0400
CI (95%)	0.0020	0.0022	0.0021	0.0020	0.0020

5.2 Feature Efficiency

The previous section demonstrated the effectiveness of our proposed CLLR model in contrast to competitive lodging recommendation baselines as well as its robustness to the removal of entire preference dimensions. In this section, we address *Q2*, by assessing the contribution of each individual feature to the effectiveness of the model. To quantify feature importance, we use two complementary metrics. *Least Square Improvement* (LSI) [13, 24] is a feature importance score commonly used to measure the discriminative power of the features in boosting regression tree learners, such as LambdaMART. LSI employs the training instances that led to the creation of the model to quantify the extent to which each feature is trusted to distinguish between relevant and non-relevant instances at different nodes in the tree. While LSI measures the discriminative capabilities of each feature, we propose *Empirical Feature Efficiency* (EFE), a simple metric aimed to measure the impact in effectiveness caused by removing the feature in an ablation study. Precisely, EFE measures the relative gain (or loss) in effectiveness (in our case, given by MRR) brought by a given feature when added to a model that lacked that very same feature. A positive EFE denotes an important feature, whereas a negative EFE denotes a noisy feature. An EFE close to zero denotes an unimportant feature.

Table 6 shows EFE/LSI scores averaged across the time windows for features which obtained a statistically significance EFE (∘ indicates a significance level $\alpha \leq 0.05$, whereas • indicates $\alpha \leq 0.01$). Whenever the EFE is statistically significant and both EFE and LSI lead to the same conclusion, we consider the corresponding feature as being important. In the following, we discuss our observations for features in different preference dimensions.

Perceived Risk. This set of features models users' perception of risk, and is composed of lodging attributes, contextual features, and lodging attributes normalized by contextual features. The review count normalized by the review counts of surrounding lodgings $\widehat{r}$ (8.07/.018) has the best contribution to the model, making it the the most informative feature. Surprisingly, the unnormalized review count r (−9.8/.010) has a negative EFE and almost 50% smaller LSI than $\widehat{r}$. Although both features contribute positively to the model (according to LSI), EFE suggests that $\widehat{r}$ is a powerful substitute of r, yet they are closely related (Pearson coefficient discards trivial correlation). These observations demonstrate the potential gains of expressing a lodging's reputation in the context of its local neighborhood. Related to this observation, we highlight the importance scores of the standard deviation of the review counts of local lodgings σ_r (5.4/.001). The location rating allows guests to endorse the convenience of the lodgings' location. The location rating is one of the few ratings that obtained positive importance scores (3.0/.001) of all rating features, alongside with the overall star-rating score (4.0/.006).

Price Sensitivity. In this preference dimension, we exclusively use information of the price dispersion of the location of a lodging, to approximate users' exposure to price variation. The lodging price normalized by the Airbnb mean-price of nearby lodgings $\overline{p}_A$ (1.6/.009) obtained greater importance scores than the unnormalized price p (−3.1/.000). Once again, these results show the discriminative power of expressing lodging attributes (less/more

Table 6: Feature Importance Scores (EFE/LSI)

Feature	(EFE/LSI)
Perceived Value (PV)	
Dist. Mean (Travel)	7.1$^\bullet$/0.001
Dist. Max (Food)	5.7$^\bullet$/0.0
Dist. Mean (Food)	4.3$^\bullet$/0.0
Security Dep.	3.9$^\bullet$/0.003
Check-ins Mean (Arts)	3.5$^\bullet$/0.0
Check-ins Min. (Arts)	2.9$^\bullet$/0.004
Check-ins Med. (Travel)	2.8$^\bullet$/0.0
Check-ins Min. (Food)	2.7°/0.017
Bedrooms	0.6°/0.002
Pets Allowed	−2.0°/0.0
Hair Dryer	−2.1$^\bullet$/0.0
Dist. Norm Max (Food)	−2.2$^\bullet$/0.017
Airbed (Bed)	−2.2$^\bullet$/0.0
Pool	−2.9$^\bullet$/0.0
Price	−3.1°/0.0
Dist. Med. (Arts)	−3.3°/0.003
Dist. Min (Food)	−4.5°/0.0
Perceived Risk (PR)	
Rev. Cnt. Norm. ($\widehat{r}$)	8.1$^\bullet$/0.018
Context Rev. Cnt. Std. (σ_r)	5.4$^\bullet$/0.001
Star Rating	4.0$^\bullet$/0.006
Location (Rating)	3.0$^\bullet$/0.001
Rev. Cnt. (r)	−9.8$^\bullet$/0.01
Perceived Sensitivity (PS)	
Price Kurtosis	4.5$^\bullet$/0.008
Airbnb Skewness	3.9°/0.0
Price Norm. Airbnb ($\overline{p}_{\mathcal{A}}$)	2.6°/0.009
Electronic Word of Mouth (EWoM)	
Comp. Skewness	6.5$^\bullet$/0.0
Pos. Skewness	6.2$^\bullet$/0.0
Neg. Med.	6.1$^\bullet$/0.009
Neg. Mean	5.1$^\bullet$/0.059
Neu. Med.	4.6°/0.0
Comp. Med.	4.1°/0.0
Comp. Max	−4.1°/0.0
Pos. Min	−5.8°/0.0
Perceived Authenticity (PA)	
Auth Min.	6.3$^\bullet$/0.0
Auth Kurtosis	4.3$^\bullet$/0.0

expensive than) relative to their neighbor lodgings. Furthermore, the feature price kurtosis $\mathcal{P}$ Kurtosis (4.5/.008) (symmetry score of the curve shaped by the prices around the accommodation) has a positive contribution to the model. Such results empirically demonstrate the utility of considering the price dispersion around an accommodation. We also observe that the skewness of the Airbnb price histogram (long-tailed score) of the area where a lodging is located obtained diverging importance scores, but EFE denoting a positive impact (3.9/0.0).

Perceived Value. This preference dimension aims to model the trade-off between the monetary sacrifice against the obtained benefits. Firstly, we discuss feature importance of PV's features that overlook the location of the lodging, followed by the results of features that leverage context information. Property type, bed type, room type, cancellation policies, and amenities obtained poor feature importance scores (such attributes are categorical and treated as indicator variables in our model). Also, lodging's traits that one would expect to be important, such as number of beds, bedrooms, and bathrooms, weekly price, and monthly price, surprisingly obtained scores indicating to be noisy or with poor discriminative power. Further experiments are needed to investigate their true usefulness. The following results refer to the usage of features obtained from information of nearby venues around a lodging (leveraging context). Contrary to previous findings where EFE and LSI converged to the same conclusions, features in this category obtained diverging EFE and LSI. A conservative interpretation would not safely attribute unconditional importance to such features. However, our findings are interesting in a way that they present promising results suggesting that it may be feasible to enhance these features' discriminative capabilities to obtain converging EFE and LSI. Some distance features were highlighted by EFE to be impactful. On the other hand, features obtained from the normalized distances were systematically highlighted by the LSI as having high importance scores (6 features for arts & entertainment venues, 3 features for food, 6 features for travel & transportation).

Electronic Word of Mouth & Perceived Authenticity. The following sets of features were obtained using the text contained in the lodging's reviews. Precisely, EWoM includes statistics from sentiment polarity scores (positive, negative, neutrality, and compound) and PA includes features computed using perceived authenticity scores that positively denote a sense of PA. The mean negative sentiment scores (5.1/.059) remarkably obtained the greatest LSI score out of all the features in our model and a congruent EFE. Excluding the latter finding, the rest of the features in both categories did not obtained converging LSI and EFE scores. Nonetheless, their EFE are interesting: compound scores' skewness (6.5/.000) and median (4.1/.000); positive scores' skewness (6.2/.000); negative scores' skewness (6.1/.000); neutrality scores' median (4.6/.000); PA scores' min (6.3/.000) and PA scores' kurtosis (4.3/.000); indicating that they enhance the accuracy of the model. Once again, these feature importance results have to be taken with caution, in order to avoid misleading conclusions. However, these results are encouraging to pursue further investigations of their true usefulness.

Recalling *Q2*, this feature importance study attests the discriminative power of using contextual information to normalize features, as demonstrated for the normalized review count (PR) and the normalized lodging price (PS). Furthermore, characterizing lodgings' surrounding area evidenced the importance of contextual information to enhance the models' accuracy (e.g. standard deviation of the review counts and price kurtosis). Finally, results suggest there is room for improving the EWoM and PA preference dimensions, which may result in a further increase in effectiveness.

5.3 Model Validation

In this section, we further extend the understanding of the preference dimensions in our CLLR model, by analyzing their interactions with one another and observing their accuracy at predicting users' purchase intention. This evaluation addresses *Q3* by drawing a parallel between our data-driven findings and the socio-economic theories of the sharing economy that inspired our study. As previously stated, the preference dimensions in our model were inspired by Liang [22]'s model of Airbnb customers' repurchase intention (Figure 6).

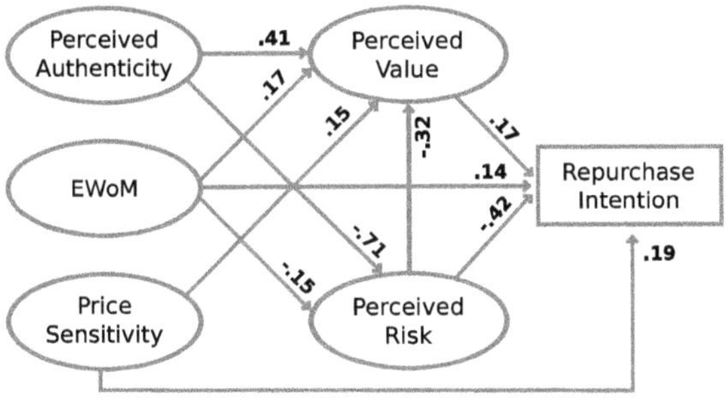

Figure 6: SEM of Airbnb Repurchase Intention (RI) [22].

Liang [22] investigated customers' intentions to reuse Airbnb as an alternative to actually predicting consumers' behavior. She relied on Structural Equation Models (SEM), a technique commonly used in socio-economic studies, which allows to analyze structural relationships based on covariance. In our work, rather than studying *repurchase* intention (RI), we are able to empirically observe Airbnb customers' *purchase* intention (PI). By measuring MRR, we can quantify how accurately each preference dimension can model PI. In particular, let $\mathcal{F} = \{PV, PR, PS, EWoM, PA\}$ denote the preference dimensions in our CLLR. When users consume an item, they implicitly state their preference towards the item's attributes. Therefore, we indirectly observe the guests' preferences for lodging's traits directly from their bookings. Given a preference dimension $\mathcal{F}_i \in \mathcal{F}$, if $\mathcal{F}_i$ shows to be discriminative when predicting users preferences, we assume that it truly implies that users give importance to $\mathcal{F}_i$. In Table 7, $\tau(\mathcal{F}_i)$ shows the MRR obtained from the evaluation of a model using solely $\mathcal{F}_i$. Additionally, $\tau(\mathcal{F}_i \cup \mathcal{F}_j)$ shows the MRR obtained from a model that combines two preference dimensions, $\mathcal{F}_i \cup \mathcal{F}_j$ (• indicates a significant difference between $\tau(\mathcal{F}_i)$ and $\tau(\mathcal{F}_i \cup \mathcal{F}_j)$ according to a two-tailed t-test with $\alpha \leq 0.05$). Finally, the column **SEM RI** indicates correlations in Liang [22]'s SEM.

The first of our findings is that PR is the factor that best explains users' PI and RI in the respective models. The risk involved in booking a lodging is the main driver for consumption and repeated consumption. Also, PV is greatly influenced by PR in both models. Furthermore, both models agree that PV does not influence PR. Our model does not support Liang [22]'s finding that there is a real interaction between PA and PR. Moreover, EWoM has a greater effect in PR than the observed in the SEM. For the rest of the edges, our model often indicates that there is a two-sided effect, not considered in Liang [22]'s research. Recalling question *Q3*, while our model supports many of the observations drawn from the socio-economic analyses conducted by Liang [22], we also find previously unseen effects, further contributing to the understanding of the drivers behind users' lodging consumption behavior in the sharing economy.

Table 7: Preference dimensions, MRR Gain/Loss

$\mathcal{F}_i$	$\tau(\mathcal{F}_i)$	$\mathcal{F}_j$	$\tau(\mathcal{F}_i \cup \mathcal{F}_j)$	SEM of RI
PR	0.038	EWoM	0.036	N/A
		PA	0.037	N/A
		PS	0.037	N/A
		PV	**0.041**	**-0.32**
PS	0.02	EWoM	0.032 •	N/A
		PA	0.037 •	N/A
		PR	0.037 •	N/A
		PV	**0.023 •**	**0.15**
EWoM	0.035	PA	0.039 •	N/A
		PR	**0.036**	**-0.15**
		PS	0.032 •	N/A
		PV	**0.036**	**0.17**
PA	0.034	EWoM	0.039 •	N/A
		PR	**0.037**	**-0.71**
		PS	0.037 •	N/A
		PV	**0.039 •**	**0.41**
PV	0.021	EWoM	0.036 •	N/A
		PA	0.039 •	N/A
		PR	0.041 •	N/A
		PS	0.023 •	N/A

6 CONCLUSIONS & FUTURE WORKS

In this work, we filled a knowledge gap in the recommender systems literature towards the sharing economy environment, precisely, in the lodging domain. We proposed a context-aware learning-to-rank model for lodging recommendation, dubbed CLLR, which demonstrated greater performance than well known state-of-the-art CF techniques and showed significant improvements compared to a real-world lodging recommender. Furthermore, the analysis of the discriminative power of the features in our model permitted the characterization of their effectiveness and demonstrated the importance that contextual information has in the lodging domain. Also, our results suggested that normalizing lodgings' attributes by leveraging context information, such as nearby lodgings' characteristics, improves the discriminative power of the devised features. In addition, we performed a characterization of the preference dimensions in our model, which highlighted the applicability of socio-economic theories of the sharing economy in a practical RS scenario. This characterization provided further evidence to state that customers' perceived risk is one of the most important factors that impacts consumption behavior, which also affects customers' perceived value of a lodging. Furthermore, our findings suggested that electronic word of mouth has a greater effect in perceived risk than the one observed in previous studies. Finally, we observed two-sided effects that were not considered by previous studies of consumption behavior on Airbnb. As future work, we intend to investigate alternative sources of contextual information in order to improve the discriminative power of the features in our model. A promising direction includes normalizing price-related features according to each individual user's perception, whenever historical data is available.

ACKNOWLEDGMENTS

This work was partially funded by projects InWeb (MCT/CNPq 573871/2008-6) and MASWeb (FAPEMIG/PRONEX APQ-01400-14), and by the authors' individual grants from CNPq, FAPEMIG, CONACYT, and COCYTEN.

REFERENCES

[1] Russell Belk. 2014. You are what you can access: Sharing and collaborative consumption online. *Journal of Business Research* 67, 8 (2014), 1595–1600.

[2] Jesús Bobadilla, Fernando Ortega, Antonio Hernando, and Abraham Gutiérrez. 2013. Recommender systems survey. *Knowledge-Based Systems* 46 (2013), 109–132.

[3] Joan Borras, Antonio Moreno, and Aida Valls. 2014. Intelligent tourism recommender systems: A survey. *Expert Systems with Applications* 41, 16 (2014), 7370–7389.

[4] Raymond C Browning, Emily A Baker, Jessica A Herron, and Rodger Kram. 2006. Effects of obesity and sex on the energetic cost and preferred speed of walking. *Journal of Applied Physiology* 100, 2 (2006), 390–398.

[5] Dimitrios Buhalis and Peter O'Connor. 2005. Information communication technology revolutionizing tourism. *Tourism recreation research* 30, 3 (2005), 7–16.

[6] Robin Burke. 2002. Hybrid recommender systems: Survey and experiments. *User modeling and user-adapted interaction* 12, 4 (2002), 331–370.

[7] Jaime Carbonell and Jade Goldstein. 1998. The use of MMR, diversity-based reranking for reordering documents and producing summaries. In *Proceedings of the 21st annual international ACM SIGIR conference on Research and development in information retrieval.* ACM, 335–336.

[8] Olivier Chapelle and Yi Chang. 2011. Yahoo! learning to rank challenge overview. In *Proceedings of the Yahoo! Learning to Rank Challenge.* 1–24.

[9] Alexandru M Degeratu, Arvind Rangaswamy, and Jianan Wu. 2000. Consumer choice behavior in online and traditional supermarkets: The effects of brand name, price, and other search attributes. *International Journal of research in Marketing* 17, 1 (2000), 55–78.

[10] Naveen Donthu and Adriana Garcia. 1999. The internet shopper. *Journal of advertising research* 39, 3 (1999), 52–52.

[11] A Felfernig, S Gordea, D Jannach, E Teppan, and M Zanker. 2007. A short survey of recommendation technologies in travel and tourism. *OEGAI Journal* 25, 7 (2007), 17–22.

[12] Samuel P Fraiberger and Arun Sundararajan. 2015. Peer-to-peer rental markets in the sharing economy. *NYU Stern School of Business Research Paper* (2015).

[13] Jerome H Friedman. 2001. Greedy function approximation: a gradient boosting machine. *Annals of statistics* (2001), 1189–1232.

[14] Michael J Gross and Graham Brown. 2008. An empirical structural model of tourists and places: Progressing involvement and place attachment into tourism. *Tourism management* 29, 6 (2008), 1141–1151.

[15] Juho Hamari, Mimmi Sjöklint, and Antti Ukkonen. 2015. The sharing economy: Why people participate in collaborative consumption. *Journal of the Association for Information Science and Technology* (2015).

[16] Clayton J Hutto and Eric Gilbert. 2014. Vader: A parsimonious rule-based model for sentiment analysis of social media text. In *Eighth International AAAI Conference on Weblogs and Social Media.*

[17] Jacob Jacoby and Leon B Kaplan. 1972. The components of perceived risk. In *SV-Proceedings of the third annual conference of the association for consumer research.*

[18] Katerina Kabassi. 2010. Personalizing recommendations for tourists. *Telematics and Informatics* 27, 1 (2010), 51–66.

[19] Rob Law, Dimitrios Buhalis, and Cihan Cobanoglu. 2014. Progress on information and communication technologies in hospitality and tourism. *International Journal of Contemporary Hospitality Management* 26, 5 (2014), 727–750.

[20] Bun Song Lee and John F McDonald. 2003. Determinants of commuting time and distance for Seoul residents: The impact of family status on the commuting of women. *Urban Studies* 40, 7 (2003), 1283–1302.

[21] Asher Levi, Osnat Mokryn, Christophe Diot, and Nina Taft. 2012. Finding a needle in a haystack of reviews: cold start context-based hotel recommender system. In *Proceedings of the sixth ACM conference on Recommender systems.* ACM, 115–122.

[22] Lena Jingen Liang. 2015. *Understanding repurchase intention of Airbnb consumers: perceived authenticity, EWoM and price sensitivity.* Ph.D. Dissertation. University of Guelph.

[23] Tie-Yan Liu and others. 2009. Learning to rank for information retrieval. *Foundations and Trends® in Information Retrieval* 3, 3 (2009), 225–331.

[24] Claudio Lucchese, Franco Maria Nardini, Salvatore Orlando, Raffaele Perego, and Nicola Tonellotto. 2015. Speeding up Document Ranking with Rank-based Features. In *Proceedings of the 38th International ACM SIGIR Conference on Research and Development in Information Retrieval.* ACM, 895–898.

[25] Mareike Möhlmann. 2015. Collaborative consumption: determinants of satisfaction and the likelihood of using a sharing economy option again. *Journal of Consumer Behaviour* 14, 3 (2015), 193–207.

[26] Mehrbakhsh Nilashi, Othman bin Ibrahim, Norafida Ithnin, and Nor Haniza Sarmin. 2015. A multi-criteria collaborative filtering recommender system for the tourism domain using Expectation Maximization (EM) and PCA–ANFIS. *Electronic Commerce Research and Applications* 14, 6 (2015), 542–562.

[27] Andreas Papatheodorou. 2001. Why people travel to different places. *Annals of tourism research* 28, 1 (2001), 164–179.

[28] Jay M Ponte and W Bruce Croft. 1998. A language modeling approach to information retrieval. In *Proceedings of the 21st annual international ACM SIGIR conference on Research and development in information retrieval.* ACM, 275–281.

[29] Daniele Quercia, Joao Paulo Pesce, Virgilio Almeida, and Jon Crowcroft. 2013. Psychological maps 2.0: a web engagement enterprise starting in London. In *Proceedings of the 22nd international conference on World Wide Web.* ACM, 1065–1076.

[30] Steffen Rendle, Christoph Freudenthaler, Zeno Gantner, and Lars Schmidt-Thieme. 2009. BPR: Bayesian personalized ranking from implicit feedback. In *Proceedings of the twenty-fifth conference on uncertainty in artificial intelligence.* AUAI Press, 452–461.

[31] Ryosuke Saga, Yoshihiro Hayashi, and Hiroshi Tsuji. 2008. Hotel recommender system based on user's preference transition. In *Systems, Man and Cybernetics, 2008. SMC 2008. IEEE International Conference on.* IEEE, 2437–2442.

[32] Raul Sanchez-Vazquez. 2017. *Repurchase Intention for Lodging Recommendation.* Master's thesis. Universidade Federal de Minas Gerais.

[33] Erika Sandow and Kerstin Westin. 2010. The persevering commuter–Duration of long-distance commuting. *Transportation Research Part A: Policy and Practice* 44, 6 (2010), 433–445.

[34] Venkatesh Shankar, Arvind Rangaswamy, and Michael Pusateri. 1999. The online medium and customer price sensitivity. *University Park: E-business Research Center* (1999).

[35] Beverley Sparks, John Bowen, and Stefanie Klag. 2003. Restaurants and the tourist market. *International Journal of Contemporary Hospitality Management* 15, 1 (2003), 6–13.

[36] Inc TranSafety. 1997. Study compares older and younger pedestrian walking speeds. *Road Management & Engineering Journal* (1997).

[37] Wen-Chin Tsao, Ming-Tsang Hsieh, Li-Wen Shih, and Tom MY Lin. 2015. Compliance with eWOM: The influence of hotel reviews on booking intention from the perspective of consumer conformity. *International Journal of Hospitality Management* 46 (2015), 99–111.

[38] Qiang Wu, Chris J. C. Burges, Krysta M. Svore, and Jianfeng Gao. 2008. *Ranking, boosting, and model adaptation.* Technical Report. Microsoft Research.

[39] Georgios Zervas, Davide Proserpio, and John Byers. 2016. The rise of the sharing economy: Estimating the impact of Airbnb on the hotel industry. *Boston U. School of Management Research Paper* 2013-16 (2016).

[40] Kai Zhang, Keqiang Wang, Xiaoling Wang, Cheqing Jin, and Aoying Zhou. 2015. Hotel recommendation based on user preference analysis. In *Data Engineering Workshops (ICDEW), 2015 31st IEEE International Conference on.* IEEE, 134–138.

Surveying User Reactions to Recommendations Based on Inferences Made by Face Detection Technology

Jennifer Marlow
FXPAL
Palo Alto, California, United States
marlow@fxpal.com

Jason Wiese
University of Utah
Salt Lake City, Utah, United States
wiese@cs.utah.edu

ABSTRACT

It is increasingly possible to use cameras and sensors to detect and analyze human appearance for the purposes of personalizing user experiences. Such systems are already deployed in some public places to personalize advertisements and recommend items. However, since these technologies are not yet widespread, we do not have a good sense of users' perception of benefits and drawbacks of public display systems that use face detection as an input for personalized recommendations. We conducted a user study with a system that inferred participants' gender and age from a facial detection and analysis algorithm and used this to present recommendations in two scenarios (finding stores to visit in a mall and finding a pair of sunglasses to buy). This work provides an initial step towards understanding user reactions to a new and emerging form of implicit recommendation based on physical appearance.

CCS CONCEPTS

H.5 Information interfaces and presentation

KEYWORDS

Face recognition; Personalization; Public displays

1 INTRODUCTION

Recommendation systems typically focus on developing algorithms and solutions to present tailored options to people online based on their online behavior (e.g. Amazon product reviews, movie recommendations, etc.). However, advances in technology are now moving the possibilities for personalization and individualized recommendations off the computer or mobile screen and out into the real world.

There is a new trend for "real-world personalization" using cameras combined with face detection and recognition to adapt and personalize information that people view in public display settings. While not yet widespread, there are examples of camera-based adaptive and personalized billboards [18], vending machines [5, 15], and even meal recommendation at fast food restaurants [7]. Currently these systems detect easily observable characteristics, (e.g. gender and age), although future sensing technologies could make more sophisticated inferences (e.g. emotional state, heart rate, or skin condition).

Given the relative recency with which camera-based public detection and personalization/recommendation systems have begun to emerge, we currently do not have a good idea of how users will react when encountering such technology. On one hand, people might see these sensing systems as beneficial (or at least as not harmful). In contrast to the online world, in a public place there is often little information about a person interacting with a public system. In these situations, even using coarse features such as age and gender to personalize an interface could help a system determine how to present more tailored information. On the other hand, people might see these types of inferences either as too invasive or as too generic to be helpful.

This work seeks to develop an understanding of user reactions to facial-recognition-based recommendations in the context of a shopping mall public display. Specifically, we explore two questions: First, how will people react to recommendations provided based on inferred gender/age? Second, what are people's attitudes towards systems that recommend items based on facial recognition in a public setting?

To explore these questions, we conducted a test of a prototype system. In this study, U.S.-based participants viewed and evaluated a personalized list of stores to visit and objects to buy. This study offers a first insight into user reactions to face-detection-driven recommender systems. Our findings suggest that in this context, participants find age to be less useful than gender as a recommendation input (with neither being considered particularly sensitive). Additionally, their comfort decreases when inaccurate detections occur, particularly of gender. These findings can help inform the design of future public displays that use facial recognition technology.

2 RELATED WORK

Providing recommendations based on an individual's preferences or characteristics can help users find relevant items in a larger item set, improve decision making, and assist a user in exploring a set of options [9]. Historically, recommendation systems have gathered information about a user's characteristics and tailored the items displayed using explicit and/or implicit feedback [21]. Explicit feedback requires an action from a user (e.g. by providing ratings on products, restaurants, or movies). Implicit

RecSys '17, August 27-31, 2017, Como, Italy

ACM ISBN 978-1-4503-4652-8/17/08...$15.00
http://dx.doi.org/10.1145/3109859.3109875

feedback, on the other hand, involves inferring interest based on online actions (such as what people are clicking on in a rating list). Each approach has pros and cons: While implicit feedback is easy to gather because it does not disrupt a user's browsing patterns, it can result in "overspecialization" where the system only recommends items that the user likes [12].

Recently, research in recommender systems has sought to move beyond making recommendations based on online behavior like clicks and browsing behavior, and has considered the role of using other (non-invasive) means of tailoring results using types of personal traits or behaviors. These have included using personality [3, 10, 20] and gaze prediction [21] as new forms of feedback to inform recommender systems. Because feedback based on physiological factors such as gaze activity is not yet widespread, it is unclear how the public will react to systems that incorporate it. For example, Zhao et al. [21] mention that gaze prediction could become commonplace, or it could face resistance from users due to privacy concerns. A similar dynamic could occur for systems that incorporate personality details – such a method requires collecting sensitive data about the user, raising the concern of privacy invasion [1].

This work focuses on assessing user reactions to recommendations based on high-level information that is detectable in public by camera: specifically, age and gender. Prior work suggests that people may be amenable to providing information about their gender and age, at least in an online context. For example, Knijnenburg and Kobsa [11] found in a survey about disclosing different types of information online that 94% of respondents did not mind disclosing their gender and 93% were willing to disclose their age. Other work has found several reasons why users of recommendation systems do not volunteer personal information like gender and age; In some cases it is intentional (to protect privacy), while other times it is unintentional (out of laziness or disinterest) [19].

It is increasingly possible to infer a user's gender and age without them agreeing to it, simply based on online behavior. Gender and other demographics can be predicted just from traces of online behavior, such as web browsing patterns [8] or posts and activity on social media [4, 13, 22] and are often used for targeting ads. Other work has shown that using gender and age outside of online ad placement might be considered less sensitive or more acceptable if users believe it actually serves a constructive purpose or will be of some benefit to them [17].

While inferring age or gender from a user's online behavior without their explicit consent is controversial, detecting this information without requiring any prior information or observations from a user (which is possible using a camera) has the potential to be even more concerning. This work explores participant reactions to exactly that type of sensing.

3 ONLINE STUDY OF USER REACTIONS

To understand user reactions to a public display that used a camera and face detection to display different kinds of information based on inferred age and gender, we first had to select a scenario to provide context to the system. We chose the scenario of a store directory in a shopping mall because shopping is a general and easily-relatable topic. We also expected that age and gender-based personalized recommendations in such a context could be useful to help shoppers explore and find relevant items in a larger item set [9].

Next, we created a simulated store directory system to investigate users' reactions after they gained a more realistic first-hand experience with the technology and its recommendations. We integrated Microsoft's Face Detection API (via webcam) into an online survey and restricted participation in the study to people who had working webcams.

We conducted the study online as a HIT on Amazon Mechanical Turk. We chose Mechanical Turk as a platform to reach a more diverse set of participants than we could using local or convenience samples [2]. Participants based within the United States who had completed over 500 tasks with a greater than 95% acceptance rate were eligible to view the HIT. They received $3.00 for participating in the 15 to 20 minute task.

Participants received the following instructions: *We are interested in getting people's reactions to a new type of technology for helping people in malls and department stores. We will show you two shopping scenarios and ask for your opinions and preferences. In order to participate in the task, we will be asking you to share your webcam (only on Page 3). This is to help simulate and give you a sense of the technology scenario.* ***Your image will not be stored or saved as part of your responses to the survey.***

The rest of the task description set up the sample scenario: Participants were asked to imagine they were on vacation in Singapore and that the airline had lost their luggage. They needed to visit an unfamiliar mall to buy (1) some clothes to wear while walking around the city and (2) a pair of sunglasses. Participants were then taken to a page representing the store directory for the mall. Instructions here were as follows: *Now we will use the webcam to recommend some items specifically for you. Make sure your face is visible below, then click the button to "verify your face appears above" - and hit "Next" in the survey. If you get an error, the webcam may not be detecting your face well so please try a few times.*

When the user clicked the button as directed, the webcam took a picture of their face and used Microsoft's Cognitive Services Face Detection API [16] to infer their gender and age from the picture (this information was used to drive the personalization of the results presented in the personalization condition). Because we did not want participants to know what the system concluded about them, (to simulate the use case where detection happens automatically and unobtrusively), we did not explicitly mention or present the system's age and gender inferences to the participant until the very end.

Participants then performed the store and sunglasses selection tasks (beginning with the store selection task). In each task, participants saw a set of 15 options (stores or sunglasses) presented together in a vertical column on one page. In the Personalized condition, the first five items in the column that corresponded to a participant's inferred gender/age category (with a yellow "recommended" banner), followed by five items labeled as being for both genders, then five items that corresponded to the opposite gender/age category. In the Unpersonalized condition, the order of the items was reversed (so there was still organization based on gender, as one would find in an ordinary mall directory,) but the most relevant items were not called out nor located at the top of the list. Approximately half of participants saw personalized stores and unpersonalized sunglasses; the other half had the reverse order of personalization.

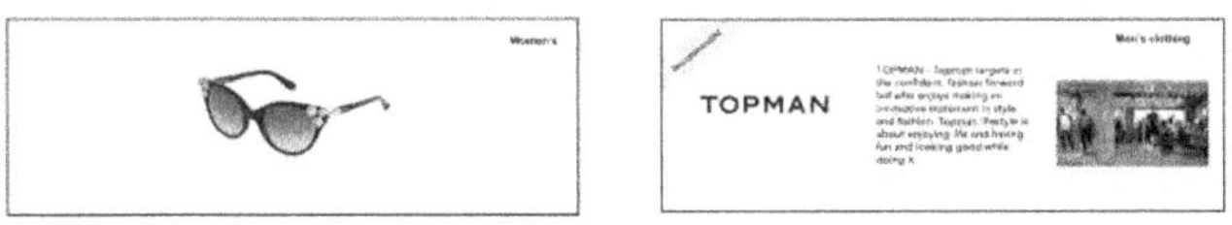

Figure 1: Sample of "unpersonalized" women's glasses and "personalized" men's clothing store

For both tasks, the study asked participants to look at the webpage listing all 15 items and then to check or select three items from the list that they were interested in trying. We recorded the position in the list of each item, and also recorded the amount of time taken to make the decision. At the end, we asked participants to rate how satisfied they were with the process of choosing stores and items within a store.

After completing the two selection tasks, we explained the purpose of the study and then showed participants what the system thought their age and gender were. Age was presented as a single number based on the Microsoft Cognitive Services API's estimate. We asked participants to rate whether or not the age was accurate within five years.

Next, the survey asked: *Now that you've experienced a sample of what it's like, how comfortable would you feel with a store directory detecting your age and gender and using this information to recommend stores/products to you? (You can assume that your picture isn't saved or recorded).* We also solicited participants' opinions about the relevance and appropriateness of using face detection for recommendations in an open-ended question. We concluded with two Likert Scale questions about the perceived benefit of the system, perceived privacy intrusion, and two questions about privacy attitudes more broadly.

4 RESULTS

In total, 44 participants took part in the study. First, we wanted to examine the role of providing recommendations on choice behavior. Figure 2 shows the percentages of participants who chose items defined as being for their "same gender" (e.g. women's items if the person was a woman), "neutral" items (things defined as being for men and women), and "opposite gender" items.

Overall, there were no significant differences of "recommending" an item for males in terms of the items they chose. Men chose "men's" items 67% of the time with no recommendations, and 61% of the time with recommendations. However, female participants were significantly more likely to choose a "female" item when it was recommended (79%) than when it was not recommended (61%) (X^2 (2,114)=7.24, p=.02). Further analysis of participants' choices showed that people in the "unpersonalized" condition frequently scrolled down to the bottom of the list to choose their own gender items. There were no significant differences in time taken to complete either task with or without the recommendations. There were also no significant differences in how easy the task was reported to be with or without recommendations.

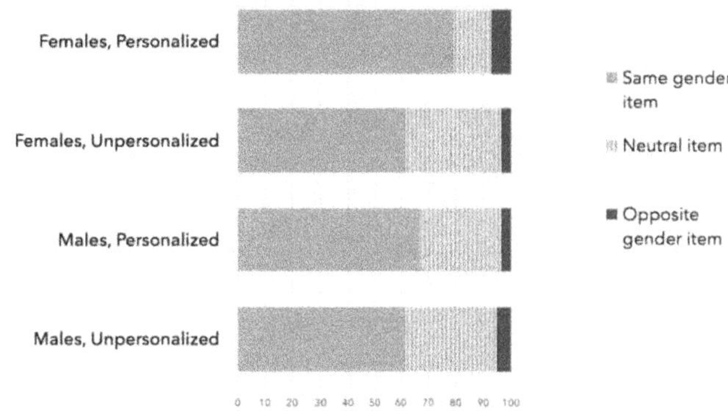

Figure 2: Percentage of participants choosing same gender, neutral, and opposite gender items

4.1 Reactions to system

Based on participants' responses, the system accurately detected the correct gender and age (+/- five years) for 24 participants. The system incorrectly detected age for an additional 14 participants, of whom the system also incorrectly classified six females as male. Table 1 presents reported comfort with gender detection and age detection by prediction accuracy (0=completely uncomfortable, 100=completely comfortable).

Table 1: Comfort with gender & age detection (Mean, SD)

Results of face detection algorithm	N	Comfort, gender detection	Comfort, age detection
Correct gender + age	24	85.3 (21.6)	67.8 (30.6)
Correct gender, Incorrect age	14	88.5 (14.9)	74.8 (21.8)
Incorrect gender, Correct age	2	49.0 (33.9)	50.0 (35.4)
Incorrect gender + age	4	25.0 (38.2)	22.50 (33.4)

Overall, participants were significantly more comfortable with a camera-based store directory system detecting information about gender (M=79.2) than they were with it detecting information about age (M=65.1) (F(1,86)=4.92, p=.03). Interestingly, there was a significant drop-off in comfort levels for people whose gender was misclassified. In these cases, they were not only less comfortable with gender detection but they were also less comfortable with age detection. Accuracy did not influence other measures such as satisfaction or ease of the task; however, this could be due to the fairly small set of choices.

We examined the open-ended responses to understand more about why people reacted as they did to the system and its recommendations. We used an open-coding process to categorize the responses as positive or negative. Then we used affinity diagramming to cluster the responses around common themes, which are presented in order of frequency in Table 2.

Table 2: Categorization of open-ended responses

Positive reaction	Negative reaction
PR1. Convenience, help narrow down options, speed up process [n=9]	NR1. Recommendations were based on stereotypes; not helpful [n=4]
PR2. Not a problem, not concerning [n=7]	NR2. Age not helpful for recommendations [n=4]
PR3. Age and gender are not sensitive info [n=5]	NR3. Prefer to make own choices when shopping [n=3]
PR4. Machine inferences are the same as what a person or salesperson could infer [n=3]	NR4. General dislike for cameras [n=2]
PR5. Recommendations were good [n=3]	NR5. Time consuming [n=1]

24 participants had only positive reactions, 10 provided a mixture of positive and negative reactions, and 9 had purely negative reactions. PR1 was the most commonly cited positive reaction, where people thought a camera-based recommendation system for shopping could be convenient in helping narrow down options, speed up the process, or filter results: *I think it's kind of cool too. I feel it could really help give me stores that would be relevant to me, and exclude stores that are more focused on the other gender or for different age groups* (P13).

The following quote exemplifies PR3 (a feeling that age and gender are not sensitive): *I don't mind it at all. age and gender aren't a secret. So I actually consider this to be an advantage. I like this idea and can see it catching on as long as it doesn't dig deeper than those two categories* (P6). Similarly, PR4 equated the inferences made by the system with a human's capabilities: *I feel fine with that information being used because any salesman in the mall can take a quick look at me and make the same recommendations based on age and gender.*

On the negative side, NR1 expressed a dislike for stereotype-based recommendations: *The system is using stereotypes to recommend things to me* (P25). NR2 had to do with the fact that age was seen as less relevant for recommendations than gender: *why would I like something just because I am a certain age. I still shop at "teen" shops even though I am almost 30!* (P35). NR3 had to do with a general preference to look around and discover things on one's own: *I think it's fine except I don't really want a machine recommending me things to buy. I have my own tastes and I doubt a machine can determine that* (P20).

Seven comments addressed the role of accuracy. People were happy to have their age underestimated (no one mentioned that their age was overestimated): *First of all, I like that it underestimated my age. I'm going to be 77 and it guessed 59.2!* (P3). In terms of gender, one woman who was misclassified as a male wrote: *I feel uncomfortable because it thought I was male. I'm actually female* (P16). People who did not experience such detrimental inaccuracies were more pleased with the results: *As it stands it cut off 13 years and got my gender correct. I liked it and it gave me some good suggestions* (P12).

5 DISCUSSION

These results seem to indicate different reactions to detecting age and gender. Gender was seen as less problematic and more helpful for recommendations when it was assessed correctly, but was problematic when assessed incorrectly. Users' reactions to misclassified age were positive when it was underestimated. As a result, in cases of uncertainty it may be beneficial to underestimate rather than overestimate. This fits with the typical cultural assumption that it is preferable to be mistaken as younger than one actually is. However, we also did not have any reactions where participant ages were overestimated, so we cannot say from this data how harmful it would be to overestimate somebody's age.

Participants' reasons for disliking the system in this study point to a potentially problematic future for these systems. These concerns seem unlikely to go away (i.e. improving the technology accuracy will not relieve the concerns). Perceived benefits may increase if privacy is ensured (e.g. systems are prevented by regulations from storing face images, recommendations are not viewable by passers-by) or the use case is convincing (using gender/age inferences for health or fitness recommendations may be more useful than for shopping).

This exploratory study has some limitations: it was done using Mechanical Turk with participants who agreed to share their webcams, and was not in a publicly-deployed context. In the future, we will try a physical instantiation of the store directory and also explore other types of scenarios (for example, health/gym kiosk, museum kiosk, movie ticket recommender) to see how participants' reactions vary in these different settings. We might encounter different reactions in different contexts, as users' information disclosure decisions are highly dependent on context and presumed benefit [14, 17]. While participants saw some value in clothing recommendations based on gender (less so on age), trying other contexts will help us explore the design space in which age and gender are seen as more or less useful and helpful for making recommendations.

REFERENCES

[1] Amos Azaria and Jason Hong. 2016. Recommender Systems with Personality. In Proceedings of the 10th ACM Conference on Recommender Systems, 207–210.

[2] Adam J. Berinsky, Gregory A. Huber, and Gabriel S. Lenz. 2012. Evaluating online labor markets for experimental research: Amazon. com's Mechanical Turk. Political Analysis 20, 3: 351–368.

[3] Shlomo Berkovsky, Ronnie Taib, and Dan Conway. 2017. How to Recommend?: User Trust Factors in Movie Recommender Systems. Proceedings of the International Conference on Intelligent User Interfaces. ACM, 287-300.

[4] Smriti Bhagat, Udi Weinsberg, Stratis Ioannidis, and Nina Taft. 2014. Recommending with an agenda: Active learning of private attributes using matrix factorization. In Proceedings of the 8th ACM Conference on Recommender systems, 65–72.

[5] Lauren Davidson. 2014. The vending machine of the future is here, and it knows who you are. http://www.telegraph.co.uk/finance/newsbysector/retailandconsumer/11274179/The-vending-machine-of-the-future-is-here-and-it-knows-who-you-are.html

[6] F. Maxwell Harper, Funing Xu, Harmanpreet Kaur, Kyle Condiff, Shuo Chang, and Loren Terveen. 2015. Putting users in control of their recommendations. In Proceedings of the 9th ACM Conference on Recommender Systems, 3–10.

[7] Amy Hawkins. 2017. KFC China is using facial recognition tech to serve customers – but are they buying it? https://www.theguardian.com/technology/2017/jan/11/china-beijing-first-smart-restaurant-kfc-facial-recognition

[8] Jian Hu, Hua-Jun Zeng, Hua Li, Cheng Niu, and Zheng Chen. 2007. Demographic prediction based on user's browsing behavior. In Proceedings of the 16th international conference on World Wide Web, 151–160.

[9] Dietmar Jannach and Gediminas Adomavicius. 2016. Recommendations with a Purpose. In Proceedings of the 10th ACM Conference on Recommender Systems, 7–10.

[10] Raghav Pavan Karumur, Tien T. Nguyen, and Joseph A. Konstan. 2016. Exploring the value of personality in predicting rating behaviors: a study of category preferences on movielens. In Proceedings of the 10th ACM Conference on Recommender Systems, 139–142.

[11] Bart P. Knijnenburg and Alfred Kobsa. 2013. Making decisions about privacy: information disclosure in context-aware recommender systems. ACM Transactions on Interactive Intelligent Systems (TiiS) 3, 3: 20.

[12] Bart P. Knijnenburg, Saadhika Sivakumar, and Daricia Wilkinson. 2016. Recommender systems for self-actualization. In Proceedings of the 10th ACM Conference on Recommender Systems, 11–14.

[13] Michal Kosinski, David Stillwell, and Thore Graepel. 2013. Private traits and attributes are predictable from digital records of human behavior. Proceedings of the National Academy of Sciences 110, 15: 5802–5805.

[14] Scott Lederer, Jennifer Mankoff, and Anind K. Dey. 2003. Who wants to know what when? privacy preference determinants in ubiquitous computing. In CHI'03 extended abstracts on Human factors in computing systems, 724–725.

[15] Elaine Lies. 2010. Japan vending machine recommends drinks to buyers. http://www.reuters.com/article/us-japan-machines-idUSTRE6AE0G720101115

[16] Microsoft Cognitive Services Face Detection API https://www.microsoft.com/cognitive-services/en-us/face-api

[17] Helen Nissenbaum. 2010. Privacy in context: Technology, policy, and the integrity of social life. Stanford University Press.

[18] Andrew Tarantola. 2015. Hey ladies, this German billboard wants to sell you a beer. https://www.engadget.com/2015/05/21/hey-ladies-this-german-billboard-wants-to-sell-you-a-beer/

[19] Udi Weinsberg, Smriti Bhagat, Stratis Ioannidis, and Nina Taft. 2012. BlurMe: Inferring and obfuscating user gender based on ratings. In Proceedings of the sixth ACM conference on Recommender systems, 195–202.

[20] Wen Wu, Li Chen, and Liang He. 2013. Using personality to adjust diversity in recommender systems. In Proceedings of the 24th ACM Conference on Hypertext and Social Media, 225–229.

[21] Qian Zhao, Shuo Chang, F. Maxwell Harper, and Joseph A. Konstan. 2016. Gaze Prediction for Recommender Systems. In Proceedings of the 10th ACM Conference on Recommender Systems, 131–138.

[22] Xin Wayne Zhao, Yanwei Guo, Yulan He, Han Jiang, Yuexin Wu, and Xiaoming Li. 2014. We know what you want to buy: a demographic-based system for product recommendation on microblogs. In Proceedings of the 20th ACM SIGKDD international conference on Knowledge discovery and data mining, 1935–1944.

An Insurance Recommendation System Using Bayesian Networks

Maleeha Qazi
American Family Insurance, Strategic Data & Analytics
mqazi@amfam.com

Glenn M. Fung
American Family Insurance, Strategic Data & Analytics
gfung@amfam.com

Katie J. Meissner
American Family Insurance, Strategic Data & Analytics
kmeissne@amfam.com

Eduardo R. Fontes
American Family Insurance, Strategic Data & Analytics
erfontes@gmail.com

ABSTRACT

In this paper we describe a deployed recommender system to predict insurance products for new and existing customers. Our goal is to give our customers personalized recommendations based on what other similar people with similar portfolios have, in order to make sure they were adequately covered for their needs. Our system uses customer characteristics in addition to customer portfolio data. Since the number of possible recommendable products is relatively small, compared to other recommender domains, and missing data is relatively frequent, we chose to use Bayesian Networks for modeling our system. Experimental results show advantages of using probabilistic graphical models over the widely used low-rank matrix factorization model for the insurance domain.

KEYWORDS

Recommender systems; Bayesian Networks; Insurance domain; Structure Learning; Deployed system

1 MOTIVATION

Our motivation for creating a recommendation system for the insurance domain stems from wanting to provide value for our customer and our company. We strive to offer products and options that are relevant to our customers, to help narrow down their set of choices to those most appropriate for them, and to improve the overall customer experience. This will increase trust and customer loyalty for the company. The company, in turn, can use the obtained knowledge of the customer base to help create actions to maximize specific company objectives.

The aim is to predict relevant insurance products for our customers based on what other similar people with similar portfolios have. We want to be able to do this for both our current customer base & the prospective customer base. Due to the shifting nature of how people choose to buy insurance, we cannot assume that customers will always have or take time to meet with agents for this purpose. The varying knowledge level of each agent for different products can also influence the customer experience. The current version of the recommender system hopes to aid our agents in providing value to our customers by generating recommendations based on customer portfolio data, and then allowing agents to act on these recommendations as they see fit. The human interaction aspect is relied on for the best possible experience for the customer. Future versions of the system will allow for direct customer interaction & offers.

RecSys '17, August 27–31, 2017, Como, Italy

ISBN 978-1-4503-4652-8/17/08...$15.00.
DOI: http://dx.doi.org/10.1145/3109859.3109907

2 RELATED WORK

To our knowledge, there are not many documented instances of recommender systems for the insurance domain. Some include: [16], [17], and [8]. [16] describes the unique properties of the insurance domain, and is focused on a system for call center reps servicing Life & Annuity policies with very limited knowledge of the products or customers. Our current system is for agents, who have higher degrees of knowledge about their customers, & is for auto, property, life, and umbrella policies (for which they might not have all the detailed information). In contrast with our system, [17] suggests that their system is based on a standard user-user collaborative filtering approach. [8] is focused on life insurance & uses association rules to create recommendations which are served directly to customers via the web.

There is documentation of a knowledge-based interactive recommender application in the financial industry [7], which was built to assist sales representatives in determining personalized financial service portfolios for their customers. The system walks a sales rep through a series of questions during a conversation with a customer, and outputs an automated summary of the advisory session.

It caught our attention, that a paper that compared some collaborative filtering algorithms [4] showed that for a wide range of conditions, Bayesian networks outperformed other methods. The preferred method depended on the nature of the data and the application, but the paper highlights that Bayesian networks have smaller memory requirements & allow for faster predictions, but require a learning phase that can take a significant amount of time (multiple hours, depending on the amount of data and features) which is not a problem in our case.

Low Rank Matrix Factorization (LRMF) models are a widely used algorithm for recommender systems. We experimented with the Boosted Inductive Matrix Completion algorithms (BIMC) as described in [15], [23], [21], and [2].

3 DESIGN CONSIDERATIONS

The following sections will describe an overview of the whole deployed system and the key design decisions made during the design process.

3.1 System Overview

Our deployed recommender system consists of the following modules, executed in-order:

(1) **The recommendation module:** This is the core recommender model, it takes the input customer data (portfolio, policy, etc.) and generates predictions for likely recommendations.
(2) **The optimization module**: it takes as an input a set of possible recommendations from the recommendation module and prioritizes recommendations based on an optimization criteria predefined by the business. Possible choices for optimization strategies are: customer retention, customer satisfaction, & customer lifetime value (prediction or estimation of the net profit attributed to the entire future relationship with a customer).
(3) **The business rule module:** This module filters recommendations according to business rules to ensure that the final recommendations are appropriate for the customer. For example, it filters out a recommendation if a similar recommendation has been presented to the customer recently (this is based on the system's business requirement).

The final goal is to have the system deployed as a service that can be used in different company applications: As a tool to assist agents (our focus in this paper), as a customer facing recommendation engine, and as a tool to assist our marketing department, among others.

3.2 Models' Scope

For the initial phase of the project, we chose to focus on 3 states: Ohio (OH), Utah (UT), & Nebraska (NE). Since the model features are line specific, we chose to create a property and an auto model per state - for a total of 6 models. All recommendations are made at the policy level.

The purpose of the system for this phase is to suggest new product offers (for both cross-sell and up-sell) for every existing customer. "Cross-sell" means a model recommends a different product line (e.g.: auto model recommends property, life, or umbrella coverage), vs. "up-sell" which means a model recommends an additional coverage in the same product line (e.g. property model recommends id fraud coverage).

Both the property and auto models have 3 cross-sell targets/products: for the auto models they are property, umbrella, and life, and for the property models they are auto, umbrella, and life. The final recommendation for the two cross-sell targets (life and umbrella) that have predictions from both the auto and property models is made by combining both predictions in an optimal way.

In addition, the auto models have 7 up-sell targets/products (comprehensive coverage, collision coverage, emergency road-side service, medical expense, rental reimbursement, death & dismemberment, and lease/loan gap coverage), and the property models have 3 up-sell targets/products (sewer/sump pump overflow coverage, itemized personal property coverage, and id fraud coverage).

3.3 Data Used by the Models

We chose to use data from four product lines: auto, property, umbrella, & life.

The auto data consisted of coverage details (limits, deductibles, discounts, etc.), customer demographics (age, gender, marital status, etc.), household characteristics, and various risk factors. The property data consisted of policy data, coverage details, options and endorsements, dwelling characteristics, household characteristics, customer demographics, sewer and wildfire risk, and geological data. In addition, we used other related policy indicators (for umbrella and life).

As described above, the data for this project came from multiple disparate sources, and the first task was to consolidate the data into a single database. We created a series of jobs to then wrangle the data into the granularity we desired for modeling: from transactional data to tables where each row contained a single policy's information. Then, we did some business analysis to determine the features that are most likely to be available at the time of execution, and contained the most relevant information for the task at hand. This analysis included data source analysis, raw/derived feature analysis, business work-flow analysis, statistical data checks, etc.

Our data contained both discrete and continuous features. Some of the continuous features were manually discretized based on business logic because that made that most sense, but most were binned using the K-Means algorithm [10]. Due to the nature of the data, missing values were kept as separate states for each node, where they were found, because their absence was considered significant.

3.4 Modeling Techniques

During the system design process, we experimented with two algorithms: (a) Bayesian networks (BN) and (b) Low rank matrix factorization (LRMF) models. We chose not to use collaborative filtering because our missing-values would cause issues with defining similarities between users which is a requirement of such algorithms.

A Bayesian network is a probabilistic generative graphical model that represents a set of variables of interest and their conditional dependencies via a directed acyclic graph (DAG). These models are intuitively easy for a human to understand due to the direct dependencies and local distributions vs. a complete joint distribution. And they have both causal and probabilistic semantics that are ideal to represent the combination of prior knowledge and data. In addition, they deal gracefully with missing values. This is one of the main reasons we considered this algorithm for our system since we want to use the methodology for both current and prospective customers for which missing data is common. A detailed introduction to graphical models can be found in [13].

The LRMF models are content-independent of the items being recommended, and they scale well with respect to the number of products added for consideration. In particular, we used a Python implementation of the Inductive Matrix Completion algorithm (IMC), the Boosted Inductive Matrix Completion algorithm (BIMC) ([15], [23], [21], and [2]). This version of LRMF allows for the incorporation of features (customer and policy characteristics) in addition to the label matrix (portfolio features).

There are several characteristics of our problem that made the Bayesian Network approach a better fit in our case:

- Most of our features derived from policy and customer data have discrete values.
- Traditional recommendation systems deal with many products, but in our case we had a limited number of products to work with.
- We had a number of missing values in our dataset that needed to be dealt with.

As we will show later in Section 4, in our initial experiments, we obtained better results with the BN approach.

3.5 Model Training

As described above, for the initial phase of the project, we created a total of 6 models: an auto and property model for each of the 3 states (OH, UT, NE) we were focusing on. The auto and property models were kept separate due to the distinct types of features used for each - the feature sets did not overlap. Also, the value ranges of the features varied by state so we choose to keep each state separate as well.

We tried various tools for BN learning: Weka BN tools [9], bnlearn for R [14, 18–20], the Python library libpgm [11], Netica [3], & BayesiaLab [1]. Due to its rich feature set, we chose BayesiaLab as the tool of choice for this phase of our system. All learning/training was done using the BayesiaLab GUI, since most of the necessary features are not provided via API. But all predictions from learned models were generated using the provided Java API.

Most available algorithms for structure learning are either unsupervised or only consider one target variable in the supervised case. Since we had multiple targets for each of the networks we wanted to learn, we tried multiple structure learning methodologies:

(1) Creating a non-empty start point by manual addition of arcs based on business & logical relationships and then running the Taboo algorithm (unsupervised learning).
(2) Learning the Augmented Markov blanket of each target separately (supervised learning), concatenating all the learned networks together, setting no targets, and using that as a non-empty starting point for running the Taboo algorithm.
(3) Running various unsupervised algorithms from a totally empty starting point (i.e. only nodes, no added arcs).
(4) Allowing for more links to the target nodes (by dropping the local structural coefficients to 0) and restricted links among other variables (by leaving the default structural coefficients), and applying various unsupervised algorithms to get the final structure.

The final auto models used the first methodology, and the final property models used a combination of the other three methodologies.

We made a 70/30 train/test split with each dataset. Recommendations were made by running inference on each target in the BN, which made it a multi-label classification problem. For each target, we evaluated the models based on the ROC (Receiver Operating Characteristic) curves [6]. The networks that gave the best test-set AUCs (Area Under Curve) across all targets were chosen as the final networks. In general, the property models had more features/nodes and were more complex than the auto models. Precision@N was not a relevant metric for us since: (a) we had a small number of possible recommendations per household and (b) for each possible recommendation type there are two possibles outcomes (recommend or not) to be shown to the agent. Hence we did not need to rank the recommendations. Since our recommendations are meant to be of the form "if you like A, then you will like B" (e.g. Amazon), time was also not a relevant factor.

Target/ State	NE Test AUC	OH Test AUC	UT Test AUC
Gap	86.99%	86.08%	82.00%
ERS	70.83%	76.99%	74.00%
RR lmt (mean)	80.06%	81.06%	77.50%
Med lmt (mean)	70.07%	74.04%	68.33%
D&D lmt (mean)	70.36%	68.77%	66.75%
Comp ded (mean)	89.87%	87.76%	84.25%
Coll ded (mean)	96.70%	94.96%	93.33%
Umbrella	90.68%	88.97%	87.00%
Property	81.89%	82.11%	88.00%
Life	97.02%	96.44%	93.00%

Table 1: Auto Test Set AUCs (BN)

Target/ State	NE Test AUC	OH Test AUC	UT Test AUC
Sewer lmt (mean)	77.77%	76.37%	79.20%
Itemized Pers Prop	74.72%	75.98%	75.87%
ID Fraud	70.38%	72.54%	74.58%
Umbrella	87.34%	85.89%	85.84%
Life	65.30%	64.65%	70.36%
Auto	64.79%	65.72%	65.11%

Table 2: Property Test Set AUCs (BN)

4 MODEL RESULTS

4.1 Pre-deployment Off-line Validation

Next, we show model validation results obtained before model deployment. The final auto networks' test-set AUCs across all targets are shown in Table 1. "Ded" stands for deductible, and "lmt" stands for limit. The final property networks' test-set AUCs across all targets are shown in Table 2. For the multi-state targets in both tables, AUCs were an average of the calculated AUC per state.

Table 3 shows comparisons between the low rank models and the BN on the UT property data (with the same data binning, and train/test data split). The best results are in bold. As it can be seen from the table, in general, the BN approach performed better. The same trend was observed for all the 6 models we built. Figure 1 shows an example of the auto network's structure for the state of OH.

4.2 Post-deployment On-line Validation

The system went live on 17 Nov 2016, and since then 4 check-points have been taken of how well the system is performing according to the operational metrics defined by business (check-points taken: 14, 56, 89, & 112 days from launch). The initial/beta roll-out went

Target/ State	IMC AUC	BIMC AUC	BN AUC
Sewer lmt	75.63%	76.51%	**79.20%**
Itemized Pers Prop	68.68%	75.08%	**75.87%**
ID Fraud	67.51%	73.49%	**74.58%**
Umbrella	81.99%	84.55%	**85.84%**
Life	71.82%	**73.14%**	70.36%
Auto	66.44%	**85.91%**	65.11%

Table 3: Low Rank Model UT Property Test Set AUCs (vs. BN). Best results in bold.

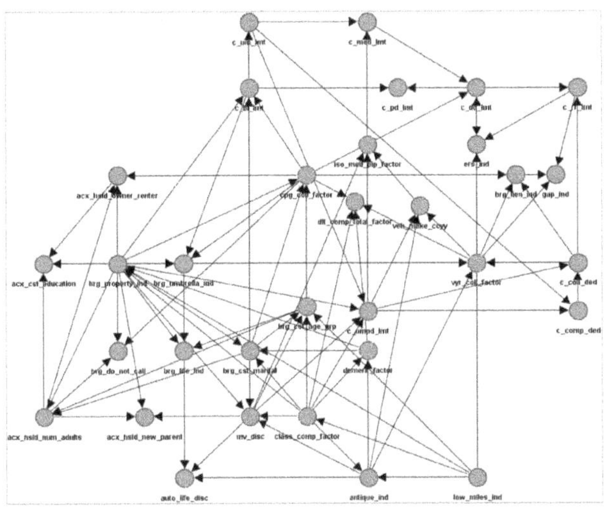

Figure 1: Example of the auto network for the state of OH. Complexity: 33 nodes, 89 arcs, avg. of 2.69 parents/children per node.

to 18 agents across the 3 states (OH, UT, NE). These individuals were the district sales representatives of those states. As of 3 Feb 2017, all remaining agents in those 3 states were given access to the recommendations generated for their accounts (only the 89 & 112 day checkpoints would be affected by this increase in number of agents; total of 619 agents licensed to sell in those 3 states).

At the last checkpoint taken (date: 3/9/2017), there were 366,998 active recommendations, 737 received agent action/feedback (accept: 104, decline: 465, defer: 56, quote initiated: 112).

Our deployed recommender has been well received in general by the agents. Some of the good feedback we have received from them includes:

- "I've increased premium volume with 3 customers in only 2 days"
- "[it] brings attention to details to every customer."
- "..is a valuable teaching tool for ourselves and our staff."

For this stage of the system, success is measured by conversion, which is the percentage of offers presented that get accepted by the customer. The conversion per state for offers generated by the system was calculated at each checkpoint, and compared to the standard industry conversion baseline of 12%, as shown in Figure 2. As expected, because NE & OH have higher recommendation

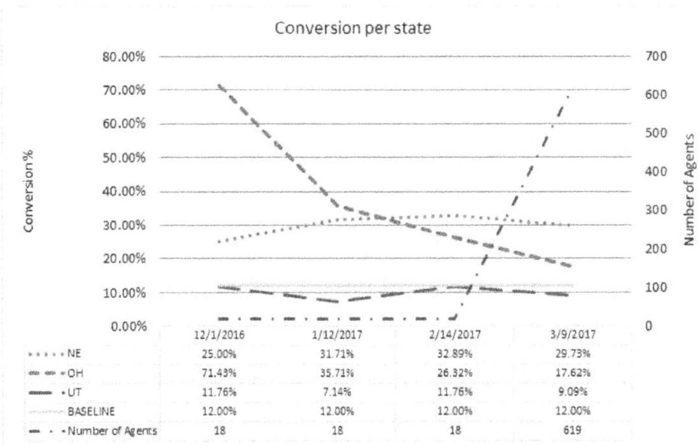

Figure 2: Conversion Across All States vs. Baseline

counts than UT, the conversion percent is higher in those states vs. UT, which is closer to the baseline.

We will wait for a year of feedback to calculate more sophisticated performance indicators (like retention) to assess the recommender's impact on the business using a test & learn methodology [12].

5 CONCLUSIONS AND LESSONS LEARNED

The recommender system we deployed aims to help the entire customer base by uniformly bringing coverage options to the attention of agents so that our customers are adequately covered for their needs. Clearly an agent tailors the recommendation coverage for each customer, but the system helps prompt this action, whereas before there were no prompts for agents.

We learned that business rules were very important. For example, the gap target didn't make sense because based on underwriting criteria this could only be added at the initial point of car purchase, and adjusting the model's thresholds for giving recommendations are very sensitive for business success.

6 FUTURE WORK

We have many things we'd like to try to improve our system, among them are:

- Create unified models for all lines instead of having separate models for auto and property
- Extend the system to prospective customers. This was one of the main reasons for our choice of Bayesian networks. There is a lot of information missing for prospective customers so the model should be able to gracefully adapt and make predictions with little available data.
- Compare our results to the deep learning approaches proposed in [5, 22].
- Roll-out recommendation models for the remaining states.
- Go beyond cross-sell and up-sell targets to "next best action" for any customer at any time. E.g., send a timely communication to the customer or grant an additional discount.

REFERENCES

- [1] Bayesialab. http://www.bayesia.com/. Versions: 5.4.3 & 6.0.2; Accessed: 1-Feb-2017.
- [2] IMC software. http://bigdata.ices.utexas.edu/software/inductive-matrix-completion/. Online; Accessed 1-Feb-2017.
- [3] Netica application. https://www.norsys.com/netica.html. Accessed: 1-Feb-2017.
- [4] J. S. Breese, D. Heckerman, and C. Kadie. Empirical analysis of predictive algorithms for collaborative filtering. In *Proceedings of the Fourteenth Conference on Uncertainty in Artificial Intelligence*, UAI'98, pages 43–52, San Francisco, CA, USA, 1998. Morgan Kaufmann Publishers Inc.
- [5] H.-T. Cheng, L. Koc, J. Harmsen, T. Shaked, T. Chandra, H. Aradhye, G. Anderson, G. Corrado, W. Chai, M. Ispir, R. Anil, Z. Haque, L. Hong, V. Jain, X. Liu, and H. Shah. Wide and deep learning for recommender systems. *arXiv:1606.07792*, 2016.
- [6] T. Fawcett. An introduction to roc analysis. *Pattern Recogn. Lett.*, 27(8):861–874, June 2006.
- [7] A. Felfernig and A. Kiener. Knowledge-based interactive selling of financial services with fsadvisor. In *Proceedings of the 17th Conference on Innovative Applications of Artificial Intelligence - Volume 3*, IAAI'05, pages 1475–1482. AAAI Press, 2005.
- [8] A. Gupta and A. Jain. Life insurance recommender system based on association rule mining and dual clustering method for solving cold-start problem. *International Journal of Advanced Research in Computer Science and Software Engineering*, 3, Oct 2013.
- [9] M. Hall, E. Frank, G. Holmes, B. Pfahringer, P. Reutemann, and I. H. Witten. The weka data mining software: An update. *SIGKDD Explor. Newsl.*, 11(1):10–18, Nov. 2009.
- [10] T. Kanungo, D. M. Mount, N. S. Netanyahu, C. D. Piatko, R. Silverman, and A. Y. Wu. An efficient k-means clustering algorithm: Analysis and implementation. *IEEE Trans. Pattern Anal. Mach. Intell.*, 24(7):881–892, July 2002.
- [11] K. R. Karkera. *Building Probabilistic Graphical Models with Python*. Packt Publishing, 2014.
- [12] D. C. Montgomery. *Design and Analysis of Experiments*. John Wiley & Sons, 2006.
- [13] K. P. Murphy. An introduction to graphical models. Technical report, 2001.
- [14] R. Nagarajan and M. Scutari. *Bayesian Networks in R with Applications in Systems Biology*. Springer, New York, 2013. ISBN 978-1-4614-6445-7, 978-1-4614-6446-4.
- [15] N. Natarajan and I. S. Dhillon. Inductive matrix completion for predicting gene-disease associations. *Bioinformatics*, 30, jun 2014.
- [16] L. Rokach, G. Shani, B. Shapira, E. Chapnik, and G. Siboni. Recommending insurance riders.
- [17] B. P. Sanghamitra Mitra, Nilendra Chaudhari. Leveraging hybrid recommendation system in insurance domain. *International Journal of Engineering and Computer Science*, 3, Oct 2014.
- [18] M. Scutari. Learning bayesian networks with the bnlearn R package. *Journal of Statistical Software*, 35(3):1–22, 2010.
- [19] M. Scutari. Bayesian network constraint-based structure learning algorithms: Parallel and optimized implementations in the bnlearn R package. *Journal of Statistical Software*, 77(2):1–20, 2017.
- [20] M. Scutari and J.-B. Denis. *Bayesian Networks with Examples in R*. Chapman and Hall, Boca Raton, 2014. ISBN 978-1-4822-2558-7, 978-1-4822-2560-0.
- [21] D. Shin, S. Cetintas, K.-C. Lee, and I. S. Dhillon. Tumblr blog recommendation with boosted inductive matrix completion. In *Proceedings of the 24th ACM International on Conference on Information and Knowledge Management*, CIKM '15, pages 203–212, New York, NY, USA, 2015. ACM.
- [22] F. Strub, R. Gaudel, and J. Mary. Hybrid Recommender System based on Autoencoders. In *the 1st Workshop on Deep Learning for Recommender Systems*, pages 11 – 16, Boston, United States, Sept. 2016.
- [23] H.-F. Yu, P. Jain, P. Kar, and I. S. Dhillon. Large-scale multi-label learning with missing labels. In *Proceedings of the 31st International Conference on International Conference on Machine Learning - Volume 32*, ICML'14, pages I–593–I–601. JMLR.org, 2014.

Getting Deep Recommenders Fit: Bloom Embeddings for Sparse Binary Input/Output Networks

Joan Serrà and Alexandros Karatzoglou
Telefónica Research
Pl. Ernest Lluch i Martín, 5
Barcelona, Spain 08019
firstname.lastname@telefonica.com

ABSTRACT

Recommendation algorithms that incorporate techniques from deep learning are becoming increasingly popular. Due to the structure of the data coming from recommendation domains (i.e., one-hot-encoded vectors of item preferences), these algorithms tend to have large input and output dimensionalities that dominate their overall size. This makes them difficult to train, due to the limited memory of graphical processing units, and difficult to deploy on mobile devices with limited hardware. To address these difficulties, we propose Bloom embeddings, a compression technique that can be applied to the input and output of neural network models dealing with sparse high-dimensional binary-coded instances. Bloom embeddings are computationally efficient, and do not seriously compromise the accuracy of the model up to 1/5 compression ratios. In some cases, they even improve over the original accuracy, with relative increases up to 12%. We evaluate Bloom embeddings on 7 data sets and compare it against 4 alternative methods, obtaining favorable results. We also discuss a number of further advantages of Bloom embeddings, such as 'on-the-fly' constant-time operation, zero or marginal space requirements, training time speedups, or the fact that they do not require any change to the core model architecture or training configuration.

CCS CONCEPTS

• **Computing methodologies** → **Neural networks**; *Learning latent representations*; • **Information systems** → *Document representation*;

KEYWORDS

Deep recommenders, sparse input/output, Bloom filters, neural network, embeddings.

1 INTRODUCTION

The size of neural network models that deal with sparse inputs and outputs is often dominated by the dimensionality of such inputs and outputs. Deep networks used for recommender systems and collaborative filtering are a paradigmatic case, as they have to deal with high-dimensional sparse vectors, typically in the order from tens of thousands to hundreds of millions, both at the input and the output of the network (e.g., [12, 26, 42, 49]). This results in large models that present a number of difficulties, both at training and prediction stages. Apart from training and prediction times, an obvious bottleneck of such models is space: their size (and even performance) is hampered by the physical memory of graphical processing units (GPUs), and they are difficult to deploy on mobile devices with limited hardware (cf. [24]).

One option to reduce the size of sparse inputs and outputs is to embed them into a lower-dimensional space. Embedding sparse high-dimensional inputs is commonplace (e.g., [5, 37, 44]). However, embedding sparse high-dimensional outputs, or even inputs and outputs at the same time, is much less common (cf. [1, 4, 48]). Importantly, typical embeddings still require the storage and processing of large matrices with the same dimensionality as the input/output (like the original neural network model would do). Thus, the gains in terms of space are limited. As mentioned, the size of such models is dominated by the input/output dimensionality, with input and output layers representing around 99.9% of the total amount of models' parameters. An example can be found in the deep recommender of Hidasi et al. [26], which uses a gated recurrent unit to perform session-based recommendations with input/output layers of dimensionality 330,000 and internal layers of dimensionality 100.

In general, an ideal embedding procedure for sparse high-dimensional inputs/outputs should produce compact embeddings, of much lower dimensionality than the original input/output. In addition, it should consume little space, both in terms of storage and memory space. Smaller sizes imply less parameters, thus training the model on embedded vectors would also be faster than with the original instances. The embedding of the output should also lead to a formulation for which the appropriate loss should be clear. Embeddings should not compromise the accuracy of the model nor the required number of training epochs to obtain that accuracy. In addition, no changes to the original core architecture of the model should be required to achieve good performance (obviously, input/output dimensions must change). The embedding should also be fast; if not to be done directly 'on-the-fly', at least fast enough so that speed improvements made during training are not lost in the embedding operation. Last, but not least, output embeddings should be easily reversible, so that the output of the model could be mapped to the original items at prediction time.

In this work, we propose an unsupervised embedding technique that fulfills all the previous requirements. It can be applied to both

RecSys '17, August 27-31, 2017, Como, Italy

ACM ISBN 978-1-4503-4652-8/17/08...$15.00
https://doi.org/10.1145/3109859.3109876

input and output layers of neural network models that deal with binary (one-hot encoded) inputs and/or outputs. In doing so, it produces lower-dimensionality binary embeddings that can be easily mapped to the original instances. Provided that the embedding dimension is not too low, the accuracy is not compromised. Furthermore, in some cases, we show that training with embedded vectors can even increase prediction accuracy (we find that is the case for three of the considered recommendation tasks). The embedding requires no changes to the core network structure nor to the model configuration, and works with a softmax output, the most common output activation for binary-coded instances. The embedding moreover preserves the ranking order of items which is crucial in recommender systems. As it is unsupervised, the embedding does not require any preliminary training. Moreover, it is a constant-time operation that can be either performed on-the-fly, requiring no disk or memory space, or can be cached in memory, occupying orders of magnitude less space than a typical embedding matrix. Lower dimensionality of input/output vectors result in faster training, and the mapping from the embedded space to the original one does not add an overwhelming amount of time to the prediction stage. The proposed embedding is based on the idea of Bloom filters [7], and therefore it inherits part of the theory developed around that idea [8, 9, 18, 38].

2 RELATED WORK

A common approach to embed high-dimensional inputs is the hashing trick [33, 41, 46]. However, the hashing trick approach does not deal with outputs, as it offers no explicit way to map back from the (dense) embedding space to the original space. A more elementary version of the hashing trick [20] can be used at the outputs by considering it as a special case of the Bloom-based methodology proposed here. A framework providing both encoding and decoding strategies is the error-correcting output codes (ECOC) framework [17]. Originally designed for single-class outputs, it can be also applied to class sets [3]. Another example of a framework offering recovery capabilities is kernel dependency estimation [48]. The compressed sensing approach of Hsu et al. [30] builds on top of ECOC to reduce multi-label regression to binary regression problems. Similarly, Cissé et al. [15] use Bloom filters to reduce multi-label classification to binary classification problems and improve the robustness of individual binary classifiers' errors.

Data-dependent embeddings that require some form of learning also exist. A typical approach is to rely on variants of latent semantic analysis or singular value decomposition (SVD), exploiting similarities or correlations that may be present in the data. Again, the issue of mapping from the embedding space to the original space is left unresolved. Nonetheless, recently, Chollet [14] has successfully applied a K-nearest neighbors (KNN) algorithm to perform such a mapping and to derive a ranking of the items in the original space. An SVD decomposition of the pairwise mutual information matrix (PMI) is used to perform the embedding, and cosine similarity is used as loss function and to retrieve neighbors. Using the KNN trick offers the possibility to exploit different types of factorization of similarity-based matrices. Canonical correlation analysis is an example that considers both inputs and outputs at the same time [28]. Other examples considering output embeddings are nuclear norm regularized learning [2], label embedding trees [4], or the WSABIE algorithm [47]. In the presence of side information, like text descriptions, item or class taxonomies, or manually-collected data, a range of approaches are applicable. Akata et al. [1] provide a comprehensive list. In our study, we assume no side information is available and focus on input/output-based embeddings.

From a more general perspective, reducing the space of (or compressing) neural network models is an active research topic, driven by the need to deploy such models in systems with limited hardware resources. A common approach is to reduce the size of already trained models by some quantization and/or pruning of the connections in dense layers [16, 24, 31]. A less frequent approach is to reduce the model size before training [11]. These methods typically do not focus on input layers and, to the best of our knowledge, none of them deals with high-dimensional outputs. It is also worth noting that a number of techniques have been proposed to efficiently deal with high-dimensional outputs, specially in the natural language processing domain. The hierarchical softmax approach [39] or the more recent adaptive softmax [22] are two examples of those. Yet, as mentioned, the focus of these works is on speed, not on space. The work of Vincent et al. [45] focuses on both aspects of very large sparse outputs but, to the best of our knowledge, cannot be directly applied to common softmax outputs.

3 BLOOM EMBEDDINGS

3.1 Bloom filters

Bloom filters [7] are a compact probabilistic data structure that is used to represent sets of items, and to efficiently check whether an item is a member of a set [38]. Since the instances we deal with represent sets of one-hot encoded items, Bloom filters are an interesting option to embed those in a compact space with good recovery (or checking) guarantees.

In essence, Bloom filters project every item of a set to k different positions of a binary array $\mathbf{u}$ of size m. Projections are done using a set of k independent hash functions $\mathsf{H} = \{H_i\}_{i=1}^{k}$, each of which with a range from 1 to m, ideally distributing the projected items uniformly at random [38]. Proper independent hash functions can be derived using enhanced double hashing or triple hashing [18]. The number of hash functions k is usually a constant, $k \ll m$, proportional to the expected number of items to be projected.

To check if an item is in $\mathbf{u}$, one feeds it to the k hash functions H to get k array positions. If any of the bits at these positions is 0, then the item is definitely not in the set. Thus, item checks return no false negatives, meaning that the structure gives an answer with 100% recall [38]. However, if all k bits at the projected positions are 1, then either the item is in the set, or the bits have by chance been set to 1 during the insertion of other set items. This implies that false positives are possible, due to collisions between projections of different items [8]. The values of m and k can be adjusted to control the probability of such collisions. However, in practice, m is usually constrained by space requirements, and $k \leq 10$ is employed, independently of the number of items to be projected, and giving less than 1% false positive probability [9].

3.2 Embedding and recovery

In the following, we describe the use of Bloom filter techniques in embedding binary high-dimensional instances, and the recovery or mapping to such instances from these embeddings. We denote our approach as Bloom embedding (BE). The idea we pursue is to embed both inputs and outputs and to perform training in the embedding space. For that, only a probability-based output activation is required, together with a loss function that is appropriate for such activations.

Let $\mathbf{x}$ be an input or output instance with dimensionality d, such that $\mathbf{x} = [x_1, \ldots x_d]$, $x_i \in \{0, 1\}$. Instances $\mathbf{x}$ are assumed to be sparse, that is, $\sum_{i=1}^{d} x_i \ll d$. Because of that, we can more conveniently (and compactly) represent $\mathbf{x}$ as set $\mathrm{p} = \{p_i\}_{i=1}^{c}$, $p_i \in \mathbb{N}_{\leq d}$, where c is the number of non-zero elements and p_i is the position of such elements in $\mathbf{x}$. For every set p, we generate an embedded instance $\mathbf{u}$ of dimensionality $m < d$, such that $\mathbf{u} = [u_1, \ldots u_m]$, $u_i \in \{0, 1\}$. To do so, we first set all m components of $\mathbf{u}$ to 0. Then, iteratively, for every position p_i, $i = 1, \ldots c$, and every projection H_j, $j = 1, \ldots k$, we assign

$$u_{H_j(p_i)} = 1. \tag{1}$$

Notice that, since H_j has a range between 1 and m, $k \geq 1$, and $m < d$, a number of original positions p_i may map to the same index in $\mathbf{u}$. Bloom filters mitigate this by properly choosing k independent hash functions H (Sec. 3.1). Notice furthermore that the process has no space requirements, as H is computed on-the-fly. Finally, notice that the embedding of a set p is constant time: the process is $O(ck)$, with c bounded by the maximum number of active items in $\mathbf{x}$, $c \ll d$, and k being a constant that is set beforehand, $k \ll m < d$. In practice, this constant time is dominated by the time spent on H to generate a hash. If we want to be faster than that, and at the same time ensure an optimal (uniform) distribution of the outputs of H, we can pre-compute a hash matrix storing the projections or hash indices for all the potential items in p. We can do it by generating vectors $\mathbf{h} = [h_1, \ldots h_k]$ for each p_i, where h_j is a uniformly randomly chosen integer between 1 and m (without replacement). This way, by pre-generating all projections for all d items, we end up with a $d \times k$ matrix $\mathbf{H}$ of integers between 1 and m, which we can easily store in random-access memory (RAM), not in the GPU memory.

We now explain how to recover a probability-based ranking of the d items at the output of the model. Assuming a softmax activation is used, we have a probability vector $\hat{\mathbf{v}} = [\hat{v}_1, \ldots \hat{v}_m]$ that, at training time, is compared to the binary embedding $\mathbf{v}$ of the ground truth $\mathbf{y}$, with its active positions q (analogously to $\mathbf{x}$ and p). To unravel the embedding $\hat{\mathbf{v}}$ and map to the d original items of $\mathbf{y}$, we can understand $\hat{\mathbf{v}}$ as a k-way factorization of every item $\hat{y}_i$ of our prediction $\hat{\mathbf{y}}$. Then, following the idea of Bloom filters, if y_i maps to v_i and $\hat{v}_i = 0$, we can confirm that that item is definitely not in the output of the model (Sec. 3.1). Otherwise, if $\hat{v}_i$ is relatively large, we want the likelihood of that item to reflect that. Specifically, given an active position q_i from q representing $\mathbf{y}$, we can compute the likelihood

$$L(q_i) = \prod_{j=1}^{k} \hat{v}_{H_j(q_i)}, \tag{2}$$

and assign outputs $\hat{y}_i = L(q_i)$. Alternatively, if a more numerically-stable output is desired, we can compute the negative log-likelihood

$$L(q_i) = -\sum_{j=1}^{k} \log\left(\hat{v}_{H_j(q_i)}\right). \tag{3}$$

Both operations, when iterated for $i = 1, \ldots d$, define a ranking over the items in $\mathbf{y}$ and from there, if needed, a probability distribution can be recovered by re-normalization. We here do not perform such re-normalization, as all the problems we consider can be mapped to a typical ranking recommendation setting.

3.3 Suitability

Note that BE, by construction, already offers a number of the aforementioned desired qualities for sparse binary high-dimensional embeddings (Sec. 1). Specifically, BE is designed for both inputs and outputs, offering a rank-based mapping between the original instances and the embedded vectors. BE yields a more compact representation of the original instance and requires no disk or memory space (at most some marginal RAM space, not GPU memory). In addition, BE can be performed on-the-fly, without training, and in constant time. In the following, we demonstrate the remaining desirable qualities using a comprehensive experimental setup: we show that the accuracy of the model remains stable or even increases given a reasonable embedding dimension, that no changes in the model architecture nor configuration are required, that training times are faster thanks to the reduction of the number of parameters of the model, that evaluation times do not carry much overhead, and that performance is generally better than a number of alternative approaches.

4 EXPERIMENTAL SETUP

4.1 General considerations

We demonstrate that BE works under several settings and that it can be applied to multiple tasks. In particular, we focus on recommendation and collaborative filtering but also demonstrate the validity of the approach on a natural language processing task. We consider a number of data sets, network architectures, configurations, and evaluation measures. In total, we define 7 different setups, which we describe in Sec. 4.2. We also demonstrate that BE is competitive with respect to the available alternatives. To this end, we consider 4 different state-of-the-art approaches, which we overview in Sec. 4.3.

Data sets are formed by inputs with n instances, corresponding to either individual instances (or one-hot encoded user profiles) or to sequences of instances (or profile lists). Outputs, also of n instances, correspond to individual instances or to class labels. Instances have an original dimensionality d, corresponding to the cardinality of all possible profile items. Given the nature of the considered problems, instances are very sparse, with all but c items being different from 0, $c \ll d$, typically with c/d in the order of 10^{-5} (Table 1).

For each data set, and based on the literature, we select an appropriate baseline neural network architecture. We experiment with both feed-forward (autoencoder-like) and recurrent networks, carefully selecting their parameters and configuration to match (or even improve) the state-of-the-art results. For the sake of comparison, we

Table 1: Data set statistics after data cleaning and splitting. From left to right: data set name, number of instances n, test split size, instance dimensionality d, median number of non-zero components c, and median density c/d.

Data set	n	Split	d	c	c/d
ML	138,224	10,000	15,405	18	$1.2 \cdot 10^{-3}$
PTB	929,589	82,430	10,001	1	$1.0 \cdot 10^{-4}$
CADE	40,983	13,661	193,998	17	$8.8 \cdot 10^{-5}$
MSD	597,155	50,000	69,989	5	$7.1 \cdot 10^{-5}$
AMZ	916,484	50,000	22,561	1	$4.4 \cdot 10^{-5}$
BC	25,816	2,500	54,069	2	$3.7 \cdot 10^{-5}$
YC	1,865,997	50,000	35,732	1	$2.8 \cdot 10^{-5}$

Table 2: Experimental setup and baseline scores. From left to right: data set name, network architecture and optimizer, evaluation measure, random score S_R, and baseline score S_0.

Data set	Architecture + Optimizer	Meas.	S_R	S_0
ML	Feed-forward + Adam	MAP	0.003	0.160
PTB	LSTM + SGD	RR	0.001	0.342
CADE	Feed-forward + RMSprop	Acc	8.5	58.0
MSD	Feed-forward + Adam	MAP	<0.001	0.066
AMZ	Feed-forward + Adam	MAP	<0.001	0.049
BC	Feed-forward + Adam	MAP	<0.001	0.010
YC	GRU + Adagrad	RR	<0.001	0.368

also choose appropriate and well-known evaluation measures [34]. Depending on the data set (Table 2), we work with mean average precision (MAP), reciprocal ranks (RR), or % of accuracy (Acc).

Each combination of data set, network architecture, configuration, and evaluation measure defines a task. For every task, we compute a baseline score S_0, corresponding to running the plain neural network model without any embedding. We then report the performance of the i-th execution with a particular embedding with respect to the baseline score using S_i/S_0. This way, we can compare the performance across different tasks using different evaluation measures, reporting relative improvement/loss with respect to the baseline. Similarly, to compare across different dimensionalities, we report the ratio of embedding dimensionality with respect to the original dimensionality, m/d, and to compare across different training and evaluation times, we report time ratios with respect to the baseline, T_i/T_0.

4.2 Tasks

We now give a brief summary of the 7 considered tasks (Tables 1 and 2). All data sets are publicly-available and, for all tasks, we make sure that the network architecture and the experimental setup is sufficient to achieve a state-of-the-art result. We use softmax outputs and categorical cross-entropy losses in all experiments.

(1) Movielens (ML): movie recommendation with the Movielens 20M data set[1] [25]. Ratings were discretized with a threshold of 3.5 and movies with less than 5 ratings and users with less than two movies were discarded. Inputs and outputs were built by splitting user profiles at a certain timestamp uniformly at random, ensuring a minimum of one movie in both input and output. To perform recommendations, we build on top of Wu et al. [49] and employ a 3-layer feed-forward neural network model with 150 rectified linear units [21] in the hidden layers. We optimize the weights of the network using cross-entropy and Adam [32], with a learning rate of 0.001 and parameters $\beta_1 = 0.9$ and $\beta_2 = 0.999$. We evaluate the accuracy of the model using MAP.

(2) Million song data set (MSD): song recommendation with the Million song data set[2] [6]. We assume that a user likes a song when he/she has listened to it a minimum of 3 times. We then remove the songs that appear less than 20 times and build user profiles with a minimum of 5 songs. Inputs and outputs are split at a uniformly random timestamp. To recommend future listens to the user we use a 3-layer feed-forward neural network and 300 rectified linear units in the hidden layers. As for the rest, we proceed as with the ML task. We evaluate the accuracy of the model with MAP.

(3) Amazon book reviews (AMZ): book recommendation with the Amazon book reviews data set[3] [35]. We proceed as with the ML data set, but this time setting the minimum number of ratings per book to 100. We employ a 4-layer feed-forward neural network with 300 rectified linear units in the hidden layers, and optimize its parameters with Adam. We evaluate the accuracy of the model with MAP.

(4) Book crossing (BC): book recommendation with the book crossing data set[4] [50]. To perform recommendations we use the same architecture and configuration as with the MSD task, but this time we use 250 units in the hidden layers.

(5) YooChoose (YC): session-based recommendation with the YooChoose RecSys15 challenge data set[5]. We work with the training set of the challenge and keep only the click events. We take the first 2 million sessions of the data set which have a minimum of 2 clicks. To predict the next click, we proceed as in Hidasi et al. [26] and consider a GRU model [13]. We set the inner dimensionality to 100 and train the network with Adagrad [19], using a learning rate of 0.01. We evaluate the accuracy of the model with RR.

(6) Penn treebank (PTB): next word prediction with the Penn treebank data set [36]. The vocabulary is limited to 10,000 words, with all other words mapped to an 'unknown' token (Table 1). We consider the end of the sentence as an additional token and form input sequences of length 10. Inspired by Graves [23], we perform next word prediction with an LSTM network [27]. We set the inner dimensionality to 250 and train the network with SGD. We use a learning rate of 0.25, a momentum of 0.99, and clip gradients to have a maximum norm of 1 [23]. We evaluate the accuracy of the model with the RR of the correct prediction.

[1] http://grouplens.org/datasets/movielens/20m/

[2] http://labrosa.ee.columbia.edu/millionsong/tasteprofile

[3] http://jmcauley.ucsd.edu/data/amazon/

[4] http://www2.informatik.uni-freiburg.de/~cziegler/BX/

[5] http://recsys.yoochoose.net

(7) CADE web directory (CADE): text categorization with the CADE web directory of Brazilian web pages[6] [10]. The data set contains around 40,000 documents assigned to one of 12 categories such as services, education, health, or culture. To perform classification we use a 4-layer feed-forward neural network with a softmax output. The number of units is, from input to output, 400, 200, 100, and 12, and we use rectified linear units as activations for the hidden layers. We train the network with RMSprop [43], a learning rate of 0.0002, and exponential decay of 0.9. Notice that this is the only considered task where output embeddings are not required (classification into 12 text categories). We use Acc as evaluation measure.

4.3 Alternative approaches

To compare the performance of BE with the state-of-the-art, we consider 4 different embedding alternatives. We base our evaluation on performance, measured at a given input/output compression ratio. It is important to note that, in general, besides performance, alternative approaches do not present some of the other desired qualities that BE offers, such as on-the-fly operation, constant-time, no supervision, or no network/configuration changes (Secs. 1 and 3.3). Note also that methods for embedding both inputs and outputs, allowing to map embedded instances to the original ones, are scarce (Sec. 2). Because of that, in some of the considered alternatives we had to perform some adaptations.

(1) Hashing trick (HT). We first consider the popular hashing trick for classifier and recommender inputs [33, 46]. In general, these methodologies only focus on inputs and are not designed to deal with any type of output. Nonetheless, in the case of binary outputs, variants like the one used by Ganchev and Dredze [20] can be adapted to map to the original items using Eqs. 2 or 3. In fact, considering this adaptation for recovery, the approach can be seen as a special case of BE with $k = 1$ (Sec. 3.2).

(2) Error-correcting output codes (ECOC). Originally designed for single-class targets [17], ECOC can be applied to class sets (inputs and outputs), with its corresponding encoding and decoding strategies [3]. Yet, in the case of training neural networks, it is not clear which loss function should be used. The obvious choice would be to use the Hamming distance. However, in pre-analysis, a Hamming loss turned out to be significantly inferior than cross-entropy. Therefore, we use the latter in our experiments. We construct the ECOC matrix with the randomized hill-climbing method of [17].

(3) Pairwise mutual information (PMI). Recently, Chollet [14] has proposed a PMI approach for embedding sets of image labels into a dense space of real-valued vectors. The approach is based on the SVD of a PMI matrix computed from counting pairwise co-occurrences. It uses cosine similarity as the loss function and, at prediction time, it performs KNN (again using cosine similarity) with the projection of individual labels to obtain a ranking.

(4) Canonical correlation analysis (CCA). CCA is a common way to learn a joint dense, real-valued embedding for both inputs and outputs at the same time [28]. CCA can be computed using SVD on a correlation matrix [29] and, similarly to PMI, we can use the KNN trick to rank items or labels at prediction time. Correlation is now the metric of choice, both for the loss function and for determining the neighbors.

[6] http://ana.cachopo.org/datasets-for-single-label-text-categorization

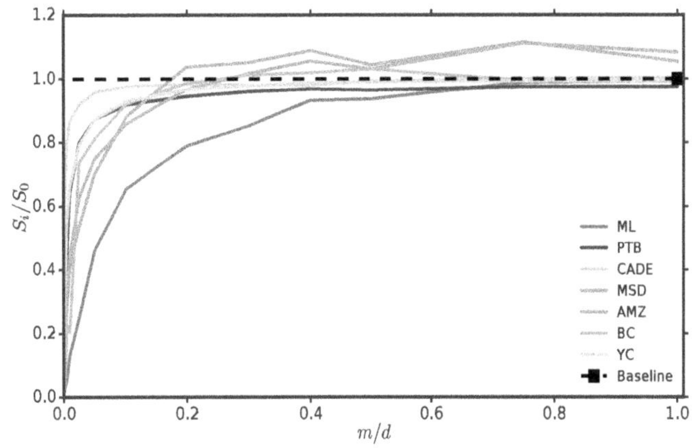

Figure 1: Score ratios S_i/S_0 as a function of dimensionality ratio m/d using $k = 4$. Qualitatively similar plots are observed for other values of k.

5 RESULTS

5.1 Compression and performance

We start by reporting on the performance of BE as a function of the embedding dimension. As mentioned, to facilitate comparisons, we report in relative terms, using score ratios S_i/S_0 and dimensionality ratios m/d. When plotting the former as a function of the latter, we see several things that are worth noting (Fig. 1). Firstly, we observe that, for most of the tasks, score ratios approach 1 as m approaches d. This indicates that the introduction of BE does not degrade the original score of the Baseline when the embedding dimension m is comparable to the original dimension d. Secondly, we observe that the lower the dimensionality ratio, the lower the score ratio. This is to be expected, as one cannot embed sets of items with their intrinsic dimensionality to an infinitesimally small m. Importantly, the reduction of S_i/S_0 should not be linear with m/d, but should maximize S_i for low m (thus getting curves close to the top left corner of Fig. 1). We see that BE fulfills this requirement. In general, we can reduce the input/output size up to 5 times ($m/d = 0.2$) and still maintain more than 92% of the value of the original score. The ML task is the only exception, which we think is due to the abnormally high density of the data (Table 1), inhibiting the embedding to low dimensions[7]. CADE is the task for which BE achieves the highest S_i for low m. Presumably, the CADE task is the easiest one we consider, as only input embeddings are required.

An additional observation is worth noting (Fig. 1). Interestingly, we find that BE can improve the scores over the Baseline for a number of tasks. That is the case for 3 out of the 7 considered tasks (all of them recommendation tasks): MSD with $m/d \geq 0.3$, AMZ with $m/d \geq 0.2$, and BC with $0.3 \leq m/d \leq 0.6$. The fact that an

[7] Note that the ML data is essentially collected through a survey-type method [25].

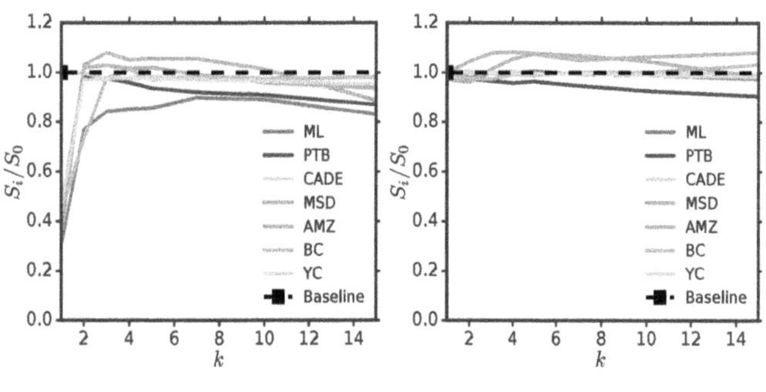

Figure 2: Score ratios S_i/S_0 as a function of the number of hash functions k: using $m/d = 0.3$ (left) and $m/d = 1$ (right).

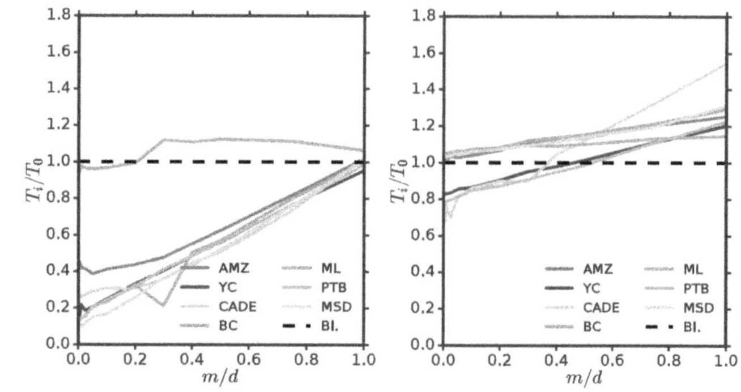

Figure 3: Time ratios T_i/T_0 as a function of dimensionality ratios m/d with $k = 4$: training time (left) and evaluation time (right). Qualitatively similar plots are observed for other values of k. Bl. denotes baseline.

embedding performs better than the original Baseline has been also observed in some other methods for specific data sets [14, 33, 48]. For instance, Chollet [14] has reported increases up to 7% using the PMI approach on the so-called JFT data set. Here, depending on the task and the embedding dimension, relative increases go from 1 to 12%. Given that the data sets where we observe these increases are some of the less dense ones (Table 1), we hypothesize that, in the case of BE, such increases come from having k times more active positions in the ground truth output (recall that one output item is projected k times using k independent hash functions, Sec. 3.2). With k more times elements set to 1 in the output, a better estimation of the gradient may be computed (larger errors that propagate back to the rest of the network).

We now focus on performance as a function of the number of projections k (Fig. 2), reporting score ratios S_i/S_0 as above. From repeating the plots for different values of m/d, we observe that S_i/S_0 is always low for $k = 1$ (Fig. 2, left), except when m approaches d, where we have an almost flat behavior (Fig. 2, right). In general, S_i/S_0 jumps up for $k \geq 2$ and remains stable until $k \approx 10$, where the decrease of S_i/S_0 becomes more apparent (Fig. 2, left). The best operating range typically corresponds to $2 \leq k \leq 4$. The ML task is again an exception, with a best operating range around $7 \leq k \leq 10$.

5.2 Training and retrieval time

Besides performance scores, it is interesting to assess whether the reduction of input and output dimensions has an effect to training and evaluation times. To this end, we plot the time ratios T_i/T_0 as a function of the dimensionality ratio m/d (Fig. 3). Regarding training times, we basically observe a linear decrease with m/d (Fig. 3, left). ML is an exception to the trend, and CADE and AMZ experiment almost no decrease for very low dimensionality ratios $m/d < 0.2$. In general, we confirm faster training times thanks to the reduction of the number of parameters of the model, dominated by input/output matrices (output dimension also affecting the time to compute the loss function). We obtain a 2 times speedup for a 2 times input/output compression and, roughly, a little bit over 3 times speedup for a 5 times input/output compression. Regarding evaluation times, we also observe a linear trend (Fig. 3, right). However, this time, T_i/T_0 is not as low, with values slightly above 1 but always below 1.5 (with the exception of CADE for $m/d > 0.6$). Overall, this indicates that, compared to the Baseline evaluation time, the mapping used by BE when reconstructing the output does not introduce an overwhelming amount of extra computation time. With the exception of ML, extra computation time is below 20% for $m/d < 0.5$.

5.3 Comparison with alternatives

Finally, we compare the performance of BE to the one of the considered alternative methods. We do so by establishing a dimensionality ratio m/d and computing the corresponding score ratio S_i/S_0 for a given task (Table 3). We see that BE is better than the alternative methods in 5 out of the 7 tasks (10 out of the 14 considered test points). PMI is better in one of the tasks (CADE) and CCA is better also in one of the tasks (AMZ). It is relevant to note that, when BE wins, it always does so by a relatively large margin (see, for instance, the ML or YC tasks). Otherwise, when an alternative approach wins, generally it does so by a smaller margin (see, for instance, the AMZ task).

These results become more relevant if we realize that PMI and CCA are both SVD-based approaches, introducing a separate degree of supervised learning to the task, exploiting pairwise item co-occurrences and correlations, respectively (Sec. 4.3). In contrast, BE does not require any learning. We formulate a co-occurrence-based version of BE below, which achieves moderate performance increments over BE and more closely approaches the performance of PMI and CCA on the two tasks where BE was not already performing best. A further interesting thing to note is that we confirm the small variation in the score ratios obtained for $2 \leq k \leq 10$ (Fig. 2). Here, score ratios for $3 \leq k \leq 5$ are often comparable in a statistical significance sense (Table 3).

6 GOING ONE STEP FURTHER WITH CO-OCCURRENCE-BASED COLLISIONS

6.1 Co-occurrence-based embedding

In Bloom filters and BE, collisions are unavoidable due to the lower embedding dimensionality and the use of multiple projections (Sec. 3). In addition, we have seen that some alternative approaches produce embeddings by exploiting co-occurrence information (Secs. 2 and 4.3). Here, we study a variant of BE that takes

Table 3: Comparison of BE with the considered alternatives. Score ratios S_i/S_0 for different combinations of data set and compression ratio m/d. Best results are highlighted in bold, up to statistical significance (Mann-Whitney U, $p > 0.05$).

Test point		Alternative methods				BE		
Data set	m/d	HT	ECOC	PMI	CCA	$k=3$	$k=4$	$k=5$
ML	0.2	0.234	0.342	0.043	0.209	**0.750**	**0.770**	0.722
ML	0.3	0.285	0.208	0.045	0.200	0.796	**0.813**	**0.815**
PTB	0.2	0.357	0.453	0.837	0.638	**0.919**	0.908	0.881
PTB	0.4	0.528	0.454	0.836	0.695	**0.942**	0.920	0.902
CADE	0.01	0.857	0.359	**0.984**	0.928	0.862	0.853	0.855
CADE	0.03	0.914	0.363	**1.002**	0.950	0.914	0.925	0.926
MSD	0.05	0.078	0.268	0.216	0.679	0.695	**0.738**	**0.738**
MSD	0.1	0.151	0.310	0.321	0.740	**0.835**	**0.841**	0.832
AMZ	0.1	0.166	0.182	0.851	**1.030**	0.864	0.881	0.861
AMZ	0.2	0.289	0.185	0.995	**1.048**	1.016	1.029	1.008
BC	0.05	0.189	0.817	0.022	0.313	0.777	0.750	**0.837**
BC	0.1	0.199	0.886	0.025	0.465	**0.965**	**0.919**	0.831
YC	0.03	0.150	0.076	0.776	0.466	**0.841**	**0.858**	**0.858**
YC	0.05	0.240	0.083	0.777	0.517	**0.919**	**0.910**	**0.928**

Algorithm 1 Pseudocode for CBE.

Input: Input and/or output instances $\mathbf{X}$ ($n \times d$ sparse binary matrix), embedding dimensionality m, number of projections k, and pre-computed hashing matrix $\mathbf{H}$ ($d \times k$ integers matrix).
Output: Co-occurrence-based hashing matrix $\mathbf{H}'$.

1: $\mathbf{C} \leftarrow \mathbf{X}^{\mathrm{T}}\mathbf{X}$
2: $\mathbf{C} \leftarrow \mathbf{C} \odot \textsc{sgn}(\mathbf{C} - \textsc{avgfreq}(\mathbf{X}))$
3: $\mathbf{c}^{\mathrm{VAL}}, \mathbf{c}^{\mathrm{ROW}}, \mathbf{c}^{\mathrm{COL}} \leftarrow \textsc{coord}(\textsc{lowtri}(\mathbf{C}))$
4: **for** i **in** $\textsc{argsort}(\mathbf{c}^{\mathrm{VAL}})$
5: $\quad a, b \leftarrow c_i^{\mathrm{ROW}}, c_i^{\mathrm{COL}}$
6: $\quad r \leftarrow \textsc{urnd}(1, m, \mathsf{h}_a \cup \mathsf{h}_b)$
7: $\quad j_a \leftarrow \textsc{urnd}(1, k, \emptyset)$
8: $\quad j_b \leftarrow \textsc{urnd}(1, k, \emptyset)$
9: $\quad h_{a,j_a}, h_{b,j_b} \leftarrow r$
10: **return H**

advantage of co-occurrence information to adjust the collisions that will inevitably take place when performing the embedding. We denote this approach by co-occurrence-based Bloom embedding (CBE).

What we propose is a quite straightforward approach to CBE, which does not add much extra pre-computation time. Training and testing times remain the same, as CBE uses a pre-computed hashing matrix **H** (Sec. 3.2). The general idea of the proposed approach is to 're-direct' the collisions of the co-occurring items to the same bits or positions of **u**. Our implementation of this idea is detailed in Algorithm 1, and briefly explained below.

First, we count pairwise co-occurrences and store them in a sparse matrix **C** (line 1). Next, we threshold **C** by the average item frequency in **X** using the Hadamard product $\odot$ and a component-wise sign function (line 2). We then get the lower triangular part of **C** and return it in coordinates format, that is, using a tuple of values, row indices, and column indices (line 3). We will use the order in $\mathbf{c}^{\mathrm{VAL}}$ to update the hash matrix **H**. To do so, we first loop over the indices of the sorted values of $\mathbf{c}^{\mathrm{VAL}}$ in increasing order (line 4). After selecting the corresponding items a and b (line 5), we then draw integers from URND (lines 6–8). The function $\textsc{urnd}(x, y, z)$ is a uniform random integer generator between x and y (both included) such that the output integer is not included in the set z, that is, $\textsc{urnd}(x, y, z) \notin z$. Rows a and b of **H** are transformed to sets h_a and h_b and its union is computed (line 6). Finally, we use the integers generated by URND to pick projections j_a and j_b from **H**, and assign them the same bit r (line 9). By updating the projections in **H** in increasing order of co-occurrence (line 4), we give priority to the pairs with largest co-occurrence, setting them to collide to the same bit r (line 9).

6.2 CBE results

Overall, the performance of CBE only provides moderate increments over the original BE approach (Fig. 4). With the exception of the BC task, the performance of CBE is always higher than the one of BE. However, with the exception of the AMZ task, we do not observe dramatic increases of CBE over BE. On average, such increases are between 0.4% and 8.4% (Table 4, right). One possible explanation for these moderate performance increases is the low co-occurrence in the considered data (Table 4, left). As it can be seen, typically less than 3% of all possible pairs show a co-occurrence. Moreover, the average co-occurrence count of such co-occurring pairs is very low, with ratios ρ to the total number of instances n in the order of 10^{-5} or 10^{-6}.

Despite being moderate on average, we observed that the increments provided by CBE were more prominent for low dimensionality ratios m/d. By relating CBE with the best approaches resulting from the previous comparison of Table 3, we see that CBE is generally better than BE, sometimes with a statistically significant difference (Table 5). Furthermore, we see that CBE, being based on co-occurrences, more closely approaches PMI and CCA in the tasks where those were performing best, and even outperforms

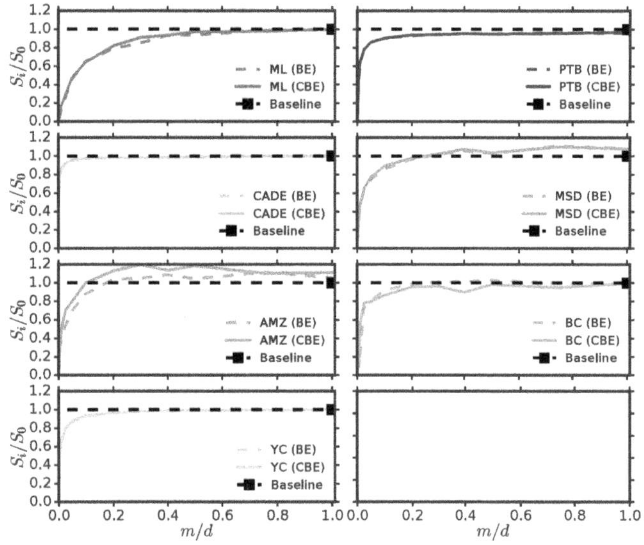

Figure 4: Comparison of score ratios S_i/S_0 as a function of dimensionality ratio m/d for BE (dashed lines) and CBE (solid lines) using $k = 4$. Qualitatively similar plots are observed for other values of k.

Table 4: Co-occurrence statistics and average score increase of CBE over BE. From left to right: data set name, input percent of co-occurrent pairs (%), input average co-occurrence ratio of co-occurrent pairs (ρ), output percent of co-occurrent pairs (%), output average co-occurrence ratio of co-occurrent pairs (ρ), and average score increases of CBE over BE (%; calculated using $100(S_j - S_i)/S_0$ and averaging over all m/d points). Co-occurrence values for PTB and YC inputs correspond to considering training sequences, not isolated sequence items.

Data set	Co-occurrence statistics				Score increase (%)	
	Input		Output			
	%	ρ	%	ρ	$k = 3$	$k = 4$
ML	25.2	$1.3 \cdot 10^{-4}$	32.9	$1.0 \cdot 10^{-4}$	+0.9	+1.7
PTB	3.3	$2.4 \cdot 10^{-5}$	0	0	+0.1	+0.9
CADE	1.3	$8.8 \cdot 10^{-5}$	N/A	N/A	−0.4	−0.1
MSD	1.3	$3.0 \cdot 10^{-6}$	1.3	$3.1 \cdot 10^{-6}$	+0.5	+1.5
AMZ	3.0	$1.8 \cdot 10^{-6}$	3.0	$1.8 \cdot 10^{-6}$	+6.6	+8.4
BC	0.8	$4.9 \cdot 10^{-5}$	0.4	$4.9 \cdot 10^{-5}$	−3.4	−1.0
YC	0.2	$1.5 \cdot 10^{-6}$	0	0	+0.4	+0.3

them in one test point (AMZ, $m/d = 0.2$). Being closer to those co-occurrence-based approaches is an indication that CBE leverages co-occurrence information to some extent.

7 CONCLUSION

We have proposed the use of Bloom embeddings to represent sparse high-dimensional binary-coded inputs and outputs. We have shown

Table 5: Comparison of CBE versus the results in Table 3. Score ratios S_i/S_0 for different combinations of data set and compression ratio m/d. Best results are highlighted in bold, up to statistical significance (Mann-Whitney-U, $p > 0.05$).

Test point		Best so far		CBE	
Data set	m/d	Method	S_i/S_0	$k = 3$	$k = 4$
ML	0.2	BE	0.770	0.760	**0.781**
ML	0.3	BE	0.815	0.812	**0.867**
PTB	0.2	BE	**0.919**	**0.915**	**0.907**
PTB	0.4	BE	**0.942**	**0.937**	0.922
CADE	0.01	PMI	**0.984**	0.854	0.853
CADE	0.03	PMI	**1.002**	0.921	0.922
MSD	0.05	BE	0.738	**0.759**	0.756
MSD	0.1	BE	0.841	0.856	**0.873**
AMZ	0.1	CCA	**1.030**	0.994	0.991
AMZ	0.2	CCA	1.048	**1.109**	**1.117**
BC	0.05	BE	**0.837**	0.774	0.808
BC	0.1	BE	**0.965**	0.880	0.878
YC	0.03	BE	0.858	0.871	**0.880**
YC	0.05	BE	0.928	0.933	**0.936**

that a compact representation can be obtained without compromising the performance of the original neural network model or, in some cases, even increasing it by a substantial factor. Due to the compact representation, the loss function and the input and output layers deal with less parameters, which results in faster training times. The approach compares favorably with respect to the considered alternatives, and offers a number of further advantages such as on-the-fly operation or zero space requirements, all this without introducing changes to the core network architecture, task configuration, or loss function.

In the future, besides continuing to exploit co-occurrences, one could enhance the proposed approach by considering further extensions of Bloom filters such as counting Bloom filters [9]. In theory, those extensions could provide a more compact representation by breaking the binary nature of the embedding. However, they could require the modification of the loss function or the mapping process (Eqs. 2 and 3). A faster mapping process using the sorted probabilities of **v** could also be studied. A detailed, comparative analysis of false positives and false negatives is also pending. Finally, it would be interesting to assess the utility of BE in combination with classical collaborative filtering approaches or factorization machines [40].

ACKNOWLEDGMENTS

We thank the curators of the data sets used in this study for making them publicly-available and Santi Pascual for his comments on a previous version of the paper.

REFERENCES

[1] Z. Akata, F. Perronnin, Z. Harchaoui, and C. Schmid. 2015. Label-embedding for image classification. *IEEE Trans. on Pattern Analysis and Machine Intelligence* 38, 7 (2015), 1425–1438.

[2] Y. Amit, M. Fink, N. Srebro, and S. Ullman. 2007. Uncovering shared structures in multiclass classification. In *Proc. of the Int. Conf. on Machine Learning (ICML)*. 17–24.

[3] G. Armano, C. Chira, and N. Hatami. 2012. Error-correcting output codes for multi-label text categorization. In *Proc. of the Italian Information Retrieval Conf. (IIR)*. 26–37.

[4] S. Bengio, J. Weston, and D. Grangier. 2010. Label embedding trees for large multi-class tasks. In *Advances in Neural Information Processing Systems (NIPS)*. Vol. 23. 163–171.

[5] Y. Bengio, R. Ducharme, and P. Vincent. 2000. A neural probabilistic language model. In *Advances in Neural Information Processing Systems (NIPS)*, T. K. Leen, T. G. Dietterich, and V. Tresp (Eds.). Vol. 13. 932–938.

[6] T. Bertin-Mahieux, D. P. W. Ellis, B. Whitman, and P. Lamere. 2011. The million song dataset. In *Proc. of the Int. Soc. for Music Information Retrieval Conf. (ISMIR)*. 591–596.

[7] B. H. Bloom. 1970. Space/time trade-offs in hash coding with allowable errors. *Commun. ACM* 13, 7 (1970), 422–426.

[8] J. Blustein and A. El-Maazawi. 2002. *Bloom filters – a tutorial, analysis, and survey.* Technical Report. Faculty of Computer Science, Dalhousie University, Halifax, Canada. https://www.cs.dal.ca/research/techreports/cs-2002-10

[9] F. Bonomi, M. Mitzenmacher, R. Panigrahy, S. Singh, and G. Varghese. 2006. An improved construction for counting Bloom filters. In *European Symposium on Algorithms (ESA)*, Y. Azar and T. Erlebach (Eds.). Lecture Notes in Computer Science, Vol. 4168. Springer-Verlag, Berlin, Germany, 684–695.

[10] A. Cardoso-Cachopo. 2007. *Improving methods for single-label text categorization.* Ph.D. Dissertation. Instituto Superior Tecnico, Universidade Tecnica de Lisboa.

[11] W. Chen, J. Wilson, S. Tyree, K. Weinberger, and Y. Chen. 2015. Compressing neural networks with the hashing trick. In *Proc. of the Int. Conf. on Machine Learning (ICML)*. 2285–2294.

[12] H.-T. Cheng, L. Koc, J. Harmsen, T. Shaked, T. Chandra, H. Aradhye, G. Anderson, G. Corrado, W. Chai, M. Ispir, R. Anil, Z. Haque, L. Hong, V. Jain, X. Liu, and H. Shah. 2016. Wide & deep learning for recommender systems. In *Proc. of the Workshop on Deep Learning for Recommender Systems (DLRS)*. 7–10.

[13] K. Cho, B. Van Merriënboer, D. Bahdanau, and Y. Bengio. 2014. On the properties of neural machine translation: encoder-decoder approaches. In *Proc. of the Workshop on Syntax, Semantics and Structure in Statistical Translation (SSST)*. 103–111.

[14] F. Chollet. 2016. Information-theoretic label embeddings for large-scale image classification. ArXiv: 1607.05691. (2016).

[15] M. Cissé, N. Usunier, T. Artières, and P. Gallinari. 2013. Robust Bloom filters for large multilabel classification tasks. In *Advances in Neural Information Processing Systems (NIPS)*. 1851–1859.

[16] M. Courbariaux, Y. Bengio, and J.-P. David. 2015. BinaryConnect: training deep neural networks with binary weights during propagations. In *Advances in Neural Information Processing Systems (NIPS)*, C. Cortes, N. D. Lawrence, D. D. Lee, M. Sugiyama, and R. Garnett (Eds.). 3123–3131.

[17] T. G. Dietterich and G. Bakiri. 1995. Solving multiclass learning problems via error-correcting output codes. *Journal of Artificial Intelligence Research* 2 (1995), 263–286.

[18] P. C. Dillinger and P. Manolios. 2004. Bloom filters in probabilistic verification. In *Proc. of the Int. Conf. on Formal Methods in Computer-Aided Design (FMCAD)*. 367–381.

[19] J. Duchi, E. Hazan, and Y. Singer. 2011. Adaptive subgradient methods for online learning and stochastic optimization. *Journal of Machine Learning Research* 12 (2011), 2121–2159.

[20] K. Ganchev and M. Dredze. 2008. Small statistical models by random feature mixing. In *ACL Workshop on Mobile Language Processing (MLP)*. 19–20.

[21] X. Glorot, A. Bordes, and Y. Bengio. 2011. Deep sparse rectifier neural networks. In *Proc. of the Int. Conf. on Artificial Intelligence and Statistics (AISTATS)*. 315–323.

[22] E. Grave, A. Joulin, M. Cissé, D. Grangier, and H. Jégou. 2016. Efficient softmax approximation for GPUs. ArXiv: 1609.04309. (2016).

[23] A. Graves. 2013. Generating sequences with recurrent neural networks. ArXiv: 1308.0850. (2013).

[24] S. Han, H. Mao, and W. J. Dally. Deep compression: compressing deep neural networks with pruning, trained quantization and Huffman coding. In *Proc. of the Int. Conf. on Learning Representations (ICLR)*. arXiv:1510.00149

[25] F. M. Harper and J. K. Konstan. 2015. The MovieLens datasets: history and context. *ACM Trans. on Interactive Intelligent Systems* 5, 4 (2015), 19.

[26] B. Hidasi, A. Karatzoglou, L. Baltrunas, and D. Tikk. Session-based recommendations with recurrent neural networks. In *Proc. of the Int. Conf. on Learning Representations (ICLR)*. arXiv:1511.06939

[27] S. Hochreiter and J. Schmidhuber. 1997. Long short-term memory networks. *Neural Computation* 9, 8 (1997), 1735–1780.

[28] H. Hotelling. 1936. Relations between two sets of variates. *Biometrika* 28, 3-4 (1936), 321–377.

[29] D. Hsu, S. M. Kakade, and T. Zhang. 2012. A spectral algorithm for learning hidden Markov models. *J. Comput. System Sci.* 78, 5 (2012), 1460–1470.

[30] D. J. Hsu, S. M. Kakade, J. Langford, and T. Zhang. 2009. Multi-label prediction via compressed sensing. In *Advances in Neural Information Processing Systems (NIPS)*, Y. Bengio, D. Schuurmans, J. D. Lafferty, C. K. I. Williams, and A. Culotta (Eds.). Vol. 22. 772–780.

[31] Y.-D. Kim, E. Park, S. Yoo, T. Choi, L. Yang, and D. Shin. Compression of deep convolutional neural networks for fast and low power mobile applications. In *Proc. of the Int. Conf. on Learning Representations (ICLR)*. arXiv:1511.06530

[32] D. P. Kingma and J. L. Ba. 2015. Adam: a method for stochastic optimization. In *Proc. of the Int. Conf. on Learning Representations (ICLR)*. arXiv:1412.6980 https://arxiv.org/abs/1412.6980

[33] J. Langford, L. Li, and A. Strehl. 2007. *Vowpal wabbit online learning project.* Technical Report. http://hunch.net/?p=309

[34] C. D. Manning, P. Raghavan, and H. Schütze. 2008. *Introduction to information retrieval.* Cambridge University Press, Cambridge, UK.

[35] J. McAuley, R. Pandey, and J. Leskovec. 2015. Inferring networks of substitutable and complementary products. In *Proc. of the ACM SIGKDD Int. Conf. on Knowledge Discovery and Data Mining (KDD)*. 785–794.

[36] T. Mikolov. 2012. *Statistical language models based on neural networks.* Ph.D. Dissertation. Brno University of Technology.

[37] T. Mikolov, K. Chen, G. S. Corrado, and J. Dean. 2013. Efficient estimation of word representations in vector space. arXiv: 1301.3781. (2013).

[38] M. Mitzenmacher and E. Upfal. 2005. *Probability and computing: randomized algorithms and probabilistic analysis.* Cambridge University Press, Cambridge, UK.

[39] F. Morin and Y. Bengio. 2005. Hierarchical probabilistic neural network language model. In *Proc. of the Int. Workshop on Artificial Intelligence and Statistics (AISTATS)*. 246–252.

[40] S. Rendle. 2010. Factorization machines. In *Proc. of the IEEE Int. Conf. on Data Mining (ICDM)*. 995–1000.

[41] Q. Shi, J. Petterson, G. Dror, J. Langford, A. Smola, and S. V. N. Vishwanathan. 2009. Hash kernels for structured data. *Journal of Machine Learning Research* 10 (2009), 2615–2637.

[42] F. Strub, R. Gaudel, and J. Mary. 2016. Hybrid recommender system based on autoencoders. In *Proc. of the Workshop on Deep Learning for Recommender Systems (DLRS)*. 11–16.

[43] T. Tieleman and G. Hinton. 2012. Lecture 6.5-RMSprop: divide the gradient by a running average of its recent magnitude. COURSERA: Neural Networks for Machine Learning 4, 2. (2012).

[44] J. Turian, L. Ratinov, and Y. Bengio. 2010. Word representations: a simple and general method for semi-supervised learning. In *Proc. of the Annual Meeting of the Association for Computational Linguistics (ACL)*. 384–394.

[45] P. Vincent, A. Brébisson, and X. Bouthilier. 2015. Efficient exact gradient update for training deep networks with very large sparse targets. In *Advances in Neural Information Processing Systems (NIPS)*. 1108–1116.

[46] K. Weinberger, A. Dasgupta, J. Attenberg, J. Langford, and A. Smola. 2009. Feature hashing for large scale multitask learning. In *Proc. of the Int. Conf. on Machine Learning (ICML)*. 1113–1120.

[47] J. Weston, S. Bengio, and N. Usunier. 2010. Large scale image annotation: learning to rank with joint word-image embeddings. *Machine Learning* 81, 1 (2010), 21–35.

[48] J. Weston, O. Chapelle, A. Elisseeff, B. Schölkopf, and V. Vapnik. 2002. Kernel dependency estimation. In *Advances in Neural Information Processing Systems (NIPS)*, S. Becker, S. Thrun, and K. Obermayer (Eds.). Vol. 15. 873–880.

[49] Y. Wu, C. DuBois, A. X. Zheng, and M. Ester. 2016. Collaborative denoising auto-Encoders for top-N recommender systems. In *Proc. of the ACM Int. Conf. on Web Search and Data Mining (WSDM)*. 153–162.

[50] C.-N. Ziegler, S. M. McNee, J. A. Konstan, and G. Lausen. 2005. Improving recommendation lists through topic diversification. In *Proc. of the Int. World Wide Web Conf. (WWW)*. 22–32.

TransNets: Learning to Transform for Recommendation

Rose Catherine
School of Computer Science
Carnegie Mellon University
rosecatherinek@cs.cmu.edu

William Cohen
School of Computer Science
Carnegie Mellon University
wcohen@cs.cmu.edu

ABSTRACT

Recently, deep learning methods have been shown to improve the performance of recommender systems over traditional methods, especially when review text is available. For example, a recent model, *DeepCoNN*, uses neural nets to learn one latent representation for the text of all reviews written by a target user, and a second latent representation for the text of all reviews for a target item, and then combines these latent representations to obtain state-of-the-art performance on recommendation tasks. We show that (unsurprisingly) much of the predictive value of review text comes from reviews of the target user for the target item. We then introduce a way in which this information can be used in recommendation, even when the target user's review for the target item is not available. Our model, called *TransNets*, extends the *DeepCoNN* model by introducing an additional latent layer representing the target user-target item pair. We then regularize this layer, at training time, to be similar to another latent representation of the target user's review of the target item. We show that TransNets and extensions of it improve substantially over the previous state-of-the-art.

1 INTRODUCTION

Using review text for predicting ratings has been shown to greatly improve the performance of recommender systems [4, 22, 24], compared to Collaborative Filtering (CF) techniques that use only past ratings [18, 33]. Recent advances in Deep Learning research have made it possible to use Neural Networks in a multitude of domains including recommender systems, with impressive results. Most neural recommender models [3, 10, 16, 21, 40] have focussed on the *content* associated with the user and the item, which are used to construct their latent representations. These representations are then fed into a CF-style architecture or a regression model to make the rating prediction.

Review text, unlike content, is not a property of only the user or only the item; it is a property associated with their joint interaction. In that sense, it is a *context* [1] feature. Only a few neural net models [2, 34, 44] have been proposed to date that use review text for predicting the rating. Of these, the most recent model, *Deep Cooperative Neural Networks* (DeepCoNN) [44] uses neural nets to learn a latent representation for the user from the text of all reviews written by her and a second latent representation for the item from the text of all reviews that were written for it, and then combines these two representations in a regression layer to obtain state-of-the-art performance on rating prediction. However, as we will show, much of the predictive value of review text comes from reviews of the target user for the target item, which can be assumed to be available only at training time, and is not available at test time. In this paper, we introduce a way in which this information can be used in training the recommender system, such that when the target user's review for the target item is not available at the time of prediction, an approximation for it is generated, which is then used for predicting the rating. Our model, called ***Trans**formational **Neural Net**works* (TransNets), extends the DeepCoNN model by introducing an additional latent layer representing an approximation of the review corresponding to the target user-target item pair. We then regularize this layer, at training time, to be similar to the latent representation of the actual review written by the target user for the target item. Our experiments illustrate that TransNets and its extensions give substantial improvements in rating prediction.

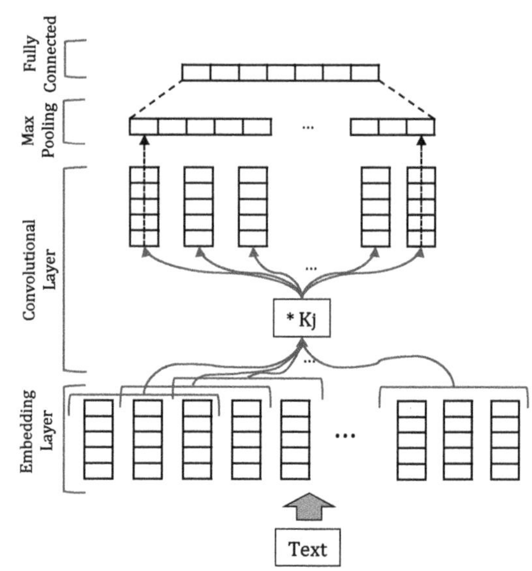

Figure 1: The *CNN Text Processor* architecture

The rest of this paper is organized as follows. The proposed model and architecture are discussed in detail in Section 2. The experiments and results are discussed in Section 3. Section 4 summarizes related work, and we conclude in Section 5.

2 PROPOSED METHOD

2.1 CNNs to process text

We process text using the same approach as the current state-of-the-art method for rating prediction, *DeepCoNN* [44]. The basic building block, referred to as a *CNN Text Processor* in the rest of

RecSys '17, August 27-31, 2017, Como, Italy

ACM ISBN 978-1-4503-4652-8/17/08...$15.00
https://doi.org/10.1145/3109859.3109878

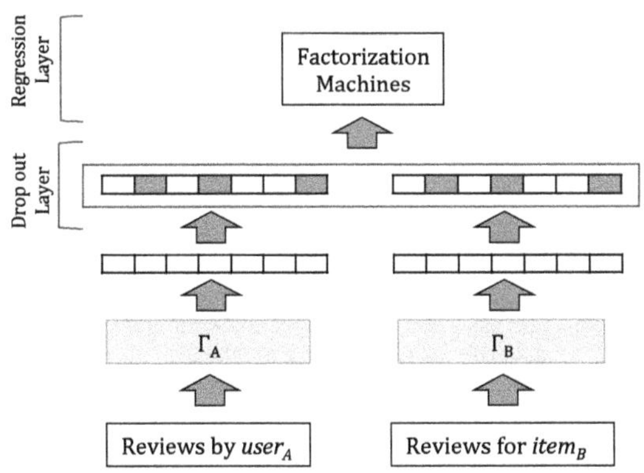

Figure 2: DeepCoNN model for predicting rating

this paper, is a Convolutional Neural Network (CNN) [20] that inputs a sequence of words and outputs a n-dimensional vector representation for the input, i.e., the *CNN Text Processor* is a function $\Gamma : [w_1, w_2, ..., w_T] \rightarrow \mathbb{R}^n$. Figure 1 gives the architecture of the *CNN Text Processor.* In the first layer, a word embedding function $f : M \rightarrow \mathbb{R}^d$ maps each word in the review that are also in its M-sized vocabulary into a d dimensional vector. The embedding can be any pre-trained embedding like those trained on the GoogleNews corpus using *word2vec*[1][27], or on Wikipedia using GloVe[2] [30]. These word vectors are held fixed throughout the training process.

Following the embedding layer is the Convolutional Layer, adapted to text processing [8]. It consists of m neurons each associated with a filter $K \in \mathbb{R}^{t \times d}$, where t is a window size, typically 2 – 5. The filter processes t-length windows of d-dimensional vectors to produce features. Let $V_{1:T}$ be the embedded matrix corresponding to the T-length input text. Then, j^{th} neuron produces its features as:

$$z_j = \alpha(V_{1:T} * K_j + b_j)$$

where, b_j is its bias, $*$ is the convolution operation and α is a non-linearity like Rectified Linear Unit (ReLU) [28] or *tanh*.

Let $z_j^1, z_j^2, ...z_j^{(T-t+1)}$ be the features produced by the jth neuron on the sliding windows over the embedded text. Then, the final feature corresponding to this neuron is computed using a max-pooling operation, defined as:

$$o_j = \max\{z_j^1, z_j^2, ...z_j^{(T-t+1)}\}$$

The max-pooling operation provides location invariance to the neuron, i.e., the neuron is able to detect the features in the text regardless of where it appears.

The final output of the Convolutional Layer is the concatenation of the output from its m neurons, denoted by:

$$O = [o_1, o_2, ...o_m]$$

This output is then passed to a fully connected layer consisting of a weight matrix $W \in \mathbb{R}^{m \times n}$ and a bias $g \in \mathbb{R}^n$, which computes the final representation of the input text as:

$$x = \alpha(W \times O + g)$$

2.2 The DeepCoNN model

To compute the rating r_{AB} that $user_A$ would assign to $item_B$, the DeepCoNN model of [44] uses two *CNN Text Processors* side by side as shown in Figure 2. The first one processes the text labeled $text_A$, which consists of a concatenation of all the reviews that $user_A$ has written and produces a representation, x_A. Similarly, the second processes the text called $text_B$, which consists of a concatenation of all the reviews that have been written about $item_B$ and produces a representation, y_B. Both outputs are passed through a dropout layer [36]. Dropout is a function $\delta : \mathbb{R}^n \rightarrow \mathbb{R}^n$, that suppresses the output of some of the neurons randomly and is a popular technique for regularizing a network. Let $\bar{x}_A = \delta(x_A)$ and $\bar{y}_B = \delta(y_B)$, denote the output of the dropout layer applied on x_A and y_B.

The model then concatenates the two representations as $z = [\bar{x}_A, \bar{y}_B]$ and passes it through a regression layer consisting of a *Factorization Machine* (FM) [32]. The FM computes the second order interactions between the elements of the input vector as:

$$\hat{r}_{AB} = w_0 + \sum_{i=1}^{|z|} w_i z_i + \sum_{i=1}^{|z|} \sum_{j=i+1}^{|z|} \langle \mathbf{v}_i, \mathbf{v}_j \rangle z_i z_j$$

where $w_0 \in \mathbb{R}$ is the global bias, $\mathbf{w} \in \mathbb{R}^{2n}$ weights each dimension of the input, and $\mathbf{V} \in \mathbb{R}^{2n \times k}$ assigns a k dimensional vector to each dimension of the input so that the pair-wise interaction between two dimensions i and j can be weighted using the inner product of the corresponding vectors $\mathbf{v}_i$ and $\mathbf{v}_j$. Note that the FM factorizes the pair-wise interaction, and therefore requires only $O(nk)$ parameters instead of $O(n^2)$ parameters which would have been required otherwise, where k is usually chosen such that $k \ll n$. This has been shown to give better parameter estimates under sparsity [32]. FMs have been used successfully in large scale recommendation services like online news[42].

FMs can be trained using different kinds of loss functions including least squared error (L_2), least absolute deviation (L_1), hinge loss and logit loss. In our experiments, L_1 loss gave a slightly better performance than L_2. DeepCoNN [44] also uses L_1 loss. Therefore, in this paper, all FMs are trained using L_1 loss, defined as:

$$loss = \sum_{(u_A, i_B, r_{AB}) \in D} |r_{AB} - \hat{r}_{AB}|$$

2.3 Limitations of DeepCoNN

DeepCoNN model has achieved impressive MSE values surpassing that of the previous state-of-the-art models that use review texts, like the Hidden Factors as Topics (HFT) model [24], Collaborative Topic Regression (CTR) [39] and Collaborative Deep Learning (CDL) [40], as well as Collaborative Filtering techniques that use only the rating information like Matrix Factorization (MF) [18] and Probabilistic Matrix Factorization (PMF) [33].

However, it was observed in our experiments that DeepCoNN achieves its best performance only when the text of the review written by the target user for the target item is available at test time. In real world recommendation settings, an item is always recommended to a user **before** they have experienced it. Therefore, it would be unreasonable to assume that the target review would be available at the time of testing.

Let rev_{AB} denote the review written by $user_A$ for an $item_B$. At training time, the text corresponding to $user_A$, denoted as $text_A$, consists of a concatenation of all reviews written by her in the training set. Similarly, the text for $item_B$, denoted by $text_B$, is a concatenation of all reviews written for that item in the training set. Both $text_A$ and $text_B$ includes rev_{AB} for all ($user_A$, $item_B$) pairs in the training set. At test time, there are two options for constructing

[1]https://code.google.com/archive/p/word2vec
[2]https://nlp.stanford.edu/projects/glove

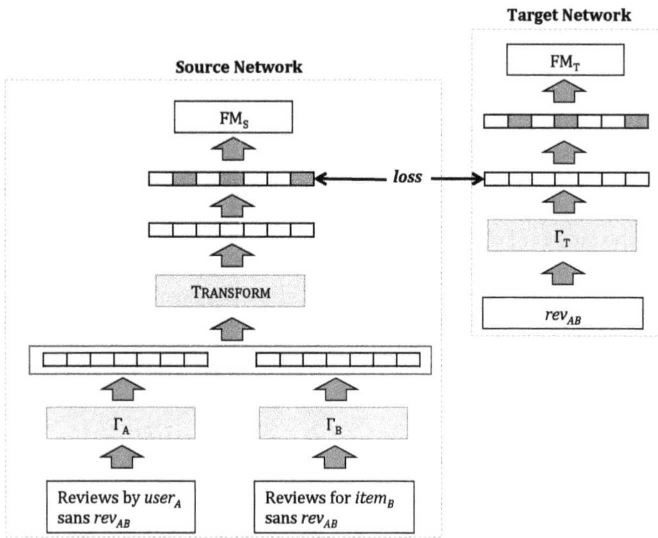

Figure 3: The TransNet architecture

the test inputs. For a test pair $(user_P, item_Q)$, their pairwise review, rev_{PQ} in the test set, could be included in the texts corresponding to the user, $text_P$, and the item, $text_Q$, or could be omitted. In one of our datasets, the MSE obtained by DeepCoNN if rev_{PQ} is included in the test inputs is only 1.21. However, if rev_{PQ} is omitted, then the performance degrades severely to 1.89. This is lower than Matrix Factorization applied to the same dataset, which has an MSE of 1.86. If we train DeepCoNN in the setting that mimics the test setup, by omitting rev_{AB} in the texts of all $(user_A, item_B)$ pairs in the training set, the performance is better at 1.70, but still much higher than when rev_{AB} is available in both training and testing.

In the setting used in this paper, reviews in the validation and the test set are never accessed at any time, i.e., assumed to be unavailable – both during training and testing – simulating a real world situation.

2.4 TransNets

As we saw in the case of DeepCoNN, learning using the target review rev_{AB} at train time inadvertently makes the model dependent on the presence of such reviews at test time, which is unrealistic. However, as shown by the experiment above, rev_{AB} gives an insight into what $user_A$ thought about their experience with $item_B$, and can be an important predictor of the rating r_{AB}. Although unavailable at test time, rev_{AB} is available during training.

TransNet consists of two networks as shown in the architecture diagram of Figure 3, a *Target Network* that processes the target review rev_{AB} and a *Source Network* that processes the texts of the $(user_A, item_B)$ pair that does not include the joint review, rev_{AB}. Given a review text rev_{AB}, the Target Network uses a CNN Text Processor, Γ_T, and a Factorization Machine, FM_T, to predict the rating as:

$$\begin{aligned} x_T &= \Gamma_T(rev_{AB}) \\ \bar{x}_T &= \delta(x_T) \\ \hat{r}_T &= FM_T(\bar{x}_T) \end{aligned}$$

Since the Target Network uses the actual review, its task is similar to sentiment analysis [19, 35].

The Source Network is like the DeepCoNN model with two CNN Text Processors, Γ_A for user text, $text_A - rev_{AB}$, and Γ_B for item text, $text_B - rev_{AB}$, and a Factorization Machine, FM_S, but with an additional TRANSFORM layer. The goal of the TRANSFORM layer is to **transform** the user and the item texts into an approximation of rev_{AB}, denoted by $\hat{rev}_{AB}$, which is then used for predicting the rating. The Source Network predicts the rating as given below:

First, it converts the input texts into their latent form as:

$$\begin{aligned} x_A &= \Gamma_A(text_A - rev_{AB}) \\ x_B &= \Gamma_B(text_B - rev_{AB}) \\ z_0 &= [x_A x_B] \end{aligned}$$

The last step above is a concatenation of the two latent representations. This is then input to the TRANSFORM sub-network, which is a L-layer deep non-linear transformational network. Each layer l in TRANSFORM has a weight matrix $G_l \in \mathbb{R}^{n \times n}$ and bias $g_l \in \mathbb{R}^n$, and transforms its input z_{l-1} as:

$$z_l = \sigma(z_{l-1} G_l + g_l)$$

where σ is a non-linear activation function. Since the input to the first layer, z_0, is a concatenation of two vectors each of n dimensions, the first layer of TRANSFORM uses a weight matrix $G_1 \in \mathbb{R}^{2n \times n}$.

The output of the Lth layer of TRANSFORM, z_L is the approximation constructed by the TransNet for rev_{AB}, denoted by $\hat{rev}_{AB}$. Note that we do not have to generate the surface form of rev_{AB}; It suffices to approximate $\Gamma_T(rev_{AB})$, the latent representation of the target review. The Source Network then uses this representation to predict the rating as:

$$\begin{aligned} \bar{z}_L &= \delta(z_L) \\ \hat{r}_S &= FM_S(\bar{z}_L) \end{aligned}$$

During training, we will force the Source Network's representation z_L to be similar to the encoding of rev_{AB} produced by the Target Network, as we discuss below.

2.5 Training TransNets

TransNet is trained using 3 sub-steps as shown in Algorithm 1. In the first sub-step, for each training example (or a batch of such examples), the parameters of the Target Network, denoted by θ_T, which includes those of Γ_T and FM_T, are updated to minimize a L_1 loss computed between the actual rating r_{AB} and the rating $\hat{r}_T$ predicted from the actual review text rev_{AB}.

To teach the Source Network how to generate an approximation of the latent representation of the original review rev_{AB} generated by the Target Network, in the second sub-step, its parameters, denoted by θ_{trans}, are updated to minimize a L_2 loss computed between the transformed representation, $\bar{z}_L$, of the texts of the user and the item, and the representation x_T of the actual review. θ_{trans} includes the parameters of Γ_A and Γ_B, as well as the weights W_l and biases g_l in each of the transformation layers. θ_{trans} does not include the parameters of FM_S.

In the final sub-step, the remaining parameters of the Source Network, θ_S, which consists of the parameters of the FM_S are updated to minimize a L_1 loss computed between the actual rating r_{AB} and the rating $\hat{r}_S$ predicted from the transformed representation, $\bar{z}_L$. Note that each sub-step is repeated for each training example (or a batch of such examples), and not trained to convergence independently. The training method is detailed in Algorithm 1.

At test time, TransNet uses only the Source Network to make the prediction as shown in Algorithm 3.

Algorithm 1 Training TransNet

procedure TRAIN(D_{train})
  while not converged **do**
    for $(text_A, text_B, rev_{AB}, r_{AB}) \in D_{train}$ **do**
      #Step 1: Train Target Network on the actual review
      $x_T = \Gamma_T(rev_{AB})$
      $\hat{r}_T = FM_T(\delta(x_T))$
      $loss_T = |r_{AB} - \hat{r}_T|$
      update θ_T to minimize $loss_T$
      #Step 2: Learn to Transform
      $x_A = \Gamma_A(text_A)$
      $x_B = \Gamma_B(text_B)$
      $z_0 = [x_A x_B]$
      z_L = TRANSFORM(z_0)
      $\bar{z}_L = \delta(z_L)$
      $loss_{trans} = ||\bar{z}_L - x_T||_2$
      update θ_{trans} to minimize $loss_{trans}$
      #Step 3: Train a predictor on the transformed input
      $\hat{r}_S = FM_S(\bar{z}_L)$
      $loss_S = |r_{AB} - \hat{r}_S|$
      update θ_S to minimize $loss_S$
  return θ_{trans}, θ_S

Algorithm 2 Transform the input

procedure TRANSFORM(z_0)
  for layer $l \in L$ **do**
    $z_l = \sigma(z_{l-1}G_l + g_l)$
  return z_L

Algorithm 3 Testing using TransNet

procedure TEST(D_{test})
  for $(text_P, text_Q) \in D_{test}$ **do**
    #Step 1: Transform the input
    $x_P = \Gamma_A(text_P)$
    $x_Q = \Gamma_B(text_Q)$
    $z_0 = [x_P x_Q]$
    z_L = TRANSFORM(z_0)
    $\bar{z}_L = \delta(z_L)$
    #Step 2: Predict using the transformed input
    $\hat{r}_{PQ} = FM_S(\bar{z}_L)$

2.6 Design Decisions and Other Architectural Choices

In this section, we describe some of the choices we have in designing the TransNet architecture and why they did not give good results in our preliminary experiments.

2.6.1 ***Training with sub-steps vs. jointly.*** While training TransNets using Algorithm 1, in each iteration (or batch), we could choose to jointly minimize a total loss, $loss_{total} = loss_T + loss_{trans} + loss_S$. However, doing so will result in parameter updates to the target network, Γ_T, resulting from $loss_{trans}$, in addition to those from $loss_T$, i.e., the Target Network will get penalized for producing a representation that is different from that produced by the Source Network. This results in both networks learning to produce sub-optimal representations and converging to a lower performance in our experiments. Therefore, it is important to separate the Target Network's parameter updates so that it learns to produce the best representation which will enable it to make the most accurate rating predictions from the review text.

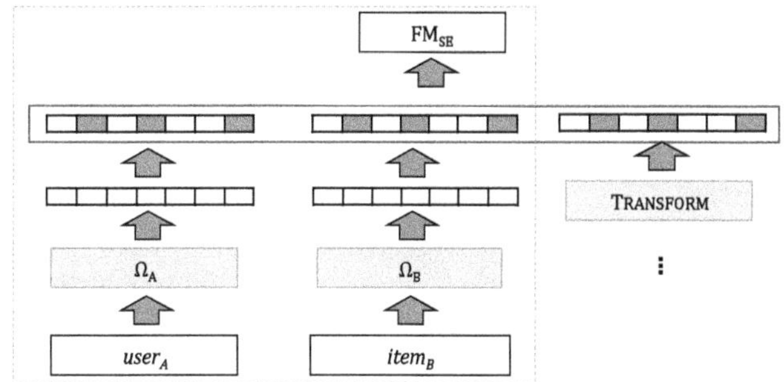

Figure 4: The Extended TransNet sub-architecture

2.6.2 ***Training Target Network to convergence independently.*** We could choose to first train the Target Network to convergence and then train the Source Network to emulate the trained Target Network. However, note that the Target Network's input is the actual review, which is unavailable for testing its performance, i.e., we do not know when the Target Network has converged with good generalization vs. when it is overfitting. The only way to measure the performance at test time is to check the output of the Source Network. Therefore, we let the Source and the Target Networks learn simultaneously and stop when the Source Network's test performance is good.

2.6.3 ***Using the same convolutional model to process text in both the Source and Target networks.*** We could choose to use the Γ_T that was trained in the Target Network to generate features from the user and the item text in the Source Network, instead of learning separate Γ_A and Γ_B. After all, we are learning to transform the latter's output into the former. However, in that case, TransNet would be constrained to generate generic features similar to topics. By providing it with separate feature generators, it can possibly learn to transform the occurrence of different features in the user text and the item text of the Source Network to another feature in the Target Network. For example, it could learn to transform the occurrence of features corresponding to say, 'love indian cuisine' & 'dislike long wait' in the user profile, and 'lousy service' & 'terrible chicken curry' in the item (restaurant) profile, to a feature corresponding to say, 'disappointed' in the target review, and subsequently predict a lower rating. Having separate feature generators in the Source Network gives TransNets more expressive power and gave a better performance compared to an architecture that reuses the Target Network's feature generator.

2.6.4 ***Training the TRANSFORM without the dropout.*** We could choose to match the output z_L of TRANSFORM with x_T instead of its dropped out version $\bar{z}_L$ in Step 2 of Algorithm 1. However, this makes the TRANSFORM layer unregularized, leading it to overfit thus giving poor performance.

2.7 Extended TransNets

TransNet uses only the text of the reviews and is user/item identity-agnostic, i.e., the user and the item are fully represented using the

Table 1: Dataset Statistics

Dataset	Category	#Users	#Items	#Ratings & Reviews
Yelp17		1,029,432	144,072	4,153,150
AZ-Elec	Electronics	4,200,520	475,910	7,820,765 (7,824,482)
AZ-CSJ	Clothing, Shoes and Jewelry	3,116,944	1,135,948	5,748,260 (5,748,920)
AZ-Mov	Movies and TV	2,088,428	200,915	4,606,671 (4,607,047)

review texts, and their identities are not used in the model. However, in most real world settings, the identities of the users and items are known to the recommender system. In such a scenario, it is beneficial to learn a latent representation of the users and items, similar to Matrix Factorization methods. The *Extended TransNet* (TransNet-Ext) model achieves that by extending the architecture of TransNet as shown in Figure 4.

The Source Network now has two embedding matrices Ω_A for users and Ω_B for items, which are functions of the form, $\Omega : id \rightarrow \mathbb{R}^n$. These map the string representing the identity of $user_A$ and $item_B$ into a n-dimensional representation. These latent representations are then passed through a dropout layer and concatenated with the output of the TRANSFORM layer before being passed to the FM regression layer. Therefore, given $user_A$ and $item_B$, TransNet-Ext computes the rating as:

$$\begin{aligned} \omega_A &= \Omega(user_A) \\ \omega_B &= \Omega(item_B) \\ \bar{z} &= [\delta(\omega_A)\ \delta(\omega_B)\ \bar{z}_L] \\ \hat{r}_{SE} &= FM_{SE}(\bar{z}) \end{aligned}$$

Computation of the loss in *Step 3* of Algorithm 1, $loss_{SE}$ is same as earlier: $loss_{SE} = |r_{AB} - \hat{r}_{SE}|$. But the parameter θ_S updated at the end now contains the embedding matrices Ω_A and Ω_B.

3 EXPERIMENTS AND RESULTS

3.1 Datasets

We evaluate the performance of the approach proposed in this paper on four large datasets. The first one, Yelp17, is from the latest Yelp dataset challenge[3], containing about 4M reviews and ratings of businesses by about 1M users. The rest are three of the larger datasets in the latest release of Amazon reviews[4] [25, 26] containing reviews and ratings given by users for products purchased on amazon.com, over the period of May 1996 - July 2014. We use the aggressively de-duplicated version of the dataset and also discard entries where the review text is empty. The statistics of the datasets are given in Table 1. The original size of the dataset before discarding empty reviews is given in brackets when applicable.

3.2 Evaluation Procedure and Settings

Each dataset is split randomly into train, validation and test sets in the ratio 80 : 10 : 10. After training on every 1000 batches of 500 training examples each, MSE is calculated on the validation and the test datasets. We report the MSE obtained on the test dataset when the MSE on the validation dataset was the lowest, similar to [24]. All algorithms, including the competitive baselines, were implemented in Python using TensorFlow[5], an open source software library for numerical computation, and were trained/tested on NVIDIA GeForce GTX TITAN X GPUs. Training TransNet on Yelp17 takes approximately 40 minutes for 1 epoch (~6600 batches) on 1 GPU, and gives the best performance in about 2–3 epochs.

Below are the details of the text processing and the parameter settings used in the experiments:

3.2.1 ***Text Pre-Processing and Embedding.*** All reviews are first passed through a Stanford Core NLP Tokenizer [23] to obtain the tokens, which are then lowercased. Stopwords (the, and, is etc.) as well as punctuations are considered as separate tokens and are retained. A 64-dimensional *word2vec*[6] [27] embedding using the Skip-gram model is pre-trained on the 50,000 most frequent tokens in each of the training corpora.

3.2.2 ***CNN Text Processor.*** We reuse most of the hyper-parameter settings reported by the authors of DeepCoNN [44] since varying them did not give any perceivable improvement. In all of the CNN Text Processors Γ_A, Γ_B and Γ_T, the number of neurons, m, in the convolutional layer is 100, the window size t is 3, and n, the dimension of the output of the CNN Text Processor, is 50. The maximum length of the input text, T, is set to 1000. If there are many reviews, they are randomly sorted and concatenated, and the first T tokens of the concatenated version are used. In our experiments, the word embedding dimension, d, is 64, and the vocabulary size, $|M|$ is 50,000. Also, the non-linearity, α, is *tanh*.

3.2.3 ***Dropout Layer and Factorization Machines.*** All dropout layers have a keep probability of 0.5. In all of the factorization machines, FM_T, FM_S and FM_{SE}, the pair-wise interaction is factorized using a $k = 8$ dimensional matrix, V. Since FM_T processes a n-dimensional input, its parameters are $\mathbf{w}_T \in \mathbb{R}^n$ and $\mathbf{V}_T \in \mathbb{R}^{n \times k}$. Similarly, since FM_{SE} processes a $3n$-dimensional input, its parameters are $\mathbf{w}_{SE} \in \mathbb{R}^{3n}$ and $\mathbf{V}_{SE} \in \mathbb{R}^{3n \times k}$. All **w**'s are initialized to 0.001, and all **V**'s are initialized from a truncated normal distribution with 0.0 mean and 0.001 standard deviation. All FMs are trained to minimize an L_1 loss.

3.2.4 ***TRANSFORM.*** The default setting for the number of layers, L, is 2. We show the performance for different values of L in Section 3.5. All weight matrices G_l are initialized from a truncated normal distribution with 0.0 mean and 0.1 standard deviation, and all biases g_l are initialized to 0.1. The non-linearity, σ, is *tanh*.

3.2.5 ***TransNet-Ext.*** The user (item) embedding matrices, Ω, are initialized from a random uniform distribution (-1.0, 1.0), and map users (items) that appear in the training set to a $n = 50$ dimensional space. New users (items) in the validation and test sets are mapped to a random vector.

3.2.6 ***Training.*** All optimizations are learned using Adam [17], a stochastic gradient-based optimizer with adaptive estimates, at a learning rate set to 0.002. All gradients are computed by automatic differentiation in TensorFlow.

[3]https://www.yelp.com/dataset_challenge
[4]http://jmcauley.ucsd.edu/data/amazon
[5]https://www.tensorflow.org
[6]https://www.tensorflow.org/tutorials/word2vec#the_skip-gram_model

3.3 Competitive Baselines

We compare our method against the current state-of-the-art, DeepCoNN [44]. Since DeepCoNN was extensively evaluated against the previous state-of-the-art models like Hidden Factors as Topics (HFT) model [24], Collaborative Topic Regression (CTR) [39], Collaborative Deep Learning (CDL) [40] and Probabilistic Matrix Factorization (PMF) [33], and shown to surpass their performance by a wide margin, we refrain from repeating those comparisons in this paper. However, we do consider some variations of DeepCoNN.

Our competitive baselines are:

(1) **DeepCoNN**: The model proposed in [44]. During training, $text_A$ and $text_B$ corresponding to the $user_A$-$item_B$ pair contains their joint review rev_{AB}, along with reviews that $user_A$ wrote for other items and what other users wrote for $item_B$ in the training set. During testing, for a $user_P$-$item_Q$ pair, $text_P$ and $text_Q$ are constructed from only the training set and therefore, does not contain their joint review rev_{PQ}.

(2) **DeepCoNN-rev$_{AB}$**: The same DeepCoNN model (1) above, but trained in a setting that mimics the test setup, i.e., during training, $text_A$ and $text_B$ corresponding to the $user_A$-$item_B$ pair **does not contain** their joint review rev_{AB}, but only the reviews that $user_A$ wrote for other items and what other users wrote for $item_B$ in the training set. Testing procedure is the same as above: for a $user_P$-$item_Q$ pair, $text_P$ and $text_Q$ are constructed from only the training set and therefore, does not contain their joint review rev_{PQ} which is present in the test set.

(3) **MF**: A neural net implementation of Matrix Factorization with $n = 50$ latent dimensions. It uses only ratings.

We also provide the performance numbers of DeepCoNN in the setting where the test reviews are available at the time of testing. i.e. the same DeepCoNN model (1) above, but with the exception that at test time, for a $user_P$-$item_Q$ pair, $text_P$ and $text_Q$ are constructed from the training set as well as the test set, and therefore, contains their joint review rev_{PQ} from the test set. This is denoted as **DeepCoNN + Test Reviews**, and its performance is provided for the sole purpose of illustrating how much better the algorithm could perform, had it been given access to the test reviews.

3.4 Evaluation on Rating Prediction

Like prior work, we use the Mean Square Error (MSE) metric to evaluate the performance of the algorithms. Let N be the total number of datapoints being tested. Then MSE is defined as:

$$MSE = \frac{1}{N}\sum_{i=1}^{N}(r_i - \hat{r}_i)^2$$

where, r_i is the ground truth rating and $\hat{r}_i$ is the predicted rating for the ith datapoint. Lower MSE indicates better performance.

The MSE values of the various competitive baselines are given in Table 2. For each dataset, the best score is highlighted in blue.

As can be seen from the Table, it is clear that TransNet and its variant TransNet-Ext perform better at rating prediction compared to the competitive baselines on all the datasets (p-$value \leq 0.05$). It can also be seen that learning a user and item embedding using only the ratings in addition to the text helps TransNet-Ext improve the performance over the vanilla TransNet (p-$value \leq 0.1$), except in the case of one dataset (AZ-CSJ).

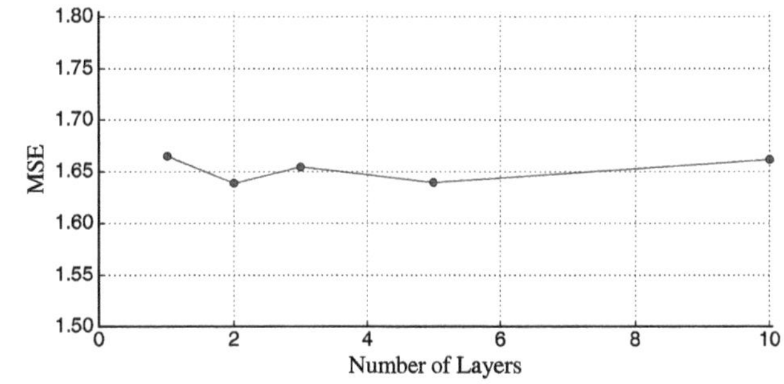

Figure 5: Variation in MSE with different Layers: TransNets on Yelp dataset

It is also interesting to note that training DeepCoNN mimicking the test setup (DeepCoNN-rev$_{AB}$) gives a large improvement in the case of Yelp, but does not help in the case of the AZ datasets.

3.5 Picking the number of TRANSFORM layers

The TRANSFORM network uses L fully connected layers. In Figure 5, we plot the MSE of TransNet on the Yelp17 dataset when varying L from 1 to 10. It can be seen from the figure that TransNets are quite robust to the choice of L, fluctuating only narrowly in its performance. Using only one layer gives the highest MSE, most probably because it doesn't have enough parameters to learn how to transform the input. Using 10 layers also gives a high MSE, probably because it overfits or because it has too many parameters to learn. From the figure, using 2 or 5 layers gives the best MSE for this particular setting of TransNets. It is known that a 2 layer non-linear neural network is sufficient to represent all the logic gates including the XOR [11]. So, using 2 layers seems like a reasonable choice.

3.6 Finding the most similar (helpful) reviews

Our primary evaluation of TransNet is quantitative, using MSE of predicted ratings. We would also like to investigate whether the learned representation is qualitatively useful—i.e., does it capture interesting high-level properties of the user's review. One possible use of learning representation would be to give the user information about her predicted reaction to the item that is more detailed than a rating. In this section, we show how TransNets could be used to find reviews that are most similar to what the user would have written, which in turn, could be helpful in making an informed decision. For example, the most helpful review for a user who is more concerned about the quality of service and wait times would be different from the most helpful review for another user who is sensitive to the price. For a test $user_P$-$item_Q$ pair, we run the Source Network with the text of their reviews from the training set to construct z_L, which is an approximation for the representation of their actual joint review. Candidate reviews are all the reviews rev_{CQ} in the training set written for $item_Q$ by other users. We pass each of them separately through the Target Network to obtain their latent representation $x_{CQ} = \Gamma_T(rev_{CQ})$. If rev_{CQ} had been most similar to what $user_P$ would write for $item_Q$, then x_{CQ} would be most similar to z_L. Therefore, the most similar review is simply the rev_{CQ} whose x_{CQ} is closest to z_L in Euclidean distance.

Some examples of such predicted most similar reviews on the Yelp17 dataset are listed in Table 3. Here, the column Original Review is the actual review that $user_P$ wrote for $item_Q$, and the

Table 2: Performance comparison using MSE metric

Dataset	DeepCoNN + Test Reviews	MF	DeepCoNN	DeepCoNN-rev$_{AB}$	TransNet	TransNet-Ext
Yelp17	1.2106	1.8661	1.8984	1.7045	1.6387	1.5913
AZ-Elec	0.9791	1.8898	1.9704	2.0774	1.8380	1.7781
AZ-CSJ	0.7747	1.5212	1.5487	1.7044	1.4487	1.4780
AZ-Mov	0.9392	1.4324	1.3611	1.5276	1.3599	1.2691

column Predicted Review gives the most similar of the candidate reviews predicted by TransNet. The examples show how the predicted reviews talk about particulars that the original reviews also highlight.

4 RELATED WORK

4.1 Recommendation Models

4.1.1 ***Non-Neural Models.*** The *Hidden Factors as Topics* (HFT) model [24] aims to find topics in the review text that are correlated with the latent parameters of users. They propose a transformation function which converts user's latent factors to the topic distribution of the review, and since the former exactly defines the latter, only one of them is learned. A modified version of HFT is the *TopicMF* model [4], where the goal is to match the latent factors learned for the users and items using MF with the topics learned on their joint reviews using a Non-Negative Matrix Factorization, which is then jointly optimized with the rating prediction. In their transformation function, the proportion of a particular topic in the review is a linear combination of its proportion in the latent factors of the user and the item, which is then converted into a probability distribution over all topics in that review. Unlike these two models, TransNet computes each factor in the transformed review from a non-linear combination of any number of factors from the latent representations of either the user or the item or both. Another extension to HFT is the *Rating Meets Reviews* (RMR) model [22] where the rating is sampled from a Gaussian mixture.

The *Collaborative Topic Regression* (CTR) model proposed in [39] is a content based approach, as opposed to a context / review based approach. It uses LDA [5] to model the text of documents (scientific articles), and a combination of MF and content based model for recommendation. The *Rating-boosted Latent Topics* (RBLT) model of [37] uses a simple technique of repeating a review r times in the corpus if it was rated r, so that features in higher rated reviews will dominate the topics. *Explicit Factor Models* (EFM) proposed in [43] aims to generate explainable recommendations by extracting explicit product features (aspects) and users' sentiments towards these aspects using phrase-level sentiment analysis.

4.1.2 ***Neural Net Models.*** The most recent model to successfully employ neural networks at scale for rating prediction is the *Deep Cooperative Neural Networks* (DeepCoNN) [44], which was discussed in detail in Section 2. Prior to that work, [2] proposed two models: *Bag-of-Words regularized Latent Factor* model (BoWLF) and *Language Model regularized Latent Factor* model (LMLF), where MF was used to learn the latent factors of users and items, and likelihood of the review text, represented either as a bag-of-words or an LSTM embedding [14], was computed using the item factors. [34] proposed a CNN based model identical to DeepCoNN, but with attention mechanism to construct the latent representations, the inner product of which gave the predicted ratings.

Some of the other past research uses neural networks in a CF setting with content, but not reviews. The *Collaborative Deep Learning* (CDL) model [40] uses a Stacked De-noising Auto Encoder (SDAE) [38] to learn robust latent representations of items from their content, which is then fed into a CTR model [39] for predicting the ratings. A very similar approach to CDL is the *Deep Collaborative Filtering* (DCF) method [21] which uses Marginalized De-noising Auto-Encoder (mDA) [7] instead. The *Convolutional Matrix Factorization* (ConvMF) model [16] uses a CNN to process the description associated with the item and feed the resulting latent vectors into a PMF model for rating prediction. The *Multi-View Deep Neural Net* (MV-DNN) model [10] uses a deep neural net to map user's and item's content into a shared latent space such that their similarity in that space is maximized. [29] proposed to generate the latent factors of items – music in this case– from the content, audio signals. The predicted latent factors of the item were then used in a CF style with the latent factors of the user. [3] also proposed a similar technique but adapted to recommending scientific-articles. [9] used a deep neural net to learn a latent representation from video content which is then fed into a deep ranking network.

Prior research has also used deep neural nets for learning latent factors from ratings alone, i.e., without using any content or review. *Collaborative De-noising Auto-Encoder* model (CDAE) [41] learns to reconstruct user's feedback from a corrupted version of the same.

4.2 Comparison to Related Architectures

4.2.1 Student-Teacher Models. Student-Teacher models [6, 13] also have two networks: a Teacher Network, which is large and complex, and typically an ensemble of different models, is first trained to make predictions, and a much simpler Student Network, which learns to emulate the output of the Teacher Network, is trained later. There are substantial differences between Student-Teacher models and TransNets in how they are structured. Firstly, in Student-Teacher models, the input to both the student and the teacher models are the same. For example, in the case of digit recognition, both networks input the same image of the digit. However, in TransNets, the inputs to the two networks are different. In the Target, there is only one input – the review by $user_A$ for an $item_B$ designated as rev_{AB}. But, in the Source, there are two inputs: all the reviews written by $user_A$ sans rev_{AB} and all the reviews written for $item_B$ sans rev_{AB}. Secondly, in Student-Teacher models, the Teacher is considerably complex in terms of width and depth, and the Student is more light-weight, trying to mimic the Teacher. In TransNets, the complexities are reversed. The Target

Table 3: Original review vs. Predicted most helpful review

Original Review	Predicted Review
my laptop flat lined and i did n't know why , just one day it did n't turn on . i cam here based on the yelp reviews and happy i did . although my laptop could n't be revived due to the fried motherboard , they did give me a full explanation about what they found and my best options . i was grateful they did n't charge me for looking into the problem , other places would have . i will definitely be coming back if needed . .	my hard drive crashed and i had to buy a new computer . the store where i bought my computer could n't get data off my old hard drive . neither could a tech friend of mine . works could ! they did n't charge for the diagnosis and only charged $ 100 for the transfer . very happy .
this place is so cool . the outdoor area is n't as big as the fillmore location , but they make up for it with live music . i really like the atmosphere and the food is pretty spot on . the sweet potato fry dip is really something special . the vig was highly recommended to me , and i 'm passing that recommendation on to all who read this .	like going on monday 's . happy hour for drinks and apps then at 6pm their burger special . sundays are cool too , when they have live music on their patio .
i have attempted at coming here before but i have never been able to make it in because it 's always so packed with people wanting to eat . i finally came here at a good time around 6ish ... and not packed but by the time i left , it was packed ! the miso ramen was delicious . you can choose from add on 's on your soup but they charge you , i dont think they should , they should just treat them as condiments . at other ramen places that i have been too i get the egg , bamboo shoot , fire ball add on 's free . so i am not sure what their deal is .	hands down top three ramen spots on the west coast , right up there with , and the line can be just as long .
this place can be a zoo !! however , with the produce they have , at the prices they sell it at , it is worth the hassle . be prepared to be pushed and shoved . this is much the same as in asia . my wife (from vietnam) says that the markets in asia are even more crowded . i agree as i have seen vietnam with my own eyes .	i enjoy going to this market on main street when i am ready to can ... the prices are great esp for onions . . broccoli and bell peppers ... a few times they have had bananas for $ 3.00 for a huge box like 30 lbs ... you can freeze them or cover in ... or make banana bread if they begin to go dark ... and ripe . the employees will talk if you say hello first ...
great spot for outdoor seating in the summer since it 's sheltered early from the sun . good service but americanos sometimes are not made right	this is my " go to " starbucks due to the location being close to where i live . i normally go through the drive-thru , which more likely than not , has a long line . . but does n't every starbucks ? i have always received great customer service at this location ! there has been a couple times that my order was n't correct - which is frustrating when you are short on time & depend on your morning coffee ! but overall you should have a good experience whether you drive-thru or dine in !
very overpriced food , very substandard food . wait staff is a joke . if you like being ignored in the front room of a one story house and being charged for it , by all means . otherwise , go to freaking mcdonald 's .	i want this place to be good but it fails me every time . i brought my parents here for dinner and was totally embarrassed with my dining choice . i tried it two more times after that and continue to be disappointed . their menu looks great but what is delivered is a total let down . to top it off , the service is painfully slow . the only thing this place has going for it is the dog friendly patio and craft beers . i hope someone reads these reviews as the poor service piece continues to be brought up as an issue .

is lean while the Source is heavy-weight, often processing large pieces of text using twice the number of parameters as the Target. Thirdly, in Student-Teacher models, the Teacher is pre-trained whereas in TransNets the Target is trained simultaneously with the Source. A recently proposed Student-Teacher model in [15] does train both the Student and the Teacher simultaneously. Also, in Student-Teacher models, the emphasis is on learning a simpler and easier model that can achieve similar results as a very complex model. But in TransNets, the objective is to learn how to transform a source representation to a target representation.

4.2.2 Generative Adversarial Networks. TransNets also bear semblance to GANs [12, 31] since both are attempting to generate an output which is similar to realistic data. But the models are fundamentally different. Firstly, unlike GAN where the Generative network generates an output from a random starting point, TransNets have a starting point for each example – the reviews written by the user and those written for the item. Secondly, the Adversarial network in GAN tries to classify if the output is real or synthetic. In TransNets, although the objective is to minimize the dissimilarity between the generated representation and that of the real input, there is no adversarial classifier that attempts to separate each out. Thirdly, in GANs, the adversarial network needs to learn a notion of 'real' outputs, which is quite generic. In TransNets, there is always a specific real output to compare to and does not need to learn what a generic real output will look like.

5 CONCLUSIONS

Using reviews for improving recommender systems is an important task and is gaining a lot of attention in the recent years. A recent neural net model, *DeepCoNN*, uses the text of the reviews written by the user and for the item to learn their latent representations, which are then fed into a regression layer for rating prediction. However, its performance is dependent on having access to the user-item pairwise review, which is unavailable in real-world settings.

In this paper, we propose a new model called *TransNets* which extends *DeepCoNN* with an additional TRANSFORM layer. This additional layer learns to transform the latent representations of user and item into that of their pair-wise review so that at test time, an approximate representation of the target review can be generated and used for making the predictions. We also showed how *TransNets* can be extended to learn user and item representations from ratings only which can be used in addition to the generated review representation. Our experiments showed that *TransNets* and its extended version can improve the state-of-the-art substantially.

ACKNOWLEDGMENTS

We would like to thank Kathryn Mazaitis for her assistance with the GPU machines. This research was supported in part by Yahoo! through the CMU-Yahoo InMind project.

REFERENCES

[1] Gediminas Adomavicius and Alexander Tuzhilin. 2008. Context-aware Recommender Systems. In *Proceedings of the 2008 ACM Conference on Recommender Systems (RecSys '08)*. 335–336.

[2] Amjad Almahairi, Kyle Kastner, Kyunghyun Cho, and Aaron Courville. 2015. Learning Distributed Representations from Reviews for Collaborative Filtering. In *Proceedings of the 9th ACM Conference on Recommender Systems (RecSys '15)*. 147–154.

[3] Trapit Bansal, David Belanger, and Andrew McCallum. 2016. Ask the GRU: Multi-task Learning for Deep Text Recommendations. In *Proceedings of the 10th ACM Conference on Recommender Systems (RecSys '16)*. 107–114.

[4] Yang Bao, Hui Fang, and Jie Zhang. 2014. TopicMF: Simultaneously Exploiting Ratings and Reviews for Recommendation. In *Proceedings of the Twenty-Eighth AAAI Conference on Artificial Intelligence (AAAI'14)*. 2–8.

[5] David M. Blei, Andrew Y. Ng, and Michael I. Jordan. 2003. Latent Dirichlet Allocation. *J. Mach. Learn. Res.* 3 (March 2003), 993–1022.

[6] Cristian Buciluǎ, Rich Caruana, and Alexandru Niculescu-Mizil. 2006. Model Compression. In *Proceedings of the 12th ACM SIGKDD International Conference on Knowledge Discovery and Data Mining (KDD '06)*. 535–541.

[7] Minmin Chen, Zhixiang Xu, Kilian Q. Weinberger, and Fei Sha. 2012. Marginalized Denoising Autoencoders for Domain Adaptation. In *Proceedings of the 29th International Coference on International Conference on Machine Learning (ICML'12)*. 1627–1634.

[8] Ronan Collobert, Jason Weston, Léon Bottou, Michael Karlen, Koray Kavukcuoglu, and Pavel Kuksa. 2011. Natural Language Processing (Almost) from Scratch. *J. Mach. Learn. Res.* 12 (Nov. 2011), 2493–2537.

[9] Paul Covington, Jay Adams, and Emre Sargin. 2016. Deep Neural Networks for YouTube Recommendations. In *Proceedings of the 10th ACM Conference on Recommender Systems (RecSys '16)*. 191–198.

[10] Ali Mamdouh Elkahky, Yang Song, and Xiaodong He. 2015. A Multi-View Deep Learning Approach for Cross Domain User Modeling in Recommendation Systems. In *Proceedings of the 24th International Conference on World Wide Web (WWW '15)*. 278–288.

[11] Ian Goodfellow, Yoshua Bengio, and Aaron Courville. 2016. *Deep Learning*. MIT Press. http://www.deeplearningbook.org.

[12] Ian J. Goodfellow, Jean Pouget-Abadie, Mehdi Mirza, Bing Xu, David Warde-Farley, Sherjil Ozair, Aaron Courville, and Yoshua Bengio. 2014. Generative Adversarial Nets. In *Proceedings of the 27th International Conference on Neural Information Processing Systems (NIPS'14)*. 2672–2680.

[13] Geoffrey E. Hinton, Oriol Vinyals, and Jeffrey Dean. 2014. Distilling the Knowledge in a Neural Network. In *Deep Learning and Representation Learning Workshop (NIPS '14)*.

[14] Sepp Hochreiter and Jürgen Schmidhuber. 1997. Long Short-Term Memory. *Neural Computation* 9, 8 (Nov. 1997), 1735–1780.

[15] Zhiting Hu, Xuezhe Ma, Zhengzhong Liu, Eduard Hovy, and Eric Xing. 2016. Harnessing Deep Neural Networks with Logic Rules. In *Proceedings of the 54th Annual Meeting of the Association for Computational Linguistics (ACL)*. 2410–2420.

[16] Donghyun Kim, Chanyoung Park, Jinoh Oh, Sungyoung Lee, and Hwanjo Yu. 2016. Convolutional Matrix Factorization for Document Context-Aware Recommendation. In *Proceedings of the 10th ACM Conference on Recommender Systems (RecSys '16)*. 233–240.

[17] Diederik P. Kingma and Jimmy Ba. 2014. Adam: A Method for Stochastic Optimization. In *Proceedings of the 3rd International Conference on Learning Representations (ICLR)*.

[18] Yehuda Koren. 2008. Factorization Meets the Neighborhood: A Multifaceted Collaborative Filtering Model. In *Proc. KDD '08*. 426–434.

[19] Quoc V Le and Tomas Mikolov. 2014. Distributed Representations of Sentences and Documents.. In *ICML*, Vol. 14. 1188–1196.

[20] Y. Lecun, L. Bottou, Y. Bengio, and P. Haffner. 1998. Gradient-based learning applied to document recognition. *Proc. IEEE* 86, 11 (1998), 2278–2324.

[21] Sheng Li, Jaya Kawale, and Yun Fu. 2015. Deep Collaborative Filtering via Marginalized Denoising Auto-encoder. In *Proceedings of the 24th ACM International on Conference on Information and Knowledge Management (CIKM '15)*. 811–820.

[22] Guang Ling, Michael R. Lyu, and Irwin King. 2014. Ratings Meet Reviews, a Combined Approach to Recommend. In *Proceedings of the 8th ACM Conference on Recommender Systems (RecSys '14)*. 105–112.

[23] Christopher D. Manning, Mihai Surdeanu, John Bauer, Jenny Finkel, Steven J. Bethard, and David McClosky. 2014. The Stanford CoreNLP Natural Language Processing Toolkit. In *Association for Computational Linguistics (ACL) System Demonstrations*. 55–60.

[24] Julian McAuley and Jure Leskovec. 2013. Hidden Factors and Hidden Topics: Understanding Rating Dimensions with Review Text. In *Proceedings of the 7th ACM Conference on Recommender Systems (RecSys '13)*. 165–172.

[25] Julian McAuley, Rahul Pandey, and Jure Leskovec. 2015. Inferring Networks of Substitutable and Complementary Products. In *Proceedings of the 21th ACM SIGKDD International Conference on Knowledge Discovery and Data Mining (KDD '15)*. 785–794.

[26] Julian McAuley, Christopher Targett, Qinfeng Shi, and Anton van den Hengel. 2015. Image-Based Recommendations on Styles and Substitutes. In *Proceedings of the 38th International ACM SIGIR Conference on Research and Development in Information Retrieval (SIGIR '15)*. 43–52.

[27] Tomas Mikolov, Ilya Sutskever, Kai Chen, Greg Corrado, and Jeffrey Dean. 2013. Distributed Representations of Words and Phrases and Their Compositionality. In *Proceedings of the 26th International Conference on Neural Information Processing Systems (NIPS'13)*. 3111–3119.

[28] Vinod Nair and Geoffrey E. Hinton. 2010. Rectified Linear Units Improve Restricted Boltzmann Machines. In *Proceedings of the 27th International Conference on Machine Learning (ICML-10), June 21-24, 2010, Haifa, Israel*. 807–814.

[29] Aäron van den Oord, Sander Dieleman, and Benjamin Schrauwen. 2013. Deep Content-based Music Recommendation. In *Proceedings of the 26th International Conference on Neural Information Processing Systems (NIPS'13)*. 2643–2651.

[30] Jeffrey Pennington, Richard Socher, and Christopher D. Manning. 2014. GloVe: Global Vectors for Word Representation. In *Empirical Methods in Natural Language Processing (EMNLP)*. 1532–1543.

[31] Scott Reed, Zeynep Akata, Xinchen Yan, Lajanugen Logeswaran, Bernt Schiele, and Honglak Lee. 2016. Generative Adversarial Text to Image Synthesis. In *Proceedings of the 33rd International Conference on International Conference on Machine Learning - Volume 48 (ICML'16)*. 1060–1069.

[32] Steffen Rendle. 2010. Factorization Machines. In *Proceedings of the 2010 IEEE International Conference on Data Mining (ICDM '10)*. 995–1000.

[33] Ruslan Salakhutdinov and Andriy Mnih. 2007. Probabilistic Matrix Factorization. In *Proceedings of the 20th International Conference on Neural Information Processing Systems (NIPS'07)*. Curran Associates Inc., USA, 1257–1264. http://dl.acm.org/citation.cfm?id=2981562.2981720

[34] Sungyong Seo, Jing Huang, Hao Yang, and Yan Liu. 2017. Representation Learning of Users and Items for Review Rating Prediction Using Attention-based Convolutional Neural Network. In *3rd International Workshop on Machine Learning Methods for Recommender Systems (MLRec) (SDM '17)*.

[35] Richard Socher, Alex Perelygin, Jean Wu, Jason Chuang, Christopher D. Manning, Andrew Y. Ng, and Christopher Potts. 2013. Recursive Deep Models for Semantic Compositionality Over a Sentiment Treebank. In *Proceedings of the 2013 Conference on Empirical Methods in Natural Language Processing*. Association for Computational Linguistics, 1631–1642.

[36] Nitish Srivastava, Geoffrey Hinton, Alex Krizhevsky, Ilya Sutskever, and Ruslan Salakhutdinov. 2014. Dropout: A Simple Way to Prevent Neural Networks from Overfitting. *J. Mach. Learn. Res.* 15, 1 (2014), 1929–1958.

[37] Yunzhi Tan, Min Zhang, Yiqun Liu, and Shaoping Ma. 2016. Rating-boosted Latent Topics: Understanding Users and Items with Ratings and Reviews. In *Proceedings of the Twenty-Fifth International Joint Conference on Artificial Intelligence (IJCAI'16)*. 2640–2646.

[38] Pascal Vincent, Hugo Larochelle, Isabelle Lajoie, Yoshua Bengio, and Pierre-Antoine Manzagol. 2010. Stacked Denoising Autoencoders: Learning Useful Representations in a Deep Network with a Local Denoising Criterion. *J. Mach. Learn. Res.* 11 (Dec. 2010), 3371–3408.

[39] Chong Wang and David M. Blei. 2011. Collaborative Topic Modeling for Recommending Scientific Articles. In *Proceedings of the 17th ACM SIGKDD International Conference on Knowledge Discovery and Data Mining (KDD '11)*. 448–456.

[40] Hao Wang, Naiyan Wang, and Dit-Yan Yeung. 2015. Collaborative Deep Learning for Recommender Systems. In *Proceedings of the 21th ACM SIGKDD International Conference on Knowledge Discovery and Data Mining (KDD '15)*. 1235–1244.

[41] Yao Wu, Christopher DuBois, Alice X. Zheng, and Martin Ester. 2016. Collaborative Denoising Auto-Encoders for Top-N Recommender Systems. In *Proceedings of the Ninth ACM International Conference on Web Search and Data Mining (WSDM '16)*. 153–162.

[42] Xing Yi, Liangjie Hong, Erheng Zhong, Nanthan Nan Liu, and Suju Rajan. 2014. Beyond Clicks: Dwell Time for Personalization. In *Proceedings of the 8th ACM Conference on Recommender Systems (RecSys '14)*. 113–120.

[43] Yongfeng Zhang, Guokun Lai, Min Zhang, Yi Zhang, Yiqun Liu, and Shaoping Ma. 2014. Explicit Factor Models for Explainable Recommendation Based on Phrase-level Sentiment Analysis. In *Proceedings of the 37th International ACM SIGIR Conference on Research & Development in Information Retrieval (SIGIR '14)*. 83–92.

[44] Lei Zheng, Vahid Noroozi, and Philip S. Yu. 2017. Joint Deep Modeling of Users and Items Using Reviews for Recommendation. In *Proceedings of the Tenth ACM International Conference on Web Search and Data Mining (WSDM '17)*. 425–434.

Interpretable Convolutional Neural Networks with Dual Local and Global Attention for Review Rating Prediction

Sungyong Seo
University of Southern California
sungyons@usc.edu

Jing Huang
Visa Research, Visa Inc.
jinhuang@visa.com

Hao Yang
Visa Research, Visa Inc.
haoyang@visa.com

Yan Liu
University of Southern California
yanliu.cs@usc.edu

ABSTRACT

Recently, many e-commerce websites have encouraged their users to rate shopping items and write review texts. This review information has been very useful for understanding user preferences and item properties, as well as enhancing the capability to make personalized recommendations of these websites. In this paper, we propose to model user preferences and item properties using convolutional neural networks (CNNs) with dual local and global attention, motivated by the superiority of CNNs to extract complex features. By using aggregated review texts from a user and aggregated review text for an item, our model can learn the unique features (embedding) of each user and each item. These features are then used to predict ratings. We train these user and item networks jointly which enable the interaction between users and items in a similar way as matrix factorization. The local attention provides us insight on a user's preferences or an item's properties. The global attention helps CNNs focus on the semantic meaning of the whole review text. Thus, the combined local and global attentions enable an interpretable and better-learned representation of users and items. We validate the proposed models by testing on popular review datasets in *Yelp* and *Amazon* and compare the results with matrix factorization (MF), the hidden factor and topical (HFT) model, and the recently proposed convolutional matrix factorization (ConvMF+). Our proposed CNNs with dual attention model outperforms HFT and ConvMF+ in terms of mean square errors (MSE). In addition, we compare the user/item embeddings learned from these models for classification and recommendation. These results also confirm the superior quality of user/item embeddings learned from our model.

KEYWORDS

Convolutional Neural Network; Attention Model; Deep Learning for Recommender Systems

RecSys'17, August 27–31, 2017, Como, Italy.

ISBN 978-1-4503-4652-8/17/08...$15.00.
DOI: http://dx.doi.org/10.1145/3109859.3109890

1 INTRODUCTION

Recommender systems are ubiquitous today at online shopping websites such as Amazon and Netflix. Ever since the famous Netflix Prize competition started ten years ago, collaborative filtering (CF) techniques have become the successful and dominant approaches for recommender systems. Many of the CF approaches are based on matrix factorization (MF) [11], which decomposes the user-item rating matrix into two matrices corresponding to latent features of users and items. The dot product between a user and an item feature vector is then used to predict the rating that the user would assign to the item.

Collaborative filtering has its own limitations and drawbacks, however. First, it is difficult to produce reliable recommendations for users with few ratings or recommend items with few ratings (the well-known cold start problem). Popular items tend to receive more recommendations, while new items are left with no chance to be exposed. Another drawback of CF/MF techniques is content-ignorance. In other words, contextual information such as properties of items or profiles of users is not considered for recommendations. Since the additional information can provide details about particular user or item, it is difficult to build personalized recommender systems without fully utilizing these data.

Using review text is one approach to alleviate the above issues. Most shopping websites encourage their users to rate shopping items and write reviews. Review text complements the rating numbers by providing rich information of items and implicit preferences of users. Review text explains why a user assigns such a rating to an item. A set of all reviews from this user allows us to derive this user's preferences; similarly, a set of reviews for an item describes prominent properties of the item rated by many users. These preferences of a user and properties of an item can then be leveraged to alleviate the cold-start problem when the ratings are few, and present explainable recommendation results to users [30]. Recently using review text information has shown to improve rating prediction accuracy, especially for users and items with few ratings [8, 14, 17].

The RMR model in [14] uses interpretable latent topic models like LDA [4] on item review text: an item document consists of all reviews of an item, and the latent topic distribution is derived from these item documents. The topics discovered from item documents may not be suitable for users. It is believed that the aggregated review text of items cannot cover the same sentimental expressions for each individual user. For example, the same word "nice" might indicate different sentimental meaning from different users, while one user links "nice" to a rating of 4, another would give it a rating of 5. Therefore, we should not discard user-specific meaning of words and ignore their effect on the ratings by just assuming the topic distribution is the same as those in the item review. Each user has their own preferences or tastes that can be discovered using all reviews written by this user. Furthermore, a topic model is specifically designed for discovering latent semantic structures in a text body and the aspect of a topic model limits generalities of extracted features.

Recently, CNNs have shown great success in many natural language processing tasks, such as text classification, sentiment analysis, neural language model and information retrieval ([9, 22, 23, 29]). From these works, it is proved that CNNs are able to extract more general contextual features from texts and the features have been successfully used to build recommender systems showing less prediction error than that of CF/MF ([6, 8]). However, it is believed that features from neural networks are not interpretable in general. Although many of the learned filters in the first convolutional layer capture features similar to *n*-grams when word embeddings input to the first convolutional layer, it becomes much more difficult to understand features come out of few more convolutional layers.

Therefore, in this paper we propose to model the user and the item separately: the aggregated review text from a user is used to build a user-specific model and the aggregated review text on an item is used to build an item-specific model. We use convolutional neural networks (CNNs) to extract embedded representations of users and items from their corresponding review text.

Furthermore, we put an attention layer after the word embedding layer and before the convolutional layer. This attention layer learns what is important from a local or global window of words by learning weights for these words. The idea of using both local and global attention modules with CNNs is inspired by the work in [15] where a local and global attention were experimented for neural machine translation. In our work, the local attention selects informative keywords from a local window before the words are fed into the convolutional layer, and the global attention aims to ignore noisy and irrelevant words from long reviews and captures the global semantic meaning. Both attention layers give us the ability to interpret and visualize what the model is doing: for example, words with higher (or lower) weights are highlighted in Table 4 and Table 5.

The main contributions of this paper are summarized as follows:

- Interpretable attention-based CNNs are used to learn user and item representations from corresponding user and item reviews; these representations are used to predict the ratings of a user for an item just like the MF technique. To the best of our knowledge, this is the first paper to use attention-based CNNs for rating prediction.
- Dual attention layers are used in our network: a local layer and a global layer. The attention layer is used before the convolutional layers to select informative words from a local or global window that contributes to the rating. These attention layers give us insight to the words that are selected by the models that highlight a user's preferences or an item's properties.
- Our model outperforms the baseline MF, HFT, and the recently proposed model, ConvMF+ on the *Yelp* Challenge dataset 2013 and the *Amazon* datasets. In addition, the representations (embeddings) learned for user/item from our model are shown to be better than those from HFT and ConvMF+ for other application purposes, such as item classification and recommendation ranked list for a query user.

The rest of this paper is organized as follows: related works are first reviewed in Section 2. Section 3 describes the components of our networks in detail . Experimental setup and result analysis are presented in Section 4 and Section 5; and finally Section 6 concludes with future work.

2 RELATED WORK

There are two lines of research related to our work: the first uses review text for recommendation, and the second is recent research on sentiment analysis using deep learning. We present brief reviews for these two research areas as follows.

Recent works on using review text for recommendations focus mostly on topic modeling from review text, such as hidden factors as topics (HFT) [17], ratings meet reviews (RMR) [14] and TopicMF [3]. HFT employs a LDA-like topic model on review text for users and items, and a matrix factorization (MF) model to fit the ratings. The two models are combined in an objective function that uses the likelihood of the review text modeling by the topic distribution as a regularization term for the latent user-item parameters. This approach is shown to improve significantly over the baselines that use ratings or reviews alone, and it also works with items with only a few reviews. RMR [14] shares the same LDA-like topic modeling on item reviews as HFT, except that RMR uses Gaussian mixtures to model the rating instead of MF-like techniques. The mixture weights are assumed to have the same distribution as the topic distribution. TopicMF [3], jointly models user ratings with MF and review text with non-negative matrix factorization (NMF) to derive topics from the reviews. A transform function is used to align the topic distribution parameters with the corresponding latent user and item factors. HFT learns the topics for each item, while topicMF learns the topics for each review. Their experimental results show topicMF improved upon HFT. However, the exponential function used as the transformation function might limit the flexibility of topic distributions. As pointed out in [3], the authors hope to model the user's preferences directly to their rating behavior in their future work, which is what our model is designed to do.

Recently, deep learning techniques have been applied to recommender systems with review content. In [1], the proposed model consists of a MF model for learning the latent factors and a recurrent neural network (RNN) for modeling the likelihood of the review using an item's latent factors. The RNN model is combined with MF via a regularization term, just like the approach used in HFT. In [26] a hierarchical Bayesian model called collaborative deep learning (CDL) is proposed to take advantage of reviews. CDL uses stacked denoising autoencoders (SDAE) to learn latent feature representations for the items. This network together with collaborative filtering for the rating matrix are jointly trained. However, the content information is only extracted from bag-of-words representations, which does not take into account word orders and context that are important for extracting semantic meaning. To improve upon the bag-of-words representation, convolutional neural networks are integrated into MF in [8] in order to capture contextual information in item reviews for the rating prediction. The proposed ConvMF+ is shown to outperform PMF and CDL. All the above works fail to explicitly link the user's preferences and sentiment in their review text to their ratings.

Another line of research closely related to recommendation on review text is sentiment analysis and text classification. Recently, there are many works on sentiment analysis and text classification using deep learning techniques that achieve impressive results as shown in [5, 7, 12, 22, 24, 25, 28, 29]. Various deep neural network configurations are used for these tasks: CNN [5, 7, 22, 25, 29], recursive neural tensor network, recurrent neural network [12, 24] and LSTM [28]. Most networks use word embeddings [12, 22, 24, 25, 28] as the input layer, while [5, 7, 29] used character embeddings, especially [5] uses very deep (29 layers) CNNs on character embeddings and shows impressive results on text classification, including the Amazon reviews.

The idea of attention in neural networks is loosely based on the visual attention mechanism found in humans. Attention-based neural networks have been applied successfully to various tasks, such as neural machine translation [2, 15], image caption generation [27] and document classification [28]. A big advantage of attention is that it gives us the ability to interpret and visualize what the model is doing. For example, in [27], a CNN is used to "encode" an image, and a recurrent neural network with attention is used to generate a caption. By visualizing the attention weights, we interpret which part of the image the model is looking at while generating a description word. While attention-based deep learning models rely on RNNs and encoder-decoders for tasks such as machine translation and image caption generation, the attention module in our model is designed to work with CNNs. It allows us to infer informative words that are linked directly to the user's rating. We put attention layers before the CNNs so that we can visualize those informative words at the end of model training and help us interpret the results (as shown in Table 4,5).

3 PROPOSED MODEL

In this section, we describe our dual attention-based model, D-Attn, for learning latent representations from review text. Figure 1 shows the overall architecture. We use the same network structure for the user and the item network. So, we describe the user network in detail: the left part is the local attention-based module (L-Attn) that learns representations of local informative keywords. The right part is the global attention-based module (G-Attn) that learns representations from the original review word sequences. These two representations are then concatenated and passed through fully-connected (FC) layers as the final learned representation for the user (and item) rating prediction.

We describe each of these modules in Figure 1. We denote scalars with italic lower-cases (x, y), vectors with bold lower-cases ($\mathbf{x}, \mathbf{z}$), and matrices or high dimensional tensors with bold upper-cases ($\mathbf{X}, \mathbf{W}$). In addition, we use MATLAB-like array indexing, thus, $\mathbf{W}(:, j)$ means elements of j-th column of the matrix $\mathbf{W}$.

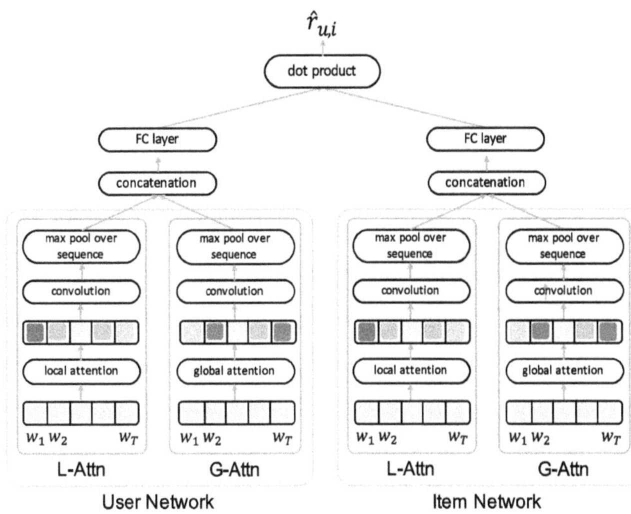

Figure 1: Architecture of D-Attn to extract latent representations of users and items. A user document D_u and an item document D_i are fed into (Left) the user network and (Right) the item network, respectively.

Embedding layer We use word embeddings for the input review document D_u: a set of reviews from user u. An embedding layer can be simply regarded as a look-up operation that reads a one-hot vector, $\mathbf{e}_t \in \mathbb{R}^{|\mathcal{V}|}$, for a word as an input, and maps it to a dense vector, $\mathbf{x}_t = (x_1, x_2, \cdots, x_d)$ and $\mathbf{x}_t \in \mathbb{R}^d$. The weight of the embedding layer is $\mathbf{W}_e \in \mathbb{R}^{d \times |\mathcal{V}|}$:

$$\mathbf{x}_t = \mathbf{W}_e \mathbf{e}_t. \quad (1)$$

and $\mathcal{V}$ is a set of words. $|\mathcal{V}|$ is the size of the vocabulary.

Local attention (L-Attn) module on the left In our model, the local attention module, L-Attn, is used to learn which words are more informative in a local window of words. Let D_u be represented as a length T word embeddings $(\mathbf{x}_1, \mathbf{x}_2, \cdots, \mathbf{x}_T)$. Then, we apply the attention through sliding kernels to this sequence. Let $\mathbf{x}_i$ be the center word and the w be the kernel width. We compute weighting scores for each word with a $\mathbf{W}^1_{l\text{-}att} \in \mathbb{R}^{w \times d}$ parameter matrix and a bias $b^1_{l\text{-}att}$ as follows:

$$\mathbf{X}_{l\text{-}att,i} = (\mathbf{x}_{i+\frac{-w+1}{2}}, \mathbf{x}_{i+\frac{-w+3}{2}}, \cdots, \mathbf{x}_i, \cdots, \mathbf{x}_{i+\frac{w-1}{2}})^\top, \quad (2)$$

$$\mathbf{s}(i) = g(\mathbf{X}_{l\text{-}att,i} * \mathbf{W}^1_{l\text{-}att} + b^1_{l\text{-}att}), \qquad i \in [1, T]. \quad (3)$$

where $*$ is an operation which means element wise multiplication and sum. We use the sigmoid function (σ) for the activation function, $g(\cdot)$.

$\mathbf{s}(i)$ are the attention scores used as a weight for i-th word embedding. Hence, if a given word has a smaller score than another word, we can interpret that the smaller score word is less important than the larger score word in our model.

$$\hat{\mathbf{x}}^L_t = \mathbf{s}(t)\mathbf{x}_t. \quad (4)$$

$\hat{\mathbf{x}}_t^L$ where $t \in [1, T]$ are a weighted sequence of word embeddings.

The weighted sequence of word embeddings are then passed through a convolutional layer with a kernel size of 1 (the 1x1 convolution was first introduced in [13]). More kernel sizes bigger than 1 could be used, but since the local attention is designed to extract individual preference or property keywords for user/item, the kernel size 1 fits exactly this purpose, and it suffers less over-fitting. A fixed length summary vector is then extracted by applying max pooling over the sequence. As a result, *local attention representation* of given text is obtained by following convolution with a matrix $\mathbf{W}_{l-att}^2 \in \mathbb{R}^{d \times n_{l-att}}$ and a bias $\mathbf{b}_{l-att}^2 \in \mathbb{R}^{n_{l-att}}$ and max pooling:

$$\mathbf{Z}_{l-att}(t, i) = g(\hat{\mathbf{x}}_t^L * \mathbf{W}_{l-att}^2(:, i) + \mathbf{b}_{l-att}^2(i)), \quad i \in [1, n_{l-att}] \tag{5}$$

$$\mathbf{z}_{l-att}(i) = \text{MAX}(\mathbf{Z}_{l-att}(:, i)). \tag{6}$$

n_{l-att} is the number of filters and $g(\cdot)$ is a tanh function.

Global attention (G-Attn) module on the right The sequence of words (with its original order) from D_u is an input to the global attention module, G-Attn. The input passes through the global attention layer by multiplying the global attention scores with themselves. This process is similar to that of L-Attn, however, the attention scores are computed from the entire input text. Let $\hat{\mathbf{x}}_t^G$ be a weighted word embedding by the G-Attn module where $t \in [1, T]$. By using the global attention layer, the effects of uninformative words are diminished and the global semantic meaning is captured more precisely through the following CNN layer. For the convolutional layer, we set the length of a filter as w_f, which means the filter operates on w_f words. If the number of filters is n_{g-att}, the convolution filters $\mathbf{W}_{g-att} \in \mathbb{R}^{w_f \times d \times n_{g-att}}$ are applied to a sequence of w_f weighted word embeddings, $\hat{\mathbf{X}}_{g-att,i} \in \mathbb{R}^{w_f \times d}$, and output features $\mathbf{Z}_{g-att} \in \mathbb{R}^{(T-w_f+1) \times n_{g-att}}$:

$$\hat{\mathbf{X}}_{g-att,i} = (\hat{\mathbf{x}}_i^G, \hat{\mathbf{x}}_{i+1}^G, \cdots, \hat{\mathbf{x}}_{i+w_f-1}^G)^\top, \tag{7}$$

$$\mathbf{Z}_{g-att}(i, j) = g(\hat{\mathbf{X}}_{g-att,i} * \mathbf{W}_{g-att}(:, :, j) + \mathbf{b}_{g-att}(j)), \quad i \in [1, T - w_f + 1], \quad j \in [1, n_{g-att}]. \tag{8}$$

$g(\cdot)$ is a tanh function and $\mathbf{b}_{g-att}$ is a bias vector. In the pooling layer, we choose heuristically a max pooling over the sequence: $\mathbf{z}_{g-att}(j) = \text{MAX}\left(\mathbf{Z}_{g-att}(:, j)\right)$. We can obtain as many $\mathbf{z}_{g-att}$ as the number of different filter length w_f. In this work, n_w different filter lengths are used.

Final layers The outputs of the local and global attention module are concatenated, and run through additional fully connected layers $\mathbf{W}_{FC}^1$ and $\mathbf{W}_{FC}^2$:

$$\mathbf{z}_{out}^1 = \mathbf{z}_{l-att} \oplus \mathbf{z}_{g-att}^1 \oplus \cdots \oplus \mathbf{z}_{g-att}^{n_w}, \tag{9}$$

$$\mathbf{z}_{out}^2 = g(\mathbf{W}_{FC}^1 \cdot \mathbf{z}_{out}^1 + \mathbf{b}_{FC}^1), \tag{10}$$

$$\gamma_u = g(\mathbf{W}_{FC}^2 \cdot \mathbf{z}_{out}^2 + \mathbf{b}_{FC}^2). \tag{11}$$

$\oplus$ is a concatenation operator. $g(\cdot)$ is a ReLU function.

Training of the network Two different channels (L-Attn and G-Attn) are used to learn two different latent representations, *local attention representation* and *global semantic representation*. These two are then merged into one attention-based semantic representation. Let γ_u be the attention-based semantic vector from the users' network and γ_i be the corresponding vector from the items' network. As in CF/MF techniques, the latent representations (γ_u, γ_i) are mapped into the same vector space ($\mathbb{R}^K$) and the ratings can be estimated by the inner product.

$$\hat{r}_{u,i} = \gamma_u^\top \gamma_i \tag{12}$$

The estimation can be considered as a regression problem and all parameters in the two networks (user network and item network) are trained jointly through the backpropagation technique. Mean Squared Error (MSE) is used as a loss function. In training time, D_u and D_i are fed into two networks respectively. At test time, a pair of a user and an item (u, i) along with their corresponding D_u and D_i are fed through the user/item networks, and the inner product of γ_u, γ_i is the estimated rating $\hat{r}_{u,i}$.

4 EXPERIMENTAL SETUP

We evaluate our proposed models using open datasets from *Yelp* and *Amazon*. In this section, we describe these datasets as well as our experimental setup.

4.1 Datasets

We use two publicly available datasets that provide user reviews and rating information. The first dataset is from the *Yelp Business Rating Prediction Challenge* 2013[1], which includes reviews on restaurants in the Phoenix, AZ metropolitan area. The second dataset is the *Amazon Product Data*[2], which contains millions of product reviews and metadata from *Amazon*. This dataset has been investigated by many researchers [17–19]. In this paper, we focus on training interpretable models rather than dealing with the cold start problem. Therefore, we start our experiments with the *5-core* subset, which has at least 5 reviews for each user or item. We use six product categories in this work. The key characteristics of these datasets are summarized in Table 1.

Table 1: Statistics of Dataset

DATASET	*Yelp*	*Amazon*
# of Users	45,980	30,759
# of Items	11,537	16,515
# of Reviews	229,900	285,644
Avg. # of Words per a review	130	104
Avg. # of Reviews per a user	5.00	9.29
Avg. # of Reviews per an item	17.30	19.93

We randomly divided each dataset into training, validation and test sets (80%, 10%, 10% respectively).

4.2 Data Preprocessing

The first step in our data processing pipeline is to remove non-contextual words such as html tags, url, or symbols. Next, we concatenate all reviews from the same user, say user u, into a document D_u. Similarly, we concatenate all reviews on the same item, say item

[1] https://www.kaggle.com/c/yelp-recsys-2013
[2] http://jmcauley.ucsd.edu/data/amazon/

i, into a document D_i. We put a delimiter between two different reviews from one user (or item) because if two reviews are concatenated without a delimiter, convolution filters will mix words which are not contextually connected. As expected, the length of these concatenated review documents follows a long-tailed distribution and we set the length of each document to conserve at least 70% of the words. The resulting documents are fed into the embedding layer as described in Section 3.

4.3 Baselines

We implemented several comparable baselines as comparisons to our proposed model. The first one is Matrix Factorization (MF)[3] [11] that characterizes both users and items by vectors of factors inferred from item rating patterns. The second baseline is Hidden Factors as Topics (HFT) [17]. We set the number of hidden topics K as 5 which is reported in [17]. We also compare our model to a recently proposed context-aware recommendation model, convolutional matrix factorization (ConvMF+) [8]. We use ConvMF+ which is based on the GloVe embedding to represent reviews as we do.

To see the effectiveness of the global attention layer, we report results from CNN-only which is a subpart of G-Attn. In addition, results from only one module, a local attention (L-Attn) or a global attention module (G-Attn), are also compared to show the synergy of the local and global attention modules. Finally, we show a naive method, Offset, which simply uses the average rating (μ) as the prediction. This baseline shows how ratings in a given dataset are biased and the upper bounds of rating estimates for each dataset.

4.4 Parameter Setting

We follow the guideline in [31] for setting initial parameters of CNN models. We use pre-trained word embedding GloVe [21] based on aggregated global word-word co-occurrence statistics from a corpus. The dimension of embedding is $d = 100$ and the most frequent 30,000 words are used. In the L-Attn module, we use $w = 5$ window size with a sigmoid function(σ) and $n_{l-att} = 200$ in $\mathbf{W}^2_{l-att}$.

In the G-Attn module, we use three different filter lengths $w_f \in [2, 3, 4]$ and $n_{g-att} = 100$ for each $\mathbf{W}_{g-att}$. These filter sizes correspond to n-gram features. Finally, to combine local and global attention representations, the fully connected layers $\mathbf{W}^1_{FC}$ and $\mathbf{W}^2_{FC}$ with the number of hidden factors, $K_1 = 500$ and $K_2 = 50$ are used, respectively. 0.5 dropout probabilities are used for the two FC layers to reduce overfitting. Activation functions of convolution layers in both L-Attn and G-Attn are tanh and ReLUs are used for the FC layers. Adam optimizer[10] is used with a 1e-4 learning rate. Our experiments are done with Theano running on GPU machines of Nvidia GeForce GTX TITAN X.

5 RESULTS AND DISCUSSION

5.1 Rating Estimation

The Mean Squared Error (MSE) of the rating estimations are shown in Table 2 for the D-Attn model as well as for other models. To obtain reliable results, we repeat our model training/testing on four random splits of the data and report the average prediction errors. The standard deviations of prediction errors are 0.004 for Yelp and 0.001 for Amazon. We can see that the D-Attn outperforms all baselines on the *Yelp* dataset and the *Amazon* datasets. This clearly confirms the effectiveness of our proposed method.

We further break down the results for the Amazon dataset by product category, as shown in Table 3. While MF and HFT each have their own strengths, our D-Attn model can achieve the best of both, which can be seen from the results on these datasets. First, the ratings in the Yelp dataset are not consistent. In other words, a user gives a broad range of ratings to different items in general. This explains why MF leads to a large MSE on this dataset. Second, the review text may also be inconsistent. On the *Automotive* dataset, HFT shows a worse result than that of MF. This is because each user is likely to use different words for different items, and each item has reviews written using a diverse set of words. As a result, it is difficult for HFT to infer proper topics for such heterogeneous corpus. Although ConvMF+ constantly shows lower MSE than those of MF and HFT, our model is even better than ConvMF+, because our model is designed to understand users' preferences and items' properties with both the local attention layer and the global attention layer in order to decide which words are more important for the rating estimation.

We also present the results of the subpart models: CNN-only, L-Attn-only, and G-Attn-only. Each model has its own limitations. First, the CNN-only model is able to capture contextual meaning by convolutional layers in the model. However, it treats every word equally in extracting contextual features. The G-Attn-only model which adds the global attention module before the CNN-only model can extract contextual features as well as diminish the influence of less important words. Thus, the results of the G-Attn-only model are better than those of the CNN-only model. Interestingly, the L-Attn-only model shows the best results among these three subpart models. This suggests that weighting words is essential and how the weights are computed makes a difference too.

The ConvMF+ model integrates two subparts: 1) Probabilistic Matrix Factorization (PMF) for combining latent user and item vectors and 2) CNN for item contextual modeling. On the other hand, our approach uses attention-based CNN models for both users and items. Next, we show visually what the local and global attention layers do, and the effectiveness of the user/item embeddings learned from our CNN models for the practical purpose of classification and recommendation.

5.2 Visualization of Attention Layers

We highlight words that have high scores computed by the local attention modules in Table 4. We randomly sample an identical review example from a user in the Yelp dataset. Words with the highest scores are colored dark-green, high scoring words are light-green, and low/medium score words are not colored. In Table 4, we compare attention scores trained by the L-Attn-only model with the D-Attn model, respectively.

We can see a few interesting patterns from these results. Overall, similar words are highlighted in the L-Attn-only model and the D-Attn model. However, the L-Attn-only model gives high scores to consecutive words including trivial pronoun words. For example, it highlights "*They are good people great atmosphere*" as high score words. On the other hand, the D-Attn model is more precise in that

[3] We use MyMediaLite package. http://www.mymedialite.net

Table 2: MSE of rating estimation for different models (the best results are starred)

Dataset	Offset	MF	HFT	ConvMF+	CNN-only	L-Attn-only	G-Attn-only	D-Attn
Yelp	1.484	1.275	1.224	1.209	1.210	1.203	1.205	1.191*
Amazon	1.011	0.876	0.871	0.858	0.864	0.860	0.861	0.855*

Table 3: Breakdown of *Amazon* dataset evaluation by product category

Dataset	Offset	MF	HFT	ConvMF+	CNN-only	L-Attn-only	G-Attn-only	D-Attn
Amazon instant video	1.256	0.968	0.957	0.950	0.952	0.950	0.951	0.946*
Automotive	0.856	0.786	0.802	0.780	0.785	0.781	0.782	0.779*
Grocery and gourmet food	1.202	1.017	1.004	1.002	1.005	1.003	1.004	0.997*
Musical instruments	0.730	0.725	0.714	0.698	0.704	0.700	0.701	0.694*
Office products	0.867	0.724	0.723	0.720	0.727	0.721	0.723	0.719*
Patio lawn and garden	1.153	1.037	1.025	1.001	1.008	1.002	1.003	0.996*

it successfully picks "*great*" from the sequence of words. Furthermore, many neutral words such as "*Arizona*", "*I've*", and "*that*" are incorrectly emphasized by the L-Attn-only windows. Hence, this example shows that the local attention modules work similarly in both models but D-Attn is more precise with the help of global attention.

Table 4: Highlighted words by local attention scores in a user's review. Top: attention scores in the L-Attn-only model. Bottom: local attention scores in the D-Attn model.

Yelp (user), L-Attn-only model: local attention
They carry some rare things that you can't find anywhere else. The staff is pretty damn cool too best in Arizona . I prefer ma-and-pa. They treat you the best and they value your business extreme . They are good people great atmosphere and music. I definitely believe that Lux has the best coffee I've ever had at this point. Screw all my previous reviews. This place has coffee down , they make damn good toast too .
Yelp (user), D-Attn model: local attention
They carry some rare things that you can't find anywhere else. The staff is pretty damn cool too best in Arizona. I prefer ma-and-pa. They treat you the best and they value your business extreme . They are good people great atmosphere and music. I definitely believe that Lux has the best coffee I've ever had at this point. Screw all my previous reviews. This place has coffee down, they make damn good toast too .

Table 5 shows words highlighted by the global attention scores from both the G-Attn-only model and the D-Attn model. In this example, we highlight *less important* words instead: words with lowest scores are red-colored, low scoring words are light-red, and high/medium score words are not colored. It seems that the global attention layer down-weighs neutral words and the later max pooling layer removes them from contributing to the final output. However, the G-Attn-only model does not do a perfect job: preference words like "rare", and "best" are grouped with their neighboring pronouns with very low scores. With the help of the local attention in the D-Attn model, the global attention in the D-Attn model synergizes with the local attention in the D-Attn by focusing on removing just the neutral words, while the local attention in the D-Attn emphasizes those preferences or attribute words.

Table 5: Highlighted words by global attention scores in a user's review. Top: attention scores in the G-Attn-only model. Bottom: global attention scores in the D-Attn model.

Yelp (user), G-Attn-only model: global attention
They carry some rare things that you can't find anywhere else . The staff is pretty damn cool too best in Arizona. I prefer ma- and -pa. They treat you the best and they value your business extreme. They are good people great atmosphere and music. I definitely believe that Lux has the best coffee I've ever had at this point. Screw all my previous reviews. This place has coffee down, they make damn good toast too.
Yelp (user), D-Attn model: global attention
They carry some rare things that you can't find anywhere else . The staff is pretty damn cool too best in Arizona. I prefer ma-and-pa. They treat you the best and they value your business extreme. They are good people great atmosphere and music. I definitely believe that Lux has the best coffee I've ever had at this point. Screw all my previous reviews. This place has coffee down, they make damn good toast too.

Table 6 shows the same text but highlighted differently by the L-Attn model in the user's network and the item's network, respectively. More words in the review are highlighted by the user network to show the user's preferences.

5.3 Embedding Analysis

Our D-Attn model maps a user or an item to a latent representation before taking the dot product for rating estimation. We consider these representations as embeddings ([20, 21]) of each user/item. We show next that these pre-trained embeddings can be used for other tasks as well.

First, we examine whether these embeddings are meaningful and useful. If the embeddings describe users or items correctly, we

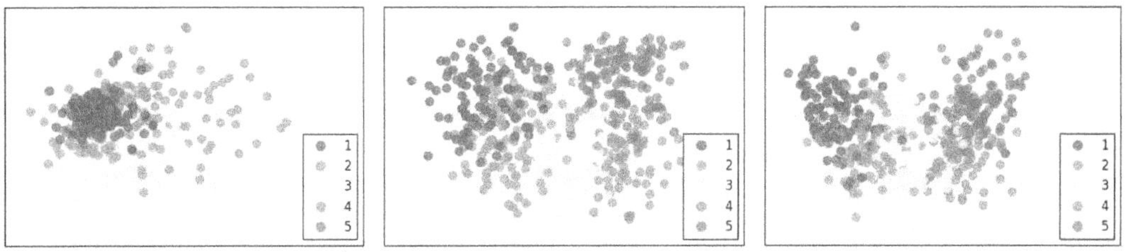

(a) HFT (K=50) (b) ConvMF+ (K=50) (c) D-Attn (K=50)

Figure 2: LDA projection of sampled item vectors of the Yelp data.

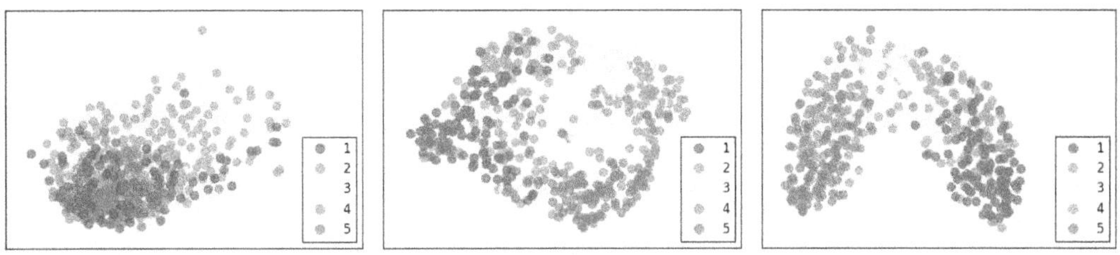

(a) HFT (K=50) (b) ConvMF+ (K=50) (c) D-Attn (K=50)

Figure 3: t-SNE embedding of sampled item vectors of the Yelp data.

Table 6: Attention words of the same review. Each network highlights different words.

Yelp (user), D-Attn: local attention
A disappointing meal and a very disappointing service . I won't be coming back anytime soon . If I was the manager I would demote the waiter and promote the busboy to a waiter as he was great tonight and he was the only reason I gave a 20% tip as it is unfair for him to suffer because of the waiters.
Yelp (item), D-Attn: local attention
A disappointing meal and a very disappointing service. I won't be coming back anytime soon. If I was the manager I would demote the waiter and promote the busboy to a waiter as he was great tonight and he was the only reason I gave a 20% tip as it is unfair for him to suffer because of the waiters.

can easily find similar users of a given user or most recommendable items to a given user. In Figure 3, we show embeddings of users and items that are trained with their ratings. Therefore, we can safely assume that items' embeddings are strongly related to their overall ratings. In other words, high-rated items would have more similar embeddings to each other than those of low-rated items. This assumption is more reasonable for an item embedding than a user embedding because ratings of a user are more dependent on what the user has purchased (or visited).

To examine the quality of item embeddings learned from HFT, ConvMF+ and our model, we sample 500 items (100 from each rating class) randomly from the Yelp dataset and classify the items (i.e. restaurants) to check whether the embeddings are good features. We apply the linear SVM for the multi-class classification of the embeddings (all with feature dimension of $K = 50$).

Table 7: Accuracy of multi-class classification.

	HFT	ConvMF+	D-Attn
Accuracy	0.482	0.580	0.602

Table 7 shows classification accuracies from three models. As we expected, both ConvMF+ and D-Attn have shown similar accuracies and D-Attn is slightly better than ConvMF+. HFT has the lowest accuracy, and it implies that the item representations of HFT are not strongly related to the average rating.

We then visualize these item embeddings in two-dimensional space to investigate subtle differences of the item embeddings. Figures 2 and 3 show the distributions of the two dimensional item embedding vectors. The top figures are obtained by Linear Discriminant Analysis (LDA) and the bottom figures are from t-distributed Stochastic Neighbor Embedding (t-SNE) with 30 perplexity [16]. Each point corresponds to each item in the dataset and the denoted number for each color is the average rating of each item.

Again, we see the item embeddings from HFT are not related to their average ratings. On the other hand, both ConvMF+ and D-Attn successfully cluster items together with the same average ratings: in the two dimensional space the five clusters are fairly distinguishable. This supports our assumption that similarly rated items are likely mapped to a closer embedding space. However, we still see the differences of the five clusters coming from ConvMF+ and our model: first, items of ConvMF+ with an average rating of 3 are more scattered over other classes than that of D-Attn (See Figure 3 (b) and (c)). This implies that D-Attn is more powerful in capturing differences between the mid-rated items and others. Second as the bottom figures show, we can see that the class (rating) distributions from D-Attn are gradually overlapped between closer

Table 8: List of recommended items

Query	Visited items	Rank	HFT Recommendations [Categories]	ConvMF+ Recommendations [Categories]	D-Attn Recommendations [Categories]
user1	**The Duce** [Bars, Nightlife, Lounges, Restaurants]	1	**Yoshi's Asian Grill** [Asian Fusion, Restaurant]	**FnB** [Gastropubs, American]	**O'connor's Pub** [Pubs, Bars, Nightlife]
		2	**Nathans Famous Hotdogs** [Hot Dogs, Restaurants]	**Petite Maison** [French, Restaurants]	**Rosie McCaffrey's** [Pubs, Bars, Nightlife, Restaurants]
		3	**Wendy's** [Fast Food, Restaurants]	**Lox Stock & Bagel** [Bagels, Breakfast & Brunch, Restaurants]	**The Vig** [Pubs, Bars, Nightlife, Restaurants]
		4	**The Coffee Bean & Tea Leaf** [Food, Coffee & Tea]	**True Food Kitchen** [American, Restaurants]	**Arcadia Tavern** [Pubs, Bars, Nightlife, Sports Bars]
user2	**Matador Restaurant** [Mexican, Greek, Restaurants]	1	**The Saguaro** [American, Mexican]	**Rocket Burger & Subs** [Burger, Hot Dogs, Sandwiches]	**Sofia's Mexican** [Mexican, Restaurants]
		2	**The Grapevine** [American, Karaoke]	**Roka Akor** [Steakhouses, Sushi Bars, Japanese]	**Tacos Jalisco** [Mexican, Restaurants]
		3	**Citizen Public House** [Gastropubs, American]	**The Fry Bread House** [American, Restaurants]	**Carolina's Mexican** [Mexican, Restaurants]
		4	**AZ 88** [Bars, American, Lounges]	**Five Guys** [Burgers, Restaurants]	**El Taco Tote** [Mexican, Restaurants]

ratings (e.g., rating 1 and 2, not 1 and 5) unlike the distributions from ConvMF+.

5.4 Recommendation

We confirm that an embedding of a given item learned from our model is correlated with the average rating of the item. Now, we investigate the possibility of using the user/item embeddings for practical recommendations. We use the Yelp dataset which has detailed information about users and items (restaurants).

First, we pick a random user who has a single review because we are going to recommend potential items to someone who does not have enough review history. The selected user is considered a query user. To recommend potential items, we first find the *nearest neighbors* to the query user in the user embedding space. Our hypothesis is that the nearest neighbors apparently have similar favorites or tastes with the query user, hence, items visited by the nearest neighbors would also be highly likely preferred by the query user.

In Table 8, we sample two users who visited only one restaurant and gave a positive rating (higher ratings than 3). We carry out the following procedure to come up with a recommended list of restaurants: first, given a query user, we find the K nearest neighbors in the user embedding space and the items that were already visited by these neighbors as candidates. Second, we compute potential ratings by the query user on these candidates. Finally, we sort the items by the rating estimations to select the most preferred ones. In Table 8, we list four restaurants from a set of candidate restaurants visited by $K = 5$ nearest neighbors.

Surprisingly there are big differences among the recommendation lists returned by HFT, ConvMF+ and D-Attn. The results show that the recommended restaurants by D-Attn and the *already visited* restaurants by the query users have common categories unlike other models. For example, D-Attn recommends *Mexican* restaurants to user2 who has already visited *Matador Restaurant* which serves Mexican foods. Moreover, we manually check that those four recommendations have common features (food menu), such as price (one $ in Yelp), or atmosphere (casual ambience and attire). Hence, these results suggest that the embeddings of user and item from the D-Attn model could be useful for the nearest-neighbors recommendation.

6 CONCLUSIONS

We have presented an interpretable, dual attention-based CNN model, D-Attn, that combines review text and ratings for product rating prediction. It learns the latent representation of users and items from the aggregated reviews, and enables the interaction between user and item models in a way similar to matrix factorization. By leveraging the best of both collaborative filtering and topic-based approaches, our model is inherently more robust to noise and inconsistency in the review and rating data by applying both local and global attention layers and combining these two in one network training. Our model is validated by experiments on both the Yelp and Amazon datasets. Our model outperforms HFT and the recently proposed ConvMF+ in terms of prediction errors. Furthermore, we show that these latent representations of users and items are meaningful and effective to provide practical applications for recommendation.

We are convinced that this work offers a new avenue to apply representation learning in the context of recommendation systems. One future direction is to use sequence learning, e.g., combine LSTM with attention network, to handle long-range dependency in the review text.

7 ACKNOWLEDGMENTS

This work is supported in part by NSF award number IIS-1254206 and Facebook Research Award. The views and conclusions are those of the authors and should not be interpreted as representing the official policies of the funding agency, or the U.S. Government.

REFERENCES

[1] Amjad Almahairi, Kyle Kastner, Kyunghyun Cho, and Aaron Courville. 2015. Learning distributed representations from reviews for collaborative filtering. In *Proceedings of the 9th ACM Conference on Recommender Systems*. ACM, 147–154.

[2] Dzmitry Bahdanau, Kyunghyun Cho, and Yoshua Bengio. 2015. Neural Machine Translation by Jointly Learning to Align and Translate. *International conference on learning representations* (2015).

[3] Yang Bao, Hui Fang, and Jie Zhang. 2014. TopicMF: Simultaneously Exploiting Ratings and Reviews for Recommendation.. In *AAAI*. 2–8.

[4] David M Blei, Andrew Y Ng, and Michael I Jordan. 2003. Latent dirichlet allocation. *Journal of machine Learning research* 3, Jan (2003), 993–1022.

[5] Alexis Conneau, Holger Schwenk, Loïc Barrault, and Yann Lecun. 2016. Very Deep Convolutional Networks for Natural Language Processing. *arXiv preprint arXiv:1606.01781* (2016).

[6] Paul Covington, Jay Adams, and Emre Sargin. 2016. Deep neural networks for youtube recommendations. In *Proceedings of the 10th ACM Conference on Recommender Systems*. ACM, 191–198.

[7] Cícero Nogueira dos Santos and Maira Gatti. 2014. Deep Convolutional Neural Networks for Sentiment Analysis of Short Texts.. In *COLING*. 69–78.

[8] Donghyun Kim, Chanyoung Park, Jinoh Oh, Sungyoung Lee, and Hwanjo Yu. 2016. Convolutional Matrix Factorization for Document Context-Aware Recommendation. In *Proceedings of the 10th ACM Conference on Recommender systems*. ACM, 223–240.

[9] Yoon Kim, Yacine Jernite, David Sontag, and Alexander M Rush. 2015. Character-aware neural language models. *arXiv preprint arXiv:1508.06615* (2015).

[10] Diederik Kingma and Jimmy Ba. 2014. Adam: A method for stochastic optimization. *arXiv preprint arXiv:1412.6980* (2014).

[11] Yehuda Koren, Robert Bell, Chris Volinsky, and others. 2009. Matrix factorization techniques for recommender systems. *Computer* 42, 8 (2009), 30–37.

[12] Jiwei Li, Minh-Thang Luong, Dan Jurafsky, and Eudard Hovy. 2015. When are tree structures necessary for deep learning of representations? *arXiv preprint arXiv:1503.00185* (2015).

[13] Min Lin, Qiang Chen, and Shuicheng Yan. 2013. Network in network. *arXiv preprint arXiv:1312.4400* (2013).

[14] Guang Ling, Michael R Lyu, and Irwin King. 2014. Ratings meet reviews, a combined approach to recommend. In *Proceedings of the 8th ACM Conference on Recommender systems*. ACM, 105–112.

[15] Minh-Thang Luong, Hieu Pham, and Christopher D. Manning. 2015. Effective Approaches to Attention-based Neural Machine Translation. In *Proceedings of the conference on empirical methods in natural language processing (EMNLP)*.

[16] Laurens van der Maaten and Geoffrey Hinton. 2008. Visualizing data using t-SNE. *Journal of Machine Learning Research* 9, Nov (2008), 2579–2605.

[17] Julian McAuley and Jure Leskovec. 2013. Hidden factors and hidden topics: understanding rating dimensions with review text. In *Proceedings of the 7th ACM conference on Recommender systems*. ACM, 165–172.

[18] Julian McAuley, Rahul Pandey, and Jure Leskovec. 2015. Inferring networks of substitutable and complementary products. In *Proceedings of the 21th ACM SIGKDD International Conference on Knowledge Discovery and Data Mining*. ACM, 785–794.

[19] Julian McAuley, Christopher Targett, Qinfeng Shi, and Anton van den Hengel. 2015. Image-based recommendations on styles and substitutes. In *Proceedings of the 38th International ACM SIGIR Conference on Research and Development in Information Retrieval*. ACM, 43–52.

[20] Tomas Mikolov, Ilya Sutskever, Kai Chen, Greg S Corrado, and Jeff Dean. 2013. Distributed representations of words and phrases and their compositionality. In *Advances in neural information processing systems*. 3111–3119.

[21] Jeffrey Pennington, Richard Socher, and Christopher D. Manning. 2014. GloVe: Global Vectors for Word Representation. In *Empirical Methods in Natural Language Processing (EMNLP)*. 1532–1543.

[22] Aliaksei Severyn and Alessandro Moschitti. 2015. Twitter sentiment analysis with deep convolutional neural networks. In *Proceedings of the 38th International ACM SIGIR Conference on Research and Development in Information Retrieval*. ACM, 959–962.

[23] Yelong Shen, Xiaodong He, Jianfeng Gao, Li Deng, and Grégoire Mesnil. 2014. A latent semantic model with convolutional-pooling structure for information retrieval. In *Proceedings of the 23rd ACM International Conference on Conference on Information and Knowledge Management*. ACM, 101–110.

[24] Richard Socher, Alex Perelygin, Jean Y Wu, Jason Chuang, Christopher D Manning, Andrew Y Ng, and Christopher Potts. 2013. Recursive deep models for semantic compositionality over a sentiment treebank. In *Proceedings of the conference on empirical methods in natural language processing (EMNLP)*, Vol. 1631. 1642.

[25] Duyu Tang, Bing Qin, and Ting Liu. 2015. Learning semantic representations of users and products for document level sentiment classification. In *Proc. ACL*.

[26] Hao Wang, Naiyan Wang, and Dit-Yan Yeung. 2015. Collaborative deep learning for recommender systems. In *Proceedings of the 21th ACM SIGKDD International Conference on Knowledge Discovery and Data Mining*. ACM, 1235–1244.

[27] Kelvin Xu, Jimmy Ba, Ryan Kiros, Kyunghyun Cho, Aaron Courville, Ruslan Salakhutdinov, Richard S Zemel, and Yoshua Bengio. 2015. Show, Attend and Tell: Neural Image Caption Generation with Visual Attention. *Proceedings of the 32nd International Conference on Machine Learning* (2015).

[28] Zichao Yang, Diyi Yang, Chris Dyer, Xiaodong He, Alex Smola, and Eduard Hovy. 2016. Hierarchical attention networks for document classification. In *Proceedings of the 2016 Conference of the North American Chapter of the Association for Computational Linguistics: Human Language Technologies*.

[29] Xiang Zhang, Junbo Zhao, and Yann LeCun. 2015. Character-level convolutional networks for text classification. In *Advances in Neural Information Processing Systems*. 649–657.

[30] Yongfeng Zhang, Guokun Lai, Min Zhang, Yi Zhang, Yiqun Liu, and Shaoping Ma. 2014. Explicit factor models for explainable recommendation based on phrase-level sentiment analysis. In *Proceedings of the 37th International ACM SIGIR Conference on Research and Development in Information Retrieval*. ACM, 83–92.

[31] Ye Zhang and Byron Wallace. 2015. A sensitivity analysis of (and practitioners' guide to) convolutional neural networks for sentence classification. *arXiv preprint arXiv:1510.03820* (2015).

When Recurrent Neural Networks meet the Neighborhood for Session-Based Recommendation

Dietmar Jannach
TU Dortmund, Germany
dietmar.jannach@tu-dortmund.de

Malte Ludewig
TU Dortmund, Germany
malte.ludewig@tu-dortmund.de

ABSTRACT

Deep learning methods have led to substantial progress in various application fields of AI, and in recent years a number of proposals were made to improve recommender systems with artificial neural networks. For the problem of making session-based recommendations, i.e., for recommending the next item in an anonymous session, Hidasi et al. recently investigated the application of recurrent neural networks with Gated Recurrent Units (GRU4REC). Assessing the true effectiveness of such novel approaches based only on what is reported in the literature is however difficult when no standard evaluation protocols are applied and when the strength of the baselines used in the performance comparison is not clear. In this work we show based on a comprehensive empirical evaluation that a heuristics-based nearest neighbor (kNN) scheme for sessions outperforms GRU4REC in the large majority of the tested configurations and datasets. Neighborhood sampling and efficient in-memory data structures ensure the scalability of the kNN method. The best results in the end were often achieved when we combine the kNN approach with GRU4REC, which shows that RNNs can leverage sequential signals in the data that cannot be detected by the co-occurrence-based kNN method.

CCS CONCEPTS

•Information systems →Recommender systems;
•General and reference →Evaluation;

KEYWORDS

Session-Based Recommendation; Deep Learning; Nearest-Neighbors

ACM Reference format:
Dietmar Jannach and Malte Ludewig. 2017. When Recurrent Neural Networks meet the Neighborhood for Session-Based Recommendation. In *Proceedings of RecSys'17, August 27–31, 2017, Como, Italy, ,* 5 pages.
DOI: http://dx.doi.org/10.1145/3109859.3109872

1 INTRODUCTION

Deep learning approaches based on artificial neural networks have recently led to significant advances in different application fields of AI like object classification in images, speech recognition, or game playing. Their success in these fields has inspired researchers to explore the potential of adapting deep learning methods for recommendation-related problems. While there are limited works yet that show the advantages of *directly* applying deep learning methods for the rating prediction task [29, 35], artificial neural networks were, for example, used to vectorize content features from audio, video or textual item data [1, 5, 6, 10] and in particular for the problem of *session-based recommendation* [14, 15, 30, 38].

The algorithmic task in the latter scenario is to predict the next action of a user given the sequence of the actions in the current session. The problem setting, while not largely explored in the research literature, is highly relevant in practical settings. Session-based approaches are usually applied when the visitors of the site are anonymous (not logged-in) and no past interactions of the users are known. Furthermore, considering the last few user actions is also important for applications where already known users often revisit the site with a specific short-term intent [18].

In their recent work, Hidasi et al. investigated the use of recurrent neural networks (RNN) for session-based next-item recommendation [14]. RNNs are a natural choice for this problem and have been successfully explored for other sequence-based prediction problems in the past [4, 8, 9, 16]. Technically, the approach in [14] uses a customized RNN with Gated Recurrent Units (GRU). An experimental evaluation on two datasets indicated that their GRU4REC method significantly outperforms other methods, including an item-based k-nearest-neighbor (kNN) method, which was the strongest baseline in their experiments. Despite these positive results, some questions regarding the effectiveness of the GRU4REC method remain open. The experiments in [14] were, for example, only conducted on two specific datasets, used baselines whose strength cannot be easily judged, and were based on a proprietary evaluation protocol without cross-validation.

To better understand the true effectiveness of the proposed approach, we conducted a series of experiments on multiple datasets in which we benchmarked the GRU4REC method with an alternative session-based nearest neighbor method, which was identified as a strong baseline in previous works on session-based music and e-commerce recommendation problems [2, 12, 21]. To achieve higher accuracy and to scale for larger datasets, our session-based kNN method incorporates heuristics to sample suitable neighbors. Our results show that the proposed kNN method leads to the same accuracy results as the best configuration reported in [14] and outperforms GRU4REC in many other tested problem setups.[1] Combining GRU4REC with the kNN methods in a weighted hybrid approach finally often led to the best results, which indicates that RNN methods are indeed capable of capturing sequential patterns in the data that the kNN approach could not identify.

[1] Recent works suggest that advanced nearest-neighbor models can lead to competitive performance also for common item-ranking tasks [34].

RecSys'17, August 27–31, 2017, Como, Italy

978-1-4503-4652-8/17/08...$15.00
DOI: http://dx.doi.org/10.1145/3109859.3109872

2 EXPERIMENT CONFIGURATIONS

2.1 Algorithms

2.1.1 GRU4REC. We used the GRU4REC implementation in Python that the authors of [14] share online.[2] The code is regularly updated by the authors and includes the implementation of the GRU4REC method, the code of their baseline algorithms, as well as the code for the evaluation procedure used in [14].

2.1.2 Session-based kNN. The kNN method takes the set of user actions in the current session, e.g., two view events for certain items, and then in a first step determines the k most similar past sessions in the training data. Then, given the current session s, the set of k nearest neighbors N_s, and a function $sim(s1, s2)$ that returns a similarity score for two sessions $s1$ and $s2$, the score of a recommendable item i is

$$score_{\text{KNN}}(i, s) = \Sigma_{n \in N_s} sim(s, n) \times 1_n(i) \tag{1}$$

where $1_n(i) = 1$ if n contains i and 0 otherwise, see also [2]. We tested different distance measures. The best results were achieved when comparing the sessions, which were encoded as binary vectors of the item space, using cosine similarity.

Determining the similarity of the current session with millions of past sessions after each user action cannot easily be accomplished under the time constraints of online recommendation. We therefore pre-process the training sessions and create an in-memory index data structure (cache) on startup. Specifically, for each item we create an index that points to the sessions in which the item appears. For each session, we furthermore have a pointer to its set of items. When recommendations for a session s are needed, we first determine the set of *possible* neighbors by creating the union of sessions in which the items of s are contained. This is a fast operation as it only involves a cache lookup and set operations. From this set of possible neighbors, we create a subsample of m sessions randomly or using a heuristic. In some experiments, we took the most recent sessions in case such information was available as focusing on recent trends has shown to be effective for recommendations in e-commerce [19]. From m we select the k nearest neighbors regarding the current session s. Again through lookup and set union operations, we create the set of recommendable items R that appear in one of the k sessions. We then compute the score for the items in R using Equation 1. The set operations, similarity computations, and the final predictions can be done very efficiently, as will be discussed later in Section 3.2.3.

2.1.3 Hybrid Approach. We tested switching, cascading, as well as weighted hybrids of the GRU4REC and the kNN method. A weighted combination led to the best results in our experiments, where in the most successful configurations the kNN score was assigned a slightly higher weight. All source code and the public datasets used in our experiments can be found online. [3]

2.2 Datasets and Evaluation Protocols

We performed experiments both on variants of the ACM RecSys 2015 Challenge dataset (*RSC15* and *RSCW*) as used in [14], on the public e-commerce dataset used in the TMall competition (*TMALL*),

[2]https://github.com/hidasib/GRU4Rec
[3]http://bit.ly/2nfNldD

Table 1: Dataset characteristics

	RSC15	RSCW	TMALL	LFM	AOTM	8T
Sessions	8M	4M	650K	120K	82K	520K
Avg. length	3.97	3.92	7.5	28.24	11.48	9.20
Items	37K	34K	300K	200K	54K	200K

as well as on three different datasets containing music playlists from the platforms last.fm (*LFM*), artofthemix.org (*AOTM*), and 8tracks.com (*8T*). Music playlists are different in nature from e-commerce user logs in various ways. Nonetheless, they are designed to be consumed in a listening session and the tracks are often arranged in a specific sequence by their creators. With the experiments on these datasets our goal is to assess if recurrent neural networks can capture sequential patterns in the data which are not leveraged by the co-occurrence-based kNN approach. The basic dataset statistics are shown in Table 1, where *RSCW* and *TMALL* correspond to the average characteristics when applying a sliding-window protocol, as will be described below. In [14], Hidasi et al. use GRU4REC to predict the next item view events in a session. They incrementally add events to the sessions in the test set and report the average hit rate (*HR*) and the Mean Reciprocal Rank (*MRR*) at list length 20. They trained the GRU4REC on six months of data and used one single day for the evaluation.

In addition to this procedure, we performed experiments where we created multiple train-test splits, consisting of 3 and 1 month of training data for the *RSC15* and TMall dataset, respectively, and the subsequent day as the test data.[4] This sliding-windows approach allows us to minimize the risk that the obtained results are specific to the single train-test split used in [14]. Furthermore, we used the algorithms to predict purchase events in the sessions, which was one of the original tasks of the ACM RecSys 2015 challenge. To investigate the performance of the methods at different stages of a session, we also measured the accuracy when predicting the *second* and the *last* view of each session. Finally, we varied the amount of the training data to see how the algorithms compare in case of more sparse data situations.

3 RESULTS

3.1 Accuracy Results

3.1.1 ACM RecSys 2015 Challenge Dataset. Table 2 shows the results when using the experimental configuration used in [14], ordered by the values for HR@20 as done in the original paper. We could reproduce their best hit rate and MRR results (using their optimal parameters) for the methods GRU4REC(1000,BPR) and GRU4REC(1000,TOP1), which use 1000 hidden units and the TOP1 and BPR's pairwise ranking loss function, respectively. In Table 2, we additionally include the results for list length ten, which might be more important in different application domains.

The method KNN_{MR}(500,1000), which uses the 500 nearest neighbors from the 1000 most recent candidate sessions, outperforms GRU4REC in all measurements except for the MRR in the TOP1

[4]Using larger training splits for the TMall dataset, due to its large number of items, led to prohibitively high computational costs by the GRU4REC method, which is why we report the results when using one month as training data for this dataset.

Table 2: Results when using the evaluation scheme of [14].

Method	HR@10	MRR@10	HR@20	MRR@20
WH(KNN,GRU,0.6,0.4)	**0.568**	0.256	**0.691**	0.265
WH(KNN,GRU,0.1,0.9)	**0.568**	**0.269**	0.666	**0.276**
KNN_{MR}(500,1000)	0.521	0.242	0.641	0.250
GRU4REC(1000,BPR)	0.517	0.235	0.636	0.243
GRU4REC(1000,TOP1)	0.517	0.261	0.623	0.268
KNN_{RAND}(500,1000)	0.499	0.235	0.616	0.242
GRU4REC(100,TOP1)	0.481	0.221	0.595	0.230

configuration. Combining the kNN-method with GRU4REC in a weighted approach (WH) leads to the best results. As in [14], the "winner" at list length 20 depends on the metric. Also, different weights for the hybrid method have to be applied to achieve the best results for a given list length.[5] The increases of the best configuration at length 20 are about 8% for the hit rate. A smaller increase was observed for the MRR when compared to the results of [14]. Even with a random sampling of candidate sessions (KNN_{RAND}(500,1000)) the kNN-method does not fall far behind and is consistently better than GRU4REC with 100 hidden units.

Table 3 shows the best results obtained with KNN_{MR}(500,1000) and GRU4REC(1000,TOP1) when using alternative measurements, including the sliding window protocol (*RSCW*), the prediction of the second (*SECOND*) and last item view (*LAST*), and the accuracy when predicting which item is purchased in a session (*BUYS*). In all experiments, the kNN method outperforms GRU4REC. For the sliding windows protocol, we applied the Wilcoxon signed-rank test over the five experiment runs, which revealed that the differences are statistically significant in terms of the hit rate ($\alpha = 0.05$).

3.1.2 Results for Other Datasets. Table 4 shows the results for the additional datasets. We again report the results at list length 20 for GRU4REC(1000,TOP1) and KNN(500,1000). For the *TMALL* dataset, we applied the sliding-window approach as for *RSCW*. Note that in this dataset each session is defined as the sequence of actions of a user during one day (resulting in a larger average session length as shown in Table 1). As the playlists have no timestamp attached, we randomly assigned each playlist to one of 31 buckets (days of the month) and used one of them as test data.

In the majority of the configurations, the kNN method outperformed GRU4REC both in terms of the hit rate and the MRR, in many cases strongly. Only on the last.fm dataset, GRU4REC worked better than the kNN approach; on the AOTM dataset, GRU4REC was furthermore better in terms of the MRR. Generally, however, the results obtained for the additional datasets indicate that the good performance of the kNN method on the *RSC15* dataset is not due to the specific nature of this dataset or the application domain.

3.2 Additional Analyses

3.2.1 Focusing on Recent Data. The *RSC15* dataset contains about 45,000 sessions per day. Since our kNN method only uses, e.g., one thousand *possible* neighbor sessions, which are not necessarily all from the same day, we were interested to what extent we can omit past sessions without compromising the accuracy results.

Figure 1 shows MRR results when we incrementally remove data from the training set, beginning with the oldest sessions. The values for the hit rate are similar. For the GRU4REC method, it seems sufficient to focus on the last 60 days. For the kNN method in contrast, it is sufficient to retain the information of the last two days. While this might come surprising, focusing on the most recent events has shown to be effective in the past in the domains of e-commerce and news recommendations [19, 23].

As mentioned above, we made additional experiments on the *RSC15* data and repeatedly sampled 1000 random neighbor sessions instead of the most recent ones. The average results were shown in the last row of Table 2. Using random neighborhood sampling leads to slightly lower accuracy results, which are however still higher than the ones obtained by GRU4REC with 100 hidden units.

3.2.2 Popularity Bias and Catalog Coverage. To assess possible recommendation biases, we measured the average popularity of the recommendations. Using a normalized popularity score for the top-20 recommendations (in the setup of [14]) we found that the kNN method tends to recommends slightly more popular items on average than GRU4REC (0.036 vs. 0.028). With respect to catalog coverage, we observed that the top-20 recommendations of GRU4REC include about 47% of the items at least once, which is slightly more than the kNN method covers (41%). This latter observation is not surprising, given the focus of the kNN method on

Table 3: Additional measurements for the RSC15 dataset.

Dataset	RSCW		SECOND		LAST		BUYS	
M@20	HR	MRR	HR	MRR	HR	MRR	HR	MRR
KNN	0.621	0.267	0.716	0.355	0.446	0.196	0.758	0.290
GRU4REC	0.587	0.261	0.655	0.300	0.388	0.174	0.542	0.215

Table 4: Results for other datasets.

Dataset	TMALL		LFM		AOTM		8T	
M@20	HR	MRR	HR	MRR	HR	MRR	HR	MRR
KNN	0.370	0.171	0.078	0.011	0.068	0.008	0.050	0.010
GRU4REC	0.223	0.117	0.121	0.053	0.035	0.012	0.019	0.008

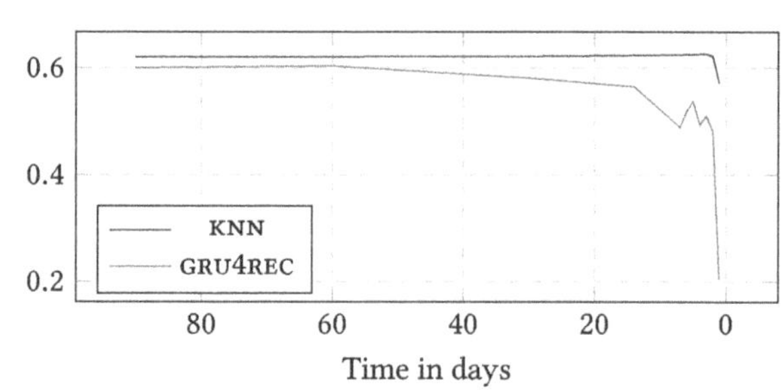

Figure 1: MRR@20 for the RSC15 when artificially reducing the size of the training set from 3 month to 1 day.

[5] In all experiments we tuned the parameters for the different algorithms using grid search. We optimized the hit rate on validation sets (subsets of the training sets). Due to the run time GRU4REC was only optimized with 100 layers as also done in [14].

the last few days. Alternative neighbor sampling strategies can however be designed to deal, e.g., with such accuracy-coverage trade-offs.

3.2.3 Computational Complexity and Memory Usage. On a desktop computer with an Intel i7-4790k processor, training GRU4REC in the best configuration needed about 23 hours for the *RSC15* dataset, which can be reduced to about 8 hours when calculations are performed by the GPU (Nvidia GeForce GTX 960). The kNN method needs about 90 seconds to build the in-memory data structures. Creating one recommendation list with GRU4REC needed about 12 ms on average and 26 ms for the kNN method. Overall, computing all (about 40,000) recommendations needs about 27 minutes with the kNN method including data structure initialization, whereas GRU4REC needs more than 8 hours in total. At the same time, the kNN method has the advantage of supporting online updates. Further speed-ups for the kNN approach can in theory be achieved when the similarity computations are parallelized, since these calculations can be done independently for individual subsets of the neighbor candidates.

The data structures of the kNN method occupy about 6.4 GB of main memory when the entire *RSC15* training dataset (2.3 GB of raw data) is used. No special data structures are used in our implementation and given the observations from above, keeping only a specific amount of the most recent log actions will help to reduce the memory requirements. For the same dataset, GRU4REC's model needs about 60 MB for 100 and 600 MB for 1000 hidden units. GRU4REC's memory demand is thus dependent of the algorithm parameters and significantly increases with the number of items. In the playlist and TMall experiments, GRU4REC's memory demands exceeded the capacity of our graphic card, making computations very slow, which is why we could only make a limited number of evaluation runs on these datasets.

4 RELATED WORK

The commonly used algorithmic approaches to leverage sequential information for predicting next user actions include Markov models and sequential pattern mining techniques. In one of the earlier works on this topic, Shani et al., for example, proposed the application of Markov Decision Processes in the scenario of an online book store [27]. More recent works that rely in Markov models include [3, 13, 17, 26] or [31]. In [31], Markov models were, for example, used with the goal to detect topic sequences in user sessions for the next-item prediction task. Detecting and leveraging sequences of topics was also the goal in [11] for the next-track music recommendation scenario. In this case, however, the authors applied sequential pattern mining techniques. Sequential patterns have been investigated earlier also for the problem of predicting the online navigation behavior of users, e.g., in [25].

Approaches based on Markov models and sequential pattern mining represent alternative baselines for session-based recommendations. Not all approaches based on Markov model however scale too well for large datasets [27]. Sequential pattern mining approaches (and association rule mining approaches in general) often require some effort to find suitable thresholds for rule learning and, depending on the application domain, do not lead to better accuracy results than co-occurrence-based kNN methods [2].

Particularly in recent years, RNNs have been applied in different ways to leverage sequence information when recommending, often based on ideas of the LSTM model proposed in [16] to avoid the vanishing or exploding gradient problem.

Zhang et al. [38] for example successfully applied RNNs in a related setting of predicting sequential advertisement clicks, in which the partitioning into sessions is less important. Hidasi et al., who proposed GRU4REC [14], were among the first to explore RNNs for session-based recommendations. Using the same evaluation protocol and *RSC15* data set, Tan et al. in [30] proposed an enhanced version of GRU4REC, which is trained on embedded item sequences with random drop-out to reduce overfitting. The models are also retrained on the most recent sessions to better adapt to short-term trends. In their paper, the authors report significant improvements over [14] which would also slightly outperform our hybrid approach. The work confirms that considering recent trends is helpful for this *RSC15* dataset and domain. Experiments on other datasets were unfortunately not reported. Since no source code was available, we re-implemented their method based on the information in the paper, but could not reproduce their results.

In [15] and [32] RNN-based approaches were recently proposed that leverage additional item features to achieve higher accuracy. Including additional information about users and items in the recommendation process is also possible for kNN based methods, but was not in the focus of our work.

Combining short-term with long-term models has shown to be a successful strategy in the past, e.g., in the e-commerce domain [18]. Song et al. [28] recently proposed an approach to predicting news click sequences, which used an RNN to model short-term interests in a combination with long-term models. The kNN method used in this paper can be combined with long-term models as well. However, in the case of the *RSC15* dataset, where sessions have no user ID attached, no long-term user models can be learned.

Yu et al. [37] use RNNs for the related task of next basket recommendations, in which, e.g., items for a shopping cart are suggested based on a user's history of past shopping carts. Although the scenario is slightly different from the one in this paper, the kNN method can be easily adapted as a baseline for this scenario.

In general, NNs have been used for a number of recommendation-related tasks in recent years. Often, such networks are used to learn embeddings of content features in compact fixed-size latent vectors, e.g., for music, for images, for video data, for documents, or to represent the user [1, 5–7, 10, 20, 24, 36]. These representations are then integrated, e.g., in content-based approaches, in variations of latent factor models, or are part of new methods for computing recommendations [6, 7, 10, 22, 29, 33, 35].

5 CONCLUSIONS

Our work shows that nearest-neighbor methods should be considered as competitive baselines for session-based recommendation scenarios. Considering a mix of co-occurrence signals and sequential patterns, as identified by recurrent neural networks, led to the best results in our experiments. In practice, however, one has to decide based on the application domain if the obtained accuracy gains justify the usage of more complex learning methods. Our future works include the comparison of the performance of additional session-based algorithms like [26] or [30].

REFERENCES

[1] Trapit Bansal, David Belanger, and Andrew McCallum. 2016. Ask the GRU: Multi-task Learning for Deep Text Recommendations. In *Proceedings of the 10th ACM Conference on Recommender Systems (RecSys '16)*. ACM, 107–114. DOI: http://dx.doi.org/10.1145/2959100.2959180

[2] Geoffray Bonnin and Dietmar Jannach. 2014. Automated Generation of Music Playlists: Survey and Experiments. *Computing Surveys* 47, 2 (Nov. 2014), 26:1–26:35. DOI: http://dx.doi.org/10.1145/2652481

[3] Shuo Chen, Josh L. Moore, Douglas Turnbull, and Thorsten Joachims. 2012. Playlist Prediction via Metric Embedding. In *Proceedings of the 18th ACM SIGKDD International Conference on Knowledge Discovery and Data Mining (KDD '12)*. ACM, 714–722. DOI: http://dx.doi.org/10.1145/2339530.2339643

[4] Junyoung Chung, Çaglar Gülçehre, KyungHyun Cho, and Yoshua Bengio. 2014. Empirical Evaluation of Gated Recurrent Neural Networks on Sequence Modeling. *CoRR* abs/1412.3555 (2014). http://arxiv.org/abs/1412.3555

[5] Paul Covington, Jay Adams, and Emre Sargin. 2016. Deep Neural Networks for YouTube Recommendations. In *Proceedings of the 10th ACM Conference on Recommender Systems (RecSys '16)*. ACM, 191–198. DOI: http://dx.doi.org/10.1145/2959100.2959190

[6] Sander Dieleman. 2016. Deep learning for audio-based music recommendation. In *Proceedings of the 1st Workshop on Deep Learning for Recommender Systems (DLRS '16)*. ACM, 1–1. DOI: http://dx.doi.org/10.1145/2988450.2991128

[7] Ali Mamdouh Elkahky, Yang Song, and Xiaodong He. 2015. A Multi-View Deep Learning Approach for Cross Domain User Modeling in Recommendation Systems. In *Proceedings of the 24th International Conference on World Wide Web (WWW '15)*. ACM, 278–288. DOI: http://dx.doi.org/10.1145/2736277.2741667

[8] Jeffrey L. Elman. 1990. Finding structure in time. *Cognitive Science* 14, 2 (1990), 179 – 211. DOI: http://dx.doi.org/10.1016/0364-0213(90)90002-E

[9] Alex Graves. 2013. Generating Sequences With Recurrent Neural Networks. *CoRR* abs/1308.0850 (2013). http://arxiv.org/abs/1308.0850

[10] Yupeng Gu, Bo Zhao, David Hardtke, and Yizhou Sun. 2016. Learning Global Term Weights for Content-based Recommender Systems. In *Proceedings of the 25th International Conference on World Wide Web (WWW '16)*. ACM, 391–400. DOI: http://dx.doi.org/10.1145/2872427.2883069

[11] Negar Hariri, Bamshad Mobasher, and Robin Burke. 2012. Context-aware Music Recommendation Based on Latenttopic Sequential Patterns. In *Proceedings of the Sixth ACM Conference on Recommender Systems (RecSys '12)*. ACM, 131–138. DOI: http://dx.doi.org/10.1145/2365952.2365979

[12] Negar Hariri, Bamshad Mobasher, and Robin Burke. 2015. Adapting to User Preference Changes in Interactive Recommendation. In *Proceedings of the 24th International Conference on Artificial Intelligence (IJCAI '15)*. AAAI, 4268–4274. http://dl.acm.org/citation.cfm?id=2832747.2832852

[13] Qi He, Daxin Jiang, Zhen Liao, Steven C. H. Hoi, Kuiyu Chang, Ee-Peng Lim, and Hang Li. 2009. Web Query Recommendation via Sequential Query Prediction. In *Proceedings of the 2009 IEEE International Conference on Data Engineering (ICDE '09)*. IEEE, 1443–1454. DOI: http://dx.doi.org/10.1109/ICDE.2009.71

[14] Balázs Hidasi, Alexandros Karatzoglou, Linas Baltrunas, and Domonkos Tikk. 2016. Session-based Recommendations with Recurrent Neural Networks. In *Proceedings of the International Conference on Learning Representations (ICLR '16)*. ACM. http://arxiv.org/abs/1511.06939

[15] Balázs Hidasi, Massimo Quadrana, Alexandros Karatzoglou, and Domonkos Tikk. 2016. Parallel Recurrent Neural Network Architectures for Feature-rich Session-based Recommendations. In *Proceedings of the 10th ACM Conference on Recommender Systems (RecSys '16)*. ACM, 241–248. DOI: http://dx.doi.org/10.1145/2959100.2959167

[16] Sepp Hochreiter and Jürgen Schmidhuber. 1997. Long Short-Term Memory. *Neural Computation* 9, 8 (Nov. 1997), 1735–1780. DOI: http://dx.doi.org/10.1162/neco.1997.9.8.1735

[17] Mehdi Hosseinzadeh Aghdam, Negar Hariri, Bamshad Mobasher, and Robin Burke. 2015. Adapting Recommendations to Contextual Changes Using Hierarchical Hidden Markov Models. In *Proceedings of the 9th ACM Conference on Recommender Systems (RecSys '15)*. ACM, 241–244. DOI: http://dx.doi.org/10.1145/2792838.2799684

[18] Dietmar Jannach, Lukas Lerche, and Michael Jugovac. 2015. Adaptation and Evaluation of Recommendations for Short-term Shopping Goals. In *Proceedings of the 9th ACM Conference on Recommender Systems (RecSys '15)*. ACM, 211–218. DOI: http://dx.doi.org/10.1145/2792838.2800176

[19] Dietmar Jannach and Malte Ludewig. 2017. Determining Characteristics of Successful Recommendations from Log Data – A Case Study. In *Proceedings of the 32th Annual ACM Symposium on Applied Computing (SAC '17)*. ACM.

[20] Donghyun Kim, Chanyoung Park, Jinoh Oh, Sungyoung Lee, and Hwanjo Yu. 2016. Convolutional Matrix Factorization for Document Context-Aware Recommendation. In *Proceedings of the 10th ACM Conference on Recommender Systems (RecSys '16)*. ACM, 233–240. DOI: http://dx.doi.org/10.1145/2959100.2959165

[21] Lukas Lerche, Dietmar Jannach, and Malte Ludewig. 2016. On the Value of Reminders Within E-Commerce Recommendations. In *Proceedings of the 2016 Conference on User Modeling Adaptation and Personalization (UMAP '16)*. ACM, 27–35. DOI: http://dx.doi.org/10.1145/2930238.2930244

[22] Sheng Li, Jaya Kawale, and Yun Fu. 2015. Deep Collaborative Filtering via Marginalized Denoising Auto-encoder. In *Proceedings of the 24th ACM International on Conference on Information and Knowledge Management (CIKM '15)*. ACM, 811–820. DOI: http://dx.doi.org/10.1145/2806416.2806527

[23] Cornelius A. Ludmann and H.-Jürgen Appelrath. 2016. Lessons Learned from Using a Data Stream Management System for Real-time Recommendation of Popular News Articles based on Real User Streams. In *Proceedings of the 4th Workshop on Large-Scale Recommender Systems at ACM RecSys 2016 (LSRS '16)*. ACM.

[24] Julian McAuley, Christopher Targett, Qinfeng Shi, and Anton van den Hengel. 2015. Image-Based Recommendations on Styles and Substitutes. In *Proceedings of the 38th International ACM SIGIR Conference on Research and Development in Information Retrieval (SIGIR '15)*. ACM, 43–52. DOI: http://dx.doi.org/10.1145/2766462.2767755

[25] Bamshad Mobasher, Honghua Dai, Tao Luo, and Miki Nakagawa. 2002. Using Sequential and Non-Sequential Patterns in Predictive Web Usage Mining Tasks. In *Proceedings of the 2002 IEEE International Conference on Data Mining (ICDM '02)*. IEEE, 669–672. DOI: http://dx.doi.org/10.1109/ICDM.2002.1184025

[26] Steffen Rendle, Christoph Freudenthaler, and Lars Schmidt-Thieme. 2010. Factorizing Personalized Markov Chains for Next-basket Recommendation. In *Proceedings of the 19th International Conference on World Wide Web (WWW '10)*. ACM, 811–820. DOI: http://dx.doi.org/10.1145/1772690.1772773

[27] Guy Shani, David Heckerman, and Ronen I. Brafman. 2005. An MDP-Based Recommender System. *The Journal of Machine Learning Research* 6 (Dec. 2005), 1265–1295. http://dl.acm.org/citation.cfm?id=1046920.1088715

[28] Yang Song, Ali Mamdouh Elkahky, and Xiaodong He. 2016. Multi-Rate Deep Learning for Temporal Recommendation. In *Proceedings of the 39th International ACM SIGIR conference on Research and Development in Information Retrieval (SIGIR '16)*. ACM Press, 909–912. DOI: http://dx.doi.org/10.1145/2911451.2914726

[29] Florian Strub, Romaric Gaudel, and Jérémie Mary. 2016. Hybrid Recommender System based on Autoencoders. In *Proceedings of the 1st Workshop on Deep Learning for Recommender Systems (DLRS '16)*. ACM, 11–16. DOI: http://dx.doi.org/10.1145/2988450.2988456

[30] Yong Kiam Tan, Xinxing Xu, and Yong Liu. 2016. Improved Recurrent Neural Networks for Session-based Recommendations. In *Proceedings of the 1st Workshop on Deep Learning for Recommender Systems (DLRS '16)*. ACM, 17–22. DOI: http://dx.doi.org/10.1145/2988450.2988452

[31] Maryam Tavakol and Ulf Brefeld. 2014. Factored MDPs for Detecting Topics of User Sessions. In *Proceedings of the 8th ACM Conference on Recommender Systems (RecSys '14)*. ACM, 33–40. DOI: http://dx.doi.org/10.1145/2645710.2645739

[32] Bart lomiej Twardowski. 2016. Modelling Contextual Information in Session-Aware Recommender Systems with Neural Networks. In *Proceedings of the 10th ACM Conference on Recommender Systems (RecSys '16)*. ACM, 273–276. DOI: http://dx.doi.org/10.1145/2959100.2959162

[33] Flavian Vasile, Elena Smirnova, and Alexis Conneau. 2016. Meta-Prod2Vec: Product Embeddings Using Side-Information for Recommendation. In *Proceedings of the 10th ACM Conference on Recommender Systems (RecSys '16)*. ACM, 225–232. DOI: http://dx.doi.org/10.1145/2959100.2959160 arXiv:1607.07326

[34] Koen Verstrepen and Bart Goethals. 2014. Unifying Nearest Neighbors Collaborative Filtering. In *Proceedings of the 8th ACM Conference on Recommender Systems (RecSys '14)*. ACM, New York, NY, USA, 177–184. DOI: http://dx.doi.org/10.1145/2645710.2645731

[35] Jeroen B. P. Vuurens, Martha Larson, and Arjen P. de Vries. 2016. Exploring Deep Space: Learning Personalized Ranking in a Semantic Space. In *Proceedings of the 1st Workshop on Deep Learning for Recommender Systems (DLRS '16)*. ACM, 23–28. DOI: http://dx.doi.org/10.1145/2988450.2988457

[36] Hao Wang, Naiyan Wang, and Dit-Yan Yeung. 2015. Collaborative Deep Learning for Recommender Systems. In *Proceedings of the 21th ACM SIGKDD International Conference on Knowledge Discovery and Data Mining (KDD '15)*. ACM, 1235–1244. DOI: http://dx.doi.org/10.1145/2783258.2783273 arXiv:1409.2944

[37] Feng Yu, Qiang Liu, Shu Wu, Liang Wang, and Tieniu Tan. 2016. A Dynamic Recurrent Model for Next Basket Recommendation. In *Proceedings of the 39th International ACM SIGIR conference on Research and Development in Information Retrieval (SIGIR '16)*. ACM, 729–732. DOI: http://dx.doi.org/10.1145/2911451.2914683

[38] Yuyu Zhang, Hanjun Dai, Chang Xu, Jun Feng, Taifeng Wang, Jiang Bian, Bin Wang, and Tie-Yan Liu. 2014. Sequential Click Prediction for Sponsored Search with Recurrent Neural Networks. In *Proceedings of the 28th AAAI Conference on Artificial Intelligence (AAAI '14)*. AAAI, 1369–1375. http://dl.acm.org/citation.cfm?id=2893873.2894086

Recommendation of High Quality Representative Reviews in e-commerce

Debanjan Paul
Indian Institute of Technology
Kharagpur
debanjan0910@gmail.com

Sudeshna Sarkar
Indian Institute of Technology
Kharagpur
sudeshna@cse.iitkgp.ernet.in

Muthusamy Chelliah
Flipkart Internet Pvt Ltd
Bangalore
muthusamy.c@flipkart.com

Chetan Kalyan
Flipkart Internet Pvt Ltd
Bangalore
chetan.k@flipkart.com

Prajit Prashant Sinai Nadkarni
Flipkart Internet Pvt Ltd
Bangalore
prajit.pn@flipkart.com

ABSTRACT

Many users of ecommerce portals commonly use customer reviews for making purchase decisions. But a product may have tens or hundreds of diverse reviews leading to information overload on the customer. The main objective of our work is to develop a recommendation system to recommend a subset of reviews that have high content score and good coverage over different aspects of the product along with their associated sentiments. We address the challenge which arises due to the fact that similar aspects are mentioned in different reviews using different natural language expressions. We use vector representations to identify mentions of similar aspects and map them with aspects mentioned in product features specifications. Review helpfulness score may act as a proxy for the quality of reviews, but new reviews do not have any helpfulness score. We address the cold start problem by using a dynamic convolutional neural network to estimate the quality score from review content. The system is evaluated on datasets from Amazon and Flipkart and is found to be more effective than the competing methods.

KEYWORDS

Review Recommendation; Content scoring; Product aspect; E-commerce

1 INTRODUCTION

Most e-commerce portals facilitate reviews and ratings by the consumers. The reviews may discuss different aspects of the product and may contain different opinions about the product or the various aspects of the product. Such reviews form an important source of information for potential buyers who use the reviews to learn about the product features and the reviewers' opinions on them and use this information to make more informed purchase decisions. However, having a large number of reviews also poses a potential challenge for the user if she has to process each review and extract useful information from them. The e-commerce system may therefore facilitate the user by recommending a small subset of reviews to the user. This subset should ideally be representative of the entire set of reviews and cover different aspects of the product along with the right balance of positive and negative opinion on them. Many e-commerce websites facilitate users to rate the review by other users by providing helpfulness score. This helpfulness score can be used as an estimate of the review quality. However, this suffers from cold start problem since new reviews do not have associated ratings. We have addressed this challenge by training a neural network to predict the helpfulness score of a review from its content. We have incorporated the representative subset computation along with the use of quality scores in selecting a subset of reviews.

RecSys '17, August 27–31, 2017, Como, Italy.

DOI: http://dx.doi.org/10.1145/3109859.3109901

2 RELATED WORK

[1] provides a survey on work that extract product aspects and their associated opinions from user reviews of products. Past works have addressed the extraction of representative summaries from review texts ([15], [4], [2], [3], [6], [14], [17], [22]). The main aim of these methods is to create a summary of the reviews of a product that is both comprehensive and statistical in nature, representing both the positive and negative sentiments on different product aspects. But these summaries lack the linguistic structure of reviews written by real users. It has been found that users give more importance to reviews written by actual customers who have used the product than some automatically generated statistical summaries while reading reviews of a product in order to make a purchase decision.

In order to recommend a set of reviews written by real users instead of statistical summaries, some methods have been proposed by ([5],[8],[19],[21]) to assign a score to each review based on helpfulness of the review, the number of aspects it covers and other parameters. These methods then produce ranked lists of reviews based on these parameters and recommend the top k reviews to the users.

But the recommended set of reviews may ignore the less popular aspects of a product. For example, all the top reviews of a mobile phone may be focused on a limited number of attributes like its camera specification and processor speed but these reviews may not address attributes like screen size or look. In order to address the above issues, another set of approaches ([10], [18]) deal with the method of representing a subset of reviews that cover as many product aspects as possible and both positive and negative opinion

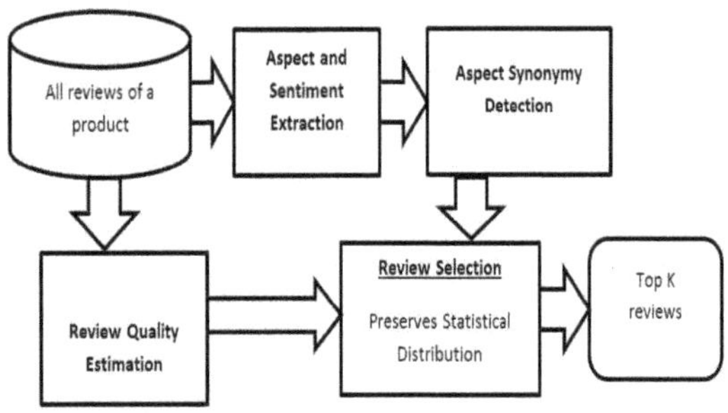

Figure 1: System Overview

sentiments associated with these aspects. The subset of reviews selected by these methods are able to represent a diverse set of aspects and opinions. However, they fail to accurately capture the proportion of opinions in the underlying corpus. This has been addressed by the method proposed by ([9]) that recommends a subset of reviews for a product which maintains the statistical distribution of product aspects along with their associated sentiments on the entire review set.

3 MOTIVATION

We wish to develop a recommendation system to recommend a small subset of reviews to the users which covers different product aspects and sentiments. We find that similar aspects are expressed in different natural language expressions in different reviews. For example, a review may speak about picture quality of a mobile phone, whereas another review may speak about the camera specifications of the same phone. However, we should be able to recognize that they are talking about the same aspect.

Most of the review recommendation systems ignore the textual content of the review and do not use review quality for recommendation. We believe that the quality of the textual content of the review should be used for review recommendation. [20] has used review helpfulness score to estimate review quality. But new reviews do not have any helpfulness score. In order to address the cold start problem, we want to develop a model to estimate the quality score of the reviews, even if they do not have any helpfulness score.

4 PROPOSED METHODOLOGY

We wish to develop a recommendation system to recommend a subset of k high quality representative reviews. The system architecture is shown in figure 1. The *Aspect and Sentiment extraction* module extracts aspect phrases (and corresponding sentiments) from review texts. It is discussed in section 4.1. Similar aspects can be mentioned by using different natural language expressions. The *Aspect Synonymy Detection* module identifies phrases that correspond to similar aspects. This is explained in section 4.2. The *Review Quality Estimation* module scores a review and is discussed in section 4.3. Section 4.4 combines our quality estimation module with the Characteristic Review Selection algorithm from [9] in order to recommend a subset of reviews to the users. Apart from recommending high quality reviews, our recommendation system also maintains the statistical distribution of product aspects along with their associated sentiments.

4.1 Aspect and Sentiment Extraction

The main task of our aspect extraction phase is to extract important aspects mentioned in the reviews along with their corresponding opinion sentiments. We extract the product aspects and opinion associated with them in a review using the double propagation method proposed by [16]. The output contains tuples of the form <review id, aspect, sentiment polarity> (for example, <1,photo quality,+>). Each aspect is a natural language phrase extracted from a review.

4.2 Aspect Synonymy Detection

Similar aspects may be mentioned using different natural language expressions in various reviews (e.g. "camera", "photo quality" and "picture quality" refer to the same product aspect "camera") and are treated as different product aspects. The main aim of synonymy detection is to identify all the similar aspects expressed in different natural language phrases and merge them together into a single aspect.

We make use of product catalogues to identify a standard set of features or aspects for each product type and try to map the different aspect phrases to one of the standard catalogue aspects. For this task, we have used the catalogue of the corresponding category from Flipkart though we have applied this to data from Amazon.

Word Vectors. We link the aspects obtained from textual expressions to the catalogue aspects by computing semantic similarity between them. We use vector representation of words to compute the semantic similarity of different aspect phrases. We train our model on the publicly available Amazon dataset ([11], [13]) for our experiment.

Merging similar aspects together . The input to this phase are the aspect phrases output from *Aspect and Synonymy Extraction* (denoted by A) and the catalogue aspects denoted by C. Algorithm 1 gives the details of Merge (A, C), which maps the extracted aspects from each review in set A with a particular catalogue aspect in set C. For each aspect $extrctd\_aspect$ in set A, if the similarity between $extrctd\_aspect$ and catalogue aspect c is maximum and is greater than a minimum threshold value $epsilon$, then $extrctd\_aspect$ is mapped to c in C. We have used $epsilon = 0.7$. The function $word2vec\_sim(extrctd\_aspect, c)$ in line 9 returns the semantic similarity between vector representation of aspect word $extrctd\_aspect$ and catalogue aspect c. Given two aspect words $extrctd\_aspect$ and catalogue aspect c, we obtain their vectors $\theta_{\text{extrctd\_aspect}}$ and θ_c from the pre-trained word vectors and we use cosine similarity to calculate the semantic similarity.

Comparing of results before and after merging similar aspect phrases. The percentage distribution of 10 out of the 35 aspects obtained from 125 reviews of "Nokia 216 (Black)" are shown in Table 1. We notice that many attributes like "audio", "sound", "speaker" are treated as distinct though they refer to the same feature of the phone. The results obtained after merging similar aspects are shown

Camera	Support	Display	Touch Screen	Price	Bluetooth Headset	Picture	Packaging	OS	Smartphone	...
10%	9%	7%	7%	6%	6%	5%	5%	4%	4%	

Table 1: Results before merging similar aspects. We obtained 35 aspects (top 10 are shown here) from 125 reviews of "Nokia 216 (Black)"". Other aspects are : Audio Quality,Video Recording, Sound Quality, photo, RAM, memory, battery life, clock speed, frequency, sim, network, internet, model, ROM, resolution, pixel, LED, button, power, configuration, processing, color, thing, formats, disk.

Algorithm 1 Merge_Similar_Aspects

procedure MERGE(A, C)
Input: Extracted aspect set A and catalogue aspect set C
Output: Aspect (and corresponding opinion) distribution for each review
  for each tuple $a \in A$ **do**
    $review\_id \leftarrow a[1]$
    $extrctd\_aspect \leftarrow a[2]$
    $opn\_pol \leftarrow a[3]$
    $max\_sim \leftarrow \Phi$
    for each aspect $c \in C$ **do**
      $sim \leftarrow word2vec\_sim(extrctd\_aspect, c)$
      if $sim > max\_sim$ **then**
        $max\_sim \leftarrow sim$
        $ctlg\_aspect \leftarrow c$
      end if
    end for
    if $max\_sim > \epsilon$ **then**
      if opn_pol is positive **then**
        map $extrtcd\_aspect$ to $ctlg\_aspect^+$
      else
        map $extrtcd\_aspect$ to $ctlg\_aspect^-$
      end if
    end if
  end for

Gene ral	Dis play	Procr essor	Mem ory	Cam era	Connec tivity	Multi media	Char ging
56%	47%	16%	6%	29%	49%	34%	36%

Table 2: Results after merging similar aspects. 29 out of 35 aspects obtained from 125 reviews of "Nokia 216 (Black)" have been mapped to 8 catalogue aspects.

Method	Percentage	Average rank
CRS	15%	2.175
CNN	25%	2.2125
COMB	60%	1.6125

Table 3: Comparison of three methods as obtained by human annotation

in Table 2. We have mapped 29 out of 35 initial aspects to 8 catalogue aspects, which results in a better percentage distribution of aspects.

Algorithms	Transactions	PPV
DEFAULT	1777	313776
COMB	1781	308782

Table 4: Comparison of COMB method against default recommendation system at Flipkart.com. Product-page visit (PPV) is defined as the number of users visiting a particular product page. Transactions (Txns) is defined as the number of users who bought the product after visiting the product page.

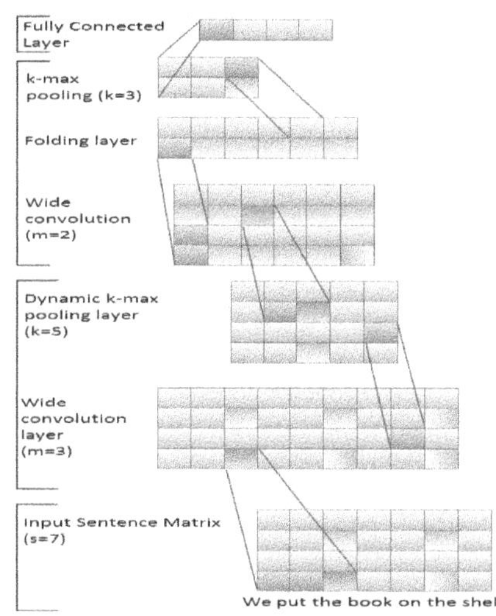

Figure 2: Dynamic convolutional neural network model for estimating review quality

4.3 Predicting review quality score from review content

We use a dynamic convolutional neural network from [7] to predict the quality score of reviews. [7] proposed this model and used this for sentiment prediction and question classification. We have used the model for estimating review quality score from review texts. The architecture is described below.

The **Input Layer** contains the reviews for a particular item. Each word in a review sentence of length s is embedded as $w_i \in \mathbb{R}^d$ corresponding to the i th position of the word in the sentence. Thus, each review is represented as a two dimensional matrix $S \in \mathbb{R}^{d \times s}$ which is given as input to the convolutional layer.

Convolutional Layer : A convolution matrix of weights $m \in \mathbb{R}^{d \times m}$ is applied to the input matrix S to obtain the next layer. We have applied one dimensional wide convolution operation to each row in the input matrix S. The resulting matrix obtained denoted by C has dimensions $d \times (s + m - 1)$.

Dynamic k-max pooling : This layer selects the k most active features from the matrix C. k is determined dynamically as a function of the length of the sentence and depth of the network i.e

$$k_l = \max(k_{\text{top}}, (L - l) \times s/L)$$

where l is the number of current convolutional layers to which the pooling is applied and L is the total number of convolutional layers in the network.

The operation described above consists of one convolution layer followed by one dynamic k-max pooling layer to obtain a first order feature map. These operations are repeated in order to obtain a higher order feature map and a network of increasing size. We have repeated the above operations 2 times in order to obtain a second order feature map and a two layer network architecture.

Folding : After a convolution operation and before dynamic pooling operation, folding is applied to reduce the dimension of the matrix. The elements in two rows of the matrix are added component wise in order to obtain a reduced matrix of dimension $d/2$.

Fully Connected Layer : After extracting the multiple features representing each sentence, the features are passed to the fully connected softmax layer where the output is probabilistically distributed and calculated using multinomial regression technique.

Training datasets and parameters. We have used 2 million reviews from six different product domains (electronics, books, shoes, musical instruments and gourmet food products) in Amazon dataset ([12], [11], [13]) to train the model. Filter sizes of 10 and 7 have been used with 6 filters in the first convolutional layer and 12 filters in the second convolutional layer. Dropout value of 0.5 has been used in the fully connected layer.

4.4 Review Selection

The main aim of this module is to recommend a subset of reviews with high content score and a proper and representative coverage of the product aspects, issues and sentiments. The ranked review list from the previous module is the input to this phase. We have used a greedy iterative algorithm from [9] for selecting a subset of reviews to have the same statistical distribution of aspects (and corresponding opinions) as that of the entire review set for the product. This algorithm greedily selects one review at a time. That review is selected next so that its inclusion makes the recommended set better representative of the entire review set.

For example, let R be the entire review set for a particular product. Let S_k be the subset of reviews which has already been formed by k iterations of the algorithm. The algorithm picks up a review r^{k+1} in the $k + 1$ th iteration such that $S_k \cup r^{k+1}$ has proportion of aspects and opinions closest to that of R.

5 EXPERIMENTAL RESULTS

5.1 Datasets

We have used reviews from the publicly available Amazon dataset ([12], [11], [13]). It includes 2 million products and 35 million reviews reviewed by 6 million users. Each review item include product title, user information, review rating, and a plaintext review. We have chosen reviews from popular product domains like Cell phone and electronics products due to the availability of a large number of products and reviews written by the users in these domains.

5.2 Comparison with existing methods

We consider the recommendation of three sets of reviews for eight items based on the three methods below:
1. **CRS**: Recommends a subset of reviews based on Characteristic Review Selection (CRS) algorithm suggested by [9].
2. **CNN**: Recommends a subset of reviews based on the quality score of each review as estimated by the DCNN model.
3.**COMB**: Recommends a subset of reviews by our combined approach as discussed in section 4.

For each of the above 8 items, we have recommended a subset of 5 reviews using the above methods. We have used 10 human annotators for this. The annotators were given the three sets of reviews (in a randomized order) and were asked to rank the methods from 1 (best) to 3 (worst). For each of the 8 items, we have given the percentage of both positive and negative opinions on each aspects of the product. This helps them to get an overall idea about the product quality and judge the representativeness of the recommended subset of reviews in a better way.

COMB method has clearly outperformed the other methods as shown in Table 3. It has been declared as the best method in 60% of the reports obtained from human annotators. Moreover, COMB approach has got a lower rank than the competing methods.

5.3 Live Evaluation on Flipkart based on Transactions

We have compared the CNN and COMB review recommendation method against the default review recommendation system implemented at a popular e-commerce website (Flipkart.com). We considered reviews from 10 random products in the mobile phone category. We have considered the top 100 sorted reviews recommended by COMB method. These reviews are shown in the most helpful tab of Flipkart product page while all other tabs shows the reviews recommended by Flipkart default algorithm. This experiment is run live for a couple of days in order to understand the impact of our methods on live users compared to their default algorithm. COMB method has clearly performed better than default recommendation system of Flipkart as seen in Table 4. The Flipkart default recommendation system resulted in 1777 product transactions out of 313776 product-page visit for 25 products from the mobile phone category. The COMB method has shown an increase in product transactions to 1781 conversions out of 308782 product-page visit, thereby increasing product sales by 1.85%.

6 CONCLUSION

We have reported the results of one preliminary evaluation of our review recommendation system. The preliminary results are encouraging but we need to improve the method for estimating review helpfulness.

REFERENCES

[1] Li Chen, Guanliang Chen, and Feng Wang. 2015. Recommender systems based on user reviews: the state of the art. *User Modeling and User-Adapted Interaction* 25, 2 (2015), 99.

[2] Kavita Ganesan, ChengXiang Zhai, and Jiawei Han. 2010. Opinosis: a graph-based approach to abstractive summarization of highly redundant opinions. In *Proceedings of the 23rd international conference on computational linguistics.* Association for Computational Linguistics, 340–348.

[3] Kavita Ganesan, ChengXiang Zhai, and Evelyne Viegas. 2012. Micropinion generation: an unsupervised approach to generating ultra-concise summaries of opinions. In *Proceedings of the 21st international conference on World Wide Web.* ACM, 869–878.

[4] Shima Gerani, Yashar Mehdad, Giuseppe Carenini, Raymond T Ng, and Bita Nejat. 2014. Abstractive Summarization of Product Reviews Using Discourse Structure.. In *EMNLP.* 1602–1613.

[5] Anindya Ghose and Panagiotis G Ipeirotis. 2007. Designing novel review ranking systems: predicting the usefulness and impact of reviews. In *Proceedings of the ninth international conference on Electronic commerce.* ACM, 303–310.

[6] Minqing Hu and Bing Liu. 2004. Mining and summarizing customer reviews. In *Proceedings of the tenth ACM SIGKDD international conference on Knowledge discovery and data mining.* ACM, 168–177.

[7] Nal Kalchbrenner, Edward Grefenstette, and Phil Blunsom. 2014. A convolutional neural network for modelling sentences. *arXiv preprint arXiv:1404.2188* (2014).

[8] Soo-Min Kim, Patrick Pantel, Tim Chklovski, and Marco Pennacchiotti. 2006. Automatically assessing review helpfulness. In *Proceedings of the 2006 Conference on empirical methods in natural language processing.* Association for Computational Linguistics, 423–430.

[9] Theodoros Lappas, Mark Crovella, and Evimaria Terzi. 2012. Selecting a characteristic set of reviews. In *Proceedings of the 18th ACM SIGKDD international conference on Knowledge discovery and data mining.* ACM, 832–840.

[10] Theodoros Lappas and Dimitrios Gunopulos. 2010. Efficient confident search in large review corpora. In *Joint European Conference on Machine Learning and Knowledge Discovery in Databases.* Springer, 195–210.

[11] Julian McAuley and Jure Leskovec. 2013. Hidden factors and hidden topics: understanding rating dimensions with review text. In *Proceedings of the 7th ACM conference on Recommender systems.* ACM, 165–172.

[12] Julian McAuley, Rahul Pandey, and Jure Leskovec. 2015. Inferring networks of substitutable and complementary products. In *Proceedings of the 21th ACM SIGKDD International Conference on Knowledge Discovery and Data Mining.* ACM, 785–794.

[13] Julian McAuley, Christopher Targett, Qinfeng Shi, and Anton Van Den Hengel. 2015. Image-based recommendations on styles and substitutes. In *Proceedings of the 38th International ACM SIGIR Conference on Research and Development in Information Retrieval.* ACM, 43–52.

[14] Xinfan Meng and Houfeng Wang. 2009. Mining user reviews: from specification to summarization. In *Proceedings of the ACL-IJCNLP 2009 Conference Short Papers.* Association for Computational Linguistics, 177–180.

[15] Thanh-Son Nguyen, Hady W Lauw, and Panayiotis Tsaparas. 2015. Review synthesis for micro-review summarization. In *Proceedings of the Eighth ACM International Conference on Web Search and Data Mining.* ACM, 169–178.

[16] Guang Qiu, Bing Liu, Jiajun Bu, and Chun Chen. 2011. Opinion word expansion and target extraction through double propagation. *Computational linguistics* 37, 1 (2011), 9–27.

[17] Kazutaka Shimada, Ryosuke Tadano, and Tsutomu Endo. 2011. Multi-aspects review summarization with objective information. *Procedia-Social and Behavioral Sciences* 27 (2011), 140–149.

[18] Panayiotis Tsaparas, Alexandros Ntoulas, and Evimaria Terzi. 2011. Selecting a comprehensive set of reviews. In *Proceedings of the 17th ACM SIGKDD international conference on Knowledge discovery and data mining.* ACM, 168–176.

[19] Oren Tsur and Ari Rappoport. 2009. RevRank: A Fully Unsupervised Algorithm for Selecting the Most Helpful Book Reviews.. In *ICWSM.*

[20] Nana Xu, Hongyan Liu, Jiawei Chen, Jun He, and Xiaoyong Du. 2014. Selecting a representative set of diverse quality reviews automatically. In *Proceedings of the 2014 SIAM International Conference on Data Mining.* SIAM, 488–496.

[21] Zhu Zhang and Balaji Varadarajan. 2006. Utility scoring of product reviews. In *Proceedings of the 15th ACM international conference on Information and knowledge management.* ACM, 51–57.

[22] Li Zhuang, Feng Jing, and Xiao-Yan Zhu. 2006. Movie review mining and summarization. In *Proceedings of the 15th ACM international conference on Information and knowledge management.* ACM, 43–50.

A Semantic-Aware Profile Updating Model for Text Recommendation

Hossein Rahmatizadeh Zagheli[1], Hamed Zamani[2], and Azadeh Shakery[1,3]
[1] School of Electrical and Computer Engineering, College of Engineering, University of Tehran, Iran
[2] Center for Intelligent Information Retrieval, University of Massachusetts Amherst, MA 01003
[3] School of Computer Science, Institute for Research in Fundamental Sciences (IPM), Iran
{rahmatizadeh,shakery}@ut.ac.ir,zamani@cs.umass.edu

ABSTRACT

Content-based recommender systems (CBRSs) rely on user-item similarities that are calculated between user profiles and item representations. Appropriate representation of each user profile based on the user's past preferences can have a great impact on user's satisfaction in CBRSs. In this paper, we focus on text recommendation and propose a novel profile updating model based on previously recommended items as well as semantic similarity of terms calculated using distributed representation of words. We evaluate our model using two standard text recommendation datasets: TREC-9 Filtering Track and CLEF 2008-09 INFILE Track collections. Our experiments investigate the importance of both past recommended items and semantic similarities in recommendation performance. The proposed profile updating method significantly outperforms the baselines, which confirms the importance of incorporating semantic similarities in the profile updating task.

KEYWORDS

Content-based recommender systems; text recommendation; adaptive filtering; word embedding; semantic similarity

1 INTRODUCTION

Text recommendation is the task of delivering sets of documents to users in order to satisfy their information needs. There exist several real-world applications for text recommendation, including applications for recommending blog and social media posts [9], news articles [3, 25, 27], scientific papers [2, 31], and products (based on their reviews) [18]. In content-based text recommender systems, the recommendation decision is made based on the similarity of user profile to the candidate documents. It has been shown that accurately modeling user profiles can lead to significant improvements in recommendation performance [7, 24].

The Rocchio's relevance feedback algorithm [30] has been extensively used for profile updating within the vector space model framework [24]. The language modeling framework for information retrieval [26] has shown theoretical and empirical advantages over the traditional vector space model [7, 16]. Relevance models proposed by Lavrenko and Croft [15] have been successfully used for profile updating in the language modeling framework [32]. All of these profile updating models use recommendation history and users' feedback in order to construct a profile for each user.

There is a large overlap between the profile updating task in text recommendation and query modeling in search engines. Recently, exploiting semantic similarities captured by distributed representation of words has attracted a lot of attention for query modeling in the information retrieval literature [13, 28, 34–36]. In this paper, we first propose to update user profiles based on recommendation history using a log-logistic model. We further propose to enrich user profiles via semantic similarity of words. The intuition behind our approach is that each user profile should be constructed based on the words extracted from the previous successful recommendations to the user that are semantically similar to the initial user profile.

We evaluate our model with the adaptive filtering setup using two standard datasets: TREC-9 Filtering Track (containing scientific publications in the field of medicine) and CLEF 2008-2009 Information Filtering Evaluation (INFLIE) Track (containing news articles) collections. The results and analysis demonstrate that the proposed log-logistic model for profile updating outperforms state-of-the-art baselines, including the mixture model and the relevance model. Our experiments also show that although updating user profiles solely based on semantic similarity of terms does not outperform the profile updating approaches based on recommendation history, constructing a semantic-aware profile updating model based on recommendation history significantly outperforms all the baselines. Our results suggest to construct semantic-aware user profiles for text recommendation.

2 RELATED WORK

Word embedding models, such as word2vec [19], have been shown to be highly effective in many natural language processing tasks. Several attempts have been made for improving the recommendation performance by employing word embedding vectors. Musto et al. [21, 22] used word embeddings for content-based recommender systems. The authors used Wikipedia as an external resource for item recommendation. Huang [11] employed word embeddings for representing job postings in a job recommendation scenario. These studies do not focus on text recommendation. Ozsoy [23] and Krishnamurthy et al. [12] used the word embedding idea to model non-textual items for the item recommendation task. Recently, Bansal et al. [2] used recurrent neural networks for text representation in a supervised manner.

Furthermore, employing semantic similarities calculated based on word embedding vectors for the query expansion task has shown significant improvements in the retrieval performance [13, 34–36].

RecSys '17, August 27–31, 2017, Como, Italy.
© 2017 ACM. 978-1-4503-4652-8/17/08...$15.00
DOI: http://dx.doi.org/10.1145/3109859.3109904

However, the effectiveness of employing such semantic similarities in profile updating for text recommendation is still relatively unstudied, which is the focus of this paper.

3 TEXT RECOMMENDATION FRAMEWORK

Text recommendation frameworks consist of three major components: text representation, filtering component, and profile learner [17]. In this section, we present how we implement the first two components in our recommendation process.

The text representation component in our recommender system is based on the language modeling framework in information retrieval [26]. Similar to prior work [16, 27, 33], each document D is represented with a unigram language model (called θ_D) smoothed using the Dirichlet prior smoothing method [38] as follows:

$$p(w|\theta_D) = \frac{|D|}{|D| + \mu} p_{ML}(w|D) + \frac{\mu}{|D| + \mu} p(w|C) \quad (1)$$

where $p_{ML}(w|D)$ and C represent the maximum likelihood estimation for document D and a reference language model, respectively. μ is the smoothing parameter.

To implement the filtering component, we use the KL-divergence retrieval model [14]. In more detail, the similarity score of each user profile P and each candidate document D is calculated as:

$$score(P, D) = -D(\theta_P || \theta_D) = -\sum_{w \in P} p(w|\theta_P) \log \frac{p(w|\theta_P)}{p(w|\theta_D)} \quad (2)$$

where $D(\cdot||\cdot)$ denotes the KL-divergence formula, and θ_P represents the profile language model. In Section 4, we present our methodology to model and update user profiles.

The recommendations are based on the similarity scores computed by the filtering component and a dissemination threshold τ. Updating the dissemination threshold plays a key role in improving the recommendation performance in text recommendation [39]. To update the threshold, we use the linear auto-adjust threshold optimization (LAUTO) algorithm [33], a simple yet effective algorithm that has recently shown relatively good performance [27, 33]. The algorithm starts with an initial threshold and is adjusted based on each user's recommendation history. Based on the LAUTO algorithm, passing a number of non-relevant documents to the user means that the dissemination threshold is probably lower than the optimal value and the threshold should be increased. In addition, rejecting a large number of continuous arrival documents by the filtering component is a signal to shows that the dissemination threshold is higher than the optimal value and should be decreased.

4 SEMANTIC-AWARE PROFILE UPDATING

In this section, we present our semantic-aware profile updating model. To do so, we first explain how we construct a profile model from the user's recommendation history. We further explain how we inject semantic similarity calculated based on distributed representation of words into our model.

In recommender systems, including this paper, the user's profile may be updated after each successful recommendation to the user. Consider a document D recommended to user u, for which an implicit or explicit feedback shows that this was a successful recommendation. We extract the weight of each term from the recommended document D using a log-logistic model. Although log-logistic has shown good performance in the pseudo-relevance feedback task in information retrieval [8, 20], to the best of our knowledge, this is the first attempt to update user profiles using this approach. In fact, the goal is to realize which term in the document is a good candidate for updating the user profile. The log-logistic score for each term w in the recommended document D is calculated as:

$$LL(w, D) = \log\left(\frac{\text{count}(w, D) * \log(1 + c\frac{avgl}{|D|}) + \lambda_w}{\lambda_w}\right) \quad (3)$$

where count(w, D) and $avgl$ denote the frequency of term w in document D and the average document length, respectively. c is a free hyper-parameter that controls the weight of document length normalization component. λ_w shows how frequent the term w is in the reference collection. In other words, λ_w is equal to N_w/N where N_w and N respectively denote the total number of documents that contain w and the total number of documents in the collection. This part of the formula models how general the term w is. The logarithm function is used to satisfy the concavity constraint for term frequency.

One of the main shortcomings of the log-logistic formulation (i.e., Equation (3)) is that it is independent of the user's original profile. In other words, $LL(w, D)$ only depends on the recommended document, while the word might not be related to the initial user profile. To address this issue, we propose to involve the semantic similarity of words to the original user profile in the profile updating model. To this aim, the profile language model θ_{P^*} is calculated as follows:

$$p(w|\theta_{P^*}) \propto score(w, F^+) p_{sem}(w|P) \quad (4)$$

where F^+ and P denote the set of past successful recommended documents and the original user profile, respectively. $score(w, F^+)$ is calculated based on the independence assumption of the recommended documents as follows:

$$score(w, F^+) \propto \sum_{D \in F^+} LL(w, D) \quad (5)$$

where $p_{sem}(w|P)$ represents the semantic similarity between the term and the original user's profile. $p_{sem}(w|P)$ can be calculated in different ways. A simple and well-known calculation is based on the similarity of the embedding vectors of w and P. We propose a translation-based probabilistic model [4] to compute this probability:

$$p_{sem}(w|P) = \sum_{p_i \in P} p_{sem}(w|p_i) p_{sem}(p_i|P) \quad (6)$$

where p_i is a profile term. The intuition behind this model is that the semantic similarities to the words that are close to the whole user's profile should get higher weights. p_{sem} is calculated based on the softmax function as follows:

$$p_{sem}(w|p_i) = \frac{\exp(\vec{w}.\vec{p_i})}{\sum_{w' \in V} \exp(\vec{w'}.\vec{p_i})} \quad (7)$$

where V denotes the vocabulary set. The vectors in Equation (7) denote the distributed representations of the given terms. The probability $p_{sem}(p_i|P)$ is estimated similarly where $\vec{P}$ is the centroid vector of all profile terms.

Table 1: Performance of the proposed method and the baselines. The best result in each column is boldfaced. The superscripts 1/2/3/4/5/6/7/8 denote that the improvements over NoUpdate/MIXTURE/RM3/LL/Cent/CombSUM/CombMNZ/CombMAX are statistically significant.

Method	OHSUMED			INFILE		
	F1-measure	Precision	Recall	F1-measure	Precision	Recall
NoUpdate	0.2007	0.301	0.3281	0.3472	0.4696	0.4932
MIX	0.2251	0.3019	0.3611	0.3598	0.4779	0.5213
RM3	0.2263	0.3031	0.3605	0.3581	0.4758	**0.5282**
LL	0.2219	0.3003	0.3706	0.3631	0.4777	0.5160
Cent	0.2134	0.3015	0.3398	0.3525	0.4897	0.5001
CombSUM	0.2052	0.3018	0.329	0.3491	0.4915	0.4985
CombMNZ	0.205	0.3032	0.3363	0.3507	**0.4927**	0.4994
CombMAX	0.2114	0.2979	0.3516	0.3451	0.4746	0.515
LL-WE	**0.2344**^{145678}	**0.3161**^{12345678}	**0.3912**^{12345678}	**0.3771**^{12345678}	0.4871^{1}	0.5272^{15678}

The final language model is estimated using the linear interpolation of the estimated profile model and the original profile model as follows:

$$p(w|\theta_P) = \alpha p_{ML}(w|P) + (1-\alpha)p(w|\theta_{P^*}) \tag{8}$$

where the parameter α controls the weight of the original profile model $p_{ML}(w|P)$ computed based on maximum likelihood estimation.

5 EXPERIMENTS

In this section, we first explain our experimental design, including the datasets that we used, the pre-processing steps, and the experimental setup details. We further introduce our evaluation metrics and finally report and discuss the results.

5.1 Experimental Design

Datasets. In our experiments, we use two standard collections: The first one is the OHSUMED collection [10] used in TREC-9 Filtering Track [29]. This collection consists of 348,566 documents collected from the United States National Library of Medicine's bibliographic database between 1987 and 1991. The TREC-9 Filtering Track's collection contains 63 topics. The second one is the INFILE collection [5] that includes around 1.5 million news articles published in a three-year period (2004-2006) by Agence France Presse (AFP). We only considered the English documents in this collection. This collection was used in CLEF 2008-2009 INFILE (INformation FILtering Evaluation) Track [6]. The INFILE collection contains 50 topics covering two different categories: 30 topics focus on general news and events and the other 20 topics include scientific and technological issues. We considered the title and keywords of each topic as the initial profile of each user.

Experimental Setup. All the experiments were carried out using the Lemur toolkit[1]. All documents were stemmed using the Porter stemmer and stopped using the INQUERY stopword list. Similar to the CLEF 2009 Filtering Track, feedback is not allowed on discarded documents and limited number of feedback documents (200 feedback documents) is allowed in our experiments [5]. The embedding vectors were trained using the word2vec model[2] [19] on the target collections.

Parameters Setting. The Dirichlet prior smoothing parameter μ is set to the average document length of each collection. The free hyper-parameters α and maximum profile size were set using 5-fold cross validation over the topics of each collection and were selected from $\{0.1, \cdots, 0.9\}$ and $\{10, 30, 50\}$, respectively. The embedding dimension was set to 100 and the parameter c of the log-logistic model was set to 1.

5.2 Evaluation Metrics

Following the evaluation methodology in CLEF 2008-2009 Filtering Track [6], we use F1-measure as the main evaluation metric. To have complete sets of evaluations, we also report precision and recall. The reported results for each metric are based on 5-fold cross validation where that metric is optimized. Statistical significance of the differences between the corresponding measures were calculated using the two-tailed paired t-test at a 95% confidence level.

5.3 Results and Discussion

In this subsection, we first introduce our baselines. We further report and discuss the results achieved by the proposed method and the baselines.

Baselines. The baselines can be categorized as follows:

- **No profile updating**: this is our simple text recommendation model with no profile updating (NoUpdate).
- **Profile updating based on recommendation history**: these baselines use the past successful recommendations to adaptively update the user profiles. We use the mixture model (MIX) [37], the relevance model (RM3) [1, 15], and the log-logistic model (LL) [8] as different profile updating models in this category.

[1] http://www.lemurproject.org/

[2] https://code.google.com/p/word2vec/

Table 2: The updated profiles for the initial topic "fight against climate change". Note that the terms were stemmed.

total number of feedback documents	top 10 profile terms in descending order
2	kyoto, climat, greenhous, gase, toothless, protocol, reduct, emiss, meaning, ecolog
5	greenhous, kyoto, climat, gase, emiss, warm, protocol, acia, reduct, ratifi
10	climat, greenhous, emiss, kyoto, gase, warm, protocol, acia, dioxid, carbon
22	emiss, climat, greenhous, kyoto, gase, protocol, warm, carbon, dioxid, environment
34	emiss, climat, greenhous, kyoto, gase, warm, protocol, carbon, environment, dioxid

- **Profile updating based on semantic similarity**: these baselines only consider the semantic similarity of vocabulary terms to the initial user profiles. All of these models are based on word embedding vectors learned from the target collection. The first baseline in this category is based on the similarity of terms to the centroid vector of the profile terms (Cent). We also consider three other baselines in this category, including CombSUM, CombMNZ, and CombMAX, that were previously used by Kuzi et al. [13] for query expansion. We used these methods for updating user profile using previously successful recommendations.

Results. The experimental results are reported in Table 1. The highest value in each column is boldfaced. According to the table, the results achieved by all the profile updating methods are higher than those obtained by the NoUpdate model (except the results of CombMAX and LL in terms of Precision in OHSUMED collection). This shows the importance of profile updating in text recommendation. Among the profile updating methods based on recommendation history (i.e., MIX, RM3, and LL), LL outperforms the other methods in terms of F1-measure in INFILE dataset. This indicates the effectiveness of the log-logistic model for profile updating. The profile updating methods solely based on semantic similarities (i.e., Cent, CombSUM, CombMNZ, and CombMAX) perform worse than those based on recommendation history. This emphasizes on the fact that the past successful recommendations provide strong signals for representing the users' information needs. Among the profile updating methods based on semantic similarities, Cent achieves the highest F1-measures in both collections. Zamani and Croft [35] have theoretically proved that this model would result in the global optimum representation in terms of likelihood.

According to Table 1, the proposed semantic-aware profile updating model, i.e., LL-WE, outperforms all the baselines in terms of F1-measure in both collections. The method also achieves higher precision and recall values in the TREC-9 Filtering Track collection. The improvements are statistically significant in nearly all cases. This shows that incorporating semantic similarity in profile updating based on recommendation history leads to significant improvements.

To have an insight into the updated profiles, Table 2 reports the updated profile obtained by the LL-WE method for a random topic from the INFILE collection. According to this table, after recommending sufficient number of relevant documents, the profile becomes stable. The updated profiles contain relevant terms that can better represent the user's information need[3].

[3] Note that the narrative for this topic is "Relevant documents will describe the climatic policy implemented at the national or international level to fight against climatic change. They will speak about international agreements relative to air pollution control and more specifically to human induced greenhouse gases emissions reduction, responsible for climate warming".

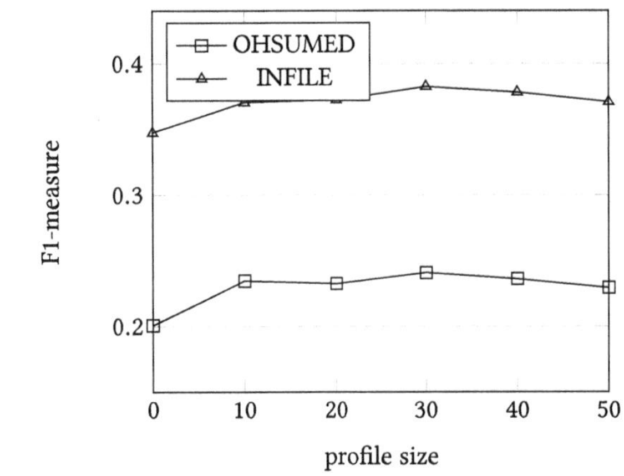

Figure 1: Sensitivity of the LL-WE method to the profile size in terms of F1-measure.

Sensitivity to the profile size. In this set of experiments, we study the sensitivity of the LL-WE method to the profile size. We sweeped the profile size from 0 to 50 terms. The results in terms of F1-measure are plotted in Figure 1. According to this figure, 30 is a reasonable profile size for the proposed profile updating model. Note that increasing the profile size does not lead to dramatic decrease in the recommendation performance.

6 CONCLUSIONS AND FUTURE WORK

In this paper, we focused on the profile updating task in text recommendation. We first proposed a log-logistic model for profile updating and further enriched our model by incorporating semantic similarities using distributed representations of words. We implemented our model in the language modeling framework and evaluated our models using two standard datasets: TREC-9 Filtering Track and CLEF 2008-2009 INFILE Track collections. The experiments demonstrated that the proposed semantic-aware log-logistic profile updating model significantly outperforms all the other profile updating models in both collections.

An interesting future direction is to consider semantic similarities in using negative feedback. In addition, this paper focused on the word embedding vectors that were learned based on term proximity. We also intend to investigate how to learn embedding vectors that are specific to the text recommendation task.

Acknowledgements. This work was supported in part by a grant from the Institute for Research in Fundamental Sciences (No. CS1396-4-51) and in part by the Center for Intelligent Information Retrieval. Any opinions, findings and conclusions or recommendations expressed in this material are those of the authors and do not necessarily reflect those of the sponsors.

REFERENCES

[1] Nasreen Abdul-jaleel, James Allan, W. Bruce Croft, Fernando Diaz, Leah Larkey, Xiaoyan Li, Donald Metzler, Mark D. Smucker, Trevor Strohman, Howard Turtle, and Courtney Wade. 2004. UMass at TREC 2004: Novelty and HARD. In *Proceedings of the 2004 Text Retrieval Conference (TREC '04)*. National Institute of Standards and Technology, Special Publication.

[2] Trapit Bansal, David Belanger, and Andrew McCallum. 2016. Ask the GRU: Multi-task Learning for Deep Text Recommendations. In *Proceedings of the 10th ACM Conference on Recommender Systems (RecSys '16)*. ACM, New York, NY, USA, 107–114.

[3] Trapit Bansal, Mrinal Das, and Chiranjib Bhattacharyya. 2015. Content Driven User Profiling for Comment-Worthy Recommendations of News and Blog Articles. In *Proceedings of the 9th ACM Conference on Recommender Systems (RecSys '15)*. ACM, New York, NY, USA, 195–202.

[4] Adam Berger and John Lafferty. 1999. Information Retrieval As Statistical Translation. In *Proceedings of the 22Nd Annual International ACM SIGIR Conference on Research and Development in Information Retrieval (SIGIR '99)*. ACM, New York, NY, USA, 222–229.

[5] Romaric Besançon, Stéphane Chaudiron, Djamel Mostefa, Ismaïl Timimi, and Khalid Choukri. 2008. The INFILE Project: a Crosslingual Filtering Systems Evaluation Campaign. In *Proceedings of the Sixth International Conference on Language Resources and Evaluation (LREC '08)*. ELRA, Marrakech, Morocco.

[6] Romaric Besançon, Stéphane Chaudiron, Djamel Mostefa, Ismaïl Timimi, Khalid Choukri, and Meriama Laïb. 2009. Information Filtering Evaluation: Overview of CLEF 2009 INFILE Track. In *Proceedings of the 10th Cross-language Evaluation Forum Conference on Multilingual Information Access Evaluation: Text Retrieval Experiments (CLEF '09)*. Springer-Verlag, Berlin, Heidelberg, 342–353.

[7] Toine Bogers and Antal van den Bosch. 2007. Comparing and Evaluating Information Retrieval Algorithms for News Recommendation. In *Proceedings of the 2007 ACM Conference on Recommender Systems (RecSys '07)*. ACM, New York, NY, USA, 141–144.

[8] Stéphane Clinchant and Eric Gaussier. 2010. Information-based Models for Ad Hoc IR. In *Proceedings of the 33rd International ACM SIGIR Conference on Research and Development in Information Retrieval (SIGIR '10)*. ACM, New York, NY, USA, 234–241.

[9] Ido Guy, Naama Zwerdling, Inbal Ronen, David Carmel, and Erel Uziel. 2010. Social Media Recommendation Based on People and Tags. In *Proceedings of the 33rd International ACM SIGIR Conference on Research and Development in Information Retrieval (SIGIR '10)*. ACM, New York, NY, USA, 194–201.

[10] William Hersh, Chris Buckley, T. J. Leone, and David Hickam. 1994. OHSUMED: An Interactive Retrieval Evaluation and New Large Test Collection for Research. In *Proceedings of the 17th Annual International ACM SIGIR Conference on Research and Development in Information Retrieval (SIGIR '94)*. Springer-Verlag New York, Inc., New York, NY, USA, 192–201.

[11] Yanbo Huang. 2016. *Exploiting Embedding in Content-Based Recommender systems.* Master's thesis. TU Delf.

[12] Balaji Krishnamurthy, Nikaash Puri, and Raghavender Goel. 2016. Learning Vector-space Representations of Items for Recommendations Using Word Embedding Models. *Procedia Computer Science* 80 (2016), 2205 – 2210.

[13] Saar Kuzi, Anna Shtok, and Oren Kurland. 2016. Query Expansion Using Word Embeddings. In *Proceedings of the 25th ACM International on Conference on Information and Knowledge Management (CIKM '16)*. ACM, New York, NY, USA, 1929–1932.

[14] John Lafferty and ChengXiang Zhai. 2001. Document Language Models, Query Models, and Risk Minimization for Information Retrieval. In *Proceedings of the 24th Annual International ACM SIGIR Conference on Research and Development in Information Retrieval (SIGIR '01)*. ACM, New York, NY, USA, 111–119.

[15] Victor Lavrenko and W. Bruce Croft. 2001. Relevance Based Language Models. In *Proceedings of the 24th Annual International ACM SIGIR Conference on Research and Development in Information Retrieval (SIGIR '01)*. ACM, New York, NY, USA, 120–127.

[16] Victor Lavrenko, Matt Schmill, Dawn Lawrie, Paul Ogilvie, David Jensen, and James Allan. 2000. Language Models for Financial News Recommendation. In *Proceedings of the Ninth International Conference on Information and Knowledge Management (CIKM '00)*. ACM, New York, NY, USA, 389–396.

[17] Pasquale Lops, Marco de Gemmis, and Giovanni Semeraro. 2011. Content-based Recommender Systems: State of the Art and Trends. In *Recommender Systems Handbook*. Springer, 73–105.

[18] Julian McAuley and Jure Leskovec. 2013. Hidden Factors and Hidden Topics: Understanding Rating Dimensions with Review Text. In *Proceedings of the 7th ACM Conference on Recommender Systems (RecSys '13)*. ACM, New York, NY, USA, 165–172.

[19] Tomas Mikolov, Ilya Sutskever, Kai Chen, Greg S. Corrado, and Jeff Dean. 2013. Distributed representations of words and phrases and their compositionality. In *Advances in Neural Information Processing Systems (NIPS '13)*. 3111–3119.

[20] Ali Montazeralghaem, Hamed Zamani, and Azadeh Shakery. 2016. Axiomatic Analysis for Improving the Log-Logistic Feedback Model. In *Proceedings of the 39th International ACM SIGIR Conference on Research and Development in Information Retrieval (SIGIR '16)*. ACM, New York, NY, USA, 765–768.

[21] Cataldo Musto, Giovanni Semeraro, Marco de Gemmis, and Pasquale Lops. 2015. Word Embedding Techniques for Content-based Recommender Systems: An Empirical Evaluation. In *Proceedings of the 9th ACM Conference on Recommender Systems (Posters) (RecSys '15)*. ACM, New York, NY, USA.

[22] Cataldo Musto, Giovanni Semeraro, Marco de Gemmis, and Pasquale Lops. 2016. Learning Word Embeddings from Wikipedia for Content-Based Recommender System. In *Proceedings of the 38th European Conference on Information Retrieval (ECIR '16)*. Springer International Publishing.

[23] Makbule Gulcin Ozsoy. 2016. From Word Embeddings to Item Recommendation. *CoRR* abs/1601.01356 (2016). http://arxiv.org/abs/1601.01356

[24] MichaelJ. Pazzani and Daniel Billsus. 2007. Content-Based Recommendation Systems. In *The Adaptive Web*. Lecture Notes in Computer Science, Vol. 4321. Springer Berlin Heidelberg, 325–341.

[25] Owen Phelan, Kevin McCarthy, and Barry Smyth. 2009. Using Twitter to Recommend Real-time Topical News. In *Proceedings of the Third ACM Conference on Recommender Systems (RecSys '09)*. ACM, New York, NY, USA, 385–388.

[26] Jay M. Ponte and W. Bruce Croft. 1998. A Language Modeling Approach to Information Retrieval. In *Proceedings of the 21st Annual International ACM SIGIR Conference on Research and Development in Information Retrieval (SIGIR '98)*. ACM, New York, NY, USA, 275–281.

[27] Hossein Rahmatizadeh Zagheli, Mozhdeh Ariannezhad, and Azadeh Shakery. 2017. Negative Feedback in the Language Modeling Framework for Text Recommendation. In *Proceedings of the 39th European Conference on Information Retrieval (ECIR '17)*. Springer International Publishing.

[28] Navid Rekabsaz, Mihai Lupu, Allan Hanbury, and Hamed Zamani. 2017. Word Embedding Causes Topic Shifting; Exploit Global Context!. In *Proceedings of the 40th Annual International ACM SIGIR Conference on Research and Development in Information Retrieval (SIGIR '17)*. ACM, New York, NY, USA.

[29] Stephen Robertson and David A. Hull. 2000. The TREC-9 filtering track final report. In *Proceedings of Ninth Text REtrieval Conference (TREC-9)*. National Institute of Standards and Technology, Special Publication, 25–40.

[30] Joseph John Rocchio. 1971. Relevance feedback in information retrieval. *The Smart retrieval system-experiments in automatic document processing* (1971), 313–323.

[31] Chong Wang and David M. Blei. 2011. Collaborative Topic Modeling for Recommending Scientific Articles. In *Proceedings of the 17th ACM SIGKDD International Conference on Knowledge Discovery and Data Mining (KDD '11)*. ACM, New York, NY, USA, 448–456.

[32] Jia Wang, Qing Li, Yuanzhu Peter Chen, Jiafen Liu, Chen Zhang, and Zhangxi Lin. 2010. News Recommendation in Forum-Based Social Media. In *Proceedings of AAAI Conference on Artificial Intelligence*. AAAI Press.

[33] Hamed Zamani. 2015. *Recommender Systems for Multi-Publisher Environments.* Master's thesis. University of Tehran.

[34] Hamed Zamani and W. Bruce Croft. 2016. Embedding-based Query Language Models. In *Proceedings of the 2016 ACM International Conference on the Theory of Information Retrieval (ICTIR '16)*. ACM, New York, NY, USA, 147–156.

[35] Hamed Zamani and W. Bruce Croft. 2016. Estimating Embedding Vectors for Queries. In *Proceedings of the 2016 ACM International Conference on the Theory of Information Retrieval (ICTIR '16)*. ACM, New York, NY, USA, 123–132.

[36] Hamed Zamani and W. Bruce Croft. 2017. Relevance-based Word Embedding. In *Proceedings of the 40th Annual International ACM SIGIR Conference on Research and Development in Information Retrieval (SIGIR '17)*. ACM, New York, NY, USA.

[37] ChengXiang Zhai and John Lafferty. 2001. Model-based Feedback in the Language Modeling Approach to Information Retrieval. In *Proceedings of the Tenth International Conference on Information and Knowledge Management (CIKM '01)*. ACM, New York, NY, USA, 403–410.

[38] ChengXiang Zhai and John Lafferty. 2004. A Study of Smoothing Methods for Language Models Applied to Information Retrieval. *ACM Trans. Inf. Syst.* 22, 2 (April 2004), 179–214.

[39] Yi Zhang and Jamie Callan. 2001. Maximum Likelihood Estimation for Filtering Thresholds. In *Proceedings of the 24th Annual International ACM SIGIR Conference on Research and Development in Information Retrieval (SIGIR '01)*. ACM, New York, NY, USA, 294–302.

A Multi-criteria Recommender System Exploiting Aspect-based Sentiment Analysis of Users' Reviews

Cataldo Musto
Dept. of Computer Science - University of Bari
cataldo.musto@uniba.it

Marco de Gemmis
Dept. of Computer Science - University of Bari
marco.degemmis@uniba.it

Giovanni Semeraro
Dept. of Computer Science - University of Bari
giovanni.semeraro@uniba.it

Pasquale Lops
Dept. of Computer Science - University of Bari
pasquale.lops@uniba.it

ABSTRACT

In this paper we propose a *multi-criteria recommender system* based on collaborative filtering (CF) techniques, which exploits the information conveyed by *users' reviews* to provide a multi-faceted representation of users' interests.

To this end, we exploited a framework for *opinion mining* and *sentiment analysis*, which automatically extracts relevant aspects and sentiment scores from users' reviews. As an example, in a *restaurant recommendation* scenario, the aspects may regard *food quality, service, position, athmosphere* of the place and so on. Such a multi-faceted representation of the user is used to feed a multi-criteria CF algorithm which predicts user interest in a particular item and provides her with recommendations.

In the experimental session we evaluated the performance of the algorithm against several state-of-the-art baselines; Results confirmed the insight behind this work, since our approach was able to overcome both single-criteria recommendation algorithms as well as more sophisticated techniques based on matrix factorization.

CCS CONCEPTS

• **Information systems → Recommender systems**;

KEYWORDS

Recommender Systems, Opinion Mining, Sentiment Analysis

ACM Reference format:
Cataldo Musto, Marco de Gemmis, Giovanni Semeraro, and Pasquale Lops. 2017. A Multi-criteria Recommender System Exploiting Aspect-based Sentiment Analysis of Users' Reviews. In *Proceedings of RecSys'17, August 27–31, 2017, Como, Italy, ,* 5 pages.
DOI: http://dx.doi.org/10.1145/3109859.3109905

1 BACKGROUND AND MOTIVATIONS

The massive spread of platforms for sharing opinions and reviews is one of the most interesting trends we are recently witnessing in the context of *Web 2.0*. Given how much data is floating around in the Web, it is quite straightforward to think about new strategies to gather and process such data, since several applications may benefit from such a better picture of what people *think* and what people *like*.

As an example, the exploitation of the information conveyed by users' reviews can be useful to tackle one of the issues Recommender Systems (RS) typically suffer from. Indeed, RSs model users' opinions about a certain item through a single discrete scale. This is a clear over-simplification, since the user who expresses the rating may have enjoyed some aspects of the item (e.g. *the quality of the food*) and may have not enjoyed others, as the *service* of the restaurant. The idea of learning users' preferences [6] by expressing several ratings, in order to evaluate different facets of the items has already been investigated in literature, and those systems fall under the name of *multi-criteria recommender systems* [2, 10]. The first attempts towards this direction [8, 9, 14, 15] showed that multi-criteria ratings can improve the predictive accuracy of the system, but they suffer from the issue of overcharging the users during the training process, by asking them to rate the same item many times.

In this work we tackle this problem by proposing a *multi-criteria RS* which automatically learns the preferences of the target user by mining the information conveyed by the reviews she wrote. To this end, we exploited a framework for *aspect extraction* and *sentiment analysis* which automatically extracts the *aspects* discussed in the review along with their *sentiment*, and we used this multi-faceted representation of users' preferences to feed a neighborhood-based CF algorithm which predicts the interest of the target user in a particular item.

As shown by Chen et al. [5], this class of RS is typically referred to as *review-based RS*. Regardless their effectiveness, such systems typically rely on a fixed set of aspects (e.g., in a restaurant scenario: *food, atmosphere, position, service*) which is statically defined and is automatically filled in by analyzing the review. As an example, Chen et al. [4] defined a set of eight different hotel-related aspects and five restaurant-related ones. Differently from such literature, in our work also the set of the aspects we used to represent the interests of the user is automatically learned from the text, as [13] proposed for Chinese restaurant reviews. Moreover, a distinguishing and novel aspect of this work lies in the ability of extracting also *couple of related aspects* (as *food-meat, food-fish*), thus building a more fine-grained representation of the preferences.

The rest of the paper is organized as follows: in Section 2 we describe the framework for aspect extraction and our multi-criteria RS.

RecSys'17, August 27–31, 2017, Como, Italy

DOI: http://dx.doi.org/10.1145/3109859.3109905

```
[Review] "I loved the food, the best
sweet and sour soup ever! Everything
was delicious and favorable. Delivery
is pretty good, nice people."

Overall: 4.0 / 5.0

Aspect          Sentiment score
food            4.0
people          4.0
food-soup       5.0
```

Figure 1: Our framework for aspect extraction at work.

Next, Section 3 shows the findings emerged from the experiments and in Section 4 we define future research directions.

2 METHODOLOGY

In the first part of this section we describe our framework for opinion mining and sentiment analysis, while in the latter we show how aspects and sentiment scores extracted from the reviews are used to feed a multi-criteria collaborative filtering algorithm.

Extracting Aspects and Sentiment from Reviews. In this work we exploit a framework for Sentiment Aspect-Based Retrieval called SABRE, proposed by Caputo et al. [3]. In a nutshell, given a set of reviews[1] $R = \{r_1, r_2 \ldots r_n\}$, SABRE produces as output a set of quintuples $\langle r_i, a_{ij}, a_{ijk}, rel(a_{ijk}, r_i), sent(a_{ijk}, r_i)\rangle$ representing the review r_i, the *j-th* aspect a_{ij} extracted from the review, the *k-th* sub-aspect a_{ijk} related to the aspect a_{ij}, the relevance $rel(a_{ijk}, r_i)$ of the aspect in the document, and its sentiment $sent(a_{ijk}, r_i)$, respectively. In order to carry out the aspect extraction process, we used the *Kullback-Leibler divergence (KL-divergence, referred to as* δ*)*, a non-symmetric measure of the difference between two distributions. Formally, given two corpora c_a and c_b and a term t, pointwise KL-divergence is calculated as:

$$\delta_t(c_a||c_b) = p(t, c_a)log\frac{p(t, c_a)}{p(t, c_b)} \tag{1}$$

Our algorithm for aspect extraction is based on the idea that the use of language differs when talking about a specific domain with respect to a general topic, then this method aims at selecting the aspects whose distributions in a specific domain (e.g. *restaurant reviews*) diverge from those in a general corpus (e.g. the British National Corpus BNC[2]). Thus, we are interested in those aspects mentioned in the review more often than usual. Our strategy for identifying the main aspects mentioned in the reviews follows:

Require: review r_i, general corpus BNC, domain corpus d
Ensure: set of main aspects A and relevance scores
  $A = \{\}$, $T = nouns(r_i)$
  for all $t_k \in T$ **do**
    if $\delta_{t_k}(d||BNC) > \epsilon$ **then**
      $a_{ij} \leftarrow t_k$
      $A = A \bigcup \{a_{ij}\}$
      $rel(a_{ij}, r_i) \leftarrow \delta_{t_k}$
    end if
  end for

[1]Documents and reviews can be used as synonyms, since the framework can be exploited to extract relevant aspects from any kind of textual document.
[2]http://www.natcorp.ox.ac.uk/

Given a review r_i we extract all the nouns from the review and we calculate KL-divergence for each of them. Those having a KL-divergence greater then a threshold ϵ are labeled as *main aspects*, and the KL-divergence is used as relevance score for that aspect.

Next, given the set A containing the main aspects, our framework identifies the sub-aspects related to each $a_{ij} \in A$. To this end, we exploited two measures already used in literature for keyphrase extraction [22], as the *phraseness* and the *informativeness* of a couple of terms. Specifically, the *phraseness* calculates how likely the terms together form a phrase, while the *informativeness* calculates how much is the gain in information when the terms are modeled together. Due to space reasons, we can't provide more details on the extraction of aspects and sub-aspects. We suggest to refer to [3] for a more thorough description of the framework.

However, given such measures, for each main aspect a_{ij} we passed again through all the terms t_k in the review r_i and we labeled as sub-aspect a_{ijk} all the t_k whose *phraseness* and *informativeness* overcome a threshold γ. At the end of the process we obtain a *hierarchy* of aspects and sub-aspects extracted from the review, as that presented in Figure 1. In this case, *soup* is automatically identified as sub-aspect of the main aspect *food*, but food is also a main aspect, so two opinions emerge from the analysis of this review: a good one about the *food* in general, and an higher one specifically related to the *soup*. As previously stated, the process of building such a hierarchy is totally unsupervised, thus we are not bound to a fixed set of aspects, as it happens in most of the current literature, but we dynamically define the *aspects* on the ground of what people actually *think* (and *write*) about a specific item.

Finally, our framework provides all the aspects and sub-aspects extracted from the review with a sentiment score $sent(a_{ijk}, r_i)$. As regards sentiment analysis, we exploited two alternative strategies: a model-based sentiment analysis algorithm included in Stanford CoreNLP[3] which uses deep learning techniques [21], and a lexicon-based algorithm [17] based on the AFINN wordlist [18], which contains about 2500 English words that have been manually tagged with a score that can range from positive (+5) to negative (−5). In both cases, the algorithms return a sentiment score associated to each aspect and sub-aspect extracted from the review, according to the sentiment of the piece of text the aspect is mentioned in.

Multi-Criteria Recommendations. Given such a pipeline, we are able to extract the aspects, the sub-aspects, their relevance (according to KL-divergence) and the sentiment they convey from each specific review. Such a representation is then used to feed a multi-criteria recommendation algorithm based on CF techniques.

Specifically, we considered the sentiment scores extracted by our framework as the *ratings* the user expressed, and we exploited the multi-dimensional euclidean distance proposed by Adomavicius et al. [1] to calculate how similar two *users* (or two *items*) are according to the opinions expressed in the reviews. In the following, we will show how our multi-criteria recommendations are generated in both *user-to-user* and *item-to-item* scenarios.

Multi-criteria User-to-User CF. Similarity between users u_j ed u_k is calculated as the opposite of the distance $dist(u_j, u_k)$, defined as:

[3]http://stanfordnlp.github.io/CoreNLP/

$$dist(u_j, u_k) = \frac{1}{|I(u_j, u_k)|} + \sum_{i \in I(u_j, u_k)} d(R(u_j, i), R(u_k, i)) \quad (2)$$

where $I(u_j, u_k)$ is the set of the co-rated items and $R(u_j, i)$ is the rating expressed by user u_j on item i. Next, if n aspects are mentioned in both reviews, the overall distance is calculated as:

$$d(R(u_j, i), R(u_k, i) = \sqrt{\sum_{a=1}^{n} |R_a(u_j, i) - R_a(u_k, i)|^2} \quad (3)$$

Finally, rating prediction of user u on item i is calculated as the *weighted sum approach* [1] on the top-k neighbors of the user, as:

$$R(u, i) = \sum_{j=1}^{k} \frac{sim(u, u_j) \cdot R(u_j, i)}{|sim(u, u_j)|} \quad (4)$$

Multi-criteria Item-to-Item CF. The similarity between two items i_j and i_k is again the opposite of their distance $dist(i_j, i_k)$ calculated as:

$$dist(i_j, i_k) = \frac{1}{|U(i_j, i_k)|} + \sum_{u \in U(i_j, i_k)} d(R(u, i_j), R(u, i_k)) \quad (5)$$

where $U(i_j, i_k)$ is the set of users who expressed a rating for both i_j and i_k. Again, if n aspects are discussed in the review, then the multi-dimensional distance is calculated as:

$$d(R(u, i_j), R(u, i_k)) = \sqrt{\sum_{c=0}^{n} |R_c(u, i_j) - R_c(u, i_k)|^2} \quad (6)$$

Finally, ratings $R(u, i)$ are predicted using the *weighted sum approach* as it happened in the user-to-user scenario.

$$R(u, i) = \frac{\sum sim(i, j) \cdot R(u, j)}{\sum_{u \in U(i,j)} |sim(i, j)|} \quad (7)$$

In the experimental session we evaluated the effectiveness of both multi-criteria algorithms on varying of different datasets as well as of different configurations of our framework for aspect extraction and sentiment analysis.

3 EXPERIMENTAL EVALUATION

Experiments were carried out on the ground of the following research questions: **(1)** Which combination of the parameters of our framework for aspect extraction and sentiment analysis leads to the best predictive accuracy of our multi-criteria RS? **(2)** How does our algorithm perform, when compared to a single-criteria CF algorithm as well as to other state-of-the-art CF techniques based on matrix factorization?

Experimental design. Experiments were carried out against three state-of-the-art datasets used for evaluating the effectiveness of review-based RS, as *Yelp*[4], *TripAdvisor*[5] and *Amazon*[6]. Table 1 reports some statistics about the datasets.

Our framework for aspect extraction and sentiment analysis was run by comparing different combinations of parameters: first, reviews were processed by removing stop-words and by identifying entities and collocations. Next, the number of aspects/sub-aspects extracted by the framework was set to 10 and 50. In order to assess about the effectiveness of *sub-aspects*, in some experimental session only the main aspects were extracted. As sentiment analysis algorithm, both CoreNLP and AFINN-based algorithms were exploited. The value ϵ, used to define threshold for KL-divergence score, was set to 0.1. As multi-criteria recommendation algorithm, we used both *user-based* and *item-based* CF. The previously introduced multi-dimensional Euclidean distance was exploited to calculate the neighborhood. Neighborhood size was set to 10, 30 and 80 for all the datasets. We used these values since bigger neighborhoods lead to a decrease in the performance of the algorithm.

[4] https://www.kaggle.com/c/yelp-recruiting/data
[5] http://www.cs.cmu.edu/ jiweil/html/hotel-review.html
[6] http://jmcauley.ucsd.edu/data/amazon/links.html

Table 1: Datasets Statistics

	Yelp	TripAdvisor	Amazon
Users	45,981	536,952	826,773
Items	11,537	3,945	50,210
Ratings/Reviews	229,906	796,958	1,324,759
Sparsity	99,95%	99,96%	99,99%

As regards the baselines, we used single-criteria *user-based* and *item-based CF* [12]. In this case, Euclidean distance and Pearson correlation was used to calculate similarities and neighborhood was set again to 10, 30 and 80. Finally, we also evaluated our algorithm against matrix factorization techniques, as the implementations of Stochastic Gradient Descent (SGD), ParallelSGD [19] and ALSWR [23] available in Mahout[7]. For each baseline we will only report the results of the best-performing combinations of parameters.

The whole experimental session was carried out as a 10-fold cross-validation. The effectiveness of our algorithms was calculated by averaging the Mean Average Error (MAE) obtained on each fold. In order to ensure the reproducibility of the results, metrics were calculated by using Rival [20] framework.

Discussion of the results. In this first experiment we evaluated different configurations of our framework for *aspect-based sentiment analysis*. Results are shown in Table 2 and 3. Due to space reasons, we only report the results obtained with AFINN sentiment analysis algorithm, since it did not emerge any significant difference with those obtained with CoreNLP algorithm. As regards *multi-criteria user-based CF*, on both *Yelp* and *Tripadvisor* the best results are obtained by extracting the *top-10 aspects* gathered from the data. Moreover, on both datasets and for all the neighborhood sizes, the results obtained with 10 aspects are better than those obtained with 50 aspects. Due to this reason, we did not evaluated a larger space of aspects. Another interesting outcome emerging on *Yelp* and *TripAdvisor* is that the use of sub-aspects further improve the performance of the framework, since in all the comparisons the extraction of sub-aspects leads to a lower MAE. However, such results are not confirmed on Amazon data. In this case, the best results are obtained by using top-50 aspects (without sub-aspects). Further investigations are needed to better understand this behavior. It is worth to note that the best-performing configurations for all datasets is that exploiting the top-10 neighbors on all the datasets.

[7] https://mahout.apache.org/

Table 2: Results of Experiment 1 for *multi-criteria user-based CF*. The best-performing configuration is highlighted in bold.

Configuration			Dataset		
#neigh.	**#asp.**	**sub-asp**	**Yelp**	**TripAdvisor**	**Amazon**
10	10	Y	**0.8362**	**0.7111**	0.6464
10	10	N	0.8410	0.7564	0.6335
10	50	Y	0.8410	0.7269	0.6346
10	50	N	0.8364	0.8007	**0.6276**
30	10	Y	0.8461	0.7677	0.7120
30	10	N	0.8473	0.7722	0.7122
30	50	Y	0.8474	0.7743	0.7101
30	50	N	0.8494	0.8003	0.7140
80	10	Y	0.8579	0.7971	0.7584
80	10	N	0.8592	0.7953	0.7554
80	50	Y	0.8590	0.7907	0.7544
80	50	N	0.8597	0.7995	0.7554

Table 3: Results of Experiment 1 for *multi-criteria item-based CF*. The best-performing configuration is highlighted in bold.

Configuration		Dataset		
#asp.	**sub-asp**	**Yelp**	**TripAdvisor**	**Amazon**
10	Y	**0.8640**	**0.8245**	**0.8110**
10	N	0.8643	0.8252	0.8117
50	Y	0.8641	0.8254	0.8118
50	N	0.8648	0.8260	0.8124

Table 4: Top-10 *main* aspects extracted for each dataset.

Yelp	place, food, service, restaurant, price menu, staff, drink, lunch, table
Tripadvisor	hotel, room, staff, location, service breakfast, restaurant, bathroom, price, view
Amazon	game, graphic, story, character, player price, gameplay, controller, level, music

Simlilar outcomes are confirmed by analyzing the results obtained by *multi-criteria item-based CF*, even if with a smaller gap. For the sake of completeness, in Table 4 we report the top-10 main aspects extracted from each dataset. Due to space reasons, it is not possible to report more aspects or sub-aspects of each main aspect.

Next, in Experiment 2 we compared the best-performing configuration to several baselines. First, we evaluated the effectiveness of single-criteria CF algorithms, as User-to-User CF (U2U) and Item-to-Item (I2I). Results are reported in Table 5. In this case, we report the values of the two similarity measures, euclidean and Pearson, obtained with the optimal number of neighbors. As we expected, our multi-criteria CF algorithm overcomes all the baselines on all the dataset. Such improvements are obtained on both U2U and I2I algorithm.

Table 5: Results of Experiment 2. The best-performing configuration is highlighted in bold. Next to each baseline we report the similarity measure used in that specific run. N.A. refers to not available results.

	Dataset		
Configuration	**Yelp**	**Tripadvisor**	**Amazon**
Multi-U2U	**0.8362**	**0.7111**	**0.6276**
U2U-Euclidean	0.8860	0.8337	0.7254
U2U-Pearson	0.9640	1.1222	0.9789
Static-Multi-U2U	N.A.	0.7980	N.A.
Multi-I2I	0.8640	0.8245	0.8110
I2I-Euclidean	0.8745	0.8429	0.8177
I2I-Pearson	1.1794	0.8644	0.9679
Static-Multi-I2I	N.A.	0.8474	N.A
RatingSGD	0.8409	0.7450	0.8859
ParallelSGD	0.8409	0.7449	0.8852
ALSWR	0.9545	0.9053	1.0354

Next, we compared our algorithm to more sophisticated baselines based on matrix factorization algorithms. Moreover, given that TripAdvisor dataset has a static set of six aspects for each review *(cleanliness, location, value, service, sleep quality* and *overall*), we also compared our approach to a (*statically defined*) multi-criteria algorithm based on such aspects. As shown in Table 5, our approach overcomes again all the baselines we took into account, those based on matrix factorization and that exploiting a static multi-criteria algorithm. These results definitely confirmed our insights, since we showed that our strategy can overcome both strategies exploiting single ratings (with or without matrix factorization) as well as multi-criteria algorithms that exploit a fixed set of pre-defined aspects. The best overall results are obtained when **multi-criteria User-to-User CF** is used as recommendation algorithm.

4 CONCLUSIONS AND FUTURE WORK

In this paper we presented a multi-criteria RS which exploits users reviews to build a multi-faceted representation of users interests. The novelty of this work lies in the fact that our framework is able to unsupervisedly extract relevant aspects from the review, and it is not bound to a fixed and static set of pre-defined aspects. Moreover, our algorithm also extracts sub-aspects related to the main aspect, thus building a finer-grained representation of the content conveyed by the review. As shown in the experiments, our framework overcame all the baselines taken into account, even those based on sophisticated techniques for matrix factorization.

As future work, we will encode the features extracted from users' reviews on context-aware recommendation algorithms [16]. Moreover, we will also evaluate the use of ontologies and rules [11], in order to implement reasoning mechanisms to better identify the most relevant aspects in the reviews. Finally, we will evaluate how our framework impacts on different evaluation metrics, as the *serendipity* of the recommendations [7]

REFERENCES

[1] Gediminas Adomavicius and YoungOk Kwon. 2007. New recommendation techniques for multicriteria rating systems. *IEEE Intelligent Systems* 22, 3 (2007).

[2] Gediminas Adomavicius and YoungOk Kwon. 2015. Multi-criteria recommender systems. In *Recommender systems handbook*. Springer, 847–880.

[3] Annalina Caputo, Pierpaolo Basile, Marco de Gemmis, Pasquale Lops, Giovanni Semeraro, and Gaetano Rossiello. 2017. SABRE: A Sentiment Aspect-Based Retrieval Engine. In *Information Filtering and Retrieval*. Springer, 63–78.

[4] Guanliang Chen and Li Chen. 2015. Augmenting service recommender systems by incorporating contextual opinions from user reviews. *User Modeling and User-Adapted Interaction* 25, 3 (2015), 295–329.

[5] Li Chen, Guanliang Chen, and Feng Wang. 2015. Recommender systems based on user reviews: the state of the art. *User Modeling and User-Adapted Interaction* 25, 2 (2015), 99–154.

[6] Marco De Gemmis, Leo Iaquinta, Pasquale Lops, Cataldo Musto, Fedelucio Narducci, and Giovanni Semeraro. 2010. Learning preference models in recommender systems. In *Preference Learning*. Springer Berlin Heidelberg, 387–407.

[7] Marco de Gemmis, Pasquale Lops, Giovanni Semeraro, and Cataldo Musto. 2015. An investigation on the serendipity problem in recommender systems. *Information Processing & Management* 51, 5 (2015), 695–717.

[8] Yanjie Fu, Bin Liu, Yong Ge, Zijun Yao, and Hui Xiong. 2014. User preference learning with multiple information fusion for restaurant recommendation. In *Proceedings of the 2014 SIAM International Conference on Data Mining*. SIAM, 470–478.

[9] Matthias Fuchs and Markus Zanker. 2012. Multi-criteria ratings for recommender systems: an empirical analysis in the tourism domain. *E-commerce and web technologies* (2012), 100–111.

[10] Dietmar Jannach, Zeynep Karakaya, and Fatih Gedikli. 2012. Accuracy improvements for multi-criteria recommender systems. In *Proceedings of the 13th ACM conference on electronic commerce*. ACM, 674–689.

[11] Loredana Laera, Valentina A. M. Tamma, Trevor J. M. Bench-Capon, and Giovanni Semeraro. 2004. SweetProlog: A System to Integrate Ontologies and Rules. In *Rules and Rule Markup Languages for the Semantic Web: Third International Workshop, RuleML 2004, Hiroshima, Japan, November 8, 2004. Proceedings (Lecture Notes in Computer Science)*, Grigoris Antoniou and Harold Boley (Eds.), Vol. 3323. Springer, 188–193.

[12] Greg Linden, Brent Smith, and Jeremy York. 2003. Amazon. com recommendations: Item-to-item collaborative filtering. *IEEE Internet computing* 7, 1 (2003), 76–80.

[13] Hongyan Liu, Jun He, Tingting Wang, Wenting Song, and Xiaoyang Du. 2013. Combining user preferences and user opinions for accurate recommendation. *Electronic Commerce Research and Applications* 12, 1 (2013), 14–23.

[14] Liwei Liu, Nikolay Mehandjiev, and Dong-Ling Xu. 2011. Multi-criteria service recommendation based on user criteria preferences. In *Proceedings of the fifth ACM conference on Recommender systems*. ACM, 77–84.

[15] Nikos Manouselis and Constantina Costopoulou. 2007. Experimental analysis of design choices in multiattribute utility collaborative filtering. *International Journal of Pattern Recognition and Artificial Intelligence* 21, 02 (2007), 311–331.

[16] Cataldo Musto, Giovanni Semeraro, Pasquale Lops, and Marco de Gemmis. 2014. Combining distributional semantics and entity linking for context-aware content-based recommendation. In *User Modeling, Adaptation, and Personalization*. Springer, 381–392.

[17] Cataldo Musto, Giovanni Semeraro, and Marco Polignano. 2014. A comparison of lexicon-based approaches for sentiment analysis of microblog posts. *DART 2014: Information Filtering and Retrieval. CEUR-WS.org, Volume 1314* (2014), 59–68.

[18] Finn Årup Nielsen. 2011. A new ANEW: Evaluation of a word list for sentiment analysis in microblogs. *arXiv preprint arXiv:1103.2903* (2011).

[19] Benjamin Recht, Christopher Re, Stephen Wright, and Feng Niu. 2011. Hogwild: A lock-free approach to parallelizing stochastic gradient descent. In *Advances in Neural Information Processing Systems*. 693–701.

[20] Alan Said and Alejandro Bellogín. 2014. Rival: a toolkit to foster reproducibility in recommender system evaluation. In *Proceedings of the 8th ACM Conference on Recommender systems*. ACM, 371–372.

[21] Richard Socher, Alex Perelygin, Jean Y Wu, Jason Chuang, Christopher D Manning, Andrew Y Ng, and Christopher Potts. 2013. Recursive deep models for semantic compositionality over a sentiment treebank. In *Proceedings of the conference on empirical methods in natural language processing (EMNLP)*, Vol. 1631. Citeseer, 1642.

[22] Takashi Tomokiyo and Matthew Hurst. 2003. A language model approach to keyphrase extraction. In *Proceedings of the ACL 2003 workshop on Multiword expressions: analysis, acquisition and treatment-Volume 18*. Association for Computational Linguistics, 33–40.

[23] Yunhong Zhou, Dennis Wilkinson, Robert Schreiber, and Rong Pan. 2008. Large-scale parallel collaborative filtering for the Netflix prize. In *International Conference on Algorithmic Applications in Management*. Springer, 337–348.

Exploring the Semantic Gap for Movie Recommendations

Mehdi Elahi
Free University of Bozen - Bolzano
Piazza Domenicani 3
Bozen - Bolzano 39100, Italy
meelahi@unibz.it

Yashar Deldjoo
Politecnico di Milano
Via Ponzio 34/5
Milan 20133, Italy
yashar.deldjoo@polimi.it

Farshad Bakhshandegan Moghaddam
Karlsruhe Institute of Technology
Karlsruhe 76131, Germany
ol5379@kit.edu

Leonardo Cella
Politecnico di Milano
Via Ponzio 34/5
Milan 20133, Italy
leonardo.cella@mail.polimi.it

Stefano Cereda
Politecnico di Milano
Via Ponzio 34/5
Milan 20133, Italy
stefano.Cereda@mail.polimi.it

Paolo Cremonesi
Politecnico di Milano
Via Ponzio 34/5
Milan 20133, Italy
paolo.cremonesi@polimi.it

ABSTRACT

In the last years, there has been much attention given to the *semantic gap* problem in multimedia retrieval systems. Much effort has been devoted to bridge this gap by building tools for the extraction of high-level, semantics-based features from multimedia content, as low-level features are not considered useful because they deal primarily with representing the perceived content rather than the semantics of it.

In this paper, we explore a different point of view by leveraging the gap between low-level and high-level features. We experiment with a recent approach for movie recommendation that extract low-level Mise-en-Scène features from multimedia content and combine it with high-level features provided by the wisdom of the crowd.

To this end, we first performed an offline performance assessment by implementing a pure content-based recommender system with three different versions of the same algorithm, respectively based on (i) conventional movie attributes, (ii) mise-en-scène features, and (iii) a hybrid method that interleaves recommendations based on movie attributes and mise-en-scène features. In a second study, we designed an empirical study involving 100 subjects and collected data regarding the quality perceived by the users. Results from both studies show that the introduction of mise-en-scène features in conjunction with traditional movie attributes improves both offline and online quality of recommendations.

CCS CONCEPTS

•Information systems → Recommender systems;

1 INTRODUCTION AND CONTEXT

In the last years, we have seen much attention given to the semantic gap problem in multimedia retrieval systems [20, 24]. The semantic gap is the gap between the high-level concepts that users expect when searching for interesting multimedia content (*e.g.*, genre, plot, actors) and the low-level features that it is possible to automatically extract from the same content (*e.g.*, brightness, contrast, *etc.*). The users' ability to comfortably and efficiently use multimedia systems is impacted as the result of the sharp discontinuity that exists between the primitive low-level features and the richness of user queries encountered in multimedia search. As a result, the multimedia information retrieval community has long struggled to *bridge* this semantic gap as several studies have confirmed the difficulty of addressing users' information needs with such low-level features, because they deal primarily with representing the perceived content rather than the semantics of it [14, 20].

Because of this gap, most movie recommender systems rely on the assumption that user preferences are mainly influenced by the high-level *semantic* features of movies (*e.g.*, plot, genre, director, actors) and, to a less extent, by the *stylistic* properties [10] (*e.g.*, color, motion, lighting key). Recommendations are automatically computed using implicit or explicit preferences of users on these attributes [1, 8]. However, recent works on RSs suggest that users' preferences when choosing a product are influenced more by the *visual* aspect of items and less by their semantic or syntactic properties [11, 19, 26, 29].

In this paper, we make a different assumption. We still believe that the semantic gap exists and limits the adoption of low-level features in information retrieval applications, where the goal is to provide a way of indexing multimedia content so that users can *explicitly* (*i.e.*, manually) query that content at the semantic level. However, we wish to investigate if this assumption holds also for recommender systems, where the goal is for the system to *automatically* find content that the user likes, without the user querying the system.

Our research hypothesis is that the semantic gap is not a problem but an opportunity. Our goal is to leverage the low-level features automatically extracted from multimedia content and complement them with the high-level features. For this purpose, we explore and evaluate a recent approach for movie recommendations that integrates traditional high-level semantic attributes, such as genre, director and cast, with low-level mise-en-scène features, *i.e.*, the design aspects of movie making that influence aesthetic and style. Examples of mise-en-scène characteristics are lighting, colors, background, and movements.

RecSys '17, August 27–31, 2017, Como, Italy.

DOI: http://dx.doi.org/10.1145/3109859.3109908

We believe that mise-en-scène features can be used to make video recommender systems more effective and useful as they help in strengthening two weak spots when working with semantic attributes: lack of diversity and novelty in video recommendations [16]. Past works show evidence that the lack of diversity and novelty in traditional recommender systems happens because recommender algorithms are designed to recommend videos similar to the ones users liked in the past [3, 16, 25]. Recommendations lacking novelty and diversity have negative consequences on user satisfaction, even if recommendations perfectly match users' tastes [4, 31]. This paper builds on previous results identifying mise-en-scène features that potentially influence accuracy of recommendations from system-centric perspective.

In this work we seek to answer the following research questions: **RQ 1.** Can the introduction of low-level mise-en-scène features in video recommender systems, combined with high-level semantic features, improve offline quality of recommendations? **RQ 2.** Can the introduction of low-level mise-en-scène features in video recommender systems, combined with high-level semantic features, induce measurable effects on the perceived utility of recommendations?

To this end, we carried out two wide and articulated empirical studies: (a) a *system-centric* evaluation to measure the offline quality of recommendations in terms of precision, novelty, diversity and coverage. (b) a *user-centric* online experiment involving 100 users, measuring different subjective metrics (*i.e.*, relevance, novelty, diversity, and satisfaction). Both studies explore the effects of recommendations under three different experimental conditions defined by one manipulated variable: the type of movie attribute used for recommendations. The studies consider (i) a content-based algorithm based on semantic movie attributes, (ii) the same algorithm based on mise-en-scène features, and (iii) a hybrid algorithm that interleaves recommendations based on attributes and mise-en-scène features.

Results show that (1) the adoption of mise-en-scène features can strongly affect precision/relevance, diversity and novelty of recommendations, determining an increased utility of recommendations and influencing the user's decision to actually watch a movie, and (2) the introduction of mise-en-scène features in conjunction with traditional attributes, tends to diversify recommendations and suggest users with less obvious choices.

2 EXPERIMENT SETUP

Table 1 summarizes the experimental conditions used in two studies.

2.1 Recommendation Algorithm

In order to generate recommendations, in both offline and online experiments, we tested a widely used pure content-based filtering (CBF) algorithm based on k-nearest neighbors, and considered 20 neighbors, cosine similarity, and log-quantile normalization of the mise-en-scène features [11].

2.2 Movie Features

In both studies, the quality of recommendations have been evaluated under three different experimental conditions defined by one manipulatable variable: the type of movie features.

Table 1: Experimental conditions used in two studies

Study	Feature Types	Quality Metrics	#Users
A: Offline	(i) semantic (ii) mise-en-scène (iii) combination of semantic and mise-en-scène	Precision Diversity Novelty Coverage	113,682
B: Online		Relevance Diversity Novelty Satisfaction	100

2.2.1 *Movie attributes.*

Content-based movie recommender systems traditionally base their recommendations on high-level attributes such as genre, director, and actors (movie attributes). Such metadata are human-generated, either editorially (*e.g.* title, cast) or by leveraging the wisdom of the crowd (*e.g.*, tags).

2.2.2 *Mise-en-Scène features.*

Recently, low-level stylistic features – such as color, motion and lighting – have been proposed for content-based video recommendations (mise-en-scène features) [11]. Mise-en-Scène features can be extracted automatically by processing the video files. Different types of visual features have been explored in the community of multimedia recommender systems [19, 21, 29].

The general procedure to extract this five categories of features comprise four steps: (a) videos are segmented into shots and for each shot, a representative key frame is extracted (this is not necessary for the shot duration); (c) for each shot, the values of the features are computed; (d) the feature values are averaged over all shots.

In our experiments, we have selected five categories of mise-en-scène low-level features described in [11, 28] as they are explainable, easy to extract from video files, and show promising results in offline experiments: *shot duration, color variance, lighting key, average motion*, and *motion variation.* The use of keyframe-based feature representation has been motivated in [9][1].

2.3 Study A: Offline Experiment

In the offline experiment, we evaluated Top-N recommendation quality of each experimental condition under a pure CBF algorithm by running a hold-out (80% train - 20% test) of a subset of the MovieLens (ML-20M) dataset. The dataset contains 113,682 users who provided 775,090 preferences (*i.e.*, ratings) to 12,573 movies. Each movie is provided with a set of 127 attributes concerning, among the others: title, genre, cast, tags. On average, each movie is labeled with six attributes. The mise-en-scène dataset contains five feature values extracted according to the procedure described in Section 2.2.2. In the offline evaluation we computed recommendation quality with respect to: *precision, diversity, novelty* and *coverage* [18].

We estimate precision by computing the percentage of movies in the recommendation list that were relevant to the user. To estimate diversity, we measure the intra-list similarity between items with

[1] The work is partially covered by a US patent application under the title of "Enhanced content based multimedia recommendation method", with application number 15/277490 [5]

respect to movie genres, *i.e.*, we compute pairwise cosine similarity between movies in the recommendation list and calculate the average similarity S. Diversity is later computed as the complement of the intra-list similarity $(1 - S)$. We compute novelty by computing the mean popularity rank of the items recommended to the user. Finally, coverage is computed by calculating the percentage of pairs of $< user, movie >$ for which we can predict a rating [2, 15, 17]. All metrics range from 0% to 100%, where 100% is the best. In our experiment, we have chosen $N = 4$ for the length of the list as it is desired to have a similar value for N in both offline and online experiments (see next section). The detailed procedure used to measure different recommendation quality metrics is similar to the one used in previous works [7, 11] maintaining compatibility with results published in other research papers.

2.4 Study B: Online Evaluation

2.4.1 Perceived Quality Metrics. The goal of the second study is to measure the user's perceived quality of the recommender system. Perceived quality is the degree to which the users judge recommendations positively and appreciate the overall experience with the recommender system. To better scope our research, we operationalize this notion in terms of fours metrics: *perceived accuracy, novelty, diversity,* and overall *user satisfaction* as defined in [15, 22, 27]: *Perceived accuracy* (also called *Relevance*) measures how much the recommendations match the users' interests, preferences and tastes; *Diversity* measures how much users perceive recommendations as different from each other, *e.g.* movies from different genres; *Novelty* measures the extent to which users receive new recommended movies; *Overall Users' Satisfaction* measures the global users' feeling of the experience with the recommender system.

2.4.2 Procedure. For the purpose of our study, we have developed *MISRec*[2], a web-centric testing framework for the movie domain, which can be easily configured to facilitate the execution of controlled empirical studies. MISRec is powered by the same pure CBF algorithm described in Section 2.1 and supports users with a wide range of functionalities that are common in online video-streaming services such as Netflix and Lovefilm (Figure 1). MISRec contains the same catalog of movies used in the first study.

Our main research audience is represented by users aged between 20 and 50 who have some familiarity with the use of the web and had never used MISRec before the study (to control for the potentially confounding factor of biases or misconceptions derived from previous uses of the system). The total number of recruited subjects who completed the task was 100 (63% men, 37% women, average age: 27.8, std 3.83).

The interaction begins with a sign-up process, where each participant (user) is initially asked to provide some basic data. Afterward, users are invited to browse the movie catalog, and then, asked to freely select five movies and rate them using a 5-level Likert scale. On the basis of these ratings, three recommendation lists are generated - one for each experimental conditions - each list containing 4 recommended movies. The user is asked to watch the trailers of the recommended movies within each of the 3 lists and reply to a set of questions related to the quality of the recommendations. Users are asked to indicate their answers to each of the questions by selecting one of the three lists. To avoid possible biases, the positions of the recommendation lists were randomized for each user. It is worth noting that since watching trailers is a time-consuming process, we decided to include 4 recommendations within each of the 3 lists.

[2] short for Mise-en-Scène Movie Recommender

Figure 1: Example screenshots of the online application

A subset of the questionnaire as reported in [15, 22] was used to measure the perceived quality of recommendations: **Acc.** Which list better understand your taste in movies? **Div.** Which list has movies that match a wider variety of moods? **Novelty.** Which list has more movies that are familiar to you? **Satisfaction.** Which list would you be more likely to recommend to your friends?

We also introduced a number of equivalent questions but formulated in a different way, in order to check for inconsistency of answers.

3 EXPERIMENTS AND RESULTS

3.1 Experiment A: Offline Evaluation

Table 2 presents the offline quality of the recommendations for each of the three experimental conditions: *movie attribute*: conventional high-level semantic attributes of movies; *mise-en-scène*: low-level visual features; *hybrid*: a combination of mise-en-scène features and movie attributes. As for the last approach, the hybridization can be done at feature-level (*e.g.* in [12]) or ensemble-level. We chose the second approach for its ease of implementation. The ensemble-level hybridization in our system was implemented by interleaving the recommendation results based on movie attributes and mise-en-scène features.

The quality has been measured with the offline methodology as described in Section 2.3. Analysis of variance suggests that the three experimental conditions (traditional movie attributes, mise-en-scène features, and hybrid) have a significant impact ($p < 0.05$) on the four variables: precision, diversity, novelty, coverage.

The *precision* metric suggests that recommendations based solely on mise-en-scène features are less accurate, while both the hybrid approach and the traditional approach are the most accurate.

If we look at *diversity* and *coverage* of recommendations, both approaches based on mise-en-scène features (either alone or in combination with traditional attributes) provide the best recommendations, *i.e.*, the most diverse recommendations, able to span almost all of the items in the catalog.

In terms of *novelty*, the approach based solely on mise-en-scène features provides the best recommendations, with the hybrid approach being marginally better than the approach based on traditional attributes.

Table 2: Results of experiment A: Offline evaluation. Results in bold are significantly different ($p < 0.05$)

Research Variables	Movie attributes	Mise-en-Scène features	Hybrid
Precision	**16.9%**	6.3%	**16.1%**
Diversity	20.8%	**21.8%**	**21.9%**
Novelty	94.9%	**96.7%**	95.7%
Coverage	75.5%	**92.7%**	**92.7%**

3.2 Experiment B: Real User Study

We first polished the collected data by removing the ones referring to subjects who showed apparent evidences of gaming with the testing system. We removed the participants who interacted with the system for less than 2 minutes, or left some questions unanswered. We also introduced a number of equivalent questions formulated in a different way, in order to check for inconsistency of answers. In the final questionnaire participants were asked to choose the preferred recommendation list. We ran multiple pair-wise Cochran Q tests on the responses from the users, as it well fits to the characteristics of the collected data [30]. All tests were run considering significance level $\alpha = 0.05$.

Table 3: Results of the experiment B: Real User Study. Results in bold are significantly different ($p < 0.05$).

Research Variables	Movie attributes	Mise-en-Scène features	Hybrid
Relevance	25%	15%	**60%**
Diversity	25%	22%	**53%**
Novelty	21%	19%	**60%**
Satisfaction	21%	22%	**57%**

The final results, presented in Table 3, show that the adoption of mise-en-scène features alone decreases almost all of the perceived quality metrics with respect to traditional semantic attributes, although not significantly (for accuracy, diversity, and novelty). This result is partially in contrast with the previous study, in which novelty and diversity with mise-en-scène recommendations are significantly better than with traditional attributes. This could be explained by previous works suggesting that offline evaluations metrics are not always good predictors of the perceived quality of recommender systems [7, 23]. However, when hybridizing recommendations based on low-level mise-en-scène features and high-level semantic attributes, they are perceived as better along all metrics. ($p < 0.05$).

4 DISCUSSION

The internal validity of our study is supported by the accuracy of our research design and by the quality of study execution. We have carefully implemented a number of mechanisms to control the accuracy of the tasks' execution. In terms of external validity, the results of our study are limited to those participants and conditions used in our study. Moreover, most services available in the market provide a user experience very similar to the one used in our study, in terms of filtering criteria and information/navigation structures [6], and it is likely that replications of our study on other systems may lead to results consistent with our findings. Finally, the high overall number of testers (100) allows us to generalize our results to a wider population of users aged 20-50.

A finer grained analysis of the statistically relevant relationships among all the different variables offers a much more articulated picture of the results, which show apparently contrasting results. More specifically, the two studies (offline and online experiment) illustrate different pictures with respect to the impact of mise-en-scène features on novelty and diversity. Our explanation is that the low accuracy of visual-only recommendations negatively affects the user opinion on the other metrics. A possible interpretation of this result is to consider that previous studies confirmed a mismatch between offline and online quality of recommendations [7, 23].

5 CONCLUSIONS

This work represents a contribution to the research and practice in the design of recommender systems, for the specific domain of movie recommendations and, from a more general perspective, for video recommendations. Our research differs from previous work in this domain for a number of aspects:

- We designed an online movie recommender system which incorporate mise-en-scène features, to be used for evaluation of recommendations with real users. In contrast, previous works on mise-en-scène features are based on only offline experiment.
- We compare three different recommendation scenarios, one of which combines recommendations based on mise-en-scène features and semantic attributes. Previous works limit their analysis to mise-en-scène features alone.
- Our results on the online evaluation of recommender systems based on mise-en-scène features (either alone or combined with semantic attributes) are totally new for the movie domain.

The results of our work can be applied to other domains where the system recommends multimedia products, such as music (e.g., Spotify, and Pandora) and images (e.g., Instagram, and Facebooks). In future, we plan to extend the range of features extracted to include both visual and audio features, using features based on the MPEG-7 standard and DNNs [13].

ACKNOWLEDGMENTS

This work has been partially funded by Telecom Italia S.p.A., Services Innovation Department, Joint Open Lab S-Cube, Milano. The work has been also partially supported by the Amazon AWS Cloud Credits for Research program.

REFERENCES

[1] Charu C Aggarwal. 2016. Content-based recommender systems. In *Recommender Systems*. Springer, 139–166.

[2] Charu C Aggarwal. 2016. *Recommender Systems*. Springer. 225–254 pages.

[3] Oscar Celma. 2010. Music recommendation. In *Music Recommendation and Discovery*. Springer, 43–85.

[4] Òscar Celma and Pedro Cano. 2008. From hits to niches?: or how popular artists can bias music recommendation and discovery. In *Proceedings of the 2nd KDD Workshop on Large-Scale Recommender Systems and the Netflix Prize Competition*. ACM, 5.

[5] Paolo Cremonesi, Mehdi Elahi, and Yashar Deldjoo. 2016. Enhanced content based multimedia recommendation method. (09 2016). http://www.polimi.it/index.php?id=6247&sel_brevetto=5093 US Patent 15/277490.

[6] Paolo Cremonesi, Mehdi Elahi, and Franca Garzotto. 2016. User interface patterns in recommendation-empowered content intensive multimedia applications. *Springer Multimedia Tools and Applications* (2016), 1–35.

[7] Paolo Cremonesi, Franca Garzotto, and Roberto Turrin. 2013. User-centric vs. system-centric evaluation of recommender systems. In *IFIP Conference on Human-Computer Interaction*. Springer, 334–351.

[8] Marco de Gemmis, Pasquale Lops, Cataldo Musto, Fedelucio Narducci, and Giovanni Semeraro. 2015. Semantics-Aware Content-Based Recommender Systems. In *Recommender Systems Handbook*. Springer, 119–159.

[9] Yashar Deldjoo, Paolo Cremonesi, Markus Schedl, and Massimo Quadrana. 2017. The effect of different video summarization models on the quality of video recommendation based on low-level visual. In *Content-Based Multimedia Indexing (CBMI), 2017 15th International Workshop on*. ACM.

[10] Yashar Deldjoo, Mehdi Elahi, Paolo Cremonesi, Franca Garzotto, and Pietro Piazzolla. 2016. Recommending movies based on mise-en-scene design. In *Proceedings of the 2016 CHI Conference Extended Abstracts on Human Factors in Computing Systems*. ACM, 1540–1547.

[11] Yashar Deldjoo, Mehdi Elahi, Paolo Cremonesi, Franca Garzotto, Pietro Piazzolla, and Massimo Quadrana. 2016. Content-based Video Recommendation System based on Stylistic Visual Features. *Journal on Data Semantics* Special Issue on Recommender Systems (2016).

[12] Yashar Deldjoo, Mehdi Elahi, Paolo Cremonesi, Farshad Bakhshandegan Moghaddam, and Andrea Luigi Edoardo Caielli. 2016. How to Combine Visual Features with Tags to Improve Movie Recommendation Accuracy?. In *International Conference on Electronic Commerce and Web Technologies*. Springer, 34–45.

[13] Yashar Deldjoo, Massimo Quadrana, Mehdi Elahi, and Paolo Cremonesi. 2017. Using Mise-En-Scene Visual Features based on MPEG7 and Deep Learning for Movie Recommendation. *arXiv preprint arXiv:1704.06109* (2017).

[14] Chitra Dorai and Svetha Venkatesh. 2003. Bridging the semantic gap with computational media aesthetics. *IEEE multimedia* 10, 2 (2003), 15–17.

[15] Michael D. Ekstrand, F. Maxwell Harper, Martijn C. Willemsen, and Joseph A. Konstan. 2014. User Perception of Differences in Recommender Algorithms. In *Proceedings of the 8th ACM Conference on Recommender Systems (RecSys '14)*. ACM, New York, NY, USA, 161–168. DOI:http://dx.doi.org/10.1145/2645710.2645737

[16] Daniel Fleder and Kartik Hosanagar. 2009. Blockbuster culture's next rise or fall: The impact of recommender systems on sales diversity. *Management science* 55, 5 (2009), 697–712.

[17] Mouzhi Ge, Carla Delgado-Battenfeld, and Dietmar Jannach. 2010. Beyond accuracy: evaluating recommender systems by coverage and serendipity. In *Proceedings of the fourth ACM conference on Recommender systems*. ACM, 257–260.

[18] Asela Gunawardana and Guy Shani. 2015. Evaluating recommender systems. In *Recommender Systems Handbook*. Springer, 265–308.

[19] Ruining He, Chen Fang, Zhaowen Wang, and Julian McAuley. 2016. Vista: A Visually, Socially, and Temporally-aware Model for Artistic Recommendation. In *Proceedings of the 10th ACM Conference on Recommender Systems (RecSys '16)*. ACM, New York, NY, USA, 309–316. DOI:http://dx.doi.org/10.1145/2959100.2959152

[20] Lu Jiang, Shoou-I Yu, Deyu Meng, Teruko Mitamura, and Alexander G Hauptmann. 2015. Bridging the ultimate semantic gap: A semantic search engine for internet videos. In *Proceedings of the 5th ACM on International Conference on Multimedia Retrieval*. ACM, 27–34.

[21] Yannis Kalantidis, Lyndon Kennedy, and Li-Jia Li. 2013. Getting the look: clothing recognition and segmentation for automatic product suggestions in everyday photos. In *Proceedings of the 3rd ACM conference on International conference on multimedia retrieval*. ACM, 105–112.

[22] Bart P Knijnenburg, Martijn C Willemsen, Zeno Gantner, Hakan Soncu, and Chris Newell. 2012. Explaining the user experience of recommender systems. *User Modeling and User-Adapted Interaction* 22, 4-5 (2012), 441–504.

[23] Joseph A Konstan and John Riedl. 2012. Recommender systems: from algorithms to user experience. *User Modeling and User-Adapted Interaction* 22, 1-2 (2012), 101–123.

[24] Hao Ma, Jianke Zhu, Michael Rung-Tsong Lyu, and Irwin King. 2010. Bridging the semantic gap between image contents and tags. *IEEE Transactions on Multimedia* 12, 5 (2010), 462–473.

[25] Sean M McNee, John Riedl, and Joseph A Konstan. 2006. Being accurate is not enough: how accuracy metrics have hurt recommender systems. In *CHI'06 extended abstracts on Human factors in computing systems*. ACM, 1097–1101.

[26] Pablo Messina, Vicente Dominquez, Denis Parra, Christoph Trattner, and Alvaro Soto. 2017. Exploring Content-based Artwork Recommendation with Metadata and Visual Features. (2017).

[27] Pearl Pu, Li Chen, and Rong Hu. 2011. A user-centric evaluation framework for recommender systems. In *Proceedings of the fifth ACM conference on Recommender systems*. ACM, 157–164.

[28] Zeeshan Rasheed, Yaser Sheikh, and Mubarak Shah. 2005. On the use of computable features for film classification. *Circuits and Systems for Video Technology, IEEE Transactions on* 15, 1 (2005), 52–64.

[29] Sujoy Roy and Sharath Chandra Guntuku. 2016. Latent Factor Representations for Cold-Start Video Recommendation. In *Proceedings of the 10th ACM Conference on Recommender Systems (RecSys '16)*. ACM, New York, NY, USA, 99–106. DOI:http://dx.doi.org/10.1145/2959100.2959172

[30] David J Sheskin. 2003. *Handbook of parametric and nonparametric statistical procedures*. crc Press.

[31] Mi Zhang and Neil Hurly. 2009. Evaluating the diversity of top-n recommendations. In *Tools with Artificial Intelligence, 2009. ICTAI'09. 21st International Conference on*. IEEE, 457–460.

Dynamic Scholarly Collaborator Recommendation via Competitive Multi-Agent Reinforcement Learning

Yang Zhang
Indiana University Bloomington
1320 E. 10th St.
Bloomington, Indiana 47408
yz90@umail.iu.edu

Chenwei Zhang
Indiana University Bloomington
1320 E. 10th St.
Bloomington, Indiana 47408
zhang334@indiana.edu

Xiaozhong Liu
Indiana University Bloomington
1320 E. 10th St.
Bloomington, Indiana 47408
liu237@indiana.edu

ABSTRACT

In an interdisciplinary environment, scientific collaboration is becoming increasingly important. Helping scholars make a right choice of potential collaborators is essential in achieving scientific success. Intuitively, the generation of collaboration relationship is a dynamic process. For instance, one scholar may first choose to work with Scholar A, and then work with Scholar B after accumulating additional academic credits. To address this property, we propose a novel dynamic collaboration recommendation method by adapting the multi-agent reinforcement learning technique to the coauthor network analysis. The collaborator selection is optimized from several different scholar similarity measurements. Unlike prior studies, the proposed method characterizes scholarly competition, a.k.a. different scholars will compete for potential collaborator at each iteration. An evaluation with the ACM data shows that multi-agent reinforcement learning plus scholarly competition modeling can be significant for collaboration recommendation.

KEYWORDS

Collaborator recommendation; dynamic; competition; reinforcement learning; multi-agent

1 INTRODUCTION

While interdisciplinary studies across multiple domains are experiencing a rapid growth in the past few decades, scientific collaboration among scholars becomes increasingly important and necessary [8]. For instance, prior studies showed that scientific collaboration can be essential for enhancing researchers' productivity [13] as well as for triggering innovation [6]. Scholar collaboration recommendation has traditionally centered on generating a ranking of potential collaborators for an author. The recommendation heavily relies on the relatedness/similarity between the source and candidate scholars. It can be estimated in different context, such as the research interest closeness [3], and the social structural proximity [4]. However, to the best of our knowledge, most existing methods only produce a static candidate collaborator list given a textual or graphical author profile. Intuitively, the generation of collaboration relationship in a scholar network should be a dynamic process. For instance, one scholar may first choose to work with Scholar A, and then work with Scholar B after accumulating additional academic credits. So, the recommendation should evolve dynamically.

In addition, recommending candidate scholars is not sufficient to guarantee the achievement of real collaboration. For most current methods, the recommendations are locally optimized—they focuses on providing a ranking list for each scholar based on their own relatedness with others. Such algorithms could recommend the same candidate to multiple scholars. Nevertheless, this candidate could not accept numerous collaborators due to the limitation of his/her time. So, scholars may need to compete for the potential candidate, even though they may not know each other. To the best of our knowledge, few existing collaboration recommendation algorithm can characterize the competition as a latent factor. In this study, we propose a novel dynamic collaboration recommendation method by adopting a multi-agent reinforcement learning technique. In this new framework, multiple authors (agents) learn the optimized chronological collaboration recommendation trajectories in a network, and they will need to compete with each other at each step. Moreover, the collaboration capacity of a candidate scholar is addressed by a function which characterizes the competition between authors, e.g., when a candidate is recommended to multiple authors, the competition function can optimize the collaboration outcome for the next iteration.

The rest of this paper is organized as follows. In Section 2 we review related work on collaboration recommendation. Section 3 explains our proposed method to address the dynamic competitive collaboration recommendation. Section 4 describes the experiments. Conclusion and future work are presented in Section 5.

2 LITERATURE REVIEW

In the literature, much attentions have been paid to collaboration recommendations. The link-based similarity and the content-based similarity are frequently used to calculate the relatedness between scholars. The former one uses the content information from the authors' publications to measure the similarity between authors (such as [3]; [7]); the latter one adopts the structure of collaboration network to measure the closeness between authors (such as [9]; [14]). Most studies combine both content-based and link-based methods and provide a ranking list of potential collaborators according to the relatedness.

For example, Chen et al. [3] designed a system that makes recommendations of collaborators based on an integration of the network structure similarity and the scholar's research interests between the source and the target authors. Similarly, Tang et al. [17] proposed

RecSys '17, August 27–31, 2017, Como, Italy.

DOI: http://dx.doi.org/10.1145/3109859.3109914

a Cross-domain Topic Learning method (CTL) to help scholars find potential collaborators from other domains. They included the "collaboration" topics detected by CTL into the collaboration graph and applied the random walk with restart algorithm to calculate the relatedness between authors from the source and the target domains. Han et al. [9] designed a regularization based method to incorporate the local network structure, the global network structure, and the content feature to provide collaboration recommendation for junior researchers, who have less collaboration information and need more collaborator recommendation. Kong et al. [12] first utilized the topic clustering model to divide scholars into different research domains and then used the random walk model to calculate the structural similarity between authors from the same domain.

However, most of the recommendation methods proposed did not reflect the evolution of collaboration–one scholar's previous collaborations can influence his/her further collaborations. The recommendation is usually a static process and only one fixed group of collaborators is finally provided. There exists some research considering the dynamic collaboration. For example, Chaiwanarom and Lursinsap [2] used the up-to-date publication data together with other factors including social proximity, friendship, complementarity skill, research interest, and seniority of researcher to measure the research trend of potential collaborators. But still only one ranked list of potential collaborators is provided. Moreover, in these methods, each scholar is provided with a list of coauthors and a same potential collaborator could be recommended to multiple scholars, in which case not all the recommendations could be achieved. Many current research only provide locally optimized recommendation results.

In this study, we use a multi-agent reinforcement learning model with a competition function to tackle these drawbacks. Multi-agent reinforcement learning has been applied in many simulation tasks [1]. It has also been successful in a few real-life domains, such as controlling traffic signals [18], robot soccer [19], automated trading [10], and recourse management [5]. As far as we know, reinforcement learning has not been used for scholar collaboration recommendation. Reinforcement learning is designed to resolve the dynamic problem. Reinforcement learning agent learns knowledge by communicating with the environment, finding out how to correspond situations to actions, and maximizing a reward in numerical representation [16]. Multi-agent reinforcement learning integrates the results of each single agent [1]. There are various types of reinforcement learning algorithms including model-free learning methods and model-based learning methods [11]. One of the well-known algorithms is Value-Iteration [16], which tries to find the optimal action selection policy based on an iteratively updated state value. These characteristics make it appropriate to address the proposed problem.

3 METHODOLOGY

In this research, we model the evolution of collaboration among scholars. One author (hereinafter referred to source author) is looking for potential collaborators (hereinafter referred to target authors). In this study, we propose two influencing factors for the match between the source author and the target author. First, the similarity/distance between the source and target authors can play a direct role. We call this a *'personal factor'*.

The second factor focuses on the target author's status in the network. To seek for collaborators, preferential attachment can be important. People would like to connect with those popular nodes in the network. The more popular one scholar is, the higher probability that others would like to collaborate with him/her. Moreover, since forming collaboration is an evolved process, if a scholar's collaborators are also popular, there exists higher chance for others to gain more collaboration after collaborating with him/her. We call it *'environmental factor'*, which guides collaborator seeking. It requires a holistic understanding of the whole collaboration network.

3.1 Network Generation

To recommend collaborators to an author A_i, his/her research interest $topic_i$ is first considered. By comparing $topic_i$ with the keywords of existing publications for all scholars in a scholarly database G, all related researchers and their articles are extracted. So a collaboration network G' is created, where the nodes represent the authors and the edges stand for the coauthorship between the authors. The total number of authors is represented by k. The network is an unweighted one (see Figure 1.1). t different relationships between authors, which are based on their personal features, such as publications are used to measure their similarities. An author A_i will have t different similarity measures with another author A_j, as shown in Figure 1.2. The overall similarity, s_{ij} between two authors, A_i and A_j can be quantified by the weighted sum of these measures, $\sum_{m=1}^{t} \theta_m \cdot s_{ij}^m$, where s_{ij}^m is the similarity measure by the mth relationship; θ_m is the weight reflecting the importance of that relationship in the overall similarity. The t weights form the vector $\vec{\theta}$. An author, A_i 's popularity, pop_i is defined by the sum of his/her overall similarities with all other authors, $\sum_{n=1,n\neq i}^{k} \sum_{m=1}^{t} (\theta_m \cdot s_{in}^m)$. It can be transformed to $\sum_{m=1}^{t} \theta_m \cdot (\sum_{n=1}^{k} s_{in}^m)$. We denote it as $\vec{\theta}^T \cdot \vec{q}_i$.

3.2 Dynamic Recommendation via Reinforcement Learning and Gradient Descent

Each author in the collaboration network is treated as a state. To guide the recommendation, the environmental factor should be learnt, i.e., the true status value of each state need to be learnt. Based on the Value Iteration algorithm [16], we propose **Gradient Value Iteration algorithm** (see Algorithm 1) to achieve this goal. Initially, the popularity of each author is assigned as his/her status value as a state. In the learning process, the status value of each state is kept updated until it reaches a stabilized value. For each iteration, $\vec{\theta}$ are updated by the gradient descent method, where the algorithm tries to minimize the Mean Squared Value Error between the current estimation of all the states' status values and their true status values. The status value of a state is updated by its original value and the discounted value of the maximum of its neighbors' status values from the collaboration network.

As Algorithm 1 shows, the proposed algorithm optimizes the composition of multiple relationships in the similarity measurement

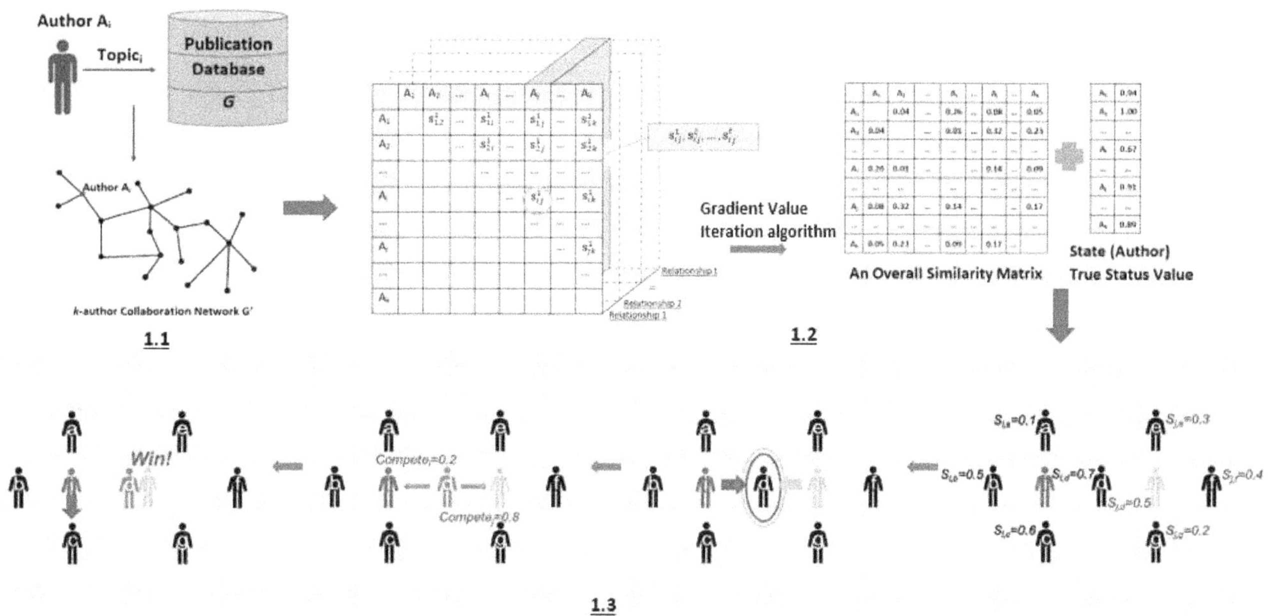

Figure 1: Toy example of the whole process

Algorithm 1 Gradient Value Iteration Algorithm for True Status Value Learning

Input: $\vec{q_1}, \vec{q_2}, ..., \vec{q_k}$
Output: $\vec{\theta}^{final}, \vec{status}^{final}$

Begin:
$\vec{\theta} \leftarrow (1, 1, ..., 1)^T$
$\vec{status}^{new} \leftarrow ((\vec{\theta}^T \cdot \vec{q_1}), (\vec{\theta}^T \cdot \vec{q_2}), ..., (\vec{\theta}^T \cdot \vec{q_k}))^T$
$\vec{status}^{old} \leftarrow (0, 0, ..., 0)^T$
while $|\vec{status}^{new} - \vec{status}^{old}| >= threshold$ **do**
$\quad \vec{status}^{old} \leftarrow \vec{status}^{new}$
$\quad \vec{\theta} \leftarrow \vec{\theta} - \alpha \cdot \vec{status}^{old} \cdot \frac{\partial \vec{status}^{old}}{\partial \vec{\theta}}$
$\quad \vec{status}^{old} \leftarrow ((\vec{\theta}^T \cdot \vec{q_1}), (\vec{\theta}^T \cdot \vec{q_2}), ..., (\vec{\theta}^T \cdot \vec{q_k}))^T$
$\quad$ **for** $i = 1$ to k **do**
$\quad\quad \vec{status}^{new}[i] \leftarrow \vec{status}^{old}[i] + \lambda \cdot max(\vec{status}^{old}[sub])$
$\quad\quad$ /*sub refers to the set of i's neighbors*/
$\quad$ **end for**
end while
$\vec{\theta}^{final} \leftarrow \vec{\theta}$
$\vec{status}^{final} \leftarrow \vec{status}^{new}$

between two authors. Thus the true status value of each state in the collaboration network is available. Each of the source authors who seeks for potential collaborators is treated as an agent. A search function is constructed for him/her to make a decision to whom he/she would like to collaborate from all the authors in the graph. In other words, this function determines which state one agent will reach. As mentioned before, the search function, $Search(A_j|A_i)$ combines the personal factor, represented by the overall similarity, s_{ij} between the source author A_i and the target author A_j, and the environmental factor, represented by the true status value, $status_j$ of the target author. As illustrated by a toy example in Figure 1.3, authors A_i and A_j are looking for potential collaborators, so they 'look for' potential collaborators via search functions.

3.3 Agent Communication and Competition

Different from previous studies, multiple agents (in one model) are allowed to seek for collaborators simultaneously, which characterizes authors' competition as well as enhances recommendation performance. Based on search function, each author will have a ranking of potential collaborators–the higher value the search function provides to collaborate with a certain author, the higher this author will rank in the list. It is very likely that multiple authors, $A_1, A_2 \dots A_h$ will reach the same candidate (state) A_e. In Figure 1.3, the author A_d is returned to A_i and A_j at the same time. In this case, A_e should choose a collaborator from this group.

To implement competition (among $A_1, A_2 \dots A_h$), a competition function is proposed to compare the social proximity between the competing authors:

$$Compete(A_e|A_1, ..., A_h) = A_i, if\, prox_{ei} = max\{prox_{e1}, ..., prox_{eh}\} \quad (1)$$

where $prox_{ei}$ stands for the social proximity between the authors A_e and A_i in the collaboration network.

Those authors, who lose the competition, will iteratively choose and compete the next candidates on the ranking list. If a candidate is recommended to multiple authors again, new competition will be conducted recursively. This process will repeat until different candidates are assigned to all the authors. The proposed method enables global recommendation optimization, and multiple source authors need to compete in each iteration. In another word, a target author is able to choose the best collaborator from the source authors who request collaborations. In the Figure 1.3, A_d selects A_j since A_j returns a higher value of competition function than A_i. So A_i needs to seek alternative candidates.

4 EXPERIMENT

4.1 Data Sets

An ACM data set including 776,295 authors and corresponding publications from 1951 to 2015 is used in this preliminary experiment. The topic *machine learning* is selected as an example and 4,420 authors and related publications are extracted. The collaboration data before 2014 are used as the training data, which includes 7,546 unweighted edges. The data from 2014 to 2015 are used for testing. Four relationships between authors are calculated: the Jaccard similarity based on the authors' publication venues and keywords, and the Cosine similarity based on the titles and abstracts.

4.2 Experimental Setup

Experimental runs are conducted on two different setting: single-agent RL (Reinforcement Learning), and multi-agent RL with competition.

(1) Single-agent RL: One agent (author) is randomly selected as the input of the reinforcement learning model. The experiment repeats twenty times.
(2) Multi-agent RL with competition: Twenty agents (authors), that are located closely to each other, are randomly selected as the input of the reinforcement learning model; each agent needs to compete with the rest agents for collaborators.

The proposed methods are compared with five baseline models, four of which adopt the content similarity method to recommend the most related scholars. The similarity measures are provided in Subsection 4.1. The other method makes recommendation according to the authors' social proximity on the collaboration network. It adopts a random-walk-based structural similarity, which has been successfully used in link prediction research[15].

4.3 Results Analysis

The significance of each relationship in the overall similarity between two authors are learned. We find that the publication venue greatly affects the similarity measure between two authors. The next important one is the research topic, reflected by the keyword adoption and it is followed by the publication title and abstract.

For each experimental setting, we run the learning for ten steps and after each step one scholar will be recommended as a collaboration candidate. The candidates from each step form a temporal sequence of recommendation. In the last step, the final ranking list of collaborations for each agent is collected. Each learning is repeated for one hundred rounds. For evaluation, if any recommended collaboration is found in the testing period, it is labeled as a correct one; otherwise it is a wrong one. For the final ranking list, the performance is evaluated in terms of MRR (Mean Reciprocal Rank), P@3 (Precision for the top 3 recommended results), P@5, P@10, NDCG@3 (Normalized Discounted Cumulative Gain for the top 3 recommended results), NDCG@5, and NDCG@10.

Table 1: Results Comparison

	MRR	P@3	P@5	P@10	NDCG@3	NDCG@5	NDCG@10
Classic Methods							
Abstract Sim.	0.246	0.246	0.122	0.075	0.166	0.195	0.214
Keyword Sim.	0.381	0.270	0.262	0.200	0.303	0.341	0.392
Title Sim.	0.339	0.200	0.174	0.112	0.269	0.297	0.330
Venue Sim.	0.485	0.333	0.290	**0.205**	0.434	0.472	0.553
Network Prox.	0.448	0.327	0.270	0.165	0.477	0.510	0.534
RL-based Methods							
Single	0.573	0.377	0.274	0.157	0.541	0.544	0.550
Multi_With	**0.601**	**0.437**	**0.321**	0.178	**0.561**	**0.560**	**0.565**

The evaluation results are listed in Table 1. It is clear that the multi-agent reinforcement learning method outperforms other methods in most of the evaluation metrics. The final ranking list obtained from the multi-agent reinforcement learning gains the highest MRR and NDCG, which demonstrates the usefulness of competition modeling in collaboration recommendation (compared with single-agent reinforcement learning and other baseline models). The multi-agent reinforcement learning also beats the other methods regarding P@3 and P@5. Thought the venue similarity and keyword similarity baseline models are superior for P@10, it reflects the precise recommendations rank higher in the multi-agent reinforcement learning method than other methods. It is also noteworthy that among the four similarity-based baseline models, the one adopting the authors' venue similarity beats the one with the keyword similarity, followed by the title similarity and the abstract similarity in most evaluation metrics. We also witness the same trend in the trained gradient descent model, which also proofs the validity of the proposed method.

Overall, evaluation shows the usefulness of the multi-agent reinforcement learning and agent competition for a scholar collaboration recommendation task, and characterizing the evolutionary nature of collaboration can be promising to enhance the recommendation performance.

5 CONCLUSION & FUTURE WORK

In this study, we propose a novel approach–Dynamic Competitive Collaborator Recommendation. Unlike the earlier studies, a multi-agent reinforcement learning is employed to predict the chronological authors collaboration. The proposed method captures the dynamic evolution of collaboration. It can be used to characterize the scholarly competition as a latent factor for optimizing the recommendation result. Preliminary experiment shows that the proposed method is promising.

Due to the computation limitation, we only include ten authors in the final ranking list. This will be addressed in the next stage. Meanwhile, currently we only consider social similarity in the competition function. In the future work, we will set different competition criteria thus measure the competition from various perspectives. For example, the match of authors' personal features, and the potential impact of collaboration. The collaboration is dynamically evolved in nature. Scholars will either repeat collaboration with their existing collaborators, or create new collaborations. Though we capture the dynamic evolution in this research, we have not yet separated the collaboration maintaining and creation. We will improve this in our next study.

REFERENCES

[1] Lucian Busoniu, Robert Babuska, and Bart De Schutter. 2008. A comprehensive survey of multiagent reinforcement learning. *IEEE Transactions on Systems Man and Cybernetics Part C Applications and Reviews* 38, 2 (March 2008), 156–172. https://doi.org/10.1109/TSMCC.2007.913919

[2] Paweena Chaiwanarom and Chidchanok Lursinsap. 2015. Collaborator recommendation in interdisciplinary computer science using degrees of collaborative forces, temporal evolution of research interest, and comparative seniority status. *Knowledge-Based Systems* 75 (Feb. 2015), 161–172. https://doi.org/10.1016/j.knosys.2014.11.029

[3] Hung-Hsuan Chen, Liang Gou, Xiaolong Zhang, and Clyde Lee Giles. 2011. CollabSeer: a search engine for collaboration discovery. In *Proceedings of the 11th Annual International ACM/IEEE Joint Conference on Digital Libraries*. ACM, Ottawa, Canada, 231–240. https://doi.org/10.1145/1998076.1998121

[4] Sara Cohen and Lior Ebel. 2013. Recommending collaborators using keywords. In *Proceedings of the 22nd International Conference on World Wide Web*. ACM, Rio de Janeiro, Brazil, 959–962. https://doi.org/10.1145/2487788.2488091

[5] Robert H Crites and Andrew G Barto. 1998. Elevator group control using multiple reinforcement learning agents. *Machine Learning* 33, 2-3 (Nov. 1998), 235–262. https://doi.org/10.1023/A:1007518724497

[6] Jonathon N Cummings and Sara Kiesler. 2005. Collaborative research across disciplinary and organizational boundaries. *Social Studies of Science* 35, 5 (Oct. 2005), 703–722. https://doi.org/10.1177/0306312705055535

[7] Sujatha Das Gollapalli, Prasenjit Mitra, and C. Lee Giles. 2012. Similar researcher search in academic environments. In *Proceedings of the 12th ACM/IEEE-CS Joint Conference on Digital Libraries*. ACM, Washington, DC, 167–170. https://doi.org/10.1145/2232817.2232849

[8] Roger Guimera, Brian Uzzi, Jarrett Spiro, and Luis A. Nunes Amaral. 2005. Team assembly mechanisms determine collaboration network structure and team performance. *Science* 308, 5722 (April 2005), 697–702. https://doi.org/10.1126/science.1106340

[9] Shuguang Han, Daqing He, Jiepu Jiang, and Zhen Yue. 2013. Supporting exploratory people search: a study of factor transparency and user control. In *Proceedings of the 22nd ACM International Conference on Information Knowledge Management*. ACM, San Francisco, CA, 449–458. https://doi.org/10.1145/2505515.2505684

[10] Wei-Tek Hsu and Von-Wun Soo. 2001. Market performance of adaptive trading agents in synchronous double auctions. In *Pacific Rim International Workshop on Multi-Agents*. Springer, 108–121.

[11] Leslie Pack Kaelbling, Michael L. Littman, and Andrew W. Moore. 1996. Reinforcement learning: a survey. *Journal of Artificial Intelligence Research* 4 (1996), 237–285. https://doi.org/10.1613/jair.301

[12] Xiangjie Kong, Huizhen Jiang, Zhuo Yang, Zhenzhen Xu, Feng Xia, and Amr Tolba. 2016. Exploiting publication contents and collaboration networks for collaborator recommendation. *PloS One* 11, 2 (Feb. 2016), e0148492. https://doi.org/10.1371/journal.pone.0148492

[13] Sooho Lee and Barry Bozeman. 2005. The impact of research collaboration on scientific productivity. *Social Studies of Science* 35, 5 (Oct. 2005), 673–702. https://doi.org/10.1177/0306312705052359

[14] Jing Li, Feng Xia, Wei Wang, Zhen Chen, Nana Yaw Asabere, and Huizhen Jiang. 2014. ACRec: a co-authorship based random walk model for academic collaboration recommendation. In *Proceedings of the 23rd International Conference on World Wide Web*. ACM, Seoul, Korea, 1209–1214. https://doi.org/10.1145/2567948.2579034

[15] Linyuan Lü and Tao Zhou. 2011. Link prediction in complex networks: A survey. *Physica A: Statistical Mechanics and its Applications* 390, 6 (March 2011), 1150–1170. https://doi.org/10.1016/j.physa.2010.11.027

[16] Richard S Sutton and Andrew G Barto. 1998. *Reinforcement learning: An introduction*. Vol. 1. MIT press, Cambridge.

[17] Jie Tang, Sen Wu, Jimeng Sun, and Hang Su. 2012. Cross-domain collaboration recommendation. In *Proceedings of the 18th ACM SIGKDD international conference on Knowledge discovery and data mining*. ACM, Beijing, China, 1285–1293. https://doi.org/10.1145/2339530.2339730

[18] Marco Wiering. 2000. Multi-agent reinforcement learning for traffic light control. In *ICML*. 1151–1158.

[19] Marco Wiering, Rafa l Sa lustowicz, and Jürgen Schmidhuber. 1999. Reinforcement learning soccer teams with incomplete world models. *Autonomous Robots* 7, 1 (1999), 77–88. https://doi.org/10.1023/A:1008921914343

Rethinking Collaborative Filtering: A Practical Perspective on State-of-the-art Research Based on Real World Insights

Noam Koenigstein
Microsoft

ABSTRACT

A decade has passed since the seminal Netflix Prize competition and Collaborative Filtering (CF) models are still at the forefront of Recommender System research. Significant progress has been achieved over this time, yet key aspects of the basic problem formulation have not been seriously challenged. Most state-of-the-art models still assume a supervised model in which the ultimate goal is to predict future user-item interactions based on the generalization of historical data.

We wish to initiate a discussion on some key assumptions behind much of the mainstream research: What is the difference between predicting future user actions and optimizing Key Performance Indicators (KPIs)? Does a trade-off between accuracy and diversity really exist? Is supervised CF based on historical data still relevant in the age of modern reinforcement learning models such as contextual bandits? What evaluation metrics can be used prior to online experimentations and what are their limitations? Our main thesis is that at the core of all these issues lies a gap between most Collaborative Filtering models and the true objective of industry systems.

1 INTRODUCTION

The seminal Netflix competition [1] brought much attention to recommender system research. The basic setting of the competition set the stage for much of the research that followed. Specifically, a dataset $\mathcal{D}$ comprising of $(user, item, rating) \in \mathcal{D}$ tuples is used to train a model that generalizes to enable future predictions. Much of the subsequent research in Collaborative Filtering (CF) has been confined to this set-up. However, the true task of real-world recommender systems is slightly different: to find a short list of items to present to the user such that the probability for a click or a purchase will be maximized. In what follows, we will discuss the gap between the classical CF problem formulation and the actual goal of most real-world recommender systems.

RecSys '17, August 27-31, 2017, Como, Italy

ACM ISBN 978-1-4503-4652-8/17/08.
https://doi.org/10.1145/3109859.3109919

2 THE GAP BETWEEN COLLABORATIVE FILTERING AND REAL WORLD RECOMMENDER SYSTEMS

One of the main differences between the CF task formulation and the real-world task of recommender systems is the fact that most real-world systems present several items simultaneously while the CF formulation models each user-item interaction separately. One of the most well-known embodiments of this gap is the apparent *"accuracy-vs-diversity trade-off"* [2, 3]. At the core of this problem is the fact CF models learn to predict ratings for single items and don't consider the diversity of the recommendation list presented to the user, hence a gap exists between the CF task and the actual goal of most real-world recommender systems which causes this apparent "trade-off".

To address this problem, we introduced the list recommendation problem [8]: given a specific user u the goal is to produce an *ordered* personalized list of K items $l_u \equiv \{i_1, i_2, \ldots, i_K\}$ that maximizes the probability that u will click on an item from l_u. Note that we assume that the same set of recommended items may yield different click probabilities when ordered differently, hence this formulation is different than that of the set recommendation problem (unordered lists). It is also different from learning to rank models [7, 9, 12] that train on pairwise relations but ignore deeper interactions between items such as item diversity etc. By considering the entire list of recommendations, we managed to formulate a supervised machine-learning model in which the trade-off between accuracy and diversity does not exist because the model automatically learns the right amount of diversity.

An additional embodiment of the gap between real-world recommender systems and CF is the apparent trade-off between accuracy and novelty or serendipity. This observation was first discussed by McNee *et al.* [5] who suggested that users prefer a certain amount of novelty and serendipity in their recommendations. Again, at the core of this apparent "trade-off" lies the fact that traditional CF models try to predict the next item the user will buy, while the actual goal of most real-world systems is to *influence* the user to consume more items than she would have without the recommendations. The output of a CF model usually consists of many popular items and lacks long tail items. However, the user is expected to consume these popular items regardless of the recommendations (even in the absence of the recommendations). Therefore, presenting these popular items is less likely to yield more purchases. Instead, it has been argued that presenting novel long tail items to the user is more effective in influencing the user to buy something she would not have considered otherwise.

The failure of current systems to actually influence the user, rather than simply predicting inevitable behavior is directly related to the optimization objective of the CF problem which differs from the actual goal of a recommender system. This gap might be mitigated by applying Reinforcement Learning (RL) algorithms such as contextual bandits [4, 11] that learn to optimize a reward function based on the user interaction with the system. Instead of predicting the user behavior, RL has the ability to learn the amount of novelty that will maximize the probability to influence the user.

Considering this major advantage of RL over CF models, one might wonder if there is any need for CF models in real-world recommender systems? CF models are exceptionally useful in learning users "taste" by training on huge datasets that expose the delicate relations between users and items. By learning user and item embeddings, this "taste" information is efficiently summarized by vectors in a latent space. Despite their clear advantage in learning to impact users, RL has a real limitation when it comes to learning these complex correlations: First, the learning process is dependent on actively querying users. Thus, learning takes a long time to converge. In contrast, CF models can easily utilize large datasets of implicit user-item interactions that are often found in abundance. Moreover, even if sufficient data can be collected, RL lacks the latent space formulation of CF which allows the efficient representation of the delicate correlations that exist in user tastes. Therefore, it is our opinion that the future of recommender systems lies in finding the correct approaches to harvest the advantages of both CF and RL.

3 THE FUTURE OF EVALUATIONS

Much has been written about evaluating recommender systems. The original Netflix competition was based on minimizing the Root Mean Squared Error (RMSE) of user ratings. In the years that have followed, research has shifted to implicit binary models, one-class formulations [6] and learning to rank [7]. Evaluation metrics have changed along with the optimization goal but one limitation has remained: the gap between CF and the actual goal of a recommender system makes it very difficult to effectively evaluate a model without performing online experiments. However, online experiments are expensive and time consuming and in many cases impossible e.g., in academic research.

Off-policy evaluation methods [10] are starting to mitigate this gap by attempting to simulate the effect of a proposed algorithm (policy) using a dataset collected from an existing system. While this approach appears promising, many challenges still remain. Most notably in cases when the proposed algorithm and the existing system have different support over the distribution of recommended items. Additional challenges lie in cases when the policies are dependent on past interactions. It is our belief that efficient evaluation of recommender systems remains an important open question that needs to be addressed in light of the gap described above.

4 CONCLUSIONS

We have reviewed some of what we consider to be key open challenges in recommender systems research. While many similar questions have been raised in the past, we have highlighted the ones that we believe to have the most significant practical implications. These insights are based on the experience gained in the development of multiple real-world recommender systems serving millions of users world-wide. Our main thesis is that at the core of all these issues lies a gap between the "Netflix problem" setup and the true objective of industry systems. Our hope is that this discussion will encourage academic researchers to understand and focus on the open problems which we consider to be the most relevant to the industry.

REFERENCES

[1] J. Bennett and S. Lanning. The Netflix Prize. In *Proc. KDD Cup and Workshop*, 2007.
[2] J. L. Herlocker, J. A. Konstan, L. G. Terveen, and J. T. Riedl. Evaluating collaborative filtering recommender systems. *ACM Transactions on Information Systems (TOIS)*, 22(1):5–53, 2004.
[3] J. A. Konstan, S. M. McNee, C.-N. Ziegler, R. Torres, N. Kapoor, and J. T. Riedl. Lessons on applying automated recommender systems to information-seeking tasks. In *Proceedings of the 21st National Conference on Artificial Intelligence - Volume 2*, AAAI'06, pages 1630–1633. AAAI Press, 2006.
[4] L. Li, W. Chu, J. Langford, and R. E. Schapire. A contextual-bandit approach to personalized news article recommendation. In *Proceedings of WWW*, 2010.
[5] S. M. McNee, J. Riedl, and J. A. Konstan. Being accurate is not enough: How accuracy metrics have hurt recommender systems. In *CHI '06 Extended Abstracts on Human Factors in Computing Systems*, pages 1097–1101, 2006.
[6] U. Paquet and N. Koenigstein. One-class collaborative filtering with random graphs. In *Proceedings of WWW*, 2013.
[7] S. Rendle, C. Freudenthaler, Z. Gantner, and L. Schmidt-Thieme. BPR: Bayesian personalized ranking from implicit feedback. In *Proceedings of the 25th Conference on Uncertainty in Artificial Intelligence*, 2009.
[8] O. Sar-Shalom, N. Koenigstein, U. Paquet, and H. P. Vanchinathan. Beyond collaborative filtering: The list recommendation problem. In *Proceedings of WWW*, 2016.
[9] Y. Shi, A. Karatzoglou, L. Baltrunas, M. Larson, N. Oliver, and A. Hanjalic. Climf: Learning to maximize reciprocal rank with collaborative less-is-more filtering. In *Proceedings of RecSys*, 2012.
[10] A. L. Strehl, J. Langford, L. Li, and S. Kakade. Learning from logged implicit exploration data. In *Proceedings of NIPS*, 2010.
[11] L. Tang, Y. Jiang, L. Li, and T. Li. Ensemble contextual bandits for personalized recommendation. In *Proceedings of RecSys*, 2014.
[12] M. Weimer, A. Karatzoglou, Q. V. Le, and A. J. Smola. Cofi rank - maximum margin matrix factorization for collaborative ranking. In *Proceedings of NIPS*, pages 1593–1600, 2008.

Recommendation Applications and Systems at Electronic Arts

Meng Wu
Electronic Arts, Inc.
209 Redwood Shores Pkwy
Redwood City, CA 94065, USA
mewu@ea.com

John Kolen
Electronic Arts, Inc.
209 Redwood Shores Pkwy
Redwood City, CA 94065, USA
jkolen@ea.com

Navid Aghdaie
Electronic Arts, Inc.
209 Redwood Shores Pkwy
Redwood City, CA 94065, USA
naghdaie@ea.com

Kazi A. Zaman
Electronic Arts, Inc.
209 Redwood Shores Pkwy
Redwood City, CA 94065, USA
kzaman@ea.com

ABSTRACT

The digital game industry has recently adopted recommendation systems to provide suitable game and content choices to players. Recommendations in digital games have several unique applications and challenges compared to other well known recommendation system such as those for movies and books. Designers must adopt different architectures and algorithms to overcome these challenges. In this talk, we describe the game recommendation system at Electronic Arts. It leverages heterogeneous player data across many games to provide intelligent recommendations. We discuss three example applications: recommending games for purchase, suitable game map, and game difficulty.

Like the movie and book recommendation problem, one application is to recommend the next favorite games for a player. Digital games fall into a wide range of genres such as first player shooting (FPS), sports, and role-playing games (RPG). Games within the same genre however tend to be unique and creative. While the recommendation item space is smaller, the recommendation system should also manage different types of contents such as games and extra downloadable contents to play, editorial videos and tutorials to watch.

The second application provides the game mode and map recommendations within a game to improve player experience. Many online digital games, especially FPS and sports games, contain different maps and game modes to provide diverse gameplay experience. Different maps and game modes often require different skill levels, strategies, or cooperation from players, and the maps and game modes are often played repeatedly. Therefore, recommending the most suitable map and game mode is important from smooth onboarding experience to retain players who are likely to churn. In the map and game mode recommendation application, the algorithms need to evaluate both the short-term actions as well as long term effects of playing different maps and game modes to optimize player's engagement.

In addition, we also use the same recommendation system to adjust in-game configurations such as difficulty. Players have a wide variety of experiences, skills, learning rates, and playing styles, and will react differently to the same difficulty setting. Second, even for an individual player, one's difficulty preference may also change over time. For example, in a level progression game, a player who loses the first several attempts to one level might feel much less frustrated compared to losing after tens of unsuccessful trials. The difficulty recommendation provides suggestions and adjustments on game configuration based on the player's previous gameplay experience to maximize the engagement. For online multiplayer games, recommending partners and opponents in matchmaking is also an effective way to improve player experience.

We developed one flexible recommendation system to satisfy the need of different applications and that executes data-driven algorithms such collaborative filtering and multi-armed bandit. The centralized system leverages entire player and game data for all recommendation applications in digital games, supports unified roll-out and update, and at the same time measures the performance together via A/B testing experiments. Moreover, the one system strategy is easy to generate consistent recommendations across multiple games and platforms. We tested these recommendation applications in EA website and games, an observed significant improvements in click-through-rate and engagement.

CCS CONCEPTS

• **Information systems → Personalization**; **Retrieval models and ranking**; **Recommender systems**; *Multimedia and multimodal retrieval*;

KEYWORDS

Recommendation system, digital game

RecSys '17, August 27-31, 2017, Como, Italy

ACM ISBN 978-1-4503-4652-8/17/08.
https://doi.org/10.1145/3109859.3109928

Search Ranking And Personalization at Airbnb

Mihajlo Grbovic
Airbnb, Inc.
888 Brannan St
San Francisco, California 94103
mihajlo.grbovic@airbnb.com

ABSTRACT

Search ranking is a fundamental problem of crucial interest to major Internet companies, including web search engines, content publishing websites and marketplaces. However, despite sharing some common characteristics a one-size-fits-all solution does not exist in this space. Given a large difference in content that needs to be ranked and the parties affected by ranking, each search ranking problem is somewhat specific. In this talk we will describe some of the key techniques used to power Search Ranking at Airbnb. Correspondingly, search ranking at Airbnb is quite unique, being a two-sided marketplace in which one needs to optimize for host and guest preferences, in a world where a user rarely consumes the same item twice and one listing can accept only one guest for a certain set of dates. In this talk, I will discuss challenges we have encountered and Machine Learning solutions we have developed for listing ranking at Airbnb. Specifically, the listing ranking problem boils down to prioritizing listings that are appealing to the guest but at the same time demoting listings that would likely reject the guest, which is not easily solvable using basic matrix completion or a straightforward linear model. I will shed the light on how we jointly optimize the two objectives by leveraging listing quality, location relevance, reviews, host response time as well as guest and host preferences and past booking history. Finally, we will talk about our recent work on using neural network models to train listing and query embeddings for purposes of enhancing search personalization, broad search and type-ahead suggestions, which are core concepts in any modern search.

CCS CONCEPTS

• **Information systems** → Content ranking; Web log analysis; Personalization; Query representation; Document representation;

KEYWORDS

Search Ranking; User Modeling; Personalization

ACM Reference format:
Mihajlo Grbovic. 2017. Search Ranking And Personalization at Airbnb. In *Proceedings of RecSys'17, Como, Italy, August 27–31, 2017,* 2 pages.
https://doi.org/10.1145/3109859.3109920

RecSys'17, August 27–31, 2017, Como, Italy

ACM ISBN ISBN 978-1-4503-4652-8/17/08.
https://doi.org/10.1145/3109859.3109920

1 INTRODUCTION

During last decade Search architectures, which were typically based on classic Information Retrieval techniques, have seen an increased application of Machine Learning to its various components [1], especially to Search Retrieval and Search Ranking that often have challenging objectives depending on the type of content that is being searched over. The main reason behind this trend is the rise in the amount of search data that can be collected and analyzed. The more data becomes available on user interaction with search retrieval and ranking systems, the more those systems can be improved, optimized and customized using Machine Learning. Furthermore, the collected data opens up possibilities for personalizing the experience for a particular user based on its previous searches or previous searches of similar users.

As we just pointed out, the objective of the search algorithm can vary depending on the platform at hand. While some platforms aim at increasing website engagement (e.g. clicks and time spent in news articles that are being searched over), some aim at maximizing conversions (e.g. purchases of goods or services that are being searched over), and in case of two sided marketplaces they often need to optimize the search results for both sides of the marketplace, i.e. sellers and buyers. The two sided marketplaces have emerged as a viable business model in many real world applications. In particular, we have moved from the social network paradigm to a network with two distinct types of participants representing supply and demand of a specific good. Examples industries include accommodation (Airbnb), video content (YouTube, Dailymotion), ride sharing (Uber, Lyft), online shops (Etsy, Ebay), music (Soundcloud), app stores (Apple App Store, Google App Store) and job sites (LinkedIn). Arguably, content discovery and search ranking for these types of marketplaces needs to satisfy both supply and demand sides of the ecosystem in order to grow and prosper.

In case of Airbnb, there is a clear need to optimize search results for both apartment hosts and apartment guests, meaning that given an input query with location and trip dates we need to rank high listings whose location, price, style, reviews, etc. are appealing to the guest and, at the same time, are a good match in terms of host preferences for trip duration and lead days. Furthermore, we need to be able to detect listings for which the host would likely reject the guest due to bad reviews, number of guests, kids, pets, smoking or any other factor, and rank these listings lower for the particular search. To achieve this type of ranking we resort to using Learning to Rank [3] techniques. Specifically, we leverage listing quality, location relevance, reviews, host response time as well as guest and host preferences and past booking history as ranking features and formulate the problem as pairwise regression with positive utilities for bookings and negative utilities for rejections, which we optimize using a modified version of Lambda Rank [2] model that conducts listing pairwise comparisons that jointly optimize ranking for both guest and host side of the marketplace.

Since guests typically conduct multiple searches, click on more than one listing and contact more than one host during their search session, we can use these in-session signals, i.e. long clicks, wishlists additions and contacts, to further personalize the future searches and show users similar content to what they already consumed. To be able to calculate similarities between listings for personalization purposes we use historical search sessions, i.e. ids of listings clicked and contacted by specific user ordered in time, to train listing embeddings [4]. These embedding algorithms are able to learn representations of listings in a low-dimensional continuous vector space using surrounding context of other listings consumed in the same session, such that listings that appeared in similar context will be close to each other in the resulting embedding space. We found that trained listing embeddings are able to capture price, room type, style, location, quality, rating and more, all in one low-dimensional vector, e.g. 32 floats, and encode similarities much better than classic representations of listings as high-dimensional sparse vectors of categorical and text features.

Given listing embeddings we are able to calculate in-session personalization features at run-time by calculating similarities between embeddings of candidate listings that need to be ranked and embeddings of listings already consumed by the guest, i.e. clicked, contacted or wishlisted listings. Consequently, our ranking model learns that the higher this similarity is the higher the candidate listing should be ranked.

Another application of embeddings at Airbnb is for purposes of search retrieval, i.e. finding a larger candidate set of listings for an input query to be later ranked by the search ranking model. While retrieval for explicit location queries, such as San Francisco, is straightforward, i.e. by calculating distances between city center and listing locations, retrieval for broad queries, such as festival names (e.g. Lollapalooza, Mardi Gras), activities (e.g. skiing in France, Costa Rica surfing) or regions (coastal Georgia, beach towns), etc., is much more involved. We found it useful to train both query and listing embeddings in the same feature space and conduct retrieval for a given query by calculating cosine similarity between its embedding and all listing embeddings from the learned vocabulary. The top listings with the highest similarity can be retrieved as broad query results. We are currently experimenting with this approach and we will share some preliminary results in this talk.

REFERENCES

[1] Ricardo Baeza-Yates, Berthier Ribeiro-Neto, et al. 1999. *Modern information retrieval.* Vol. 463. ACM press New York.

[2] Christopher J Burges, Robert Ragno, and Quoc V Le. 2007. Learning to rank with nonsmooth cost functions. In *Advances in neural information processing systems.* 193–200.

[3] Olivier Chapelle and Yi Chang. 2011. Yahoo! learning to rank challenge overview. In *Proceedings of the Learning to Rank Challenge.* 1–24.

[4] Mihajlo Grbovic, Nemanja Djuric, Vladan Radosavljevic, Fabrizio Silvestri, Ricardo Baeza-Yates, Andrew Feng, Erik Ordentlich, Lee Yang, and Gavin Owens. 2016. Scalable semantic matching of queries to ads in sponsored search advertising. In *Proceedings of the 39th International ACM SIGIR conference on Research and Development in Information Retrieval.* ACM, 375–384.

Bootstrapping a Destination Recommender System

Neal Lathia
Skyscanner Ltd.
London, United Kingdom
neal.lathia@skyscanner.net

ABSTRACT

Across different web services, we hear about recommendation systems that help users tackle information overload. Travel is different: the world does not have millions of cities, but finding new, interesting places to inspire people to travel is still a challenge. What are the factors that make traveling to destinations appealing, and how do those factors change based on your origin? What data, algorithms, and interactions do we need to surface destinations as recommendations? Moreover, how can a recommender system be built in a domain where typical users will book a flight, anonymously, less than a handful of times per year?

Years ago, Skyscanner[1] started it's 'everywhere' search, allowing users to find the cheapest countries to travel to. This feature evolved into an 'inspiration feed;' a stream of destinations, again ordered by price. However, price is just one of many factors that can make a place attractive. In this talk, I'll discuss how we've bootstrapped a destination recommender system to augment Skyscanner's destination feeds with wisdom-of-the-crowd recommendations, and give an overview of experiments that gauge how localised and personalised recommendations affects user engagement in different parts of the Android and iOS apps.

There are a variety of challenges that we had to tackle in this domain, ranging from data sourcing, sampling, and segmenting, to metric and algorithm selection, and building a pipeline that could facilitate rapid online and offline experimentation. We now have a system that uses the rich implicit data generated by Skyscanner's millions of users alongside a set of diverse algorithmic approaches to compute destination recommendations. Experimental features that use this pipeline are also collecting unique interaction data that is being analysed to further personalise users' recommendations. This talk will give an overview of the journey so far and some potential future directions and research challenges for recommendation in the travel domain.

Bio. Dr Neal Lathia is a Senior Data Scientist in Skyscanner's London office. Prior to that, he was a Senior Research Associate in the Computer Laboratory, University of Cambridge and a postdoctoral researcher at University College London. Neal has a PhD in recommender systems from the Department of Computer Science, University College London.

[1]http://www.skyscanner.net

RecSys'17, , August 27–31, 2017, Como, Italy.

ACM ISBN 978-1-4503-4652-8/17/08.
http://dx.doi.org/10.1145/3109859.3109924

Figure 1: Recommended destinations from London in the Skyscanner iOS app.

ACKNOWLEDGMENTS

Thanks to the all the current and former members of the Vespa squad, in London, who all contributed to building the data pipeline, interfaces, and online experiments described in this presentation.

Déjà Vu: The Importance of Time and Causality in Recommender Systems

Justin Basilico
Netflix, Inc.
Los Gatos, CA
jbasilico@netflix.com

Yves Raimond
Netflix, Inc.
Los Gatos, CA
yraimond@netflix.com

ABSTRACT

Time plays a key role in recommendation. Handling it properly is especially critical when using recommender systems in real-world applications, which may not be as clear when doing research with historical data. In this talk, we will discuss some of the important challenges of handling time in recommendation algorithms at Netflix. We will focus on challenges related to how our users, items, and systems all change over time. We will then discuss some strategies for tackling these challenges, which revolves around proper treatment of causality in our systems.

One clear way that time impacts recommendations is that users and items change over time. Users and items come and go from a service. Individual user interests also change, which could be someone picking up a new interest or even just people maturing and their tastes changing. Many recommendation approaches are based on historical co-occurrence, in which case they tend to lag with such changes instead of anticipating them. An item that is new to the system may start cold but then develop a lot of interest because it is new. So the level of interest in an item fluctuates across time, which can be additionally impacted by trends such as external events and seasonality.

Beyond these, the system itself changes over time. Feedback loops in the system, where users actions are influenced by the output of the recommendation system, cause the data that the system uses for recommendations to evolve over time. These feedback loops also can degrade the quality of the recommendations because it becomes hard to tease apart when a user is playing something because they enjoy it versus when they are playing it because it was shown prominently. These loops also can make it difficult for new algorithms to be trained and evaluated due to the influence of the production system. Different components of the system also can change over time, which can impact the data seen by other components. Time also becomes a tradeoff for how accurate a model can be against the time it takes to learn or compute recommendations for a certain request. A model giving very promising results offline but taking weeks to learn might be outperformed online by a model with weaker results but more responsive. On the other hand, changing fast may improve online accuracy by being responsive but may also confuse users when everything changes quickly.

RecSys '17, August 27-31, 2017, Como, Italy

ACM ISBN 978-1-4503-4652-8/17/08.
https://doi.org/10.1145/3109859.3109932

Since time is fundamental to the recommendation problem, we seek to optimize our handling of time in our systems. This includes designing experimentation around time by splitting across time and avoiding time-traveling data. It means introducing controlled stochasticity and counterfactuals to break feedback loops and understand causality. It means treating time as a first-class citizen in algorithms. It also means that we often want to optimize our recommendation systems such that a user minimizes the time a user needs to interact with it so that they can find something great to watch.

KEYWORDS

Recommender Systems; Time; Causality; Netflix

BIOS

Justin Basilico is a Research/Engineering Manager for Page Algorithms Engineering at Netflix. He leads an applied research team focused on developing the next generation of algorithms used to generate the Netflix homepage through machine learning, ranking, recommendation, and large-scale software engineering. He has also developed machine learning approaches that yielded significant improvements in the personalized ranking algorithms that drive the Netflix recommendation system. Prior to Netflix, he worked on machine learning in the Cognitive Systems group at Sandia National Laboratories. He is also the co-creator of the Cognitive Foundry, an open-source software library for building machine learning algorithms and applications.

Yves Raimond is a Research/Engineering Director at Netflix, where he leads the Search, Targeting & Recommendations Algorithm Engineering team: a mixed team of researchers and engineers building the next generation of Machine Learning algorithms used to drive the Netflix experience. Before that, he was a Lead Research Engineer in BBC R&D, working on information extraction from Multimedia content. He holds a PhD from Queen Mary, University of London.

Building Recommender Systems for Fashion

Industry Talk Abstract

Nick Landia
Dressipi
nick@dressipi.com

ABSTRACT

There has been a lot of recent interest in building recommender systems for fashion, with increased attention and investment from the retail industry. For academia, the fashion domain presents new challenges and opportunities that have not been explored before.

Dressipi is a personalisation and style advice engine for women's fashion. We work with some of the biggest retailers in the UK who have integrated our service into their site, and are currently expanding to the US and Australia. Since our launch in 2011 we have been helping millions of users find the clothes that they will love, buy and keep.

In this talk I will discuss the unique characteristics of the fashion domain and some of the most interesting challenges they pose for recommender systems. Fashion is inherently social and public: we dress not only for ourselves but also for the appropriateness of the environment we are in. When a user buys clothes it is not only important that they like the items themselves, but also that they feel confident and comfortable in the situation they are in. Fashion recommendations must satisfy two sometimes competing objectives: identifying the user's personal preference from their past behaviour and giving advice on what changes to their style would make them look better. Unlike other domains, recommendations should not be purely based on the user's personal taste and past activity. They must also take public perception into account by being aware of fashion rules, outfit guidelines and current trends.

Many companies providing recommendations in this space have realised that the user-item interaction data alone can only get you so far. We have started gathering additional personal information about the users in questionnaires, if they wish to provide it. Examples of this include body shape, age, favourite colours, lifestyle etc. These additional data points allow for some exciting applications such as giving style advice and generating high quality recommendation reasons that are useful to the user. For example: 'A bodycon dress is a figure flaunting style for your slender frame'.

The main challenges addressed in this talk are:

- Users are looking for guidance and validation that their fashion choices present the best version of themselves.
- There are objective fashion do's and dont's that professional stylists know about but users might not.
- Trends and popular culture events influence user preference and public perception quickly and sometimes drastically.
- Good recommendation reasons are extremely important, especially when trying to give advice and recommend items outside of the user's comfort zone.
- Outfits: a big factor in the decision to buy an item is the user's existing wardrobe. It is important for them to know whether they can wear the new item together with garments they already own to create good outfits.

RecSys '17, August 27-31, 2017, Como,Italy

ACM ISBN 978-1-4503-4652-8/17/08.
https://doi.org/10.1145/3109859.3109929

CCS CONCEPTS

• **Information systems → Recommender systems;**

KEYWORDS

Fashion, Dressipi, Recommendation Reasons, Outfits, User Features

ACM Reference format:
Nick Landia. 2017. Building Recommender Systems for Fashion. In *Proceedings of RecSys '17, Como,Italy, August 27-31, 2017,* 1 pages.
https://doi.org/10.1145/3109859.3109929

SPEAKER BIO

Nick Landia is the Chief Data Scientist at Dressipi where he has been working on recommendation algorithms for fashion for over three years. He is not only in charge of the recommendation and analytics teams, but also interacts with fashion domain experts on a regular basis to help guide the development of new approaches. The current areas of focus of his work are relating item features to user features, generating recommendation reasons and whole page optimisation. Previously he completed a PhD in the area of recommender systems at the University of Warwick, UK under the supervision of Dr. Sarabjot Singh Anand, and has co-founded two startups.

Boosting Recommender Systems with Deep Learning

João Gomes
Farfetch
Porto, Portugal
joao.gomes@farfetch.com

ABSTRACT

Farfetch is a global fashion marketplace with a catalog that, at any time, has over 200 000 products spanning over 2000 brands from luxury boutiques all around the world. Finding the right product to the right customer is a challenge that, we, as Data Scientists working on the Recommendations team, are trying to solve using state-of-the art algorithms and disruptive technologies. Deep learning (DL) is an area of Machine Learning that has recently been brought to the spotlight for its breakthrough results across several domains. In this talk, we will provide an overview of some ongoing projects in which Deep Learning methods play a major role.

A common problem in online marketplaces with large catalogs such as ours is the lack of detailed metadata about the products. Particularly, features such as style, colors, pattern, occasion, sizing, etc., are known to drive customers intent but are hard to catalog manually, in a consistent way. We explain how we use our extensive dataset of normalized product images together with state of the art convolutional neural networks to extract visual features. These can then be used to provide better recommendations and improve other applications across the platform.

Another application of DL is to capture relationships between products which are stylistically complementary. We leverage data from thousands of hand-curated outfits to model these intangible fashion concepts only a human specialist can provide, and generalize a method of recommending complementary products using deep siamese neural networks. This an alternative recommendation strategy that can be used to drive cross-sell opportunities.

These are merely a sample of problems we are tackling using DL at Farfetch. We believe that there are plenty of opportunities for application of these techniques to recommender systems and we look forward to discussing the potentials of this stream of research with the RecSys community.

KEYWORDS

Recommender systems; Deep Learning; Visual similarity; Feature extraction; E-commerce; Fashion.

ABOUT THE AUTHOR

João Gomes is the Lead Data Scientist for the Recommendations team at Farfetch. Since joining the company in 2015 he has helped design and develop new algorithms that power personalized recommendations and discoverability across the multiple channels of the Farfetch platform. His team's mission is to leverage large amounts of data to know, understand and ultimately inspire its customers. He holds a PhD in computational physics from the University of Aveiro, Portugal.

RecSys '17, August 27-31, 2017, Como, Italy

ACM ISBN 978-1-4503-4652-8/17/08.
https://doi.org/10.1145/3109859.3109926

Personalization Challenges in e-Learning

Roberto Turrin, PhD
Cloud Academy Inc.
Head of Technology
roberto.turrin@cloudacademy.com

ABSTRACT

Online learning is a hot trend in the education industry, as testified by the proliferation of e-learning platforms and MOOCs on a huge variety of topics, from science and technology to foreign language learning and musical instruments playing.

In this talk we will present some of the common challenges in the e-learning industry that we are personally facing at Cloud Academy, an on-line continuous training platform for Cloud technologies.

First, the nature of recommendation objects is quite diversified. Typically an e-learning platform comprises several content types, such as video lessons, reading material, quizzes, practical exercises (e.g., hands-on laboratories), etc. Also, they can be organized into composite objects, such as whole courses (groups of lessons) or exams (topic-specific quizzes and exercises).

Signals are very heterogeneous, too. Users can trigger all sorts of events while interacting with the learning platform, such as time spent on a given lesson video, outcome of a quiz or a test after a specific number of attempts, natural language feedback, etc. Such variety can be an important and comprehensive source of information but it must be normalized and handled within an appropriate common framework.

The objectives of recommendation in e-learning differ from the case of more well-established targets. Although enjoyment remains a driving force (e.g., proposing new interesting courses to an old user), the focus is on learning specific skills or topics for specific goals. In this scenario, recommendation seeks to suggest the new best lesson, exercise, or course to acquire the desired skill while keeping the user engaged, assembling a personalized study path in the process. The pace of the learning activity must be tailored on the user's needs and commitments, like deadlines (e.g., the user plans to get a certification by a certain date), specific goals (e.g., objectives of an employee might be defined by the user's manager) or learning prerequisites (e.g., a course can be consumed only after the student has acquired the needed knowledge, either via other more basic courses or pre-existing skills).

Consequently, recommendations must take into account the initial user skills and knowledge as well as her learning objectives (e.g., improving the skills of a non-beginner student requires recommending more advanced material). Transparency plays an important role in the e-learning domain as users are willing to continuously monitor and inspect their progress and understand which training resources better fit their learning goals.

Finally, the online learning environment can be made even more complex by "social features" such as virtual classes of multiple users, a context that recommender systems both can exploit and need to take into account.

ABOUT THE SPEAKER

Roberto is a well-known researcher in the recommendation community, with a record of relevant scientific publications, some of them also presented at RecSys.

He already organized some successful activities at RecSys: the ACM RecSys challenge in 2014, the RecSysTV workshop in 2015, and the CrowdRec workshop in 2015.

Roberto coordinated the research activities of ContentWise for several years, where he was also involved in the three-year FP7 European project CrowdRec as responsible of the work package dedicated to the development of recommendation algorithms.

Roberto currently works as Head of Technology at Cloud Academy, an online learning platform focused on cloud technologies, where he leads the research team focused on data-driven tasks such as (i) simplify, scale, and automate content operations and (ii) improve the customer experience.

RecSys '17, August 27-31, 2017, Como, Italy

ACM ISBN 978-1-4503-4652-8/17/08.
http://dx.doi.org/10.1145/3109859.3109927

Personalized Job Recommendation System at LinkedIn: Practical Challenges and Lessons Learned

Krishnaram Kenthapadi
LinkedIn Corporation, USA
kkenthapadi@linkedin.com

Benjamin Le
LinkedIn Corporation, USA
ble@linkedin.com

Ganesh Venkataraman
LinkedIn Corporation, USA
ghvenkataraman@linkedin.com

ACM Reference format:
Krishnaram Kenthapadi, Benjamin Le, and Ganesh Venkataraman. 2017. Personalized Job Recommendation System at LinkedIn: Practical Challenges and Lessons Learned. In *Proceedings of RecSys'17, August 27–31, 2017, Como, Italy.*, , 2 pages.
DOI: http://dx.doi.org/10.1145/3109859.3109921

1 PERSONALIZED JOB RECOMMENDATION: PRACTICAL CHALLENGES

Online professional social networks such as LinkedIn play a key role in helping job seekers find right career opportunities and job providers reach out to potential candidates. LinkedIn's job ecosystem has been designed to serve as a marketplace for efficient matching between potential candidates and job postings, and to provide tools to connect job seekers and job providers. LinkedIn's job recommendations product is a crucial mechanism to help achieve these goals, wherein personalized sets of recommended job postings are presented for members based on the structured, context data present in their profiles.

The problem of recommending jobs to LinkedIn members poses several unique information retrieval, system, and modeling challenges. (1) Personalized recommendations need to be computed in real-time by scoring millions of structured candidate job documents associated with each query while providing a high degree of data freshness and meeting strict latency requirements. Here, the query incorporates the member context / interests expressed through member profile, and hence can become very large, comprising of thousands of Boolean clauses over hundreds of document attributes. Consequently, candidate selection techniques need to be applied since it is infeasible to retrieve and score all matching jobs from the underlying inverted index. (2) Typically, the underlying retrieval systems may use content-based recommendation models, which are primarily based on the explicit member context / interests obtained from the profile, and may not take into account the implicit context in the form of user interactions. Hence, we may face the challenge of incorporating different types of user interaction signals as part of the relevance model. (3) The job recommendation problem is fundamentally different from traditional recommendation system problems such as recommending books, products, or movies to users. While all of the above have a common objective to maximize the engagement rate of the users, one key difference is that a job posting is typically meant to hire one or a few employees only, whereas the same book, product, or movie could be potentially recommended to hundreds of thousands of users for consumption.

RecSys'17, August 27–31, 2017, Como, Italy.

DOI: http://dx.doi.org/10.1145/3109859.3109921

As LinkedIn's job posters pay to post jobs on the site, on the one hand it is critical to deliver sufficient number of applications from qualified candidates to each job, such that the job poster can interview the top candidates and finally hire one or a few of them. On the other hand, it is not desirable either for the system to deliver too many applications to any posted jobs with one or a few openings, as the amount of effort for the job poster to interview would become much greater than expected. Also, if too many job seekers compete for the same job posting, each job seeker's chances of getting that job will be dramatically reduced.

In this talk, we will present how we formulated and addressed the above problems, the overall system design and architecture, the challenges encountered in practice, and the lessons learned from the production deployment of these systems at LinkedIn. By presenting our experiences of applying techniques at the intersection of recommender systems, information retrieval, machine learning, and statistical modeling in a large-scale industrial setting and highlighting the open problems, we hope to stimulate further research and collaborations with the RecSys community.

2 OVERVIEW OF SYSTEMS DEVELOPED AND DEPLOYED AT LINKEDIN

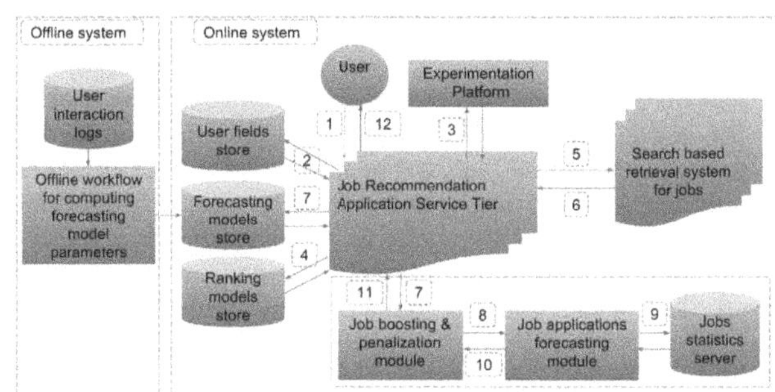

Figure 1: Architecture of LinkedIn's job recommendation engine.

The overall architecture of LinkedIn's job recommendation engine is shown in Figure 1. Our system can be subdivided into an online system for serving job recommendations and an offline workflow for updating different machine learned and statistical forecasting models (not fully shown).

We now provide a description of the overall flow for how a client request (query) is processed in our online job serving system. It makes use of a multi-tier service architecture, wherein the recommendation request queries are handled in a distributed fashion across hundreds of production servers. The online query processing proceeds as follows:

- Whenever a job recommendation needs to be shown to a user, the client application issues a query containing the userId and other metadata to the backend distributed job recommendation application service tier (step 1).

- The job recommendation application service then retrieves relevant structured user data from the user fields store (step 2), determines the appropriate A/B testing experimental treatment that the user falls under (step 3), and fetches the necessary ranking models based on the experimental treatment (step 4). Then, it creates a request object containing the user data and the models, which is issued to the distributed search service tier (step 5).
- Our search based retrieval system is built on top of LinkedIn's Galene search platform [5]. This system is responsible for applying the candidate selection model [1] [4] to the user data to generate a corresponding Galene query, issuing this query to the distributed search index service, scoring the resulting jobs using the final-pass GLMix ranking model [7], and returning back the top ranked job recommendation results (step 6).
- The job recommendation application service then performs post-processing (such as applying filters and certain business rules), and in particular, invokes the job boosting and penalization module [2] (steps 7–11).

We will focus on three sub-systems in this talk:

Candidate Selection: Inspired by our prior work in *CaSMoS* [1] , we present a new machine learning framework to construct effective queries as part of candidate selection in personalized search and recommendation systems via decision trees [4]. Query construction is done by converting the branch paths in the decision tree to corresponding Weighted AND (WAND) clauses [3]. The deployment of the prior candidate selection system resulted in up to 25% reduction in latency without sacrificing recommendation quality. Iterating on top of this system by introducing decision trees and early termination with static rank further reduced p99 latency by 56%. These system efficiency improvements paved the way for usage of more sophisticated scoring models, including GLMix.

Personalized Relevance Models: *Dionysius* was our first work for incorporating user interactions to personalize job recommendations in a system originally built as a content-based recommender [6]. Designed to leverage existing recommendation infrastructure, we learned the hidden fields for each user by considering the hierarchy of interaction signals and replaced the user profile-based fields with them to use in our ranking model. Through improved modeling and ranking infrastructure, we have replaced *Dionysius* with large-scale generalized linear mixed models (GLMix) containing millions of parameters [7]. In order to capture user's personal preferences on items and the item's specific attraction, we introduce member and job level regression coefficients in addition to the global regression coefficients. The global regression coefficients act as our prior prediction given a member profile and job posting. The posterior is estimated through fitting the per-member and per-job regression coefficients, which becomes more effective as a member interacts with more jobs and a job receives more attention. The end result is tailored job recommendations for a member given their profile, activity, and activity of similar members. Deploying the GLMix model increased job applications by 20% to 40% per day.

LiJAR: *LiJAR* is LinkedIn's job applications forecasting and redistribution system, designed with the goal of ensuring that job postings do not receive too many or too few applications, while providing job recommendations to users with *the same level* of relevance as the system that purely optimizes for user engagement [2]. This system uses a dynamic forecasting model to estimate the expected number of applications at the job expiration date, and algorithms to either promote or penalize jobs based on the output of the forecasting model in real time. Our online A/B testing experiments demonstrate the effectiveness of our approach in increasing the engagement of users for underserved jobs by 6.5%, while keeping the user engagement in terms of the total number of job applications the same.

3 AUTHOR BIOS

Krishnaram Kenthapadi is a Staff Software Engineer and Applied Researcher at LinkedIn. He shaped the technical roadmap and led the privacy/modeling efforts for LinkedIn Salary product, and prior to that, served as the relevance lead for the LinkedIn Careers and Talent Solutions Relevance team, which powers search/recommendation products at the intersection of members, recruiters, and career opportunities. Previously, he was a Researcher at Microsoft Research Silicon Valley. He received his PhD degree in Computer Science from Stanford University in 2006. He received the SODA best student paper award and the WWW best paper award nomination. He has published 35+ papers, with 2500+ citations and filed 110+ patents.

Benjamin Le is a Senior Software Engineer at LinkedIn. His contributions to jobs relevance include candidate selection in job search through multi-pass ranking and deploying generalized linear mixed models for reducing poor job recommendation impressions. Currently, he is focusing on the deployment of deep and wide models for job recommendations. He is a recent graduate of the University of California, Berkeley, where he received both his Master of Engineering and Bachelor of Science Degrees.

Ganesh Venkataraman currently leads all AI powering jobs relevance at LinkedIn. His contributions at LinkedIn include, leading a multi group effort that led to 50% improvement in job applications at LinkedIn, leading end to end re-architecture of job search, machine learned ranking for people search typeahead (system that allows members to search for 400MM+ users via instant results), introducing machine learned ranking towards skills search at LinkedIn (ex: searching for people skilled at "information retrieval"). He co-authored a paper on personalized ranking which won the best paper award at the IEEE Big Data Conference 2015. He holds a Ph.D. from Texas A&M in Electrical & Computer Engineering where he was the recipient of the Dean's graduate merit scholarship. He has several publications with 200+ citations including one fundamental contribution to graph theory.

REFERENCES

[1] F. Borisyuk, K. Kenthapadi, D. Stein, and B. Zhao. CaSMoS: A framework for learning candidate selection models over structured queries and documents. In *KDD*, 2016.

[2] F. Borisyuk, L. Zhang, and K. Kenthapadi. LiJAR: A system for job application redistribution towards efficient career marketplace. In *KDD*, 2017.

[3] A. Z. Broder, D. Carmel, M. Herscovici, A. Soffer, and J. Zien. Efficient query evaluation using a two-level retrieval process. In *CIKM*, 2003.

[4] A. Grover, D. Arya, and G. Venkataraman. Latency reduction via decision tree based query construction. LinkedIn Technical Report, 2017.

[5] S. Sriram and A. Makhani. LinkedIn's Galene Search engine, 2014. http://engineering.linkedin.com/search/did-you-mean-galene.

[6] J. Wang, K. Kenthapadi, K. Rangadurai, and D. Hardtke. Dionysius: A framework for modeling hierarchical user interactions in recommender systems. LinkedIn Technical Report, available at https://arxiv.org/abs/1706.03849, 2016.

[7] X. Zhang, Y. Zhou, Y. Ma, B.-C. Chen, L. Zhang, and D. Agarwal. GLMix: Generalized linear mixed models for large-scale response prediction. In *KDD*, 2016.

Online Learning to Rank for Recommender Systems

Daan Odijk
Blendle Research
daan@blendle.com

Anne Schuth
Blendle Research
anneschuth.com

ABSTRACT

Blendle is a New York Times backed startup that builds a platform where users can explore and support the world's best journalism. Users can read all content from 120 publications and only pay for what they read. Every morning, at Blendle, we have a huge cold-start problem when over 8.000 new articles from the latest editions of newspapers arrive in our system. At that moment, these articles are read by virtually no-one and we are tasked with sending out personalised newsletters to over 1 million users. We can thus not rely on collaborative filtering type of recommendations, nor can we use the popularity of the articles as clues for what our user might want to read. We overcome our cold-start problem by a mix of curation by our editorial team and an automated analysis of the content of these articles. We extract named entities, semantic links, authors, the language and plenty of stylometrics. For each of our users, we build a very fine grained profile based on the attributes of the articles that they read. The combination of enriched articles and user profiles is fed into our machine learning pipeline. We are currently experimenting with an online learning to rank setup, where each of our users is exposed to a slightly perturbed version of our ranking model. We observe the interactions of our users to infer in which direction we should be updating the model. Our editorial team gets up at around 5am every morning to read what was published over night. They are done reading and recommending their selection of articles around 8am, which is also the time we would ideally send out the newsletter so that our users, on their commute to work, can read our newsletter. These timing restrictions pose yet another challenge: our content analysis and machine learning pipeline needs to be really fast. We solve this by using a streaming infrastructure build on Kafka. In this infrastructure, an article is analysed and scored for relevance towards each of our users as soons as it arrives. This has the advantage that at 8am, when our editorial team is done reading, personalisation is much more lightweight. We use the precomputed relevance scores and balance them with diversity to arrive at a unique ranking for each of our users. In this talk, I will detail how we enrich articles in a streaming fashion and how we use online learning methods to learn a ranking model. I will also talk about how we deal with the time constraints of the problem we are trying to solve.

KEYWORDS

Recommender Systems, Journalism, Online Learning to Rank

RecSys '17, August 27-31, 2017, Como, Italy

ACM ISBN 978-1-4503-4652-8/17/08.
https://doi.org/10.1145/3109859.3109925

DAAN ODIJK

Daan Odijk is lead data scientist at Blendle and heads a team of eight data scientists and engineers who work on personalised recommendations. Daan has a PhD in information retrieval and has worked on leveraging context when searching for news. Daan was a research intern at Microsoft Research, where he worked on understanding struggling in web search.

ANNE SCHUTH

Anne Schuth is data scientist at Blendle. Last year, Anne obtained his PhD in Computer Science from the University of Amsterdam. His research focused on online learning to rank: optimizing search engine algorithms based on the interactions with users. Anne published over 30 peer-reviewed scholarly articles; including full papers at major information retrieval venues such as CLEF, ECIR, CIKM, WSDM, and SIGIR. Anne was research intern at Yandex in Moscow and Microsoft Research in Cambridge. At Yandex, Anne worked on evaluating bandit algorithms for retrieving fresh documents about current events. At Microsoft, Anne worked on making online evaluation methods more sensitive so that experiments need less traffic. At Blendle, Anne is responsible for the learning aspects of a recommendation engine for journalism.

Bandit Algorithms for e-Commerce Recommender Systems*

Extended Abstract

Björn Brodén
Apptus Technologies
Trollebergsvägen 5
Lund, Sweden SE-222 29
bjorn.broden@apptus.com

Mikael Hammar
Apptus Technologies
Trollebergsvägen 5
Lund, Sweden SE-222 29
mikael.hammar@apptus.com

Bengt J. Nilsson
Dept. of Computer Science
Malmö University
Malmö, Sweden SE-205 06
bengt.nilsson.TS@mah.se

Dimitris Paraschakis
Dept. of Computer Science
Malmö University
Malmö, Sweden SE-205 06
dimitris.paraschakis@mah.se

ABSTRACT

We study bandit algorithms for e-commerce recommender systems. The question we pose is whether it is necessary to consider reinforcement learning effects in recommender systems. A key reason to introduce a recommender system for a product page on an e-commerce site is to increase the order value by improving the chance of making an upsale. If the recommender system merely predicts the next purchase, there might be no positive effect at all on the order value, since the recommender system predicts sales that would have happened independent of the recommender system. What we really are looking for are the false negatives, i.e., purchases that happen as a consequence of the recommender system. These purchases entail the entire uplift and should be present as reinforcement learning effects. This effect cannot be displayed in a simulation of the site, since there are no reinforcement learning effects present in a simulation. The attribution model must capture the uplift to guarantee an increased order value. However, such an attribution model is not practical, due to data sparsity. Given this starting point, we study some standard attribution models for e-commerce recommender systems, and describe how these fare when applied in a reinforcement learning algorithm, both in a simulation and on live sites.

CCS CONCEPTS

• **Information systems** → **Recommender systems**; **Collaborative filtering**;

*This research is part of the research projects "Automated System for Objectives Driven Merchandising", funded by the VINNOVA innovation agency; `http://www.vinnova.se/en/`

RecSys'17, August 27-31, 2017,Como, Italy
 978-1-4503-4652-8/17/08.
DOI: http://dx.doi.org/10.1145/3109859.3109930

KEYWORDS

Recommender systems, e-commerce, multi-arm bandits, Thompson sampling, ensemble learning

1 DESCRIPTION

We extend the Thompson sampling (TS) bandit policy for orchestrating the collection of base recommendation algorithms for e-Commerce. We focus on the problem of item-to-item recommendations, for which multiple behavioral and content based predictors are provided to an ensemble learner. The extended TS-based policy must be able to handle situations when bandit arms are non-stationary and non-answering.

The talk covers the following topics:

(1) Bandit algorithms and attribution models for e-commerce recommender systems. We show that the click-through attribution model is prone to click attractors that may harm site performance. This is quite interesting, since many business models for recommender systems are based on the number of clicks that can be attributed to recommendations. We also show the effects of using a click-to-purchase attribution model. Finally, we discuss how to devise an attribution model that attacks the uplift.

(2) We analyze the bandit problem where we allow multiple responses, as well as retries if an arm does not answer a query. We show how the standard sampling method in this case correlates to a greedy solution for a specific problem in combinatorial optimization.

(3) The last area deals with non-stationary arms. The Thompson sampling method cannot handle these types of arms. We demonstrate that this property entails devastating practical issues and show a simple trick that transforms arms into both relatively homogenous and stationary arms that improve system performance drastically in practice.

We give results from simulations as well as results from live sites. The emphasis is to make the recommender system work in practice, and that it should answer any given query.

You are what apps you use - Transfer Learning for Personalized Content and Ad Recommendation

Zhixian Yan, Lai Wei, Yunshan Lu, Zhongqiang Wu, Bo Tao
Cheetah Mobile - Palo Alto, California, US
{zhixian.yan,lai.wei,luke.lu,jerry.wu,bo.tao}@cmcm.com

ABSTRACT

Cold start is always a key challenge for building real-life recommendation systems. Thanks to the ever-growing multi-modal data in the mobile Internet age and the latest deep learning techniques, transfer-learning based cross-domain recommendation starts to play a crucial role in tackling the cold start problem and to provide "warm-start" recommendation for new users. At Cheetah Mobile, we apply transfer learning to build personalized recommendation systems for both advertisement and content scenarios, serving 600+ millions monthly active mobile users. In particular, we leveraged the app install & usage and many other mobile data, built a *Unified User Profile* (UUP) by the state-of-the-art deep learning techiniques, and developed cross-domain personalized Ad and news recommendation. Our approaches enable us to solve the cold start problem with close to full coverage of our user base while yielding significant CTR increase and better user experience.

KEYWORDS

User Profile, Personalized Recommendation, Transfer Learning

1 INTRODUCTION

Cheetah Mobile is a leading mobile Internet company developing utility and content mobile applications, e.g., *Clean Master*, the number one Android optimizing tool for junk-file cleaning and antivirus. In addition to utility apps, Cheetah further developed a number of content apps in recent years, including news aggregator (i.e., *News Republic*), social live video streaming (i.e., *Live.me*), mobile games (e.g., *Piano Tiles*), and many more. These are top-downloaded apps at Google Play or Apple App Store in their own categories. As a result, Cheetah serves billions of requests per day for content or advertisement from its apps. One of the key challenges as well as a big potential at Cheetah now is how to connect such a big portfolio of different mobile apps. In particular, how to transfer users & study inter-app behaviors across different utility and content apps.

In order to address these challenges and to achieve our business goals, we leveraged petabytes of mobile data, applied transfer learning & deep learning, and built a rich user profile at Cheetah to serve hundreds of millions of users for both utility and content applications. Below are our three main contributions:

- Analyze massive mobile data from hundreds of millions of users, and build *Unified User Profile* using deep learning.
- Develop transfer learning that can cross-learn user behaviors through various utility or content apps about Ad or news engagement.
- Apply the *UUP* to solve the cold start problem in order to build real-time personalized Ad and content recommendation.

2 UUP - TRANSFER LEARNING

Approach. There has been much recent progress in transfer learning in both academy and industry [3][2][5]. Similarly, we have compiled massive daily logs from dozens of mobile apps at Cheetah, analyzed both intra- and inter- app user behaviors, and applied transfer learning to build a *Unified User Profile* (UUP) that is able to support cross-domain recommendation for various content and advertising applications. We built UUP to model users from different aspects, e.g., *basic profile, Ad profile, news profile.* More importantly, the UUP system provides end-to-end supports for personalized Ad and news recommendation for our utility and content apps. The UUP system unfolds its full tech stack with four layers, i.e., apps, data ETL, model learning and serving pipeline:

- *App Layer.* Various utility & content apps and their logging systems.
- *ETL Layer.* Clean, preprocess massive mobile logs, conduct daily and multi-day aggregation, build cross-domain data joins.
- *Learning Layer.* Define model targets, refine training data, develop transfer learning and wide & deep learning models.
- *UUP Serving Layer.* Develop diverse user profiles capturing user demographics and preference on Ads & news contents.

Results. The talk will include key features and models we developed to support personalized news & Ad recommendation. We will elaborate how various user profiles from UUP can achieve a warm-start recommendation for new users. By using UPP, the system can automatically learn user behaviors and recommend the most appropriate Ad or news for different app platforms. For the model part, we applied FastText [1] "as a fast and reasonable baseline" and the wide-deep neural networks [4]. In the talk, we will present offline and A/B test results. For example, our news app achieved 12% CTR increase for new users without click history; we were able to boost personalization from initial 30% users to a full coverage of 600+ million. In addition, we will share experiences and performance tricks in building real-life large scale recommendation engine that serves hundreds of millions of users in production.

REFERENCES

[1] Piotr Bojanowski, Edouard Grave, Armand Joulin, and Tomas Mikolov. 2016. Enriching Word Vectors with Subword Information. *CoRR* (2016).
[2] Paul Covington, Jay Adams, and Emre Sargin. 2016. Deep Neural Networks for YouTube Recommendations. In *RecSys.* 191–198.
[3] Ali Mamdouh Elkahky, Yang Song, and Xiaodong He. 2015. A Multi-View Deep Learning Approach for Cross Domain User Modeling in Recommendation Systems. In *WWW.*
[4] Heng-Tze Cheng et al. 2016. Wide & Deep Learning for Recommender Systems. In *DLRS.*
[5] Jie Tang, Sen Wu, Jimeng Sun, and Hang Su. 2012. Cross-domain Collaboration Recommendation. In *KDD.*

RecSys'17, August 27–31, 2017, Como, Italy.
 ISBN 978-1-4503-4652-8/17/08.
DOI: http://dx.doi.org/10.1145/3109859.3109923

CheckInShop.eu : A Sensor-based Recommender System for micro-location Marketing

Panagiotis Symeonidis
Faculty of Computer Science
Free University of Bolzano, Italy
psymeonidis@unibz.it

Stergios Chairistanidis
Department of Informatics
Aristotle University of Thessaloniki, Greece
hericonejito@gmail.com

ABSTRACT

CheckInShop is an app that employs sensors to capture the user preferences in physical stores and provide either micro-location marketing or product recommendations. By utilizing iBeacon technology and with the exploitation of a mobile app, we keep track of customer's preferences in physical stores. Then, based on the time that a product is viewed by a customer and his micro-location inside the store, we send to him either product offers or recommendations of similar products to the ones he is looking at. These recommendations are accurate because they are provided at the right time and in the right place. A video that demonstrates our system can be found in the following link: https://www.youtube.com/watch?v=Z99IMCHowAA

KEYWORDS

ibeacon; Recommender System

1 INTRODUCTION

Beacons are transmitters that broadcast Bluetooth Low Energy (BLE) signal with their identifier to nearby portable electronic devices. The technology enables smartphones, tablets and other devices to perform actions when in close proximity to a Beacon. They have the ability, using an appropriate app, to capture the moment a user enters and exits their region (the first time the application gets the beacon's signal and the last time it does). Thus, we know how much time a customer spends in a beacon's region. Consequently, we are able to cluster time into intervals, and in the end we can assign an implicit rating, which expresses the customer's preference on a product that belongs in a beacon's region, based on the time that the product is viewed by the customer and her micro-location inside the shop. Based on these implicit ratings, we can provide products recommendations.

A simple utilization matrix example of a sensor-based recommender system for a physical shop is illustrated in Table 1. Users are represented by their user IDs, whereas the items are represented by the beacon's major number. Some cells of Table 1 are left blank, which indicates that the three users have never been to the corresponding sections. The implicit preference values in our example are the actual number of seconds a user spends in a store section or views the details of a specific product. For example, a user with ID 234 passes from three different sections in a physical shop where beacons have been installed. Specifically, his app detects the signal of a beacon with major number equal to 54132 (Apple section) for 50 seconds, whereas the user stays in the Samsung store section for 80 seconds and in the camera store section for 2000 seconds. We can conclude that this specific potential buyer shows more interest for cameras than for mobile phones.

User ID	Beacon's major numbers / Store Section			
	54132 (Apple)	11353 (Samsung)	86766 (TV Section)	33377 (Camera)
1	122 sec	255 sec	-	-
4	-	-	600 sec	-
234	50 sec	80 sec	-	2000 sec

Table 1: Mapping preference between user and item

Our goal is to predict more accurately the customer's preferences on products, by analyzing the real time correlations between customers and products. Moreover, we can perform real-time product pricing and marketing. An example of our CheckInShop.eu system is shown in Figure 1. As shown, a store contains 4 beacons, which are assigned to 4 different store sections. The first one, B1, is installed in the entrance to keep track of users' enter and exit, and to provide them with general discounts and other deals. The other three beacons (B2, B3, B4) are assigned to jeans, shirts and shoes sections, respectively. Let's assume there are two users, visiting this store, having our CheckInShop app installed on their devices. As shown in Figure 1(a), user U_1 visits firstly the jeans section and afterwards, he goes to the shoes section. In both sections, he stays for more than 15 minutes, which is assumed as a positive preference rating to the products that belong in these sections. Next, as shown in Figure 1(a) a second user, U_2, enters the store and visits the shoes section for more than 15 minutes. Thus, when he decides to leave the shoes section, the following notification message appears on his smart phone that recommends him the jeans section, which is also shown in Figure 1(b) : "We recommend you to visit the jeans section because U_1 visited it in the past and you both have visited the shoes section for more than 15 minutes".

The rest of this paper is organized as follows. Section 2 summarizes the related work, Section 3 summarizes the system's architecture. Finally, Section 4 concludes this paper.

2 RELATED WORK

Our CheckInShop.eu system captures similarity among users based on the link analysis of the user-product bipartite graph. The "link prediction problem", as denoted by Liben-Nowell and Kleinberg [2],

RecSys '17, August 27-31, 2017, Como, Italy

ACM ISBN 978-1-4503-4652-8/17/08.
https://doi.org/10.1145/3109859.3109977

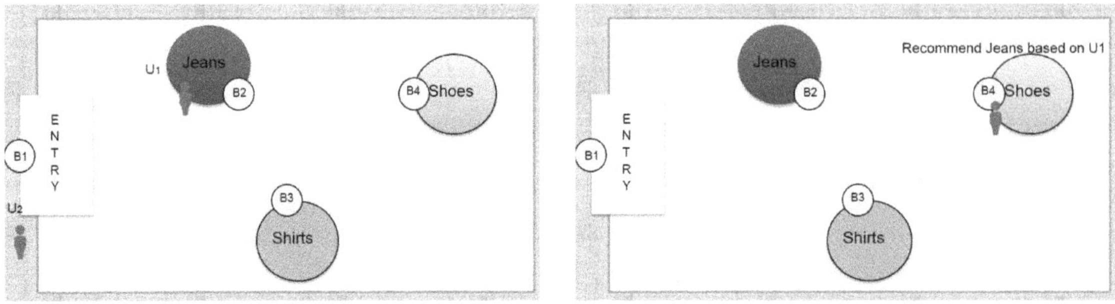

(a) Recommendation Scenario (b) Recommendation Scenario

Figure 1: Example of a context-aware recommender system based on beacons

exists in several networks (social networks, protein-protein networks, user-products networks, etc.). There is a lot of research work in the domain of link prediction in graphs. We can distinguish two different algorithms for computing the similarity between nodes in such a network. The first one is SimRank [1] and the second one is P-Rank [3]. By exploiting these algorithms, we provide context-aware recommendations based on the sensor technology and the smart phone devices.

3 SYSTEM'S ARCHITECTURE

Figure 2 demonstrates the architecture of our CheckInShop system. It consists of a website for the shop owners, a mobile application for iOS devices named CheckInShop, a JAVA servlet which is the web-server of our system, and a MySQL web-based database.

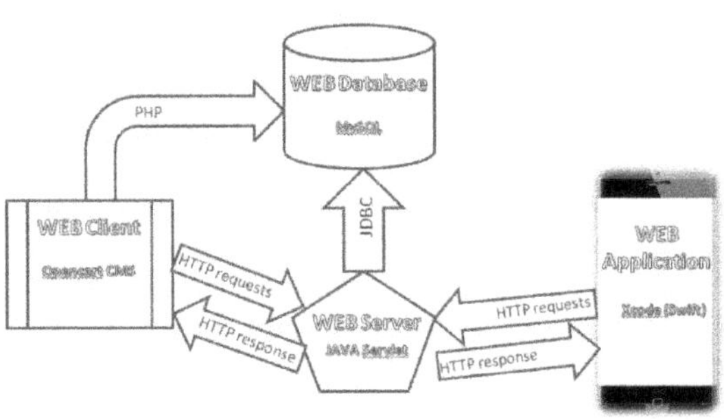

Figure 2: CheckInShop.eu System's architecture

Our CheckInShop.eu website offers a friendly interface to shop owners for uploading their products' information and correlating them with beacons. On the other hand, our CheckInShop App keeps track of the time a customer spends for viewing a product and can provide to him other recommendations of similar products either based on the item-based or the user-based recommendation styles, which are shown in Fig. 3. The user-based recommendation style is shown in Fig. 3(a). User-based style employs users' similarities for generating product recommendations. Moreover, Fig. 3(b) shows the Item-based recommendation style, which is based on an item-item similarity matrix to generate recommendations of similar products.

Please notice that the user-user and item-item similarity matrices can be build based on either SimRank or P-Rank algorithms.

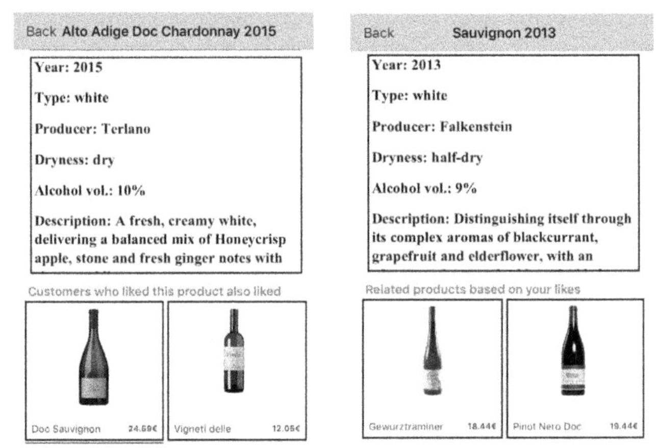

(a) User-based recommendation style (b) Item-based recommendation style

Figure 3: Recommended Products

4 CONCLUSIONS

In this demo paper, we proposed CheckInShop.eu, which provides either micro-location marketing or product recommendations based on the contextual (i.e., micro-location, time, etc.) information of the customer. In future, we want to test experimentally our system to check its accuracy effectiveness.

REFERENCES

[1] G. Jeh and J. Widom. Simrank - a measure of structural-context similarity. *Proceedings of the ACM SIGKDD International Conference on Knowledge Discovery and Data Mining*, pages 271 – 279, 2002.
[2] D. Liben-Nowell and J. Kleinberg. The link prediction problem for social networks. *Proceedings of the twelfth international conference on Information and knowledge management*, 2003.
[3] P. Zhao, J. Han, and Y. Sun. P-rank: a comprehensive structural similarity measure over information networks. *Proceeding of the 18th ACM Conference on Information and Knowledge Management*, pages 553 – 562, 2009.

A Research Tool for User Preferences Elicitation with Facial Expressions

Marko Tkalčič
Faculty of Computer Science
University of Bozen-Bolzano
Piazza Domenicani 3
Bolzano, Italy 39100
marko.tkalcic@unibz.it

Nima Maleki
Politecnico di Milano
Piazza Leonardo da Vinci, 32
Milano, Italy 20133
nima.maleki@mail.polimi.it

Matevž Pesek
Faculty of Computer Science
University of Ljubljana
Večna pot 113
Ljubljana, Slovenia 1000
matevz.pesek@fri.un-lj.si

Mehdi Elahi
Faculty of Computer Science
University of Bozen-Bolzano
Piazza Domenicani 3
Bolzano, Italy 39100
meelahi@unibz.it

Francesco Ricci
Faculty of Computer Science
University of Bozen-Bolzano
Piazza Domenicani 3
Bolzano, Italy 39100
francesco.ricci@unibz.it

Matija Marolt
Faculty of Computer Science
University of Ljubljana
Večna pot 113
Ljubljana, Slovenia 1000
matija.marolt@fri.uni-lj.si

ABSTRACT

We present a research tool for user preference elicitation that collects both explicit user feedback and unobtrusively acquired facial expressions. The concrete implementation is a web-based user interface where the user is presented with two music excerpts. After listening to both, the user provides a pairwise score (i.e. which of the two items is preferred) for each pair of music excerpts. The novelty of the demo is the integration of the unobtrusive acquisition of facial expressions through the webcam. During the listening of the music excerpts, the system extracts features related to the facial expressions of the user several times per second. The interaction runs as a web application, which allows for a large-scale remote acquisition of emotional data. Up to now, such acquisitions were usually done in controlled environments with few subjects, hence being of little use for the recommender systems community.

CCS CONCEPTS

• **Human-centered computing** → *Interaction devices*; *Empirical studies in HCI*; • **Computing methodologies** → *Machine learning*;

KEYWORDS

pairwise scores, implicit preference elicitation, facial expressions, emotions

ACM Reference format:
Marko Tkalčič, Nima Maleki, Matevž Pesek, Mehdi Elahi, Francesco Ricci, and Matija Marolt. 2017. A Research Tool for User Preferences Elicitation with Facial Expressions. In *Proceedings of RecSys '17, Como, Italy, August 27-31, 2017,* 2 pages.
https://doi.org/10.1145/3109859.3109978

ACM ISBN 978-1-4503-4652-8/17/08...$15.00
https://doi.org/10.1145/3109859.3109978

1 INTRODUCTION

This demo addresses elicitation of user preferences. Preference elicitation deals with retrieving user feedback about items. The feedback is usually provided in the form of explicitly entered ratings of some numerical form (e.g., one to five stars) or signals of implicit preferences, such as click, preview, purchase etc. Furthermore, feedback can be acquired as a single judgment or in the form of pairwise comparison [4]. These forms of feedback reflect the opinions of users about items. However, these opinions are not based only on rational thinking but are often fast, intuitive and emotionally charged, as described by the two-systems model [3]. This model describes human decision making as an aggregation of a fast, emotional (System I) and a slow, rational, cognitive process. When the preferences are acquired explicitly, content-based recommender systems [6] exploit well the rational part, i.e. the relationship between item characteristics and expressed user preferences. Still, the relationship between the user's emotional state and the expressed preference and its impact on the performance of recommender systems is a less explored area. Research on emotions-based recommender systems have been done on a smaller scale [1, 9] as the acquisition of such data has been traditionally difficult.

In recent years, the unobtrusive acquisition of emotional user responses has become more accessible. Algorithms, that take advantage of multiple modalities, such as facial expressions, voice and physiological responses, have become robust and accurate [7]. Furthermore, a number of off-the-shelf products have become available, such as the Affectiva API[1].

This demo showcases a tool for researchers in the form of a web interface, which allows preference elicitation both in the forms of (i) explicit comparison of item pairs and (ii) unobtrusively acquired affective responses of users. The added value of extracting facial features, related to emotions, from the web camera allows to pursue new research directions: (i) development of unobtrusive acquisition of user ratings from facial expressions and (ii) new multidimensional models of user preferences.

[1] https://developer.affectiva.com/

2 TECHNICAL DESCRIPTION

The demo user interface is available at the URL https://recsys.musiclab.si/PairwiseComparisonsStudy/ while a video walkthrough is available at the URL http://www.inf.unibz.it/~tkalcic/RecSysDemo2017Walkthrough/. It is written in PHP using the CodeIgniter framework and using JavaScript on the client side. The information flow is shown in Fig. 1. The facial expressions are acquired through the webcam video stream. The stream is sent to the Affectiva API directly using Javascript. In this way our server is not burdened with proxying the multiple video streams. The Affectiva API returns to the web browser a JSON file containing the extracted facial features. The sampling frequency is not constant through time but in practice it fluctuates around 11 frames per second. The features are then sent from the web browser to our server and stored in a database. The database also stores the user-entered pairwise scores and other user characteristics, acquired through pre- and post-questionnaires, such as personality and the Music Sophistication Index [5].

The music excerpts are taken from the Moodo dataset [8], which consists of 200 snippets of songs, each lasting approximately 15 seconds. The songs are not widely known to the general public, which reduces the popularity bias. The selection of song pairs for comparison was done randomly, however, we used a weighting schema to simulate the short-head, long-tail effect.

Each music comparison, which is defined by the tuple $(user, song1, song2, score)$ contains several database entries. The pairwise score $score$ is on the scale $\{-2, -1, 0, 1, 2\}$, where $-2(2)$ means the user preferred the left-most (right-most) song and 0 means both songs were equal. Each entry within the same comparison contains the facial features acquired at a sampling point while the user was comparing the two items. In the study conducted up to this point, we had 27 users (10 males, median age 27 years) who completed the interaction. On average, each user compared 9.4 pairs of songs. The average comparison lasted 27.9 seconds. The average facial features sampling frequency was 11.2 times per second. Hence, for each comparison we had on average 312 database entries with facial features.

From the Affectiva API we collect a total of 47 features for each video frame. Examples of concrete features are

- **appearance**: gender, age, glasses, ethnicity
- **low-level facial features**: innerBrowRaise, browFurrow, noseWrinkle, upperLipRaise, lipCornerDepressor, eyeClosure, chinRaise, jawDrop etc.
- **emotions**: joy, sadness, disgust, contempt, anger, fear, surprise, valence, engagement

The low-level facial features and the emotions are integers on the scale $[0, 100]$.

Beside the pairwise music preference elicitation part, the users are asked to fill-in a pre- and post-questionnaires. In the pre-questionnaire, we inquired about the user demographics, while in the post-questionnaires we inquired about the user personality (using the TIPI questionnaire[2]) and the Music Sophistication Index (using the MSI [5] questionnaire).

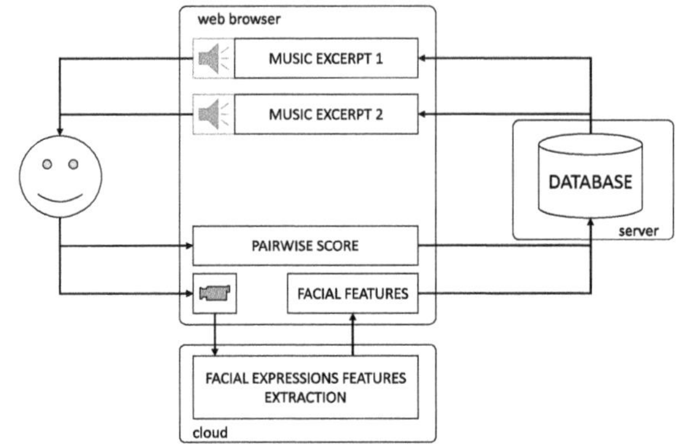

Figure 1: Demo flow: the user listens to two music snippets and then provides a pairwise score. During the listening to the music, a web camera streams the video to an API that extracts the facial features.

3 IMPLICATIONS FOR RECOMMENDER SYSTEMS RESEARCH AND FUTURE WORK

The demo presented in this paper is targeted primarily at researchers, who are interested in advanced preference elicitation techniques. The data collected with this system allows to pursue new research directions, such as (i) development of unobtrusive acquisition of user ratings from facial expressions and (ii) new multidimensional models of user preferences.

An open issue is privacy. Systems, that extract sensitive information, such as emotions, should be carefully designed, but this is beyond the scope of this demo.

REFERENCES

[1] Sergio Benini, Luca Canini, and Riccardo Leonardi. 2011. A Connotative Space for Supporting Movie Affective Recommendation. *IEEE Transactions on Multimedia* 13, 6 (dec 2011), 1356–1370. https://doi.org/10.1109/TMM.2011.2163058
[2] Samuel D Gosling, Peter J Rentfrow, and William B Swann. 2003. A very brief measure of the Big-Five personality domains. *Journal of Research in Personality* 37, 6 (dec 2003), 504–528. https://doi.org/10.1016/S0092-6566(03)00046-1
[3] Daniel Kahneman. 2003. A perspective on judgment and choice: mapping bounded rationality. *The American psychologist* 58, 9 (sep 2003), 697–720. https://doi.org/10.1037/0003-066X.58.9.697
[4] Saikishore Kalloori, Francesco Ricci, and Marko Tkalcic. 2016. Pairwise Preferences Based Matrix Factorization and Nearest Neighbor Recommendation Techniques. *Proceedings of the 10th ACM Conference on Recommender Systems - RecSys '16* (2016), 143–146. https://doi.org/10.1145/2959100.2959142
[5] Daniel Müllensiefen, Bruno Gingras, Lauren Stewart, and Jason Ji. 2013. *Goldsmiths Musical Sophistication Index (Gold-MSI) v1.0: Technical Report and Documentation Revision 0.3.* Technical Report. University of London Goldsmiths.
[6] Francesco Ricci, Lior Rokach, and Bracha Shapira. 2015. Recommender Systems: Introduction and Challenges. In *Recommender Systems Handbook*. Vol. 54. Springer US, Boston, MA, 1–34. https://doi.org/10.1007/978-1-4899-7637-6_1
[7] Björn W Schuller. 2016. Acquisition of Affect. In *Emotions and Personality in Personalized Services: Models, Evaluation and Applications*, Marko Tkalčič, Berardina De Carolis, Marco de Gemmis, Ante Odić, and Andrej Košir (Eds.). Springer International Publishing, Cham, 57–80. https://doi.org/10.1007/978-3-319-31413-6_4
[8] Gregor Strle, Matevž Pesek, and Matija Marolt. 2016. Towards User-Aware Music Information Retrieval: Emotional and Color Perception of Music. 327–353. https://doi.org/10.1007/978-3-319-31413-6_16
[9] Marko Tkalčič, Urban Burnik, and Andrej Košir. 2010. Using affective parameters in a content-based recommender system for images. *User Modelling and User-Adapted Interaction* 20, 4 (sep 2010), 279–311. https://doi.org/10.1007/s11257-010-9079-z

Data-Driven Repricing Strategies in Competitive Markets: An Interactive Simulation Platform

Martin Boissier¶, Rainer Schlosser¶, Nikolai Podlesny§, Sebastian Serth§, Marvin Bornstein§, Johanna Latt§, Jan Lindemann§, Jan Selke§, Matthias Uflacker¶
Hasso Plattner Institute, University of Potsdam, Germany
¶{firstname.lastname}@hpi.de, §{firstname.lastname}@student.hpi.de

ABSTRACT

Modern e-commerce platforms pose both opportunities as well as hurdles for merchants. While merchants can observe markets at any point in time and automatically reprice their products, they also have to compete simultaneously with dozens of competitors. Currently, retailers lack the possibility to test, develop, and evaluate their algorithms appropriately before releasing them into the real world. At the same time, it is challenging for researchers to investigate how pricing strategies interact with each other under heavy competition. To study dynamic pricing competition on online marketplaces, we built an open simulation platform. To be both flexible and scalable, the platform has a microservice-based architecture and handles large numbers of competing merchants and arriving consumers. It allows merchants to deploy the full width of pricing strategies, from simple rule-based strategies to more sophisticated data-driven strategies using machine learning. Our platform enables analyses of how a strategy's performance is affected by customer behavior, price adjustment frequencies, the competitors' strategies, and the exit/entry of competitors. Moreover, our platform allows to study the long-term behavior of self-adapting strategies.

KEYWORDS

dynamic pricing; simulation; oligopoly competition; demand learning; microservice architecture

1 SIMULATING PRICING COMPETITION

Online marketplaces are highly dynamic and competitive. Merchants are allowed to automatically adjust prices to react to changing market situations. To derive effective pricing strategies is challenging considering that thousands of products have to be managed and demand information is limited (cf. Chen and Chen [1]).

As testing automated pricing strategies is potentially hazardous when done in production, simulating the performance of competing repricing strategies is important. However, little effort has been made to build flexible simulation platforms that ease the development and evaluation of repricing algorithms. Existing platforms (e.g., [2, 3]) are limited in their capabilities: Simulations run on a single machine, offer a limited set of consumer behaviors, simulate solely finite sales horizons, and pricing updates are restricted to discrete points in time that are predefined by the system.

In other areas simulation platforms are also used to study complex systems, e.g., in the field of real-time bidding [8], marketing [5], or electricity markets [3].

We built a continuous time framework (mimicking production marketplaces such as Amazon or eBay) to simulate dynamic pricing competition for the sale of durable goods. This setup allows to define a random stream of potential customers whose buying decisions for a specific product can arbitrarily depend on the current market situation determined by the competitors' offers which include price and quality. Evaluating the mutual price reactions of competing strategies, we obtain price trajectories and simulate realized sales events. By visualizing various performance measures (e.g., short and long-term profits), the user can easily compare different types of repricing strategies.

Our simulation marketplace has an HTTP/REST-based interface. That enables our platform to allow an arbitrary number of merchants to compete simultaneously. Each merchant can run his preferred repricing strategy to adjust prices on the marketplace. The platform logs each interaction (such as price updates, new offers, sales, etc.), which can be requested and analyzed by each merchant. This way, merchants can deploy both rule-based strategies as well as data-driven strategies that leverage various demand learning approaches to estimate customers' buying behavior (Figure 1 depicts the platform's components for both pricing strategies).

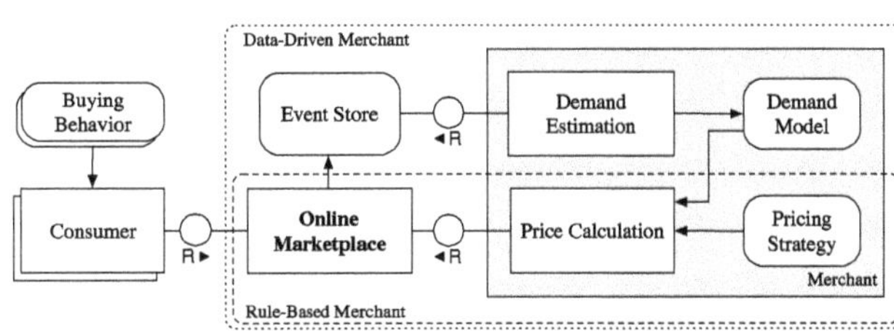

Figure 1: Platform architecture showing the different components used by rule-based and data-driven merchants (FMC notation [6]).

Our framework also makes it possible to measure the influence of the customers' buying behavior, price adjustment frequencies, and the exit or entry of competitors on a strategy's performance. In addition, demand learning techniques can be compared regarding their accuracy and efficiency.

RecSys '17, August 27-31, 2017, Como, Italy

ACM ISBN 978-1-4503-4652-8/17/08.
https://doi.org/10.1145/3109859.3109979

2 DESCRIPTION OF THE PLATFORM

The platform was built with a microservice-based architecture for scalability and flexibility. Each service implements one business artifact, whereby services can be scaled out for large simulations. By having separated services, additional components can be added during running simulations at any time.

Most importantly, merchants can be easily added to the simulation or updated as long as they confirm to the HTTP/REST interface of the platform. Merchants update their products' prices based on the current market situation which they can request at any time. Arbitrary strategies, e.g., rule-based or data-driven strategies, can be applied. Data of observed market situation as well as a merchant's sales data can be used to estimate sales probabilities using various machine learning techniques (e.g., Q-learning [7]).

The centre of the simulation is the *marketplace* which manages all product offers. Offers include price and quality. The marketplace is the access point for the *consumer* component which creates a random stream of interested customers. Any customer choice behavior can be defined. The decision whether a customer buys a product and which offer is chosen, is modelled by probabilities that can depend on all parameters of the current market situation. The *log store* logs platform events (e.g., price adjustments and sales) and provides CSV files for data-driven merchants. The *producer* is responsible for the replenishment. Merchants are provided with new products according to a (fair) distribution. This way the performances of competing strategies are not affected by asymmetric reordering strategies. However, the model also allows to let merchants choose their replenishment on their own. The *HTML-based front end* enables the user to configure customer behavior, merchants, as well as replenishment rules.

The front end shown in Figure 2 allows to observe the evolution of market situations and price trajectories over time. The strategies' short-term and long-term performances are measured by different KPIs, including profits, revenues (see Figure 3), sales, etc.

A detailed description of the platform, its architecture, and the components can be found in [4].

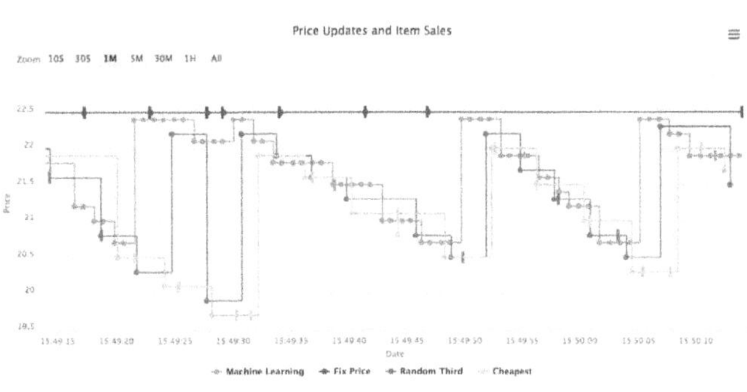

Figure 2: Competitors' price trajectories over time.

3 RESULTS

The platform allows to simulate strategic interaction of various rule-based and data-driven strategies in different market scenarios characterized by product portfolios, customer behaviors, oligopoly

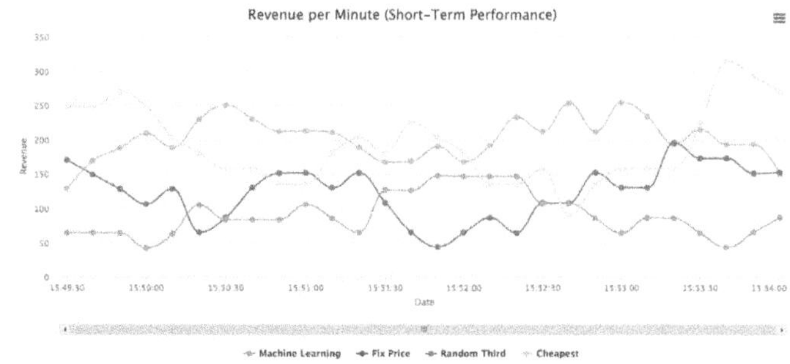

Figure 3: Comparison of short-term revenue (moving window aggregation over last minute) over time.

settings, and price adjustment frequencies. We found that adjustment frequencies have a major impact on expected profits and data-driven strategies often vastly outperform rule-based ones after a sufficiently large data set has been gathered. Moreover, the platform can be used to study short-term as well as long-term performance of self-adapting strategies that iteratively improve their pricing strategies.

4 CONCLUSION

The presented dynamic pricing simulation is a distributed and scalable platform mimicking real-world e-commerce applications. With this toolkit, both practitioners and researchers can directly participate and study various pricing strategies under competition and develop, test, and evaluate own approaches. Furthermore, our model can be easily extended in several ways: (i) additional offer dimensions (ratings, shipping time, etc.), (ii) joint replenishment decisions for sellers, (iii) the consideration of perishable products, and (iv) substitution effects between different products.

The source code and its technical documentation is publicly available at GitHub[1]. A screen cast of the simulation is available under https://vimeo.com/epicchair/pricewars.

REFERENCES

[1] Ming Chen and Zhi-Long Chen. 2015. Recent Developments in Dynamic Pricing Research: Multiple Products, Competition, and Limited Demand Information. *Production and Operations Management* 24, 5 (2015), 704–731.

[2] DiMicco et al. 2003. Learning Curve: A Simulation-based Approach to Dynamic Pricing. *Electronic Commerce Research* 3, 3-4 (2003), 245–276.

[3] Pinto et al. 2014. Adaptive learning in agents behaviour: A framework for electricity markets simulation. *Integrated Computer-Aided Engineering* 21, 4 (2014), 399–415.

[4] Serth et al. 2017. An Interactive Platform to Simulate Dynamic Pricing Competition on Online Marketplaces. In *21st IEEE International Enterprise Distributed Object Computing Conference, EDOC 2017, Québec City, Canada, October 10-13, 2017.* To appear.

[5] Tkachenko et al. 2016. Customer Simulation for Direct Marketing Experiments. In *2016 IEEE International Conference on Data Science and Advanced Analytics, DSAA 2016, Montreal, QC, Canada, October 17-19, 2016.* 478–487.

[6] Andreas Knöpfel, Bernhard Gröne, and Peter Tabeling. 2005. Fundamental modeling concepts. *Effective Communication of IT Systems, England* (2005).

[7] Erich Kutschinski, Thomas Uthmann, and Daniel Polani. 2003. Learning competitive pricing strategies by multi-agent reinforcement learning. *Journal of Economic Dynamics and Control* 27, 11 (2003), 2207–2218.

[8] Wush Chi-Hsuan Wu, Mi-Yen Yeh, and Ming-Syan Chen. 2015. Predicting Winning Price in Real Time Bidding with Censored Data. In *Proceedings of the 21th ACM SIGKDD International Conference on Knowledge Discovery and Data Mining, Sydney, NSW, Australia, August 10-13, 2015.* 1305–1314.

[1] Platform repository: https://github.com/hpi-epic/masterproject-pricewars

5 THUMBNAIL

Thumbnail Caption: "Price Wars" is a distributed simulation platform for large dynamic pricing competitions. The platform is open source (https://github.com/hpi-epic/masterproject-pricewars) and provides means to develop and evaluate data-driven pricing strategies.

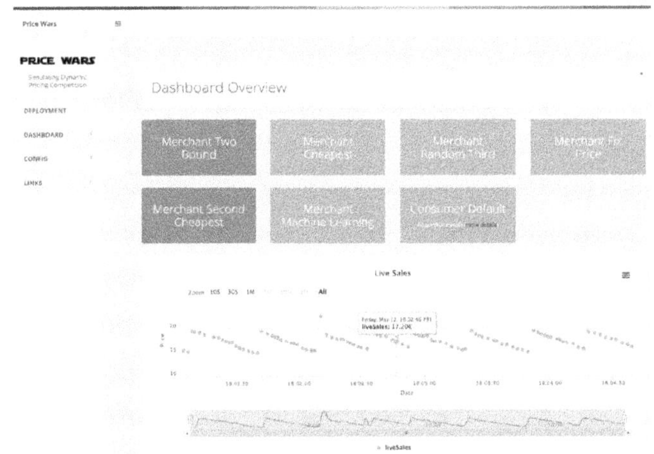

Figure 4: ACM DL Thumbnail.

Pokedem: an Automatic Social Media Management Application

Francesco Corcoglioniti[1], Claudio Giuliano[1], Yaroslav Nechaev[1,2], Roberto Zanoli[1]

[(1)] Fondazione Bruno Kessler, Via Sommarive 18, 38123 Trento, Italy
[(2)] University of Trento, Via Sommarive 14, 38123 Trento, Italy
{corcoglio,giuliano,nechaev,zanoli}@fbk.eu

ABSTRACT

Typically, the task of managing the social media presence of a company or a public person is the job of a dedicated social media account manager. While many attempts have been made in recent years to provide more automation to account managers, complete workflow automation has still to be achieved. *Pokedem* is a social media management application that aims at filling this gap, recommending actions that could be performed by the account manager to increase the popularity of a Twitter account and the engagement of its audience. By casting the problem in the setting of recommendation systems, Pokedem is able to provide account managers with a complete tool for automating their daily activities.

KEYWORDS

Recommender system; Social media management; Machine learning

1 INTRODUCTION

Social media account managers perform a wide range of daily activities including content generation, engagement of target audience, data analytics and any other account promotion activity, for all of which little workflow automation support is currently available.

The goal of Pokedem[1] is to automate those daily activities to reduce the burden, required time and skills for account managers, allowing them to focus on activities needing human judgment and creativity. Focusing on Twitter, Pokedem provides an account manager with comprehensive data analytics about the performances of the account as well as the profiling of the target audience. The main feature of Pokedem, however, is its *recommendation system* that suggests possible actions to perform on the account (tweet/retweet, follow/unfollow, like/unlike), with the business-relevant goal [6] of improving account popularity and audience engagement, rather than suggesting people and contents that the user may like as typically considered in Twitter recommendation literature [3].

In this demo, we showcase the capabilities of Pokedem, highlighting through a use case deployment (@esseredeltoro account) how its use allows managing social media presence with little effort.

[1]Demonstration video at http://pokedem.futuro.media/

RecSys '17, August 27-31, 2017, Como, Italy

ACM ISBN 978-1-4503-4652-8/17/08.
https://doi.org/10.1145/3109859.3109980

2 POKEDEM OVERVIEW

Pokedem consists of three main components, corresponding to distinct tabs in the web interface it provides to social media account managers (Figure 1): *Recommendations*, *User Profiling*, and *Analytics*.

Recommendations This tab (excerpt in Figure 1a) provides a ranked, always up-to-date list of recommended social media actions, with explanations of why they are recommended. The account manager may reject, execute immediately, or schedule a recommended action for later execution at an optimal time chosen by the system.

Recommendations are generated using *content-based recommendation techniques* [4] based on rich *user profile* features, tailored to each type of action, and aimed at improving account reputation rather than mimicking the account manager's behavior. Therefore, actions are proposed based on the likelihood of a positive feedback on social media—follow-back for follow or like actions, likes or retweets for tweet actions—estimated from previous actions done by the account. The execute/reject feedback of the account manager for past actions is currently ignored. Pokedem recommends:

- following users that may follow back the account (top box in Figure 1a), based on several user profile features that are compared in a content-based way with the ones of followers;
- tweeting links to relevant news articles (bottom box in Figure 1a), chosen from configurable RSS feeds based on news popularity (e.g., number of comments) and topicality;
- tweeting different charts comparing the social media performances (activity level, influence) of users on configurable topics, to engage them and improve followers retention.

For tweeting actions, Pokedem also recommends trending hashtags to increase tweet visibility, and supports replacing proper names with corresponding Twitter accounts (to notify them of the tweet).

User Profiling This tab (excerpt in Figure 1b) shows the rich user profiles collected by Pokedem to support recommendations. Profiles are computed for the target Twitter audience of the account, identified by navigating the social network from representative seed accounts. In addition to basic attributes (e.g., language, creation date, followers count), the following attributes are extracted from public social media data via state-of-the-art classification techniques and the linking of popular Twitter accounts to Wikipedia/DBpedia [5]:

- user gender/type (person, org.), via rules and gazetteers;
- user location, either gathered explicitly from the user or estimated via supervised classifiers trained on explicit data;
- user influence score, consisting in a *h-index* like measure based on the number of user tweets and their retweets/likes;
- user activity level, based on number and recency of tweets;
- domain-specific attributes like the user's favourite football team, estimated mainly based on followed accounts.

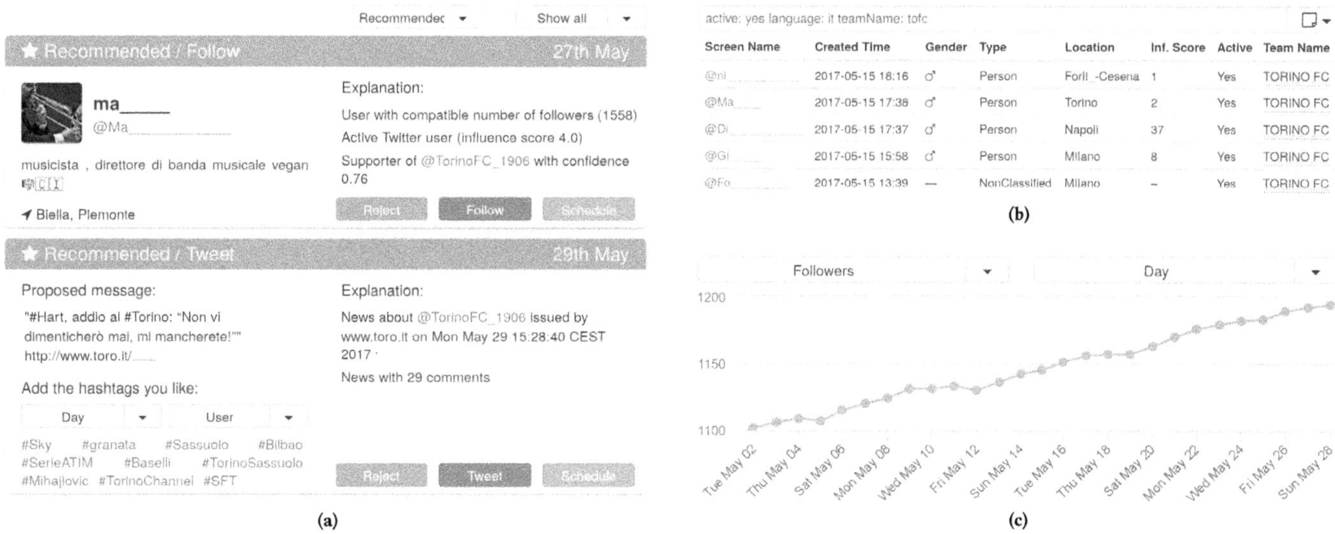

Figure 1: Pokedem user interface for @esseredeltoro: (a) Recommendations tab, (b) User Profiling tab, (c) Analytics tab.

Filtering facilities and attribute distribution charts support demographic analyses and *microtargeting* [1], i.e., the selection and engagement of specific users on the basis of their attributes.

Analytics This tab (graph example in Figure 1c) leverages the metrics gathered for recommending actions (e.g., numbers of followers, likes, retweets) to offer charts and other analytics services. They allow comparing the performances of the managed account and of competitor accounts (listed by the account manager) along time and different dimensions, to identify the metrics needing improvement.

3 POKEDEM IN ACTION

We deployed Pokedem to @esseredeltoro, a Twitter account that we created on August 2016 to support the development and testing of Pokedem and that we use here to demonstrate its capabilities.

Account @esseredeltoro acts as a non-personal, community-like account targeting the supporters of Torino Football Club, a professional football team playing in the Italian top football division (Serie A). Similarly to other "competitor" Twitter accounts, @esseredeltoro aims at becoming a popular account among Torino's supporters, acquiring followers and fostering interaction with them.

Challenge As @esseredeltoro account managers needing followers and reputation starting from scratch, we look for interesting news to publish and people to follow. However, surfing social networks and websites to find good contents, and going over users accounts who might follow @esseredeltoro and spread its contents, are time consuming tasks. Deciding when to tweet to maximize impressions and interacting with users are other expensive tasks.

Strategy We delegated to Pokedem all the activities that could be automated: (i) keeping track of the latest Twitter trending topics related to Torino; (ii) recommending interesting and influential people to follow; (iii) discovering and recommending relevant contents about the team; (iv) creating and recommending charts about Torino's supporters most active on Twitter and their comparison with supporters of the opposite team in a match; and (v) assessing the impact of actions performed on the account. This let us concentrate on tasks requiring creativity and reasoning, like creating original contents and interacting with people that we follow or like.

Results ~50% of tweets and ~95% of follow actions done so far by @esseredeltoro were recommended by Pokedem, with considerable time savings for the account managers. 26% of users followed via Pokedem recommendations followed back (vs. 8% for Twitter recommendations [2], tested by executing all recommended actions for 1 month). Together with the engaging posts recommended by Pokedem, this allowed @esseredeltoro to jump from 100 to 1000 followers in ~6 months (4.3 new followers/day, vs 1.0 avg. of competitors for the same 100 to 1000 followers growth), approaching competitors in terms of popularity and interaction rates (0.015 replies+retweets+likes/follower/day, vs 0.019 avg. of competitors).

4 CONCLUSIONS

Pokedem can be deployed on different accounts to effectively improve reputation and audience engagement with its recommendations. For the future, we plan to support other social media apart Twitter, to extend the actions being recommended, and to improve recommendations using feedback data from similar accounts.

ACKNOWLEDGEMENTS

This work is partially supported by the EC Commission through EIT Digital's High Impact Initiative Street Smart Retail (HII SSR).

REFERENCES

[1] Oana Barbu. 2014. Advertising, Microtargeting and Social Media. *Procedia - Social and Behavioral Sciences* 163 (2014), 44 – 49.
[2] Pankaj Gupta, Ashish Goel, Jimmy Lin, Aneesh Sharma, Dong Wang, and Reza Zadeh. 2013. WTF: The Who to Follow Service at Twitter. In *WWW*. 505–514.
[3] Su Mon Kywe, Ee-Peng Lim, and Feida Zhu. 2012. A Survey of Recommender Systems in Twitter. In *Proc. of Int. Conf. on Social Informatics (SocInfo)*. 420–433.
[4] Pasquale Lops, Marco de Gemmis, and Giovanni Semeraro. 2011. *Content-based Recommender Systems: State of the Art and Trends*. 73–105.
[5] Yaroslav Nechaev, Francesco Corcoglioniti, and Claudio Giuliano. 2017. Linking Knowledge Bases to Social Media Profiles. In *Proc. of ACM SAC*. 145–150.
[6] Jordi Paniagua and Juan Sapena. 2014. Business performance and social media: Love or hate? *Business Horizons* 57, 6 (2014), 719 – 728.

Citolytics - A Link-based Recommender System for Wikipedia

Malte Schwarzer[1], Corinna Breitinger[2], Moritz Schubotz[2], Norman Meuschke[2], Bela Gipp[2]
[1]National Institute of Informatics, Tokyo, Japan & Technical University Berlin, Germany
[2]University of Konstanz, Germany
ms@mieo.de, {first.last}@uni-konstanz.de

ABSTRACT

We present Citolytics - a novel link-based recommendation system for Wikipedia articles. In a preliminary study, Citolytics achieved promising results compared to the widely used text-based approach of Apache Lucene's MoreLikeThis (MLT). In this demo paper, we describe how we plan to integrate Citolytics into the Wikipedia infrastructure by using Elasticsearch and Apache Flink to serve recommendations for Wikipedia articles. Additionally, we propose a large-scale online evaluation design using the Wikipedia Android app. Working with Wikipedia data has several unique advantages. First, the availability of a very large user sample contributes to statistically significant results. Second, the openness of Wikipedia's architecture allows making our source code and evaluation data public, thus benefiting other researchers. If link-based recommendations show promise in our online evaluation, a deployment of the presented system within Wikipedia would have a far-reaching impact on Wikipedia's more than 30 million users.

CCS CONCEPTS

•General and reference → Evaluation; •Information systems → Recommender systems; *Wikis;* Evaluation of retrieval results;

KEYWORDS

Recommender System; Link-based; Wikipedia; Co-Citation Proximity Analysis; Online Evaluation

1 INTRODUCTION

Recommender systems (RS) are a crucial filtering and discovery tool to manage the vast and continuously increasing volume of items available in digital libraries and on the Web. However, RS are inherently difficult to evaluate: User-studies are expensive to conduct and are thus often small-scale. Offline evaluations, on the other hand, have been criticized for not accurately representing true user satisfaction [2]. Hence, our aim is to conduct a large-scale online evaluation for Citolytics, an open source RS framework designed for recommending related Wikipedia articles.

Working with Wikipedia data offers several benefits: (1) *Openness.* The corpus is publicly available and both source code and collected evaluation data can be published. This contributes to reproducibility. (2) *Size.* Wikipedia's very large user base contributes to statistical significance. (3) *Diversity.* Several million articles in 296 languages cover various topics. (4) *Transferability.* Wikis are widely used. This research can impact other domains and all websites using the MediaWiki[1] software.

In this work, we expand on our previous research on link-based RS [3], in which we conducted two independent large-scale *offline* evaluations using Wikipedia. In these previous evaluations, we investigated whether the two citation-based similarity measures Co-Citation (Co-Cit) and Co-Citation Proximity Analysis (CPA), the later of which Bela Gipp proposed in prior research [1], could be applied to the links in Wikipedia articles. We benchmarked these citation-based measures against the TF-IDF approach of MLT[2], which is currently being used by Wikipedia.

Both Co-Cit and CPA consider articles that are co-cited by other articles, or in the case of Wikipedia, co-linked. For example, if an article links to two other articles, article A and article B, then articles A and B are considered semantically related. The more frequently two articles are co-linked, the more likely they are semantically related. CPA additionally takes into account link proximity, i.e. the in-text placement of links. The closer two articles are co-linked in a text, e.g. sentence level vs. paragraph level, the more likely they are highly related. Relatedness is measured using the Co-Citation Proximity Index (CPI) [1].

The outcome of our initial study suggested that CPA and MLT performed similarly well in offline evaluations, while an additional manual analysis favored CPA. While MLT performed well in identifying narrowly similar articles that shared similar words and structure, CPA was better able to identify topically related information, such as information on the city of a certain university, or other technical universities in the region. However, the small scale of our previous manual analyses, and the shortcomings of offline evaluations, prevented us from arriving at definitive conclusions. Hence, we aim to conduct a large-scale online evaluation to arrive at a more conclusive judgment on the effectiveness of link-based recommendations.

2 SYSTEM OVERVIEW

To integrate Citolytics with Wikipedia, we must modify or access four components from the Wikipedia system as shown in Fig. 1:

(1) Wikipedia's Android app. The mobile app acts as the frontend in which recommendations are presented to users. The recommendations are shown under the heading "Read more" at the bottom of each article page. By default, three recommendations with their corresponding preview images are presented (Fig. 2). A screen capture video is available on YouTube[3]. The evaluation will be implemented as an A/B test: Users will randomly be assigned to one of two groups. While group A will use the current MLT

[1]http://mediawiki.org/
[2]http://lucene.apache.org/
[3]https://youtu.be/gb09Z7PAlLU

RecSys '17, August 27–31, 2017, Como, Italy.
© 2017 Copyright held by the owner/author(s). 978-1-4503-4652-8/17/08.
DOI: http://dx.doi.org/10.1145/3109859.3109981

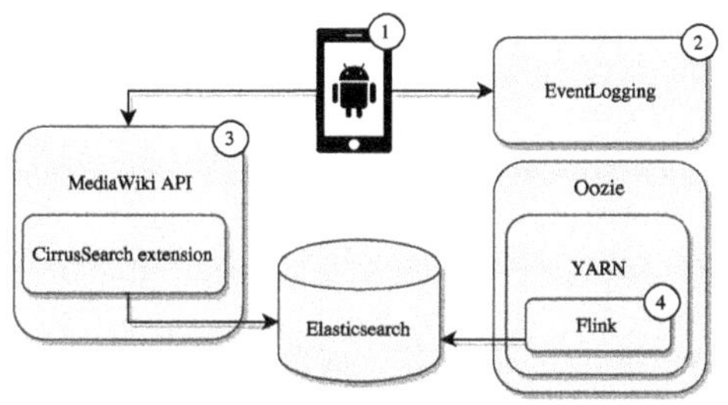

Figure 1: A Flink job scheduled by Oozie generates the recommendations and stores them in ES. An Android app accesses the recommendations via the MediaWiki API.

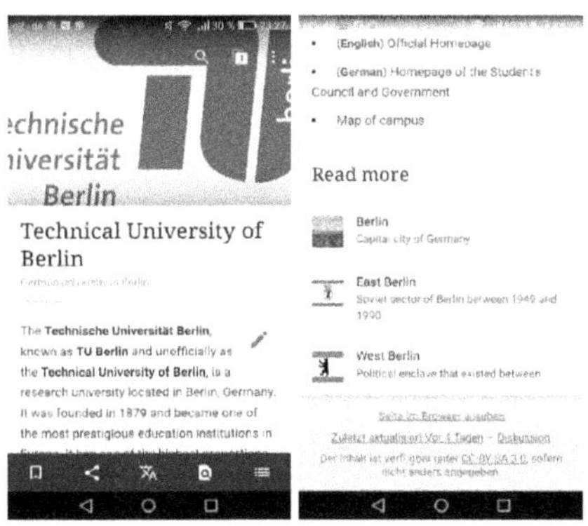

Figure 2: Screenshots of the recommender system within the Wikipedia Android app. Three recommendations are presented at the bottom of each article page.

implementation in Wikipedia, group B will receive the Citolytics recommendations.

(2) EventLogging. We must read from the EventLogging system, which logs user behavior in the Android app.

(3) MediaWiki. Recommendations must be made accessible via the MediaWiki API, which is the software that runs the Wikipedia website, and its CirrusSearch extension. Therefore, our modification must fulfill Wikipedia's scalability requirements.

(4) Oozie & YARN pipeline. The frequent generation of recommendations is ensured by an Apache Flink job[4] that is scheduled and executed in a pipeline based on Apache Oozie and YARN. The generated recommendations are written to Elasticsearch (ES), from where CirrusSearch reads the recommendations.

The Apache Flink job computes the article recommendations in batch fashion, whereby a Wikipedia XML dump is used as data source and an ES dump is the data sink, which is used to populate the recommendations to Wikipedia's ES index. The use of a big data processing framework like Flink is crucial for this task, since we must process all co-linked Wikipedia articles. For the English version of Wikipedia alone, this leads to intermediate results consisting of 11.8 billion records with a size of 0.8 TB. Fig. 3 shows the schema and descriptions of the involved Flink operators. While our demo setup uses a ten node cluster, Flink has been shown to be scalable to 1,000+ nodes.

[4]http://flink.apache.org/

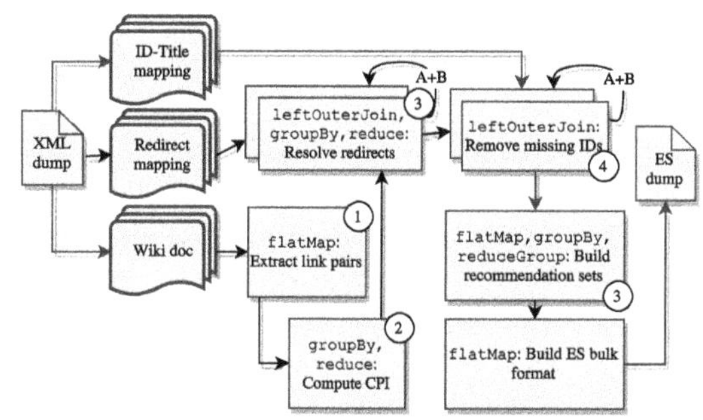

Figure 3: Schema of the Citolytics Flink job that generates the article recommendations. Operators marked with *A+B* are executed twice on each recommendation pair, once per recommendation direction.

The essential steps for the recommendation generation are: (1) extracting link pairs, (2) computing CPI, which is based on the original CPA concept [1], and (3) building recommendation sets. Additional steps, which mainly serve to tweak the recommendation performance include (4) redirection resolver, and (5) removal of missing IDs. **The Citolytics source code and documentation is available on GitHub[5].**

3 EVALUATION & CONTRIBUTION

The main contribution of this research will be its openly accessible and reproducible evaluation on a large scale. This online evaluation will be conducted using the data from Wikipedia's EventLogging system, which allows for detailed user tracking. Metrics such as click-through-rate, session length, and reading time of recommended articles will be collected.

4 CONCLUSION

With Citolytics we presented an open source RS for Wikipedia articles, and a proposal for its large-scale online evaluation. The ability to gather a large volume of user data will provide significant evidence to determine the best performing RS for the Wikipedia use case. Furthermore, the detailed categorization of Wikipedia articles will enable a granular evaluation of the strengths and weaknesses of each RS approach. The use of Wikipedia as a test system allows for the publication of the evaluation data, contributing to reproducibility. Finally, we would like to encourage other researchers to adapt our Citolytics framework[5] to their own RS needs.

REFERENCES

[1] Bela Gipp and Joeran Beel. 2009. Citation Proximity Analysis (CPA) - A new approach for identifying related work based on Co-Citation Analysis. *ISSI '09: Proc. of the 12th Int. Conf. on Scientometrics and Informetrics* 2 (2009), 571–575.

[2] Bart P. Knijnenburg, Martijn C. Willemsen, Zeno Gantner, Hakan Soncu, and Chris Newell. 2012. Explaining the user experience of recommender systems. *User Modeling and User-Adapted Interaction* 22, 4-5 (2012), 441–504. DOI: http://dx.doi.org/10.1007/s11257-011-9118-4

[3] Malte Schwarzer, Moritz Schubotz, Norman Meuschke, Corinna Breitinger, Volker Markl, and Bela Gipp. 2016. Evaluating Link-based Recommendations for Wikipedia. *Proc. of the 16th ACM/IEEE Joint Conf. on Digital Libraries (JCDL '16)* (2016), 191–200. DOI: http://dx.doi.org/10.1145/2910896.2910908

[5]https://github.com/wikimedia/citolytics

Visual Analysis of Recommendation Performance

Ludovik Çoba, Panagiotis Symeonidis, Markus Zanker
{lucoba,psymeonidis,mzanker@unibz.it}
Free University of Bozen
Faculty of Computer Science
Piazza Domenicani, 3
Bozen, Italy 39100

ABSTRACT

rrecsys is a novel library in R for developing and assessing recommendation algorithms. In this demo, we extend rrecsys with functions for visual analytics of recommendation performance, that is one of the strong capabilities of the R environment. In particular, we show how the library can be used to depict dataset characteristics, train and test recommendation algorithms and to visually assess, for instance, their capability to exploit long-tail items for making correct predictions.

KEYWORDS

Recommendation algorithms; R; evaluation; Visualization

1 INTRODUCTION

In a market economy, the Pareto principle is also known as the 80/20 rule, which is based on the probability of a power-law distribution, and states that a small proportion (e.g., 20%) of products in a market often results in a large proportion (e.g., 80%) of sales, whereas the many niche products only lead to a small share of overall sales. In this context, the promise of Recommender Systems (RS) is to make this large proportion of relatively unknown products accessible to consumers by, for instance, pointing them to niche items that nicely match their interest, i.e. making *serendipitous* recommendations. Thus, businesses can avoid customer churn or increase profits, since these non-popular items usually might have higher profit margins. Figure 1, for instance, depicts the popularity distribution of a popular rating dataset, MovieLens 1ML [5], where items are ranked depending on how frequently they have been rated by users, which nicely depicts a power-law distribution.

Current offline evaluation practice in recommender systems research predominantly focuses on averaged accuracy metrics (i.e, RMSE, MAE, precision, recall etc.), without putting much emphasis on how these results may relate to item popularity, number of ratings per user or average rating values.

In addition, they miss to analyze extensively the dataset characteristics [1]. Obviously the accuracy results of a proposed recommendation technique do also depend on the characteristics and the structure of a dataset and up to now little research is dedicated to analyze what effects dataset characteristics might have on the performance of an algorithm.

In this demo, we therefore extend rrecsys [2] library with additional graphical functionalities, that enable visual representations and analysis of the performance of recommendation algorithms. rrecsys is an open source library for R. It has a modular structure and expansion capabilities. The core of the package includes several popular algorithms and an evaluation component. In summary, we extend *rrecsys*, by incorporating also graphical evaluation capabilities, to help researchers better analyze and understand RS algorithms.

2 RELATED WORK

Jannach et al. [6] mention in their research that RS aim at boosting recommendations from the long tail as it increases sales of new and niche items. Meanwhile, they claimed that many algorithms do not take under consideration the afore mentioned fundamental aspect. Even though recommending popular items is a strong baseline in terms of precision and recall [3, 8], it seems that it cannot fully support the purpose of RSs. They also analyzed and evaluated the recommended items of different algorithms with respect to their popularity distribution and demonstrated how it impacts measured accuracy results. In the same direction, this demo uses graphical visualizations for assessing algorithms' performance in recommending either popular items or items from the long tail distribution as the guiding example.

Listing 1: Overview of a dataset

```
> d <- defineData(ml1m, sparse=TRUE)
> summary(d)
# of items: 3706
Minimum # of ratings per item: 1
Average # of ratings per item: 269.8891
Maximum # of ratings per item: 3428
# of users: 6040
Minimum # of ratings per user: 20
Average # of ratings per user: 165.5975
Maximum # of ratings per user: 2314
# of ratings: 1000209
Average rating: 3.581564
Sparsity: 95.53%
> dataChart(d, x = "items", y = "num_of_ratings")
```

3 VISUALIZING ALGORITHMS' BEHAVIOR

In this Section, we present how rrecsys can be used for training a model and for evaluating two exemplary and well-understood algorithms, namely User-based and Item-based Collaborative Filtering (CF) using graph visualizations.

Listing 1 demonstrates how a dataset that resides within R's environment can be quickly analyzed. For example, the predefined

RecSys '17, August 27–31, 2017, Como, Italy.
 978-1-4503-4652-8/17/08.
DOI: http://dx.doi.org/10.1145/3109859.3109982

function *summary* provides basic dataset characteristics as outlined in [4]. In particular, in the last line of Listing 1, the function *data_chart* plots the popularity distribution of the Movielens 1ML dataset, which is shown in Figure 1. As shown in Figure 1, the dataset follows a power law distribution for the number of ratings per item. That is, there is a small number of items which have many ratings, and many items with just a few ratings.

Listing 2 presents just a 2-fold cross validation process (for reasons of space) for measuring the effectiveness of User-based CF and Item-based CF algorithms in terms of precision and recall. As shown both algorithms have relatively similar accuracy performance (e.g, Item-based prec@3 = 0.268 and User-based prec@3 = 0.293). Please notice that the generation of the top-N recommendation list is based on the Most Frequent (MF) item recommendation method, which counts the frequency of each item inside the identified neighborhood, and recommends the N most frequent ones [7].

In the next step, since both algorithms have almost similar precision/recall, we want to understand if these *True Positives* (hits) recommendations are coming from the same sources w.r.t. the popularity distribution of items (see Figure 1). In Listing 3, the function *plot* plots the frequency of *True Positives* versus the ordered items by popularity for both algorithms. Surprisingly, as shown in Figures 2a and 2b, the User-based CF algorithm heavily exploits popular items coming from the short-head of the popularity distribution, whereas the Item-based CF recommends more items from the long tail distribution, which could be considered to be more effective since these niche items might actually constitute novel and serendipitous recommendations.

Listing 2: Evaluating precision/recall.

```
> e <- evalModel(d, folds = 2)
> resIB <- evalRec(e, "ibknn", topN = 3, neigh = 100,
simFunct = "cos", positiveThreshold = 3, topNGen = "MF")
> resIB
         prec.   recall   ex.time
1-fold   0.266   0.0169   58.023
2-fold   0.269   0.0173   57.338
Average  0.268   0.0171   57.680
> resUB <- evalRec(e, "ubknn", topN = 3, neigh = 100,
simFunct = "cos", positiveThreshold = 3, topNGen = "MF")
> resUB
         prec.   recall   ex.time
1-fold   0.292   0.0180   63.779
2-fold   0.294   0.0185   65.284
Average  0.293   0.0182   64.531
```

Listing 3: Plotting True Positives vs. items' Popularity.

```
> evalChart(resIB, x = "items", y = "TP")
> evalChart(resUB, x = "items", y = "TP")
```

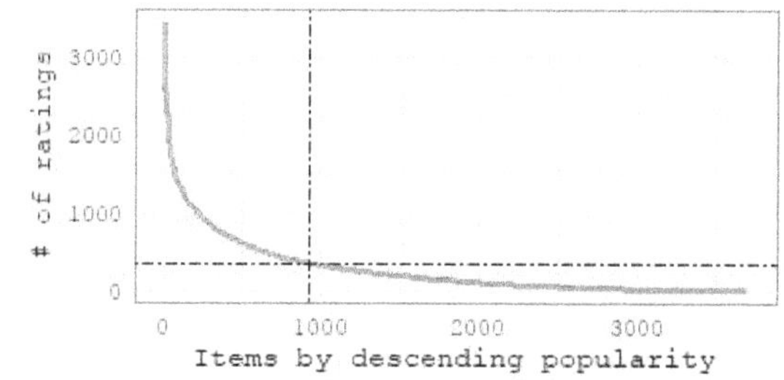

Figure 1: Popularity distribution of items.

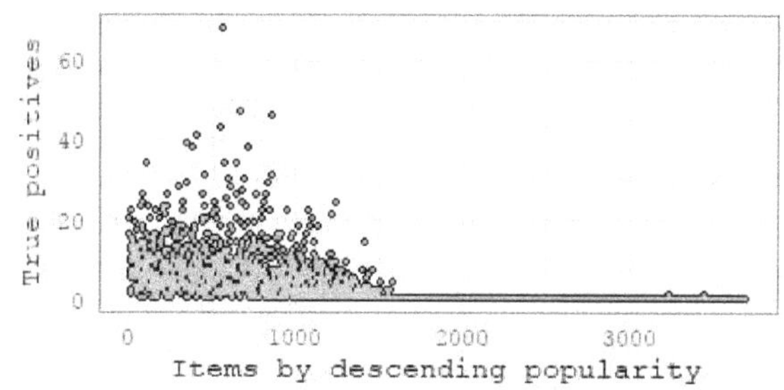

(a)

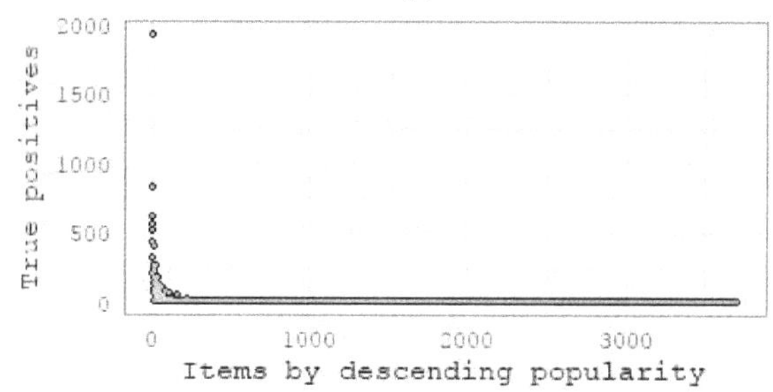

(b)

Figure 2: Frequency of *True Positives* of (a) the Item-based CF and (b) the User-based CF algorithms.

4 CONCLUSIONS

In this paper, we demonstrate the extension of rrecsys library with graphical functionalities in order to support visual analysis of recommendation algorithm performance and dataset characteristics.

5 ACKNOWLEDGEMENTS

We thank Damiana Salvalai for her contribution in the implementation of the visualization features.

REFERENCES

[1] G. Adomavicius and J. Zhang. Impact of data characteristics on recommender systems performance. *ACM Transactions on Management Information Systems (TMIS)*, 3(1):3, 2012.

[2] L. Çoba and M. Zanker. rrecsys: an r-package for prototyping recommendation algorithms. In I. Guy and A. Sharma, editors, *Poster Track of the 10th ACM Conference on Recommender Systems (RecSys 2016) (RecSysPosters)*, number 1688 in CEUR Workshop Proceedings, Aachen, 2016.

[3] P. Cremonesi, Y. Koren, and R. Turrin. Performance of recommender algorithms on top-n recommendation tasks. In *Proceedings of the Fourth ACM Conference on Recommender Systems*, RecSys '10, pages 39–46, New York, NY, USA, 2010. ACM.

[4] S. Dooms, A. Bellogín, T. D. Pessemier, and L. Martens. A framework for dataset benchmarking and its application to a new movie rating dataset. *ACM Trans. Intell. Syst. Technol.*, 7(3):41:1–41:28, Feb. 2016.

[5] F. M. Harper and J. A. Konstan. The movielens datasets: History and context. *ACM Transactions on Interactive Intelligent Systems (TiiS)*, 5(4):19, 2016.

[6] D. Jannach, L. Lerche, I. Kamehkhosh, and M. Jugovac. What recommenders recommend: An analysis of recommendation biases and possible countermeasures. *User Modeling and User-Adapted Interaction*, 25(5):427–491, 2015.

[7] G. Karypis. Evaluation of item-based top-n recommendation algorithms. In *Proceedings of the Tenth International Conference on Information and Knowledge Management*, CIKM '01, pages 247–254, New York, NY, USA, 2001. ACM.

[8] H. Steck. Item popularity and recommendation accuracy. In *Proceedings of the Fifth ACM Conference on Recommender Systems*, RecSys '11, pages 125–132, New York, NY, USA, 2011. ACM.

PathRec: Visual Analysis of Travel Route Recommendations

Dawei Chen*†, Dongwoo Kim*, Lexing Xie*†, Minjeong Shin*, Aditya Krishna Menon†*,
Cheng Soon Ong†*, Iman Avazpour‡, John Grundy‡
*The Australian National University, †Data61/CSIRO, ‡Deakin University
{u5708856,dongwoo.kim,lexing.xie,minjeong.shin,aditya.menon,chengsoon.ong}@anu.edu.au
{iman.avazpour,j.grundy}@deakin.edu.au

ABSTRACT

We present an interactive visualisation tool for recommending travel trajectories. This system is based on new machine learning formulations and algorithms for the sequence recommendation problem. The system starts from a map-based overview, taking an interactive query as starting point. It then breaks down contributions from different geographical and user behavior features, and those from individual points-of-interest versus pairs of consecutive points on a route. The system also supports detailed quantitative interrogation by comparing a large number of features for multiple points. Effective trajectory visualisations can potentially benefit a large cohort of online map users and assist their decision-making. More broadly, the design of this system can inform visualisations of other structured prediction tasks, such as for sequences or trees.

CCS CONCEPTS

• **Information systems → Learning to rank**; • **Human-centered computing → Visualization**;

KEYWORDS

Route Visualisation, Travel Recommendation, Learning to rank

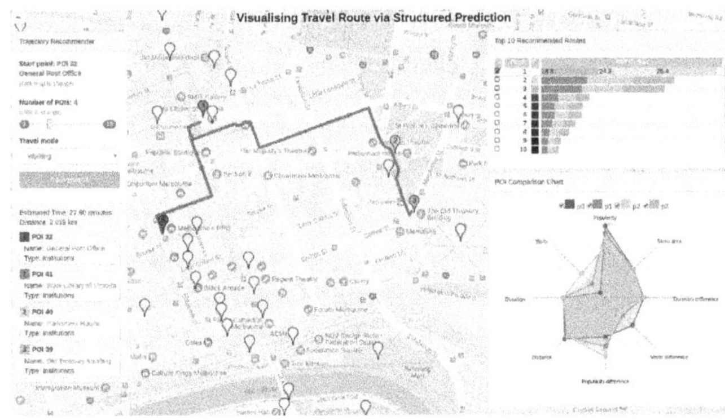

Figure 1: Travel route visualisation system[1]. Given a starting POI and the number of POIs to be visited, the system recommends multiple routes from travel history of tourists. Shown above: recommendation in central Melbourne.

1 INTRODUCTION

Sequence recommendation has emerged as an important framework for modelling diverse problems such as travel route and music playlist recommendation [2]. Unlike classical ranking algorithms where items are considered independently [6], a sequence recommendation algorithm requires modelling a structure between items and suggests a set of items as a whole. For example, consider recommending a trajectory of *points-of-interest* (POIs) in a city to a visitor. While a classical ranking algorithm can learn a user's preference for each individual location, it may ignore the distances between them and could suggest a longer trajectory than is optimal. Several sequence recommendation algorithms have been proposed to solve this problem and demonstrated superior performance compared to classical ranking algorithms [2, 7]. Nonetheless, recommendation algorithms for sequences and trajectories [1, 2] have many components and can be difficult for a user to understand. This is part of the general challenge of introducing transparency and accountability for machine learning algorithms [3].

In this paper, we tackle the problem of sequence visualisation, specifically focussing on travel routes recommendation. A travel route is a sequence of POIs, and the sequence recommendation problem can be formulated as a structured prediction problem [2]. Based on a diverse set of features for individual and pairs of POIs, we train the prediction model with trajectory data extracted from geotagged photos taken in Melbourne [1]. To visualise the suggested routes, we develop a novel tool that efficiently displays multiple suggested routes, which helps users understand the process behind the recommendations. Specifically, our system decomposes a total score of each route into a set of features and their corresponding scores, and shows the total score as a stacked bar plot of the features. The system also visualises the differences between POIs in a single route to show how POIs in that route can exhibit vast diversity.

This visualisation helps tourists who want diverse experiences by choosing the best route among multiple recommendations. Generalising to a broader class of routes, such a visualisation could also help users of online mapping apps to make decisions on suggested travel routes, such as by trading off distance, traffic, and scenery.

2 TRAVEL ROUTE RECOMMENDATION

The travel route recommendation problem involves a set of POIs in a city. Given a trajectory query $\mathbf{x} = (s, l)$, comprising a start POI s and trip length l, the goal is to suggest one or more sequences of POIs that maximise some notion of utility.

RecSys '17, August 27-31, 2017, Como, Italy

ACM ISBN 978-1-4503-4652-8/17/08.
https://doi.org/10.1145/3109859.3109983

[1] http://www.pathrec.ml

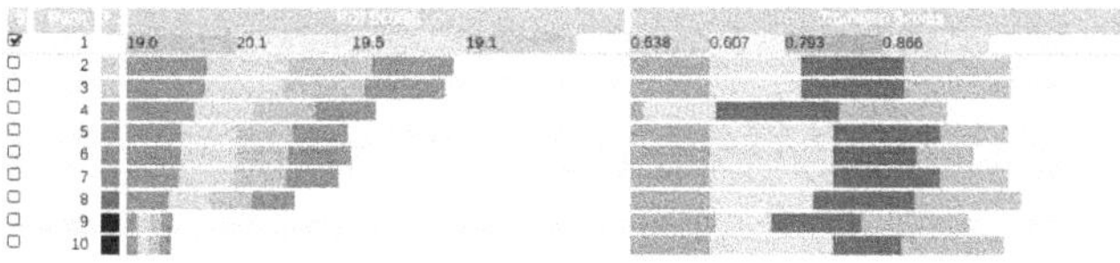

Figure 2: Visualisation of POI and transition scores for top 10 recommended routes. Each bar from left to right represents a relative score of each POI or transition along the route. The length of stacked bars represents the total score of the suggested route.

Following [2], we first cast travel recommendation as a structured prediction problem, which allows us to leverage the well-studied literature of structured SVMs (SSVM) [5]. From a visualisation perspective, an advantage of the SSVM is the explicit representation of feature scores in its final decision process. Specifically, we can disassemble the final score of a route into feature scores of each POI and the transition between two adjacent POIs. We use hand-crafted POI features such as the category, popularity, and average visit duration of previous tourists. We also crafted transition features such as the distance and neighbourhood of two POIs to maximise the interpretability of the outcome.

3 VISUALISATION

Our goal is to design an interactive visualisation system on top of the structured prediction framework. Figure 1 shows the overview of a live demo system, which consists of five major components: a map to display the suggested routes, an input box for user query (upper left), a stacked score of routes (upper right), a POI list box (lower left), and a radar chart to compare features of multiple POIs (lower right). The role and the construction of the four major components, besides the main map, are as follows:

Query input: A query consists of a starting POI and a trip length. Users can choose the starting POI by clicking icons on the map and can adjust the slide to set the trip length. In addition, three different travelling modes (e.g. bicycling, driving and walking) are supported, and we optimise the suggested routes for each mode.

Route score visualisation: The SSVM evaluates relevance scores of POIs and transitions in a candidate route to the given query and uses the sum of the relevance scores to determine the ranks of the routes. To visualise the POI and transition scores, we adopt a stacked bar representation [4], designed to support the visualisation of multi-attribute ranking. In Figure 2, the system decompose the scores of top 10 recommended routes into POI and transition scores via the stacked bar representation, where the size of each bar is proportional to the relevance score of the corresponding POI and transition in the route. Note that the POI and transition scores are scaled differently to support better visual discrimination[2]. For a seamless match between a route on the map and the corresponding POI scores in the bar plot, we use the same colour for both POI score and POI icon on the map. We also allow users to select multiple rows to visualise the corresponding routes on the map.

POI list: The POI list box provides the list of POI names and categories along the recommended route. The list is sorted according to the suggested visiting order, and again, the same POI colour is used to match the corresponding POI on the map. On top of the list, the system also provides an estimated travel time and total distance of the route. The POI list box is updated whenever a user selects a different route or the system makes a new recommendation. If more than one route is selected, the system displays the information of the most recent chosen route.

[2]See Appendix for details at http://arxiv.org/abs/1707.01627

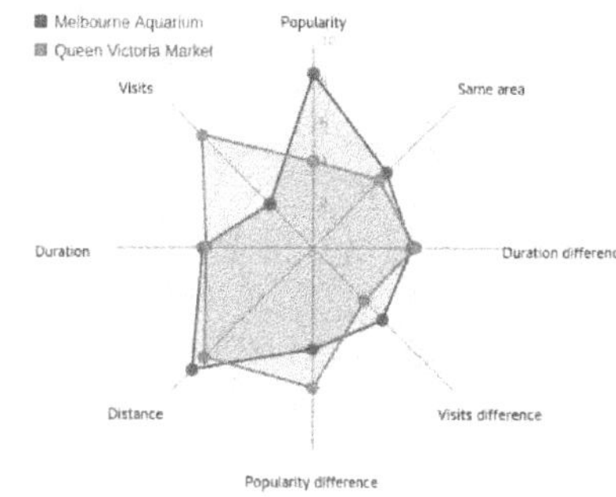

Figure 3: POI feature comparison between *Melbourne Aquarium* and *Queen Victoria Market*: the former scores higher on *Popularity* and *Visits difference* features whereas the latter scores higher on *Visits* and *Popularity difference* features.

POI feature visualisation: We further provide a radar chart to analyse the variation between POIs in a single route. For example, in Figure 3, we compare two POIs (*Melbourne Aquarium* and *Queen Victoria Market*) in terms of POI features and their importance in the suggested route. The radar chart shows the corresponding POI feature scores when a user selects a route. In particular, the user can check/uncheck any POI in the selected route, and the feature scores of all checked POIs will be shown in the chart.

4 CONCLUSION

In this demonstration, we detail an interactive route analyser which helps the interaction between users and a route recommendation system. The system benefits from the explicit feature construction of the structured prediction model, and visualises recommended routes in terms of information on both the routes and the POIs.

Acknowledgements. We thank the National Computational Infrastructure (NCI), supported by the Australian Government, for computational resources. This work is supported in part by the Australian Research Council via Discovery Project program DP140102185.

REFERENCES

[1] Dawei Chen, Cheng Soon Ong, and Lexing Xie. 2016. Learning Points and Routes to Recommend Trajectories. In *Proceedings of the 25th ACM International on Conference on Information and Knowledge Management*. ACM, 2227–2232.

[2] Dawei Chen, Lexing Xie, Aditya Krishna Menon, and Cheng Soon Ong. 2017. Structured Recommendation. *CoRR* abs/1706.09067 (2017). https:arxiv.org/abs/1706.09067

[3] FAT/ML. 2017. Fairness, Accountability, and Transparency in Machine Learning. (2017). http://www.fatml.org, retrieved May 2017.

[4] Samuel Gratzl, Alexander Lex, Nils Gehlenborg, Hanspeter Pfister, and Marc Streit. 2013. Lineup: Visual analysis of multi-attribute rankings. *IEEE transactions on visualization and computer graphics* 19, 12 (2013), 2277–2286.

[5] Thorsten Joachims, Thomas Hofmann, Yisong Yue, and Chun-Nam Yu. 2009. Predicting structured objects with support vector machines. *Commun. ACM* 52, 11 (2009), 97–104.

[6] Yehuda Koren, Robert Bell, and Chris Volinsky. 2009. Matrix factorization techniques for recommender systems. *Computer* 42, 8 (2009).

[7] Kwan Hui Lim, Jeffrey Chan, Christopher Leckie, and Shanika Karunasekera. 2015. Personalized tour recommendation based on user interests and points of interest visit durations *(IJCAI '15)*.

The 1st Workshop on Intelligent Recommender Systems by Knowledge Transfer & Learning (RecSysKTL)

Yong Zheng
School of Applied Technology
Illinois Institute of Technology
Chicago, Illinois, USA 60616
yzheng66@iit.edu

Weike Pan
College of Computer Science & Software Engineering
Shenzhen University
Shenzhen, Guangdong, China 518060
panweike@szu.edu.cn

Shaghayegh (Sherry) Sahebi
Department of Computer Science
University at Albany, SUNY
Albany, NY, USA 12222
ssahebi@albany.edu

Ignacio Fernández
NTENT
Almogàvers 123
Barcelona, Spain 08018
ignacio.fernandezt@uam.es

ABSTRACT

Cross-domain recommender systems and transfer learning approaches are useful to help integrate knowledge from different places, so that we alleviate some existing problems (such as the cold-start problem), or improve the quality of recommender systems. With the advantages of these techniques, we host the first international workshop on intelligent recommender systems by knowledge transfer and learning (RecSysKTL) to provide such a forum for academia researchers and application developers from around the world to present their work and discuss exciting research ideas or outcomes. The workshop is held in conjunction with the ACM Conference on Recommender Systems 2017 on August 27th at Como, Italy.

CCS CONCEPTS

• **Information systems → Recommender systems**;

KEYWORDS

cross-domain, knowledge transfer, recommender system

1 BACKGROUND AND MOTIVATIONS

Recommender systems, as one of well-known Web intelligence applications, aim to alleviate the information overload problem and produce item suggestions tailored to user preferences. Typically, user preferences or tastes are collected through usersŠ implicit or explicit feedback in various formats, such as user ratings, online behaviors, text reviews, etc. Also, user feedback on different items can be collected from several systems or domains. The diversity of feedback formats and domains provides multiple views to usersŠ preferences, and thus, can be helpful in recommending more related items to users. Cross-domain recommender systems and transfer learning approaches propose to take advantage of such diversity of viewpoints to provide better-quality recommendations and resolve issues such as the cold-start problem.

The emerging research on cross-domain, context-aware and multi-criteria recommender systems, has proved to be successful. Given the recent availability of cross-domain datasets and novelty of the topic, we organize the 1st workshop on intelligent recommender systems by knowledge transfer and learning (RecSysKTL) held in conjunction with the 11th ACM Conference on Recommender Systems. The definition of "*domain*" may vary in different applications, e.g., it could be (but not limited to):

- **From one application to another**: We may utilize user behaviors on social networks to predict their preferences on movies (e.g., Netflix, Youtube) or music (e.g., Pandora, Spotify).
- **From one category to another**: We may predict a userŠs taste on electronics by using his or her preference history on books based on the data collected from Amazon.com.
- **From one context to another**: We may collect a userŠs preferences on the items over different time segment (e.g., weekend or weekday) and predict her preferences on movie watching within another context (e.g., companion and location).
- **From one task to another**: It may be useful for us to predict how a user will select hotels for his or her vocations by learning from how he or she books the tickets for transportation.
- **From one structure to another**: It could be also possible for us to infer social connections by learning from the structure of heterogeneous information network.

2 OBJECTIVES

This workshop intends to create a medium to generate more practical and efficient predictive models or recommendation approaches by leveraging user feedbacks or preferences from multiple domains.

This workshop will be beneficial for both researchers in academia and data scientists in industry to explore and discuss different definition of domains, interesting applications, novel predictive models or recommendation approaches to serve the knowledge transfer and learning from one domain to another.

As this is the first time to host such a workshop on knowledge transfer and learning in the area of recommender systems, we also

RecSys'17, August 27–31, 2017, Como, Italy.
 978-1-4503-4652-8/17/08.
DOI: http://dx.doi.org/10.1145/3109859.3109951

expect to collect feedbacks from the workshop, so that we can better organize the workshop in the future.

3 TOPICS OF INTEREST

The topics of interest include (but are not limited to):

Applications of Knowledge Transfer for RecSys

- Cross-domain recommendation
- Context-aware or time-aware recommendation
- Multi-criteria recommender systems
- Novel applications

Methods for Knowledge Transfer in RecSys

- Knowledge transfer for content-based filtering
- Knowledge transfer in user- and item-based collaborative filtering
- Transfer learning of model-based approaches to collaborative filtering
- Deep Learning methods for knowledge transfer

Challenges in Knowledge Transfer for Recommendation

- Addressing user feedback heterogeneity from multiple domains (e.g. implicit vs. explicit, binary vs. ratings, etc.)
- Multi-domain and multi-task knowledge representation and learning
- Detecting and avoiding useless knowledge transfer
- Ranking and selection of auxiliary sources of knowledge to transfer from
- Performance and scalability of knowledge transfer approaches for recommendation

Evaluation of RecSys based on Knowledge Transfer

- Beyond accuracy: novelty, diversity, and serendipity of recommendations supported by the transfer of knowledge
- Performance of knowledge transfer systems in cold-start scenarios
- Impact of the size and quality of transferred data on target recommendations
- Analysis of the amount of domain overlap on recommendation performance

4 PROGRAM COMMITTEES

We thank the contributions by the following workshop program committee members:

- Alejandro Bellogín, Universidad Autónoma de Madrid
- Steve Bourke, Schibsted Media Group
- Iván Cantador, Universidad Autónoma de Madrid
- Liang Dong, Google, Inc.
- Mehdi Elahi, Free University of Bozen
- Negar Hariri, Apple, Inc.
- Mahesh Joshi, Linkedin
- Bin Li, Data61, Australia
- Zhongqi Lu, Hong Kong University of Science and Technology, Hong Kong, China
- Cataldo Musto, University of Bari "Aldo Moro"
- Denis Parra, Pontificia Universidad Catolica de Chile
- Alan Said, University of Skövde, Sweden
- Yue Shi, Facebook, USA
- Fatemeh Vahedian, DePaul University
- Saúl Vargas, Mendeley
- Tong Yu, Carnegie Mellon University, USA
- Fuzhen Zhuang, Chinese Academy of Sciences, China
- Yong Zhuang, Carnegie Mellon University, USA

5 WORKSHOP PROGRAMS

This year, we received 11 valid submissions. The workshop is expected to be featured with paper presentations and invited talks. The copyrights of the accepted papers are held by the owner/author(s). All of the accepted papers will be published by CEUR workshop proceedings[1]. Hopefully, we can collaborative with some journals, and invite the extended version of the accepted papers to a special issue in the journal.

6 ACKNOWLEDGMENTS

We thank the workshop organizing committee for giving us the opportunity to host this workshop in conjunction with ACM RecSys 2017. And we appreciate the contributions by the authors and program committee members.

[1] http://ceur-ws.org/

The 1st International Workshop on Temporal Reasoning in Recommender Systems

Maria Bielikova
Slovak University of Technology in Bratislava
Slovakia
maria.bielikova@stuba.sk

Veronika Bogina
University of Haifa
Israel
sveron@gmail.com

Tsvi Kuflik
University of Haifa
Israel
tsvikak@is.haifa.ac.il

Roy Sasson
Google & Tel Aviv University
Israel
roy.sasson@gmail.com

ABSTRACT

The workshop focus is on considering temporal aspects for recommender systems in general, regardless of the specific domain and application, trying to develop a holistic approach for dealing with temporal aspects in recommender systems, like personal assistants, news, tourism, health care, TV, e-commerce, social networks and so on.

CCS CONCEPTS

Information retrieval -> Retrieval tasks and goals -> Recommender systems

KEYWORDS

Recommender systems, temporal aspects, temporal sequence, concept drift, recurrent neural networks, time-aware recommendations

ACM Reference format:

M.Bielikova, V.Bogina, T.Kuflik and R.Sassion. 2017. SIG Proceedings Paper in word Format. In *Proceedings of ACM RecSys '17, August 27–31, 2017, Como, Italy,* 2 pages.
DOI: 10.1145/3109859.3109952

1 INTRODUCTION

Hitherto, temporal aspects of user activity in Recommender Systems (RecSys) were used in two different scenarios: explicit feedback and implicit feedback. The first one is related to explicitly expressing ratings for movies, for example: Netflix prize data set contains timestamps associated with the ratings. As it was shown using them improved rating prediction.

ACM ISBN 978-1-4503-4652-8/17/08.
http://dx.doi.org/10.1145/3109859.3109952

On the other hand, there is an implicit feedback data (e.g. e-commerce logs that describe user shopping behavior), which contain timestamps that also can be used in identifying user patterns (when the user tends to purchase more in the morning and towards the evening; on Mondays rather than the middle of the week, before the holidays on August rather than other months and so on), building user profiles, identifying similar users (for CF) and use all this useful information for items to purchase recommendations. Not only e-commerce, but other domains with web clickstreams, can be analyzed considering temporal components. In recent years' Markovian model and sequential pattern-mining methods were frequently used for such tasks. Recently temporal graphs and Recurrent Neural Networks are also considered for sequential data analyses and providing recommendations for people, communities, locations, etc.

The workshop aimed at bringing together researchers and practitioners working on temporal aspects in recommender systems domain in order to look at the challenges from the point of view of the temporal aspects in recommender systems and user modelling in order to provide relevant (often personalized) recommendations regarding the representation and reasoning about temporal aspects. All in all, the workshop aims at attracting presentations of novel ideas for addressing these challenges and how to advance the current state of the art in this field.

Having a specific workshop focused on temporal aspects in all its aspects ranging from user profiling through context modelling to recommendation algorithms will provide an opportunity for RecSys participants working in these different domains to discuss specific temporal issues of interest. We also hope to attract additional, domain specific professionals that initially might not consider attending RecSys.

2 SUBMISSIONS

The primary goal of this workshop was to gather researchers and practitioners from different fields, e.g., recommender systems, user modelling, user interaction, mobile, ubiquitous and ambient technologies, artificial intelligence and web information systems in various domains such as media, e-commerce, music, health care, personal assistants, social networks, tourism, technology enhanced learning,, so as to explore various practical use cases of significance of temporal aspects in recommender systems in these domains. During the workshop, we aim to identify the typical user groups, tasks and roles in order to achieve an adequate personalization and recommendation relying on temporal aspects.

Important aspects and topics to be discussed evolve around:

- Specific applications and case studies where temporal aspects were considered (evaluation)
- Temporal aspects in Session-based recommendations
- Specific methods and techniques for integrating temporal aspects into the recommendations
- Integrating data
- Exploiting data from various sources, i.e., catalogues, Linked Open Data, and usage logs
- Context and Mobility
- Cold-Start Problem
- Preference Elicitation
- Temporal Personalization
- Temporal aspects in group recommendations
- Cross domain temporal patterns
- Metrics for evaluating temporal aspects in recommendations

The submissions to the workshop varied greatly and included the following aspects: temporal aspects in session-based recommendations, recommendations based on temporal item popularity, time-aware tag recommendations, concept drift of user's communities, the short-term behavior modelling, the duration of adequate news recommendations, fashion recommendations based on temporal sequence of sales events (LSTM-based model), Collaborative Filtering for temporal scenarios, concept drifts in music tastes and ranking prediction in non-stationary environments.

Few relevant domains with timestamp data were covered: e-commerce, media, social tagging, music and movies.

Since most of the papers incorporate time series data into baseline algorithms, they require datasets containing timestamps. Therefore, such available datasets as: RecSys Challenge 2015[1], 30Music[2], MovieLens[3], Netflix and Bibsonomy [4], NewsREEL 2017[5] and few more were used in the evaluation phases.

3 SUMMARY

Almost all the methods and frameworks presented in the papers strive to solve an ad hoc problem, whether in e-commerce, media, social tagging or music domains, considering sequence of events or various concept drifts. Since neural networks algorithms become widely used and popular, RNN-based model processes sequential data and is frequently used in such tasks. Though CF, based on Matrix Factorization and taking into account the fact that users and items evolve over time, is still relevant in recommendations and yields good results.

The intent of the workshop is to have a fruitful discussion on using different temporal aspects in various domains. Furthermore, the desire is to come up with directions to some general solution for incorporating temporal aspects in recommender systems.

COMMITTEES

Organizing committee

Maria Bielikova, Slovak University of Technology in Bratislava
Veronika Bogina, University of Haifa
Tsvi Kuflik, University of Haifa
Roy Sasson, Google and Tel-Aviv University

Program committee

Shlomo Berkovsky, CSIRO
Robin Burke, DePaul University
Peter Dolog, Aalborg University
Dietmar Jannach, TU Dortmund
Judy Kay, University of Sydney
David Konopnicki, IBM
Bamshad Mobasher, DePaul University
Osnat Mokryn, University of Haifa
Robert Moskovitch, Deutsche Telekom Laboratories at Ben-Gurion University
Giuseppe Sansonetti, Roma Tre University
Amit Tiroshi, Atlassian

[1] http://2015.recsyschallenge.com/challenge.html
[2] http://crowdrec.eu/2015/11/30music-dataset-release/
[3] https://grouplens.org/datasets/movielens/
[4] https://www.kde.cs.uni-kassel.de/bibsonomy/dumps/
[5] http://www.clef-newsreel.org/dataset/

DLRS 2017 - Second Workshop on Deep Learning for Recommender Systems

Balázs Hidasi
Gravity R&D
Budapest, Hungary
balazs.hidasi@gravityrd.com

Alexandros Karatzoglou
Telefonica Research
Barcelona, Spain
alexk@tid.es

Oren Sar-Shalom
IBM Research
Haifa, Israel
orensr@il.ibm.com

Sander Dieleman
Google DeepMind
London, United Kingdom
sanderdieleman@gmail.com

Bracha Shapira
Ben Gurion University of the Negev
Beersheba, Israel
bshapira@bgu.ac.il

Domonkos Tikk
Gravity R&D
Budapest, Hungary
domonkos.tikk@gravityrd.com

ABSTRACT

Deep learning methods became widely popular in the recommender systems community in 2016, in part thanks to the previous event of the DLRS workshop series. Now, deep learning has been embedded in the main conference as well and initial research directions have started forming, so the role of DLRS 2017 is to encourage starting new research directions, incentivize the application of very recent techniques from deep learning, and provide a venue for specialized discussion of this topic.

KEYWORDS

deep learning, neural networks, recommender systems

1 INTRODUCTION

Deep learning techniques achieved great success in complex domains, such as computer vision, natural language processing, machine translation, speech recognition and reinforcement learning. The uptake of deep learning by the recommender systems community was relatively slow, as the topic became popular only in 2016. The first Deep Learning for Recommender Systems workshop (DLRS 2016 [11]) – which was the workshop with the highest demand at RecSys 2016 – also took its share to propagate the topic. The popularity of this topic is still in its growing phase demonstrated – beside others – by the $\sim 25\%$ increase in the number of submissions received by DLRS compared to last year.

As deep learning methods gradually become part of the main conference, accordingly changes the role of DLRS. From being the primary venue for any RecSys related deep learning research, DLRS will gradually become a forum of discussing pioneering work that uses recent techniques from deep learning or proposes novel recommendation related problems that can be solved with deep learning. Fortunately, we see both among this year's submission.

DLRS 2017 builds upon the positively received traits of DLRS 2016. DLRS 2017 is a fast paced workshop with a focus on high quality paper presentations and keynote. We welcome original research using deep learning technology for solving recommender systems related problems. The workshop centers around the use of Deep Learning technology in Recommender Systems and algorithms.

2 STATE OF THE ART

While using neural networks for recommender systems is not a recent trend – e.g. see the application of Restricted Boltzmann Machines for collaborative filtering [15] from ten years ago – the recent boom of deep learning revitalized this topic in the last two years. With deep learning for recommender related tasks becoming more and more popular, we have seen distinct research directions forming within the area during last year. The topics form around few seminal papers with subsequent work extending or improving upon those. Here we give a very brief overview of these research directions that can be considered as the state-of-the-art of this area.

Embeddings & 2vec models: Several papers focus on finding good embeddings (also known as distributed representations, or latent features) for items. This direction is not foreign for the recommendation domain, e.g. matrix factorization methods are also latent models that find "embeddings" for items and users[1]. Recent methods focus on item embeddings without user identification and can be used as the basis of more advanced methods or as item-to-item recommenders. Most of the models use some variation of Word2Vec [13] – originally devised for word embeddings – on event data [6]. Subsequent papers extend the model (e.g. with side information [19]) or examine the latent space [20].

Extracting features from heterogenous data: Hybrid factorization algorithms in the past often relied on constraining item features on metadata to overcome the weaknesses of pure collaborative filtering, e.g. the cold-start. With deep learning, it became easier to reliably extract useful features directly from content and use them in CF. Depending on the domain the content and thus its processing can greatly differ. [18] used convolutional neural networks (CNNs) to extract features from music to be used in a factor model. More recently [1] used recurrent neural networks (RNNs) to include textual data in their end-to-end CF model. Using

[1]MF can also be represented as a very simplistic neural network with one hidden layer without any nonlinearities. The input is the one-hot encoded user ID, the hidden layer is the user feature vector and the output is the user's preference over the items.

RecSys'17, August 27–31, 2017, Como, Italy.
 ISBN 978-1-4503-4652-8/17/08.
DOI: http://dx.doi.org/10.1145/3109859.3109953

images is also a popular choice to enhance recommendations in domains like fashion [7, 12] or video recommendation [10].

Deep collaborative filtering: A natural application of deep models is collaborative filtering. Leveraging the versatility of deep models, multiple types of interaction and/or context is often integrated. [4] describes the deep learning algorithm behind YouTube's related video recommendation. [2] combines deep models with a wide logistic regression model to find a balance between generalization and memorization in the app recommendation domain. [5] proposes a model in which user and item features co-evolve and follow the conceptional drift in the interaction data.

Autoencoders for CF: A subclass of deep CF methods use denoising autoencoders as the central component of their model. This approach is popular with several different variants proposed [21, 23, 24]. These models can also be extended with additional information sources, such as text [22].

Session-based recommendations with RNNs: Session-based recommendation is a good example for a task that is very important in real life applications, yet was hardly addressed due to its complexity when using classic methods. However, [9] showed that gated RNN (such as the Gated Recurrent Unit, GRU [3]) can be adapted to be a perfect fit for this task. Subsequent papers building on this idea either improve the original algorithm by (1) proposing loss functions suiting the problem better [8], (2) data augmentation [16]; or other extend it e.g. by adding context [17] or personalization [14].

3 THE WAY FORWARD

This area of research is very young, thus there is much room for improvement in the aforementioned research directions. Besides, up to this point only a fraction of well established deep learning models have been used for recommendations. We expect the community to delve into exploring the use of more recent approaches (e.g. generative models) in the near future. We also expect that novel or previously discarded recommendation problems will come forward now that the toolset for tackling them is available; similarly to how session-based recommendation was revitalized by [8]. The submissions to DLRS 2017 show traits of all three types of research.

4 SUMMARY

After its success in other domains, deep learning became popular in the recommender systems community last year. As researchers started to use deep learning methods in the RecSys domain, different research directions revealed themselves, such as creating better item embeddings or session based recommendations with recurrent neural networks. The DLRS workshop series aims to further speed up the acceptance of deep learning methods in the RecSys community. Even though deep learning papers are now also present at the main conference, DLRS 2017 is the venue for discussing novel research directions, applications of recent techniques of deep learning and bringing together researchers from the deep learning and recommender systems communities.

REFERENCES

[1] Trapit Bansal, David Belanger, and Andrew McCallum. 2016. Ask the GRU: Multi-task Learning for Deep Text Recommendations. In *Proceedings of the 10th ACM Conference on Recommender Systems (RecSys '16)*. 107–114.

[2] Heng-Tze Cheng, Levent Koc, Jeremiah Harmsen, Tal Shaked, Tushar Chandra, Hrishi Aradhye, Glen Anderson, Greg Corrado, Wei Chai, Mustafa Ispir, and others. 2016. Wide & deep learning for recommender systems. In *Proceedings of the 1st Workshop on Deep Learning for Recommender Systems*. ACM, 7–10.

[3] Kyunghyun Cho, Bart van Merrienboer, Çaglar Gülçehre, Fethi Bougares, Holger Schwenk, and Yoshua Bengio. 2014. Learning Phrase Representations using RNN Encoder-Decoder for Statistical Machine Translation. *CoRR* 1406.1078 (2014). http://arxiv.org/abs/1406.1078

[4] Paul Covington, Jay Adams, and Emre Sargin. 2016. Deep Neural Networks for YouTube Recommendations. In *Proceedings of the 10th ACM Conference on Recommender Systems (RecSys '16)*. 191–198.

[5] Hanjun Dai, Yichen Wang, Rakshit Trivedi, and Le Song. 2016. Recurrent coevolutionary latent feature processes for continuous-time recommendation. In *Proceedings of the 1st Workshop on Deep Learning for Recommender Systems*. ACM, 29–34.

[6] Mihajlo Grbovic, Vladan Radosavljevic, Nemanja Djuric, Narayan Bhamidipati, Jaikit Savla, Varun Bhagwan, and Doug Sharp. 2015. E-commerce in your inbox: Product recommendations at scale. In *Proceedings of the 21th ACM SIGKDD International Conference on Knowledge Discovery and Data Mining*. ACM, 1809–1818.

[7] Ruining He and Julian McAuley. 2016. VBPR: Visual Bayesian Personalized Ranking from Implicit Feedback.. In *AAAI*. 144–150.

[8] Balázs Hidasi and Alexandros Karatzoglou. 2017. Recurrent Neural Networks with Top-k Gains for Session-based Recommendations. *arXiv preprint arXiv:1706.03847* (2017).

[9] Balázs Hidasi, Alexandros Karatzoglou, Linas Baltrunas, and Domonkos Tikk. 2015. Session-based recommendations with recurrent neural networks. *arXiv preprint arXiv:1511.06939; ICLR 2016* (2015).

[10] Balázs Hidasi, Massimo Quadrana, Alexandros Karatzoglou, and Domonkos Tikk. 2016. Parallel Recurrent Neural Network Architectures for Feature-rich Session-based Recommendations. In *Proceedings of the 10th ACM Conference on Recommender Systems (RecSys '16)*. 241–248.

[11] Alexandros Karatzoglou, Balázs Hidasi, Domonkos Tikk, Oren Sar-Shalom, Haggai Roitman, Bracha Shapira, and Lior Rokach. 2016. RecSys'16 Workshop on Deep Learning for Recommender Systems (DLRS). In *Proceedings of the 10th ACM Conference on Recommender Systems (RecSys '16)*. 415–416.

[12] Julian McAuley, Christopher Targett, Qinfeng Shi, and Anton Van Den Hengel. 2015. Image-based recommendations on styles and substitutes. In *Proceedings of the 38th International ACM SIGIR Conference on Research and Development in Information Retrieval*. ACM, 43–52.

[13] Tomas Mikolov, Ilya Sutskever, Kai Chen, Greg Corrado, and Jeffrey Dean. 2013. Distributed Representations of Words and Phrases and their Compositionality. *CoRR* 1310.4546 (2013). http://arxiv.org/abs/1310.4546

[14] Massimo Quadrana, Alexandros Karatzoglou, Balázs Hidasi, and Paolo Cremonesi. 2017. Personalizing Session-based Recommendations with Hierarchical Recurrent Neural Networks. *arXiv preprint arXiv:1706.04148* (2017).

[15] Ruslan Salakhutdinov, Andriy Mnih, and Geoffrey Hinton. 2007. Restricted Boltzmann machines for collaborative filtering. In *ICML'07: 24th Int. Conf. on Machine Learning*. 791–798.

[16] Yong Kiam Tan, Xinxing Xu, and Yong Liu. 2016. Improved Recurrent Neural Networks for Session-based Recommendations. In *Proceedings of the 1st Workshop on Deep Learning for Recommender Systems (DLRS 2016)*. 17–22.

[17] Bartłomiej Twardowski. 2016. Modelling Contextual Information in Session-Aware Recommender Systems with Neural Networks. In *Proceedings of the 10th ACM Conference on Recommender Systems (RecSys '16)*. 273–276.

[18] Aaron Van den Oord, Sander Dieleman, and Benjamin Schrauwen. 2013. Deep content-based music recommendation. In *Advances in Neural Information Processing Systems*. 2643–2651.

[19] Flavian Vasile, Elena Smirnova, and Alexis Conneau. 2016. Meta-Prod2Vec: Product Embeddings Using Side-Information for Recommendation. In *Proceedings of the 10th ACM Conference on Recommender Systems (RecSys '16)*. 225–232.

[20] Jeroen B. P. Vuurens, Martha Larson, and Arjen P. de Vries. 2016. Exploring Deep Space: Learning Personalized Ranking in a Semantic Space. In *Proceedings of the 1st Workshop on Deep Learning for Recommender Systems (DLRS 2016)*. 23–28.

[21] Hao Wang, Naiyan Wang, and Dit-Yan Yeung. 2015. Collaborative deep learning for recommender systems. In *Proceedings of the 21th ACM SIGKDD International Conference on Knowledge Discovery and Data Mining*. ACM, 1235–1244.

[22] Hao Wang, SHI Xingjian, and Dit-Yan Yeung. 2016. Collaborative recurrent autoencoder: Recommend while learning to fill in the blanks. In *Advances in Neural Information Processing Systems*. 415–423.

[23] Yao Wu, Christopher DuBois, Alice X Zheng, and Martin Ester. 2016. Collaborative denoising auto-encoders for top-n recommender systems. In *Proceedings of the Ninth ACM International Conference on Web Search and Data Mining*. ACM, 153–162.

[24] Yin Zheng, Cailiang Liu, Bangsheng Tang, and Hanning Zhou. 2016. Neural Autoregressive Collaborative Filtering for Implicit Feedback. In *Proceedings of the 1st Workshop on Deep Learning for Recommender Systems*. ACM, 2–6.

RecSys Challenge 2017: Offline and Online Evaluation

Fabian Abel
XING AG
Hamburg, Germany
fabian.abel@xing.com

Yashar Deldjoo
Politecnico di Milano
Milan, Italy
yashar.deldjoo@polimi.it

Mehdi Elahi
Free University of Bozen - Bolzano
Bozen - Bolzano, Italy
meelahi@unibz.it

Daniel Kohlsdorf
XING AG
Hamburg, Germany
daniel.kohlsdorf@xing.com

ABSTRACT

The ACM Recommender Systems Challenge 2017[1] focused on the problem of job recommendations: given a new job advertisement, the goal was to identify those users who are both (a) interested in getting notified about the job advertisement, and (b) appropriate candidates for the given job. Participating teams had to balance between user interests and requirements for the given job as well as dealing with the cold-start situation. For the first time in the history of the conference, the RecSys challenge offered an online evaluation: teams first had to compete as part of a traditional offline evaluation and the top 25 teams were then invited to evaluate their algorithms in an online setting, where they could submit recommendations to real users. Overall, 262 teams registered for the challenge, 103 teams actively participated and submitted together more than 6100 solutions as part of the offline evaluation. Finally, 18 teams participated and rolled out recommendations to more than 900,000 users on XING[2].

CCS CONCEPTS

• **Information systems → Recommender systems**; *Data mining*; *Test collections*;

KEYWORDS

Recommender Systems; Challenge; Cold Start

1 INTRODUCTION

The ACM Recommender Systems Challenge is an annual competition that focuses on the design and development of the best performing recommendation algorithms for a particular scenario. From its inception in 2010 until the eighth iteration in 2017, the challenge has experienced a substantial gain in interest and has drawn a lot of participants from industry and academia. It thus became a key part of the ACM RecSys Conference series [3].

[1]http://2017.recsyschallenge.com
[2]https://xing.com

RecSys'17, , August 27–31, 2017, Como, Italy.

ACM ISBN 978-1-4503-4652-8/17/08.
https://doi.org/10.1145/3109859.3109954

The 2017 edition of the challenge is organized jointly by XING, Politecnico di Milano[3] and Free University of Bozen - Bolzano[4]. This edition focused on a reciprocal recommendation problem: recommending job advertisements to people who are interested in the job and who are at the same time also good candidates for the job role that needs to be filled in the corresponding company. This problem had to be tackled in the cold-start situation [2].

XING, as an industrial organizer of the challenge, is a career-oriented social networking site, with around 20 Million users and around one Million open job offers on the platform. For the challenge, we published large training datasets of anonymized user profiles, job postings, and interactions between them.

The RecSys challenge 2017 started with an offline evaluation round. The top 25 teams qualified for the subsequent online evaluation round during which the participating teams were actually pushing recommendations to real XING users.

2 DATASET

For both offline and online evaluation, we provided a dataset that features the following details[5]:

- **interactions:** all transactions between a user and an item such as impressions, clicks, bookmarks, deletions and recruiter interests (= recruiter interacted with the candidate).
- **users:** details about users such as job title, skills, career level, location, estimated willingness to change jobs, etc.
- **items:** details about the job advertisement including fields such as job title, required skills, location, etc.
- **target items:** list of item IDs which the teams were allowed to push to interested users and for which the teams were supposed to identify matching candidates.
- **target users:** set of user IDs for which the teams were allowed to recommend items and which were allowed to appear as candidates.

During the online evaluation (see Section 4), the list of target items and target users changed on a daily basis. The training datasets were enriched with noise and anonymized in the same way as during the RecSys Challenge 2016 [1]. Basic statistics about the training datasets, that were handed out for the offline evaluation and shortly before the online evaluation, are listed in Table 1.

[3]https://www.polimi.it
[4]https://www.unibz.it
[5]http://2017.recsyschallenge.com/#dataset

Table 1: Statistics about datasets, used in offline and online evaluations.

	Offline	Online
users	1,497,020	963,346
items	1,306,054	853,058
impressions	314,501,101	88,719,060
clicks	6,867,579	3,552,973
bookmarks	281,672	184,061
replies	117,843	96,907
deletes	906,836	360,645
recruiter interests	100,971	35,715

3 CHALLENGES

During RecSys Challenge 2016, teams had to focus solely on estimating how relevant a job is for a given user [1]. In 2017, teams had to tackle multiple challenges at once.

Balancing user interest and recruiter demands: job recommendations should be relevant to the users. However, at the same time the users who receive those job recommendations also need to be appropriate candidates for the given job, i.e. the corresponding recruiter should show an interest in the candidate.

Balancing relevance and revenue: for some of the job advertisements, companies actually paid money to publish the ad on XING. Moreover, some users pay for premium subscriptions. Teams had to balance between relevance of recommendations and monetary aspects, i.e. the money that is earned with a successful recommendation.

Novelty / sparsity: recommendations had to be computed particularly for newly created job postings (new items). At the time a posting was supposed to be recommended to users, most of the postings did not receive any interaction yet.

Smart targeting of recommendations: also, the participating teams had to estimate how likely it is that a user is actually interested in job recommendations, e.g. users that are not interested in job recommendations may delete recommendations or disable notifications about recommendations in case they receive too many. The latter was primarily relevant for the teams that participated in the online challenge.

4 EVALUATION

The above challenges were also reflected in the evaluation metrics[6]. For example, recommendations for which the candidate and recruiter showed mutual interest led to a higher score compared to recommendations that just triggered the candidate to click on the job advertisement. Furthermore, successfully recommending paid content to premium users also led to higher scores. The same evaluation metrics is used in both offline evaluation phase and the subsequent online evaluation phase:

offline evaluation: during this phase which started on March 3rd 2017 and ended on April 16th, teams trained their algorithms on a fixed historic dataset and had to submit their solutions for a fixed set of target items and users (see Table 1).

online evaluation: this part of the challenge started on May 1st 2017 and ended on June 4th. Participating teams were equipped with an up-to-date training dataset before the start of the online challenge to prepare and re-train their algorithms and models. New target job advertisements, new interactions, etc. were then handed out on a daily basis. The teams had 24 hours time to submit their recommendations which were then actually rolled out on XING (Web, mobile apps and emails). The evaluation metric was applied on the interaction data that was collected within seven days after the recommendations were submitted[7].

[6] http://2017.recsyschallenge.com/#evaluation

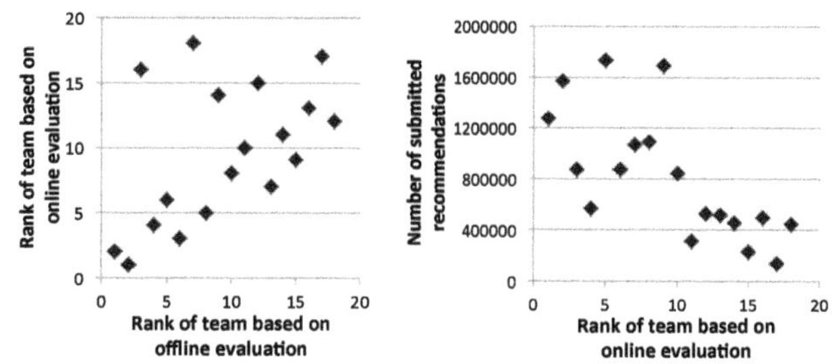

(a) offline vs. online (b) submitted recommendations

Figure 1: Correlation between: (a) ranks achieved during the offline and online evaluations and (b) ranks and the number of submitted recommendations (online)

5 RESULTS AND CONCLUSION

Figure 1a compares the performance of the teams during the offline evaluation and online evaluation: for most teams, we observe that they managed to confirm their offline evaluation performance also during the online challenge. Only for a few teams, the performance dropped strongly, e.g. one team lost more than 10 positions in the ranking. The recommendations contributed by that team also showed the lowest specificity regarding user targeting: one item was, on average, recommended, to 86 users. Other teams typically recommended the same item to 4-11 users.

We also see that the pure amount of recommendations that were submitted during the online challenge did not decide about the winner (see Figure 1b), for example: the team that submitted the highest number of recommendations ended up at rank 5.

In summary, we saw that there was high engagement among the participants: 103 teams were active during the challenge. As part of the offline evaluation, each team submitted, on average, 59.4 different solutions. During the online evaluation, the qualified teams successfully proved that their algorithms also work in a live system. Overall, the participants managed to rolled out more than 14.7 Million recommendations to more than 900,000 XING users.

REFERENCES

[1] Fabian Abel, András Benczúr, Daniel Kohlsdorf, Martha Larson and Róbert Pálovics. 2016. RecSys Challenge 2016: Job Recommendations. In *Proceedings of the 10th ACM Conference on Recommender Systems* (RecSys '16). ACM, New York, NY, USA, 425–426.

[2] Mehdi Elahi, Francesco Ricci, and Neil Rubens. 2016. A survey of active learning in collaborative filtering recommender systems. In *Computer Science Review* 20, 29–50.

[3] Alan Said. 2016. A Short History of the RecSys Challenge. In *AI Magazine*, 37, 4.

[7] https://github.com/recsyschallenge/2017/tree/master/online-evaluation

Second Workshop on Health Recommender Systems (HealthRecSys 2017)

David Elsweiler
University of Regensburg
Germany
david.elsweiler@ur.de

Santiago Hors-Fraile
Uni. of Seville, Maastricht Uni.
Spain & The Netherlands
sanhorfra@gmail.com

Bernd Ludwig
University of Regensburg
Germany
bernd.ludwig@ur.de

Alan Said
University of Skövde
Sweden
alansaid@acm.org

Hanna Schäfer
Technical University of Munich
Germany
hanna.schaefer@tum.de

Christoph Trattner
MODUL University Vienna
Austria
trattner.christoph@gmail.com

Helma Torkamaan
University of Duisburg-Essen
Germany
h.torkamaan@acm.org

André Calero Valdez
RWTH Aachen
Germany
calero-valdez@comm.rwth-aachen.de

ABSTRACT

The 2017 Workshop on Health Recommender Systems was held in conjunction with the 2017 ACM Conference on Recommender Systems in Como, Italy. Following the fists workshop in 2016, the focus of this workshop was on enhancing the results of the first workshop by elaborating discussions on the topics, attracting scientist from other domains, finding cross-domain collaboration, and establishing shared infrastructures.

KEYWORDS

Health Recommender System; Health-aware computing; Health-aware information systems; Recommender Systems; Well-being;

ACM Reference format:
David Elsweiler, Santiago Hors-Fraile, Bernd Ludwig, Alan Said, Hanna Schäfer, Christoph Trattner, Helma Torkamaan, and André Calero Valdez. 2017. Second Workshop on Health Recommender Systems (HealthRecSys 2017). In *Proceedings of RecSys'17, Como, Italy., August 27–31, 2017,* 2 pages.
DOI: http://dx.doi.org/10.1145/3109859.3109955

1 INTRODUCTION

Health is at the center of our everyday lives. During the 1st Health Recommender Systems workshop[1] we elaborated a great variety of fields in which recommender systems can improve our awareness, understanding and behavior regarding our own health. At the same time these application areas bring new challenges into the recommender community. Recommendations that influence the health status of a patient, need to be either liable or accompanied by domain experts. To make the recommender liable, complex domain specific user models need to be created, which on the other hand creates privacy issues. While trust in a recommendation needs to be explicitly earned via transparency, explanations and empowerment, other systems might want to persuade users into beneficial actions that would not be willingly chosen otherwise. The variety of those challenges also results from the number and diversity of stakeholders involved in health systems. Taking the patient perspective, simple interaction and safety against harmful recommendations might be the prior concern. For clinicians and experts, on the other hand, what matters is precise and accurate content. Finally, health care providers, insurance companies, and clinics are interested in success rates, study results, and financial benefits of the new systems. In this workshop, we wish to extend and deepen the discussions initiated last year with the aim of establishing a roadmap of possible research topics in Health Recommender Systems.

Our aim is to enhance the results of the first workshop in the following areas:

- Elaborate discussion topics of the first workshop
- Strengthen the community of researchers working on Health in RecSys
- Attract scientists from other domains to RecSys (e.g. health, psychology, ...)
- Find cross-domain collaboration projects and funding targets
- Establish shared infrastructure (datasets and tools)

2 WORKSHOP FORMAT

The workshop was conducted as a full-day interactive workshop in conjunction with the 2017 ACM Conference on Recommender Systems in Como, Italy. The morning session started of with a keynote by Xavier Amatriain from "Dr.Assist". The rest of the morning session consisted of lightning presentation for selected research submissions and poster presentations for the other submission. Between each presentation plentiful time for discussion and feedback on the ideas presented was given. Prominent topics were discussed via social media and a shared document that all participants could edit. The afternoon session was highly interactive, since we received great feedback on that approach last year. The sessions included, idea generation sessions, focused group discussions and open fish-bowl discussions.

3 ACCEPTED CONTRIBUTIONS

The workshop accepted short research papers (4 pages) and short position papers (2 pages), both in the ACM conference paper style. Papers were either selected for lightning presentations, or otherwise discussed in the form of poster presentations. Overall approximately 10 contributions were accepted and presented during the HealthRecSys workshop 2017. The topics of discussed in the workshop include but are not limited to:

- Algorithms for HRS
- Domain Knowledge Representation
- Regulations and Standards
- Behavioral Change
- Medical evaluation techniques
- User Profiling
- Pervasive Systems
- Personalization
- Persuasion
- Social Motivation
- Gamification
- Empowerment
- Trust
- Explanations
- Nudging
- Patient Needs/Satisfaction
- User Interaction Design
- Expert-in-the-Loop
- Privacy
- Ethics

4 PROGRAM COMMITTEE

We thank the program committee for supporting this workshop:

- Tim Althoff
- Shlomo Berkovsky
- Aysegl Dogangün
- Michael Ekstrand
- Mehdi Elahi
- Alexander Felfernig
- Georg Groh
- Morgan Harvey
- Kjetil Nørvåg
- Toon De Pessemier
- Francesco Ricci
- Markus Rokicki
- Ingmar Weber
- Robert West
- Martin Wiesner
- Martijn Willemsen
- Longqi Yang

5 ACKNOWLEDGMENTS

We thank the RecSys 2017 organizing committee for giving us the opportunity to host this workshop in conjunction with RecSys 2017 in Como, Itly. We would also like to thank the authors, presenters, and reviewers, whose efforts made the workshop possible.

REFERENCES

[1] David Elsweiler, Bernd Ludwig, Alan Said, Hanna Schaefer, and Christoph Trattner. 2016. Engendering Health with Recommender Systems. In *Proceedings of the 10th ACM Conference on Recommender Systems (RecSys '16)*. ACM, New York, NY, USA, 409–410. DOI: http://dx.doi.org/10.1145/2959100.2959203

KidRec: Children & Recommender Systems

Workshop Co-located with ACM Conference on Recommender Systems (RecSys 2017)

Jerry Alan Fails
Dept. of Computer Science
Boise State University
Boise, Idaho, USA
jerryfails@boisestate.edu

Maria Soledad Pera
People and Information Research Team
Dept. of Computer Science
Boise State University
Boise, Idaho, USA
solepera@boisestate.edu

Franca Garzotto
Computer Engineering at the Politecnico di Milano
Dept. of Electronics, Information, and Bioengineering
Milan, Italy
franca.garzotto@polimi.it

Mirko Gelsomini
Computer Engineering at the Politecnico di Milano
Dept. of Electronics, Information, and Bioengineering
Milan, Italy
mirko.gelsomini@polimi.it

ABSTRACT

The 1st Workshop on Children and Recommender Systems (KidRec) is taking place in Como, Italy August 27th, 2017 in conjunction with the ACM RecSys 2017 conference. The goals of the workshop are threefold: (1) discuss and identify issues related to recommender systems used by children including specific challenges and limitations, (2) discuss possible solutions to the identified challenges and plan for future research, and (3) build a community to directly work on these important issues.

CCS CONCEPTS

• **Information systems → Recommender systems**; • **Social and professional topics → Children**;

KEYWORDS

Children, recommender systems, technology for children

1 RATIONALE

Recommender systems have been studied for the past few decades [9, 10]. Recommendation strategies detailed in the literature [1, 2, 5] – for the most part – have been developed to serve traditional users: adult individuals who often offer explicit feedback, write reviews, or purchase items themselves.

Children's access to technology has dramatically increased in the past fifteen years [3, 8]. This includes children's access to and use of popular recommender systems when they search using websites such as Google or when they are recommended related content when they browse and watch videos on YouTube. While recommendation systems for adults have been studied for several years, recommendation systems for children are only recently beginning to be studied and are primarily limited to recommenders in education-related environments [6, 7]. When focused on this particular audience, the role of a recommendation system needs to be reformulated, as it is not sufficient for recommenders to identify items that match users' preferences and interests. Instead, it is imperative that they also explicitly consider their needs from multiple perspectives: educational, developmental, and engagement, to name a few.

Considering these particular needs opens a rich set of questions for the research community to answer:

- What are the benefits of child-specific recommendations?
- What role does personal history, age, developmental stage, or even curricular standards have in recommendation systems for children?
- What are the goals of recommendation systems for children: persuade, educate, guide, and support their well-being, or something else entirely?
- What are the ethical or privacy challenges associated with this type of recommendation?
- What are the domains in which recommendations make sense for children? Are they the same as for adults?
- How should we model personalization given that traditional mechanisms of explicit feedback, writing reviews, and purchasing items (directly) do not match this particular population whose literacy levels are growing and who generally do not directly have the ability to purchase items?
- Are their specifics concern, from the point of view of developing technology that should be considered?

In addition, the interests and needs of this population are rapidly evolving, as children are in formative stages of development and are still refining their interests as they get to know new things, and enhance their educational context.

Given the increasing use of technology by children, and the breadth of issues already identified, we feel it is necessary to bring this community together to work to build the community, collectively map out the field of recommendation systems for children, and to begin to address these issues together.

RecSys'17, August 27–31, 2017, Como, Italy.

ACM ISBN ISBN 978-1-4503-4652-8/17/08.
https://doi.org/10.1145/3109859.3109956

2 WORKSHOP DESCRIPTION

We offer below the goal, objectives and activities proposed for the workshop, as well as research communities that have a direct impact of the outcomes of the proposed meeting, in terms of shaping priorities for this emerging domain.

2.1 Goal

The goal of this interactive workshop is to congregate researchers and experts from multiple disciplines, in order to understand the ethical, pedagogical, and technical implications of designing and developing recommendation systems that can be of use for children, whether for leisure or educational activities.

2.2 Objectives

The main workshop objectives include sharing and discussing research and projects that reach beyond classic recommender techniques and discuss the many child related challenges of recommender systems.

2.3 Areas of Interest

Recommender systems for children relates to a variety of research communities, including:

- Technology for children
- Recommender algorithms for children
- Recommendation explanations, transparency,
- Expert-in-the-Loop (e.g., teacher, parent)
- Child-centered content domains (e.g., leisure, education)
- User Profiling
- Personalization
- Gamification
- Ethics
- Privacy
- Information Retrieval
- Human Computer Interaction
- Education

By inviting members from these varied communities and building a community of KidRec researchers, we foster a multidisciplinary perspective that can initiate a conversation of the challenges, limitations, and needs related to the design and development of recommendation systems that can be directly and widely adopted by children.

2.4 Activities

We aim to facilitate a highly participatory [4] workshop in which attendees can discuss the limitations and challenges of recommendation systems for children and identify possible solutions and avenues of research. We propose to accomplish this through an interactive format, including: community building exercises, informal interactions, facilitated group work, and short and position paper presentations.

3 ACCEPTED PAPERS

For this first meeting, we have accepted six submissions. The topics of the accepted papers are varied and come from researchers in informatics, human computer interaction, gaming, music, design, and visualization, to name a few.

The accepted papers will start the discussion on how aesthetic relevance influence the decision making process, when it comes to recommend multimedia items for children; how to enhance children's book recommendations; how attention patterns can bias the recommendation selection of items in the movie domain; how to tailor music recommendation for young children and adolescents; how to depend upon gaming to generate recommendation that promote vocabulary development; and, how to evaluate recommendations when it comes to children, given the lack of existing benchmarks.

The accepted paper presentations and following discussions, along with the interactive activitites the KidRec's organizing commitee has planned will help build community and start an important conversation on the needs, challenges, and limitations of recommendation systems designed to benefit children both through direct use, and that indirectly meet children's needs by guiding an adult to interact with children (e.g a teacher or a librarian).

4 OUTCOMES AND FUTURE

The primary benefit of this workshop will be to start to formally build a community of researchers who directly work with one another to address the particular needs of children with regards to recommender systems. We invite and welcome researchers from disparate research areas to openly acknowledge and work towards addressing the particular issues related to recommender systems that impact children.

ACKNOWLEDGMENTS

We would like to thank Program Committee members for their prompt and insightful reviews, which directly impacts the level of the workshop discussions. We also thank the Organizing Committee for RecSys 2017 for giving us the opportunity to host this workshop in conjunction with the main RecSys 2017 conference.

REFERENCES

[1] Gediminas Adomavicius and Alexander Tuzhilin. 2005. Toward the next generation of recommender systems: A survey of the state-of-the-art and possible extensions. *IEEE transactions on knowledge and data engineering* 17, 6 (2005), 734–749.
[2] Michael D Ekstrand, John T Riedl, Joseph A Konstan, et al. 2011. Collaborative filtering recommender systems. *Foundations and Trends® in Human–Computer Interaction* 4, 2 (2011), 81–173.
[3] James M Ernest, Cora Causey, Allison B Newton, Kimberly Sharkins, Jennifer Summerlin, and Najla Albaiz. 2014. Extending the global dialogue about media, technology, screen time, and young children. *Childhood Education* 90, 3 (2014), 182–191.
[4] Seeds for Change. 2017. Facilitating Participatory Workshops. *Seedsforchange.org.uk* (2017).
[5] Pasquale Lops, Marco De Gemmis, and Giovanni Semeraro. 2011. Content-based recommender systems: State of the art and trends. In *Recommender systems handbook*. Springer, 73–105.
[6] Nikos Manouselis, Hendrik Drachsler, Riina Vuorikari, Hans Hummel, and Rob Koper. 2011. Recommender systems in technology enhanced learning. In *Recommender systems handbook*. Springer, 387–415.
[7] Maria Soledad Pera and Yiu-Kai Ng. 2014. Automating readers' advisory to make book recommendations for k-12 readers. In *Proceedings of the 8th ACM Conference on Recommender systems*. ACM, 9–16.
[8] Lydia Plowman. 2015. Researching young children's everyday uses of technology in the family home. *Interacting with Computers* 27, 1 (2015), 36–46.
[9] Paul Resnick and Hal R Varian. 1997. Recommender systems. *Commun. ACM* 40, 3 (1997), 56–58.
[10] Francesco Ricci, Lior Rokach, and Bracha Shapira. 2011. *Introduction to recommender systems handbook*. Springer.

VAMS 2017: Workshop on Value-Aware and Multistakeholder Recommendation

Robin Burke
School of Computing
DePaul University
Chicago, Illinois
rburke@cs.depaul.edu

Gediminas Adomavicius
Department of Information and Decision Science
University of Minnesota
Minneapolis, Minnesota
gedas@umn.edu

Ido Guy
eBay
Netanya, Israel
idoguy@acm.org

Jan Krasnodebski
Expedia
Geneva, Switzerland
jkrasnodebski@expedia.com

Luiz Pizzato
Commonwealth Bank of Australia
Sydney, Australia
luiz@pizzato.cc

Yi Zhang
Department of Technology Management
University of California, Santa Cruz
Santa Cruz, California
yiz@soe.ucsc.edu

Himan Abdollahpouri
School of Computing
DePaul University
Chicago, Illinois
habdolla@depaul.edu

ABSTRACT

In this paper, we summarize VAMS 2017 – a workshop on value-aware and multistakeholder recommendation co-located with RecSys 2017. The workshop encouraged forward-thinking papers in this new area of recommender systems research and obtained a diverse set of responses ranging from application results to research overviews.

KEYWORDS

Recommender systems; Value-aware Recommendation; Multistakeholder Recommendation; Multiobjective; Multicriteria

1 INTRODUCTION

Personalization is an essential characteristic of recommender systems; they are designed to find items that meet user needs and tastes. However, the receiver of the recommendation may sometimes be only one of several parties whose goals are relevant in recommendation computation and evaluation. Also, in many contexts, such as retail and digital advertising, the business value associated with recommendation delivery may need to be included in the recommendation calculation.

The purpose of the VAM 2017 workshop was to bring together researchers to formulate a common vision for research progress in this emerging area. The workshop invited submissions on a range of topics:

- Reciprocal recommendation: the context in which a recommendation must satisfy both the target user and recommended party, such as person-to-person recommendation.
- Strategic recommendation: the context in which the system has its own recommendation objectives, not necessarily shared by the user, for example, pedagogical goals in educational recommendation.
- Multi-objective recommendation, especially where the objectives represent the interests of different parties, and where the objectives may vary by context.
- Recommendation in multisided platforms.
- Mechanisms to represent and resolve conflicting interests among recommendation stakeholders.

2 WORKSHOP PROGRAM

The VAMS workshop was organized as a set of interactive working sessions, aimed at exploring the important questions and problems in this area of research. The workshop accepted a small number of papers, proposing key research areas for value-aware and multistakeholder recommendation and presenting relevant application results. These were presented in "campfire sessions" with short presentations followed by extended discussion. Participants were encouraged to read the papers in advance and were expected to be active participants in the discussion.

In the first session, three papers were presented and discussed. In [4], Jannach and Adomavicius introduce the "value-aware" aspect of the problem by examining the tradeoff between profit and accuracy, and discuss the challenge of assessing long-term and short-term consequences of recommendation decisions. Burke and Abdollahpouri [2] develop a taxonomy of different types of multistakeholder recommender systems based on the ways in which systems optimize the utilities of different parties: users, providers, and the recommender system itself. In [6], Zheng also examines different classes of multistakeholder recommendation problems and suggests different types of possible solutions.

RecSys '17, August 27-31, 2017, Como, Italy

ACM ISBN 978-1-4503-4652-8/17/08.
https://doi.org/10.1145/3109859.3109957

The second session examined two application papers. The paper by Ekman et al. [3] examines the problem of task allocation for complex tasks in a crowd-sourced work distribution environment such as Amazon Mechanical Turk. This is a multicriteria problem under uncertainty in which the workers' skills and the task requirements may not be known accurately, and in which some workers may have an incentive to misrepresent their abilities. This tension between different stakeholders also arises in the hotel recommendation scenario described in [5]. In this application, a learning-to-rerank solution is deployed to find a solution point optimizing a multicriterion performance function including user satisfaction, provider sales, and system margin / profitability. Adding to the application discussion was a statement of interest contributed by Abdollahpouri and Essinger [1] introducing a sequential recommendation problem involving multiple stakeholders: the integration of advertising into streaming audio services.

The third session of the workshop was a joint panel with the RecSys Challenge workshop. The 2017 RecSys Challenge was notable in that the recommendation problem posed by the organizers was inherently a multistakeholder one – job recommendation using data from the XING online business network. The function to be optimized included user-oriented criteria (user click probability), system-oriented criteria (whether a given user is a (paid) premium user or not), and provider-oriented criteria (whether a user was selected by a recruiter for follow-up). The purpose of the panel was to explore the overlap in the two workshops: the demands of the specific multistakeholder recommendation task posed by the Challenge and the benefits of an explicitly multistakeholder approach as explored in the VAMS workshop.

3 CONCLUSION

While recommender systems research maintains a strong focus on the end user, there are a number of applications where it is essential to recognize the multistakeholder nature of recommendation and to integrate the concerns of the different parties appropriately. This workshop highlights some of those applications, and attempts to synthesize prior work in reciprocal and multi-objective recommendation that has pointed in this direction. The multistakeholder paradigm generates new challenges for the recommender systems field: challenges in evaluation, in algorithm design and implementation, and in transparency and user trust. We plan to summarize the state of the field in a survey article, bringing together the insights gained from this workshop to provide a foundation for future research.

REFERENCES

[1] Himan Abdollahpouri and Steve Essinger. 2017. Multiple Stakeholders in a Music Recommender System. In *1st International Workshop on Value-Aware and Multistakeholder Recommendation at RecSys 2017*. 3 pages.
[2] Robin Burke and Himan Abdollahpouri. 2017. Patterns of Multistakeholder Recommendation. In *1st International Workshop on Value-Aware and Multistakeholder Recommendation at RecSys 2017*. 5 pages.
[3] Philip Ekman, Sebastian Bellevik, Christos Dimitrakakis, and Aristide Tossou. 2017. Learning to match. In *1st International Workshop on Value-Aware and Multistakeholder Recommendation at RecSys 2017*. 5 pages.
[4] Dietmar Jannach and Gediminas Adomavicius. 2017. Price and Profit Awareness in Recommender Systems. In *1st International Workshop on Value-Aware and Multistakeholder Recommendation at RecSys 2017*. 5 pages.
[5] Phong Nguyen, John Dines, and Jan Krasnodebski. 2017. A Multi-Objective Learning to re-Rank Approach to Optimize Online Marketplaces for Multiple Stakeholders. In *1st International Workshop on Value-Aware and Multistakeholder Recommendation at RecSys 2017*. 5 pages.
[6] Yong Zheng. 2017. Multi-Stakeholder Recommendation: Applications and Challenges. In *1st International Workshop on Value-Aware and Multistakeholder Recommendation at RecSys 2017*. 5 pages.

Workshop on Recommendation in Complex Scenarios (ComplexRec 2017)

Toine Bogers
Department of Communication & Psychology
Aalborg University Copenhagen
Denmark
toine@hum.aau.dk

Marijn Koolen
Huygens ING, Royal Netherlands Academy of Arts and Sciences
Netherlands
marijn.koolen@huygens.knaw.nl

Bamshad Mobasher
School of Computing
DePaul University
United States
mobasher@cs.depaul.edu

Alan Said
University of Skövde
Sweden
alansaid@acm.org

Alexander Tuzhilin
Stern School of Business
New York University
United States
atuzhili@stern.nyu.edu

ABSTRACT

Recommendation algorithms for ratings prediction and item ranking have steadily matured during the past decade. However, these state-of-the-art algorithms are typically applied in relatively straightforward scenarios. In reality, recommendation is often a more complex problem: it is usually just a single step in the user's more complex background need. These background needs can often place a variety of constraints on which recommendations are interesting to the user and when they are appropriate. However, relatively little research has been done on these complex recommendation scenarios. The ComplexRec 2017 workshop addressed this by providing an interactive venue for discussing approaches to recommendation in complex scenarios that have no simple one-size-fits-all-solution.

KEYWORDS

Complex recommendation

1 INTRODUCTION

Over the past decade, recommendation algorithms for ratings prediction and item ranking have steadily matured, spurred on in part by the success of data mining competitions such as the Netflix Prize, the 2011 Yahoo! Music KDD Cup, and the RecSys Challenges. Matrix factorization and other latent factor models emerged from these competitions as the state-of-the-art algorithms to apply in both existing and new domains. However, these state-of-the-art algorithms are typically applied in relatively straightforward and static scenarios: given information about a user's past item preferences in isolation, can we predict whether they will like a new item or rank all unseen items based on predicted interests?

In reality, recommendation is often a more complex problem: the evaluation of a list of recommended items never takes place in a vacuum, and it is often only a single step in the user's more complex background task or need. These background needs can often place a variety of constraints on which recommendations are interesting to the user and when they are appropriate. However, relatively little research has been done on how to elicit rich information about these complex background needs or how to incorporate it into the recommendation process. Furthermore, while state-of-the-art algorithms typically work with user preferences aggregated at the item level, real users may prefer some of an item's features more than others or attach more weight in general to certain features. Finally, providing accurate and appropriate recommendations in such complex scenarios comes with a whole new set of evaluation and validation challenges.

The current generation of recommender systems and algorithms are good at addressing straightforward recommendation scenarios, yet more complex scenarios as described above have been underserved. The **ComplexRec 2017** workshop addressed this by providing an interactive venue for discussing approaches to recommendation in complex scenarios that have no simple one-size-fits-all solution.

While ComplexRec 2017 was the first edition of this workshop, in recent years other workshops have been organized on related topics. Examples include the CARS (Context-aware Recommender Systems) workshop series (2009-2012) organized in conjunction with RecSys [1–4], the CARR (Context-aware Retrieval and Recommendation) workshop series (2011-2015) organized in conjunction with IUI, WSDM, and ECIR [5–8, 11], as well as the SCST (Supporting Complex Search Tasks) workshop series (2015, 2017) organized in conjunction with ECIR and CHIIR [9, 10].

2 FORMAT & TOPICS

ComplexRec was organized as an interactive, half-day workshop. The workshop started with a keynote presentation by Dietmar Jannach about his work on session-aware recommendation, where a recommender system has to adapt its suggestions instantly to the assumed short-term interests of each user, usually based on the user's most recent interactions with the site or app. In his keynote, discussed existing approaches and challenges in this area

RecSys'17, August 27–31, 2017, Como, Italy.
 ISBN 978-1-4503-4652-8/17/08.
DOI: http://dx.doi.org/10.1145/3109859.3109958

based on examples from the domains of e-commerce and music recommendation. The keynote presentation was followed by a single paper session, for which short papers and position papers of 2-4 pages in length were solicited. Accepted submissions received short 10-minute presentations with 5 minutes for discussion. Evaluation criteria for acceptance included novelty, diversity, significance, quality of presentation, and the potential for sparking interesting discussion at the workshop. All submitted papers were reviewed by the Program Committee. The second half of the workshop featured 3-4 breakout groups corresponding to the participant's interests in addition to the topics of the contributed papers. Afterwards, the breakout groups reported back for more discussion on what was learned.

2.1 Topics of interest

Relevant topics for the ComplexRec workshop included:

- **Task-based recommendation** (Approaches that take the user's background tasks and needs into account when generating recommendations)
- **Feature-driven recommendation** (Techniques for eliciting, capturing and integrating rich information about user preferences for specific product features)
- **Constraint-based recommendation** (Approaches that successfully combine state-of-the-art recommendation algorithms with complex knowledge-based or constraint-based optimization)
- **Query-driven recommendation** (Techniques for eliciting and incorporating rich information about the user's recommendation need (e.g., need for accessibility, engagement, socio-cultural values, familiarity, etc.) in addition to the standard user preference information)
- **Context-aware recommendation** (Methods for the extraction and integration of complex contextual signals for recommendation)
- **Complex data sources** (Approaches to dealing with complex data sources and how to infer user preferences from these sources)
- **Evaluation & validation** (Approaches to the evaluation and validation of recommendation in complex scenarios)

3 ACCEPTED PAPERS

A total of 7 papers were submitted to the workshop, which were all reviewed by a program committee of international experts in the field. Five of these papers were accepted for presentation at the workshop, resulting in an acceptance rate of 71.4%.

The accepted papers focused on a variety of complex recommendation problems. Delgado et al. discussed the complexity inherent in personalized voice search for Internet TV, which requires the generation of fresh, domain-specific, relevant and contextual recommendations under a variety of personal and general constraints.

Piazza et al. investigate the usefulness of 3D body scans for fashion product recommendations. They extracted a variety of different body measures from this complex data source and showed that it significantly improved the recommendation performance.

Campos et al. describe the construction and composition of a semi-automatically constructed context taxonomy for extracting context data from user reviews for recommendation. The taxonomy is composed of semantic entities from DBpedia and can be manually adjusted through a proprietarily developed software tool.

Lofi & Tintarev discuss a first step towards analogy-based recommendation by benchmarking the semantics of perceived analogies. Their results show that current word embedding approaches are still not not suitable to sufficiently deal with deeper analogy semantics.

Finally, Wiwobo et al. et al. tackle the complex problem of package recommendation where utility of combinations of items must also be considered, such as travel or fashion. They introduce both a new data set for this domain and propose several extensions to the existing matrix factorization framework.

4 WEBSITE & PROCEEDINGS

The workshop material (list of accepted papers, invited talk, and the workshop schedule) can be found on the ComplexRec workshop website at http://complexrec2017.aau.dk. The proceedings are available as a CEUR Workshop Proceedings volume, a link to which can be found on the workshop website. A summary of the workshop will appear in SIGIR Forum to increase cross-disciplinary awareness of recommender systems research.

REFERENCES

[1] Gediminas Adomavicius, Linas Baltrunas, Ernesto William de Luca, Tim Hussein, and Alexander Tuzhilin. 2012. 4th Workshop on Context-aware Recommender Systems (CARS 2012). In *Proceedings of RecSys '12*. ACM, New York, NY, USA, 349–350.

[2] Gediminas Adomavicius, Linas Baltrunas, Tim Hussein, Francesco Ricci, and Alexander Tuzhilin. 2011. 3rd Workshop on Context-aware Recommender Systems (CARS 2011). In *Proceedings of RecSys '11*. ACM, New York, NY, USA, 379–380.

[3] Gediminas Adomavicius and Francesco Ricci. 2009. RecSys'09 Workshop 3: Workshop on Context-aware Recommender Systems (CARS-2009). In *Proceedings of RecSys '09*. ACM, New York, NY, USA, 423–424.

[4] Gediminas Adomavicius, Alexander Tuzhilin, Shlomo Berkovsky, Ernesto W. De Luca, and Alan Said. 2010. Context-awareness in Recommender Systems: Research Workshop and Movie Recommendation Challenge. In *Proceedings of RecSys '10*. ACM, New York, NY, USA, 385–386.

[5] Matthias Böhmer, Ernesto W. De Luca, Alan Said, and Jaime Teevan. 2013. 3rd Workshop on Context-awareness in Retrieval and Recommendation. In *Proceedings of WSDM '13*. ACM, New York, NY, USA, 789–790.

[6] Ernesto William De Luca, Matthias Böhmer, Alan Said, and Ed Chi. 2012. 2nd Workshop on Context-awareness in Retrieval and Recommendation: (CaRR 2012). In *Proceedings of IUI '12*. ACM, New York, NY, USA, 409–412.

[7] Ernesto William De Luca, Alan Said, Matthias Böhmer, and Florian Michahelles. 2011. Workshop on Context-awareness in Retrieval and Recommendation. In *Proceedings of IUI '11*. ACM, New York, NY, USA, 471–472.

[8] Ernesto W. De Luca, Alan Said, Fabio Crestani, and David Elsweiler. 2015. 5th Workshop on Context-awareness in Retrieval and Recommendation. In *Proceedings of ECIR '15*. Springer, 830–833.

[9] Maria Gäde, Mark Michael Hall, Hugo C. Huurdeman, Jaap Kamps, Marijn Koolen, Mette Skov, Elaine Toms, and David Walsh. 2015. First Workshop on Supporting Complex Search Tasks. In *Proceedings of the First International Workshop on Supporting Complex Search Tasks, co-located with ECIR 2015*.

[10] Marijn Koolen, Jaap Kamps, Toine Bogers, Nicholas J. Belkin, Diane Kelly, and Emine Yilmaz. 2017. Current Research in Supporting Complex Search Tasks. In *Proceedings of the Second Workshop on Supporting Complex Search Tasks, co-located with CHIIR 2017*. 1–4.

[11] Alan Said, Ernesto W. De Luca, D. Quercia, and Matthias Böhmer. 2014. 4th Workshop on Context-awareness in Retrieval and Recommendation. In *Proceedings of ECIR '14*. Springer, 802–805.

FATREC Workshop on Responsible Recommendation

Michael D. Ekstrand
People and Information Research Team (PIReT)
Department of Computer Science
Boise State University
Boise, Idaho, USA
michaelekstrand@boisestate.edu

Amit Sharma
Microsoft Research
New York, New York, USA
amshar@microsoft.com

ABSTRACT

The first Workshop on Responsible Recommendation (FATREC) was held in conjunction with the 11th ACM Conference on Recommender Systems in August, 2017 in Como, Italy. This full-day workshop brought together researchers and practitioners to discuss several topics under the banner of *social responsibility* in recommender systems: fairness, accountability, transparency, privacy, and other ethical and social concerns.

CCS CONCEPTS

• **Information systems** → **Recommender systems;** • **Security and privacy** → *Human and societal aspects of security and privacy;* • **Social and professional topics** → *User characteristics;* • **Applied computing** → *Law, social and behavioral sciences;* • **Human-centered computing** → HCI design and evaluation methods;

KEYWORDS

recommender systems, fairness, transparency, ethics

ACM Reference format:
Michael D. Ekstrand and Amit Sharma. 2017. FATREC Workshop on Responsible Recommendation. In *Proceedings of RecSys '17, Como, Italy, August 27–31, 2017,* 2 pages.
https://doi.org/10.1145/3109859.3109960

1 INTRODUCTION

We sought, with this workshop, to foster a discussion of various topics that fall under the general umbrella of *responsible recommendation*: ethical considerations in recommendation, bias and discrimination in recommender systems and their emergent effects, transparency and accountability, social impact of recommenders, user privacy, and other related concerns. Our goal was to encourage the community to think about how we build and study recommender systems in a socially-responsible manner.

Recommendation systems are increasingly impacting people's decisions in different walks of life including commerce, employment, dating, health, education and governance. As the impact and scope of recommendations increase, developing systems that tackle issues of fairness, transparency and accountability becomes important. This workshop was held in the spirit of FATML (Fairness, Accountability, and Transparency in Machine Learning)[1], DAT (Data and Algorithmic Transparency)[2], and similar workshops in related communities. With "Responsible Recommendation", we brought that conversation to RecSys.

RecSys '17, August 27–31, 2017, Como, Italy

ACM ISBN 978-1-4503-4652-8/17/08.
https://doi.org/10.1145/3109859.3109960

2 BACKGROUND

Fairness, accountability, transparency, and related topics around the ethical deployment of machine learning have seen increasing attention in the last several years. From formalizing fairness and designing algorithms to improve it [1] to black-box verification of nondiscrimination [3] and external audits of deployed applications [5], significant progress has been made on how to evaluate and improve the fairness of machine learning systems in general.

Much of this work has focused on systems connected to domains historically recognized as susceptible for discrimination, such as criminal justice, lending, and employment, and many of the machine learning techniques have focused on classification. There has been significantly less work on what constitutes fair or unfair recommendations, or how the fairness of such systems can be improved. Some of this has existed in the recommender systems literature, with a history of work on topics such as privacy [8] and diversity [4]. It is not obvious what the key problems and questions around recommender fairness even are, as there are many different stakeholders in the recommendation process who may experience very different impacts. Work is needed, therefore, to better define the questions and problems around fairness and responsibility in recommendation, and then to address those issues; this workshop was intended to be a catalyst for that conversation.

3 TOPICS

As this is the first workshop and we sought to get a sense for what all questions the community had around responsibility in recommender systems, we cast the list of interesting topics very broadly, including (but not limited to):

- Bias and discrimination in recommendations
- Meeting the needs of different groups of users [6]
- Balancing needs of users, recommender system owners, and other stakeholders [2]
- Ethics of explore/exploit strategies or A/B testing
- "Filter bubble" [7] or "balkanization" [10] effects
- Clickbait

[1] http://www.fatml.org
[2] http://datworkshop.org/

- Transparent and accurate explanations for recommendations [9]
- User data privacy [8]

We went in to the workshop with two desired outcomes:

- Collecting ideas currently in the recommender systems and fairness communities around what kinds of fairness, responsibility, and ethical problems face recommender systems.
- A set of open problems and a research agenda for making recommender systems more socially responsible.

4 PAPER TRACK

We solicited three types of submissions:

Position papers 2–4-page position papers on what it means for recommender systems to be socially responsible and how we might measure or evaluate such responsibility.

Practical abstracts 2-page abstracts on practical issues in building responsible recommender systems in either research industry.

Research papers 6-page papers presenting empirical or analytical results related to the social impact of recommender systems or algorithms. These could be explorations of bias in recommender systems (either live systems or sandboxed algorithms), explainability and transparency of recommender systems, experiments regarding the impact of the recommender on its users or others, etc.

We received 14 submissions that were reviewed by a 12-person program committee. The accepted papers can be found at http://scholarworks.boisestate.edu/cs_facpubs/98/.

5 WORKSHOP PROGRAM

The workshop schedule allocated the morning to paper presentations and discussion, with the papers grouped into two panels each moderated by a discussant from the program committee.

The afternoon saw a keynote address and a group discussion of open issues and a desired research agenda.

6 FURTHER READING

The workshop proceedings are published in the Boise State University ScholarWorks repository and available at http://scholarworks.boisestate.edu/cs_facpubs/98/.

A report on the outcomes of the workshop is in preparation for publication in a suitable forum, and will be linked from the workshop proceedings as well as the workshop web site at http://piret.gitlab.io/fatrec/.

REFERENCES

[1] Cynthia Dwork, Moritz Hardt, Toniann Pitassi, Omer Reingold, and Richard Zemel. 2012. Fairness Through Awareness. In *Proceedings of the 3rd Innovations in Theoretical Computer Science Conference (ITCS '12)*. ACM, New York, NY, USA, 214–226. https://doi.org/10.1145/2090236.2090255

[2] Michael D Ekstrand and Martijn C Willemsen. 2016. Behaviorism is Not Enough: Better Recommendations Through Listening to Users. In *Proceedings of the 10th ACM Conference on Recommender Systems (RecSys '16)*. ACM, New York, NY, USA, 221–224. https://doi.org/10.1145/2959100.2959179

[3] Michael Feldman, Sorelle A Friedler, John Moeller, Carlos Scheidegger, and Suresh Venkatasubramanian. 2015. Certifying and Removing Disparate Impact. In *Proceedings of the 21th ACM SIGKDD International Conference on Knowledge Discovery and Data Mining*. ACM, 259–268. https://doi.org/10.1145/2783258.2783311

[4] Daniel M Fleder and Kartik Hosanagar. 2009. Blockbuster Culture's Next Rise or Fall: The Impact of Recommender Systems on Sales Diversity. *Manage. Sci.* 55, 5 (May 2009), 697–712. https://doi.org/10.1287/mnsc.1080.0974

[5] Aniko Hannak, Claudia Wagner, David Garcia, Markus Strohmaier, and Christo Wilson. 2016. Bias in Online Freelance Marketplaces: Evidence from TaskRabbit. In *Proceedings of the Workshop on Data and Algorithm Transparency*. http://datworkshop.org/papers/dat16-final22.pdf

[6] Rishabh Mehrotra, Ashton Anderson, Fernando Diaz, Amit Sharma, Hanna Wallach, and Emine Yilmaz. 2017. Auditing Search Engines for Differential Satisfaction Across Demographics. In *Proceedings of the 26th International Conference on World Wide Web Companion (WWW '17 Companion)*. International World Wide Web Conferences Steering Committee, Republic and Canton of Geneva, Switzerland, 626–633. https://doi.org/10.1145/3041021.3054197

[7] Eli Pariser. 2011. *The Filter Bubble: How the New Personalized Web Is Changing What We Read and How We Think.* Penguin.

[8] N Ramakrishnan, B J Keller, B J Mirza, A Y Grama, and G Karypis. 2001. Privacy risks in recommender systems. *Internet Computing, IEEE* 5, 6 (2001), 54–63. https://doi.org/10.1109/4236.968832

[9] N Tintarev and J Masthoff. 2007. A Survey of Explanations in Recommender Systems. In *IEEE ICDE Workshop*. IEEE Computer Society, 801–810. https://doi.org/10.1109/ICDEW.2007.4401070

[10] Marshall van Alstyne and Erik Brynjolfsson. 2005. Global Village or Cyber-Balkans? Modeling and Measuring the Integration of Electronic Communities. *Manage. Sci.* 51, 6 (1 June 2005), 851–868. https://doi.org/10.1287/mnsc.1050.0363

RecSys'17 Joint Workshop on Interfaces and Human Decision Making for Recommender Systems

Peter Brusilovsky
School of Information Sciences
University of Pittsburgh
USA
peterb@pitt.edu

Marco de Gemmis
Department of Computer Science
University of Bari
Italy
marco.degemmis@uniba.it

Alexander Felfernig
Institute for Software Technology
Graz University of Technology
Austria
afelfernig@ist.tugraz.at

Pasquale Lops
Department of Computer Science
University of Bari
Italy
pasquale.lops@uniba.it

John O'Donovan
Department of Computer Science
University of California
Santa Barbara, USA
jod@cs.ucsb.edu

Nava Tintarev
Department of Software Technology
Delft University of Technology
The Netherlands
n.tintarev@tudelft.nl

Martijn Willemsen
Human-Technology Interaction
Eindhoven University of Technology
The Netherlands
m.c.willemsen@tue.nl

ABSTRACT

As intelligent interactive systems, recommender systems focus on determining predictions thatfi t the wishes and needs of users. Still, a large majority of recommender systems research focuses on accuracy criteria and much less attention is paid to how users interact with the system, and in which way the user interface has an influence on the selection behavior of the users. Consequently, it is important to look beyond algorithms. The main goals of the IntRS workshop are to analyze the impact of user interfaces and interaction design, and to explore human interaction with recommender systems from a human decision making perspective. Methodologies for evaluating these aspects are also within the scope of the workshop.

1 INTRODUCTION

The complexity of decision tasks, limited cognitive resources of recommender systems users, and a tendency to keep decision efforts as low as possible are related to the phenomenon of bounded rationality [12], i.e., users tend to employ decision heuristics rather than exhaustive search for optimal decisions. Furthermore, preferences of users are typically constructed within, and often changed throughout a recommendation session [1].

Decision making under bounded rationality is a door opener for different types of influences on decision outcomes. There exist different psychological theories that describe settings that can lead to suboptimal decisions. The manner in which alternatives are presented via a user interface, including accompanying information, can have an impact on the decision outcome.

Recently, these issues have gained some attention in the recommender systems community [4, 8]. Cosely et al. [6] show that user ratings can be manipulated by the predictions shown by the system. Chang et al. [3] show that preference elicitation can be completed more efficiently if the interface does not support initial personalization by letting users express their preferences on individual items but rather on groups of items. Stettinger et al. [10] analyze anchoring effects in the preference acquisition phase of group decision scenarios. The earlier the preferences of other group members are visible the lower is the standard deviation of individual user ratings. The later preferences are disclosed, the higher is the satisfaction with thefi nal group decision and the perceived degree of decision support. Teppan and Felfernig [13] analyze the impact of decoy effects in recommendation scenarios where disliked items as part of a result set can have an impact on the selection behavior of the user. Chen and Pu [5] and O'Donovan et al. [11] show the positive impact of explanations on the trustworthiness of recommender systems. For an overview of different explanation approaches in recommender systems see e.g., [14]. Bollen et al. [2] show that larger recommendation sets that contain solely good items do not necessarily trigger higher choice satisfaction since increased difficulty in selection choice counteracts the attractiveness of the recommendation set. Willemsen et al.[16] showed that such choice difficulty can be reduced by latent feature diversification, an algorithm adaptation based on psychological theory. Finally, Tkalcic et al. provide an overview of the role of emotions in recommender systems. Specifically, they discuss models and acquisition methods for emotions and personality [15]. For further related discussions see e.g., [8, 9].

IntRS aims to bring together researchers and practitioners focusing on topics of designing and developing novel intelligent interfaces and evaluating their impact in terms of different dimensions

RecSys'17, August 27–31, 2017, Como, Italy.
 ISBN 978-1-4503-4652-8/17/08.
DOI: http://dx.doi.org/10.1145/3109859.3109961

such as usability, perceived recommendation quality, time needed to take a decision, decision quality and degree of subjective well-being [7]. A primary goal of the workshop is to foster a community with a strong focus on recommendation-related decision making and user interface design issues.

2 TOPICS AND CONTRIBUTIONS

The workshop covers *three interrelated themes*:

(1) *user interfaces* (e.g., visual interfaces, explanation interfaces, natural language interfaces, trust-aware and social interfaces, context-aware interfaces, ubiquitous and mobile interfaces, and decision making interfaces);
(2) *interaction mechanisms, user modeling, and decision making* (e.g., cognitive modeling for recommender systems, human - recommender interaction, controllability, decision theories, preference construction, interfaces that take into account the role of emotions, argumentation and persuasive recommendation, cultural differences, approaches to high-quality group decision making, and the detection and avoidance of decision biases);
(3) *evaluation* (e.g., case studies, empirical studies, new interfaces and interaction designs, and evaluation methods).

Topics of *contributions submitted* to this year's workshop include:

- learning binary preference relations;
- rating by ranking;
- personalized presentation of recommendations;
- review-based filtering for interactive recommender systems;
- simplifying user privacy experience;
- cognition-based evaluation models;
- diversity-enhancing interfaces for recommender systems;
- user control and cognitive load;
- human choice support;
- guided course recommendations for students;
- personalized explanations in recommender systems.

3 WORKSHOP FORMAT

The 4th *Joint Workshop on Interfaces and Human Decision Making for Recommender Systems (IntRS'17)* is a result of merging two original RecSys workshops: *Human Decision Making and Recommender Systems (Decisions@RecSys – 2010–2013)* and *Interfaces for Recommender Systems (InterfaceRS'12)*. The idea of merging the two workshops was motivated by the strong inter-relationship between user interface and human decision making topics. The combination of these two aspects seems to be highly attractive, for example, the IntRS'15 workshop in Vienna had 60 participants and IntRS'16 in Boston had similar attendance.

IntRS'17 accepted both long (8 pages max) and short (4 pages max) papers. For short papers, alternative modes of presentation were encouraged, such as demos, playing out of scenarios, mock-ups, and alternate media such as video. Each accepted contribution was included in the workshop proceedings and presented in a workshop session.

An invited talk by Dietmar Jannach titled "*Interacting with Recommenders - Overview and Research Directions*" enriched the workshop program.

The list of accepted IntRS'17 papers and the workshop schedule can be found at: *intrs17.wordpress.com.*

4 CONCLUSIONS

IntRS aims to bring together researchers and practitioners from areas related to users interfaces and decision making in recommender systems. This year's contributions are high quality and are expected to attract a large audience.

REFERENCES

[1] R. Bettman, M. Luce, and J. Payne. 1998. Constructive Consumer Choice Processes. *Journal of Consumer Research* 25 (1998), 187–217.
[2] D. Bollen, B. Knijnenburg, M. Willemsen, and M. Graus. 2010. Understanding choice overload in recommender systems. In *4th ACM Conference on Recommender Systems*. Barcelona, Spain, 63–70.
[3] S. Chang, F. Harper, and L. Terveen. 2015. Using Groups of Items for Preference Elicitation in Recommender Systems. In *18th ACM Conference on Computer Supported Cooperative Work & Social Computing*. 1258 – 1269.
[4] L. Chen, M. deGemmis, A. Felfernig, P. Lops, F. Ricci, and G. Semeraro. 2013. Human Decision Making and Recommender Systems. *ACM Transactions on Interactive Intelligent Systems* 3, 3 (2013), 17.
[5] L. Chen and P. Pu. 2005. Trust Building in Recommender Agents. In *International Workshop on Web Personalization, Recommender Systems and Intelligent User Interfaces (WPRSIUI'05)*. Reading, UK, 135–145.
[6] D. Cosley, S. Lam, I. Albert, J. Konstan, and J. Riedl. 2003. Is seeing believing? How recommender interfaces affect users' opinions. In *Conference on Human Factors in Computing Systems*. 585–592.
[7] E. Diener. 2000. The science of happiness and a proposal for a national index. *Am. Psychol.* 55, 1 (2000), 34–43.
[8] A. Jameson, M. Willemsen, A. Felfernig, M. de Gemmis, P. Lops, G. Semeraro, and L. Chen. 2015. Human Decision Making and Recommender Systems. *Recommender Systems Handbook* (2015), 619–655.
[9] B. Knijnenburg, M. Willemsen, Z. Gantner, H. Soncu, and C. Newell. 2012. Explaining the User Experience of Recommender Systems. *User Modeling and User-Adapted Interaction (UMUAI)* (2012), 441–504.
[10] G. Leitner M. Stettinger, A. Felfernig and S. Reiterer. 2015. Counteracting Anchoring Effects in Group Decision Making. In *23rd Conference on User Modeling, Adaptation, and Personalization*. Dublin, Ireland, 118–130.
[11] John O'Donovan, Barry Smyth, Brynjar Gretarsson, Svetlin Bostandjiev, and Tobias Höllerer. 2008. PeerChooser: Visual Interactive Recommendation. In *Proceedings of the SIGCHI Conference on Human Factors in Computing Systems (CHI '08)*. ACM, New York, NY, USA, 1085–1088. https://doi.org/10.1145/1357054.1357222
[12] H. Simon. 1955. A Behavioural Model of Choice. *Quarterly Journal of Economics* 69, 1 (1955), 99–118.
[13] E. Teppan and A. Felfernig. 2012. Minimization of Decoy Effects in Recommender Result Sets. *Web Intelligence and Agent Systems* 1, 4 (2012), 385–395.
[14] Nava Tintarev and Judith Masthoff. 2015. Explaining recommendations: Design and evaluation. In *Recommender Systems Handbook*. Springer, 353–382.
[15] M. Tkalcic, M. deGemmis, and G. Semeraro. 2014. Personality and emotions in decision making and recommender systems. In *1st International Workshop on Decision Making and Recommender Systems*. Bolzano, Italy, 14–18.
[16] Martijn C. Willemsen, Mark P. Graus, and Bart P. Knijnenburg. 2016. Understanding the role of latent feature diversification on choice difficulty and satisfaction. *User Modeling and User-Adapted Interaction* 26, 4 (01 Oct 2016), 347–389. https://doi.org/10.1007/s11257-016-9178-6

RecTour 2017: Workshop on Recommenders in Tourism

Julia Neidhardt
TU Wien
Vienna, Austria
julia.neidhardt@ec.tuwien.ac.at

Daniel R Fesenmaier
University of Florida
Gainesville, FL, USA
drfez@ufl.edu

Tsvi Kuflik
The University of Haifa
Haifa, Israel
tsvikak@is.haifa.ac.il

Wolfgang Wörndl
Technical University of Munich
Garching, Germany
woerndl@in.tum.de

ABSTRACT

The Workshop on Recommenders in Tourism (RecTour) 2017, which is held in conjunction with the eleventh Conference on Recommender Systems (RecSys), addresses specific challenges for recommender systems within the tourism domain. In this overview, we summarize our motivations to organize such a workshop and give an overview of the submissions that we received. The main topics discussed in this yearfis Workshop include context-aware recommender systems, group recommender systems, and the impact of itinerary, sequence, and trust on travel-related recommendations.

CCS CONCEPTS

•Information systems → Recommender systems; •Human-centered computing → User models;

KEYWORDS

Tourism recommender systems; context-aware recommender systems; group decisions; itinerary recommendations; sequence recommendations; trust.

ACM Reference format:
Julia Neidhardt, Daniel R Fesenmaier, Tsvi Kuflik, and Wolfgang Wörndl. 2017. RecTour 2017: Workshop on Recommenders in Tourism. In *Proceedings of RecSys'17, August 27–31, 2017, Como, Italy.*, , 2 pages.
DOI: http://dx.doi.org/10.1145/3109859.3109962

1 INTRODUCTION

RecTour 2017 focuses on a variety of challenges specific to recommender systems for travellers. In this domain, there are considerably more complicated scenarios than finding the best product for a user. Planning a vacation usually involves searching for a bundle of products that are interconnected (e.g., means of transportation, accommodations, attractions, and activities) with a rather limited availability, and where contextual aspects (e.g., spatiotemporal context, social context, activity sequence, and environment) may have a major impact. In addition, travel related products are emotionally "loaded" and largely experiential in nature; therefore, decision taking is often not based on rational or objective criteria [3, 6]. As such, providing the right information to visitors of a tourism site at the right time about the site itself and various services nearby is challenging. Additionally, and in contrast to many other domains related to recommender systems, information providers are usually small-medium enterprises (SMEs) that do not have the capacity or access to basic recommender systems. Moreover, there is no single, standard format to house information which might be included in these systems. Last, much of the tourism experience is co-produced, i.e., it occurs during the consumption of the product and interaction with the provider. Therefore, the context of the recommendation is extremely important [2]. Thus given this diversity, building effective recommender systems within the tourism domain is extremely challenging [4].

The rapid development of information and communication technologies (ICT) in general and the web in particular has transformed the tourism domain whereby most travellers rely little on travel agents or agencies [5]. Indeed, recent studies indicate that travellers now actively search for information using ICT in order to compose their vacation packages according to their specific emotionally driven preferences. Additionally when onsite, they search for freely available information about the site itself rather than renting a visitor guide that may be available, but considered to be expensive and sometimes outdated.

However, like in many other cases, the blessing of the web comes with a curse; the curse of information overload. As such, recommender systems have been suggested as a practical tool for overcoming this information overload. However, because the tourism domain is extremely complicated, those designing tourism-focused recommenders face huge challenges.

2 WORKSHOP GOALS

This workshop brings together researchers and practitioners from different fields (e.g., tourism, recommender systems, user modelling, user interaction, mobile, ubiquitous and ambient technologies, artificial intelligence and web information systems) working in the tourism recommendation domain. The workshop aims to provide a forum for these people to discuss novel ideas for addressing the specific challenges for recommender systems in tourism with the goal to advance the current state-of-the-art in this field. A secondary goal of the workshop is to identify practical applications of these technologies within tourism settings from the point of view of the user interactions, service providers, as well as from additional

RecSys'17, August 27–31, 2017, Como, Italy.
 ISBN 978-1-4503-4652-8/17/08.
DOI: http://dx.doi.org/10.1145/3109859.3109962

stakeholders (e.g., destination management organizations). Finally, RecTour 2017 aims to continue the community building processes and discussions started at RecTour 2016 [1].

3 WORKSHOP TOPICS

The main topics of this year's workshop can be summarized as follows.

Context-aware recommender systems. Proposing relevant points-of-interests (POIs) is a central function of many tourism recommender systems. The aim is to not only to adapt the recommended POIs to the current location of a specific user but to consider other contextual attributes as well, e.g. weather, season, date, time of visits and user history. Several approaches are proposed which retrieve and analyse data from social network sources such as Twitter or Foursquare. The results presented in these papers indicate that context-aware solutions can outperform baseline algorithms without context.

Trustworthiness of recommendations. An important issue in recommender systems is the degree to which users trust information which relies on user-generated content such as reviews and ratings of items from social networks. These networks can be analyzed to find interesting items but also increase the trustworthiness of recommendations.

Itinerary recommendations. Combining POIs to a suitable path to follow is an instance of the Tourist Trip Design Problem (TTDP), which involves moving from recommending single items to personalized sets or sequences of relevant items. Within TTDP, users choose from a large number of items (in the context of leisure activities), but then figure out how to combine them into a practical itinerary. Several papers discuss this issue wherein they incorporate various constraints such as time and budget so as to provide personalized solutions adapted to user preferences.

Additional topics of interest. RecTour 2017 received papers which discuss the cold start problem, group recommender systems, location prediction, and the visualization of recommendations and the consideration of public transportation. The last part of the workshop will be specifically dedicated to a panel session and an interactive discussion of project ideas and related challenges.

4 CONCLUSIONS

The contributions at RecTour 2017 highlight many fundamental challenges for recommender systems in the tourism domain. They offer useful and well-considered approaches for addressing these challenges and therefore, provide a relevant foundation for future research. The workshop proceedings can be found on the website of the workshop (i.e., at http://www.ec.tuwien.ac.at/rectour2017/).

REFERENCES

[1] Daniel R Fesenmaier, Tsvi Kuflik, and Julia Neidhardt. 2016. RecTour 2016: Workshop on recommenders in tourism. In *Proceedings of the 10th ACM Conference on Recommender systems*. ACM, 417–418.
[2] Carlos Lamsfus, Dan Wang, Aurkene Alzua-Sorzabal, and Zheng Xiang. 2015. Going mobile: Defining context for on-the-go travelers. *Journal of Travel Research* 54, 6 (2015), 691–701.
[3] Julia Neidhardt, Rainer Schuster, Leonhard Seyfang, and Hannes Werthner. 2014. Eliciting the users' unknown preferences. In *Proceedings of the 8th ACM Conference on Recommender systems*. ACM, 309–312.
[4] Francesco Ricci. 2002. Travel recommender systems. *IEEE Intelligent Systems* 17, 6 (2002), 55–57.
[5] Hannes Werthner, Aurkene Alzua-Sorzabal, Lorenzo Cantoni, Astrid Dickinger, Ulrike Gretzel, Dietmar Jannach, Julia Neidhardt, Birgit Pröll, Francesco Ricci, Miriam Scaglione, and others. 2015. Future research issues in IT and tourism. *Information Technology & Tourism* 15, 1 (2015), 1–15.
[6] Hannes Werthner and Francesco Ricci. 2004. E-commerce and tourism. *Commun. ACM* 47, 12 (2004), 101–105.

CitRec 2017: International Workshop on Recommender Systems for Citizens

Jie Yang
Delft University of Technology
j.yang-3@tudelft.nl

Zhu Sun
Nanyang Technological University
sunzhu@ntu.edu.sg

Alessandro Bozzon
Delft University of Technology
a.bozzon@tudelft.nl

Jie Zhang
Nanyang Technological University
zhangj@ntu.edu.sg

Martha Larson
Radboud University Nijmegen
m.a.larson@tudelft.nl

ABSTRACT

The "International Workshop on Recommender Systems for Citizens" (CitRec) is focused on a novel type of recommender systems both in terms of ownership and purpose: recommender systems run by citizens and serving society as a whole.

CCS CONCEPTS

• **Information systems → Information retrieval; Recommender systems;**

KEYWORDS

Recommender Systems; Citizens; Smart Cities; Spatio-temporal Context-aware Recommendation

ACM Reference format:
Jie Yang, Zhu Sun, Alessandro Bozzon, Jie Zhang, and Martha Larson. 2017. CitRec 2017: International Workshop on Recommender Systems for Citizens. In *Proceedings of RecSys '17, Como, Italy, August 27-31, 2017,* 2 pages.
https://doi.org/10.1145/3109859.3109969

1 INTRODUCTION

With the growing number of people living in ever denser areas, there is an increasing demand for novel Information and Communication Technology (ICT) to support the complex social and environmental interactions of citizens, and to improve their quality of life. A typical example is the concept and construct of the "smart city" [3, 5], which has been introduced to highlight the importance of ICT for enhancing the competitive profile of a city (e.g., liveability, to attract and retain talents).

This workshop focuses on citizens' recommender systems. This particular type of recommender systems, while still belonging to the broad area of recommendation, differs from conventional recommender systems both in terms of ownership and purpose. Unlike conventional recommender systems driven by a per-click business model, citizens' recommender systems are run by citizen themselves and serve the society as a whole.

RecSys '17, August 27-31, 2017, Como, Italy

ACM ISBN 978-1-4503-4652-8/17/08.
https://doi.org/10.1145/3109859.3109969

Motivation. When restricted to the application for citizens, a large body of literature on recommender systems could be found on Point-Of-Interest (POI) recommendation [1, 12], tourist location recommendation [14], and orthogonally, spatio-temporal context-aware recommendation [6, 7]. However, existing literature primarily focuses on a single domain (e.g., POI recommendation) from an algorithmic perspective [12, 13], without considering the user perspective and the specific activities of citizens, which form a continuous experience. Citizen activities in daily life, including transportation, working, sports, entertainment, shopping, are not only diverse, but also closely related to each other [10]. Together they form the integrated, unbroken experience of a citizen living in an urban environment. The specific needs of citizens calls for scientific investigation on the relationships among citizens' daily activities, in order to better understand their behaviors.

More importantly, the target user of conventional recommender systems are individuals, while recommender systems for citizens are expected to serve the society as a whole. To optimize the effectiveness of recommendations for society, recommender systems for citizens require deep understanding of citizen-environment and citizen-citizen interactions. For example, to optimally recommend driving routes to a community of citizens, the system should be able to understand how the effectiveness of recommendations is influenced by the environment (e.g., road condition) and how the recommendations provided to different citizens affect each other (e.g., to avoid traffic congestion). This example illustrates the need for either algorithmic design that enables recommendations to benefit society as a whole, or incentive mechanisms that balance personal and societal interests.

Challenges and Opportunities. The success of citizens' recommender systems heavily depends on the amount and quality of citizens' behavioral data, which have typically been scarce. The scarcity, on the one hand, can be compensated by engaging citizens to actively contribute their behavioral data to the system, i.e., citizen crowdsourcing via effective incentive schemes.

On the other hand, the emergence of social data, i.e., data generated by people during their societal activities, available through new sources (e.g., social media, mobile phones, sensor networks), brings both opportunities and challenges to the development of citizens' recommender systems. Such data, when well-integrated, contain a multitude of dimensions, such as the targeted urban population, the purpose of use, the spatio-temporal context, etc. [2]. Thus they describe comprehensively citizens' behaviors and their relationships with the environment, providing opportunities for recommendation based techniques to enhance citizens' living experiences. At the same time, social data are characterized by an intrinsic diversity, manifested through each of the relevant dimensions [9, 11]. It remains an open question how to leverage such diversity for optimally enhancing citizens' living experiences. Another notable challenge is citizen privacy, i.e., how to effectively preserve citizen privacy when capitalizing on social data that are descriptive of citizen behaviors.

Recent studies have shown that recommender systems can actively change citizen mobility patterns, reducing traffic congestion [8] and improve urban mobility [4]. By exploiting social data and addressing the challenges, recommender systems have the potential to largely expand their impact and play an important role in today's society, in improving citizens' living experiences and the effectiveness of environmental use.

Purpose. This workshop on "Recommender Systems for Citizens" aims at bringing together researchers and practitioners from different disciplines to explore the challenges and opportunities of novel approaches to recommender systems that address the intrinsic diversity of social data as a core element of their scientific study and design principles for improving citizen living experiences.

2 THEME AND TOPICS

In order to effectively address the social and environmental aspects of recommender systems for enhancing citizens' living experience, the workshop solicited contributions from researchers from computer science (in particular, recommender systems and related sub-fields), citizen science, and urban science working at the intersections of studying the described classes of recommender systems. We put an emphasis on novel recommender system research that contributes to a better understanding of citizen behaviors and needs, and novel approaches to recommender systems that enhance citizen living experiences that go beyond classic recommendation techniques.

The topics of interest include but are not limited to:

- Requirements definition, design and implementation for citizen recommendation
- Collection, integration, exploration of social data for citizen recommendation
- Citizen user modeling and behavioral analysis
- Mining social data, social urban data for citizen recommendation
- Crowdsourcing for citizen recommendation
- Group recommendation in citizens' recommender systems
- Algorithms for citizen recommendation
- Incentivazation in citizen recommendation
- Spatio-temporal context in citizen recommendation
- Cross-domain recommendation for citizens' continuous living experiences
- Citizen recommendation for smart urban environment
- Design, implementation of citizen knowledge base, and knowledge transfer to citizen recommendation
- User interface for citizen recommendation
- Ethical, cultural issues related to citizen recommendation
- Privacy and policy in citizen recommendation

3 FORMAT AND ACTIVITIES

The half-day workshop includes a keynote presentation (Daniel Gatica-Perez from Idiap Research Institute and EPFL, Switzerland), two sessions of presentations by selected papers, and an interactive discussion panel.

Through discussions on the social and environmental aspects of recommender systems and relating them to experiences from the practice of citizen science and urban science (i.e., in terms of specific problems, conceptual models and use cases), we expect the workshop to facilitate the exchange of experiences between typically disparate research communities from different fields but which are working on related problems.

After the workshop, the participants will come together to write a position paper about the potential and challenges of citizen recommendation. We expect to identify the major challenges and opportunities that will shape the research on recommender systems for citizens in the future.

Acknowledgments

We thank the Social Urban Data Lab (SUDL) of the Amsterdam Institute for Advanced Metropolitan Solutions (AMS) and Delft Data Science (DDS) for supporting the workshop.

REFERENCES

[1] Marco Balduini, Alessandro Bozzon, Emanuele Della Valle, Yi Huang, and Geert-Jan Houben. 2014. Recommending Venues Using Continuous Predictive Social Media Analytics. *IEEE Internet Computing* 18, 5 (2014), 28–35.

[2] Stefano Bocconi, Alessandro Bozzon, Achilleas Psyllidis, Christiaan Titos Bolivar, and Geert-Jan Houben. 2015. Social Glass: A Platform for Urban Analytics and Decision-making through Heterogeneous Social Data. In *Proceedings of the 24th International Conference on World Wide Web (WWW 2015)*. ACM, 175–178.

[3] Annalisa Cocchia. 2014. Smart and digital city: A systematic literature review. In *Smart city*. Springer, 13–43.

[4] Sergio Di Martino and Silvia Rossi. 2016. An Architecture for a Mobility Recommender System in Smart Cities. *Procedia Computer Science* 98 (2016), 425–430.

[5] Robert G Hollands. 2008. Will the real smart city please stand up? Intelligent, progressive or entrepreneurial? *City* 12, 3 (2008), 303–320.

[6] Longke Hu, Aixin Sun, and Yong Liu. 2014. Your neighbors affect your ratings: on geographical neighborhood influence to rating prediction. In *Proceedings of the 37th international ACM SIGIR Conference on Research & Development in Information Retrieval (SIGIR 2014)*. ACM, 345–354.

[7] Yehuda Koren. 2010. Collaborative filtering with temporal dynamics. *Commun. ACM* 53, 4 (2010), 89–97.

[8] Rod McCall, Vincent Koenig, Romain Martin, and Thomas Engel. Changing Mobility Behaviour through Recommendations. In *ACM RecSys Workshop on Crowdsourcing and Human Computation for Recommender Systems (CrowdRec 2015)*.

[9] Zhu Sun, Jie Yang, Alessandro Bozzon, and Jie Zhang. 2017. Exploiting both Vertical and Horizontal Dimensions of Feature Hierarchy for Effective Recommendation. In *The 31st AAAI Conference on Artificial Intelligence (AAAI 2017)*. AAAI.

[10] Jie Yang, Claudia Hauff, Geert-Jan Houben, and Christiaan Titos Bolivar. 2016. Diversity in urban social media analytics. In *International Conference on Web Engineering (ICWE 2016)*. Springer, 335–353.

[11] Jie Yang, Zhu Sun, Alessandro Bozzon, and Jie Zhang. 2016. Learning Hierarchical Feature Influence for Recommendation by Recursive Regularization. In *Proceedings of 10th ACM Conference on Recommender Systems.(RecSys 2016)*. ACM, 51–58.

[12] Mao Ye, Peifeng Yin, Wang-Chien Lee, and Dik-Lun Lee. 2011. Exploiting Geographical Influence for Collaborative Point-of-Interest Recommendation. In *Proceedings of the 34th international ACM SIGIR conference on Research and development in Information Retrieval (SIGIR 2011)*. ACM, 325–334.

[13] Quan Yuan, Gao Cong, Zongyang Ma, Aixin Sun, and Nadia Magnenat Thalmann. 2013. Time-aware Point-of-Interest Recommendation. In *Proceedings of the 36th international ACM SIGIR Conference on Research and Development in Information Retrieval (SIGIR 2013)*. ACM, 363–372.

[14] Yu Zheng and Xing Xie. 2011. Learning Travel Recommendations from User-generated GPS Traces. *ACM Transactions on Intelligent Systems and Technology (TIST)* 2, 1 (2011), 2.

LSRS'17: Workshop on Large-Scale Recommender Systems

Tao Ye
Pandora Inc.
2101 Webster St., Suite 700, Oakland, CA 94612, USA
tye@pandora.com

Denis Parra
Pontificia Universidad Católica de Chile (PUC Chile),
Vicuña Mackenna 4860, Santiago, Chile
dparra@ing.puc.cl

Vito Ostuni
Pandora Inc.
2101 Webster St., Suite 700, Oakland, CA 94612, USA
vostuni@pandora.com

Tao Wang
Apple Inc.
Infinite loop, Cupertino, CA 95014, USA
tao_wang@apple.com

ABSTRACT

With the increase of data collected and computation power available, modern recommender systems are ever facing new challenges. While complex models are developed in academia, industry practice seems to focus on relatively simple techniques that can deal with the magnitude of data and the need to distribute the computation. The workshop on large-scale recommender systems (LSRS) is a meeting place for industry and academia to discuss the current and future challenges of applied large-scale recommender systems.*

CCS CONCEPTS

• **Database Management** → **Database Applications**; *Datamining* • **System and Software** → Distributed Systems

KEYWORDS

Recommendation systems; big data; scalability; machine learning

1 BACKGROUND AND MOTIVATION

This is the 5th installment of a mini-conference style workshop that focuses on practical and scaling issues for recommender systems. Modern recommender systems face greatly increased data volume and complexities. Computational models and experience on small data may not hold for millions of users, thus, how to build an efficient and robust system has become an important issue for many practitioners. Even well known models might have different performance on different domains' data. Meanwhile, there is an increasing gap between academia research of recommendation systems focusing on complex models, and industry practice focusing on solving problems at large scale using relatively simple techniques. Evaluation of models have diverged as well. While most publications focus on fixed datasets and offline ranking measures, industry practitioners tend to use long term engagement metrics to make final judgments.

The motivation of this workshop is to bring together researchers and practitioners working on large-scale recommender system in order to: (1) share experience, techniques and methodologies used to develop effective large-scale recommender, from architecture, algorithms, programming model, to evaluation (2) challenge conventional wisdom (3) identify key challenges and promising trends in the area, and (4) identify collaboration opportunities among participants.

2 OBJECTIVES

This workshop aims to foster discussions in several fields that are of interest to our growing community of recommendation system builders. On the practical side, we would like to encourage sharing of architecture best practices in large-scale recommender systems as they are practiced in industry, as well as particular challenges and pain points. We hope this will guide future research that is system aware. On the research side, we focus on bringing in ideas and evaluations on scaling beyond the current generation of big data systems, with improved recommendation metrics. We believe the brightest minds from both sides will mutually benefit from the discussions and accelerate problem solving.

3 TOPICS OF INTEREST

We solicited submissions from industrial level recommendation system practitioners in either a short paper or slides format on large scale system practice, as well as from recommendation systems researchers on their new research related to system aspect of recommendation with Big Data.

We focused on the following topics:

Data & Algorithms in Large-scale RS:

- Scalable deep learning algorithm
- Big data processing in offline/near-line/online modules

RecSys '17, August 27-31, 2017, Como, Italy

ACM ISBN 978-1-4503-4652-8/17/08. http://dx.doi.org/10.1145/3109859.3109970

- Data platforms for recommendation
- Large, unstructured and social data for recommendation
- Heterogeneous data fusion
- Sampling techniques
- Parallel algorithms
- Algorithm validation and correctness checking

Systems of Large-scale RS:

- Architecture
- Programming Model
- Cloud platforms best for recommenders
- Real-time recommendation
- Online learning for recommendation
- Scalability and Robustness

Evaluation of Large-scale RS:

- Comparison of algorithms' application and effectiveness in different domains
- Offline optimization and online measurement consistency
- Evaluation metrics alignment with product/project goal
- Large user studies
- A/B testing methodology

4 PROGRAM COMMITTEE

We are grateful for the help of our program committee to review submissions:
Leandro Balby Marinho, Federal University of Campina Grande
Gianmarco De Francisci Morales, Qatar Computing Research Institute
Tommaso Di Noia, Polytechnic University of Bari
Liang Dong, Google
Zhenhua Dong, Noah's ark lab, Huawei Technologies
Alexandros Karatzoglou, Telefonica Research
Pasquale Lops, University of Bari
Zhen Qin, UC-Riverside
Paolo Tomeo, Polytechnic University of Bari
Massimo Quadrana, Polytechnic University of Milan
Rodrygo Santos, Universida de Federal de Minas Gerais
Yong Zhuang, Carnegie Mellon University
Dávid Zibriczky, Trivago GmbH

5 WORKSHOP FORMAT

The workshop features one keynote and three to four presentation sessions. We expect a mix of peer reviewed contributions to be presented along with invited talks. In addition, we will again include two 40min breakout discussions, based positive feedback from the 2016 LSRS workshop.

At the time of this summary, the submissions reviewing process for 2017 is not yet completed. We provide the 2016 program for reference.

[09:00 - 10:30] Large scale recommender architecture

- Opening remarks
- Lessons Learned from Using a Data Stream Management System for Real-time Recommendation of Popular News Articles based on Real User Streams

Cornelius A. Ludmann and H.-Jürgen Appelrath, University of Oldenburg, Germany

- Ranking and Recommendation for Billions of Users at Facebook: Need for Hybrid Solutions

Dr. Komal Kapoor, Research scientist, Facebook

- Brazil-Europe project on Big Data and Recommendations

Prof. Leandro Balby-Marinho, Federal University of Campina Grande, Brasil

[10:30 - 11:00] Coffee break

[11:00 - 12:30] Scaling with Distributed Learning

- The Pitfalls of Distributed Learning

Dr. Yves Raimond, Research/Engineering Manager - Machine Learning, Netflix

- Scaling Verizon IPTV Recommendations with a Full Stack in Scala and Spark

Diana Hu, Data science architect, OnCue TV (Verizon)

- Breakout discussion of morning talks

[12:30 - 14:00] Lunch

[14:00 - 15:30] Algorithms

- **Keynote:** Matrix factorization and factorization machine for recommendations

Prof. Chih-Jen Lin, Distinguished professor, Department of Computer Science, National Taiwan University

- A New Likelihood-Based Similarity Score For Collaborative Filtering

Veronika Strnadova-Neeley, Aydin Buluc, John Gilbert, Leonid Oliker and Weimin Ouyang, UC Santa Barbara, Lawrence Berkeley National Lab

[15:30 - 16:00] Coffee break

[16:00 - 17:30] Case studies

- Scaling Recommendations at Quora

Nikhil Dandekar, Senior Engineering Manager, Quora

Iron: Keyword Grouping Model for Text Ads Bidding in Paid Search

Suxin Guo, Xutong Liu, Angelo Restificar and James Zhang, eBay

Breakout discussion of afternoon talks

ACKNOWLEDGMENTS

We thank the RecSys 2017 organizing committee for giving us the opportunity to host this workshop in conjunction with RecSys 2017 in Como, Italy.

New Paths in Music Recommender Systems Research

Markus Schedl
Johannes Kepler University Linz
Linz, Austria
markus.schedl@jku.at

Peter Knees
TU Wien
Vienna, Austria
peter.knees@tuwien.ac.at

Fabien Gouyon
Pandora Inc.
Oakland, CA, USA
fgouyon@pandora.com

ABSTRACT

The particularities of musical data and its multiple modalities make original contributions possible in many core RecSys topics such as content-based and hybrid recommendation, user modeling, interfaces, and context-aware and mobile recommendations. But more urgently, the current revolution in the music industry represents major opportunities and challenges for recommendation systems in general. Recommendation systems are now central to music streaming platforms, which are rapidly increasing in listenership and becoming the top source of revenue for the music industry. It is increasingly more common for a music listener to simply access music than to purchase and own it in a personal collection. In this scenario, recommendation calls no longer for a one-shot recommendation for the purpose of a track or album purchase, but for a recommendation of a listening experience, comprising a very wide range of challenges, such as sequential recommendation, or conversational and contextual recommendations. Recommendation technologies now impact all actors in the rich and complex music industry ecosystem (listeners, labels, music makers and producers, concert halls, advertisers, etc.). To highlight these developments, we focus on three use cases: automatic playlist generation, context-aware music recommendation, and recommendation in the creative process of music making.

ACM Reference format:
Markus Schedl, Peter Knees, and Fabien Gouyon. 2017. New Paths in Music Recommender Systems Research. In *Proceedings of RecSys'17, August 27–31, 2017, Como, Italy.*, , 2 pages.
DOI: http://dx.doi.org/10.1145/3109859.3109934

MOTIVATION

In the RecSys community, music is too often treated as "just another item". Yet, the particularities of music data and its multiple modalities open many opportunities, e.g., to leverage content-based audio features or to build comprehensive listener models that go beyond simple user-item interactions. Furthermore, since it is now increasingly more common for a music listener to simply stream music rather than to purchase and own it, todayfis music recommenders need to focus on recommending a listening experience. As a consequence, Music Recommender Systems (MRS) [17] research has to face a wide range of challenges, such as sequential recommendation/automatic radio stationing, sound recommendation to music producers, conversational and contextual recommendation (cf. Google Home, Siri, or Alexa), or even tasks such as recommending *concerts to users* or *fans to artists*.

While recommender systems in other domains, such as movies, have already been extensively researched, the still underrepresented topic of music recommendation is a highly important research area for its particularities which require specific considerations beyond application of constantly improving collaborative filtering methods. We argue that the music domain should receive increased attention as it provides more diverse use cases than just the typical user-item recommendation scenario that was at the core of previous tutorials on music recommendation [5].

To this end, we focus on three use cases: automatic playlist generation, context-aware music recommendation, and recommendation in the creative process of music making. We incorporate both academic and industrial points of view into the tutorial and echo some of the research directions highlighted in the "Past, Present and Future" session at RecSys 2016, in particular in [1, 3, 7, 13]. The tutorial is accompanied by a set of slides published online.[1]

1 BACKGROUND

Since the development of audio compression techniques and mobile music players, the music industry has been in constant turmoil. The first decade of the 2000's witnessed an explosion of music content availability. The overwhelming choices implied by having most of the world's music only a few clicks away did set the stage for the birth of music recommendation technologies. The last tutorial on Music Recommendation at RecSys [5], held in 2011, highlighted the progress at the time towards alleviating this issue.

More recently, we are witnessing a revolution in the very way music is consumed. It is increasingly more common to *access* music than to *purchase* and *own* it in a personal collection. Indeed, in the US, the amount of music listening happening on streaming platforms has dramatically increased in the last few years and is now the top source of revenue for the music industry.

This evolution represents major opportunities and challenges for MRS technologies. Recommending music calls no more for a one-shot recommendation for the purpose of a *product* purchase, but instead for an "infinite recommendation loop", where what is recommended is a listening *experience* and where the recommendation of a specific item to a user never really ends. Further, recommendation technologies can now impact a multitude of complementary use cases, including all actors in the music production and consumption chain. It is therefore in a unique position to contribute significantly to recommender systems research as a whole, as it touches many core topics, e.g., *user modeling, user interaction and interfaces*, or *context-aware and mobile recommendations.*

RecSys'17, August 27–31, 2017, Como, Italy.
 ISBN 978-1-4503-4652-8/17/08.
DOI: http://dx.doi.org/10.1145/3109859.3109934

[1] http://www.cp.jku.at/tutorials/mrs_recsys_2017

2 IT'S ALL ABOUT THE USE CASE

The current evolution of the music industry results in an explosion of use cases for recommender systems, much beyond the traditional item-to-user use case, cf. [13]. This includes scenarios such as automatic playlist/radio generation, context-aware recommendations, and recommendations in the creative process, which we address in more detail.

2.1 Playlist generation

The task of playlist generation is a core recommendation task in the music domain, with particular relevance for the industry. In order to address this important task, we discuss the question of *what makes a good playlist?* and highlight specificities in terms of requirements and methods. This comprises challenges of *exploration vs. exploitation* and *giving a playlist a focus*, e.g., a genre, (re)discovery, or newly released music, together with a discussion of different *methods* for playlist generation, e.g., curatorial, collaborative filtering, content-based, and/or personalized, and practical aspects of *evaluation* (offline vs. A/B testing).

2.2 Context-aware music recommendation

Regarding the music recommendation task as dependent on the context of the listener, we present examples and discuss *methodology* and *evaluation* strategies of context-aware MRS. This is supported by a review of *context categories*, e.g., time, location, activity, weather, and social context, and elaborated in a discussion on *cultural and regional specificities* in which we summarize findings on country-specific differences in music preferences and requirements for MRS.

2.3 Recommendation in the creative processes of music making

To highlight the role of recommendation in the process of music *making*, we review recent and ongoing projects in this area, with a focus on user-centric requirement identification, theoretic future systems, and user-centric evaluation strategies [2, 7, 10]. This comprises a rather traditional role of recommendation to *facilitate collaborations*, presented through a real-world use case from an online jam community, as well as more emerging scenarios originating from interviews with international music producers, often differing in their requirements from consumer-based systems in terms of a *stronger need for serendipity, preservation of originality, and systems embodying opposition*, cf. [2, 3].

3 WHAT'S NEXT?

Beside a rich variety of other use cases, such as user-centric MRS (e.g., emotion- and personality-aware), recommending fans to artists, artists to labels, concert venues to performers, or tracks to listener groups, we reflect on social implications of music recommendation growth, such as filter bubble, ethics, and influence on popular culture, and on the challenges ahead from both academic and industry perspectives.

THE BAND

Markus Schedl is an Associate Professor at the Department of Computational Perception of the Johannes Kepler University Linz, Austria.[2] Recent publications on the topic include [9, 12, 15–17, 19].

Peter Knees is an Assistant Professor of the Institute of Software Technology and Interactive Systems of the TU Wien, Austria.[3] Recent publications on the topic include [2, 10–12, 17, 19].

Fabien Gouyon is Principal Scientist at the internet radio Pandora.[4] Recent and less recent publications on the topic include [4, 6, 8, 14, 18].

ACKNOWLEDGMENTS

Supported by the Austrian Science Fund (FWF): P25655 and the Austrian FFG: BRIDGE 1 project *SmarterJam* (858514).

REFERENCES

[1] Xavier Amatriain and Justin Basilico. 2016. Past, Present, and Future of Recommender Systems: An Industry Perspective. In *Proc. RecSys.* Boston, MA, USA.
[2] Kristina Andersen and Peter Knees. 2016. Conversations with Expert Users in Music Retrieval and Research Challenges for Creative MIR. In *Proc. ISMIR.* New York, NY, USA.
[3] Amos Azaria and Jason Hong. 2016. Recommender Systems with Personality. In *Proc. RecSys.* Boston, MA, USA.
[4] Pedro Cano, Markus Koppenberger, Nicolas Wack, et al. 2005. An Industrial-strength Content-based Music Recommendation System. In *Proc. SIGIR.* Salvador, Brazil.
[5] Òscar Celma and Paul Lamere. 2011. Music Recommendation and Discovery Revisited. In *Proc. RecSys.* Chicago, IL, USA.
[6] Marcos Aurélio Domingues, Fabien Gouyon, Alípio Mário Jorge, et al. 2013. Combining usage and content in an online recommendation system for music in the Long Tail. *International Journal of Multimedia Information Retrieval* 2 (2013).
[7] Michael D. Ekstrand and Martijn C. Willemsen. 2016. Behaviorism is Not Enough: Better Recommendations Through Listening to Users. In *Proc. RecSys.* Boston, MA, USA.
[8] Fabien Gouyon, Bob L. Sturm, João Lobato Oliveira, Nuno Hespanhol, and Thibault Langlois. 2014. On Evaluation Validity in Music Autotagging. *CoRR* abs/1410.0001 (2014). http://arxiv.org/abs/1410.0001
[9] Marius Kaminskas, Francesco Ricci, and Markus Schedl. 2013. Location-aware Music Recommendation Using Auto-Tagging and Hybrid Matching. In *Proc. RecSys.* Hong Kong, China.
[10] Peter Knees and Kristina Andersen. 2017. Building Physical Props for Imagining Future Recommender Systems. In *Proc. HUMANIZE.* Limassol, Cyprus.
[11] Peter Knees, Kristina Andersen, and Marko Tkalčič. 2015. "I'd like it to do the opposite": Music-Making Between Recommendation and Obstruction . In *Proc. DMRS.* Bolzano, Italy.
[12] Peter Knees and Markus Schedl. 2016. *Music Similarity and Retrieval: An Introduction to Audio- and Web-based Strategies.* Springer.
[13] Tamas Motajcsek, Jean-Yves Le Moine, Martha Larson, et al. 2016. Algorithms Aside: Recommendation As The Lens Of Life. In *Proc. RecSys.* Boston, MA, USA.
[14] Matthew Prockup, Andreas F. Ehmann, Fabien Gouyon, et al. 2015. Modeling Genre with the Music Genome Project: Comparing Human-Labeled Attributes and Audio Features. In *Proc. ISMIR.* Málaga, Spain.
[15] Markus Schedl. 2015. Listener-aware Music Recommendation from Sensor and Social Media Data. In *Proc. ECML PKDD.* Porto, Portugal.
[16] Markus Schedl, Emilia Gómez, and Julián Urbano. 2014. Music Information Retrieval: Recent Developments and Applications. *Foundations and Trends in Information Retrieval* 8, 2–3 (2014), 127–261.
[17] Markus Schedl, Peter Knees, Brian McFee, Dmitry Bogdanov, and Marius Kaminskas. 2015. Music Recommender Systems. In *Recommender Systems Handbook* (2nd ed.), Francesco Ricci, Lior Rokach, Bracha Shapira, and Paul B. Kantor (Eds.). Springer.
[18] Mohamed Sordo, Fabien Gouyon, Luís Sarmento, Òscar Celma, and Xavier Serra. 2013. Inferring Semantic Facets of a Music Folksonomy with Wikipedia. *Journal of New Music Research* 42 (December 2013), 346–363. Issue 4.
[19] Andreu Vall, Marcin Skowron, Peter Knees, and Markus Schedl. 2015. Improving Music Recommendations with a Weighted Factorization of the Tagging Activity. In *Proc. ISMIR.* Málaga, Spain.

[2] http://www.cp.jku.at/people/schedl
[3] http://www.ifs.tuwien.ac.at/~knees
[4] http://www.fabiengouyon.org

Privacy for Recommender Systems

Tutorial Abstract

Bart P. Knijnenburg
Clemson University School of Computing
215 McAdams Hall
Clemson, SC 29631, USA
bartk@clemson.edu

Shlomo Berkovsky
CSIRO Data61
Epping
New South Wales, Australia
shlomo.berkovsky@data61.csiro.au

ABSTRACT

It is important for recommender system designers and service providers to learn about ways to generate accurate recommendations while at the same time respecting the privacy of their users. In this tutorial, we analyze common privacy risks imposed by recommender systems, survey privacy-enhanced recommendation techniques, and discuss implications for users.

CCS CONCEPTS

• **Information systems → Recommender Systems**
• **Security and privacy**

KEYWORDS

Privacy; recommender systems

1 INTRODUCTION

Recommender systems collect behavioral data, context, social connections, or demographics to provide users with tailored recommendations [17]. These data collection practices may pose a threat to user privacy [13]. At the same time, though, we count only two papers about privacy (cf. [4,25]) at the three most recent installments of the Recommender Systems conference! To promote research on privacy in recommender systems, this tutorial gives an overview of the privacy threats faced by recommender system users, surveys technical approaches to address privacy in recommender systems, and discusses ways to provide users with privacy decision support.

2 PRIVACY THREATS

While users are generally willing to give up some personal data for recommendation purposes [3,8,22,33], they may worry that systems collect too much information about them, could make incorrect inferences, or may use the data for unacceptable purposes [29]. In this tutorial, we give an overview of these threats from the perspective of three types of adversaries:

1. *The recommender system itself*, which may engage in unsolicited data collection, targeted advertising, and discrimination [14,19,27]
2. *Other users of the system*, who might be able to exploit the outputs of the recommender to uncover private information regarding a target user [5,31].
3. *External entities*, which may try to access the collected data or intervene in the interaction between the system and its users [28].

RecSys '17, August 27-31, 2017, Como, Italy

ACM ISBN 978-1-4503-4652-8/17/08.
http://dx.doi.org/10.1145/3109859.3109935

3 TECHNICAL SOLUTIONS

Given these threats, how can systems protect their users' privacy without compromising recommendation quality? In the tutorial, we provide a detailed discussion of three categories of approaches to address privacy in recommender systems:

1. *Architectures, platforms, and standards*, designed specifically to minimize data leakage. These include distributed architectures, portable user profiles, and client-side recommendation techniques that provide limited access to and linkability of user data [9,16,23].
2. *Algorithmic techniques* for data protection. These include anonymization, obfuscation, differential privacy, and homomorphic encryption [6,12,24,30].
3. *Legislations, policies,* and *regulations*, which may be imposed by governments and legislative bodies, or adopted as self-regulatory industry practices [22,34].

4 PRIVACY DECISION SUPPORT

The concept of privacy is an inherently human attitude associated with the collection, distribution and use of disclosed data. Since recommenders rely on users to disclose information about themselves, our tutorial discusses existing research concerning users' privacy attitudes and behaviors. Moreover, we discuss the benefits and drawbacks of three popular paradigms for providing users with privacy decision support:

1. *Notice and choice*, which argues that giving users information about and control over their privacy will empower them to regulate their privacy at the desired level [7,32]. This paradigm is hampered, though, by the fact that users eschew the hassle of exploiting control [10,20], have misconceptions about the implications of their settings [26] and do not follow rational economic principles in making privacy decisions [2,21].
2. *Privacy nudging*, which suggests giving users a subtle yet persuasive cue that makes them more likely to make the right privacy choices [1]. Privacy nudges,

however, take a one-size-fits-all approach to privacy, which means that they rarely work for all users, since their privacy preferences tend to vary extensively [15]

3. *User-tailored privacy*, an approach in which a system measures users' privacy-related characteristics and behaviors, uses this as input to model their privacy preferences, and then adapts the system's privacy settings to these preferences [11,18,35].

4 DISCUSSION AND CONCLUSION

We end our tutorial on a discussion of privacy in new recommendation scenarios, such as cross-domain recommender systems, mobile and context-aware recommendations, group recommenders, and social web recommenders. We note that the available patchwork of technical and non-technical solutions can each address specific privacy risks regarding these scenarios, but that future work needs to focus on holistic solutions to privacy. While companies often do not feel comfortable to talk about privacy [13], we hope that our tutorial can inspire a more conscientious discussion about privacy in recommender systems.

REFERENCES

[1] Alessandro Acquisti. 2009. Nudging Privacy: The Behavioral Economics of Personal Information. *IEEE Security and Privacy* 7: 82–85. DOI: http://doi.org/10.1109/MSP.2009.163

[2] Alessandro Acquisti and Jens Grossklags. 2005. Privacy and Rationality in Individual Decision Making. *IEEE Security & Privacy* 3, 1: 26–33. DOI: http://doi.org/10.1109/MSP.2005.22

[3] Naveen Farag Awad and M. S. Krishnan. 2006. The personalization privacy paradox: An empirical evaluation of information transparency and the willingness to be profiled online for personalization. *MIS Quarterly* 30, 1: 13–28.

[4] Arnaud Berlioz, Arik Friedman, Mohamed Ali Kaafar, Roksana Boreli, and Shlomo Berkovsky. 2015. Applying Differential Privacy to Matrix Factorization. In *Proceedings of the 9th ACM Conference on Recommender Systems*, 107–114. DOI: http://doi.org/10.1145/2792838.2800173

[5] Joseph A. Calandrino, Ann Kilzer, Arvind Narayanan, Edward W. Felten, and Vitaly Shmatikov. 2011. You Might Also Like: Privacy Risks of Collaborative Filtering. In *Proceedings of the 2011 IEEE Symposium on Security and Privacy*, 231–246. DOI: http://doi.org/10.1109/SP.2011.40

[6] John Canny. 2002. Collaborative Filtering with Privacy. In *Proceedings of the 2002 IEEE Symposium on Security and Privacy*, 45–57. DOI: http://doi.org/10.1109/SECPRI.2002.1004361

[7] Fred H. Cate and Viktor Mayer-Schönberger. 2013. Notice and consent in a world of Big Data. *International Data Privacy Law* 3, 2: 67–73.

[8] R. K Chellappa and R. G Sin. 2005. Personalization versus privacy: An empirical examination of the online consumer's dilemma. *Inform. Tech. and Mgmt.* 6, 2: 181–202. DOI: http://doi.org/10.1007/s10799-005-5879-y

[9] Richard Cissée and Sahin Albayrak. 2007. An Agent-based Approach for Privacy-preserving Recommender Systems. In *Proceedings of the 6th International Joint Conference on Autonomous Agents and Multiagent Systems*, 182:1–182:8. DOI: http://doi.org/10.1145/1329125.1329345

[10] Ramón Compañó and Wainer Lusoli. 2010. The Policy Maker's Anguish: Regulating Personal Data Behavior Between Paradoxes and Dilemmas. In *Economics of Information Security and Privacy*, Tyler Moore, David Pym and Christos Ioannidis (eds.). Springer US, New York, NY, 169–185. DOI: http://doi.org/10.1007/978-1-4419-6967-5_9

[11] Cailing Dong, Hongxia Jin, and Bart P. Knijnenburg. 2016. PPM: A Privacy Prediction Model for Online Social Networks. In *Social Informatics*, 400–420. DOI: http://doi.org/10.1007/978-3-319-47874-6_28

[12] Cynthia Dwork and Moni Naor. 2008. On the Difficulties of Disclosure Prevention in Statistical Databases or The Case for Differential Privacy. *Journal of Privacy and Confidentiality* 2, 1.

[13] Arik Friedman, Bart P. Knijnenburg, Kris Vanhecke, Luc Martens, and Shlomo Berkovsky. 2015. Privacy Aspects of Recommender Systems. In *Recommender Systems Handbook* (2nd ed.), Francesco Ricci, Lior Rokach and Bracha Shapira (eds.). Springer US, 649–688. DOI: http://doi.org/10.1007/978-1-4899-7637-6_19

[14] Avi Goldfarb and Catherine E Tucker. 2011. Online advertising, behavioral targeting, and privacy. *Commun. ACM* 54, 5: 25–27. DOI: http://doi.org/10.1145/1941487.1941498

[15] Harris Interactive inc. 2000. *A Survey of Consumer Privacy Attitudes and Behaviors.* Harris Interactive, Inc., New York, NY. Retrieved from http://www.bbbonline.org/UnderstandingPrivacy/library/harrissummary.pdf

[16] Benjamin Heitmann, James G Kim, Alexandre Passant, Conor Hayes, and Hong-Gee Kim. 2010. An architecture for privacy-enabled user profile portability on the web of data. In *Proceedings of the 1st International Workshop on Information Heterogeneity and Fusion in Recommender Systems* (HetRec '10), 16–23. DOI: http://doi.org/10.1145/1869446.1869449

[17] Arjan J.P. Jeckmans, Michael Beye, Zekeriya Erkin, Pieter Hartel, Reginald L. Lagendijk, and Quiang Tang. 2013. Privacy in Recommender Systems. In *Social Media Retrieval*, Naeem Ramzan, Roelof van Zwol, Jong-Seok Lee, Kai Clüver and Xian-Sheng Hua (eds.). Springer.

[18] Bart P. Knijnenburg. 2015. A user-tailored approach to privacy decision support. University of California, Irvine, Irvine, CA.

[19] Bart P. Knijnenburg and Alfred Kobsa. 2013. Making Decisions about Privacy: Information Disclosure in Context-Aware Recommender Systems. *ACM Trans. Interact. Intell. Syst.* 3, 3: 20:1-20:23. DOI: http://doi.org/10.1145/2499670

[20] Bart P. Knijnenburg, Alfred Kobsa, and Hongxia Jin. 2013. Counteracting the Negative Effect of Form Auto-completion on the Privacy Calculus. In *ICIS 2013 Proceedings.*

[21] Bart P. Knijnenburg, Alfred Kobsa, and Hongxia Jin. 2013. Preference-based location sharing: are more privacy options really better? In *Proceedings of the SIGCHI Conference on Human Factors in Computing Systems*, 2667–2676. DOI: http://doi.org/10.1145/2470654.2481369

[22] Alfred Kobsa. 2007. Privacy-Enhanced Web Personalization. In *The Adaptive Web: Methods and Strategies of Web Personalization*, Peter Brusilovsky, Alfred Kobsa and Wolfgang Nejdl (eds.). Springer Verlag, Berlin/Heidelberg/New York, 628–670. Retrieved from 10.1007/978-3-540-72079-9_21

[23] Alfred Kobsa, Bart P. Knijnenburg, and Benjamin Livshits. 2014. Let's Do It at My Place Instead? Attitudinal and Behavioral Study of Privacy in Client-side Personalization. In *Proceedings of the SIGCHI Conference on Human Factors in Computing Systems*, 81–90. DOI: http://doi.org/10.1145/2556288.2557102

[24] Alfred Kobsa and Jörg Schreck. 2003. Privacy through pseudonymity in user-adaptive systems. *ACM Transactions on Internet Technology* 3, 2: 149–183. DOI: http://doi.org/10.1145/767193.767196

[25] Ziqi Liu, Yu-Xiang Wang, and Alexander Smola. 2015. Fast Differentially Private Matrix Factorization. In *Proceedings of the 9th ACM Conference on Recommender Systems*, 171–178. DOI: http://doi.org/10.1145/2792838.2800191

[26] M. Madejski, M. Johnson, and S.M. Bellovin. 2012. A study of privacy settings errors in an online social network. In *4th Intl. Workshop on Security and Social Networking*, 340–345. DOI: http://doi.org/10.1109/PerComW.2012.6197507

[27] Jakub Mikians, László Gyarmati, Vijay Erramilli, and Nikolaos Laoutaris. 2012. Detecting Price and Search Discrimination on the Internet. In *Proceedings of the 11th ACM Workshop on Hot Topics in Networks* (HotNets-XI), 79–84. DOI: http://doi.org/10.1145/2390231.2390245

[28] Arvind Narayanan and Vitaly Shmatikov. 2009. Myths and fallacies of "personally identifiable information." *Commun. ACM* 53: 24–26. DOI: http://doi.org/10.1145/1743546.1743558

[29] OECD. 1980. Recommendation of the Council Concerning Guidelines Governing the Protection of Privacy and Transborder Flows of Personal Data. Organization for Economic Co-operation and Development.

[30] Huseyin Polat and Wenliang Du. 2005. Privacy-Preserving Collaborative Filtering. *International Journal of Electronic Commerce* 9, 4: 9–35.

[31] Naren Ramakrishnan, Benjamin J. Keller, Batul J Mirza, Ananth Y Grama, and George Karypis. 2001. Privacy Risks in Recommender Systems. *IEEE Internet Computing*, Nov-Dec.: 54–62.

[32] David Taylor, Donna Davis, and Ravi Jillapalli. 2009. Privacy concern and online personalization: The moderating effects of information control and compensation. *Electronic Commerce Research* 9, 3: 203–223. DOI: http://doi.org/10.1007/s10660-009-9036-2

[33] Eran Toch, Yang Wang, and L. F. Cranor. 2012. Personalization and Privacy: A Survey of Privacy Risks and Remedies in Personalization-Based Systems. *User Modeling and User-Adapted Interaction* 22, 1–2: 203–220. DOI: http://doi.org/10.1007/s11257-011-9110-z

[34] Yang Wang and Alfred Kobsa. 2006. Impacts of Privacy Laws and Regulations on Personalized Systems. In *Proceedings of the CHI 2006 Workshop on Privacy-Enhanced Personalization*, 44–46.

[35] Daricia Wilkinson, Saadhika Sivakumar, David Cherry, Bart P. Knijnenburg, Elaine M. Raybourn, Pamela Wisniewski, and Henry Sloan. 2017. User-Tailored Privacy by Design. In *Proceedings of the Usable Security Mini Conference 2017.* DOI: http://doi.org/10.14722/usec.2017.23007

Deep Learning for Recommender Systems

Alexandros Karatzoglou
Telefonica Research
Barcelona, Spain
alexk@tid.es

Balázs Hidasi
Gravity R&D
Budapest, Hungary
hidasi.balazs@gravityrd.com

ABSTRACT

Deep Learning is one of the next big things in Recommendation Systems technology. The past few years have seen the tremendous success of deep neural networks in a number of complex machine learning tasks such as computer vision, natural language processing and speech recognition. After its relatively slow uptake by the recommender systems community, deep learning for recommender systems became widely popular in 2016.

We believe that a tutorial on the topic of deep learning will do its share to further popularize the topic. Notable recent application areas are music recommendation, news recommendation, and session-based recommendation. The aim of the tutorial is to encourage the application of Deep Learning techniques in Recommender Systems, to further promote research in deep learning methods for Recommender Systems.

CCS CONCEPTS

• **Information systems → Information retrieval**; • **Computing methodologies → Artificial intelligence**; **Machine learning**;

KEYWORDS

Deep Learning, Recommender Systems

1 INTRODUCTION

The aim of the tutorial is dual, 1) we would like to introduce Deep Learning techniques that have been used in recommender systems such as Recurrent Neural Networks and Convolutional Networks etc. 2) we would like to present the current state-of-the-art methods that use deep learning techniques to provide recommendations.

Machine learning methods such as matrix factorization and tensor factorization have been frequently used in the area of recommender systems deep learning methods. These methods share in fact some similarities to deep learning such as e.g. the use of Stochastic Gradient Descend (SGD) for optimization. One can in fact cast matrix factorization as a neural network. In that respect the use of deep learning methods in the recommender systems community represents a natural step.

Deep Learning provides a new toolkit for recommender systems practitioners to extract features and to model user generated data and item data that has the potential to provide large improvements in the quality of the recommendations provided to users. Part of the power of deep learning techniques in recommender systems stems from the fact that deep learning methods allow for much better feature extraction from item characteristics such as image, video and audio compared to traditional techniques. This allows for a more accurate modeling of items based on their content, thus one can potentially expect hybrid and content-based methods to perform better compared to traditional content based techniques whenever deep learning is used. Another advantage deep learning methods provide is that they allow for different views of the data, standard collaborative filtering techniques such as matrix factorization have often treated user-item interaction as flat matrix structured data often ignoring the temporal structure and order in the data. Deep learning techniques like convolutions and recurrent neural networks allow us to model the temporal structure in this data leading to significant performance improvements.

RecSys'17, August 27–31, 2017, Como, Italy.
 ISBN 978-1-4503-4652-8/17/08.
DOI: http://dx.doi.org/10.1145/3109859.3109903

2 DEEP LEARNING TECHNIQUES FOR RECOMMENDER SYSTEMS

Deep Learning has become popular after a 2006 paper by Hinton [7] described how to train deep neural networks using unsupervised layer-wise training (Deep Belief Networks). Since then there has been an immense amount of research in the area with impressive results in ares such as computer vision, speech recognition and natural language processing. The uptake of deep networks in the recommender systems community has been relatively slow but recent advances in the area of deep learning and recommender systems have encouraged researchers and practitioners to use these methods. Deep neural networks are now used in a range of recommender systems algorithms and form a considerable part of the program of many Information Retrieval conferences and indeed of the ACM RecSys conference.

Over the last 3-4 years there has been a number of notable publications in the area of deep learning for recommender systems. This deep learning work can be broadly grouped into the following categories:

- **Embedding methods**. This class of methods utilize embedding techniques inspired by deep learning methods such as word2vec [8] to embed user, item,[11], [13] or context profiles in latent spaces. These embeddings can then be used either directly to provide recommendations or as input to other (typically supervised) (deep learning) methods that provide the recommendations. While matrix factorization can be also viewed as an embedding technique, 2vec type embedding techniques are often somewhat more flexible then the matrix factorization models often employed in collaborative filtering.

- **Feedforward Networks and Autoencoders for Collaborative Filtering**. These methods use either Feedforward or Autoencoder [9], [14] networks directly on the user-item interactions in order to build collaborative filtering models that can then be used for recommendations. These methods can also be seen as a form of deep factorization methods. Deep Factorization Machines [2] can be seen as an example of this class of methods. These methods often outperform standard model-based collaborative filtering methods.
- **Deep Feature extracting methods**. This class of deep learning for recommenders methods focuses on using deep networks to perform feature extraction on the item features. These features are then either used in a more standard (hybrid) collaborative filtering methods or often the feature extractor is part of a larger deep architecture that also models other aspects of the data. Examples of this class of methods includes convolutional methods for image feature extraction for hybrid collaborative filtering methods [3], or convolutional networks for audio and music feature extraction [10] or even text-based recommendations with neural feature extractors (RNN's or convolutional networks).
- **Session-based Recommendation with Recurrent Neural Networks**.

  These methods are based on the fact that often user interactions with content are in sessions, e.g. music listening, shopping. Moreover one often does not have a reliable user-identifier to model user preferences. In this case on can resort to model sessions as sequential data and one of the best performing models for sequential data are Recurrent Neural Networks. Typically GRU's are used in these models as they seem to perform equivalently to LSTM's and have slightly less memory usage. These models have been shown to outperform traditional methods by a large margin [5], [6], [4].

3 FUTURE

Deep Learning techniques are constantly progressing and several new techniques have been recently introduced such as e.g. Adversarial Training, Siamese Networks, one-shot learning and much more. While the application of these techniques to the recommender systems domain is not obvious at the moment we do believe that these and other techniques will eventually be adopted by the recommender systems community.

We also expect a significant increase in deployment of deep learning models with content-based methods becoming more popular due to increased quality of features that can be extracted with these methods. Another area where we believe that deep learning methods will become instrumental is the area of conversational recommender systems [1]. Deep models are used in conversational agents (bots) [12] and it is only natural that they will eventually be used in conversational recommender systems.

REFERENCES

[1] Konstantina Christakopoulou, Filip Radlinski, and Katja Hofmann. 2016. Towards Conversational Recommender Systems. In *Proceedings of the 22Nd ACM SIGKDD International Conference on Knowledge Discovery and Data Mining (KDD '16)*. ACM, New York, NY, USA, 815–824. https://doi.org/10.1145/2939672.2939746

[2] Huifeng Guo, Ruiming Tang, Yunming Ye, Zhenguo Li, and Xiuqiang He. 2017. DeepFM: A Factorization-Machine based Neural Network for CTR Prediction. *CoRR* abs/1703.04247 (2017). http://arxiv.org/abs/1703.04247

[3] Ruining He and Julian McAuley. 2016. VBPR: Visual Bayesian Personalized Ranking from Implicit Feedback. In *Proceedings of the Thirtieth AAAI Conference on Artificial Intelligence (AAAI'16)*. AAAI Press, 144–150. http://dl.acm.org/citation.cfm?id=3015812.3015834

[4] Balázs Hidasi and Alexandros Karatzoglou. 2017. Recurrent Neural Networks with Top-k Gains for Session-based Recommendations. abs/1706.03847 (2017). https://arxiv.org/abs/1706.03847

[5] Balázs Hidasi, Alexandros Karatzoglou, Linas Baltrunas, and Domonkos Tikk. 2016. Session-based recommendations with recurrent neural networks. *International Conference on Learning Representations (ICLR)* (2016).

[6] Balázs Hidasi, Massimo Quadrana, Alexandros Karatzoglou, and Domonkos Tikk. 2016. Parallel recurrent neural network architectures for feature-rich session-based recommendations. In *Proceedings of the 10th ACM Conference on Recommender Systems*. ACM, 241–248.

[7] Geoffrey E Hinton, Simon Osindero, and Yee-Whye Teh. 2006. A fast learning algorithm for deep belief nets. *Neural computation* 18, 7 (2006), 1527–1554.

[8] Tomas Mikolov, Ilya Sutskever, Kai Chen, Greg S Corrado, and Jeff Dean. 2013. Distributed representations of words and phrases and their compositionality. In *Advances in neural information processing systems*. 3111–3119.

[9] Suvash Sedhain, Aditya Krishna Menon, Scott Sanner, and Lexing Xie. 2015. Autorec: Autoencoders meet collaborative filtering. In *Proceedings of the 24th International Conference on World Wide Web*. ACM, 111–112.

[10] Aaron van den Oord, Sander Dieleman, and Benjamin Schrauwen. 2013. Deep content-based music recommendation. In *Advances in Neural Information Processing Systems 26*, C. J. C. Burges, L. Bottou, M. Welling, Z. Ghahramani, and K. Q. Weinberger (Eds.). Curran Associates, Inc., 2643–2651. http://papers.nips.cc/paper/5004-deep-content-based-music-recommendation.pdf

[11] Flavian Vasile, Elena Smirnova, and Alexis Conneau. 2016. Meta-Prod2Vec: Product Embeddings Using Side-Information for Recommendation. In *Proceedings of the 10th ACM Conference on Recommender Systems*. ACM, 225–232.

[12] Oriol Vinyals and Quoc Le. 2015. A neural conversational model. *arXiv preprint arXiv:1506.05869* (2015).

[13] Jeroen BP Vuurens, Martha Larson, and Arjen P de Vries. 2016. Exploring Deep Space: Learning Personalized Ranking in a Semantic Space. In *Proceedings of the 1st Workshop on Deep Learning for Recommender Systems*. ACM, 23–28.

[14] Yao Wu, Christopher DuBois, Alice X Zheng, and Martin Ester. 2016. Collaborative denoising auto-encoders for top-n recommender systems. In *Proceedings of the Ninth ACM International Conference on Web Search and Data Mining*. ACM, 153–162.

Product Recommendations Enhanced with Reviews

Muthusamy Chelliah
Flipkart, Bangalore
muthusamy.c@flipkart.com

Sudeshna Sarkar
Indian Institute of Technology Kharagpur
sudeshna@cse.iitkgp.ernet.in

ABSTRACT

User-written product reviews contain rich information about user preferences for product features and provide helpful explanations that are often used by shoppers to make their purchase decisions. E-commerce recommender systems can benefit enormously by also exploiting experiences of multiple customers captured in product reviews. In this tutorial, we present a range of techniques that allow recommender systems in e-commerce websites to take full advantage of reviews. This includes text mining methods for feature-specific sentiment analysis of products, topic models and distributed representations that bridge the vocabulary gap between user reviews and product descriptions. We present recommender algorithms that use review information to address the cold-start problem and generate recommendations with explanations. We discuss examples and experiences from an online marketplace (i.e., Flipkart).

KEYWORDS

Recommender System; Review Based Recommendation; Text Mining; Sentiment Analysis; Explainable Recommendation

1 INTRODUCTION

E-commerce websites commonly deploy recommender systems that make use of user activity (e.g., ratings, views, and purchases) or content (product descriptions). Recommender systems based on collaborative filtering make use of user activity to identify latent user-item factors to suggest new products to a user. However such systems are often unable to identify these rating dimensions when a user or item has too few ratings due to data sparsity. On the other hand content based recommender systems make use of product descriptions, but they do not consider the user views on the products.

User-generated reviews are enabled by the portals of most e-commerce companies. The reviews contain details reflecting the experiences of consumers and many shoppers use product reviews to support their purchasing decisions [2]. But a product on a popular e-commerce site may have a large number of diverse reviews leading to information overload on the user.

This tutorial explains algorithms for using the reviews for making recommendations and discusses how such algorithms are evaluated. The benefits of using review texts in large scale recommendation systems is discussed.

RecSys '17, August 27-31, 2017, Como, Italy

ACM ISBN 978-1-4503-4652-8/17/08.
https://doi.org/10.1145/3109859.3109936

2 OUTLINE OF THE TUTORIAL

2.1 Introduction and Motivation

We first outline the important concepts and terminologies relevant to recommendation and reviews. We define different elements of the review such as product features, review contexts, review sentiments, feature specific sentiments and comparative opinions. We also discuss the major recommendation approaches. To make effective use of reviews, it is important to understand not just the overall sentiment on a product, but also the opinions about the different features of the product. For this, the unique features of a product and the associated opinions need to be identified and aggregated from multiple reviews. Reviews also provide valuable information about the features of the product that a particular user cares about more, and can be used to make personalized recommendations to a user. We motivate why reviews should be used for making accurate and interpretable recommendations.

2.2 Feature and Opinion Mining

In this part, we discuss how product features, opinions on product features and review contexts may be extracted from user reviews of products and used to build product and user profiles.

Since different natural language expressions may be used to refer to the same product feature in reviews, it is important to group the feature mentions into unique product features. Topic models have been used [9, 14] to leverage words co-occurring in review sentences for doing feature normalization. More recently, vector representations of words and text segments have been used [4, 15] in order to cluster the contexts of feature mentions.

Product specifications, unlike user-generated review comments, have less noise and are useful for extracting various product features. We discuss how the vocabulary gap between both forms of text may be bridged so as to map review features from user-generated content to product features from seller descriptions [3, 12, 13].

This analysis enables the representation of product information in terms of user opinions on the entire product as well as on the fine grained product features and their values. User profiles may also be represented based on the importance that a user attaches to the different product features and their preferences on their values. Further, review contexts may be extracted from reviews which are required for making context-aware recommendations.

2.3 Handling data sparsity

When a new user or item is introduced in the system, there is little data available to learn rating dimensions of the user or the item profile. This is known as the cold-start problem and this results in poor shopping experience in online marketplaces. Collaborative filtering based recommendation systems that make use of ratings to infer hidden product-item features, fail for products and items with insufficient number of ratings. Product reviews which contain the justifications of user opinions on products and indicate user preferences can help tackle the sparsity challenge by using product features and associated sentiments articulated in reviews.

We discuss algorithms that incorporate product and user profiles obtained from reviews into recommendation algorithms that can handle the cold-start problem and also provide more informed recommendations. [5] provides a comprehensive survey on using profiles obtained from review elements in different recommendation algorithms. Even when there are few reviews associated with a product or a user, the feature specific information mined from the review texts or obtained from topic models may be mapped to the latent features of a matrix factorization model and can address the cold start problem [7, 11]. [10] applies LDA on the review texts and finds a transformation to align the latent topics with the rating dimensions. The rating dimensions are made interpretable by mapping them to explicit features or word clouds and can be used to recommend absolutely new products for which prior content or tags are available. Further, the product features of interest to a reviewer and consumer preferences thus uncovered, can help personalized recommendation of related products to users with similar tastes.

Recent research has explored neural network based approaches to incorporate review texts into recommendation algorithms. Deep neural networks architectures such as recurrent neural network and cooperative neural networks with convolutional layers [1, 18] have been used for this. Representing review texts using word embedding is shown to improve the representation quality.

2.4 Explainable product recommendation

It is difficult to know how users translate their judgment of various product features into ratings, and even more difficult to understand why an item may not be recommended by the system. Even when different users assign a similar overall product rating, each may care about different features of the product as is evident from review comments. Mining explicit user opinions on product features from reviews helps infer user preferences at a finer granularity.

In this part, we discuss how to make use of knowledge about which features are of particular interest to a user. This is used in order to predict ratings specific to the user thereby resulting in personalized recommendation of products. By explaining transparently how a product is suggested, recommender systems can help their users make faster and better informed purchase decisions. The detailed explanations have been found to make the recommendations have better influence on a user's decision making. This approach in turn can help in making intuitively explainable recommendations as well as dis-recommendations by providing feature level explanations and correlating review snippets with product suggestions [8, 16]. [17] designed a template based and a word cloud based explanation after identifying the product aspects and user preferred features.

[6] proposes an explanation interface to present the tradeoffs between multiple recommended products in terms of their static features as well as sentiments.

2.5 Industry use cases

Throughout the different parts in the tutorial, we will motivate the problem with real-life use cases from our experience with an online marketplace Flipkart. Flipkart is an e-commerce pioneer in India and we present results from a Web-scale system and opportunities for further research.

REFERENCES

[1] Amjad Almahairi, Kyle Kastner, Kyunghyun Cho, and Aaron Courville. 2015. Learning distributed representations from reviews for collaborative filtering. In *Proceedings of the 9th ACM Conference on Recommender Systems*. ACM, NY, USA, 147–154.

[2] Georgios Askalidis and Edward C Malthouse. 2016. The Value of Online Customer Reviews.. In *Proceedings of the 10th ACM Conference on Recommender Systems*. ACM, NY, USA, 155–158.

[3] Lidong Bing, Tak-Lam Wong, and Wai Lam. 2016. Unsupervised extraction of popular product attributes from e-commerce web sites by considering customer reviews. *ACM Transactions on Internet Technology (TOIT)* 16, 2 (2016), 12:1–12:17.

[4] Huimin Chen, Maosong Sun, Cunchao Tu, Yankai Lin, and Zhiyuan Liu. 2016. Neural sentiment classification with user and product attention. In *Proceedings of the 2016 Conference on Empirical Methods in Natural Language Processing*. ACL, 1650–1659.

[5] Li Chen, Guanliang Chen, and Feng Wang. 2015. Recommender systems based on user reviews: the state of the art. *User Modeling and User-Adapted Interaction* 25, 2 (2015), 99–154.

[6] Li Chen and Feng Wang. 2017. Explaining Recommendations Based on Feature Sentiments in Product Reviews. In *Proceedings of the 22nd International Conference on Intelligent User Interfaces*. ACM, Cyprus, 17–28.

[7] Qiming Diao, Minghui Qiu, Chao-Yuan Wu, Alexander J Smola, Jing Jiang, and Chong Wang. 2014. Jointly Modeling Aspects, Ratings and Sentiments for Movie Recommendation (JMARS). In *Proceedings of the 20th ACM SIGKDD international conference on Knowledge discovery and data mining*. ACM, 193–202.

[8] Xiangnan He, Tao Chen, Min-Yen Kan, and Xiao Chen. 2015. Trirank: Review-aware explainable recommendation by modeling aspects. In *Proceedings of the 24th ACM International on Conference on Information and Knowledge Management*. ACM, 1661–1670.

[9] Himabindu Lakkaraju, Chiranjib Bhattacharyya, Indrajit Bhattacharya, and Srujana Merugu. 2011. Exploiting coherence for the simultaneous discovery of latent facets and associated sentiments. In *Proceedings of the 2011 SIAM international conference on data mining*. SIAM, AZ, USA, 498–509.

[10] Guang Ling, Michael R Lyu, and Irwin King. 2014. Ratings meet reviews, a combined approach to recommend. In *Proceedings of the 8th ACM Conference on Recommender systems*. ACM, USA, 105–112.

[11] Julian McAuley and Jure Leskovec. 2013. Hidden factors and hidden topics: understanding rating dimensions with review text. In *Proceedings of the 7th ACM conference on Recommender systems*. ACM, Hong Kong, 165–172.

[12] Dae Hoon Park, ChengXiang Zhai, and Lifan Guo. 2015. Speclda: Modeling product reviews and specifications to generate augmented specifications. In *Proceedings of the 2015 SIAM International Conference on Data Mining*. SIAM, Vancouver, 837–845.

[13] Debanjan Paul, Sudeshna Sarkar, Muthusamy Chelliah, Chetan Kalyan, and Prashant Nadkarni. 2017. Recommendation of high quality representative reviews in e-commerce. In *Proceedings of the 11th ACM Conference on Recommender Systems*. ACM, Italy, Accepted.

[14] Shuai Wang, Zhiyuan Chen, and Bing Liu. 2016. Mining aspect-specific opinion using a holistic lifelong topic model. In *Proceedings of the 25th International Conference on World Wide Web*. International World Wide Web Conferences Steering Committee, Geneva, Switzerland, 167–176.

[15] Yequan Wang, Minlie Huang, Xiaoyan Zhu, and Li Zhao. 2016. Attention-based LSTM for Aspect-level Sentiment Classification. In *Proceedings of the 2016 Conference on Empirical Methods in Natural Language Processing*. Austin, USA, 606–615.

[16] Yao Wu and Martin Ester. 2015. Flame: A probabilistic model combining aspect based opinion mining and collaborative filtering. In *Proceedings of the Eighth ACM International Conference on Web Search and Data Mining*. ACM, Shanghai, 199–208.

[17] Yongfeng Zhang, Guokun Lai, Min Zhang, Yi Zhang, Yiqun Liu, and Shaoping Ma. 2014. Explicit factor models for explainable recommendation based on phrase-level sentiment analysis. In *Proceedings of the 37th international ACM SIGIR conference on Research & development in information retrieval*. ACM, Australia, 83–92.

[18] Lei Zheng, Vahid Noroozi, and Philip S Yu. 2017. Joint deep modeling of users and items using reviews for recommendation. In *Proceedings of the Tenth ACM International Conference on Web Search and Data Mining*. ACM, Cambridge, UK, 425–434.

Tutorial on Open Source Online Learning Recommenders

Róbert Pálovics Domokos Kelen András A. Benczúr
Institute for Computer Science and Control
Hungarian Academy of Sciences (MTA SZTAKI)
{rpalovics,kelen.domokos.miklos,benczur}@sztaki.hu

ABSTRACT

Recommender systems have to serve in online environments that can be non-stationary. Traditional recommender algorithms may periodically rebuild their models, but they cannot adjust to quick changes in trends caused by timely information. In contrast, online learning models can adopt to temporal effects, hence they may overcome the effect of concept drift.

In our tutorial, we present open source systems capable of updating their models on the fly after each event: Apache Spark, Apache Flink and Alpenglow, a C++ based Python recommender framework. Participants of the tutorial will be able to experiment with all the three systems by using interactive Jupyter and Zeppelin Notebooks. Our final objective is to compare and then blend batch and online methods to build models providing high quality top-k recommendation in non-stationary environments.

KEYWORDS

open source recommender systems; temporal evaluation; ranking prediction by online learning; streaming; concept drift

TARGET AUDIENCE

Recommender systems researchers and practitioners. Basic Python and/or Scala programming skills are required.

EXPERIENCE OF THE PRESENTERS

The presenters have been using Jupyter for international courses on data science relying on tools such as Scikit-learn, Spark, Flink and formerly GraphLab Create. They participated in the organization of the RecSys Challenges 2016 and 2017. In addition, they contribute to the Apache Flink Machine Learning Library.

TUTORIAL URL

https://github.com/rpalovics/recsys-2017-online-learning-tutorial

SUPPORT

From the *EU H2020* research and innovation program under grant agreement *Streamline No 688191* and the "Big Data—Momentum" grant of the Hungarian Academy of Sciences.

RecSys '17, , August 27-31, 2017, Como, Italy

ACM ISBN 978-1-4503-4652-8/17/08.
http://dx.doi.org/10.1145/3109859.3109937

INTRODUCTION

In a real recommender system, users request one or a few items at a time, and may get exposed to new information that can change their needs and taste before they return to the service the next time. Therefore, *top item recommendation by online learning* is usually more relevant than the Netflix Prize style batch rating prediction [3, 8]. In this tutorial, we consider top-k recommendation in highly non-stationary environments. Our goal is to promptly update recommender models after user interactions by online learning methods, and investigate whether performance gains in batch experiments carry over to online environments. In addition, we consider data sets with *implicit feedback* [3].

We set up environments, in which events and requests for recommendation arrive in a continuous data stream. The difficulty of evaluating *streaming recommenders* [5] was first mentioned in [6], although they split the stream into a training and a testing part instead of evaluating continuously online. Ideas for *online evaluation metrics* appeared first in [7, 8, 12]. An important part of the tutorial considers the framework for evaluating recommender systems over streaming data. We rely on ideas of [1, 8] for the online DCG measure.

The objectives of the tutorial are to

- provide evaluation measures suited to non-stationary environments that may also indicate which algorithm would work well on a particular data set,
- present open source online learning recommender systems in Jupyter and Zeppelin notebooks,
- compare the performance of simpler algorithms that can be updated online—and hence use the most recent data as well—with more complex algorithms that can be updated only periodically,
- experiment with combinations of batch and online training to improve accuracy.

TEMPORAL EVALUATION

In a time-aware or online recommender that potentially re-trains its model after each new item, we have to generate a new top-k recommendation list for every single event in the evaluation period [1]. In an online setting, as seen in Figure 1, whenever we see a new user-item pair, we assume that the user becomes active and requests a recommendation. We recommend items of potential interest for the user, which then we match against the actual item consumed. After this evaluation step, we may update the model. Following [2], we propose DCG instead of precision and recall for measuring the quality of top-k recommendation. Furthermore, in our time-aware ranking evaluation setting DCG is computed individually for each event and then averaged in time[7, 8].

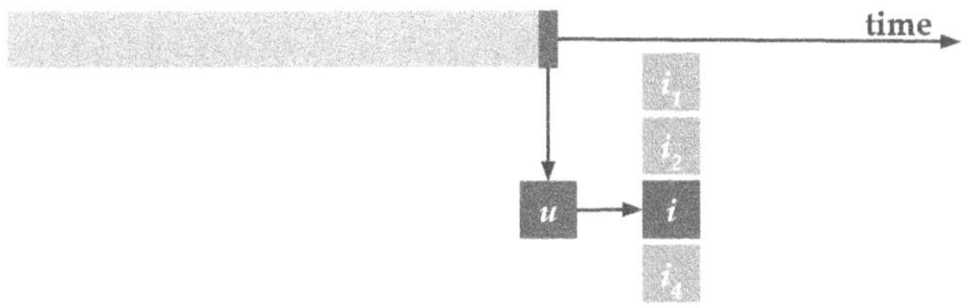

Figure 1: Temporal evaluation of the online ranking prediction problem.

OPEN SOURCE RECOMMENDERS

The tutorial covers recommender algorithms both by batch and by online learning. Participants have the opportunity to install and evaluate the following systems and algorithms in Jupyter and Zeppelin notebooks:

Alpenglow[1] is a free and open source C++ based framework with easy-to-use Python API especially suited for conjoint batch and online learning. We experiment in Aplenglow with
- non-personalized temporal popularity and item-to-item recommender models,
- time-aware variants of nearest neighbor [10],
- SGD based batch and online matrix factorization [11],
- asymmetric matrix factorization [9].

Flink[2] matrix factorization algorithms are available only as pull requests. We experiment both with batch and online factorization models,
- batch iALS[3] [11],
- batch DSGD[4] [4],
- parameter server based asynchronous online SGD[5].

The first two methods use the Flink batch API while the third uses the Flink streaming API.

SparkML[6] provides batch iALS[7] that we compare to the batch models of Alpenglow and Flink.

TUTORIAL OUTLINE

All material (slides, readings, Jupyter and Zeppelin notebooks, code) used in the tutorial will be publicly available after the conference. The instructors aid the participants with the installation. Basic knowledge of Python and Scala is assumed. The material includes
- slides explaining the online ranking prediction problem, the temporal evaluation framework, and the models,
- installation guides for Alpenglow, Flink and SparkML,
- experiments in Jupyter and Zeppelin notebooks,
- public research data collections.

[1]https://github.com/rpalovics/Alpenglow
[2]https://flink.apache.org/
[3]https://github.com/apache/flink/pull/2542
[4]https://github.com/apache/flink/pull/2819
[5]https://github.com/gaborhermann/\flink-parameter-server
[6]https://spark.apache.org/docs/latest/ml-guide.html
[7]https://spark.apache.org/docs/latest/ml-guide.html

The tutorial consists of two independent sessions, with the first one focusing on the main concepts and Alpenglow, and the the second one focusing on Apache Spark and Flink recommenders. In the first part, participants may
- install Alpenglow,
- experiment with various batch and online recommendation models and evaluate them in a temporal setting,
- compare and then combine batch and online matrix factorization methods.

In the second session, we provide distributed recommendation models that may learn from potentially large data sets *and* update their models by online learning. The audience will

- install Flink and Spark, and compare their batch iALS implementations and the batch DSGD included in the Flink Batch API,
- compare the performance of the above batch models to the Parameter Server based asynchronous online SGD in Flink,
- combine batch and online matrix factorization using the Flink Streaming API.

REFERENCES

[1] Jacob Abernethy, Kevin Canini, John Langford, and Alex Simma. 2007. Online collaborative filtering. *University of California at Berkeley, Tech. Rep* (2007).

[2] Azzah Al-Maskari, Mark Sanderson, and Paul Clough. 2007. The relationship between IR effectiveness measures and user satisfaction. In *Proceedings of the 30th annual international ACM SIGIR conference on Research and development in information retrieval.* ACM, 773–774.

[3] Xavier Amatriain and Justin Basilico. 2016. Past, Present, and Future of Recommender Systems: An Industry Perspective. In *Proceedings of the 10th ACM Conference on Recommender Systems.* ACM, 211–214.

[4] Rainer Gemulla, Erik Nijkamp, Peter J Haas, and Yannis Sismanis. 2011. Large-scale matrix factorization with distributed stochastic gradient descent. In *Proceedings of the 17th ACM SIGKDD international conference on Knowledge discovery and data mining.* ACM, 69–77.

[5] Frank Hopfgartner, Benjamin Kille, Tobias Heintz, and Roberto Turrin. 2015. Real-time recommendation of streamed data. In *Proceedings of the 9th ACM Conference on Recommender Systems.* ACM, 361–362.

[6] Neal Lathia, Stephen Hailes, and Licia Capra. 2009. Temporal collaborative filtering with adaptive neighbourhoods. In *Proceedings of the 32nd international ACM SIGIR conference on Research and development in information retrieval.* ACM, 796–797.

[7] Róbert Pálovics and András A Benczúr. 2013. Temporal influence over the Last.fm social network. In *Proceedings of the 2013 IEEE/ACM International Conference on Advances in Social Networks Analysis and Mining.* ACM, 486–493.

[8] Róbert Pálovics, András A Benczúr, Levente Kocsis, Tamás Kiss, and Erzsébet Frigó. 2014. Exploiting temporal influence in online recommendation. In *Proceedings of the 8th ACM Conference on Recommender systems.* ACM, 273–280.

[9] Arkadiusz Paterek. 2007. Improving regularized singular value decomposition for collaborative filtering. In *Proc. KDD Cup Workshop at SIGKDD'07, 13th ACM Int. Conf. on Knowledge Discovery and Data Mining.* 39–42.

[10] Badrul Sarwar, George Karypis, Joseph Konstan, and John Reidl. 2001. Item-based collaborative filtering recommendation algorithms. In *WWW '01: Proceedings of the 10th international conference on World Wide Web.* ACM Press, New York, NY, USA, 285–295. https://doi.org/10.1145/371920.372071

[11] G. Takács, I. Pilászy, B. Németh, and D. Tikk. 2008. Investigation of various matrix factorization methods for large recommender systems. In *Proceedings of the 2nd KDD Workshop on Large-Scale Recommender Systems and the Netflix Prize Competition.* ACM, 1–8.

[12] João Vinagre, Alípio Mário Jorge, and João Gama. 2014. Evaluation of recommender systems in streaming environments. In *Workshop on Recommender Systems Evaluation: Dimensions and Design (REDD 2014), held in conjunction with RecSys 2014. October 10, 2014, Silicon Valley, United States.*

Recommending a Sequence of Points of Interest to a Group of Users in a Mobile Context

Daniel Herzog
Department of Informatics
Technical University of Munich
Boltzmannstr. 3
85748 Garching bei München, Germany
herzogd@in.tum.de

ABSTRACT

Recommender systems (RSs) recommend points of interest (POIs), such as restaurants, museums or monuments, to users. In practice, tourists often travel in groups and want to visit a sequence of POIs along an enjoyable route. Recommending such a sequence of items to a group complicates the problem of travel recommendations because the preferences of all group members have to be taken into account. In this work, we want to examine how a RS can solve the so-called Tourist Trip Design Problem (TTDP) for a group of users. We present the most important components of our work and the research questions we want to be answered. We summarize the results we achieved so far and outline future work.

KEYWORDS

Group Recommender System; Tourist Trip Design Problem; Sequence; Point of Interest; Algorithm; User Interaction

1 INTRODUCTION AND MOTIVATION

Most Recommender Systems (RSs) provide personalized recommendations for single items, such as movies, books or points of interest (POIs). When planning a trip, tourists usually want to visit a sequence of POIs along an enjoyable route. The problem of finding such a tourist trip is called the Tourist Trip Design Problem (TTDP) [18]. Applications solving the TTDP for single users already exist but in practice, tourists often travel in groups. A Group RS (GRS) for tourist trips has to consider the preferences and constraints of all group members.

Different strategies exist for recommending items or sequences of items to groups. Basic approaches, such as calculating the average of the users' preferences, are easy to implement but might not be optimal. For example, if one user really dislikes a certain item, this item should not be recommended even if the majority of group members likes the item. It should be noted that there is no perfect way to aggregate the individual preferences. Instead, the group's intrinsic characteristics and the problem's nature have to be considered [4].

RecSys '17, August 27-31, 2017, Como, Italy
© 2017 ACM. 978-1-4503-4652-8/17/08...$15.00
DOI: 10.1145/3109859.3109860

In this PhD work, we want to examine how to recommend a sequence of items to a group of users, which is still an unexplored topic [13]. Our work focuses on tourist trips, sequences of POIs along enjoyable routes. Compared to other sequences of items, tourist trip recommendations are a more complex issue. The order of POIs in a trip is not very flexible because the recommended route should avoid disproportionate detours. Furthermore, it is likely that some POIs cannot be visited, for example, if they are too expensive or if the remaining time is insufficient. Recommending tourist trips to a group of users is a particular challenge. So far, no research has been done to evaluate which group recommendation strategies work best for recommending tourist trips. Simply combining existing preference aggregation strategies with TTDP algorithms for single users might not guarantee a high group satisfaction or work at all. An average strategy cannot be implemented when some POIs, e.g., bars or night clubs, are not suitable for special group members such as children. It is also conceivable that new group recommendation strategies have to be developed for the tourist trip scenario. For example, if the group members have very different travel preferences, the group could split up during the trip and meet again at a later point of time to avoid dissatisfaction.

The overall research question we want to answer in this work is: *How can RSs solve the TTDP for a group of users?* We want to investigate the problem from two perspectives: how to generate a recommendation for a group and how a group can interact with a tourist trip GRS. The rest of this paper is organized as follows: Section 2 summarizes related work. In Section 3, the different components of our work and research questions we want to be answered are presented. We outline our first results in Section 4. We describe our evaluation methodology and present an outlook on future work in Section 5. This work finishes with a short conclusion.

2 RELATED WORK

Early travel RSs suggested single items such as hotels and destinations or bundled such items to travel plans [16] [19]. They did not recommend items to a group of users or suggested a sequence of POIs along enjoyable routes.

Recommending sequences of items has been researched in different domains, such as music or television [13]. Algorithms solving the TTDP represent one solution to recommending sequences of POIs. Many algorithms and heuristics solving different variants of the TTDP have been developed over the past years. Some researchers integrated their algorithms in practical tourist trip applications. The City Trip Planner is a web-based tourist trip RS recommending single and multi-day trips [17]. CompRecTrip is another similar system recommending either sets or sequences of POIs [21]. The web and mobile application called DailyTRIP, presented by Gavalas et al. [6], can recommend multi-day trips around a common start/end point but it was evaluated with a simulation and a focus on efficiency only. The presented applications show how the TTDP can be solved in practical applications but none of them recommends trips to a group of users.

A few GRSs in tourism exist but to the best of our knowledge, no GRS generates tourist trips composed of multiple POIs. INTRIGUE recommends a list of POIs the user should visit but without combining them along a route [2]. The Travel Decision Forum supports users in agreeing on attributes of a trip, such as desired room facilities or leisure activities [8]. CATS is a case based RS proposing ski packages consisting of several attributes such as the locations, ski lift systems or hotel features [14]. Another GRS recommending single POIs is STSGroup [15].

In contrast to previous work, we want to show how to recommend sequences of POIs to a group of users. We will present solutions how to generate tourist trip recommendations for groups and develop different interaction styles. We want to integrate our findings in a practical application and evaluate them with real groups in user studies.

3 RESEARCH QUESTIONS

Jameson and Smyth [9] present four subtasks that have to be performed by a GRS:

(1) The system acquires information about the members' preferences.
(2) The system generates recommendations.
(3) The system presents recommendations to the members.
(4) The system helps the members arrive at a consensus about which recommendation (if any) to accept.

In the following, we present our research questions for each of the four subtasks. We outline how to evaluate the research questions in user studies in Section 5.

3.1 The System Acquires Information about the Members' Preferences

A GRS can either generate individual recommendations for all group members and combine them to a group recommendation or aggregate the users' preferences to create a virtual group user and recommend an item to this virtual user [13]. A user's preferences depend on the preferences of other group members and the group itself. In some scenarios, a user might accept a recommendation to do a close person a favor. Furthermore, a user might not want other group members to know which POIs she or he likes or dislikes. Revealing preferences to other users in a GRS may allow users to better understand what the best choice for the group is but this knowledge also enables manipulation [8].

Research questions we want to answer in this subtask:

(1) Which group types exist and which information about the group and its members is relevant for a tourist trip GRS?
(2) Which recommendation strategies work best when recommending tourist trips to a group of users?
(3) Which preferences should be revealed to other group members to maximize the quality of the recommendations without enabling manipulation or social embarrassment?

3.2 The System Generates Recommendations

TTDP algorithms perform two steps: At first, POIs are fetched from a data source and assigned a score. Then, a route containing some of the POIs and maximizing the total score of the trip without violating constraints has to be found [20]. Experiments showed that consuming recommended items can have a large impact on the ratings of other items in the same sequence [12]. While this has been proven for news recommendations, we assume that this is even more critical for POI recommendations. For example, when recommending two restaurants in a row, the second restaurant will not be appreciated by the users. Tourist trip algorithms have to identify appreciated and unwanted combinations of POI and consider them during the recommendation process [7].

Research questions we want to answer in this subtask:

(1) Which TTDP algorithms recommend the trips with the highest user satisfaction?
(2) How can the selection and order of POIs in tourist trips be optimized?
(3) How can existing TTDP algorithms be extended to generate recommendations for groups?

3.3 The System Presents Recommendations to the Members

Different approaches to presenting item sequences to users exist. In a tourist trip GRS, either the whole trip or only the upcoming POI can be presented. Travelers often change their plans spontaneously, e.g., stay longer at a POI. In this case, the rest of the trip has to be adapted accordingly. Using a conversational approach by proposing different alternatives successively and collecting feedback on every suggestion can help to better understand the user's preferences and improve the recommendation even after the trip has started. Some GRSs use public screens to present recommendations and to interact with the users. The advantage of such a screen is that it provides an extensive overview of the recommendations for all group members at the same time. On the other side, the use of public screens in recommendations raises privacy issues [1]. People may not like their recommendation to be seen by a broad audience. User interfaces for tourist trip GRS have to find a compromise between privacy and transparency and hide parts of the recommendation from the group or the public.

Research questions we want to answer in this subtask:

(1) How can tourist trip recommendations be presented to a group on mobile devices?
(2) How can public displays be integrated into the recommendation process to improve the user experience?
(3) How do the composition of the group and the relations between the group members influence the individuals' requirements towards privacy and transparency?

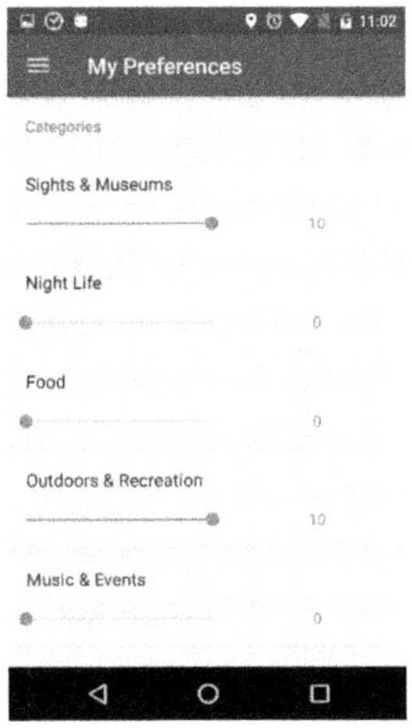

Figure 1: Travel preferences elicitation

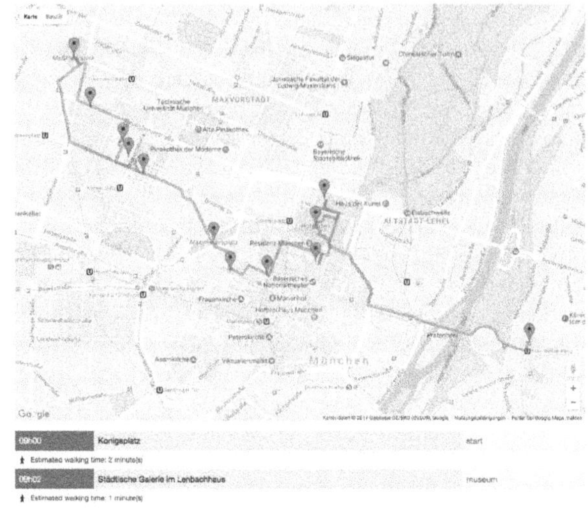

Figure 2: TourRec recommendation

3.4 The System Helps the Members Arrive at a Consensus about which Recommendation to Accept

In our scenario, users receive a recommendation with explanations and can provide feedback on the recommended trips by either using a personal device or a public screen, or both. Again, a good compromise between privacy and transparency has to be found. Users might feel more comfortable sharing their feedback on their personal devices but transparent explanations and open debates about the recommendations can help users to understand the preferences of other users and thus support them in finding a consensus.

Research questions we want to answer in this subtask:

(1) How can tourist trip recommendations be explained to a group?
(2) How much information can be revealed to ensure a high transparency while not violating the users' privacy?
(3) How can the group members provide feedback on a trip using their personal device or a public screen, or both?

4 RECENT RESULTS

We started to develop and evaluate first components of a tourist trips GRS.

4.1 Preference Elicitation

Figure 1 shows a basic approach we implemented to elicit a user's travel preferences [11]. This approach is limited to single users and works solely on the user's personal device.

A user interface as illustrated in Figure 1 allows users to easily indicate their travel preferences. One drawback is that this approach allows only to elicit very basic travel preferences, in this case, how much the user likes very general categories such as *Sights & Museums*. We are currently developing conversational interfaces to elicit the user's travel preferences in a more precise manner.

4.2 Tourist Trip Algorithms

We developed three tourist trip algorithms. The first approach (DB) is an extension of the algorithm presented in [20]. It uses Dijkstra's algorithm to maximize $\frac{total\ score}{distance}$ for each subpath. We developed an extension of this algorithm considering the distance to the destination for each subpath (DBDD). The third algorithm is a Greedy Randomised Adaptive Search Procedure (GRASP), a metaheuristic that performs a number of independent iterations to eventually return the best iteration results [5].

All algorithms were extended by item dependencies because the score of each POI is dependent on the presence or absence of other POIs in the same trip. In addition, we consider suitable times for visiting POIs. For example, a restaurant receives a higher score when recommended for lunch or dinner than in the afternoon. In a small pilot study, we compared our algorithms to our previous solution presented in [20]. A few users tested our system and emphasized that item dependencies and suitable times improve the recommendations by optimizing the ordering of POIs. Venues, such as restaurants or bars, are recommended at more appropriate times of the day.

Furthermore, we developed a responsive web application to evaluate our three TTDP algorithms in a preliminary user study. Every time a user requests a recommendation, one of the three algorithms is randomly chosen and a tourist trip as illustrated in Figure 2 is presented to the user on a map and as a list with arrival and walking times. After every recommendations, the users were asked to rate the following statements on a 5-point Likert scale (1: strongly disagree, 5: strongly agree):

(S1) Overall, I am satisfied with the recommended trip.
(S2) The number of places in my route is well chosen.
(S3) The selection of different categories in the trip is satisfying.
(S4) Places are suggested at the right times during the trip.
(S5) The route is feasible for a walking tourist.

During the preliminary user study, our tourist trip planner suggested 62 trips which were rated by the participants. Table 1 shows the average ratings for every statement.

Table 1: User study results

Algorithm	∅S1	∅S2	∅S3	∅S4	∅S5	# responses
DB	3.33	3.22	3.44	3.28	3.33	18
DBDD	3.13	3.33	3.29	2.88	4.08	24
GRASP	3.10	3.15	3.15	3.25	3.35	20

The results in Table 1 and the feedback we received from the participants show that the users like the general idea of the RS and are mainly satisfied with the recommendations. The average ratings of S5 show that routes generated by the DBDD algorithm are more feasible for walking tourists. This algorithm considers the distance to the final destination before adding a POI to the trip and therefore allows a more even distribution of POIs along the route. By contrast, the DB algorithm and GRASP tend to recommend trips where the majority of POIs are located in a small area. This is recommended for trips in small areas with many POIs, such as city centers. Otherwise, the connection to the final destination can be perceived as too large.

4.3 An Architecture for Tourist Trip Recommender Systems

We developed a multi-tier architecture which is partitioned into a presentation tier, an application logic tier and a data tier [11]. This architecture is the basis for our developments. The main advantages of this architecture for our work are:

- Reusability of functionality. For example, when developing new components such as clients, we do not have to re-implement the whole application logic.
- Modularity. Our system is composed of individual modules such as dedicated microservices for each TTDP algorithm. This architecture allows us to easily add, exchange or remove POI sources, algorithms and clients. Figure 1 and Figure 2 show the two clients our RSs currently uses to recommend tourist trips to single users.
- Developer friendliness. Single modules are easier to understand and teams can work on different components at the same time.
- Scalability. The modular design facilitates scalability.

5 EVALUATION METHODOLOGY AND FUTURE WORK

In this section, we summarize the next steps of our research and explain how we want to evaluate the different parts of our work. As explained, we want to investigate the problem from the two perspectives algorithms and user interaction and will therefore conduct user studies for both parts.

We will continue the user study described in Section 4.2 over a longer period of time to gather more feedback on the developed TTDP algorithms. In this study, the manipulated variable is the selection of the algorithm. Each user request is handled by a randomly selected algorithm. Apart from the different recommendations, the user is not able to distinguish between the algorithms as the other test conditions remain the same. The dependent variables are the answers to the questions S1 to S5 in Section 4.2 and will be extended by some implicit feedback, e.g., if the user exports or saves a recommendation. The gathered feedback will help us find out which algorithms promise the highest user satisfaction and how we can improve them to optimize the sequences.

Furthermore, the TTDP algorithms for single users will serve as a baseline for the evaluation of the TTDP group recommendation algorithms we develop. The simplest approach is to execute the single user TTDP algorithms with the aggregated group preferences. As explained, more sophisticated approaches should be evaluated when recommending tourist trips to different types of groups. We will develop alternatives approaches considering, for example, split groups and compare them against the baseline. The dependent variables are the individual's satisfaction with the recommendation (as in the single user study) as well as the perceived group satisfaction since group members have to compromise when using a GRS.

Our clients currently work for single users only. We will extend them to support group recommendations. This can be done by connecting multiple mobile devices, using a public display or combining both approaches. We will conduct usability tests to evaluate which of these interaction types is preferred by the users in the scenario of tourist trip planning. The manipulated variable in this scenario is the selected interaction type. The dependent variables are the time a group needs to find a tourist trip, the number of clicks and how many errors the users make. In addition, questionnaires such as the SUS can be used to measure usability [3]. Another manipulated variable in this user study is, besides different options for providing feedback on the different devices, the selected explanation style. We will investigate if a higher privacy level has a significant influence on the user experience.

User studies with groups of three to five users require a higher number of participants than studies with a single user. This is why we choose an within-subject design where each participant is exposed to all conditions of the manipulated variable [10]. We will randomize the order of the selected interaction type in each test to minimize the learning effect. We will perform a power analysis to determine the number of participants we need for our studies [10].

A major drawback of previous research in the field of GRS is that studies were either conducted on a small scale, in a contrived setting or used synthetic groups which can lead to falsified results [13]. This is why we want to conduct user studies with real groups and reach as many groups as possible. We want to achieve this goal by placing a public screen at a crowded place, among other things.

6 CONCLUSION

Recommending a sequence of items to a group of users remains a big challenge. Tourist trip recommendations are a particularly complex example of a sequence of items and will hence be the focus of our work. We want to tackle the problem from two perspectives: algorithms and user interaction. Therefore, we will develop new strategies for recommending tourist trips to groups as well as user interfaces for different devices. We will evaluate our results in user studies with real groups.

REFERENCES

[1] Florian Alt, Stefan Schneegaß, Albrecht Schmidt, Jörg Müller, and Nemanja Memarovic. 2012. How to Evaluate Public Displays. In *Proceedings of the 2012 International Symposium on Pervasive Displays (PerDis '12)*. ACM, New York, NY, USA, Article 17, 6 pages. DOI: http://dx.doi.org/10.1145/2307798.2307815

[2] Liliana Ardissono, Anna Goy, Giovanna Petrone, Marino Segnan, and Pietro Torasso. 2002. Tailoring the Recommendation of Tourist Information to Heterogeneous User Groups. In *Revised Papers from the Nternational Workshops OHS-7, SC-3, and AH-3 on Hypermedia: Openness, Structural Awareness, and AdaptivityÆŠ.* Springer-Verlag, London, UK, UK, 280–295. http://dl.acm.org/citation.cfm?id=648105.746696

[3] John Brooke. 1996. SUS-A quick and dirty usability scale. *Usability evaluation in industry* (1996), 189–194.

[4] Sérgio R. de M. Queiroz and Francisco de A.T. de Carvalho. 2004. Making Collaborative Group Recommendations Based on Modal Symbolic Data. In *Advances in Artificial Intelligence – SBIA 2004: 17th Brazilian Symposium on Artificial Intelligence, Sao Luis, Maranhao, Brazil, September 29-Ocotber 1, 2004. Proceedings*, Ana L. C. Bazzan and Sofiane Labidi (Eds.). Springer Berlin Heidelberg, Berlin, Heidelberg, 307–316. DOI: http://dx.doi.org/10.1007/978-3-540-28645-5_31

[5] Thomas A Feo and Mauricio G.C Resende. 1989. A probabilistic heuristic for a computationally difficult set covering problem. *Operations Research Letters* 8, 2 (1989), 67 – 71. DOI: http://dx.doi.org/10.1016/0167-6377(89)90002-3

[6] Damianos Gavalas, Michael Kenteris, Charalampos Konstantopoulos, and Grammati Pantziou. 2012. Web application for recommending personalised mobile tourist routes. *Software, IET* 6, 4 (2012), 313–322.

[7] Daniel Herzog and Wolfgang Wörndl. 2016. Exploiting Item Dependencies to Improve Tourist Trip Recommendations. In *Proceedings of the Workshop on Recommenders in Tourism co-located with 10th ACM Conference on Recommender Systems (RecSys 2016), Boston, MA, USA, September 15, 2016.* 55–58. http://ceur-ws.org/Vol-1685/paper10.pdf

[8] Anthony Jameson. 2004. More Than the Sum of Its Members: Challenges for Group Recommender Systems. In *Proceedings of the Working Conference on Advanced Visual Interfaces (AVI '04)*. ACM, New York, NY, USA, 48–54. DOI: http://dx.doi.org/10.1145/989863.989869

[9] Anthony Jameson and Barry Smyth. 2007. Recommendation to Groups. In *The Adaptive Web*, Peter Brusilovsky, Alfred Kobsa, and Wolfgang Nejdl (Eds.). Springer, Berlin, Heidelberg, 596–627. http://dl.acm.org/citation.cfm?id=1768197.1768221

[10] Bart P Knijnenburg and Martijn C Willemsen. 2015. Evaluating recommender systems with user experiments. In *Recommender Systems Handbook*. Springer, 309–352.

[11] Christopher Laß, Wolfgang Wörndl, and Daniel Herzog. 2016. A Multi-Tier Web Service and Mobile Client for City Trip Recommendations. In *The 8th EAI International Conference on Mobile Computing, Applications and Services (MobiCASE)*. ACM. DOI: http://dx.doi.org/10.4108/eai.30-11-2016.2267194

[12] Judith Masthoff. 2004. Group Modeling: Selecting a Sequence of Television Items to Suit a Group of Viewers. *User Modeling and User-Adapted Interaction* 14, 1 (Feb. 2004), 37–85. DOI: http://dx.doi.org/10.1023/B:USER.0000010138.79319.fd

[13] Judith Masthoff. 2015. Group Recommender Systems: Aggregation, Satisfaction and Group Attributes. In *Recommender Systems Handbook*, Francesco Ricci, Lior Rokach, and Bracha Shapira (Eds.). Springer US, Boston, MA, 743–776. DOI: http://dx.doi.org/10.1007/978-1-4899-7637-6_22

[14] Kevin McCarthy, Lorraine McGinty, Barry Smyth, and Maria Salamó. 2006. The Needs of the Many: A Case-based Group Recommender System. In *Proceedings of the 8th European Conference on Advances in Case-Based Reasoning (ECCBR'06)*. Springer-Verlag, Berlin, Heidelberg, 196–210. DOI: http://dx.doi.org/10.1007/11805816_16

[15] Thuy Ngoc Nguyen and Francesco Ricci. 2016. Supporting Group Decision Making with Recommendations and Explanations. In *Late-breaking Results, Posters, Demos, Doctoral Consortium and Workshops Proceedings of the 24th ACM Conference on User Modeling, Adaptation and Personalisation (UMAP 2016), Halifax, Canada, July 13-16, 2016.* http://ceur-ws.org/Vol-1618/Poster2.pdf

[16] Francesco Ricci. 2002. Travel Recommender Systems. *IEEE Intelligent Systems* (2002), 55–57.

[17] Pieter Vansteenwegen, Wouter Souffriau, Greet Vanden Berghe, and Dirk Van Oudheusden. 2011. The City Trip Planner. *Expert Syst. Appl.* 38, 6 (June 2011), 6540–6546. DOI: http://dx.doi.org/10.1016/j.eswa.2010.11.085

[18] Pieter Vansteenwegen and Dirk Van Oudheusden. 2007. The mobile tourist guide: an OR opportunity. *OR Insight* 20, 3 (2007), 21–27.

[19] Adriano Venturini and Francesco Ricci. 2006. Applying Trip@Dvice Recommendation Technology to www.visiteurope.com. In *Proceedings of the 2006 Conference on ECAI 2006: 17th European Conference on Artificial Intelligence August 29 – September 1, 2006, Riva Del Garda, Italy.* IOS Press, Amsterdam, The Netherlands, The Netherlands, 607–611. http://dl.acm.org/citation.cfm?id=1567016.1567148

[20] Wolfgang Wörndl, Alexander Hefele, and Daniel Herzog. 2017. Recommending a sequence of interesting places for tourist trips. *Information Technology & Tourism* (2017), 1–24. DOI: http://dx.doi.org/10.1007/s40558-017-0076-5

[21] M. Xie, L. V. S. Lakshmanan, and P. T. Wood. 2011. CompRec-Trip: A composite recommendation system for travel planning. In *2011 IEEE 27th International Conference on Data Engineering*. 1352–1355. DOI: http://dx.doi.org/10.1109/ICDE.2011.5767954

Deep Cross-Domain Fashion Recommendation

Shatha Jaradat
KTH - Royal Institute of Technology
Sweden
shatha@kth.se

ABSTRACT

With the increasing number of online shopping services, the number of users and the quantity of visual and textual information on the Internet, there is a pressing need for intelligent recommendation systems that analyze the user's behavior amongst multiple domains and help them to find the desirable information without the burden of search. However, there is little research that has been done on complex recommendation scenarios that involve knowledge transfer across multiple domains. This problem is especially challenging when the involved data sources are complex in terms of the limitations on the quantity and quality of data that can be crawled. The goal of this paper is studying the connection between visual and textual inputs for better analysis of a certain domain, and to examine the possibility of knowledge transfer from complex domains for the purpose of efficient recommendations. The methods employed to achieve this study include both design of architecture and algorithms using deep learning technologies to analyze the effect of deep pixel-wise semantic segmentation and text integration on the quality of recommendations. We plan to develop a practical testing environment in a fashion domain.

CCS CONCEPTS

•**Human-centered computing** →*Social recommendation;*

KEYWORDS

Fashion recommendation; deep learning; cross-domain knowledge transfer; transfer learning; domain adaptation; CNN

1 INTRODUCTION AND MOTIVATION

Intelligent fashion analysis and recommendation is receiving a great deal of attention in computer vision and machine learning communities, due to the huge profit potential in fashion industry [2]. Many algorithms have been developed recently to analyze users' taste of fashion and recommend them personalized looks and outfits. On the other hand, analysis of users' preferred fashion styles also gives insights to clothing companies of what customers like and helps them to achieve greater connectivity with their clients [18]. However, there are major challenges in fashion recommendation: (a) diversity of fashion styles and extremely large amounts of online clothes, which makes it difficult to retrieve accurate options close to users' preferences, (b) evaluation of fashion recommendation algorithms has to be done in time-based large datasets due to seasonality effects, (c) fashion analysis requires usage of effective image-based clothing recognition, retrieval and segmentation computer vision techniques. Therefore, this research direction deserves further attention.

Relying solely on users' online shopping history for fashion recommendation ignores the implicit tastes of users that get reflected on their photos and interactions in social media. Thus, developing recommendation systems that seamlessly integrate information form both sources can open up novel possibilities for retrieving more accurate recommendations. One of the effective social media platforms in fashion domain is Instagram [1], which became the favorite new tool for both designers and models who gain more popularity through publishing photos and connecting with their fans. With over 400 million users in Instagram, fashion retailers and designers started to promote hashtags to encourage audiences to share photos and engage with the brand community [1]. Moreover, casual users caption photos, write description and hashtags about the brands they wear. This let them play an active role in selling the brands to their friends.

Apparently, analysis of the user's visual and textual information from multiple domains is necessary to achieve more interactive recommendations with better quality. However, there is little research that has been done on complex recommendation scenarios that involves knowledge transfer across domains. Knowledge transfer has to deal with the situations when there is insufficient amount of information in a certain domain, but plenty of supplementary data in other related domains. To give an example from our work, clothes in Instagram fashion photos can be analyzed and mapped to similar or exact items in online shopping websites. This will further facilitate the detection of the user's favorite brands and style, and help in building a rich user's fashion profile. In our work, we plan to analyze Instagram photos for the following purposes: (a) getting deep understanding about users' favorite styles and brands, (b) recommending them clothes from similar styles or brands according to season and trends, (c) recommending them clothes similar to their favorite fashion models or trusted friends who have a similar taste of fashion, which up to our knowledge has not been explored before in previous researches. To achieve this, we apply transfer learning together with the recent improvements provided by deep learning technologies in both image and natural language processing, to enhance the development of more efficient and practically applicable cross-domain recommendation system.

RecSys '17, August 27–31, 2017, Como, Italy.
© 2017 ACM. 978-1-4503-4652-8/17/08...$15.00
DOI: http://dx.doi.org/10.1145/3109859.3109861

[1] Instagram.com

We propose a domain adaptation strategy with two Convolutional neural sub-networks framework for integrating visual inputs with user feedback as an enhancing factor of image multi-label prediction. This in turn, will be used to analyze the user's preferred fashion brands and styles. We perform pixel-wise segmentation and integrate text as a correction factor to enhance image semantic segmentation. The rest of the paper is organized as follows: Section 2 provides a background study on the related research. In Section 3, the proposed methodology and research plan are illustrated in detail. Finally, conclusions are presented in Section 4.

2 RELATED WORK

To get an insight into fashion analysis techniques, we have done the following: (a) an extensive survey about current approaches of clothing retrieval, semantic segmentation and recommendation, (b) a comparative study of traditional computer vision and deep learning approaches for image analysis.

2.1 Fashion Analysis Research Categories

Fashion analysis research could be classified into multiple categories. The first category is clothing recognition and retrieval, which is the process of matching clothes with available online clothes and retrieving similar or same clothes from photos. Another category is clothing parsing and semantic segmentation: which is image decomposition and labeling of semantically meaningful parts, e.g. jackets, dresses. Finally, clothing style and features extraction, which is a type of analysis of popular clothing features that could be very helpful for clothing recommendation and advertising. These tasks are considered to be challenging due to the large number of possible garment items to match, variations in photos' configurations and lighting, occlusions from other humans or objects, similarity between items, garments appearance, and layering. Most of the works on clothing analysis relied on handcrafted features such as SIFT, HOG, LBP, and color histogram. Research examples in the above categories are [6, 15, 21].

2.2 Deep Learning for Fashion Analysis

In recent years, a number of deep Convolutional Neural Networks (CNN) [11] models have been introduced to learn more discriminative representation of clothing to handle cross-scenario variations and enhance the performance of clothing recognition and retrieval [16]. Deep CNN models have achieved dramatic accuracy improvements in image classification and many other computer vision areas [3]. To reduce the complexity in CNN training, transfer learning is incorporated in several recent works. Transfer learning, which has shown effectiveness is based on fine-tuning pre-trained models on large-scale datasets. This is based on the assumption that the low or middle level features are common across different problem domains. To give an example, in [12] they fine-tuned a pre-trained GoogleLeNet CNN architecture [20] on their training set for clothing feature extraction. Another direction of transfer learning between a source and target domains is domain adaptation. Domain adaptation can be achieved by learning a transformation that aligns the source and target domains representations into a common feature space. It can be useful for situations where there is only a limited amount of labeled data available in the target domain. [10] Introduced a deep domain adaptation methodology to measure the similarity between street and shop photos. They compute CNN features on the entire shop image, then they compare the similarity between the query features and all shop image features and rank shop retrievals based on this similarity. Other recent examples are [8, 16].

2.3 Fashion Recommendation

Online recommendation has become a common way of satisfying users' needs of clothes. Image-based clothing retrieval plays a very important role in building an online recommendation system and offering a convenient way for customers to identify their favorite items. Based on the idea that the fashion choices are influenced by factors such as seasons, brands, location and occasion: [9] proposed a visual context based fashion recommendation system. In another work [14], they proposed an occasion-oriented clothing recommendation system using human body parsing detectors and latent Support Vector Machine (SVM) model.

2.4 Advanced CNN architectures for Image Analysis

The detection and localization of the elements that appear in an image has been always a useful and challenging technique in image processing. Object localization is not only about predicting a class label of the image, but also a bounding box that describes where the object is located. The process of localization can be split into two general components: the region proposal step and the classification step. A recent example of effective CNN architectures that were proposed to solve the problem of objects detection and localization is faster R-CNN (2015) [17]. Semantic segmentation, which is sometimes referred to as pixel classification, is more precise than object localization and detection. In this task, an outline of every object in the input image is decided, and classified for semantic segmentation. Several proposals have been studied concerning the usage of CNNs to perform segmentation. To name a few: Multi-task Network Cascades (MNCs) [5] and Human Parsing techniques using CNN [13]. Some of these approaches offer the benefits of working with a pixel resolution and aggregating information from different Convolutional layers, while others focus on the efficient detection and classification of more than one instance in the input image. All these approaches are interesting. However, in our project, we propose a more detailed-level segmentation where we include parsed text for enhanced pixel-wise prediction. We also focus on pixel classification on localized regions to increase the accuracy of our work

3 METHODOLOGIES AND RESEARCH PLAN

3.1 Cross-Domain Adaptation Strategy for Fashion Recommendation

We aim to develop an interactive hybrid recommendation system that integrates visual inputs from multiple domains with user feedback for a better quality of recommendation. To achieve this goal, the first part of our work is focused on the development of a framework that adapts a non-ideal domain such as Instagram where there

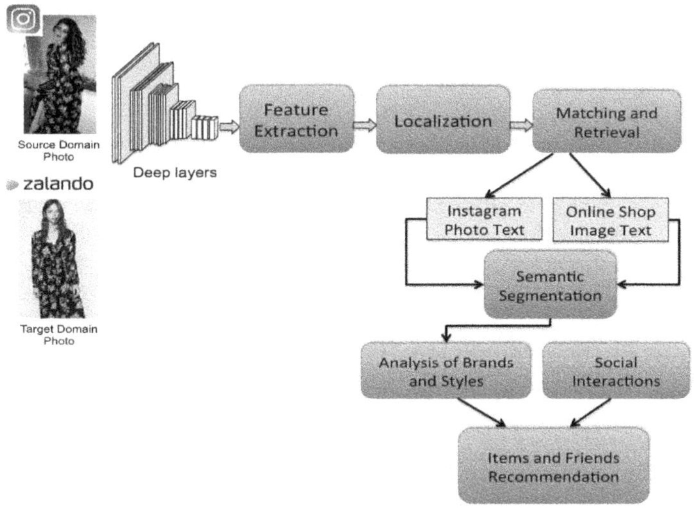

Figure 1: Illustration of the main procedures of image and text processing for item and friends recommendation

might be lack or absence of labeled data, to an ideal domain such as an online shopping website where there are labels associated with each image. For this, we apply a deep CNN domain adaptation methodology to measure the similarity between Instagram and online shopping website images. Domain adaptation can be achieved by learning a transformation that aligns the source and target domains representations into a common feature space. The two models will be connected through several layers where we compute the similarity between extracted features from these layers. This will help in retrieving the most similar images from the online shopping website, and then the brand could be detected from Instagram image and the text associated with the online shopping website image and Instagram storytelling text could be used, and integrated in the main architecture to help in better semantic segmentation of the images (within the same architecture).
Figure 1 [2] illustrates the main procedures in our architecture.

The integrated parsed text will be used as a correction factor of the image multi-label prediction. The deep pixel-wise segmentation that we perform will help in analyzing the detailed style preferences such as length of dresses, patterns of jackets, etc. This will further facilitate the recommendation of items along the time.

3.2 Deep Pixel-Wise Segmentation Effect On Recommendation Quality

According to the general research goals, our first step will be working on the problem of integrating text input as a factor of correction in the pixel resolution segmentation process in the CNN architecture. Our hypothesis for such analysis is as follows. In order to perform a correct segmentation with high accuracy, some tasks have to be performed: localization, mask generation, instance categorization, features upsampling and pixel-wise segmentation. The localization task proposes a set of region proposals where an object is supposed to appear. The output of this stage will be then used in the matching process between the two domains. In this case, we will consider the exceptional scenarios, when an image from one domain might be mapped to more than one image in the other domain. The localized regions which resulted from the previous step (localization) will be used in the following stage - mask generation - which we will decide through training if it is essential or not. The idea is that the masks are only generated in the regions where an object is supposed to appear; therefore, the region proposals from the previous stage provide great help. Concerning the process of mask generation, it must be noted that it is nothing but segmentation with only two categories: foreground and background, i.e. object or non-object.

For a detailed segmentation of the image with only this foreground and background generation it is not enough. That is the reason why the following stage is introduced: given the foreground regions: a more concrete segmentation is computed. This level of details will be achieved by performing segmentation in a pixel resolution. This is achieved by upsampling the features to a pixel resolution and performing a pixel-wise segmentation. The text retrieved after matching the images between the two domains (ideal target domain and source real-world domain), will be used as a factor of correction in the pixel-wise prediction to ensure the correct operation of the whole segmentation process.

In order to have an initial check of the hypothesis, we are developing a model that merges and modifies two advance semantic segmentation architectures: MNC [5] and Human Parsing using CNN [13]. We modified the merged architecture in four ways. First, we introduce the multi-label retrieval (matching) process, which output we use to retrieve auxiliary text from two domains. Second, we apply the segmentation indirectly, we upsample the features to a pixel resolution and perform a pixel-wise segmentation (this part is inspired from Human parsing approach [13]). Third, as opposed to other approaches, we focus on certain localized regions during upsampling. We expect that this will save more computational resources and enhance the accuracy. Fourth, we introduce two correction factors from the text we retrieve from images to be used to ensure the correct operation of the whole segmentation process. The CNN architecture will be a modification of VGG 19 [19], and later we plan to evaluate on other advanced architectures such as Microsoft ResNet [7].

3.3 Text Analysis for Enhanced Style Detection

We are going to analyze the text that we retrieve with images. Here we plan to use methods and tools for text translation (when needed) and topic modeling. To achieve this, we will use a deep learning framework for natural language processing or one of the topic modeling algorithms such as a version of labeled Latent Dirichlet Allocation (LDA).

3.4 Fashion Recommendation Engine

Recently, deep learning has been employed in multiple recommendation scenarios, such as music and movies recommendation [4].

[2]Instagram image taken from a fashionista account

Our recommendation system will be comprised of two neural networks: one for predicting user's outfit preferences from the available categories in an online shop, and another one for recommending Instagram friends who are similar in the taste of fashion and have mutual friends with the user. The output from the semantic segmentation and text analysis framework previously introduced will be interpreted as scores of user's preferences for each clothing category and user's favorite brands. The clothing prediction neural network takes these scores as input, in addition to some controlling factors such as season, to produce personalized predictions of the possible outfits in which the user might be interested. The analyzed interactions between users through likes and comments on photos will be used as scores for the second neural network, together with the user's style preferences scores to produce predictions of possible future friends. The detailed design of our recommendation engines will be illustrated in future work.

3.5 Evaluation Plan

We plan to evaluate our work by implementing an experimental framework in fashion analysis that will include the following functions: (a) detection of clothing brands and style preferences for a community of users from Instagram OSN, (b) the brand and style detection analysis to be used for prediction of highly demanded brands on coming seasons, (c) recommendation of clothing items that combine the personal preferences and recommended styles from the people with whom we interact a lot , (d) recommendation of friends who have similar taste of fashion (e) advising the user about highly favored items by performing sentiment analysis on the comments that people add in userfis profile. We plan to develop an experimental framework to evaluate our architecture in intelligent fashion item recommendation and link prediction scenarios.

In order to implement and evaluate our proposed methods, we are in the process of gathering a sufficiently large Instagram dataset over a one year period, and another dataset from an online shopping website (Zalando) [3]. From theoretical point of view, our architecture should demonstrate better performance and accuracy of the developed methods when compared to the state of the art. From the practical point of view, we believe that our results will open opportunities for industrial applications for intelligent recommendation based on visual and textual analysis.

4 CONCLUSIONS

In this paper, we propose a domain adaptation methodology with two Convolutional neural sub-networks framework for image and text analysis. As a practical result of the project, we are going to implement an experimental framework in fashion analysis that will include the following functions: detection of brands and styles, item recommendation and link prediction based on similarity in taste of fashion. Significance of our work lays in improving quality of image and text analysis and, as a consequence, improving quality of recommendations based on the results of such analysis.

[3] Zalando.com

ACKNOWLEDGMENTS

This research is conducted in cooperation with Marc Ros-Marti, who provided valuable expertise in computer vision techniques, which greatly assisted in the architecture design. Deep thanks go to Nima Dokoohaki for his notable ideas that greatly improved the work and aided in guiding the work to the right direction. I would like to express sincere gratitude to Mihhail Matskin for his guidance through the work and his vital support in providing the required equipment.

REFERENCES

[1] Nicole Alter. 2016. Launch Metrics - Four ways Instagram is Redefining The Fashion Industry. (2016). https://www.launchmetrics.com/resources/blog/four-ways-instagram-is-redefining-the-fashion-industry
[2] Eric Bowman. 2017. MinuteTack - Fashion's Next Revolution Is All About Machine Learning. (2017). http://minutehack.com/opinions/fashions-next-revolution-is-all-about-machine-learning
[3] Qiang Chen, Junshi Huang, Rogerio Feris, Lisa M. Brown, Jian Dong, and Shuicheng Yan. 2015. Deep domain adaptation for describing people based on fine-grained clothing attributes. In *CVPR*.
[4] Paul Covington, Jay Adams, and Emre Sargin. 2016. Deep Neural Networks for YouTube Recommendations. In *Recsys*.
[5] Jifeng Dai, Kaiming He, and Jian Sun. 2016. Instance-aware semantic segmentation via multi-task network cascades. In *CVPR*.
[6] Jian Dong, Qiang Chen, Wei Xia, Zhongyang Huang, and Shuicheng Yan. 2013. A deformable mixture parsing model with parselets. In *ICCV*. 3408–3415.
[7] Kaiming He, Xiangyu Zhang, Shaoqing Ren, and Jian Sun. 2016. Deep residual learning for image recognition. In *CVPR*.
[8] Junshi Huang, Rogerio Feris, Qiang Chen, and Shuicheng Yan. 2015. Cross-domain image retrieval with a dual attribute-aware ranking network. In *CVPR*. 1062–1070.
[9] Vignesh Jagadeesh, Robinson Piramuthu, Anurag Bhardwaj, Wei Di, and Neel Sundaresan. 2014. Large scale visual recommendations from street fashion images. arXiv:1401.1778.
[10] M. Hadi Kiapour, Xufeng Han, Svetlana Lazebnik, Alexander C. Berg, and Tamara L. Berg. 2015. Where to buy it: Matching street clothing photos in online shops. In *ICCV*.
[11] Yann LeCun and Yoshua Bengio. 1995. *The Handbook of Brain Theory and Neural Networks*. MIT Press, Chapter Convolutional networks for images speech and time series, 255–258.
[12] Zhi Li, Yubao Sun, Feng Wang, and Qingshan Liu. 2015. Convolutional Neural Networks for Clothes Categories. In *CCF*. 120–129.
[13] Xiaodan Liang. 2015. Human parsing with contextualized convolutional neural network. In *Proceedings IEEE Int. Conf. Comput. Vis.* 136–139.
[14] Si Liu, Jiashi Feng, Zheng Song, Tianzhu Zhang, Hanqing Lu, Changsheng Xu, and Shuicheng Yan. 2012. Hi, magic closet, tell me what to wear!. In *ACM*. 619–628.
[15] Si Liu, Zheng Song, Guangcan Liu, Changsheng Xu, Hanqing Lu, and Shuicheng Yan. 2012. Street-to-shop: Cross-scenario clothing retrieval via parts alignment and auxiliary set. In *Proceedings of the 20th ACM international conference on Multimedia*. 619–628.
[16] Ziwei Liu, Ping Luo, Shi Qiu, Xiaogan Wang, and Xiaoou Tang. 2016. Deepfashion: powering robust clothes recognition and retrieval with rich annotations. In *CVPR*. 1096–1104.
[17] Shaoqing Ren, Kaiming He, Ross Girshick, and Jian Sun. 2015. Faster R-CNN: Towards real-time object detection with region proposal networks. In *NIPS*.
[18] Michael D. Shaw. 2017. Huffingtion Post - Machine Learning and Fashion: The New Fashion of the Times. (2017). http://www.huffingtonpost.com/michael-d-shaw/machine-learning-and-fash_b_14204376.html
[19] Karen Simonyan and Andrew Zisserman. 2015. Very deep convolutional networks for large-scale image recognition. In *ICLR*.
[20] Christian Szegedy, Wei Liu, Yangqing Jia, Pierre Sermanet, Scott Reed, Dragomir Anguelov, Dumitru Erhan, and Andrew Rabinovich. 2015. Going deeper with convolutions. In *CVPR*. 1–9.
[21] Kota Yamaguchi, M. Hadi Kiapour, Luis E. Ortiz, and Tamara L. Berg. 2012. Parsing clothing in fashion photographs. In *CVPR*. 3570–3577.

Online Recommender System for Personalized Nutrition Advice

Rodrigo Zenun Franco
Computer Science
University of Reading
Reading, United Kingdom
rodrigo.zenun.franco@pgr.reading.ac.uk

ABSTRACT

The general recommendations for addressing non-communicable diseases, which are responsible for two thirds of deaths globally, are mainly related to lifestyle changes, such as diet and physical activity. Challenges with encouraging healthy diets include gathering accurate information about dietary intake and delivering interventions that can influence behavior. Internet technologies offer excellent potential for addressing these challenges. Furthermore, personalized recommendations are more effective than general population-based recommendations at modifying health-related behavior in nutrition interventions.

The overall aim of this project is to design, develop and evaluate a recommender system able to assess dietary intake, using a validated Food Frequency Questionnaire (FFQ), and propose valid personalized nutrition advice for adults. It is investigating an effective way of providing personalized online dietary recommendations to increase diet quality at population-level and of considering an individual user's preferences, population data and experts' knowledge in the recommendation. The system is envisaged to be a web-based service, built with commercially available technologies, scalable, replicable, inexpensive and independent of any bespoke device (e.g. proprietary activity trackers).

Different levels of personalized advice will be evaluated via an online Randomised Control Trial (RCT) and surveys with nutrition professionals will be used for rating the advice proposed by the recommender system.

KEYWORDS

Nutrition; Diet; Food; Health; Personalization; Recommender systems; Behavior change

1 INTRODUCTION

Non-communicable diseases such as diabetes and cardiovascular diseases account for almost two thirds of deaths globally. The general recommendations for addressing these epidemics are related to lifestyle changes, mainly encouraging healthy diets, physical activity (PA) and the reduction of tobacco use and alcohol consumption [24]. The majority of face-to-face nutrition consultations in public services are only available to people with diagnosed conditions such as diabetes and obesity. There is a need for preventative initiatives for the general population, which are currently focused on public guidelines only.

A nutrition consultation cycle can be simplified as comprising three main steps: Assessment, Decision-making and provision of Advice. Typically, a person's dietary intake is assessed and then used as an input for decision-making, in order to provide feedback to the person. In developing an online system for personalized nutrition, all three steps are important to address.

Regarding the assessment stage, a valid method for online dietary intake recording is key. An important and long-established retrospective nutrition assessment method is the Food Frequency Questionnaire (FFQ). It has been used in epidemiological studies for decades [22]. With this method, participants are asked to indicate frequencies and portion sizes for foods that they have consumed during a period of time (e.g. over the last month). FFQs have some accuracy limitations (e.g. calorie estimation), but, relative to some other methods such as 4-day food diaries, are more appropriate for initial dietary assessments aiming at personalized nutrition; FFQs are able to capture habitual dietary intake patterns, can be completed in a relatively short time by participants, and lend themselves to automated data processing [8].

After a person has completed an FFQ, researchers and nutrition professionals typically use guidelines to evaluate the diet quality of an individual. They may calculate the energy and nutrient content of the person's diet and compare this with current nutritional guidelines, in order to guide decision-making. However, food composition tables can contain more than a hundred nutrients and analysis of a person's nutrient profile can be complex and difficult to summarize into useful dietary advice. To address this challenge, a number of indexes of diet quality have been developed over the last decades (see [4] for a comprehensive report containing existing indexes of diet quality, published in 2005). Some of the indexes focus on local guidelines and others on specific target groups or diseases. One particular index of interest for this project is the United States Department of Agriculture (USDA)'s Healthy Eating Index (HEI), whose most recent version was published in 2010 [11]. In some cases, specific indexes have been created to correlate with particular diseases, such as the Alternative Healthy Eating Index (AHEI) which claims to predict the risk of chronic diseases [5], which is the

RecSys '17, August 27-31, 2017, Como, Italy

ACM ISBN 978-1-4503-4652-8/17/08.
http://dx.doi.org/10.1145/3109859.3109862

main nutritional issue to be targeted by the system proposed in this project.

2 RELATED WORK

2.1 Personalized nutrition

Recent work in personalized nutrition intervention studies have shown that personalized recommendations based on diet are more effective than general population-based recommendations at modifying health-related behavior change [4]. In the Food4Me project, the advice was based on a decision tree, executed manually (i.e. by humans) during the study, and subsequently automated [7]. Details of the decision tree have not been published.

There are also studies investigating the personalization of recipes [10] and nutrition decisions [21], aiming to increase the acceptability of recommendations to the user.

2.2 Diet and meal planning

Experts Systems have been used in the nutrition field, mainly for meal planning [3][12]. Some systems applied Case-Based Reasoning (CBR) to propose a nutrient balanced meal plan [20]. Diet modeling was recently approached using constraint optimization techniques [19]. Besides meeting the nutritional guidelines, it is imperative to recommend recipes that individuals will like. Some systems proposed solutions based on recipes collected from the Internet [13]. The decision making process for nutrition advice is not discrete, opening an opportunity for addressing this challenge via fuzzy logic [16] .

2.3 Dietary patterns in nutrition surveys

Population surveys, such as the National Diet and Nutrition Survey (NDNS) in the UK [18], can provide insightful information for tailoring nutrition recommendations. The NDNS covers a representative sample of around 1,000 British residents per year. This type of survey offers potential for analyzing eating behaviors, using for example Topic Models [23]. Factor Analysis has potential to support the identification of food groups that correlate with each other and Cluster Analysis can identify clusters of individuals with similar dietary patterns [15].

3 PROBLEM STATEMENTS

The core challenge of this research is to design an online system that can automatically provide personalized nutrition advice that will be effective in changing people's diets. Besides factoring in an individual's dietary intake relative to general recommended dietary guidelines, it is important that the intervention takes into account personal information (e.g. phenotype, health conditions, dietary restrictions, etc.), population data (e.g. food availability and popularity) and users' preferences (e.g. preferred foods) in defining advice/feedback.

It is particularly important that this recommender system be able to consider participant's actual willingness to change their behavior. For instance, one could want to improve nutrition and yet be unwilling to decrease alcohol consumption, so the cost of the path for reducing the alcohol component would need to be recognized as higher than an alternative method for increasing the diet quality index, such as including more fruit for example. In other words, the system would need to take into account participants' interactions and propose different paths for increasing their diet quality.

Another key challenge in designing a nutrition recommendation system is the problem of how to train the system. In a typical recommender system, for example a medical diagnosis system, there is available data on the inputs (e.g. symptoms) and corresponding outputs (i.e. diagnosis/treatment). One of the main differences with a nutrition recommender system is that there is no existing openly-available dataset with people's case histories and the corresponding proposed diet modifications from nutrition professionals that could be used for training. Furthermore, differently from many common recommender systems (e.g. online shopping based on previous purchases), the food items that users like and consume the most are not necessarily the healthiest. In other words, the recommender system must consider factors other than users' preferences and prior consumption.

4 RESEARCH QUESTIONS

Considering the knowledge in this field obtained from other studies, this project proposes to answer a number of novel research questions:

- How to provide valid online personalized nutrition advice based only on individual's dietary intake and preferences (e.g. food likes and dislikes)?
- How to capture intelligence from nutrition experts and consider it in the recommender system?
- How to increase its level of personalization and improve its acceptability using historical data (e.g. other users of the system) and population data (e.g. national surveys)?

5 METHODS

My PhD research plan comprises three main stages, reflecting the questions presented in the previous section.

5.1 Recommender system based on individual's dietary intake and preferences

In my PhD research to date, I have designed and deployed an online personalized nutrition advice system called e-Nutri. It asks users to complete a FFQ (Fig. 1) which is based on one that has been previously validated [6], converts the dietary intake into nutrients, calculates the components of the AHEI (e.g. vegetables, fruits and sugar) [5], derives a personalized nutrition recommendation based on the AHEI score, and presents the recommendation (Fig. 2), together with a progress report (Fig. 3). It also calculates the ideal weight range of the participants, based on the Body Mass Index (BMI), and provides feedback on their physical activity level, based on the Baecke questionnaire [1].

The design of the user interface takes advantage of an existing design guideline (i.e. Google Material Design [17]) to present web components that are familiar to the participants. It is a fully responsive web application and uses professional cloud computing services.

In a deployment study, 163 participants positively evaluated a previous version of this system and the results are reported in [9]. Currently, the feedback is driven purely by the diet data, and the question of how best to balance nutritional healthiness against users' preferences in a way that maximizes the likelihood

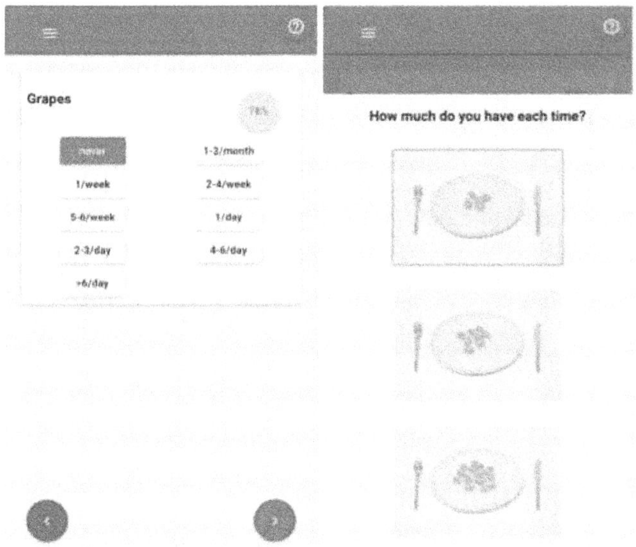

Figure 1: e-Nutri - Food frequencies and portion selections in smartphones

Figure 2: e-Nutri - Personalized report with nutrition advice, ideal weight range and physical activity level

of the user adopting healthier choices remains an open research challenge. A possible solution is to evaluate the quality of a diet using the AHEI, to identify multiple foods that can improve the AHEI score and to let the user choose from the multiple modifications. If the system also allows the users to rate the proposed modifications, that could act as further input to improve the recommendations. This type of approach seems to

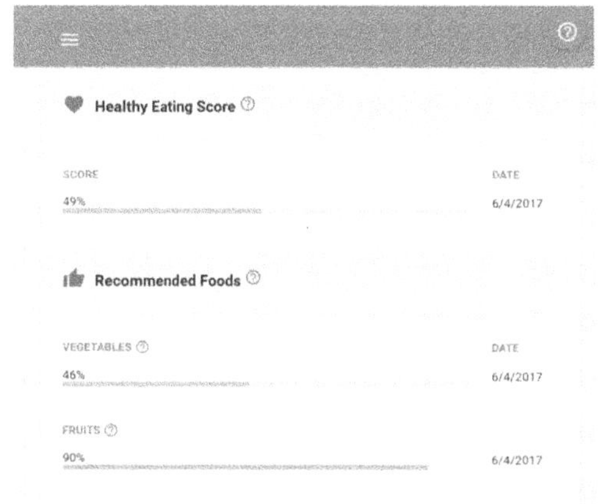

Figure 3: e-Nutri presenting the progress during the study

lend itself well to the use of node graphs, where the nodes represent the dietary intakes and vertices the possible changes [3]. Different from basic meal planning, it is important to have different weights (i.e. change acceptability) for the vertices, similar to map routing with different traffic conditions.

The system is also able to collect timestamps and device details directly from the web browser, and this data can offer insight about how people are using the system. After completing the FFQ, participants are requested to complete the System Usability Scale (SUS) [2] questionnaire for measuring acceptability of the nutrition assessment stage.

5.2 Incorporating intelligence from nutrition experts

Regarding incorporating intelligence from nutrition experts, the project also includes conducting a dietary feedback survey validating the advice provided by the e-Nutri software against professional nutrition standards. The dietary feedback survey will explore professional (Registered Dietitians and Nutritionists) agreement with the e-Nutri automated personalized nutrition advice. Participants (n=32) will be recruited via professional associations (British Dietetic Association, UK Voluntary Register for Nutritionists) and invited to complete the survey online. The survey will present each participant with 2 scenarios, each comprising dietary intake analysis, individual characteristics and the designated advice. The scenarios (n=16) will be drawn from a pool of FFQ responses (available to us from the Food4Me study [7]) based on four features (age, gender, BMI and HEI), and so have good ecological validity. The participants will be asked to audio record (via an online form) the most relevant nutrition recommendations to that hypothetical individual, using their professional judgment. After this stage, the participants will be allowed to access the nutrition advice generated by our recommender system and asked to rate their level of agreement, considering appropriateness, relevance and suitability, via 5-star style questions. Additional feedback will also be collected via audio or free text boxes. The results from this study will be used to refine and improve the recommendations provided by the system.

5.3 Incorporating intelligence from population data

One alternative for addressing the lack of initial data to train the system is to capture intelligence from national nutrition surveys, which provide detailed dietary intake (e.g. food diaries) and socio-demographic (e.g. gender and age) data. It opens a possibility for detecting correlations, such as the most consumed fruits by a specific age range and gender, or for assessing which food substitutions are more likely to be acceptable.

Differently from FFQs, which use a limited food list, the nutrition surveys contain complete food diaries linked with extensive food composition tables (i.e. thousands of items). This type of dataset contains information that would not be captured even after intensive use of the system based only on the FFQ.

5.4 Randomized Control Trial

At the final stage of the project, the effectiveness of the nutrition recommendation will be evaluated, via an online RCT with the following groups (n=100 per group):

- Level 0 (Control group): web-based delivery of non-personalized dietary and physical activity exercise based on the UK general healthy eating guidelines.
- Level 1: Web-based delivery of personalized nutrition information and physical activity advice based on the individual's dietary intake, anthropometrics and physical activity levels.
- Level 2: As in Level 1, plus recommendations based on group/population preferences, as a way to improve the acceptability of the recommendation.

The effectiveness of the recommender system will be captured in terms of users' actual diet change, using the AHEI as an outcome measure. As well, the recommender system will be evaluated via questions regarding the users' perceived system effectiveness and quality [14] and the report design.

6 CONCLUSIONS

This project proposes to increase the acceptability, effectiveness and adoption of online nutrition services. This project will investigate an effective way of providing automated personalized online dietary recommendations in order to increase the diet quality of the population and ways considering user's preferences during the online recommendation.

This proposed system aims to increase effectiveness and acceptability using the following dimensions: dietary intake, user's preferences, other users' responses, population data and nutrition experts' knowledge.

To date, the PhD work has addressed a number of important challenges in usability of assessing dietary intake assessment, and proposing basic personalized diet recommendations based on dietary intake only. The remainder of the PhD research aims to design an intelligent system for personalized nutrition advice. Although the previous version of the system can be very useful and potentially contribute to healthier dietary habits, its decision engine is elementary computationally and deterministic (i.e. if two individuals have the same dietary intake information, they will receive the same advice, even if they have different preferences). In addition, the previous decision engine does not take into account important data sources, such as population data, historical data or individual's preferences. The hypothesis of the final study in the PhD is that these other data sources, combined with recommender system algorithms can increase both the acceptability and effectiveness of the nutrition advice.

ACKNOWLEDGMENTS

Thanks to Dr Faustina Hwang, Professor Julie A Lovegrove and Dr Rosalind Fallaize for the valuable support during my PhD. Thanks to Keith Tam and Julia Castillo for the review of the report design. Thanks to the Food4Me (http://food4me.org) consortium for use of their portion size photographs. Rodrigo Zenun Franco is sponsored by CNPq (National Counsel of Technological and Scientific Development), from the Brazilian Government.

REFERENCES

[1] Baecke, J.A.J.A.H., Burema, J. and Frijters, J.E. 1982. A short questionaire for the measuremnet of habitual physical activity in epidemiological studies. *The American journal of clinical nutrition.* 36, November (Nov. 1982), 936–942.

[2] Brooke, J. 1996. SUS—a quick and dirty usability scale. 1996. *Usability evaluation in industry.* B.W. and A.M. PW Jordan, B. Thomas, ed. 4–7.

[3] Buisson, J.-C. 2008. Nutri-Educ, a nutrition software application for balancing meals, using fuzzy arithmetic and heuristic search algorithms. *Artificial intelligence in medicine.* 42, 3 (Mar. 2008), 213–27.

[4] Celis-Morales, C. et al. 2016. Effect of personalized nutrition on health-related behaviour change: evidence from the Food4me European randomized controlled trial. *International Journal of Epidemiology.* August (2016), dyw186.

[5] Chiuve, S.E., Fung, T.T., Rimm, E.B., Hu, F.B., McCullough, M.L., Wang, M., Stampfer, M.J. and Willett, W.C. 2012. Alternative dietary indices both strongly predict risk of chronic disease. *Journal of Nutrition.* 142, C (2012), 1009–1018.

[6] Fallaize, R., Forster, H., Macready, A.L., Walsh, M.C., Mathers, J.C., Brennan, L., Gibney, E.R., Gibney, M.J. and Lovegrove, J.A. 2014. Online dietary intake estimation: Reproducibility and validity of the Food4Me food frequency questionnaire against a 4-day weighed food record. *Journal of Medical Internet Research.* 16, 8 (Aug. 2014), e190.

[7] Forster, H. et al. 2016. A dietary feedback system for the delivery of consistent personalized dietary advice in the web-based multicenter Food4Me study. *Journal of Medical Internet Research.* 18, 6 (Jun. 2016), e150.

[8] Forster, H., Fallaize, R., Gallagher, C., O'Donovan, C.B., Woolhead, C., Walsh, M.C., Macready, A.L., Lovegrove, J.A., Mathers, J.C., Gibney, M.J., Brennan, L. and Gibney, E.R. 2014. Online dietary intake estimation: the Food4Me food frequency questionnaire. *Journal of medical Internet research.* 16, 6 (Jan. 2014), e150.

[9] Franco, R.Z., Fallaize, R., Alwadhi, B., Lovegrove, J.A., Hwang, F., Alawadhi, B., Fallaize, R., Lovegrove, J.A. and Hwang, F. 2017. Design, Development and Usability Metrics of a Web-based Graphical Food Frequency Assessment System. *JMIR Human Factors.* 4, 2 (May 2017), e13.

[10] Freyne, J. and Berkovsky, S. 2010. Intelligent Food Planning: Personalized Recipe Recommendation. *Proceedings of the 15th international conference on Intelligent user interfaces.* (2010), 321–324.

[11] Guenther, P.M., Casavale, K.O., Reedy, J., Kirkpatrick, S.I., Hiza, H.A.B., Kuczynski, K.J., Kahle, L.L. and Krebs-Smith, S.M. 2013. Update of the Healthy Eating Index: HEI-2010. *Journal of the Academy of Nutrition and Dietetics.* 113, 4 (Apr. 2013), 569–80.

[12] Harvey, M. and Elsweiler, D. 2015. Automated Recommendation of Healthy , Personalised Meal Plans. *RecSys 2015: Proceedings of the 9th ACM conference on Recommender systems.* (2015), 327–328.

[13] Harvey, M., Ludwig, B. and Elsweiler, D. 2013. You Are What You Eat: Learning User Tastes for Rating Prediction. Springer, Cham. 153–164.

[14] Knijnenburg, B.P. and Willemsen, M.C. 2015. Evaluating recommender systems with user experiments. *Recommender Systems Handbook, Second Edition.* (2015), 309–352.

[15] Krebs-Smith, S.M., Subar, A.F. and Reedy, J. 2015. Examining dietary patterns in relation to chronic disease: Matching measures and methods to questions of interest. *Circulation.* 132, 9 (2015), 790–793.

[16] Lee, C.-S., Wang, M.-H. and Lan, S.-T. 2014. Adaptive Personalized Diet Linguistic Recommendation Mechanism Based on Type-2 Fuzzy Sets and Genetic Fuzzy Markup Language. *IEEE Transactions on Fuzzy Systems.* 23, 5 (Oct. 2014), 1777–1802.

[17] Material design - Material design guidelines: 2016. *https://material.google.com/.* Accessed: 2016-10-26.

[18] National Diet and Nutrition Survey: 2016. *https://www.gov.uk/government/collections/national-diet-and-nutrition-survey*. Accessed: 2017-06-28.

[19] Probst, Y., Morrison, E., Sullivan, E. and Dam, H.K. 2016. First-Stage Development and Validation of a Web-Based Automated Dietary Modeling Tool: Using Constraint Optimization Techniques to Streamline Food Group and Macronutrient Focused Dietary Prescriptions for Clinical Trials. *Journal of Medical Internet Research*. 18, 7 (Jul. 2016), e190.

[20] Ravana, S.D., Rahman, S.A. and Chan, H.Y. 2006. Web-Based Diet Information System with Case-Based Reasoning Capabilities. *International Journal of Web Information Systems*. 2, 3/4 (2006), 154–163.

[21] Schäfer, H. 2016. Personalized Support for Healthy Nutrition Decisions. *Proceedings of the 10th ACM Conference on Recommender Systems* (2016).

[22] Welch, A.A., Luben, R., Khaw, K.T. and Bingham, S.A. 2005. The CAFE computer program for nutritional analysis of the EPIC-Norfolk food frequency questionnaire and identification of extreme nutrient values. *Journal of Human Nutrition and Dietetics*. 18, 2 (2005), 99–116.

[23] White, R., Harwin, W.S., Holderbaum, W. and Johnson, L. 2015. Investigating Eating Behaviours Using Topic Models. *2015 IEEE 14th International Conference on Machine Learning and Applications (ICMLA)* (Dec. 2015), 265–270.

[24] WHO 2010. *Global status report on noncommunicable diseases 2010*.

Improving Similarity Measures Using Ontological Data

Özge Sürer
Northwestern University
Robert R. McCormick School of Engineering and Applied Science Technological Institute 2145 Sheridan Road
Evanston, Illinois 60208-2101
ozgesurer2019@u.northwestern.edu

ABSTRACT

The representation of structural data is important to capture the pattern between features. Interrelations between variables provide information beyond the standard variables. In this study, we show how ontology information may be used in a recommender systems to increase the efficiency of predictions. We propose two alternative similarity measures that incorporates the structural data representation. Experiments show that our ontology-based approach delivers improved classification accuracy when the dimension increases.

KEYWORDS

ontology, metadata, recommender systems

ACM Reference format:
Özge Sürer. 2017. Improving Similarity Measures Using Ontological Data. In *Proceedings of RecSys'17, August 27–31, 2017, Como, Italy, ,* 5 pages.
DOI: http://dx.doi.org/10.1145/3109859.3109863

1 INTRODUCTION

The distribution of TV content has been developing via many services such as live TV, video on demand (VOD), catch-up TV and IP-TV. These services offer users the opportunity to watch programs of interest at any time and place. As a consequence, TV viewers typically have hundreds of programs available. However, this creates information overload. Thus, recommendation systems (RS) are important to help consumers find the best content to increase their satisfaction and retain them longer.

TV content distributors analyze viewers' past interaction with TV programs to understand the implicit preference of users. Since the number of programs is large, recommendations are made by first constructing a rating matrix from the length of time spent viewing genres, subgenres, etc. [9, 10]. Then, the similarity between users or items can be calculated by using different similarity metrics. In general, these metrics consider the number of common features that the users or items share. The shortcoming of these metrics is that known interrelations between features are ignored. Similarity between (sub)genres may contribute to the training of RS algorithms. In this study, we generate a hierarchical structure using the ontologies of the information on TV programs. The ontology consists of multiple hierarchical subontologies and the subclass describes the upper class in more details. In TV RS, genres are classified into subgenres based on the content. Moreover, ontology information is not unique to TV programs. Many other areas such as video streaming (e.g., Netflix, Youtube, Hulu, Amazon Video), music streaming (e.g., Spotify, Pandora) and selling products and services (e.g., Amazon, Booking.com) have ontological information. We investigate whether the structured representation of data using ontological taxonomies may be used to improve RS.

In this study, we incorporate ontological information of TV programs into the similarity measures to improve accuracy of TV program preference predictions. We propose and evaluate two approaches by introducing the concepts of *tree-structured covariance matrices* and *path-based similarity* in TV RS. Previous research has been done for similar concepts in text mining and graph classification. However, to the best of our knowledge, there is no previous research exploring how these concepts can be used to improve TV RS. Our experiments show that the new metrics based on ontologies outperform the *cosine similarity* metric.

RecSys'17, August 27–31, 2017, Como, Italy
© 2017 ACM. ISBN 978-1-4503-4652-8/17/08...$15.00
DOI: http://dx.doi.org/10.1145/3109859.3109863

2 LITERATURE REVIEW

In RS, there are four different classes of recommendation techniques: collaborative, content-based, demographic and knowledge-based [4, 5]. These methods can be combined in hybrid recommenders to improve performance. While user ratings for each item is the basis of typical collaborative recommenders, content-based recommenders rely on the features present in items the user has rated. Our approach is a hybrid one, since it uses the knowledge of existing TV program ontology to construct user profiles. This structure is called as the *ontological user profile* [16]. Instead of using viewing time per TV program as an indicator of preference, user profiles are defined based on users' viewing time associated with relevant (sub)genres in the TV program ontology. Therefore, user similarities are computed based on their preference across (sub)genres in the TV program ontology. Our work combines content-knowledge based on the taxonomy of TV programs with collaborative filtering using feature combination strategy.

The ontological user profiling is used in various fields and it is shown that the use of ontology information is successful to address the cold-start problem. Previously, the ontological user profile is used in web personalization [15]. In web search, recommender systems are important to prevent ambiguity in keyword queries and information overload. Sieg et al. [15] create a dynamic ontological profile for each user based on the concepts in domain ontology. They use a spreading activation technique to update the interest weights. Hawalah and Fasli [11] build contextual and personalized ontological user profiles based on the user's interests and context information. Rather than using a reference ontology, they extract hidden semantic information from user profiles to define ontological profiles for each user. Ontological information is incorporated into top-N item recommender in graph-based setting [14]. In this study, path-based features are extracted using the existing ontology and then the learning-to-rank algorithm is used to construct top-N recommendations.

The TV domain varies from other fields, since a broadcast TV program is available for a particular time period. In TV RS, the use of combined recommendation approach is the key for TV service providers. At a specific time and day, a hundreds of TV channels and thousands of TV programs are available, which causes the information overload problem. The use of content-based approaches reduces the diversity, since the recommended items tend to be similar to the past items. On the other hand, collaboration filtering suffers from latency problem [17]. In the TV domain, new programs occur regularly and these programs should be considered even though we do not have enough initial information. Therefore, hybrid recommendation strategies should be considered for TV RS. In addition, TV RS suffers from scalability and sparsity problems, since the number of programs and TV viewers is large at a specific time. Ontological user profiles based on (sub)genre preferences instead of individual TV program preferences help to overcome these problems by using a feature combination strategy. The hidden user problem is another issue for personalized TV RS since we cannot identify who is watching a program at a specific time [12]. All of these issues should be considered for personalized TV program listings.

There has been a lot of research in TV RS to develop more effective algorithms. The cold-start problem is analyzed in [6, 7]. Cremonesi and Turrin [6] use SVD- and item-based algorithms to solve the cold start problem by using data from an IP-TV provider. In their dataset, pay-per-view movies purchased are used implicitly to denote the preferences of users. Cremonesi and Turrin [7] evaluate the performance of different CF algorithms over time to see the effect of time on cold-start problem. The learning-to-rank approach is presented for a cable TV operator that provides live and catch-up TV services by [9]. They compare their algorithm with a baseline algorithm in terms of different metrics such as diversity, novelty and accuracy. Turrin et al. [18] proposed a new metric called *top channel per user per slot*. The algorithm uses the number of minutes watched by a user on a specific channel during a particular slot to find the popularity of a channel. Then, the most popular channel during a particular slot is recommended to a user. However, the resulting models do not take advantage of patterns in the structural data set. Our proposed method based on ontologies may be incorporated into existing methodologies.

In our case, there are two classes of entities: users and TV program genres. Here, $U = \{u_1, u_2, \ldots, u_N\}$ and $I = \{i_1, i_2, \ldots, i_M\}$ are the sets of users and genres, respectively. In the experiments, m represents the size of M genres. User-rating matrix R includes the preferences of users for each genre. Each element r_{ui} in R denotes the log watch time of user u on genre i.

One common approach is to find similarities using the cosine similarity function:

Figure 1: Tree structure for a user

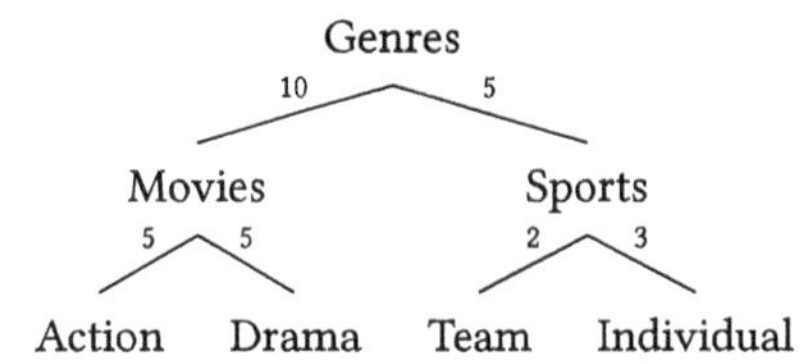

$$\kappa_C(u_i, u_j) = \frac{u_i' u_j}{||u_i|| ||u_j||} \quad \forall i, j \in U \tag{1}$$

Here, the measure of similarity between two TV viewers is derived from the cosine of the angle between them.

By using the ontological profile of programs, we can represent each user profile as a weighted tree structure in which the nodes represent the genres at different levels and the weight of edges represent the viewing time. Figure 1 shows a user tree structure with four leaves. The root of the tree corresponds to the set of all genres and leaf nodes define the final layer of features used in the prediction. This figure will be discussed further below.

2.1 Tree-structured covariance matrices

Kernel functions based on the structure of data have been widely used in text categorization [1, 2]. Hierarchically structured semantic relations are used to increase the accuracy of text classification. In our study, we use ontology information about genres to construct the tree- structured covariance matrix. Once the tree-structured covariance matrix of movie genres is defined over a tree, similar to the text classification, tree structure can be informative in RS.

The kernel for two items is defined by $\kappa(x, y) = x'Gy, \forall x, y \in X$ where X corresponds to the input vector space and G is a positive-definite matrix. Since G is positive-definite, it can be decomposed as $G = ZZ'$. Then, in the simplest case, kernels have the form $\kappa(x, y) = x'Z'Zy$.

The proposed measure of similarity is defined as follows:

$$\kappa_T(u_i, u_j) = \frac{u_i' Z' Z u_j}{||u_i|| ||u_j||} \quad \forall i, j \in U, \tag{2}$$

where Z is the tree-structured covariance matrix of the leaf nodes. The tree-structured covariance matrix of the example in Figure 1 can be given as:

$$Z = \begin{array}{c} \\ Action \\ Drama \\ Team \\ Individual \end{array} \begin{array}{c} \begin{array}{cccc} Action & Drama & Team & Individual \end{array} \\ \begin{pmatrix} 1 & 0.5 & 0.25 & 0.25 \\ 0.5 & 1 & 0.25 & 0.25 \\ 0.25 & 0.25 & 1 & 0.5 \\ 0.25 & 0.25 & 0.5 & 1 \end{pmatrix} \end{array}.$$

Here, the row of the covariance matrix corresponds to the leaf nodes in the tree-structured covariance matrix. It is constructed based on the distances between leaf nodes. If the two leaf nodes belong to the same parent node, the correlation between these nodes will be 0.5. Otherwise, the correlation between the leaf nodes is 0.25. In our small example, since action and drama belong to the same superclass, the covariance between them is higher compared to the covariance between, for example action and team sports. Therefore, two TV viewers show higher similarity if the two tree structures have a common last ancestor of leaf nodes.

2.2 Path-based similarity

The goal of graph classification is to learn a model to identify the class of a graph. Various features of graphs are widely used in graph classification [3, 13]. In this study, each user profile is represented as a weighted tree that is a directed, acyclic graph. Our aim is to predict a program preference of a user based on the structural properties of a tree.

The structure of a tree can be explored through the weighted paths from root to leaf. In our example, if we consider the length of time spent viewing the genres at the leaf node as a feature vector, the user profile can be given as [5 5 2 3]. When the weighted paths from root node to leaf nodes are considered, the user profile is given as [15 15 7 8].

Once we calculate the weighted paths for each user, the similarity between two user profile is calculated as:

$$\kappa_P(u_i, u_j) = \frac{p_i' p_j}{||p_i|| ||p_j||} \quad \forall i, j \in U, \tag{3}$$

where $P = \{p_1, p_2, \ldots, p_N\}$ is the set of paths for all the users. This representation enables supergenres to contribute the similarity of two users beyond the leaf nodes.

3 METHODS AND RESULTS

3.1 Data description

We use data from a leading multi-system operator (MSO) in the US, which provides cable TV, phone and Internet services to multiple communities. The firm has more than one million subscribers from 15 states. The dataset is comprised of TV programming and watching data collected over a period of nine months from April to December 2015. We have two main tables. The entity of the first table is a TV program. The metadata for each program in the EPG (Electronic Programming Guide) is its unique program code, title, start time, end time and TV channel. The second table records every "tuning" action of each household and includes the fields user id, start time, end time and TV program.

In this study, the upper level of categorization describes the content of a program and we call it the *supergenre* of a program. A program is categorized into the following supergenres: movies, current affairs, game show, sports, children, music/ballet/dance, arts, social/political issues, education, leisure hobbies and other [8]. Each supergenre is split into various mutually exclusive *genres*. For example, the movie supergenre has subcategories such as drama, adventure, science fiction, comedy, soap, romance, historical, adult movie and others. In total, we have 11 different supergenres and 62 genres. The description of a program is a combination of different keywords that describes the topic of a program. For instance, if the description of a program (subgenre) is "children, adventure, animated," then the tags of this program are "children," "adventure" and "animated." In our data set, we have 195 different program tags and 4011 different subgenres. As a subclass of the tag of a program, the subgenre class is used.

In this study, we see the effects of hierarchical structure of the dataset on prediction accuracy. We use watching behavior as an implicit profile of each household. A view is defined to be a program watched consecutively for more than two minutes since a short viewing duration does not denote the users' interests.

3.2 Results

First, we construct the rating matrix R. Each row of R corresponds to the user profile. User profiles are encoded as vectors whose dimensions correspond to the total log watch time of different genres at the specific level. In this study, we use cosine similarity κ_C and naive Bayes approach as a baseline algorithm and compare the results with the proposed measures of similarity κ_T and κ_P. The TV program preferences of a user are found by means of a k-NN (k-nearest-neighborhood) approach.

The rating matrix R is constructed with three different distance functions: κ_C, κ_T and κ_P. Then, for each user, the k closest users are identified and the predicted preference is given by the majority vote of the associated responses of the k closest neighbors. We have tested 10 different values of the number k. After calculating the test error with varying value of k, the optimal value of k is chosen as the one that gives the lowest test error. Naive Bayes approach is trained with three different hierarchy levels of data set and then test error is calculated. The data is divided into two parts. Test set includes 1000 households selected at random. In order to see the effect of sample size on the prediction accuracy, we have tested the methods with three different sample sizes N=1000, 2000, 4000.

In Figure 2, the test error rate is given at the best optimal value of k for each method at different levels at the hierarchical structure. For N=2000, the test error at different values of k is given in Figure 3. For N=1000 and 4000, we do not provide the results due to the page limit. In Figure 2, the best setting occurs at m=195 with the path-based similarity measure. At this level of hierarchy, the path-based similarity measure is superior to the other similarity measures. As N increases, the performance of the path-based similarity measure and kernel function based on tree-structured covariance matrices becomes closer. At the upper level of hierarchy corresponding to 62 genres, the cosine similarity metric performs better as the sample size increases. At the lowest level of hierarchy, with m=4011, the accuracy of path-based similarity measure is better compared to the remaining methods. As the sample size increases, the cosine similarity performs better than the tree-covariance matrix.

The performance of three metrics at various values of k is shown in in Figure 3. We can see that the performance of three metrics is closer to each other at the upper level of hierarchy. When the dimension increases from m=62 to m=195, the performance of path-based similarity measure improves substantially. This shows that we can integrate the ontological data into predictive models to increase the accuracy of algorithms. At m=4011, although the path-based similarity metric provides the best setting, the improvement compared to m=95 is not significant. We can conclude that the contribution of ontological information is much more influential, when the dimension increases from the lowest level to moderate level. The best test error obtained is %35 with m=62 and N=4000

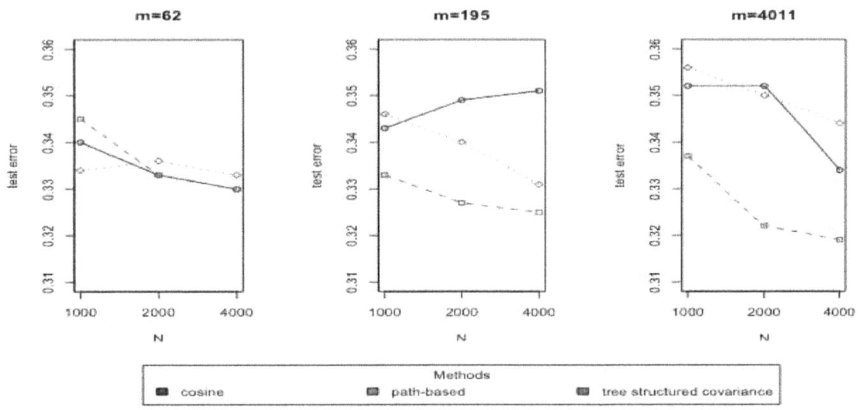

Figure 2: Test error at the optimal value of k.

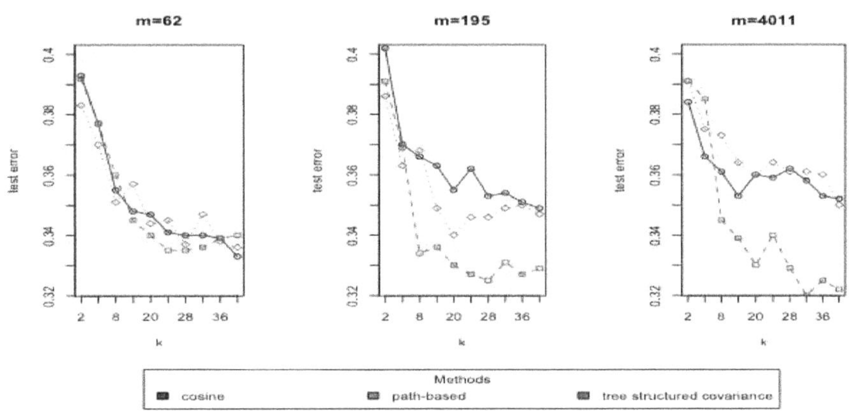

Figure 3: Test error with varying value of k.

using naive Bayes approach. Our approach is superior to naive Bayes approach in terms of classification accuracy.

4 DISCUSSION

This study shows how ontologies can be integrated into techniques used for TV recommendation. In our experiments, the performance of k-NN algorithm is improved with the use of ontological data. When the dimension of the data increases from the lowest level to the moderate level, the performance of the path-based similarity measure increases significantly. In addition to k-NN algorithm, we have tested the performance of logistic regression, LASSO, ridge regression and random forests with the same data set. The performance of these algorithms improve with increasing dimension. These experiments show that ontological information can be used to supplement classical machine learning and statistical approaches.

The defining characteristics of this problem are that there is (1) a large number (e.g., millions) of users, (2) a large number (e.g., hundreds of thousands) of items, and (3) an ontology describing hierarchical relationships between the items. This problem exists in many different fields such as bioinformatics and text mining. The focus of our research is on developing methods for using and refining the ontological information in RS and predictive analytics situations. This work opens up fruitful directions for future research. We would like to investigate the use of existing ontologies to extract the hidden ontology in the data set. In general, a few components of input variables can explain the outcome variation. However, it is hard to identify the groups of variables that have high explanatory power. The hidden ontology will be helpful to identify these groups in a reduced feature space. In addition, the ontological information exists in different fields with the increase of digital information. Therefore, the algorithmic and theoretical developments can be applied to other fields.

5 ACKNOWLEDGEMENT

I thank Northwestern University's Spiegel Center for Digital and Database Marketing for giving me access to the data and financial support.

REFERENCES

[1] Matthew B. Blaschko, Wojciech Zaremba, and Arthur Gretton. 2013. *Taxonomic Prediction with Tree-Structured Covariances.* Springer Berlin Heidelberg, Berlin, Heidelberg, 304–319. DOI: http://dx.doi.org/10.1007/978-3-642-40991-2_20

[2] Stephan Bloehdorn, Roberto Basili, Marco Cammisa, and Alessandro Moschitti. 2006. Semantic Kernels for Text Classification Based on Topological Measures of Feature Similarity. In *Sixth International Conference on Data Mining (ICDM'06).*

[3] Christopher Bowles and James Hogan. 2014. Weighted tree kernels for sequence analysis. In *ESANN.*

[4] Robin Burke. 2002. Hybrid Recommender Systems: Survey and Experiments. *User Modeling and User-Adapted Interaction* 12, 4 (2002), 331–370.

[5] Robin Burke. 2007. *Hybrid Web Recommender Systems.* Springer Berlin Heidelberg, Berlin, Heidelberg, 377–408. DOI: http://dx.doi.org/10.1007/978-3-540-72079-9_12

[6] Paolo Cremonesi and Roberto Turrin. 2009. Analysis of Cold-Start Recommendations in IPTV Systems. In *Proceedings of the Third ACM Conference on Recommender Systems (RecSys '09).* ACM, 233–236.

[7] Paolo Cremonesi and Roberto Turrin. 2010. Time-evolution of IPTV Recommender Systems. In *Proceedings of the 8th International Interactive Conference on Interactive TV&Video.*

[8] Digital Video Broadcasting (DVB) Specification for Service Information (SI) in DVB systems V1.11.1 2010. *ETSI EN 300 468.* Digital Video Broadcasting (DVB) Specification for Service Information (SI) in DVB systems V1.11.1.

[9] Diogo Gonçalves, Miguel Costa, and Francisco M. Couto. 2016. A Flexible Recommendation System for Cable TV. In *3rd Workshop on Recommendation Systems for Television and online Video (RecSysTV).*

[10] Diogo Gonçalves, Miguel Costa, and Francisco M. Couto. 2016. A Large-Scale Characterization of User Behaviour in Cable TV. In *3rd Workshop on Recommendation Systems for Television and online Video (RecSysTV).*

[11] Ahmad Hawalah and Maria Fasli. 2014. Utilizing contextual ontological user profiles for personalized recommendations. *Expert Systems with Applications* 41, 10 (2014), 4777 – 4797. DOI: http://dx.doi.org/10.1016/j.eswa.2014.01.039

[12] Myung-Won Kim, Eun-Ju Kim, Won-Moon Song, Sung-Yeol Song, and A. Ra Khil. 2012. *Efficient Recommendation for Smart TV Contents.* Springer Berlin Heidelberg, Berlin, Heidelberg, 158–167. DOI: http://dx.doi.org/10.1007/978-3-642-35542-4_14

[13] Geng Li, Murat Semerci, Bulent Yener, and Mohammed J. Zaki. 2012. Effective Graph Classification Based on Topological and Label Attributes. *Statistical Analysis and Data Mining* 5, 4 (2012), 265–283.

[14] Vito Claudio Ostuni, Tommaso Di Noia, Eugenio Di Sciascio, and Roberto Mirizzi. 2013. Top-N Recommendations from Implicit Feedback Leveraging Linked Open Data. In *Proceedings of the 7th ACM Conference on Recommender Systems (RecSys '13).* ACM, New York, NY, USA, 85–92. DOI: http://dx.doi.org/10.1145/2507157.2507172

[15] Ahu Sieg, Bamshad Mobasher, and Robin Burke. 2007. Web Search Personalization with Ontological User Profiles. In *Proceedings of the Sixteenth ACM Conference on Conference on Information and Knowledge Management (CIKM '07).* ACM, New York, NY, USA, 525–534. DOI: http://dx.doi.org/10.1145/1321440.1321515

[16] Ahu Sieg, Bamshad Mobasher, and Robin Burke. 2010. Improving the Effectiveness of Collaborative Recommendation with Ontology-based User Profiles. In *Proceedings of the 1st International Workshop on Information Heterogeneity and Fusion in Recommender Systems (HetRec '10).* ACM, New York, NY, USA, 39–46. DOI: http://dx.doi.org/10.1145/1869446.1869452

[17] Barry Smyth and Paul Cotter. 2000. A personalised TV listings service for the digital TV age. *Knowledge-Based Systems* 13, 2 (2000), 53 – 59. DOI: http://dx.doi.org/10.1016/S0950-7051(00)00046-0

[18] Roberto Turrin, Andrea Condorelli, Paolo Cremonesi, and Roberto Pagano. 2014. Time-based TV programs prediction. In *RecSysTV Workshop at ACM RecSys 2014.*

Improving the Trustworthiness of Recommendations in Collaborative Filtering under the Belief Function Framework

Raoua Abdelkhalek*
LARODEC, Institut Supérieur de Gestion de Tunis
Université de Tunis, Tunis, Tunisia
abdelkhalek_raoua@live.fr

ABSTRACT

Collaborative Filtering (CF) consists of filtering data, predicting users' preferences and providing recommendations accordingly. Commonly, neighborhood-based CF methods predict the future ratings based on similar users (user-based) or similar items (item-based) to perform recommendations. However, the reliability of the information provided by these pieces of evidence as well as the final predictions cannot be fully trusted. Incorporating trust in the recommendation process can be argued to be an important challenge in Recommender Systems (RSs). To tackle these issues, we propose new CF approaches under the belief function framework. The final prediction is obtained by fusing evidences from similar items or similar users using Dempster's rule of combination. The prediction process of our evidential approaches is able to provide the users with a global overview of their possible preferences. This would lead to increase their confidence towards the system as well as their satisfaction. In this paper, we mainly highlight the benefits of incorporating uncertainty in CF approaches using the belief function theory. We present the preliminary results and also discuss our ongoing works, as well as the challenges in the future.

CCS CONCEPTS

•**Retrieval tasks and goals → Recommender systems;**

KEYWORDS

Collaborative Filtering, Uncertainty, Trust, Reliability, Belief Function Theory

1 INTRODUCTION

Collaborative Filtering (CF) [29] is an effective and a popular approach in the field of Recommender Systems (RSs). An important class for this kind of RS is the neighborhood-based CF approaches [2], also referred to memory-based CF. Typically, these approaches are divided into user-based [12] and item-based [22]. User-based predicts the user's preferences based on the users sharing similar interests. Item-based, on the other hand, relies on the ratings of similar items rather than similar users to predict the final rating. Neighborhood-based CF are widely used in commercial systems since they are simple, easy to implement and highly effective [29]. Despite their simplicity and popularity, these approaches exhibit some limitations since they do not take into account the uncertainty behind the final recommendations. The reliability of the information sources as well as the final ratings provided to the active user cannot be fully trusted. An effective recommendation approach must inspire trust in the system and provide reliable and credible recommendations. While making decisions, users may speculate about the uncertainty pervaded behind the given recommendation. For instance, if a user receives a prediction indicating whether or not to visit a given country, he might wonder about his possible preferences towards this destination. In this situation, the predicted ratings may help him to make the best decision possible since this area is unfamiliar to him. Furthermore, he might prefer a reliable prediction that gives him a complete overview about his preferences rather than a risky one that may not fit his interests and goals. Hence, increasing intelligibility and transparency of the provided predictions is a crucial challenge to improve the users' confidence as well as their satisfaction [21].

Aiming to overcome the limitations mentioned above, we propose in this paper new CF approaches that quantify this uncertainty using the belief function theory [6, 24, 27]. Such theory represents a general framework to deal with uncertainty and offers a rich representation about all situations ranging from complete knowledge to complete ignorance. Our approaches tend to take into account both information imperfection and source reliability to form more valuable evidence. The final prediction is obtained by fusing different pieces of evidence using Dempster's rule of combination. The prediction process is able to provide the users with a global overview of their possible preferences that the traditional CF approaches fail to consider. We assume that such representation provide a convenient way for the users to put the recommendations in the right perspectives and help them to take a better decision.

The research goals can be summarized as follows:

- Dealing with uncertainty pervaded in the predictions made by the Recommender System.
- Building a trustworthy recommender and providing faithful predictions to improve the users' confidence and enhance the chance to succeed for such systems.
- Helping the users making a better decision by allowing them to get a closer picture about their potentially future ratings.

The remainder of this paper is organized as follows: In Section 2, we recall the basic concepts and tools related to the belief function theory. Section 3 presents briefly some related works focusing on trustworthiness in Recommender Systems. In Section 4, we

*

RecSys '17, August 27–31, 2017, Como, Italy.
© 2017 ACM. 978-1-4503-4652-8/17/08...$15.00
DOI: http://dx.doi.org/10.1145/3109859.3109864

introduce a new item-based CF approach under the belief function theory. In Section 5, we highlight our ongoing works and we explain the challenges considered in each work. Finally, the paper is concluded and potential future works are depicted in Section 6.

2 BELIEF FUNCTION THEORY

The Belief Function Theory [6, 24, 27] is one of the most used theories for representing and reasoning under uncertainty. Let Θ be the frame of discernment. It represents a finite set including exhaustive and mutually exclusive events associated to the problem domain. Such set contains hypotheses concerning the given problem. All the possible values that each subset of Θ can take is called the power set of Θ and denoted by 2^Θ such that: $2^\Theta = \{A : A \subseteq \Theta\}$. The belief committed to each element of Θ is expressed by a basic belief assignment (*bba*). It is a mapping function $m : 2^\Theta \longrightarrow [0, 1]$ such that:

$$\sum_{A \subseteq \Theta} m(A) = 1 \quad (1)$$

Each mass $m(A)$, called a basic belief mass (*bbm*), quantifies the degree of belief exactly assigned to the event A of Θ.

Two useful operations in the manipulation of belief functions are the *Shafer's discounting operation* and *Dempster's rule of combination* [24].

Considering two *bba*'s m_1 and m_2 induced from two independent information sources, the pieces of evidence can be combined using Dempster's rule of combination defined as:

$$(m_1 \oplus m_2)(A) = k. \sum_{B,C \subseteq \Theta : B \cap C = A} m_1(B) \cdot m_2(C) \quad (2)$$

$$where \ (m_1 \oplus m_2)(\emptyset) = 0 \ and \ k^{-1} = 1 - \sum_{B,C \subseteq \Theta : B \cap C = \emptyset} m_1(B) \cdot m_2(C)$$

In most cases, the information provided by the pieces of evidence are not fully reliable. A discounting mechanism could therefore be performed on m as following:

$$m^\alpha(A) = (1 - \alpha) \cdot m(A), \text{ for } A \subset \Theta \quad (3)$$
$$m^\alpha(\Theta) = \alpha + (1 - \alpha) \cdot m(\Theta)$$

where the coefficient $\alpha \in$ [0,1] is called the discounting factor.

While holding beliefs tends to represent knowledge, we can use such beliefs to make a decision by transforming them into a probability distribution called the pignistic probability $BetP$ [27] defined as:

$$BetP(A) = \sum_{B \subseteq \Theta} \frac{|A \cap B|}{|B|} \frac{m(B)}{(1 - m(\emptyset))} \ for \ all \ A \in \Theta \quad (4)$$

3 RELATED WORK

Recommender System can be evaluated according to its ability to predict accurate ratings and to provide relevant items. Besides, trustworthiness is another important factor that can deeply affect the recommendations success. In fact, Pu et al.[19] have emphasized that users' perception of recommendations is directly related to their trust in the system. They also highlighted in [20] the benefits of raising perceived trustworthiness of predictions and how recommended results could affect users' confidence. They affirmed that if the provided recommendation succeeds in inspiring users' confidence, users will increasingly like the RS. Sinha and Swearingen [26] pointed out that an effective recommendation approach must inspire trust in the system and increase transparency of the recommendations. They assumed that providing familiar recommendations plays an important role in increasing the user's trust. Komiak et al. [14] have also focused on the effects of personalization and familiarity on trust and adoption of recommendation agents. The influence of transparency on user trust has also been explored in [5]. A study performed by Herlocker et al. [11] showed that explanations provide a suitable solution to build trust in the RS. They proved that the users are more likely to trust the recommender when they know the reasons behind the provided recommendations. In the same context, Schaffer et al. [23] have investigated how the explanations and dynamic feedback given to the user during the recommendation process can influence user experience. Similarly, Wang et al. highlighted in [31] the effects of explanation facilities on users initial trusting on Recommender Systems. More recently, Chen and Wang [4] proposed to provide explanations while recommending items based on feature sentiments in product reviews. A deep analysis concerning the effect of explanations in Recommender Systems can also be found in [30]. Harman et al. [9] carried out cognitive experiments and found that users trust the RS and react more strongly to personalized recommendations even when they provide inaccurate predictions. Likewise, Knijnenburg et al. [13] proposed a user-centric evaluation framework for Recommender Systems where they studied recommenders from a user-centric perspective. They provided a detailed description of how to conduct offline user experiments beyond accuracy measures. In [25], Shani et al. invoked that users build trust when systems provide a display of confidence alongside a recommendation. They assumed that confidence displays can also be considered as a part of the broader recommendation explanation area. This can be explained by the fact that users may speculate about the uncertainty pervaded behind the given recommendation. Based on these assumptions, we are interested in our work to improve the performance of neighborhood-based Collaborative Filtering approaches by quantifying and representing this uncertainty using the belief function theory. The relevance of this theory has been emphasized in several fields including RSs ([16],[17], [18]).

4 CURRENT STATE OF THE RESEARCH

In this section, we mainly introduce our current work on handling uncertainty in CF based on the belief function theory.

4.1 Evidential Item-Based CF

In this approach, we aim to infer more reliable and trustworthy predictions while maintaining a good recommendations performance. To do this, we resort to the belief function theory in order to model conveniently the uncertainty in the final recommendations. We define the frame of discernment Θ as following: $\Theta = \{\rho_1, \rho_2, \cdots, \rho_n\}$ where n is the number of the possible ratings ρ that can be provided by the users. In this work, we opt for the Evidential K-Nearest Neighbors classifier [7]. This machine learning technique allows the objects to belong to more than only one class. This concept is referred to credal classification which leads to a richer information content of the classifier's output. Thereupon, we draw on an evidential item-based CF based on the ratings of similar items. Using the terminology of the belief function theory, we assume the K-similar items to provide pieces of evidence supporting a particular hypothesis about the final prediction. The rating provided by each similar item will be transformed into a mass function $m(\{\rho_i\})$ based on the formalism proposed in [7] such that:

$$m_{x,y}(\{\rho_i\}) = \alpha_0 \exp^{-(\gamma_{\rho_i}^2 \times (D(x,y))^2)} \qquad (5)$$

$$m_{x,y}(\Theta) = 1 - \alpha_0 \exp^{-(\gamma_{\rho_i}^2 \times (D(x,y))^2)}$$

where α_0 is fixed to the value 0.95 as invoked in [7], γ_{ρ_i} is the inverse of the mean distance between each pair of items sharing the same rating value ρ_i and $D(x,y)$ is the distance between the item x and the item y defined as:

$$D(x,y) = \frac{\sqrt{\sum_{u \in u_x \cap u_y} (r_{u,x} - r_{u,y})^2}}{|u_x \cap u_y|} \qquad (6)$$

Where $r_{u,x}$ and $r_{u,y}$ are the ratings given by user u for the items x and y, u_x and u_y are the users who have rated respectively the items x and y.

Once the *bba*'s are generated for each similar item, we aggregate these *bba*'s using the following expression:

$$m(\{\rho_i\}) = \frac{1}{R}(1 - \prod_{i \in i_K}(1 - \alpha_{\rho_i})) \cdot \prod_{\rho_j \neq \rho_i} \prod_{i \in i_K}(1 - \alpha_{\rho_j}) \qquad (7)$$

$$\forall \rho_i \in \{\rho_1, \cdots, \rho_n\}$$

$$m(\Theta) = \frac{1}{R}\prod_{i=1}^{n}(1 - \prod_{i \in i_K}(1 - \alpha_{\rho_i}))$$

where $i_K = \{i_1, i_2, \cdots, i_K\}$ is the set containing the indexes of the K-nearest neighbors of the target item over the user-item matrix, n is the number of the ratings provided by the similar items, α_{ρ_i} is the belief committed to the rating ρ_i, α_{ρ_j} is the belief committed to the rating $\rho_j \neq \rho_i$, R is a normalized factor defined by:

$$R = \sum_{i=1}^{n}(1 - \prod_{i \in i_K}(1 - \alpha_{\rho_i}) \prod_{\rho_j \neq \rho_i} \prod_{i \in i_K,}(1 - \alpha_{\rho_j}) + \prod_{i=1}^{n}(\prod_{i \in i_K}(1 - \alpha_{\rho_j})) \qquad (8)$$

The main advantage behind this representation is that the final prediction must be a basic belief assignment which reflects more credible results. The decision about the final rating that should be provided to the active user is made with the pignistic probability (Eq. 4). We assume that the rating having the greatest pignistic probability is more likely to be the potential future one. On the other hand, all the other possible preferences generated by this approach are also displayed to the active user as illustrated in Figure 1.

In this example, the results given to the active user predict for him that a *bbm* of 0.5033 supports that he will extremely like the current item . Otherwise, the evidence that he will never be interested in such item has a value of 0.2472. Furthermore, a moderate satisfaction towards this suggestion is around 0.179. The rest of the belief is allocated to Θ which reflects the case of total ignorance. The user, in this case, understands the reasons behind the provided

	⋆	⋆⋆	⋆⋆⋆	⋆⋆⋆⋆	⋆⋆⋆⋆⋆	Θ
 Active User	0.2472	-	0.179	-	0.5033	0.0706

Figure 1: A New Prediction Process Under the Belief Function Theory

recommendation. He may tend to further research the item before making a decision. Indeed, a recent work in [10] found that putting users in control of their recommendations results in more positive evaluations.

4.2 Experimental Evaluation

We have successfully evaluated in our preliminary work [1], the evidential item-based CF approach using MovieLens dataset [1]. In order to assess its prediction's accuracy, we used three evaluation metrics: the *Mean Absolute Error* (MAE), the *Root Mean Squared Error* (RMSE) and the *Distance criteron* (dist_crit) proposed by [8]. However, since we are dealing with recommendation as a classification problem, we can also make use of well-known measures for classifier evaluation such as precision, recall and F-Measure [3]. We followed the same experimental protocol in [28]. We ranked the movies according to the number of their ratings. Then, we progressively increased the number of the missing ratings to obtain 10 different subsets. Hence, each subset contains a specific number of ratings leading to different degrees of sparsity. Note that each subset contains the ratings given of the 943 users for 20 movies. Further details about the experimental protocol can be found in [28]. For each subset, we varied the number of neighborhood size K from 1 to 10 then we note the overall value. We used 80% of the available ratings for training our approach and 20% for testing. The results are depicted in Table 1 and compared to state of the art CF approaches. As can be seen, the evidential item-based CF (EVIB-CF) has practically better Precision, Recall and F-Measure comparing to Pearson Item-Based CF (PIB-CF) and Cosine Item-Based CF (CIB-CF). The precision of our approach remains the highest over the different sparsity degrees. For instance, at 80.8%, the precision of our evidential approach (equal to 0.778) is significantly higher than the precision of PIB-CF (equal to 0.729) and CIB-CF (equal to 0.718). Similarly for the Recall, the new approach achieves the best results for 9 out of 10 subsets with a small difference at a sparsity level of 59.8% (0.725 compared to 0.726). For the three CF approaches, a remarkable drop is observed for the last subset corresponding to the highest sparsity degree (95.9%). This can be explained by the lack of available ratings which we tend to tackle in future works.

5 ONGOING-WORKS AND CHALLENGES

Until now, we showed the relevance of handling uncertainty in item-based CF throughout the prediction process. Another direction of our research work is to consider the reliability of information sources under the belief function theory. Before combining the *bba*'s provided by each neighbor, we incorporate a reliability

[1] http://movielens.org

Table 1: Comparison Result in Terms of Precision, Recall and F-Measure

Evaluation Metric	Sparsity Degree	PIB-CF	CIB-CF	EVIB-CF
Precision Recall F-Measure	53%	0,774 0.691 0.73	0,778 0.686 0.729	**0,79** **0.732** **0.759**
Precision Recall F-Measure	56.83%	0,737 0.655 0.693	0,739 0.677 0.706	**0,76** **0.717** **0.737**
Precision Recall F-Measure	59.8%	0,752 **0.726** 0.738	0,749 0.718 0.733	**0,77** 0.725 **0.746**
Precision Recall F-Measure	62.7%	0,746 0.705 0.724	0,745 0.709 0.726	**0,763** **0.77** **0.766**
Precision Recall F-Measure	68.72%	0,707 0.657 0.681	0.69 0.699 0.694	**0,741** **0.764** **0.752**
Precision Recall F-Measure	72.5%	0,732 0.639 0.682	0,733 0.665 0.697	**0,735** **0.68** **0.706**
Precision Recall F-Measure	75%	0,752 0.737 0.744	0,745 0.698 0.711	**0,78** **0.718** **0.747**
Precision Recall F-Measure	80.8%	0,729 0.666 0.696	0.718 0.673 0.694	**0,778** **0.696** **0.734**
Precision Recall F-Measure	87.4%	0,665 0.59 0.625	0,653 0.737 0.692	**0,707** **0.747** **0.726**
Precision Recall F-Measure	95.9%	0,463 0.6 0.522	0,509 0.685 0.584	**0,513** **0.716** **0.597**

measure into the mass function using the discounting method. The idea is to weight most heavily the evidence of the items having the lowest distances and conversely for the less reliable ones. We divide the obtained distance for each similar item by the maximum value in order to get normalized values in [0,1] to be used in the the reliability computation. Hence, we obtain the discounting factor that we denote by β. Note that the smaller the discounting, the higher the reliability. Finally, the discounted *bba's* are combined using Dempster's rule of combination. On the other hand, uncertainty reigns also in the second category of the CF approach namely the user-based CF. Based on the same intuition behind the evidential item-based apprach, we conceived a new user-based CF approach under the belief function framework. Similar users have been considered as different pieces of evidence leading to the final prediction. We represent their contributions through a basic belief assignment and aggregate their evidences using Dempster's rule of combination. The induced *bba* encodes the evidence of the active user' neighbors regarding the rating that should be provided to him. In both cases, a lot of heavy computations are needed which reflects a scalability problem. That is why, we are oriented to tackle this issue by grouping the most similar items into different clusters and the predictions are then performed. However, an item may potentially belong to more than only one cluster. This concept is referred as soft clustering. We assume that this uncertainty may impact the relationship between the items and therefore the final prediction. In this context, we have developed recently an evidential clustering item-based CF which relies on items clusters rather than the user-item matrix. In our approach, we involved the Evidential C-Means [15] which is a clustering technique under the belief function theory. According to the current experiments, execution time has been significantly improved, along with better prediction and recommendation performance.

ACKNOWLEDGMENTS

Special thanks to my advisor Professor Zied Elouedi and my co-advisor Doctor Imen Boukhris for their valuable support and guidance.

6 CONCLUSIONS AND FUTURE WORKS

In this paper, we propose several methods through which Collaborative Filtering systems could be improved. The uncertainty pervaded in the prediction task is considered in both item-based and user-based CF. The active user gets a closer picture about his potentially future ratings which reflects more credible, flexible and transparent results. We also handle the scalability problem in CF as well the uncertainty in the clusters membership. Future research directions will focus on conceiving further evidential approaches under this theory to handle other challenges imposed from the CF framework such as the cold start and the sparsity problems. We tend also to conduct more experiments online with real test users and to perform more complete comparisons with previous methods.

REFERENCES

[1] Raoua Abdelkhalek, Imen Boukhris, and Zied Elouedi. 2016. Evidential Item-Based Collaborative Filtering. In *International Conference on Knowledge Science, Engineering and Management.* Springer, 628–639.
[2] Charu C Aggarwal. 2016. Neighborhood-Based Collaborative Filtering. In *Recommender Systems.* Springer, 29–70.
[3] Xavier Amatriain and Josep M Pujol. 2015. Data Mining Methods for Recommender Systems. In *Recommender Systems Handbook.* Springer, 227–262.
[4] Li Chen and Feng Wang. 2017. Explaining Recommendations Based on Feature Sentiments in Product Reviews. In *International Conference on Intelligent User Interfaces.* ACM, 17–28.
[5] Henriette Cramer, Vanessa Evers, Satyan Ramlal, Maarten Van Someren, Lloyd Rutledge, Natalia Stash, Lora Aroyo, and Bob Wielinga. 2008. The effects of transparency on trust in and acceptance of a content-based art recommender. *User Modeling and User-Adapted Interaction* 18, 5 (2008), 455–496.
[6] Arthur P Dempster. 2008. A generalization of Bayesian inference. In *Classic works of the dempster-shafer theory of belief functions.* Springer, 73–104.
[7] Thierry Denoeux. 1995. A k-nearest neighbor classification rule based on Dempster-Shafer theory. *IEEE transactions on systems, man, and cybernetics* 25, 5 (1995), 804–813.
[8] Zied Elouedi, Khaled Mellouli, and Philippe Smets. 2004. Assessing sensor reliability for multisensor data fusion within the transferable belief model. *IEEE Transactions on Systems, Man, and Cybernetics, Part B (Cybernetics)* 34, 1 (2004), 782–787.
[9] Jason L Harman, John O'Donovan, Tarek Abdelzaher, and Cleotilde Gonzalez. 2014. Dynamics of human trust in recommender systems. In *ACM Conference on Recommender systems.* ACM, 305–308.
[10] F Maxwell Harper, Funing Xu, Harmanpreet Kaur, Kyle Condiff, Shuo Chang, and Loren Terveen. 2015. Putting users in control of their recommendations. In *ACM Conference on Recommender Systems.* ACM, 3–10.
[11] Jonathan L Herlocker, Joseph A Konstan, and John Riedl. 2000. Explaining collaborative filtering recommendations. In *ACM conference on Computer supported cooperative work.* ACM, 241–250.
[12] Rong Jin, Joyce Y Chai, and Luo Si. 2004. An automatic weighting scheme for collaborative filtering. In *International ACM SIGIR conference on Research and development in information retrieval.* ACM, 337–344.
[13] Bart P Knijnenburg and Martijn C Willemsen. 2015. Evaluating recommender systems with user experiments. In *Recommender Systems Handbook.* Springer, 309–352.
[14] Sherrie YX Komiak and Izak Benbasat. 2006. The effects of personalization and familiarity on trust and adoption of recommendation agents. *MIS quarterly* (2006), 941–960.
[15] Marie-Hélène Masson and Thierry Denoeux. 2008. ECM: An evidential version of the fuzzy c-means algorithm. *Pattern Recognition* 41, 4 (2008), 1384–1397.

[16] Van-Doan Nguyen and Van-Nam Huynh. 2014. A community-based collaborative filtering system dealing with sparsity problem and data imperfections. In *Pacific Rim International Conference on Artificial Intelligence*. Springer, 884–890.

[17] Van-Doan Nguyen and Van-Nam Huynh. 2015. A reliably weighted collaborative filtering system. In *European Conference on Symbolic and Quantitative Approaches to Reasoning and Uncertainty*. Springer, 429–439.

[18] Van-Doan Nguyen and Van-Nam Huynh. 2017. Two-probabilities focused combination in recommender systems. *International Journal of Approximate Reasoning* 80 (2017), 225–238.

[19] Pearl Pu and Li Chen. 2007. Trust-inspiring explanation interfaces for recommender systems. *Knowledge-Based Systems* 20, 6 (2007), 542–556.

[20] Pearl Pu, Li Chen, and Rong Hu. 2012. Evaluating recommender systems from the user's perspective: survey of the state of the art. *User Modeling and User-Adapted Interaction* 22, 4 (2012), 317–355.

[21] Francesco Ricci, Lior Rokach, and Bracha Shapira. 2015. Recommender systems: Introduction and challenges. In *Recommender Systems Handbook*. Springer, 1–34.

[22] Badrul Sarwar, George Karypis, Joseph Konstan, and John Riedl. 2001. Item-based collaborative filtering recommendation algorithms. In *International conference on World Wide Web*. ACM, 285–295.

[23] James Schaffer, Tobias Höllerer, and John O'Donovan. 2015. Hypothetical Recommendation: A Study of Interactive Profile Manipulation Behavior for Recommender Systems.. In *FLAIRS Conference*. 507–512.

[24] Glenn Shafer and others. 1976. *A mathematical theory of evidence*. Vol. 1. Princeton university press Princeton.

[25] Guy Shani, Lior Rokach, Bracha Shapira, Sarit Hadash, and Moran Tangi. 2013. Investigating confidence displays for top-N recommendations. *Journal of the American Society for Information Science and Technology* 64, 12 (2013), 2548–2563.

[26] Rashmi Sinha and Kirsten Swearingen. 2002. The role of transparency in recommender systems. In *CHI'02 extended abstracts on Human factors in computing systems*. ACM, 830–831.

[27] Philippe Smets. 1998. The transferable belief model for quantified belief representation. In *Quantified Representation of Uncertainty and Imprecision*. Springer, 267–301.

[28] Xiaoyuan Su and Taghi M Khoshgoftaar. 2008. Collaborative filtering for multiclass data using bayesian networks. *International Journal on Artificial Intelligence Tools* 17, 01 (2008), 71–85.

[29] Xiaoyuan Su and Taghi M Khoshgoftaar. 2009. A survey of collaborative filtering techniques. *Advances in artificial intelligence* 2009 (2009), 4.

[30] Nava Tintarev and Judith Masthoff. 2007. A survey of explanations in recommender systems. In *Data Engineering Workshop, 2007 IEEE 23rd International Conference on*. IEEE, 801–810.

[31] Weiquan Wang and Izak Benbasat. 2007. Recommendation agents for electronic commerce: Effects of explanation facilities on trusting beliefs. *Journal of Management Information Systems* 23, 4 (2007), 217–246.

Unsupervised Context-Driven Recommendations Based On User Reviews

Francisco J. Peña
Insight-Centre for Data Analytics
Department of Computer Science
University College Cork
Cork, Ireland
francisco.pena@insight-centre.org

ABSTRACT

In this work we present Rich-Context, a context-driven recommender system that extracts contextual information using topic modeling without the need to define keywords. Our system uses the mined context to produce recommendations. We propose a methodology to measure the quality of context topic models along with a novel way to represent context that allows it to be used as side-information in a recommendation engine. Results show that Rich-Context makes more accurate predictions than five well-established recommendation algorithms.

CCS CONCEPTS

• **Information systems → Collaborative filtering; Recommender systems;** • **Computing methodologies → Topic modeling;** *Natural language processing; Unsupervised learning;*

KEYWORDS

Context-driven recommender system, context-aware recommender systems, topic modeling, review-mining

ACM Reference format:
Francisco J. Peña. 2017. Unsupervised Context-Driven Recommendations Based On User Reviews. In *Proceedings of RecSys '17, Como, Italy, August 27-31, 2017,* 5 pages.
https://doi.org/10.1145/3109859.3109865

1 INTRODUCTION

User reviews have become a source of additional information for recommender systems to work with besides ratings. Many recommender systems have successfully extracted information from user reviews in order to make better recommendations ([6]).

Additionally, [1] has also shown that including contextual information into recommender systems leads to improved recommendations. Since context has an influence on how a user perceives a product or service, the same user could rate the same item with totally different (1 to 5) ratings depending on the context in which the item is consumed. For instance, if a user is on a business trip, she could rate a small hotel room with 5 stars because she is mainly concerned about the quality of the Wi-Fi, whereas if she goes to the same hotel with her husband and kids, she could rate it with 2 stars because of the room size and the lack of a swimming pool for the children. When users rate services, they are not just rating the facilities, but their overall experience.

Approaches such as [11, 17, 18] have successfully incorporated contextual information into their recommendation models to produce more accurate recommendations. They have used datasets that contain explicit information about the context in which the items were consumed. The problem with many real-world systems is that contextual information is not often available or it is very limited. This happens because users are often not bothered about stating the context in which they visited a restaurant or hotel, and web portals normally limit what they ask users for to a couple of contextual features (typically the purpose of the trip/meal and the companion). To overcome this lack of extra contextual information, several context-aware recommender systems have started to incorporate contextual information from user-generated reviews in order to improve the recommendation models ([5, 10]).

When users write reviews, they tend to do it in two styles: giving detailed stories about their visit, or writing general overviews of a place. Detailed stories are told when users are describing past experiences in a hotel or restaurant. On the other hand, most of the time general overviews cannot be related to a particular visit in the past. Since every experience happens under a context (there is no such thing as a context-less experience), we assume that reviews that describe experiences are going to contain more contextual information than the ones that do not describe experiences. We call reviews that describe experiences *specific* and the ones that give general descriptions *generic* ([2]). Reviews in which the author is describing an experience with a product or service are specific; for instance: *"During the summer, we like to take a mini staycation. This year it was extra special as we also got engaged. Our stay at the Biltmore was just fantastic. The service was exceptional, and the food was amazing"*. Generic reviews just give general opinions and do not describe an experience with the product or service; for instance: *"Nice hotel, all the amenities you need, great complex of pools"*.

In this paper we present Rich-Context, a recommender system that extracts contextual information from user reviews using unsupervised topic modeling algorithms. This has the benefit of not having to predefine keywords that describe context, capturing contextual situations that were not considered before, such as wheelchair accessibility, parking facilities or pet friendliness, we call this *latent*

ACM ISBN 978-1-4503-4652-8/17/08...$15.00
https://doi.org/10.1145/3109859.3109865

context. We introduce a new way to measure the quality of topic models in terms of their context-richness and present a novel way to represent contextual information. Tests on multiple datasets show that our system can beat several other well-known recommenders in terms of rating prediction.

The remainder of this paper is organized as follows: Section 2 discusses related work, followed in Section 3 by the methodology to create a Context-Driven Recommender System. Section 4 introduces a series of metrics to measure the quality of topic models in terms of context-richness. Section 5 presents the results and Section 6 contains the conclusions and the future work.

2 RELATED WORK

Our work relies heavily in two areas, review-based recommender systems and topic modeling. Latent Dirichlet Allocation ([4, 9, 16]) is arguably the most popular topic modeling algorithm. LDA is a generative probabilistic model in which documents are represented as random mixtures of latent topics, and each topic is characterized by a distribution over words. The main problem with LDA is that due to its stochastic nature, it produces different topic models on separate runs over the same data when using distinct random seeds. To overcome this issue, [3] proposed a technique called Ensemble Topic Modeling that is based on Non-negative Matrix Factorization and it factorizes a stacked matrix composed of several runs of the same topic model using different random seeds. Results show that it reduces variability, producing more stable and reliable topic models.

[12] link LDA with matrix factorization via a transformation function to learn more accurately the parameters that lead to better recommendations. [8] presents an unsupervised model that mines aspects from movie reviews using topic modeling and integrates the mined aspects into the recommendation engine. [5] uses heuristics to extract contextual information from reviews along with item aspects and sentiment. [10] uses a supervised topic modeling method (Labeled-LDA) to classify reviews based on their context. These last two methods are the most similar to ours because they also extract contextual information from user-generated reviews. The problem with these methods is that all of them have to predefine the possible types of contextual variables and their values, thus leaving out many other contextual possibilities.

[2] presents a method to extract contextual information from user-generated reviews through topic modeling and word similarities. We borrow some of their ideas to build our recommender system, such as the separation of reviews into specific and generic, and the use of topic modeling to discover contextual information.

3 METHODOLOGY

Rich-Context is a query-based context-driven recommender system ([13]). In our system the users write queries stating the context in which they intend to travel and then receive a list of recommendations. It has three main components: RCClassifier, RCMiner and RCRecommender. RCClassifier separates reviews into specific and generic, RCMiner creates topic models using only specific reviews and then labels topics as contextual or non-contextual. Finally, RCRecommender applies the topic model to the input query and uses the contextual information contained in the query as side-information to produce recommendations. An example of a query for hotels can be *"summer holidays children"*. Here the user is indicating the context under she wants to travel.

3.1 Classifying Reviews

To classify reviews we first created a training set of manually labeled reviews. We manually labeled 300 reviews from each of our datasets, assigning two classes: *specific* or *generic*. Reviews that told particular experiences during a visit were labeled as specific and reviews that gave a general overview of a place were labeled as generic ([2]).

We perform part-of-speech tagging on those reviews and then give them to a logistic regression classifier. The features we use in our classifier are a subset of the features specified in [2] that, after running several tests, helped us achieve the best classification performance, viz:

- *LogWords*: log of number of words in the sentence + 1
- *Vsum*: log of number of verbs in the sentence + 1
- *VBDSum*: log of number of verbs in the past tense in the sentence + 1
- *ProRatio*: ratio of log of number of personal pronouns + 1 to *LogWords*

3.2 Creating Contextual Topic Models

To obtain contextual information from user-generated reviews, we use topic modeling. The basic idea behind this is to generate a topic model from a set of documents and then distinguish between topics that contain contextual information and topics that do not.

In topic modeling documents are expressed as a mixture of topics. Algorithms such as Latent Dirichlet Allocation take a probabilistic view of topic modeling, in which the documents are represented as a probability vector of topics. Other authors have used Non-negative Matrix Factorization (NMF) for topic modeling. Using NMF we have a document-term matrix $\mathbf{A} \in \mathbb{R}^{d \times t}$, where d is the number of documents and t is the number of terms. Matrix $\mathbf{A}$ can be factorized into two matrices $\mathbf{H} \in \mathbb{R}^{d \times k}$ and $\mathbf{W} \in \mathbb{R}^{k \times t}$ so that $\mathbf{A} \approx \mathbf{WH}$. The $\mathbf{H}$ matrix may be seen as a document-topic matrix and the $\mathbf{W}$ matrix can be seen as the topic-term matrix.

To create the topic models, we use the methodology of ensemble topic modeling proposed by [3]. The goal of this methodology is to reduce the variability that is characteristic of topic models built using stochastic algorithms. Since stochastic methods are used, two topic models that are created using the same dataset but different random seeds can be quite different. The goal of ensemble topic modeling is to reduce that variability. This is done by creating a set of base topic models by executing NMF r times applied to the same document-term matrix $\mathbf{A}$, then the r generated matrices are stacked together in one matrix and a final run of NMF is applied to the stacked matrix in order to obtain the ensembled topic model ([3]).

After we have classified reviews as specific or generic using RCClassifier, RCMiner creates a topic model using the ensemble topic model approach proposed by [3] using only specific reviews. Once the topic model has been created, we apply the topic model to all the reviews (specific and generic) to obtain the vector of topic weights for each review and then normalize the vector so its sum adds up to 1.0. Then, we calculate which topics appear more frequently in specific reviews than in generic ones. We do so by using a variation of the approach proposed in [2] in which, instead of computing cardinalities, we sum weights for each topic. We say that topics that appear more frequently in specific reviews than in generic ones, are contextual topics and those that appear more in generic reviews are non-contextual topics.

$$w^s(t_k) = \frac{\sum_{S \in specific} T[k]}{|S : S \in specific|} \tag{1}$$

We make a similar calculation for generic reviews:

$$w^g(t_k) = \frac{\sum_{S \in generic} T[k]}{|S : S \in generic|} \tag{2}$$

Finally, the likely contextual topics, CT, are those where the ratio of the two proportions exceeds a threshold β:

$$CT = \left\{ t_k \mid \frac{w^s(t_k)}{w^g(t_k)} > \beta \right\} \tag{3}$$

The topic models are created using only the nouns of the specific reviews, as these capture most of the contextual information. As we will show in the results sections, using only nouns translates into more context-rich topic models compared to using words from all part-of-speech.

3.3 Making Context-driven Recommendations

Once we have created the topic models and separated contextual topics from non-contextual topics, we transform our original dataset of records from $\langle\langle u, i, R_{ui}, \rangle, r_{ui}\rangle$ into records where the contextual information is represented by a vector of contextual topics weights $\langle\langle u, i, c_1, \ldots, c_{|CT|}\rangle, r_{ui}\rangle$. We do this by applying the topic model to the review, which will give us a vector with the weights for each topic; we normalize that vector so all the weights add up to 1.0 and then we discard the weights of all the topics that have been marked as non-contextual. We use the vector of contextual topic weights as side-information and include it into the recommendation model. For the recommendations we use the LibFM implementation of Factorization Machines algorithm ([14]). Since we are assuming a context-driven approach, the user supplies a query containing her intended context, similarly represented as a vector of weights.

4 TOPIC MODEL METRICS

To evaluate how good our model is, we measured the quality of the topic models produced. Given that there is not a well-established methodology to measure the quality of topic models in terms of their context-richness that we are aware of, we designed our own metrics. We came up with three metrics to do this: the topic score, the topic model score and the separation score. We also had to manually create a vocabulary of contextual words to help us see if a topic was composed of many contextual words or not. This vocabulary was used only in this evaluation: it is not used in the RC system.

4.1 Topic Score

The topic score measures how rich is a topic in terms of context and is given by $ts(t) = \sum_{v \in V} x_{vt} \cdot b_{vt}$, where x_{vt} denotes the weight that the word v has in topic t, V is the vocabulary of all words, and b_{vt} is a binary variable that indicates if the word v belongs to the manually defined vocabulary of contextual words.

Dataset	Reviews	Users	Items	Sparsity
Yelp Hotels	4085	3408	102	0.988
Yelp Restaurants	148161	35054	2552	0.998

Table 1: Description of the datasets.

4.2 Topic Model Score

The topic model score is just the average of all the topic scores in the topic model, and is given by $tms = \frac{\sum_{t \in T} ts(t)}{|T|}$, where T is the set of all topics in the topic model.

4.3 Separation Score

The separation score measures how well our algorithm separates context-rich topics from non-context-rich topics. It is the average score of the context-rich topics multiplied by a constant γ plus the average score of the non-context-rich topics multiplied by $1 - \gamma$:

$$ss = \left[\gamma \cdot \frac{\sum_{c \in CT} ts(c)}{|CT|} + (1 - \gamma) \cdot \left(1 - \frac{\sum_{n \in N} ts(n)}{|NCT|}\right)\right] \tag{4}$$

where CT is the set of the topics marked as contextual by RCMiner and NCT is the set of the topics marked as non-contextual ($NCT = T \setminus CT$) and γ is a weight that balances the importance of getting high scores on context topics versus getting low scores on non-context topics.

5 RESULTS

To evaluate RCMiner, we used the hotels and restaurants dataset from Yelp that were provided for the RecSys 2013 competition. We removed records that contained items that had less than 10 reviews. Table 1 contains a description of the data after the records were removed.

5.1 Topic Model Quality

In Table 2 we can see the topic model created from the restaurants dataset with 10 topics. The contextual words are highlighted. Since topics 1 to 5 appear more frequently on specific reviews than in generic ones, they have been labeled by RCMiner as contextual, the remaining are labeled as non-contextual. The first column of the Table 2 shows the ratio of frequency appearance of topics within reviews. For instance Topic 1 appears 2.03 times more in specific reviews than in generic ones. As we can see in Table 2 contextual words appear more frequently in topics with high ratio than in topics with lower ratio.

Table 3 shows that topic models that are richer in contextual words are obtained if topic models are created only with nouns of reviews compared to using all the types of words of reviews. Using only specific reviews leads to context-richer topics in the hotels dataset, but in the restaurants dataset the same does not hold. For separation scores there is not a big difference between using nouns or all types of words. For separation scores we use a value of $\gamma = 0.5$. The baselines in Table 3 are the topic models created from all reviews using all types of words, we can see that there is an improvement on creating topic models with just nouns. Note that for the cases where all reviews are used for building the

Ratio	Word 1	Word 2	Word 3	Word 4	Word 5
2.03	night	dinner	friend	saturday	friday
1.61	lunch	today	day	friend	yesterday
1.34	time	couple	week	minute	hour
1.10	breakfast	morning	sunday	club	day
1.07	review	yelp	experience	star	read
0.99	scottsdale	location	town	experience	tempe
0.93	restaurant	phoenix	area	mexican	week
0.85	chicken	pizza	burger	sandwich	cheese
0.75	place	area	bar	love	home
0.72	food	service	mexican	atmosphere	price

Table 2: Yelp Restaurant topic model (Top-5 words)

Dataset	Part-of-speech	Review Type	Topic Model Score	Separation Score
Yelp Hotel	All	All	0.019	-
Yelp Hotel	All	Specific	0.025	**0.509**
Yelp Hotel	Nouns	All	0.037	-
Yelp Hotel	Nouns	Specific	**0.046**	0.504
Yelp Restaurant	All	All	0.003	-
Yelp Restaurant	All	Specific	0.007	**0.498**
Yelp Restaurant	Nouns	All	**0.019**	-
Yelp Restaurant	Nouns	Specific	0.014	0.494

Table 3: Topic model scores across the different datasets

topic model, the separation score can not be calculated since all the topics would be marked as contextual, having $|NCT| = 0$, which makes Equation 4 fail.

5.2 Recommendations

To evaluate our system and compare it with others, we opted to use the RiVal [15] evaluation framework for recommender systems. Each record in the dataset $\langle\langle u, i, R_{ui}\rangle, r_{ui}\rangle$ is transformed to one in which reviews are represented by their corresponding contextual topic vectors, $\langle\langle u, i, c_1, \ldots, c_{|CT|}\rangle, r_{ui}\rangle$. Then, we split the dataset into training and testing sets. First, we train the recommender using only the records of the training set. Then, we test, in which we simulate that the query the user writes is the review R_{ui}, and measure the RMSE and MAE using only the elements in the test set. We repeat this step 5 times, doing 5-fold cross validation. We compared ourselves against several non-context-aware recommender systems algorithms contained in CARSKit ([19]).

In Tables 4 and 5 we can see the results of comparing Rich-Context against five well known recommender systems. We can see that in both datasets we are able to achieve the best rating prediction. The difference between our approach and the pure factorization machines approach is that ours uses the contextual vector as side information, along with the ratings, whereas the factorization machines just uses the ratings. The implementation is the same, the difference lies in that for factorization machines the dataset is composed of records in the form of $\langle\langle u, i\rangle, r_{ui}\rangle$ and for Rich-context the records are $\langle\langle u, i, c_1, \ldots, c_{|CT|}\rangle, r_{ui}\rangle$.

Algorithm	RMSE	MAE
Rich-Context 50 Topics	**0.964**	**0.762**
Rich-Context 30 Topics	0.966	0.753
Rich-Context 10 Topics	0.967	0.759
Factorization-Machines	0.986	0.771
BiasedMF	1.090	0.847
SlopeOne	1.165	0.909
BPMF	1.322	1.049
NMF	1.489	1.143

Table 4: Rating prediction performance on the Yelp Hotels dataset

Algorithm	RMSE	MAE
Rich-Context 50 Topics	**1.019**	**0.803**
Rich-Context 30 Topics	1.019	0.802
Factorization-Machines	1.047	0.824
Rich-Context 10 Topics	1.048	0.824
SlopeOne	1.278	0.973
BPMF	1.305	1.018
BiasedMF	1.333	1.033
NMF	1.378	1.055

Table 5: Rating prediction performance on the Yelp Restaurants dataset

For evaluating the Top-N performance of RCRecommender we are currently running experiments using a methodology based on [7], with results expected soon.

6 CONCLUSIONS

We have presented Rich-Context, a context-driven recommender system that can mine contextual information from users reviews without the need of keywords. The fact that we do not need to define keywords allows the recommender to have a wider range of contextual situations and make more accurate recommendations. We also introduced new metrics to measure the quality of topic models in terms of context-richness. Tests show that Rich-Context has better performance compared against five other well established recommendation algorithms in terms of rating prediction.

Our immediate plans are to evaluate the Top-N performance of Rich-Context and to compare it against context-aware recommenders from CARSKit. We also want to include sentiment analysis as side-information along with context and test it on other recommendation engines that support side-information besides Factorization Machines. To continue our work in building topic models, we would like to find how to improve topic models in terms of their separation scores. We would also like to use the generated topic models to produce explanations of recommendations. Finally, we would like to explore how our recommender performs in cold-start scenarios.

ACKNOWLEDGMENTS

This work is supported by the Science Foundation Ireland(SFI) under Grant Number SFI/12/RC/2289. I would also like to thank my supervisor Dr. Derek Bridge for his contributions.

REFERENCES

[1] Gediminas Adomavicius and Alexander Tuzhilin. 2011. Context-Aware Recommender Systems. In *Recommender Systems Handbook*, Francesco Ricci, Lior Rokach, Bracha Shapira, and Paul B. Kantor (Eds.). Springer US, 217–253. https://doi.org/10.1007/978-0-387-85820-3_7

[2] Konstantin Bauman and Alexander Tuzhilin. 2014. Discovering contextual information from user reviews for recommendation purposes. In *1st Workshop on New Trends in Content-based Recommender Systems co-located with the 8th ACM Conference on Recommender Systems.* ACM, Foster City, Silicon Valley, California, USA, 2–9.

[3] Mark Belford, Brian Mac Namee, and Derek Greene. 2016. Ensemble Topic Modeling via Matrix Factorization. In *24th Irish Conference on Artificial Intelligence and Cognitive Science.*

[4] David M. Blei, Andrew Y. Ng, and Michael I. Jordan. 2003. Latent Dirichlet Allocation. *J. Mach. Learn. Res.* 3 (March 2003), 993–1022. http://dl.acm.org/citation.cfm?id=944919.944937

[5] Guanliang Chen and Li Chen. 2015. Augmenting service recommender systems by incorporating contextual opinions from user reviews. *User Modeling and User-Adapted Interaction* 25, 3 (2015), 295–329. https://doi.org/10.1007/s11257-015-9157-3

[6] Li Chen, Guanliang Chen, and Feng Wang. 2015. Recommender systems based on user reviews: the state of the art. *User Modeling and User-Adapted Interaction* 25, 2 (2015), 99–154. https://doi.org/10.1007/s11257-015-9155-5

[7] Paolo Cremonesi, Yehuda Koren, and Roberto Turrin. 2010. Performance of Recommender Algorithms on Top-n Recommendation Tasks. In *Proceedings of the Fourth ACM Conference on Recommender Systems (RecSys '10).* ACM, New York, NY, USA, 39–46. https://doi.org/10.1145/1864708.1864721

[8] Qiming Diao, Minghui Qiu, Chao-Yuan Wu, Alexander J. Smola, Jing Jiang, and Chong Wang. 2014. Jointly Modeling Aspects, Ratings and Sentiments for Movie Recommendation (JMARS). In *Proceedings of the 20th ACM SIGKDD International Conference on Knowledge Discovery and Data Mining (KDD '14).* ACM, New York, NY, USA, 193–202. https://doi.org/10.1145/2623330.2623758

[9] T. L. Griffiths and M. Steyvers. 2004. Finding scientific topics. *Proceedings of the National Academy of Sciences* 101, Suppl. 1 (April 2004), 5228–5235.

[10] Negar Hariri, Yong Zheng, Bamshad Mobasher, and Robin Burke. 2011. Context-aware recommendation based on review mining. *Proceedings of the 9th Workshop on Intelligent Techniques for Web Personalization & Recommender Systems..* http://ceur-ws.org/Vol-756/

[11] Alexandros Karatzoglou, Xavier Amatriain, Linas Baltrunas, and Nuria Oliver. 2010. Multiverse Recommendation: N-dimensional Tensor Factorization for Context-aware Collaborative Filtering. In *Proceedings of the Fourth ACM Conference on Recommender Systems (RecSys '10).* ACM, New York, NY, USA, 79–86. https://doi.org/10.1145/1864708.1864727

[12] Julian McAuley and Jure Leskovec. 2013. Hidden Factors and Hidden Topics: Understanding Rating Dimensions with Review Text. In *Proceedings of the 7th ACM Conference on Recommender Systems (RecSys '13).* ACM, New York, NY, USA, 165–172. https://doi.org/10.1145/2507157.2507163

[13] Roberto Pagano, Paolo Cremonesi, Martha Larson, Balázs Hidasi, Domonkos Tikk, Alexandros Karatzoglou, and Massimo Quadrana. 2016. The Contextual Turn: From Context-Aware to Context-Driven Recommender Systems. In *Proceedings of the 10th ACM Conference on Recommender Systems (RecSys '16).* ACM, New York, NY, USA, 249–252. https://doi.org/10.1145/2959100.2959136

[14] Steffen Rendle. 2012. Factorization Machines with libFM. *ACM Trans. Intell. Syst. Technol.* 3, 3, Article 57 (May 2012), 22 pages. https://doi.org/10.1145/2168752.2168771

[15] Alan Said and Alejandro Bellogín. 2014. Comparative Recommender System Evaluation: Benchmarking Recommendation Frameworks. In *Proceedings of the 8th ACM Conference on Recommender Systems (RecSys '14).* ACM, New York, NY, USA, 129–136. https://doi.org/10.1145/2645710.2645746

[16] Mark Steyvers and Tom Griffiths. 2007. *Probabilistic Topic Models.* Lawrence Erlbaum Associates. http://www.worldcat.org/isbn/1410615340

[17] Yong Zheng, Robin Burke, and Bamshad Mobasher. 2013. Recommendation with Differential Context Weighting. In *User Modeling, Adaptation, and Personalization*, Sandra Carberry, Stephan Weibelzahl, Alessandro Micarelli, and Giovanni Semeraro (Eds.). Lecture Notes in Computer Science, Vol. 7899. Springer Berlin Heidelberg, 152–164. https://doi.org/10.1007/978-3-642-38844-6_13

[18] Yong Zheng, Bamshad Mobasher, and Robin Burke. 2014. CSLIM: Contextual SLIM Recommendation Algorithms. In *Proceedings of the 8th ACM Conference on Recommender Systems (RecSys '14).* ACM, New York, NY, USA, 301–304. https://doi.org/10.1145/2645710.2645756

[19] Yong Zheng, Bamshad Mobasher, and Robin Burke. 2015. Carskit: A Java-Based Context-Aware Recommendation Engine. In *Data Mining Workshop (ICDMW), 2015 IEEE International Conference on.* IEEE, 1668–1671.

The Exploration-Exploitation Trade-off in Interactive Recommender Systems

Andrea Barraza-Urbina
Insight Centre for Data Analytics, NUI Galway, Ireland
andrea.barraza@insight-centre.org

ABSTRACT

Recommender Systems (RS) help users discover interesting products by means of relevant proactive suggestions. To accomplish this, RS must learn about user's unknown/unclear tastes, and constantly adapt to the dynamic nature of their environment. In this research, I focus on the notion that RS are faced with an optimization problem when generating recommendations: exploit the known user model, or explore other preferences the user might have. My PhD work aims to define the role of exploitation and exploration in RS, and propose mechanisms that would allow to balance and control this trade-off. In this extended abstract I present the motivation, related work and research plan that guide the project.

KEYWORDS

Recommendation System; Reinforcement Learning; Exploration Exploitation Trade-off; Multi-Armed bandits; Information Discovery.

1 INTRODUCTION

In face of information overload, Recommender Systems (RS) have emerged as tools that aim to guide users when navigating a large product space, ideally subtlety pushing the user outside their exploitative comfort zone towards relevant areas that he/she could explore. By offering suggestions of novel and useful products/services, a RS encourages serendipity, allowing users to "fortuitously" stumble more often on something they did not know existed, much less wanted, and might not have found on their own. Indeed, the heart and value of RS lies on notions related to discovery, such as novelty (unknown item), serendipity (unknown and useful item) and unexpectedness (unknown, useful and non-obvious item)[12].

In [2], the RS task is formalized as offering to a user item recommendations that maximize the user's utility. The challenge is that user-item utility information is mostly unknown, and RS techniques differ in their approach towards estimating unknown item relevance. In general, RS depend on explicit (e.g. a numeric rating) or implicit (e.g. click behavior) feedback about items offered by users, which serve as training examples to build over time user models of interests, preferences and likes/dislikes. In most scenarios, the RS task is depicted within the framework of supervised learning, where the goal is to predict the unknown utility of an item for a user given past samples of correct utility data. Using predictions, a conventional RS would offer suggestions in a greedy fashion, by offering products with the highest predicted utility.

This research is founded on the notion that a supervised learning approach does not take into account that RS are faced with an optimization problem: exploit the known user model, or actively explore other preferences the user might have by delivering products for which little information is known [18][13][23]. Taking the risk of exploring might reduce user short term satisfaction, nonetheless gathering more information can empower the RS so it can make better decisions in the long run.

The overall goal of this PhD work will take on the challenge of representing the RS as an open-ended Reinforcement Learning (RL) task, where the concepts of exploitation and exploration are key. This extended abstract is organized as follows: first, we introduce RL and the exploitation-exploration dilemma of interactive learning. Second, we discuss in-depth the motivation of our research and present related work. Next, we define the research questions and methods that define our thesis. Finally, we offer concluding remarks.

2 THEORETICAL BACKGROUND

In this section we will establish the conceptual foundations of the Reinforcement Learning field needed to understand the motivation and problem definition of the current research.

2.1 Reinforcement Learning

Reinforcement Learning (RL) is a branch of machine learning inspired by how humans and animals learn from trial-and-error experiences. In the RL context, a goal-oriented agent must perform a task without receiving any examples of the correct actions to perform in diverse situations. Instead, the agent receives feedback in terms of positive or negative reward signals. Examples of RL from psychological behaviorism include training a dog or in the computation field teaching a flying helicopter stunt manoeuvres [16].

The RL problem can be formalized under the following framework [21]: The learner or decision-making *agent* interacts in a sequence of discrete time steps t with an *environment*: the agent performs an *action* a_t and the environment presents the agent with its new *state* s_{t+1} and a *reward* r_{t+1}. The environment in RL is often described as a Markov Decision Process (MDP) which defines the dynamics of the world in response to the agent's actions. The agent behaves following a *policy* that determines for all states/situations an action to perform. The agent's goal is to learn from experience an optimal policy that when followed would maximize rewards received in the long run. It is important to highlight that each performed action has long-term consequences as it influences the environment and determines the information the agent can observe to update its policy going forward. A simplified version of the RL setting is defined by the Multi-Armed Bandit Problem [21].

RecSys '17, August 27-31, 2017, Como, Italy

ACM ISBN 978-1-4503-4652-8/17/08...$15.00
https://doi.org/10.1145/3109859.3109866

2.2 The Multi-Armed Bandit Problem

The Multi-Armed Bandit Problem (MAB) depicts a gambler/learning agent faced with the sequential decision making challenge of betting on an N-armed bandit (slot machine with N levers) for a period of t plays/steps in order to maximize its profit. The pay-off or reward offered by each arm $a \in \mathcal{A}$ is guided by a stationary and independent probability distribution R_a unknown to the gambler. The agent's final goal is to maximize its expected total cumulative reward.

At each step t, the gambler chooses one arm a to bet on and receives feedback only on the reward offered by that arm. In other words, the agent receives one sample from R_a. In this manner, the gambler's knowledge about the environment (i.e. the N-armed bandit) depends on the sequence of actions/bets it chooses during the course of its lifetime. The main challenge is, given that reward distributions are unknown to the gambler: How to discover which is the best next action to take? How to learn the real pay-off for arms?

2.3 The Exploration-Exploitation Dilemma

Given reward samples for different actions, the agent could estimate the true value or expected reward of choosing each arm/action. A natural value estimate is to use the sample mean of received rewards for action a up to time step t. Using this statistic and given enough samples, the agent's estimates would eventually converge to the true expected reward for actions given the law of large numbers. Lets define the value function $Q_t(a)$ as the agent's estimated value for action a at time step t.

In order to maximize its received reward, a potential strategy for the agent could be to always choose the arm with the greatest estimated value $\max_a Q_t(a)$ i.e. the greedy action. This is an *exploitative* strategy as the agent is in fact exploiting its current knowledge of the environment. However, though an exploitative strategy could lead to short-term high reward, the agent's knowledge is imprecise and it could mistakenly be choosing a sub-optimal action due to misleading action value estimates. Alternatively, selecting non-greedy actions would help improve the agent's value estimates for arms that otherwise might not have been chosen. This is an *exploratory* strategy. Exploration could sacrifice immediate reward in order to refine the agent's knowledge, thus improving the agent's chances of finding the true optimal action and increasing long term reward.

Overall, the agent must explore to search for the optimal action, but also, it must use what it has learned and choose the best action as often as possible to maximize reward [4]. There is a clear trade-off between exploration and exploitation: both are necessary to achieve the agent's goal but cannot be carried out at the same time [21].

2.4 Action Selection Strategies

Balancing the trade-off between exploitation and exploration is a key and distinctive challenge in RL, and has been studied for a long time. This section will present action selection strategies which aim to balance the trade-off and are the most relevant to our work.

A simple approach is provided by the *ϵ-greedy* policy. This strategy selects the greedy action (exploits) with probability $1-\epsilon$ and selects a random action (explores) with probability ϵ, where $0 \leq \epsilon \leq 1$ [21][4]. A disadvantage of the ϵ-greedy approach is that exploration is random and chooses equally between actions. This strategy runs the risk of over-exploring actions that have proven to be inferior and overlooking promising actions. The *Upper Confidence Bound* (UCB) algorithm offers an alternative that explores in accordance to the agent's confidence of estimated values [4]. UCB chooses at time step t the arm a that maximizes the value for $Q_t(a) + \sqrt{\frac{2\ln t}{t_a}}$, where t_a is the total number of samples the agent has acquired for arm a. UCB considers exploitation by favoring arms with high value estimates, and as well considers exploration by favoring arms for which the agent knows less about in comparison to other arms. The UCB algorithm practices *"optimism in the face of uncertainty"* by prioritizing arms that have the highest potential to provide high pay-off. As the agent gathers more samples the confidence bounds become tighter, and thus the agent would select more often greedy actions. Finally, *Thompson Sampling* offers a Bayesian approach towards balancing the trade-off [7][3][8]. Given rewards, the posterior probability of success for each arm is estimated. At each iteration, the algorithm samples each arm and chooses the action that maximizes expected reward.

3 MOTIVATION AND RELATED WORK

We believe that RL can offer a proper framework to represent RS that learn from evaluative feedback when interacting with an uncertain environment. In this section we identify how the exploration-exploitation trade-off already plays an important role in current research towards solving RS challenges.

Firstly, from an exploitation-exploration lens, we would like to address all RS solutions aiming to maximize user immediate satisfaction as *exploitative strategies* given their greedy nature. These type of solutions have already been well worked in the RS area. However, exploitative strategies alone have been shown not to manage well issues such as the cold-start problem [13], active learning [18], and achieving beyond accuracy metrics [12]. In order to enhance exploitative strategies, *exploratory strategies* have been proposed. Exploratory strategies are focused on encouraging the user to browse unknown sections of the product catalog, while attempting to gain new and useful information about user preferences. We motivate our work in the need to balance exploratory and exploitative goals in order to achieve high long-run RS performance.

3.1 Learning to Adapt

Core challenges arise as complexity is added to the RS problem definition to better reflect real-world use cases. In practice, user preferences are generally unclear and evolving, and thus the user can shift their opinion about an item, e.g. given contextual factors [8], changing user interests, conflicting short-term and long-term user preferences [18], among others. In this case, it does not make sense to consider a user's feedback for an item to be a static, independent and true indicator of the item's utility. As well, we should consider the RS's environment to be dynamic: the product catalog can change as items are added, updated and removed and new users constantly arrive. Given the dynamic and nondeterministic nature of the RS's environment, it has become clear that a successful RS must continuously and quickly learn to adapt in order to achieve its goals.

In many domains, such as computational advertisement and news, the product catalog undergoes frequent changes and new visitors arrive constantly. As a result, services must regularly learn to overcome nonstop cold-start issues. In [13], the authors model news recommendation as a MAB (view section 2.2) that can consider contextual information about users and items in order to maximize total user clicks. The authors adapt the context-free UCB to propose the LinUCB algorithm, which can handle changing arms (news stories) and multiple users. Evaluating a contextual bandit can be "frustratingly difficult", given its dependence on the individual decisions at each time step [13]. The authors highlight that online evaluation is costly and evaluating based on simulated data can introduce bias [13]. One of the main contributions of [13] is their offline evaluation approach based on i.i.d. logged data.

Another adaptive approach is proposed in [22], where Amazon Stream is presented as a visual browsing tool that aims to replicate the in-store browsing experience. Authors use Thompson Sampling to learn the contribution of item features towards an item's click probability. The algorithm balances the selection of exploitative (relevant/popular) or explorative (new/underexposed) item features to generate a mixed list of items for the user to navigate.

Alternatively, in [20], the authors view the RS problem as a sequential optimization problem and model the dynamics of the RS as a Markov Decision Process (MDP). The authors highlight that MDPs are better suited to consider the long-term value of a recommendation and the sequential nature of user choices. As well, [14] use an MDP approach, in their case to adaptively select the appropriate interaction strategy for a conversational RS.

Work in adopting techniques from RL for RS has been carried out for specific domains and use cases as early as 1997, when [10] proposed Q-Learning for web page recommendations. Still, we believe that valuable work can be found in expanding current research to consider a more holistic view towards defining the role of exploitation and exploration in the overall framework of RS research.

3.2 Exploration and Active learning

Active Learning (AL) is concerned with achieving the exploratory goal of learning about users' tastes, and is especially important when facing sparsity and cold-start problems [19]. It is a type of semi-supervised learning, where the system actively chooses the most informative items to query the user for feedback. The goal is to retrieve the most useful information about a user in the least amount of queries to achieve a better representation of the user's preferences. In order to choose items, AL must take into account several considerations, for example [18]: How to learn without compromising the user's experience? Is the user able to evaluate the item? What is the cost for evaluating an item?

AL solutions generally focus on eliciting feedback from new users by preselecting a set of items that once rated can help bootstrap the user profile [17][18]. Other approaches focus on methods to select items for AL, for example in [19], the authors propose a mechanism to determine an item's explorative value by its capacity to reduce uncertainty and increase coverage. However, according to [18]: "Traditionally AL does not consider the trade-off of exploration (learning user's preferences) and exploitation (utilizing user's preferences)". Owing to the potential of AL techniques as exploratory strategies and the need for exploration across the lifetime of the RS, we view important work in defining solutions that can embed AL seamlessly with exploitative approaches by defining adaptive solutions that can select which type of exploration is needed in different situations.

3.3 Exploratory and Exploitative Evaluation

There is a growing consensus in RS research that standard metrics focused on rating prediction accuracy are not enough to measure the real-world value of RS [12][9][15]. Thus, beyond accuracy objectives have been defined to better quantify the quality of RS from different perspectives, mainly: diversity, novelty, serendipity and coverage. From our exploitation-exploration lens, we could view accuracy-based metrics as those that measure the quality of exploitative RS strategies, and beyond accuracy metrics as those measuring the quality of explorative RS strategies. Intuitively, this separation could make sense, and various works have identified trade-off situations indicating that an increase of beyond accuracy metrics generally incurs in a loss of accuracy [5][12][11][18]. However, trade-off situations have also been identified between beyond accuracy metrics themselves [12], or cases in which both types of metrics can be increased at the same time [1]. In general, the relation between types of metrics has not been fully determined, and we cannot state their is a clear-cut separation between explorative and exploitative types. Nonetheless, it seems reasonable to conjecture that each metric can have a mixture of exploitative and explorative characteristics.

For example, in [5], we studied the role of exploration and exploitation in relation to diversity and introduced the XPLODIV diversification technique [5][6]. Our approach can be tuned to either offer: (a) diverse exploitation: by offering recommendations that would cover the variety of the user's known preferences, or (b) diverse exploration: by offering diverse novel products to discover what other preferences the user could have and to incentivize users to explore the unknown.

Though an absolute separation between explorative and exploitative measures might not be possible, if we accept that proposed RS quality metrics measure the system's ability to achieve both exploratory and exploitative goals, then it should be expected for the RS to be required an ability of balancing exploratory and exploitative strategies across its lifetime. Towards this goal, it can be valuable to study both the short-term and long-term relations between metrics considering their explorative/exploitative characteristics. As well, this point of view could help to better understand trade-off situations, define which are the tolerable compromises between metrics and even the desired metric values to obtain long-term high performance for different types of users given different situations.

4 RESEARCH QUESTIONS

We have argued that balancing the exploitation-exploration dilemma is key to the long-term success of a RS. Also, we introduced the notion of exploratory and exploitative RS strategies in section 3. However, these strategies can be seen as two extremes of a spectrum of strategies, which progresses from those that generate item recommendations which are: purely exploratory, through those that offer a mixture of both explore-exploit characteristics to finally those that offer items that are purely exploitative. We will refer to strategies that intentionally generate item recommendations with both explore-exploit characteristics as *hybrid explore-exploit strategies*.

We propose our first research questions around three possible approaches to incorporate the exploration-exploitation trade-off, considering the defined explore-exploit strategies, in a RS: (1) Naive switching: chooses in a naive/simple way between a pure exploration or a pure exploitation strategy, (2) Adaptive switching: chooses between a pure exploration or a pure exploitation strategy based on an informed heuristic, (3) Adaptive mixture: smoothly transitions along the spectrum of exploitative and exploratory item recommendations by using a hybrid explore-exploit strategy. Lastly, our final research question aims to investigate how the user can influence the exploration/exploitation trade-off. More specifically, we address the following research questions:

(RQ1) *Do recommender systems that offer naive switching between pure exploration and pure exploitation perform better than those that do not consider exploration at all?* We want to address the need for a naive strategy to enhance exploitative RS approaches. Our hypothesis is that a simple switching hybrid RS can perform better in the long run than a purely exploitative RS. In this case, the RS can alternate between the two strategies: pure exploration $\epsilon\%$ of the time and pure exploitation otherwise. Diverse experiment set-ups for different strategy combinations and values of ϵ should be defined. In order to carry out any type of tests we need to define an evaluation methodology that will serve our purpose across the different stages of our research project. The initial design of this methodology is presented in section 5. In attacking RQ1 we will aim to test and refine our evaluation methodology which in itself will work as a contribution of the PhD thesis.

(RQ2) *Do recommender systems that offer adaptive switching between pure exploration and pure exploitation perform better than those that offer naive switching?* We aim to study solutions that can dynamically switch between explore and exploit strategies in an adaptive manner, given the current situation and domain characteristics. Towards this, we can find inspiration in context-aware mechanisms (e.g. by exploring when a contextual change is detected as in [8]) and in MAB approaches (exploratory or exploitative strategies as arms). For all experiments we would use our evaluation methodology.

(RQ3) *Do recommender systems that offer an adaptive mixture of both exploration and exploitation perform better than strategies switching between pure exploitation and pure exploration?* We would like to study solutions that are not purely explorative nor exploitative (as in RQ1 and RQ2) but that merge in a single strategy both exploratory and exploitative characteristics. In this case, exploration can be seamlessly embedded to a RS approach without being a separate strategy. Amazon Stream [22] is an example, as each item recommendation could have both exploitative and exploratory characteristics. In relation to these approaches we would continue our study of RL literature in order to identify other potential solutions that can smoothly integrate and balance exploration with exploitation. To compare approaches we would use our evaluation methodology.

(RQ4) *Can exploitation-exploration aware recommender systems be extended to allow for user guided navigation?* This research question intends to study mechanisms by which the previously studied methods can be extended to allow for user guided navigation. A complementary question can be: Can exploitation-exploration aware RS be tuned to optimize different metrics? Our aim is to define how these approaches can be controlled or influenced directly by the user in order to offer different levels of exploration and exploitation. Any proposed approach would have to be evaluated in an online fashion.

5 EVALUATION METHODOLOGY

We propose to set-up an experimental framework that would allow us to study the role of exploration and exploitation for a RS approach when interacting with a given RS use case. Our setting will reflect the RL framework (view section 2.1) where time will be defined as discrete time steps.

Goals. The goal of our experimental evaluation is to compare different RS approaches across time in terms of final performance and consistency for a set of metrics. Given a rigorous evaluation we will analyze gain/loss values among metrics across time steps and observe trade-off situations between the cumulative value of metrics. We would address questions such as: What is the rate of learning measured in terms of coverage? Which strategy achieves the highest final cumulative reward? For the purpose of analysis, we will take inspiration from [5] and separate recommended items in to exploratory and exploitative items. With this separation we can answer questions such as: What percentage of each type is recommended the most? Which type received higher reward? In which situations are each type recommended? As well, we could analyze: What is the cost of exploration/exploitation in terms of a given metric? For example, If the RS policy decides to exploit is there a loss in novelty? Finally, as a side goal, we can study the exploratory or exploitative characteristics of metrics themselves, addressing challenges introduced in section 3.3.

Experimental Set-Up. In first place, we map the elements of the RL framework (view section 2.1) to a RS scenario as follows: the RS is a learning agent which at each time step suggests an item given a context/state from the environment. The environment represents the dynamics of items and users across time steps. After recommending an item, the RS agent will receive a reward. The agent's policy will be determined by the RS strategy being studied. In our simplest configuration, the context received by the agent will be a user for which the recommendation is intended, and the reward will be in the form of a binary feedback. Complexity can be added to the model, e.g. to consider delayed rewards. We do not aim to evaluate the predictive capacity of the RS approach. The learning agent will initialize without knowledge about its environment and we must model different types of environments for the agent to interact with. We aim to evaluate the agent with three types of environments: (1) static ratings, (2) dynamic ratings and (3) online users. For each environment we assume to have complete information of the world and its dynamics e.g. we have complete knowledge of user preferences. This is only true for the case of online users. To model the static rating world, we plan to use current rating data sets by applying matrix completion strategies or by selecting subsections of the rating matrix that have close to full coverage. More work needs to be carried out to model the dynamic world potentially looking in to agent simulations. Monte Carlo simulations will be run for each experiment set-up as described in [24].

6 CONCLUSIONS

In this paper we have argued that the RS task should be modeled as an RL problem and not only under the view of supervised learning. We have argued that balancing the exploitation and exploration dilemma is key to the long-term success of a RS, leading to benefits such as: (a) increase novelty/serendipity thereby facing the filter bubble, (b) improve catalog coverage and increase overall item visibility, (c) deal with both user and item cold-start problems (d) respond to dynamic user preferences or evolving user intent (e) react to contextual changes, and (f) dynamically adapt to changing business goals. Overall, this PhD thesis aims to contribute an in-depth study on the role of exploration and exploitation in RS, an RL-based RS approach that can seamlessly balance exploitation and exploration and finally the use of the proposed approach in the use case of an exploratory search system.

ACKNOWLEDGMENTS

This publication has emanated from research supported in part by a research grant from Science Foundation Ireland (SFI) under Grant Number SFI/12/RC/2289 (Insight).

REFERENCES

[1] Panagiotis Adamopoulos and Alexander Tuzhilin. 2011. On Unexpectedness in Recommender Systems: Or How to Expect the Unexpected.. In *DiveRS@ RecSys*. 11–18.

[2] Gediminas Adomavicius and Alexander Tuzhilin. 2005. Toward the next generation of recommender systems: A survey of the state-of-the-art and possible extensions. *IEEE transactions on knowledge and data engineering* 17, 6 (2005), 734–749.

[3] Shipra Agrawal and Navin Goyal. 2013. Thompson Sampling for Contextual Bandits with Linear Payoffs.. In *ICML (3)*. 127–135.

[4] Peter Auer, Nicolo Cesa-Bianchi, and Paul Fischer. 2002. Finite-time analysis of the multiarmed bandit problem. *Machine learning* 47, 2-3 (2002), 235–256.

[5] Andrea Barraza-Urbina, Benjamin Heitmann, Conor Hayes, and Angela Carrillo Ramos. 2015. XPLODIV: An Exploitation-Exploration Aware Diversification Approach for Recommender Systems.. In *FLAIRS Conference*. 483–488.

[6] Andrea Barraza-Urbina, Benjamin Heitmann, Angela Carrillo Ramos, and Conor Hayes. 2015. *XploDiv: Diversification Approach for Recommender Systems*. Technical Report. INSIGHT Centre for Data Analytics, National University of Ireland, Galway.

[7] Olivier Chapelle and Lihong Li. 2011. An empirical evaluation of thompson sampling. In *Advances in neural information processing systems*. 2249–2257.

[8] Negar Hariri, Bamshad Mobasher, and Robin Burke. 2015. Adapting to User Preference Changes in Interactive Recommendation.. In *IJCAI*. 4268–4274.

[9] Dietmar Jannach and Gediminas Adomavicius. 2016. Recommendations with a Purpose. In *Proceedings of the 10th ACM Conference on Recommender Systems (RecSys '16)*. ACM, New York, NY, USA, 7–10. https://doi.org/10.1145/2959100.2959186

[10] Thorsten Joachims, Dayne Freitag, Tom Mitchell, et al. 1997. Webwatcher: A tour guide for the world wide web. In *IJCAI (1)*. Citeseer, 770–777.

[11] Marius Kaminskas and Derek Bridge. 2014. Measuring surprise in recommender systems. In *Proceedings of the Workshop on Recommender Systems Evaluation: Dimensions and Design (Workshop Programme of the 8th ACM Conference on Recommender Systems)*. Citeseer.

[12] Marius Kaminskas and Derek Bridge. 2016. Diversity, Serendipity, Novelty, and Coverage: A Survey and Empirical Analysis of Beyond-Accuracy Objectives in Recommender Systems. *ACM Transactions on Interactive Intelligent Systems (TiiS)* 7, 1 (2016), 2.

[13] Lihong Li, Wei Chu, John Langford, and Robert E Schapire. 2010. A contextual-bandit approach to personalized news article recommendation. In *Proceedings of the 19th international conference on World wide web*. ACM, 661–670.

[14] Tariq Mahmood and Francesco Ricci. 2007. Learning and adaptivity in interactive recommender systems. In *Proceedings of the ninth international conference on Electronic commerce*. ACM, 75–84.

[15] Sean M McNee, John Riedl, and Joseph A Konstan. 2006. Being accurate is not enough: how accuracy metrics have hurt recommender systems. In *CHI'06 extended abstracts on Human factors in computing systems*. ACM, 1097–1101.

[16] Andrew Y Ng. 2003. *Shaping and policy search in reinforcement learning*. Ph.D. Dissertation. University of California, Berkeley.

[17] Al Mamunur Rashid, Istvan Albert, Dan Cosley, Shyong K Lam, Sean M McNee, Joseph A Konstan, and John Riedl. 2002. Getting to know you: learning new user preferences in recommender systems. In *Proceedings of the 7th international conference on Intelligent user interfaces*. ACM, 127–134.

[18] Francesco Ricci, Lior Rokach, and Bracha Shapira (Eds.). 2015. *Recommender Systems Handbook*. Springer.

[19] Neil Rubens and Masashi Sugiyama. 2007. Influence-based collaborative active learning. In *Proceedings of the 2007 ACM conference on Recommender systems*. ACM, 145–148.

[20] Guy Shani, David Heckerman, and Ronen I Brafman. 2005. An MDP-based recommender system. *Journal of Machine Learning Research* 6, Sep (2005), 1265–1295.

[21] Richard S Sutton and Andrew G Barto. 1998. *Reinforcement learning: An introduction*. Vol. 1. MIT press Cambridge.

[22] Choon Hui Teo, Houssam Nassif, Daniel Hill, Sriram Srinivasan, Mitchell Goodman, Vijai Mohan, and SVN Vishwanathan. 2016. Adaptive, Personalized Diversity for Visual Discovery. In *Proceedings of the 10th ACM Conference on Recommender Systems*. ACM, 35–38.

[23] Xinxi Wang, Yi Wang, David Hsu, and Ye Wang. 2014. Exploration in interactive personalized music recommendation: a reinforcement learning approach. *ACM Transactions on Multimedia Computing, Communications, and Applications (TOMM)* 11, 1 (2014), 7.

[24] John White. 2012. *Bandit algorithms for website optimization*. " O'Reilly Media, Inc.".

User Preferences Analysis using Visual Stimuli

Peter Gaspar*
Slovak University of Technology in Bratislava
Bratislava, Slovakia
name_surname@stuba.sk

ABSTRACT

Recommender systems aim at enhancing user experience on the Web by employing the results of users behavior analysis for recommending items. However, user behavior is usually influenced by various aspects. Even though visual stimuli greatly influence almost every part of our life, it is yet poorly reflected in the domain of recommendation. In our work, we study the impact of visual stimuli (specifically images) on recommendation process on the Web. We focus on the domains where the impact of images is substantial (e.g., movies and shopping). First results of our experiments suggest that features extracted from the images are able to improve the ranking of the current recommendation approaches.

CCS CONCEPTS

• **Information systems** → **Recommender systems**; *Personalization*; • **Computing methodologies** → *Ranking*; *Learning to rank*; Image representations;

KEYWORDS

Top-N recommender; content-based; hybrid; image features; rank; learning to rank

1 INTRODUCTION AND RELATED WORK

Study of user behavior on the Web has been a widely-researched topic for many years. Researchers are trying to analyze how people interact with the content and which decision-makers influence them the most. Such knowledge allows us to design qualitatively better methods for adaptation and personalization tasks.

Recommender systems have been used as one of the methods to enhance user experience on the Web. Their main goal is to provide a user the suggestions of items he would likely consume. Recommender systems are particularly useful in those decision-making processes that suffer from the problem of information overload, such as which movies to watch, which items to buy, what music to listen, or what news to read [25].

Collaborative filtering aims to find a similarity between the behavior of two or more users. In other words, for a given user, we try to find users that have a similar taste (user-based collaborative filtering) or for a given item, we try to find items that are consumed similarly by other users (item-based collaborative filtering). Other recommendations coming from these users are then considered to be relevant for a given user.

Content-based recommenders rely on the item and user descriptions in order to build user model and capture user preferences [25]. Many state-of-the-art approaches focus on extracting *textual features*: the properties of items (extracted from the metadata), or item text content (relevant words from text description). This is specifically important in the domains where textual features play an important role and are able to describe items [14, 23, 24].

Recommenders often suffer from the problem of the lack of information about the items (or users) – also called *the cold-start problem*. In case of content-based recommenders, it is necessary to have enough features in order to sufficiently represent the item – such as categories, keywords, or item descriptions. These item descriptors are commonly represented as a text. However, there are some domains (such as movies, e-shops, or fashion) where multimedia is present and can serve as a good source to describe the items. These domains may actually benefit from features extracted from the multimedia (e.g., images, audio or video [1, 2, 22]).

As discussed in [6], the major problem with approaches relying on textual features is the reliability of such features. One example are e-shops where people choose between many items based on their properties. In this case users are limited in the interaction with items (physical contact) and have to rely on the information provided by the seller. Textual descriptions of the products are not always sufficient enough to describe, how the product actually looks like. Since the images (of the products) are usually connected to these items and presented simultaneously with the item textual descriptions, they can be considered to be visual stimuli and make a user's attention. Then, features extracted from images can be used to describe the user preferences. Moreover, these images may have an impact on users' behavior.

There have been many studies that discuss the importance of visual stimuli on the user preferences. Di. et al. [6] reported that a product's salability could be improved by showing a user more product images with higher-quality. He et. al studied in [11] the visualization patterns that can influence users while choosing from fashion products. They extracted visual preferences and built a personalized user model that was also able to reflect the temporal fashion trends.

Deldjoo el al. [4] used the movie tags with the low-level visual features (e.g., motion, color, lighting) from the movies to build a content-based recommender. They also employed a fusion method to combine these features. Yu et al. [31] recommended goods images using low-level visual features. These features were also weighted

*Supervisors: Maria Bielikova, Michal Kompan, Slovak University of Technology in Bratislava

RecSys '17, August 27-31, 2017, Como, Italy

ACM ISBN 978-1-4503-4652-8/17/08...$15.00
https://doi.org/.1145/3109859.3120955

and tailored to various user preferences (e.g., the color of the product). Neidhardt et al. focused on the problem of eliciting user preferences in the travel domain [21].

We believe that images have an impact on user's behavior on the Web. However, in the domain of recommenders, this issue has not been properly addressed in current approaches yet.

We study the user behavior in the domain of recommender systems, analyze how to capture visual features, and how these visual features could be incorporated into the recommendation generation. We have identified the potential in improving existing content-based recommendation approaches.

To summarize, to achieve our goals, in my thesis we:

- analyze the influence of visual stimuli on the user during the decision-making process,
- use visual features extracted from the items in the selected domain to enhance item descriptions,
- study the impact of visual features on user behavior in Top-N list of items,
- propose and evaluate a personalized Top-N recommender that uses visual features.

In this paper, we analyze how the visual stimuli can be used to enrich item content descriptions. We present our first analysis and conducted experiments to support our assumptions.

2 VISUAL FEATURES ANALYSIS

Prior to method proposal, we opted for the analysis of the movies features. We aimed to reveal whether the visual features can describe a movie in the similar manner than content features or these features can be rather used to extract more information about a movie.

Here we focus on the *genre* attribute of a movie. An importance of genres in movie recommendation task has been reported by many researches (e.g., [20]). In content-based recommendation genres play an important role, since they reflect user preferences. However, genres are still too abstract characteristics of the movies.

We defined the following research questions:

- Can we utilize the visual features to represent the movie genres?
- Can visual features be used to extend the basic movie's metadata (e.g., genre) in the recommendation task?

To answer these questions, we conducted the analysis of visual features extracted from the movie posters. Our goal was to compare the similarity of movies within genres.

2.1 Feature extraction

We pick the MovieLens 20M Dataset [10], which contains 27 278 movies and corresponding 20 millions usersâĂŹ ratings. Each movie is labelled with one or more genres (dataset contains 19 unique genres; each movie is labelled in average with 2 genres). Using The Movie Database public API[1] we extended the dataset by adding the main poster and a plot (of a movie). Although the dataset does not contain information about whether a user sees a particular poster, we do not need to take this information into consideration. Here, we focus on the extraction of the visual features from the images in order to be able to compare them with the content features.

To analyze posters, we need to extract suitable image features. We consider two types of the features:

(1) *low-level features* (e.g., based on the color characteristics),
(2) *high-level features* (e.g., based on the content of the image).

To extract *low-level features*, we opt for the Hue-Saturation-Value (HSV) color space, since we want to have a representation that is close to the human vision system (based on the [8, 28]). For each of these color dimensions (i.e., hue, saturation, value) we calculate the following features (adopted from [8]):

- mean (of values of all the pixels),
- standard deviation (of values of all the pixels),
- mean value of pixels on both diagonals.

Moreover, we analyze a share of six basic colors (red, green, blue, orange, yellow, and violet) based on the hue value. Valdez et al. investigated [29] the impact of color characteristics on user emotions using the Pleasure-Arousal-Dominance model. The Pleasure-Arousal-Dominance model is used especially in the field of psychology to estimate user emotional state by combining its components (i.e., pleasure, arousal, dominance). Based on their study we adopt coefficients that are used to calculate each emotional state.

To overcome issues such as the image rotation or the reflection, we divide the whole image matrix into 20 equally sized rectangles and calculate these features for each rectangle separately. Additionally, for each feature we apply a normalization into $\langle 0, 1 \rangle$. Finally, we end up with totally 255 low-level features for each image. High-level visual features are extracted using the pre-trained convolutional neural network Inception-v3 [27] by Google, which is based on the ImageNet dataset [5]. Convolutional neural networks have gained a lot of attraction recently, especially in the domain of object recognition (for instance, food recognition [13]). However, they are also suitable for extracting latent features [7], which may reflect user preferences and may be further used for various classification tasks.

Inception-v3 was trained to classify input image into 1000 classes that were meant to describe the content of a particular image. These classes can be utilized as the vectors of latent features for each image. In other words, instead of representing the image using pixels, image can be represented using the weights extracted from the neural network.

Inspired by [16], for each movie we pick a movie poster and let the neural network predict the probabilities of assignment into 1000 classes. Then we extract the weights of the next-to-last layer of the neural network and consider these weights to be *the high-level visual features of the movie.* For each movie, we store the vector of a total of 2048 features (normalized to $\langle 0, 1 \rangle$).

2.2 Genres analysis

By analyzing the genres of movies, we wanted to reveal whether the image features can be used to represent genres of movies. Our assumption was that if visual features are related to content features, movies falling into the same genre should be more similar than all the movies (regardless of the genre). In other words, two movies having the same genre should be more visually similar than the two movies having different genres.

[1] https://www.themoviedb.org

Table 1: Results of the analyzed movie genres (based on the low-level and high-level features extracted from images). avg_D **denotes an average distance within each pair of movies in genre,** σ **denotes a standard deviation of all the distances within genre.**

Genre	Low-level features		High-level features		No. of movies
	avg_D	σ	avg_D	σ	
Children	0.09	0.06	0.35	0.07	1 139
Animation	0.10	0.07	0.40	0.09	1 027
Adventure	0.11	0.06	0.36	0.07	2 329
Musical	0.12	0.06	0.37	0.07	1 036
Comedy	0.13	0.07	0.37	0.06	8 374
Fantasy	0.13	0.08	0.37	0.06	1 412
Romance	0.13	0.08	0.37	0.06	4 127
Sci-Fi	0.13	0.07	0.37	0.06	1 743
Horror	0.14	0.11	0.37	0.07	2 611
Drama	0.15	0.09	0.38	0.06	13 344
IMAX	0.15	0.08	0.37	0.07	196
Mystery	0.17	0.09	0.37	0.07	1 514
Action	0.19	0.10	0.34	0.06	3 520
Thriller	0.19	0.10	0.37	0.06	4 178
Documentary	0.21	0.10	0.40	0.07	2 471
Film-Noir	0.21	0.11	0.33	0.08	330
Crime	0.22	0.11	0.36	0.06	2 939
War	0.23	0.13	0.37	0.07	1 194
Western	0.33	0.15	0.34	0.07	676
ALL	0.19	0.09	0.38	0.06	26 521

We put the movies into 19 groups based on the genres assigned to them. Since in the dataset some movies are assigned to more than one genre, they appear in more than one genre group.

To analyze created groups, we compute a pairwise cosine distance between each movie from the group. The cosine distance is computed using the vectors of image features (low-level and high-level, separately). Finally, we calculate an average distance and standard deviation for each genre.

As we can see from the Table 1 low-level features can reflect the genre of the movie, since the average distance is rather low (in comparison to average distance calculated over the whole dataset) in many groups (e.g., children of musical movies). These results suggest that the similarity of movie genres can be identified using low-level features extracted from the images.

In counterpart, for the high-level features (Table 1), an average similarity in each genre group does not change significantly and does not seem to be depending on the genre of the movie. This result suggests that high-level image features may capture hidden (latent) features that are not present in the content features (e.g., genres).

3 TOWARDS A BETTER TOP-N RANK

The main task of the recommender is to generate a list of items the user would be likely interested in. However, the number of presented items is usually constrained, since the user receiving a recommendation has a limited time. Therefore, the result of recommendation is presented in the form of a list of N items sorted by the user interest, such that the most attractive item is the first in the list.

There, when evaluating the performance of a recommender, we are not only interested in whether the recommended item is really attractive for the user, but also what the position of an item in the Top-N list is [3]. Moreover, there are other metrics that study the items in a different manner than accuracy, such as the diversity of the items [32].

3.1 Hybrid recommendation approach

In our preliminary study, we developed a personalized hybrid recommender that relies on visual features to improve the results of baseline content-based Top-N recommender in terms of the rank of the recommended items. Firstly, the content-based recommender calculates the candidates. Next, the returned candidates are re-ranked using visual features extracted from the images.

Content-based recommender relies on the movies similarity calculated from the *content features* (e.g., overview, genres). Firstly, a single vector of content features for each movie is created using the standard TF-IDF model. Then, for a particular user a recommendation is done by finding the most similar movies (i.e., documents) to the movies user had previously seen (all the movies from the his profile). We employ the state-of-the-art ranking function Okapi BM25 [26], which calculates a similarity score for each movie-to-movie pair. As a result, content-based recommender creates a list of Top-N movies having the highest similarity to the movies user

Table 2: Comparison of content-based and proposed hybrid recommender. The Normalised Discounted Cumulative Gain (nDCG) and Mean Average Precision ($\overline{P}$).

	$\overline{P}$	$nDCG@10$
Content-only	0.1735	0.2463
Hybrid	0.1773	0.2504

had previously seen. A list of Top-N movies is considered to be the *candidates.*

High-level visual features extracted from the movie poster (discussed in Section 2.1) are utilized in order to re-rank candidates. Firstly, a pair-wised cosine similarity is calculated between each movie poster in the dataset. Then, a candidate generated by the content-based recommender is compared to the movies that user previously had seen, and a *visual similarity* is calculated. We compute the visual similarity between two movies as a cosine similarity between the vectors of high-level image features of the main movie posters.

We have already evaluated our approach on the MovieLens dataset (further described in the Section 2.1). For each user in the dataset we generate N movies (currently $N = 10$) from the content-based recommender (candidates) and then re-rank them using visual features. Finally, a list of N movies is returned to the user as a recommendation.

The main goal of this approach is to improve the ranking of the items generated by the baseline content-based recommender. This is closely related to the task of *learning to rank* [17], where the main goal is to enhance baseline ranking using additional knowledge about items in the list.

We evaluated the results using the metrics that are applied in the field of learning to rank, namely mean average precision and normalized discounted cumulative gain. We present the results in Table 2. Proposed hybrid recommender achieved statistically significant improvement in both metrics (p-value < 0.01).

Also we investigated the metrics on per user basis, where we found that the more ratings users have, the better results were returned by the hybrid recommender. For example, for the users having at least 1 400 ratings the hybrid recommender outperformed the content-only approach by more than 3% (an average number of ratings per user in the whole dataset was 143, maximum 9 190).

Although these results are yet preliminary, we believe that they are promising and visual features play an important role during the recommendation task.

3.2 Learning to rank using visual features

The task of Top-N recommender usually does not end up with the presentation of results. Recommender usually takes into consideration the user's behavior and the interaction with the presented items – in a form of an implicit or explicit feedback.

User feedback in the domain of recommender systems has been a well-studied area [12, 18, 19, 30]. However, existing approaches do not take into consideration the form of the presented item.

Suppose we present a result of Top-N recommendation in a form a text (e.g. list of news articles). By clicking on the n-th item in the list, we should penalize all the previous items (having rank lower than n) and improve future ranking [17]. One reasoning behind this idea is that the user has to scan all the items up-to-n until he clicks, and also, he considers these items not relevant for him (and therefore he do not seek to select any of them). Another problem occurs when the relevant item is placed too low in the presented list and the user may miss it completely [9].

However, in the case of Top-N lists where the images are also present we are not further able to rely on such assumptions. As we discussed before, by browsing the list with images, one can be influenced by the several visual stimuli. There, the decision of the user can be influenced by his preference, which is invoked by seeing a particular image.

Here we hypothesize that the ranking approach should take into consideration the visual stimuli and distinguish between (a) the case a user has not clicked on the item because of his disinterest and (b) the case that the item has not invoked his attention (due to the visual appearance).

4 CONCLUSIONS

In my thesis, we focus on the analysis of user decision-making process. We examine the influence of visual stimuli (in a form of images) on the user behavior on the Web. Using the features extracted from the images we study how images influence and invoke user preferences.

Some of our ideas are already validated by performing the analysis in the domain of movies. We propose a hybrid content-based recommender that re-ranks recommendations generated by the baseline content-based recommender. First experiments prove that visual features are able to improve both mean average precision and normalized discounted cumulative gain.

Based on the results, we believe that visual stimuli should be taken into account not only in the learning-to-rank tasks, but also in the recommendation process. However, our analysis also reveals that this approach should be personalized. Therefore, we plan to further analyze user's behavior and propose methods that would take into account different user preferences and behavior patterns. We will also analyze another existing approaches dedicated to feature extraction from the images (e.g., [15]).

Also, we plan to investigate how a different presentation of recommendations may affect user's behavior (i.e., present recommendations using only text, images, and using both elements). During this process, we will conduct not only offline, but also online experiments using the eye-tracking technology.

ACKNOWLEDGMENTS

This work was partially supported by Human Information Behavior in the Digital Space, the Slovak Research and Development Agency under the contract No. APVV-15-0508, and by Adaptation of access to information and knowledge artifacts based on interaction and collaboration within web environment, the Scientific Grant Agency of the Slovak Republic, grant No. VG 1/0646/15.

The authors would also like to thank for financial contribution from the STU Grant scheme for Support of Young Researchers.

REFERENCES

[1] Dmitry Bogdanov, MartÃŋn Haro, Ferdinand Fuhrmann, Anna XambÃş, Emilia GÃşmez, and Perfecto Herrera. 2013. Semantic audio content-based music recommendation and visualization based on user preference examples. *Information Processing & Management* 49, 1 (2013), 13 – 33. https://doi.org/10.1016/j.ipm.2012.06.004

[2] Pedro Cano, Markus Koppenberger, and Nicolas Wack. 2005. Content-based Music Audio Recommendation. In *Proceedings of the 13th Annual ACM International Conference on Multimedia (MULTIMEDIA '05)*. ACM, New York, NY, USA, 211–212. https://doi.org/10.1145/1101149.1101181

[3] Paolo Cremonesi, Yehuda Koren, and Roberto Turrin. 2010. Performance of Recommender Algorithms on Top-n Recommendation Tasks. In *Proceedings of the Fourth ACM Conference on Recommender Systems (RecSys '10)*. ACM, New York, NY, USA, 39–46. https://doi.org/10.1145/1864708.1864721

[4] Yashar Deldjoo, Mehdi Elahi, and Paolo Cremonesi. 2016. Using visual features and latent factors for movie recommendation. *CBRecSys 2016* (2016), 15.

[5] J. Deng, W. Dong, R. Socher, L. J. Li, Kai Li, and Li Fei-Fei. 2009. ImageNet: A large-scale hierarchical image database. In *2009 IEEE Conference on Computer Vision and Pattern Recognition*. 248–255. https://doi.org/10.1109/CVPR.2009.5206848

[6] Wei Di, Neel Sundaresan, Robinson Piramuthu, and Anurag Bhardwaj. 2014. Is a Picture Really Worth a Thousand Words?: - on the Role of Images in e-Commerce. In *Proceedings of the 7th ACM International Conference on Web Search and Data Mining (WSDM '14)*. ACM, New York, NY, USA, 633–642. https://doi.org/10.1145/2556195.2556226

[7] Jeff Donahue, Yangqing Jia, Oriol Vinyals, Judy Hoffman, Ning Zhang, Eric Tzeng, and Trevor Darrell. 2013. DeCAF: A Deep Convolutional Activation Feature for Generic Visual Recognition. *CoRR* abs/1310.1531 (2013). http://arxiv.org/abs/1310.1531

[8] Bruce Ferwerda, Markus Schedl, and Marko Tkalcic. 2015. Predicting Personality Traits with Instagram Pictures. In *Proceedings of the 3rd Workshop on Emotions and Personality in Personalized Systems 2015 (EMPIRE '15)*. ACM, New York, NY, USA, 7–10. https://doi.org/10.1145/2809643.2809644

[9] Zhiwei Guan and Edward Cutrell. 2007. An Eye Tracking Study of the Effect of Target Rank on Web Search. In *Proceedings of the SIGCHI Conference on Human Factors in Computing Systems (CHI '07)*. ACM, New York, NY, USA, 417–420. https://doi.org/10.1145/1240624.1240691

[10] F. Maxwell Harper and Joseph A. Konstan. 2015. The MovieLens Datasets: History and Context. *ACM Trans. Interact. Intell. Syst.* 5, 4, Article 19 (Dec. 2015), 19 pages. https://doi.org/10.1145/2827872

[11] Ruining He and Julian McAuley. 2016. Ups and Downs: Modeling the Visual Evolution of Fashion Trends with One-Class Collaborative Filtering. *CoRR* abs/1602.01585 (2016). http://arxiv.org/abs/1602.01585

[12] Gawesh Jawaheer, Martin Szomszor, and Patty Kostkova. 2010. Comparison of Implicit and Explicit Feedback from an Online Music Recommendation Service. In *Proceedings of the 1st International Workshop on Information Heterogeneity and Fusion in Recommender Systems (HetRec '10)*. ACM, New York, NY, USA, 47–51. https://doi.org/10.1145/1869446.1869453

[13] Yoshiyuki Kawano and Keiji Yanai. 2014. Food Image Recognition with Deep Convolutional Features. In *Proceedings of the 2014 ACM International Joint Conference on Pervasive and Ubiquitous Computing: Adjunct Publication (UbiComp '14 Adjunct)*. ACM, New York, NY, USA, 589–593. https://doi.org/10.1145/2638728.2641339

[14] Michal Kompan and Mária Bieliková. 2010. *Content-Based News Recommendation*. Springer Berlin Heidelberg, Berlin, Heidelberg, 61–72. https://doi.org/10.1007/978-3-642-15208-5_6

[15] Eduard Kuric and Maria Bielikova. 2015. ANNOR: Efficient image annotation based on combining local and global features. *Computers & Graphics* 47 (2015), 1–15.

[16] Kernix Lab. 2016. Image classification with a pre-trained deep neural network. https://www.kernix.com/blog/image-classification-with-a-pre-trained-deep-neural-network_p11. (2016).

[17] Tie-Yan Liu et al. 2009. Learning to rank for information retrieval. *Foundations and Trends® in Information Retrieval* 3, 3 (2009), 225–331.

[18] Xin Liu and Karl Aberer. 2014. Towards a Dynamic top-N Recommendation Framework. In *Proceedings of the 8th ACM Conference on Recommender Systems (RecSys '14)*. ACM, New York, NY, USA, 217–224. https://doi.org/10.1145/2645710.2645720

[19] Walid Maalej, Hans-Jörg Happel, and Asarnusch Rashid. 2009. When Users Become Collaborators: Towards Continuous and Context-aware User Input. In *Proceedings of the 24th ACM SIGPLAN Conference Companion on Object Oriented Programming Systems Languages and Applications (OOPSLA '09)*. ACM, New York, NY, USA, 981–990. https://doi.org/10.1145/1639950.1640068

[20] Marcelo G. Manzato. 2012. Discovering Latent Factors from Movies Genres for Enhanced Recommendation. In *Proceedings of the Sixth ACM Conference on Recommender Systems (RecSys '12)*. ACM, New York, NY, USA, 249–252. https://doi.org/10.1145/2365952.2366006

[21] Julia Neidhardt, Leonhard Seyfang, Rainer Schuster, and Hannes Werthner. 2015. A picture-based approach to recommender systems. *Information Technology & Tourism* 15, 1 (2015), 49–69. https://doi.org/10.1007/s40558-014-0017-5

[22] Aäron van den Oord, Sander Dieleman, and Benjamin Schrauwen. 2013. Deep Content-based Music Recommendation. In *Proceedings of the 26th International Conference on Neural Information Processing Systems (NIPS'13)*. Curran Associates Inc., USA, 2643–2651. http://dl.acm.org/citation.cfm?id=2999792.2999907

[23] Owen Phelan, Kevin McCarthy, and Barry Smyth. 2009. Using Twitter to Recommend Real-time Topical News. In *Proceedings of the Third ACM Conference on Recommender Systems (RecSys '09)*. ACM, New York, NY, USA, 385–388. https://doi.org/10.1145/1639714.1639794

[24] István Pilászy and Domonkos Tikk. 2009. Recommending New Movies: Even a Few Ratings Are More Valuable Than Metadata. In *Proceedings of the Third ACM Conference on Recommender Systems (RecSys '09)*. ACM, New York, NY, USA, 93–100. https://doi.org/10.1145/1639714.1639731

[25] Francesco Ricci, Lior Rokach, and Bracha Shapira. 2015. *Recommender Systems Handbook* (2nd ed.). Springer US, New York, NY, USA.

[26] Stephen E Robertson and K Sparck Jones. 1976. Relevance weighting of search terms. *Journal of the American Society for Information science* 27, 3 (1976), 129–146.

[27] Christian Szegedy, Vincent Vanhoucke, Sergey Ioffe, Jonathon Shlens, and Zbigniew Wojna. 2015. Rethinking the Inception Architecture for Computer Vision. *CoRR* abs/1512.00567 (2015). http://arxiv.org/abs/1512.00567

[28] M. Tkalcic and J. F. Tasic. 2003. Colour spaces: perceptual, historical and applicational background. In *The IEEE Region 8 EUROCON 2003. Computer as a Tool.*, Vol. 1. 304–308 vol.1. https://doi.org/10.1109/EURCON.2003.1248032

[29] Patricia Valdez and Albert Mehrabian. 1994. Effects of color on emotions. *Journal of experimental psychology: General* 123, 4 (1994), 394.

[30] Hastagiri P. Vanchinathan, Isidor Nikolic, Fabio De Bona, and Andreas Krause. 2014. Explore-exploit in top-N Recommender Systems via Gaussian Processes. In *Proceedings of the 8th ACM Conference on Recommender Systems (RecSys '14)*. ACM, New York, NY, USA, 225–232. https://doi.org/10.1145/2645710.2645733

[31] Li Yu, Fangjian Han, Shaobing Huang, and Yiwen Luo. 2017. A content-based goods image recommendation system. *Multimedia Tools and Applications* (2017), 1–15. https://doi.org/10.1007/s11042-017-4542-z

[32] Mi Zhang. 2009. Enhancing Diversity in Top-N Recommendation. In *Proceedings of the Third ACM Conference on Recommender Systems (RecSys '09)*. ACM, New York, NY, USA, 397–400. https://doi.org/10.1145/1639714.1639798

Constructive Recommendation

Paolo Dragone*
University of Trento, Italy
TIM-SKIL
paolo.dragone@unitn.it

ABSTRACT

Constructive recommendation is the task of recommending object "configurations", i.e. objects that can be assembled from their components on the basis of the user preferences. Examples include: PC configurations, recipes, travel plans, layouts, and other structured objects. Recommended objects are created by maximizing a learned utility function over an exponentially (or even infinitely) large combinatorial space of configurations. The utility function is learned through preference elicitation, an interactive process for collecting user feedback about recommended objects. Constructive recommendation systems can help users make good decisions over complex configuration spaces. Our goal is to adapt existing machine learning techniques, or devise new ones, in order to build recommendation systems suitable for constructive tasks.

1 INTRODUCTION

When faced with complex choices, humans can hardly make optimal decisions due to their *bounded rationality* [12]. Recommendation systems give computational aid to users in making good decisions over a set of heterogeneous choices. These systems usually leverage a mix of domain knowledge and preference data to infer interesting choices for the user. Nowadays recommendation systems are widely employed in online marketing to suggest books, movies, songs and many other products. Thanks to the large amount of available data in these domains, recommendation systems are often "data-driven", using techniques such as collaborative or content-based filtering [11]. These techniques are, however, not well suited when preference data is scarce and the set of items is very large.

We focus on decision problems involving a very large combinatorial set of possible choices or objects. Feasible objects, are represented as sets of attributes, or components, e.g. shape, size, color, and other basic properties of the object itself. These attributes can be combined in many different ways. The size of the set of possible combinations is exponential in the number of attributes. When considering unbounded numerical attributes, the configuration space can also be infinitely large. In this setting, the decision task consists in searching for a good combination of basic components inside this very large space of choices. This kind of decision tasks are called "constructive", as the combinatorial search over the configuration set equates, in a sense, to creating from scratch a new object by assembling it from its components. Constructive recommendation systems create novel objects on the basis of the user preferences.

Consider, for instance, planning a trip around Italy. This task involves deciding which city to visit, in which order, how long to stop and which activity to do in each city, all subject to the available time and budget. Each combination of city, travel and activity is a feasible trip, and thus the set of possible trips is a very large combinatorial space. Handling this problem without computational aid could lead to severe sub-optimal decisions. However, designing a collaborative or a content-based recommendation system for this task is hard, as scarce or no user preference data is available for most of the possible trips. One approach could be to use a constraint-based recommender system [6], gradually specifying tighter constraints to reduce the space of alternatives. However, asking users to specify constraints over a complex domain is not ideal, as they cannot consider all the implications of these constraints over the set of choices, thereby possibly excluding good or optimal candidates.

Decision making in a constructive scenario can be solved by a *preference elicitation* system. Preference elicitation [9] is a iterative process in which, at each iteration, the system selects a recommendation and the user provides a feedback, which is then used by the system to update the user preference model. The goal of preference elicitation systems is to produce good recommendations while keeping the user involvement low. State-of-the-art preference elicitation systems are based on Bayesian estimation of the user preferences [7, 18], but they have been shown not to scale to large constructive domains [15].

Preference elicitation in constructive domains differs from the standard recommendation setting as it has to deal with structured objects coming from a combinatorial domain. This implies that, in the constructive case, recommendation is a structured-output prediction task [1]. Moreover, the interactive nature of the preference elicitation process requires the underlying preference model to be updated as soon as a new user feedback comes by, thereby making it akin to an online machine learning process. Perhaps the best existing online structured prediction technique for preference learning is the Coactive Learning framework [13], which adapts the structured perceptron [4] and online gradient descent techniques [19] to learn a preference model from manipulative feedback. Coactive Learning has already been successfully applied to constructive tasks [5, 14].

Constructive recommendation raises new challenging research problems, ranging from the unprecedented complexity of the inference problem (creating new recommendations) to the nontrivial development of efficient learning models for preference elicitation over combinatorial domains. Our aim is to develop constructive recommendation systems either by leveraging existing techniques, e.g. Coactive Learning, or by developing new learning algorithms for estimating user preferences over large constructive domains.

*PD is a fellow of TIM-SKIL Trento and is supported by a TIM scholarship.

RecSys '17, August 27–31, 2017, Como, Italy.

DOI: http://dx.doi.org/10.1145/3109859.3109867

2 LEARNING MODEL

As most structured prediction systems based on e.g. SSVM [17], constructive recommendation systems are composed of a learning algorithm and an inference procedure.

The preference model in constructive recommendation is a *utility* function $u : \mathcal{X} \times \mathcal{Y} \rightarrow \mathbb{R}$ that maps each object $y \in \mathcal{Y}$ to a real-valued score representing its level of desirability for the user. The utility of an object also depends on the "context" $x \in \mathcal{X}$, i.e. additional (implicit or explicit) side information available at recommendation time. The true user utility function $u^*(x, y)$ is unknown and never directly observed by the system. The system needs to collect preference information by interacting iteratively with the user. At each iteration t, as new preference information is acquired, the system can refine its estimate $u^t(x, y)$ of the true utility function. The utility function is often assumed to be the type $u^t(x, y) = \langle \mathbf{w}^t, \boldsymbol{\phi}(x, y)\rangle$ where $\mathbf{w}^t \in \mathbb{R}^m$ is the current estimate of the weight parameters of the utility model and $\boldsymbol{\phi} : \mathcal{X}\times\mathcal{Y} \rightarrow \mathbb{R}^m$ is a feature map from the joint context-object space to an m-dimensional feature space. To estimate a utility function from the user preference feedback, we employ online preference learning algorithms. In our previous work, we employed Coactive Learning algorithms [13]. Coactive Learning is a framework for learning a utility function from the user manipulative feedback. After receiving a recommendation, the user is asked to provide a slightly improved version of the recommended object. Algorithm 1 shows the Preference Perceptron algorithm, which is one the simplest, but rather effective, Coactive Learning algorithms. At each iteration t, the algorithm receives a context $x^t \in \mathcal{X}$, which may include side information or a user query. The system then makes a recommendation $y^t \in \mathcal{Y}$ by maximizing the current estimate of the user utility. The system then receives an improvement $\bar{y}^t \in \mathcal{Y}$ from the user, such that $u^*(x^t, \bar{y}^t) \geq u^*(x^t, y^t)$. Using the ranking information provided by the pair $(y^t, \bar{y}^t)$, the algorithm can update the current estimate of the weights.

The objective of the Preference Perceptron is to minimize the average *regret* of the system:

$$\mathrm{REG}^T = \frac{1}{T}\sum_{t=1}^{T} u^*(x^t, y_t^*) - u^*(x^t, y^t)$$

where $y_t^* = \mathrm{argmax}_{y\in\mathcal{Y}}\, u^*(x^t, y)$ is the optimal object for the user in context x^t. In Coactive Learning [13] the user is assumed to behave according to the following α-informative feedback model:

$$u^*(x^t, \bar{y}^t) - u^*(x^t, y^t) = \alpha(u^*(x^t, y_t^*) - u^*(x^t, y^t)) - \xi^t$$

This model requires the user feedback $\bar{y}^t$ to improve y^t of a fraction α of the regret, modulo a slack ξ^t. When the user behaves according to this model, the average regret of the Preference Perceptron is guaranteed to decrease as $O(1/\sqrt{T})$. In particular, the average regret is upper-bounded by (proof in [13]):

$$\mathrm{REG}^T \leq \frac{2R\|\mathbf{w}^*\|}{\alpha\sqrt{T}} + \frac{1}{T}\sum_{t=1}^{T}\xi^t \qquad (1)$$

where $\mathbf{w}^*$ are the true weights of the user and R is the radius of the smallest ball enclosing the feature space, i.e. $\|\boldsymbol{\phi}(x, y)\| \leq R$.

3 OBJECT SYNTHESIS

The second component needed to build a constructive recommendation system is an inference procedure that, given the current utility

Algorithm 1 The Preference Perceptron algorithm [13].

1: **for** $t = 1, \ldots, T$ **do**
2: Receive context x^t
3: $y^t \leftarrow \mathrm{argmax}_{y\in\mathcal{Y}}\langle \mathbf{w}^t, \boldsymbol{\phi}(x^t, y)\rangle$
4: Receive user feedback $\bar{y}^t$
5: $\mathbf{w}^{t+1} \leftarrow \mathbf{w}^t + \boldsymbol{\phi}(x^t, \bar{y}^t) - \boldsymbol{\phi}(x^t, y^t)$

model, generates new objects with high utility. In the Preference Perceptron, the recommendation step consists in finding the object with highest utility in the space $\mathcal{Y}$ of feasible configurations:

$$y^t = \mathrm{argmax}_{y\in\mathcal{Y}}\langle \mathbf{w}^t, \boldsymbol{\phi}(x^t, y)\rangle$$

The configuration space $\mathcal{Y}$ is a combinatorial space defined by the domains of the attributes and the imposed constraints. Attributes may be boolean or numerical (integer or real) variables. Maximize the utility function over this space equates to solving a constrained optimization problem. To keep computational complexity low, we usually require constraints and features to depend linearly in the attributes. This makes the inference problem a mixed integer linear program (MILP). While being NP-hard in the general case, modern solvers can find exact solutions to large problems in reasonable time. In many cases, however, exact solutions are too computationally expensive to find and thus approximation techniques may be used.

4 PRELIMINARY RESULTS

This section describes two of our already achieved results. The first is an applicative constructive recommendation system to recommend layouts. The second is an extension of Coactive Learning to allow feature elicitation in constructive domains.

4.1 Constructive Layout Synthesis

In this work [5], we presented a constructive recommendation system to recommend layouts, i.e. 2D arrangements of objects. Examples of recommendation problems involving layout synthesis are recommendation of furniture arrangements, space division, or urban planning. This system is able to learn the "style" of a designer or an architect and recommend new configurations on the basis of their preferences. Coactive Learning is particularly well suited in this setting because we imagine the system to be able to learn from designers sketches as improvements to recommended configurations. We instantiated this system on a furniture arrangement task, in which the goal of the system is to learn to arrange tables in a room. The contexts x include the shape of the room and the number of tables, whereas the attributes of y consist in the coordinates and the sizes of all the tables in the room. Features $\boldsymbol{\phi}(x, y)$ include different high-level properties of the table arrangement, such as the maximum and minimum distances between the tables and the maximum and minimum distances between the tables and the walls. Several constraints are imposed to ensure the tables fit into the room and they do not overlap.

The difficulty of the inference problem grows with the number of tables, as more variables and constraints are added for each table. When the running time becomes unfeasibly long, we employ an approximation heuristic consisting in setting a time cutoff on the solver and retaining the best solution found. We tested this system

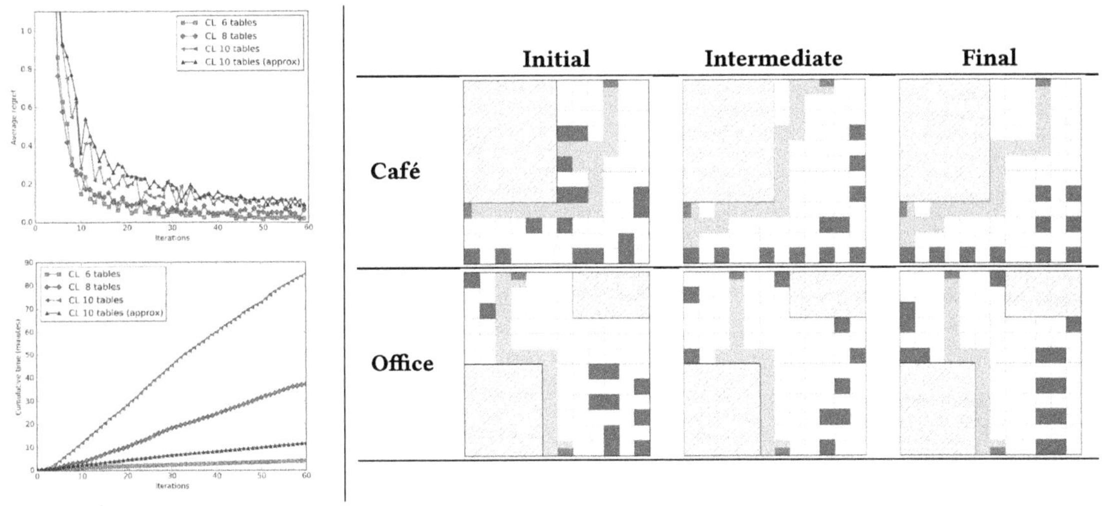

Figure 1: Left: average regret (top) cumulative running time (bottom) of the layout synthesis system [5]; Right: Two examples of configurations built by our system when used by users who are furnishing a café or an office. The figure shows different stages of algorithm while learning the user preferences. The tables are colored in brown and the doors in red. An automatically generated path between the doors is showed in grey the walls are represented with black striped sections. Best viewed in colors.

with 6, 8, and 10 tables with exact inference, and 10 tables with approximate inference over 20 randomly selected weight vectors. We can see from the plots on the left in Figure 1 that the regret follows the same descending pattern for all settings with exact inference, with minor differences as the problem complexity grows. The running times, however, become quickly unfeasible for the case with 10 tables. The approximate version, instead, has predictable running time for a small loss in recommendation quality.

We also make a qualitative evaluation by comparing the configurations produced by the system while interacting with very different users. We run how algorithm with two synthetic users, one furnishing a café and another furnish an office. We run our algorithm on these users and we show, in the right block of Figure 1, different stages of the two elicitation processes. The initial configuration is random in both cases. In the intermediate configuration we can see some emerging patterns, for instance the choice of mostly 1×1 tables in the café. In the final configurations, the café has all 1×1 positioned along the walls, while the office contains mostly 1×2 desks positioned in a regular fashion across the room.

4.2 Coactive Critiquing

Feature selection is an important but quite daunting task. Particularly so in constructive recommendation systems. In general, relevant preference criteria (i.e. features) may differ from user to user. Engineering all the relevant features for all users is expensive and error prone. Moreover, learning and solving inference in a high-dimensional feature space requires more data and more computing time. In this work, we proposed a procedure to elicit relevant features as additional user feedback. We modified the Preference Perceptron algorithm to allow the system to ask *critiques* to the user. Critiques are "explanations" that are asked when the system receives ambiguous improvements. Given an example pair $(y^t, \bar{y}^t)$, a critique is a function discriminating $\bar{y}^t$ from y^t.

Algorithm 2 The Critiquing Preference Perceptron algorithm.

for $t = 1, \ldots, T$ **do**
  Receive query x^t from the user
  $y^t \leftarrow \text{argmax}_{y \in \mathcal{Y}} \langle \boldsymbol{w}^t, \boldsymbol{\phi}(x^t, y) \rangle$
  User provides improvement $\bar{y}^t$
  if NeedCritique$(x^t, y^t, \bar{y}^t)$ **then**
    Receive critique ρ from the user
    $\boldsymbol{\phi}^t \leftarrow \boldsymbol{\phi}^t \circ [\rho]$
    $\boldsymbol{w}^t \leftarrow \boldsymbol{w}^t \circ [0]$
  $\boldsymbol{w}^{t+1} \leftarrow \boldsymbol{w}^t + \boldsymbol{\phi}^t(x^t, \bar{y}^t) - \boldsymbol{\phi}^t(x^t, y^t)$
  $\boldsymbol{\phi}^{t+1} \leftarrow \boldsymbol{\phi}^t$

Algorithm 1 lists our Critiquing Perceptron algorithm. At each iteration t, after receiving the improvement $\bar{y}^t$ the system has the option of asking the user to provide a critique for the example. To decide whether a critique is needed, we check if the feedback is consistent with all the previous ones. If this check fails, the algorithm asks the user for a critique of the last example, which is then used to enlarge the feature vector with a new feature. In this way, the feature space grows only when necessary, keeping the learned model simple and inference time low.

We found that the Critiquing Perceptron enjoys a regret upper-bound analogous to that of the Preference Perceptron (Eq 1). For a α-informative user the average regret of the Critiquing Perceptron is upper-bounded by (proof in [14]):

$$\text{REG}^T \leq \frac{2R\|\boldsymbol{w}^*\|}{\alpha\sqrt{T}} + \frac{1}{T}\sum_{t=1}^{T}(\xi^t + \eta^t)$$

where

$$\eta^t = \langle \boldsymbol{w}^*, \boldsymbol{\phi}^*(x^t, \bar{y}^t) - \boldsymbol{\phi}^*(x^t, y^t) \rangle - \langle \boldsymbol{w}^*, \boldsymbol{\phi}^t(x^t, \bar{y}^t) - \boldsymbol{\phi}^t(x^t, y^t) \rangle$$

is the amount of utility gain the Critiquing Perceptron "misses out" by having only a subset $\boldsymbol{\phi}^t$ of the relevant user features $\boldsymbol{\phi}^*$.

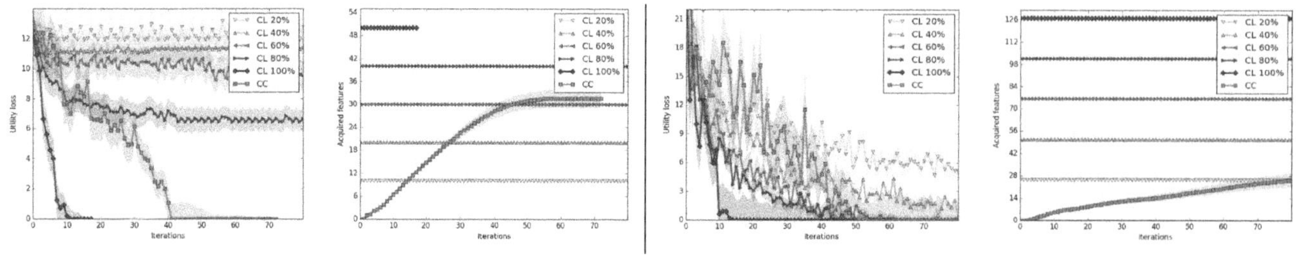

Figure 2: Regret and acquired features for the synthetic problem (left) and the trip planning problem (right) in Coactive Critiquing [14]. Best viewed in color.

We also tested our algorithm on two simulated constructive settings, a synthetic problem and a realistic problem involving trip plan recommendations. We compared the Critiquing Perceptron (CC) with the standard Preference Perceptron (CL) using different percentages of user features. The former starts with only basic features and elicits more during the interaction, whereas the latter starts with a percentage of additional features on top of the basic ones but does not elicit more. As we can see in Figure 2, in both settings the Critiquing Perceptron is able to rapidly decrease the regret as CL 60% or 80% while eliciting only a fraction of the total user features.

5 RESEARCH DIRECTIONS

This section outlines few research problems we are investigating.

5.1 Online preference learning

Learning algorithms used in constructive recommendation systems should be fast and scalable to large volumes of data, as typical of modern recommendation systems. Online preference learning algorithms are well suited candidates. There is, however, little work in online preference learning when it comes to defining the right interaction protocol with the user and the best policy to select the recommendation maximizing both the satisfaction of the user and the information gained by the feedback. Both these aspects are crucial in the constructive scenario. Furthermore, in the case of Coactive Learning, while this framework is well suited in some scenarios, manipulative feedback may not be easy to acquire from the user in many constructive tasks. An alternative to the coactive feedback is the choice set feedback, a well studied type of user interaction in the literature of algorithmic decision theory and preference elicitation [8, 10, 16]. Choice set feedback is often deemed less effort demanding for the user [7]. In a recent work, we developed an online algorithm, specifically designed for constructive tasks, to learn from choice set feedback. Differently from Coactive Learning, the use of choice set feedback brings up the problem of how to select recommendation sets. In this work, we developed a theoretically-driven selection strategy and we produced empirical results favouring our approach over existing preference elicitation techniques both in recommendation quality and running times. Future work in this direction include: [i] increase expressiveness of our preference models by employing long-standing preference elicitation tools, such as GAI utility functions and CP-nets [2]; [ii] generalize local feedback on portions of the objects (a.k.a. "sketches") by exploiting structural properties, e.g. generalize improvements over a single room to the entire house in layout synthesis tasks [5].

5.2 Feature selection and elicitation

As pointed out in Section 4.2, feature selection is a crucial aspect in constructive recommendation systems and Coactive Critiquing is one possible approach to learn relevant user features by eliciting them as additional critiquing feedback. While being quite effective, this approach requires further user involvement in providing critiques, which may be too cognitively expensive. An alternative that we are developing is to automatically learn new features directly from the user improvements or some other source of high-level feedback. Other possible approaches that we are investigating include reducing the space of relevant features via a sparsifying L_1 norm or by exploiting structural properties of the features, such as their *inheritance* [3].

5.3 Inference over combinatorial domains

Recommendations in constructive domains are selected by solving some kind of constrained optimization problem. As detailed in Section 3, the inference problem is a MILP problem when constraints and features are linear in the attributes. With increasing domain complexity solving inference exactly becomes impractical. As in Section 4.1 [5], a viable option is relying on some kind of approximate inference. However, we are still looking for some more reliable approximation technique with some guarantee on the final recommendation quality, instead of the somewhat unreliable solving time cutoff. Another interesting research question in this direction is whether we can go beyond linear programs and address inference in quadratically constrained domains. This would allow us to describe domains involving areas and euclidean distances, such as layout synthesis [5].

6 CONCLUSION

This abstract presented the topic of Constructive Recommendation, a framework for recommending objects created from scratch on the basis of the user preferences. Constructive recommendation systems may be devised using online structured prediction algorithms and a constraint programming solver as inference oracle. The abstract outlined some of the accomplished work in this research line and mentioned some future directions we are currently investigating.

REFERENCES

[1] GH Bakir, T Hofmann, B Schölkopf, AJ Smola, B Taskar, and SVN Vishwanathan. 2007. Predicting Structured Data. (2007).

[2] Craig Boutilier, Fahiem Bacchus, and Ronen I Brafman. 2001. UCP-networks: A directed graphical representation of conditional utilities. In *UAI*. 56–64.

[3] Hugh Chipman. 1996. Bayesian variable selection with related predictors. *CJS* 24, 1 (1996), 17–36.

[4] Michael Collins. 2002. Discriminative training methods for hidden markov models: Theory and experiments with perceptron algorithms. In *ACL'02*, Vol. 10. 1–8.

[5] Paolo Dragone, Luca Erculiani, Maria Teresa Chietera, Stefano Teso, and Andrea Passerini. 2016. Constructive Layout Synthesis via Coactive Learning. In *Constructive Machine Learning workshop, NIPS*.

[6] Alexander Felfernig and Robin Burke. 2008. Constraint-based recommender systems: technologies and research issues. In *Proceedings of the 10th international conference on Electronic commerce*. ACM, 3.

[7] Shengbo Guo and Scott Sanner. 2010. Real-time multiattribute Bayesian preference elicitation with pairwise comparison queries. In *AISTATS*. 289–296.

[8] Jordan J Louviere, David A Hensher, and Joffre D Swait. 2000. *Stated choice methods: analysis and applications*. Cambridge University Press.

[9] Gabriella Pigozzi, Alexis Tsoukiàs, and Paolo Viappiani. 2016. Preferences in artificial intelligence. *Annals of Mathematics and Artificial Intelligence* (2016).

[10] Pearl Pu and Li Chen. 2009. User-involved preference elicitation for product search and recommender systems. *AI magazine* 29, 4 (2009), 93.

[11] Francesco Ricci, Lior Rokach, and Bracha Shapira. 2011. *Introduction to recommender systems handbook*. Springer.

[12] Ariel Rubinstein. 1998. *Modeling bounded rationality*. MIT press.

[13] Pannaga Shivaswamy and Thorsten Joachims. 2015. Coactive Learning. *JAIR* 53 (2015), 1–40.

[14] Stefano Teso, Paolo Dragone, and Andrea Passerini. 2017. Coactive Critiquing: Elicitation of Preferences and Features. In *AAAI*.

[15] Stefano Teso, Andrea Passerini, and Paolo Viappiani. 2016. Constructive Preference Elicitation by Setwise Max-Margin Learning. In *IJCAI*. 2067–2073.

[16] Olivier Toubia, John R Hauser, and Duncan I Simester. 2004. Polyhedral methods for adaptive choice-based conjoint analysis. *Journal of Marketing Research* 41, 1 (2004), 116–131.

[17] Ioannis Tsochantaridis, Thomas Hofmann, Thorsten Joachims, and Yasemin Altun. 2004. Support vector machine learning for interdependent and structured output spaces. In *ICML*. ACM, 104.

[18] Paolo Viappiani and Craig Boutilier. 2010. Optimal Bayesian recommendation sets and myopically optimal choice query sets. In *NIPS*. 2352–2360.

[19] Martin Zinkevich. 2003. Online convex programming and generalized infinitesimal gradient ascent. In *Proceedings of the 20th International Conference on Machine Learning (ICML-03)*. 928–936.

Author Index

NOTES

www.ingramcontent.com/pod-product-compliance
Ingram Content Group UK Ltd.
Pitfield, Milton Keynes, MK11 3LW, UK
UKHW051413290926
15471UKWH00009B/1577